HOW TO WIN FRIENDS AND INFLUENCE PEOPLE
HOW TO STOP WORRYING AND START LIVING
THE QUICK AND EASY WAY TO EFFECTIVE SPEAKING

英汉双语

卡耐基励志经典

人性的弱点 • 人性的优点 • 语言的突破

[美] 戴尔·卡耐基 ⊙ 著
刘 祜 ⊙ 译

中国城市出版社
·北京·

图书在版编目（CIP）数据

英汉双语卡耐基励志经典：人性的弱点·人性的优点·语言的突破/（美）卡耐基（Carnegie，D.）著；刘祜译. 北京：中国城市出版社，2009.1（2012.6 重印）

ISBN 978-7-5074-2061-6

Ⅰ.英… Ⅱ.①卡…②刘… Ⅲ.①英语—汉语—对照读物②成功心理学—通俗读物③演讲学 Ⅳ.H319.4：B

中国版本图书馆 CIP 数据核字（2008）第 171992 号

选题策划	徐昌强（greatbook@sina.com 13661335586）
责任编辑	华 风
装帧设计	美信书籍设计工作室
责任技术编辑	张建军
出版发行	中国城市出版社
地　　址	北京市西城区广安门南街甲 30 号（邮编 100053）
网　　址	www.citypress.cn
发行部电话	（010）63454857 63289949
发行部传真	（010）63421417 63400635
总编室电话	（010）68171928
总编室信箱	citypress@sina.com
经　　销	新华书店
印　　刷	北京集惠印刷有限责任公司
字　　数	1200 千字 印张 37.5
开　　本	850×1168（毫米） 1/16
版　　次	2009 年 1 月第 1 版
印　　次	2012 年 6 月第 3 次印刷
定　　价	48.00 元

CONTENTS

HOW TO WIN FRIENDS AND INFLUENCE PEOPLE

目 录

人性的弱点

Part Three How to Win People to Your Way of Thinking

第三篇 如何赢得别人的赞同

Part Four Be a Leader: How to Change People without Giving Offense or Arousing Resentment

Part Five Letters That Produced Miraculous Results / 191

Part Six Seven Rules for Making Your Home Life Happier

第四篇 领导艺术:如何改变他人而不招致反感或怨恨

第五篇 创造奇迹的信 / 191

第六篇 使你的家庭生活更幸福

HOW TO STOP WORRYING AND START LIVING

Part One Fundamental Facts You Should Know about Worry

Part Two Basic Techniques in Analysing Worry

人性的优点

第一篇 了解忧虑的基本事实

第二篇 分析忧虑的基本技巧

Part Three How to Break the Worry Habit Before It Breaks You

Part Four Seven Ways to Cultivate A Mental Attitude That Will Bring You Peace and Happiness

第三篇 如何改变忧虑的习惯

第四篇 培养平安快乐的心理

Part Eight How to Lessen Your Financial Worries

Part Nine "How I Conquered Worry"— 32 True Stories / 405

THE QUICK AND EASY WAY TO EFFECTIVE SPEAKING

Part One Fundamentals of Effective Speaking

Part Two Speech, Speaker, and Audience

第八篇 如何减少金钱的烦恼

第九篇 克服忧虑的真实故事 / 405

语言的突破

第一篇 高效演讲的基本原则

第二篇 演讲、演讲者和听众

Part Three The Purpose of Prepared and Impromptu Talks

Part Four The Art of Communicating

Part Five The Challenge of Effective Speaking

第三篇 成功发表商务演讲

第四篇 沟通的艺术

第五篇 接受成功演讲的挑战

HOW TO WIN FRIENDS AND INFLUENCE PEOPLE

人性的弱点

Eight Things This Book Will Help You Achieve

1. Get out of a mental rut, think new thoughts, acquire new visions, discover new ambitions.
2. Make friends quickly and easily.
3. Increase your popularity.
4. Win people to your way of thinking.
5. Increase your influence, your prestige, your ability to get things done.
6. Handle complaints, avoid arguments, keep your human contacts smooth and pleasant.
7. Become a better speaker, a more entertaining conversationalist.
8. Arouse enthusiasm among your associates.

This book has done all these things for more than ten million readers in thirty-six languages.

本书将帮你达到的八项技能

1. 走出思想的窠臼，思考新观念，获得新视野，发现新抱负。
2. 快速容易地赢得朋友。
3. 让你更受人欢迎。
4. 让别人赞同你的观点。
5. 增加你的影响、你的名声以及处理事情的能力。
6. 处理抱怨，避免争论，让你的人际关系融洽愉悦。
7. 成为一个出色的说话者，一个更令人愉悦的交谈者。
8. 在你的同伴中激发出热情。

本书已翻译成 36 种语言，让 1000 多万读者拥有了上述技能。

How This Book Was Written—And Why By Dale Carnegie

During the first thirty–five years of the twentieth century, the publishing houses of America printed more than a fifth of a million different books. Most of them were deadly dull, and many were financial failures. "Many," did I say? The president of one of the largest publishing houses in the world confessed to me that his company, after seventy–five years of publishing experience, still lost money on seven out of every eight books it published.

Why, then, did I have the temerity to write another book? And, after I had written it, why should you bother to read it?

Fair questions, both; and I'll try to answer them.

I have, since 1912, been conducting educational courses for business and professional men and women in New York. At first, I conducted courses in public speaking only—courses designed to train adults, by actual experience, to think on their feet and express their ideas with more clarity, more effectiveness and more poise, both in business interviews and before groups.

But gradually, as the seasons passed, I realized that as sorely as these adults needed training in effective speaking, they needed still more training in the fine art of getting along with people in everyday business and social contacts.

I also gradually realized that I was sorely in need of such training myself. As I look back across the years, I am appalled at my own frequent lack of finesse and understanding. How I wish a book such as this had been placed in my hands twenty years ago! What a priceless boon it would have been.

Dealing with people is probably the biggest problem you face, especially if you are in business. Yes, and that is also true if you are a housewife, architect or engineer. Research done a few years ago under the auspices of the Carnegie Foundation for the Advancement of Teaching uncovered a most important and significant fact—a fact later confirmed by additional studies made

本书的形成，为什么是由戴尔·卡耐基写成的

在20世纪前35年当中，美国的出版商曾出版过20多万种图书，但这些书大多数都乏味至极，许多都是赔本买卖。“许多。”是我说的吗？世界上最大之一的一家书店的老板就对我说，虽然他的公司拥有75年的出版经验，但还是每出版8本书就有7本亏本。

既然如此，那我为什么还敢冒险来再写一本书呢？而且在我写完之后，你又何必去读它呢？

这两个问题都很有道理，就让我来一一回答！

从1912年开始，我就在纽约为那些商业和专业男士及女士开教育讲座。最初我只开了演讲的课程，用实际经验来训练成年人，使他们在商业洽谈及公共场合中沉着自若，更清楚、更有效、更镇定地发表他们的意见。

经过一段时间，我逐渐发现这些人虽然需要高效演讲的训练，但是他们更需要在日常事务和社会交往中与人相处的技巧训练。

我也逐渐发现我自己也非常需要这种训练。当我回忆起那时的情形时，就会对自己贫乏的知识感到惶恐不安。我真希望在20年前手中就有这么一本书！这将是一件珍宝！

你所面临的最大困难可能是如何与人打交道，尤其当你是一位商人时更是如此。当然，如果你是一位家庭主妇、建筑师或工程师，同样也是如此。几年前由卡内基基金会赞助的一项调查研究，显示了一个最为重要的事实——后来被卡内基技术研究院所做的其他研究证实的事实。这些调查表明，即使在工程技术工作方面，一个人所获得的高额薪水中，

at the Carnegie Institute of Technology.These investigations revealed that even in such technical lines as engineering, about 15 percent of one's financial success is due to one's technical knowledge and about 85 percent is due to skill in human engineering—to personality and the ability to lead people.

For many years, I conducted courses each season at the Engineers' Club of Philadelphia, and also courses for the New York Chapter of the American Institute of Electrical Engineers.A total of probably more than fifteen hundred engineers have passed through my classes.They came to me because they had finally realized, after years of observation and experience, that the highest-paid personnel in engineering are frequently not those who know the most about engineering.One can for example, hire mere technical ability in engineering, accountancy, architecture or any other profession at nominal salaries.But the person who has technical knowledge *plus* the ability to express ideas, to assume leadership, and to arouse enthusiasm among people—that person is headed for higher earning power.

In the heyday of his activity, John D.Rockefeller said that "the ability to deal with people is as purchasable a commodity as sugar or coffee.And I will pay more for that ability," said John D., "than for any other under the sun."

Wouldn't you suppose that every college in the land would conduct courses to develop the highest-priced ability under the sun? But if there is just one practical, common-sense course of that kind given for adults in even one college in the land, it has escaped my attention up to the present writing.

The University of Chicago and the United Y.M.C.A.Schools conducted a survey to determine what adults want to study.

That survey cost $25,000 and took two years.The last part of the survey was made in Meriden, Connecticut.It had been chosen as a typical American town.Every adult in Meriden was interviewed and requested to answer 156 questions—questions such as "What is your business or profession? Your education? How do you spend your spare time? What is your income? Your hobbies? Your ambitions? Your problems? What subjects are you most interested in studying?" And so on.That survey revealed that health is the prime interest of adults—and that their second interest is people;

大概只有 15%是因为他的技术知识，而大约 85%则是因为他的为人处世技巧，也就是他的个人品质和领导才能。

许多年来，我每个季度都要在费城的工程师俱乐部开设讲座，同时还在美国电机工程学会纽约分会开设讲座。大约有 1500 多人听过我的讲座。他们之所以到我这里来，是因为他们经过多年的观察发现，工程师得到的报酬最高的，通常不是那些工程学知识最多的人。例如，我们可以以正常的薪水雇用工程、会计、建筑或其他专业方面的技术人才。但是既有技术知识，又善于表达自己内心思想、同时又具备领导才能和激发他人热情的人，他们就会获得更高的收入。

洛克菲勒在事业达到巅峰的时候，曾这样说："与人打交道的能力也是一种可以购买的商品，这正如同糖和咖啡一样。我愿意付出比世界上其他任何东西都要高的代价来购买这种能力。"

难道你不认为每个大学都应该开设这种实用课程，来开发我们这个世界上最宝贵的能力吗？但是直到我写这本书为止，我还没有发现哪个大学开设了这种既实用又需求迫切的课程。

芝加哥大学和青年会联合学校曾经做过一项调查，以考察成年人关心哪些事情。

这项调查耗资 25000 美元，花了两年时间。调查的最后部分是在康涅狄格州的米利顿进行的。这是一个典型的美国城镇。镇上的每个成年人都被调查过，他们被要求回答 156 个问题，例如"你的职业和专业是什么？""你接受过什么教育？""你如何打发闲暇时间？""你的收入是多少？""你有什么爱好？""你的志向是什么？""你有什么问题？""你最喜欢什么学科？"……调查表明，成年人最关心的问题是健康——接下来的问题就是人，包括如何了解人、如何与人相处、如何让别人喜欢你、如何使别人赞同你的意见。

于是，这个调查委员会决定在米利顿为成年人开设这样一门课程。他们努力寻找这方面的

how to understand and get along with people; how to make people like you; and how to win others to your way of thinking.

So the committee conducting this survey resolved to conduct such a course for adults in Meriden.They searched diligently for a practical textbook on the subject and found—not one.Finally they approached one of the world's outstanding authorities on adult education and asked him if he knew of any book that met the needs of this group. "No,"he replied, "I know what those adults want.But the book they need has never been written."

I knew from experience that this statement was true,for I myself had been searching for years to discover a practical,working handbook on human relations.

Since no such book existed,I have tried to write one for use in my own courses.And here it is.I hope you like it.

In preparation for this book,I read everything that I could find on the subject—everything from newspaper columns,magazine articles,records of the family courts,the writings of the old philosophers and the new psychologists.In addition,I hired a trained researcher to spend one and a half years in various libraries reading everything I had missed,plowing through erudite tomes on psychology,poring over hundreds of magazine articles,searching through countless biographies, trying to ascertain how the great leaders of all ages had dealt with people.We read their biographies,we read the life stories of all great leaders from Julius Caesar to Thomas Edison.I recall that we read over one hundred biographies of Theodore Roosevelt alone.We were determined to spare no time,no expense,to discover every practical idea that anyone had ever used throughout the ages for winning friends and influencing people.

I personally interviewed scores of successful people,some of them world-famous—inventors like Marconi and Edison; political leaders like Franklin D.Roosevelt and James Farley; business leaders like Owen D.Young; movie stars like Clark Gable and Mary Pickford; and explorers like Martin Johnson—and tried to discover the techniques they used in human relations.

From all this material,I prepared a short talk.I called it "How to Win Friends and Influence People."I say "short."It was short in the beginning,but it soon expanded to a lecture that consumed one hour and thirty minutes.For years,I gave this talk each season to the adults in the Carnegie

实用教材，但一本都没有找到。最后他们找到一位世界著名的成人教育权威，问他是否知道有什么书符合成年人的这些需求。“没有，”他说，“我知道这些成年人需要什么，但是他们所需要的书至今都没人写。”

据我所知，他的话是对的，因为我自己也花了许多年的时间来寻找这种人际关系方面的实效书。既然这种书至今还没有，于是我就尝试着写了一本，用于我自己的课程。这就是你眼前的这本书。希望你们喜欢它。

为了写好这本书，我读了能找到的所有材料，包括报纸专栏、杂志文章、家庭法庭记录，以及旧哲学家和新心理学家的著作。而且我还雇了一位训练有素的研究员，花了一年半的工夫，在图书馆阅读我所遗漏的东西，研究各种心理学专著，翻阅了成百上千篇杂志文章，还抄录了许许多多的传记，以了解各个时代的伟大人物是如何与他人打交道的。我们读过从恺撒到爱迪生的各个时代的伟人传记。我还记得，仅西奥多·罗斯福的传记我们就看了100多本。我们决定不惜花费时间和金钱，一定要找到各个时代都曾用过的有关赢得朋友和影响他人的高效实用的方法。

我自己还拜访过几十位成功人士，其中一些人还是世界著名人物——例如发明家马可尼和爱迪生；政治领袖富兰克林·罗斯福和詹姆斯·弗雷；商业领袖欧文·扬；电影明星克拉克·盖博尔和玛丽亚·毕克馥；探险家马丁·约翰逊——尽力了解他们的为人处世之道。

我在这些材料的基础上准备了一篇简短的演讲稿，题目就叫《如何赢得朋友以及影响他人》。我说它短，因为它最初确实很短，但不久就扩充成一篇一个半小时的演讲稿。多年来我每个季度都在纽约的卡内基研究所为成年人做这篇演讲。

我为听众演讲，鼓励他们走出去，在工作、社会交往中试验，然后回到班上讲述他们的经验和取得的成果。这是一项多么有趣的工作啊！这些渴望成功的男男女女完全被这种新型的实

Institute courses in New York.

I gave the talk and urged the listeners to go out and test it in their business and social contacts, and then come back to class and speak about their experiences and the results they had achieved. What an interesting assignment! These men and women, hungry for self-improvement, were fascinated by the idea of working in a new kind of laboratory—the first and only laboratory of human relationships for adults that had ever existed.

This book wasn't written in the usual sense of the word. It grew as a child grows. It grew and developed out of that laboratory, out of the experiences of thousands of adults.

Years ago, we started with a set of rules printed on a card no larger than a postcard. The next season we printed a larger card, then a leaflet, then a series of booklets, each one expanding in size and scope. After fifteen years of experiment and research came this book.

The rules we have set down here are not mere theories or guesswork. They work like magic. Incredible as it sounds, I have seen the application of these principles literally revolutionize the lives of many people.

To illustrate: A man with 314 employees joined one of these courses. For years, he had driven and criticized and condemned his employees without stint or discretion. Kindness, words of appreciation and encouragement were alien to his lips. After studying the principles discussed in this book, this employer sharply altered his philosophy of life. His organization is now inspired with a new loyalty, a new enthusiasm, a new spirit of teamwork. Three hundred and fourteen enemies have been turned into 314 friends. As he proudly said in a speech before the class, "When I used to walk through my establishment, no one greeted me. My employees actually looked the other way when they saw me approaching. But now they are all my friends and even the janitor calls me by my first name."

This employer gained more profit, more leisure and—what is infinitely more important—he found far more happiness in his business and in his home.

Countless numbers of salespeople have sharply increased their sales by the use of these principles. Many have opened up new accounts—accounts that they had formerly solicited in vain. Executives have been given increased authority, increased pay. One executive reported a large

验室迷住了——这也是有史以来为成年人创设的最早的、也是唯一的人际关系实验室。

这本书并不是像普通的书那样写成的，它像个孩子一样逐渐成长。它在实践中成长发育，并吸收了成百上千人的经验及智慧。

许多年以前，我刚开始只是把这些规则写在和明信片差不多大小的卡片上；在下一个季度，又将它们印在较大的卡片上；然后是印在一本小册子中；再往后就成了一小套书。它的篇幅和内容每次都有所扩充。经过 15 年的实验和研究之后，终于成了现在这本书。

这本书所说的不仅仅是理论或猜测，它们就像魔法一样有效。这听起来似乎难以置信，但我确确实实看见这些规则改变了许多人的生活。

例如，有一个人参加了这些课程，他手下有 314 名员工。长期以来，他总是不停地批评和责难他的员工，对他们从来没有赞扬和鼓励。当他学了这本书所讨论的各项规则以后，这位雇主的人生观得到了很大的改变。现在，他的公司充满了新的精诚合作的精神，314 个敌人变成了 314 个朋友。他在一次班级演讲中得意地说道："以前我在我的公司中走动的时候，没有人跟我打招呼。我的员工看到我走近时，会立即转过脸去。但现在他们都成了我的朋友，甚至连看门员都直接叫我的名字。"

这位老板现在获得了更多的利润，也有了更多的闲暇时间——而且更加重要的是，他在工作和家庭中得到了更多的幸福。

还有数不清的推销员因为采用了这些规则，从而迅速增加了他们的销售额。例如许多人找到了新的客户，而这些客户他们以前是根本找不到的。那些公司高级职员也因此得到了晋升，获得了更多的薪水。例如有一位高级职员就说，因为采用了这些规则，他的薪水大大增加。还有费城煤气公司的一位高级职员，因为喜欢争强好胜，又加上领导无方，65 岁时被公司决定降职。接受这项训练之后，他不仅没有被降职，而且还晋升了职

increase in salary because he applied these truths. Another, an executive in the Philadelphia Gas Works Company, was slated for demotion when he was sixty-five because of his belligerence, because of his inability to lead people skillfully. This training not only saved him from the demotion but brought him a promotion with increased pay.

On innumerable occasions, spouses attending the banquet given at the end of the course have told me that their homes have been much happier since their husbands or wives started this training.

People are frequently astonished at the new results they achieve. It all seems like magic. In some cases, in their enthusiasm, they have telephoned me at my home on Sundays because they couldn't wait forty-eight hours to report their achievements at the regular session of the course.

One man was so stirred by a talk on these principles that he sat far into the night discussing them with other members of the class. At three o'clock in the morning, the others went home. But he was so shaken by a realization of his own mistakes, so inspired by the vista of a new and richer world opening before him, that he was unable to sleep. He didn't sleep that night or the next day or the next night.

Who was he? A naïve, untrained individual ready to gush over any new theory that came along? No. Far from it. He was a sophisticated, blasé dealer in art, very much the man about town, who spoke three languages fluently and was a graduate of two European universities.

While writing this chapter, I received a letter from a German of the old school, an aristocrat whose forebears had served for generations as professional army officers under the Hohenzollerns. His letter, written from a transatlantic steamer, telling about the application of these principles, rose almost to a religious fervor.

Another man, an old New Yorker, a Harvard graduate, a wealthy man, the owner of a large carpet factory, declared he had learned more in fourteen weeks through this system of training about the fine art of influencing people than he had learned about the same subject during his four years in college. Absurd? Laughable? Fantastic? of course, you are privileged to dismiss this statement with whatever adjective you wish. I am merely reporting, without comment, a declaration made by a conservative and eminently successful Harvard graduate in a public address to approximately six

务，增加了薪水。

还有许多次，那些参加毕业聚会的妻子或丈夫对我说，自从她们的丈夫(或他们的妻子)开始这种训练之后，他们的家庭变得更加快乐了。

人们常常对自己所获得的新成就感到惊异。这一切就像魔术一样！有时他们甚至会在星期天激动万分地打电话到我家来，迫不及待地报告他们所取得的成就。

有一名学员就这些规则和班上的学员激动地一直谈到深夜。凌晨3点钟，其他人都回家了，他这才发现了自己的失误。但经过这次谈话，他发现自己面前有一条美好的前程，这使得他好几天都无法入睡。

这个人是谁呢？难道是一个没有经过什么训练、遇到任何新的东西就会兴奋难耐的人吗？不，当然不是！他是一个拥有高学历的、历尽沧桑的艺术商，社会交际很广，可以流利地说3种外语，还获得了两所欧洲大学的学位。

在写这章的时候，我收到了以前班上一名德国学员的来信。这是一位德国贵族，他的祖先曾在德国贵族霍亨佐勒恩的帐下世代担任终身军官。他这封信是在一艘横渡大西洋的轮船上写的，讲了他运用这些规则的情况，怀着一种近乎宗教的热情。

还有一位学员，他是一位老纽约人，哈佛大学毕业，而且非常富有，有一个地毯公司。他说他在14个星期中通过这种方法学到的关于影响他人的艺术，比大学4年中所学到的还要多。很荒唐吗？可笑吗？难以置信吗？你当然可以不相信这种说法，但我只是如实地告诉你一位守旧的、成就卓著的哈佛毕业生1933年2月23日(星期四)晚上在纽约的雅尔俱乐部面对大约600人的公开演讲中所说的内容。

“和我们所应该取得的成就相比，”哈佛大学著名教授威廉·詹姆斯曾这样说道，“我们不过是半醒着。现在我们只利用了我们身心资源的一小部分。从广义上来说，人类生活在自身潜能

hundred people at the Yale Club in New York on the evening of Thursday, February 23, 1933.

"Compared to what we ought to be," said the famous Professor William James of Harvard, "compared to what we ought to be, we are only half awake. We are making use of only a small part of our physical and mental resources. Stating the thing broadly, the human individual thus lives far within his limits. He possesses powers of various sorts which he habitually fails to use."

Those powers which you "habitually fail to use"! The sole purpose of this book is to help you discover, develop and profit by those dormant and unused assets.

"Education," said Dr. John G. Hibben, former president of Princeton University, "is the ability to meet life's situations."

If by the time you have finished reading the first three chapters of this book—if you aren't then a little better equipped to meet life's situations, then I shall consider this book to be a total failure so far as you are concerned. For "the great aim of education," said Herbert Spencer, "is not knowledge but action."

And this is an action book.

DALE CARNEGIE(1936)

远远没有开发的狭小天地中。人类具有各种潜能,但却不曾开发和利用。"

开发你所拥有的"但却不曾利用的"的潜能！本书唯一的目的就是帮助你发现、发展、利用自身潜在的却又未曾利用的资源。

普林斯顿大学前任校长希本博士也说道:"教育才是应对生活中各种问题的有效手段。"

如果你读了这本书的前三章之后,还感到难以应对生活中的各种情况,那么我认为,这本书至少对你来说是完全失败的,因为斯宾塞曾说:"教育的伟大目的,不是知识,而是行动。"

这是一本教人如何行动的书。

戴尔·卡耐基(1936)

Nine Suggestions on How to Get the Most out of This Book

1. If you wish to get the most out of this book, there is one indispensable requirement, one essential infinitely more important than any rule or technique. Unless you have this one fundamental requisite, a thousand rules on how to study will avail little. And if you do have this cardinal endowment, then you can achieve wonders without reading any suggestions for getting the most out of a book.

What is this magic requirement? Just this: a deep, driving desire to learn, a vigorous determination to increase your ability to deal with people.

How can you develop such an urge? By constantly reminding yourself how important these principles are to you. Picture to yourself how their mastery will aid you in leading a richer, fuller, happier and more fulfilling life. Say to yourself over and over: "My popularity, my happiness and sense of worth depend to no small extent upon my skill in dealing with people."

2. Read each chapter rapidly at first to get a bird's-eye view of it. You will probably be tempted then to rush on to the next one. But don't—unless you are reading merely for entertainment. But if you are reading because you want to increase your skill in human relations, then go back and reread each chapter thoroughly. In the long run, this will mean saving time and getting results.

3. Stop frequently in your reading to think over what you are reading. Ask yourself just how and when you can apply each suggestion.

4. Read with a crayon, pencil, pen, magic marker or highlighter in your hand. When you come across a suggestion that you feel you can use, draw a line beside it. If it is a four-star suggestion, then underscore every sentence or highlight it, or mark it with "* * * *." Marking and underscoring a book makes it more interesting, and far easier to review rapidly.

5. I knew a woman who had been office manager for a large insurance concern for fifteen years.

从本书获得最大教益的九条建议

1. 如果你想通过本书获得最大教益，有一个必不可少的条件，一个比任何规则或技术都重要的基本条件。除非你具备了这种基本条件，否则即使再多的规则也毫无意义。假如你真的具备这种异常重要的天资，那么你将创造出奇迹，而不必去读书中提出来的最大限度地获益的建议。

这种奇妙的条件是什么？那就是深入学习的强烈欲望，一种提高你的为人处世能力的决心。

如何才能使这种欲望获得滋长的营养呢？那就是经常性地提醒自己这些原则对你多么重要。你可以不断地想象，如果能够自如地应用这些规则，将会使你的生活变得更加富有，更加多彩，更加快乐充实。要一而再、再而三地对自己说："我之所以受人欢迎，我之所以幸福，我的收入之所以增加，大部分都是因为我的为人处世的技巧。"

2. 首先快速阅读完每一章，以获得整体概念。然后你可能会急着读下一章，但是不要这样做——除非你只是为了消遣。如果你是为了提高自己的为人处世技巧，那么你应该再返回去，将读过的内容再详细阅读。这才是既省时间又能取得效果的好办法。

3. 阅读的时候经常停下来，思考自己所读的内容。还要问自己什么时候、如何运用各项建议。

4. 阅读时手里拿一支笔。当遇到一条你认为可以采用的建议时，就在旁边画一条线。如果这是一条极妙的建议，那么你还要在句子的下面划一道线或星号。这将使你的阅读更有意思，也更容易快速复习。

5. 我认识一个女士，她曾在某家大保险公司担任经理达 15 年之久。她每个月都要翻看公

Every month, she read all the insurance contracts her company had issued that month. Yes, she read many of the same contracts over month after month, year after year. Why? Because experience had taught her that that was the only way she could keep their provisions clearly in mind.

I once spent almost two years writing a book on public speaking and yet I found I had to keep going back over it from time to time in order to remember what I had written in my own book. The rapidity with which we forget is astonishing.

So, if you want to get a real, lasting benefit out of this book, don't imagine that skimming through it once will suffice. After reading it thoroughly, you ought to spend a few hours reviewing it every month. Keep it on your desk in front of you every day. Glance through it often. Keep constantly impressing yourself with the rich possibilities for improvement that still lie in the offing. Remember that the use of these principles can be made habitual only by a constant and vigorous campaign of review and application. There is no other way.

6. Bernard Shaw once remarked, "If you teach a man anything, he will never learn." Shaw was right. Learning is an active process. We learn by doing. So, if you desire to master the principles you are studying in this book, do something about them. Apply these rules at every opportunity. If you don't you will forget them quickly. Only knowledge that is used sticks in your mind.

You will probably find it difficult to apply these suggestions all the time. I know because I wrote the book, and yet frequently I found it difficult to apply everything I advocated. For example, when you are displeased, it is much easier to criticize and condemn than it is to try to understand the other person's viewpoint. It is frequently easier to find fault than to find praise. It is more natural to talk about what you want than to talk about what the other person wants. And so on. So, as you read this book, remember that you are not merely trying to acquire information. You are attempting to form new habits. Ah yes, you are attempting a new way of life. That will require time and persistence and daily application.

So refer to these pages often. Regard this as a working handbook on human relations; and whenever you are confronted with some specific problem—such as handling a child, winning your spouse to your way of thinking, or satisfying an irritated customer—hesitate about doing the natural thing, the impulsive thing. This is usually wrong. Instead, turn to these pages and review the

司当月签订的保险合同。是的，她每个月、每年都会这样翻看同样的保险合同。为什么她要这样做呢?因为经验告诉她，这是让她清楚地记住保险条款的唯一有效的方法。

有一次，我曾花了将近两年的时间写一本当众演讲的书。但是我发现，为了记住我在书中写了些什么，必须经常性地返回去看。我们遗忘的速度实在太惊人了！

所以，如果你想从本书获得真实持久的教益，就不要以为匆匆浏览一遍就管用了。在仔细阅读之后，你每个月还应该花几个小时温习。把它放在你每天用的桌子上，经常看看它。这样你才会注意到深藏在你身体内部的、可以大大改进的潜能。要记住，只有通过长期深切地温习与实践，你才会习惯性地应用这些原则。除此之外没有其他办法。

6. 萧伯纳曾说："如果你是去教某个人做某事，他永远学不会。"他说得很对。学习是一个自动的过程，我们总是在一边做一边学。因此，如果你想掌握从本书学到的原则，那么只要有机会，就应该将所学知识应用到实践中去；否则，你将很快遗忘它们。记住，只有用过的知识才会给你的脑海留下深刻的印象。

你或许会觉得，要想每时每刻都应用这些原则非常困难。我当然知道这一点。在我写这本书的时候，我也觉得很难按照我提出来的每一项建议去做。例如，当别人令你不高兴的时候，批评和斥责显然要比了解对方的观点更加容易。挑毛病总比称赞要容易得多；而且谈论你自己所需要的远比谈论对方所需要的要自然得多。其他的例子也很多。所以，你在读这本书时，不要忘了你不是仅需要获得一些知识，更需要养成一种新的习惯。你是在尝试一种新的生活方法，这需要时间、毅力和亲身实践。

所以要经常看这本书，把它当作一本为人处世的实用手册，无论你在什么时候遇到特殊问题——例如管教孩子、让你的配偶同意你的观点，或者让一个愤怒的顾客心满意足——都不要有冲动之举，这通常是不对的。相反，你可以求助于本书，看你划了重点的段落。然后试

paragraphs you have underscored.Then try these new ways and watch them achieve magic for you.

7. Offer your spouse,your child or some business associate a dime or a dollar every time he or she catches you violating a certain principle.Make a lively game out of mastering these rules.

8. The president of an important Wall Street bank once descried,in a talk before one of my classes,a highly efficient system he used for self-improvement.This man had little formal schooling; yet he had become one of the most important financiers in America,and he confessed that he owed most of his success to the constant application of his homemade system.This is what he does,I'll put it in his own words as accurately as I can remember.

"For years I have kept an engagement book showing all the appointments I had during the day. My family never made any plans for me on Saturday night,for the family knew that I devoted a part of each Saturday evening to the illuminating process of self-examination and review and appraisal. After dinner I went off by myself,opened my engagement book,and thought over all the interviews, discussions and meetings that had taken place during the week.I asked myself:

'What mistakes did I make that time?' 'What did I do that was right—and in what way could I have improved my performance?'

'What lessons can I learn from that experience?'

"I often found that this weekly review made me very unhappy.I was frequently astonished at my own blunders.Of course,as the years passed,these blunders became less frequent.Sometimes I was inclined to pat myself on the back a little after one of these sessions.This system of self-analysis,self-education,continued year after year,did more for me than any other one thing I have ever attempted.

"It helped me improve my ability to make decisions—and it aided me enormously in all my contacts with people.I cannot recommend it too highly."

Why not use a similar system to check up on your application of the principles discussed in this book? If you do,two things will result.

First,you will find yourself engaged in an educational process that is both intriguing and priceless.

Second,you will find that your ability to meet and deal with people will grow enormously.

着应用这些方法,观察它们为你创造的奇迹。

7. 每次当你的配偶、孩子或同事发现你没有遵守某一原则时,不妨给他一点钱,以示对自己的处罚。这将使得掌握这些规则成为一项有趣的游戏。

8. 华尔街一家重要银行的董事长曾在我的一个班上发表过一次演讲，介绍他是如何自我完善的。这个人接受的正规教育很少,但他现在是美国最重要的金融家之一。他认为自己之所以成功,大部分都应该归功于经常运用自我克制。下面就是他的做法,我凭记忆用他自己的话叙述如下:

"我这些年一直保存着一本约会的小册子,上面记录了我所有的约会。我的家人从不会在星期六晚上与我订约会,因为他们知道我会在每个星期六的晚上进行自省。晚饭之后,我一个人关在房间,翻开我的约会簿,回想这一周所有的会谈、讨论及集会。我会问自己:

"'我做错了什么?''我做的哪些是对的?怎样才能有所改进?'

"'从这些经验中我能获得什么教训?'

"我常常发现,这种每周的自我反省让我很不愉快。我对自己的错误常常感到痛心。但是几年之后,这些错误也就不怎么出现了。现在,有时我在这种自省之后,会感到极大的宽慰。这样长期坚持下来,这种自我分析、自我教育的方法,比我所试用过的任何方法都更有效。

"这种方法帮助我增强了决断能力——对我的为人处世也有很大的帮助。我非常乐意推荐这种方法。"

为什么不用类似的方法,来检验你是如何应用本书所介绍的原则的?如果你这样做,就会有两种效果:

第一,你将会发现,自己所接受的是一种有趣而宝贵的教育。

第二,你将会发现,自己的为人处世能力将大大提高。

9. You will find at the end of this book several blank pages on which you should record your triumphs in the application of these principles. Be specific. Give names, dates, results. Keeping such a record will inspire you to greater efforts; and how fascinating these entries will be when you chance upon them some evening years from now!

In order to get the most out of this book:

a. Develop a deep, driving desire to master the principles of human relations.

b. Read each chapter twice before going on to the next one.

c. As you read, stop frequently to ask yourself how you can apply each suggestion.

d. Underscore each important idea.

e. Review this book each month.

f. Apply these principles at every opportunity. Use this volume as a working handbook to help you solve your daily problems.

g. Make a lively game out of your learning by offering some friends a dime or a dollar every time he or she catches you violating one of these principles.

h. Check up each week on the progress you are making. Ask yourself what mistakes you have made, what improvement, what lessons you have learned for the future.

i. Keep notes in the back of this book showing how and when you have applied these principles.

9. 你将会发现,本书最后有几页白纸,你可以写下运用这些原则所取得的成果。注意将姓名、日期和结果写清楚。这样将会激励你更加努力。当你在多年之后再翻看这些时,将会觉得其乐无穷!

为了从本书获得最大教益:

a. 培养一种深刻而强烈的、掌握为人处世原则的欲望。

b. 在阅读下一章之前,将前面的章节读两遍。

c. 阅读的时候,要经常停下来问自己,如何才能运用各项建议。

d. 在每个重要的观点旁边做记号。

e. 每个月温习本书一次。

f. 抓住每一个可以运用这些原则的机会。将本书作为帮助你解决日常问题的实用手册。

g. 每当你违反某一项原则而被你的朋友抓到时,给他一点钱,使你的学习成为一种活泼有趣的游戏。

h. 每个星期对你的进步检查一次。问自己曾犯了什么错,有什么改进,有什么教训,将来该如何做。

i. 在书后面做记录,写下你是在什么时候以及如何应用这些原则的。

Part One
Fundamental Techniques in Handling People

1 "If You Want to Gather Honey, Don't Kick over the Beehive"

On May 7,1931,the most sensational manhunt New York City had ever known had come to its climax.After weeks of search, "Two Gun"Crowley—the killer,the gunman who didn't smoke or drink—was at bay,trapped in his sweetheart's apartment on West End Avenue.

One hundred and fifty policemen and detectives laid siege to his top—floor hideaway.They Chopped holes in the roof;they tried to smoke out Crowley,the "Cop killer,"With tear gas.Then they mounted their machine guns on surrounding buildings,and for more than all hour one of New York's fine residential areas reverberated with the crack of pistol fire and the rat-tat-tat of machine guns.Crowley,crouching behind ail over-stuffed chair,fired incessantly at the police. Ten thousand excited people watched the battle.Nothing like it had ever been seen before on the sidewalks of New York.

When Crowley was captured,Police Commissioner E. P.Mulrooney declared that the two-gun desperado was one of the most dangerous criminals ever encountered in the history of New York. "He will kill,"said the Commissioner,"at the drop of a feather."

But how did "Two Gun" Crowley regard himself? We know,because while the police were firing into his apartment,he wrote a letter addressed "To whom it may concern." And,as he wrote, the blood flowing from his wounds left a crimson trail on the paper.In his letter Crowley said, "Under my coat is a weary heart,but a kind one—one that would do nobody any harm."

A short time before this,Crowley had been having a necking party with his girl friend on a

第一篇 人际交往的基本技巧

第1章 要想采蜜,就不要踢翻蜂巢

1931年5月7日,在纽约市发生了一场有史以来最让人震惊的剿匪事件。经过好几个星期的侦察,"双枪手"科洛雷——一个烟酒不沾的凶手——陷入了重围,被包围在西尾街他情人的公寓中。

150名警察和侦探包围了他在顶楼的藏身之处。他们在屋顶上打了个洞,试图使用催泪瓦斯将这位"杀害警察的人"熏出来。然后他们在四周的建筑物上架起了机关枪,在一个多小时里,在纽约这个环境最优美的住宅小区中,手枪和机关枪声持续不断。科洛雷躲在一张堆满了杂物的椅子后面,不断地向警察开火。一万多名惊恐万状的老百姓目击了这场枪战。在纽约的人行道上还从来没有出现过这种情况。

在科洛雷被抓到的时候,警察总监马洛尼说:这位暴徒是纽约有史以来最危险的罪犯之一。"他杀人,"总监说,"连眼睛都不眨一下。"

但是"双枪手"科洛雷又是如何看待自己的呢?这一点我们已经知道了,因为在警察朝他的公寓开火的时候,他写了一封公开信。在写这封信时,鲜血从他的伤口涌了出来,染红了信纸。他在信中说:"在我的衣服之下是一颗疲惫的心,但这颗心是仁慈的——它不会伤害任何人。"

此前不久,科洛雷在长岛的一条乡村公路上和他的女友调情。突然有一个警察朝他的汽车

country road out on Long Island.Suddenly a policeman walked up to the car and said,"Let me see your license."

Without saying a word,Crowley drew his gun and cut the policeman down with a shower of lead.As the dying officer fell,Crowley leaped out of the car,grabbed the officer's revolver,and fired another bullet into the prostrate body.And that was the killer who said,"Under my coat is a weary heart,but a kind one—one that would do nobody any harm."

Crowley was sentenced to the electric chair.When he arrived at the death house in Sing Sing, did he say,"This is what I get for killing people"? No,he said:"This is what I get for defending myself."

The point of the story is this,"Two Gun" Crowley didn't blame himself for anything.

Is that an unusual attitude among criminals? If you think so,listen to this:

"I have spent the best years of my life giving people the lighter pleasures,helping them have a good time,and all I get is abuse,the existence of a hunted man."

That's Al Capone speaking.Yes,America's most notorious Public Enemy—the most sinister gang leader who ever shot up Chicago.Capone didn't condemn himself.He actually regarded himself as a public benefactor—an unappreciated and misunderstood public benefactor.

And so did Dutch Schultz before he crumpled up under gangster bullets in Newark.Dutch Schultz,one of New York's most notorious rats,said in a newspaper interview that he was a public benefactor.And he believed it.

I have had some interesting correspondence with Lewis Lawes,who was warden of New York's infamous Sing Sing prison for many years,on this subject,and he declared that "few of the criminals in Sing Sing regard themselves as bad men.They are just as human as you and I.So they rationalize,they explain.They can tell you why they had to crack a safe or be quick on the trigger finger.Most of them attempt by a form of reasoning,fallacious or logical,to justify their antisocial acts even to themselves, consequently stoutly maintaining that they should never have been imprisoned at all."

If A1 Capone,"Two Gun" Crowley,Dutch Schultz,and the desperate men and women behind prison walls don't blame themselves for anything—what about the people with whom you and I come in contact?

走过来说:“让我看看你的驾照。”

科洛雷二话不说就拔出了手枪,向那位警察连开几枪。当警察倒地之后,科洛雷跳出汽车,抓起警察的枪,又朝着俯卧的尸体连开数枪。这就是那位声称“在我的衣服之下是一颗疲惫的心,但这颗心是仁慈的——它不会伤害任何人”的凶手。

科洛雷被判坐电椅处死。当他被押到星星监狱死刑室时,他是否说过“这就是因为杀人而得到的下场”呢?没有,他说的是:“这就是我为了保卫自己而得到的结果。”

可见,“双枪手”科洛雷并没有觉得自己有任何不对的地方。

这是犯罪分子一种不寻常的态度吗? 如果你是这样想的,请听这段话:

“我将我一生中最美好的时光,都奉献给了为别人提供轻松的娱乐,帮助他们得到快乐上。而我所得到的只是耻辱,一种被捕者的生活。”

这就是阿尔·卡普的自白。是的,他是美国最臭名昭著的公敌——一位横行于芝加哥的最凶狠的匪徒。他从不责怪自己。他真的自以为是一个对公众有益的大好人——一个不被人们感激,反而被人误会的大好人。

苏尔兹,纽约最臭名昭著的罪犯之一,当他在纽瓦克被匪徒枪击倒地之前,也是这样的。在一次和新闻记者的谈话中,他声称自己是一个对大众有恩的人。而且他对此深信不疑。

就此问题, 我曾和星星监狱的监狱长刘易斯进行过几次有趣的通信。他说:“在星星监狱,几乎没有哪个罪犯会认为自己是坏人。他们和你我一样,同样是人。因此他们会为自己辩护和解释。他们会告诉你为什么他们必须撬开保险箱,为什么会扣动扳机。而且他们大多数人都有意识地以一种错误的逻辑来为自己的反社会行为作辩护, 都坚称自己不应该被关人监狱。”

如果阿尔·卡普、“双枪手”科洛雷、苏尔兹以及监狱中的那些亡命之徒,他们都毫不自责,

John Wanamaker, founder of the stores that bear his name, once confessed, "I learned thirty years ago that it is foolish to scold. I have enough trouble overcoming my own limitations without fretting over the fact that God has not seen fit to distribute evenly the gift of intelligence."

Wanamaker learned this lesson early, but I personally had to blunder through this old world for a third of a century before it even began to dawn upon me that ninety-nine times out of a hundred, people don't criticize themselves for anything, no matter how wrong it may be.

B.F.Skinner, the world-famous psychologist, proved through his experiments that an animal rewarded for good behavior will learn much more rapidly and retain what it learns far more effectively than an animal punished for bad behavior. Later studies have shown that the same applies to humans. By criticizing, we do not make lasting changes and often incur resentment.

Hans Selye, another great psychologist, said, "As much as we thirst for approval, we dread condemnation."

The resentment that criticism engenders can demoralize employees, family members and friends, and still not correct the situation that has been condemned.

George B.Johnston of Enid, Oklahoma, is the safety coordinator for an engineering company. One of his responsibilities is to see that employees wear their hard hats whenever they are on the job in the field. He reported that whenever he came across workers who were not wearing hard hats, he would tell them with a lot of authority of the regulation and that they must comply. As a result he would get sullen acceptance, and often after he left, the workers would remove the hats.

He decided to try a different approach. The next time he found some of the workers not wearing their hard hat, he asked if the hats were uncomfortable or did not fit properly. Then he reminded the men in a pleasant tone of voice that the hat was designed to protect them from injury and suggested that it always be worn on the job. The result was increased compliance with the regulation with no resentment or emotional upset.

You will find examples of the futility of criticism bristling on a thousand pages of history. Take, for example, the famous quarrel between Theodore Roosevelt and President Taft—a quarrel that split the Republican party, put Woodrow Wilson in the White House, and wrote bold, luminous lines across the First World War and altered the flow of history. Let's review the facts quickly. When

那么我们所接触的人又如何呢？

华纳梅克百货公司的创始人约翰·华纳梅克曾经承认："我在30年前就已经明白，批评别人是愚蠢的。我并不埋怨上帝对智慧的分配不均，因为要克服自己的缺陷都已经非常困难了。"

华纳梅克早就领悟到了这一点，但是我自己在这个古老的世界中探索了30多年，才有所醒悟：一个人不论做错了什么事，100次中有99次不会自责。

世界著名心理学家史京纳用实验证明，一只动物如果在学习方面表现良好就可以得到奖励，要比学习不好就受到斥责的动物学得更快，而且能够记住所学的东西。进一步研究还显示，人类有同样的情况。我们采取批评的方法并不能使别人永久改变，相反只会引起嫉恨。

另一位伟大的心理学家席勒也说道："我们总是渴望赞扬，同样我们也害怕指责。"

批评所引起的嫉恨，只会降低员工、家人以及朋友的士气和情感，同时指责的事情也不会有任何改善。

俄克拉荷马州的乔治·约翰逊是一家工程公司的安全检查员，其职责之一就是检查工人在野外工作时戴没戴安全帽。他说，每当他看见工人不戴安全帽时，他就会以权威的口气命令工人必须改正。结果工人很不高兴，常常是他一走开，工人就会摘掉帽子。

他决定改变方式。当他再次看到工人不戴安全帽时，就会问是否是戴帽子不舒服，或者是不合适。然后他又以愉快的口气提醒工人，安全帽是保护他们不受伤害的，并建议工人在工作时戴上安全帽。这样的效果大大增加，再也没有抵触或不高兴的工人了。

批评毫无益处，你会发现这种例子在历史上多得是。例如在西奥多·罗斯福和塔夫脱总统之间就有一场著名的争论——这场争论分裂了共和党，使威尔逊入主白宫，并在第一次世界大战中写下了辉煌的一页。让我们来简单地回顾这一情况：1908年，当西奥多·罗斯福总统走出白宫的时候，他让塔夫脱当了总统，自己则去非洲猎狮。当他回来的时候，暴跳如雷。他批评塔

Theodore Roosevelt stepped out of the White House in 1908, he supported Taft, who was elected President. Then Theodore Roosevelt went off to Africa to shoot lions. When he returned, he exploded. He denounced Taft for his conservatism, tried to secure the nomination for a third term himself, formed the Bull Moose party, and all but demolished the G.O.P. In the election that followed, William Howard Taft and the Republican party carried only two states—Vermont and Utah. The most disastrous defeat the party had ever known.

Theodore Roosevelt blamed Taft, but did President Taft blame himself? Of course not, with tears in his eyes, Taft said, "I don't see how I could have done any differently from what I have."

Who was to blame? Roosevelt or Taft? Frankly, I don't know, and I don't care. The point I am trying to make is that all of Theodore Roosevelt's criticism didn't persuade Taft that he was wrong. It merely made Taft strive to justify himself and to reiterate with tears in his eyes, "I don't see how I could have done any differently from what I have."

Or, take the Teapot Dome oil scandal. It kept the newspapers ringing with indignation in the early 1920s. It rocked the nation! Within the memory of living men, nothing like it had ever happened before in American public life. Here are the bare facts of the scandal: Albert B. Fall, Secretary of the interior in Harding's cabinet, was entrusted with the leasing of government oil reserves at Elk Hill and Teapot Dome—oil reserves that had been set aside for the future use of the Navy. Did Secretary Fall permit competitive bidding? No sir. He handed the fat, juicy contract outright to his friend Edward L. Doheny. And what did Doheny do? He gave Secretary Fall what he was pleased to call a "loan" of one hundred thousand dollars. Then, in a high-handed manner, Secretary Fall ordered United States Marines into the district to drive off competitors whose adjacent wells were sapping oil out of the Elk Hill reserves. These competitors, driven off their ground at the ends of guns and bayonets, rushed into court—and blew the lid off the Teapot Dome scandal. A stench arose so vile that it mined the Harding Administration, nauseated an entire nation, threatened to wreck the Republican party, and put Albert B. Fall behind prison bars.

Fall was condemned viciously—condemned as few men in public life have ever been. Did he repent? Never! Years later Herbert Hoover intimated in a public speech that President Harding's death had been due to mental anxiety and worry because a friend had betrayed him. When Mrs. Fall

夫脱总统过于保守，试图使自己第三次当选总统，就组建了一个公麋党。但是这几乎毁了共和党。在这次选举中，塔夫脱和共和党只得到两个州的选票——佛蒙特州和犹他州。这是共和党的空前惨败。

西奥多·罗斯福责怪塔夫脱，但是塔夫脱对自己是否责怪呢？当然没有，而是眼中饱含着泪水为自己辩解道："我不知道我怎样做才能够和以前有所不同。"

这件事得怪谁呢？是罗斯福，还是塔夫脱？老实说我也不知道，而且我也不用去管它。现在我要指出来的是，西奥多·罗斯福所有的批评都不能让塔夫脱承认自己错了。这只能让塔夫脱竭力为自己辩护，而且眼中饱含着泪水说："我不知道我怎样做才能够和以前有所不同。"

或者再拿"茶壶盖油田"舞弊案来说吧。大家还记得这个案子吗？舆论为此批评了许多年，整个国家都为之震惊。在这代人的记忆中，在美国政坛上还没有出现过这类丑闻。这桩赤裸裸的丑闻是这样的：哈定总统的内政部长弗尔负责主管政府在阿尔克山丘和茶壶盖地区油田的出租——这块油田是保留给海军将来使用的。弗尔部长是不是进行了公开招标呢？没有。他干脆把这份优厚的合同交给了他的朋友杜亨尼。而杜亨尼干了些什么呢？他给了弗尔部长10万美元的"贷款"。然后，弗尔部长又令美国海军进入该区，以高压手段把那些竞争者赶走，免得他们位于周围的油井吸干阿尔克山丘的原油。这些竞争者被强行赶走了，他们只好走上法庭，揭发茶壶盖油田舞弊案。结果这件事的影响非常恶劣，几乎毁了哈定总统的政府，使整个国家极其反感，共和党也几乎垮台，弗尔部长则锒铛入狱。

弗尔部长遭到了公众的谴责，以前很少有公众人物遭到这样的谴责。他反悔了吗？没有！许多年以后，胡佛总统在一次公开演讲中暗示哈定总统之死是由于精神刺激和忧虑，因为一个朋友出卖了他。弗尔的夫人听到后，从椅子上跳了起来，她大叫大嚷，攥紧了拳头尖叫道："什么？哈定是被弗尔出卖的吗？不，我的丈夫从来没有辜负过任何人。即使这整座房间都堆满了黄金，

heard that, she sprang from her chair, she wept, she shook her fists at fate and screamed, "What! Harding betrayed by Fall? No! My husband never betrayed anyone. This whole house full of gold would not tempt my husband to do wrong. He is the one who has been betrayed and led to the slaughter and crucified."

There you are; human nature in action, wrongdoers, blaming everybody but themselves. We are all like that. So when you and I are tempted to criticize someone tomorrow, let's remember Al Capone, "Two Gun" Crowley and Albert Fall. Let's realize that criticisms are like homing pigeons. They always return home. Let's realize that the person we are going to correct and condemn will probably justify himself or herself, and condemn us in return; or, like the gentle Taft, will say, "I don't see how I could have done any differently from what I have."

On the morning of April 15, 1865, Abraham Lincoln lay dying in a hall bedroom of a cheap lodging house directly across the street from Ford's Theater, where John Wilkes Booth had shot him. Lincoln's long body lay stretched diagonally across a sagging bed that was too short for him. A cheap reproduction of Rosa Bonheur's famous painting The Horse Fair hung above the bed, and a dismal gas jet flickered yellow light.

As Lincoln lay dying, Secretary of War Stanton said, "There lies the most perfect ruler of men that the world has ever seen."

What was the secret of Lincoln's success in dealing with people? I studied the life of Abraham Lincoln for ten years and devoted all of three years to writing and rewriting a book entitled Lincoln the Unknown. I believe I have made as detailed and exhaustive a study of Lincoln's personality and home life as it is possible for any being to make. I made a special study of Lincoln's method of dealing with people. Did he indulge in criticism? Oh, yes. As a young man in the Pigeon Creek Valley of Indiana, he not only criticized but he wrote letters and poems ridiculing people and dropped these letters on the country roads where they were sure to be found. One of these letters aroused resentments that burned for a lifetime.

Even after Lincoln had become a practicing lawyer in Springfield, Illinois, he attacked his opponents openly in letters published in the newspapers. But he did this just once too often.

In the autumn of 1842 he ridiculed a vain, pugnacious politician by the name of James Shields.

都不会让我的丈夫干任何蠢事。他才是被人出卖而被钉上十字架的。"

你看,这就是人类的天性!做错了事的人只知道责怪别人,绝不会责怪自己。我们都是这样。因此,当你和我以后想要批评别人的时候,请记住阿尔·卡普、"双枪手"科洛雷和弗尔。我们要明白,批评就好比家养的鸽子,它们总是要飞回家的。我们还应该清楚,我们所要纠正和指责的人总是会为他们作自我辩护,并反过来指责我们;或者他们会像温和的塔夫脱总统那样,会说:"我不知道我该怎样做才能和以前有所不同。"

1865 年 4 月 15 日早晨,林肯奄奄一息地躺在福特戏院对面一家简陋公寓的卧室中,他在戏院遭到了布思的枪袭。林肯那瘦长的身躯斜躺在一张松垮的床上,这床对他来说太小了。在床的上方挂的是波纳尔的名画《马市》的廉价复制品,一盏煤气灯散发出惨淡的黄晕光圈。

就在林肯即将咽气时,陆军部长史丹顿说:"这里躺着的,是人类有史以来最完美的元首。"

林肯为人处世的成功秘诀是什么呢?我曾花了 10 年时间研究林肯的一生,并用了整整 3 年时间撰写和修改了一本名叫《世人所未知的林肯》的书。我相信我已尽了一切可能,对林肯的性格及家庭生活作了详细透彻的研究。而对于林肯的为人处世之道,我更是作了特殊研究。他是否喜欢动不动就批评别人?啊,确实是这样。在他年轻的时候住在印第安纳的鸽溪谷时,他不仅喜欢指责别人,还写信做诗来挖苦别人,把这些信扔在一定会被人发现的路上。其中有一封信竟致使对方终生都痛恨他。

即使林肯在伊里诺伊州的斯普林菲尔德镇当上律师之后,他还在报纸上发表文章,公开攻击他的对手。不过这给他也带来了不少麻烦。

1842 年秋天,林肯在《斯普林菲尔德日报》发表了一封匿名信,讥讽一位自高自大的政客詹姆斯·谢尔兹。所有读过它的人都捧腹大笑。谢尔兹是个敏感而自负的人,恼怒万分。他一查出是谁写的这封信之后,立即跳上马去找林肯,提出要和他决斗。林肯不想打架,反对决斗,但

Lincoln lampooned him through an anonymous letter published in the *Springfield Journal*. The town roared with laughter.Shields, sensitive and proud, boiled with indignation.He found out who wrote the letter, leaped on his horse, started after Lincoln, and challenged him to fight a duel.Lincoln didn't want to fight.He was opposed to dueling, but he couldn't get out of it and save his honor.He was given the choice of weapons.Since he had very long arms, he chose cavalry broadswords and took lessons in sword fighting from a West Point graduate; and, on the appointed day, he and Shields met on a sandbar in the Mississippi River, prepared to fight to the death; but, at the last minute, their seconds interrupted and stopped the duel.

That was the most lurid personal incident in Lincoln's life.It taught him an invaluable lesson in the art of dealing with people.Never again did he write an insulting letter.Never again did he ridicule anyone.And from that time on, he almost never criticized anybody for anything.

Time after time, during the Civil War, Lincoln put a new general at the head of the Army of the Potomac, and each one in turn—McClellan, Pope, Burnside, Hooker, Meade—blundered tragically and drove Lincoln to pacing the floor in despair.Half the nation savagely condemned these incompetent generals, but Lincoln, "with malice toward none, with charity for all," held his peace. One of his favorite quotations was "Judge not, that ye be not judged."

And when Mrs.Lincoln and others spoke harshly of the southern people, Lincoln replied, "Don't criticize them; they are just what we would be under similar circumstances."

Yet if any man ever had occasion to criticize, surely it was Lincoln.Let's take just one illustration:

The Battle of Gettysburg was fought during the first three days of July 1863.During the night of July 4, Lee began to retreat southward while storm clouds deluged the country with rain.When Lee reached the Potomac with his defeated army, he found a swollen, impassable river in front of him, and a victorious Union Army behind him.Lee was in a trap.He couldn't escape.Lincoln saw that. Here was a golden, heaven-sent opportunity—the opportunity to capture Lee's army and end the war immediately.So, with a surge of high hope, Lincoln ordered Meade not to call a council of war but to attack Lee immediately.Lincoln telegraphed his orders and then sent a special messenger to Meade demanding immediate action.

为了保全面子只好接受决斗的要求。对手让他选择武器。由于林肯双臂较长，他就选择了骑兵用的长剑，并向西点军校一位毕业生学剑术。决斗那天，他和谢尔兹在密西西比河的一个沙滩上对峙，准备决战至死。但就在决斗即将开始的最后一分钟，他们的同伴阻止了这场决斗。

这是林肯人生当中最难堪的一件事。这给他在为人处世方面上了宝贵的一课。从此以后，他再也没有写过任何侮辱他人的信，也不再讥笑别人了。从那时起，他不再因为任何事而批评别人。

在美国内战期间，林肯屡屡委派新的将领统帅波多马克的军队作战，麦克里兰、波普、伯恩塞德、胡克、米德——全都相继惨败。这使得林肯在房间里绝望地来回走动。全国有一半的人都在痛骂这些不中用的将军，但林肯却始终一声不吭，不作任何表态。他最喜欢引用的一句格言是"不要议论别人，别人才不会议论你"。

当林肯夫人和其他人都在非议南方佬时，林肯回答道："不要批评他们。如果我们处在他们同样的情况下，也会跟他们一样的。"

可是如果说谁有资格批评的话，这个人肯定是林肯。我们来看一个例子：

葛底斯堡战役发生在1863年7月的头3天。7月4日晚，南方的李将军开始向南撤退。当时乌云笼罩，大雨倾盆而下。当李将军率领败军之师退到波多马克时，一条大河拦住了去路，难以通行；而在他身后则是乘胜追击的北方联军。李将军已经被围困了，无路可逃。林肯看到这正是天赐良机——可以俘获李将军的军队并立即结束战争。于是他满怀希望地命令米德将军，不必召开军事会议，而是立即进攻李将军。林肯用电报下命令，又派出特使，要求立即行动。

而米德将军又是怎么做的呢?他所做的与林肯命令的恰恰相反。他违背了林肯的命令，召开了一次军事会议。他一再拖延，犹豫不决。他还打电话以各种借口来解释。他甚至一口回绝了进攻李将军。最后，河水退却，李将军和他的军队从波多马克逃走了。

And what did General Meade do? He did the very opposite of what he was told to do.He called a council of war in direct violation of Lincoln's orders.He hesitated.He procrastinated.He telegraphed all manner of excuses.He refused point-blank to attack Lee.Finally the waters receded and Lee escaped over the Potomac with his forces.

Lincoln was furious, "What does this mean?" Lincoln cried to his son Robert. "Great God! What does this mean? We had them within our grasp, and had only to stretch forth our hands and they were ours; yet nothing that I could say or do could make the army move.Under the circumstances, almost any general could have defeated Lee.If I had gone up there, I could have whipped him myself."

In bitter disappointment, Lincoln sat down and wrote Meade this letter.And remember, at this period of his life Lincoln was extremely conservative and restrained in his phraseology.So this letter coming from Lincoln in 1863 was tantamount to the severest rebuke.

My dear General,

I do not believe you appreciate the magnitude of the misfortune involved in Lee's escape.He was within our easy grasp, and to have closed upon him would, in connection with our other late successes, have ended the war.As it is, the war will be prolonged indefinitely.If you could not safely attack Lee last Monday, how can you possibly do so south of the river, when you can take with you very few—no more than two-thirds of the force you then had in hand? It would be unreasonable to expect and I do not expect that you can now effect much.Your golden opportunity is gone, and I am distressed measurably because of it.

What do you suppose Meade did when he read the letter?

Meade never saw that letter.Lincoln never mailed it.It was found among his papers after his death.

My guess is—and this is only a guess—that after writing that letter, Lincoln looked out of the window and said to himself, "Just a minute.Maybe I ought not to be so hasty.It is easy enough for me to sit here in the quiet of the White House and order Meade to attack; but if I had been up at Gettysburg, and if I had seen as much blood as Meade has seen during the last week, and if my ears had been pierced with the screams and shrieks of the wounded and dying, maybe I wouldn't be so

林肯异常恼怒。"这是什么意思?"林肯朝儿子罗伯特大声叫嚷。"天啊! 这是什么意思?敌军已落入我们掌心,只需一伸手,他们就会完蛋了! 但我不论说什么做什么,却不能让军队前进一步。在这种形势下,几乎任何一位将军都能击败李将军。如果我在那里,我自己就可以消灭他!"

在痛苦失望之余,林肯坐下来给米德将军写了封信。要记住,林肯这时已经非常克制自己的脾气了。因此林肯这封写于 1863 年的信算是最严厉的斥责了。

我亲爱的将军:

我想你肯定体会不到李将军的逃脱所带来的严重不幸。本来他已经处于我们的绝对掌控之中,如果抓住了他,再加上最近我们在其他方面的胜利,战争就可以结束了。可是现在,战争恐怕会无限期拖延。假如你不能在上周一成功地击败李将军,你又怎么能在渡河之后进攻他?因为那时你手中的兵力可能不到现在的2/3。期盼你会成功是不明智的,我已不再期盼你会做得更好。你已经失去了大好时机,我深感痛惜。

你猜猜米德读了这封信后会是什么反应?

结果米德一直没有看到这封信,因为林肯并没有将它寄出去。林肯遇刺身亡后,从他的文件中找到了这封信。

我猜想——这仅仅是猜想——林肯在写完这封信后,向窗外远望,自言自语道:"等等。也许我不该这么着急。我坐在这宁静的白宫中,命令米德进攻是件很容易的事;但我当时如果到了葛底斯堡,如果我也和米德上周一样见过遍地鲜血,如果我的耳边也听到了伤亡士兵的哀号和呻吟,也许我不会急着进攻了。如果我的性格和米德一样柔弱,我的做法可能会与他相同。无论如何,现在生米已经煮成熟饭了。如果我寄出这封信,固然可以发泄我的不快,但米德不会为自己辩护吗?他甚至会反过来斥责我。这将会产生厌恶心理,损害他的军队统帅的威信,甚至会使他干脆辞职不干了。"

anxious to attack either.If I had Meade's timid temperament, perhaps I would have done just what he had done.Anyhow, it is water under the bridge now.If I send this letter, it will relieve my feelings, but it will make Meade try to justify himself.It will make him condemn me.It will arouse hard feelings, impair all his further usefulness as a commander, and perhaps force him to resign from the army."

So, as I have already said, Lincoln put the letter aside, for he had learned by bitter experience that sharp criticisms and rebukes almost invariably end in futility.

Theodore Roosevelt said that when he, as President, was confronted with a perplexing problem, he used to lean back and look up at a large painting of Lincoln which hung above his desk in the White House and ask himself, "What would Lincoln do if he were in my shoes? How would he solve this problem?"

The next time we are tempted to admonish somebody, let's pull a five-dollar bill out of our pocket, look at Lincoln's picture on the bill, and ask "How would Lincoln handle this problem if he had it?"

Mark Twain lost his temper occasionally and wrote letters that turned the paper brown.For example, he once wrote to a man who had aroused his ire: "The thing for you is a burial permit.You have only to speak and I will see that you get it." On another occasion he wrote to an editor about a proofreader's attempts to "improve my spelling and punctuation." He ordered: "Set the matter according to my copy hereafter and see that the proofreader retains his suggestions in the mush of his decayed brain."

The writing of these stinging letters made Mark Twain feel better.They allowed him to blow off steam, and the letters didn't do any real harm, because Mark's wife secretly lifted them out of the mail.They were never sent.

Do you know someone you would like to change and regulate and improve? Good! That is fine.I am all in favor of it.But why not begin on yourself?From a purely selfish standpoint, that is a lot more profitable than trying to improve others—yes, and a lot less dangerous. "Don't complain about the snow on your neighbor's roof," said Confucius, "when your own doorstep is unclean."

When I was still young and trying hard to impress people, I wrote a foolish letter to Richard Harding Davis, an author who once loomed large on the literary horizon of America.I was preparing

于是，就像我上面所说的，林肯将信放在一边，因为他已从痛苦的经验中体会到：尖刻的批评和斥责是无济于事的。

西奥多·罗斯福总统曾说，在他当总统时，只要碰到难以解决的问题，他总是往后一靠，抬头仰望他白宫办公室墙上挂着的林肯巨幅画像，问他自己："如果林肯处在我的困境中，他会怎么办?他将怎么解决这个问题?"

当你下次想要批评某人的时候，就从口袋中掏出一张 5 美元的钞票来，凝视上面的林肯头像，然后问："如果林肯遇到这种问题，他会如何处理呢?"

马克·吐温常常会大发脾气，写的信足以烧掉信纸。例如，他有一次写信给一位让他生气的人："你想要得到的应该是死亡人葬书。只要你开口，我一定会帮你搞到。"又有一次他写信给一位编辑，提到有一位校对人员企图"改正我的拼写和标点"，他以命令的口气写道："以后这种情况必须按我的底稿做，而且让那位校对员把他的建议留在他那已经腐烂的脑壳里。"

写这种令人痛苦的信使马克·吐温感到很爽快，这样他的怒气也出来了，这些信也不会造成任何真实伤害，因为他的夫人早已在寄信的时候把信悄悄拿走了，信根本就没有寄出去。

你是否想劝你所认识的人改掉一些不好的习惯?这可真是太好了，我非常赞同。但是为什么不先从你自己开始呢?从纯粹自私的角度而言，那也比改进别人要收益更大——而且所冒的风险也会小许多。孔子就说过："各人自扫门前雪，休管他人瓦上霜。"

当我还很年轻时，很想在人面前表现自我。我曾给查哈丁·戴维斯——一位曾在美国文坛红得发紫的作家写了一封愚蠢的信。当时我正准备给某家杂志社写一篇关于作家的文章，我就请戴维斯告诉我他的写作方法。在此之前几个星期，我曾收到一封信，信的末尾写道："口述信，未曾读过。"我觉得这种办法很好，认为写这封信的人一定是个了不起的大忙人。尽管我一点儿都不忙，但我迫切地想给戴维斯留下深刻的印象，就在短信的末尾写上了"口述

a magazine article about authors, and I asked Davis to tell me about his method of work. A few weeks earlier, I had received a letter from someone with this notation at the bottom: "Dictated but not read." I was quite impressed. I felt that the writer must be very big and busy and important. I wasn't the slightest bit busy, but I was eager to make an impression on Richard Harding Davis, so I ended my short note with the words: "Dictated but not read."

He never troubled to answer the letter. He simply returned it to me with this scribbled across the bottom: "Your bad manners are exceeded only by your bad manners." True, I had blundered, and perhaps I deserved this rebuke. But, being human, I resented it. I resented it so sharply that when I read of the death of Richard Harding Davis ten years later, the one thought that still persisted in my mind—I am ashamed to admit—was the hurt he had given me.

If you and I want to stir up a resentment tomorrow that may rankle across the decades and endure until death, just let us indulge in a little stinging criticism—no matter how certain we are that it is justified.

When dealing with people, let us remember we are not dealing with creatures of logic. We are dealing with creatures of emotion, creatures bristling with prejudices and motivated by pride and vanity.

Bitter criticism caused the sensitive Thomas Hardy, one of the finest novelists ever to enrich English literature, to give up forever the writing of fiction. Criticism drove Thomas Chatterton, the English poet, to suicide.

Benjamin Franklin, tactless in his youth, became so diplomatic, so adroit at handling people, that he was made American Ambassador to France. The secret of his success? "I will speak ill of no man," he said, "...and speak all the good I know of everybody."

Any fool can criticize, condemn and complain—and most fools do.

But it takes character and self-control to be understanding and forgiving.

"A great man shows his greatness," said Carlyle, "by the way he treats little men."

Bob Hoover, a famous test pilot and frequent performer at air shows, was returning to his home in Los Angeles from an air show in San Diego. As described in the magazine Flight Operations, at three hundred feet in the air, both engines suddenly stopped. By deft maneuvering he managed to

信，未曾读过"的字样。

但是戴维斯根本没有给我回信。他只是将信退回给我，并在下面草草写了几个字："态度倨傲，无以复加。"我确实是弄巧成拙了，这也是我自作聪明所应得的斥责。但我当时对此却不以为然，甚至深怀厌恨，以至于10年后我得知戴维斯的死讯时，心里所想到的仍然是他对我的伤害——虽然我羞于承认！

因此，如果你我想要激起怨恨，让人怀恨几十年，至死才消失的话，那么只需说些恶毒的批评之语就可以了——不论我们多么肯定这些话本身是多么的合理。

与人相处时，一定要切记：与我们交往的不是理性的生物，而是充满了感情的，带有偏见、傲慢和虚荣的人。

刻薄的批评曾使得英国大文学家、敏感的托马斯·哈代永远放弃了小说创作；批评还促使英国诗人托马斯·卡德登自杀。

本杰明·富兰克林青年时期并不是很聪明伶俐，但后来却变得非常精明能干，结果被委任为美国驻法大使。他成功的秘诀是什么？"我不愿意说任何人的坏话，"他说，"……只说我所认识的每个人的一切优点。"

任何傻子都会批评、指责和抱怨——而且大多数傻子也正是这样做的。

要了解和宽容别人，就要有良好的品德和自我克制。

"伟人之所以伟大，"卡莱尔说，"就是通过对待卑微者的方式来体现的。"

鲍伯·胡佛是一位著名的试飞员，常常在各种航空展览中作飞行表演。有一天，他在圣地亚哥航空展中表演完飞行后，朝洛杉矶家中飞回。正如《飞行作业》杂志所描述的那样，当飞机飞到300英尺的高度时，两具引擎突然熄灭了。幸亏胡佛的技术娴熟，他驾驶飞机着了陆，虽然飞机严重毁坏，所幸无人受伤。

land the plane, but it was badly damaged although nobody was hurt.

Hoover's first act after the emergency landing was to inspect the airplane's fuel. Just as he suspected, the World War II propeller plane he had been flying had been fueled with jet fuel rather than gasoline.

Upon returning to the airport, he asked to see the mechanic who had serviced his airplane. The young man was sick with the agony of his mistake. Tears streamed down his face as Hoover approached. He had just caused the loss of a very expensive plane and could have caused the loss of three lives as well.

You can imagine Hoover's anger. One could anticipate the tongue-lashing that this proud and precise pilot would unleash for that carelessness. But Hoover didn't scold the mechanic; he didn't even criticize him. Instead, he put his big arm around the man's shoulder and said, "To show you I'm sure that you'll never do this again, I want you to service my F-51 tomorrow."

Often parents are tempted to criticize their children. You would expect me to say "don't." But I will not, I am merely going to say, "Before you criticize them, read one of the classics of American journalism, 'Father Forgets.'" It originally appeared as an editorial in the People's Home Journal. We are reprinting it here with the author's permission, as condensed in the Reader's Digest:

"Father Forgets" is one of those little pieces which—dashed off in a moment of sincere feeling—strikes an echoing chord in so many readers as to become a perennial reprint favorite. Since its first appearance, "*Father Forgets* has been reproduced," writes the author, W. Livingston Lamed, "in hundreds of magazines and house organs, and in newspapers the country over. It has been reprinted almost as extensively in many foreign languages. I have given personal permission to thousands who wished to read it from school, church, and lecture platforms. It has been 'on the air' on countless occasions and programs. Oddly enough, college periodicals have used it, and high-school magazines. Sometimes a little piece seems mysteriously to 'click'. This one certainly did."

FATHER FORGETS

W. Livingston Lamed

Listen, son: I am saying this as you lie asleep, one little paw crumpled under your cheek

胡佛在飞机迫降之后所做的第一件事，就是检查飞机的燃料。结果正如他预料的那样，他所驾驶的这架二战时期的螺旋桨飞机里面装的竟然是喷气机燃油，而不是汽油。

胡佛回机场后，要求见为他的飞机做保养的机械师。这个年轻人还在为他所犯的错误而难过不已呢。当胡佛向他走去的时候，他泪流满面。他使一架昂贵的飞机受到了损坏，还差点要了3个人的性命。

你可以想象胡佛的愤怒，并猜想这位荣誉心极强、做事认真的飞行员一定会痛斥机械师的粗心大意。然而，胡佛并没有责骂他，甚至连一句批评的话都没有说。相反，他伸出双手，抱住这位机械师的肩膀，说道："为了表明我相信你不会再犯错误，我要你明天再给我的F-51飞机做保养。"

许多父母动不动就批评他们的孩子。你一定以为我会说"不要批评"。但我并不想这么说，而是说"在你批评孩子之前，请先读一读《父亲错了》这篇美国典型的新闻教育文章。"这篇文章最初发表在《家庭纪事》的社论栏。经过作者同意，我按照《读者文摘》的节写版，将它放在下面。

这是篇小短文，是在一时的内心冲动之下写出来的，但它却打动了许多读者，以至于成为众人都喜欢的一再被转载的文章。这篇文章首次发表之后，作者利文斯登·拉米德说："全美国成百上千家报纸杂志和家庭组织都刊登过，在国外也差不多如此。我自己也允许过好几千人在学校、教堂和演讲台上宣读这篇文章。它还被电视和收音机转播或广播过无数次。令人奇怪的是，大学刊物转载它，中学刊物也转载。有时，一篇小文章竟能够深深地引起人们的共鸣。这篇文章确实产生了这样的效果。"

父亲错了

利文斯登·拉米德

听着，儿子：我想在你熟睡的时候和你说上几句。你躺在床上，小手按在脸颊上，湿湿

and the blond curls stickily wet on your damp forehead.I have stolen into your room alone.Just a few minutes ago,as I sat reading my paper in the library,a stifling wave of remorse swept over me.Guiltily I came to your bedside.

There are the things I was thinking,son: I had been cross to you.I scolded you as you were dressing for school because you gave your face merely a dab with a towel.I took you to task for not cleaning your shoes.I called out angrily when you threw some of your things on the floor.

At breakfast I found fault,too.You spilled things.You gulped down your food.You put your elbows on the table.You spread butter too thick on your bread.And as you started off to play and I made for my train,you turned and waved a hand and called,"Goodbye,Daddy!" and I frowned,and said in reply,"Hold your shoulders back!"

Then it began all over again in the late afternoon.As I came up the road I spied you,down on your knees,playing marbles.There were holes in your stockings.I humiliated you before your boyfriends by marching you ahead of me to the house.Stockings were expensive—and if you had to buy them you would be more careful! Imagine that,son,from a father!

Do you remember,later,when I was reading in the library,how you came in timidly,with a sort of hurt look in your eyes? When I glanced up over my paper,impatient at the interruption, you hesitated at the door."What is it you want?" I snapped.

You said nothing,but ran across in one tempestuous plunge,and threw your arms around my neck and kissed me,and your small arms tightened with an affection that God had set blooming in your heart and which even neglect could not wither.And then you were gone, pattering up the stairs.

Well,son,it was shortly afterwards that my paper slipped from my hands and a terrible sickening fear came over me.What has habit been doing to me? The habit of finding fault,of reprimanding—this was my reward to you for being a boy.It was not that I did not love you; it was that I expected too much of youth.I was measuring you by the yardstick of my own years.

And there was so much that was good and free and true in your character.The little heart of you was as big as the dawn itself over the wide hills.This was shown by your spontaneous

的金黄色卷发粘在你那出了些许汗水的额头上。我刚才一个人悄悄地走进你的房间。当我几分钟以前在书房读报时,突然感到十分懊悔。我是怀着愧疚之心来到你床边的。

我的儿子,我想到了许许多多的事情:我对你确实太粗暴了。在你穿衣服上学的时候我会呵斥你,因为你只是用毛巾随便擦了把脸;在你没有擦干净鞋子的时候,我也会对你大发雷霆;当你把东西丢在地板上时,我又会冲着你怒吼。

在早餐时,我又发现了你的毛病:你把食物溅在了桌上,吃饭时没有一点修养,还把胳膊肘放在桌子上,甚至在面包上涂了厚厚的一层黄油。当你出门去玩,而我要去赶火车的时候,你转身朝我挥挥手,响亮地说:"爸爸再见!"可是我却皱着眉头告诉你:"挺起胸膛!"

晚上,一切又重新开始。我在路上就看见你跪在地上打弹珠,你的长统袜子磨出了好几个洞。我当着你的伙伴押你回家,让你感到了羞辱。我还对你说:"袜子是要花钱买的,如果你自己掏钱,你就会在意了。"唉,这竟出自一位父亲之口!

你还记得吗?没过多久,当我在书房看书时,你小心地走进来,眼里带着委屈的样子。我从报纸上面看到了你,对你的打搅十分不悦。你站在门口,有些犹豫。"你想干什么?"我恶狠狠地说。

你什么也没说,只是突然朝我跑过来,搂住我的脖子亲吻着我。你的小手紧紧地抱了我一下。满含情爱,那是上帝种在你心田里的,任何漠视都不能使它枯萎。之后你离开了,快步上了楼梯。

在你离开不久,儿子,报纸从手中滑落在地,一阵令人难受的强烈愧疚涌上了我的心头。我真是受习惯之害匪浅!吹毛求疵,并且动不动就斥责——这就是我对你这个小男孩的报偿!我不是不爱你,而是对你的期望太高,并以我自己的年龄标准来要求你。

在你的天性中充满了真、善、美。你那幼小的心灵就好像包含并照亮了群山的清晨的

impulse to rush in and kiss me good night.Nothing else matters tonight,son.I have come to your bedside in the darkness,and I have knelt there,ashamed!

It is a feeble atonement; I know you would not understand these things if I told them to you during your waking hours.But tomorrow I will be a real daddy! I will chum with you,and suffer when you suffer,and laugh when you laugh.I will bite my tongue when impatient words come.I will keep saying as if it were a ritual:"He is nothing but a boy—a little boy!"

I am afraid I have visualized you as a man.Yet as I see you now,son,crumpled and weary in your cot,I see that you are still a baby.Yesterday you were in your mother's arms,your head on her shoulder.I have asked too much,too much.

Instead of condemning people,let's try to understand them.Let's try to figure out why they do what they do.That's a lot more profitable and intriguing than criticism; and it breeds sympathy, tolerance and kindness."To know all is to forgive all."

As Dr.Johnson said, "God himself,sir,does not propose to judge man until the end of his days."

Why should you and I?

Principle 1:Don't criticize,condemn or complain.

阳光——你跑进来亲吻我,向我道晚安的内在冲动表明了这一切。其他都不重要了!我的儿子!我在黑暗中来到你的床边,内心充满愧疚地跪在这里。

我这不过是一种没什么作用的忏悔。我知道,当我在你醒来的时候告诉你这些时,你也不会明白。但是我从明天开始要做一个真正的父亲。我要成为你的好伙伴,在你痛苦时帮你分担,在你欢笑时和你共同分享。我不会再说那些不耐烦的话,我会每天告诉自己:"他只是个孩子——一个小男孩!"

我想我以前是将你当大人来对待的。但是,我的儿子,当我现在看到你蜷缩着睡在你的小床上时,你仍然是个婴儿。你在母亲的怀里,头靠在她肩上,此情此景犹如发生在昨天。我以前对你太苛刻了,太苛刻了!

因此,我们不要去责怪别人,而要试着去了解他们,弄明白他们为什么会那么做。这会比批评更有益,而且还能产生同情、容忍以及仁慈。"了解了一切,就会宽恕一切!"

正如约翰逊博士所说的:"要知道, 即使是上帝, 如果不到世界末日, 也不会轻易审判世人。"为什么你我要批评别人呢?

第一项规则:不要批评、指责或抱怨。

2 The Big Secret of Dealing with People

There is only one way under high heaven to get anybody to do anything.Did you ever stop to think of that? Yes,just one way.And that is by making the other person want to do it.

Remember,there is no other way.

Of course,you can make someone want to give you his watch by sticking a revolver in his ribs. You can make your employees give you cooperation—until your back is turned—by threatening to fire them.You can make a child do what you want it to do by a whip or a threat.But these crude methods have sharply undesirable repercussions.

The only way I can get you to do anything is by giving you what you want.

What do you want?

Sigmund Freud said that everything you and I do springs from two motives: the sex urge and the desire to be great.

John Dewey,one of America's most profound philosophers,phrased it a bit differently.Dr.Dewey said that the deepest urge in human nature is "the desire to be important." Remember that phrase: "the desire to be important." It is significant.You are going to hear a lot about it in this book.

What do you want? Not many things,but the few things that you do wish,you crave with an insistence that will not be denied.Some of the things most people want include:

1. Health and the preservation of life.
2. Food.
3. Sleep.
4. Money and the things money will buy.
5. Life in the hereafter.
6. Sexual gratification.
7. The well-being of our children.
8. A feeling of importance.

Almost all these wants are usually gratified—all except one.But there is one longing—almost as deep,almost as imperious,as the desire for food or sleep—which is seldom gratified.It is what Freud calls "the desire to be great."It is what Dewey calls the "desire to be important."

Lincoln once began a letter saying: "Everybody likes a compliment."William James said: "The deepest principle in human nature is the craving to be appreciated." He didn't speak,mind you,of the

第2章 与人交往的秘诀

在这个世界上,只有一个方法能够让任何人去做任何事。你是否静下心来想过这一点呢?是的,只有一个方法,那就是让别人愿意去做那件事。

请记住,除此之外没有别的方法。

当然,你可以用枪威逼某人把他的手表给你。你可以用解雇来威胁你的雇员,使他听你的话,哪怕你并不在身边。你还可以用鞭子或恫吓的方法使一个孩子做你交给他的事。但这些粗暴的做法显然只会导致极其不良的反应。

而我能够促使你做任何事的唯一方法,就是满足你的需要。那么,你需要什么呢?弗洛伊德说:"你我所做的任何事情都起源于两种动机:性冲动以及成为伟人的欲望。"美国大哲学家杜威的观点与此稍有不同。杜威博士说:人类天性中最深层的冲动就是"显要感"。记住,是"显要感"。这是非常重要的。你将在这本书中看到许多有关的内容。

你所需要的是什么呢?并不多。但不可否认,有少数东西的确是你所需要并且迫切渴望的。大多数人想要的东西包括:

1.健康与生命的保障。 2.食物。 3.睡眠。 4.金钱及金钱所能买到的东西。
5.长寿。 6.性欲的满足。 7.子女的幸福。 8.显要感。

除去一点之外,几乎所有这些需要都能满足。还有一项需要如同食物或睡眠一样重要却很难满足,那就是弗洛伊德所说的"成为伟人的欲望",也就是杜威所说的"显要感"。

林肯曾在一封信的开头说:"每个人都喜欢别人的恭维。"威廉·詹姆斯也说:"在人类天性中,最深层的本性就是渴望得到重视。"一定要注意,他并没有说"愿望"、"欲望"或"希望",而是说"渴望"得到重视。

"wish" or the "desire" or the "longing" to be appreciated.He said the "craving" to be appreciated.

Here is a gnawing and unfaltering human hunger, and the rare individual who honestly satisfies this heart hunger will hold people in the palm of his or her hand and "even the undertaker will be sorry when he dies."

The desire for a feeling of importance is one of the chief distinguishing differences between mankind and the animals.To illustrate: When I was a farm boy out in Missouri, my father bred fine Duroc-Jersey hogs and pedigreed white-faced cattle.We used to exhibit our hogs and white-faced cattle at the country fairs and livestock shows throughout the Middle West.We won first prizes by the score.My father pinned his blue ribbons on a sheet of white muslin, and when friends or visitors came to the house, he would get out the Long sheet of muslin.He would hold one end and I would hold the other while he exhibited the blue ribbons.

The hogs didn't care about the ribbons they had won.But Father did.These prizes gave him a feeling of importance.

If our ancestors hadn't had this flaming urge for a feeling of importance, civilization would have been impossible.Without it, we should have been just about like animals.

It was this desire for a feeling of importance that led an uneducated, poverty-stricken grocery clerk to study some law books he found in the bottom of a barrel of household plunder that he had bought for fifty cents.You have probably heard of this grocery clerk.His name was Lincoln.

It was this desire for a feeling of importance that inspired Dickens to write his immortal novels. This desire inspired Sir Christopher Wren to design his symphonies in stone.This desire made Rockefeller amass millions that he never spent! And this same desire made the richest family in your town build a house far too large for its requirements.

This desire makes you want to wear the latest styles, drive the latest cars, and talk about your brilliant children.

It is this desire that lures many boys and girls into joining gangs and engaging in criminal activities.The average young criminal, according to E.P.Mulrooney, onetime police commissioner of New York, is filled with ego, and his first request after arrest is for those lurid newspapers that make him out a hero.The disagreeable prospect of serving time seems remote so long as he can gloat over

这是一种令人痛苦而且迫切需要解决的人类的饥饿，只有极少数能满足这种人类内心饥饿的人才能把握别人,“甚至在他去世的时候,连殡仪馆的人也会为之叹息”。

出人头地的“显要感”这种欲望是人与动物之间的一种主要差别。例如,当我还是密苏里州的一个农村孩童时,我父亲就在饲养良种杜罗·杰赛猪和白脸牛。我们经常在中西部的集市及家畜展销会上出售我们的猪和牛。我们获得过几十个头等奖。我父亲用别针把蓝缎带奖章别在一条白布上,当朋友或客人来我家时,他就取出这条长带。他拿着这一端,而我则持着那一端,为客人展示蓝缎带奖章。

这些猪并不关心它们得了什么奖章。但是我父亲却很在意,因为这些奖章给他一种显要感。假如我们的祖先对于这种显要感并没有强烈欲求的话,那么人类文明也就无法产生。而没有文明,我们和动物就没什么区别。

正是这种追求显要感的强烈欲望,推动着一位没有受过什么教育的、极其贫困的杂货店伙计去研究一本法律书,这本书是他在一只堆满了杂物的大木桶底下找出来,并花了 50 美分买下的。也许你已经听说过这位杂货店的伙计,他的名字叫林肯。正是这种追求显要感的强烈欲望,激励着狄更斯完成了不朽的作品。这种欲望还激励克里斯托弗·雷恩设计出了“石之和音”。这种欲望还促使洛克菲勒创造了他一辈子都花不完的财富。也正是这种欲望促使城里那些大富豪们建造起一栋栋大别墅,这些别墅远远超过了其实际需要。也正是这种欲望促使你想要穿最时髦的衣服,驾驶最新款式的汽车,和别人谈论你聪明伶俐的孩子。也正是这种欲望,诱使许多孩子成为匪徒。“如今的青年罪犯,”纽约市前任警察总监马洛尼说,“非常自负。被捕以后,他的第一个反应是要求看那份骇人听闻的、使他成为‘英雄’的报纸。他们只想看见自己的照片与那些体育明星、影视明星和政治家的照片同时见诸报端,而对于以后的牢狱生活却毫不在意,认为这似乎是不可能的事情。”

如果你将自己如何获得显要感的方式告诉我,我就能说出你是怎样的人。凭这一点就可以

his likeness sharing space with pictures of sports figures, movie and TV stars and politicians.

If you tell me how you get your feeling of importance, I'll tell you what you are. That determines your character. That is the most significant thing about you. For example, John D. Rockefeller got his feeling of importance by giving money to erect a modem hospital in Peking, China, to care for millions of poor people whom he had never seen and never would see. Dillinger, on the other hand, got his feeling of importance by being a bandit, a bank robber and killer. When the FBI agents were hunting him, he dashed into a farmhouse up in Minnesota and said, "I'm Dillinger!" He was proud of the fact that he was Public Enemy Number One. "I'm not going to hurt you, but I'm Dillinger!" he said.

Yes, the one significant difference between Dillinger and Rockefeller is how they got their feeling of importance.

History sparkles with amusing examples of famous people struggling for a feeling of importance. Even George Washington wanted to be called "His Mightiness, the President of the United States"; and Columbus pleaded for the title "Admiral of the Ocean and Viceroy of India." Catherine the Great refused to open letters that were not addressed to "Her Imperial Majesty"; and Mrs. Lincoln, in the White House, turned upon Mrs. Grant like a tigress and shouted, "How dare you be seated in my presence until I invite you!"

Our millionaires helped finance Admiral Byrd's expedition to the Antarctic in 1928 with the understanding that ranges of icy mountains would be named after them; and Victor Hugo aspired to have nothing less than the city of Paris renamed in his honor. Even Shakespeare, mightiest of the mighty, tried to add luster to his name by procuring a coat of arms for his family.

People sometimes became invalids in order to win sympathy and attention, and get a feeling of importance. For example, take Mrs. McKinley. She got a feeling of importance by forcing her husband, the President of the United States, to neglect important affairs of state while he reclined on the bed beside her for hours at a time, his arm about her, soothing her to sleep. She fed her gnawing desire for attention by insisting that he remain with her while she was having her teeth fixed, and once created a stormy scene when he had to leave her alone with the dentist while he kept an appointment with John Hay, his secretary of state.

确定你的性格，因为这是你生活中最重要的事情。例如，"石油大王"洛克菲勒在中国北京出资建新式医院，为千百万他从来都没有见过，而且今后也永远不会见到的贫民治病，以此获得显要感。相反，狄林格则通过当强盗抢劫银行和杀人来获得显要感。当联邦调查局的人追捕他的时候，他闯进明尼苏达州一个农民的家中，说："我是狄林格！"他竟然以自己是头号公敌而感到荣耀。他说："我不会伤害你，但我是狄林格！"

是的，狄林格与洛克菲勒之间最重要的差别，就在于他们获得显要感的手段不同。

在历史上，一些名人为了获得显要感而上演了许多有趣的事情。即使是乔治·华盛顿也愿意被称为"至高无上的美国总统"；哥伦布为了得到"海军上将兼印度总督"的名号而不惜远涉重洋；女皇凯瑟琳干脆拒绝拆阅那些没有称她为"女皇陛下"的信件；而林肯夫人曾在白宫对格兰特夫人大发雷霆，说："你怎么敢在我请你坐下以前，在我面前坐下！"

1928年，那些百万富翁出钱赞助拜德大将去南极探险时，附加了一个条件，那就是以他们的名字命名冰山。雨果甚至希望将巴黎改成他的名字。连"名人中的名人"莎士比亚，为了光宗耀祖，也想方设法为他的家族弄到了一枚象征荣誉的徽章。

有时候，人们还会通过装病来博得同情和注意力，以此获得显要感。例如麦金利总统夫人，她曾强迫她丈夫——美国总统——将手中重要的国家事务放下，斜倚在她的床边抱着她，抚慰她进入梦乡，而且每次长达几小时，以此来获得显要感。她在治疗牙齿的时候，坚持让丈夫陪着她，以此来满足她希望得到关注的强烈欲望。有一次，由于总统和国务卿约翰·海有要事相商而不得不让她一个人呆在牙医那里，于是她大发脾气。

作家玛丽·莱恩哈特也曾告诉过我，为了获得显要感，一位聪明活泼的少妇突然装起病来。"总有一天，"莱恩哈特夫人说，"这个人将不得不面对这一现实，那就是她将逐渐衰老。她的未来将是一片寂寞，她已经没什么希望了。

The writer Mary Roberts Rinehart once told me of a bright, vigorous young woman who became an invalid in order to get a feeling of importance. "One day," said Mrs. Rinehart, "this woman had been obliged to face something, her age perhaps. The lonely years were stretching ahead and there was little left for her to anticipate."

"She took to her bed; and for ten years her old mother traveled to the third floor and back, carrying trays, nursing her. Then one day the old mother, weary with service, lay down and died. For some weeks, the invalid languished; then she got up, put on her clothing, and resumed living again."

Some authorities declare that people may actually go insane in order to find, in the dreamland of insanity, the feeling of importance that has been denied them in the harsh world of reality. There are more patients suffering from mental diseases in the United States than from all other diseases combined.

What is the cause of insanity?

Nobody can answer such a sweeping question, but we know that certain diseases, such as syphilis, break down and destroy the brain cells and result in insanity. In fact, about one-half of all mental diseases can be attributed to such physical causes as brain lesions, alcohol, toxins and injuries. But the other half—and this is the appalling part of the story—the other half of the people who go insane apparently have nothing organically wrong with their brain cells. In post-mortem examinations, when their brain tissues are studied under the highest-powered microscopes, these tissues are found to be apparently just as healthy as yours and mine.

Why do these people go insane?

I put that question to the head physician of one of our most important psychiatric hospitals. This doctor, who has received the highest honors and the most coveted awards for his knowledge of this subject, told me frankly that he didn't know why people went insane. Nobody knows for sure. But he did say that many people who go insane find in insanity a feeling of importance that they were unable to achieve in the world of reality. Then he told me this story:

"I have a patient right now whose marriage proved to be a tragedy. She wanted love, sexual gratification, children and social prestige, but life blasted all her hopes. Her husband didn't love her. He refused even to eat with her and forced her to serve his meals in his room upstairs. She had no children, no social standing. She went insane; and, in her imagination, she divorced her husband and

"整整10年,她一直躺在床上,由她那年迈的母亲在楼梯上艰难地爬上爬下,端茶倒水地服侍她。终于有一天,这位老迈的母亲因劳累过度而离开了人世。这个装病的女人伤心了几个星期之后,不得不爬起来,穿上衣服,重新开始生活。"

有些专家认为人的确会精神失常,这是因为他们需要在癫狂的梦境中获得在残酷的现实世界所得不到的显要感。在美国,精神病患者多于其他一切患者的总数。

精神失常的原因是什么呢?

无人能够回答这个大问题,不过我们知道有些病——例如梅毒,能够使脑细胞受到损伤,从而造成精神失常。事实上,大约有一半的精神病是由于生理原因造成的,如脑部受损伤、酒精、中毒,以及躯体受到创伤。但令人惶惑不安的是,另一半患上精神病的人在脑细胞等机体上并没有明显的毛病。对这些人死后所进行的尸检中,即使用最高倍的显微镜检查他们的脑部神经,也难以查出有什么问题,他们的脑部神经和你我的一样健全。

那么,这些人为什么会精神失常呢?

我向一家精神病院的一位著名的主任医生请教了这一问题。这位医生曾因为在这方面的突出贡献而获得过最高荣誉及最著名的奖章。他坦率地对我说,他也不知道人为什么会变疯,根本就没有人知道确切原因。不过他又说,许多患上精神病的人,能够在癫狂中找到真实世界中难以获得的显要感。他向我讲了这样一个故事:

"现在,我有一位病人,她的婚姻是个悲剧。她渴求爱情和性欲的满足,而且希望有个孩子及社会声誉,但是她所有的希望都被现实生活打破了——她的丈夫不爱她,甚至拒绝和她一同吃饭,并强迫她在楼上的房间服侍他吃饭。她没有孩子,没有社会地位。于是,她疯了。在她的幻想中,她已经和丈夫离婚,并且恢复了婚前的姓名。她现在相信自己已经嫁给了一位英国贵族,并坚持让别人称她为史密斯夫人。

resumed her maiden name. She now believes she has married into English aristocracy, and she insists on being called Lady Smith.

"And as for children, she imagines now that she has had a new child every night. Each time I call on her she says, 'Doctor, I had a baby last night.'"

Life once wrecked all her dream ships on the sharp rocks of reality; but in the sunny, fantasy isles of insanity, all her barkentines race into port with canvas billowing and winds singing through the masts.

Tragic? Oh, I don't know. Her physician said to me: "If I could stretch out my hand and restore her sanity, I wouldn't do it. She's much happier as she is."

If some people are so hungry for a feeling of importance that they actually go insane to get it, imagine what miracle you and I can achieve by giving people honest appreciation this side of insanity.

One of the first people in American business to be paid a salary of over a million dollars a year (when there was no income tax and a person earning fifty dollars a week was considered well off) was Charles Schwab. He had been picked by Andrew Carnegie to become the first president of the newly formed United States Steel Company in 1921, when Schwab was only thirty-eight years old. (Schwab later left U.S.Steel to take over the then-troubled Bethlehem Steel Company, and he rebuilt it into one of the most profitable companies in America.)

Why did Andrew Carnegie pay a million dollars a year, or more than three thousand dollars a day, to Charles Schwab? Why? Because Schwab was a genius? No. Because he knew more about the manufacture of steel than other people? Nonsense. Charles Schwab told me himself that he had many men working for him who knew more about the manufacture of steel than he did.

Schwab says that he was paid this salary, largely because of his ability to deal with people. I asked him how he did it. Here is his secret set down in his own words—words that ought to be cast in eternal bronze and hung in every home and school, every shop and office in the land—words that children ought to memorize instead of wasting their time memorizing the conjugation of Latin verbs or the amount of the annual rainfall in Brazil—words that will all but transform your life and mine if we will only live them:

"I consider my ability to arouse enthusiasm among my people," said Schwab, "the greatest asset I possess, and the way to develop the best that is in a person is by appreciation and encouragement.

"至于孩子,她现在幻想着每个晚上都会生下一个新的婴儿。当我每次去看她的时候,她都会说:'医生,我昨晚上生了个孩子。'"

残酷的现实曾经摧毁了她的梦幻之舟,但在想象的阳光灿烂的美丽海岛边,她的梦幻之舟再度扬帆,驶进快乐的港湾。

这是悲剧吗?唉,我可不知道。不过她的医生对我说:"即使我能伸手治好她的精神症,我也不愿那样做。她现在这样生活更加快乐。"

试想一下,如果有人如此渴求显要感,甚至真的变成了疯子,那么我们在他还没有变疯之前就给予真诚的赞许,将会创造出什么奇迹呢?

查尔斯·施瓦伯是美国少数年收入超过100万美元的商人(当时没有个人所得税,一个人一周挣50美元就被认为很富有)。1921年,他被卡内基提拔为新成立的联合钢铁公司首任总经理,那时他38岁。(后来他离开联合钢铁公司,接管当时陷入困境的贝氏拉罕钢铁公司,重新将它经营成美国最盈利的公司之一。)

安德鲁·卡内基为什么付给施瓦伯100万美元的年薪,也就是一天3000多美元的薪水呢?是因为施瓦伯是个天才吗?不。是因为他所掌握的钢铁制造知识比别人更多吗?那绝对是瞎说。施瓦伯自己就曾告诉过我,在他手下做事的许多人比他在这方面知道得更多。

施瓦伯说,他之所以能获得这么高的薪水,主要是他为人处世的本领。我问他是如何与人相处的,他亲口说出了自己的秘诀——应该将这些话镌刻在传之久远的铜牌上,悬挂在全国的每个家庭、学校、商店以及办公室中——这些话每个儿童都应该背下来,而不是浪费他们的时间去背诵拉丁动词的变形或巴西每年的降雨量——如果我们真的能够按照这些话去做的话,你我的生活必然会大不相同。

施瓦伯说:"我认为鼓动、激发职工热情的能力,才是我所拥有的最大资本。而充分发挥一

"There is nothing else that so kills the ambitions of a person as criticisms from superiors.I never criticize any one.I believe in giving a person incentive to work.So I am anxious to praise but loath to find fault.If I like anything, *I am hearty in my approbation and lavish in my praise.*"

That is what Schwab did.But what do average people do? The exact opposite.If they don't like a thing, they bawl out their subordinates; if they do like it, they say nothing.As the old couplet says: "Once I did bad and that I heard ever/Twice I did good, but that I heard never."

"In my wide association in life, meeting with many and great people in various parts of the world," Schwab declared, "I have yet to find the person, however great or exalted his station, who did not do better work and put forth greater effort under a spirit of approval than he would ever do under a spirit of criticism."

That he said, frankly, was one of the outstanding reasons for the phenomenal success of Andrew Carnegie.Carnegie praised his associates publicly as well as privately.Carnegie wanted to praise his assistants even on his tombstone.He wrote an epitaph for himself which read: "Here lies one who knew how to get around him men who were cleverer than himself."

Sincere appreciation was one of the secrets of the first John D.Rockefeller's success in handling men.For example, when one of his partners, Edward T.Bedford, lost a million dollars for the firm by a bad buy in South America, John D.might have criticized; but he knew Bedford had done his best—and the incident was closed.So Rockefeller found something to praise; he congratulated Bedford because he had been able to save 60 percent of the money he had invested. "That's splendid," said Rockefeller."We don't always do as well as that upstairs."

I have among my clippings a story that I know never happened, but it illustrates a truth, so I'll repeat it:

According to this silly story, a farm woman, at the end of a heavy day's work, set before her menfolks a heaping pile of hay.And when they indignantly demanded whether she had gone crazy, she replied, " Why, how did I know you'd notice? I've been cooking for you men for the last twenty years and in all that time I ain't heard no word to let me know you wasn't just eating hay."

When a study was made a few years ago on runaway wives, what do you think was discovered to be the main reason wives ran away? It was "lack of appreciation." And I'd bet that a similar

个人才能的方法，正是欣赏和鼓励。

"上司的批评最容易扼杀一个人的雄心壮志。我从来都不批评任何人。我认为应给人以工作方面的激励。所以我更加乐于称赞，而不喜欢挑剔。如果说我有什么偏好的话，那就是我'诚于嘉许，宽于称道'。"

这就是施瓦伯的做法。但一般人又是如何做的呢?正好相反。如果他们不喜欢某件事，他们就会挑剔毛病；如果他们真的喜欢它，他们也会闭口不谈，就好像俗话说的："好事不出门，坏事传千里。"

"我这一辈子交际很广，见过世界各地的许多著名人物，"施瓦伯说，"我发现所有的人，无论他如何伟大，地位如何高，当他在得到赞许的情况下工作时，总是会比在被批评时工作更出色，成就也更大。"

其实，他所说的也正是安德鲁·卡内基成功的一个重要原因。卡内基不仅仅是私下里，而且还在许多公开场合称赞他的雇员。甚至在他的墓碑上还不忘称赞他的雇员。他给自己写了一句这样的碑文："长眠于此处的，是一个知道如何与比自己更聪明的人相处的人。"

真诚的欣赏也是洛克菲勒与人打交道的成功秘诀之一。例如，当一位名叫爱德华·贝弗德的合伙人在南美做砸了一大笔买卖，使公司损失上百万美元时，洛克菲勒本来可以批评的，但他知道贝弗德的确尽了最大的努力——更不用说这件事已经发生了。因此洛克菲勒将这件事情朝好的一面来看。他祝贺贝弗德挽回了60%的投资。"这已经很不错了，"他说，"我们不可能每件事情都不出错。"

在我的剪报中有个故事，我知道并不是真的，但它揭示了一条真理，所以我想复述一下：

这个故事说，一位农妇劳累了一天，在家里的男人们面前放了一堆干草。当他们愤怒地问她是否疯了时，她说："怎么了？我怎么知道你们会在意呢？20年来，我一直为你们男人做饭，你们却一声不吭，也没告诉我你们不吃干草啊。"

几年前，有人对离家出走的妻子进行研究。你认为妻子离家出走的主要原因是什么？这

study made of runaway husbands would come out the same way.We often take our spouses so much for granted that we never let them know we appreciate them.

A member of one of our classes told of a request made by his wife.She and a group of other women in her church were involved in a self-improvement program.She asked her husband to help her by listing six things he believed she could do to help her become a better wife.He reported to the class, "I was surprised by such a request.Frankly, it would have been easy for me to list six things I would like to change about her—my heavens, she could have listed a thousand things she would like to change about me—but I didn't.I said to her, 'Let me think about it and give you an answer in the morning.'

"The next morning I got up very early and called the florist and had them send six red roses to my wife with a note saying, 'I can't think of six things I would like to change about you.I love you the way you are.'

"When I arrived at home that evening, who do you think greeted me at the door? That's right. My wife! She was almost in tears.Needless to say, I was extremely glad I had not criticized her as she had requested.

"The following Sunday at church, after she had reported the results of her assignment, several women with whom she had been studying came up to me and said, 'that was the most considerate thing I have ever heard.' It was then I realized the power of appreciation."

Florenz Ziegfeld, the most spectacular producer who ever dazzled Broadway, gained his reputation by his subtle ability to "glorify the American girl." Time after time, he took drab little creatures that no one ever looked at twice and transformed them on the stage into glamorous visions of mystery and seduction.Knowing the value of appreciation and confidence, he made women feel beautiful by the sheer power of his gallantry and consideration.He was practical: he raised the salary of chorus girls from thirty dollars a week to as high as one hundred and seventy-five.And he was also chivalrous; on opening night at the Follies, he sent telegrams to the stars in the cast, and he deluged every chorus girl in the show with American Beauty roses.

I once succumbed to the fad of fasting and went for six days and nights without eating.It wasn't difficult.I was less hungry at the end of the sixth day than I was at the end of the second.Yet I

就是“没有人欣赏”。我敢打赌,离家出走的男人也是同样的情况。我们常将配偶所做的事情认为是理所当然的,却从不让他们知道我们的感激之情。

我班上一位学员讲了他妻子对他的一个要求。她和其他一群妇女参加了一项自我提升的训练。她要求她丈夫帮她列出6项让她变得更聪明的事项。他在班上说:“我对这项要求很惊讶。坦白地说,要我列出将会改变她的6件事很容易——天啊!我太太可是能列出上千个希望我能变得更好的事项来——但我没这么做。我对她说:‘让我想想,明天早上再告诉你。’

“第二天早上我起得很早,打电话给花店,让他们给我妻子送6朵玫瑰花来,并在上面写道:‘我想不出有哪6件事希望你改变。我喜欢你现在的样子。’

“我晚上回家时,你想谁在门口迎接我?对了,我妻子。她几乎成了泪人。不必说什么,我很高兴没照她要求的那样去批评她。

“下个星期天她去教堂时,她把事情经过讲了出来,和她一起上课的几位女士走过来对我说:‘这是我听说过的最善解人意的事。’我也体会到了赞美的力量。”

佛罗伦兹·齐科菲——这位最富盛名的歌舞剧团老板,在百老汇可谓风光无限,他因为能让一个美国女子在一夜之间扬名四海而享有盛誉。他经常能把人们不愿多看一眼的平凡女子,魔幻般地变成舞台上富有魅力的名角。他深知赞赏和自信的价值,他总是会用那种热切的殷勤和体贴的关怀来使那些女子相信自己的美丽。他很现实,为那些歌女增加薪金,从每星期30美元增加到175美元;他还很懂感情,在福立士歌舞剧开始上演的晚上,向剧中明星们发电报祝贺,并将美丽迷人的玫瑰花赠送给每一位表演的歌舞女郎。

记得我有一次迷上了流行的节食风潮,竟6天6夜没有吃一点儿东西。不过这并没有什么难的。尤其是在第六天结束时,我反而不觉得比第二天更饥饿难耐。但我知道,而且你也知道,如果有人强迫他们的家人或雇员6天不许吃东西,那么这就是在犯罪;然而我们经常6天、6

know, as you know, people who would think they had committed a crime if they let their families or employees go for six days without food; but they will let them go for six days, and six weeks, and sometimes sixty years without giving them the hearty appreciation that they crave almost as much as they crave food.

When Alfred Lunt, one of the great actors of his time, played the leading role in *Reunion in Vienna*, he said, "There is nothing I need so much as nourishment for my self-esteem."

We nourish the bodies of our children and friends and employees, but how seldom do we nourish their self-esteem? We provide them with roast beef and potatoes to build energy, but we neglect to give them kind words of appreciation that would sing in their memories for years like the music of the morning stars.

Paul Harvey, in one of his radio broadcasts, "The Rest of the Story," told how showing sincere appreciation can change a person's life. He reported that years ago a teacher in Detroit asked Stevie Morris to help her find a mouse that was lost in the classroom. You see, she appreciated fact that nature had given Stevie something no one else in the room had. Nature had given Stevie a remarkable pair of ears to compensate for his blind eyes. But this was really the first time Stevie had been shown appreciation for those talented ears. Now, years later, he says that this act of appreciation was the beginning of a new life. You see, from that time on he developed his gift of hearing and went on to become, under the stage name of Stevie Wonder, one of the great pop singers and songwriters of the seventies.

Some readers are saying right now as they read these lines, "Oh, phooey! *Flattery! Bear oil!* I've tried that stuff. It doesn't work—not with intelligent people."

Of course flattery seldom works with discerning people. It is shallow, selfish and insincere. It ought to fail and it usually does. True, some people are so hungry, so thirsty, for appreciation that they will swallow anything, just as a starving man will eat grass and fishworms.

Even Queen Victoria was susceptible to flattery. Prime Minister Benjamin Disraeli confessed that he put it on thick in dealing with the Queen. To use his exact words, he said he "spread it on with a trowel." But Disraeli was one of the most polished, deft and adroit men who ever ruled the far-flung British Empire. He was a genius in his line. What would work for him wouldn't necessarily work for you

星期，或60年都不给人以真诚的赞美，而这种赞美却和食物一样重要。

当年阿尔弗雷德(他那个时代最伟大的演员)在《维也纳团聚》一剧中担任主角时曾说："我最迫切需要的东西，就是我的自尊。"

我们供养我们的孩子、朋友和雇员，但我们对他们自尊心的关注却少得可怜；我们为他们提供烤牛排、土豆，以增加他们的体力，但我们却不知道给他们以赞赏的语言，而这恰恰是生活中的晨曲，将会永远铭记在他们的心灵深处。

保尔·哈维在他的一次广播《故事启示》中讲了真诚的赞美是如何改变一个人的生活的。他说，几年前底特律一位老师请史蒂维·莫里斯帮她找一只在教室丢失的老鼠。你看，她赞美上帝给了史蒂维其他同学所没有的才能———对灵感的耳朵，以弥补失明的缺陷。但这却是史蒂维第一次有人赞美他的听力。现在，好几年过去了，他说这次赞美成了他新生活的开始。你看，从那以后他就开发自己的听力才能，并以史蒂维·王德尔的艺名而成为70年代顶尖的歌唱家和词作者。

有些读者读到这些话时，也许会说："老一套！阿谀奉承！拍马屁！那一套我已试过了，根本就不管用——对有知识的人根本就没有任何用处。"

当然，对于有自知之明的人来说，拍马屁很难起作用。因为拍马屁不过是肤浅、自私和虚伪的表现，它应该而且也常常遭到失败。可是，有些人确实非常渴望得到别人的赞美，甚至到了饥不择食的地步，正如即将饿死之人会吃草或鱼饵一样。

甚至连维多利亚女王也愿意被人恭维。曾经担任英国首相的狄斯累利承认，他常常在女王面前极力施展恭维之术。用他自己的话来说就是"尽力奉承"。狄斯累利是最文雅、最机巧、最老练的人之一，他曾经统治着幅员辽阔的英国。他也是一个天才。但他对维多利亚女王有效的方法不一定对你我有效。总的来说，恭维的弊端要多于益处。恭维是一种假象，正如假钞一样。如果你想用它，最终将会招来厄运。

赞赏和恭维区别何在呢?这其实很简单。一个是真诚的，而另一个是虚伪的。一个是出自

and me.In the long run,flattery will do you more harm than good.Flattery is counterfeit,and like counterfeit money,it will eventually get you into trouble if you pass it to someone else.

The difference between appreciation and flattery? That is simple.One is sincere and the other insincere.One comes from the heart out; the other from the teeth out.one is unselfish; the other selfish.One is universally admired; the other universally condemned.

I recently saw a bust of Mexican hero General Alvaro Obregon in the Chapultepec palace in Mexico City.Below the bust are carved these wise words from General Obregon's philosophy, "Don't be afraid of enemies who attack you.Be afraid of the friends who flatter you."

No! No! No! I am not suggesting flattery! Far from it.I'm talking about a new way of life.Let me repeat.I am talking about a new way of life.

King George V had a set of six maxims displayed on the walls of his study at Buckingham Palace.One of these maxims said, "Teach me neither to proffer nor receive cheap praise." That's all flattery is—cheap praise.I once read a definition of flattery that may be worth repeating, "Flattery is telling the other person precisely what he thinks about himself."

"Use what language you will," said Ralph Waldo Emerson, "you can never say anything but what you are."

If all we had to do was flatter,everybody would catch on and we should all be experts in human relations.

When we are not engaged in thinking about some definite problem,we usually spend about 95 percent of our time thinking about ourselves.Now,if we stop thinking about ourselves for a while and begin to think of the other person's good points,we won't have to resort to flattery so cheap and false that it can be spotted almost before it is out of the mouth.

One of the most neglected virtues of our daily existence is appreciation.Somehow,we neglect to praise our son or daughter when he or she brings home a good report card,and we fail to encourage our children when they first succeed in baking a cake or building a birdhouse.Nothing pleases children more than this kind of parental interest and approval.

The next time you enjoy filet mignon at the club,send word to the chef that it was excellently prepared,and when a tired salesperson shows you unusual courtesy,please mention it.

内心的，而另一个只不过是口头上的。一个是没有丝毫自私目的的，而另一个是出自个人私利的。一个将会得到天下人的钦佩，而另一个只会被天下人唾弃。

最近，我在墨西哥城的查普特佩克宫看到墨西哥英雄奥伯根将军的一座半身像。在像的下面刻着奥伯根将军的哲理名言："不要怕那些攻击你的敌人；而要小心那些恭维你的朋友。"

在此我绝不是想提倡恭维！绝对不是。我只是在讲一种新的生活方式。让我再说一遍吧，我只是在讲一种新的生活方式。

英国的乔治五世国王也有一套共计6条的格言，被挂在白金汉宫书房的墙上。其中有一条格言说："不要恭维他人，也不要接受不值钱的赞美。"恭维就是那种"不值钱的赞美"。我曾读过一句关于恭维的话，也许值得重复："恭维就是巧妙地告诉别人他是如何看待自己的。"

"无论你说什么话，"爱默生说，"也无法欺骗你自己的本心。"

假如靠恭维就可以达到目的，那么每个人都会争着去学习恭维之术了，而且我们都可以成为人际关系专家了。

当我们没有思考某个确定的问题时，我们常有95%的时间在考虑个人的事情。现在，如果我们暂且不想我们自己，而是去想想别人的优点，那么我们就不会，也没有必要刻意造出那些廉价而尚未出口的虚假恭维了。

在日常生活中，我们最容易忽略的美德之一就是赞美。有时候，孩子从学校带回好成绩，我们忘了赞扬他们；当孩子第一次烤好一块蛋糕或做好一个鸟笼时，我们也忘了鼓励他们。父母的关注和赞扬是最令孩子高兴的。

下一次，当你在餐厅见到盘中漂亮的装饰时，不妨告诉厨师他们做得多好。当疲惫的售货员耐心地给你取货物时，也别忘了称赞。

每一位牧师、演讲者和公共发言人都知道，当他们倾其所有对听众讲话却得不到一丝赞美时会多么

Every minister, lecturer and public speaker knows the discouragement of pouring himself or herself out to an audience and not receiving a single ripple of appreciative comment. What applies to professionals applies doubly to workers in offices, shops and factories and our families and friends. In our interpersonal relations we should never forget that all our associates are human beings and hunger for appreciation. It is the legal tender that all souls enjoy.

Try leaving a friendly trail of little sparks of gratitude on your daily trips. You will be surprised how they will set small flames of friendship that will be rose beacons on your next visit.

Pamela Dunham of New Fairfield, Connecticut, had among her responsibilities on her job the supervision of a janitor who was doing a very poor job. The other employees would jeer at him and litter the hallways to show him what a bad job he was doing. It was so bad, productive time was being lost in the shop.

Without success, Pam tried various ways to motivate this person. She noticed that occasionally he did a particularly good piece of work. She made a point to praise him for it in front of the other people. Each day the job he did all around got better, and pretty soon he started doing all his work efficiently. Now he does an excellent job and other people give him appreciation and recognition. Honest appreciation got results where criticism and ridicule failed.

Hurting people not only does not change them, it is never called for. There is an old saying that I have cut out and pasted on my mirror where I cannot help but see it every day:

I shall pass this way but once; any good, therefore, that I can do or any kindness that I can show to any human being, let me do it now. Let me not defer nor neglect it, for I shall not pass this way again.

Emerson said: "Every man I meet is my superior in some way. In that, I learn of him."

If that was true of Emerson, isn't it likely to be a thousand times more true of you and me? Let's cease thinking of our accomplishments, our wants. Let's try to figure out the other person's good points. Then forget flattery. Give honest, sincere appreciation. Be "hearty in your approbation and lavish in your praise," and people will cherish your words and treasure them and repeat them over a lifetime—repeat them years after you have forgotten them.

Principle 2: Give honest and sincere appreciation.

沮丧。同样的情形发生在办公室、店铺和工厂员工,甚至我们家人和朋友身上,他们也会有同样感受,甚至加倍难受。不要忘了,我们接触的是渴望赞美的人。赞美是所有人都喜欢的一种合情合理的美德。

在你每天的生活之旅中,要努力留下赞美的温馨。你将惊讶地发现,这一点小火花会点燃友谊的火焰,当你下次再访时就会看见其痕迹。

康涅狄格州新费尔菲尔德市的帕米拉·杜哈姆的职责之一,便是监督一位可怜的看门员的工作。其他员工总是讥讽他,在过道里乱扔东西,让他知道他的工作多么下贱。这对他来说太惨了,大好时光被耗费在了商场里。

帕米拉试了各种办法去激励这个人,都徒劳无功。她注意到他偶尔也会做一件非常出色的事情,于是她立即就此当众表扬了他。自此,他每天的工作都干得更好了,不久他所有的工作都非常有效率。现在他干的是一份优秀的工作,其他人都会给他赞美和认可。真诚的赞美所获得的结果是批评和嘲笑所难以达到的。

伤害别人不仅不能改变他们,更不能鼓舞他们。下面是一则古老的格言,我剪下来贴在镜子上,这样每天都能看见:

人生只有一次;所以,任何能奉献出来的美德和善行,现在就要去做。不要迟缓,不要忘记,因为人生只有一次。

爱默生说:"凡是我所遇见的人,都在某方面比我强。在这方面,我应该向他学习。"

爱默生都尚且如此,那么对你我来说不更应该这样去做吗?我们先别忙着表述自己的功绩和自己的需要。让我们先看看别人的优点,然后抛弃恭维,给人以真挚诚恳的赞美吧。"诚于嘉许,宽于称道",那么人们将视你的每一句话为珍宝,终身不忘——即使你自己早已经忘到九霄云外了,但别人仍然会铭记在心。

第二项规则:给予真挚诚恳的赞美。

3 "He Who Can Do This Has the Whole World with Him. He Who Cannot Walks a Lonely Way"

I often went fishing up in Maine during the summer.Personally I am very fond of strawberries and cream,but I have found that for some strange reason,fish prefer worms.So when I went fishing, I didn't think about what I wanted.I thought about what they wanted.I didn't bait the hook with strawberries and cream.Rather,I dangled a worm or a grasshopper in front of the fish and said, "Wouldn't you like to have that?"

Why not use the same common sense when fishing for people?

That is what Lloyd George,Great Britain's Prime Minister during World War I,did.When someone asked him how he managed to stay in power after the other wartime leaders—Wilson,Orlando and Clemenceau—had been forgotten,he replied that if his staying on top might be attributed to any one thing,it would be to his having learned that it was necessary to bait the hook to suit the fish.

Why talk about what we want? That is childish.Absurd.Of course,you are interested in what you want.You are eternally interested in it.But no one else is.The rest of us are just like you: we are interested in what we want.

So the only way on earth to influence other people is to talk about what *they* want and show them how to get it.

Remember that tomorrow when you are trying to get somebody to do something.If,for example, you don't want your children to smoke,don't preach at them,and don't talk about what you want; but show them that cigarettes may keep them from making the basketball team or winning the hundred-yard dash.

This is a good thing to remember regardless of whether you are dealing with children or calves or chimpanzees.For example: one day Ralph Waldo Emerson and his son tried to get a calf into the barn. But they made the common mistake of thinking only of what they wanted: Emerson pushed and his son pulled.But the calf was doing just what they were doing; he was thinking only of what he wanted; so he stiffened his legs and stubbornly refused to leave the pasture.The Irish housemaid saw their

第3章 激发他人的强烈需求

每年夏天,我都要去缅因州钓鱼。我自己很喜欢吃草莓和奶油,但是我发现鱼儿却喜欢吃小虫子。所以我钓鱼时,不会想我所喜欢吃的东西,而是琢磨这些鱼儿喜欢吃什么。我不会在鱼钩上挂上草莓和奶油,而是穿上一条蚯蚓或一只蚱蜢,垂到鱼儿面前,说:"你想吃这个吗?"

当你"钓"人时,为什么不试试同样的道理呢?第一次世界大战期间,英国首相劳埃德·乔治就采用了这种方式。有人问他,当其他在战争年代成为领袖的人,例如威尔逊、奥兰多及克里孟梭都被世人遗忘时,为什么他还能够大权在握。他回答说,如果他执权有术,那可能是因为他很早就明白了一个道理:要想钓到鱼,鱼饵必须适合鱼的口味!

为什么我们总是对自己的需要大加谈论呢?这可是孩子似的荒谬做法。当然,你关心的是自己的需要,而且对自己的需要永远都会感兴趣。但别人却不这样。别人都像你一样,只会对自己的需要感兴趣。

所以,世界上能够影响他人的唯一方法,就是谈论他们的需要,并告诉他们如何去获得它。

当你明天打算让某个人去做什么事的时候,一定要记住这一点。例如,当你不希望你的孩子吸烟时,那么不要训斥他,也不要对他讲你想什么。你只需让他知道,吸烟会使他不能加入篮球队,或不能赢得百米赛跑。

不论你是对待孩子还是小牛或黑猩猩,这条原则都必须牢记。例如,有一天爱默生和他的儿子想将一头小牛赶进牛棚。但他们犯了一个常识性的错误,他们只想达到自己的目的:爱默生在后面推小牛,他儿子则在前面拉小牛。但正如他们自己一样,这头小牛也只想它自己所要的,所以它蹬紧四腿,顽固地不肯离开原来的地方。一位爱尔兰女仆看到了这个僵持的场面。

predicament.She couldn't write essays and books; but,on this occasion at least,she had more horse sense,or calf sense,than Emerson had.She thought of what the calf wanted; so she put her maternal finger in the calf's mouth and let the calf suck her finger as she gently led him into the barn.

Every act you have ever performed since the day you were born was performed because you wanted something.How about the time you gave a large contribution to the Red Cross? Yes,that is no exception to the rule.You gave the Red Cross the donation because you wanted to lend a helping hand; you wanted to do a beautiful,unselfish,divine act."Inasmuch as ye have done it unto one of the least of these my brethren,ye have done it unto me."

If you hadn't wanted that feeling more than you wanted your money,you would not have made the contribution.Of course,you might have made the contribution because you were ashamed to refuse or because a customer asked you to do it.But one thing is certain.You made the contribution because you wanted something.

Harry A.Overstreet in his illuminating book *Influencing Human Behavior* said,"Action springs out of what we fundamentally desire...and the best piece of advice which can be given to would-be persuaders,whether in business,in the home,in the school,in politics,is: First,arouse in the other person an eager want.He who can do this has the whole world with him.He who cannot walks a lonely way."

Andrew Carnegie,the poverty-stricken Scotch lad who started to work at two cents an hour and finally gave away $365 million,learned early in life that the only way to influence people is to talk in terms of what the other person wants.He attended school only four years; yet he learned how to handle people.

To illustrate: His sister-in-law was worried sick over her two boys.They were at Yale,and they were so busy with their own affairs that they neglected to write home and paid no attention whatever to their mother's frantic letters.

Then Carnegie offered to wager a hundred dollars that he could get an answer by return mail, without even asking for it.Someone called his bet; so he wrote his nephews a chatty letter, mentioning casually in a postscript that he was sending each one a five-dollar bill.

He neglected,however,to enclose the money.

Back came replies by return mail thanking "Dear Uncle Andrew" for his kind note and—you

尽管她不会写什么东西,但她至少比爱默生更了解马和牛的性格。她知道小牛想要什么,于是她把拇指伸进小牛的口中,一边让小牛吮吸她的手指,一边将它轻轻地引进牛棚。

从你来到这个世界起,你的每一种行为都是出自你的需求。你为什么要给红十字会捐一大笔钱?不错,这个行为仍不例外。你之所以捐钱给红十字会,是因为你也想伸出援助之手,要做一件善良无私的神圣之事。《圣经》中说:“既然你此举是为我的弟兄们做的,也就是为我做的。”

假如你行善的感觉比不上你对钱的喜爱,那你绝对不会捐款。当然,你也许会因为不好意思拒绝,或因为一个主顾请你捐,你才去捐款。但有一点是可以肯定的,那就是你是为了满足某种需要而捐款的。

奥弗斯特里特在他那本极具启发性的著作《影响人类的行为》中说:“行动源于我们的基本欲望……无论是在商业、家庭、学校中,还是在政治中,对那些想劝导别人的人来说,我所能给的最好的建议,就是首先要激发别人的需求。如果能做到这点,就可以如鱼得水;否则办不成任何事情。”

安德鲁·卡内基是一个贫苦的苏格兰少年。他刚开始工作的时候,每小时只挣两美分,可是他后来竟捐赠了3.65亿美元。这是因为他很早就明白,影响他人的唯一方法,就是谈论对方的需要。尽管他只读过4年书,但他学会了如何与人相处。

例如,他的嫂嫂因为她的两个儿子而忧劳成疾。他们在耶鲁大学读书,但却一心忙自己的事情,连信都不给家里写,而他们母亲写给他们的充满焦虑的信,他们也不愿回复。

于是,卡内基打了100美元的赌,说他不必请求回信,就可以得到他们的回信。有人和他打了这个赌。他给两个侄子写了一封信,在信后附带说给他们每人寄一张5美元的钞票。

不过,卡内基并没将钱装入信封里面。他们果然回信了,信中谢谢“亲爱的安德鲁叔叔给我们的来信,但……”——我想下面的内容读者一猜就知道了。

另一个例子来自我班上一位俄亥俄州克利夫兰市的学员史丹·诺瓦克。一天晚上,史丹下

can finish the sentence yourself.

Another example of persuading comes from Stan Novak of Cleveland, Ohio, a participant in our course. Stan came home from work one evening to find his youngest son, Tim, kicking and screaming on the living room floor. He was to start kindergarten the next day and was protesting that he would not go. Stan's normal reaction would have been to banish the child to his room and tell him had just better make up his mind to go. He had no choice. But tonight, recognizing that this would not really help Tim start kindergarten in the best frame of mind, Stan sat down and thought, "If I were Tim, why would I be excited about going to kindergarten?" He and his wife made a list of all the fun things Tim would do such as finger painting, singing songs, making new friends. Then they put them into action. "We all started finger-painting on the kitchen table—my wife, Lil, my other son Bob, and myself, all having fun. Soon Tim was peeping around the corner. Next he was begging to participate. 'Oh, no! You have to go to kindergarten first to learn how to finger-paint.' With all the enthusiasm I could muster I went through the list talking in terms he could understand—telling him all the fun he would have in kindergarten. The next morning, I thought I was the first one up. I went downstairs and found Tim sitting sound asleep in the living room chair. 'What are you doing here?' I asked. 'I'm waiting to go to kindergarten. I don't want to be late.' the enthusiasm of our entire family had aroused in Tim an eager want that no amount of discussion or threat could have possibly accomplished."

Tomorrow you may want to persuade somebody to do something. Before you speak, pause and ask yourself, "How can I make this person want to do it?"

That question will stop us from rushing into a situation heedlessly, with futile chatter about our desires.

At one time I rented the grand ballroom of a certain New York hotel for twenty nights in each season in order to hold a series of lectures.

At the beginning of one season, I was suddenly informed that I should have to pay almost three times as much rent as formerly. This news reached me after the tickets had been printed and distributed and all announcements had been made.

Naturally, I didn't want to pay the increase, but what was the use of talking to the hotel about what I wanted? They were interested only in what they wanted. So a couple of days later I went to see the manager.

班回家后，发现小儿子迪米在客厅的地板上打滚，又哭又闹的。原来，迪米第二天就要去幼儿园了，但他不愿去。如果是平时，史丹肯定会将迪米叫到房间，命令他最好还是去幼儿园，他别无选择。但史丹这天晚上意识到这样并不能让迪米带着好心情去幼儿园。于是史丹坐了下来，心想："如果我是迪米，为什么会高高兴兴地去幼儿园呢？"他和夫人一起将迪米将在幼儿园所乐意做的事情列了一张表，例如手指画画、唱歌、交朋友等。然后，他们开始采取行动。"我和我夫人、我的另一个儿子鲍勃开始在厨房的桌子上用手指画画，而且很开心。没过多久，迪米就站在墙角偷看我们，然后请求参加我们的活动。'不行，你必须先去幼儿园学习用手指画画。'我用他能够听得懂的话，以最大的热情向他解释那张表上所列的各种有趣的事情，并告诉他会在幼儿园得到这些乐趣。第二天早上，我本以为我是第一个起床的人，可是下楼后发现迪米竟坐在客厅的沙发上睡了一个晚上。我问：'你怎么睡在这里？'他说：'我在等着去幼儿园。我可不想迟到。'你看，我们全家已经激起了迪米内心强烈的愿望，而若采取讨论或强迫的办法是根本无济于事的。"

也许你明天打算劝某人做某事。在你开口之前，不妨先问问自己："我怎样才能使他心甘情愿做这件事？"

这问题可以使我们不至于冒冒失失、毫无结果地去同别人谈论我们的各种愿望。

有一段时间，我每个季度都要租纽约某大饭店的大舞厅用20个晚上，举行一系列演讲。

在某一季开始的时候，我忽然接到饭店的通知，必须支付几乎比以前高3倍的租金。我得知这个消息时，入场券已经印发，而且通告已经公布了。

我当然不愿意支付这增加的部分租金，但是和饭店谈我的想法又有何用呢？他们只关心他们所需要的。于是，几天之后我找到了饭店经理。

"我接到你的信时有点吃惊，"我说，"但我一点都不怪你。如果换成是我，恐怕也会写一

"I was a bit shocked when I got your letter," I said, "but I don't blame you at all. If I had been in your position, I should probably have written a similar letter myself. Your duty as the manager of the hotel is to make all the profit possible. If you don't do that, you will be fired and you ought to be fired. Now, let's take a piece of paper and write down the advantages and the disadvantages that will accrue to you, if you insist on this increase in rent."

Then I took a letterhead and ran a line through the center and headed one column "Advantages" and the other column "Disadvantages."

I wrote down under the head "Advantages" these words: "Ballroom free." Then I went on to say, "You will have the advantage of having the ballroom free to rent for dances and conventions. That is a big advantage, for affairs like that will pay you much more than you can get for a series of lectures. If I tie your ballroom up for twenty nights during the course of the season, it is sure to mean a loss of some very profitable business to you.

"Now, lets' consider the disadvantages. First, instead of increasing your income from me, you are going to decrease it. In fact, you are going to wipe it out because I cannot pay the rent you are asking. I shall be forced to hold these lectures at some other place.

"There's another disadvantage to you also. These lectures attract crowds of educated and cultured people to your hotel. That is good advertising for you, isn't it? In fact, if you spent five thousand dollars advertising in the newspapers, you couldn't bring as many people to look at your hotel as I can bring by these lectures. That is worth a lot to a hotel, isn't it?"

As I talked, I wrote these two "disadvantages" under the proper heading, and handed the sheet of paper to the manager, saying, "I wish you would carefully consider both the advantages and disadvantages that are going to accrue to you and then give me your final decision."

I received a letter the next day, informing me that my rent would be increased only 50 percent instead of 300 percent.

Mind you, I got this reduction without saying a word about what I wanted. I talked all the time about what the other person wanted and how he could get it.

Suppose I had done the human, natural thing; suppose I had stormed into his office and said, "What do you mean by raising my rent three hundred percent when you know the tickets have been printed and

封相似的信。你身为饭店经理,有责任为饭店创造利润。如果你不那样做,你就要被辞掉,并且应当被辞掉。现在,且让我们拿一张纸来,将你坚持增加租金而给你带来的利弊一一列出来。"

说完,我拿出一张信纸,在中间画好一条竖线,一栏的上端写明"利",另一栏则写上"弊"。

在"利"的一栏我写上"舞厅空出来"几个字,然后接着说:"你可以随便出租舞厅开舞会和聚会。收益会相当可观,因为这类活动比租给演讲所得的租金要多得多。如果我在这一季度占用你的舞厅 20 个晚上,你一定会失去这笔利润。

"现在,让我们来看看'弊'。首先,将舞厅租给我并不能增加你的收入,相反你还会减少收入。事实上,你将一点收入都没有,因为我付不起你所要求的租金。我只能到别处举行演讲。

"对你还有另一个不利。这些演讲会吸引那些受过高等教育的人士来你的饭店,这对你可是一种极好的广告,难道不是吗?事实上,你就是花上 5000 美元在报纸上做广告,也不能使来你饭店的人数和来听我演讲的人那样多。而这对于一家饭店来说是很有价值的,对不对?"

我一边讲,一边将这两种不利写在相应的栏目中,然后将那张纸递给经理,说:"我希望你好好考虑一下,然后将最后的决定告诉我。"

第二天,我收到一封信,通知我租金只加一半,而不是当初的 3 倍。

请注意,我对于我的愿望没有谈一个字,就达到了减少租金的目的。因为我一直在讲对方所需要的东西,以及他怎样才能得到它。

假设我像普通人那样,直接闯进他的办公室说:"你这是什么意思?明明知道入场券已经印好,而且通知已经公告,却要增加我的租金 3 倍?3 倍!太可笑了!太荒谬了!我可不会付给你!"

然后情况会怎样呢?那一定会引发激烈的争论,甚至是白热化的争吵——而你知道会造成

the announcements made? Three hundred percent! Ridiculous! Absurd! I won't pay it! "

What would have happened then? An argument would have begun to steam and boil and sputter—and you know how arguments end.Even if I had convinced him that he was wrong,his pride would have made it difficult for him to back down and give in.

Here is one of the best bits of advice ever given about the fine art of human relationships. "If there is any one secret of success," said Henry Ford, "it lies in the ability to get the other person's point of view and see things from that person's angle as well as from your own."

That is so good,I want to repeat it: "*If there is any one secret of success,it lies in the ability to get the other person's point of view and see things from that person's angle as well as from your own.*"

That is so simple,so obvious,that anyone ought to see the truth of it at a glance; yet 90 percent of the people on this earth ignore it 90 percent of the time.

An example? Look at the letters that come across your desk tomorrow morning,and you will find that most of them violate this important canon of common sense.Take this one,a letter written by the head of the radio department of an advertising agency with offices scattered across the continent.This letter was sent to the managers of local radio stations throughout the country.(I have set down,in brackets,my reactions to each paragraph.)

Mr.John Blank,
Blankville,
Indiana
Dear Mr.Blank:

The company desires to retain its position in advertising agency leadership in the radio field.

[Who cares what your company desires? I am worried about my own problems.The bank is foreclosing the mortgage on my house,the bugs are destroying the hollyhocks,the stock market tumbled yesterday.I missed the eight-fifteen this morning,I wasn't invited to the Jones's dance last night,the doctor tells me I have high blood pressure and neuritis and dandruff.And then what happens? I come down to the office this morning worried,open my mail and here is some little whippersnapper off in New York yapping about what his company wants.Bah! If he only realized what sort of impression his letter makes,he would get out of the advertising business

什么后果。即使我能让他相信他是错的,他的自尊也不会让他屈服和退让。

关于为人处世,这里有一句至理名言。"如果成功有什么秘诀的话","汽车大王"亨利·福特说,"那就是站在对方的立场看问题,如同从你自己的立场看问题一样。"

这话真是棒极了!我要重述一次:"如果成功有什么秘诀的话,那就是站在对方的立场看问题,如同从你自己的立场看问题一样。"

这话实在是再简单、再浅显不过了,任何人都应该一眼就看出其中的道理,但我们这个世界上90%的人在90%的时候都忽略了它。

例子呢? 明天早上看看你桌上的信, 你就会发现大多数信都违反了这种常识性的道理。就拿其中一封信来说吧——这封信是一家在全国各地都有分公司的广告公司的无线电部主任写的,它分发给全国各地的无线电台经理。(我将在括号中表明我对每一段文字的想法)。

约翰·布兰克先生
布兰克维尔,印第安纳州
亲爱的布兰克先生:

本公司希望保持在无线电界广告业务的领袖地位。

(谁关心你的公司希望什么? 我正担心我自己的问题呢! 银行正准备没收我的房产抵押,害虫正在咬花草,昨天交易市场大跌。今天早上我又误了8:15的火车,昨晚琼斯家举办舞会没有邀请我,而且医生告诉我说我患有高血压、神经炎、头屑过多等毛病。然后呢,又发生了什么?今天早上我心烦意乱地走进办公室,打开信件,竟然看到纽约一个名不见经传的家伙在啰啰嗦嗦地讲他公司的什么希望。这真是一派胡言!假如他知道他的信会给人什么印象的话,他就会知趣地离开广告界,改行干别的了。)

and start manufacturing sheep dip.]

This agency's national advertising accounts were the bulwark of the network.Our subsequent clearances of station time have kept us at the top of agencies year after year.

[You are big and rich and right at the top, are you? So what? I don't give two whoops in Hades if you are as big as General Motors and General Electric and the General Staff of the U.S.Army all combined.If you had as much sense as a half-witted hummingbird, you would realize that I am interested in how big I am—not how big you are.All this talk about your enormous success makes me feel small and unimportant.]

We desire to service our accounts with the last word on radio station information.

[You desire! You desire.You unmitigated ass.I'm not interested in what you desire or what the President of the United States desires.Let me tell you once and for all that I am interested in what I desire—and you haven't said a word about that yet in this absurd letter of yours.]

Will you, therefore, put the—company on your preferred list for weekly station information—every single detail that will be useful to an agency in intelligently booking time.

["Preferred list." You have your nerve! You make me feel insignificant by your big talk about your company —and then you ask me to put you on a "preferred" list, and you don't even say "please" when you ask it.]

A prompt acknowledgment of this letter, giving us your latest "doings," will be mutually helpful.

[You fool! You mail me a cheap form letter—a letter scattered far and wide like the autumn leaves—and you have the gall to ask me, when I am worried about the mortgage and the hollyhocks and my blood pressure, to sit down and dictate a personal note acknowledging your form letter—and you ask me to do it "promptly." What do you mean, "promptly"? Don't you know I am just as busy as you are—or, at least, I like to think I am.And while we are on the subject, who gave you the lordly right to order me around?...You say it will be "mutually helpful." At last, at last, you have begun to see my viewpoint.But you are vague about how it will be to my advantage.]

Very truly yours,

John Doe
Manager Radio Department

本公司在全国的广告客户,是各无线电台的保护伞。本公司每年的营业额都位居前列。

(你是不是又大又富,而且遥遥领先?但那又怎么样?即使你的公司有通用汽车公司、通用电气公司以及美国陆军总部合起来那么大,也不关我什么事。只要你有蜂鸟那么一点儿一知半解的大脑,你就应该清楚我只关心"我"有多大——而不是你有多大。关于你的伟大成功的所有这些言论,在我看来都非常渺小,而且毫不重要。)

我们希望将各家无线电台最新的消息提供给我们的客户。

(你希望!你希望!你这笨驴。我才不管你或美国总统有什么希望。我不妨干脆地告诉你,我只对我自己的事情感兴趣——而在你这封荒谬无比的信中却没有提到一个字。)

所以,你可将本公司列为你们告知每周消息的优先对象——凡是广告公司在刊登广告信息时有用的每一个细节都告诉我们。

("优先对象。"你胆子可不小!你在大吹大擂自己的公司,使我觉得微不足道——然后你要我将你列入"优先"名单,可是你却连个"请"字都不说。)

即刻回信,告诉我们你最近的"活动",这对彼此都会有好处。

(你这笨蛋!你将这样一封像秋天落叶般的信随随便便地寄给我,还在全国各地分送,竟然还好意思要我在担心房产被抵押、花草遭到害虫、血压太高的情况下,坐下来单独给你写一封回信,来回答你的复写信,而且还要我"即刻"回答——"即刻"是什么意思?难道你不知道我和你一样忙吗——或者我至少会想象和你一样忙?还有就是既然我们在谈某个问题,是谁给你这种权力来指使我干这干那的?……你说这件事将会使双方受益,可是你直到最后才想到我的利益。但怎样才对我有益你却又含混不清。)

你的朋友

无线电部主任 约翰·杜伊

P.S.The enclosed reprint from the Blankville Journal will be of interest to you, and you may want to broadcast it over your station.

[Finally, down here in the postscript, you mention something that may help me solve one of my problems. Why didn't you begin your letter with—but what's the use? Any advertising man who is guilty of perpetrating such drivel as you have sent me has something wrong with his medulla oblongata. You don't need a letter giving our latest doings. What you need is a quart of iodine in your thyroid gland.]

Now, if people who devote their lives to advertising and who pose as experts in the art of influencing people to buy—if they write a letter like that, what can we expect from the butcher and baker or the auto mechanic?

Here is another letter, written by the superintendent of a large freight terminal to a student of this course, Edward Vermylen. What effect did this letter have on the man to whom it was addressed? Read it and then I'll tell you.

A.Zerega's Sons, Inc.
28 Front St.
Brooklyn, N.Y.11201
Attention: Mr.Edward Vermylen
Gentlemen:

The operations at our outbound-rail-receiving station are handicapped because a material percentage of the total business is delivered us in the late afternoon. This condition results in congestion, overtime on the part of our forces, delays to trucks, and in some cases delays to freight. On November 10, we received from your company a lot of 510 pieces, which reached here at 4:20 p.m.

We solicit your cooperation toward overcoming the undesirable effects arising from late receipt of freight. May we ask that, on days on which you ship the volume which was received on the above date, effort be made either to get the truck here earlier or to deliver us part of the freight during the morning?

The advantage that would accrue to you under such an arrangement would be that of more expeditious discharge of your trucks and the assurance that your business would go forward on

再启：附上《布兰克维尔日报》的副本，你也许会感兴趣，愿在你的电台播放。

（在这最后的附言中，你是提到了可以帮助我解决一个问题。但是这又有什么用呢？为什么一开始不用这个呢？任何广告商如果犯了你这种毛病，一定是神经错乱。你并不需要我们最近活动的消息。你所要的不过是一品脱碘，好注射进你的甲状腺。）

现在，假如一生都投身于广告事业的人自以为是专家，能左右他人的购买决策，可是却写出那样一封信来，对于其他行业的人，我们还能指望他们会写出什么来呢？

这儿还有另一封由一个大货运公司的总监给我班上一位名叫维米兰的学员写的信。对于收信人来说，这封信会有什么影响呢？先来读这封信，然后我再告诉你。

齐瑞格公司
前街28号，布洛克林，纽约，11201
爱德华·维米兰先生收
尊敬的先生：

本公司外运收货站的工作常常受到阻碍，因为大部分货物都是在傍晚才送过来给我们，结果就导致了交通拥挤，员工也不得不加班，卡车也被堵塞，致使货物延迟发送。11月10日，我们收到贵公司需要发运的510件货物，但这些货物直到下午4:20才送到我们这里。

为了避免货物延迟送达所产生的不利影响，我们请求你们进行合作。你们以后如果需要发送上面这类大宗货物时，能不能尽量让卡车提早过来，或者在上午时先送过来一部分货物？

这样对你们会有好处：你们的卡车可以迅速返回，并且可以保证你们的货物在收到的当天就可以发出去。

the date of its receipt.

Very truly yours,

J—B—, Supt.

After reading this letter, Mr.Vermylen, sales manager for A.Zerega's Sons, Inc., sent it to me with the following comment:

This letter had the reverse effect from that which was intended.The letter begins by describing the Terminal's difficulties, in which we are not interested, generally speaking.Our cooperation is then requested without any thought as to whether it would inconvenience us, and then, finally, in the last paragraph, the fact is mentioned that if we do cooperate it will mean more expeditious discharge of our trucks with the assurance that our freight will go forward on the date of its receipt.

In other words, that in which we are most interested is mentioned last and the whole effect is one of raising a spirit of antagonism rather than of cooperation.

Let's see if we can't rewrite and improve this letter.Let's not waste any time talking about our problems.As Henry Ford admonishes, let's "get the other person's point of view and see things from his or her angle, as well as from our own."

Here is one way of revising the letter.It may not be the best way, but isn't it an improvement?

Mr.Edward Vermylen
A.Zerega's Sons, Inc.
28 Front St.
Brooklyn, N.Y.11201
Dear Mr.Vermylen:

Your company has been one of our good customers for fourteen years.Naturally, we are very grateful for your patronage and are eager to give you the speedy, efficient service you deserve. However, we regret to say that it isn't possible for us to do that when your trucks bring us a large shipment late in the afternoon, as they did on November 10.Why? Because many other customers make late afternoon deliveries also.Naturally, that causes congestion.That means your trucks are held up unavoidably at the pier and sometimes even your freight is delayed.

你的朋友

总监 J-B-

读完这封信以后，担任齐瑞格公司销售经理的维米兰先生写了下面这些意见给我：

“这封信所产生的实际效果，与其初衷正好相反。这封信在一开头就讲货运站的困难，但是一般来说，我们并不关心这些。然后是要求我们合作，却一点也没有想到对我们是否有任何的不便。在最后一段，总算是提到，如果我们合作，可以使我们的卡车迅速返回，并保证我们的货物可以在收到之日发送出去。

“换言之，我们最关注的事情，对方却在最后才提到，因此这封信的整体效果，只会产生敌对，而不是合作的心理。”

我们来看看是否可以重写并完善这封信。我们不应该浪费时间讲我们的问题。正如亨利·福特所建议的，我们应该“站在对方的立场看问题，如同从你自己的立场看问题一样”。

下面就是一种修改方法。这也许不是最好的方法，但是不是可以有所改善呢？

爱德华·维米兰先生
齐瑞格公司
前街 28 号，布洛克林，纽约，11201
亲爱的维米兰先生：

14 年来，贵公司一直是我们的好主顾。对于你们的光顾，我们当然非常感谢，并非常乐意为你们提供迅速高效的服务。但让我们感到遗憾的是，如果你们的卡车还是像 11 月 10 日那样在傍晚给我们送过来大批的货物，那么我们就很难为贵公司提供迅速高效的服务。为什么呢？因为其他许多顾客也在傍晚给我们送货。这样，经常会造成交通拥堵，你们的卡车就会在码头受阻，甚至会导致你们的货物不能按时发出。

That's bad, but it can be avoided. If you make your deliveries at the pier in the morning when possible, your trucks will be able to keep moving, your freight will get immediate attention, and our workers will get home early at night to enjoy a dinner of the delicious macaroni and noodles that you manufacture.

Regardless of when your shipments arrive, we shall always cheerfully do all in our power to serve you promptly.

You are busy. Please don't trouble to answer this note.

Yours truly,

J—B—, Supt.

Barbara Anderson, who worked in a bank in New York, desired to move to Phoenix, Arizona, because of the health of her son. Using the princiles she had learned in our course, she wrote the following letter to twelve banks in Phoenix:

Dear Sir:

My ten years of bank experience should be of interest to a rapidly growing bank like yours.

In various capacities in bank operations with the Bankers Trust Company in New York, leading to my present assignment as Branch Manager, I have acquired skills in all phases of banking including depositor relations, credits, loans and administration.

I will be relocating to Phoenix in May and I am sure I can contribute to your growth and profit. I will be in Phoenix the week of April 3 and would appreciate the opportunity to show you how I can help your bank meet its goals.

Sincerely,

Barbara L. Anderson

Do you think Mrs. Anderson received any response from that letter? Eleven of the twelve banks invited her to be interviewed, and she had a choice of which bank's offer to accept. Why? Mrs. Anderson did not state what *she* wanted, but wrote in the letter how she could help them, and focused on *their* wants, not her own.

Thousands of salespeople are pounding the pavements today, tired, discouraged and underpaid. Why? Because they are always thinking only of what they want. They don't realize that neither you

这种情况实在是太糟糕了，但它是可以避免的。如果你们尽可能在上午把货物运到我们的码头，你们的卡车就会畅通无阻，货物也可以即刻发送出去，而我们的员工每天晚上也可以早点回家，吃到贵公司生产的鲜美的馄饨和面条。

当然，无论你们的货物何时到达，我们都会竭力而迅速地为贵公司服务。

你公务繁忙，请不必费工夫回信。

你的朋友

总监 J–B–

芭贝拉·安德森在纽约一家银行工作，但为了儿子的身体健康，她打算搬到亚利桑那州的凤凰城。她利用在我们班上学到的原则，给凤凰城的 12 家银行写了下面这封信。

敬上启信者：

我在银行工作，已有 10 年经验，对于像你们这样快速发展的银行，对我应该会感兴趣。

我曾就职于一家纽约银行的信托公司，现在已经升为分部经理，对银行各部门的业务十分熟悉，包括与储户的关系、信用、贷款以及行政。

我将十 5 月份搬到凤凰城居住，深信能够对贵银行的发展与盈利有所帮助。我将在 4 月 3 日那个星期抵达凤凰城。如果能被给予机会，使我显示如何有助于贵银行发展，则不胜感激。

你的朋友

芭贝拉·安德森

你认为安德森夫人这封信会得到答复吗？这 12 家银行中有 11 家请她去面谈，这足够她选择的了。为什么会这样呢？安德森夫人并没有说她想要什么，她只是在信中说自己可以帮助银行，强调银行的需要，而不是她自己的需要。

nor I want to buy anything.If we did,we would go out and buy it.But both of us are eternally interested in solving our problems.And if salespeople can show us how their services or merchandise will help us solve our problems,they won't need to sell us.We'll buy.And customers like to feel that they are buying—not being sold.

Yet many salespeople spend a lifetime in selling without seeing things from the customer's angle.For example,for many years I lived in Forest Hills,a little community of private homes in the center of Greater New York.One day as I was rushing to the station,I chanced to meet a real-estate operator who had bought and sold property in that area for many years.He knew Forest Hills well,so I hurriedly asked him whether or not my stucco house was built with metal lath or hollow tile.He said he didn't know and told me what I already knew—that I could find out by calling the Forest Hills Garden Association.The following morning,I received a letter from him.Did he give me the information I wanted? He could have gotten it in sixty seconds by a telephone call.But he didn't.He told me again that I could get it by telephoning,and then asked me to let him handle my insurance.

He was not interested in helping me.He was interested only in helping himself.

J.Howard Lucas of Birmingham,Alabama,tells how two salespeople from the same company handled the same type of situation,He reported:

"Several years ago I was on the management team of a small company.Headquartered near us was the district office of a large insurance company.Their agents were assigned territories,and our company was assigned to two agents,whom I shall refer to as Carl and John.

"One morning,Carl dropped by our office and casually mentioned that his company had just introduced a new life insurance policy for executives and thought we might be interested later on and he would get back to us when he had more information on it.

"The same day,John saw us on the sidewalk while returning from a coffee break,and he shouted, 'Hey Luke,hold up,I have some great news for you fellows.'He hurried over and very excitedly told us about an executive life insurance policy his company had introduced that very day.(It was the same policy that Carl had casually mentioned.)He wanted us to have one of the first issued.He gave us a few important facts about the coverage and ended saying, 'the policy is so new,I'm going to have someone from the home office come out tomorrow and explain it.Now,in the

现在有成千上万的推销员在路上疲于奔命,心情沮丧而且入不敷出。这是什么原因呢?因为他们一直在想的只是自己的需要,却不知道你和我都不想买任何东西。如果我们需要的话,我们会出去购买。我们总是在想着如何解决自己的问题。所以如果推销员能告诉我们,他们的服务或商品将会帮助我们解决问题,那么他们就不必向我们推销,我们会主动购买。顾客喜欢感到是自己主动要买——而不是被人推销。

但是,许多干了一辈子推销的人,却从不知道应该从顾客的角度来看问题。例如,我曾长期住在纽约中心的林丘住宅小区。有一天我正急匆匆地赶去车站, 碰巧遇到了一位房地产经纪人,他在那一带推销房地产已有许多年。由于他对林丘很熟悉,所以我急忙问他我的水泥房是用钢筋造的,还是用空心砖造的。他说他不知道,并告诉我一大堆我早已知道的东西。他说我可以打电话给林丘公司协会询问我房子的事。次日一早,我就收到了他的信。他是不是给了我需要的东西呢?他只需花 60 秒钟打一个电话就可以得到这些信息的,可是他并没有那样做。他再次告诉我自己打电话去咨询,然后请我让他来为我办理保险业务。

他并不是真的想帮助我。他只对帮助自己感兴趣。

亚拉巴马州伯明翰市的卢卡斯介绍了同一个公司两名推销员在处理同一类事情时是如何做的。他说:

"几年前,我在一个小公司任管理职务。在我们附近有一家大保险公司的分公司。他们的业务员按区域分配任务,而我们公司由两名业务员负责。我姑且称他们为卡尔和约翰。

"一天早上,卡尔来我们办公室,偶然谈到他的公司刚计划为高级职员办理人身保险,也许我们会对此感兴趣,并说等他得到更详细的资料之后再来看我们。

"同一天,我们喝完咖啡往回走时,约翰看见我们,他大声说:'等等,我有好消息告诉你们!'他追了过来,兴冲冲地告诉我们,说他公司新设了一项人身保险业务(其实卡尔在闲谈中

meantime, let's get the applications signed and on the way so he can have more information to work with.' His enthusiasm aroused in us an eager want for this policy even though we still did not have details. When they were made available to us, they confirmed John's initial understanding of the policy, and he not only sold each of us a policy, but later doubled our coverage.

"Carl could have had those sales, but he made no effort to arouse in us any desire for the policies."

The world is full of people who are grabbing and self-seeking. So the rare individual who unselfishly tries to serve others has an enormous advantage. He has little competition. Owen D. Young, a noted lawyer and one of America's great business leaders, once said, "People who can put themselves in the place of other people, who can understand the workings of their minds, need never worry about what the future has in store for them."

If out of reading this book you get just one thing—an increased tendency to think always in terms of other people's point of view, and see things from their angle—if you get that one thing out of this book, it may easily prove to be one of the building blocks of your career.

Looking at the other person's point of view and arousing in him an eager want for something is not to be construed as manipulating that person so that he will do something that is only for your benefit and his detriment. Each party should gain from the negotiation. In the letters to Mr. Vermylen, both the sender and the receiver of the correspondence gained by implementing what was suggested. Both the bank and Mrs. Anderson won by her letter in that the bank obtained a valuable employee and Mrs. Anderson a suitable job. And in the example of John's sale of insurance to Mr. Lucas, both gained through this transaction.

Another example in which everybody gains through this principle of arousing an eager want comes from Michael E. Whidden of Warwick, Rhode Island, who is a territory salesman for the Shell Oil Company. Mike wanted to become the Number One salesperson in his district, but one service station was holding him back. It was run by an older man who could not be motivated to clean up his station. It was in such poor shape that sales were declining significantly.

This manager would not listen to any of Mike's pleas to upgrade the station. After many exhortations and heart-to-heart talks—all of which had no impact—Mike decided to invite the

已经提到过它)。约翰要我们成为首批投保人员。他给了我们一些重要资料,还说:'这种保险是最新的。我会请总公司明天派人来作详细介绍。现在就请在申请单上签名,这样就会有更多的资料供那人作分析了。'尽管我们还不了解这项保险的具体情况,但他的热情已经激发出我们对这项保险的强烈需要。等保险合同送达我们时,我们发现它和约翰所说的完全相符。因此他不但让我们每个人都购买了这项保险,后来还增加了保额!"

"本来卡尔也可以卖出这些保险的,但他并没有想办法激起我们购买保险的欲望。"

世界上到处都是充满贪求和欲望的人,所以那少数不存私心帮助别人的人,能够大有收获。他几乎遇不到竞争。欧文·扬这位著名律师及伟大商业领袖曾说:"能够设身处地为别人着想、洞察别人心理的人,永远不必担心自己的前途。"

如果你从本书中学到了一件事——"永远从别人的立场去思考, 并从他们的角度来看问题"——如果你从本书学到了这一点,那么你这一生就会有一个新的里程碑。

分析别人的观点,并激发他对某件东西的强烈需求,并不是为控制这个人,使他做出对你有利而对他不利的事。任何一方都应在这种情况下有所得。例如就前面给维米兰先生的信来说,写信者和收信者都会因为所建议的事情而有所收获。安德森夫人的信,也使她和银行均有所得,银行得到了一位经验丰富的职员,而安德森夫人则找到了理想的工作。约翰将保险推销给卢卡斯的例子中,双方也都有所得。

激发别人的迫切需求,使双方都从中受益,这样的例子还有。下面这个例子就是由罗得岛威克市的麦克尔·威登先生说出来的。威登是壳牌石油公司一名地区推销员。他希望成为区域内最优秀的推销员, 但一个加油站使他受到了挫折。这个加油站的经理是一个上了年纪的老人,尽管威登想尽了办法,但老人仍然不能让加油站保持清洁,结果这里的汽油销售大大减少。

不论威登如何劝说,老人就是不动手清理加油站。在多次恳谈和劝说都以失败告终之后,

manager to visit the newest Shell station in his territory.

The manager was so impressed by the facilities at the new station that when Mike visited him the next time, his station was cleaned up and had recorded a sales increase. This enabled Mike to reach the Number One spot in his district. All his talking and discussion hadn't helped, but by arousing an eager want in the manager, by showing him the modem station, he had accomplished his goal, and both the manager and Mike benefited.

Most people go through college and learn to read Virgil and master the mysteries of calculus without ever discovering how their own minds function. For instance: I once gave a course in Effective Speaking for the young college graduates who were entering the employ of the Carrier Corporation, the large air-conditioner manufacturer. One of the participants wanted to persuade the others to play basketball in their free time, and this is about what he said, "I want you to come out and play basketball. I like to play basketball, but the last few times I've been to the gymnasium there haven't been enough people to get up a game. Two or three of us got to throwing the ball around the other night—and I got a black eye. I wish all of you would come down tomorrow night. I want to play basketball."

Did he talk about anything you want? You don't want to go to a gymnasium that no one else goes to, do you? You don't care about what he wants. You don't want to get a black eye.

Could he have shown you how to get the things you want by using the gymnasium? Surely. More pep. Keener edge to the appetite. Clearer brain. Fun. Games. Basketball.

To repeat Professor Overstreet's wise advice: *First, arouse in the other person an eager want. He who can do this has the whole world with him. He who cannot walks a lonely way.*

One of the students in the author's training course was worried about his little boy. The child was underweight and refused to eat properly. His parents used the usual method. They scolded and nagged. "Mother wants you to eat this and that." "Father wants you to grow up to be a big man."

Did the boy pay any attention to these pleas? Just about as much as you pay to one fleck of sand on a sandy beach.

No one with a trace of horse sense would expect a child three years old to react to the viewpoint of a father thirty years old. Yet that was precisely what that father had expected. It was

威登决定请他去参观区域内的另一处壳牌加油站。

老人对这个加油站的整洁美观印象深刻。当威登再次来找他时，只见他的加油站已经整理得干干净净，而且汽油销量也创下纪录。威登由此成为地区销售业绩最佳的员工。他以前的劝说和恳谈都没有打动老人，但他激发了老人内心的迫切愿望，并带他去观察另一家加油站，终于达到了他的目标——他和老人也都从中获益。

许多人上大学研读维吉尔的作品，并精通微积分，却从不知道他们的内心活动。例如，我有一次给一些年轻的大学生讲授《高效演讲》，他们即将去卡瑞尔公司工作，这是一家大型空调器生产公司。有一个学生劝别人闲暇时和他一起去打篮球，他是这样说的："我希望你们去打篮球。我喜欢打篮球，但我最近几次去体育馆时，人数不够，不能打比赛。前天晚上，我们两三个人玩投篮，结果把我眼睛都打肿了。我希望你们明天晚上都来。我想打篮球。"

他提到了你想要的任何东西吗？你不想去一个没人愿去的体育馆，对不对？你不愿关心他想要什么，你也不希望自己的眼睛被打肿。他本来能够让你明白如何利用体育馆来满足你的需要吗？当然能。例如，让你精神焕发、食欲更好、头脑更清醒，得到消遣和锻炼等。

再重复一次奥弗斯特里特教授的明智建议："首先激发别人的需求。如果能做到这点，就可以如鱼得水；否则办不成任何事情。"

在我的训练班上有一位学员，他非常担心他的儿子。这孩子很瘦，还不愿好好吃饭。他父母为此常采取责备的方法："妈妈要你吃这个、吃那个！""爸爸希望你长得又高又大。"

孩子理会这些吗？不会，一点儿都不会。

任何稍有常识的人，都不会指望一个3岁的孩子能够对30岁的父亲的规劝有什么积极反应，但这正是父亲本来期望的。这真是有些可笑！这位父亲最后领悟了，于是他问自己："这孩子想要什么？怎样才能将我所要的和他所要的结合起来？"

absurd.He finally saw that.So he said to himself,"What does that boy want? How can I tie up what I want to what he wants?"

It was easy for the father when he started thinking about it.His boy had a tricycle that he loved to ride up and down the sidewalk in front of the house in Brooklyn.A few doors down the street lived a bully—a bigger boy who would pull the little boy off his tricycle and ride it himself.

Naturally,the little boy would run screaming to his mother,and she would have to come out and take the bully off the tricycle and put her little boy on again.This happened almost every day.

What did the little boy want?It didn't take a Sherlock Holmes to answer that one.His pride,his anger,his desire for a feeling of importance—all the strongest emotions in his makeup—goaded him to get revenge,to smash the bully in the nose.And when his father explained that the boy would be able to wallop the daylights out of the bigger kid someday if he would only eat the things his mother wanted him to eat—when his father promised him that—there was no longer any problem of dietetics.That boy would have eaten spinach,sauerkraut,salt mackerel—anything in order to be big enough to whip the bully who had humiliated him so often.

After solving that problem,the parents tackled another: the little boy had the unholy habit of wetting his bed.

He slept with his grandmother.In the morning,his grandmother would wake up and feel the sheet and say,"Look,Johnny,what you did again last night."

He would say,"No,I didn't do it.You did it."

Scolding,spanking,shaming him,reiterating that the parents didn't want him to do it—none of these things kept the bed dry.So the parents asked,"How can we make this boy want to stop wetting his bed?"

What were his wants? First,he wanted to wear pajamas like Daddy instead of wearing a nightgown like Grandmother.Grandmother was getting fed up with his nocturnal iniquities,so she gladly offered to buy him a pair of pajamas if he would reform.Second,he wanted a bed of his own.Grandma didn't object.

His mother took him to a department store in Brooklyn,winked at the salesgirl,and said,"Here is a little gentleman who would like to do some shopping."

The salesgirl made him feel important by saying,"Young man,what can I show you?"

一旦父亲开始思考这个问题时,一切就容易多了。他儿子有辆三轮脚踏车,小家伙总喜欢在家门口的人行道上来回骑车。在他家附近住着一个小坏蛋——一个比他稍大些的孩子,他常常把这小孩拉下车,自己骑上去。当然,这小男孩会哭着告诉母亲。母亲便会立刻出来,将小坏蛋拉下车,再将她儿子抱上去。这种情况几乎每天都会发生。

这孩子需要什么呢?这并不需要福尔摩斯来解答。他需要的是自尊、发泄怒火,以及得到显要感——所有最强烈的情感——都在驱使他去"复仇",揍扁那个坏蛋的鼻子。于是,当父亲告诉他,只要他不挑食,乖乖地吃饭的话,终有一天他会把那坏蛋打得落花流水——当父亲向他作了这种保证之后,他果然不再挑食了。他开始愿意吃菠菜、白菜、咸鱼以及任何其他食物,想让自己快些长大,好狠狠地揍那个经常羞辱他的坏蛋一顿。

解决这个问题之后,这对父母又面临着另一件麻烦——这小男孩有尿床的坏习惯。

他和奶奶睡一张床。每天早上,奶奶醒了之后会摸摸床单,说:"你看,约翰,你昨晚又干了什么?"

小孩会说:"没有,不是我干的,是你。"

打他、骂他,甚至羞辱他,一再强调父母不许他尿床——都无济于事。于是,父母开始自问:"怎样才能让他愿意停止尿床呢?"他想要什么?第一,他想和父亲一样穿睡衣,而不是像奶奶那样穿睡袍。由于奶奶受够了他半夜尿床之苦,她答应如果他不再尿床的话,会很高兴地为他买一套睡衣。第二,他想要一张自己的床。奶奶当然也不反对。

于是,他母亲把他带到布鲁克林的一家百货商店,用眼光示意售货员小姐,说:"这位小先生想买点东西。"

售货员小姐以一种让男孩颇感受尊重的口气说:"小伙子,我能为你效劳吗?"

他站在那里,立刻像长高了两寸的样子,说:"我要给自己买张床。"

当他看过他母亲看中的一张床之后,母亲冲着售货员小姐使了个眼神。在售货员小姐的劝

He stood a couple of inches taller and said, "I want to buy a bed for myself."

When he was shown the one his mother wanted him to buy, she winked at the salesgirl and the boy was persuaded to buy it.

The bed was delivered the next day; and that night, when Father came home, the little boy ran to the door shouting, "Daddy! Daddy! Come upstairs and see my bed that I bought!"

The father, looking at the bed, obeyed Charles Schwab's injunction: he was "hearty in his approbation and lavish in his praise."

"You are not going to wet this bed, are you?" the father said.

"Oh, no, no! I am not going to wet this bed." The boy kept his promise, for his pride was involved. That was his bed. He and he alone had bought it. And he was wearing pajamas now like a little man. He wanted to act like a man. And he did.

Another father, K.T.Dutschmann, a telephone engineer, a student of this course, couldn't get his three-year-old daughter to eat breakfast food. The usual scolding, pleading, coaxing methods had all ended in futility. So the parents asked themselves, "How can we make her want to do it?"

The little girl loved to imitate her mother, to feel big and grown up; so one morning they put her on a chair and let her make the breakfast food. At just the psychological moment, Father drifted into the kitchen while she was stirring the cereal and she said, "Oh, look, Daddy, I am making the cereal this morning."

She ate two helpings of the cereal without any coaxing, because she was interested in it. She had achieved a feeling of importance; she had found in making the cereal an avenue of self-expression.

William Winter once remarked that "self-expression is the dominant necessity of human nature." Why can't we adapt this same psychology to business dealings? When we have a brilliant idea, instead of making others think it is ours, why not let them cook and stir the idea themselves? They will then regard it as their own; they will like it and maybe eat a couple of helpings of it.

Remember: "First, arouse in the other person an eager want. He who can do this has the whole world with him. He who cannot walks a lonely way."

Principle 3: Arouse in the other person an eager want.

说下,小男孩"买"了这张床。

第二天,床送到了。父亲晚上回家时,小男孩跑到门口,叫道:"爸爸,爸爸!快上楼来看我给自己买的床。"

当父亲看到那张床之后,遵循施瓦伯"诚于嘉许,宽于称道"的规诫,问儿子:"你不会尿湿这张床,是不是?"

"啊,是的,是的!我当然不会。"为了自尊,小男孩果然遵守住了诺言。这是"他"的床,而且是"他"自己买来的。他现在穿着睡衣,就像个小大人。他希望自己像个大人,而他也做到了。

另一个名叫德施曼的父亲,他是一位电话工程师,也是我班上一位学员,很难让他3岁的女儿吃早餐。普通的手段,如责骂、请求、哄骗等都不奏效。于是父母就问自己:"我们怎样才能使她'要'吃早餐?"

这小女孩喜欢模仿她母亲,喜欢让自己看上去像个大人。于是一天早上,他们把她放在一张椅子上,让她来做早餐。就在她搅拌早餐的时候,父亲走进厨房。她说:"瞧,爸爸,今天早上我自己做的早餐。"

那天早上,她没用任何诱哄就吃了两碗粥,因为她对早餐已经产生了兴趣。她从中获得了自重,从做早餐中找到了表现自我的方式。

威廉·温特尔曾说过:"自我表现是人类天性中最重要的因素。"为什么我们不在工作中应用同样的心理学呢?当我们有了一个好主意时,何不让对方说出来,而不让对方认为这是我们想到的?这样,他们会认为这是他们的主意而异常喜欢的,或许还会吃上两大碗呢!

记住:"首先激发别人的需求。如果能做到这点,就可以如鱼得水,否则办不成任何事情。"

第三项规则:激发别人的强烈需求。

Part Two
Six Ways to Make People Like You

1 Do This and You'll Be Welcome Anywhere

Why read this book to find out how to win friends? Why not study the technique of the greatest winner of friends the world has ever known? Who is he? You may meet him tomorrow coming down the street.When you get within ten feet of him,he will begin to wag his tail.If you stop and pat him, he will almost jump out of his skin to show you how much he likes you.And you know that behind this show of affection on his part,there are no ulterior motives: he doesn't want to sell you any real estate,and he doesn't want to marry you.

Did you ever stop to think that a dog is the only animal that doesn't have to work for a living? A hen has to lay eggs,a cow has to give milk,and a canary has to sing.But a dog makes his living by giving you nothing but love.

When I was five years old,my father bought a yellow-haired pup for fifty cents.He was the light and joy of my childhood.Every afternoon about four-thirty,he would sit in the front yard with his beautiful eyes staring steadfastly at the path,and as soon as he heard my voice or saw me swinging my dinner pail through the buck brush,he was off like a shot,racing breathlessly up the hill to greet me with leaps of joy and barks of sheer ecstasy. Tippy was my constant companion for five years.Then one tragic night—I shall never forget it—he was killed within ten feet of my head, killed by lightning.Tippy's death was the tragedy of my boyhood.

You never read a book on psychology,Tippy.You didn't need to.You knew by some divine instinct that you can make more friends in two months by becoming genuinely interested in other

第二篇 让别人喜欢你的 6 种方法

第 1 章 这样做你就会到处受欢迎

为什么要通过读本书来学习如何赢得朋友呢？为什么不向世界上最善于交友的人学习这种技巧呢?他又是谁?当你明天走到街上时,你也许会遇到他。当你走到距他 10 英尺之内的地方时,他就会开始摇尾巴。如果你停下来轻轻地抚摸他,他就会异常高兴地跳起来,向你表示他是多么的喜欢你。而且你也知道,在他这种亲热表现的背后,并没有其他的目的:他并不是想将一块地产推销给你,也不是要和你结婚。

你是否曾静下心来想过,狗是唯一不需要为生活而工作的动物呢?母鸡需要下蛋、母牛需要产奶、金丝雀必须唱歌。而狗只需要把它的爱给你,就可以生活无忧。

当我 5 岁的时候，我父亲花 50 美分给我买了一只小黄毛狗。它是我童年时代的光明和快乐源泉。每天下午大约 4 点半,它就会坐在院子前面,用它那美丽的眼睛静静地望着小道,只要一听到我的声音,或看见我晃着饭盒穿过矮树林时,它就会像箭飞一般,气喘吁吁地跑上小山,又跳又叫地欢迎我。蒂比和我做了 5 年的好朋友。然后,在一个悲惨的晚上——我永远也不会忘记的晚上——在离我 10 英尺远的地方,它被电击死了。蒂比的死是我童年时代的悲剧。

蒂比,你从来都没有读过心理学。你也不必去读。你可以通过你的直觉知道这点。如果你

people than you can in two years by trying to get other people interested in you.Let me repeat that. You can make more friends in two months by becoming interested in other people than you can in two years by trying to get other people interested in you.

Yet I know and you know people who blunder through life trying to wigwag other people into becoming interested in them. Of course, it doesn't work.People are not interested in you.They are not interested in me.They are interested in themselves—morning, noon and after dinner. The New York Telephone Company made a derailed study of telephone conversations to find out which word is the most frequently used.You have guessed it: it is the personal pronoun "I." "I." "I."It was used 3900 times in 500 telephone conversations. "I." "I." "I." "I." When you see a group photograph that you are in, whose picture do you look for first? If we merely try to impress people and get people interested in us, we will never have many true, sincere friends.Friends, real friends, are not made that way.

Alfred Adler, the famous Viennese psychologist, wrote a book entitled *What Life Should Mean to You.* In that book he says, "It is the individual who is not interested in his fellow men who has the greatest difficulties in life and provides the greatest injury to others.It is from among such individuals that all human failures spring."

You may read scores of erudite tomes on psychology without coming across a statement more significant for you and for me.Adler's statement is so rich with meaning that I am going to repeat it in italices: *It is the individual who is not interested in his fellow men who has the greatest difficulties in life and provides the greatest injury to others.It is from among such individuals that all human failures spring.*

I once took a course in short-story writing at New York University, and during that course the editor of a leading magazine talked to our class.He said he could pick up any one of the dozens of stories that drifted across his desk every day and after reading a few paragraphs he could feel whether or not the author liked people."If the author doesn't like people," he said, "people won't like his or her stories."

This hard - boiled editor stopped twice in the course of his talk on fiction writing and apologized for preaching a sermon."I am telling you," he said, "the same things your preacher

真的关心别人，那么你在两个月内所交到的朋友要比一个总想让别人关心他的人在两年内所交的朋友还要多。让我再重复一遍：如果你关心别人，你在两个月内所交到的朋友会比一个总想让别人关心他的人在两年之内所交的朋友还要多。

但是你和我都知道，有的人就是一辈子都难以醒悟过来，总是想让别人对他们感兴趣。当然，这种方法是行不通的。因为别人并不在意你。他们对我也不关心。他们只关心自己——无论是在早晨、中午，还是晚上。纽约电话公司曾对电话中的谈话内容做过详细研究，以了解哪些词在电话中最常用。你已经猜到了，那就是"我"、"我"、"我"。在500次电话谈话中，这个词曾被用过3990次。当你看一张你也在里面的团体照片时，你会先看谁呢?假如我们只想引起别人的注意，让别人对我们留下印象，我们永远不会有许多真挚而诚恳的朋友。朋友，真正的朋友，不是用那种方法交来的。

维也纳已故著名心理学家阿尔弗雷德·阿德勒写过一本书叫《生活的意义》。在那本书中，他说："对别人漠不关心的人，他的一生困难最多，对别人的伤害也最大。所有人类的失败，都是由这些人造成的。"

你也许读过几十卷关于心理学方面的书，但是却再也找不到比这句话对你和我更重要的了。阿德勒这句话太具有深意了，所以我重录于下："对别人漠不关心的人，他的一生困难最多，对别人的伤害也最大。所有人类的失败，都是由这些人造成的。"

我曾在纽约大学选修一门关于短篇小说写作的课。上课时，一家重要杂志的一位编辑为我们上课。他说当他每天拿起桌子上堆着的几十篇小说的任何一篇，只需要读完几段，就能感觉出作者是否喜欢人。"如果作者不喜欢别人，"他说，"别人也不会喜欢他的小说。"

这位阅历很深的编辑在他的讲课中曾停下来两次，为他所讲的那些大道理道歉。"现在我告诉你们的，"他说，"和你们的牧师告诉你们的一样。但是请记住，如果你要做一个成功的小说

would tell you, but remember, you have to be interested in people if you want to be a successful writer of stories."

If that is true of writing fiction, you can be sure it is true of dealing with people face-to-face.

I spent an evening in the dressing room of Howard Thurston the last time he appeared on Broadway—Thurston was the acknowledged dean of magicians. For forty years he had traveled all over the world, time and again, creating illusions, mystifying audiences, and making people gasp with astonishment. More than 60 million people had paid admission to his show, and he had made almost $2 million in profit.

I asked Mr. Thurston to tell me the secret of his success. His schooling certainly had nothing to do with it, for he ran away from home as a small boy, became a hobo, rode in boxcars, slept in haystacks, begged his food from door to door, and learned to read by looking out of boxcars at signs along the railway.

Did he have a superior knowledge of magic? No, he told me hundreds of books had been written about legerdemain and scores of people knew as much about it as he did. But he had two things that the others didn't have. First, he had the ability to put his personality across the footlights. He was a master showman. He knew human nature. Everything he did, every gesture, every intonation of his voice, every lifting of an eyebrow had been carefully rehearsed in advance, and his actions were timed to split seconds. But, in addition to that, Thurston had a genuine interest in people. He told me that many magicians would look at the audience and say to themselves, "Well, there is a bunch of suckers out there, a bunch of hicks; I'll fool them all right." But Thurston's method was totally different. He told me that every time he went on stage he said to himself, "I am grateful because these people come to see me. They make it possible for me to make my living in a very agreeable way. I'm going to give them the very best I possibly can."

He declared he never stepped in front of the footlights without first saying to himself over and over, "I love my audience. I love my audience." Ridiculous? Absurd? You are privileged to think anything you like. I am merely passing it on to you without comment as a recipe used by one of the most famous magicians of all time.

George Dyke of North Warren, Pennsylvania, was forced to retire from his service station

家,你必须关心别人。"

如果写小说是那样的话,那么在待人接物方面就更应该如此了。

当塞斯顿最后一次在百老汇演出时,我曾去他的化妆室呆了一整晚——塞斯顿被认为是"魔术之王"。他周游世界40年,一再创造出各种幻象,令观众如痴如醉,使人惊奇不已。总共有超过6000万的人掏钱观看他的表演,而他也得到了大约200万美元的收入。

我请塞斯顿先生将他的成功秘诀告诉我。当然,他的学校教育与此毫无关系,因为他在幼年时就离家出走,成了一个流浪儿,沿途搭乘货车,睡在草堆上,一路上乞讨为生,靠坐在车上观看铁路沿线的标识而学会了认字。

是他的魔术知识高人一筹吗?不是。他告诉我:关于魔术的书已经有几百种,而且有几十个人知道的魔术同他一样多。但他有两点是其他人所没有的。首先,他在舞台上能够展现自己的个性。他是一位表演天才,了解人类的天性。因此他的每个手势、每种声调、每一次提起眼眉,都是提前演习好了的,而他的每一个动作也都配合得不差分秒。但除此之外,塞斯顿还有一点就是对人有热情。他告诉我,许多魔术家会面对观众,而对他们自己说:"好,那里是一群笨蛋,一群乡巴佬。我可以把他们骗得团团转。"但塞斯顿却完全不同。他告诉我,每次上台时,他都会对自己说:"我很感动,因为这些人来看我的表演。是他们使我过上了舒适的生活。我一定尽力为他们演出最好的节目。"

他说他每次走到台前时,总会对自己说:"我爱我的观众。我爱我的观众。"可笑吗?荒诞不经吗?你怎么想都可以。但我只不过是不加评论地把有史以来最著名的魔术家所用的方法传授给了你。

住在宾夕法尼亚州北华伦城的乔治·戴克,由于他的服务站被一条高速公路抢走了好位置而不得不提前退休。没过多久,无聊的退休生活就让他难以忍受,于是他开始演奏他那把旧小

business after thirty years when a new highway was constructed over the site of his station.It wasn't long before the idle days of retirement began to bore him,so he started filling in his time trying to play music on his old fiddle.Soon he was traveling the area to listen to music and talk with many of the accomplished fiddlers.In his humble and friendly way he became generally interested in learning the background and interests of every musician he met.Although he was not a great fiddler himself, he made many friends in this pursuit.He attended competitions and soon became known to the country music fans in the eastern part of the United States as "Uncle George,the Fiddle Scraper from Kinzua County." When we heard Uncle George, he was seventy-two and enjoying every minute of his life. By having a sustained interest in other people,he created a new life for himself at a time when most people consider their productive years over.

That,too,was one of the secrets of Theodore Roosevelt's astonishing popularity.Even his servants loved him.His valet,James E.Amos,wrote a book about him entitled *Theodore Roosevelt, Hero to His Valet.* In that book Amos relates this illuminating incident:

> My wife one time asked the President about a bobwhite.She had never seen one and he described it to her fully.Sometime later,the telephone at our cottage rang.[Amos and his wife lived in a little cottage on the Roosevelt estate at Oyster Bay.]My wife answered it and it was Mr.Roosevelt himself.He had called her,he said,to tell her that there was a bobwhite outside her window and that if she would look out she might see it.Little things like that were so characteristic of him.Whenever he went by our cottage,even though we were out of sight,we would hear him call out,"Oo-oo-oo,Annie?" or "Oo-oo-oo,James! " It was just a friendly greeting as he went by.

How could employees keep from liking a man like that? How could anyone keep from liking him?

Roosevelt called at the White House one day when the President and Mrs.Taft were away.His honest liking for humble people was shown by the fact that he greeted all the old White House servants by name,even the scullery maids.

"When he saw Alice,the kitchen maid," writes Archie Butt,"he asked her if she still made corn bread.Alice told him that she sometimes made it for the servants,but no one ate it upstairs.

提琴来打发时日。不久,他到处旅行,到处听音乐,向那些修养极高的小提琴家请教。尽管他不是什么伟大的提琴家,但是他以谦虚友善的态度去了解别人,结交他所认识的每一位音乐家,结果他交到了许多朋友。他去参加比赛,不久美国东部的那些乡村音乐迷很快就知道了"来自金兹阿乡村的拉小提琴的乔治叔叔"。这时乔治已经72岁了,但他还在享受自己生命中的每一分钟。由于对别人具有持续的热情和兴趣,当大多数人都认为他们已经行将就木时,他却为自己创造了一个崭新的生命。

这也正是西奥多·罗斯福深受爱戴的秘诀之一。即使他的仆人也敬爱他。他的男仆詹姆斯·阿莫斯曾写过一本关于他的书,名叫《西奥多·罗斯福,他仆人的英雄》。在那本书中,阿莫斯提到了一件很具有启发性的事:

> "有一次我妻子问总统鹑鸟的事。她从来没有见过这种鸟。他给她作了详细描述。过了没多久,我屋里的电话响了(阿莫斯和他妻子住在牡蛎湾罗斯福住宅的一间小屋里)。我妻子去接电话,打电话的是罗斯福先生本人。他说他打来电话,就是要告诉她,在她的窗外正好有一只鹑鸟,如果她向窗外面看的话,也许可以看见它。许多这样的小事情,正是他的特点。无论他什么时候经过我们屋,虽然看不见我们,但我们总是能听见他'哦,哦,哦……安妮!'或'哦,哦,哦……詹姆斯!'的招呼声。那是他经过我们时对我们的友善问候。"

作为仆人,怎么会不喜欢这样的人呢?谁会不喜欢他呢?

有一天,罗斯福去白宫,恰好塔夫脱总统和夫人出去了。他那真诚地喜欢身份卑微者的善良品性这时得到了鲜明的表现:他向白宫所有原来当差的伙伴们,甚至做杂务的女仆直呼姓名,向他们问好。

"当他看见厨房的女仆艾丽斯时,"亚奇·巴特这样写道,"他问她是否还做玉米面包。艾丽斯告诉他说她有时候做给仆人们吃,但楼上已经不再有人吃了。"

"'they show bad taste,' Roosevelt boomed, 'and I'll tell the President so when I see him.'"

"Alice brought a piece to him on a plate, and he went over to the office eating it as he went and greeting gardeners and laborers as he passed...

"He addressed each person just as he had addressed them in the past. Ike Hoover, who had been head usher at the White House for forty years, said with tears in his eyes, 'It is the only happy day we had in nearly two years, and not one of us would exchange it for a hundred-dollar bill.'"

The same concern for the seemingly unimportant people helped sales representative Edward M. Sykes, Jr., of Chatham, New Jersey, retain an account. "Many years ago," he reported, "I called on customers for Johnson and Johnson in the Massachusetts area. One account was a drugstore in Hingham. Whenever I went into this store I would always talk to the soda clerk and sales clerk for a few minutes before talking to the owner to obtain his order. One day I went up to the owner of the store, and he told me to leave as he was not interested in buying J&J products anymore because he felt they were concentrating their activities on food and discount stores to the detriment of the small drugstore. I left with my tail between my legs and drove around the town for several hours. Finally, I decided to go back and try at least to explain our position to the owner of the store.

"When I returned I walked in and as usual said hello to the soda clerk and sales clerk. When I walked up to the owner, he smiled at me and welcomed me back. He then gave me double the usual order. I looked at him with surprise and asked him what had happened since my visit only a few hours earlier. He pointed to the young man at the soda fountain and said that after I had left, the boy had come over and said that I was one of the few salespeople that called on the store that even bothered to say hello to him and to the others in the store. He told the owner that if any salesperson deserved his business, it was I. The owner agreed and remained a loyal customer. Inever forgot that to be genuinely interested in other people is a most important quality for a salesperson to possess—for any person, for that matter."

I have discovered from personal experience that one can win the attention and time and cooperation of even the most sought-after people by becoming genuinely interested in them. Let me illustrate.

"'他们没口福,'罗斯福大声说,'等我见到总统时,我会告诉他。'

"艾丽斯拿了一块玉米面包放在托盘上递给他,他边走边吃,一直来到办公室。当走过那些园丁或工役面前时,便向他们问好……

"他向每个人问好,正如他从前所做的那样。一个名叫艾克·胡福的人在白宫服务 40 年,他眼中含泪地说:'这是我们最近两年中唯一快乐的日子。我们谁都不会将它与一张 100 美元的钞票交换。'"

也正是这种对普通人的关怀,新泽西州查特汉市一位销售代表爱德华·赛克斯重新赢得了一笔生意。"许多年前,"赛克斯说,"在马萨诸塞,我为强生公司前去拜访一位客户。这是一个住在印姆的杂货店经销商。每次我去这家商店时,总是先和店伙计说几句话,再和店主谈订单的事。有一次我正想和店主谈订单,他突然让我走开,还说他再也不想买强生公司的东西了,因为他觉得强生公司几乎将全部精力放在了食品店和折扣店上,而对小杂货店造成了损害。我赶紧离开了,进城兜了几圈。后来我决定再返回去,因为我至少得向店主解释一下我们的情况。

"我回来后,像平时一样先和店伙计打了个招呼。我走近店主时,店主笑着欢迎我回来,并且给了我比平时多两倍的订单。我惊讶地看着他,问他我离开的几个小时发生了什么事情。店主指着卖冷饮的店伙计说,我走之后,店伙计说我是少数向他和其他店伙计打招呼的推销员。他告诉店主,如果有某人值得与其做生意的话,那就是我了。店主觉得也对,仍旧成为我忠实的客户。我永远都不会忘记,真心关注别人,会是推销员应拥有的最重要的品格——对任何人都一样,不只是就这件事来说如此。"

我从个人的经验中也已经发现,一个人凭着对他人的真诚关心,能够获得即使是最忙的人的注意,占有他们的时间,并赢得他们的合作。让我举例说明。

许多年前,我在布鲁克林文理学院开设了一门小说创作课。我们打算邀请一些知名而且

Years ago I conducted a course in fiction writing at the Brooklyn Institute of Arts and Sciences, and we wanted such distinguished and busy authors as Kathleen Norris, Fannie Hurst, Ida Tarbell, Albert Payson Terhune and Rupert Hughes to come to Brooklyn and give us the benefit of their experiences. So we wrote them, saying we admired their work and were deeply interested in getting their advice and learning the secrets of their success.

Each of these letters was signed by about a hundred and fifty students. We said we realized that these authors were busy—too busy to prepare a lecture. So we enclosed a list of questions for them to answer about themselves and their methods of work. They liked that. Who wouldn't like it? So they left their homes and traveled to Brooklyn to give us a helping hand.

By using the same method, I persuaded Leslie M. Shaw, secretary of the treasury in Theodore Roosevelt's cabinet; George W. Wickersham, attorney general in Taft's cabinet; William Jennings Bryan; Franklin D. Roosevelt and many other prominent men to come to talk to the students of my courses in public speaking.

All of us, be we workers in a factory, clerks in an office or even a king upon his throne—all of us like people who admire us. Take the German Kaiser, for example. At the close of World War I he was probably the most savagely and universally despised man on this earth. Even his own nation turned against him when he fled over into Holland to save his neck. The hatred against him was so intense that millions of people would have loved to tear him limb from limb or burn him at the stake. In the midst of all this forest fire of fury, one little boy wrote the Kaiser a simple, sincere letter glowing with kindliness and admiration. This little boy said that no matter what the others thought, he would always love Wilhelm as his Emperor. The Kaiser was deeply touched by his letter and invited the little boy to come to see him. The boy came, so did his mother—and the Kaiser married her. That little boy didn't need to read a book on how to win friends and influence people. He knew how instinctively.

If we want to make friends, let's put ourselves out to do things for other people—things that require time, energy, unselfishness and thoughtfulness. When the Duke of Windsor was Prince of Wales, he was scheduled to tour South America, and before he started out on that tour he spent months studying Spanish so that he could make public talks in the language of the country; and the

十分忙碌的作家，例如凯瑟琳·诺里斯、凡尼·赫斯德、伊达·塔贝尔、亚尔伯特·德恩、卢伯特·休斯到布鲁克林来为我们讲授经验。我们给他们写信，说我们仰慕他们的作品，并深切地希望获得他们的指导，学习他们成功的秘诀。

每封信都由大约150名学员签名。我们说我们知道他们很忙——忙得没有时间准备演讲稿。所以我们在信里面附上了一份问卷，好让他们介绍他们自己及他们的工作方法。他们喜欢我们那样做。谁会不喜欢呢?所以他们都特意从家里赶到布鲁克林，来给我们提供帮助。

用同样的方法，我曾邀请到西奥多·罗斯福总统任期内的财政部长莱斯利·肖，塔夫脱总统任期内的司法部长乔治·威格萨姆，还有威廉·拜伦、富兰克林·罗斯福以及其他许多名人来给我班上的学员演讲。

我们所有的人——无论是工厂工人、办公室职员，或是宝座上的君王——任何人都喜欢那些尊敬我们的人。就以德国皇帝凯瑟为例。在第一次世界大战结束的时候，他大概是世界上最受轻视的人。因为即使他的国民在他为了保住性命而打算逃亡荷兰时全都反对他。人们如此憎恨他，以至于成千上万的人都希望把他手足撕裂，或钉在火刑柱上烧死。在这怒火难以抑制的时候，有一个小孩给德国皇帝写了一封简单而诚恳的信，信中充满了仁爱和钦佩。这个小孩说，不论其他人是怎么想的，他都永远希望敬爱的威廉当他的皇帝。皇帝被他的信深深感动，邀请小男孩去看他。小男孩来了，他母亲也来了——德国皇帝娶了她。这个小孩根本就没有必要去读一本如何交友以及如何影响他人的书，因为他天生就知道这些。

如果我们想要交朋友的话，我们就应该去为别人效劳——去做那些需要花时间、精力、奉献和思考的事。当温莎公爵还是威尔士王储的时候，就计划周游南美。他在出发以前，花了好几个月的时间学习西班牙语言，这样他才能够用当地语言演讲。南美人也因此而喜欢他。

许多年来，我一直都在打听我那些朋友的生日。怎样才能做到这点呢?尽管我根本就不相

South Americans loved him for it.

For years I made it a point to find out the birthdays of my friends.How? Although I haven't the foggiest bit of faith in astrology,I began by asking the other party whether he believed the date of one's birth has anything to do with character and disposition.I then asked him or her to tell me the month and day of birth.If he or she said November 24,for example,I kept repeating to myself, "November 24,November 24." The minute my friend's back was turned,I wrote down the name and birthday and later would transfer it to a birthday book.At the beginning of each year,I had these birthday dates scheduled in my calendar pad so that they came to my attention automatically.When the natal day arrived,there was my letter or telegram.What a hit it made! I was frequently the only person on earth who remembered.

If we want to make friends,let's greet people with animation and enthusiasm.When somebody calls you on the telephone use the same psychology.Say "Hello" in tones that bespeak how pleased you are to have the person call.Many companies train their telephone operators to greet all callers in a tone of voice that radiates interest and enthusiasm.The caller feels the company is concerned about them.Let's remember that when we answer the telephone tomorrow.

Showing a genuine interest in others not only wins friends for you,but may develop in its customers a loyalty to your company.In an issue of the publication of the National Bank of North America of New York,the following letter from Madeline Rosedal,a depositor,was published:

"I would like you to know how much I appreciate your staff.Everyone is so courteous,polite and helpful.What a pleasure it is,after waiting on a long line,to have the teller greet you pleasantly.

"Last year my mother was hospitalized for five months.Frequently I went to Marie Petrucello,a teller.She was concerned about my mother and inquired about her progress."

Is there any doubt that Mrs.Rosedale will continue to use this bank?

Charles R.Walters,of one of the large banks in New York City,was assigned to prepare a confidential report on a certain corporation.He knew of only one person who possessed the facts he needed so urgently.As Mr.Walters was ushered into the president's office,a young woman stuck her head through a door and told the president that she didn't have any stamps for him that day.

信星相学,但我总是会先问对方,是否相信一个人的生辰与性格有关。然后我就会请他将他的生辰告诉我。例如,如果他或她说11月24日,我就会反复地说:"11月24日,11月24日。"等他转过身时,我会立即记下他的姓名和生日,然以再誊到我的日历上,到时它就会引起我的注意。到了某个人生日那天,我会给他写信或发电报。他们多么兴奋啊!我恐怕是这个世界上唯一记住他生日的人。

如果我们想要交朋友的话,就要用生机和热情去应对别人。当别人给你打电话时,你也应该用同样的心理学。你和他说话的声音要表示出你多么喜欢他给你打电话。许多公司训练他们的接线员,要求他们接电话时语气要透出关心和热情,让打电话过来的人感觉公司对他们的关注。明天我们接电话时,也要记住这一点。

这种哲学在商业中管用吗?我们可以举出几十个例子来,但我们只有工夫举出几个。

对别人表达你的真诚关注,不但可以让你交到许多朋友,还可以为你的公司增加客户的忠诚度。纽约的北美国家银行一份出版物中,刊登了一位储户梅德兰·罗斯黛的来信:

"我真希望您能知道我是多么的欣赏贵公司的员工。他们每个人都这么热情有礼,助人为乐。当我在排了长长的队之后,会有一位员工来向我亲切地打个招呼,这令人感到很愉快。

"去年,我母亲生病住了5个月的院。我那时经常遇到贵公司一位员工玛丽。她很关心我的母亲,问了她的病情。"

罗斯黛是否和这家银行继续往来呢?

查尔斯·华尔德是纽约市一家大银行的员工,有一次受命准备一份关于某公司的机密文件。他知道只有某个人掌握了他急需的这些材料。当华尔德被引进这位董事长办公室时,一位年轻女子从门外伸进头来,告诉董事长说她今天没有什么可给他的邮票。

董事长对华尔德解释道:"我正在为我12岁的儿子收集邮票。"

"I am collecting stamps for my twelve-year-old son,"the president explained to Mr.Walters.

Mr.Walters stated his mission and began asking questions.The president was vague,general, nebulous.He didn't want to talk,and apparently nothing could persuade him to talk.The interview was brief and barren.

"Frankly,I didn't know what to do," Mr.Walters said as he related the story to the class."Then I remembered what his secretary had said to him—stamps,twelve-year-old son...And I also recalled that the foreign department of our bank collected stamps—stamps taken from letters pouring in from every continent washed by the seven seas.

"The next afternoon I called on this man and sent in word that I had some stamps for his boy. Was I ushered in with enthusiasm? Yes sir,He couldn't have shaken my hand with more enthusiasm if he had been running for Congress.He radiated smiles and good will.'My George will love this one,' he kept saying as he fondled the stamps.'And look at this! This is a treasure.'

"We spent half an hour talking stamps and looking at a picture of his boy,and he then devoted more than an hour of his time to giving me every bit of information I wanted—without my even suggesting that he do it.He told me all he knew,and then called in his subordinates and questioned them.He telephon some of his associates.He loaded me down with facts,figures,reports and correspondence.In the parlance of newspaper reporters,I had a scoop."

Here is another illustration:

C.M.Knaphle,Jr.,of Philadelphia had tried for years to sell fuel to a large chain-store organization.But the chain-store company continued to purchase its fuel from an out-of-town dealer and haul it right past the door of Knaphle's office.Mr.Knaphle made a speech one night before one of my classes,pouring out his hot wrath upon chain stores,branding them as a curse to the nation. And still he wondered why he coulddn't sell them. I suggested that he try different tactics.To put it briefly,this is what happened.We staged a debate between members of the course on whether the spread of the chain stores is doing the country more harm than good.

Knaphle,at my suggestion,took the negative side; he agreed to defend the chain stores,and then went straight to an executive of the chain-store organization that he despised and said,"I am not here to try to sell fuel.I have come to ask you to do me a favor." He then told about his debate

华尔德说明自己的来意,开始问问题。这位董事长的回答含混不清——很明显,他不愿讲话,没有什么事情能够让他开口的。因此这次会谈变得简短而枯燥。

"说实话,我当时不知如何是好,"华尔德在我班上讲这件事时说,"然后,我想起他的秘书对他说过的话——邮票,12岁的儿子……同时我又想起我们银行的外汇兑换部经常收集邮票——世界各地寄来的信上取下的邮票。

"第二天下午,我再次去拜访这位董事长,并请人传话进去,说我有些邮票要给他的儿子。我是不是受到了热烈欢迎呢?当然。即使是他要竞选国会议员,也不可能那么热情地握着我的手了。他发出善意的微笑说,'我的乔治肯定会喜欢的,'他抚摸着邮票不断地说,'看这张!这可是无价之宝啊!'

"我们花了一个小时谈论邮票,并看了他儿子的照片。然后,他用了一个多小时的时间,谈了我所需要的一切情况——我没有要求他那样做。他讲了他知道的一切,又把他的下属叫进来询问。他还给几位常有来往的人打了电话。他把所有的事实、数字、报告以及信件全都给了我。用一位新闻记者的话来说,我得了一个'大丰收'。"

下面还有另外一个例子:

多年来,费城的克纳夫尔先生一直想将煤推销给一家大型连锁公司。但这家公司仍旧愿意经过克纳夫尔先生的办公室门口,向市外一个煤商采购燃煤。一天晚上,克纳夫尔先生在我的班上作了一次演讲,对连锁公司大加指责,认为他们的行为是国家的一颗毒瘤。可是,他依然不知道他为什么不能把煤卖给他们。我建议他试试其他手段。简而言之,后来的情形是这样的。我将班上的学员分成两支队伍,就"连锁公司的广泛分布对国家是否害多益少"进行辩论。

按照我的建议,克纳夫尔先生加入反对方,他同意为连锁公司做辩护。于是,他径直去找那家被他大加指责的连锁公司的经理,对他说:"我来这里并不是向你推销煤的。我只是来请你帮

and said, "I have come to you for help because I can't think of anyone else who would be more capable of giving me the facts I want. I'm anxious to win this debate, and I'll deeply appreciate whatever help you can give me."

Here is the rest of the story in Mr. Knaphle's own words:

I had asked this man for precisely one minute of his time. It was with that understanding that he consented to see me. After I had stated my case, he motioned me to a chair and talked to me for exactly one hour and forty-seven minutes. He called in another executive who had written a book on chain stores. He wrote to the National Chain Store Association and secured for me a copy of a debate on the subject. He feels that the chain store is rendering a real service to humanity. He is proud of what he is doing for hundreds of communities. His eyes fairly glowed as he talked, and I must confess that he opened my eyes to things I had never even dreamed of. He changed my whole mental attitude.

As I was leaving, he walked with me to the door, put his arm around my shoulder, wished me well in my debate, and asked me to stop in and see him again and let him know how I made out. The last words he said to me were, "Please see me again later in the spring. I should like to place an order with you for fuel."

To me that was almost a miracle. Here he was offering to buy fuel without my even suggesting it. I had made more headway in two hours by becoming genuinely interested in him and his problems than I could have made in ten years trying to get him interested in me and my product.

You didn't discover a new truth, Mr. Knaphle, for a long time ago, a hundred years before Christ was born, a famous old Roman poet, Publilius Syrus, remarked: "We are interested in others when they are interested in us."

A show of interest, as with every other principle of human relations, must be sincere. It must pay off not only for the person showing the interest, but for the person receiving the attention. It is a two-way street—both parties benefit.

Martin Ginsberg, who took our course in Long Island, New York, reported how the special interest a nurse took in him profoundly affected his life:

我一个忙。"于是他讲了这场辩论赛,并说:"我来请你帮忙,因为我想没有什么人会比你更适合为我提供我所需要的材料。我非常想赢得这场辩论赛;无论你能给我什么帮助,我都将非常感激。"

下面是克纳夫尔先生对后来情况的介绍:

"我请他给我一分钟的时间。由于讲了这个条件,他才答应见我。但是当我说明来意之后,他让我坐下,和我谈了1小时47分钟。他还叫进来另一位曾写过一本关于连锁经营的书的高级职员向我介绍相关情况。他还给全国连锁公司联合会写信,替我要了一份这方面的资料。他觉得连锁公司是真正为人们服务的,他对于能够为成千上万的人服务而自豪。他谈话的时候,精神焕发;而我也必须承认,他开阔了我的眼界,使我看见了我以前连做梦都没有想过的事。他改变了我的整个想法。

"当我离开的时候,他把我送到门口,搂着我的肩,祝我辩论胜利,并请我再来看他,将辩论的结果告诉他。他最后对我说的是:'请你在春末的时候再来看我。我愿意订购你的煤。'

"对我来说,这几乎是一件不可思议的事。我对于卖煤一个字都没有说,可是他却要买我的煤。我只不过因为对他及他的问题真的感兴趣,因此在不到两个小时内所取得的成果,比我在过去10年当中试图让他对我及我的煤发生兴趣所得的还多。"

克纳夫尔先生并不是发现了一条新真理,因为很久以前,在基督诞生100年以前,古罗马一位著名的诗人西拉斯就曾说过:"我们对别人产生兴趣的时候,恰好是别人对我们产生兴趣的时候。"

对他人表示关心,这与其他人际关系一样必须真诚。这不仅使得付出关心的人会得到相应的回报,而得到这种关心的人也会同样有所收获。这是一条双向大道,在这条道路上的当事人都会受益。

"It was Thanksgiving Day and I was ten years old.I was in a welfare ward of a city hospital and was scheduled to undergo major orthopedic surgery the next day.I knew that I could only look forward to months of confinement,convalescence and pain.My father was dead; my mother and I lived alone in a small apartment and we were on welfare.My mother was unable to visit me that day.

"As the day went on,I became overwhelmed with the feeling of loneliness,despair and fear.I knew my mother was home alone worrying about me,not having anyone to be with,not having anyone to eat with and not even having enough money to afford a Thanksgiving Day dinner.

"The tears welled up in my eyes,and I stuck my head under the pillow and pulled the covers over it.I cried silently,but oh so bitterly,so much that my body racked with pain.

"A young student nurse heard my sobbing and came over to me.She took the covers off my face and started wiping my tears.She told me how lonely she was,having to work that day and not being able to be with her family.She asked me whether I would have dinner with her.She brought two trays of food: sliced turkey,mashed potatoes,cranberry sauce and ice cream for dessert.She talked to me and tried to calm my fears.Even though she was scheduled to go off duty at 4 P.M.,she stayed on her own time until almost 11 P.M.She played games with me,talked to me and stayed with me until I finally fell asleep.

"Many Thanksgivings have come and gone since I was ten,but one never passes without me remembering that particular one and my feelings of frustration,fear,loneliness and the warmth and tenderness of the stranger that somehow made it all bearable."

If you want others to like you,if you want to develop real friendships,if you want to help others at the same time as you help yourself,keep this principle in mind:

Principle 1:Become genuinely interested in other people.

马丁·金斯伯参加了我们纽约长岛的课程,他说一位护士给他的关怀深深地影响了他的一生。他说:"那天是感恩节,我当时只有10岁,由于生病住进了市里面一家医院,而且第二天就要做手术了。我知道在以后的几周会很痛苦,而且行动都会受到限制。我父亲早已过世了,只有我和母亲相依为命,住在一家小公寓中,靠社会救济金生活。可是那天母亲却不能来看我。

"那天,我陷入了无边无际的寂寞、失望和恐惧中。我也知道母亲正在为我担心,而且也是一个人孤零零地在家里,没有人陪她一同吃饭,甚至没钱买感恩节的晚餐。

"泪水一直在我的眼眶中打转,我把头埋进了枕头下面,一个人暗中伤心哭了起来,全身颤抖着。

"一位年轻的实习护士听到了我的哭声,就到这边来看我。她从我脸上将枕头拿开,替我擦干了眼泪。她说她也很寂寞,那天她必须在医院工作,不能和家人一同吃饭。她又问我愿不愿意和她一同吃晚餐。她拿来了两盘食物:火鸡肉片、马铃薯泥、草莓酱、冰激凌等。她和我聊天,努力安抚我。虽然她下午4点就应该下班回家的,可是她一直陪我到晚上将近11点。她一直和我做游戏、聊天,等我入睡后才走。

"我在10岁以前过了许多感恩节,可是这个感恩节我永远都不会忘记。我还记得当时那种失落、恐惧和孤独。突然一个陌生人的温暖关怀使得这一切都消失得无踪无影了。"

如果你想让别人喜欢你,或者培养真正的友情,或是既帮助别人又帮助自己,那么就要牢记——

第一项规则:真诚地关心别人。

2 A Simple Way to Make a Good First Impression

At a dinner party in New York, one of the guests, a woman who had inherited money, was eager to make a pleasing impression on everyone. She had squandered a modest fortune on sables, diamonds and pearls. But she hadn't done anything whatever about her face. It radiated sourness and selfishness. She didn't realize what everyone knows: namely, that the expression one wears on one's face is far more important than the clothes one wears on one's back.

Charles Schwab told me his smile had been worth a million dollars. And he was probably understating the truth. For Schwab's personality, his charm, his ability to make people like him, were almost wholly responsible for his extraordinary success; and one of the most delightful factors in his personality was his captivating smile.

Actions speak louder than words, and a smile says, "I like you. You make me happy. I am glad to see you."

That is why dogs make such a hit. They are so glad to see us that they almost jump out of their skins. So, naturally, we are glad to see them.

A baby's smile has the same effect.

Have you ever been in a doctor's waiting room and looked around at all the glum faces waiting impatiently to be seen? Dr. Stephen K. Sproul, a veterinarian in Raytown, Missouri, told of a typical spring day when his waiting room was full of clients waiting to have their pets inoculated. No one was talking to anyone else, and all were probably thinking of a dozen other things they would rather be doing than "wasting time" sitting in that office. He told one of our classes: "There were six or seven clients waiting when a young woman came in with a nine-month-old baby and a kitten. As luck would have it, she sat down next to a gentleman who was more than a little distraught about the long wait for service. The next thing he knew, the baby just looked up at him with that great big Smile that is so characteristic of babies. What did that gentleman do? Just what you and I would do, of course; he smiled back at the baby. Soon he struck up a conversation with the woman about her

第2章 产生良好印象的简单方法

在纽约的一次晚宴上，有一位客人——她是一位继承了大笔遗产的女士，因为迫切想给每个人留下良好的印象，就花费重金买了貂皮、钻石和珍珠。但是，她对自己的面孔却没做任何打扮。她的脸上充满了尖酸刻薄以及自私。她并不明白每个人都知道的道理——那就是一个人脸上的神色，要远远比她身上所穿的衣服重要得多。

施瓦伯告诉我，他的微笑价值百万。他大概深谙这一真理，因为施瓦伯的性格、他的魅力、他那令人欢喜的能力，几乎正是他超常成功的最主要原因。而他的个性中最可爱的因素之一，就是他那能够打动一切人的微笑。

行动胜于言论。微笑会让人明白："我喜欢你。你使我快乐。我很高兴见到你。"

这就是狗为什么讨人喜欢的原因。它们是那么高兴见到我们，以至于心都要从肚子里跳出来似的。所以，我们当然也高兴看见它们。

婴儿的微笑也有同样的效果。

你是否曾在医院的候诊室里待过？是否注意到四周的人都阴沉着脸，十分厌烦的样子？住在密苏里州雷顿市的兽医史蒂芬·史波尔曾说过这样一件事：有一年的春天，在他的候诊室中挤满了人，等着给他们的宠物注射疫苗。没有一个人说话，也许每个人都在想该干些什么，而不是坐在那儿浪费时间。他在我们一个班上讲道："候诊室有六七个人在等着，这时进来一位女士，她带了一个9个月大的孩子和一只小猫。她坐在一位男士的边上，而这位男士正等得不耐烦了。当他朝边上看时，那个孩子正注视着他，并天真无邪地向他笑着。这位男士的反应如何呢？和你我一样，他也对那个孩子笑了笑。然后他就和那位母亲聊了起来，谈到了她的孩子和他

baby and his grandchildren, and soon the entire reception room joined in, and the boredom and tension were converted into a pleasant and enjoyable experience."

An insincere grin? No. That doesn't fool anybody. We know it is mechanical and we resent it. I am talking about a real smile, a heartwarming smile, a smile that comes from within, the kind of smile that will bring a good price in the marketplace.

Professor James V. McConnell, a psychologist at the University of Michigan, expressed his feelings about a smile. "People who smile," he said, "tend to manage teach and sell more effectively, and to raise happier children. There's far more information in a smile than a flown. That's why encouragement is a much more effective teaching device than punishment."

The employment manager of a large New York department store told me she would rather hire a sales clerk who hadn't finished grade school, if he or she has a pleasant smile, than to hire a doctor of philosophy with a somber face.

The effect of a smile is powerful—even when it is unseen. Telephone companies throughout the United States have a program called "phone power" which is offered to employees who use the telephone for selling their services or products. In this program they suggest that you smile when talking on the phone. Your "smile" comes through in your voice.

The chairman of the board of directors of one of the largest rubber companies in the United States told me that, according to his observations, people rarely succeed at anything unless they have fun doing it. This industrial leader doesn't put much faith in the old adage that hard work alone is the magic key that will unlock the door to our desires, "I have known people," he said, "who succeeded because they had a rip-roaring good time conducting their business. Later, I saw those people change as the fun became work. The business had grown dull. They lost all joy in it, and they failed."

You must have a good time meeting people if you expect them to have a good time meeting you.

I have asked thousands of business people to smile at someone every hour of the day for a week and then come to class and talk about the results. How did it work? Let's see...Here is a letter from William B. Steinhardt, a New York stockbroker. His case isn't isolated. In fact, it is typical of

的孙子。很快,整个候诊室的人都聊了起来,气氛活跃了,每个人都有了一种愉快的体验。"

小孩的笑是否不诚意呢?绝对不是。不诚意的笑是骗不了人的。我们知道那种笑是机械的,我们会厌恶它。我是在讲一种真正的微笑、热心的微笑、发自内心的微笑,那种在人际交往中极具价值的微笑。

密歇根大学心理学教授詹姆斯·麦克奈尔谈了他对微笑的看法。他说:"那些笑脸常在的人,在教育和推销当中会更容易成功,更容易培养快乐的下一代。笑容比皱眉头更能传情达意,这正是鼓励比惩罚更能起到有效教育的原因所在。"

纽约一家大百货商店的人事经理告诉我,他情愿雇一个带着可爱微笑的小学未毕业的职员,也不愿雇一位面孔冷淡的哲学博士。

即使我们不能看到笑的本质,但它的影响却是很大的。遍布全美国的电话公司有一个栏目叫"声音的威力",这个栏目是为用电话推销产品和服务的业务员提供的。在这个栏目中,电话公司建议在你打电话时,应该保持微笑,但是这种微笑只能通过你的声音来传达。

美国一家最大的橡胶公司的董事长告诉我,根据他的观察,一个人无论做什么事,除非他对此很感兴趣,否则将很难成功。这位实业界的领袖对"十年寒窗可以成就功名"那句老话并不太相信。"我认识一些人,"他说,"他们起初成功了,因为他们对他们的事业极其感兴趣。后来,我看见那些人开始变成工作的奴隶,工作对他们而言变得异常无聊,他们失掉了所有工作中的乐趣,于是他们失败了。"

如果你希望别人看到你的时候很愉快,那么当你看见别人时,你也一定要心情愉悦。

我曾建议成千上万的商界人士,花上一个星期的时间,每天的每小时都要对人微笑,然后再回到班上来谈结果。效果怎样呢?就让我们来看看……这是纽约证券交易所会员威廉·史丹哈德的一封信。他的情况并不是个别现象。事实上,它是好几百人中的代表。

hundreds of cases.

"I have been married for over eighteen years," wrote Mr.Steinhardt, "and in all that time I seldom smiled at my wife or spoke two dozen words to her from the time I got up until I was ready to leave for business.I was one of the worst grouches who ever walked down groadway.

"When you asked me to make a talk about my experience with smiles, I thought I would try it for a week.So the next morning, while combing my hair, I looked at my glum mug in the mirror and said to myself, 'Bill, you are going to wipe the scowl off that sour puss of yours today.You are going to smile.And you are going to begin right now.' As I sat down to breakfast, I greeted my wife with a 'Good morning, my dear,' and smiled as I said it.

"You warned me that she might be surprised.Well, you underestimated her reaction.She was bewildered.She was shocked.I told her that in the future she could expect this as a regular occurrence, and I kept it up every morning.

"This changed attitude of mine brought more happiness into our home in the two months since I started than there was during the last year.

"As I leave for my office, I greet the elevator operator in the apartment house with a 'Good morning' and a smile, I greet the doorman with a smile.I smile at the cashier in the subway booth when I ask for change.As I stand on the floor of the Stock Exchange, I smile at people who until recently never saw me smile.

"I soon found that everybody was smiling back at me.I treat those who come to me with complaints or grievances in a cheerful manner, I smile as I listen to them and I find that adjustments are accomplished much easier.I find that smiles are bringing me dollars, many dollars every day.

"I share my office with another broker.One of his clerks is a likable young chap, and I was so elated about the results I was getting that I told him recently about my new philosophy of human relations.He then confessed that when I first came to share my office with his firm he thought me a terrible grouch—and only recently changed his mind.He said I was really human when I smiled.

"I have also eliminated criticism from my system.I give appreciation and praise now instead of condemnation.I have stopped talking about what I want.I am now trying to see the other person's

"我已经结婚18年多了,"史丹哈德写道,"在此期间,我从起床到准备好出门上班,我都难得对我妻子的微笑,或说上一两句话。我是那些在大街上奔波的人当中脾气最坏的一个。

"因为你建议我们讲对微笑的感受,于是我就想试一个星期。所以,第二天早上,当我梳头的时候,我就看着镜中那副阴沉的面孔,对自己说:'比尔,你今天必须把你的愁容从脸上扫除。你要微笑。你现在就应该开始。'我坐下吃早餐的时候,对妻子说:'亲爱的,早上好!'我说的时候,脸上带着微笑。

"你曾提醒过我,她可能会感到惊讶。可是,你低估了她的反应。她不仅迷惑不已,甚至惊呆了。我告诉她,她将来可以每天都看到这种愉快的事情。从此以后,我每天早上都这样。

"由于我改变了态度,使得我们家在这两个月中所得到的快乐,比过去一年的还多。

"当我去办公室的时候,我会对大楼开电梯的人说'早上好!'并且对他微笑。我还和看门人微笑着打招呼。我在地铁售票处兑换零钱的时候,也会以微笑和服务员打招呼。当我站在交易所大厅的时候,还会对那些以前从未见我微笑的人微笑。

"不久,我就发现每个人都对我报以微笑。我微笑地接待那些发牢骚和抱怨的人。当我听他们抱怨的时候,我会保持微笑,于是问题的解决更容易了。我发现微笑给我带来了财富,我每天都会收获许多财富。

"我同另一位经纪人共用一间办公室。他的一位秘书是一个可爱的小伙子。我很为我所取得的进展而高兴,所以将自己最近学到的人际关系新哲学告诉了他。他承认说,当我最初与他共用办公室的时候,他还以为我是个郁郁寡欢的人呢——直到最近他才改变这一看法。他说,当我微笑的时候非常亲切。

"现在我改掉了批评的习惯。我只是欣赏和称赞别人,而不指责。我也不再谈论自己的需要,我现在总是从别人的立场来分析问题。这些做法,真的改变了我的生活。我现在已经变成另

viewpoint.And these things have literally revolutionized my life.I am a totally different man,a happier man,a richer man,richer in friendships and happiness—the only things that matter much after all."

You don't feel like smiling? Then what? Two things.First,force yourself to smile.If you are alone,force yourself to whistle or hum a tune or sing.Act as if you were already happy,and that will tend to make you happy.Here is the way the psychologist and philosopher William James put it:

"Action seems to follow feeling,but really action and feeling go together; and by regulating the action,which is under the more direct control of the will,we can indirectly regulate the feeling, which is not.

"Thus the sovereign voluntary path to cheerfulness,if our cheerfulness be lost,is to sit up cheerfully and to act and speak as if cheerfulness were already there ...."

Everybody in the world is seeking happiness—and there is one sure way to find it.That is by controlling your thoughts.Happiness doesn't depend on outward conditions.It depends on inner conditions.

It isn't what you have or who you are or where you are or what you are doing that makes you happy or unhappy.It is what you think about it.For example,two people may be in the same place, doing the same thing; both may have about an equal amount of money and prestige—and yet one may be miserable and the other happy.Why? Because of a different mental attitude.I have seen just as many happy faces among the poor peasants toiling with their primitive tools in the devastating heat of the tropics as I have seen in air-conditioned offices in New York,Chicago or Los Angeles.

"There is nothing either good or bad," said Shakespeare,"but thinking makes it so."

Abe Lincoln once remarked that "most folks are about as happy as they make up their minds to be." He was right.I saw a vivid illustration of that truth as I was walking up the stairs of the Long Island Railroad station in New York.Directly in front of me thirty or forty crippled boys on canes and crutches were struggling up the stairs.One boy had to be carried up.I was astonished at their laughter and gaiety.I spoke about it to one of the men in charge of the boys."Oh,yes," he said,"when a boy realizes that he is going to be a cripple for life,he is shocked at first; but after he gets over the

一个人了,一个更快乐、更充实的人,而且富有友谊和快乐——而这些才是最重要的。"

你不愿意微笑吗?那该怎么办呢?有两个办法:第一,强迫自己微笑。第二,如果你一个人独处,不妨强迫自己吹吹口哨,或哼一支小曲,或唱唱歌,就好像你很快乐的样子,那就能使你快乐。心理学家、哲学家威廉·詹姆斯曾这样说:

"行动就好像是跟随感觉之后而产生的,但它与感觉其实是同时进行的,这就足以使直接受意志控制的行动有规律,而且也间接地使不直接受意志控制的情感有一定的规律。

"因此,如果我们不愉快的话,那么得到它的主动途径就是让自己高兴起来,就好像你已经得到了快乐一样……"

世界上的每一个人都在追求幸福——而获得幸福的一个可靠的方法,就是控制你的思想。幸福并不取决于外界的因素,而是取决于你内心的状态。

幸福并不取决于你拥有什么,你是谁,你在何处,或者你在做什么事;决定你是否幸福的关键,在于你怎么想。例如,两个人在同一地方做同一事情,两人都有同样的金钱与名声——可是一个人会痛苦,另一个人会快乐。这是为什么呢?因为他们的内心想法不同。我从那些在酷热之下流着汗做苦工的人那里看到了快乐的脸孔,就像我在纽约、芝加哥或洛杉矶的空调办公室所看到的一样。

"事无善恶,"莎士比亚说,"思想使然。"

林肯也曾说:"大多数人的快乐,和他们内心所想到的快乐相差无几。"他说得确实没错。我最近看到了这一真理的生动的例子。当时我正在爬纽约长岛火车站的台阶。在我前面有三四十个拄着拐杖的残疾儿童正用力登上台阶,有一个男孩还必须由人抱上去。但他们的欢笑和快乐使我吃惊极了。我对带领这些儿童的管理员说了我个人的感受。

"哦,是的,"他说,"当一个孩子知道自己将终生残疾时,他最初往往是惊慌失措;但在惊慌

shock, he usually resigns himself to his fate and then becomes as happy as normal boys."

I felt like taking my hat off to those boys. They taught me a lesson I hope I shall never forget.

Working all by oneself in a closed-off room in an office not only is lonely, but it denies one the opportunity of making friends with other employees in the company. Senora Maria Gonzalez of Guadalajara, Mexico, had such a job. She envied the shared comradeship of other people in the company as she heard their chatter and laughter. As she passed them in the hall during the first weeks of her employment, she shyly looked the other way.

After a few weeks, she said to herself, "Maria, you can't expect those women to come to you. You have to go out and meet them." The next time she walked to the water cooler, she put on her brightest smile and said "Hi, how are you today" to each of the people she met. The effect was mediate. Smiles and hellos were returned, the hallway seemed brighter, the job friendlier. Acquaintanceships developed and some ripened into friendships. Her job and her life became more pleasant and interesting.

Peruse this bit of sage advice from the essayist and publisher Elbert Hubbard—but remember, perusing it won't do you any good unless you apply it:

> Whenever you go out-of-doors, draw the chin in, carry the crown of the head high, and fill the lungs to the utmost; drink in the sunshine; greet your friends with a smile, and put soul into every handclasp. Do not fear being misunderstood and do not waste a minute thinking about your enemies. Try to fix firmly in your mind what you would like to do; and then, without veering off direction, you will move straight to the goal. Keep your mind on the great and splendid things you would like to do, and then, as the days go gliding away, you will find yourself unconsciously seizing upon the opportunities that are required for the fulfillment of your desire, just as the coral insect takes from the running tide the element it needs. Picture in your mind the able, earnest, useful person you desire to be, and the thought you hold is hourly transforming you into that particular individual ....Thought is supreme. Preserve a right mental attitude—the attitude of courage, frankness, and good cheer. To think rightly is to create. All things come through desire and every sincere prayer is answered. We become like that on which our hearts are fixed. Carry your chin in and the crown of your head high. We are gods in the

之后,常常会接受命运的安排,并和正常儿童一样快乐。"

我真觉得要向那些孩子致敬。他们给我上了一堂我永远都不会忘记的课。

一个人独自在一间封闭的办公室工作,不仅会感到寂寞,还会失去和公司其他人交朋友的机会。在墨西哥的瓜达拉拉加拉市,西罗拉·玛丽亚就是一个人一间办公室。当她听到其他同事的聊天和欢笑声时,她非常羡慕。上班的头一个星期,当她经过大家时,她害羞地掉过头去。

几个星期之后,她告诉自己:"玛丽亚,你不能指望别人先和你打招呼,你应该先向别人问好。"于是,当她下一次出去倒冷饮时,脸上总是呈现出最迷人的微笑,并和她遇到的每个人打招呼:"嗨,你好!"这样做立即有效了。别人都对她回应了笑容和欢呼,过道好像也明亮了许多,工作气氛友善多了。熟人越来越多,有的人甚至成了玛丽亚的好朋友。她的工作和生活变得更加愉快和有趣了。

让我们细读随笔作家、出版家阿尔伯特·哈伯德下面这段睿智的忠告吧——请记住,除非你把它付诸实践,否则光是阅读对你并无益处。

> "每次出去的时候,都要收缩下巴,抬起头,挺起胸膛深呼吸;在阳光中沐浴;以微笑来招呼每一个人,每次握手时都应该使出力气。不要怕被误会,不要将时间浪费在想你的仇敌。要在你心中明确你喜欢做什么,然后坚持不懈,勇往直前,集中精力大展宏图。日后,在时光流逝之中,你会发觉你于不知不觉中抓住了机会,实现了你的欲望,正如珊瑚虫由潮水中吸取所需要的营养一样。在脑海中想象你希望成为的那个有能力的、诚恳的、有作为的人,这种想象会每时每刻改造你,成为你所希望的那种人……思想是至高无上的。必须保持正确的人生观——一种勇敢、诚实、愉悦的态度。正确的思想本身就是创造。一切都来源于希望,每一次真诚的祈祷都会有所应验。我们内心希望成为什么,我们就会变成什么。请收缩你的下巴,抬高你的头,我们就是破蛹而出。"

chrysalis.

The ancient Chinese were a wise lot—wise in the ways of the world; and they had a proverb that you and I ought to cut out and paste inside our hats.It goes like this: "A man without a smiling face must not open a shop."

Your smile is a messenger of your good will.Your smile brightens the lives of all who see it.To someone who has seen a dozen people frown, scowl or turn their faces away, your smile is like the sun breaking through the clouds.Especially when that someone is under pressure from his bosses, his customers, his teachers or parents or children, a smile can help him realize that all is not hopeless—that there is joy in the world.

Some years ago, a department store in New York City, in recognition of the pressures its sales clerks were under during the Christmas rush, presented the readers of its advertisements with the following homely philosophy:

The Value of a Smile at Christmas

It costs nothing, but creates much.

It enriches those who receive, without impoverishing those who give.

It happens in a flash and the memory of it sometimes lasts forever,

None are so rich they can get along without it, and none so poor but are richer for its benefits.

It creates happiness in the home, fosters good will in a business, and is the countersign of friends.

It is rest to the weary, daylight to the discouraged, sunshine to the sad, and Nature's best antidote for trouble.

Yet it cannot be bought, begged, borrowed, or stolen, for it is something that is no earthly good to anybody till it is given away.

And if in the last-minute rush of Christmas buying some of our salespeople should be too tired to give you a smile, may we ask you to leave one of yours?

For nobody needs a smile so much as those who have none left to give!

Principle 2: Smile.

中国的古人真是非常睿智——通达世事；他们有一句格言，你我都应该剪下来贴在帽子里。这格言就是"和气生财"。

你的微笑是善意的信使。你的微笑会照亮所有看见它的人的人生。对那些见多了冷漠面孔的人来说,你的微笑就像穿透云层的阳光。尤其当人处于重重压力之下时,一个微笑可以让他看到一切并非毫无希望——世界还有欢快！

许多年前,纽约一家百货商店在圣诞购物狂潮中,它的员工压力很大,就为读者张贴了下面这份实用的哲学:

圣诞节的微笑

它无所耗费,但收获却很多。

它让得到者获益,而施舍者却丝毫无损。

它出现在眨眼之间,但却给人永恒的记忆。

没有人会富得不需要它,也没有人穷到不能因它而致富。

它给家庭带来快乐,在生意场上使人产生好感,又是朋友间的亲热问候。

它是疲倦者的港湾,沮丧者的曙光,悲伤者的太阳,又是大自然的良药。

它买不到,求不来,借不到,偷不着,因为你将它送人之前,它对谁都没用。

而假如在圣诞节最后一分钟的忙碌采购中,我们的售货员也许太疲倦而不能给你微笑时,我们能请你留下你的微笑吗?

因为,那些没有微笑的人更需要微笑。

第二项规则:微笑。

3 If You Don't Do This, You Are Headed for Trouble

Back in 1898, a tragic thing happened in Rockland County, New York. A child had died, and on this particular day the neighbors were preparing to go to the funeral. Jim Farley went out to the barn to hitch up his horse. The ground was covered with snow, the air was cold and snappy; the horse hadn't been exercised for days; and as he was led out to the watering trough, he wheeled playfully, kicked both his heels high in the air, and killed Jim Farley. So the little village of Stony Point had two funerals that week instead of one.

Jim Farley left behind him a widow and three boys, and a few hundred dollars in insurance.

His oldest boy, Jim, was ten, and he went to work in a brickyard, wheeling sand and pouring it into the molds and turning the brick on edge to be dried by the sun. This boy Jim never had a chance to get much education. But with his natural geniality, he had a flair for making people like him, so he went into politics, and as the years went by, he developed an uncanny ability for remembering people's names.

He never saw the inside of a high school; but before he was forty-six years of age, four colleges had honored him with degrees and he had become chairman of the Democratic National Committee and Postmaster General of the United States.

I once interviewed Jim Farley and asked him the secret of his success. He said, "Hard work," and I said, "Don't be funny."

He then asked me what I thought was the reason for his success. I replied, "I understand you can call ten thousand people by their first names."

"No. You are wrong," he said. "I can call fifty thousand people by their first names."

Make no mistake about it. That ability helped Mr. Farley put Franklin D. Roosevelt in the White House when he managed Roosevelt's campaign in 1932.

During the years that Jim Farley traveled as a salesman for a gypsum concern, and during the years that he held office as town clerk in Stony Point, he built up a system for remembering names.

第3章 牢记他人的名字

1898 年,在纽约的洛克兰乡发生了一件悲剧:一个孩子死了。这天,邻居正准备去参加葬礼。吉姆·法莱到马厩中去牵他那匹马。地上满是积雪,寒风刺骨,那匹马有好几天都没有运动了,因此当它被拉到水槽边的时候,欢欣鼓舞,奋起双蹄向空中踢去,结果将吉姆·法莱踢死。因此在那个星期,在这个小小的镇子里有两个葬礼,而不是一个。

吉姆·法莱死后,留下了他的妻子和 3 个孩子,以及几百美元的保险金。

他最大的儿子小吉姆,这时才只有 10 岁,到砖厂去工作,运沙子,将沙子倒入砖模中,将砖坯翻过来在太阳底下晒干。这个小吉姆从来都没有机会接受什么教育,但因为具有天生的愉快品性,他有一种使别人喜欢他的才能。因此当他从政以后,随着岁月的流逝,他培养起一种记住别人名字的奇特能力。

他从未上过中学,但在他 46 岁以前,已经有 4 所大学授予他名誉学位;他还成为美国民主党全国委员会的主席,当上了美国邮政总监。

有一次,我去拜访小吉姆·法莱,问他成功的秘诀。他说:"卖力地工作。"我说:"别开玩笑了。"

于是他问我,我认为他成功的原因是什么。我说:"我知道你可以叫出一万人的名字。"

"不,不。你错了,"他说,"我能叫出 5 万人的名字。"

千万不要小看这一点。正是这种能力,才使得小吉姆·法莱于 1932 年辅佐富兰克林·罗斯福时,使他顺利地入主白宫。

当小吉姆·法莱为一家石膏公司担任推销员而到处奔波的那些年,当他在家乡小镇担任乡间公务员的那段时间,他就找到了一种记住别人姓名的有效方法。

In the beginning, it was a very simple one. Whenever he met a new acquaintance, he found out his or her complete name and some facts about his or her family, business and political opinions. He fixed all these facts well in mind as part of the picture, and the next time he met that person, even if it was a year later, he was able to shake hands, inquire after the family, and ask about the hollyhocks in the backyard. No wonder he developed a following!

For months before Roosevelt's campaign for President began, Jim Farley wrote hundreds of letters a day to people all over the western and northwestern states. Then he hopped onto a train and in nineteen days covered twenty states and twelve thousand miles, traveling by buggy, train, automobile and boat. He would drop into town, meet his people at lunch or breakfast, tea or dinner, and give them a "heart-to-heart talk." Then he'd dash off again on another leg of his journey.

As soon as he arrived back East, he wrote to one person in each town he had visited, asking for a list of all the guests to whom he had talked. The final list contained thousands and thousands of names; yet each person on that list was paid the subtle flattery of getting a personal letter from James Farley. These letters began "Dear Bill" or "Dear Jane," and they were always signed "Jim."

Jim Farley discovered early in life that the average person is more interested in his or her own name than in all the other names on earth put together. Remember that name and call it easily, and you have paid a subtle and very effective compliment. But forget it or misspell it—and you have placed yourself at a sharp disadvantage. For example, I once organized a public-speaking course in Paris and sent off letters to all the American residents in the city. French typists with apparently little knowledge of English filled in the names and naturally they made blunders. One man, the manager of a large American bank in Paris, wrote me a scathing rebuke because his name had been misspelled.

Sometimes it is difficult to remember a name, particularly if it is hard to pronounce. Rather than even try to learn it, many people ignore it or call the person by an easy nickname. Sid Levy called on a customer for some time whose name was Nicodemus Papadoulos. Most people just called him "Nick." Levy told us, "I made a special effort to say his name over several times to myself before I made my call. When I greeted him by his full name, 'Good afternoon, Mr. Nicodemus Papadoulos,' he was shocked. For what seemed like several minutes there was no reply from him at all. Finally, he said with tears rolling

刚开始的时候,这种方法非常简单。每当他接触一个陌生人的时候,总是要问清对方的姓名、他家中有几个人、他的职业和政治观点,并认真地记住这一切,将这些和其本人的面貌联系起来。当下次再遇到那个人时,即使是在一年以后,他都能够和对方握手,问候他的家人,以及他家后院的花草等。难怪有这么多人拥戴他!

在富兰克林·罗斯福开始竞选总统的前几个月,小吉姆一天要写好几百封信给西部及西北部各个州的人。然后他登上火车,在19天内足迹遍及20个州,行程12000公里,用轻便马车、火车、汽车、快艇代步。他每到一个城镇,就要和人们共进午餐或早点、茶点或晚餐,同他们作一番亲切的交谈,然后再奔向下一站。

等他一回到东部,就立刻给他到过的每个城镇的某个人写信,请对方将与他谈过话的客人的名单寄给他。最后名单上的名字就多得数不清了,但名单中的每个人都收到了小吉姆一封表达赞美的私人信函。这些信都是用"亲爱的比尔"或"亲爱的简"开头的,而最后总是签着"吉姆"的名字。

小吉姆·法莱早就发现普通人对自己的名字总是很感兴趣,甚至比对世上其他所有名字加起来还要感兴趣。记住一个人的姓名,并且能很容易就叫出来,你就是给对方一种巧妙而有效的恭维。但假若你忘了或记错了某个人的名字——你就会处于极其不利的境地。例如,我曾在巴黎开设了一门公共演讲课程,并向居住在城中的所有美国人寄了信。但法国打字员的英文水平很低,因此在打姓名时自然会出现错误。有一个人是巴黎一家美国大银行的经理,他给我写了一封毫不留情面的责备我的信,因为他的名字拼错了。

要想记住一个人的名字有时很难,尤其是当这个名字不太好念的时候。一般人都不愿记这种名字,而情愿叫对方的昵称。希德·李维曾经拜访过一位顾客,这位顾客的名字叫尼古德马斯·帕帕杜拉斯。由于这个名字太难记,大多数人都叫他"尼克"。李维告诉我:"拜访之前,我特

down his cheeks, 'Mr.Levy, in all the fifteen years I have been in this country, nobody has ever made the effort to call me by my right name.' "

What was the reason for Andrew Carnegie's success?

He was called the Steel King; yet he himself knew little about the manufacture of steel.He had hundreds of people working for him who knew far more about steel than he did.

But he knew how to handle people, and that is what made him rich.Early in life, he showed a flair for organization, a genius for leadership.By the time he was ten, he too had discovered the astounding importance people place on their own name.And he used that discovery to win cooperation.To illustrate: When he was a boy back in Scotland, he got hold of a rabbit, a mother rabbit.Presto! He soon had a whole nest of little rabbits—and nothing to feed them.But he had a brilliant idea.He told the boys and girls in the neighborhood that if they would go out and pull enough clover and dandelions to feed the rabbits, he would name the bunnies in their honor.

The plan worked like magic, and Carnegie never forgot it.

Years later, he made millions by using the same psychology in business.For example, he wanted to sell steel rails to the Pennsylvania Railroad.J.Edgar Thomson was the president of the Pennsylvania Railroad then.So Andrew Carnegie built a huge steel mill in Pittsburgh and called it the "Edgar Thomson Steel Works."

Here is a riddle.See if you can guess it.When the Pennsylvania Railroad needed steel rails, where do you suppose J.Edgar Thomson bought them?From Sears, Roebuck? No.No.You're wrong. Guess again.

When Carnegie and George Pullman were battling each other for supremacy in the railroad sleeping-car business, the Steel King again remembered the lesson of the rabbits.

The Central Transportation Company, which Andrew Carnegie controlled, was fighting with the company that Pullman owned.Both were struggling to get the sleeping-car business of the Union Pacific Railroad, bucking each other, slashing prices, and destroying all chance of profit.Both Carnegie and Pullman had gone to New York to see the board of directors of the Union Pacific. Meeting one evening in the St.Nicholas Hotel, Carnegie said, "Good evening, Mr.Pullman, aren't we making a couple of fools of ourselves?"

别用心记住了他的名字。当我用全称和他打招呼'早上好，尼古德马斯·帕帕杜拉斯先生'时，他呆在那里，好几分钟都没有反应。最后，他流着泪说：'李维先生，我在这个国家已经呆了15年，可是从来没有人用我真正的名字来称呼我！'"

安德鲁·卡内基成功的原因是什么？

尽管他被誉为"钢铁大王"，但他自己对于钢铁制造的知识知之甚少。他有成千上万的人为他工作，他们在钢铁制造方面懂得的都比他要多得多。

但是他知道如何为人处世，而这正是他发财致富的原因。小时候，他就显露出组织方面的本领和领导天赋。10岁那年，他就发现人们对自己的名字非常重视。于是他就利用这一发现去赢得合作。例如，当他童年时代住在苏格兰的时候，抓到了一只怀孕的母兔。很快，他就有了一窝小兔子——可是他没有东西给它们吃。但是他有一个很妙的办法。他对邻近的孩子们说，如果他们愿意出去采集足够的苜蓿和蒲公英来喂这些小兔子，他就用他们的名字来给它们取名字。

这个方法太神奇了，安德鲁·卡内基永远也忘不了。

许多年以后，他在商业上应用同样的心理学，赚了好几百万美元。例如，他希望将钢轨卖给宾夕法尼亚铁路公司。当时埃格·汤姆森正好是这家公司的董事长。于是安德鲁·卡内基在匹兹堡建了一家巨型钢铁厂，就取名为"埃格·汤姆森钢铁厂"。

你是否能猜出来，当宾夕法尼亚铁路公司需要钢轨的时候，埃格·汤姆森会去哪里买呢？是西尔斯公司？是鲁巴克公司？不！错了，再猜猜！

当卡内基与普尔曼之间为了获得卧车生意而开展激烈竞争时，这位钢铁大王又想起了兔子的故事。

卡内基控制的中央运输公司正在和普尔曼的公司火拼这场生意，双方都希望获得太平洋

"What do you mean?" Pullman demanded.

Then Carnegie expressed what he had on his mind—a merger of their two interests.He pictured in glowing terms the mutual advantages of working with,instead of against,each other.Pullman listened attentively,but he was not wholly convinced.Finally he asked, "What would you call the new company?" and Carnegie replied promptly, "Why,the Pullman Palace Car Company,of course."

Pullman's face brightened."Come into my room," he said."Let's talk it over."That talk made industrial history.

This policy of remembering and honoring the names of his friends and business associates was one of the secrets of Andrew Carnegie's leadership.He was proud of the fact that he could call many of his factory workers by their first names,and he boasted that while he was personally in charge,no strike ever disturbed his flaming steel mills.

Benton Love,chairman of Texas Commerce Bankshares,believes that the bigger a corporation gets,the colder it becomes."One way to warm it up," he said,"is to remember people's names."

Karen Kirsech of Rancho Palos Verdes,California,a flight attendant for TWA,made it a practice to learn the names of as many passengers in her cabin as possible and use the name when serving them.This resulted in many compliments on her service expressed both to her directly and to the airline.One passenger wrote:"I haven't flown TWA for some time,but I'm going to start flying nothing but TWA from now on.You make me feel that your airline has become a very personalized airline and that is important to me."

People are so proud of their names that they strive to perpetuate them at any cost.Even blustering,hardboiled old P.T.Barnum,the greatest showman of his time,disappointed because he had no sons to carry on his name,offered his grandson,C.H.Seeley, $25,000 if he would call himself "Barnum" Seeley.

For many centuries,nobles and magnates supported artists,musicians and authors so that their creative works would be dedicated to them.

Libraries and museums owe their richest collections to people who cannot bear to think that their names might perish from the memory of the race.The New York Public Library has its Astor

铁路联合公司的这笔卧车订单，于是两家公司互相排挤、大杀其价，最后到了无利可图的地步。卡内基与普尔曼都亲自去太平洋联合公司在纽约的董事局。一天晚上，在圣尼古拉大饭店中，卡内基遇到了普尔曼，他说："晚上好，普尔曼先生！我们不是在自己出洋相吗?"

"你这是什么意思?"普尔曼问。

于是，卡内基把自己心中想了许久的话说了出来——将他们双方的利益合在一起。两家公司互相合作而不竞争的好处，被他描述得天花乱坠。普尔曼认真地听着，但并没有完全赞同。最后他问道："这家新公司你怎么取名呢?"卡内基立刻回答说："哦！当然是普尔曼皇宫卧车公司。"

普尔曼立刻神采飞扬。"到我房里来，"他说，"我们来详细谈谈。"那次谈话改写了美国工业史。

安德鲁·卡内基这种记住并尊敬他的朋友及同行名字的习惯，正是他成为商界领袖的秘诀之一。他能叫出他手下许多工人的名字，这也是他引以为豪的。他还非常得意地说，当他亲自管理公司的时候，从未发生过罢工的事件。

得克萨斯州商业股份有限公司董事长班顿·拉夫认为，公司越大就越冷漠。"唯一能够使公司变得温暖一些的办法，"他说，"就是记住人们的名字。"

加利福尼亚兰克帕罗市的凯伦·科瑟奇是一位空姐，她经常练习记住飞机上旅客的名字，并在为他们服务时称呼他们的名字。因此，有的顾客会当面表扬她，也有的顾客会告诉公司。有一位顾客曾写信说："我许久没有坐你们公司的飞机了。但从现在开始，我一定要等你们公司的飞机才乘坐。你们让我觉得你们的航空公司好像专属化了，而这对我非常重要。"

人们如此重视他们的名字，因此他们会不惜代价地使之永垂不朽。就连脾气暴躁而且富可敌国的伯纳姆，也曾因为没有儿子继承其姓氏而心灰意冷，以至于答应他的外孙西雷，如果他愿意称自己为"伯纳姆·西雷"的话，情愿给他 25000 美元。

几百年来，有钱人常常出钱资助那些艺术家、音乐家和作家，希望他们的作品献给他们。

and Lenox collections.The Metropolitan Museum perpetuates the names of Benjamin Altman and J. P.Morgan.And nearly every church is beautiful by stained-glass windows commemorating the names of their donors.Many of the buildings on the campus of most universities bear the names of donors who contributed large sums of money for this honor.

Most people don't remember names,for the simple reason that they don't take the time and energy necessary to concentrate and repeat and fix names indelibly in their minds.They make excuses for themselves; they are too busy.

But they were probably no busier than Franklin D.Roosevelt,and he took time to remember and recall even the names of mechanics with whom he came into contact.

To illustrate: The Chrysler organization built a special car for Mr.Roosevelt,who could not use a standard car because his legs were paralyzed.W.F.Chamberlain and a mechanic delivered it to the White House.I have in front of me a letter from Mr.Chamberlain relating his experiences."I taught President Roosevelt how to handle a car with a lot of unusual gadgets,but he taught me a lot about the fine art of handling people.

"When I called at the White House," Mr.Chamberlain writes,"the President was extremely pleasant and cheerful.He called me by name,made me feel very comfortable,and particularly impressed me with the fact that he was vitally interested in things I had to show him and tell him. The car was so designed that it could be operated entirely by hand.A crowd gathered around to look at the car; and he remarked,'I think it is marvelous.All you have to do is to touch a button and it moves away and you can drive it without effort.I think it is grand—I don't know what makes it go. I'd love to have the time to tear it down and see how it works.'

"When Roosevelt's friends and associates admired the machine,he said in their presence: 'Mr.Chamberlain,I certainly appreciate all the time and effort you have spent in developing this car.It is a mighty free job.'He admired the radiator,the special rear-vision mirror and clock,the special spotlight,the kind of upholstery,the sitting position of the driver's seat,the special suitcases in the trunk with his monogram on each suitcase.In other words,he took notice of every detail to which he knew I had given considerable thought.He made a point of bringing these various pieces of equipment to the attention of Mrs.Roosevelt,Miss Perkins,the Secretary of Labor,and his

图书馆和博物馆最有价值的收藏品，常常是由那些担心他们的姓名日后被遗忘的人捐赠的。纽约公共图书馆有爱斯德家族与李诺克斯家族的藏书；大都会博物馆则永远保存着本杰明·爱特曼与摩根的名字。几乎每一个教堂都镶嵌上了彩色玻璃，以纪念捐赠者。许多大学校园的建筑物也刻有捐赠者的名字，他们捐赠了大笔钱来获得此荣耀。

大多数人之所以不记得别人的姓名，只是因为他们不想花时间和精力去用心记。他们总是为自己寻找各种借口，例如说他们太忙了。

但他们大概不会比富兰克林·罗斯福更忙了，然而罗斯福却能花时间去记那些他曾经接触过的机械师的名字。

例如，克莱斯勒汽车公司曾为罗斯福先生特制了一辆汽车，因为他的腿瘫痪了不能开标准型号的车。张伯伦和一位机械师将汽车送到了白宫。我这里有一封张伯伦的信，讲了他当时的经历："我教罗斯福总统如何驾驶一辆配置了许多特殊部件的汽车，但他也教给我许多为人处世的知识。

"当我被召到白宫的时候，"张伯伦先生写道，"总统非常高兴。他叫出了我的名字，使我感到非常欣慰。令我印象尤其深刻的，是他确实很注意我对他所说明的事项。这辆汽车设计成完全可以用手操作。一群人围在汽车四周观看。他说：'我认为这辆汽车真是太棒了。只要按下这开关就可以开动，毫不费力。实在是太好了——我不知道它是如何工作的。我真希望有时间拆开来，看看它是如何工作的。'

"当罗斯福的朋友和同事都在称赞这辆车时，他当着他们的面说：'张伯伦先生，我真的非常感谢你为了设计这辆车所花的时间和精力。这简直太棒了。'他对散热器、特制反光镜、时钟、特制照明灯、椅垫的式样、驾驶座的位置、车厢内标有他姓名缩写字母的特制衣箱等，都大加赞赏。换句话说，他注意到了每个细节，知道我所付出的心血。他还特别让罗斯福夫人、波金女士、

secretary.He even brought the old White House porter into the picture by saying, 'George, you want to take particularly good care of the suitcases.'

"When the driving lesson was finished, the President turned to me and said, 'Well, Mr. Chamberlain, I have been keeping the Federal reserve Board waiting thirty minutes.I guess I had better get back to work.'

"I took a mechanic with me to the White House.He was introduced to Roosevelt when he arrived.He didn't talk to the President, and Roosevelt heard his name only once.He was a shy chap, and he kept in the background.But before leaving us, the President looked for the mechanic, shook his hand, called him by name, and thanked him for coming to Washington.And there was nothing perfunctory about his thanks.He meant what he said.I could feel that.

"A few days after returning to New York, I got an autographed photograph of President Roosevelt and a little note of thanks again expressing his appreciation for my assistance.How he found time to do it is a mystery to me."

Franklin D.Roosevelt knew that one of the simplest, most obvious and most important ways of gaining good will was by remembering names and making people feel important—yet how many of us do it?

Half the time we are introduced to a stranger, we chat a few minutes and can't even remember his or her name by the time we say goodbye.

One of the first lessons a politician learns is this: "To recall a voter's name is statesmanship.To forget it is oblivion."

And the ability to remember names is almost as important in business and social contacts as it is in politics.

Napoleon the Third, Emperor of France and nephew of the great Napoleon, boasted that in spite of all his royal duties he could remember the name of every person he met.

His technique? Simple.If he didn't hear the name distinctly, he said, "So sorry. I didn't get the name clearly." Then, if it was an unusual name, he would say, "How is it spelled?"

During the conversation, he took the trouble to repeat the name several times, and tried to associate it in his mind with the person's features, expression and general appearance.

劳工部长和他的秘书注意这些部件。他甚至还让那位白宫老搬运工也格外小心,他说:'乔治,你可要小心这些衣箱。'

"在上完驾驶课之后,总统转向我说:'好了,张伯伦先生,我已经让联邦储备委员会等我30分钟了。我想我该回去工作了。'

"我带了一位机械师去白宫。他刚到白宫时曾被介绍给罗斯福总统。他没有和总统说过一句话,而罗斯福总统也只听过他的名字一次。他是一个害羞的人,总是退缩在后面。但是在离开以前,总统找到这位机械师,和他握了握手,还叫出了他的名字,对他来到华盛顿表示感谢。他的这种感谢绝非做作,而是出自真心诚意。我能感觉到这一点。

"回到纽约几天后,我就收到了一张由罗斯福总统亲笔签名的照片,照片上还有简短的谢辞,再次对我的帮助表示感谢。他如何有时间做这样的事,可真让我难以理解。"

富兰克林·罗斯福知道一个最简单、最明显、最重要的使人获得好感的方法,那就是记住别人的姓名,使人感觉受到了重视——但我们有多少人能够这样做呢?

有一半情形是这样的:我们被介绍给一位陌生人,和对方谈了几分钟,可是在分手的时候连对方的姓名都不记得。

作为一名政治家,所要学的第一课就是:"记住选民的姓名就是政治才能。倘若忘记,你将会被遗忘。"

在个人事业与商业交往中,记住姓名的能力与在政治领域中几乎同样重要。

法国皇帝拿破仑三世——也就是伟大的拿破仑的侄子,曾自我炫耀地说,虽然国务很忙,但是他能记住他所见过的每一个人的姓名。

他的方法呢?很简单。如果他没有听清楚对方的姓名,就会说:"对不起。我没听清楚姓名。"如果这是一个不常见的姓名,他就会问:"这是如何拼的?"

If the person was someone of importance, Napoleon went to even further pains. As soon as His Royal Highness was alone, he wrote the name down on a piece of paper, looked at it, concentrated on it, fixed it securely in his mind, and then tore up the paper. In this way, he gained an eye impression of the name as well as an ear impression.

All this takes time, but "Good manners," said Emerson, "are made up of petty sacrifices."

We should be aware of the *magic* contained in a name and realize that this single item is wholly and completely owned by the person with whom we are dealing...and nobody else. The name sets the individual apart; it makes him or her unique among all others. The information we are imparting or the request we are making takes on a special importance when we approach the situation with the name of the individual. From the waitress to the senior executive, the name will work magic as we deal with others.

Principle 3: Remember that a person's name is to that person the sweetest and most important sound in any language.

在谈话的过程中,他会将那个人的名字反复记几次,并在大脑中将这个姓名和这个人的面孔、神色以及外观对应起来。

如果对方是个很重要的人物,拿破仑三世就会更费心思记住他。在他单独一人的时候,会将这人的姓名写在一张纸上,仔细观看,牢牢记住,确信记住后将那张纸撕掉。这样,他对那个人的印象就会更深了。

所有这些事都要费一定的功夫,但爱默生认为:"礼貌,是由小小的牺牲换来的。"

我们应注意名字中包含的魔力,明白这正是我们与之打交道的人所完全拥有的东西,而不是属于别人的。名字使人们与他人有所区别,在众人中与众不同。当我们记住某人的姓名后,我们传递给对方的信息就会非常重要了。从服务员到高级经理,如果记住了他们的名字,我们与之交往时就会收到奇效。

第三项规则:记住一个人的姓名,对他来说这是所有语言中最甜蜜、最重要的声音。

4 An Easy Way to Become a Good Conversationalist

Some time ago, I attended a bridge party. I don't play bridge—and there was a woman there who didn't play bridge either. She had discovered that I had once been Lowell Thomas' manager before he went on the radio and that I had traveled in Europe a great deal while helping him prepare the illustrated travel talks he was then delivering. So she said, "Oh, Mr. Carnegie, I do want you to tell me about all the wonderful places you have visited and the sights you have seen."

As we sat down on the sofa, she remarked that she and her husband had recently returned from a trip to Africa. "Africa!" I exclaimed. "How interesting! I've always wanted to see Africa, but I never got there except for a twenty-four-hour stay once in Algiers. Tell me, did you visit the big-game country? Yes? How fortunate. I envy you. Do tell me about Africa."

That kept her talking for forty-five minutes. She never again asked me where I had been or what I had seen. She didn't want to hear me talk about my travels. All she wanted was an interested listener, so she could expand her ego and tell about where she had been.

Was she unusual? No. Many people are like that.

For example, I met a distinguished botanist at a dinner party given by a New York book publisher. I had never talked with a botanist before, and I found him fascinating. I literally sat on the edge of my chair and listened while he spoke of exotic plants and experiments in developing new forms of plant life and indoor gardens (and even told me astonishing facts about the humble potato). I had a small indoor garden of my own—and he was good enough to tell me how to solve some of my problems.

As I said, we were at a dinner party. There must have been a dozen other guests, but I violated all the canons of courtesy, ignored everyone else, and talked for hours to the botanist.

Midnight came, I said good night to everyone and departed. The botanist then turned to our host and paid me several flattering compliments. I was "most stimulating." I was this and I was that, and he ended by saying I was a "most interesting conversationalist."

第4章 如何成为优秀的谈话家

最近,我参加了一次桥牌聚会。我不会打桥牌——恰好有一位美丽的女士也不会打桥牌。她知道我在罗维尔·托马斯从事无线电行业之前曾经担任过他的助理。当时,我去欧洲各地旅行,帮助他整理即将播出的旅行演讲。所以她说:"啊!卡耐基先生,你能不能将你所见过的名胜古迹告诉我?"

当我们在沙发上坐下的时候,她说她同她丈夫最近刚从非洲旅行回来。"非洲,"我说,"这可是一个非常有趣的地方!我总想去看看非洲,但我除了在阿尔及尔呆过24小时外,没有到过其他任何地方。告诉我,你是否到过野兽出没的国度?是吗?真是幸运极了!我太羡慕你了!请讲讲非洲的情况吧!"

这让她说了45分钟。她不再问我到过什么地方或看见过什么东西。她并不是想听我谈论我的旅行,她想要的,是一个认真的倾听者,她可以借此机会讲她到过的地方,以扩大她的自我感。

她很特殊吗?不。许多人都是这样的。

例如,我在纽约一位出版商举行的宴会上遇到了一位著名的植物学家。我以前从来没有和植物学家交谈过,我觉得他具有极强的吸引力。我真的坐在椅子边上,静静地听他介绍大麻、室内花园,甚至廉价马铃薯的惊人事实。我自己有一个室内小花园,他非常热情地告诉我如何解决我的问题。

我已经说过,我们这是在宴会中。还有十几位其他客人,但我违反了所有的礼节规矩,没有注意到其他人,而与这位植物学家谈了好几个小时。

An interesting conversationalist? Why, I had said hardly anything at all. I couldn't have said anything if I had wanted to without changing the subject, for I didn't know any more about botany than I knew about the anatomy of a penguin. But I had done this: I had listened intently. I had listened because I was genuinely interested. And he felt it. Naturally that pleased him. That kind of listening is one of the highest compliments we can pay anyone. "Few human beings," wrote Jack Woodford in *Strangers in Love* "few human beings are proof against the implied flattery of rapt attention." I went even further than giving him rapt attention. I was "hearty in my approbation and lavish in my praise."

I told him that I had been immensely entertained and instructed—and I had. I told him I wished I had his knowledge—and I did. I told him that I should love to wander the fields with him—and I have. I told him I must see him again—and I did.

And so I had him thinking of me as a good conversationalist when, in reality, I had been merely a good listener and had encouraged him to talk.

What is the secret, the mystery, of a successful business interview? Well, according to former Harvard president Charles W. Eliot, "There is no mystery about successful business intercourse... Exclusive attention to the person who is speaking to you is very important. Nothing else is so flattering as that."

Self-evident, isn't it? You don't have to study for four years in Harvard to discover that. Yet I know and you know department store owners who will rent expensive space, buy their goods economically, dress their windows appealingly, spend thousands of dollars in advertising and then hire clerks who haven't the sense to be good listeners—clerks who interrupt customers, contradict them, irritate them, and all but drive them from the store.

A department store in Chicago almost lost a regular customer who spent several thousand dollars each year in that store because a sales clerk wouldn't listen. Mrs. Henrietta Douglas, who took our course in Chicago, had purchased a coat at a special sale. After she had brought it home she noticed that there was a tear in the lining. She came back the next day and asked the sales clerk to exchange it. The clerk refused even to listen to her complaint. "You bought this at a special sale," she said. She pointed to a sign on the wall. "Read that," she exclaimed. "'*All sales are final.*' Once

到了深夜，我向众人告辞。这时这位植物学家转身面对主人，对我大加赞扬，说我是“最富激励性的人”，我在某方面这样，在某方面那样……他最后说我是一个“最有意思的谈话家”。

一个有意思的谈话家？我几乎没有说什么话。如果我不改变话题的话，我也说不出什么来，因为我对于植物学的知识就像对企鹅的解剖学一样全然无知。但是我做到了认真倾听。我专注地听着，因为我真的有了兴趣。他也察觉到了，这当然让他很高兴。这种倾听是我们对任何人的一种最高的恭维。伍德福德在《相爱的人》中写道：“很少有人能拒绝那种隐藏于专心倾听中的恭维。”而我却比专心致志还要更进一步。我这是“诚于嘉许，宽于称道”。

我告诉他，我已经得到了极其周到的款待和指导——我确实感到如此。我告诉他，我真的希望自己能有他的知识——我也确实希望如此。我还告诉他，我希望和他一起去田野漫步——我真的希望是这样。我还告诉他，我必须再见到他——我真的这样想。

就因为这样，我使他认为我是一个善于谈话的人。可是说实话，我不过是一个善于倾听的人，并鼓励他谈话而已。

成功的商业会谈的神奇秘诀是什么呢？根据前哈佛大学校长伊利亚特的观点，那就是：“成功的商业交往并没有什么神秘的……专心致志地倾听正在和你讲话的人，这是最重要的。没有别的东西会比这更使人开心的。”

这个道理很明显，是不是？你不必去哈佛大学读4年书才能领悟它。但是你和我也都知道，有的商人出重金租用豪华的店面做生意，橱窗的设计也很吸引人，他们还不惜投入巨资做广告，可是他们雇的却是那些不知道做倾听者的服务员——这些服务员甚至会打断顾客的谈话，反驳他们，激怒他们，有的甚至还将顾客赶出店去。

芝加哥市一家百货商场，由于员工不善倾听而差点儿失去了一位常客，这位顾客每年都要在这家商场消费几千美元。亨利塔·道格拉斯女士上了我们在芝加哥的课。她买了一件特价的

you bought it, you have to keep it. Sew up the lining yourself."

"But this was damaged merchandise," Mrs. Douglas complained.

"Makes no difference," the clerk interrupted. "Final's final."

Mrs. Douglas was about to walk out indignantly, swearing never to return to that store ever, when she was greeted by the department manager, who knew her from her many years of patronage. Mrs. Douglas told her what had happened.

The manager listened attentively to the whole story, examined the coat and then said, "Special sales are 'final', so we can dispose of merchandise at the end of the season. But this 'no return' policy does not apply to damaged goods. We will certainly repair or replace the lining, or if you prefer, give you your money back."

What a difference in treatment! If that manager had not come along and listened to the customer, a long-term patron of that store could have been lost forever.

The chronic kicker, even the most violent critic, will frequently soften and be subdued in the presence of a patient, sympathetic listener—a listener who will be silent while the irate fault-finder dilates like a king cobra and spews the poison out of his system. To illustrate: The New York Telephone Company discovered a few years ago that it had to deal with one of the most vicious customers who ever cursed a customer service representative. And he did curse. He raved. He threatened to tear the phone out by its roots. He refused to pay certain charges that he declared were false. He wrote letters to the newspapers. He fried innumerable complaints with the Public Service Commission, and he started several suits against the telephone company.

At last, one of the company's most skillful "troubleshooters" was sent to interview this stormy petrel. This "troubleshooter" listened and let the cantankerous customer enjoy himself pouring out his tirade. The telephone representative listened and said "yes" and sympathized with his grievance.

"He raved on and I listened for nearly three hours," the "troubleshooter" said as he related his experiences before one of the author's classes. "Then I went back and listened some more. I interviewed him four times, and before the fourth visit was over I had become a charter member of an organization he was starting. He called it the 'Telephone Subscribers' Protective Association. I am still a member of this organization, and, so far as I know, I'm the only member in the world

衣服。可是买回家后注意到领子撕开了口，第二天她将衣服带回百货公司，要求售货员换货。可是售货员却不听她说话。“你买的是特价衣服。”售货员说，并指着墙上的标识说，“看，‘尾货概不退换。’如果你买了，就自己留着。你可以自己把领子缝好。”

“但这件衣服是坏的。”道格拉斯女士说。

“也一样，”售货员打断说，“尾货就是尾货。”

道格拉斯女士正要愤怒地离开，发誓再也不光顾这家商场了。这时市场部经理过来和她打招呼，他已认识她许多年了。道格拉斯女士讲了事情的经过。

这位经理认真地听了整个经过，检查了衣服，然后说：“特价品是尾货，所以我们在季度末会处理一些商品。但这并不是说卖劣等品。我们当然会修好或更换衣领，或者如果你愿意，你可以退款。”

多么不同的处理呀！如果那位经理不来倾听，商场将会永远失去一位长期客户。

喜欢挑剔的人，甚至最激烈的批评，也常常会在一个具有忍耐心和同情心的倾听者面前变得软化——当怒火万丈的寻衅者像一条大毒蛇张嘴咬人的时候，这位倾听者应当保持缄默。例如，纽约电话公司在几年前不得想办法去安抚一位曾凶言恶语咒骂客服代表的顾客。他可是真的咒骂。他简直有些歇斯底里，甚至威胁毁掉电话线路。他不仅拒绝支付某些不合理的费用，还写信给各家报纸，并多次向公众服务委员会投诉，好几次向法院起诉这家电话公司。

最后，电话公司派了一位经验最丰富的调解员去见这位暴怒的顾客。这位调解员只是静静地听着，听凭这位好辩的老先生大发牢骚。这位电话公司的调解员倾听着，不断说“是”，并同情他的冤屈。

“他继续毫无顾忌地说了将近3个小时，”这位调解员在我的班上叙述他的经历时说，“以后我又多次去他那里听他抱怨。我见过他4次，而在第四次访问结束时，我已经成为他正在创

today besides Mr.—

"I listened and sympathized with him on every point that he made during these interviews.He had never had a telephone representative talk with him that way before,and he became almost friendly.The point on which I went to see him was not even mentioned on the first visit,nor was it mentioned on the second or third,but upon the fourth interview,I closed the case completely,he paid all his bills in full,and for the first time in the history of his difficulties with the telephone company he voluntarily withdrew his complaints from the Public Service Commission."

Doubtless Mr.—had considered himself a holy crusader,defending the public rights against callous exploitation.But in reality,what he had really wanted was a feeling of importance.He got this feeling of importance at first by kicking and complaining.But as soon as he got his feeling of importance from a representative of the company,his imagined grievances vanished into thin air.

One morning years ago,an angry customer stormed into the office of Julian F.Detmer,founder of the Detmer Woolen Company,which later became the world's largest distributor of woolens to the tailoring trade.

"This man owed us a small sum of money," Mr.Detmer explained to me."The customer denied it,but we knew he was wrong.So our credit department had insisted that he pay.After getting a number of letters from our credit department,he packed his grip,made a trip to Chicago,and hurried into my office to inform me not only that he was not going to pay that bill,but that he was never going to buy another dollar's worth of goods from the Detmer Woolen Company.

"I listened patiently to all he had to say.I was tempted to interrupt,but I realized that would be bad policy.So I let him talk himself out.When he finally simmered down and got in a receptive mood,I said quietly,'I want to thank you for coming to Chicago to tell me about this.You have done me a great favor,for if our credit department has annoyed you,it may annoy other good customers,and that would be just too bad.Believe me,I am far more eager to hear this than you are to tell it.'

"That was the last thing in the world he expected me to say.I think he was a trifle disappointed,because he had come to Chicago to tell me a thing or two,but here I was thanking him instead of scrapping with him.I assured him we would wipe the charge off the books and forget

办的一个组织的主要会员了。他称之为'电话用户权益保障协会'。我现在仍然是这个组织的会员。然而,据我所知,除了这位老先生之外,我是这个组织在这个世界上唯一的会员。

"每次拜访时,我都是倾听他谈话,并且赞同他的每一个观点。他从来没有遇到过电话公司的人像我这样和他谈话,这使得他变得几乎友善起来。我在第一次拜访中并没有提到见他的目的,在第二次、第三次也没有提到我的目的。但在第四次,我妥善处理了案件——老先生将所有的欠费都付清了,并使他自从与电话公司作对以来,第一次撤销了向公众服务委员会的投诉。"

显然,这位老先生自认为是在为公益而战,是在保护公众的权利不被无情地剥夺。但实际上他是在追求一种自重感。他先是通过挑剔和抱怨来得到这种自重感。但是,当他从电话公司的代表那里得到了自重感时,他那并不真实的冤屈立即化为乌有。

好几年前的一个早上,一位怒气冲冲的客户闯进了德第摩尔毛料公司——这家公司后来成了世界上服装行业最大的毛料供应公司——创始人德第摩尔先生的办公室。

"这个人欠我们公司15美元,"德第摩尔先生向我解释说。"尽管这位顾客不承认,但我们知道他错了。所以我们公司信用部坚持要他付款。他在收到我们信用部的几封信之后,穿戴整齐地来到芝加哥,怒气冲冲地闯进我的办公室,说他不但不会付那笔钱,而且今后再也不会订购德第摩尔公司任何货物。

"我耐心地听他说完一切。我好几次都想打断他,但我知道那只会弄僵,所以我就让他尽情发泄。当他最后怒气消尽,能够静下心来听别人的意见时,我平静地说:'你到芝加哥来告诉我这件事,我得向你表示感谢。你已帮了我一个大忙,因为我们信用部如果使您不愉快的话,它也可能会让别的顾客不高兴,那可真是太糟了。你一定要相信我,我比你更想听到这件事。'

"他大概怎么也没有料到我会这样说。我想他可能还会有一点失望,因为他到芝加哥来,本来是想和我大干一番的,可是我却向他表示感谢,而不是和他争论。我明白地告诉他,我们要勾

it, because he was a very careful man with only one account to look after, while our clerks had to look after thousands. Therefore, he was less likely to be wrong than we were.

"I told him that I understood exactly how he felt and that, if I were in his shoes, I should undoubtedly feel precisely as he did. Since he wasn't going to buy from us anymore, I recommended some other woolen houses.

"In the past, we had usually lunched together when he came to Chicago, so I invited him to have lunch with me this day. He accepted reluctantly, but when we came back to the office he placed a larger order than ever before. He returned home in a softened mood and, wanting to be just as fair with us as we had been with him, looked over his bills, found one that had been mislaid, and sent us a check with his apologies.

"Later, when his wife presented him with a baby boy, he gave his son the middle name of Detmer, and he remained a friend and customer of the house until his death twenty-two years afterwards."

Years ago, a poor Dutch immigrant boy washed the windows of a bakery shop after school to help support his family. His people were so poor that in addition he used to go out in the street with a basket every day and collect stray bits of coal that had fallen in the gutter where the coal wagons had delivered fuel. That boy, Edward Bok, never got more than six years of schooling in his life; yet eventually he made himself one of the most successful magazine editors in the history of American journalism. How did he do it? That is a long story, but how he got his start can be told briefly. He got his start by using the principles advocated in this chapter.

He left school when he was thirteen and became an office boy for Western Union, but he didn't for one moment give up the idea of an education. Instead, he started to educate himself. He saved his carfares and went without lunch until he had enough money to buy an encyclopedia of American biography—and then he did an unheard-of thing. He read the lives of famous people and wrote them asking for additional information about their childhoods. He was a good listener. He asked famous people to tell him more about themselves. He wrote General James A. Garfield, who was then running for President, and asked if it was true that he was once a tow boy on a canal; and Garfield replied. He wrote General Grant asking about a certain battle, and Grant drew a map for him and

销那笔 15 美元的账，并忘掉这件事，因为他是一个很细心的人，而且只是涉及这一份账目，而我们的员工却要负责几千份账目，所以和我们的员工相比，他不大可能出错。

"我告诉他，我十分清楚他的感受；如果我处在他的位置，我也会和他的感受一样。由于他不想再买我们的产品了，于是我给他推荐了其他几家公司。

"以往他每次来芝加哥时，我们总是一同吃午餐，所以那天我照例请他吃午餐，他勉强答应了，但是当我们回到办公室的时候，他订了比以往更多的货物，然后平心静气地回去了。为了回报我们如此宽厚地对待他，他检查了他的账单，找到了一张他以前放错了地方的账单。于是，他给我们公司寄来了一张支票，并表达了他的歉意。

"后来，他的妻子生了一个男孩，他为他的儿子取名德第摩尔。他一直是我们公司的朋友和顾客，直到 22 年后去世。"

多年前，有一个贫困的荷兰移民少年，他每天都在放学后为一面包店擦窗户，好挣点钱养家。他家非常贫困，因此他每天都必须挎上一个篮子，去街上拾运煤车送煤时落在沟里的碎煤块。这个孩子名叫巴克，一生只在学校读过 6 年书，但他最后竟成为美国新闻界有史以来最成功的杂志编辑。他是怎么做的呢?说来话长，但关于他是如何开始的可以做个简单的介绍。他正是利用本章所提出的原则而走向成功的。

巴克 13 岁就离开了学校，去西联公司做了一名童工，但他从来都没有放弃过求学的念头。他开始自学。他平时不坐车，不吃午饭，最后用省下来的钱买了一部《美国名人传记大全》——然后他做了一件人们未曾听说过的事情。他读了这些名人传记后，开始给他们写信，请求得到他们童年时代的补充材料。他是一个善于倾听的人，他恳请这些名人谈论他们自己。他又给当时正在竞选总统的加飞大将写信，问他以前是否真的在一条运河上当过纤夫，加飞给他回了信。他还给格兰特将军写信，询问某一次战役的有关情况，格兰特将军为他画了一张地图，并邀

invited this fourteen-year-old boy to dinner and spent the evening talking to him.

Soon our Western Union messenger boy was corresponding with many of the most famous people in the nation: Ralph Waldo Emerson, Oliver Wendell Holmes, Longfellow, Mrs. Abraham Lincoln, Louisa May Alcott, General Sherman and Jefferson Davis. Not only did he correspond with these distinguished people, but as soon as he got a vacation, he visited many of them as a welcome guest in their homes. This experience imbued him with a confidence that was invaluable. These men and women fired him with a vision and ambition that shaped his life. And all this, let me repeat, was made possible solely by the application of the principles we are discussing here.

Isaac F. Marcosson, a journalist who interviewed hundreds of celebrities, declared that many people fail to make a favorable impression because they don't listen attentively. "They have been so much concerned with what they are going to say next that they do not keep their ears open ... Very important people have told me that they prefer good listeners to good talkers, but the ability to listen seems rarer than almost any other good trait."

And not only important personages crave a good listener, but ordinary folk do too. As the *Reader's Digest* once said, "Many persons call a doctor when all they want is an audience."

During the darkest hours of the Civil War, Lincoln wrote to an old friend in Springfield, Illinois, asking him to come to Washington. Lincoln said he had some problems he wanted to discuss with him. The old neighbor called at the White House, and Lincoln talked to him for hours about the advisability of issuing a proclamation freeing the slaves. Lincoln went over all the arguments for and against such a move, and then read letters and newspaper articles, some denouncing him for not freeing the slaves and others denouncing him for fear he was going to free them. After talking for hours, Lincoln shook hands with his old neighbor, said good night, and sent him back to Illinois without even asking for his opinion. Lincoln had done all the talking himself. That seemed to clarify his mind. "He seemed to feel easier after that talk," the old friend said. Lincoln hadn't wanted advice. He had wanted merely a friendly, sympathetic listener to whom he could unburden himself. That's what we all want when we are in trouble. That is frequently all the irritated customer wants, and the dissatisfied employee or the hurt friend.

If you want to know how to make people shun you and laugh at you behind your back and even

请这位14岁的少年和他共进晚餐，和他谈了整整一晚上。

不久，这位西联公司的信童便和国内最著名的人通起信来：爱默生、温德勒·霍尔摩斯、朗费罗、林肯夫人、露易莎·奥尔科特、谢尔曼将军和杰弗逊·戴维斯。他不仅和这些著名人士通信，而且一到休息日或节假日就去拜访他们中的许多人，成了他们家中受欢迎的客人。这些经历使他培养出一种价值连城的自信心。这些著名人士激发了他的理想和志向，改变了他的人生。而所有这一切，让我再说一遍吧，都只是因为实行了我们在本章所讨论的原则而成为可能。

马可逊访问过几百位著名人物。他说许多人之所以不能给别人留下良好的印象，就是因为他们不注意倾听。“他们极其关心的是他们自己下面要说什么，他们从来都不会侧耳倾听……许多名人曾告诉我，和善于谈话者相比，他们更喜欢善于倾听者。但是，善于倾听的能力好像比任何其他能力都要少。”

不仅仅是重要人物愿意和善于倾听的人打交道，就连普通人也不例外。这正像《读者文摘》中曾说过的：“许多人去看医生，他们需要的不过是一个善于倾听的人。”

在美国内战最激烈的时候，林肯写信给在伊利诺伊州斯普林菲尔德镇的一位朋友，请他来华盛顿。林肯说他想和他探讨一些问题。这位老朋友到了白宫，于是林肯就关于解放黑奴是否合适这个问题，和他谈了好几个小时。林肯详细分析了赞成或反对这项措施的各种观点，又读了一些信件及报纸上的文章——其中有的谴责他不解放黑奴，但也有的谴责他要解放黑奴。谈论几个小时之后，林肯与这位老朋友握了握手，说了声“晚安”之后，就派人将他送回了伊利诺伊，竟然没有征求他的意见。所有的话都是林肯一个人说的，似乎这样才能使他平静下来。“谈完之后，他似乎稍稍感到舒适些。”这位老朋友说。林肯并不想要建议。林肯所需要的只是一位友善的、同情的倾听者，使他可以宣泄内心的苦闷——而这正是我们每个人在困难中都需要

despise you, here is the recipe: Never listen to anyone for long. Talk incessantly about yourself. If you have an idea while the other person is talking, don't wait for him or her to finish, bust right in and interrupt in the middle of a sentence.

Do you know people like that? I do, unfortunately; and the astonishing part of it is that some of them are prominent.

Bores, that is all they are—bores intoxicated with their own egos, drunk with a sense of their own importance.

People who talk only of themselves think only of themselves. And "those people who think only of themselves," Dr. Nicholas Murray Butler, longtime president of Columbia University, said, "are hopelessly uneducated. They are not educated," said Dr. Butler, "no matter how instructed they may be."

So if you aspire to be a good conversationalist, be an attentive listener. To be interesting, be interested. Ask questions that other persons will enjoy answering. Encourage them to talk about themselves and their accomplishments.

Remember that the people you are talking to are a hundred times more interested in themselves and their wants and problems than they are in you and your problems. A person's toothache means more to that person than a famine in China which kills a million people. A boil on one's neck interests one more than forty earthquakes in Africa. Think of that the next time you start a conversation.

Principle 4: Be a good listener. Encourage others to talk about themselves.

的；这也正是那些忿怒的顾客所需要的；不满意的雇员、伤感的朋友也都是这样。

如果你想知道如何让别人躲避你，在背后讥笑你，甚至轻视你，这里就有一个好方法，那就是永远不要长时间地倾听别人谈话，而是不断地谈论你自己；如果你在别人谈话过程中有了一个想法，大可不必等他说完，只要立即插嘴说你自己的事情，就可以让他住口。

你认识这种人吗？不幸得很，我认识；但最让人感到震惊的是，他们中一些人还是知名人士。

他们正是那种令人厌恶的人——被他们的自私及他们的自重感所麻醉了的、令人厌恶的人。

一心只谈自己的人只会为自己着想。而"只为自己着想的人，"哥伦比亚大学校长巴德勒博士说，"是无可救药的，也是不可教育的。"巴德勒博士说，"无论他接受过什么样的教育。"

所以，如果你希望成为一个善于谈话的人，就要做一个善于倾听的人。要使别人对你感兴趣，首先就要对别人感兴趣。不妨问问别人喜欢回答的问题，鼓励他们开口谈他们自己以及他们所取得的成就。

要记住，那个正在与你谈话的人对他自己、他的需要、他的问题比对你及你的问题感兴趣超过上百倍。一个人的牙痛对他来说，比中国死亡百万人的灾难还重要；一个人对自己脖子上一点儿痒痒的在意也要远远超过对非洲 40 次地震的关注。在你下次开始谈话的时候，请不要忘了这一点。

第四项规则：做一个善于倾听的人，鼓励别人谈论他们自己。

5 How to Interest People

Everyone who was ever a guest of Theodore Roosevelt was astonished at the range and diversity of his knowledge.Whether his visitor was a cowboy or a Rough Rider,a New York politician or a diplomat,Roosevelt knew what to say.And how was it done? The answer was simple. Whenever Roosevelt expected a visitor,he sat up late the night before,reading up on the subject in which he knew his guest was particularly interested.

For Roosevelt knew,as all leaders know,that the royal road to a person's heart is to talk about the things he or she treasures most.

The genial William Lyon Phelps,essayist and professor of literature at Yale,learned this lesson early in life.

"When I was eight years old and was spending a weekend visiting my Aunt Libby Linsley at her home in Stratford on the Housatonic," he wrote in his essay on *Human Nature*,"a middle-aged man called one evening,and after a polite skirmish with my aunt,he devoted his attention to me.At that time,I happened to be excited about boats,and the visitor discussed the subject in a way that seemed to me particularly interesting.After he left,I spoke of him with enthusiasm.What a man! My aunt informed me he was a New York lawyer,that he cared nothing whatever about boats—that he took not the slightest interest in the subject.'But why then did he talk all the time about boats?'

"'Because he is a gentleman.He saw you were interested in boats,and he talked about the things he knew would interest and please you.He made himself agreeable.'"

And William Lyon Phelps added,"I never forgot my aunt's remark."

As I write this chapter,I have before me a letter from Edward L.Chalif,who was active in Boy Scout work.

"One day I found I needed a favor," wrote Mr.Chalif."A big Scout jamboree was coming off in Europe,and I wanted the president of one of the largest corporations in America to pay the expenses of one of my boys for the trip.Fortunately,just before I went to see this man,I heard that

第5章 如何让别人对你感兴趣

每一个拜访过西奥多·罗斯福总统的人,都会对他那渊博的知识感到惊讶。不论是牧童还是骑士,或纽约的政客和外交家,罗斯福都知道该和他说些什么。那么,罗斯福又是如何做的呢?答案很简单——不论罗斯福要见什么人,他总是会在头天晚上晚些入睡,翻阅一些来访者会特别感兴趣的知识。

因为罗斯福和所有领袖人物一样,深知通达对方内心的妙方,就是和对方谈论他最感兴趣的事情。

散文家、耶鲁大学文学教授菲尔普斯先生是个非常和蔼的人,他在早年就学到了这个道理。

"我8岁那年,有一次去姑姑林斯莉家过周末,"菲利普在他一篇谈论人性的小品文中这样写道,"有一天晚上,一位中年人来访。在和姑姑随便聊了几句之后,他就把注意力转移到了我身上。当时我对船的兴趣正浓,而这位客人和我谈论了这方面的知识,令我产生了特殊的兴趣。他离开之后,我还对他赞赏不已。多么了不起啊!姑姑告诉我,他是纽约一位律师,本来他对有关船的事情是不应该如此热心的,甚至应该是毫无兴趣可言的。'可是,他为什么自始至终都在谈论有关船的问题呢?'

"'因为他是一位绅士。他见你对船很感兴趣,就谈论他认为能使你注意并高兴的话题。这使得他成为一个受欢迎的人。'"

菲尔普斯教授又补充说:"我永远也忘不了我姑姑的话。"

就在我写这章的时候,我面前放着一封查立夫先生的来信,他是一位热心于童子军事业的人。

"一天,我感到我需要帮助。"查立夫先生写道,"欧洲将举办童子军夏令营活动,我想邀请

he had drawn a check for a million dollars, and that after it was canceled, he had had it framed. So the first thing I did when I entered his office was to ask to see the check. A check for a million dollars! I told him I never knew that anybody had ever written such a check, and that I wanted to tell my boys that I had actually seen a check for a million dollars. He gladly showed it to me; I admired it and asked him to tell me all about how it happened to be drawn."

You notice, don't you, that Mr. Chalif didn't begin by talking about the Buy Scouts, or the jamboree in Europe, or what it was he wanted? He talked in terms of what interested the other man. Here's the result:

"Presently, the man I was interviewing said, 'Oh, by the way, what was it you wanted to see me about?' So I told him.

"To my vast surprise," Mr. Chalif continues, "he not only granted immediately what I asked for, but much more. I had asked him to send only one boy to Europe, but he sent five boys and myself, gave me a letter of credit for a thousand dollars and told us to stay in Europe for seven weeks. He also gave me letters of introduction to his branch presidents, putting them at our service, and he himself met us in Paris and showed us the town. Since then, he has given jobs to some of the boys whose parents were in want, and he is still active in our group.

"Yet I know if I hadn't found out what he was interested in, and got him warmed up first, I wouldn't have found him one-tenth as easy to approach."

Is this a valuable technique to use in business? Is it? Let's see. Take Henry G. Duvernoy of Duvernoy and Sons, a wholesale baking firm in New York.

Mr. Duvernoy had been trying to sell bread to a certain New York hotel. He had called on the manager every week for four years. He went to the same social affairs the manager attended. He even took rooms in the hotel and lived there in order to get the business. But he failed.

"Then," said Mr. Duvernoy, "after studying human relations, I resolved to change my tactics. I decided to find out what interested this man—what caught his enthusiasm.

"I discovered he belonged to a society of hotel executives called the Hotel Greeters of America. He not only belonged, but his bubbling enthusiasm had made him president of the organization, and president of the International Greeters. No matter where its conventions were held,

美国某家大公司的经理赞助一位童子军的旅行。幸运的是,在拜访他之前,我听说他曾开出了一张 100 万美元的支票。这张支票退回来后,他把它放在了镜框中。所以我进他办公室的第一件事就是请他给我展示那张支票。我告诉他,我这辈子从来都没有听说有人开过数额如此巨大的支票;我还要告诉我的童子军,说我的确看到过一张 100 万美元的支票。他愉快地把那张支票给我看。我赞叹不已,并请他把开这张支票的详细情况告诉我。"

请注意,查立夫先生在刚开始时并没有谈有关童子军或欧洲夏令营的事,也没有谈他想要对方帮助的事。他只是谈对方感兴趣的话题。下面就是结果:

"过了一会儿,我拜访的那位经理问我:'哦,请问你来找我有什么事?'我就把我的事情告诉了他。

"令我吃惊的是,他不但立即答应了我的请求,还给了我更多的资助。我本来只请他赞助一名童子军去欧洲,可是他资助了 5 名童子军和我本人,给我开了一张 1000 美元的支票,并建议我们在欧洲玩上 7 个星期。然后,他又给我一封介绍信,把我引荐给他在欧洲分公司的经理,请他们到时候帮助我们,他又亲自去巴黎接我们,带领我们游览了这座城市。从此以后,他就经常为家庭贫困的童子军提供工作的机会,对我们童子军事业非常热心。

"但是我也很清楚,如果我当时没有找到他感兴趣的话题,让他高兴起来,那么我大概连 1/10 的机会都没有。"

这种方法在商业活动中也有价值吧?我们就举个例子,来看看纽约一家高级面包公司——杜弗诺公司的经理杜弗诺先生是怎样做的吧:

杜弗诺先生一直想把面包推销给纽约某家大饭店。连续 4 年,杜弗诺先生几乎每个星期都要去拜访这家饭店的经理,并且经常参加这位经理出席的各种社交聚会。为了促成这笔生意,他甚至在这家饭店租了一个房间住在那里。但是他仍未做成生意。

he would be there.

"So when I saw him the next day, I began talking about the Greeters. What a response I got. What a response! He talked to me for half an hour about the Greeters, his tones vibrant with enthusiasm. I could plainly see that this society was not only his hobby, it was the passion of his life. Before I left his office, he had 'sold' me a membership in his organization.

"In the meantime, I had said nothing about bread. But a few days later, the steward of his hotel phoned me to come over with samples and prices.

"'I don't know what you did to the old boy,' the steward greeted me, 'but he sure is sold on you!'

"Think of it! I had been drumming at that man for four years—trying to get his business—and I'd still be drumming at him if I hadn't finally taken the trouble to find out what he was interested in, and what he enjoyed talking about."

Talking in terms of the other person's interests pays off for both parties. Howard Z. Herzig, a leader in the field of employee communications, has always followed this principle. When asked what reward he got from it, Mr. Herzig responded that he not only received a different reward from each person but that in general the reward had been an enlargement of his life each time he spoke to someone.

Principle 5: Talk in terms of the other person's interests.

"后来,"杜弗诺先生说,"我研究了人际关系,决定改变策略。我决定找到这个人的兴趣所在,找出他最热衷的事业。

"我发现他是美国饭店业协会的会员。不仅如此,由于他在这方面的浓厚兴趣,使他被推举为这个组织的主席。每次只要开会或举行什么活动,他都会参加。

"于是,当我再次去拜访他的时候,我开始和他谈论饭店业协会的事情。你猜他怎么了?他的反应简直令人吃惊!他和我谈了半小时饭店业协会的事情,而且精神饱满,充满热情。我可以明确看出他不仅对饭店业协会的事情感兴趣,而且将自己的全部精力都投入在这上面。就在我离开他的办公室之前,他劝我加入了这个协会。

"在这次会谈中,我没有提有关面包的半个字。可是没过几天,我就接到他饭店主管人员的电话,让我把面包的货样和报价单送过去。

"'我真不知道你对这老先生用了什么魔法,'这位主管人员对我说,'他可是真的被你打动了!'

"试想一下!我和这位经理打了4年交道,一心想把面包卖给他。如果不是设法找到他感兴趣的事,了解他愿意讨论的问题,恐怕我现在还一无所获!"

谈论别人感兴趣的话题,双方都不会有损失。霍华德·赫齐兹是雇员通讯领域的领袖,他曾奉行着这项法则。当被问到从中有何受益时,他说他不仅从不同的人那里获益;而且每次与人谈话时,这种获益从整体上丰富了他的生活。

第五项规则:谈论别人感兴趣的话题。

6 How to Make People Like You Instantly

I was waiting in line to register a letter in the post office at Thirty-third Street and Eighth Avenue in New York.I noticed that the clerk appeared to be bored with the job—weighing envelopes,handing out stamps,making change,issuing receipts—the same monotonous grind year after year.So I said to myself,"I am going to try to make that clerk like me.Obviously,to make him like me,I must say something nice,not about myself,but about him." So I asked myself,"What is there about him that I can honestly admire?" That is sometimes a hard question to answer,especially with strangers; but,in this case,it happened to be easy.I instantly saw something I admired no end.

So while he was weighing my envelope,I remarked with enthusiasm,"I certainly wish I had your head of hair."

He looked up,half-startled,his face beaming with smiles."Well,it isn't as good as it used to be," he said modestly.I assured him that although it might have lost some of its pristine glory, nevertheless it was still magnificent.He was immensely pleased.We carried on a pleasant little conversation and the last thing he said to me was,"Many people have admired my hair."

I'll bet that person went out to lunch that day walking on air.I'll bet he went home that night and told his wife about it.I'll bet he looked in the mirror and said,"It is a beautiful head of hair."

I told this story once in public and a man asked me afterwards,"What did you want to get out of him?"

What was I trying to get out of him!!! What was I trying to get out of him!!!

If we are so contemptibly selfish that we can't radiate a little happiness and pass on a bit of honest appreciation without trying to get something out of the other person in return—if our souls are no bigger than sour crab apples,we shall meet with the failure we so richly deserve.

Oh yes, I did want something out of that chap.I wanted something priceless.And I got it. I got the feeling that I had done something for him without his being able to do anything whatever in return for me.That is a feeling that flows and sings in your memory long after the incident is past.

第6章 如何使人马上喜欢你

有一次,我在纽约第33大街和第8大道交叉处的邮局排队,准备寄出一封挂号信。我注意到那位邮局员工对他的工作很不耐烦——秤信、取邮票、找零钱、开收据——这样年复一年的单调而重复的工作。于是我对自己说:"我一定要让那个人喜欢我。显然,要让他喜欢我,我必须说些让他高兴的话,不是关于我的,而是关于他的。"所以我问自己:"他有什么值得我真诚赞美的呢?"这个问题有时候可不好回答,尤其是对一个陌生人。但是这次却很巧,我很快就发现了一件值得赞美的东西。

就在他给我秤信的时候,我热情地对他说:"我真希望自己也有您这样一头好头发。"

他有些惊讶地抬起头来,脸上露出了欢欣的微笑。"不过现在没以前好了。"他很谦虚地说。我诚恳地对他说:"虽然它比以前稍减光泽,但还是那样好。"他显得非常高兴。于是我们愉快地谈了一会儿,最后他对我说:"有许多人羡慕我的头发。"

我敢打赌,他那天吃午饭的时候一定非常愉快;那天晚上他回家后一定会把这件事告诉他妻子;他甚至会对着镜子自夸:"这头发实在太漂亮了。"

有一次,我在某个公共场所讲到了这件事。一个人问我:"你想从他那里获得什么?"

我想从他那里获得什么!!! 我想从他那里获得什么!!!

假如我们是这么自私,一心只想着得到回报,那我们就不会给人任何快乐,不会给人一点儿真诚的赞美——假如我们的气度如此小,那我们只会遭到应有的失败。

不错,我确实想从他那里得到某些东西,想得到某些难以用金钱衡量的东西,而我也得到了!我赞美了他,可是他对我却难以回报。你会在这件事情过去许久之后,仍在记忆中得到一种美妙如歌的体验。

在人类行为中,有一条至关重要的法则,如果我们遵守它,就会万事如意;实际上,如果我们遵

There is one all-important law of human conduct.If we obey that law,we shall almost never get into trouble.In fact,that law,if obeyed,will bring us countless friends and constant happiness.But the very instant we break the law,we shall get into endless trouble.The law is this: Always make the other person feel important.John Dewey,as we have already noted,said that the desire to be important is the deepest urge in human nature; and William James said,"The deepest principle in human nature is the craving to be appreciated." As I have already pointed out,it is this urge that differentiates us from the animals.It is this urge that has been responsible for civilization itself.

Philosophers have been speculating on the roles of human relationships for thousands of years,and out of all that speculation,there has evolved only one important precept.It is not new.It is as old as history.Zoroaster taught it to his followers in Persia twenty-five hundred years ago.Confucius preached it in China twenty-four centuries ago.Lao-tse,the founder of Taoism,taught it to his disciples in the Valley of the Pan.Buddha preached it on the bank of the Holy Ganges five hundred years before Christ. The sacred books of Hinduism taught it a thousand years before that.Jesus taught it among the stony hills of Judea nineteen centuries ago.Jesus summed it up in one thought—probably the most important rule in the world:"Do unto others as you would have others do unto you."

You want the approval of those with whom you come in contact.You want recognition of your true worth.You want a feeling that you are important in your little world.You don't want to listen to cheap, insincere flattery,but you do crave sincere appreciation.You want your friends and associates to be,as Charles Schwab put it,"hearty in their approbation and lavish in their praise." All of us want that.

So let's obey the Golden Rule,and give unto others what we would have others give unto us.

How? When? Where? The answer is: All the time,everywhere.

David G.Smith of Eau Claire,Wisconsin,told one of our classes how he handled a delicate situation when he was asked to take charge of the refreshment booth at a charity concert.

"The night of the concert I arrived at the park and found two elderly ladies in a very bad humor standing next to the refreshment stand.Apparently each thought that she was in charge of this project. As I stood there pondering what to do,one of the members of the sponsoring committee appeared and handed me a cash box and thanked me for taking over the project. She introduced Rose and Jane as my helpers and then ran off.

守这条法则,将会得到无数朋友和无穷无尽的快乐。可是,如果我们违背这条法则,就会招致数不清的挫折。这条法则就是:“永远使对方获得自重感。”这正如杜威教授所说的,自重是人类天性中最强烈的欲望;也正如詹姆斯教授所说的:“在人类天性中,最深层的欲望就是渴望得到别人的重视。”我也曾指出,这种冲动正是我们区别于动物的特征,正是这种欲望才推动了人类文明的发展。

千百年来,哲学家们一直在思考人类关系的准则,终于悟出一种观念。这并不是什么新东西,它和历史一样古老。2500 年前索罗亚斯特在波斯告诉过他的追随者, 孔子也在 2400 多年前在中国提倡过,道家创始人老子也在函谷关这么说过,基督降生前 500 年佛陀在神圣的恒河边倡导过,1000 多年前的印度教经典也这么教导。耶稣 19 世纪以前在犹大的石头山教导过,并将它概括成一句话——也许是世界上最重要的一句话:“你希望别人怎么待你,就先怎样待别人。”

你希望周围的人赞同你,希望自己的价值得到认同,希望在你的小圈子里得到重视;你不愿听到不值钱的卑贱的谄媚,但渴求得到真诚的赞美。你希望你的朋友和同事都能像施瓦伯所说的“诚于嘉许,宽于称道”——我们都希望这样。

那么,就让我们遵守这条黄金法则:你希望别人怎么待你,就先怎样待别人。

怎么做?什么时候做?在什么地方做?答案是:随时随地去做。

威斯康星州犹卡莱尔市的戴维·史密斯在我们一个班上讲了他的经历。当时他负责一个慈善音乐会的饮料摊,巧妙地处理了一次纠纷。

“音乐会那天晚上,我到了公园,发现两个大女孩相互敌视地站在饮料摊边上。显然她们都认为自己应该负责这一摊事。我站在那里想对策,这次活动发起组织的一位成员来了,给了我一个现金盒子,并谢谢我照料此事。她将那两个女孩——罗丝和简介绍给我,说是我助手,然后就走了。

“一阵沉寂之后,我发现那个现金盒子是一种权威象征,就把它给了罗丝,并说我整理不清那些钱,如果她能负责此事,我会很感谢她。然后我又告诉简,去教两个负责饮料机的十几岁的

"A great silence ensued.Realizing that the cash box was a symbol of authority (of sorts),I gave the box to Rose and explained that I might not be able to keep the money straight and that if she took care of it I would f eel better.I then suggested to Jane that she show two teenagers who had been assigned to refreshments how to operate the soda machine,and I asked her to be responsible for that part of the project.

"The evening was very enjoyable with Rose happily counting the money,Jane supervising the teenagers,and me enjoying the concert."

You don't have to wait until you are ambassador to France or chairman of the Clambake Committee of your lodge before you use this philosophy of appreciation.You can work magic with it almost every day.

If,for example,the waitress brings us mashed potatoes when we have ordered French fried,let's say: "I'm sorry to trouble you,but I prefer French fried." She'll probably reply, "No trouble at all" and will be glad to change the potatoes,because we have shown respect for her.

Little phrases such as "I'm sorry to trouble you," "Would you be so kind as to—?" "Won't you please?" "Would you mind?" "Thank you"—little courtesies like these oil the cogs of the monotonous grind of everyday life—and,incidentally,they are the hallmark of good breeding.

Let's take another illustration.Hall Caine's novels—*The Christian*, *The Deemster*, *The Manxman*,among them—were all best-sellers in the early part of this century.Millions of people read his novels,countless millions.He was the son of a blacksmith.He never had more than eight years' schooling in his life; yet when he died he was the richest literary man of his time.

The story goes like this: Hall Caine loved sonnets and ballads; so he devoured all of Dante Gabriel Rossetti's poetry.He even wrote a lecture chanting the praises of Rossetti's artistic achievement—and sent a copy to Rossetti himself.Rossetti was delighted."Any young man who has such an exalted opinion of my ability," Rossetti probably said to himself, "must be brilliant." So Rossetti invited this blacksmith's son to come to London and act as his secretary.That was the mining point in Hall Caine's life; for,in his new position,he met the literary artists of the day. Profiting by their advice and inspired by their encouragement,he launched upon a career that emblazoned his name across the sky.

His home,Greeba Castle,on the Isle of Man,became a Mecca for tourists from the far corners

孩子如何操作,并让她负责那件事。

"那天晚上,罗丝快乐地数着钱,简看管那两个孩子,我则在享受那场音乐会。"

其实,你大可不必等自己当上大官之后,再去奉行这条赞美法则。你几乎每天都可以运用它产生奇迹。

例如,我们进餐馆时要了一份法式炸薯条,而女服务员却端给我们一盘薯泥,我们不妨说:"对不起,给你添麻烦了,但我更喜欢法式炸薯条。"她也许会说:"一点也不麻烦。"由于我们对她表示了尊敬,所以她会很高兴地给我们换炸薯条。

"对不起, 给你添麻烦了"、"请你……"、"能不能……"、"谢谢"——这些细微平常的礼貌短语,就像是每天单调生活中的润滑剂,会给我们的生活平添几分色彩,同时也是我们优良品质的体现。

让我们再看另一个例子。霍尔·凯恩的小说《基督教徒》、《法官》、《男人岛的男人》是本世纪初最畅销的小说,有成千上万的人读过他的小说。凯恩是个铁匠的儿子,一生只上过 8 年学,但他去世时已成为他那个时代最富有的作家。

大概情况是这样的:由于凯恩酷爱十四行诗和叙事诗,所以他将大诗人罗斯迪所有的诗都读了一遍。他还写了一篇演说辞,歌颂罗斯迪在诗歌方面的艺术成就,并送了一份给罗斯迪本人。罗斯迪很高兴,"任何一个青年能对我的才华有如此高深的见解,"也许罗斯迪会说,"一定是个非常聪明的人。"于是,罗斯迪将凯恩请到伦敦的家中来担任自己的秘书。这可是凯恩人生的转折点——因为他凭借这一新的身份,接触了许多当代著名的文学家。他从他们那里接受有益的建议,并受到他们的鼓励和激发,开始了写作生涯,最终名闻世界。

凯恩的故乡英国曼岛的格里巴堡,现在已经成为世界各地旅游者的胜地。他留下来的财产高达几百万美元! 可是,又有谁知道,如果他当初没有写那篇真诚赞美罗斯迪的演讲词,他或许会穷困潦倒地死去呢?

of the world, and he left a multimillion dollar estate. Yet—who knows—he might have died poor and unknown had he not written an essay expressing his admiration for a famous man.

Such is the power, the stupendous power, of sincere, heartfelt appreciation.

Rossetti considered himself important. That is not strange. Almost everyone considers himself important, very important.

The life of many a person could probably be changed if only someone would make him feel important. Ronald J. Rowland, who is one of the instructors of our course in California, is also a teacher of arts and crafts. He wrote to us about a student named Chris in his beginning—crafts class:

Chris was a very quiet, shy boy lacking in self-confidence, the kind of student that often does not receive the attention he deserves.

On Wednesday, Chris was diligently working at his desk. I really felt there was a hidden fire deep inside him. I asked Chris if he would like to be in the advanced class. How I wish I could express the look in Chris's face, the emotions in that shy fourteen-year-old boy, trying to hold back his tears.

"Who me, Mr. Rowland? Am I good enough?"

"Yes, Chris, you are good enough."

I had to leave at that point because tears were coming to my eyes.

As Chris walked out of class that day, seemingly two inches taller, he looked at me with bright blue eyes and said in a positive voice, "Thank you, Mr. Rowland."

Chris taught me a lesson I will never forget—our deep desire to feel important. To help me never forget this rule, I made a sign which reads "YOU ARE IMPORTANT." This sign hangs in the front of the classroom for all to see and to remind me that each student I face is equally important.

The unvarnished truth is that almost all the people you meet feel themselves superior to you in some way, and a sure way to their hearts is to let them realize in some subtle way that you recognize their importance, and recognize it sincerely.

Remember what Emerson said, "Every man I meet is my superior in some way. In that, I learn of him."

And the pathetic part of it is that frequently those who have the least justification for a feeling

这就是发自内心地真诚赞美的力量,这是一种伟大的力量!

罗斯迪认为自己很重要,这并不奇怪——几乎每个人都认为自己很重要,非常非常重要。

有的人的人生仅仅因为某人使他获得了自重感而发生改变。罗纳尔德·罗兰是我们在加州的一位律师,也教美工课。他给我们写信,讲到了他的初级手工艺班一个学生克里斯的故事。

克里斯是个文静、害羞、缺乏自信的男孩,平静很少引人注意。

一个星期三,克里斯正在案头用功。我感到他内心深处有一股看不见的火焰。我问他是否喜欢进高级班。我多么希望能表达出他的表情呀!这个14岁的害羞男孩的表情太感人了!他努力控制住了泪水。

"是我吗?罗兰先生?我行吗?"

"是的,克里斯,你棒极了。"

我必须立即走开,因为我的眼泪快要出来了。

那天,克里斯走出教室,似乎长高了两英寸。他用那双明亮的蓝眼睛看着我,肯定地说:"谢谢你,罗兰先生。"

克里斯教了我永难忘怀的一课——我们对自重的渴望。为了不使自己忘记这条法则,我做了一条标语——"你是重要的!"这条标语挂在教室前面,每个人都能看见,并提醒我,我所面对的每个学生都是同等重要的。

一个不容否认的事实就是,凡是你遇见的人,都会觉得他们在某些方面比你强。巧妙地承认对方的重要性,并由衷地表达出来,就会使你得到他的友谊。

要记住爱默生的话:"凡是我所遇见的人都有比我优秀之处。在这方面,我正好可以向他学习。"

但可悲的是,那些无所作为却自以为很成功的人,整天都在用令人恶心的浮华夸饰之词来掩饰他们内心的不安。这种人正像莎士比亚所说的:"……人!狂傲的人!借着那么一点儿

of achievement bolster up their egos by a show of tumult and conceit which is truly nauseating.As Shakespeare put it, "...man, proud man, Drest in a little brief authority, ...Plays such fantastic tricks before high heaven, As make the angels weep."

I am going to tell you how business people in my own courses have applied these principles with remarkable results.Let's take the case of a Connecticut attorney (because of his relatives he prefers not to have his name mentioned).

Shortly after joining the course, Mr.R—drove to Long Island with his wife to visit some of her relatives.She left him to chat with an old aunt of hers and then rushed off by herself to visit some of the younger relatives.Since he soon had to give a speech professionally on how he applied the principles of appreciation, he thought he would gain some worthwhile experience talking with the elderly lady.So he looked around the house to see what he could honestly admire.

"This house was built about 1890, wasn't it?" he inqured.

"Yes," she replied, "that is precisely the year it was built."

"It reminds me of the house I was born in," he said. "It's beautiful.Well built.Roomy, You know, they don't build houses like this anymore."

"You're right," the old lady agreed. "The young folks nowadays don't care for beautiful homes. All they want is a small apartment, and then they go off gadding about in their automobiles.

"This is a dream house," she said in a voice vibrating with tender memories. "This house was built with love.My husband and I dreamed about it for years before we built it.We didn't have an architect.We planned it all ourselves."

She showed Mr.R—about the house, and he expressed his hearty admiration for the beautiful treasures she had picked up in her travels and cherished over a lifetime—paisley shawls, an old English tea set, Wedgwood china, French beds and chairs, Italian paintings, and silk draperies that had once hung in a French chateau.

After showing Mr.R—through the house, she took him out to the garage.There, jacked up on blocks, was a Packard car—in mint condition.

"My husband bought that car for me shortly before he passed on," she said softly. "I have never ridden in it since his death ...You appreciate nice things, and I'm going to give this car to you."

才能,竟然在上天面前胡作非为,骗得天使们都流下了眼泪。"

下面我要告诉你,我班上那些从事商业的学员应用这些法则而获得成功的故事。我先讲一位康涅狄格州律师的故事(由于他亲属方面的原因,他不想让别人知道他的姓名)。

R先生参加课程后不久,就和他妻子驾车去长岛看望她的亲戚。妻子将他留下来,陪同她年迈的姑妈聊天,而她自己则去看另几家亲戚。由于R先生要在班上做一次关于如何运用赞美法则的演讲,所以他打算从与这位老太太的谈话中获得宝贵体验。于是他在房子四周巡视了一番,希望能找到一些他可以真诚赞美的东西。

"这栋房子建于1890年前后,对吗?"他问。

"是的,"老太太回答说,"正是那一年建的。"

"它使我回想起我出生的老家的房子。"他说,"它真是太好了,真漂亮,里面真宽敞!您知道,人们现在再也不建这种房子了。"

"一点都不错,"老太太赞同道,"现在的年轻人可不怎么在乎漂亮的房子。他们所想要的不过是一套小公寓,然后开着汽车到处去兜风。"

"这是一所梦想之屋。"老太太的声音有些颤抖,陷入了回忆,"这房子是我和我丈夫爱情的结晶。我丈夫和我在建这栋房子之前,梦想了许多年。我们没有请建筑师,它完全是我们自己设计的。"

她领着R先生参观了房子。房子里放满了老太太在世界各地旅行时搜集到的纪念珍品:波斯披肩、英国老茶具、威格瓷器、法式寝具、意大利油画,以及曾风靡于法国封建王朝时期的装饰丝帷。R先生对这些东西表示了真诚的赞美。

领R先生参观完房子后,她又带他到车库去。那里放着一辆几乎全新的别克高级汽车。

"那辆车是我丈夫去世前不久为我买的。"老太太慢声细语地说,"他离我而去之后,我再也没有用过它……你很会欣赏美丽的东西,我准备把这辆车送给你。"

"Why, aunty," he said, "you overwhelm me.I appreciate your generosity, of course; but I couldn't possibly accept it.I'm not even a relative of yours.I have a new car, and you have many relatives that would like to have that Packard."

"Relatives!" she exclaimed."Yes, I have relatives who are just waiting till I die so they can get that car.But they are not going to get it."

"If you don't want to give it to them, you can very easily sell it to a secondhand dealer."he told her.

"Sell it!" she cried."Do you think I would sell this car? Do you think I could stand to see strangers riding up and down the street in that car—that car that my husband bought for me? I wouldn't dream of selling it.I'm going to give it to you.You appreciate beautiful things."

He tried to get out of accepting the car, but he couldn't without hurting her feelings.

This lady, left all alone in a big house with her paisley shawls, her French antiques, and her memories, was starving for a little recognition.She had once been young and beautiful and sought after. She had once built a house warm with love and had collected things from all over Europe to make it beautiful.Now, in the isolated loneliness of old age, she craved a little human warmth, a little genuine appreciation—and no one gave it to her.And when she found it, like a spring in the desert, her gratitude couldn't adequately express itself with anything less than the gift of her cherished Packard.

Let's take another case: Donald M.McMahon, who was superintendent of Lewis and Valentine, nurserymen and landscape architects in Rye, New York, related this incident.

"Shortly after I attended the talk on 'How to Win Friends and Influence People,' I was landscaping the estate of a famous attorney.The owner came out to give me a few instructions about where he wished to plant a mass of rhododendrons and azaleas.

"I said, 'Judge, you have a lovely hobby.I've been admiring your beautiful dogs.I understand you win a lot of blue ribbons every year at the show in Madison Square Garden.'

"The effect of this little expression of appreciation was striking.

"'Yes,' the judge replied, 'I do have a lot of fun with my dogs.Would you like to see my kennel?'

"He spent almost an hour showing me his dogs and the prizes they had won.He even brought out their pedigrees and explained about the bloodlines responsible for such beauty and intelligence.

"哦，姑妈!"他说，"您太抬举我了。对于您这番盛情，我当然感激不尽。可是我不能接受它。我不是您的直系亲属，我也有一辆汽车，您的许多亲戚也很喜欢这辆别克车呢。"

"亲戚!"她大声喊道。"是的，我确实有亲戚。可是他们都正等着我死呢，这样他们就好得到我的车了。但他们谁也甭想得到它。"

"如果您不愿将它送给他们，您可以把它卖给旧车公司。"他告诉老太太。

"卖掉它!"老太太叫了起来。"你以为我想卖掉它吗?你以为我愿意让那些和我素不相识的陌生人坐在我丈夫给我买的车中，到处跑来跑去吗?年轻人，我做梦都不会卖的。我只想把它送给你，因为你是个懂得欣赏美丽东西的人。"

R 先生尽力拒绝接受汽车，然而他最后不得不收下，因为拒绝只会使她更伤心。

这位老太太一个人孤独地住在这栋空荡荡的老房子里;伴随她的只有她的波斯披肩、法国古董以及她的回忆。她渴望赞美。她也曾经年轻而美丽，拥有许许多多的追求者。她曾经建起了温暖的爱巢，还从欧洲各国搜集到各种珍品来装饰它。可是现在，她已经老迈而孤独，她渴望得到一点人性的温暖，得到一点真诚的赞美——但没有人给她。现在 R 先生给了她这一切，她的心犹如久旱逢甘露，充满了感激，以至于即使将她珍爱的别克车送给他，也不能完全表达她的感激之情。

让我们再举一个例子。露易斯—维仑特公司总经理麦克马洪先生，是纽约市著名的园艺专家，他讲了下面这件事：

"我听了'人性的弱点——如何赢得朋友并影响他人'的演讲之后不久，有一天我正在一位知名法官家中布置园林。主人出来向我提了几项建议，说他想在哪里栽一些杜鹃花。

"我说：'法官先生，你有一个很好的业余爱好。我很羡慕你那几条狗，它们漂亮极了。我听说你获得了许多在麦迪逊广场公园举行的狗选美大赛蓝丝带奖。'

"这短短几句赞美，产生了惊人的效果!

"Finally, turning to me, he asked, 'Do you have any small children?'

"'Yes, I do,' I replied, 'I have a son.'

"'Well, wouldn't he like a puppy?' the judge inquired.

"'Oh, yes, he'd be tickled pink.'

"'All right, I'm going to give him one,' the judge announced.

"He started to tell me how to feed the puppy. Then he paused. 'You'll forget it if I tell you. I'll write it out.' So the judge went in the house, typed out the pedigree and feeding instructions, and gave me a puppy worth several hundred dollars and one hour and fifteen minutes of his valuable time largely because I had expressed my honest admiration for his hobby and achievements."

George Eastman, of Kodak fame, invented the transparent film that made motion pictures possible, amassed a fortune of a hundred million dollars, and made himself one of the most famous businessmen on earth. Yet in spite of all these tremendous accomplishments, he craved little recognitions even as you and I.

To illustrate: When Eastman was building the Eastman School of Music and also Kilbourn Hall in Rochester, James Adamson, then president of the Superior Seating Company of New York, wanted to get the order to supply the theater chairs for these buildings. Phoning the architect, Mr. Adamson made an appointment to see Mr. Eastman in Rochester.

When Adamson arrived, the architect said, "I know you want to get this order, but I can tell you right now that you won't stand a ghost of a show if you take more than five minutes of George Eastman's time. He is a strict disciplinarian. He is very busy. So tell your story quickly and get out."

Adamson was prepared to do just that.

When he was ushered into the room he saw Mr. Eastman bending over a pile of papers at his desk. Presently, Mr. Eastman looked up, removed his glasses, and walked toward the architect and Mr. Adamson, saying, "Good morning, gentlemen, what can I do for you?"

The architect introduced them, and then Mr. Adamson said, "While we've been waiting for you, Mr. Eastman, I've been admiring your office I wouldn't mind working in a room like this myself. I'm in the interior-woodworking business, and I never saw a more beautiful office in all my life."

George Eastman replied, "You remind me of something I had almost forgotten. It is beautiful,

"'是的。'法官回答道,'我确实对我的狗有着至爱。你愿不愿看看我的狗?'

"他花了近一个小时,让我看他的狗和这些狗所获得的各种奖项。他甚至为我讲解它们的血统如何影响狗的外貌和智慧。

"最后,他转过身问我:'你有儿子吗?'

"'是的,我有个儿子,先生。'我回答说。

"'啊,那他想不想要只小狗呢?'法官又问我。

"'当然,他一定会非常高兴的。'

"'那太好了,我打算送他一只小狗。'法官大声说。

"他又开始教我怎样喂养小狗。然后,他又停了下来:'我只是用嘴说,你会记不住的。我还是给你写下来吧。'于是他走进屋,打印好谱系以及喂养方法,又送给我一只价值几百美元的小狗,并和我共同度过了对他而言十分宝贵的1小时15分钟,这是因为我真诚地赞美了他的爱好和他所取得的成就。"

乔治·伊斯曼是著名的柯达公司的总经理,他发明了透明胶片,从而使活动电影变成了现实,他也因此而成为亿万富翁,成为全世界最著名的企业家之一。然而,尽管有如此大的成就,他仍然渴望得到别人的赞美,就像你和我一样。

例如,当伊斯曼在罗切斯特建造伊斯曼音乐学院和基尔伯恩大剧院时,纽约的优美座椅公司经理亚当斯想获得这些建筑物中的座椅业务。他给建筑师打了电话去罗切斯特拜访伊斯曼。

亚当斯抵达后,建筑师说:"我知道你想获得这笔订单。但我可以告诉你,如果你占用他的时间超过5分钟,就别指望得到这笔业务了。他是个很严厉的人,他很忙。所以你最好是长话短说,说完就出来。"

亚当斯准备照此去做。

当他被领进房间时,他看见伊斯曼正俯身看文件。过了片刻,伊斯曼抬起头来,摘下眼镜,

isn't it? I enjoyed it a great deal when it was first built.But I come down here now with a lot of other things on my mind and sometimes don't even see the room for weeks at a time."

Adamson walked over and rubbed his hand across a panel."This is English oak,isn't it? A little different texture from Italian oak."

"Yes," Eastman replied."Imported English oak.It was selected for me by a friend who specializes in fine woods."

Then Eastman showed him about the room,commenting on the proportions,the coloring,the hand carving and other effects he had helped to plan and execute.

While drifting about the room,admiring the wood-work,they paused before a window,and George Eastman,in his modest,soft-spoken way,pointed out some of the institutions through which he was trying to help humanity: the University of Rochester,the General Hospital,the Homeopathic Hospital,the Friendly Home,the Children's Hospital.Mr.Adamson congratulated him warmly on the idealistic way he was using his wealth to alleviate the sufferings of humanity.Presently,George Eastman unlocked a glass case and pulled out the first camera he had ever owned—an invention he had bought from an Englishman.

Adamson questioned him at length about his early struggles to get started in business,and Mr. Eastman spoke with real feeling about the poverty of his childhood,telling how his widowed mother had kept a boardinghouse while he clerked in an insurance office.The terror of poverty haunted him day and night,and he resolved to make enough money so that his mother wouldn't have to work.Mr. Adamson drew him out with further questions and listened,absorbed,while he related the story of his experiments with dry photographic plates.He told how he had worked in an office all day,and sometimes experimented all night,taking only brief naps while the chemicals were working, sometimes working and sleeping in his clothes for seventy-two hours at a stretch.

James Adamson had been ushered into Eastman's office at ten-fifteen and had been warned that he must not take more than five minutes; but an hour had passed,then two hours passed.And they were still talking.

Finally,George Eastman turned to Adamson and said,"The last time I was in Japan I bought some chairs,brought them home,and put them in my sun porch.But the sun peeled the paint,so I

走到建筑师和亚当斯跟前,说道:"两位好,请问有何指教?"

建筑师作了简单介绍之后,亚当斯说:"伊斯曼先生,当我们等候你的时候,我一直在欣赏你的办公室;如果我也有你这样的办公室,我也一定会很高兴在里面工作的。我干的是室内木工装潢,可是我一辈子还没有见过这么漂亮的办公室。"

伊斯曼说:"如果不是你提醒,我倒真的想不起这些了。这办公室是不是很漂亮?当初装好之后,我就非常喜欢它。可是我现在事务缠身,因此许久以来都没有注意到它。"

亚当斯走上前来,摸了摸壁板,说:"这是英国橡木,对吧?它与意大利橡木在质地上有点儿差异。"

"是的。"伊斯曼回答说,"那是进口的英国橡木。这是我一位对硬质木材很有研究的朋友特意为我挑选的。"

随后,伊斯曼带着亚当斯参观了整个办公室,还给他详细介绍了各种物品的大小比例、颜色、精细雕刻以及某些在他的参与下设计完成的装饰。

他们一边在办公室随意走动,一边欣赏木艺装饰,这时来到一扇窗户前停了下来。伊斯曼温和地说起了他正要捐赠的一些机构,如罗切斯特大学、公众医院、顺势治疗医院、慈善养老院、儿童医院。亚当斯巧妙地赞赏了他用自己创造的财富来解救人类疾苦的崇高行为。过了一会儿,伊斯曼打开一个上了锁的玻璃柜,取出了他所拥有的世界上第一架照相机,这是他从一个英国人那里买来的一件发明。

亚当斯又详细询问他早期艰苦创业的经过。伊斯曼先生充满感慨地讲了他幼年的贫困生活,说到他守寡的母亲出租房屋,而他则去一家保险公司当业务员。贫困的恐惧日夜纠缠着他,他决心赚到足够多的钱,让他母亲不再劳累。亚当斯静静地听着这些,听得着了迷。他又向伊斯曼问起试验胶片的经历。伊斯曼说,他整天都在试验室做各种试验,只有在化学药品进行反应的时候打个盹;有一次他竟连续工作 72 小时,由于劳累交加,他工作时就睡着了。

亚当斯在 10 点一刻进到伊斯曼的办公室,还被警告不要超过 5 分钟。可是一小时过去了、

went downtown the other day and bought some paint and painted the chairs myself. Would you like to see what sort of a job I can do painting chairs? All right. Come up to my home and have lunch with me and I'll show you."

After lunch, Mr. Eastman showed Adamson the chairs he had brought from Japan. They weren't worth more than a few dollars, but George Eastman, now a multimillionaire, was proud of them because he himself had painted them.

The order for the seats amounted to $90,000. Who do you suppose got the order—James Adamson or one of his competitors?

From the time of this story until Mr. Eastman's death, he and James Adamson were close friends.

Claude Marais, a restaurant owner in Rouen, France, used this principle and saved his restaurant the loss of a key employee. This woman had been in his employ for five years and was a vital link between Mr. Marais and his staff of twenty-one people. He was shocked to receive a registered letter from her advising him of her resignation.

Mr. Marais reported: "I was very surprised and, even more, disappointed, because I was under the impression that I had been fair to her and receptive to her needs. In as much as she was a friend as well as an employee, I probably had taken her too much for granted and maybe was even more demanding of her than of other employees.

"I could not, of course, accept this resignation without some explanation. I took her aside and said, 'Paulette, you must understand that I cannot accept your resignation. You mean a great deal to me and to this company, and you are as important to the success of this restaurant as I am.' I repeated this in front of the entire staff, and I invited her to my home and reiterated my confidence in her with my family present.

"Paulette withdrew her resignation, and today I can rely on her as ever before. I frequently reinforce this by expressing my appreciation for what she does and showing her how important she is to me and to the restaurant."

"Talk to people about themselves," said Disraeli, one of the shrewdest men who ever ruled the British Empire. "Talk to people about themselves and they will listen for hours."

Principle 6: Make the other person feel important–and do it sincerely.

两小时过去了……他们还在继续交谈。

最后，伊斯曼转身对亚当斯说："我上次在日本时买了几张椅子回来，放在我家的阳台上。但它们已被太阳晒脱油漆了，我就到街上去买了些油漆，亲自把它们给漆了一遍。你愿去我家看看我漆得怎么样吗？好了，就到我家来，和我一同吃午饭，看看我油漆的那几张椅子。

午饭之后，伊斯曼让亚当斯看了看他从日本买来的椅子。这些椅子值不了几个钱，但对于亿万富翁伊斯曼先生来说可是值得骄傲的事，因为他"亲自"油漆了这些椅子。

伊斯曼先生这次要订购的座椅价值9万美元。你猜谁得到了这笔生意？是亚当斯还是他的竞争对手？

从那以后，直到伊斯曼先生去世，他和亚当斯成了亲密朋友。

克劳德·马雷是法国劳恩市一家饭店主人，他应用这项法则挽留了一位重要员工。这位女子为他工作了5年，成为马雷先生和他21位员工的重要纽带。当他接到她的辞职信时，他很震惊。

马雷先生说："我很吃惊，甚至更多的是失望，因为我觉得对她很平等，并满足了她的许多需求。她不仅是员工，还是朋友，所以我可能认为她做的是理所当然的，甚至对她的要求比其他员工更高。

"我当然不能接受不加解释的辞职。我把她叫到一边说：'葆丽，你必须明白，我不能接受你的辞职。你对我和这个公司非常重要，你对它的成功和我一样重要。'我将这些话当着所有员工的面重复了一遍，又请她去我家，当着全家人说出了我对她的信任。

"葆丽撤回了辞呈，现在我又和以前一样可以倚重于她了。我会经常赞美她所做的一切，并向她表达她对我和饭店多么重要。"

"和人们谈论他们自己，"狄斯累利说（他是曾统治大英帝国的最聪明人士之一），"和人们谈论他们自己，他们就会听上几个小时。"

第六项法则：让别人感到自己重要——并真诚地照此去做。

Part Three
How to Win People to Your Way of Thinking

1 You Can't Win an Argument

Shortly after the close of World War I,I learned an invaluable lesson one night in London.I was manager at the time for Sir Ross Smith.During the war,Sir Ross had been the Australian ace out in Palestine; and shortly after peace was declared,he astonished the world by flying halfway around it in thirty days.No such feat had ever been attempted before.It created a tremendous sensation.The Australian government awarded him fifty thousand dollars; the King of England knighted him; and,for a while,he was the most talked-about man under the Union Jack.I was attending a banquet one night given in Sir Ross's honor; and during the dinner,the man sitting next to me told a humorous story which hinged on the quotation"There's a divinity that shapes our ends, roughhew them how we will."

The raconteur mentioned that the quotation was from the Bible.He was wrong.I knew that,I knew it positively.There couldn't be the slightest doubt about it.And so,to get a feeling of importance and display my superiority,I appointed myself as an unsolicited and unwelcome committee of one to correct him.He stuck to his guns.What?From Shakespeare?Impossible! Absurd! That quotation was from the Bible.And he knew it.

The storyteller was sitting on my right; and Frank Gammond,an old friend of mine,was seated at my left.Mr.Gammond had devoted years to the study of Shakespeare.So the storyteller and I agreed to submit the question to Mr.Garamond.Mr.Gammond listened,kicked me under the table, and then said,"Dale,you are wrong.The gentleman is right.It is from the Bible."

第三篇 如何赢得别人的赞同

第1章 你赢不了争论

在第一次世界大战结束不久的一个晚上,我在伦敦学到了一个极有价值的教训。当时,我担任罗斯·史密斯爵士的经纪人。在战争时期,史密斯爵士曾担任澳大利亚飞行员,被派往巴勒斯坦。宣布和平不久之后,他因为在30天之内飞行了半个世界而轰动了全世界。在此之前,还从来没有过如此壮举,这件事轰动一时。澳大利亚政府奖励他5万美元,英国国王封他为爵士,于是一时间他成了英国境内最受关注的人。有一天晚上,我参加了欢迎罗斯·史密斯爵士的宴会。席间有一位坐在我旁边的先生讲了一个幽默的故事,这故事正好应验了一句格言:"谋事在人,成事在天。"

这位讲故事的先生提到这句话出自《圣经》。他错了,我敢肯定。于是,为了显示我的自重感和优越,我讨人嫌地想纠正他。他坚持他的说法:什么?出自莎士比亚?不可能! 绝对不可能! 那句话确实出自《圣经》。他非常自信。这位讲故事的先生坐在我右边,而我的一位老朋友弗兰克·加蒙坐在我左边。加蒙先生潜心研究莎士比亚的著作已有多年。所以这位讲故事的先生和我同意请加蒙先生做裁判。加蒙先生静静地听着,用脚在桌下踢我,然后说道:"戴尔,你错了。这位先生是对的。那句话确实出自《圣经》。"

那天晚上回家的时候,我对加蒙先生说:"弗兰克,你知道那句话出自莎士比亚。"

On our way home that night, I said to Mr.Gammond, "Frank, you knew that quotation was from Shakespeare."

"Yes, of course," he replied, "*Hamlet*, Act Five, Scene Two.But we were guests at a festive occasion, my dear Dale.Why prove to a man he is wrong?Is that going to make him like you?Why not let him save his face?He didn't ask for your opinion.He didn't want it.Why argue with him? Always avoid the acute angle."The man who said that taught me a lesson I'll never forget.I not only had made the storyteller uncomfortable, but had put my friend in an embarrassing situation.How much better it would have been had I not become argumentative.

It was a sorely needed lesson because I had been an inveterate arguer.During my youth, I had argued with my brother about everything under the Milky Way.When I went to college, I studied logic and argumentation and went in for debating contests.Later, I taught debating and argumentation in New York; and once, I am ashamed to admit, I planned to write a book on the subject.Since then, I have listened to, engaged in, and watched the effect of thousands of arguments. As a result of all this, I have come to the conclusion that there is only one way under high heaven to get the best of an argument—and that is to avoid it.Avoid it as you would avoid rattlesnakes and earthquakes.

Nine times out of ten, an argument ends with each of the contestants more firmly convinced than ever that he is absolutely right.

You can't win an argument.You can't because if you lose it, you lose it; and if you win it, you lose it.Why?Well, suppose you triumph over the other man and shoot his argument full of holes and prove that he is *non compos mentis*. Then what?You will feel fine.But what about him?You have made him feel inferior.You have hurt his pride.He will resent your triumph.And—

A man convinced against his will
Is of the same opinion still.

Years ago Patrick J.O'Haire joined one of my classes.He had had little education, and how he loved a scrap! He had once been a chauffeur, and he came to me because he had been trying, without much success, to sell trucks.A little questioning brought out the fact that he was continually scrapping with and antagonizing the very people he was trying to do business with.If a prospect said

"是的,当然,"他回答说,"《哈姆雷特》第五幕的第二场。但是亲爱的戴尔,我们只不过是参加一次盛会的客人。为什么非要证明一个人是错的呢?那样做难道就能使他喜欢你吗?为什么不给他留点面子呢?他并没有征求你的意见,而且也不需要你的意见。你为什么要和他争辩呢?应该永远避免争辩。"说这句话的先生给我的教训难以磨灭。我不仅让讲故事的人不舒服,而且让我的朋友处境尴尬。如果我不争辩,那该多好呀!

那个教训对我来说极其重要,因为我向来是一个非常固执的辩论者。在我青年时期,我曾和我哥哥就天下所有的事争论过。上了大学以后,我又研究了逻辑学和辩论术,并参加了许多辩论赛。后来我又在纽约教授辩论课;不好意思的是,我还打算写一本辩论方面的书。从那时起,我曾听过、参加过好几千场辩论赛,并注意到了它们的影响。通过这些活动,我得出一个结论:天底下只有一种赢得争论的方法——那就是避免争论,就像避免毒蛇和地震一样避免它。

十之八九,争论的结果只会使双方都比以前更加坚信自己是绝对正确的。

你赢不了争论。要是输了,你也就输了;但即使你赢了,你还是失败的。为什么?如果你胜了对方,把他驳得体无完肤,证明他毫无是处,那又能怎样?你也许会觉得很好。但是他呢?你只会让他觉得受到了羞辱。既然你伤了他的自尊心,他自然会怨恨你的胜利。而且——

一个人即使口头认输,但心里根本不服。

多年以前,帕特里克·哈里参加了我的辅导班。他受过的教育很少,但却非常喜欢争论!他当过汽车司机,后来又尝试推销卡车,但是并不怎么成功,便到我这里来求助。我稍微问了他几句,就可以看出他总是同他的顾客争论,并冒犯他们。假如有某位买主对他推销的卡车有所挑剔,他就会怒火难捺地和对方争论,直到对方哑口无言。那时他的确赢过不少次争论。正如他后来对我说的:"每当我走出人家的办公室时,总会对自己说:'我总算把那家伙教训了一顿。'我的确教训了他,可是我什么也没有卖出去。"

anything derogatory about the trucks he was selling, Pat saw red and was right at the customer's throat. Pat won a lot of arguments in those days. As he said to me afterward, "I often walked out of an office saying: 'I told that bird something.' Sure I had told him something, but I hadn't sold him anything."

My first problem was not to teach Patrick J.O'Haire to talk. My immediate task was to train him to refrain from talking and to avoid verbal fights.

Mr.O'Haire became one of the star salesmen for the White Motor Company in New York. How did he do it? Here is his story in his own words: "If I walk into a buyer's office now and he says: 'What? A White truck? They're no good! I wouldn't take one if you gave it to me. I'm going to buy the Whose-It truck.' I say, 'the Whose-It is a good truck. If you buy the Whose-It, you'll never make a mistake. The Whose-Its are made by a free company and sold by good people.'

"He is speechless then. There is no room for an argument. If he says the Whose-It is best and I say sure it is, he has to stop. He can't keep on all afternoon saying, 'It's the best' when I'm agreeing with him. We then get off the subject of Whose-It and I begin to talk about the good points of the White truck.

"There was a time when a remark like his first one would have made me see scarlet and red and orange. I would start arguing against the Whose-It; and the more I argued against it, the more my prospect argued in favor of it; and the more he argued, the more he sold himself on my competitor's product.

"As I look back now I wonder how I was ever able to sell anything. I lost years of my life in scrapping and arguing. I keep my mouth shut now. It pays."

As wise old Ben Franklin used to say:

If you argue and rankle and contradict, you may achieve a victory sometimes; but it will be an empty victory because you will never get your opponent's good will.

So figure it out for yourself. Which would you rather have, an academic, theatrical victory or a person's good will? You can seldom have both.

The Boston *Transcript* once printed this bit of significant doggerel:

Here lies the body of William Jay,

我的第一个难题不是教哈里如何与人交谈，我立即要做的是训练他如何克制自己不要讲话，避免与人争执。

现在，哈里先生已经是纽约怀特汽车公司的一位明星推销员。他是怎么成功的呢？下面是他自己叙述的："假如我现在走进一个顾客的办公室，而他却说：'什么？怀特卡车？它们可不怎么样！你白白送给我，我都不要。我只买某某牌的汽车。'我说：'那种卡车的确很不错，你买那种卡车绝对错不了。那家公司的车质量可靠，而且推销员也很优秀。'

"于是他就无话可说了。他没有争辩的余地了。如果他说某某牌卡车最好，我说确实不错，他就只好住嘴了。既然我同意他的看法，他当然不能整个下午不停地说'某某牌卡车最好'了。于是，我们不再谈某某牌卡车，我开始向他介绍怀特卡车的优点。

"我若是在当年听到他刚开始说的话，一定会大发脾气。我会立即和他吵起来，挑剔某某牌卡车。而我越挑剔，顾客则会越卖力地辩护；他越辩护，就越喜欢竞争对手的产品。

"现在回想起来，我真的不知道我一辈子究竟能卖出多少东西。我把自己一生中的许多时间都耗费在争论上了。现在我缄口克己，很是有效。"

正如睿智的本杰明·富兰克林常说的：

"如果你争强好胜，喜欢争论，以反驳他人为乐趣，或许能赢得一时的胜利；但这种胜利毫无意义，因为你永远得不到对方的好感。"

所以，你自己应该考虑好：你是要一个毫无实质意义的、理论上的胜利？还是得到一个人的好感？你不能两者兼得。

有一次，波士顿《临摹》杂志刊登了一首很有意义的顺口溜：

威廉·杰的尸体躺在这里，他死去之时还认为他是正确的——

他是正确的，绝对正确的，当他匆匆而去时，但就像他的错误一样，他已经死了。

Who died maintaining his right of way—
He was right, dead right, as he sped along,
But he's just as dead as if he were wrong.

You may be right, dead right, as you speed along in your argument; but as far as changing another's mind is concerned, you will probably be just as futile as if you were wrong.

Frederick S.Parsons, an income tax consultant, had been disputing and wrangling for an hour with a government tax inspector. An item of nine thousand dollars was at stake. Mr.Parsons claimed that this nine thousand dollars was in reality a bad debt, that it would never be collected, that it ought not to be taxed. "Bad debt, my eye! "retorted the inspector. "It must be taxed."

"This inspector was cold, arrogant and stubborn," Mr.Parsons said as he told the story to the class. "Reason was wasted and so were facts...The longer we argued, the more stubborn he became. So I decided to avoid argument, change the subject, and give him appreciation.

"I said, 'I suppose this is a very petty matter in comparison with the really important and difficult decisions you're required to make. I've made a study of taxation myself. But I've had to get my knowledge from books. You are getting yours from the firing line of experience. I sometime wish I had a job like yours. It would teach me a lot.' I meant every word I said.

"'Well.' The inspector straightened up in his chair, leaned back, and talked for a long time about his work, telling me of the clever frauds he had uncovered. His tone gradually became friendly, and presently he was telling me about his children. As he left, he advised me that he would consider my problem further and give me his decision in a few days.

"He called at my office three days later and informed me that he had decided to leave the tax return exactly as it was filed."

This tax inspector was demonstrating one of the most common of human frailties. He wanted a feeling of importance; and as long as Mr.Parsons argued with him, he got his feeling of importance by loudly asserting his authority. But as soon as his importance was admitted and the argument stopped and he was permitted to expand his ego, he became a sympathetic and kindly human being.

Buddha said, "Hatred is never ended by hatred but by love," and a misunderstanding is never

在你与人争论的时候，你或许是对的，甚至绝对正确，但你若想改变对方的想法，你可能会一无所得，正如你错了一样。

巴森是一位所得税顾问，他因为一项9000美元账目发生了问题，而与政府一位税收稽查员争论了一个小时。巴森先生认为这9000美元实际上是一笔呆账，永远不会收上来，所以不应该征税。"呆账?胡说！"那位稽查员反驳说，"这税非征不可。"

"这位稽查员非常冷漠、傲慢，而且固执，"巴森先生在我班上讲述经过时说，"我和他讲道理摆事实，都没有用……我们越是争论，他越是固执。于是，我决定不再和他争论，而是改变话题，给予他赞赏。

"我说：'与你所要处理的其他重要而困难的事相比，这件事简直微不足道。我也曾研究过税务问题，但我只是从书本上获得的知识。而你的经验和知识全都来自实践。有时我真希望能有你这样的工作。它可以让我学到许多东西。'我说得非常认真。

"'啊！'那位稽查员在椅子上伸了伸腰，向椅背上一靠，兴奋地讲起他的工作来。他告诉我他发现过许多在税务上巧妙舞弊的鬼花招。他的口气逐渐变得友善起来；接着他又谈起他的孩子来。临走时，他告诉我说，他会再考虑我的问题，并在几天之内给我决定。

"三天之后，他来我的办公室，说他决定不征收那笔税了。"

这位税务稽查员正表现出了一种人类最常见的弱点。他需要一种自重感；巴森先生越是和他辩论，他就越强调他的权威，以获得自重感。一旦巴森承认了他的权威，争论立即偃旗息鼓。自重感得到了满足，他也就变成一个富有同情心的、和善的人。

佛祖说："恨不止恨，唯爱能止。"误会永远不能靠争论来消除，只有靠技巧、调解、宽容，以及用同情的眼光来看待对方的观点。

有一次，林肯责罚一位与同事发生了激烈争执的青年军官。"凡是决心想要成功的人，"林

ended by an argument but by tact, diplomacy, conciliation and a sympathetic desire to see the other person's viewpoint.

Lincoln once reprimanded a young army officer for indulging in a violent controversy with an associate. "No man who is resolved to make the most of himself," said Lincoln, "can spare time for personal contention. Still less can he afford to take the consequences, including the vitiation of his temper and the loss of self-control. Yield larger things to which you show no more than equal rights; and yield lesser ones though clearly your own. Better give your path to a dog than be bitten by him in contesting for the right. Even killing the dog would not cure the bite."

In an article in *Bits and Pieces*, some suggestions are made on how to keep a disagreement from becoming an argument:

Welcome the disagreement. Remember the slogan, "When two partners always agree, one of them is not necessary." If there is some point you haven't thought about, be thankful if it is brought to your attention. Perhaps this disagreement is your opportunity to be corrected before you make a serious mistake.

Distrust your first instinctive impression. Our first natural reaction in a disagreeable situation is to be defensive. Be careful. Keep calm and watch out for your first reaction. It may be you at your worst, not your best.

Control your temper. Remember, you can measure the size of a person by what makes him or her angry.

Listen first. Give your opponents a chance to talk. Let them finish. Do not resist, defend or debate. This only raises barriers. Try to build bridges of understanding. Don't build higher barriers of misunderstanding.

Look for areas of agreement. When you have heard your opponents out, dwell first on the points and areas on which you agree.

Be honest. Look for areas where you can admit error and say so. Apologize for your mistakes. It will help disarm your opponents and reduce defensiveness.

Promise to think over your opponents' ideas and study them carefully. And mean it. Your opponents may be right. It is a lot easier at this stage to agree to think about their points than to

肯说,"绝不能在私人成见上浪费时间。争论的结果是他无法承受的,包括脾气变坏、丧失自制。如果你们各自都有正确的一面,你不妨多让步些;即使是你完全正确,也不妨做些让步,哪怕少让一点。与其同狗争道而被狗咬,还不如让狗先走。因为即使将狗杀死,也治不好伤口。"

在一篇《点点滴滴》的文章中提出了一些如何使不同意见避免争论的建议:

1. 欢迎不同的意见。应该记住这句话:"当两个合作者总是意见一致时,其中一人就不再需要了。"如果有些问题你没有想到,而有人向你提出来了,你就应该表示感谢。也许这种不同的意见是使你避免犯大错的最好机会。

2. 不要相信你的直觉。当有人提出不同意见时,我们的第一反应,也是自然反应,就是自卫。但是一定要小心。要保持平常之心,并且警惕你的直觉反应。因为这种直觉可能是你最致命的错误,而不是最好的决策。

3. 自我克制。记住,你可以根据一个人在什么情况下会发脾气来推测这个人的气量和成就有多大。

4. 倾听。让你的反对者有机会说话。让他把话说完,不要抵制、不要自卫或争论,否则只会加深矛盾。努力建立了解的桥梁,而不是再加深误解。

5. 寻找共同点。当你听完反对者的意见之后,应该先想想哪些意见是你可以同意的。

6. 待人以诚。承认错误,坦诚地说出来。就你的错误向人道歉,这样有助于解除反对者的武装,减少他们的防卫。

7. 认真考虑反对者的意见。要发自内心。你的反对者可能是对的,这时认真考虑他们的意见无疑是明智之举。如果等到对方这样说:"我早就告诉你这件事了,可你就是听不进去!"那时你可就无地自容了。

move rapidly ahead and find yourself in a position where your opponents can say: "We tried to tell you, but you wouldn't listen."

Thank your opponents sincerely for their interest. Anyone who takes the time to disagree with you is interested in the same things you are. Think of them as people who really want to help you, and you may turn your opponents into friends.

Postpone action to give both sides time to think through the problem. Suggest that a new meeting be held later that day or the next day, when all the facts may be brought to bear. In preparation for this meeting, ask yourself some hard questions:

Could my opponents be right? Partly right? Is there truth or merit in their position or argument? Is my reaction one that will relieve the problem, or will it just relieve any frustration? Will my reaction drive my opponents further away or draw them closer to me? Will my reaction elevate the estimation good people have of me? Will I win or lose? What price will I have to pay if I win? If I am quiet about it, will the disagreement blow over? Is this difficult situation an opportunity for me?

Opera tenor Jan Peerce, after he was married nearly fifty years, once said, "My wife and I made a pact a long time ago, and we've kept it no matter how angry we've grown with each other. When one yells, the other should listen—because when two people yell, there is no communication, just noise and bad vibrations."

Principle 1: The only way to get the best of an argument is to avoid it.

8. 感谢反对者的关心。任何人只要愿意花时间来表达他的不同意见,就一定是和你一样关心同一件事情的。如果你把他们这种不同意见当成是对你的帮助,那你也许会将反对者变成你的朋友。

9. 三思而后行。建议你在当天稍晚些时间,或次日再开会讨论,把问题考虑清楚。在准备下次开会的时候,要问自己下面这些问题:

"反对者的意见是不是对的?部分是对的?他们的立场和论点是否站得住?我的反应是在解决问题,还是为了自尊而不愿接受对方意见?我的反应是使反对者亲近我,还是让他们更远离我?我的反应是不是能够提高别人对我的评价?我将成功还是失败?如果我能成功,代价是什么?如果我不说话,反对者的意见会消失吗?这是不是我的新机会?"

男高音歌唱家杰恩·皮尔斯结婚近50年了,他有一次说:"我夫人和我在很早以前就订了一条协议,不论我们如何不满对方,都必须遵守这条协议:当一个人大吼大叫的时候,另一个人应该安静地听着——因为当两个人都大吼大叫时,就毫无沟通可言,有的只是噪音和震动。"

第一项规则:赢得争论的唯一方法是避免争论。

2 A Sure Way of Making Enemies—And How to Avoid It

When Theodore Roosevelt was in the White House, he confessed that if he could be right 75 percent of the time, he would reach the highest measure of his expectation.

If that was the highest rating that one of the most distinguished men of the twentieth century could hope to obtain, what about you and me?

If you can be sure of being right only 55 percent of the time, you can go down to Wall Street and make a million dollars a day. If you can't be sure of being right even 55 percent of the time, why should you tell other people they are wrong?

You can tell people they are wrong by a look or an intonation or a gesture just as eloquently as you can in words—and if you tell them they are wrong, do you make them want to agree with you? Never! For you have struck a direct blow at their intelligence, judgment, pride and self-respect. That will make them want to strike back. But it will never make them want to change their minds. You may then hurl at them all the logic of a Plato or an Immanuel Kant, but you will not alter their opinions, for you have hurt their feelings.

Never begin by announcing "I am going to prove so-and-so to you." That's bad. That's tantamount to saying: "I'm smarter than you are, I'm going to tell you a thing or two and make you change your mind."

That is a challenge. It arouses opposition and makes the listener want to battle with you before you even start.

It is difficult, under even the most benign conditions, to change people's minds. So why make it harder? Why handicap yourself?

If you are going to prove anything, don't let anybody know it. Do it so subtly, so adroitly, that no one will feel that you are doing it. This was expressed succinctly by Alexander Pope:

Men must be taught as if you taught them not
And things unknown proposed as things forgot.

第2章 如何避免树敌招怨

当西奥多·罗斯福入主白宫时，他承认如果能有75%的时候不出错，就达到了他的最高期望标准。

如果这是这位20世纪最杰出人物希望达到的最高标准，那何况你我呢？

如果你能确信你有55%的正确率，你大可以去华尔街，一天赚100万美元。如果你没有这样的把握，你又凭什么说别人错了？

你可以用眼神、声调或手势指责别人说他们错了，就像用话一样说他们错了，你以为他们会同意你吗？绝对不会！因为你直接打击了他们的智慧、判断力、自豪和自尊。这只会使他们起来反击，但永远不会使他们改变他们的看法。即使你搬用所有柏拉图或康德式的逻辑与他们辩论，也改变不了他们的看法，因为你伤了他们的感情。

永远不要这样说："我要给你证明……"那就糟了。因为那等于在说："我比你聪明。我要告诉你怎样怎样，使你改变看法。"

那是一种挑战。它只会引起反抗，甚至使对方在你还没说话之前就和你争论起来。

即使是在最温和的情况下，也不容易改变别人的主意，那为什么要将事情弄得更糟呢？为什么要自找麻烦呢？

如果你想要证明什么事，大可不必声张宣扬，而要讲究策略方法，不要让任何人看出来，使其在不知不觉中接受你的观点。

"教导他人时，不能使其发现是在受教导；指出人所不知的事，使其觉得那只是他一时忘记的事。"

Over three hundred years ago Galileo said:

You cannot teach a man anything; you can only help him to find it within himself.

As Lord Chesterfield said to his son:

Be wiser than other people if you can;
but do not tell them so.

Socrates said repeatedly to his followers in Athens:

One thing only I know, and that is
that I know nothing.

Well, I can't hope to be any smarter than Socrates, so I have quit telling people they are wrong. And I find that it pays.

If a person makes a statement that you think is wrong—yes, even that you know is wrong—isn't it better to begin by saying: "Well, now, look, I thought otherwise, but I may be wrong. I frequently am. And if I am wrong, I want to be put right. Let's examine the facts."

There's magic, positive magic, in such phrases as: "I may be wrong. I frequently am. Let's examine the facts."

Nobody in the heavens above or on the earth beneath or in the waters under the earth will ever object to your saying: "I may be wrong. Let's examine the facts."

One of our class members who used this approach in dealing with customers was Harold Reinke, a Dodge dealer in Billings, Montana. He reported that because of the pressures of the automobile business, he was often hard-boiled and callous when dealing with customers' complaints. This caused flared tempers, loss of business and general unpleasantness.

He told his class, "Recognizing that this was getting me nowhere fast, I tried a new tack. I would say something like this: 'Our dealership has made so many mistakes that I am frequently ashamed. We may have erred in your case. Tell me about it.'

"This approach becomes quite disarming, and by the time the customer releases his feelings, he is usually much more reasonable when it comes to settling the matter. In fact, several customers have thanked me for having such an understanding attitude. And two of them have even brought in friends to buy new cars. In this highly competitive market, we need more of this type of customer, and I

300多年前，伽利略说：

“你不可能教会一个人任何事情；你只能帮助他自己学会处理这种事情。”

正如查斯特菲尔德勋爵对他儿子所说的：

“如果可能，应该比别人聪明；但绝不能对人说你比他聪明。”

苏格拉底在雅典一再告诫他的门徒说：

“我只知道一件事，那就是我什么也不知道。”

我可不敢奢望比苏格拉底更高明，所以我也尽量避免告诉别人说他们错了。我发现这么做很有用。

如果一个人说了一句你认为错的话——是的，即使你肯定是错的——但这样说也许更好：“噢，是的！不过我还有另一种想法，但我也许不对。我总是这样。如果我错了，还请你指正。让我们来看看问题所在。”

用这类话，如“我也许不对”，“我常常会出错”，“让我们来看看问题所在”，会收到神奇的功效。

无论在什么地方，永远不会有人反对你说“我也许不对，让我们来看看问题所在”。

我班上有一位名叫哈罗德·伦克的学员，他是道奇汽车公司在蒙大拿州比林斯县的代理商。他曾采用了这种方法与顾客打交道。他说在汽车销售行业压力非常大，因此他以往在处理顾客抱怨时，常常以自我为中心，导致发生冲突，生意锐减，同时还会出现其他不愉快的事情。

他在班上这样说：“当我认识到这样做对我并没有什么好处时，我开始尝试新的方法。我这样对顾客说：‘我们确实犯了许多错误，真是万分抱歉。关于你的问题，我们也可能有错误，请你告诉我。’

“这办法在解除顾客的对立情绪方面很有效。顾客平静下来之后，往往会很讲道理，问题也

believe that showing respect for all customers' opinions and treating them diplomatically and courteously will help beat the competition."

You will never get into trouble by admitting that you may be wrong.That will stop all argument and inspire your opponent to be just as fair and open and broad-minded as you are.It will make him want to admit that he,too,may be wrong.

If you know positively that a person is wrong,and you bluntly tell him or her so,what happens? Let me illustrate.Mr.S—a young New York attorney,once argued a rather important case before the United States Supreme Court (*Lustgarten v.Fleet Corporation* 280 U.S.320).The case involved a considerable sum of money and an important question of law.During the argument,one of the Supreme Court justices said to him, "The statute of limitations in admiralty law is six years,is it not?"

Mr.S—stopped,stared at the Justice for a moment,and then said bluntly, "Your Honor,there is no statute of limitations in admiralty."

"A hush fell on the court,"said Mr.S—as he related his experience to one of the author's classes, "and the temperature in the room seemed to drop to zero.I was right.Justice—was wrong. And I had told him so.But did that make him friendly?No.I still believe that I had the law on my side.And I know that I spoke better than I ever spoke before.But I didn't persuade.I made the enormous blunder of telling a very learned and famous man that he was wrong."

Few people are logical.Most of us are prejudiced and biased.Most of us are blighted with preconceived notions,with jealousy,suspicion,fear,envy and pride.And most citizens don't want to change their minds about their religion or their haircut or communism or their favorite movie star. So,if you are inclined to tell people they are wrong,please read the following paragraph every morning before breakfast.It is from James Harvey Robinson's enlightening book *The Mind in the Making.*

> We sometimes find ourselves changing our minds without any resistance or heavy emotion,but if we are told we are wrong,we resent the imputation and harden our hearts.We are incredibly heedless in the formation of our beliefs,but find ourselves filled with an illicit passion for them when anyone proposes to rob us of their companionship.It is obviously not the

就容易解决了;甚至还有许多顾客感谢我,因为他们获得了自重感。其中还有两个人带他们的朋友来买新车。在这竞争激烈的商场上,我们需要更多的这种顾客。我认为尊重顾客的所有意见,并且采取灵活礼貌的方式来处理,就会帮助你打败对手。"

承认或许是你错了,那么你永远不会惹来麻烦。这样做不仅可以避免所有争论,而且还能使对方和你一样宽宏大度,承认他也难免会犯错。

如果你确实肯定某人错了,并直接告诉他,会怎样呢?我可以举一个例子。某先生是纽约一位青年律师,有一次参加由美国最高法院审理的一个重要案件的辩论。这个案件涉及一大笔金钱与一项重要的法律问题。在辩论中,最高法院的一位法官对他说:"《海事法》的追诉期限是6年,是不是?"

某先生顿了顿,注视该法官许久,然后直率地说:"审判长,《海事法》中没有关于追诉期的条文。"

"法庭立即寂静下来。"某先生在我的班上叙述他的经历时说,"法庭中的温度好似降到了零度。我是对的,这位法官是错的,而我也告诉了他。但那能够使他变得友善吗?不。尽管我相信法律可以作为我的后盾,而且我也很清楚当时我的发言比以往任何时候都更精彩,可是我并没有说服他。我犯了个大错,当众指出一位学识渊博的、极有声望的人错了。"

很少有人会进行逻辑思考。我们大多数人都是主观而偏见的。多数人都会因为成见、嫉妒、猜疑、恐惧以及傲慢等而受挫折。许多人都不会改变他们的信仰、发型或喜爱的电影明星。所以,如果你习惯于指出别人的错误,就请你在每天早餐前,坐下来读读下面这段文字。它摘自詹姆斯·哈维·鲁滨逊教授那本富有启迪意义的《决策的过程》一书。

> "有时候我们会毫无抵触或反感地改变自己的思想,但是如果有人指出我们的错误,我们反而会固执己见,并迁怒于对方。我们不会特别在意自己的某些愿望,但如果有人指

ideas themselves that are dear to us, but our serf-esteem which is threatened ...The little word "my" is the most important one in human affairs, and properly to reckon with it is the beginning of wisdom. It has the same force whether it is "my" dinner, "my" dog, and "my" house, or "my" father, "my" country, and "my" God. We not only resent the imputation that our watch is wrong, or our car shabby, but that our conception of the canals of Mars, of the pronunciation of "Epictetus," of the medicinal value of salicin, or of the date of Sargon I is subject to revision. We like to continue to believe what we have been accustomed to accept as true, and the resentment aroused when doubt is cast upon any of our assumptions leads us to seek every manner of excuse for clinging to it. The result is that most of our so-called reasoning consists in finding arguments for going on believing as we already do.

Carl Rogers, the eminent psychologist, wrote in his book *On Becoming a Person*:

I have found it of enormous value when I can permit myself to understand the other person. The way in which I have worded this statement may seem strange to you. Is it necessary to permit oneself to understand another? I think it is. Our first reaction to most of the statements (which we hear from other people) is an evaluation or judgment, rather than an understanding of it. When someone expresses some feeling, attitude or belief, our tendency is almost mediately to feel "That's right," or "That's stupid," "that's abnormal," "that's unreasonable," "that's incorrect," "that's not nice." Very rarely do we permit ourselves to *understand* precisely what the meaning of the statement is to the other person.

I once employed an interior decorator to make some draperies for my home. When the bill arrived, I was dismayed.

A few days later, a friend dropped in and looked at the draperies. The price was mentioned, and she exclaimed with a note of triumph: "What? That's awful. I am afraid he put one over on you."

True? Yes, she had told the truth, but few people like to listen to truths that reflect on their judgment. So, being human, I tried to defend myself. I pointed out that the best is eventually the cheapest, that one can't expect to get quality and artistic taste at bargain-basement prices, and so on and on.

The next day another friend dropped in, admired the draperies, bubbled over with enthusiasm,

正我们这些愿望,我们反而会极力维护它。很明显,这并不是那些观念本身非常宝贵,而是我们的自尊心受到了伤害……在为人处世时,'我的'是最重要的词。妥善地用好这个词,才是智慧之源。无论是'我的'饭,'我的'狗,'我的'屋子,'我的'父亲,'我的'国家,还是'我的'上帝,都有着同样的力量。我们不但不喜欢别人说我们的手表不准,或我们的汽车太破旧,也不喜欢别人纠正我们对于火星上水道的概念,对于"爱比克泰德"的读音,对于水杨素药效的认识,或对于萨尔根大帝生卒年月的错误。我们总是愿意相信以往所习惯的东西,当我们所相信的任何事物受到怀疑时,我们就会反感,并寻找各种理由来辩护。结果呢,我们所谓的理智就变成了维系我们所惯于相信的事物的借口。"

著名心理学家卡尔·罗吉斯在他的《怎样做人》一书中说:

"当我尝试了解别人的时候,我发现这实在是太有意义了。你对我这样说也许会觉得奇怪。我们真的有必要这样做吗?我以为这是绝对必要的。我们听别人说话的时候,第一反应一般是进行判断或评价,而不是理解这些话。当别人说出他的某种感觉、态度或者信念的时候,我们总是会做出各种判断:'不错'、'太可笑了'、'这正常吗'、'这不合乎道理'、'这太离谱了'、'这可不对'……而很少真正了解这些话对别人有什么意义。"

有一次,我雇了一位室内装饰设计师,为我家中装一些窗帘。当账单送给我时,我大吃一惊。

过了几天,一位朋友来我家,看到这些窗帘,问了问价钱,然后她带着得意的口气大叫道:"什么?太过分了。我想你大概上了他的当。"

真的吗?是的,她说的是实话,但很少有人愿听别人羞辱自己判断力的实话。所以,作为常人,我竭力为自己辩护。我说最好的东西总是最贵的,一个人不可能希望用便宜的价格买到既品质优良,又具有艺术特色的东西等。

and expressed a wish that she could afford such exquisite creations for her home.My reaction was totally different."Well,to tell the truth,"I said,"I can't afford them myself.I paid too much.I'm sorry I ordered them."

When we are wrong,we may admit it to ourselves.And if we are handled gently and tactfully, we may admit it to others and even take pride in our frankness and broad-mindedness. But not if someone else is trying to ram the unpalatable fact down our esophagus.

Horace Greeley,the most famous editor in America during the time of the Civil War,disagreed violently with Lincoln's policies.He believed that he could drive Lincoln into agreeing with him by a campaign of argument,ridicule and abuse.He waged this bitter campaign month after month,year after year.In fact,he wrote a brutal,bitter,sarcastic and personal attack on President Lincoln the night Booth shot him.

But did all this bitterness make Lincoln agree with Greeley?Not at all.Ridicule and abuse never do.

If you want some excellent suggestions about dealing with people and managing yourself and improving your personality,read Benjamin Franklin's autobiography—one of the most fascinating life stories ever written,one of the classics of American literature.Ben Franklin tells how he conquered the iniquitous habit of argument and transformed himself into one of the most able,suave and diplomatic men in American history.

One day,when Ben Franklin was a blundering youth,an old Quaker friend took him aside and lashed him with a few stinging truths,something like this:

> Ben,you are impossible.Your opinions have a slap in them for everyone who differs with you.They have become so offensive that nobody cares for them.Your friends find they enjoy themselves better when you are not around.You know so much that no man can tell you anything.Indeed,no man is going to try,for the effort would lead only to discomfort and hard work.So you are not likely ever to know any more than you do now,which is very little.

One of the finest things I know about Ben Franklin is the way he accepted that smarting rebuke.He was big enough and wise enough to realize that it was true,to sense that he was headed for failure and social disaster.So he made a right-about-face.He began immediately to change his

第二天,另一朋友来我家。她赞赏那些窗帘,并表示她也希望有能力为家里买这么精美的窗帘。我的反应完全不同了。"哦,说老实话,"我说,"我也没钱买那些窗帘,它们实在太贵了。我现在还后悔买了它们。"

当我们犯错的时候,我们或许会自己承认。如果对方待我们非常和善友好,我们也会向别人承认,甚至会对我们的直率坦诚感到自豪。但如果有人要将难以下咽的东西塞进我们喉咙,那可办不到。

美国南北内战时最著名的编辑赫雷斯·格里莱激烈地反对林肯的政策。他相信用辩论、讥笑、谩骂等办法可以迫使林肯同意他的观点。于是他月复一月、年复一年地持续使用这种苛刻的办法。事实上,就在林肯遇刺的那天晚上,他还写了一篇粗暴而苛刻的文章来讽刺攻击林肯。

但所有这些尖刻的攻击使林肯妥协了吗?丝毫没有。讥笑、谩骂永远于事无补。

如果你想要得到一些关于为人处世、自我控制、增进品德修养的有益建议,不妨读读本杰明·富兰克林的自传——这是一本极吸引人的传记,也是美国文学经典之一。富兰克林讲述了他如何克服好争辩的陋习,使他成为美国历史上最能干、最和蔼、最善于外交的人。

当富兰克林还是一个冒冒失失的青年时,有一天,一位教友会老教友将他拉到一边,用尖酸刻薄的话训斥了他一顿。那几句话大致如下:

> "本,你真是无药可救。你攻击每一个和你意见不同的人。你的意见太让人讨厌了,没人会接受。如果你不在场,你的朋友觉得更加自在。你知道得太多了,没有人能再教你什么,而且也没有人愿做这种费力不讨好的事。所以你不可能再学到新知识了,而你现在所知却又十分有限。"

据我所知,富兰克林最大的优点之一,是他接受尖刻责备的态度。他已经成熟,也很明智,

insolent, opinionated ways.

"I made it a rule," said Franklin, "to forbear all direct contradiction to the sentiment of others, and all positive assertion of my own, I even forbade myself the use of every word or expression in the language that imported a fix'd opinion, such as 'certainly,' 'undoubtedly,' etc., and I adopted, instead of them, 'I conceive,' 'I apprehend,' or 'I imagine' a thing to be so or so, or 'it so appears to me at present.' When another asserted something that I thought an error, I deny'd myself the pleasure of contradicting him abruptly, and of showing immediately some absurdity in his proposition: and in answering I began by observing that in certain cases or circumstances his opinion would be right, but in the present case there appear'd or seem'd to me some difference, etc. I soon found the advantage of this change in my manner; the conversations I engag'd in went on more pleasantly. The modest way in which I propos'd my opinions procur'd them a readier reception and less contradiction; I had less mortification when I was found to be in the wrong, and I more easily prevaile'd with others to give up their mistakes and join with me when I happened to be in the right.

"And this mode, which I at first put on with some violence to natural inclination, became at length so easy, and so habitual to me, that perhaps for these fifty years past no one has ever heard a dogmatical expression escape me. And to this habit (after my character of integrity) I think it principally owing that I had earned so much weight with my fellow citizens when I proposed new institutions, or alterations in the old, and so much influence in public councils when I became a member; for I was but a bad speaker, never eloquent, subject to much hesitation in my choice of words, hardly correct in language, and yet I generally carried my points."

How do Ben Franklin's methods work in business? Let's take two examples.

Katherine A, Allred of Kings Mountain, North Carolina, is an industrial engineering supervisor for a yarn-processing plant. She told one of our classes how she handled a sensitive problem before and after taking our training:

"Part of my responsibility," she reported, "deals with setting up and maintaining incentive systems and standards for our operators so they can make more money by producing more yarn. The system we were using had worked free when we had only two or three different types of yarn, but recently we had expanded our inventory and capabilities to enable us to run more than twelve

知道那是事实，并发现这样下去，他将面临前途及社交失败的危险。于是，他改掉了陋习，立刻抛弃了骄傲、固执的态度。

"我订下一条规矩，"富兰克林说，"绝对不许伤害别人的感情，不许武断。我甚至不允许自己在语言文字中使用过于肯定意思的字眼，例如'当然'、'无疑'等，而代之以'我想'、'我猜'或'我想象'一件事可能是这样或那样，或'目前在我看来是这样'。当别人说了些我明知其错误的话，我也不再冒冒失失地反驳他，不再立即指出他的错误。我会在回答时，先说'在某种情况下，你的意见不错；但在现在的条件之下，我认为事情或许会……'很快我就看出我这种改变带来的收获；我所参与的许多谈话，气氛都愉快多了。我以谦逊的态度表达自己的意见，不仅更容易让人接受，而且还减少了冲突。当我犯了错误时，我也很少会难堪；而我自己碰巧对的时候，更容易使对方不再固执己见而赞同我。

"我最初采用这种方法时，的确与我的本性有冲突，但是我后来越来越习惯了。在过去 50 年中，可能还没有人听到我说出一句武断的话。当年我提议新法案或修改旧条文的时候，之所以能得到民众的重视，并且当我成为议员后能具有相当大的影响，大都要归功于这一习惯。虽然我并不善于辞令，也没有什么口才，谈吐也比较迟疑，甚至还会说错话，但一般说来，我的意见还是得到了广泛的支持。"

如何将富兰克林的方法用在商业领域中呢？我们可以举两个例子：

凯瑟琳是北卡罗莱纳州王山市一家纺纱厂的工程总监。她在我班上讲述了她接受训练之前和之后，处理敏感问题的不同方法：

"我工作的一部分，"她介绍说，"就是设计并保持各种方法和标准来激励员工，使员工能生产更多的纱线，挣更多的钱。当我们只生产两三种纱线时，我们采用的方法还算过得去。但我们最近扩大了项目，提高了生产量，计划生产 12 种以上的纱线，这时原来的方法就不管用了，员

different varieties.The present system was no longer adequate to pay the operators fairly for the work being performed and give them an incentive to increase production.I had worked up a new system which would enable us to pay the operator by the class of yarn she was running at any one particular time.With my new system in hand,I entered the meeting determined to prove to the management that my system was the right approach.I told them in detail how they were wrong and showed where they were being unfair and how I had all the answers they needed.To say the least,I failed miserably! I had become so busy defending my position on the new system that I had left them no opening to graciously admit their problems on the old one.The issue was dead.

"After several sessions of this course,I realized all too well where I had made my mistakes.I called another meeting and this time I asked where they felt their problems were.We discussed each point,and I asked them their opinions on which was the best way to proceed.With a few low-keyed suggestions,at proper intervals,I let them develop my system themselves.At the end of the meeting when I actually presented my system,they enthusiastically accepted it.

"I am convinced now that nothing good is accomplished and a lot of damage can be done if you tell a person straight out that he or she is wrong.You only succeed in stripping that person of self-dignity and making yourself an unwelcome part of any discussion."

Let's take another example—and remember these cases I am citing are typical of the experiences of thousands of other people.R.V.Crowley was a salesman for a lumber company in New York.Crowley admitted that he had been telling hard-boiled lumber inspectors for years that they were wrong.And he had won the arguments too.But it hadn't done any good."For these lumber inspectors,"said Mr.Crowley,"are like baseball umpires.Once they make a decision,they never change it,"

Mr. Crowley saw that his firm was losing thousands of dollars through the arguments he won.So while taking my course,he resolved to change tactics and abandon arguments.With what results?Here is the story as he told it to the fellow members of his class:

"One morning the phone rang in my office.A hot and bothered person at the other end proceeded to inform me that a car of lumber we had shipped into his plant was entirely unsatisfactory.His firm had stopped unloading and requested that we make immediate arrangements

工既不能按要求生产出所需要的纱线，而且她们也拿不到原有的报酬了。于是，我设计了一套新标准，这样员工可以根据她们生产的纱线质量获得合理的报酬，产量也会随之上升。我在一次会议上向公司的主管层介绍了这套新标准，打算证明它是正确的。我从各方面指出了以前那套老办法的错误之处，希望得到他们的赞同。可是，我完全错了！我急于为新的方法辩护，没有给这些人留面子，使他们认识到以前的错误。这样，我的新标准还没采用就寿终正寝了。

"参加辅导班几堂课之后，我就意识到了我的错误。我建议再召开一次会议。这一次，我请他们指出问题到底出在何处。我们就每一个要点展开讨论，并请他们拿出最佳解决方案，而我则在适当的时候引导他们按照我的思路来提建议。当会议结束时，我所要提的方案实际上也就出来了，而他们也非常赞同。

"现在，我相信如果你径直指出某个人的错误，那么不仅不会收效，而且还会适得其反。你这样做只会剥夺别人的自尊，并使自己成为不受欢迎的人。"

让我们另外再举一例——别忘了，我所举的这些例子代表了成千上万人的经验。克洛里是纽约一家木材公司的推销员。克洛里承认，多年来他总是对那些脾气大的木料检验员挑毛病，而他也常常赢得争论。但这一点好处都没有。"因为那些木材检验员，"克洛里先生说，"和棒球裁判员一样，一旦他们做出裁判，就不再更改。"

克洛里先生发现因为他争辩得胜而使公司损失了成千上万收入。所以，他在参加我的培训班时，决定改变方法，放弃争论。结果如何呢?下面是他对同班学员的叙述：

"一天早上，我办公室的电话响了。一位气恼万分的顾客在电话中抱怨说，我们送到他厂里的一车木料完全不合乎要求。他的公司已经停止卸货，并要求我们立刻将这些木料从他们那里运走。他们的木料检验员说，在木料卸下 1/4 之后，发现有 55%不合格。在这种情况下，他们拒绝接受。

to remove the stock from their yard. After about one-fourth of the car had been unloaded, their lumber inspector reported that the lumber was running 55 percent below grade. Under the circumstances, they refused to accept it.

"I immediately started for his plant and on the way turned over in my mind the best way to handle the situation. Ordinarily, under such circumstances, I should have quoted grading rules and tried, as a result of my own experience and knowledge as a lumber inspector, to convince the other inspector that the lumber was actually up to grade, and that he was misinterpreting the rules in his inspection. However, I thought I would apply the principles learned in this training.

"When I arrived at the plant, I found the purchasing agent and the lumber inspector in a wicked humor, both set for an argument and a fight. We waited out to the car that was being unloaded, and I requested that they continue to unload so that I could see how things were going. I asked the inspector to go right ahead and lay out the rejects, as he had been doing, and to put the good pieces in another pile.

"After watching him for a while it began to dawn on me that his inspection actually was much too strict and that he was misinterpreting the rules. This particular lumber was white pine, and I knew the inspector was thoroughly schooled in hard woods but not a competent, experienced inspector on white pine. White pine happened to be my own strong suit, but did I offer any objection to the way he was grading the lumber? None whatever. I kept on watching and gradually began to ask questions as to why certain pieces were not satisfactory. I didn't for one instant insinuate that the inspector was wrong. I emphasized that my only reason for asking was in order that we could give his firm exactly what they wanted in future shipments.

"By asking questions in a very friendly, cooperative spirit, and insisting continually that they were right in laying out boards not satisfactory to their purpose, I got him warmed up, and the strained relations between us began to thaw and melt away. An occasional carefully put remark on my part gave birth to the idea in his mind that possibly some of these rejected pieces were actually within the grade that they had bought, and that their requirements demanded a more expensive grade. I was very careful, however, not to let him think I was making an issue of this point.

"Gradually his whole attitude changed. He finally admitted to me that he was not experienced

“我立刻动身去他的工厂。在路上我一直想着处理这种情况的最佳方法。在这种情况下，我一般会引用木材等级的规则，并以我自己担任检验员的经验与知识，来说服那位检验员木料确实符合标准，是他在检验时误解了规则。不过我想我还是试试我在训练中所学的法则。

“当我到达工厂时，只见采购经理及木料检验员一脸不高兴，全都准备争辩的样子。我们走到正在卸货的卡车边上，我要求他们继续卸货，让我看看具体情况。我请检验员照常检查，把不合格的木料放在一旁，合格的则另放一堆。

“看了一会儿以后，我发现他的检查确实太挑剔了，而且他又误解了规则。这次的木料是白松，我知道这位检验员在硬木方面知识丰富，但在检验白松时却经验不足。检查白松正是我的强项，但我是不是对他提出了反对意见呢？绝对没有。我继续观看，渐渐地开始问他为什么有些木料不合格。我丝毫没有暗示这位检验员他错了。我郑重地向他表明，我之所以问他，只是希望将来能以他们要求的标准给他的公司供货。

“用一种友善合作的精神请教，并坚持将他们不满意的木料挑出来，结果他很高兴，而我们之间的紧张关系也开始缓和下来。不过我也会时不时地提醒他几句，在被拒绝的木材中实际上有些还是符合他们购买的标准的。但是我非常小心，不让他知道我指出了这一点。

“渐渐地，他的整个态度有所改变。最后他承认他对于白松并没有多少经验，并在每根木料从车上搬下来时问我是否合格。我就向他解释为什么这根是合乎标准的；但我仍然坚持说，如果木料不合乎他们的需要，他们可以不接受。终于，每当他挑出一根他认为不合格的木料时，就感到不安了。最后，他意识到错误在他们，因为他们没有规定木料的等级标准。

“最后的结果是，在我走之后，他重新检验了全车木料，并且全部接受，我们收到了一张全额支票。

“就这件事来看，讲究一点技巧，尽量不指责对方的错误，可以使我公司减少一大笔收入损

on white pine and began to ask me questions about each piece as it came out of the car, I would explain why such a piece came within the grade specified, but kept on insisting that we did not want him to take it if it was unsuitable for their purpose. He finally got to the point where he felt guilty every time he put a piece in the rejected pile. And at last he saw that the mistake was on their part for not having specified as good a grade as they needed.

"The ultimate outcome was that he went through the entire carload again after I left, accepted the whole lot, and we received a check in full.

"In that one instance alone, a little tact, and the determination to refrain from telling the other man he was wrong, saved my company a substantial amount of cash, and it would be hard to place a money value on the good will that was saved."

Martin Luther King was asked how, as a pacifist, he could be an admirer of Air Force General Daniel "Chappie" James, then the nation's highest-ranking black officer. Dr. King replied, "I judge people by their own principles—not by my own."

In a similar way, General Robert E. Lee once spoke to the president of the Confederacy, Jefferson Davis, in the most glowing terms about a certain officer under his command. Another officer in attendance was astonished. "General," he said, "do you not know that the man of whom you speak so highly is one of your bitterest enemies who misses no opportunity to malign you?" "Yes," replied General Lee, "but the president asked my opinion of him; he did not ask for his opinion of me."

By the way, I am not revealing anything new in this chapter. Two thousand years ago, Jesus said, "Agree with thine adversary quickly."

And 2,200 years before Christ was born, King Akhtoi of Egypt gave his son some shrewd advice—advice that is sorely needed today. "Be diplomatic," counseled the King. "It will help you gain your point."

In other words, don't argue with your customer or your spouse or your adversary. Don't tell them they are wrong, don't get them stirred up. Use a little diplomacy.

Principle 2: Show respect for the other person's opinions. Never say, "You're wrong."

失，而给人留下良好的印象更非金钱所能衡量。”

有一次，有人问马丁·路德·金，作为一位和平使者，为什么他那么崇拜当时官阶最高的黑人空军将军丹尼尔·詹姆斯，他回答说：“我判断别人是根据他们的原则，而不是我自己的原则。”

同样，罗伯特·李将军曾向南部联邦“总统”杰斐逊·戴维斯极力赞扬他手下一位军官。另一位在场军官十分吃惊地说：“你知道吗，将军？你所称赞的那个人对你可不客气呀！他总是动不动就攻击你。”“是的。”李将军回答道，“但总统问的是我对他的看法，而不是他对我的看法。”

顺便说一下，我在本章并没有讲什么新观念。2000年以前，耶稣就说：“尽快与你的对手握手言和。”

在基督降生2200多年以前，古代埃及国王阿克图给了他儿子一条英明的忠告——一条今天仍然十分重要的忠告。阿克图国王说：“谦虚而有策略，你将无所不能。”

换言之，不要同你的顾客或你的配偶，或你的对手争论。不要指责他们错了，也不要刺激他们，而是讲究一点儿技巧。

第二项规则：尊重别人的意见。千万不要指责别人的错误。

3 If You're Wrong, Admit It

Within a minute's walk of my house there was a wild stretch of virgin timber, where the blackberry thickets foamed while in the springtime, where the squirrels nested and reared their young, and the horseweeds grew as tall as a horse's head. This unspoiled woodland was called Forest Park—and it was a forest, probably not much different in appearance from what it was when Columbus discovered America. I frequently walked in this park with Rex, my little Boston bulldog. He was a friendly, harmless little hound; and since we rarely met anyone in the park, I took Rex along without a leash or a muzzle.

One day we encountered a mounted policeman in the park, a policeman itching to show his authority.

"What do you mean by letting that dog run loose in the park without a muzzle and leash?" he reprimanded me. "Don't you know it's against the law?"

"Yes, I know it is," I replied softy, "but I didn't think he would do any harm out here."

"You didn't think! You didn't think! The law doesn't give a tinker's damn about what you think. That dog might kill a squirrel or bite a child. Now, I'm going to let you off this time; but if I catch this dog out here again without a muzzle and a leash, you'll have to tell it to the judge."

I meekly promised to obey.

And I did obey—for a few times. But Rex didn't like the muzzle, and neither did I; so we decided to take a chance. Everything was lovely for a while, and then we struck a snag. Rex and I raced over the brow of a hill one afternoon and there, suddenly—to my dismay—I saw the majesty of the law, astride a bay horse. Rex was out in front, heading straight for the officer.

I was in for it. I knew it. So I didn't wait until the policeman started talking. I beat him to it. I said, "Officer, you've caught me red-handed. I'm guilty. I have no alibis, no excuses. You warned me last week that if I brought the dog out here again without a muzzle you would fine me."

"Well, now," the policeman responded in a soft tone. "I know it's a temptation to let a little dog

第3章 勇于承认自己的错误

从我家步行不到一分钟，就是一片原始森林。当春天来临时，那里野花盛开，松鼠在树林中筑巢生子，草长得与马头齐高。这块完整的原始林地叫森林公园——它的确是一片森林，恐怕和哥伦布发现美洲时没有什么不同。我常带着我的波士顿哈巴狗瑞克斯去公园散步。这是一只友善而不会伤人的小狗，并且因为在公园中很少遇见人，因此我带瑞克斯散步时，没有给它系狗链或戴口罩。

一天，我们在公园遇见了一位骑马的警察，他好像急于显示他的威权。

"你不给狗戴口罩，不系链子，让它在公园中乱跑，想干什么？"他责问我说，"你难道不知道那是违法的吗？"

"是的，我知道，"我轻柔地回答，"但我想它在这里不至于伤到人。"

"你想不至于！你想不至于！法律才不管你怎样想呢。这只狗也许会伤害松鼠，或咬伤小孩。这次我就算了，但如果我下回再在这里发现这狗不戴口罩，不系链子，你就必须去和法官解释了。"

我小心客气地答应遵守他的命令。

我的确遵守了——而且遵守了好几次。但是瑞克斯不喜欢戴口罩，我也不喜欢那样，所以我们决定碰碰运气。起初一切都很顺利，后来我们就遇到了麻烦。一天下午，瑞克斯和我正跑过一个小山丘，就在那里，忽然——不幸得很——我看见那位法律的权威正骑着一匹棕红色的马。瑞克斯在前面跑，直向那位警察冲过去。

我知道这回肯定麻烦了。所以，我还没等警察开口说话，就先发制人。我说："警官先生，这次你当场抓住了我，我是违了法。我没有推辞，没有借口。你在上星期已经警告过我，如果我再

like that have a run out here when nobody is around."

"Sure it's a temptation,"I replied,"but it is against the law."

"Well,a little dog like that isn't going to harm anybody."the policeman remonstrated.

"No,but he may kill squirrels."I said.

"Well now,I think you are taking this a bit too seriously,"he told me."I'll tell you what you do.You just let him run over the hill there where I can't see him—and we'll forget all about it."

That policeman,being human,wanted a feeling of importance; so when I began to condemn myself,the only way he could nourish his self-esteem was to take the magnanimous attitude of showing mercy.

But suppose I had tried to defend myself—well,did you ever argue with a policeman?

But instead of breaking lances with him,I admitted that he was absolutely right and I was absolutely wrong; I admitted it quickly,openly,and with enthusiasm.The affair terminated graciously in my taking his side and his taking my side.Lord Chesterfield himself could hardly have been more gracious than this mounted policeman,who,only a week previously,had threatened to have the law on me.

If we know we are going to be rebuked anyhow,isn't it far better to beat the other person to it and do it ourselves?Isn't it much easier to listen to self-criticism than to bear condemnation from alien lips?

Say about yourself all the derogatory things you know the other person is thinking or wants to say or intends to say—and say them before that person has a chance to say them.The chances are a hundred to one that a generous,forgiving attitude will be taken and your mistakes will be minimized just as the mounted policeman did with me and Rex.

Ferdinand E.Warren,a commercial artist,used this technique to win the good will of a petulant,scolding buyer of art.

"It is important,in making drawings for advertising and publishing purposes,to be precise and very exact."Mr.Warren said as he told the story.

"Some art editors demand that their commissions be executed immediately; and in these cases,some slight error is liable to occur.I knew one art director in particular who was always

将小狗不戴口罩就带到这里,你就要罚我。"

"是的,现在,"警察用温柔的声调说,"我也知道,在这周围没有人的时候,谁都忍不住想带着这样一只小狗在这儿溜达。"

"那真是一种诱惑,"我回答说,"但那也是违法的。"

"像这样一只小狗不会伤人的。"警察替我辩护说。

"不,它也许会伤害松鼠。"我说。

"哦,我想也许你对这事太认真了。"他告诉我说,"让我告诉你怎么办吧。你只要让它跑过那山丘,我看不见它,我们就可以将这事忘了。"

和平常人一样,那位警察也渴望得到重视,所以当我开始责怪自己时,唯一能增加他的自尊的方法,就是对我表现得宽宏大度。

但假如我为自己辩护的话,那结果又将会怎样呢?

但我没有和他正面争论,我承认他是绝对正确的,我是绝对错误的;我爽快地、坦白地、真诚地承认这一点。我站在他的立场说话,于是他也为我说话,这件事就这样化解了。即使是查斯特菲尔德勋爵,也不会比这位骑马的警察更仁慈了,而仅在一个星期之前,这位警察还曾以法律来威胁我。

假如我们知道我们免不了要受责备的话,为什么不积极主动地认错呢?难道自己责备自己,不比别人的斥责要好受得多?

要是你知道别人正想指责你的错误时,你就应该在他有机会说出来之前,自己把他要说的说出来。很有可能,他就会采取宽厚谅解的态度宽恕你的错误,正如那位骑马的警察对我和瑞克斯一样。

费迪南·华伦是一位商业艺术家,他就曾用这种方法获得了一位粗鲁无礼、爱训斥人的雇

delighted to find fault with some little thing.I have often left his office in disgust,not because of the criticism,but because of his method of attack.Recently I delivered a rush job to this editor,and he phoned me to call at his office immediately.He said something was wrong.When I arrived,I found just what I had anticipated—and dreaded.He was hostile,gloating over his chance to criticize.He demanded with heat why I had done so and so.My opportunity had come to apply the self-criticism I had been studying about.So I said,'Mr.So-and-so,if what you say is true,I am at fault and there is absolutely no excuse for my blunder.I have been doing drawings for you long enough to know better.I'm ashamed of myself.'

"Immediately he started to defend me.'Yes,you're right,but after all,this isn't a serious mistake.It is only—'

"I interrupted him.'Any mistake,'I said,'may be costly and they are all irritating.'

"He started to break in,but I wouldn't let him.I was having a grand time.For the first time in my life,I was criticizing myself—and I loved it.

"'I should have been more careful,'I continued.'You give me a lot of work,and you deserve the best; so I'm going to do this drawing all over.'

"'No! No! 'he protested.'I wouldn't think of putting you to all that trouble.'He praised my work,assured me that he wanted only a minor change and that my slight error hadn't cost his firm any money; and,after all,it was a mere detail—not worth worrying about.

"My eagerness to criticize myself took all the fight out of him.He ended up by taking me to lunch; and before we parted,he gave me a check and another commission."

There is a certain degree of satisfaction in having the courage to admit one's errors.It not only clears the air of guilt and defensiveness,but often helps solve the problem created by the error.

Bruce Harvey of Albuquerque,New Mexico,had incorrectly authorized payment of full wages to an employee on sick leave.When he discovered his error,he brought it to the attention of the employee and explained that to correct the mistake he would have to reduce his next paycheck by the entire amount of the overpayment.The employee pleaded that as that would cause him a serious financial problem,could the money be repaid over a period of time?In order to do this,Harvey explained,he would have to obtain his supervisor's approval."And this I

主的好感。

"简洁明快,是为广告及出版物作画的最重要的原则。"华伦先生讲这故事的时候说。

"有些美术编辑要求将他们的工作立即做好。在这种情况下,出现细小的错误在所难免。我认识的某位美术主任,总是喜欢鸡蛋里面挑骨头。我每次离开他的办公室时总会感到不舒服,这并不是因为他的批评,而是因为他攻击我的方法。最近,我交了一份万分火急的画稿给这位编辑,他打电话让我立刻去他办公室,说是出了问题。当我赶到时,不出所料——麻烦事来了。他满怀敌意,正得意有了批评的机会。他恶意地质问我为什么如此如此。这正好是运用我新学到的自我认错方法的大好机会,于是我说:'先生,如果你说的是真的,那么我错了。我绝不是推托过错。我为你作画这么多年,应该知道如何做才会更好些。我自己也觉得很惭愧。'

"他立刻开始为我辩护了。'是的,你说得没错,但这毕竟还不是一个严重的错误。只不过是——'

"我打断了他。'无论什么错误,'我说,'都必须付出代价,都会让人生气。'

"他想要插嘴,但我没给他机会。我很高兴。我有生以来第一次批评自己——我很喜欢这样做。

"'我今后应该更小心些,'我继续说。'你给我了许多工作,我应尽力做得更好。所以我要重画一次。'

"'不!不!'他反对说。'我绝不想那样麻烦你。'他称赞了我的作品,并且对我说他只不过想做个小小的改动,我这点儿小错误对他的公司没有什么损失;而且,那毕竟不过是一个小节,不值得担心。

"我急切地自我批评,使他怒气全消。最后他还请我吃了午饭;在我们分手以前,他又给了我一张支票和另外一件工作。"

勇于承认自己的错误,可以得到某种满足感。这不仅只是消除罪恶感和自我辩护,而且有

knew," reported Harvey, "would result in a boss-type explosion. While trying to decide how to handle his situation better, I realized that the whole mess was my fault and I would have to admit it to my boss.

"I walked into his office, told him that I had made a mistake and then informed him of the complete facts. He replied in an explosive manner that it was the fault of the personnel department. I repeated that it was my fault. He exploded again about carelessness in the accounting department. Again I explained it was my fault. He blamed two other people in the office. But each time I reiterated it was my fault. Finally, he looked at me and said, 'Okay, it was your fault. Now straighten it out.' the error was corrected and nobody got into trouble. I felt great because I was able to handle a tense situation and had the courage not to seek alibis. My boss has had more respect for me ever since."

Any fool can try to defend his or her mistakes—and most fools do—but it raises one above the herd and gives one a feeling of nobility and exultation to admit one's mistakes. For example, one of the most beautiful things that history records about Robert E. Lee is the way he blamed himself and only himself for the failure of Pickett's charge at Gettysburg.

Pickett's charge was undoubtedly the most brilliant and picturesque attack that ever occurred in the Western world. General George E. Pickett himself was picturesque. He wore his hair so long that his auburn locks almost touched his shoulders; and, like Napoleon in his Italian campaigns, he wrote ardent love-letters almost daily while in the battlefield. His devoted troops cheered him that tragic July afternoon as he rode off jauntily toward the Union lines, his cap set at a rakish angle over his right ear. They cheered and they followed him, man touching man, rank pressing rank, with banners flying and bayonets gleaming in the sun. It was a gallant sight. Daring. Magnificent. A murmur of admiration ran through the Union lines as they beheld it.

Pickett's troops swept forward at any easy trot, through orchard and cornfield, across a meadow and over a ravine. All the time, the enemy's cannon was tearing ghastly holes in their ranks, but on they pressed, grim, irresistible.

Suddenly the Union infantry rose from behind the stone wall on Cemetery Ridge where they had been hiding and fired volley after volley into Pickett's onrushing troops. The crest of the hill

利于解决由失误造成的问题。

新墨西哥州阿布库克市的布鲁斯·哈威在给一位请病假的员工核准薪水时，错误地给了他全薪。他发现这个错误之后，告诉这位员工他有必要纠正，而且在下次发放工资时再予减扣。这位员工说这会给他造成严重的财务困难，请求分多期扣除多发的工资。哈威说这必须由他的上司批准。"我知道这样做，"哈威说，"会使老板不满。当我考虑如何更好地处理这个问题时，我意识到这一切都是由我的失误造成的，因此我必须向老板承认错误。

"我走进老板的办公室，把我的错误告诉了他，并讲了整个过程，但他大发脾气地说这应该是人事部门的错误，我重申这是我的错误；他又大声指责财会部门的粗心，我仍说这是我的错误；他又责怪办公室另外两个人，但我每次都坚持是我的错误。最后，他看着我说：'好的，是你的错误，那你就去改正吧！'结果，这个错误改正了，而且没有给任何人带来麻烦。我自认为很不错，因为我可以处理这种紧急事件，而且有勇气承认自己的错误。从那以后，老板更重视我了。"

任何傻瓜都会为他的错误辩解——而且大多数傻瓜正是这样做的——而敢于承认自己错误的人，都会获得别人的谅解，给人以谦恭而高尚的印象。例如，美国历史上记载的一个极好的例证，便是关于罗伯特·李将军的——他把毕克德进攻葛底斯堡的失败完全归咎于自己，并为此而自责。

毕克德的那次进攻，无疑是西方世界最辉煌显赫的一次战斗。毕克德将军本人就是个光彩照人的显赫人物。他长发披肩，而且像拿破仑在意大利的战役中一样，几乎每天在战场上写热烈的情书。在那惨痛的七月的一个下午，当他把军帽斜戴在右耳上方，骑马冲向联军战线时，他那军心大振的将士们为他喝起彩来。他们欢呼着，跟随着他，一路上浩浩荡荡，军旗飞扬，刺刀闪烁。那壮伟的一幕，以及那支勇敢出色的队伍，连北军也不禁为之惊叹。

毕克德的军队迈着轻捷的步伐，穿过果园和玉米地，踏过草地，翻过山峡。北军的大炮一直

was a sheet of flame, a slaughterhouse, a blazing volcano. In a few minutes, all of Pickett's brigade commanders except one were down, and four-fifths of his five thousand men had fallen.

General Lewis A. Armistead, leading the troops in the final plunge, ran forward, vaulted over the stone wall, and, waving his cap on the top of his sword, shouted:

"Give'em the steel, boys!"

They did. They leaped over the wall, bayoneted their enemies, smashed skulls with clubbed muskets, and planted the battleflags of the South on Cemetery Ridge.

The banners waved there only for a moment. But that moment, brief as it was, recorded the high-water mark of the Confederacy.

Pickett's charge—brilliant, heroic—was nevertheless the beginning of the end. Lee had failed. He could not penetrate the North. And he knew it.

The South was doomed.

Lee was so saddened, so shocked, that he sent in his resignation and asked Jefferson Davis, the president of the Confederacy, to appoint "a younger and abler man." If Lee had wanted to blame the disastrous failure of Pickett's charge on someone else, he could have found a score of alibis. Some of his division commanders had failed him. The cavalry hadn't arrived in time to support the infantry attack. This had gone wrong and that had gone awry.

But Lee was far too noble to blame others. As Pickett's beaten and bloody troops struggled back to the Confederate lines, Robert E. Lee rode out to meet them all alone and greeted them with a self-condemnation that was little short of sublime. "All this has been my fault," he confessed. "I and I alone have lost this battle."

Few generals in all history have had the courage and character to admit that.

Elbert Hubbard was one of the most original authors who ever stirred up a nation, and his stinging sentences often aroused fierce resentment. But Hubbard with his rare skill for handling people frequently turned his enemies into friends.

For example, when some irritated reader wrote in to say that he didn't agree with such and such an article and ended by calling Hubbard this and that, Elbert Hubbard would answer like this:

在向他们发起猛攻。但他们毫不退缩,勇往直前。

突然,北军的步兵从他们隐伏的墓山脊的石墙后面冲了出来,朝毕克德正在行进的军队开火。山上硝烟四起,变成了一片火海,犹如屠场。几分钟之内,毕克德所有的旅长除一人幸存之外,其余的全部阵亡,他的5000名士兵有4000人阵亡。

阿密斯坦将军率领残军,拼死冲杀。他冲向前去,跃过石墙,把军帽顶在他的指挥刀上挥动着,大呼道:

"孩子们,杀啊!"

他们全都豁出去了。他们跃过墙头,用刺刀和枪托与他们的敌人肉搏,终于把南军的军旗插上了墓地山脊。

尽管大旗只在那里飘扬了一会儿,但那短暂的一会儿却记录了南方同盟军的辉煌战功。

毕克德的冲锋——虽然光荣、勇敢,然而却是战争进入尾声的前奏。李将军失败了。他知道他没法深入北方。

南方失败的命运早就注定了。

李将军悲痛万分,震惊不已,他向同盟政府总统戴维斯提出了辞呈,请求改派"一位更加年轻有为之士"。如果李将军要将毕克德的冲锋所导致的惨痛失败归罪于其他人的话,他可以找出数十个借口,例如有些军官不称职、马队到得太迟、不能协助步兵进攻。总之,这事错了,那事也不对。

但是李将军太高尚了,他没有责怪别人。当毕克德的残兵败将从前线退回南方阵线的时候,李将军单身骑马亲自迎接他们,并自我谴责。"这都是我的过失,"他承认说,"我,我一个人在这场战斗中战败了。"

历史上很少有将军有这种勇气和情操承认自己的错误。

Come to think it over, I don't entirely agree with it myself. Not everything I wrote yesterday appeals to me today. I am glad to learn what you think on the subject. The next time you are in the neighborhood you must visit us and we'll get this subject threshed out for all time. So here is a handclasp over the miles, and I am,

Yours sincerely.

What could you say to a man who treated you like that?

When we are right, let's try to win people gently and tactfully to our way of thinking, and when we are wrong—and that will be surprisingly often, if we are honest with ourselves—let's admit our mistakes quickly and with enthusiasm. Not only will that technique produce astonishing results; but, believe it or not, it is a lot more fun, under the circumstances, than trying to defend oneself.

Remember the old proverb: "By fighting you never get enough, but by yielding you get more than you expected."

Principle 3: If you are wrong, admit it quickly and emphatically.

阿尔伯特·哈伯德是一位全国都为之震动不已的最具创造性的作家，他那讽刺性的文字常引起别人的强烈反感。但哈伯德常常会采用他那罕有的待人处世技巧，将他的仇敌转变为朋友。

例如，当一些恼怒的读者写信来表示不同意他的某篇文章，并在末尾把他臭骂一顿时，他会这样回答对方：

细想起来，我自己也不完全同意我自己。我昨天所写的东西，今天我也不一定全都满意。我很高兴知道你对这类问题的看法。如果下次你到附近来，欢迎大驾光临，我们可以相互交流。遥祝平安。

哈伯德谨上

面对一个如此待你的人，你还能说什么？

当我们是对的时候，我们要温和巧妙地使别人赞同我们；当我们错的时候——如果我们对自己诚实，这是很常见的——我们就要迅速而诚挚地承认。这不但能产生惊人的效果，而且在许多情况下要远远胜过自我辩护。信不信由你。

请记住这句古语："用争斗的方法，你永远不会得到满足；但用让步的方法，你收获的会比你所期望的更多。"

第三项规则：如果你错了，迅速坦诚地承认。

4 A Drop of Honey

If your temper is aroused and you tell'em a thing or two, you will have a fine time unloading your feelings. But what about the other person? Will he share your pleasure? Will your belligerent tones, your hostile attitude, make it easy for him to agree with you?

"If you come at me with your fists doubled," said Woodrow Wilson, "I think I can promise you that mine will double as fast as yours; but if you come to me and say, 'Let us sit down and take counsel together, and, if we differ from each other, understand why it is that we differ, just what the points at issue are,' we will presently find that we are not so far apart after all, that the points on which we differ are few and the points on which we agree are many, and that if we only have the patience and the candor and the desire to get together, we will get together."

Nobody appreciated the truth of Woodrow Wilson's statement more than John D. Rockefeller, Jr. Back in 1915, Rockefeller was the most fiercely despised man in Colorado. One of the bloodiest strikes in the history of American industry had been shocking the state for two terrible years. Irate, belligerent miners were demanding higher wages from the Colorado Fuel and Iron Company; Rockefeller controlled that company. Property had been destroyed, troops had been called out. Blood had been shed. Strikers had been shot, their bodies riddled with bullets.

At a time like that, with the air seething with hatred, Rockefeller wanted to win the strikers to his way of thinking. And he did it. How? Here's the story. After weeks spent in making friends, Rockefeller addressed the representatives of the strikers. This speech, in its entirety, is a masterpiece. It produced astonishing results. It calmed the tempestuous waves of hate that threatened to engulf Rockefeller. It won him a host of admirers. It presented facts in such a friendly manner that the strikers went back to work without saying another word about the increase in wages for which they had fought so violently.

The opening of that remarkable speech follows. Note how it fairly glows with friendliness. Rockefeller, remember, was talking to men who, a few days previously, had wanted to hang him by

第4章 一切从友善开始

假如你生气时,对人家发一顿火,你固然会觉得舒服了,但对方又会怎样呢?他也能分享到你的痛快吗?你那充满火药味的声调、仇视的态度,能使他赞同你吗?

"如果你握紧两个拳头来找我,"伍德罗·威尔逊总统说,"我敢保证我的拳头会握得比你的更紧。但如果你到我这儿来说:'让我们坐下来一起商量,看看为什么我们意见不同,问题出在哪里。'那么不久我们就会发现,我们的分歧其实并不大,我们的看法大同小异。因此,只要我们有耐心相互沟通,我们就能相互理解。"

最欣赏威尔逊这些至理名言的,要数小约翰·洛克菲勒了。1915年,洛克菲勒还是科罗拉多州最受轻视的人。美国工业史中流血最多的罢工潮在科罗拉多州持续了动荡不安的两年。愤怒而粗野的矿工要求科罗拉多煤铁公司增加薪水, 而这家公司正归洛克菲勒所有。当时,房产被毁坏,军队也被调动出来,发生了多起流血事件。罢工者遭到枪杀,许多尸体遍体枪伤。

在那样一种充满仇恨的情况下,洛克菲勒却要赢得罢工者的赞同,而且他做到了。他又是怎样做的呢?大致的情形是这样的:他先是花了数星期和工人交涉,然后又对工人代表发表演说。这篇演说可算得上一篇杰作,它产生了惊人的效果:不仅平息了要把洛克菲勒吞下去的仇恨,而且使他赢得了许多崇拜者。他用极其友善的态度来阐明事实,使罢工者回去工作,而不再提增加工资,而这曾是他们强烈要求的。

这是那篇著名演讲的开始部分,且看它所流露出来的友善精神。要知道,洛克菲勒这次演讲的对象几天前还打算将他吊死在酸苹果树上。然而他却再仁慈、再友善不过了,好像是

the neck to a sour apple tree; yet he couldn't have been more gracious, more friendly if he had addressed a group of medical missionaries. His speech was radiant with such phrases as I am *proud* to be here, having *visited* in *your homes*, met many of your wives and children, we meet here not as strangers, but as *friends*...spirit of *mutual friendship*, *our common interests*, it is only by *your courtesy* that I am here.

"This is a red-letter day in my life," Rockefeller began. "It is the first time I have ever had the good fortune to meet the representatives of the employees of this great company, its officers and superintendents, together, and I can assure you that I am proud to be here, and that I shall remember this gathering as long as I live. Had this meeting been held two weeks ago, I should have stood here a stranger to most of you, recognizing a few faces. Having had the opportunity last week of visiting all the camps in the southern coal field and of talking individually with practically all of the representatives, except those who were away; having visited in your homes, met many of your wives and children, we meet here not as strangers, but as friends, and it is in that spirit of mutual friendship that I am glad to have this opportunity to discuss with you our common Interests.

"Since this is a meeting of the officers of the company and the representatives of the employees, it is only by your courtesy that I am here, for I am not so fortunate as to be either one or the other; and yet I feel that I am intimately associated with you men, for, in a sense, I represent both the stockholders and the directors."

Isn't that a superb example of the fine art of making friends out of enemies?

Suppose Rockefeller had taken a different tack. Suppose he had argued with those miners and hurled devastating facts in their faces. Suppose he had told them by his tones and insinuations that they were wrong. Suppose that, by all the rules of logic, he had proved that they were wrong. What would have happened? More anger would have been stirred up, more hatred, more revolt.

If a man's heart is rankling with discord and ill feeling toward you, you can't win him to your way of thinking with all the logic in Christendom. Scolding parents and domineering bosses and husbands and nagging wives ought to realize that people don't want to change their minds. They can't he forced or driven to agree with you or me. But they may possibly be led to, if we are gentle and friendly, ever so gentle and ever so friendly.

在对一群传道医生演讲。他的演讲因为这些言辞而散发出光芒：我很高兴在这儿，参观你们的家，看望你们的妻子儿女，我们是以朋友而不是陌生人的身份在此相聚，我们共同的利益，正因为你们的好意而使我有幸在此。

“这是我一生中值得纪念的日子，”洛克菲勒说，“这是我第一次这样幸运地会见这家伟大公司的劳工代表、职员及监督们。说心里话，我很荣幸能到这里来，而且在我有生之年绝不会忘了这次聚会。如果这次聚会在两个星期前举行，我对你们中大多数人来说一定是一个陌生人，而且我也只认识少数人。上星期我有机会访问南矿区所有的住户，除去出外的代表，我差不多和所有代表谈过话；我见过你们的家庭，看望你们的妻子儿女。我们在这里见面，不再是陌生人，而是朋友。也正是在这种互相友善的精神中，我很幸运有这种机会，和你们讨论我们共同的利益。

“这是由公司职员及工人代表参加的集会。我之所以能来这里，全都是因为你们的厚爱。我既不是公司职员，也不是工人代表，但我仍然觉得与你们关系亲密，因为从某方面说，我代表了股东及董事双方。”

这不是一个化敌为友的最佳技巧的例子吗？

假如洛克菲勒采用别的方法；假如他和那些矿工争论，态度强硬地当着他们的面举出毁坏矿场的事实来；假如他用暗示的语气告诉他们，说他们是错的；假如他运用逻辑规则来证明他们是错误的，结果会如何？必然会激起更多的愤怒、更多的仇恨和更多的反抗。

如果一个人因为与你不和，并对你怀有恶感而对你心怀不满，那么你用任何办法都不能使他赞同你。责骂的父母、强硬的上司及丈夫，以及唠叨不休的妻子们应该明白：人们不愿改变他们的想法，不能勉强或迫使他们与你我意见一致。但如果我们温柔友善——非常温柔，非常友善——就能引导他们和我们走向一致。

Lincoln said that, in effect, over a hundred years ago. Here are his words:

It is an old and true maxim that "a drop of honey catches more flies than a gallon of gall." So with men, if you would win a man to you cause, first convince him that you are his sincere friend. Therein is a drop of honey that catches his heart; which, say what you will, is the great high road to his reason.

Business executives have learned that it pays to be friendly to strikers. For example, when 2,500 employees in the White Motor Company's plant struck for higher wages and a union shop, Robert F. Black, then president of the company, didn't lose his temper and condemn and threaten and talk of tryanny and Communists. He actually praised the strikers. He published an advertisement in the Cleveland papers, complimenting them on "the peaceful way in which they laid down their tools." Finding the strike pickets idle, he bought them a couple of dozen baseball bats and gloves and invited them to play ball on vacant lots. For those who preferred bowling, he rented a bowling alley.

This friendliness on Mr. Black's part did what friendliness always does: it begot friendiness. So the strikers borrowed brooms, shovels, and rubbish carts, and began picking up matches, papers, cigarette stubs, and cigar butts around the factory. Imagine it! Imagine strikers tidying up the factory grounds while battling for higher wages and recognition of the union. Such an event had never been heard of before in the long, tempestuous history of American labor wars. That strike ended with a compromise settlement within a week—ended without any ill feeling or rancor.

Daniel Webster, who looked like a god and talked like Jehovah, was one of the most successful advocates who ever pleaded a case; yet he ushered in his most powerful arguments with such friendly remarks as: "It will be for the jury to consider," "This may perhaps be worth thinking of," "Here are some facts that I trust you will not lose sight of," or "You, with your knowledge of human nature, will easily see the significance of these facts." No bulldozing. No high-pressure methods. No attempt to force his opinions on others. Webster used the soft-spoken, quiet, friendly approach, and it helped to make him famous.

You may never be called upon to settle a strike or address a jury, but you may want to get your rent reduced. Will the friendly approach help you then? Let's See.

其实，100多年前，林肯就说过这些。下面是他的原话：

“一句古老的格言说：‘一滴蜂蜜比一加仑胆汁能捕到更多的苍蝇。’对人也是这样。如果你要让别人同意你的观点，首先要让他相信你是他真正的朋友。这就像一滴蜂蜜，用一滴蜂蜜赢得了他的心，那么，你就能使他走在理智的大道上。”

商人们正日渐明白，对罢工者态度友善是很值的。例如，当怀特汽车公司的2500名工人为增加工资而组织工会罢工的时候，公司经理罗伯特·布兰克没有生气和责罚、恫吓。相反，他还称赞罢工者。他在《克里夫兰报》上登广告，颂扬他们“放下工具的和平方式”。当他看见罢工纠察队的人闲得无聊时，他还给他们买了棒球棍及手套，请他们在空地上打棒球。为了讨好那些喜欢打地球的人，他甚至为他们租了一间地球室。

布兰克的友善态度产生了良好的效果，唤起了罢工者的友善。于是罢工者借来扫帚、铁铲、垃圾车，开始清扫工厂。想想看！当罢工者要求涨工资并组织起来时，竟然打扫工厂。在美国罢工史上，这种事情从未出现过。那次罢工事件在一星期之内达成和解——没有任何怀恨或怨恶情绪地结束了。

丹尼尔·韦伯斯特相貌出众，谈吐如耶和华，是一位能言善辩而且非常有成就的辩护律师。他善于用友善温和的词句在法庭上表达他那强有力的观点，例如“这一点应该请陪审团考虑”，“这也许值得想一想”，“这几件事实，我相信你们是不会忽略的”，或“由于你们对人性的了解，很容易看出这些事实的重要”。没有威逼，也没有高压的手段，他从不将自己的意见强加于人。韦伯斯特用的是轻声细语和安详友善的方式，而这正是他闻名遐迩的原因。

你或许永远不必去调解罢工，或对陪审团发言，但是你或许会希望房东减少你的房租。友善的方法能帮助你吗？我们来看下面的例子。

一位工程师施特劳伯希望减少房租，而他知道他的房东脾气不好。“我写了封信给他，”施

O.L.Straub, an engineer, wanted to get his rent redued. And he knew his landlord was hard-boiled. "I wrote him," Mr.Straub said in a speech before the class, "notifying him that I was vacating my apartment as soon as my lease expired. The truth was, I didn't want to move. I wanted to stay if I could get my rent reduced. But the situation seemed hopeless. Other tenants had tried—and failed. Everyone told me that the landlord was extremely difficult to deal with. But I said to myself, 'I am studying a course in how to deal with people, so I'll try it on him—and see how it works.'

"He and his secretary came to see me as soon as he got my letter. I met him at the door with a friendly greeting. I fairly bubbled with good will and enthusiasm. I didn't begin talking about how high the rent was. I began talking about how much I liked his apartment house. Believe me, I was 'hearty in my approbation and lavish in my praise.' I complimented him on the way he ran the building and told him I should like so much to stay for another year but I couldn't afford it.

"He had evidently never had such a reception from a tenant. He hardly knew what to make of it.

"Then he started to tell me his troubles. Complaining tenants. One had written him fourteen letters, some of them positively insulting. Another threatened to break his lease unless the landlord kept the man on the floor above from snoring. 'What a relief it is,' he said, 'to have a satisfied tenant like you.' And then, without my even asking him to do it, he offered to reduce my rent a little. I wanted more, so I named the figure I could afford to pay, and he accepted without a word.

"As he was leaving, he turned to me and asked, 'What decorating can I do for you?'

"If I had tried to get the rent reduced by the methods the other tenants were using, I am positive I should have met with the same failure they encountered. It was the friendly, sympathetic, appreciative approach that won."

Dean Woodcock of Pittsburgh, Pennsylvania, is the superintendent of a department of the local electric company. His staff was called upon to repair some equipment on top of a pole. This type of work had formerly been performed by a different department and had only recently been transferred to Woodcock's section. Although his people had been trained in the work, this was the first time they had ever actually been called upon to do it. Everybody in the organization was

特劳伯在我班上的一次演讲中说,“通知他在租期将满时,我就会搬出我的公寓。事实上我并不想搬走。如果能减少房租,我还会住下去。但这似乎希望不大。别的房客也试过——都失败了。每个人都告诉我,这个房东是极难对付的。但我对自己说:‘我正在研究如何与人相处,所以我要对他试一试——看有没有用’。

“他接到我的信以后,就同他的秘书一起来找我。我在门前友好地欢迎他,充满了善意与热心。我没有一开口就说房租多么高。我只是说我如何喜欢他的公寓。请相信,我真是‘诚于嘉许,宽于称道’。我称赞他管理有方,并告诉他我很乐意再住上一年,可是我支付不起房租。

“很明显,他从来没有从一个房客那儿得到这种欢迎和赞扬。他简直不知如何是好了。

“然后他开始向我大倒苦水,并抱怨那些房客。曾有一位房客给他写过14封信,有的话简直是侮辱。还有一位房客威胁说,如果房东不能让上面一层楼的人睡觉时停止打鼾,他就取消租约。他说:‘有你这样满意的一位房客,多么令人愉快。’接着,我没有请求,他就自动减少了一部分租金。但我想再多减些,于是我提出了我所能负担的数目,他二话没说就答应了。

“离开的时候,他转身问我:‘你有什么装饰需要我做的吗?’

“如果我用别的房客曾用过的方法来降低房租,我肯定会遇到他们同样的困难。正是这种友善、同情、欣赏的方法使我赢得了一切。”

宾夕法尼亚州匹兹堡市的狄恩·伍德科克是当地电力公司的一个部门主管。他手下两个员工被叫去修理一根电线杆上的某种器件。以前这类工作是由另一个部门负责的,最近才由伍德科克这个部门负责。虽然这两个人曾经接受过这方面的训练,但却是第一次实际去做这项工作。公司的每一个人都想看看他们是否能把这件事情做好。伍德科克先生、他下面的几个组长以及公司其他部门的一些人都去看这两人工作的情况。许多车停在那里,一大群人围在四周看灯杆上的两个人工作。

interested in seeing if and how they could handle it.Mr.Woodcock,several of his subordinate managers,and members of other departments of the utility went to see the operation.Many cars and trucks were there,and a number of people were standing around watching the two lone men on top of the pole.

Glancing around,Woodcock noticed a man up the street getting out of his car with a camera. He began taking pictures of the scene.Utility people are extremely conscious of public relations, and suddenly Woodcock realized what this setup looked like to the man with the camera–overkill dozens of people being called out to do a two-person job.He strolled up the street to the photographer.

"I see you're interested in our operation."

"Yes,and my mother will be more than interested.She owns stock in your company.This will be an eye-opener for her.She may even decide her investment was unwise.I've been telling her for years there's a lot of waste motion in companies like yours.This proves it.The newspapers might like these pictures,too."

"It does look like it,doesn't it?I'd think the same thing in your position.But this is a unique situation ..."And Dean Woodcock went on to explain how this was the first job of this type for his department and how everybody from executives down was interested.He assured the man that under normal conditions two people could handle the job.The photographer put away his camera,shook Woodcock's hand,and thanked him for taking the time to explain the situation to him.

Dean Woodcock's friendly approach saved his company much embarrassment and bad publicity.

Another member of one of our classes,Gerald H.Winn of Littleton,New Hampshire,reported how by using a friendly approach,he obtained a very satisfactory settlement on a damage claim.

"Early in the spring,"he reported,"before the ground had thawed from the winter freezing, there was an unusually heavy rainstorm and the water,which normally would have run off to nearby ditches and storm drains along the road,took a new course onto a building lot where I had just built a new home.

"Not being able to run off,the water pressure built up around the foundation of the house.The

伍德科克看了看四周,只见一个人拿着照相机走出汽车,拍下了当时的场面。像电力公司这样的公用事业公司,其成员一般都很注意公共关系,而伍德科克这时突然意识到,在那位带照相机的人看来,他们这些人是在磨洋工。于是,他过街走近那位带照相机的人。

"好像你对我们的作业很感兴趣。"

"不错,不过我母亲可能更感到兴趣。她买了你们公司的股票,这可以让她更清楚地认识你们。她看到之后,或许会认为买你们公司的股票是不明智的。我这些年一直都对她说你们这种公司存在的浪费太多了,这证明我说的确实没错。报纸对这些照片也会感兴趣。"

"看起来确实如此,不是吗?如果我站在你的立场,也会有同样的想法。但这次情况有所不同……"狄恩·伍德科克向这人解释,这是他部门的人第一次执行这类工作,而且公司上下都很关心。他还向那个人保证,通常情况下只需两个人就可以做好这项工作。那个人收起了照相机,和伍德科克握手,谢谢他花时间向他说明这些。

伍德科克的友善态度,使他的公司免除了尴尬和不好的名声。

新罕布什尔州李特顿市的吉拉德·文恩,是我班上另一位学员,他讲了他怎样运用友善的态度,解决了一项损毁赔偿的案子。

"春季开始的时候,"他说,"地面尚未解冻,却出人意料地下了一场大雨。由于雨水不能像平常那样沿着附近的水沟排泄,只好另寻途径,朝我刚建好的一栋新房子的所在地流了过去。

"雨水流不走,对地基形成了压力。雨水渗进了房屋底层的水泥地板中,使地板出现裂缝,水淹没了地下室,地下室的火炉和热水器被毁坏。修理这些东西要花2000多美元,而我买的保险并不包含这一类损坏。

"不过,不久我就发现,由于承建商设计上的疏忽,没有在房子附近修建排污沟。如果有这道排污沟,就可以防止这类问题。我约好去找他。在前往他办公室的路上,我仔细地考虑了这

water forced itself under the concrete basement floor, causing it to explode, and the basement filled with water. This ruined the furnace and the hot-water heater. The cost to repair this damage was in excess of two thousand dollars. I had no insurance to cover this type of damage.

"However, I soon found out that the owner of the subdivision had neglected to put in a storm drain near the house which could have prevented this problem. I made an appointment to see him. During the twenty-five-mile trip to his office, I carefully reviewed the situation and, remembering the principles I learned in this course, I decided that showing my anger would not serve any worthwhile purpose. When I arrived, I kept very calm and started by talking about his recent vacation to the West Indies; then, when I felt the timing was right, I mentioned the 'little' problem of water damage. He quickly agreed to do his share in helping to correct the problem.

"A few days later he called and said he would pay for the damage and also put in a storm drain to prevent the same thing from happening in the future.

"Even though it was the fault of the owner of the subdivision, if I had not begun in a friendly way, there would have been a great deal of difficulty in getting him to agree to the total liability."

Years ago, when I was a barefoot boy walking through the woods to a country school out in northwest Missouri, I read a fable about the sun and the wind. They quarreled about which was the stronger, and the wind said, "I'll prove I am. See the old man down there with a coat? I bet I can get his coat off him quicker than you Can."

So the sun went behind a cloud, and the wind blew until it was almost a tornado, but the harder it blew, the tighter the old man clutched his coat to him.

Finally, the wind calmed down and gave up, and then the sun came out from behind the clouds and smiled kindly on the old man. Presently, he mopped his brow and pulled off his coat. The sun then told the wind that gentleness and friendliness were always stronger than fury and force.

The use of gentleness and friendliness is demonstrated day after day by people who have learned that a drop of honey catches more flies than a gallon of gall. F. Gale Connor of Lutherville, Maryland, proved this when he had to take his four-month-old car to the service department of the car dealer for the third time. He told our class, "It was apparent that talking to, reasoning with or shouting at the service manager was not going to lead to a satisfactory resolution of my problems.

件事情，并且想到了我在班上所学到的法则，知道光发火肯定不管用。当我到达后，我保持冷静，先和他谈了谈他最近去西印度群岛度假的事；然后在适当的时候提到了雨水淹没地下室这个‘小’问题。他很爽快地答应解决。

“几天以后，他打来电话说，他会支付修理损坏设备的费用，并且要建一道排污沟，防止以后再发生同样的事情。

“这虽然是承建商的责任，但我如果不是一开始就态度友善，要他同意承担全部责任恐怕不会这么顺利了。”

多年以前，当我还是个孩子，光着脚穿过密苏里西北部的树林，去一个乡村学校读书时，曾读过一则关于太阳与风的寓言。它们在争论谁更强有力，风说：“我可以证明我更加强大。你看见那边那个穿大衣的老人吗？我敢打赌，我能比你更快地使他脱去大衣。”

于是太阳躲到云后，风开始刮起来，几乎变成一场飓风，但它吹得越厉害，老人越是将大衣裹得紧紧的。

最后，风放弃了，平静下来。然后太阳从云后钻出来，对老人和善地“微笑”。不久，老人开始擦前额的汗水，脱下了他的大衣。太阳告诉风说：“温柔、友善永远比愤怒、暴力更强大。”

温柔友善的作用，每天都能从那些深谙“一滴蜂蜜比一加仑胆汁能捕到更多苍蝇”这一道理的人身上得到验证。马里兰州路德维尔市的盖尔·康纳先生就证明了这句话的真理性。当时，康纳先生必须将他买了4个月的汽车第三次送去经销商那里进行维修。他在我们班上说：“很明显，和维修厂的经理谈话、说理或指责他，都不能圆满地解决我的问题。

“于是，我进入汽车展销大厅，要求见老板怀特先生。我稍等了一会儿，就被领进了怀特先生的办公室。我先做了自我介绍，向他说明我之所以买他的汽车，是由于我朋友的推荐。他们都买了他的汽车，认为价格合理，而且服务也很出色。怀特先生满意地听着，笑了起来。然后，我又

"I walked over to the showroom and asked to see the agency owner, Mr.White. After a short wait, I was ushered into Mr.White's office. I introduced myself and explained to him that I had bought my car from his dealership because of the recommendations of friends who had had previous dealings with him. I was told that his prices were very competitive and his service was outstanding. He smiled with satisfaction as he listened to me. I then explained the problem I was having with the service department. 'I thought you might want to be aware of any situation that might tarnish your fine reputation,' I added. He thanked me for calling this to his attention and assured me that my problem would be taken care of. Not only did he personal get involved, but he also lent me his car to use while mine was being repaired."

Aesop was a Greek slave who lived at the court of Croesus and spun immortal fables six hundred years before Christ. Yet the truths he taught about human nature are just as true in Boston and Birmingham now as they were twenty-six centuries ago in Athens. The sun can make you take off your coat more quickly than the wind; and kindliness, the friendly approach and appreciation can make people change their minds more readily than all the bluster and storming in the world.

Remember what Lincoln said: "A drop of honey catches more flies than a gallon of gall."

Principle 4: Begin in a friendly way.

向他说明我的问题。我进一步指出：'我想你一定会非常关心那些不利于你的良好声誉的事情。'他感谢我告诉他这件事，并向我保证一定会解决我的问题。他不但亲自为我处理好了这件事，而且还在我的汽车送修期间，将他自己的车借给我使用。"

伊索是希腊克诺索斯王宫的一名奴隶，在基督降生之前600年他就说过许多不朽的寓言，其中有关人性的真理现在仍适用于我们，正如它在26个世纪以前适用于雅典一样。太阳能比风更快地使你脱下大衣；友谊和赞赏远比任何强权暴力更容易改变人的心意。

请记住林肯说的："一滴蜂蜜比一加仑胆汁能捕到更多的苍蝇。"

第四项法则：用友善的方法开始。

5 The Secret of Socrates

In talking with people, don't begin by discussing the things on which you differ. Begin by emphasizing—and keep on emphasizing—the things on which you agree. Keep emphasizing, if possible, that you are both striving for the same end and that your only difference is one of method and not of purpose.

Get the other person saying "Yes, yes" at the outset. Keep your opponent, if possible, from saying "No."

A "No" response, according to Professor Overstreet, is a most difficult handicap to overcome. When you have said "No," all your pride of personality demands that you remain consistent with yourself. You may later feel that the "No" was ill-advised; nevertheless, there is your precious pride to consider! Once having said a thing, you feel you must stick to it. Hence it is of the very greatest importance that a person be started in the affirmative direction.

The skillful speaker gets, at the outset, a number of "Yes" responses. This sets the psychological process of the listeners moving in the affirmative direction. It is like the movement of a billiard ball. Propel in one direction, and it takes some force to deflect it; far more force to send it back in the opposite direction.

The psychological patterns here are quite clear. When a person says "No" and really means it, he or she is doing far more than saying a word of two letters. The entire organism—glandular, nervous, muscular—gathers itself together into a condition of rejection. There is, usually in minute but sometimes in observable degree, a physical withdrawal or readiness for withdrawal. The whole neuromuscular system, in short, sets itself on guard against acceptance. When, to the contrary, a person says "Yes," none of the withdrawal activities takes place. The organism is in a forward-moving, accepting, open attitude. Hence the more "Yeses" we can, at the very outset, induce, the more likely we are to succeed in capturing the attention for our ultimate proposal.

It is a very simple technique—this yes response. And yet, how much it is neglected! It often

第5章 苏格拉底的秘诀

与人交谈时，不要一开始就讨论你们有分歧的事。刚开始应先强调——并且不断地强调——你们都同意的事。继而强调——如果可能的话——你们双方都在追求同一目标，你们之间的唯一差别只是在方法上，而不是在目标上。

应该让对方在刚开始的时候就说“是，是”。如果有可能，应该使他避免说“不”。

一个“不”的反应，根据奥弗斯特里特教授的观点，是最难克服的障碍。一旦你说出“不”以后，你所有的自尊都会促使你固执己见。过后你也许觉得“不”是不甚恰当的，然而你得考虑自己那宝贵的自尊！一旦一句话说出口，你觉得就要坚持到底。所以，一开始就使人采取肯定的态度极为重要。

善于讲话的人，常常一开始就会获得“是”的反应，从而将听者的心理导向肯定的方向。这就好比打弹子球：向前方击球之后，要使其转向就得费些力气；要使其反向弹回就需要更大的力气了。

人的心理模式在此明显可见。当一个人说“不”，而且内心也确实否定的话，那么他的所作所为远非一两个词所能包容。他全身的组织——腺体、神经系统、肌肉——全都会协调起来，进入抗拒状态，并且常常伴有细微的、时而可见的身体收缩，或准备收缩的状态。简而言之，他的整个神经和肌肉系统会处于一种紧急抗拒的状态。相反，当一个人说“是”的时候，就不会出现这种收缩现象，而且他的身体处于前进、接受和开放状态。因此，如果我们在一开始的时候越能造成“是的，是的”谈话气氛，就越容易使对方同意我们的观点。

这是一种很简单的方法，但是却很容易被人忽略！一般来说，人们一开始即采取反对态度，

seems as if people get a sense of their own importance by antagonizing others at the outset.

Get a student to say "No"at the beginning,or a customer,child,husband,or wife,and it takes the wisdom and the patience of angels to transform that bristling negative into an affirmative.

The use of this "yes,yes"technique enabled James Eberson,who was a teller in the Greenwich Savings Bank,in New York City,to secure a prospective customer who might otherwise have been lost.

"This man came in to open an account,"said Mr.Eberson,"and I gave him our usual form to fill out.Some of the questions he answered willingly,but there were others he flatly refused to answer.

"Before I began the study of human relations,I would have told this prospective depositor that if he refused to give the bank this information,we should have to refuse to accept this account.I am ashamed that I have been guilty of doing that very thing in the past.Naturally,an ultimatum like that made me feel good.I had shown who was boss,that the bank's rules and regulations couldn't be flouted.But that sort of attitude certainly didn't give a feeling of welcome and importance to the man who had walked in to give us his patronage.

"I resolved this morning to use a little horse sense.I resolved not to talk about what the bank wanted but about what the customer wanted.And above all else,I was determined to get him saying 'yes,yes'from the very start.So I agreed with him.I told him the information he refused to give was not absolutely necessary.

"'However,'I said,'suppose you have money in this bank at your death.Wouldn't you like to have the bank transfer it to your next of kin,who is entitled to it according to law?'

"'Yes,of course,'he replied.

"'don't you think,'I continued,'that it would be a good idea to give us the name of your next of kin so that,in the event of your death,we could carry out your wishes without error or delay?'

"Again he said,'Yes.'

"The young man's attitude softened and changed when he realized that we weren't raking for this information for our sake but for his sake.Before leaving the bank,this young man not only gave

这样似乎能得到一种自重感。

如果一开始就使一名学生或顾客、孩子、丈夫或妻子说"不",那恐怕要有神仙般的智慧和耐心,才能使那种绝对否定变为肯定。

正是用这种"是,是"的方法,使得纽约格林威治储蓄所的一位出纳员詹姆斯·艾伯森挽回了一位差点儿流失的顾客。

"这个人进来要开一个账户,"艾伯森先生说,"我让他填写一些常规表格,其中有些问题他愿意回答,但有些问题他却根本不想回答。

"在我开始学习人际关系之前,我会告诉这位顾客说,如果他不向银行提供这些材料,我们就拒绝为他开户。我对我以前这样做感到很惭愧。自然,那样的最后通牒使我觉得很痛快。我显示了这里究竟是谁说话算数,银行的规章制度不能违反。但那样的态度显然让那些来我们银行的人得不到一种受欢迎和重视的感觉。

"那天早晨,我决定采用待人处世的常识。我决定不谈银行的规矩,而谈顾客的需要。最重要的是,我决意使他从一开始就说'是,是'。所以我同意了他的做法。我告诉他,他拒绝填写的那些材料并不是绝对必要的。

"'然而,'我说,'假如你把钱存在银行,而你不幸去世了,你不希望银行将钱转移给你依照法律有权继承的直系亲属吗?'

"'不,当然希望。'他回答说。

"'难道你不认为,'我继续说,'将你的直系亲属的名字告诉我们,使我们在你万一去世的时候准确无误地实现你的愿望,不是一个很好的办法吗?"

"他又说:'是的。'

"当他明白我们需要这些材料不是为了我们,而是为了他的时候,他的态度软化下来,改变

me complete information about himself but he opened, at my suggestion, a trust account, naming his mother as the beneficiary for his account, and he had gladly answered all the questions concerning his mother also.

"I found that by getting him to say 'yes, yes' from the outset, he forgot the issue at stake and was happy to do all the things I suggested."

Joseph Allison, a sales representative for Westinghouse Electric Company, had this story to tell: "There was a man in my territory that our company was most eager to sell to. My predecessor had called on him for ten years without selling anything. When I took over the territory, I called steadily for three years without getting an order. Finally, after thirteen years of calls and sales talk, we sold him a few motors. If these proved to be all right, an order for several hundred more would follow. Such was my expectation.

"Right? I knew they would be all right. So when I called three weeks later, I was in high spirits.

"The chief engineer greeted me with this shocking announcement, 'Allison, I can't buy the remainder of the motors from you.'

"'Why?' I asked in amazement. 'Why?'

"'Because your motors are too hot. I can't put my hand on them.'

"I knew it wouldn't do any good to argue. I had tried that sort of thing too long. So I thought of getting the 'yes, yes' response.

"'Well, now look, Mr. Smith,' I said. 'I agree with you a hundred percent; if those motors are running too hot, you ought not to buy any more of them. You must have motors that won't run any hotter than standards set by the National Electrical Manufacturers Association. Isn't that so?'

"He agreed it was. I had gotten my first 'yes.'

"'the Electrical Manufacturers Association regulations say that a properly designed motor may have a temperature of 72 degrees Fahrenheit above room temperature. Is that correct?'

"'Yes,' he agreed. 'that's quite correct. But your motors are much hotter.'

"I didn't argue with him. I merely asked: 'How hot is the mill room?'

"'Oh,' he said, 'about 75 degrees Fahrenheit.'

了。在离开银行以前,这年轻人不仅将关于他自己的全部材料告诉了我,并且根据我的建议,还开了一个信托账户,指定他的母亲为受益人,而且十分高兴地回答了关于他母亲的各种问题。

"我发现一旦让他开始就说'是,是'时,他便忘了我们之间的争执,并且愿意做我所建议的事。"

约瑟夫·爱立森是西屋电气公司的销售代表,他讲了这个故事:"在我负责的区域中有一个人,我们公司极想将商品推销给他。我的前任曾拜访了他 10 年,但没有卖出任何东西。当我接管这片区域以后,我继续拜访了 3 年,也没得到一份订单。最后,在 13 年的拜访和交易会谈之后,我们卖了几台发动机给他。如果这些发动机不出毛病,我相信一定可以再得到几百台的订货单。而这正是我期望的。

"正常吗?我知道这些发动机不会有问题。所以,当我在 3 个星期后去拜访时,我很高兴。

"但那位总工程师令我吃惊地说:'爱立森,我不能向你订购剩余的发动机了。'

"'为什么?'我惊讶地问,'为什么?'

"'因为你的发动机太热了,我的手都不能放在上面。'

"我知道争论是没有用的,那种方法我已经试过很久了。所以我想到了获得'是,是'的反应。

"'噢,现在,史密斯先生,'我说,'我完全同意你的看法。如果那些发动机工作起来太热了,你就不应再买。你当然不会购买超过全国电气制造协会标准热度的发动机,是不是?'

"他同意这一点。我已经得到了我的第一个'是'。

"'电气制造协会的规定要求,正确设计的发动机可以比室内温度高华氏 72 度。对不对?'

"'是,'他同意说,'的确是那样。但你的发动机热多了。'

"我没有同他争论。我只问:'厂房有多热?'

"'Well,' I replied, 'if the mill room is 75 degrees and you add 72 to that, that makes a total of 147 degrees Fahrenheit. Wouldn't you scald your hand if you held it under a spigot of hot water at a temperature of 147 degrees Fahrenheit?'

"Again he had to say 'yes.'

"'Well,' I suggested, 'wouldn't it be a good idea to keep your hands off those motors?'

"'Well, I guess you're right,' he admitted. We continued to chat for a while. Then he called his secretary and lined up approximately $35,000 worth of business for the ensuing month.

"It took me years and cost me countless thousands of dollars in lost business before I finally learned that it doesn't pay to argue, that it is much more profitable and much more interesting to look at thing from the other person's viewpoint and try to get that person saying 'yes, yes.'"

Eddie Snow, who sponsors our courses in Oakland, California, tells how he became a good customer of a shop because the proprietor got him to say "yes, yes." Eddie had become interested in bow hunting and had spent considerable money in purchasing equipment and supplies from a local bow store. When his brother was visiting him he wanted to rent a bow for him from this store. The sales clerk told him they didn't rent bows, so Eddie phoned another bow store. Eddie described what happened:

"A very pleasant gentleman answered the phone. His response to my question for a rental was completely different from the other place. He said he was sorry but they no longer rented bows because they couldn't afford to do so. He then asked me if I had rented before. I replied, 'Yes, several years ago.' He reminded me that I probably paid $25 to $30 for the rental. I said 'yes' again. He then asked if I was the kind of person who liked to save money. Naturally, I answered 'yes.' He went on to explain that they had bow sets with all the necessary equipment on sale for $34.95. I could buy a complete set for only $4.95 more than I could rent one. He explained that is why they had discontinued renting them. Did I think that was reasonable? My 'yes' response led to a purchase of the set, and when I picked it up I purchased several more items at this shop and have since become a regular customer."

Socrates, "the gadfly of Athens," was one of the greatest philosophers the world has ever known. He did something that only a handful of men in all history have been able to do: he sharply

"'啊,'他说,'大约华氏 75 度。'

"'好,'我回答说,'如果厂房是 75 度,你再加上 72 度,总计华氏 147 度。如果你将手放在华氏 147 度的热水塞门下面,是不是烫手?'

"他还得说'是'。

"'那么,'我建议说,'别把手放在发动机上面,是不是更好呢?'

"'对,我想你是对的。'他承认说。接着我们又谈了片刻。然后他叫来他的秘书,给下一个月订了差不多价值 35000 美元的货物。

"我费了多年的工夫,丢了许多生意,损失了数不清的钱,最后才明白争论是没有用的。只有从别人的立场来分析问题,使他说'是,是',才会有更多的收益,才会更有乐趣。"

爱迪·史诺是我们在加州奥克兰克的课程负责人。他讲了他是如何成为一家商店的忠诚顾客的,因为店主让他说"是,是"。爱迪对弓箭狩猎很感兴趣,花了不少钱在当地一个弓箭商店购置器材和装备。有一次他弟弟来看他,他想去商店为弟弟租一套弓。店伙计说他们不租借,于是爱迪给另一家商店打电话租用弓箭。他描述了经过:

"一位温和的男士接的电话。他对我租借弓箭的回答与其他商店完全不同。他表示非常遗憾,因为他们已经不提供这种服务了。然后他问我以前是否租过,我说:'是的,几年前租过。'他提醒我,当时租金应该是 25 至 30 美元。我又说:'是的。'他又问我是不是喜欢节约的人,我当然说'是的'。他继续解释他们有一种弓(包括所有小装备)只售 34.95 美元。我只需比租金多付 4.95 美元就可以买到一整套。他解释这就是他们不再租借的缘故,并问我这是不是很合理。我的肯定回答使我买了一套。当我买下那套弓时,又买了其他东西,并成为一位常客。"

"雅典的牛蝇"苏格拉底,是世界上最伟大的哲学家。他所做的事情在历史上只有几个人能够做到:他彻底改变了人类思想的进程;而现在,在他死去 24 个世纪后,他仍被尊为世界上最

changed the whole course of human thought; and now, twenty-four centuries after his death, he is honored as one of the wisest persuaders who ever influenced this wrangling world.

His method? Did he tell people they were wrong? Oh, no, not Socrates. He was far too adroit for that. His whole technique, now called the "Socratic method," was based upon getting a "yes, yes" response. He asked questions with which his opponent would have to agree. He kept on winning one admission after another until he had an armful of yeses. He kept on asking questions until finally, almost without realizing it, his opponents found themselves embracing a conclusion they would have bitterly denied a few minutes previously.

The next time we are tempted to tell someone he or she is wrong, let's remember old Socrates and ask a gentle question—a question that will get the "yes, yes" response.

The Chinese have a proverb pregnant with the age-old wisdom of the Orient: "He who treads softly goes far."

They have spent five thousand years studying human nature, those cultured Chinese, and they have garnered a lot of perspicacity: "*He who treads softly goes far.*"

Principle 5: Get the other person saying "yes, Yes" immediately.

有才智的劝说者。

他的方法是什么?他是否告诉别人他们是错误的?啊,没有,苏格拉底才不会那样做呢。他是如此老练,绝不会那样做。他的整套方法现在被称为"苏格拉底方法",以得到"是,是"的反应为基础。他问的问题都是反对者必然会同意的。他持续不断地得到一个又一个同意,直到得到许多"是"。他持续不断地发问,最后反对者不知不觉地发现自己得出的结论竟是他们在几分钟前坚决反对的。

如果我们下次想告诉某人是错误的时候,不要忘了苏格拉底,问一个温和的问题——一个能得到"是,是"的回答的问题。

中国人有句格言,充满了东方人悠久的智慧:"轻履者行远。"

中国人花了5000年研究人类的天性,因而学问至深,积累了极其丰富的人生经验。

第五项法则:使对方立刻说"是,是"。

6 The Safety Valve in Handling Complaints

Most people trying to win others to their way of thinking do too much talking themselves.Let the other people talk themselves out.They know more about their business and problems than you do.So ask them questions.Let them tell you a few things.

If you disagree with them you may be tempted to interrupt.But don't.It is dangerous.They won't pay attention to you while they still have a lot of ideas of their own crying for expression.So listen patiently and with an open mind.Be sincere about it.Encourage them to express their ideas fully.

Does this policy pay in business?Let's see.Here is the story of a sales representative who was *forced* to try it.

One of the largest automobile manufacturers in the United States was negotiating for a year's requirements of upholstery fabrics.Three important manufacturers had worked up fabrics in sample bodies.These had all been inspected by the executives of the motor company,and notice had been sent to each manufacturer saying that,on a certain day,a representative from each supplier would be given an opportunity to make a final plea for the contract.

G.B.R.,a representative of one manufacturer,arrived in town with a severe attack of laryngitis."When it came my turn to meet the executives in conference,"Mr.R—said as he related the story before one of my classes,"I had lost my voice.I could hardly whisper.I was ushered into a room and found myself face to face with the textile engineer,the purchasing agent,the director of sales and the president of the company.I stood up and made a valiant effort to speak,but I couldn't do anything more than squeak.

"They were all seated around a table,so I wrote on a pad of paper:'Gentlemen,I have lost my voice.I am speechless.'

"'I'll do the talking for you,'the president said.He did.He exhibited my samples and praised their good points.A lively discussion arose about the merits of my goods.And the president,since he was talking for me,took the position I would have had during the discussion.My sole participation consisted of smiles, nods and a few gestures.

第6章 处理抱怨的灵丹妙药

大多数人想使别人同意他们的观点，可是他们自己的话却说得太多了。让别人畅所欲言吧！对于他们自己的事及他们自己的问题，他们一定知道得比你多。所以你应向他们提些问题，让他们告诉你几件事。

如果你不同意他们的观点，你可能想打断他们。但不要这样做，那是危险的。因为当他们还有许多意见急于发表的时候，他们是不会注意你的。所以，要以宽广的胸襟耐心倾听，要诚恳地鼓励对方充分地发表他们的意见。

在商场上这种策略有用吗？我们来看看。这是一位推销员被迫试行这一策略的经历。

美国最大的一家汽车制造公司，正在洽谈订购下一年度所需要的汽车坐垫布。三个重要的厂家已经做好了垫布的样品。这些样布都已经得到汽车公司高级职员的检验，并发通知给各厂家，说各厂家的代表有机会在某一天进行最后陈述。

其中一个厂家的业务代表R先生在抵达时，正患着严重的喉炎。“轮到我上会与高级职员面谈时，”R先生在我班上叙述他的经历时说，“我嗓子哑了。我几乎发不出一点声音。我被领到一个房间，与纺织工程师、采购经理、推销经理以及公司的总经理会晤。我站起来想尽力说话，但只能发出嘶哑的声音。

“他们都围坐在一张桌子边上，所以我在纸上写道：‘各位，我的嗓子哑了，不能说话。’

“‘让我替你说吧，’总经理说。他真的在替我说话。他展示了我的样品，并称赞了它们的优点。围绕我的样品的优点，展开了一场热烈的讨论。由于那位总经理代表我说话，因此在这场讨论中，他站在我这一边。而我在整个过程中只是微笑、点头以及做几个手势。

"As a result of this unique conference, I was awarded the contract, which called for over half a million yards of upholstery fabrics at an aggregate value of $1,600,000—the biggest order I had ever received.

"I know I would have lost the contract if I hadn't lost my voice, because I had the wrong idea about the whole proposition. I discovered, quite by accident, how richly it sometimes pays to let the other person do the talking."

Letting the other person do the talking helps in family situations as well as in business. Barbara Wilson's relationship with her daughter, Laurie, was deteriorating rapidly. Laurie, who had been a quiet, complacent child, had grown into an uncooperative, sometimes belligerent teenager. Mrs. Wilson lectured her, threatened her and punished her, but all to no avail.

"One day," Mrs. Wilson told one of our classes, "I just gave up. Laurie had disobeyed me and had left the house to visit her girl friend before she had completed her chores. When she returned I was about to scream at her for the ten-thousandth time, but I just didn't have the strength to do it. I just looked at her and said sadly, 'Why, Laurie, Why?'

"Laurie noted my condition and in a calm voice asked, 'do you really want to know?' I nodded and Laurie told me, first hesitantly, and then it all flowed out. I had never listened to her. I was always telling her to do this or that. When she wanted to tell me her thoughts, feelings, ideas, I interrupted with more orders. I began to realize that she needed me—not as a bossy mother, but as a confidante, an outlet for all her confusion about growing up. And all I had been doing was talking when I should have been listening. I never heard her.

"From that time on I let her do all the talking she wanted. She tells me what is on her mind, and our relationship has improved immeasurably. She is again a cooperative person."

A large advertisement appeared on the financial page of a New York newspaper calling for a person with unusual ability and experience. Charles T. Cubellis answered the advertisement, sending his reply to a box number. A few days later, he was invited by letter to call for an interview. Before he called, he spent hours in Wall Street finding out everything possible about the person who had founded the business. During the interview, he remarked, "I should be mighty proud to be associated with an organization with a record like yours. I understand you started twenty-eight years ago with

“这个特殊会议的结果，是我得到了这份合同，和对方签订了 50 万码的坐垫布，总价值为 160 万美元——这是我曾获得的最大的订单。

“我知道，如果我的嗓子没有哑，我就会失掉那份合同，因为我对于整个情况的看法是错误的。我很偶然地发现，有时候让别人多说话是多么有益！”

让别人说话，不仅适用于商业方面，而且适用于家庭事务。例如，芭芭拉·威尔逊和她的女儿洛瑞的关系迅速恶化。洛瑞以前是个文静乖巧的小孩，现在却成了一个缺乏合作精神，有时还会为自己辩护的孩子。威尔逊夫人曾用各种办法威吓、教训和惩罚她，但都无济于事。

“一天，”威尔逊夫人在我班上说，“我放弃了。洛瑞根本不听我的话，家务活还没做完就去找她的朋友。她回家时，我准备像往常那样骂她一顿，但我已经没有力气了。我看着她，伤心地说：‘为什么会这样呢？为什么？’

“洛瑞看出了我的痛苦，平静地问我：‘你真想知道？’我点点头。于是她告诉我一切情况：我从来没想过去听她的意见，总是命令她做这做那；当她想与我谈心时，我总是打断她，并给她更多的命令。我开始认识到，她其实很需要我——不是一个爱命令的母亲，而是一个亲密的朋友，使她可以倾诉成长的烦恼。而我过去在该听的时候却只顾说我自己的，我从来没听过她要说什么。

“从那以后，我总是让她畅所欲言。她告诉我她的心事，我们的关系大大改善。她也再次成为一个愿意合作的孩子。”

最近，纽约一家报纸的财经栏目中刊登了一幅巨大的广告，聘请一位有特殊能力和经验的人。查尔斯·科贝利斯应聘了，将资料寄给了信箱。几天以后，他接到了回信，约他面谈。去面谈之前，他在华尔街花了许多时间打听那个公司老板的有关情况。在面试的时候，他说：“如果能在你这家有着不凡经历的公司做事，我将十分自豪。我听说你在 28 年前开始创建这家公司时

nothing but desk room and one stenographer.Is that true?"

Almost every successful person likes to reminisce about his early struggles.This man was no exception.He talked for a long time about how he had started with $450 in cash and an original idea.He told how he had fought against discouragement and battled against ridicule,worked on Sundays and holidays,twelve to sixteen hours a day; how he had finally won against all odds until now the most important executives on Wall Street were coming to him for information and guidance. He was proud of such a record.He had a right to be,and he had a splendid time telling about it. Finally,he questioned Mr.Cubellis briefly about his experience,then called in one of his vice presidents and said,"I think this is the person we are looking for."

Mr.Cubellis had taken the trouble to frind out about the accomplishments of his prospective employer.He showed an interest in the other person and his problems.He encouraged the other person to do most of the talking—and made a favorable impression.

Roy G.Bradley of Sacramento,California,had the opposite problem.He listened as a good prospect for a sales position talked himself into a job with Bradley's firm.Roy reported:

"Being a small brokerage firm,we had no fringe benefits,such as hospitalization,medical insurance and pensions.Every representative is an independent agent.Richard Pryor had the type of experience we wanted for this position,and he was interviewed first by my assistant,who told him about all the negatives related to this job.He seemed slightly discouraged when he came into my office.I mentioned the one benefit of being associated with my firm,that of being an independent contractor and therefore virtually being self-employed.

"As he talked about these advantages to me,he talked himself out of each negative thought he had when he came in for the interview.Several times it seemed as though he was half talking to himself as he was thinking through each thought.At times I was tempted to add to his thoughts; however,as the interview came to a close I felt he had convinced himself,very much on his own, that he would like to work for my firm.

"Because I had been a good listener and let Dick do most of the talking,he was able to weigh both sides fairly in his mind,and he came to the positive conclusion,which was a challenge he created for himself.We hired him and he has been an outstanding representative for our firm."

什么也没有,只有一张桌子、一间办公室、一位速记员。那是真的吗?"

差不多每个成功的人都喜欢回忆他早年的奋斗。这个老板也不例外。他谈了许久,例如他如何依靠450美元现金及富有创意的思想开始创业。他还讲了他如何与失望、讥笑作斗争,如何在星期日及节假日照常工作,每天工作12~16小时,以及他最后如何战胜所有的厄运,直到现在华尔街的一些要人都来向他请教。他对自己的过去很自豪。他有这种权力,并且很高兴地讲述这些事。最后,他简单地问了问科贝利斯的经历,然后把一位副经理叫进来,说:"我想这就是我们正在寻找的人。"

科贝利斯先生不厌其烦地调查他未来老板的成就,而且对对方及对方的问题表示出感兴趣。他鼓励对方多说话,因此给对方留下了很好的印象。

加利福尼亚州圣克拉蒙托市的洛伊·布莱德雷,正好遇到了一件相反的事。当一个很适合担任公司推销工作的人在做自我说服工作时,他只是静静地听着。洛伊说:

"作为一家小中介公司,我们没有什么福利,如住院、医疗保险和养老金等。每个代表都是独立代理商。理查德·普莱尔具有担任这项工作的经验。他先是和我的助手面谈,我的助手把这项工作所有的不利之处都告诉了他。当他走进我的办公室时,好像无精打采的样子。但我提到了一个与我公司合作的有利之处,即我们公司是一个独立承包商,因此他实际上也是一个老板。

"当他分析了这方面的有利之处以后,他抛弃了当初面试时一切不利的想法。在他谈话的过程中,几乎常常是在对自己说那些话。我也不时地肯定他的想法;不过,当面谈结束时,我认为他已经说服了他自己,并决定来我公司工作。

"由于我当了一个好听众,使他可以畅所欲言,可以在内心进行权衡,并做出了积极的结论。这正是他对自己的一次挑战。因此,我录用了他,而他也成为我们公司杰出的代表。"

Even our friends would much rather talk to us about their achievements than listen to us boast about ours.

La Rochefoucauld, the French philosopher, said, "If you want enemies, excel your friends; but if you want friends, let your friends excel you."

Why is that true? Because when our friends excel us, they feel important; but when we excel them, they—or at least some of them—will feel inferior and envious.

By far the best-liked placement counselor in the Midtown Personnel Agency in New York City was Henrietta G—. It hadn't always been that way. During the first few months of her association with the agency, Henrietta didn't have a single friend among her colleagues. Why? Because every day she would brag about the placements she had made, the new accounts she had opened, and anything else she had accomplished.

"I was good at my work and proud of it," Henrietta told one of our classes. "But instead of my colleagues sharing my triumphs, they seemed to resent them. I wanted to be liked by these people. I really wanted them to be my friends. After listening to some of the suggestions made this course, I started to talk about myself less and listen more to my associates. They also had things to boast about and were more excited about telling me about their accomplishments than about listening to my boasting. Now, when we have some time to chat, I ask them to share their joys with me, and I only mention my achievements when they ask."

Principle 6: Let the other person do a great deal of the talking.

即使是我们的朋友,也宁愿只谈论他们的成就,而不愿意听我们夸显自己。

法国哲学家拉·罗什弗科说:"如果你想结下仇人,那你可以比你的朋友表现得更出色;但如果你想要赢得朋友,就要让你的朋友胜过你。"

为什么这是对的呢?因为当我们的朋友胜过我们时,他们就会获得自重感;但是当我们胜过他们时,就会使他们感到自卑和妒忌。

在纽约市中区人事局,与别人关系最融洽的就业顾问是亨丽塔女士。但过去情况可不是这样的。当亨丽塔刚到人事局时,她有好几个月都没有在同事中交到一个朋友。原因何在?因为她每天都在谈她工作上的业绩、她在银行新开的户头,以及她所做的每一件事。

"我的工作干得确实不错,我一直感到很骄傲。"亨丽塔在我班上说。"但我那些同事不但不愿与我分享我的成就,而且好像还很不高兴。我渴望得到这些人的喜欢,真的想使他们成为我的朋友。在听了辅导课中提出来的建议之后,我开始少谈我自己,而多听我的同事说话。其实,他们也有许多值得夸耀的事,把他们的事情告诉我,比听我吹自己更让他们高兴。现在,每当我们在一起聊天时,我会让他们多说话,与他们共同分享快乐。只有他们问我的时候,我才说我的情况。"

第六项法则:让别人多说话。

7 How to Get Co-operation

Don't you have much more faith in ideas that you discover for yourself than in ideas that are handed to you on a silver platter?If so,isn't it bad judgment to try to ram your opinions down the throats of other people?Isn't it wiser to make suggestions—and let the other person think out the conclusion?

Adolph Seltz of Philadelphia,sales manager in an automobile showroom and a student in one of my courses,suddenly found himself confronted with the necessity of injecting enthusiasm into a discouraged and disorganized group of automobile salespeople.Calling a sales meeting,he urged his people to tell him exactly what they expected from him.As they talked,he wrote their ideas on the blackboard.He then said,"I'll give you all these qualities you expect from me.Now I want you to tell me what I have a right to expect from you."The replies came quick and fast:loyalty,honesty, initiative,optimism,teamwork,eight hours a day of enthusiastic work.The meeting ended with a new courage,a new inspiration—one salesperson volunteered to work fourteen hours a day—and Mr. Seltz reported to me that the increase of sales was phenomenal.

"The people had made a sort of moral bargain with me,"said Mr.Seltz,"and as long as I lived up to my part in it,they were determined to live up to theirs.Consulting them about their wishes and desires was just the shot in the arm they needed."

No one likes to feel that he or she is being sold something or told to do a thing.We much prefer to feel that we are buying of our own accord or acting on our own ideas.We like to be consulted about our wishes,our wants,our thoughts.

Take the case of Eugene Wesson.He lost countless thousands of dollars in commissions before he learned this truth.Mr.Wesson sold sketches for a studio that created designs for stylists and textile manufacturers.Mr.Wesson had called on one of the leading stylists in New York once a week,every week for three years."He never refused to see me,"said Mr.Wesson,"but he never bought.He always looked over my sketches very carefully and then said,'No,Wesson,I guess we Don't get together today.'"

After 150 failures,Wesson realized he must be in a mental rut,so he resolved to devote one

第7章 如何赢得合作

你对于自己发现的思想是不是比别人的思想更为信仰？即使别人的思想放在一只银盘子里递给你。如果是这样,那么你想将你的想法硬塞进别人的喉咙,岂不是一厢情愿?提出建议,再让别人去想出结论,这是不是更明智?

费城的阿道夫·塞尔兹先生是一家汽车展示中心的销售经理,也是我班上学员,他迫切地感到有必要给一群沮丧而散漫的汽车推销员打气加油。于是,他召开了一次销售会议,鼓励他的部下如实说出他们对他的期望。在他们说这些的时候,他将他们的想法都写在黑板上。然后他说:"我可以满足你们对我的全部要求。现在，请你们告诉我，我有权利从你们那里得到什么?"大家的回答很迅速:忠心、诚实、主动、乐观、合作,以及每天8小时的热情工作。会议开得十分成功,给人以新的勇气、新的激励。有一个人甚至自告奋勇地要求每天工作14个小时。塞尔兹告诉我,销售很自然就上升了。

塞尔兹先生说:"他们实际上是在和我做一种道德交易。在我保证尽我所能时,他们也决定尽其所能。和他们商讨他们的愿望和希望,正是他们所需要的精神食粮。"

没有人喜欢觉得自己是在被迫去买什么东西或被命令去做某件事。我们宁愿觉得我们是自愿购买的,或遵循自己的意念在做事。我们喜欢别人关心我们的愿望、需要及想法。

就拿尤金·威森来说吧。在懂得这一真理之前,他不知损失了多少收入。威森替一家专门为时装设计师及纺织品制造商设计花样的画室推销图样。威森曾连续3年每周一次地拜访纽约一位时装设计领军人物。"他从未拒绝见我。"威森说,"但也从来没有买过我的图样。他总是仔细地看我的图样,然后说:'不行,威森。我想今天我们不能要你的东西。'

evening a week to the study of influencing human behavior, to help him develop new ideas and generate new enthusiasm.

He decided on this new approach. With half a dozen unfinished artists' sketches under his arm, he rushed over to the buyer's office. "I want you to do me a favor, if you will," he said. "Here are some uncompleted sketches. Won't you please tell me how we could finish them up in such a way that you could use them?"

The buyer looked at the sketches for a while without uttering a word. Finally he said, "Leave these with me for a few days, Wesson, and then come back and see me."

Wesson returned three days later, got his suggestions, took the sketches back to the studio and had them finished according to the buyer's ideas. The result? All accepted.

After that, this buyer ordered scores of other sketches from Wesson, all drawn according to the buyer's ideas. "I realized why I had failed for years to sell him," said Mr. Wesson. "I had urged him to buy what I thought he ought to have. Then I changed my approach completely. I urged him to give me his ideas. This made him feel that he was creating the designs. And he was. I didn't have to sell him. He bought."

Letting the other person feel that the idea is his or hers not only works in business and politics, it works in family life as well. Paul M. Davis of Tulsa, Oklahoma, told his class how he applied this principle:

"My family and I enjoyed one of the most interesting sightseeing vacation trips we have ever taken. I had long dreamed of visiting such historic sites as the Civil War battlefield in Gettysburg, Independence Hall in Philadelphia, and our nation's capital. Valley Forge, Jamestown and the restored colonial village of Williamsburg were high on the list of things I wanted to see.

"In March my wife, Nancy, mentioned that she had ideas for our summer vacation which included a tour of the western states, visiting points of interest in New Mexico, Arizona, California and Nevada. She had wanted to make this trip for several years. But we couldn't obviously make both trips.

"Our daughter, Anne, had just completed a course in U.S. history in junior high school and had become very interested in the events that had shaped our country's growth. I asked her how she would like to visit the places she had learned about on our next vacation. She said she would love to.

"Two evenings later as we sat around the dinner table, Nancy announced that if we all agreed,

经历了150次失败以后，威森终于明白自己一定是陷于心理故辙之中，于是他决定每星期用一个晚上的时间学习为人处世的技巧，努力培养新观念，激发新的热情。

他决定尝试一种新的方法。他拿了6张画家们还没有完成的图样，跑到那位设计师的办公室。“我想请你帮我一个忙。”他说，“这里有一些还没有完成的图样。你能不能告诉我，我们应该怎样完成才能使你满意?’

这位设计师默默地看了图样一会儿，然后说：“将图样放在我这里，你过几天再来找我。”

威森3天之后又去找他，听取了他的建议，取回了图样，并按照设计师的意见把它们画完。结果呢?它们全都被买下了。

从那以后，这位买主又订了几十张图样，全都是按照他的意见画的。“我现在明白，为什么我这么多年不能和这位买主做成生意了，”威森先生说。“以前我一味劝他购买我以为他应该买的。后来我改变策略，请他告诉我他的想法。这使他觉得是他在创造图样，并且也的确是这样。我不必向他推销，他会主动来买。”

让别人认为某个主意是他的，这种策略不仅可以用在商业和政坛中，还可以用在家庭生活中。俄克拉荷马州吐萨市的保罗·戴维斯就在他班上讲了他是如何运用这一法则的。

“我家人和我共同度过了一次最有意义的旅行。我早就想能去游览葛底斯堡内战战场、费城独立大厅等历史古迹，以及我们国家的首都。就连法吉谷、詹姆斯镇以及威廉斯堡遗留至今的殖民时代的村庄，也被我列入了游览的名单中。

“三月份，我妻子南茜向我提出了她的暑假计划，包括游览西部各州，以及新墨西哥州、伊利桑那州、加利福尼亚州、内华达州的旅游胜地。她已经有好几年都在想着去这些地方了。但是，我们显然不能达成一致。

“我们的女儿安妮刚上完初中的美国历史，对于美国历史上的重大事件极感兴趣。我问她

the summer's vacation would be to the eastern states, that it would be a great trip for Anne and thrilling for all of us. We all concurred."

This same psychology was used by an X-ray manufacturer to sell his equipment to one of the largest hospitals in Brooklyn. This hospital was building an addition and preparing to equip it with the finest X-ray department in America. Dr. L—, who was in charge of the X-ray department, was overwhelmed with sales representatives, each caroling the praises of his own company's equipment.

One manufacturer, however, was more skillful. He knew far more about handling human nature than the others did. He wrote a letter something like this:

> Our factory has recently completed a new line of X-ray equipment. The first shipment of these machines has just arrived at our office. They are not perfect. We know that, and we want to improve them. So we should be deeply obligated to you if you could find time to look them over and give us your ideas about how they can be made more serviceable to your profession. Knowing how occupied you are, I shall be glad to send my car for you at any hour you specify.

"I was surprised to get that letter," Dr. L—said as he related the incident before the class. "I was both surprised and complimented. I had never had an X-ray manufacturer seeking my advice before. It made me feel important. I was busy every night that week, but I canceled a dinner appointment in order to look over the equipment. The more I studied it, the more I discovered for myself how much I liked it.

"Nobody had tried to sell it to me. I felt that the idea of buying that equipment for the hospital was my own. I sold myself on its superior qualities and ordered it installed."

Ralph Waldo Emerson in his essay *"Self-Reliance"* stated: "In every work of genius we recognize our own rejected thoughts; they come back to us with a certain alienated majesty."

Colonel Edward M. House wielded an enormous influence in national and international affairs while Woodrow Wilson occupied the White House. Wilson leaned upon Colonel House for secret counsel and advice more than he did upon even members of his own cabinet.

What method did the Colonel use in influencing the President? Fortunately, we know, for House himself revealed it to Arthur D. Howden Smith, and Smith quoted House in an article in *The Saturday Evening Post*.

"'After I got to know the President,' House said, 'I learned the best way to convert him to an

是否喜欢在度假时去看看她学到的那些地方，她说非常喜欢。

“两天后，我们一家围桌而坐。南茜说，如果我们都同意的话，那么夏天暑假就去东部各州，这不仅对安妮很有意义，而且对大家也是一件值得高兴的事。我们都同意了。”

一位X光机器制造商也利用同样的心理策略，把他的机器卖给了布鲁克林最大的一家医院。这家医院正在扩建，准备设置全美国最好的X光科。L博士是X光部的主任，他被推销员重重包围，每个人都极力吹嘘自己的机器。

但是，有一位制造商却更有技巧。他比其他人更了解为人处世之道。他写了下面这封信：

> 我们公司最近研制成功一种新型X光机器。这种机器的第一批货刚运到我们办公室。它们还不是十全十美。我们深知这一点，因此希望能改进。所以，如果你能抽空来看一看，为我们提出你的宝贵意见，使它们更适合你们这个行业，我们将不胜感激。我知道你很忙，我很乐意在你指定的任何时间派车来接你。

“我接到那封信时很惊讶，”L博士在班上叙述这件事时说，“又觉得备受恭维。以前从来没有一个X光设备制造商征求过我的意见。这使我觉得很受重视。那个星期我每天晚上都在忙着，但为了去看那机器，我取消了一次约会。我越研究，就越发现我很喜欢那机器。

“没有人试图向我推销。我觉得为医院买那套设备完全是我自己的主意。我对那台设备的优点很满意，买了下来，把它装在医院。”

爱默生在他的散文《依靠自己》中说：“在天才的每一项创造中，我们都看到了被我们排斥的想法；这些想法再次展现在我们面前时，却显得相当伟大。”

爱德华·豪斯上校在伍德罗·威尔逊总统执政时期，在国内外事务方面具有很大的影响。威尔逊对豪斯的秘密策划及建议的依赖，比对他自己的内阁成员还多。

豪斯上校是用什么方法影响总统的呢？我们有幸得知答案，因为豪斯自己曾对亚瑟·豪登·史密斯

idea was to plant it in his mind casually, but so as to interest him in it so as to get him thinking about it on his own account. The first time this worked it was an accident. I had been visiting him at the White House and urged a policy on him which he appeared to disapprove. But several days later, at the dinner table, I was amazed to hear him trot out my suggestion as his own.'"

Did House interrupt him and say, "That's not your idea. That's mine"? Oh, no. Not House. He was too adroit for that. He didn't care about credit. He wanted results. So he let Wilson continue to feel that the idea was his. House did even more than that. He gave Wilson public credit for these ideas.

Let's remember that everyone we come in contact with is just as human as Woodrow Wilson. So let's use Colonel House's technique.

A man up in the beautiful Canadian province of New Brunswick used this technique on me and won my patronage. I was planning at the time to do some fishing and canoeing in New Brunswick. So I wrote the tourist bureau for information. Evidently my name and address were put on a mailing list, for I was immediately overwhelmed with scores of letters and booklets and printed testimonials from camps and guides. I was bewildered. I didn't know which to choose. Then one camp owner did a clever thing. He sent me the names and telephone numbers of several New York people who had stayed at his camp and he invited me to telephone them and discover for myself what he had to offer.

I found to my surprise that I knew one of the men on his list. I telephoned him, found out what his experience had been, and then wired the camp the date of my arrival.

The others had been trying to sell me on their service, but one let me sell myself. That organization won.

Twenty-five centuries ago, Lao-tse, a Chinese sage, said some things that readers of this book might use today:

"*The reason why rivers and seas receive the homage of a hundred mountain streams is that they keep below them. Thus they are able to reign over all the mountain streams. So the sage, wishing to be above men, putteth himself below them; wishing to be before them, he putteth himself behind them. Thus, though his place be above men, they do not feel his weight; though his place be before them, they do not count it an injury.*"

Principle 7: Let the other person feel that the idea is his or hers.

说过,而史密斯又在《星期天晚报》的一篇文章中引用了他的话。

"'认识总统以后,'豪斯说,'我发现,要使他相信某一种观念的最好方法,就是将它很自然地植于他心中,并巧妙地使他对此产生兴趣,并经常思考。这方法第一次奏效纯属巧合。我曾去白宫拜访他,劝他推行某项他似乎不太赞成的政策。但几天以后在一次聚餐的时候,我很惊讶地听到他把我的那个提议当作他自己的意见说了出来。'"

豪斯是否阻止了总统,说"那不是你的意见,而是我的"呢?哦,没有。豪斯不会那样。他非常聪明,不屑于居功,只求行事有效。所以他使威尔逊继续认为那意见是他自己想出来的。不仅如此,他还使威尔逊因为公开了这些意见而获得了世人的赞誉。

一定要记住,我们接触的人也许正像威尔逊一样。所以,我们应采用豪斯上校的做法。

一个住在加拿大美丽的新布伦斯维克省的人就对我用了这一方法,由此得到了我的光顾。那时我正计划去那里划船钓鱼,所以我写信给旅行社打听相关情况。我的姓名、住址显然被列入了公开信息中,因为我立刻就收到了从野营处与向导处寄来的几十封信、小册子和印刷品。我差点儿糊涂了,不知该选择哪一家。不久,有一位野营处的主人做了一件很聪明的事。他送给我几个他曾接待过的纽约人的姓名及电话号码,请我给他们打电话,让我自己调查他的情况。

我很惊异地发现,我竟然认识名单上的一个人。我打电话给他,打听他对这个野营处的印象和感受,然后打电话给野营处,告诉了我到达的日期。

其他人都强行向我推销,但这个野营处却让我自己做出安排,因此他胜利了。

2500 年以前,中国的一位圣人老子曾讲了本书的读者今天仍然可以应用的话:

"江海所以能为百谷王者,以其善下之,故能为百谷王。是以欲上民,必以言下之;欲先民,必以身后之。是以圣人处上而民不重,处前而民不害。"

第七项法则:使别人觉得那是他的主意。

8 A Formula That Will Work Wonders for You

Remember that other people may be totally wrong.But they don't think so.Don't condemn them. Any fool can do that.Try to understand them.Only wise,tolerant,exceptional people even try to do that.

There is a reason why the other man thinks and acts as he does.Ferret out that reason—and you have the key to his actions,perhaps to his personality.

Try honestly to put yourself in his place.

If you say to yourself, "How would I feel,how would I react if I were in his shoes?"you will save yourself time and irritation,for "by becoming interested in the cause,we are less likely to dislike the effect."And,in addition,you will sharply increase your skill in human relationships.

"Stop a minute,"says Kenneth M.Goode in his book *How to Turn People Into Gold*, "stop a minute to contrast your keen interest in your own affairs with your mild concern about anything else.Realize then,that everybody else in the world feels exactly the same way! Then,along with Lincoln and Roosevelt,you will have grasped the only solid foundation for interpersonal relationships; namely,that success in dealing with people depends on a sympathetic grasp of the other person's viewpoint."

Sam Douglas of Hempstead,New York,used to tell his wife that she spent too much time working on their lawn,pulling weeds,fertilizing,cutting the grass twice a week when the lawn didn't look any better than it had when they moved into their home four years earlier.Naturally,she was distressed by his remarks,and each time he made such remarks the balance of the evening was ruined.

After taking our course,Mr.Douglas realized how foolish he had been all those years.It never occurred to him that she enjoyed doing that work and she might really appreciate a compliment on her diligence.

One evening after dinner,his wife said she wanted to pull some weeds and invited him to keep

第8章 从对方的立场看问题

要记住,别人也许完全错了,但他们却不这么想。不要指责别人,任何傻子都会那样做;而要尽量了解别人,那才是明智大度、超凡不俗的人应该做的。

对方之所以会那样思考和行动,自有其道理。如果能找出那个原因,你就找到了理解他的行为和人格的钥匙。

试着真诚地站在别人的立场思考问题。

假如你对自己说:"如果我处在他的情况下,我将有何感受,有何反应?"那么你就可省去许多时间与不必要的烦恼,因为"如果对原因发生兴趣,我们就不会厌恶结果"。而且除此之外,你还可以大大增加你的为人处世技巧。

"暂停一分钟,"肯尼斯·古德在他的作品《如何使人变得高贵》中说,"暂停一分钟,比较一下你对自己事情的浓厚兴趣和对别的事情的漠不关心。然后你就会明白,世界上任何其他人也都是同样的态度。然后,你就会像林肯、罗斯福一样,能从容应对任何事情了。换句话说,为人处世成功与否,全在于你能否以同情之心接受别人的观点。"

萨姆·道格拉斯住在纽约的汉普斯特市,他以前总是指责妻子浪费太多时间去修整家中的草地、拔杂草、施肥和剪花草,还每个星期做两遍,可是草地看上去并不比4年前他们搬来住时更好看。这种话当然让他妻子十分不高兴,因此每当他这样批评她时,整个晚上家中就会笼罩一片乌云。

在参加我们的课程之后,道格拉斯先生认识到了他这些年的错误。他从来都没有想过,她在修整草地时也会从中获得快乐,以及她渴望由此得到的夸奖。

her company.He first declined,but then thought better of it and went out after her and began to help her pull weeds.She was visibly pleased,and together they spent an hour in hard work and pleasant conversation.

After that he often helped her with the gardening and complimented her on how fine the lawn looked,what a fantastic job she was doing with a yard where the soil was like concrete.Result:a happier life for both because he had learned to look at things from her point of view—even if the subject was only weeds.

In his book *Getting Through to People*,Dr.Gerald S.Nirenberg commented,"Cooperativeness in conversation is achieved when you show that you consider the other person's ideas and feelings as important as your own.Starting your conversation by giving the other person the purpose or direction of your conversation,governing what you say by what you would want to hear if you were the listener,and accepting his or her viewpoint will encourage the listener to have an open mind to your ideas."

I have always enjoyed walking and riding in a park near my home.Like the Druids of ancient Gaul,I all but worship an oak tree,so I was distressed season after season to see the young trees and shrubs killed off by needless fires.These fires weren't caused by careless smokers.They were almost all caused by youngsters who went out to the park to go native and cook a frankfurter or an egg under the trees.Sometimes,these fires raged so fiercely that the fire department had to be called out to fight the conflagration.

There was a sign on the edge of the park saying that anyone who started a fire was liable to fine and imprisonment,but the sign stood in an unfrequented part of the park,and few of the culprits ever saw it.A mounted policeman was supposed to look after the park; but he didn't take his duties too seriously,and the fires continued to spread season after season.On one occasion,I rushed up to a policeman and told him about a fire spreading rapidly through the park and wanted him to notify the fire department,and he nonchalantly replied that it was none of his business because it wasn't in his precinct! I was desperate,so after that when I went riding,I acted as a self-appointed committee of one to protect the public domain.In the beginning,I am afraid I didn't even attempt to see the other people's point of view.When I saw a fire blazing under the trees,I was so

一天晚上晚饭之后，妻子说要去除杂草，并想让他陪她。道格拉斯先是拒绝了，但过后他想了一下，又陪她出去帮她拔草。她显得非常兴奋，两个人一同干了一个多小时，过了一个愉快的晚上。

从那以后，他经常陪妻子修整草坪，并夸奖妻子说草坪修整得很好看，而且院子里的泥土地整得像水泥地一样光滑。结果他们俩都从中获得了快乐，因为他学会了从妻子的观点来看事情。

吉拉德·尼仁堡博士在他的作品《深入人心》中评论说："当你认为别人的观念、感觉与你自己的同等重要，并向对方表示这一点时，你和别人的交谈才会轻松愉快。在谈话开始的时候，要尽量使对方提出这次谈话的目的或方向。如果你是听者，就要克制自己不要随意说话。接受对方的观点，将会使对方大受鼓舞，与你开怀畅谈，并接受你的观念。"

多年来，我常喜欢在离家不远的公园里散步骑马。和古代高卢人的传教士一样，我很喜欢橡树，所以每当我看见小树苗和灌木被火灾毁灭时，就非常痛心。这些火灾并不是由粗心的吸烟者造成的，它们大都是那些到园中来过野外生活而在树下做饭烧烤的儿童引发的。有时这些火烧的太大，不得不出动消防队。

在公园的一个角落里有一布告牌，上面写着："凡导致火灾的肇事者，将处以罚款及拘禁。"但这布告牌放在少有人迹的地方，很少有人能看到它。虽然有一位骑马的警察在公园里面巡逻，但他很不尽职，因此火灾时常发生并向四周蔓延。有一次，我跑到那个警察那里，告诉他说公园有一处失火了，火势正急速地蔓延，要他立即通知消防队，但他却冷漠地说那不关他的事，因为那不是他的管辖区域。我失望了，从那以后，每当我骑马去公园时，便自成"单人委员会"，来保护公园的公共财产。最初，我根本不想了解别人的观点。当我看见树下起火时，便非常不高兴，我急于做好事，但结果却做错了。我总是骑马过去，警告他们会引起火灾并会被拘禁。我还

unhappy about it, so eager to do the right thing, that I did the wrong thing. I would ride up to the boys, warn them that they could be jailed for starting a fire, order with a tone of authority that it be put out; and, if they refused, I would threaten to have them arrested. I was merely unloading my feelings without thinking of their point of view.

The result? They obeyed—obeyed sullenly and with resentment. After I rode on over the hill, they probably rebuilt the fire and longed to burn up the whole park.

With the passing of the years, I acquired a trifle more knowledge of human relations, a little more tact, a somewhat greater tendency to see things from the other person's standpoint. Then, instead of giving orders, I would ride up to a blazing fire and begin something like this:

"Having a good time, boys? What are you going to cook for supper?...I loved to build fires myself when I was a boy—and I still love to. But you know they are very dangerous here in the park. I know you boys don't mean to do any harm, but other boys aren't so careful. They come along and see that you have built a fire; so they build one and don't put it out when they go home and it spreads among the dry leaves and kills the trees. We won't have any trees here at all if we aren't more careful. You could be put in jail for building this fire. But I don't want to be bossy and interfere with your pleasure. I like to see you enjoy yourselves; but won't you please rake all the leaves away from the fire right now—and you'll be careful to cover it with dirt, a lot of dirt, before you leave, won't you? And the next time you want to have some fun, won't you please build your fire over the hill there in the sandpit? It can't do any harm there ....Thanks so much, boys. Have a good time."

What a difference that kind of talk made! It made the boys want to cooperate. No sullenness, no resentment. They hadn't been forced to obey orders. They had saved their faces. They felt better and I felt better because I had handled the situation with consideration for their point of view.

Seeing things through another person's eyes may ease tensions when personal problems become overwhelming. Elizabeth Novak of New South Wales, Australia, was six weeks late with her car payment. "On a Friday," she reported, "I received a nasty phone call from the man who was handling my account informing me if I did not come up with $122 by Monday morning I could anticipate further action from the company. I had no way of raising the money over the weekend, so when I received his phone call first thing on Monday morning I expected the worst. Instead of becoming upset

用权威的口气,命令他们把火扑灭;而且如果他们拒绝,我便威胁要将他们抓起来。我只顾发泄我的怒气,全然不理会他们的想法。

结果呢?他们表面上遵从了。可是当我骑马跑过山后,他们很可能又重新生火,并极想把整个公园烧光。

许多年过去以后,我对人际关系的知识有了更多的了解,更懂得从对方的立场来看问题。于是我不再下命令了,我会骑马来到火前,然后这样说:

"孩子们,玩得高兴吗?你们在做什么晚餐?……当我还是个孩子时,我也喜欢生火——我至今还很喜欢。但你们知道,在公园中生火是非常危险的。我知道你们这些孩子不会造成损失的,但别的孩子可不像你们这样小心。他们走过来见你们生了火,于是他们也点起火来,回家的时候忘了扑灭,结果火在公园中蔓延,烧毁了树木。如果我们不再加小心些,我们这儿的树就会烧得精光了。因此,你们可能会因为这堆火而被捕入狱。但我不想干涉你们,扫你们的兴。我喜欢看到你们快乐地生活,但请你们立刻将旁边的枯树叶拨得离火远些,好不好?在你们离开以前,要小心地多用些泥土把火盖起来,好不好?你们下次还想来玩时,去山那边的沙坑生火好不好? 那就不会有危险了……多谢了,孩子们。祝你们快乐。"

这种说法效果很好!孩子们非常合作。他们没有怨恨,也没有反感。他们并没有被强制服从什么命令,他们保住了面子,他们觉得能够接受,我也觉得很满意,因为我先考虑了他们的想法再来处置这事情的。

当个人的问题显得更加急迫的时候, 如果能从别人的立场来看问题, 就可以缓解紧张气氛。澳大利亚新南威尔士的伊丽莎白·诺瓦克已有6个星期未支付分期购车的钱款。"在某个星期五,"她说,"一个负责我账户的男人给我打来电话,很不礼貌地告诉我,如果我在下周一早晨还不缴付122美元,他们公司将采取进一步措施。周末我自然筹不到这笔钱,因此星期一一大

I looked at the situation from his point of view. I apologized most sincerely for causing him so much inconvenience and remarked that I must be his most troublesome customer as this was not the first time I was behind in my payments. His tone of voice changed immediately, and he reassured me that I was far from being one of his really troublesome customers. He went on to tell me several examples of how rude his customers sometimes were, how they lied to him and often tried to avoid talking to him at all. I said nothing. I listened and let him pour out his troubles to me. Then, without any suggestion from me, he said it did not matter if I couldn't pay all the money immediately. It would be all right if I paid him $20 by the end of the month and made up the balance whenever it was convenient for me to do so."

Tomorrow, before asking anyone to put out a fire or buy your product or contribute to your favorite charity, why not pause and close your eyes and try to think the whole thing through from another person's point of view? Ask yourself: "Why should he or she want to do it?" True, this will take time, but it will avoid making enemies and will get better results—and with less friction and less shoe leather.

"I would rather walk the sidewalk in front of a person's office for two hours before an interview," said Dean Donham of the Harvard business school, "than step into that office without a perfectly clear idea of what I was going to say and what that person—from my knowledge of his or her interests and motives—was likely to answer."

That is so important that I am going to repeat it in italics for the sake of emphasis.

I would rather walk the sidewalk in front of a person's office for two hours before an interview than step into that office without a perfectly clear idea of what I was going to say and what that person—from my knowledge of his or her interests and motives—was likely to answer.

If, as a result of reading this book, you get only one thing—an increased tendency to think always in terms of the other person's point of view, and see things from that person's angle as well as your own—if you get only that one thing from this book, it may easily prove to be one of the stepping-stones of your career.

Principle 8: Try honestly to see things from the other person's point of view.

早我就接到了那个男人的电话。不过我并没有发火，而是从他的立场来看这件事。我真诚地向他道歉给他带来了这么大的麻烦，而且我已经不是头一次逾期未付款，因此我一定很让他为难。他的语气立即缓和下来，并说我根本不是令他头疼的顾客。他还举了好几个例子，说有些人更不讲理，不仅信口胡说，还躲着不见他。我没有说更多的话，只是听着，让他说出了心中的不愉快。然后，根本不需我请求，他就说即使我不能立刻缴付欠款也问题不大；还说如果月底之前我能先缴付20美元，然后在手头方便时付清余额，一切都好说。"

所以，当你明天请人熄火，或请他买你的东西，或捐钱给红十字会以前，为什么不先停一下，闭上眼睛，从对方的角度将整个事情想一想？问问你自己："他为什么要这样做？"当然，那要费点儿时间，但能使你赢得朋友，培养情谊，并且减少摩擦，少惹麻烦。

"在与人会谈以前，我情愿在他办公室的过道上多走两小时，"哈佛商学院院长唐哈姆说，"而不愿贸然走进他的办公室，如果我对于我所要说的，以及他——根据我对他的兴趣及动机的认识来推断——可能会做出什么答复都没有很清晰的认识的话。"

这话非常重要，为了强调，我再重复一次：

"在与人会谈以前，我情愿在他办公室的过道上多走两小时，而不愿贸然走进他的办公室，如果我对于我所要说的，以及他——根据我对他的兴趣及动机的认识来推断——可能会做出什么答复都没有很清晰的认识的话。"

如果你读完这本书后，只学到一件事——养成从对方的角度去思考，从他人的立场出发的习惯，如同从你自己的立场出发一样——如果你从本书只学到这一点，它也会成为你人生的基石。

第八项法则：真诚地从别人的立场来看问题。

9 What Everybody Wants

Wouldn't you like to have a magic phrase that would stop arguments, eliminate ill feeling, create good will, and make the other person listen attentively?

Yes? All right. Here it is: "I don't blame you one iota for feeling as you do. If I were you I would undoubtedly feel just as you do."

An answer like that will soften the most cantankerous old cuss alive. And you can say that and be 100 percent sincere, because if you were the other person you, of course, would feel just as he does. Take A1 Capone, for example. Suppose you had inherited the same body and temperament and mind that Al Capone had. Suppose you had had his environment and experiences. You would then be precisely what he was—and where he was. For it is those things—and only those things—that made him what he was. The only reason, for example, that you are not a rattlesnake is that your mother and father weren't rattlesnakes.

You deserve very little credit for being what you are—and remember, the people who come to you irritated, bigoted, unreasoning, deserve very little discredit for being what they are. Feel sorry for the poor devils. Pity them. Sympathize with them. Say to yourself, "There, but for the grace of God, go I."

Three-fourths of the people you will evermeet are hungering and thirsting for sympathy. Give it to them, and they will love you.

I once gave a broadcast about the author of *Little Women*, Louisa May Alcott. Naturally, I knew she had lived and written her immortal books in Concord, Massachusetts. But, without thinking what I was saying, I spoke of visiting her old home in Concord, New Hampshire. If I had said New Hampshire only once, it might have been forgiven. But, alas and alack! I said it twice, I was deluged with letters and telegrams, stinging messages that swirled around my defenseless head like a swarm of hornets. Many were indignant. A few insulting. One Colonial Dame, who had been reared in Concord, Massachusetts, and who was then living in Philadelphia, vented her scorching

第9章 每个人都需要的东西

你不希望拥有一个神奇的句子,它既可以阻止争执,去除厌恶感,带来和谐融洽,又可以使对方注意倾听你吗?

希望?太好了。这就是那个神奇的句子:"我一点都不会责怪你有那种感受。如果我是你,我也会和你的感受一样。"

这样一句话,即使再固执的人也会软化。而且你完全要发自内心,因为假如你是对方,你的感受当然会同他一样。还以卡普恩为例吧。假如你遗传所得的躯体、性情、思想和卡普恩的完全相同;假如你的环境与经历和他一样,那么你就会同他完全一样——也会落到他的下场。例如,你之所以不是一条响尾蛇,唯一的原因就是你的父母不是响尾蛇。

你之所以成为你目前的样子,你没什么可居功自傲的——要记住,那个让你愤怒的、固执的、不可理喻的人,错误也并不全在他自己。要对这可怜的人表示惋惜、怜恤、同情。要对自己说:"如果不是上帝的恩典,我也会像他们一样。"

你明天将要遇见的人中,有3/4都渴望得到同情。如果你能给他们同情,他们就会喜欢你。

我曾做过一次关于《小妇人》的作者露易莎·梅·奥尔科特的广播。我当然知道她生长在马萨诸塞州的康科特,并在此写出了她这本不朽的名作。但是,我竟然粗心地说曾到新罕布什尔州的康科特去凭吊过她的故居。如果我只说了一次,或许还可以原谅。但是,天啊!我竟说了两次。于是,无数信件、电报包围了我,激烈的言辞就像一群毒蜂绕着我这毫无防范的脑袋打转。这些信函大多是愤怒的,有些则是侮辱我的。有一位名叫卡洛尼亚·达姆的人,她从小在马萨诸塞的康科特长大,当时她住在费城,对我发泄了强烈的怒火。即使我将奥尔科特女士误说成来

wrath upon me.She couldn't have been much more bitter if I had accused Miss Alcott of being a cannibal from New Guinea.As I read the letter,I said to myself,"Thank God,I am not married to that woman."I felt like writing and telling her that although I had made a mistake in geography, she had made a far greater mistake in common courtesy.That was to be just my opening sentence. Then I was going to roll up my sleeves and tell her what I really thought.But I didn't.I controlled myself.I realized that any hotheaded feel could do that—and that most fools would do just that.

I wanted to be above fools.So I resolved to try to turn her hostility into friendliness.It would be a challenge,a sort of game I could play.I said to myself,"After all,if I were she,I would probably feel just as she does."So,I determined to sympathize with her viewpoint.The next time I was in Philadelphia,I called her on the telephone.The conversation went something like this:

ME:Mrs.So-and-So,you wrote me a letter a few weeks ago,and I want to thank you for it.

SHE:(in incisive,cultured,well-bred tones)To whom have I the honor of speaking?

ME:I am a stranger to you.My name is Dale Carnegie.You listened to a broadcast I gave about Louisa May Alcott a few Sundays ago,and I made the unforgivable blunder of saying that she had lived in Concord,New Hampshire.It was a stupid blunder,and I want to apologize for it.It was so nice of you to take the time to write me.

SHE:I am sorry,Mr.Carnegie,that I wrote as I did.I lost my temper.I must apologize.

ME:No! No! You are not the one to apologize; I am.Any school child would have known better than to have said what I said.I apologized over the air the following Sunday,and I want to apologize to you personally now.

SHE:I was bom in Concord,Massachusetts.My family has been prominent in Massachusetts affairs for two centuries,and I am very proud of my native state.I was really quite distressed to hear you say that Miss Alcott had lived in New Hampshire.But I am really ashamed of that letter.

ME:I assure you that you were not one-tenth as distressed as I am.My error didn't hurt Massachusetts,but it did hurt me.It is so seldom that people of your standing and culture take the time to write people who speak on the radio,and I do hope you will write me again if you detect an error in my talks.

自新几内亚的食人族,她大概也不会那么愤怒了。我在读信时,对自己说:"感谢上帝,幸好我没有娶这老太太。"我觉得应写一封信告诉她,虽然我犯了一个地理上的错误,但她在通常的礼貌上犯了一个更大的错误。我准备就用这两句话作为开头。于是,我卷起袖子,准备告诉她我这些真心话。但我没有那样做,我克制住自己。我知道,任何昏了头的傻子都会那样做——而大多数傻子也只会那样做。

我当然不愿做傻子,所以我决定把她的仇视变为友善。这将是一次挑战,也是我喜欢玩的游戏。我对自己说:"说实话,如果我是她,我的感受大概会和她一样。"所以,我决定对她的观点表示认同。当我后来到费城的时候,便给她打电话。电话大致是这样的:

我:夫人,你在几个星期之前给我写了一封信,我要为此感谢你。

她:(用清晰、文雅、有教养的声调)请问你是谁?我有此荣幸和你说话?

我:你并不认识我这个陌生人。我叫戴尔·卡耐基。在几个星期之前,你听过我关于奥尔科特的广播;而我犯了一个不可宽恕的大错,说她生长在新罕布什尔州的康科特。那实在是一个低级错误;我要为此道歉。你花时间给我写信,实在太好了。

她:我很抱歉,卡耐基先生。我写那封信,发了那么大的火,我必须向你道歉。

我:不!不!不是你应道歉,而是我。任何上了学的小孩都不会犯我那样的错误。在第二个星期日的广播里我已经道了歉。现在我要亲自对你个人道歉。

她:我出生在马萨诸塞州的康科特。两个世纪以来,我的家族在马萨诸塞州很有声望,而且我以我的家乡而自豪。听你说奥尔科特女士生在新罕布什尔州,实在让我太难过了。不过,我对那封信真是感到很抱歉。

我:我敢对你说,我比你还要难受10倍。我的错误对于马萨诸塞州来说没有任何损害,但却伤害了我自己。像你这样有地位、有教养的人,难得花工夫给无线电台的人写信。

SHE: You know, I really like very much the way you have accepted my criticism. You must be a very nice person. I should like to know you better.

So, because I had apologized and sympathized with her point of view, she began apologizing and sympathizing with my point of view, I had the satisfaction of controlling my temper, the satisfaction of returning kindness for an insult. I got infinitely more real fun out of making her like me than I could ever have gotten out of telling her to go and take a jump in the Schuylkill River.

Every man who occupies the White House is faced almost daily with thorny problems in human relations. President Taft was no exception, and he learned from experience the enormous chemical value of sympathy in neutralizing the acid of hard feelings. In his book *Ethics in Service*, Taft gives rather an amusing illustration of how he softened the ire of a disappointed and ambitious mother.

"A lady in Washington," wrote Taft, "whose husband had some political influence, came and labored with me for six weeks or more to appoint her son to a position. She secured the aid of Senators and Congressmen in formidable number and came with them to see that they spoke with emphasis. The place was one requiring technical qualification, and following the recommendation of the head of the Bureau, I appointed somebody else. I then received a letter from the mother, saying that I was most ungrateful, since I declined to make her a happy woman as I could have done by a turn of my hand. She complained further that she had labored with her state delegation and got all the votes for an administration bill in which I was especially interested and this was the way I had rewarded her.

"When you get a letter like that, the first thing you do is to think how you can be severe with a person who has committed an impropriety, or even been a little impertinent. Then you may compose an answer. Then if you are wise, you will put the letter in a drawer and lock the drawer. Take it out in the course of two days—such communications will always bear two days' delay in answering—and when you take it out after that interval, you will not send it. That is just the course I took. After that, I sat down and wrote her just as polite a letter as I could, telling her I realized a mother's disappointment under such circumstances, but that really the appointment was not left to my mere personal preference, that I had to select a man with technical qualifications, and had, therefore, to follow the recommendations of the head of the Bureau. I expressed the hope that her son would go

如果你今后再在我的讲话中发现错误，我非常希望你给我写信指正。

她：你知道吗？我真的很高兴你接受批评的态度。你一定是个很好的人，我愿和你交朋友。

就这样，因为我向她道歉，并同意了她的观点，她也向我道了歉，并同意我的观点。我对自己的自我克制和以德报怨很满意。让她喜欢我，而不是激怒她，使我获得了更多的快乐。

凡入主白宫的人，差不多每天都会遇到棘手的人际关系问题。塔夫脱总统也不例外，但他从自己的经验中学到，同情对于中和"酸性的恶感"有极大的化学功能。在他的《服务道德》一书中，塔夫脱举了一个很有趣的例子，说明他如何使一位野心勃勃却又满怀失望的母亲平息愤怒的。

"华盛顿一位妇人，"塔夫脱写道，"她丈夫在政界很有影响。她来找我，与我纠缠了6个多星期，想为她儿子安排一个职位。她得到了许多参议员的支持，并请他们一起来见我，讲了他们对她的支持。因为这个位置需要技术能力，于是我根据该部部长的举荐安排了别人。不久，我接到这位母亲的一封信，说我是这个世界上最无情无义的人，因为我拒绝让她成为一个快乐的母亲，而对我来说这本来是易如反掌的。她进一步抱怨说，她与她的州代表费尽了心思，为我特别关注的一项行政议案赢得了所有的投票，而我却这样报答她。

"当你收到那样一封信时，你想到的第一件事，就是何必跟一个失礼或甚至有些唐突的人那么较真。于是你可能会写一封回信。然后，如果你够聪明的话，就应该把这信锁抽屉里，过两天之后再拿出来——这类书信一般要迟两天再写——当你经过几天再取出信时，你就不会把它寄出去了。我采取的正是这种做法。于是，我给她写了一封极其客气的回信，告诉她我很明白在这种情况下一个做母亲的会很失望的，但这件事实在不能只凭我个人的好恶，我必须选择一个有技术资格的人，所以我只能接受这位部长的推荐。我又希望她的儿子能在他目前的职位上

on to accomplish what she had hoped for him in the position which he then had.That mollified her and she wrote me a note saying she was sorry she had written as she had.

"But the appointment I sent in was not confirmed at once, and after an interval I received a letter which purported to come from her husband; though it was in the the same handwriting as all the other.I was therein advised that, due to the nervous prostration that had followed her disappointment in this case, she had to take to her bed and had developed a most serious case of cancer of the stomach.Would I not restore her to health by withdrawing the first name and replacing it by her son's?I had to write another letter, this one to the husband, to say that I hoped the diagnosis would prove to be inaccurate, that I sympathized with him in the sorrow he must have in the serious illness of his wife, but that it was impossible to withdraw the name sent in.The man whom I appointed was confirmed, and within two days after I received that letter, we gave a musicale at the White House.The first two people to greet Mrs.Taft and me were this husband and wife, though the wife had so recently been *in articulo mortis*."

Jay Mangum represented an elevator-escalator maintenance company in Tulsa, Oklahoma, which had the maintenance contract for the escalators in one of Tulsa's leading hotels.The hotel manager did not want to shut down the escalator for more than two hours at a time because he did not want to inconvenience the hotel's guests.The repair that had to be made would take at least eight hours, and his company did not always have a specially qualified mechanic available at the convenience of the hotel.

When Mr.Mangum was able to schedule a topflight mechanic for this job, he telephoned the hotel manager and instead of arguing with him to give him the necessary time, he said:

"Rick, I know your hotel is quite busy and you would like to keep the escalator shutdown time to a minimum.I understand your concern about this, and we want to do everything possible to accommodate you.However, our diagnosis of the situation shows that if we do not do a complete job now, your escalator may suffer more serious damage and that would cause a much longer shutdown.I know you would not want to inconvenience your guests for several days."

The manager had to agree that an eight-hour shut down was more desirable than several days'. By sympathizing with the manager's desire to keep his patrons happy, Mr.Mangum was able to win the hotel manager to his way of thinking easily and without rancor.

完成她对他的期望。这封回信使她终于息怒了，她给我写了一封短信，为她的信表示道歉。

“但我推荐的人选没有立即确定。过了一段时间，我接到一封据说是由她丈夫写的信，但笔迹却跟她的信完全相同。信中告诉我，因为她在这件事情上的失望，导致神经衰弱，卧床不起，并得了严重的胃癌；并问我能不能将第一个人的名字撤回来，换上她儿子，以使她恢复健康。我不得不再写一封信，这次是给她丈夫的，说我希望这次诊断是不准确的，他夫人的重病必然让他非常忧虑，对此我很同情，但将已送报的名字撤回来是不可能的。不久，我任命的人选终于获准通过。在接到那封信的两天之后，我在白宫举行了一次音乐会。音乐会上最先向我夫人和我致意的就是这对夫妇，虽然这位夫人不久前差点儿‘重病而死’！”

杰伊·孟古是俄克拉荷马州图尔萨市一家电梯维修公司的经理。这家公司与该市最好的一家饭店签有电梯维修合同。饭店经理在每次电梯维修期间，为了不给旅客带来不便，规定电梯最多只能停开两小时。但是，电梯维修最少要 8 小时，而且在停开电梯的那两个小时之内，公司也不一定能派出人手来维修。

当孟古先生能够为修理工作安排一位最好的技工时，他给这家饭店的经理打电话，也不和这位经理争辩，只是说：

“瑞克，我知道你们饭店客人非常多，你希望尽量减少电梯停开的时间。我知道你很在意这一点，我们应该尽量配合你的要求。不过，我们检查你们的电梯之后，发现如果我们现在不能将电梯彻底修理好，那么电梯损坏可能会更加严重，到时候停开的时间会更长。我知道，你不会希望让客人好几天都不方便。”

这位经理不得不同意，电梯停开 8 个小时总比停开几天要好。由于孟古对这位经理方便客人的愿望表示了理解，因此他很容易而且没有争议地赢得了这位经理的同意。

杰西·诺瑞丝是密苏里州圣路易市的一位钢琴教师。她讲述了她如何处理钢琴教师与十几

Joyce Norris, a piano teacher in St, Louis, Missouri, told of how she had handled a problem piano teachers often have with teenage girls. Babette had exceptionally long fingernails. This is a serious handicap to anyone who wants to develop proper piano-playing habits.

Mrs. Norris reported, "I knew her long fingernails would be a barrier for her in her desire to play well. During our discussions prior to her starting her lessons with me, I did not mention anything to her about her nails. I didn't want to discourage her from taking lessons, and I also knew she would not want to lose that which she took so much pride in and such great care to make attractive.

"After her first lesson, when I felt the time was right, I said, 'Babette, you have attractive hands and beautiful fingernails. If you want to play the piano as well as you are capable of and as well as you would like to, you would be surprised how much quicker and easier it would be for you, if you would trim your nails shorter. Just think about it, Okay?' She made a face which was definitely negative. I also talked to her mother about this situation, again mentioning how lovely her nails were. Another negative reaction. It was obvious that Babette's beautifully manicured nails were important to her.

"The following week Babette returned for her second lesson. Much to my surprise, the fingernails had been trimmed. I complimented her and praised her for making such a sacrifice. I also thanked her mother for influencing Babette to cut her nails. Her reply was 'Oh, I had nothing to do with it. Babette decided to do it on her own, and this is the first time she has ever trimmed her nails for anyone.'"

Did Mrs. Norris threaten Babette? Did she say she would refuse to teach a student with long fingernails? No, she did not. She let Babette know that her fingernails were a thing of beauty and it would be a sacrifice to cut them. She implied, "I sympathize with you—I know it won't be easy, but it will pay off in your better musical development."

Sol Hurok was probably America's number one impresario. For almost half a century he handled artists—such world-famous artists as Chaliapin, Isadora Duncan, and Pavlova. Mr. Hurok told me that one of the first lessons he had learned in dealing with his temperamental stars was the necessity for sympathy, sympathy and more sympathy with their idiosyncrasies.

岁女孩子之间经常出现的一个问题。贝贝蒂从小就留了一手很长的指甲，而任何人要想弹好钢琴，就不能留长指甲。

诺瑞丝太太说："我知道她的长指甲会妨碍她学好弹钢琴。在开始教她钢琴课之前，我们俩谈话的时候，我根本没有提到她指甲的问题。我不能打击她学钢琴的愿望，我也知道她不想失去她以此为傲，并且花了许多时间去修饰的长指甲。

"在上了第一堂课之后，我觉得时机成熟了，就说：'贝贝蒂，你有双很漂亮的手，指甲也很美。如果你想把钢琴弹得如你所能够的以及你所希望的那么好，那么我认为，如果你能把指甲修得稍短一点，你就会发现弹好钢琴真是太容易了。你好好想一想，好不好？'她向我做了一个鬼脸，表示她绝对不会修短指甲。我也和她的母亲谈了这一情况，提到她的指甲确实很美丽。但我从她母亲那里又得到了否定回答。显然，贝贝蒂仔细修剪过的美丽指甲对她很重要。

"第二个星期，贝贝蒂来上第二堂课。让我很惊讶的是，她的指甲修短了。我称赞她做出这样的舍弃，同时对她母亲给她的影响也表示了感谢。她母亲回答说：'啊，我没有做什么。这是贝贝蒂自己决定的。这也是她第一次为了别人而修短了她的指甲。'"

诺瑞丝太太是否强迫贝贝蒂了呢？她有没有说她不愿教留有长指甲的学生呢？没有，她并没有这么说。她告诉贝贝蒂，说她的指甲很美丽，要她修短指甲是她的一种牺牲。她只是暗示："我很同情你——我知道对你来说修短指甲不是一件容易的事；但是这会让你的钢琴练得更好。"

索尔·休洛也许是美国第一位音乐经纪人。在近半个世纪中，他一直和艺术家们——如查利亚宾、邓肯和帕弗洛娃等世界著名的艺术家保持往来。休洛先生告诉我，要和这些性情无常的艺术家打交道，最关键的第一课就是必须同情，同情！而且对他们那些荒谬可笑的古怪脾气必须给予更多的同情。

For three years, he was impresario for Feodor Chaliapin—one of the greatest bassos who ever thrilled the ritzy boxholders at the Metropolitan. Yet Chaliapin was a constant problem. He carried on like a spoiled child. To put it in Mr. Hurok's own inimitable phrase, "He was a hell of a fellow in every way."

For example, Challapin would call up Mr. Hurok about noon of the day he was going to sing and say, "Sol, I feel terrible. My throat is like raw hamburger. It is impossible for me to sing tonight." Did Mr. Hurok argue with him? Oh, no. He knew that an entrepreneur couldn't handle artists that way. So he would rush over to Chaliapin's hotel, dripping with sympathy. "What a pity," he would mourn. "What a pity! My poor fellow. Of course, you cannot sing. I will cancel the engagement at once. It will only cost you a couple of thousand dollars, but that is nothing in comparison to your reputation."

Then Chaliapin would sigh and say, "Perhaps you had better come over later in the day. Come at five and see how I feel then."

At five o'clock, Mr. Hurok would again rush to his hotel, dripping with sympathy. Again he would insist on canceling the engagement and again Challapin would sigh and say, "Well, maybe you had better come to see me later. I may be better then."

At seven-thirty the great basso would consent to sing, only with the understanding that Mr. Hurok would walk out on the stage of the Metropolitan and announce that Challapin had a very bad cold and was not in good voice. Mr. Hurok would lie and say he would do it, for he knew that was the only way to get the basso out on the stage.

Dr. Arthur I. Gates said in his splendid book *Educational Psychology*: "Sympathy the human species universally craves. The child eagerly displays his injury; or even inflicts a cut or bruise in order to reap abundant sympathy. For the same purpose adults show their bruises, relate their accidents, illness, especially details of surgical operations. 'Self - pity' for misfortunes real or imaginary is in some measure, practically a universal practice."

So, if you want to win people to your way of thinking, put in practice...

Principle 9: Be sympathetic with the other person's ideas and desires.

他曾给查利亚宾担任音乐经纪人达3年之久——查利亚宾是最伟大的男低音歌唱家之一,大都会歌剧院高贵的观众无不为之倾倒。但查利亚宾总是给人出难题,他的行为处事就像一个被宠坏了的孩子。用休洛先生的话来说:"他是一个各方面都令人头疼的家伙。"

例如,查利亚宾可能会在他将要演唱的那天中午,给休洛先生打电话说:"索尔,我觉得不舒服。我的喉咙像生牛排一样。今晚我不能演唱了。"休洛先生是否同他辩论呢?哦,没有。他知道自己作为艺术经纪人,不能那样对待艺术家。于是他赶到查利亚宾下榻的宾馆,对他表示同情。"多么不幸!"他会忧伤地说,"多么不幸!我可怜的朋友。当然,你不能唱了,我会立即取消这场演唱会。那只不过损失你几千美元,但这和你的名誉相比算不得什么。"

然后,查利亚宾会叹息说:"也许你下午最好再来一趟。看到5点钟时我觉得怎样。"

到了5点钟,休洛先生再次来到他的旅馆,对他表示同情。休洛一再坚持取消演唱会,查利亚宾会再叹气说:"好吧。你再晚点儿来看我!那时我或许会感到好一点。"

到7点半,这位伟大的男低音歌唱家答应演唱了,但有一个条件,就是休洛先生要登上大都会歌剧院的戏台,宣布查利亚宾患有重感冒,嗓子不太好。休洛先生会谎称照他说的去办,因为他知道,那是使这位歌唱家上台的唯一方法。

亚瑟·盖茨博士在他的名著《教育心理学》中说:"所有的人都普遍地渴求同情。例如小孩急于展示他所受的伤害,甚至故意割伤或弄伤自己,以期获得大量的同情。出于同样的原因,成人也会向别人显示他们的伤痕,叙述他们的意外、疾病,特别是动手术开刀的详情。为真实的或想象中的不幸而'自怜',这几乎是普遍的心理现象。"

所以,如果你想使人同意你的看法……

第九项规则:同情别人的想法和愿望。

10 An Appeal That Everybody Likes

I was reared on the edge of the Jesse James country out in Missouri, and I visited the James farm at Kearney, Missouri, where the son of Jesse James was then living. His wife told me stories of how Jesse robbed trains and held up banks and then gave money to the neighboring farmers to pay off their mortgages. Jesse James probably regarded himself as an idealist at heart, just as Dutch Schultz, "Two Gun" Crowley, A1 Capone and many other organized crime "godfathers" did generations later. The fact is that all people you meet have a high regard for themselves and like to be fine and unselfish in their own estimation.

J.Pierpont Morgan observed, in one of his analytical interludes, that a person usually has two reasons for doing a thing: one that sounds good and a real one.

The person himself will think of the real reason. You don't need to emphasize that. But all of us, being idealists at heart, like to think of motives that sound good. So, in order to change people, appeal to the nobler motives.

Is that too idealistic to work in business? Let's see. Let's take the case of Hamilton J.Farrell of the Farrell-Mitchell Company of Glenolden, Pennsylvania. Mr.Farrell had a disgruntled tenant who threatened to move. The tenant's lease still had four months to run; nevertheless, he served notice that he was vacating immediately, regardless of lease.

"These people had lived in my house all winter—the most expensive part of the year," Mr. Farrell said as he told the story to the class, "and I knew it would be difficult to rent the apartment again before fall. I could see all that rent income going over the hill and believe me, I saw red.

"Now, ordinarily, I would have waded into that tenant and advised him to read his lease again. I would have pointed out that if he moved, the full balance of his rent would fall due at once—and that I could, *and would*, move to collect.

"However, instead of flying off the handle and making a scene, I decided to try other tactics. So I started like this: 'Mr.Doe,' I said, 'I have listened to your story, and I still don't believe you

第10章 激发高尚的动机

我在密苏里州杰西·詹姆斯活动的乡间长大，我曾造访过詹姆斯的农场，那时詹姆斯的儿子还活着。他的妻子对我说起杰西·詹姆斯如何抢劫火车及银行，然后将这些钱分给邻近的农夫们去赎回抵押物。杰西·詹姆斯大概在心中把自己当成了一个理想主义者，正如几十年之后的苏尔兹、"双枪手"克洛雷、卡朋恩及其他许多有组织的犯罪分子所想的一样。事实上，你遇见的每一个人都会过高估计自己，并认为自己是善良而无私的人。

摩根在他的一篇短文中分析说，一个人做任何事，通常有两种理由：一种是动听的，另一种是真实的。

每个人都会想到那个真实的理由，因此你不必过分强调它。而我们每个人心中又大都是理想主义者，总喜欢听到那个说来动听的动机。所以，要改变人们，就需要激起他们高尚的动机。

要在商业中实践这一点是否太理想化了？我们就以宾夕法尼亚州格利诺顿的法莱尔-密歇尔公司的汉密尔顿·法莱尔先生的一件事为例吧。法莱尔先生有一位不满意的房客威胁要搬走。但这位房客的合同还有4个月，而他却通知说马上就要搬走，而不顾合同。

"这些人已在我的屋子里住了整整一个冬季——这是一年中房租最高的时期。"法莱尔先生在班上讲述这件事时说，"而且我知道，要在秋季以前再将这些公寓租出去是很难的。眼看这就要到手的租金将泡汤了，我真着急了。

"现在，要照从前的情况，我会跑到那位房客那儿，让他把那份合同再看一遍。我可以向他指出，如果他搬走，应付清合同规定的余款——我会那样做，并且会立刻收款。

"可是，那样做只会弄得更僵，我决定试试别的方法。于是我这样对他说：'杜伊先生，我已

intend to move.Years in the renting business have taught me something about human nature,and I sized you up in the first place as being a man of your word.In fact,I'm so sure of it that I'm willing to take a gamble.'

"'Now,here's my proposition.Left your decision on the table for a few days and think it over.If you come back to me between now and the first of the month,when your rent is due,and tell me you still intend to move,I give you my word I will accept your decision as final.I will privilege you to move and admit to myself I've been wrong in my judgment.But I still believe you're a man of your word and will live up to your contract.For after all,we are either men or monkeys—and the choice usually lies with ourselves!'

"Well,when the new month came around,this gentleman came to see me and paid his rent in person.He and his wife had talked it over,he said—and decided to stay.They had concluded that the only honorable thing to do was to live up to their lease."

When the late Lord Northcliffe found a newspaper using a picture of him which he didn't want published,he wrote the editor a letter.But did he say,"Please do not publish that picture of me any more;I don't like it"?No,he appealed to a nobler motive.He appealed to the respect and love that all of us have for motherhood.He wrote,"Please do not publish that picture of me any more.My mother doesn't like it."

When John D.Rockefeller,Jr.,wished to stop newspaper photographers from snapping pictures of his children,he too appealed to the nobler motives.He didn't say,"I don't want their pictures published."No,he appealed to the desire,deep in all of us,to refrain from harming children.He said,"You know how it is,boys.You've got children yourselves,some of you.And you know it's not good for youngsters to get too much publicity."

When Cyrus H.K.Curtis,the poor boy from Maine,was starting on his meteoric career,which was destined to make him millions as owner of *The Saturday Evening Post* and the *Ladies' Home Journal*,he couldn't afford to pay his contributors the prices that other magazines paid.He couldn't afford to hire first-class authors to write for money alone.So he appealed to their nobler motives.For example,he persuaded even Louisa May Alcott,the mortal author of *Little Women*,to write for him when she was at the flood tide of her fame;and he did it by offering to send a check for a hundred

经知道了你的计划,但我还是相信你真想搬走。从事多年房屋租赁生意,使我学到不少观人料事的经验,我从一开始就看出你是一个有信用的人。对此我确信不疑,我情愿和你打赌。'

"'现在,我提议这样。你不妨再想想你的决定。如果你在下个月的1号租房到期之前,到我这里来告诉我你仍想搬走,那我愿意接受你的决定。我将给你搬走的权利,并承认我的判断有误。但我仍相信你是一个讲信用的人,一定会住到合同期满。因为,说到底,我们是人还是猴子——这个选择全在我们自己。'

"好了!当下个月来到时,这位先生亲自来我这里支付房租。他说他已经和他的妻子商量过,决定再住下去。他们得出的结论是,唯一光荣的就是履行契约。"

当已故的诺斯克立夫勋爵发现一家报纸刊登了他不愿公开的照片时,便给编辑写了一封信。他是否说"请不要再刊登我那张照片,因为我不喜欢它"吗?没有,他找到了高尚的动机——我们每个人对于母亲的敬爱心理。他写道:"请不要再刊登那张照片,我母亲不喜欢它。"

当小约翰·洛克菲勒想阻止那些摄影记者为他的孩子拍照时,他也诉诸更高尚的动机。他没有说:"我不希望将他们的照片刊登出来。"不,他是出于深藏在我们心中的爱护儿童的欲望。他说:"诸位,你们都明白,你们之中有些人也有孩子。而你们也知道,小孩子太出风头并没有什么好处。"

当来自缅因州的穷小子希鲁斯·克蒂斯开始为他的光辉事业而奋斗,并成为百万富翁,拥有《星期六晚邮》与《妇女家庭杂志》的时候,他既付不出其他杂志那么高的稿酬,也无法请那些一流作家来为他的杂志撰稿,所以他就设法激发他们的高尚动机。例如,他甚至说动了《小妇人》的不朽作者奥尔科特女士为他撰稿,当时她的声望正如日中天。他送了一张100美元的支票,但不是给她,而是给她热心的慈善事业。

说到这里,有人会怀疑说:"啊!这套把戏对于诺斯克立夫及洛克菲勒,或对富有情感的小

dollars, not to her, but to her favorite charity.

Right here the skeptic may say, "Oh, that stuff is all right for Northcliffe and Rockefeller or a sentimental novelist. But, I'd like to see you make it work with the tough babies I have to collect bills from!" You may be right. Nothing will work in all cases—and nothing will work with all people. If you are satisfied with the results you are now getting, why change? If you are not satisfied, why not experiment? At any rate, I think you will enjoy reading this true story told by James L. Thomas, a former student of mine:

Six customers of a certain automobile company refused to pay their bills for servicing. None of the customers protested the entire bill, but each claimed that some one charge was wrong. In each case, the customer had signed for the work done, so the company knew it was right—and said so. That was the first mistake.

Here are the steps the men in the credit department took to collect these overdue bills. Do you suppose they succeeded? 1. They called on each customer and told him bluntly that they had come to collect a bill that was long past due. 2. They made it very plain that the company was absolutely and unconditionally right; therefore he, the customer, was absolutely and unconditionally wrong. 3. They intimated that they, the company, knew more about automobiles than he could ever hope to know. So what was the argument about? 4. Result: They argued.

Did any of these methods reconcile the customer and settle the account? You can answer that one yourself.

At this stage of affairs, the credit manager was about to open fire with a battery of legal talent, when fortunately the matter came to the attention of the general manager. The manager investigated these defaulting clients and discovered that they all had the reputation of paying their bills promptly. Something was wrong here—something was drastically wrong about the method of collection. So he called in James L. Thomas and told him to collect these "uncollectible" accounts.

Here, in his words, are the steps Mr. Thomas took: 1. My visit to each customer was likewise to collect a bill long past due—a bill that we knew was absolutely right. But I didn't say a word about that. I explained I had called to find out what it was the company had done, or failed to do. 2. I made it clear that, until I had heard the customer's story, I had no opinion to offer. I told him the

说家也许可行。但是,对那些我不得不向其讨账的不可理喻的家伙管用吗?"或许你是对的。没有什么东西能在任何情况下都有效——也没有什么东西对任何人都有效。如果你对自己的现状很满意,为什么要改变呢?但如果你不满意,又何不试一试呢?不管怎样,我想你将会乐意听我从前一位学员詹姆斯·托马斯讲的故事:

某家汽车公司有6位顾客拒付汽车修理费。但没有一个人拒付整个账单,而是都说账单上某一项有错误。每次修理工作顾客都签过字,所以公司知道这些账目不会出错——并且公司也对顾客这么说。但这犯了第一个错误。

下面是该公司信贷部职员催讨这些过期账款所采取的步骤。你想他们会成功吗?

1. 他们拜访每一位顾客,直截了当地告诉他,他们是来收已经拖欠很久的账款的。

2. 他们明确表示,公司的账目绝对没错,所以肯定是顾客错了。

3. 他们暗示顾客,公司对汽车的知识无论如何都要比他懂得多。所以顾客无须狡辩。

4. 结果:他们吵了起来。

这些方法能使顾客乐意付款吗?你可以自己回答这个问题。

事情到了这一步,信贷部经理已准备诉诸法律,幸而这事传到总经理那里。总经理调查了这些欠账的顾客,发现他们向来付款很爽快。这就有问题了——或许是收账的方法有问题。所以他叫来托马斯,让他去收这些"不能收回的欠款"。

下面是托马斯先生采取的步骤:1. 我拜访了每一位顾客,同样是要收回一笔过期很久的欠款——一笔我们知道绝对不会错的钱。但我对此没有提一个字。我对他们说,我来拜访是想要调查公司曾做了什么事,或什么事未曾做到。2. 我明确地表示,在我听完他们的叙述之前,我没有任何要说的。我告诉他们,公司并不认为自己完美无缺。3. 我告诉他,我只关心他的汽车,而他对自己的汽车比世界上其他任何人都知道得多,他是这问题的权威。4. 我让他尽量讲

company made no claims to being infallible. 3. I told him I was interested only in his car, and that he knew more about his car than anyone else in the world; that he was the authority on the subject. 4. I let him talk, and I listened to him with all the interest and sympathy that he wanted—and had expected. 5. Finally, when the customer was in a reasonable mood, I put the whole thing up to his sense of fair play. I appealed to the nobler motives. "First," I said, "I want you to know I also feel this matter has been badly mishandled. You've been inconvenienced and annoyed and irritated by one of our representatives. That should never have happened. I'm sorry and, as a representative of the company, I apologize. As I sat here and listened to your side of the story, I could not help being impressed by your fairness and patience. And now, because you are fair-minded and patient, I am going to ask you to do something for me. It's something that you can do better than anyone else, something you know more about than anyone else. Here is your bill; I know it is safe for me to ask you to adjust it, just as you would do if you were the president of my company. I am going to leave it all up to you. Whatever you say goes."

Did he adjust the bill? He certainly did, and got quite a kick out of it. The bills ranged from $150 to $400—but did the customer give himself the best of it? Yes, one of them did! One of them refused to pay a penny of the disputed charge; but the other five all gave the company the best of it! And here's the cream of the whole thing: we delivered new cars to all six of these customers within the next two years!

"Experience has taught me," says Mr. Thomas, "that when no information can be secured about the customer, the only sound basis on which to proceed is to assume that he or she is sincere, honest, truthful and willing and anxious to pay the charges, once convinced they are correct. To put it differently and perhaps more clearly, people are honest and want to discharge their obligations. The exceptions to that rule are comparatively few, and I am convinced that the individuals who are inclined to chisel will in most cases react favorably if you make them feel that you consider them honest, upright and fair."

Principle 10: Appeal to the nobler motives.

话，倾听他的意见，对他的想法表示关注与同情。5. 最后，顾客变得理智了，我使他觉得整个事情的交涉是公平的。我激发了他们高尚的动机。"首先，"我说，"我想使你明白，我也觉得这事情处理不当。我们公司的一个代表已经烦忧、激怒了你，并使你不愉快。那是不应发生的。我很抱歉，并以公司代表的资格表示道歉。我坐在这里听你阐述你的理由，不禁为你的公正与耐心感动。现在，因为你的公正和耐心，我想请你帮我一个忙，我想这件事你比谁都做得更好，因为你比谁都了解得多。这是你的账单，请你核查一下，我知道你会像我公司经理一样，我完全放心。我全部托付给你，你说多少就多少。"

顾客核查了账单吗?他的确这样做了，并且非常高兴。这些账单从150美元至400美元不等，但顾客为自己捞了便宜吗?是的，有一位确实因为对某一项存有疑问而拒付这笔钱，但其余5位顾客都慷慨地付清了欠账！这件事还有更妙的结果——在以后的两年内，这6位顾客都向我们公司买了新汽车！

"经验告诉我，"托马斯先生说，"在不了解顾客的确切情况之前，唯一妥善的办法就是假定他是一个真诚、诚实、可靠的人，一旦使他相信账目是准确无误的，他就会自愿付款。换一个更明晰的说法，人都是诚实的，都愿意履行应尽的义务。这一规则的例外非常少。而且我相信那些有意欺骗的人，如果你让他觉得你认为他是诚实、正直、公道的，那么大多数时候他就会做出积极的反应。"

第十项法则：激发人们高尚的动机。

11 The Movies Do It.Tv Does It.Why Don't You Do It?

Many years ago, the *Philadelphia Evening Bulletin* was being maligned by a dangerous whispering campaign.A malicious rumor was being circulated.Advertisers were being told that the newspaper was no longer attractive to readers because it carried too much advertising and too little news.Immediate action was necessary.The gossip had to be squelched.

But how?

This is the way it was done.

The *Bulletin* cliped from its regular edition all reading matter of all kinds on one average day, classified it, and published it as a book.The book was called *One Day*. It contained 307 pages—as many as a hard-covered book; yet the *Bulletin* had printed all this news and feature material on one day and sold it, not for several dollars, but for a few cents.

The printing of that book dramatized the fact that the *Bulletin* carried an enormous amount of interesting reading matter.It conveyed the facts more vividly, more interestingly, more impressively, than pages of figures and mere talk could have done.

This is the day of dramatization.Merely stating a truth isn't enough.The truth has to be made vivid, interesting, dramatic.You have to use showmanship.The movies do it.Television does it.And you will have to do it if you want attention.

Experts in window display know the power of dramatization.For example, the manufacturers of a new rat poison gave dealers a window display that included two live rats.The week the rats were shown, sales zoomed to five times their normal rate.

Television commercials abound with examples of the use of dramatic techniques in selling products.Sit down one evening in front of your television set and analyze what the advertisers do in each of their presentations.You will note how an antacid medicine changes the color of the acid in a test tube while its competitor doesn't, how one brand of soap or detergent gets a greasy shirt clean when the other brand leaves it gray.You'll see a car maneuver around a series of turns and curves—

第11章 戏剧化地表达你的意见

几年前,《费城晚报》受到一种危险的谣言恶意中伤。一则恶意的谣言正在四处散布。有人警告登广告的客户说,这家报纸刊登的广告太多,新闻太少,对于读者已经没有了吸引力。必须立即行动,以戳穿谣言。

但怎么做呢?

《费城晚报》采取的方法如下:

《晚报》将所有版面上每天的各种阅读资料全部剪下来,加以分类,出版成书,书名就叫《一天》,共有307页——与一本精装书一样多。但《晚报》将每天的新闻及文章印出来,售价不是几美元,而是几美分。

那本书的印行,证明《晚报》刊登了大量有趣的文章。这种方法远比列举数字及空谈更清楚、更有趣,给人印象更深刻。

这是一个富有戏剧色彩的时代,仅仅是叙述真理还远远不够,必须使之更生动、更有趣、更戏剧化。你必须使用吸引人的方法。电影是如此,广播是如此,所以,如果你想引起别人的注意,你也必须这样做。

橱窗展示专家非常了解戏剧化的威力。例如,灭鼠药制造商开发出一种新鼠药后,专门为经销商提供了一个橱窗展览,包括两只活老鼠。结果在展示活鼠的那个星期,销量比平时增加了5倍。

在各种电视广告中,更是有许多运用戏剧化的技巧促销产品的例子。当你晚上坐在电视机前,分析广告专家在每一个广告中的表现手法,你就会看到一种解酸剂在试管中如何改变酸的

far better than just being told about it.Happy faces will show contentment with a variety of products. All of these dramatize for the viewer the advantages offered by whatever is being sold—and they do get people to buy them.

You can dramatize your ideas in business or in any other aspect of your life.It's easy.Jim Yeamans,who sells for the NCR company (National Cash Register) in Richmond,Virginia,told how he made a sale by dramatic demonstration.

"Last week I called on a neighborhood grocer and saw that the cash registers he was using at his checkout counters were very old-fashioned.I approached the owner and told him: 'You are literally throwing away pennies every time a customer goes through your line.' With that I threw a handful of pennies on the floor.He quickly became more attentive.The mere words should have been of interest to him,but the sound of Pennies hitting the floor really stopped him.I was able to get an order from him to replace all of his old machines."

It works in home life as well.When the old-time lover proposed to his sweetheart,did he just use words of love?No! He went down on his knees.That really showed he meant what he said.We don't propose on our knees any more,but many suitors still set up a romantic atmosphere before they pop the question.

Dramatizing what you want works with children as well.Joe B.Fant,Jr.,of Birmingham, Alabama,was having difficulty getting his five-year-old boy and three-year-old daughter to pick up their toys,so he invented a"train."Joey was the engineer (Captain Casey Jones) on his tricycle. Janet's wagon was attached,and in the evening she loaded all the"coal"on the caboose (her wagon) and then jumped in while her brother drove her around the room.In this way the room was cleaned up—without lectures,arguments or threats.

Mary Catherine Wolf of Mishawaka,Indiana,was having some problems at work and decided that she had to discuss them with the boss.On Monday morning she requested an appointment with him but was told he was very busy and she should arrange with his secretary for an appointment later in the week.The secretary indicated that his schedule was very tight,but she would try to fit her in.

Ms.Wolf described what happened:

颜色,而另一种解酸剂却做不到;一种品牌的肥皂或洗衣粉如何洗干净油污的衣服,而另一种品牌还会留下污渍;你会看到一辆汽车在转弯飞驰——比只用嘴说的还要表现得好;以及快乐的面孔显示对各种产品的满意。所有这些,都是为了戏剧化地表现产品所能提供的好处——而且确实能够吸引观众购买这些东西。

你可以用戏剧化手法来表现你所能想到的任何经商观念或生活中的任何事物。这很容易。弗吉尼亚州瑞奇蒙市的吉姆·伊曼斯是国家现金注册公司的推销员,他讲了他如何用戏剧化的示范手法来达到促销目的的。

"上个星期,我拜访了我家附近一家杂货店的老板,看到他用的收银机是一种非常过时的老古董。我走近老板,对他说:'你实际上是在每一位顾客每次走过你柜台的时候,把钱丢出去。'同时我把一些硬币扔在了地上。他马上注意起我来。我只说一句话就引起了他的兴趣,但硬币丢在地上的声音使他停了下来。我从他那里得到了更新所有旧机器的订单。"

戏剧化的手法也适用于家庭生活中。过去男人向情人求婚时,是不是只说些情话呢?不是!他还会跪下来,这才真正地表示他是认真的。尽管我们现在不再下跪求婚了,但是还有很多男人在向情人求婚之前,会先布下罗曼蒂克的氛围。

把你所要的东西以戏剧化手法表现出来,对小孩也会有用。亚拉巴马州伯明翰市的乔·冯特先生很难让他5岁的儿子和3岁的女儿收拾玩具,因此他发明了一列"火车"。儿子乔伊当司机,骑着他那辆三轮车,女儿珍妮的篷车连接在后面。晚上,当她哥哥骑着车子绕室而行的时候,她则把所有的"煤"装上她的篷车改装成的"货车",然后,她也跳进车去。这样一来,屋内到处乱扔的玩具收拾好了——不需要教训、斥责或恐吓。

印第安纳州密莎瓦卡市的玛丽·伍尔夫,在工作上遇到了一些问题,认为必须和老板谈谈。星期一早晨,她要求和他面谈,但是他告诉她说他很忙,让她先和他的秘书联系,本周晚些时候再谈。秘书说

"I did not get a reply from her all week long.Whenever I questioned her,she would give me a reason why the boss could not see me.Friday morning came and I had heard nothing definite.I really wanted to see him and discuss my problems before the weekend,so I asked myself how I could get him to see me.

"What I finally did was this.I wrote him a formal letter.I indicated in the letter that I fully understood how extremely busy he was all week,but it was important that I speak with him.I enclosed a form letter and a self-addressed envelope and asked him to please fill it out or ask his secretary to do it and return it to me.The form letter read as follows:

Ms.Wolf—I will be able to see you on ___ at ___ A.M./P.M.I will give you ___ minutes of my time.

"I put this letter in his in-basket at 11 A.M.At 2 P.M.I checked my mailbox.There was my self-addressed envelope.He had answered my form letter himself and indicated he could see me that afternoon and could give me ten minutes of his time.I met with him,and we talked for over an hour and resolved my problems.

"If I had not dramatized to him the fact that I really wanted to see him,I would probably be still waiting for an appointment."

James B.Boynton had to present a lengthy market report.His firm had just finished an exhaustive study for a leading brand of cold cream.Data were needed immediately about the competition in this market; the prospective customer was one of the biggest—and most formidable—men in the advertising business.

And his first approach failed almost before he began.

"The first time I went in,"Mr.Boynton explains,"I found myself sidetracked into a futile discussion of the methods used in the investigation.He argued and I argued.He told me I was wrong,and I tried to prove that I was right.

"I finally won my point,to my own satisfaction—but my time was up,the interview was over,and I still hadn't produced results.

"The second time,I didn't bother with tabulations of figures and data,I went to see this man,I dramatized my facts.

他的日程表已经排满了,但是会想办法安排好。

伍尔夫夫人描述了经过:

"整个一星期,我一直没有得到那位秘书的通知。每当我问她时,她都找出老板没时间见我的各种理由。到了星期五早上,我还是没有得到确实的消息。我必须在周末之前见到他,和他谈我的问题,因此我就问自己怎样才能使老板接见我。

"最后我想了这样一个办法:我给他写了一封正式的信。我在信中表示我完全了解他整个星期都很忙,但是我要和他面谈的事也极为重要。我随信附了一张表和一个写了我自己名字的信封,请他或由他叫秘书把这张表填好,然后寄给我。这张表的内容是这样的:

伍尔夫夫人:我将在___月___日___点抽出___分钟和你见面讨论问题。

"我上午11点钟把这封信放在他的公文盒里面。下午两点钟我去看我的信箱,就收到了我自己写上名字的信封。他亲自给我回了信,表示当天下午就可以接见我,并且给我10分钟的时间谈话。我和他见了面,而且谈了一个多小时,解决了我的问题。

"如果我不把我要见他的事以戏剧化的方式表达出来,我可能现在还在等他。"

詹姆斯·普顿要作一个长篇市场报告。他的公司刚刚为一家最著名的润肤膏品牌完成了一项详尽的市场调研。对手的数据必须马上提交,而客户正是广告界资产实力最雄厚——也最让人头疼的人。

但是他的第一次报告还没开始就失败了。

"我第一次走进去时,"普顿先生说,"我竟跑题了,讨论起调查方法来。我们吵了起来。他说我错了,而我则竭力想证明我是对的。

"最后,我赢得了胜利,我自己也很满意——但我的时间正好到了。会谈完了,可是我仍然没有谈出什么结果。

"As I entered his office, he was busy on the phone. While he finished his conversation, I opened a suitcase and dumped thirty-two jars of cold cream on top of his desk—all products he knew—all competitors of his cream.

"On each jar, I had a tag itemizing the results of the trade investigation. And each tag told its story briefly, dramatically.

"What happened?

"There was no longer an argument. Here was something new, something different. He picked up first one and then another of the jars of cold cream and read the information on the tag. A friendly conversation developed. He asked additional questions. He was intensely interested. He had originally given me only ten minutes to present my facts, but ten minutes passed, twenty minutes, forty minutes, and at the end of an hour we were still talking.

"I was presenting the same facts this time that I had presented previously. But this time I was using dramatization, showmanship—and what a difference it made."

Principle 11: Dramatize your ideas.

"第二次,我没有再费神将数字及资料制成表格。我直接去找那人,戏剧化地表达我调查到的事实。

"当我走进他的办公室时,他正忙着接电话。他接完电话后,我打开一只手提箱,取出32瓶润肤膏,放在了他的桌上——这些都是他知道的产品——全都是他的竞争产品。

"我在每个瓶子上都贴上了标签,列出商业调查的结果。但每张标签都简明扼要,生动地说明了一切。

"结果如何呢?

"我们不再争论了。这是一种全新的、完全不同的结果。他先拿起一瓶又一瓶的润肤膏,阅读标签上的文字说明。我们开始了友善的交谈。他问了一些另外的问题,显然产生了极大的兴趣。他本来只给我10分钟时间报告结果,但现在10分钟过去了,20分钟、40分钟、1个小时过去了,我们却还在交谈。

"我这次报告的内容和上次的完全一样,但这次我采用了戏剧化的表现方法,其效果截然不同。"

第十一条法则:戏剧化地表现你的想法。

12 When Nothing Else Works, Try This

Charles Schwab had a mill manager whose people weren't producing their quota of work.

"How is it, "Schwab asked him, "that a manager as capable as you can't make this mill run out what it should?"

"I don't know, "the manager replied. "I've coaxed the men, I've pushed them, I've sworn and cussed, I've threatened them with damnation and being fired. But nothing works. They just won't produce."

This conversation took place at the end of the day, just before the night shift came on. Schwab asked the manager for a piece of chalk, then, turning to the nearest man, asked: "How many heats did your shift make today?"

"Six."

Without another word, Schwab chalked a big figure six on the floor, and walked away.

When the night shift came in, they saw the "6" and asked what it meant.

"The big boss was in here today, "the day people said. "He asked us how many heats we made, and we told him six. He chalked it down on the floor."

The next morning Schwab walked througt the mill again. The night shift had rubbed out "6" and replaced it with a big "7".

When the day shift reported for work the next morning, they saw a big "7" chalked on the floor. So the night shift thought they were better than the day shift, did they? Well, they would show the night shift a thing or two. The crew pitched in with enthusiasm, and when they quit that night, they left behind them an enormous, swaggering "10". Things were stepping up.

Shortly this mill, which had been lagging way behind in production, was turning out more work than any other mill in the plant.

The principle?

Let Charles Schwab say it in his own words, "The way to get things done, "say Schwab, "is to

第12章 提出有意义的挑战

有一次,查尔斯·施瓦伯下面一位钢厂经理来找他,因为他的工人完不成生产任务。

“怎么回事?”施瓦伯问,“像你这样能干的人,竟无法让钢厂运行?”

“我不知道。”这位经理回答说,“我曾以利诱导他们,也曾鼓动他们,或发誓、责骂,甚至用开除来威胁他们。但无论怎样都不管用,他们就是不愿工作。”

当时正巧白班刚下,夜班即将开始。施瓦伯向经理要了一支粉笔,然后转向最近的一个工人问道:“你们这班今天生产了多少炉?”

“6 炉。”

施瓦伯一声不响,只用粉笔在地上写了一个大大的“6”就走了。

上夜班的工人进来时,看见了“6”,就问是什么意思。

“大老板今天来了这里,”上日班的工人说,“他问我们产了几炉,我们告诉他 6 炉,他便在地板上写下了这数字。”

次日早晨,施瓦伯又来到这家钢厂,发现夜班工人已将“6”抹去,换上了一个大大的“7”。

早晨,白班工人来上班的时候,看见了地板上那个大大的“7”。夜班工人是要证明他们比白班强?是不是?那好,他们决定给夜班工人一点儿颜色看看。于是,他们热情地工作,在那晚下班时,留下了一个神气活现的大“10”。从此,情况好转起来。

不久,这家生产一度落后的钢厂比公司任何其他工厂产量都高。

原因在哪里呢?

且用施瓦伯自己的话来说:“使生产圆满完成的方法,就是激起竞争。我并不是指鄙贱、谋

stimulate competition.I do not mean in a sordid,money-getting way,but in the desire to excel."

The desire to excel! The challenge! Throwing down the gauntlet! An infallible way of appealing to people of spirit.

Without a challenge,Theodore Roosevelt would never have been President of the United States. The Rough Rider,just back from Cuba,was picked for governor of New York State.The opposition discovered he was no longer a legal resident of the state,and Roosevelt,frightened,wished to withdraw.Then Thomas Collier Platt,then U.S.Senator from New York,threw down the challenge. Turning suddenly on Theodore Roosevelt,he cried in a ringing voice:"Is the hero of San Juan Hill a coward?"

Roosevelt stayed in the fight—and the rest is history.A challenge not only changed his life; it had a real effect upon the future of his nation.

"All men have fears,but the brave put down their fears and go forward,sometimes to death,but always to victory"was the motto of the King's Guard in ancient Greece.What greater challenge can be offered than the opportunity to overcome those fears?

When Al Smith was governor of New York,he was up against it.Sing Sing,at the time the most notorious penitentiary west of Devil's Island,was without a warden.Scandals had been sweeping through the prison walls,scandals and ugly rumors.Smith needed a strong man to rule Sing Sing—an iron man.But who?He sent for Lewis E. Lawes of New Hampton.

"How about going up to take charge of Sing Sing?"he said jovially when Lawes stood before him."They need a man up there with experience."

Lawes was flabbergasted.He knew the dangers of Sing Sing.It was a political appointment, subject to the vagaries of political whims.Wardens had come and gone—one had lasted only three weeks.He had a career to consider.Was it worth the risk?

Then Smith,who saw his hesitation,leaned back in his chair and smiled."Young fellow,"he said,"I don't blame you for being scared.It's a tough spot.It'll take a big person to go up there and stay."

So Smith was throwing down a challenge,was he?Lawes liked the idea of attempting a job that called for someone"big".

利的竞争,而是超越对手的欲望。"

超越的欲望!挑战!这才是激励人的精神的可靠方法。

如果不是挑战,西奥多·罗斯福不会当上美国总统。当时,这位英勇的骑士刚从古巴归来,就被推选出来竞选纽约州长。当反对党人发现他并不是那个州的合法居民时,罗斯福慌了,想退出竞选。于是来自纽约的议员托马斯·普拉特向他提出了挑战。他突然转向罗斯福,大声叫道:"难道你这位圣巨思山的英雄竟是懦夫?"

罗斯福接受了挑战,继续奋斗,这才改写了历史。这项挑战不仅改变了罗斯福的一生,同时也对美国的历史产生了重大的影响!

"每个人都有害怕的时候,但是勇敢者会将畏惧放置一边,继续勇往直前,结果或许会走向死亡,但更多的则是通向胜利。"这是古希腊一位先哲的名言。还有什么东西比克服困难更具有挑战性呢?

当艾尔·史密斯担任纽约州长时,就用过这一方法。星星监狱——位于魔鬼岛西部的最负恶名的一个监狱,没有领导,丑闻在狱中满天飞。因此,史密斯需要一位强有力的人——一位铁人去治理星星监狱。但是找谁呢?他找来了新汉普顿的刘易斯·劳斯。

"去管理星星,如何?"当劳斯站在他面前的时候,他愉快地说,"那里需要一个有经验的人。"

劳斯非常为难。他知道星星的危险,那可是一项政治任务,极易受政治变化的影响,监狱长曾一再更换,有一位监狱长在职只有3个星期。他必须考虑他的前途。值得冒险吗?

史密斯看出了他的犹豫,便往椅背上一靠,露出了微笑。"年轻人,"他说,"我并不怪你的犹豫,那个地方是不太平,那儿需要一个大人物坐镇。"

史密斯提出了一个挑战,不是吗?而劳斯内心当然喜欢尝试出任一个大人物的工作。

So he went.And he stayed.He stayed,to become the most famous warden of his time.His book *20,000 Years in Sing Sing* sold into the hundreds of thousands of copies.His broadcasts on the air and his stories of prison life have inspired dozens of movies.His "humanizing"of criminals wrought miracles in the way of prison reform.

"I have never found,"said Harvey S.Firestone,founder of the great Firestone Tire and Rubber Company,"that pay and pay alone would either bring together or hold good people.I think it was the game itself."

Frederic Herzberg,one of the great behavorial scientists,concurred.He studied in depth the work attitudes of thousands of people ranging from factory workers to senior executives.What do you think he found to be the most motivating factor—the one facet of the jobs that was most stimulating?Money?Good working conditions?Fringe benefits?No—not any of those.The one major factor that motivated people was the work itself.If the work was exciting and interesting,the worker looked forward to doing it and was motivated to do a good job.

That is what every successful person loves:the game.The chance for self-expression.The chance to prove his or her worth,to excel,to win.That is what makes footraces and hog-calling and pie-eating contests.The desire to excel.The desire for a feeling of importance.

Principle 12:Throw down a challenge.

所以他去了,他待了下来,成了当今美国最著名的监狱长,他的著作《星星两万年》售出了几十万册。他曾在电台讲他在狱中的生活故事——它们被拍成了几十部电影。他对罪犯的"人道化"也创造了许多监狱改革的奇迹。

"我从不以为,"哈维·费尔斯通——伟大的火石轮胎公司的创始人说,"薪水,仅靠薪水,就能吸引那些优秀的员工。我想那要靠工作本身的竞争。"

伟大的行为科学家弗里德里克·赫兹伯也同意这种观点。他对上千名工厂员工及高级经理的工作态度作了深入的研究。你认为他发现的最富激励性的因素是什么?是工作具有刺激性?钞票?良好的工作条件?福利待遇?不,都不是!激励人们工作的主要因素正是工作本身。如果某项工作令人兴奋和感兴趣,那么人们就会渴望去做它,而且尽力做好它。

这正是每个成功者所喜爱的:竞争和表现自我的机会,证明他自己的价值、超越对手、获取胜利——渴望超越,渴望有一种重要的感觉。

第十二项法则:提出一个挑战。

Part Four
Be a Leader: How to Change People without Giving Offense or Arousing Resentment

1 If You Must Find Fault, This is the Way to Begin

A friend of mine was a guest at the White House for a weekend during the administration of Calvin Coolidge. Drifting into the President's private office, he heard Coolidge say to one of his secretaries, "That's a pretty dress you are wearing this morning, and you are a very attractive young woman."

That was probably the most effusive praise Silent Cal had ever bestowed upon a secretary in his life. It was so unusual, so unexpected, that the secretary blushed in confusion. Then Coolidge said, "Now, don't get stuck up. I just said that to make you feel good. From now on, I wish you would be a little bit more careful with your punctuation."

His method was probably a bit obvious, but the psychology was superb. It is always easier to listen to unpleasant things after we have heard some praise of our good points.

A barber lathers a man before he shaves him; and that is precisely what McKinley did back in 1896, when he was running for President. One of the prominent Republicans of that day had written a campaign speech that he felt was just a trifle better than Cicero and Patrick Henry and Daniel Webster all rolled into one. With great glee, this chap read his immortal speech aloud to McKinley. The speech had its fine points, but it just wouldn't do. It would have raised a tornado of criticism. McKinley didn't want to hurt the man's feelings. He must not kill the man's splendid enthusiasm, and yet he had to say "no". Note how adroitly he did it.

"My friend, that is a splendid speech, a magnificent speech," McKinley said. "No one could

第四篇 领导艺术:如何改变他人而不招致反感或怨恨

第1章 从赞美和欣赏开始

卡尔文·柯立芝总统在任的时候,我的一位朋友应邀于周末去白宫做客。当他踱入总统的私人办公室时,他听到柯立芝对他的一位秘书说:"你今天早上穿的衣服漂亮极了,你真是一位美貌迷人的姑娘。"

这可能是沉默寡言的柯立芝一生当中对一位秘书的最高称赞了。这事如此出乎寻常,以至于那位女秘书面红耳赤。然后,柯立芝说:"不要太高兴了。我说那话只是为了让你觉得好过些。从现在起,我希望你对标点符号稍加注意些。"

他的方法似乎太明显了一点儿,但这种心理却很巧妙。在我们听到别人对我们优点的称赞以后,再去听令人不愉快的话总会好受些。

理发师在给客人刮脸之前,先要在客人脸上涂肥皂。麦金利在1896年竞选总统时,采用的方法正是这种方法。当时一位著名的共和党成员写了一篇竞选演讲词,自认为比西西洛、亨利和韦伯斯特等人合起来所写的还要高明。他非常高兴地把他这篇不朽的演讲词大声朗读给麦金利听。尽管这篇演讲词有很多优点,但不适合竞选,因为那将会引起一场批评的风波。但麦金利不愿伤这人的感情,他知道自己不能挫伤这人的高度热忱,但他又不得不说"不"。看看他是怎样巧妙地处理此事的。

have prepared a better one.There are many occasions on which it would be precisely the right thing to say,but is it quite suitable to this particular occasion? Sound and sober as it is from your standpoint,I must consider its effect from the party's standpoint.Now you go home and write a speech along the lines I indicate,and send me a copy of it."

He did just that.McKinley blue-penciled and helped him rewrite his second speech,and he became one of the effective speakers of the campaign.

Here is the second most famous letter that Abraham Lincoln ever wrote.(His most famous one was written to Mrs.Bixby,expressing his sorrow for the death of the five sons she had lost in battle.) Lincoln probably dashed this letter off in five minutes; yet it sold at public auction in 1926 for twelve thousand dollars,and that,by the way,was more money than Lincoln was able to save during half a century of hard work.The letter was written to General Joseph Hooker on April 26,1863, during the darkest period of the Civil War.For eighteen months,Lincoln's generals had been leading the Union Army from one tragic defeat to another.Nothing but futile,stupid human butchery.The nation was appalled.Thousands of soldiers had deserted from the army,and even the Republican members of the Senate had revolted and wanted to force Lincoln out of the White House."We are now on the brink of destruction," Lincoln said."It appears to me that even the Almighty is against us.I can hardly see a ray of hope."Such was the period of black sorrow and chaos out of which this letter came.

I am printing the letter here because it shows how Lincoln tried to change an obstreperous general when the very fate of the nation could have depended upon the general's action.

This is perhaps the sharpest letter Abe Lincoln wrote after he became President; yet you will note that he praised General Hooker before he spoke of his grave faults.

Yes,they were grave faults,but Lincoln didn't call them that.Lincoln was more conservative, more diplomatic.Lincoln wrote:"There are some things in regard to which I am not quite satisfied with you." Talk about tact! And diplomacy!

Here is the letter addressed to General Hooker:

> I have placed you at the head of the Army of the Potomac.Of course,I have done this upon what appears to me to be sufficient reasons,and yet I think it best for you to know that

"朋友,这是一篇极其精彩、极其伟大的演讲词。"麦金利说,"再也没有人能写得比这篇更好的。它在许多场合都适用,不过对这次特殊的场合是否十分合适呢?从你的立场来看,那是非常合理而切题的,但我必须从整体角度来考虑它的影响。现在,请你回家去,根据我所指示的要点重写一篇演讲词,并送给我一份。"

他那样照办了。麦金利又帮他做了修改,并帮他重新写了第二篇演讲词。后来,他成为竞选班子中一位最得力的演说员。

下面是林肯总统所有信件中第二著名的信。(他最著名的一封信是写给贝克斯贝夫人的,对她在战争中丧失了5个儿子表示哀悼。)这封信林肯大约只花了5分钟就写完了,但在1926年公开拍卖时卖到了12000美元。顺便说一下,这比林肯辛苦工作50年的积蓄还要多。这封信是在1863年4月26日,也即内战最黑暗时期写给约瑟夫·胡克将军的。接连18个月,林肯的将军率领的联军连遭惨败,到处都是无益的、愚蠢的相互残杀。全国上下人心惶惶。数千名士兵开小差逃走,甚至连参议院的共和党议员都犯乱,强迫林肯让出白宫。"我们现今处在生死存亡的边缘,"林肯说,"我看连上帝都在反对我们。我几乎看不到一丝希望的曙光。"就在这黑暗、忧愁、混乱的局势下,林肯写了这封信。

我将这封信附在这里,因为它展示了林肯是如何改变一位哗闹作乱的将军的,而当时全国的成败系于这位将军的行动。

这恐怕是林肯担任总统以后所写的最严厉的一封信, 但你会看到他在指出胡克将军的严重错误以前,先称赞了他。

是的,那些错误确实很严重,但林肯并没有指明。林肯非常谨慎,而且很有策略。林肯写道:"对于有些事,我对你并不十分满意。"多么圆滑,多么机智!

下面就是林肯写给胡克将军的信:

there are some things in regard to which I am not quite satisfied with you.

I believe you to be a brave and skillful soldier, which, of course, I like. I also believe you do not mix politics with your profession, in which you are right. You have confidence in yourself, which is a valuable if not an indispensable quality.

You are ambitious, which, within reasonable bounds, does good rather than harm. But I think that during General Burnside's command of the army you have taken counsel of your ambition and thwarted him as much as you could, in which you did a great wrong to the country and to a most meritorious and honorable brother officer.

I have heard, in such a way as to believe it, of your recently saying that both the army and the Government needed a dictator. Of course, it was not for this, but in spite of it, that I have given you command.

Only those generals who gain successes can set up as dictators. What I now ask of you is military success and I will risk the dictatorship.

The Government will support you to the utmost of its ability, which is neither more nor less than it has done and will do for all commanders. I much fear that the spirit which you have aided to infuse into the army, of criticizing their commander and withholding confidence from him, will now turn upon you. I shall assist you, as far as I can, to put it down.

Neither you nor Napoleon, if he were alive again, could get any good out of an army while such spirit prevails in it, and now beware of rashness. Beware of rashness, but with energy and sleepless vigilance go forward and give us victories.

You are not a Coolidge, a McKinley or a Lincoln. You want to know whether this philosophy will operate for you in everyday business contacts. Will it? Let's see. Let's take the case of W.P.Gaw of the Wark Company, Philadelphia.

The Wark Company had contracted to build and complete a large office building in Philadelphia by a certain specified date. Everything was going along well; the building was almost finished, when suddenly the subcontractor making the ornamental bronze work to go on the exterior of this building declared that he couldn't make delivery on schedule. What! An entire building held up! Heavy penalties! Distressing losses! All because of one man!

我已经任命你为波多马克军队的首长。当然,我之所以这样做,自然有我认为很充分的理由。不过我想最好还是让你知道,有些事我对你并不十分满意。

我相信你是一位勇敢多谋的将军,那当然是我喜欢的。我也相信你不会将政治与你的军职混淆起来,在这件事情上,你做得很不错。你对自己很有信心,这正是一种极有价值同时也是不可或缺的性格。

你有雄心壮志,这在相当范围内是有益而无害的。但我认为,在伯恩赛将军统领军队时,你曾表现出你自己的个人野心,竭力地阻挠他,你在这件事情上,对国家以及对一位功勋卓著、享有盛誉的军官来说,都是极大的过错。

我曾听说,并因为言之确凿而不得不相信,你最近曾说军队与政府都需要一位独裁者。当然,我并不是因为这个原因,而是我并不顾及这个原因,才授予你军队统帅权的。

只有赢得胜利的将领才有可能成为独裁者。我现在对你要求的是军事上的胜利,所以不惜冒独裁的危险。

政府将尽一切能力帮助你,正如以往及今后对于所有将领的支持一样。我十分担心你以前带到军队中的那些思想——批评及不信任将领,现在它将回报到你的身上。我会尽力帮助你肃清这种思想。

当这种思想在军队中蔓延时,无论对你还是对拿破仑——如果他还活着,都绝不会有什么好处。现在,你千万要小心,绝不可轻率从事。绝不可轻率从事,但要以充沛的精力和永不疲倦的努力前进,并带给我们胜利。

你不是柯立芝、麦金利或林肯。你想知道的是这些哲学是否能在你的日常生活中应用,是吗?让我们拿费城华克公司的高伍先生为例来说吧。

华克公司在费城承包了一项建筑工程,并要求在指定的日期内完工。一切都进展顺利,这

Long-distance telephone calls. Arguments! Heated conversations! All in vain. Then Mr. Gaw was sent to New York to beard the bronze lion in his den.

"Do you know you are the only person in Brooklyn with your name?" Mr. Gaw asked the president of the subcontracting firm shortly after they were introduced. The president was surprised. "No, I didn't know that."

"Well," said Mr. Gaw, "when I got off the train this morning, I looked in the telephone book to get your address, and you're the only person in the Brooklyn phone book with your name."

"I never knew that," the subcontractor said. He checked the phone book with interest. "Well, it's an unusual name," he said proudly. "My family came from Holland and settled in New York almost two hundred years ago." He continued to talk about his family and his ancestors for several minutes. When he finished that, Mr. Gaw complimented him on how large a plant he had and compared it favorably with a number of similar plants he had visited. "It is one of the cleanest and neatest bronze factories I ever saw," said Gaw.

"I've spent a lifetime building up this business," the subcontractor said, "and I am rather proud of it. Would you like to take a look around the factory?"

During this tour of inspection, Mr. Gaw complimented the other man on his system of fabrication and told him how and why it seemed superior to those of some of his competitors. Gaw commented on some unusual machines and the subcontractor announced that he himself had invented those machines. He spent considerable time showing Gaw how they operated and the superior work they turned out. He insisted on taking his visitor to lunch. So far, mind you, not a word had been said about the real purpose of Gaw's visit.

After lunch, the subcontractor said, "Now, to get down to business. Naturally, I know why you're here. I didn't expect that our meeting would be so enjoyable. You can go back to Philadelphia with my promise that your material will be fabricated and shipped, even if other orders have to be delayed."

Mr. Gaw got everything that he wanted without even asking for it. The material arrived on time, and the building was completed on the day the completion contract specified.

Would this have happened had Mr. Gaw used the hammer-and-dynamite method generally

项工程就快要完成了。这时,负责供应外部装饰铜器的承包商突然说他不能按期交货。什么?整个建筑工程都要搁浅?而这巨额的罚金、惨重的损失,都因为一个人?

长途电话、争论、激烈的争吵,全都没有用。于是高伍先生被派往纽约解决难题。

"你知道你的姓名在布鲁克林区是独一无二的吗?"在互作介绍之后,高伍先生这样问道。这位经理很惊异:"不,我可不知道。"

"哦,"高伍先生说,"当我今天早上走下火车后,查看电话簿找你的住址时,在布鲁克林区的电话簿中只有你一个人叫你这姓名的。"

"我可一直都不知道,"这位经理说。他开始很有兴趣地查看电话簿。"啊,那不是普通的姓名,"他自豪地说,"我的家庭大约在200年前从荷兰迁到纽约来的。"他接着谈论他的家庭及祖先,长达几分钟。当他说完后,高伍先生又恭维他有那么大的一个工厂,并且比他曾参观过的几家同样的公司更好。"这是我所见过的最清洁的铜器厂。"高伍先生说。

"我花了一生的心血经营它。"这位经理说,"对此我很自豪。你愿意参观一下工厂吗?"

在参观的时候,高伍先生又赞扬了他的管理组织系统,并告诉他为什么他的工厂看来比他的几家竞争者要好,以及好在哪里。高伍先生提到了工厂中几种特殊的机器,这位经理说那些机器是他自己发明的。他特别花了许多时间带高伍先生去看那些机器,解释它们如何工作,以及产品如何精良等。他坚持要请高伍先生吃午餐。注意,高伍先生对他的目的还只字未提。

吃完午餐后,这位经理说:"现在,我们谈正事吧。自然,我知道你是为什么来的。我没有想到我们的聚会如此愉快。你可以回费城转达我的承诺,即使其他生意我不得不延迟,你们的材料我也将保证按期做好并运到。"高伍先生甚至没有任何请求,就得到了他所需要的东西。结果,材料按期交到,建筑工程在合同期满的那天竣工了。

如果高伍先生采用平常人在这种情形下所用的争执吵闹的方法,会有这样的结果吗?

employed on such occasions?

Dorothy Wrublewski, a branch manager of the Fort Monmouth, New Jersey, Federal Credit Union, reported to one of our classes how she was able to help one of her employees become more productive.

"We recently hired a young lady as a miler trainee. Her contact with our customers was vary good. She was accurate and efficient in handling individual transactions. The problem developed at the end of the day when it was time to balance out.

"The head teller came to me and strongly suggested that I fire this woman. 'She is holding up everyone else because she is so slow in balancing out. I've shown her over and over, but she can't get it. She's got to go.'

"The next day I observed her working quickly and accurately when handling the normal everyday transactions, and she was very pleasant with our customers.

"It didn't take long to discover why she had trouble balancing out. After the office closed, I went over to talk with her. She was obviously nervous and upset. I praised her for being so friendly and outgoing with the customers and complimented her for the accuracy and speed used in that work. I then suggested we review the procedure we use in balancing the cash drawer. Once she realized I had confidence in her, she easily followed my suggestions and soon mastered this function. We have had no problems with her since then."

Beginning with praise is like the dentist who begins his work with Novocain. The patient still gets a drilling, but the Novocain is pain-killing. A leader will use...

Principle 1: Begin with praise and honest appreciation.

新泽西州福特蒙马斯市有一位联邦信用合作社支行经理桃乐丝·鲁布卢斯基，她在我班上讲了她如何帮助手下员工提高工作效率的事。

“最近，我们雇了一位年轻女孩当实习出纳。她与顾客的关系很好，处理问题时效率很高。但有一天结账时，却出了问题。

“出纳部经理来找我，强烈要求解雇她：‘她耽误了大家的工作。我不知教了她多少次，可她太笨了。一定得辞掉她。’

“第二天，我见她处理业务时确实非常迅速准确，而且与顾客相处很愉快。

“但没过多久，我就发现她在结账时为何出问题的。下班以后，我找到她。她显得很是不安。我夸奖了她的友善和工作热情，以及她工作时的准确和速度。我建议她将现金平衡过程复习一下。她明白了我对她的信任，照我的建议做了，很快就掌握了。以后，她再也没有出过错。”

用赞美的方式开始，就好像牙科医生用麻醉剂一样，病人仍然要受钻牙之苦，但麻醉剂却能消除这种痛苦。作为领导者，应该用……

第一项法则：从赞美和真诚的欣赏着手。

2 How to Criticize—and Not Be Hated for It

Charles Schwab was passing through one of his steel mills one day at noon when he came across some of his employees smoking.Immediately above their heads was a sign that said "No Smoking." Did Schwab point to the sign and say,"Can't you read?" Oh,no not Schwab.He walked over to the men,handed each one a cigar,and said,"I'll appreciate it,boys,if you will smoke these on the outside." They knew that he knew that they had broken a role—and they admired him because he said nothing about it and gave them a little present and made them feel important, couldn't keep from loving a man like that,could you?

John Wanamaker used the same technique.Wanamaker used to make a tour of his great store in Philadelphia every day.Once he saw a customer waiting at a counter.No one was paying the slightest attention to her.The salespeople? Oh,they were in a huddle at the far end of the counter laughing and talking among themselves.Wanamaker didn't say a word.Quietly slipping behind the counter,he waited on the woman himself and then handed the purchase to the salespeople to be wrapped as he went on his way.

Public officials are often criticized for not being accessible to their constituents.They are busy people,and the fault sometimes lies in overprotective assistants who don't want to overburden their bosses with too many visitors.Carl Langford,who has been mayor of Orlando,Florida,the home of Disney World,for many years,frequently admonished his staff to allow people to see him.He clamed he had an "open-door" policy; yet the citizens of his community were blocked by secretaries and administrators when they called.

Finally the mayor found the solution.He removed the door from his office! His aides got the message,and the mayor has had a truly open administration since the day his door was symbolically thrown away.

Simply changing one three-letter word can often spell the difference between failure and success in changing people without giving offense or arousing resentment.

第2章 间接提醒对方的错误

查尔斯·施瓦伯有一天中午经过他的一个钢厂,看见几个工人正在吸烟。而在他们头顶上方就悬挂着一块"禁止吸烟"的牌子。施瓦伯是否指着牌子说:"你们不识字吗?"不!施瓦伯绝不会这么做。他走到这些人跟前,发给每人一支雪茄,说道:"孩子们,如果你们到外边吸烟,我会感激不尽。"他们知道他们违反了规定——但他们赞赏他,因为他什么也没有说,还送给他们一点小礼物,使他们感受到了尊重。你能不喜欢像施瓦伯那样的人吗?

约翰·华纳梅克也使用过同样的方法。华纳梅克习惯每天去他在费城的大百货商场巡视一次。有一次,他看见一位顾客在柜台前无人服务,而店员正在柜台另一端聊天。于是他一声不响地轻轻溜入柜台后面,自己接待了这位顾客,然后将商品交给售货员包扎,自己就走开了。

官员们经常被批评不接见民众。他们非常忙碌,但有时候由于助手们过度保护他的上司,不想让他接见太多的来访者而产生负担。卡尔·兰福特曾担任迪斯尼世界所在地佛罗里达州奥兰多市的市长许多年。他时常告诫部属,要让民众来见他。他宣称自己打算推行"开门政策"。然而,当他社区的民众来拜访他时,都被秘书和行政官员挡在了门外。

最后,这位市长找到了解决的办法。他拆掉了办公室的大门。他的助手们知道了这件事。从此以后,这位市长真正做到了"行政公开"。

若想不惹人生气并改变别人,只要换两个字,就会产生截然不同的效果。

许多人在开始批评之前,都先真诚地赞美对方,然后接下来会说"但是",再进行批评。例如,要改变某个孩子读书不专心的态度,我们可能会说:"乔尼,我们真的以你为荣,这学期你成绩有了进步。'但是',假如你的代数再努力一些的话,就会更好了。"

Many people begin their criticism with sincere praise followed by the word "but" and ending with a critical statement.For example,in trying to change a child's careless attitude toward studies, we might say,"We're really proud of you,Johnnie,for raising your grades this term.*But* if you had worked harder on your algebra,the results would have been better."

In this case,Johnnie might feel encouraged until he heard the word "but".He might then question the sincerity of the original praise.To him,the praise seemed only to be a contrived lead-into a critical inference of failure.Credibility would be strained,and we probably would not achieve our objectives of changing Johnnie's attitude toward his studies.

This could be easily overcome by changing the word "but" to "and." "We're really proud of you,Johnnie,for raiseing your grades this term,*and* by continuing the same conscientious efforts next term,your algebra grade can be up with all the others."

Now,Johnnie would accept the praise because there was no follow-up of an inference of failure.We have called his attention to the behavior we wished to change indirectly,and the chances are he will try to live up to our expectations.

Calling attention to one's mistakes indirectly works wonders with sensitive people who may resent bitterly any direct criticism.Marge Jacob of Woonsocket,Rhode Island,told one of our classes how she convinced some sloppy construction workers to clean up after themselves when they were building additions to her house.

For the first few days of the work,when Mrs.Jacob returned from her job,she noticed that the yard was strewn with the cut ends of lumber.She didn't want to antagonize the builders,because they did excellent work.So after the workers had gone home,she and her children picked up and neatly piled all the lumber debris in a corner.The following morning she called the foreman to one side and said,"I'm really pleased with the way the front lawn was left last night; it is nice and clean and does not offend the neighbors." From that day forward the workers picked up and piled the debris to one side,and the foreman came in each day seeking approval of the condition the lawn was left in after a day's work.

One of the major areas of controversy between members of the army reserves and their regular army trainers is haircuts.The reservists consider themselves civilians (which they are most of the

在这个例子里,可能约翰在听到“但是”之前会感觉很高兴。而当他听到“但是”时,马上就会怀疑这称赞的可信度。对他而言,这种称赞只是批评他失败的一种开头而已。由于可信度遭到了曲解,我们也许就不能达到改变他的学习态度的目的。

只要把“但是”改为“而且”,就可以轻易解决这个问题了。“我们真的以你为荣,乔尼,这学期你的成绩有了进步;而且,只要你下学期继续努力,你的代数就会赶上别人了。”

这样乔尼就会接受这种称赞,因为你没有把失败的推论放在后面。我们已经间接地让他知道我们想使他有所改变,因此他会尽力实现我们的期望。

对那些不愿接受直接批评的人,如果能间接地让他们认识自己的错误,就会收到非常神奇的效果。住在罗得岛温沙克的玛姬·雅克布在我班上讲述了她是如何使得一群磨洋工的建筑工人帮她盖房子之后清理干净的。

最初几天,当雅克布夫人下班回家之后,发现满院子都是锯木屑。她不想找那些工人争论,因为他们的工程做得很好。所以当这些工人走了之后,她和孩子们捡好碎木块,并整整齐齐地堆放在角落里。次日早晨,她把领班叫到旁边说:“我很高兴昨天晚上地上这么干净,又没有让邻居感到不方便。”从那天起,工人们每天都会捡好木屑堆在一边,领班也每天都来看看。

在预备役军人和正规军训练人员之间,最大的差异就是理发,预备役军人认为他们只是老百姓,因此非常不愿把头发剪短。

美国陆军第542分校的士官长哈雷·凯塞在带预备役军官时,就面临着这一问题。跟以前正规军的士官长一样,他可以向他的士兵怒吼或威胁。但他不愿这样做。

“先生们,”他开始说,“你们都是领导。当你们以身教导时,那是最有效的。你们必须为自己领导的人做出榜样。你们应该了解军队对理发的规定。今天我也要去理发,而我的头发却比某些人的头发要短多了。你们不妨对着镜子看看,如果你们要做个榜样的话,我们会帮你们安排

time) and resent having to cut their hair short.

Master Sergeant Harley Kaiser of the 542nd USAR School addressed himself to this problem when he was working with a group of reserve noncommissioned officers.As an old-time regular-army master sergeant,he might have been expected to yell at his troops and threaten them.Instead he chose to make his point indirectly.

"Gentlemen," he started, "you are leaders.You will be most effective when you lead by example.You must be the example for your men to follow.You know what the army regulations say about haircuts.I am going to get my hair cut today,although it is still much shorter than some of yours.You look at yourself in the mirror,and if you feel you need a haircut to be a good example, we'll arrange time for you to visit the post barbership."

The result was predictable.Several of the candidates did look in the mirror and went to the barbershop that afternoon and received "regulation" haircuts.Sergeant Kaiser commented the next morning that he already could see the development of leadership qualities in some of the members of the squad.

On March 8,1887,the eloquent Henry Ward Beecher died.The following Sunday,Lyman Abbott was invited to speak in the pulpit left silent by Beecher's passing.Eager to do his best,he wrote,rewrote and polished his sermon with the meticulous care of a Flaubert.Then he read it to his wife.It was poor—as most written speeches are.She might have said,if she had had less judgment, "Lyman,that is terrible. That'll never do.You'll put people to sleep.It reads like an encyclopedia.You ought to know better than that after all the years you have been preaching.For heaven's sake,why don't you talk like a human being? Why don't you act natural? You'll disgrace yourself if you ever read that stuff."

That's what she *might* have said.And,if she had,you know what would have happened.And she knew too.So,she merely remarked that it would make an excellent article for the *North American Review*. In other words,she praised it and at the same time subtly suggested that it wouldn't do as a speech.Lyman Abbott saw the point,tore up his carefully prepared manuscript and preached without even using notes.

An effective way to correct others' mistakes is...

Principle 2:Call attention to people's mistakes indirectly.

时间去营区理发部理发。"

结果是可以预料的。有几个人自动去镜子前看了看,然后下午去理发部按规定理了发。次日早晨,凯塞讲评时说,他已经看到队伍中有些人已经具备了领导者的气质。

1887年3月8日,口才大师亨利·华德·毕切尔去世了。在下一个星期日,莱曼·阿伯特应邀向那些因毕切尔去世而伤心不已的牧师演讲。他急于取得成功,把演讲词改了又改,就像福楼拜一样小心地进行润饰。然后他将演讲词读给他妻子听。演讲词写得并不好,就像大多数演讲词一样。如果他妻子缺乏见识,她可能会这样说:"莱曼,糟极了,绝对不能用。你会让听众都睡着的,那听起来像一本百科全书。你传道这么多年,应该知道写得更好。天啊!你为什么不像普通人那样去讲呢?你为什么不自然点儿?你如果念那篇东西,一定会搞糟的。"

她可能会这样说的。如果她真的那样说了,你也知道结果会怎样。她也知道。所以,她只这样说:如果演讲词寄给《北美评论》,一定是一篇极好的文章。换言之,她称赞了这篇演讲词,同时又巧妙地暗示不能用这篇演讲词。莱曼·阿伯特看出了这点,干脆将他精心准备的底稿撕碎,没用讲稿就自然地作了演讲。

有效地改正别人错误的方法是……

第二项法则:间接提醒别人注意他的错误。

3 Talk about Your Own Mistakes First

My niece, Josephine Carnegie, had come to New York to be my secretary. She was nineteen, had graduated from high school three years previously, and her business experience was a trifle more than zero. She became one of the most proficient secretaries west of Suez, but in the beginning, she was—well, susceptible to improvement. One day when I started to criticize her, I said to myself, "Just a minute, Dale Carnegie; just a minute. You are twice as old as Josephine. You have had ten thousand times as much business experience. How can you possibly expect her to have your viewpoint, your judgment, your initiative—mediocre though they may be? And just a minute, Dale, what were you doing at nineteen? Remember the asinine mistakes and blunders you made? Remember the time you did this...and that...?"

After thinking the matter over, honestly and impartially, I concluded that Josephine's batting average at nineteen was better than mine had been—and that, I'm sorry to confess, isn't paying Josephine much of a compliment.

So after that, when I wanted to call Josephine's attention to a mistake, I used to begin by saying, "You have made a mistake, Josephine, but the Lord knows, it's no worse than many I have made. You were not born with judgment. That comes only with experience, and you are better than I was at your age. I have been guilty of so many stupid, silly things myself, I have very little inclination to criticize you or anyone. But don't you think it would have been wiser if you had done so and so?"

It isn't nearly so difficult to listen to a recital of your faults if the person criticizing begins by humbly admitting that he, too, is far from impeccable.

E.G. Dillistone, an engineer in Brandon, Manitoba, Canada, was having problems with his new secretary. Letters he dictated were coming to his desk for signature with two or three spelling mistakes per page. Mr. Dillistore reported how he handled this:

"Like many engineers, I have not been noted for my excellent English or spelling. For years I

第3章 先谈你自己的错误

我侄女约瑟芬·卡耐基来纽约当我的秘书。她才19岁，高中毕业刚3年，几乎没有任何工作经验。而现在，她却是苏伊士运河以西最称职的秘书之一。但在刚开始时，她——哦，尚待改进。有一天，我正要批评她的时候，我对我自己说："且慢，戴尔·卡耐基，且慢。你的年纪比约瑟芬大一倍，经验比她多一万倍。你怎么可能希望她有你的观点，有你的判断，有你的精力呢——虽然这些都是很平凡的？等等，戴尔，你在19岁时正干什么？还记得你那时呆笨的举动、愚蠢的错误吗？记得你……的时候吗？"

经过真诚而公平地考虑之后，我得出结论：约瑟芬19岁的能力比我那时可要强多了——尽管如此，我很惭愧地承认，我并没有经常称赞约瑟芬。

所以，从那以后，当我要让约瑟芬注意她的错误时，我就会这样开始："约瑟芬，你做错了一件事，但老天知道，我所做的许多事比这更糟糕。你并非天生就具有判断力，那只能从经验中得来，而且你比我在你这年纪时强多了。我自己也曾犯过许多愚蠢的错误，所以我不愿意批评你或任何人。但如果你这样去做，你想那不是更聪明吗？"

如果你一开始就承认自己的错误，然后再指出别人的错误，那么情形就会好得多。

迪利斯通是加拿大曼尼托巴省布兰顿市一位工程师，在与秘书相处时遇到了问题。秘书送给他的口授信件每页总会有两三处拼错的。他讲了他是如何处理此事的：

"和许多工程师一样，我的英文或拼写也不好。多年来，我总是带着一个小本子，记下我拼错的词。当我发现仅仅指出错误并不能提高秘书的拼写水平时，我决定另想办法。当我下一次发现错误时，就坐到打字机旁说：

have kept a little black thumb-index book for words I had trouble spelling. When it became apparent that merely pointing out the errors was not going to cause my secretary to do more proofreading and dictionary work, I resolved to take another approach. When the next letter came to my attention that had errors in it, I sat down with the typist and said:

"Somehow this word doesn't look right. It's one of the words I always have had trouble with. That's the reason I started this spelling book of mine. [I opened the book to the appropriate page.] Yes, here it is. I'm very conscious of my spelling now because people do judge us by our letters and misspellings make us look less professional.

"I don't know whether she copied my system or not, but since that conversation, her frequency of spelling errors has been significantly reduced."

The polished Prince Bernhard von Bülow learned the sharp necessity of doing this back in 1909. Von Bülow was then the Imperial Chancellor of Germany, and on the throne sat Wilhelm II—Wilhelm, the haughty; Wilhelm the arrogant; Wilhelm, the last of the German Kaisers, building an army and navy that he boasted could whip their weight in wildcats.

Then an astonishing thing happened. The Kaiser said things, incredible things, things that rocked the continent and started a series of explosions heard around the world. To make matters infinitely worse, the Kaiser made silly, egotistical, absurd announcements in public, he made them while he was a guest in England, and he gave his royal permission to have them printed in the *Daily Telegraph*. For example, he declared that he was the only German who felt friendly toward the English; that he was constructing a navy against the menace of Japan; that he, and he alone, had saved England from being humbled in the dust by Russia and France; that it had been his campaign plan that enabled England's Lord Roberts to defeat the Boers in South Africa; and so on and on.

No other such amazing words had ever fallen from the lips of a European king in peacetime within a hundred years. The entire continent buzzed with the fury of a hornet's nest. England was incensed. German statesmen were aghast. And in the midst of all this consternation, the Kaiser became panicky and suggested to Prince von Bülow, the Imperial Chancellor, that he take the blame. Yes, he wanted von Bülow to announce that it was all his responsibility, that he had advised

"这个字似乎不对，它也是我常拼错的词之一。这就是我开始做这个拼写本的原因。(我打开它，翻到那一页。)哦，就在这里。我现在对拼写很注意，因为别人常通过我们的信件来评判我们，而拼错会让我们显得很不专业。

"我不知道她是否采用了我的方法，但从那次谈话以后，她的拼写错误明显少了。"

风度优雅的布洛亲王早在1909年就明白这样做很有必要。当时，布洛亲王是德国总理大臣，而德国皇帝则是威廉二世——傲慢自大的威廉，也是德国凯萨王朝最后一位皇帝——他建立了陆军和海军，并自夸能征服一切。

于是，震惊世人的事情发生了。这位德国皇帝竟然说了许多令人难以置信、震惊世人的话。例如他是唯一一位对英国友好的德国人，为了对抗日本的威胁他建立了一支海军，他一人挽救了英国，使之免于向俄、法称臣，由于他的征讨计划，使英国得以在南非战胜土著人等。更糟糕的是，他竟然允许《每日电讯报》将他这些丧失理智的自吹自擂的言论公之于众。于是，这些爆炸性的新闻震动了整个欧洲，波及全世界。

在100多年的和平时期里，还没有一位欧洲君主说过这样的话。整个欧洲立即轰动了，如激怒的野蜂；英国也被激怒了，德国政治家更是惊骇万分。在这种形势下，德国皇帝也惶恐不安，提议由总理大臣布洛来处理此事。是的，他希望布洛亲王宣布这一切责任都是他的，是他建议他的君主说这些令人难以相信的话。

"但是陛下，"布洛反对说，"在我看来，不论在德国或英国，绝对不会有任何人相信我会建议陛下说这些话的。"

布洛一说出这句话，就意识到自己犯了一个严重的错误。德皇果然大为恼火。

他咆哮着说："你以为我是一头笨驴，只会犯你永远都不会犯的错！"

布洛知道他应先称赞皇帝再提出批评意见，但事已至此，他只得退而求其次。他在批评之

his monarch to say these incredible things.

"But Your Majesty," von Bülow protested, "it seems to me utterly impossible that anybody either in Germany or England could suppose me capable of having advised Your Majesty to say any such thing."

The moment those words were out of von Bülow's mouth, he realized he had made a grave mistake. The Kaiser blew up.

"You consider me a donkey," he shouted, "capable of blunders you yourself could never have committed!"

Von Bülow's knew that he ought to have praised before he condemned; but since that was too late, he did the next best thing. He praised after he had criticized. And it worked a miracle.

"I'm far from suggesting that," he answered respectfully. "Your Majesty surpasses me in many respects; not only, of course, in naval and military knowledge, but above all, in natural science. I have often listened in admiration when Your Majesty explained the barometer, or wireless telegraphy, or the Roentgen rays. I am shamefully ignorant of all branches of natural science, have no notion of chemistry or physics, and am quite incapable of explaining the simplest of natural phenomena. But," von Bülow continued, "in compensation, I possess some historical knowledge and perhaps certain qualities useful in politics, especially in diplomacy."

The Kaiser beamed. Von Bülow had praised him. Von Bülow had exalted him and humbled himself. The Kaiser could forgive anything after that. "Haven't I always told you," he exclaimed with enthusiasm, "that we complete one another famously? We should stick together, and we will!"

He shook hands with von Bülow, not once, but several times. And later in the day he waxed so enthusiastic that he exclaimed with doubled fists, "If anyone says anything to me against Prince von Bülow, *I shall punch him in the nose*."

Von Bülow saved himself in time—but, canny diplomat that he was, he nevertheless had made one error: he should ,have *begun* by talking about his own shortcomings and Wilhelm's superiority—not by intimating that the Kaiser was a half-wit in need of a guardian.

If a few sentences humbling oneself and praising the other party can turn a haughty, insulted Kaiser into a staunch friend, imagine what humility and praise can do for you and me in our daily

后再予称赞。结果极其神妙。

"我绝不会有那样的意思,"他恭敬地回答说,"陛下在许多方面都胜过我,这不只是就海陆军知识而言,尤为重要的是在自然科学方面。每次倾听陛下解释晴雨表、无线电报或伦琴射线时,我总是对自己对各种自然科学一无所知而深感惭愧,我不懂化学或物理,不能解释最简单的自然现象,因此对陛下万分钦佩。但是,"布洛接着说,"作为补偿,我知道一些历史知识,以及一些在政治上,特别是在外交上有用的知识。"

德皇高兴了。布洛亲王称赞了他。布洛赞扬了他而使自己显得卑微。这时的德皇已经能宽容任何事。"我不是常告诉你,"他热情地说,"我们应互相取长补短吗?我们应齐心协力,而且我们愿意这样!"

他与布洛握了握手,不只是一次,而是多次。那天下午,他尤其激动,握紧双拳喊道:"如果任何人对我说布洛亲王不好,我将一拳砸扁他的鼻子!"

布洛及时救了自己——但像他这样机敏的外交家还是犯了一个错误:他应该一开始先谈自己的短处和威廉的长处——而不要暗示德皇是一个智力不足、需要保护的人。

如果仅仅说几句自我谦恭、称赞对方的话,就能使一位傲慢孤僻的德国皇帝变成一个牢固可靠的朋友,那你就可以想象得到谦逊与称赞在我们的日常生活中多么有用。如果运用得当,它们必然有助于我们在人际关系上创造奇迹。

一个人即使还没有改正他的错误,但只要承认自己的错误,就有助于帮助另一个人改变其行为。最近这句话从马里兰州提蒙尼姆市的克拉伦斯·周哈森那里得到了验证,当时他发现他15岁的儿子正在尝试抽烟。

"当然,我不希望大卫吸烟,"周哈森先生说,"但我和他妈妈都吸烟,我们给他树立了一个不好的榜样。我向大卫解释,说我在他这么大时就开始抽烟,尼古丁最终战胜了我,使我上了

contacts.Rightfully used, they will work veritable miracles in human relations.

Admitting one's own mistakes—even when one hasn't corrected them—can hell convince somebody to change his behavior.This was illustrated more recently by Clarence Zerhusen of Timonium, Maryland, when he discovered his fifteen -year -old son was experimenting with cigarettes.

"Naturally, I didn't want David to smoke," Mr.Zerhusen told us, "but his mother and I smoked cigarettes; we were giving him a bad example all the time.I explained to Dave how I started smoking at about his age and how the nicotine had gotten the best of me and how it was nearly impossible for me to stop.I reminded him how irritating my cough was and how he had been after me to give up cigarettes not many years before.

"I didn't exhort him to stop or make threats or warn him about their dangers.All I did was point out how I was hooked on cigarettes and what it had meant to me.

"He thought about it for a while and decided he wouldn't smoke until he had graduated from high school.As the years went by David never did start smoking and has no intention of ever doing so.

"As a result of that conversation I made the decision to stop smoking cigarettes myself, and with the support of my family, I have succeeded."

A good leader follows this principle:

Principle 3: Talk about your own mistakes before criticizing the other person.

瘾。我还提醒他，我的咳嗽很厉害；如果他也吸烟，很快就会和我一样。

"我并没有劝他不要吸烟，或警告他吸烟的害处。我只是告诉他我如何吸上烟并深受其害的。

"他想了一会儿，然后决定在高中毕业前不吸烟。直到现在他也确实没有吸过烟。

"那次谈话的结果，是我也决定戒烟。由于家人的支持，我戒烟成功了。"

一个好的领导会遵守下面这项法则：

第三项法则：在批评别人之前，先谈你自己的错误。

4 No One Likes to Take Orders

I once had the pleasure of dining with Miss Ida Tarbell, the dean of American biographers. When I told her I was writing this book, we began discussing this all-important subject of getting along with people, and she told me that while she was writing her biography of Owen D.Young, she interviewed a man who had sat for three years in the same office with Mr.Young. This man declared that during all that time he had never heard Owen D.Young give a direct order to anyone. He always gave suggestions, not orders. Owen D.Young never said, for example, "Do this or do that," or "Don't do this or don't do that." He would say, "You might consider this," or "Do you think that would work?" Frequently he would say, after he had dictated a letter, "What do you think of this?" In looking over a letter of one of his assistants, he would say, "Maybe if we were to phrase it this way it would be better." He always gave people the opportunity to do things themselves; he never told his assistants to do things; he let them do them, let them learn from their mistakes.

A technique like that makes it easy for a person to correct errors. A technique like that saves a person's pride and gives him or her a feeling of importance. It encourages cooperation instead of rebellion.

Resentment caused by a brash order may last a long time—even if the order was given to correct an obviously bad situation. Dan Santarelli, a teacher at a vocational school in Wyoming, Pennsylvania, told one of our classes how one of his students had blocked the entrance way to one of the school's shops by illegally parking his car in it. One of the other instructors stormed into the classroom and asked in an arrogant tone, "Whose car is blocking the driveway?" When the student who owned the car responded, the instructor screamed, "Move that car and move it right now, or I'll wrap a chain around it and drag it out of there."

Now that student was wrong. The car should not have been parked there. But from that day on, not only did that student resent the instructor's action, but all the students in the class did everything they could to give the instructor a hard time and make his job unpleasant.

第4章 没有人喜欢接受命令

我曾荣幸地同美国著名传记作家伊达·塔贝尔小姐一起吃饭。我告诉她我正在写这本书,于是我们开始讨论"为人处世"这个重要话题。她告诉我,她在写欧文·扬的传记时,访问了曾与扬先生在同一房间办公3年的一位先生。这人说,在那期间,他从未听到欧文·扬给任何人下达过直接命令。他总是"建议",而不是"命令"。例如,欧文·扬从未说过"做这个或那个",或"别做这个别做那个"。他总是说:"你可以考虑这个"或"你以为那样合适吗?"当他口述一封信后,常这样说:"你认为如何?"在看完他的助手写的信以后,他会说:"也许这样措辞会更好些。"他总给别人机会亲自动手做事,而从不告诉他的助手该如何去做事;他让他们自己去做,让他们从自己的错误中学习。

像这种方法,能使人更容易改正错误。像这种方法,能维持一个人的自尊,给他一种自重感,使他乐于合作而非对立。

无礼的命令所引起的愤怒可能会持续很长时间——即便是想纠正一个很明显的错误。丹·桑塔瑞利是宾夕法尼亚州怀俄明市一所职业学校的老师,他在我班上说了一件事:有一个学生因为违章停车而堵住了学校的大门。有一位老师冲进教室,以非常凶悍的口吻问:"谁的车堵住了大门?"当那个学生回答时,那位老师怒吼道:"马上把车开走,否则我就用铁链把它绑上拖走。"

这位学生确实错了,汽车不该停在那儿。可是从那天以后,不只是这位学生对那位老师的举止感到愤怒,全班的学生也总是和他作对,使得他的工作很不愉快。

他可以用完全不同的方式来处理这件事吗?假如他友善一点地问:"门口的车是谁

How could he have handled it differently? If he had asked in a friendly way, "Whose car is in the driveway?" and then suggested that if it were moved, other cars could get in and out, the student would have gladly moved it and neither he nor his classmates would have been upset and resentful.

Asking questions not only makes an order more palatable; it often stimulates the creativity of the persons whom you ask. People are more likely to accept an order if they have had a part in the decision that caused the order to be issued.

When Ian Macdonald of Johannesburg, South Africa, the general manager of a small manufacturing plant specializing in precision machine parts, had the opportunity to accept a very large order, he was convinced that he would not meet the promised delivery date. The work already scheduled in the shop and the short completion time needed for this order made it seem impossible for him to accept the order.

Instead of pushing his people to accelerate their work and rush the order through, he called everybody together, explained the situation to them, and told them how much it would mean to the company and to them if they could make it possible to produce the order on time. Then he started asking questions:

"Is there anything we can do to handle this order?"

"Can anyone think of different ways to process it through the shop that will make it possible to take the order?"

"Is there any way to adjust our hours or personnel assignments that would help?"

The employees came up with many ideas and insisted that he take the order. They approached it with a "We can do it" attitude, and the order was accepted; produced and delivered on time.

An effective leader will use…

Principle 4: Ask questions instead of giving direct orders.

的?"并建议说如果能把它开走,那别人的车就可以进出了,这位学生一定会很乐意地把车开走,而且他和他的同学也就不会那么生气和反感了。

向对方问些问题,不但能接到一张订单,更能激发对方的创造力。假如人们能参与决定是否开出某张订单,他们会更有可能接受订单。

南非约翰内斯堡一家专门生产精密机件的小工厂,经理伊安·麦克唐纳有幸接到一份大订单,但他知道自己不能按期交货。尽管工作已在工厂排定好了,可是这份订单所要求的时间实在太短了,他不太可能承接这份订单。

他并没有催促工人们加速工作来赶订单,他只是把大家召集起来,对他们解释情况,并对他们说,假如能按时完成订单,对他们和公司的意义将有多大。然后他问了些问题:

"我们有什么办法来完成这份订单吗?"

"有没有人能想出别的办法解决它,使我们能接这份订单?"

"有没有别的办法帮助调整我们的工作时间和工作安排?"

员工们提出了许多意见,并坚持让他接下订单。他们用一种"我们可以办到"的态度,终于获得了这份订单,并如期交货。

所以,一位有影响力的领导会使用……

第四项法则:建议对方,而不是直接下命令。

5 Let the Other Person Save Face

Years ago the General Electric Company was faced with the delicate task of removing Charles Steinmetz from the head of a department.Steinmetz,a genius of the first magnitude when it came to electricity,was a failure as the head of the calculating department.Yet the company didn't dare offend the man.He was indispensable—and highly sensitive.So they gave him a new title.They made him Consulting Engineer of the General Electric Company—a new title for work he was already doing—and let someone else head up the department.

Steinmetz was happy.

So were the officers of G.E.They had gently maneuvered their most temperamental star,and they had done it without a storm—by letting him save face.

Letting one save face! How important,how vitally important that is! And how few of us ever stop to think of it! We ride roughshod over the feelings of others,getting our own way,finding fault,issuing threats,criticizing a child or an employee in front of others,without even considering the hurt to the other person's pride.Whereas a few minutes'thought,a considerate word or two,a genuine understanding of the other person's attitude,would go so far toward alleviating the sting!

Let's remember that the next time we are faced with the distasteful necessity of discharging or reprimanding an employee.

"Firing employees is not much fun.Getting fired is even less fun." (I'm quoting now from a letter written me by Marshall A.Granger,a certified public accountant.) "Our business is mostly seasonal.Therefore we have to let a lot of people go after the income tax rush is over.

"It's a byword in our profession that no one enjoys wielding the ax.Consequently,the custom has developed of getting it over as soon as possible,and usually in the following way:'Sit down,Mr. Smith.The season's over,and we don't seem to see any more assignments for you.Of course,you understood you were only employed for the busy season anyhow,etc.,etc.'

"The effect on these people is one of disappointment and a feeling of being 'let down.'Most of

第5章 让对方保住面子

多年前,通用电气公司遇见一件很麻烦的事:免除查尔斯·斯坦梅兹某部门主管的职务。斯坦梅兹是电器方面第一流的天才,但是担任会计部主管却很外行。但公司又不敢得罪他,因为他是不可或缺的人才——并且极其敏感。所以公司决定授予他一个新的头衔。他们让他担任通用电气公司顾问工程师的职务——他还干老本行,但换了一个新头衔——并让他人担任会计部主管。

斯坦梅兹很高兴。

通用电气公司的主管人员也很高兴。他们巧妙地调动了这位最喜怒无常的明星人物,没有引起任何风波——因为他们让他保住了面子。

使人保住面子,这实在是太重要了!而我们中却极少有人能够想到这一点。我们无情地蹂躏别人的感情,为所欲为,挑差错,发出威胁,当着别人的面批评孩子或员工,而不考虑对别人自尊的伤害!然而,几分钟的思考、一两句体贴的话、对别人态度的宽容,对于减少这种伤害都大有帮助!

当我们下次再想解雇员工时,一定要记住这一点。

"辞退员工并没有什么乐趣,而被辞退更是如此。"(我现在正引用会计师格兰吉尔的来信)"由于我们的工作具有季节性,所以我们必须在税收忙完之后让许多人离开。

"在我们行业有一句老话叫'没有人喜欢抡斧头'。因此,我们养成了一种习惯,将此事处理得越利索越好。我们通常采用这种方法:'请坐,史密斯先生。这个季度已完,我们似乎再没有什么工作给你干了。当然,你也明白,你只是在最忙的季节受雇。'等等。

them are in the accounting field for life, and they retain no particular love for the firm that drops them so casually.

"I recently decided to let our seasonal personnel go with a little more tact and consideration. So I call each one in only after carefully thinking over his or her work during the winter. And I've said something like this, 'Mr. Smith, you've done a fine job (if he has). That time we sent you to Newark, you had a tough assignment. You were on the spot, but you came through with flying colors, and we want you to know the firm is proud of you. You've got the stuff—you're going a long way, wherever you're working. This firm believes in you, and is rooting for you, and we don't want you to forget it.'

"Effect? The people go away feeling a lot better about being fired. They don't feel 'let down.' they know if we had work for them, we'd keep them on. And when we need them again, they come to us with a keen personal affection."

At one session of our course, two class members discussed the negative effects of faultfinding versus the positive effects of letting the other person save face.

Fred Clark of Harrisburg, Pennsylvania, told of an incident that occurred in his company: "At one of our production meetings, a vice president was asking very pointed questions of one of our production supervisors regarding a production process. His tone of voice was aggressive and aimed at pointing out faulty performance on the part of the supervisor. Not wanting to be embarrassed in front of his peers, the supervisor was evasive in his responses. This caused the vice president to lose his temper, berate the supervisor and accuse him of lying.

"Any working relationship that might have existed prior to this encounter was destroyed in a few brief moments. This supervisor, who was basically a good worker, was useless to our company from that time on. A few months later he left our firm and went to work for a competitor, where I understand he is doing a fine job."

Another class member, Anna Mazzone, related how a similar incident had occurred at her job—but what a difference in approach and results! Ms. Mazzone, a marketing specialist for a food packer, was given her first major assignment—the test-marketing of a new product. She told the class: "When the results of the test came in, I was devastated. I had made a serious error in my planning, and the entire test had to be done all over again. To make this worse, I had no time to discuss it

"这会给这些人带来失望,给他们造成一种'被遗弃'的感觉。他们中大多数人终身从事会计工作,对这样草率辞退他们的公司,他们自然不会怀有特别的爱心。

"最近我决定多用一点技巧与体谅来遣散季节性人员。因此,在仔细考察每个人冬季的工作表现之后,我把他们召进来,这样说:'史密斯先生,你的工作干得很好(如果真好的话)。那次我们派你去纽瓦克,给了你一项艰苦的任务。虽然困难重重,但你仍然顺利完成,我们希望你能知道,公司以你为荣。你有真实本领——不论你在哪里工作,都将前途远大。公司相信你,并将支持你。希望你不要忘记这一切!

"结果呢?这些人走以后,对于被辞退的感觉要好了许多。他们不觉得是'被遗弃',他们知道,如果我们有工作给他们做,我们一定会留下他们的。而当我们需要再用他们的时候,他们会带着深切的私人感情重新投靠我们。"

有一个学期,我班上两位学员曾讨论挑剔错误的负面效果和让人保住面子的正面效果。

宾夕法尼亚州哈里斯堡的弗雷德·克拉克讲了一件发生在他公司的事:"在我们的一次生产会议中,一位副总经理就某个非常尖锐的问题质问一位负责生产的监督员。他的语调不仅充满了攻击性,而且指责监督员处置不当。为了不让自己在攻击前受羞辱,这位监督员回答含混不清。这使得这位副总经理发起火来,痛斥这位监督员,并指责他说谎。

"公司以前再好的工作关系,都毁于这一刻。这位监督员本来是很负责的人,可是从那一刻起他再也不想待下去了。几个月之后,他离开了我们公司,为一家竞争对手工作。据我所知,他在那里非常称职。"

另一位学员安娜·马佐尼则讲了她工作中一件非常相似的事,不同的是处理的方式和结果。马佐尼小姐是一位食品包装业的市场行销专家,她的第一份工作是某项新产品的市场调查。她在班上说:"当结果出来时,我可惨了。由于我在计划时犯了一个严重错误,整个调查都必

with my boss before the meeting in which I was to make my report on the project.

"When I was called on to give the report, I was shaking with fright. I had all I could do to keep from breaking down, but I resolved I would not cry and have all those men make remarks about women not being able to handle a management job because they are too emotional. I made my report briefly and stated that due to an error I would repeat the study before the next meeting. I sat down, expecting my boss to blow up.

"Instead, he thanked me for my work and remarked that it was not unusual for a person to make an error on a new project and that he had confidence that the repeat survey would be accurate and meaningful to the company. He assured me, in front of all my colleagues, that he had faith in me and I knew I had done my best, and that my lack of experience, not my lack of ability, was the reason for the failure.

"I left that meeting with my head up in the air and with the determination that I would never let that boss of mine down again."

Even if we are right and the other person is definitely wrong, we only destroy ego by causing someone to lose face. The legendary French aviation pioneer and author Antoine de Saint-Exupéry wrote, "I have no right to say or do anything that diminishes a man in his own eyes. What matters is not what I think of him, but what he thinks of himself. Hurting a man in his dignity is a crime."

A real leader will always follow...

Principle 5: Let the other person save face.

须重做。更糟的是,我在下次开会提交项目报告之前,没有时间和我的老板讨论。

"轮到我作报告时,我非常不安。我尽力不使自己崩溃,因为我知道我绝不能哭,否则会让那些男人以为女人太情绪化而无法担任管理工作。我那次报告很简短,并指出因为发生了一个错误,我会在下次会议前重新递交报告。我坐下后,心想老板一定会发火。

"但是,他只是感谢我的工作,并强调说在一个新计划中犯错并不稀奇。而且他有信心,我的第二次调查会更准确,对公司更有意义。他在众人面前肯定我,相信我已尽力了,并说我缺少经验,而非能力。

"我挺直胸膛离开了会场。我下定决心,不会再让老板失望。"

假使我们是对的,别人绝对是错的,我们也会因为使别人失去颜面而毁其自尊。法国传奇性飞行先锋和作家安东尼·圣埃克叙佩里曾写道:"我没有权利去做或说任何事来贬低一个人的自尊。重要的不是我觉得他怎么样,而是他觉得自己如何。伤害人的自尊是一种犯罪。"

所以,一位真正的领导者会遵行……

第五项法则:让别人保住面子。

6 How to Spur People on to Success

Pete Barlow was an old friend of mine.He had a dog-and-pony act and spent his life traveling with circuses and vaudeville shows.I loved to watch Pete train new dogs for his act.I noticed that the moment a dog showed the slightest improvement,Pete patted and praised him and gave him meat and made a great to-do about it.

That's nothing new.Animal trainers have been using that same technique for centuries.

Why,I wonder,don't we use the same common sense when trying to change people that we use when trying to change dogs? Why don't we use meat instead of a whip? Why don't we use praise instead of condemnation? Let us praise even the slightest improvement.That inspires the other person to keep on improving.

In his book *I Ain't Much,Baby—But I'm All I Got*,the psychologist Jess Lair comments, "Praise is like sunlight to the warm human spirit; we cannot flower and grow without it.And yet, while most of us are only too ready to apply to others the cold wind of criticism,we are somehow reluctant to give our fellow the warm sunshine of praise."

I can look back at my own life and see where a few words of praise have sharply changed my entire future.Can't you say the same thing about your life? History is replete with striking illustrations of the sheer witchery of praise.

For example,many years ago a boy of ten was working in a factory in Naples.He longed to be a singer,but his first teacher discouraged him."You can't sing," he said."You haven't any voice at all.It sounds like the wind in the shutters."

But his mother,a poor peasant woman,put her arms about him and praised him and told him she knew he could sing,she could already see an improvement,and she went barefoot in order to save money to pay for his music lessons.That peasant mother's praise and encouragement changed that boy's life.His name was Enrico Caruso,and he became the greatest and most famous opera singer of his age.

第6章 称赞最微小的进步

我和彼特·巴洛是老朋友了。他从事驯狗工作，一生都随同马戏团及杂技表演团到处旅行表演。我很喜欢看他的驯狗表演。我注意到每当狗儿稍有进步时，他就会轻轻地拍拍它，称赞它几句，并给它肉吃，好像它做了一件了不起的大事。

这并不是什么新鲜事。驯兽师几百年来都是用同样的方法。

我一直很奇怪，为什么我们要改变一个人时却不用驯狗的常识?为什么我们不以肉代鞭?为什么我们不用称赞代替斥责?即使是微小的进步我们也要称赞，这样可以激励别人不断进步。

心理学家杰斯·莱尔在其作品《我没什么了不起，但却是真我》中评论道："赞美对于人的精神就像温暖的阳光，没有它我们就不能开花成长。但是，我们大多数人却只想给别人冷酷的批评，而不愿给我们的伙伴赞美的温暖阳光。"

我可以从回顾我自己的生活中看出：几句称赞的话会深刻地改变我的一生。在你的人生中是否也有同样的情形呢?历史上因称赞而成功的奇迹数不胜数。

例如，许多年前，一个10来岁的孩子在那不勒斯一家工厂工作。他渴望成为一名歌唱家，但他的第一位老师却打击他。"你不能唱歌，"他说，"你天生就没有好嗓子。你的嗓音就像风穿过百叶窗一样难听。"

但他的母亲——一位贫苦的农家妇女，却热烈地拥抱着他，称赞他，并告诉他，她知道他能唱歌，她已经看到了他的进步。她节衣缩食，省钱付他的音乐学费。那位农家母亲的称赞与鼓励改变了这个孩子的一生。他的名字叫恩瑞克·卡鲁索，他成了他那个时代最伟大、最著名的歌剧

In the early nineteenth century, a young man in London aspired to be a writer. But everything seemed to be against him. He had never been able to attend school more than four years. His father had been flung in jail because he couldn't pay his debts, and this young man often knew the pangs of hunger. Finally, he got a job pasting labels on bottles of blacking in a rat-infested warehouse, and he slept at night in a dismal attic room with two other boys—guttersnipes from the slums of London. He had so little confidence in his ability to write that he sneaked out and mailed his first manuscript in the dead of night so nobody would laugh at him. Story after story was refused. Finally the great day came when one was accepted. True, he wasn't paid a shilling for it, but one editor had praised him. One editor had given him recognition. He was so thrilled that he wandered aimlessly around the streets with tears rolling down his cheeks.

The praise, the recognition, that he received through getting one story in print, changed his whole life, for if it hadn't been for that encouragement, he might have spent his entire life working in rat-infested factories. You may have heard of that boy. His name was Charles Dickens.

Another boy in London made his living as a clerk in a dry-goods store. He had to get up at five o'clock, sweep out the store, and slave for fourteen hours a day. It was sheer drudgery and he despised it. After two years, he could stand it no longer, so he got up one morning and, without waiting for breakfast, tramped fifteen miles to talk to his mother, who was working as a housekeeper.

He was frantic. He pleaded with her. He wept. He swore he would kill himself if he had to remain in the shop any longer. Then he wrote a long, pathetic letter to his old schoolmaster, declaring that he was heartbroken, that he no longer wanted to live. His old schoolmaster gave him a little praise and assured him that he really was very intelligent and fitted for finer things and offered him a job as a teacher.

That praise changed the future of that boy and made a lasting impression on the history of English literature. For that boy went on to write innumerable best-selling books and made over a million dollars with his pen. You've probably heard of him. His name: H.G.Wells.

Use of praise instead of criticism is the basic concept of B.F.Skinner's teachings. This great contemporary psychologist has shown by experiments with animals and with humans that when criticism is minimized and praise emphasized, the good things people do will be reinforced and the

音乐家。

19 世纪早期,伦敦有一位青年希望成为一名作家。但似乎事事都跟他过不去:他顶多上过 4 年学,他父亲因为还不起债而被投入大牢,因此这位青年常常饱受饥饿之苦。最后,他找到了一份工作,在一间老鼠穿梭的库房中粘贴黑油瓶标签。晚上,他和两个来自伦敦贫民窟的脏小孩一起睡在一间阴暗的小阁楼中。他对自己的写作能力毫无信心,在深夜溜出去,将他的第一篇稿件寄出去,以免别人笑话他。尽管一篇篇稿件都被退了回来,但他最后迎来了伟大的一天,他的一篇文章被录用了。事实上,他没有得到一先令报酬,不过有一位编辑称赞了他。他如此兴奋,在街上毫无目的地游荡,兴奋得泪流满面。

一篇故事被刊出而获得称赞及认可,改变了他的整个人生,如果没有那次鼓励,他很可能会在那家老鼠成灾的工厂中过一辈子。你也许早已知道那个孩子,他的名字叫查尔斯·狄更斯。

伦敦的另一个孩子,在一家干货店当店员。他每天早上必须 5 点钟起床,把店铺打扫干净,还得像奴隶般工作 14 个小时。那简直是在做苦役,他看不起这份工作。过了两年,他实在忍受不下去了。一天早上,他起床之后没吃早饭,步行 15 里去找他母亲,她在别人家里当管家。

他几乎发狂了。他请求她,他哭泣,他发誓:如果他必须再留在这家商店,他一定会自杀。然后,他写了一封长长的且带有悲剧色彩的信给他的老校长,说他的心已经破碎,不愿再活下去了。老校长给了他一些勉励,并肯定他是个很聪明的孩子,应得到一份更好的工作,并给了他一个教员的工作。

这次鼓励改变了那个孩子的前途,使他在英国文学史上写出了不朽的一页。因为他后来写了许多畅销作品,挣得了 100 多万美元。你大概已经听说过他,他的名字就是赫伯特·韦尔斯。

以赞扬代替批评,是史金纳教授的核心观点。这位世界上最伟大的心理学家以动物和人做

poorer things will atrophy for lack of attention.

John Ringelspaugh of Rocky Mount, North Carolina, used this in dealing with his children. It seemed that, as in so many families, mother and dad's chief form of communication with the children was yelling at them. And, as in so many cases, the children became a little worse rather than better after each such session—and so did the parents. There seemed to be no end in sight for this problem.

Mr. Ringelspaugh determined to use some of the principles he was learning in our course to solve this situation. He reported, "We decided to try praise instead of harping on their faults. It wasn't easy when all we could see were the negative things they were doing; it was really tough to find things to praise. We managed to find something, and within the first day or two some of the really upsetting things they were doing quit happening. Then some of their other faults began to disappear. They began capitalizing on the praise we were giving them. They even began going out of their way to do things right. Neither of us could believe it. Of course, it didn't last forever, but the norm reached after things leveled off was so much better. It was no longer necessary to react the way we used to. The children were doing far more right things than wrong ones." All of this was a result of praising the slightest improvement in the children rather than condemning everything they did wrong.

This works on the job too. Keith Roper of Woodland Hills, California, applied this principle to a situation in his company. Some material came to him in his print shop which was of exceptionally high quality. The printer who had done this job was a new employee who had been having difficulty adjusting to the job. His supervisor was upset about what he considered a negative attitude and was seriously thinking of terminating his services.

When Mr. Roper was informed of this situation, he personally went over to the print shop and had a talk with the young man. He told him how pleased he was with the work he had just received and pointed out it was the best work he had seen produced in that shop for some time. He pointed out exactly why it was superior and how important the young man's contribution was to the company.

Do you think this affected that young printer's attitude toward the company? Within days there

实验，证明当减少批评并且多加夸赞时，被实验者就会多做好事，而相对不好的方面则会大大减少。

北卡罗莱纳州落基山的约翰·林杰波夫就采取这种方式来对待他的孩子。像许多家庭一样，父母对孩子动不动就大声吼叫。许多情况显示，在经历了这样一段时期之后，孩子和父母的关系恶化了。

林杰波夫先生决定试试在我班上学到的方法来解决这一问题。他说："我们决定以称赞来代替挑错。当我们看到他们经常做错时，这一点很难做到；要找些事情来真心称赞真的太难了。我们就想办法找他们值得赞扬的事情。第一天，他们以前做过的那些令人不愉快的事情真的不再发生了。接着，他们其他的错误也消失了，并开始按照我们的赞许去行事。结果事情出乎意料，连我们都不敢相信。当然，这种情况并没有一直持续下去，但比以前要好得多。我们现在不必像以前那样。孩子们做对的事情远远多于做错的事情。"这全都是赞美最细小的进步，而不是斥责过失的结果。

这在工作中也有效。凯斯·罗伯在加利福尼亚州木林山公司工作，也运用了这一道理。他的印刷厂承接的业务，有许多品质很精细。有一位印刷工是新手，不太适应工作，导致他的上司很不高兴，打算解雇他。

罗伯先生知道了这一情况后，亲自来到印刷厂，和这位年轻人谈了一次。他说他对他刚接手的工作非常满意，并告诉他这是他曾在公司看到的最好的产品。他还指出这些东西好在哪里，以及年轻人对公司的重要性。

你想这能不影响那年轻人对公司的态度吗？几天以后，情况大为改观。他后来告诉他的同事，罗伯先生非常欣赏他生产的产品。从那天起，他就成了一位忠诚细心的员工。

罗伯先生并没有奉承年轻印刷工，说"你很不错"。他特意指出了他的工作好在何处。由于

was a complete turnabout.He told several of his co-workers about the conversation and how someone in the company really appreciated good work.And from that day on,he was a loyal and dedicated worker.

What Mr.Roper did was not just flatter the young printer and say "You're good." He specifically pointed out how his work was superior.Because he had singled out a specific accomplishment,rather than just making general flattering remarks,his praise became much more meaningful to the person to whom it was given.Everybody likes to be praised,but when praise is specific,it comes across as sincere—not something the other person may be saying just to make one feel good.

Remember,we all crave appreciation and recognition,and will do almost anything to get it.But nobody wants insincerity.Nobody wants flattery.

Let me repeat: The principles taught in this book will work only when they come from the heart.I am not advocating a bag of tricks.I am talking about a new way of life.

Talk about changing people.If you and I will inspire the people with whom we come in contact to a realization of the hidden treasures they possess,we can do far more than change people.We can literally transform them.

Exaggeration? Then listen to these sage words from William James,one of the most distinguished psychologists and philosophers America has ever produced:

Compared with what we ought to be,we are only half awake.We are making use of only a small part of our physical and mental resources.Stating the thing broadly,the human individual thus lives far within his limits.He possesses powers of various sorts which he habitually fails to use.

Yes,you who are reading these lines possess powers of various sorts which you habitually fail to use; and one of these powers you are probably not using to the fullest extent is your magic ability to praise people and inspire them with a realization of their latent possibilities.

Abilities wither under criticism; the blossom under encouragement.To become a more effective leader of people,apply...

Principle 6:Praise the slightest improvement and praise every improvement.Be "hearty in your approbation and lavish in your praise."

指出了具体的成就,所以他的赞美对被赞美者尤具意义。每个人都喜欢被赞美,但这种赞美必须具体真诚——而不是为了让某人高兴而说的泛泛之词。

我们都渴望赞美和认可,而且会尽一切努力得到它。但没有人希望得到那种不诚恳的阿谀奉承。

让我再重复一遍,本书所教导的各项原则,只有真心诚意实践才有用。我不是在推荐阴谋诡计。我谈的是一种新的生活方式。

讲到改变人,假如你我愿意鼓励我们所接触的每一个人,使他们认识并挖掘自己所拥有的内在宝藏,那么,我们不仅可以改变他,甚至可以使他脱胎换骨。

夸张吗?来听听美国有史以来最杰出的心理学家及哲学家威廉·詹姆斯的名言吧:

"与我们应有的成就相比,我们不过半醒着。我们现在只利用了我们身心资源的一小部分。广义地说,人类的能力远未开发。人拥有各种能力,却不曾利用它们。"

是的,读到这句话的你就具有各种潜能,但你却不习惯于运用。这些你大概没有充分发挥出来的才能之一,就是称赞别人、激励别人,使其认识到他们的潜能。

能力会在批评下萎缩,赞美会开出美丽的花朵。所以,要想成为高效率领导,就要应用……

第六项法则:称赞最微小的进步,并称赞每一次进步。要"诚于嘉许,宽于称道"。

7 Give a Dog a Good Name

What do you do when a person who has been a good worker begins to turn in shoddy work? You can fire him or her, but that really doesn't solve anything. You can berate the worker, but this usually causes resentment. Henry Henke, a service manager for a large truck dealership in Lowell, Indiana, had a mechanic whose work had become less than satisfactory. Instead of bawling him out or threatening him, Mr. Henke called him into his office and had a heart-to-heart talk with him.

"Bill," he said, "you are a fine mechanic. You have been in this line of work for a good number of years. You have repaired many vehicles to the customers' satisfaction. In fact, we've had a number of compliments about the good work you have done. Yet, of late, the time you take to complete each job has been increasing and your work has not been up to your own old standards. Because you have been such an outstanding mechanic in the past, I felt sure you would want to know that I am not happy with this situation, and perhaps jointly we could find some way to correct the problem."

Bill responded that he hadn't realized he had been falling down in his duties and assured his boss that the work he was getting was not out of his range of expertise and he would try to improve in the future.

Did he do it? You can be sure he did. He once again became a fast and thorough mechanic. With that reputation Mr. Henke had given him to live up to, how could he do anything else but turn out work comparable to that which he had done in the past.

"The average person," said Samuel Vauclain, then president of the Baldwin Locomotive Works, "can be led readily if you have his or her respect and if you show that you respect that person for some kind of ability."

In short, if you want to improve a person in a certain respect, act as though that particular trait were already one of his or her outstanding characteristics. Shakespeare said, "Assume a virtue, if you have it not." And it might be well to assume and state openly that other people have the virtue you

第7章 送人一顶高帽子

如果一个好工人开始变得不负责任，你会怎么办?你可以解雇他，但这却解决不了任何问题。你也可以责骂他，但这通常会引起怨恨。亨利·哈克是印第安纳州洛威市一家大型卡车经销公司的服务部经理，他手下一个技工的工作每况愈下。但哈克并没有对他怒吼或威胁，而是叫他到办公室，跟他做了一次坦诚的谈话。

他说："比尔，你是一名出色的技工。你在这条生产线上已经工作好几年了。你修的车顾客也都很满意。其实，有很多人都赞赏你干的活。不过你最近完成一项工作需要的时间加长了，而且质量也不如你以前的水平。以前你是个优秀的技工，我想你一定知道我不太满意你目前这种情况。也许我们可以一起想办法改进这个问题。"

比尔回答说，他并不知道他没有做好他的工作，并且保证以后一定会改进。

他做到了没有?你可以肯定他做到了。他再次成为优秀而敏捷的技工。有了哈克先生给他的名声，他会去努力，而不会做不如从前的事。

"对普通人来说，"鲍德文铁路机车厂总经理华克莱说，"如果你能得到他的敬重，并且你对他的某种能力也表示敬重，那么他们会很乐意接受你的领导。"

总之，如果你要在某方面改变一个人，就必须认为某项特殊品质是他早就具备的优秀品质之一。莎士比亚说："假定一种美德，如果你没有的话。"如果你希望某人具备一种美德，你可以认为并公开宣称他早就拥有这一美德了。给别人一个好名声，让他们去实现，他们便会尽量努力，而不愿看到你失望。

吉尔吉特·利布兰克在她的作品《我与马德林的一生》中，描述了一个卑贱的比利时女仆的

want them to develop.Give them a fine reputation to live up to,and they will make prodigious efforts rather than see you disillusioned.

Georgette Leblanc,in her book *Souvenirs,My Life with Maeterlinck*,describes the startling transformation of a humble Belgian Cinderella.

"A servant girl from a neighboring hotel brought my meals," she wrote."She was called'Marie the Dishwasher'because she had started her career as a scullery assistant.She was a kind of monster,cross-eyed,bandy-legged,poor in flesh and spirit.

"One day,while she was holding my plate of macaroni in her red hand,I said to her point-blank,'Marie,you do not know what treasures are within you.'

"Accustomed to holding back her emotion,Marie waited a few moments,not daring to risk the slightest gesture for fear of a catastrophe.Then she put the dish on the table,sighed and said ingenuously,'madame,I would never have believed it.'She did not doubt,she did not ask a question.She simply went back to the kitchen and repeated what I had said,and such is the force of faith that no one made fun of her.From that day on,she was even given a certain consideration.But the most curious change of all occurred in the humble Marie herself.Believing she was the tabernacle of unseen marvels,she began taking care of her face and body so carefully that her starved youth seemed to bloom and modestly hide her plainness.

"Two months later,she announced her coming marriage with the nephew of the chef.'I'm going to be a lady,'she said,and thanked me.A small phrase had changed her entire life."

Georgette Leblanc had given "Marie the Dishwasher" a reputation to live up to—and that reputation had transformed her.

Bill Parker,a sales representative for a food company in Daytona Beach,Florida,was very excited about the new line of products his company was introducing and was upset when the manager of a large independent food market turned down the opportunity to carry it in his store.Bill brooded all day over this rejection and decided to return to the store before he went home that evening and try again.

"Jack," he said,"since I left this morning I realized I hadn't given you the entire picture of our new line,and I would appreciate some of your time to tell you about the points I omitted.I have

惊人变化。

"隔壁旅馆的一个女仆来给我送饭,"她写道,"人们叫她'洗碗的玛莉',因为她一开始只是做厨房里的杂工。她好像是一个怪物,斜眼、弯腿,无论从肉体还是从精神上来说都是天生的可怜人。

"一天,当她用红红的双手给我端来一盘面时,我直爽地对她说:'玛莉,你知不知道你有许多内在的美?'

"习惯于压抑情感的她,因害怕失误而惹下大祸,呆在那里好几分钟。然后,她将盘子放在桌上,叹了口气,认真地说:'夫人,我以前从来不敢相信。'她没有怀疑,也没有发问。她只是回到厨房,重复我的话。由于那些人很相信我,没有人取笑她。从那天起,甚至开始有人体恤她。但最奇怪的变化发生在卑微的玛莉本人身上。她确实相信她拥有一些自己看不见的优点,她开始注意自己的容貌及身体,这使她干瘪的身体焕发出青春的魅力,并掩盖了她的缺陷。

"两个月以后,她宣布她将和厨师长的侄子结婚。她说:'我要做太太了。'并向我致谢。一句小小的赞美就改变了她整个人生。"

利布兰克给了"洗碗的玛莉"一个好名声,让她努力奋斗——而那名声的确改变了她。

比尔·帕克是佛罗里达州德托纳海滩一家食品公司的推销员,他对公司新推出的系列产品感到非常兴奋,但一家大食品公司的经理取消了产品展销,这使得比尔很不高兴。他想这件事想了一整天,决定在下午回家之前再去那家公司试试。

他说:"杰克,今天早上我走时,还没有让你真正了解我们最新推出的产品。假如你能再给我一些时间为你介绍我还没说完的几点,我会很感激。我敬重你听人谈话的雅量,而且你宽容大度,当事实需要你改变时,你会改变你的决定。"

杰克会拒绝再听帕克的话吗?为了这个好名声,他不会拒绝的。

respected the fact that you are always willing to listen and are big enough to change your mind when the facts warrant a change."

Could Jack refuse to give him another hearing? Not with that reputation to live up to.

One morning Dr.Martin Fitzhugh, a dentist in Dublin, Ireland, was shocked when one of his patients pointed out to him that the metal cup holder which she was using to rinse her mouth was not very clean.True, the patient drank from the paper cup, not the holder, but it certainly was not professional to use tarnished equipment.

When the patient left, Dr.Fitzhugh retreated to his private office to write a note to Bridgit, the charwoman, who came twice a week to clean his office.He wrote:

My dear Bridgit,

I see you so seldom, I thought I'd take the time to thank you for the fine job of cleaning you've been doing.By the way, I thought I'd mention that since two hours, twice a week, is a very limited amount of time, please feel free to work an extra half hour from time to time if you feel you need to do those "once-in-a-while" things like polishing the cup holders and the like. I, of course, will pay you for the extra time.

"The next day, when I walked into my office," Dr.Fitzhugh reported, "My desk had been polished to a mirror-like finish, as had my chair, which I nearly slid out of.When I went into the treatment room I found the shiniest, cleanest chrome-plated cup holder I had ever seen nestled in its receptacle.I had given my charwoman a fine reputation to live up to, and because of this small gesture she outperformed all her past efforts.How much additional time did she spend on this? That's right—none at all."

There is an old saying: "Give a dog a bad name and you may as well hang him." But give him a good name—and see what happens!

When Mrs. Ruth Hopkins, a fourth-grade teacher in Brooklyn, New York, looked at her class roster the first day of school, her excitement and joy of starting a new term was tinged with anxiety. In her class this year she would have Tommy T., the school's most notorious "bad boy." His third-grade teacher had constantly complained about Tommy to colleagues, the principal and anyone else who would listen.He was not just mischievous; he caused serious discipline problems in the class,

一天早晨,爱尔兰都柏林的一位牙科医生马丁·费兹夫对一位病人挑剔她用的漱口杯托盘不干净感到很震惊——不错,他用的是纸杯,而不是托盘,但那些设备都生锈了,这当然不够专业。

病人离开后,费兹夫医生将私人诊所关了,并写了一封信给布利基特——一位女佣,她一个星期为他打扫两次卫生。他写道:

亲爱的布利基特:

我最近很少看到你。我想我应该抽时间感谢你为我做的清洁工作。顺便说一下,一周两个小时的时间并不算多。假如你愿意,我想请你随时来我这里工作半个小时,做些你认为应该经常做的事,例如清理漱口杯托盘等。当然,我会支付这额外的费用。

"当我第二天走进办公室时,"他说,"我的桌子和椅子擦得几乎和镜子一样光亮,我差点儿滑了下去。当我走进诊室时,看到铬制杯托放在储存器里,从未那么干净、光亮过。我给了女佣一个美誉,使她去努力,而且只为了这么一个小小的赞美,她尽了最大的努力。她额外用了多少时间呢?对了,一点都没有!"

有一句古话说:"给人一个坏名声,你就会让他上吊。"但是给他一个好名声呢?看看会发生什么!

纽约市布鲁克林镇一位四年级的老师露丝·霍普金斯太太在新学期的第一天看到班上的学生名册时,就有了某种忧虑:今年她班上有一个全校最顽皮的"坏孩子"汤姆。汤姆读三年级的老师总是向同事或校长抱怨。汤姆不仅恶作剧,严重违纪,跟男同学打架,还捉弄女同学,对老师无礼,而且好像愈来愈恶劣。他唯一值得称赞的品质是他能很快掌握学校的功课,而且非常熟练。

霍普金斯太太决定直面这个"问题汤姆"。当她第一次见到新学生时,她对每个人做了些评

picked fights with the boys, teased the girls, was fresh to the teacher, and seemed to get worse as he grew older. His only redeeming feature was his ability to learn rapidly and master the school work easily.

Mrs. Hopkins decided to face the "Tommy problem" immediately. When she greeted her new students, she made little comments to each of them: "Rose, That's a pretty dress you are wearing," "Alicia, I hear you draw beautifully." When she came to Tommy, she looked him straight in the eyes and said, "Tommy, I understand you are a natural leader. I'm going to depend on you to help me make this class the best class in the fourth grade this year." She reinforced this over the first few days by complimenting Tommy on everything he did and commenting on how this showed what a good student he was. With that reputation to live up to, even a nine-year-old couldn't let her down—and he didn't.

If you want to excel in that difficult leadership role of changing the attitude or behavior of others, use...

Principle 7: Give the other person a fine reputation to live up to.

论:“罗丝,你的衣服很漂亮。”“爱丽西亚,我听说你的画画得很好。”当她说到汤姆时,她双眼直视汤姆,说:“汤姆,我知道你是个天生的领导。今年我要依靠你来帮助我把这个班变成四年级最好的班。”在头几天,她一直强调这一点,并夸奖汤姆所做的一切,还说他的行为表明他是一个很好的学生。由于有了这种值得奋斗的美名,即使一个 9 岁大的男孩也不会令人失望——而他真的做到了。

如果你想改变别人的态度或行为,成为一个优秀领导者,就要使用……

第七项法则:给人一个好名声,让他为此而努力。

8 Make the Fault Seem Easy to Correct

A bachelor friend of mine, about forty years old, became engaged, and his fiancée persuaded him to take some belated dancing lessons. "The Lord knows I needed dancing lessons," he confessed as he told me the story, "for I danced just as I did when I first started twenty years ago. The first teacher I engaged probably told me the truth. She said I was all wrong; I would just have to forget everything and begin all over again. But that took the heart out of me. I had no incentive to go on. So I quit her.

"The next teacher may have been lying, but I liked it. She said nonchalantly that my dancing was a bit old-fashioned perhaps, but the fundamentals were all right, and she assured me I wouldn't have any trouble learning a few new steps. The first teacher had discouraged me by emphasizing my mistakes. This new teacher did the opposite. She kept praising the things I did right and minimizing my errors. 'You have a natural sense of rhythm,' she assured me. 'You really are a natural-born dancer.' Now my common sense tells me that I always have been and always will be a fourth-rate dancer; yet, deep in my heart, I still like to think that *maybe* she meant it. To be sure, I was paying her to say it; but why bring that up?

"At any rate, I know I am a better dancer than I would have been if she hadn't told me I had a natural sense of rhythm. That encouraged me. That gave me hope. That made me want to improve."

Tell your child, your spouse, or your employee that he or she is stupid or dumb at a certain thing, has no gift for it, and is doing it all wrong, and you have destroyed almost every incentive to try to improve. But use the opposite technique—be liberal with your encouragement, make the thing seem easy to do, let the other person know that you have faith in his ability to do it, that he has an undeveloped flair for it—and he will practice until the dawn comes in the window in order to excel.

Lowell Thomas, a superb artist in human relations, used this technique. He gave you confidence, inspired you with courage and faith. For example, I spent a weekend with Mr. and Mrs. Thomas; and on Saturday night, I was asked to sit in on a friendly bridge game before a roaring fire. Bridge? Oh, no! No! No! Not me. I knew nothing about it. The game had always been a black

第8章 使错误更容易改正

我的一位近40岁的单身朋友订婚了，他的未婚妻劝他去学跳舞。“上帝知道我要学跳舞，”他在告诉我这事的时候说，“因为我的舞技与20年前我第一次跳舞时一样没有长进。第一位教师告诉我，我跳的全都不对，我必须忘掉一切，重新开始。这可能是真话。但那让我灰心丧气。我没有勇气再跳下去，所以我放弃了。

“第二位教师或许在说谎，但我很喜欢。她满不在乎地说，我跳的舞或许有点过时，但基本上还是不错的，她还让我确信我不必花多少工夫就可以学会几种新式步法。第一位教师因为挑我的毛病而伤了我的心。而这位新教师正好相反，她不断地称赞我的正确之处，忽视我的错误。‘你有天生的节奏感，’她向我保证，‘你真是一位天生的舞蹈家。’现在，我的常识告诉我，我以往是、将来也是一个四流的跳舞者；但在内心深处，我仍愿意相信她说的是真话。确实，我是用钱买她说那些话的，但又何必说穿呢？

“无论如何，我知道我现在跳舞比以前好多了，这都是因为她说我有天生的节奏感。这句话鼓励了我，给了我希望，使我努力进步。”

如果你告诉你的孩子、配偶或下属，他在某件事上很愚笨，没有一点天分，做的全都错了，你就扼杀了他所有进步的动力。但用相反的方法，多加鼓励，就可以使事情变得更容易，使对方知道你相信他有能力做好一件事，他在这件事上很有潜力可挖——那么他就会努力做得更好。

这正是罗维尔·托马斯所用的方法，他是一位了不起的人际关系专家。他会给你自信，给你勇气和信任，以此激励你。例如，我最近同托马斯夫妇共度周末。星期六晚上，他们请我在一堆旺火边打友谊桥牌比赛。打桥牌？我？不！不！不！我可不会，我对此一窍不通。这游戏对

mystery to me. No! No! Impossible!

"Why, Dale, it is no trick at all," Lowell replied. "There is nothing to bridge except memory and judgment. You've written articles on memory. Bridge will be a cinch for you. It's right up your alley."

And presto, almost before I realized what I was doing, I found myself for the first time at a bridge table. All because I was told I had a natural flair for it and the game was made to seem easy.

Speaking of bridge reminds me of Ely Culbertson, whose books on bridge have been translated into a dozen languages and have sold more than a million copies. Yet he told me he never would have made a profession out of the game if a certain young woman hadn't assured him he had a flair for it.

When he came to America in 1922, he tried to get a job teaching in philosophy and sociology, but he couldn't.

Then he tried selling coal, and he failed at that.

Then he tried selling coffee, and he failed at that, too.

He had played some bridge, but it had never occurred to him in those days that someday he would teach it. He was not only a poor card player, but he was also very stubborn. He asked so many questions and held so many post-mortem examinations that no one wanted to play with him.

Then he met a pretty bridge teacher, Josephine Dillon, fell in love and married her. She noticed how carefully he analyzed his cards and persuaded him that he was a potential genius at the card table. It was that encouragement and that alone, Culbertson told me, that caused him to make a profession of bridge.

If you want to help others to improve, remember...

Principle 8: Use encouragement. Make the fault seem easy to correct.

我来说永远是神秘的。不！不！我一点都不会。

“啊！戴尔，这没什么神秘的，”罗维尔说，“桥牌除记忆及判断以外，并没有什么。你写过记忆方面的文章。桥牌对你来说再容易不过，而且这正对你的胃口。”

立刻，我还没有弄清楚到底是怎么回事时，我就惊讶地发现我竟然第一次坐在桌上打桥牌了。这都是因为有人告诉我，我在打桥牌上有天生的能力，并使这游戏好像很容易。

说起打桥牌，我想起了赫伯逊先生。他写的桥牌书，已经被翻译成12种语言，并卖出了100多万册。但他告诉我，如果不是一位年轻妇人肯定地告诉他，他有这方面的天才，他永远不会以这种游戏为职业。

他1922年来到美国时，想得到一份教哲学或社会学的工作，但他没有找到。

后来他试着卖煤，但也失败了。

以后他又试着卖咖啡，又失败了。

他也打过桥牌，但他从未想过有朝一日要教桥牌。他不仅牌技很差，并且很固执。他总是向别人提各种问题，并且每次玩牌过后还要扯一大堆别的事，所以没有人愿意和他玩。

后来，他遇见一位美貌的桥牌教师约瑟芬·狄伦，并对她产生了爱情，和她结了婚。她发现他每次都小心地分析他的牌，于是对他说，他是桥牌桌上尚未崭露头角的天才。赫伯逊告诉我，正是那种鼓励，也只有那种鼓励，才使他成为桥牌专家。

所以，如果你想帮助别人进步，就要记住……

第八项规则：多用鼓励，使别人的错误更容易改正。

9 Making People Glad to Do What You Want

Back in 1915, America was aghast. For more than a year, the nations of Europe had been slaughtering one another on a scale never before dreamed of in all the bloody annals of mankind. Could peace be brought about? No one knew. But Woodrow Wilson was determined to try. He would send a personal representative, a peace emissary, to counsel with the warlords of Europe.

William Jennings Bryan, secretary of state, Bryan, the peace advocate, longed to go. He saw a chance to perform a great service and make his name immortal. But Wilson appointed another man, his intimate friend and advisor Colonel Edward M. House; and it was House's thorny task to break the unwelcome news to Bryan without giving him offense.

"Bryan was distinctly disappointed when he heard I was to go to Europe as the peace emissary," Colonel House records in his diary. "He said he had planned to do this himself... I replied that the President thought it would be unwise for anyone to do this officially, and *that his going would attract a great deal of attention* and people would wonder why he was there ..." You see the intimation? House practically told Bryan that he was too *important* for the job—and Bryan was satisfied. Colonel House, adroit, experienced in the ways of the world, was following one of the important rules of human relations: *Always make the other person happy about doing the thing you suggest.*

Woodrow Wilson followed that policy even when inviting William Gibbs McAdoo to become a member of his cabinet. That was the highest honor he could confer upon anyone, and yet Wilson extended the invitation in such a way as to make McAdoo feel doubly important. Here is the story in McAdoo's own words: "He [Wilson] said that he was making up his cabinet and that he would be very glad if I would accept a place in it as Secretary of the Treasury. He had a delightful way of putting things; he created the impression that by accepting this great honor I would be doing him a favor." Unfortunately, Wilson didn't always employ such tact. If he had, history might have been different.

I knew a man who had to refuse many invitations to speak, invitations extended by friends, invitations coming from people to whom he was obligated; and yet he did it so adroitly that the

第9章 使人乐意做你建议的事

1915年,美国人心惶惶。仅仅一年时间,欧洲各国就相互残杀,规模之大在人类血战史上从未有过。和平能实现吗?没有人知道。但伍德罗·威尔逊总统决意一试。他派了一位私人代表作为和平特使,与欧洲列强磋商。

国务卿威廉·布莱恩是和平倡导者,他很希望做这件事。他认为这是一个建功扬名的大好机会。但威尔逊派了另一个人——他的挚友和智囊霍斯上校。对于霍斯来说,这可是一件麻烦事,因为他必须将这不好的消息告知布莱恩,还不能让他不高兴。当他听说我要去欧洲做和平特使时,布莱恩极其失望,"霍斯上校在他的日记中写道,"他说他早就打算亲自去斡旋……我回答说,总统认为任何人以官方身份去正式处理此事都不合适。如果派他去,将会引起许多人的注意,人们会觉得奇怪,为什么布莱恩去那里……"你看出内在含义了吗?霍斯实际上告诉布莱恩他太重要了,以至于不适合那项工作——于是布莱恩满意了。霍斯上校老于世故,遵从了处理人际关系的一项重要规则——永远使别人乐于做你建议的事。

威尔逊总统在请麦卡杜担任他的内阁成员的时候,也运用了同一策略。任何人与总统共事都会觉得是一种荣誉,但威尔逊的方法更使人觉得自己加倍重要。下面是麦卡杜自己叙述的经过:"他(威尔逊)说他正在组阁,如果我能接受内阁中的某个位置,担任财政部长,他会非常高兴。他说话令人愉快,而且给人一种印象,如果我接受这个荣誉,就帮了他一个大忙。"不幸的是,威尔逊并没有一贯运用这种技巧。如果他能这样做,历史或许要重写。

我认识一个人,他必须拒绝许多演讲邀请、来自朋友的邀请,以及来自盛情难却的人们的邀请,但他做得很巧妙,使对方感到很满意。他是怎样做的呢?他并不是说太忙,太这样或太那

other person was at least contented with his refusal.How did he do it? Not by merely talking about the fact that he was too busy and too-this and too-that.No, after expressing his appreciation of the invitation and regretting his inability to accept it, he suggested a substitute speaker.In other words, he didn't give the other person any time to feel unhappy about the refusal.He immediately changed the other person's thoughts to some other speaker who could accept the invitation.

Gunter Schmidt, who took our course in West Germany, told of an employee in the food store he managed who was negligent about putting the proper price tags on the shelves where the items were displayed.This caused confusion and customer complaints.Reminders, admonitions, confrontations, with her about this did not do much good.Finally, Mr.Schmidt called her into his office and told her he was appointing her Supervisor of Price Tag Posting for the entire store and she would be responsible for keeping all of the shelves properly tagged.This new responsibility and title changed her attitude completely, and she fulfilled her duties satisfactorily from then on.

Childish? Perhaps.But that is what they said to Napoleon when he created the Legion of Honor and distributed 15,000 crosses to his soldiers and made eighteen of his generals "Marshals of France" and called his troops the "Grand Army." Napoleon was criticized for giving "toys" to war-hardened veterans, and Napoleon replied, "Men are ruled by toys."

This technique of giving titles and authority worked for Napoleon and it will work for you.For example, a friend of mine, Mrs.Ernest Gent of Scarsdale, New York, was troubled by boys running across and destroying her lawn.She tried criticism.She tried coaxing.Neither worked.Then she tried giving the worst sinner in the gang a title and a feeling of authority.She made him her "detective" and put him in charge of keeping all trespassers off her lawn.That solved her problem.Her "detective" built a bonfire in the backyard, heated an iron red hot, and threatened to brand any boy who stepped on the lawn.

The effective leader should keep the following guidelines in mind when it is necessary to change attitudes or behavior:

1. Be sincere.Do not promise anything that you cannot deliver.Forget about the benefits to yourself and concentrate on the benefits to the other person.
2. Know exactly what it is you want the other person to do.

样。不,他会在拒绝邀请并对此表示感谢与致歉后,会提议一位代替他的人。换言之,他不会让对方对他的推辞感到不快。他会立刻让对方想到可以邀请别人做演讲。

冈特·斯密特上了我们在西德的课,讲了他管理的一家食品店的一位员工常把价签和陈列的商品贴错。这造成了混乱和顾客抱怨。提醒、责备、对抗,都不管用。最后,斯密特先生把她叫到办公室,告诉她他将任命她为整个商店的价签监督员,她必须让所有货价上的商品标价准确。这项新的工作和头衔完全改变了她的态度,从那以后她的工作都很令人满意。

是不是孩子气?或许是。但当拿破仑创立荣誉勋章,并给他的士兵颁发了15000枚这样的勋章,提升他的18位将军为"法国元帅",称他的部队为"大陆军"的时候,人们也说有些孩子气。还有人批评拿破仑把"玩具"赠送给那些久经沙场的勇士,而拿破仑却回答说:"人就是受玩具支配的。"

这种给人以名誉和头衔的方法能为拿破仑所用,也能为你所用。例如,我一位朋友、住在纽约斯加斯台尔的琴德夫人,因为孩子们经常在她家的草地上乱跑、毁坏草地而烦恼。她批评、哄劝都不管用。然后,她试着授予这些孩子中最坏的一个孩子一个头衔,让他有权威的感觉。她让他当她的"侦探",管理她的草地,不让别人践踏。于是,一切都解决了,她的"侦探"在后院生了一堆火,把铁棒烧得红红的,威胁说谁要践踏草地,就会用铁棒烫谁。

作为一位优秀的领导者,要想改变别人的态度或举止,应该把下面的大纲记在心里:

1. 诚恳待人。不要答应无法办到的事,忘掉自己的个人利益,专心为别人的利益着想。
2. 要确切地知道你希望别人做什么。
3. 有同情心。问你自己别人真正需要什么。
4. 要想想如果别人照你的建议去做会得到什么。
5. 将那些利益与人们的需要协调起来。

3. Be empathetic. Ask yourself what is it the other person really wants.

4. Consider the benefits that person will receive from doing what you suggest.

5. Match those benefits to the other person's wants.

6. When you make your request, put it in a form that will convey to the other person the idea that he personally will benefit. We could give a curt order like this: "John, we have customers coming in tomorrow and I need the stockroom cleaned out. So sweep it out, put the stock in neat piles on the shelves and polish the counter." Or we could express the same idea by showing John the benefits he will get from doing the task: "John, we have a job that should be completed right away. If it is done now, we won't be faced with it later. I am bringing some customers in tomorrow to show our facilities. I would like to show them the stockroom, but it is in poor shape. If you could sweep it out, put the stock in neat piles on the shelves, and polish the counter, it would make us look efficient and you will have done your part to provide a good company image."

Will John be happy about doing what you suggest? Probably not very happy, but happier than if you had not pointed out the benefits. Assuming you know that John has pride in the way his stockroom looks and is interested in contributing to the company image, he will be more likely to be cooperative. It also will have been pointed out to John that the job would have to be done eventually and by doing it now, he won't be faced with it later.

It is naïve to believe you will always get a favorable reaction from other persons when you use these approaches, but the experience of most people shows that you are more likely to change attitudes this way than by not using these principles—and if you increase your successes by even a mere 10 percent, you have become 10 per cent more effective as a leader than you were before—and that is *your* benefit.

People are more likely to do what you would like them to do when you use...

Principle 9: Make the other person happy about doing the thing you suggest.

6. 当你提出你的要求时，要让别人感到他将会因此而获益。我们可以这么说："约翰，明天将有客人来，我希望仓库干净些。所以，请你把它打扫一下，把货物摆好放在货架上，把柜台擦干净。"或者我们可以另换一种方式，让他知道从中得到的利益："约翰，我们有一件事必须马上完成。假如我们现在做好了，以后就不必做了。我明天会带一些客人来参观我们的设备，我想带他们参观一下仓库，但那儿很乱，如果你能打扫一下，把货物摆好放在架子上，并擦擦柜台，这样我们看起来就很有效率，你也为公司的良好形象尽了一份力。"

约翰会按照你建议的去做吗？可能他不会很快乐；但假如你不说出其利益，他会更不高兴。假如你知道约翰以仓库的清洁为荣，并对公司形象很在意的话，他会更乐意合作的。这也能让约翰知道，这件工作是一定要做的，如果他现在做了，以后就不用做了。

如果你以为用这些方法都会得到愉快的反应，那可就太无知了。但大多数人的经验显示，用这个方法比不用这个方法更能改变人的态度。假如你只增加了10%的成功，那你就比原来提高了10%的领导效率——而这正是你的利益所在。

如果你使用了这种方法，人们更有可能做你想让他们做的事……

第九项规则：使别人乐意做你所建议的事。

Part Five
Letters That Produced Miraculous Results

I'll Bet I know what you are thinking now.You are probably saying to yourself something like this:"'Letters that produced miraculous results!'Absurd! Smacks of patent-medicine advertising!" It you are thinking that,I don't blame you.I would probably have thought that myself if I had picked up a book like this fifteen years ago. Sceptical?

Let's be honest.Is the title,"Letters That Produced Miraculous Results," accurate? No,to be frank with you,it isn't.The truth is,it is a deliberate understatement of fact.Some of the letters reproduced in this chapter harvested results that were rated twice as good as miracles.Rated by whom? By Ken R. Dyke,one of the best-known sales promotion men in America,formerly sales promotion manager for Johns-Manville,and now advertising manager for Colgate-Palmolive Peet Company and Chairman of the Board of the Association of National Advertisers.

Mr.Dykes says that letters he used to send out,asking for information from dealers,seldom brought more than a return of 5 to 8 per cent.He said he would have regarded a 15 per cent response as most extraordinary,and told me that,if his replies had ever soared to 20 per cent,he would have regarded it as nothing short of a miracle. But one of Mr.Dyke's letters,printed in this chapter,brought 42 1/2 percent; in other words,that letter was twice as good as a miracle. You can't laugh that off.And this letter wasn't a sport,a fluke,an accident.Similar results were obtained from scores of other letters.

How did he do it? Here is the explanation in Ken Dyke's own words:"This astonishing increase in the effectiveness of letters occurred immediately after I attended Mr.Carnegie's course in 'Effective Speaking and Human Relations.'I saw that the approach I had formerly used was all wrong.I tried to apply the principles taught in this book—and they resulted in an increase of from 500 to 800 per cent in the effectiveness of my letters asking for information."Here is the letter.It pleases the other man by asking him to do the writer a small favour—a favour that makes him feel important.My own comments on the letter appear in parentheses.

Dear Mr.Blank:

第五篇 创造奇迹的信

我敢打赌,我知道你现在正想什么。你大概在对你自己这样说:"'创造奇迹的信?!'可笑!这是在自吹自擂!"如果你那样想,我不会责怪你。如果我在15年前拿起这样一本书,我可能也会这样想的。你是不是在怀疑?

我们需要诚实。"创造奇迹的信"这个题目准确吗?不,说老实话,这个题目并不准确。实际上,这种说法还是很审慎的、低估了事实的呢。本章收入的某些信件,所获得的效果比奇迹还要更加神奇。这是谁说的?这个人就是肯·戴克,美国最著名的推销专家之一,他曾经担任约翰—梅维尔公司的推销部经理,现在担任比德公司的广告经理,同时还担任全美广告联合会主席。

戴克先生说,他以前寄给那些经销商进行市场行情调查的信件,很少得到5%~8%以上的回信。他认为15%的回信就已经是非常好的结果了。他告诉我说,如果他的回信升至20%,他将认为是奇迹。但这一章所附的一封戴克先生的信,竟得到了42.5%的回信。换一句话说,这封信比奇迹还要好上一倍!对此,你可不能一笑置之。而且这封信并不是什么小孩子的游戏、侥幸或偶然结果。还有几十封别的信件,也都达到了同样的效果。

他是怎样做的呢?这是戴克先生自己的解释:"在我参加了卡耐基先生的《高效演讲技巧与人际关系》的课程以后,我的信件的效力立刻惊人地增加。我认识到了我以前所用的方法是完全错误的。我开始采用本书所教的各种原则——结果我调查市场行情信息的信件,增加了5~8倍的效力。"下面是原信。它请求对方稍微给写信者一些帮助——这会使对方感觉受到了重视,自然让对方喜欢。我自己对这封信的注释放在括号内。

亲爱的布兰克先生:

I wonder if you would mind helping me out of a little difficulty?

(Let's get the picture clear.Imagine a lumber dealer in Indiana receiving a letter from an executive of the Johns-Manville Company; and in the first line of the letter, this high-priced executive in New York asks the other fellow to help him out of a difficulty.I can imagine the dealer in Indiana saying to himself something like this: "Well, if this chap in New York is in trouble, he has certainly come to the right person.I always try to be generous and help people. Let's see what's wrong with him! ")

Last year, I succeeded in convincing our company that what our dealers needed most to help increase their re-roofing sales was a year round direct-mail campaign paid for entirely by Johns-Manville.

(The dealer out in Indiana probably says, "Naturally, they ought to pay for it.They're hogging most of the profit as it is.They're making millions while I'm having hard scratchin' to pay the rent ...Now what is this fellow in trouble about?")

Recently I mailed a questionnaire to the 1,600 dealers who had used the plan and certainly was very much pleased with the hundreds of replies which showed that they appreciated this form of cooperation and found it most helpful.

On the strength of this, we have just released our new direct-mail plan which I know you'll like still better.

But this morning our president discussed with me my report of last year's plan and, as presidents will, asked me how much business I could trace to it.Naturally, I must come to you to help me answer him.

(That's a good phrase: "I must come to you to help me answer him." The big shot in New York is telling the truth, and he is giving the Johns-Manville dealer in Indiana honest, sincere recognition.Note that Ken Dyke doesn't waste any time talking about how important his company is.Instead, he immediately shows the other fellow how much he has to lean on him.Ken Dyke admits that he can't even make a report to the president of Johns-Manville without the dealer's help.Naturally, the dealer out in Indiana, being human, likes that kind of talk.)

What I'd like you to do is: (1) to tell me, on the enclosed postcard, how many roofing and re-

我不知道你是否愿意帮助我解决一点困难?

(我们要认清情况。试想一下,如果是印第安纳州的一个木材商收到梅维尔公司一位高级职员的来信,而且在这信的第一行,这位纽约的高级职员就请求他帮助解决困难,我可以想象,这位印第安纳州的木材经销商一定会这样对自己说:“好的,如果这位纽约人真的有什么困难,他算是找对人了。我永远是宽厚待人,助人为乐的。看看他出了什么事!”)

去年,我成功地使我们公司相信,为了帮助经销商增加他们屋顶装修材料的销售,最需要在年终进行直接的函件宣传,并由公司完全负担费用。

(这位印第安纳州的经销商可能会说:“自然,他们应该负担这笔费用。他们获得了大部分的利润,他们赚了好几百万美元,而我连房租都难以支付……现在,这位朋友的困难是什么呢?”)

最近,我向1600位采用这函寄推销方法的经销商寄出了调查表,有幸得到数百名经销商的回信,表示他们赞成这种合作,认为这种方法很有帮助。

根据这种情况,我们刚刚发布我们新的直接函寄计划,我知道你将会非常喜欢它的。

但是,今天早上我们经理和我讨论我去年的这一计划时,他像一般经理那样,问我由此能获得多少业务。因此,我必须请你替我来回答他。

(这句话说得太妙了:“我必须请你替我来回答他。”这位纽约的高级职员说实话了,他向梅维尔公司在印第安纳的经销商说出了实情。注意,戴克并没有将时间浪费在说他的公司是多么多么的重要;相反,他直接向对方表明,他是多么依赖他。戴克承认,如果没有经销商的帮忙,他甚至不能向公司的经理汇报工作。当然,因为共有的人性,印第安纳的经销商会喜欢那样的话。)

我期望你做的是:(1)在附上的明信片中告诉我,去年的直接函寄计划帮助你赢得了多少建造屋顶及屋顶装修的生意;(2)给我这些业务的总营业额,越确切越好(根据所得工程的总价)。

如果你能够这样做,我将感激不尽。你能给我这份资料,谢谢你的好意。

roofing jobs you feel last year's direct–mail plan helped you secure,and (2) give me,as nearly as you can,their total estimated value in dollars and cents (based on the total cost of the jobs applied).

If you'll do this,I'll surely appreciate it and thank you for your kindness in giving me this information.

Sincerely,

KEN R.DYKE, Sales Promotion Manager

(Note how,in the last paragraph,he whispers "I" and shouts "You." Note how generous he is in his praise:"Surely appreciate," "thank you," "your kindness.")

Simple letter,isn't it? But it produced "miracles" by asking the other person to do a small favour—the performing of which gave him a feeling of importance. That psychology will work,regardless of whether you are selling asbestos roofs or touring Europe in a Ford. To illustrate.Homer Croy and I once lost our way while motoring through the interior of France.Halting our old Model T,we asked a group of peasants how we could get to the next big town. The effect of the question was electrical.These peasants,wearing wooden shoes,regarded all Americans as rich.And automobiles were rare in those regions,extremely rare. Americans touring through France in a car! Surely we must be millionaires.Maybe cousins of Henry Ford.But they knew something we didn't know.We had more money than they had; but we had to come to them hat in hand to find out how to get to the next town.And that gave them a feeling of importance.They all started talking at once.One chap,thrilled at this rare opportunity,commanded the others to keep quiet.He wanted to enjoy all alone the thrill of directing us.

Try this yourself.The next time you are in a strange city,stop someone who is below you in the economic and social scale and say:"I wonder if you would mind helping me out of a little difficulty. Won't you please tell me how to get to such and such a place?"

Benjamin Franklin used this technique to turn a caustic enemy into a lifelong friend.Franklin,a young man at the time,had all his savings invested in a small printing business.He managed to get himself elected clerk of the General Assembly in Philadelphia.That position gave him the job of doing the official printing.There was good profit in this job,and Ben was eager to keep it.But a menace loomed ahead.One of the richest and ablest men in the assembly disliked Franklin bitterly. He not only disliked Franklin,but he denounced him in a public talk.

推销经理 肯·戴克

(注意,他在最后一段非常谦虚而轻微地说"我",却十分强调"你";还要注意他的称赞多么宽厚:"将感激不尽","谢谢","你的好意"。)

这封信是不是很简单?它不过是请对方帮个小忙,但产生了"奇迹"——这种做法会让对方得到一种自重感。不论你是出售海绵屋顶材料,还是乘坐福特汽车去欧洲旅行,这种心理学都会有效。例如,有一次我和克罗伊在法国内地乘坐汽车旅行时迷了路。我们停下老式T型车,向一群乡下人打听如何才能到达下一个镇子。这样一个问题却产生了轰动。这些全都穿着木鞋的乡下人,以为所有美国人都是有钱人,而汽车在那些地方极其少见。美国人竟然乘汽车在法国旅行!所以我们必定是百万富翁,或许还是亨利·福特的堂兄弟。但他们知道我们所不知道的事情。尽管我们比他们有钱,我们仍然得摘下帽子,向他们打听道路。这给了他们一种自重感,于是所有的人都立即接口回答。其中一人甚至担心这机会被别人抢走,就让别人不要说话,他想独享为我们指路给他带来的愉悦。

你不妨自己试一试。下次当你到一个陌生地方时,走到一个经济、社会等级都比你低的人面前,对他说:"不知道你愿不愿帮我一个忙?请告诉我如何到某个地方去?"

富兰克林就曾采用这方法,将一位苛刻的仇敌变成了他终身的朋友。富兰克林青年时期,将他所有的积蓄投入到了一小印刷厂。他又设法使自己被选举为费城议会的秘书。这个位置帮他揽到了许多承印公函的业务。这工作获利可观,富兰克林很想保住它。但他的前途发生了危机:议会中最富有、最有能力的一个人对富兰克林极其反感,他不仅不喜欢富兰克林,还在各种公开讲话中诽谤他。

这可是一件很危险的事情。所以富兰克林决定要让那个人喜欢他。但是这该怎样办呢?这是一个难题。奉承他的仇人?不,那样做会引起他的怀疑,或是遭到他的轻视。富兰克林是个非常聪明、非常细致的人,绝不会被这种困境难倒。所以,他做了恰好相反的事。他请他的敌人帮

That was dangerous, very dangerous. So Franklin resolved to make the man like him. But how? That was a problem. By doing a favour for his enemy? No, that would have aroused his suspicions, maybe his contempt. Franklin was too wise, too adroit to be caught in such a trap. So he did the very opposite. He asked his enemy to do him a favour. Franklin didn't ask for a loan of ten dollars. No! No! Franklin asked a favour that pleased the other man—a favour that touched his vanity, a favour that gave him recognition, a favour that subtly expressed Franklin's admiration for his knowledge and achievements. Here is the balance of the story in Franklin's own words:

Having heard that he had in his library a certain very scarce and curious book, I wrote a note to him, expressing my desire of perusing that book and requesting that he would do me the favour of lending it to me for a few days. He sent it immediately, and I returned it in about a week with another note expressing strongly my sense of the favour. When next we met in the House, he spoke to me (which he had never done before) and with great civility and he ever afterward manifested a readiness to serve me on all occasions, so that we became great friends and our friendship continued to his death.

Ben Franklin has been dead now for a hundred and fifty years, but the psychology that he used, the psychology of asking the other man to do you a favour, goes marching right on.

For example, it was used with remarkable success by one of my students, Albert B. Amsel. For years, Mr. Amsel, a salesman of plumbing and heating materials, had been trying to get the trade of a certain plumber in Brooklyn. This plumber's business was exceptionally large and his credit unusually good. But Amsel was licked from the beginning. The plumber was one of those disconcerting individuals who pride themselves on being rough, tough, and nasty. Sitting behind his desk with a big cigar tilted in the corner of his mouth, he snarled at Amsel every time he opened the door, "Don't need a thing today! Don't waste my time and yours! Keep moving!"

Then one day Mr. Amsel tried a new technique, a technique that split the account wide open, made a friend, and brought many fine orders. Amsel's firm was negotiating for the purchase of a new branch store in Queens Village on Long Island. It was a neighbourhood the plumber knew well, and one where he did a great deal of business. So this time, when Mr. Amsel called, he said: "Mr. C—, I'm not here to sell you anything today. I've got to ask you to do me a favour, if you will. Can you spare

他一个忙。富兰克林并没有请求对方借给他10美元。没有！绝不是这样的！富兰克林只是请对方做了一件令他高兴的事——一件能够触动他的虚荣心，并且能表达对他的仰慕，又可以巧妙地展示富兰克林对他的知识和成就表示钦佩的事。下面是富兰克林对这件事的描述：

听说在他的书房有一本神奇的书，于是我就写了一张便条给他，表达了我想借阅那本书的愿望，并请求他帮忙借给我看几天。他立刻给我送来了这本书。大约过了一个星期，我把它送回给他，并写了另一张便条，热切地表达了我的感谢之意。当我们下一次在会议厅中见面的时候，他主动和我交谈起来，(以前他可从来没有这样，)而且非常客气。从那以后，他表示愿意在任何时候帮助我。所以我们成了好朋友，我们的友谊一直持续到他去世。

现在，富兰克林去世已经150年了，但他所运用的心理学知识，以及请对方帮忙的心理策略，对于我们都大有教益。

例如，我的学员爱姆塞在运用这种方法时就非常成功。爱姆塞多年来一直担任某公司的铅管热气材料推销员，他一直想和布鲁克林一位铅管匠做生意。这位铅管匠的生意相当忙，而且他的信用非常好，但爱姆塞一开始就碰了一鼻子灰。这位铅管匠是一个没什么文化的人，对于粗暴下流之事很感自豪。他坐在桌子后面，嘴角斜叼着一支粗大的雪茄，每次当爱姆塞开门进去的时候，他就会立刻大声怒吼："我今天什么也不要！别耽误我和你的时间！滚开！"

后来，有一天，爱姆塞试了一个新方法——一个使他既可以大做生意，又能够交到朋友，并得到许多高额订单的方法。当时，爱姆塞的公司正准备在长岛的皇后村开设一家新分店。那位铅管匠对这一带非常熟悉，而且在那里有不少生意。所以，当爱姆塞再次拜访时，他说："先生，我今天不是来向你推销的。我只想请你帮我一个忙，如果你愿意的话。你能抽出一分钟吗？"

"哼——好吧，"铅管匠用手摆弄了一下他的雪茄说，"你有什么话？快说吧。"

"我的公司正想在皇后村开一家分店，"爱姆塞说，"你现在对那地方的了解比谁都多。所以

me just a minute of your time?" "H'm— well," said the plumber, shifting his cigar. "What's on your mind? Shoot." "My firm is thinking of opening up a branch store over in Queens Village," Mr. Amsel said. "Now, you know that locality as well as anyone living. So I've come to you to ask what you think about it. Is it a wise move—or not?"

Here was a new situation! For years this plumber had been getting his feeling of importance out of snarling at salesmen and ordering them to keep moving. But here was a salesman begging him for advice; yes, a salesman from a big concern wanting his opinion as to what they should do.

"Sit down," he said, pulling forward a chair. And for the next hour, he expatiated on the peculiar advantages and virtues of the plumbing market in Queens Village. He not only approved the location of the store, but he focused his intellect on outlining a complete course of action for the purchase of the property, the stocking of supplies, and the opening of trade. He got a feeling of importance by telling a wholesale plumbing concern how to run its business. From there, he expanded into personal grounds. He became friendly, and told Mr. Amsel of his intimate domestic difficulties and household wars.

"By the time I left that evening," Mr. Amsel says, "I not only had in my pocket a large initial order for equipment, but I had laid the foundations of a solid business friendship. I am playing golf now with this chap who formerly barked and snarled at me. This change in his attitude was brought about by my asking him to do me a little favour that made him feel important."

Let's examine another of Ken Dyke's letters, and again note how skilfully he applies this "do-me-a-favour" psychology.

A few years ago, Mr. Dyke was distressed at his inability to get business men, contractors, and architects to answer his letters asking for information.

In those days, he seldom got more than 1 per cent return from his letters to architects and engineers. He would have regarded 2 per cent as very good, and 3 per cent as excellent. And 10 per cent? Why, 10 per cent would have been hailed as a miracle. But the letter that follows pulled almost 50 per cent ...Five times as good as a miracle. And what replies! Letters of two and three pages! Letters glowing with friendly advice and cooperation.

Here is the letter. You will observe that in the psychology used—even in the phraseology in

我特意前来向你请教。这是否明智?"

于是,出现了一种新场景!多年来,这位铅管匠对所有的推销员总是怒吼连连,以赶走他们而获得自重感。然而现在竟然有一位推销员向他请教。是的,一位大公司的推销员亲自来向他征求他们应该怎样做的意见。

"坐下吧,"他说,并拉过来一张椅子。在接下来的一个小时,他详细说明了皇后村铅管市场的特殊地位和优点。他不仅赞成开店的地点,还竭尽全力为爱姆塞在购买房屋、存储货物、开业等方面作了一个完整的计划——他由此获得了一种自重感。从这件事情谈起,他又谈到了个人生活。他开始变得和善了,并把他家庭的困难及家庭纠纷告诉了爱姆塞。

"在我那天晚上离开的时候,"爱姆塞说,"我不但在我的口袋里装进了第一次得到的一大笔订单,并且为我的业务建立了一个坚固的友谊基础。现在,我和这位从前对我怒吼咆哮的人一起打高尔夫球。他的这种态度的改变,是由我请他给我帮忙,使他获得了自重感而得到的。"

再来看看戴克先生的另一封信,请注意他是如何巧妙地运用这种"请帮我一个忙"的心理学知识的。

几年前,因为得不到商人、承包商和建筑师对他调查函件的复信,戴克先生非常沮丧。

那时他寄给建筑师和工程师的信很少得到1%以上的回复。他认为2%的回复率就很好,而3%就非常好了。至于10%的回复率呢?啊!那就可以称之为奇迹了。但下面这封信得到了将近50%的回复——比奇迹还要好上5倍。多么令人满意的结果!这信只有两三页!但是它充满了友好的建议及合作精神。

这里是原信。你将会发现它所运用的心理学——甚至有些地方词句的用法——这些都和本书前面所列举的相同。当你读这封信时,要尽力分析收信人从字里行间所获得的感觉,找出为什么会发生比奇迹还要好5倍的原因。

some places—the letter is almost identical with that quoted on pages 188–89. As you peruse this letter, read between the lines, try to analyze the feeling of the man who got it. Find out why it produced results five times as good as a miracle.

Dear Mr. Doe:

I wonder if you'll help me out of a little difficulty? About a year ago I persuaded our company that one of the things architects most needed was a catalogue which would give them the whole story of all J–M building materials and their part in repairing and remodelling homes.

The attached catalogue resulted—the first of its kind. But now our stock is getting low, and when I mentioned it to our president he said (as presidents will) that he would have no objection to another edition provided / furnished satisfactory evidence that the catalogue had done the job for which it was designed.

Naturally, I must come to you for help, and 7 am therefore taking the liberty of asking you and forty-nine other architects in various parts of the country to be the jury.

To make it quite easy for you, I have written a few simple questions on the back of this letter. And I'll certainly regard it as a personal favour if you'll check the answers, add any comments that you may wish to make, and then slip this letter into the enclosed stamped envelope. Needless to say, this won't obligate you in any way, and I now leave it to you to say whether the catalogue shall be discontinued or reprinted with improvements based on your experience and advice.

In any event, rest assured that I shall appreciate your cooperation very much. Thank you!

Sincerely yours,

KEN R. DYKE, Sales Promotion Manager

Another word of warning. I know from experience that some men, reading this letter, will try to use the same psychology mechanically. They will try to boost the other man's ego, not through genuine, real appreciation, but through flattery and insincerity. And their technique won't work. Remember, we all crave appreciation and recognition, and will do almost anything to get it. But nobody wants insincerity. Nobody wants flattery.

Let me repeat: the principles taught in this book will work only when they come from the heart. I am not advocating a bag of tricks. I am talking about a new way of life.

亲爱的杜伊先生：

不知你肯不肯帮我解决一个小困难？

大约一年前，我建议我们公司说，建筑师们最需要的东西之一就是一本列举本公司所有建筑材料的目录，并说明这些材料在建造或改装房屋时的各种用途。

于是我们出版了这本随信附上的目录——这是这类出版物的第一种。但是我们现在所存的目录不多了，我向我们的经理提起这事，他说（就像所有经理一样）他并不反对再印一次目录，但是我必须提供令他满意的证据，证明这种目录确实已经达到了出版的目的。

现在，我必须向你求助，所以我一大早就冒昧地请你及全国各地其他49位建筑师来为我们这件事担任裁判。

为尽可能使你感到方便，我已经在这信的背面写了几个简单的问题。如果你愿意写上答案，加上你所愿意加上的任何评语，然后装入随信附上的已经贴好邮票的信封中，我将感激不尽。当然，这件事你不是非做不可。只是这本目录是否应该停印，或根据你的经验与建议而修改重印，均需你的裁定。

无论如何，我都很感激你的合作。谢谢！

推销经理 戴克

根据我的经验，还有一点需要注意的就是，有些人读了这封信，会呆板地照搬同样的方法。他们只是为了鼓起对方的虚荣，并不是出自真诚的欣赏，相反却充满了谄媚和虚伪。他们这种方法是不会奏效的。要记住，我们都渴求欣赏与承认，为了得到它，几乎什么都可以做。但是，没有人要虚伪，也没有人要谄媚。

让我再重复一遍：本书所提倡的各项原则，只有发自内心，才会收到实效。我并不是在教骗人的伎俩，我是在讲一种新的生活方法。

Part Six
Seven Rules for Making Your Home Life Happier

1 How to Dig Your Marital Grave in the Quickest Possible Way

Seventy-Five years ago, Napoleon III of France, nephew of Napoleon Bonaparte, fell in love with Marie Eugenic Ignace Augustine de Montijo, Countess of Teba, the most beautiful woman in the world—and married her. His advisors pointed out that she was only the daughter of an insignificant Spanish count. But Napoleon retorted: "What of it?" Her grace, her youth, her charm, her beauty filed him with divine felicity. In a speech hurled from the throne, he defied an entire nation: "I have preferred a woman I love and respect," he proclaimed, "to a woman unknown to me."

Napoleon and his bride had health, wealth, power, fame, beauty, love, adoration—all the requirements for a perfect romance. Never did the sacred fire of marriage glow with a brighter incandescence. But, alas, the holy flame soon flickered and the incandescence cooled—and turned to embers. Napoleon could make Eugenic an empress; but nothing in all la belle France, neither the power of his love nor the might of his throne, could keep her from nagging.

Bedeviled by jealousy, devoured by suspicion, she flouted his orders, she denied him even a show of privacy. She broke into his office while he was engaged in affairs of state. She interrupted his most important discussions. She refused to leave him alone, always fearing that he might be consorting with another woman. Often she ran to her sister, complaining of her husband, complaining, weeping, nagging, and threatening. Forcing her way into his study, she stormed at him and abused him. Napoleon, master of a dozen sumptuous palaces, Emperor of France, could not find a cupboard in which he could call his soul his own.

第六篇 使你的家庭生活更幸福

第1章 不要挖掘婚姻的坟墓

75年前，法国的拿破仑三世——拿破仑·波拿巴的侄子，爱上了全世界最美貌的女人、德伯女伯爵玛丽·尤琴，并和她结了婚。他的顾问指出，她不过是一位地位并不显赫的西班牙伯爵之女，但拿破仑三世反驳说："这有什么关系?"她的高雅、青春及迷人的美貌使他感觉如神仙般幸福，他甚至在一篇皇家公告中公然宣称，即使全国人民反对，他也绝不后悔。"我已经爱上了一位我敬重的女士，"他说，"我从未见过她这样的女士。"

拿破仑和他的新娘拥有健康、财富、势力、名声、美丽、爱情和敬仰——所有这一切都完全符合浪漫的情调。婚姻的圣火在人世间从来没有燃烧得如此炽热。然而，这"圣火"很快就摇曳不定，而且热度也有所下降，终于只剩下灰烬。尽管拿破仑可以让尤琴当上皇后，但即使他倾尽美丽的法国全部财富，献出他全身心的爱和皇帝的权威，也无法阻止这个女人的唠叨。

由于嫉妒和猜疑，尤琴根本无视拿破仑的命令，甚至不许他有一点个人隐私。有时他正在处理国务，她会冲进他的办公室；当他正讨论重要事务时，她也会进来干扰。她不想让他一个人独处，担心他会和别的女人鬼混。她经常去她姐姐家，埋怨自己的丈夫，不停地唠叨哭闹，还会说些威胁性的话。她还会强行冲进他的书房，大发雷霆，辱骂丈夫。拿破仑虽然贵为法国皇帝，拥有无数财富，却没有一处安身之地。

And what did Eugenic accomplish by all this? Here is the answer.I am quoting now from E.A. Rheinhardt's engrossing book,*Napoleon and Eugenic*: *The Tragicomedy of an Empire*: "So it came about that Napoleon frequently would steal out by a little side door at night, with a soft hat pulled over his eyes, and, accompanied by one of his intimates, really betake himself to some fair lady who was expecting him, or else stroll about the great city as of old, passing through streets of the kind which an Emperor hardly sees outside a fairy tale, and breathing the atmosphere of might-have-beens." That is what nagging accomplished for Eugenic.True, she sat on the throne of France.True, she was the most beautiful woman in the world.But neither royalty nor beauty can keep love alive amidst the poisonous fumes of nagging.Eugenic could have raised her voice like Job of old and have wailed: "The thing which I greatly feared is come upon me." Come upon her? She brought it upon herself, poor woman, by her jealousy and her nagging.Of all the sure-fire, infernal devices ever invented by all the devils in hell for destroying love, nagging is the deadliest.It never fails.Like the bite of the king cobra, it always destroys, always kills.

The wife of Count Leo Tolstoy discovered that—after it was too late. Before she passed away, she confessed to her daughters: "I was the cause of your father's death." Her daughters didn't reply. They were both crying.They knew their mother was telling the truth.They knew she had killed him with her constant complaining, her eternal criticisms, and her eternal nagging.Yet Count Tolstoy and his wife ought, by all odds, to have been happy.He was one of the most famous novelists of all time. Two of his masterpieces, *War and Peace* and *Anna Karenina* will forever shine brightly among the literary glories of earth.

Tolstoy was so famous that his admirers followed him around day and night and took down in shorthand every word he uttered.Even if he merely said, "I guess I'll go to bed"; even trivial words like that, everything was written down; and now the Russian Government is printing every sentence that he ever wrote; and his combined writings will fill one hundred volumes. In addition to fame, Tolstoy and his wife had wealth, social position, children.No marriage ever blossomed under softer skies.In the beginning, their happiness seemed too perfect, too intense, too endure.So kneeling together, they prayed to Almighty God to continue the ecstasy that was theirs.Then an astonishing thing happened.Tolstoy gradually changed.He became a totally different person.He became ashamed

尤琴这样做的结果是什么呢？下面就是答案。我就引用莱哈德的巨著《拿破仑三世与尤琴——一个帝国的悲剧》来说吧："从此以后，拿破仑经常三更半夜在一个亲信的陪伴之下，从一个小侧门悄悄溜出去，用一个小软帽遮住双眼，真的去找一位正在等他的美貌女士；或者是去游览巴黎这座古老的城市，欣赏神仙故事中连皇帝也见不到的街道美景，呼吸本来应该拥有自由的空气。"这就是尤琴唠叨的结果。不错，她是坐在法国皇后的宝座上，她也的确是全世界最美丽的女人，但在她的喋喋不休中，美丽和尊贵都不能维持爱情。尤琴失声痛哭，说："我最害怕的事情终于发生了。"这种事降临到她身上了吗？这是她自找的。可怜的女人，一切都起源于她的嫉妒和唠叨。地狱中的魔鬼所发明的破坏爱情的所有恶毒手段，最厉害的要算唠叨了。这种方法总是会得逞，它就像眼镜蛇毒一样，总是置人于死地。

托尔斯泰伯爵的妻子也发现了这点——可惜太晚了。她在临死前向女儿们坦承："你们的父亲是因我而死的。"她的女儿们没有回答，全都失声痛哭，她们清楚母亲是在说实话。她们知道，正是她用那没完没了的埋怨、批评以及唠叨，才使丈夫走向死亡的。然而，照常理来说，托尔斯泰伯爵及其夫人本应该是幸福美满的一对。托尔斯泰是世界上最著名的小说家之一，他的《战争与和平》、《安娜·卡列尼娜》，将在世界文学中永放光芒。

托尔斯泰太有名了，以至于他的崇拜者整天追随左右，记下他所说的每一句话。哪怕他只是说"我想我要上床睡觉了"这样的日常碎语，也会被逐字记录下来。现在，俄国政府正计划印行他所写的每一句话，合计有100卷。除了名声之外，托尔斯泰和他的夫人还拥有财产、社会地位及孩子。可以说天底下没有比这更美好的婚姻了。起初，他们的幸福似乎完美至极，也甜蜜至极，他们相信一定会白头到老。所以他们甚至一同跪拜在地，祈祷万能的上帝永远将这种幸福赐予他们。然而，不幸的怪事发生了。托尔斯泰慢慢变了，几乎完全不同于以前了。他对自己所写的鸿篇巨著感到羞耻，并从那时开始专心写作宣传和平的小册子，呼吁废除战争与贫穷。这

of the great books that he had written, and from that time on he devoted his life to writing pamphlets preaching peace and the abolition of war and poverty. This man who had once confessed that in his youth he had committed every sin imaginable—even murder—tried to follow literally the teachings of Jesus. He gave all his lands away and lived a life of poverty. He worked in the fields, chopping wood and pitching hay. He made his own shoes, swept his own room, ate out of a wooden bowl, and tried to love his enemies.

Leo Tolstoy's life was a tragedy, and the cause of his tragedy was his marriage. His wife loved luxury, but he despised it. She craved fame and the plaudits of society, but these frivolous things meant nothing whatever to him. She longed for money and riches, but he believed that wealth and private property were a sin. For years, she nagged and scolded and screamed because he insisted on giving away the right to publish his books freely without paying him any royalties whatever. She wanted the money those books would produce. When he opposed her, she threw herself into fits of hysteria, rolling on the floor with a bottle of opium at her lips, swearing that she was going to kill herself and threatening to jump down the well. There is one event in their lives that to me is one of the most pathetic scenes in history. As I have already, said, they were gloriously happy when they were first married; but now, forty-eight years later, he could hardly bear the sight of her. Sometimes of an evening, this old and heartbroken wife, starving for affection, came and knelt at his knees and begged him to read aloud to her the exquisite love passages that he had written about her in his diary fifty years previously. And as he read of those beautiful, happy days that were now gone forever, both of them wept. How different, how sharply different, the realities of life were from the romantic dreams they had once dreamed in the long ago.

Finally, when he was eighty-two years old, Tolstoy was unable to endure the tragic unhappiness of his home any longer so he fled from his wife on a snowy October night in 1910—fled into the cold and darkness, not knowing where he was going. Eleven days later, he died of pneumonia in a railway station. And his dying request was that she should not be permitted to come into his presence. Such was the price Countess Tolstoy paid for her nagging and complaining and hysteria. The reader may feel that she had much to nag about. Granted. But that is beside the point. The question is: did nagging help her, or did it make a bad matter infinitely worse? "I really think I was insane." That is

个曾经承认在年轻时犯过各种可以想象得出的罪恶——甚至包括谋杀的人，想要真正遵奉耶稣的教导。他捐出了所有的财产，过着清贫的生活。他在田里耕作，砍柴堆草。他自己动手做鞋子，打扫房间，用木碗吃饭，并尽量爱他的敌人。

托尔斯泰的一生是个悲剧，其根源正在于他的婚姻。他夫人喜欢奢华，而他对此却不屑一顾。她渴望名声和社会的赞誉，但对他而言这些虚浮之物毫无意义。她渴求金钱与财富，而他认为财富及私产是罪恶的东西。多年以来，由于他坚持放弃作品的出版权，不收任何版税，因此她一直吵闹不休。她希望得到这些著作能赚到的钱。当他反对时，她就歇斯底里在地上打滚，拿着一瓶鸦片，发誓要自杀，并威胁要跳井。在他们的生活中，有一幕我认为是历史上最凄惨的场面。我已经说过，他们结婚之初非常幸福；但48年过后，他一看到她就不舒服。有一天晚上，这位年老色衰的女人渴望得到丈夫的爱情，就跪在他的面前，请求他为她大声朗读50年前他写给她的日记，这份日记饱含了浓情厚意。当他读完那早已一去不复返的美丽而愉快的往事时，两个人都哭了。生活的现实和他们许久以前所拥有的浪漫梦想简单天差地别！

最后，当托尔斯泰82岁时，他再也忍受不了家庭的悲惨和不快，就在1910年10月的一个大雪之夜，逃离了他的夫人——闯进了寒冷的黑夜，不知去向。11天之后，托尔斯泰因肺炎在一个火车站死去。他临死的要求，竟然是不让她来到他身边！这就是托尔斯泰伯爵夫人喋喋不休、抱怨及疯狂所付出的代价。你也许会认为她的唠叨是应该的。当然！但这并不是要点。问题在于，唠叨对她有什么好处？是不是把事情弄得更糟了呢？"我想我真的是神经错乱了。"这是托尔斯泰伯爵夫人对那段经历的看法，但太晚了。

林肯一生最大的悲剧，也是他的婚姻。请注意，不是他的被刺，而是他的婚姻。布司开枪之后，林肯甚至不知道自己遇刺了，因为他几乎每天都活在痛苦中。23年来，林肯的处境正像他的律师合伙人赫登所说的，是"婚姻不幸的苦果"。说"婚姻不幸"还是轻描淡写的，因为林肯夫

what Countess Tolstoy herself thought about it—after it was too late.

The great tragedy of Abraham Lincoln's life also was his marriage.

Not his assassination, mind you, but his marriage. When Booth fired, Lincoln never realized he had been shot; but he reaped almost daily, for twenty-three years, what Herndon, his law partner, described as "the bitter harvest of conjugal infelicity." "Conjugal infelicity?" That is putting it mildly. For almost a quarter of a century, Mrs. Lincoln nagged and harassed the life out of him.

She was always complaining, always criticizing her husband; nothing about him was ever right. He was stoop-shouldered, he walked awkwardly and lifted his feet straight up and down like an Indian. She complained that there was no spring in his step, no grace to his movement; and she mimicked his gait and nagged at him to walk with his toes pointed down, as she had been taught at Madame Mentelle's boarding school in Lexington. She didn't like the way his huge ears stood out at right angles from his head. She even told him that his nose wasn't straight, that his lower lip stuck out, and he looked consumptive, that his feet and hands were too large, his head too small. Abraham Lincoln and Mary Todd Lincoln were opposites in every way: in training, in background, in temperament, in tastes, in mental outlook. They irritated each other constantly.

"Mrs. Lincoln's loud, shrill voice," wrote the late Senator Albert J. Beveridge, the most distinguished Lincoln authority of this generation—"Mrs. Lincoln's loud shrill voice could be heard across the street, and her incessant outbursts of wrath were audible to all who lived near the house. Frequently her anger was displayed by other means than words, and accounts of her violence are numerous and unimpeachable."

To illustrate: Mr. and Mrs. Lincoln, shortly after their marriage, lived with Mrs. Jacob Early—a doctor's widow in Springfield who was forced to take in boarders. One morning Mr. and Mrs. Lincoln were having breakfast when Lincoln did something that aroused the fiery temper of his wife. What, no one remembers now. But Mrs. Lincoln, in a rage, dashed a cup of hot coffee into her husband's face. And she did it in front of the other boarders. Saying nothing, Lincoln sat there in humiliation and silence while Mrs. Early came with a wet towel and wiped off his face and clothes.

Mrs. Lincoln's jealousy was so foolish, so fierce, so incredible, that merely to read about some of the pathetic and disgraceful scenes she created in public—merely reading about them seventy-five

人20多年来一直对他喋喋不休，让他难得安宁。

她总是抱怨，总是批评自己的丈夫，认为他的一切都不对：他伛背缩肩、走路难看，抬脚放步简直呆板得像个印第安人。她数落他走路没有弹性，举止不优雅。她会模仿他走路的样子讥笑他，并让他走路时先将脚尖着地，就像她从莱克星顿市孟德尔夫人的寄宿学校学到的那样。她还不喜欢他那两只大耳朵和他的头长成直角的模样；甚至告诉他说他的鼻子不直，嘴唇前突，而且外表看上去像个肺结核病人，手和脚太大，而头又太小。林肯和他夫人玛丽·托德几乎在每个方面都完全相反：教育、出身、性格、爱好以及思想观念。他们常常会厌恨对方。

"林肯夫人那高而尖锐的声音，"当代最著名的林肯研究权威专家、已故参议员阿尔伯特·贝弗里奇写道，"在街的对面都能听得见。她愤怒的责骂声，所有邻居家都能听到。而且她的暴怒常常不只是通过言语来表达，她发泄暴怒的方式多得难以胜数。"

举例来说吧：林肯夫妇结婚不久，和欧莉夫人住在一起——她是斯普林菲尔德镇一个医生的遗孀，因生活所迫而不得不出租房屋维生。一天早上，林肯夫妇正在吃早餐，林肯可能做错了某件事，立即使他夫人暴跳如雷。究竟什么原因，现在已经无人记得。只见林肯夫人在盛怒之下，将一杯热咖啡泼到了丈夫脸上，而当时还有许多房客在场。林肯忍气吞声地呆坐在那里，一言不发。欧莉夫人进来了，用一块湿毛巾替他擦净了脸和衣服。

林肯夫人的嫉妒是如此的愚蠢和凶暴，让人难以相信，只要读到她在公众场合所做的这些有失风度的事情——即使是在75年后的今天看到这些，也会让人惊讶不已。最后她终于精神失常。对于她这个人，我们用一句最宽容的说法，只能认为她是"性情使然"。

所有这些唠叨、斥责和发怒是否改变了林肯呢？从某些方面来说确实如此，那就是改变了他对她的态度，使他后悔自己婚姻的不幸，并竭力避免和她见面。

当时，斯普林菲尔德镇有11位律师，在那里谋生并不容易。所以，当大法官大卫·戴维斯去

years later makes one gasp with astonishment.She finally went insane; and perhaps the most charitable thing one can say about her is that her disposition was probably always affected by incipient insanity.

Did all this nagging and scolding and raging change Lincoln? In one way, yes.It certainly changed his attitude toward her.It made him regret his unfortunate marriage, and it made him avoid her presence as much as possible.

Springfield had eleven attorneys, and they couldn't all make a living there; so they used to ride horseback from one county seat to another, following Judge David Davis while he was holding court in various places.In that way, they managed to pick up business from all the county seat towns throughout the Eighth Judicial District. The other attorneys always managed to get back to Springfield each Saturday and spend the weekend with their families.But Lincoln didn't.He dreaded to go home: and for three months in the spring, and again for three months in the autumn, he remained out on the circuit and never went near Springfield.He kept this up year after year.Living conditions in the country hotels were often wretched; but, wretched as they were, he preferred them to his own home and Mrs.Lincoln's constant nagging and wild outbursts of temper.

Such are the results that Mrs.Lincoln, the Empress Eugenic, and Countess Tolstoy obtained by their nagging.They brought nothing but tragedy into their lives.They destroyed all that they cherished most.

Bessie Hamburger, who has spent eleven years in the Domestic Relations Court in New York City, and has reviewed thousands of cases of desertion, says that one of the chief reasons men leave home is because their wives' nag.Or, as the *Boston Post* puts it: "Many a wife has made her own marital grave with a series of little digs."

So, if you want to keep your home life happy,

Rule 1 is: Don't, Don't nag.

各地开庭审理案件的时候，这些律师就会骑马从一个县到另一个县地追随他，因为他们只有这样才能设法找到一些业务。每当星期六来临时，其他律师都会尽量赶回斯普林菲尔德，和家人共度周末。但是林肯却不想回去，他害怕回家：每年春季3个月，秋季又是3个月，他都跟随巡回法庭到各地审案，从不走近斯普林菲尔德。他就这样年复一年地生活。尽管乡村旅馆的条件非常恶劣，但林肯情愿呆在这里，而不愿回家面对妻子那喋喋不休的话语和暴怒的脾气。

这就是林肯夫人、尤琴皇后、托尔斯泰伯爵夫人唠叨不休所获得的结果。她们给自己的生活所带来的，除了悲剧，什么也没有。她们毁坏了她们最珍爱的一切。

贝丝·亨博格在纽约一家家政法庭工作11年，审理过好几千个案子。她说男人离弃家庭的一个重要原因，就是他们妻子的唠叨。或者像《波士顿邮报》所说的："许多妻子正在慢慢地挖掘她们自己婚姻的坟墓。"

因此，如果你想使你的家庭生活幸福，就请记住

第一项原则：千万不要唠叨!

2 Love and Let Live

"I May Commit many follies in life," Disraeli said, "but I never intend to marry for love." And he didn't.He stayed single until he was thirty-five, and then he proposed to a rich widow, a widow fifteen years his senior; a widow whose hair was white with the passing of fifty winters.Love? Oh, no.She knew he didn't love her.She knew he was marrying her for her money! So she made just one request: she asked him to wait a year to give her the opportunity to study his character.And at the end of that time, she married him.

Sounds pretty prosaic, pretty commercial, doesn't it? Yet paradoxically enough, Disraeli's marriage was one of the most glowing successes in all the battered and bespattered annals of matrimony.

The rich widow that Disraeli chose was neither young, nor beautiful, nor brilliant.Far from it. Her conversation bubbled with a hugh-provoking display of literary and historical blunders.For example, she "never knew which came first, the Greeks or the Romans." Her taste in clothes was bizarre; and her taste in house furnishings was fantastic.But she was a genius, a positive genius at the most important thing in marriage: the art of handling men.

She didn't attempt to set up her intellect against Disraeli's.When he came home bored and exhausted after an afternoon of matching repartee with witty duchesses, Mary Anne's frivolous patter permitted him to relax.Home, to his increasing delight, was a place where he could ease into his mental slippers and bask in the warmth of Mary Anne's adoration.These hours he spent at home with his ageing wife were the happiest of his life.She was his helpmate, his confidante, his advisor. Every night he hurried home from the House of Commons to tell her the day's news.And—this is important—whatever he undertook, Mary Anne simply did not believe he could fail.

For thirty years, Mary Anne lived for Disraeli, and for him alone.Even her wealth she valued only because it made his life easier.In return, she was his heroine.He became an Earl after she died; but, even while he was still a commoner, he persuaded Queen Victoria to elevate Mary Anne

第2章 爱对方,并给他自由

"我一生会做出许多愚蠢的事,"狄斯累利说,"但我从来没有想过为爱情而结婚。"他确实没有为爱情而结婚。35岁以前,他一直过着单身汉的生活,然后才向一位有钱的寡妇求婚。这位寡妇竟比他大15岁,已经年过半百,而且满头白发。他娶她是出于爱情吗?才不是呢。她知道他并不爱她,而且也知道他是为了她的财产而娶她的。因此,她只有一个要求:她让他再等一年,以便她有机会研究他的人品。一年之后,她嫁给了他。

这故事听起来很俗气,特别商业化,是不是?但令人奇怪的是,在所有破碎而污浊的婚姻中,狄斯累利的婚姻却是最闪光的成功典范之一。

狄斯累利选择的这位有钱寡妇,既不年轻也不漂亮,更不聪明,甚至还差得很远。她的谈话常常错误百出,显示出她在文学和历史知识方面的贫乏。例如,她"从来都不知道历史上是先有希腊人,还是先有罗马人"。她对服饰的审美观也十分古怪,她对家庭装饰的偏好也很奇特。但是在处理婚姻生活中最重要的事情——如何对待男人方面,她却是一个天才,一个真正的天才。

她并不想在智慧方面和狄斯累利一较高低。当狄斯累利和那些机智百出的女公爵们周旋了一个下午,精疲力竭地回到家中以后,妻子玛丽·安妮说的那些家常话能让他放松。家变成了狄斯累利求得心神安宁的地方,而且他还可以沐浴在玛丽宠爱的温暖之中。他越来越喜欢这个家了。和年长的妻子在家中共同相处,成了狄斯累利一生中最快乐的时光。她是他的伴侣,是他的亲信,是他的顾问。每天晚上,他从众议院匆匆忙忙赶回家,把这一天的新闻告诉她。而且重要的是,不论他做什么事情,玛丽都相信他不会失败。

30年来,玛丽只为狄斯累利一个人而活着。甚至她所有的财产也只是因为让他生活更加

to the peerage.And so, in 1868, she was made Viscountess Beaconsfield.

No matter how silly or scatterbrained she might appear in public, he never criticized her; he never uttered a word of reproach; and if anyone dared to ridicule her, he sprang to her defence with ferocious loyalty.Mary Anne wasn't perfect, yet for three decades she never tired of talking about her husband, praising him, admiring him.Result? "We have been married thirty years," Disraeli saki, "and I have never been bored by her." (Yet some people thought because Mary Anne didn't know history, she must be stupid!)

For his part, Disraeli never made it any secret that Mary Anne was the most important thing in his life.Result? "Thanks to his kindness," Mary Anne used to tell their friends, "my life has been simply one long scene of happiness." Between them, they had a little joke. "You know," Disraeli would say, "I only married you for your money anyhow." And Mary Anne, smiling, would reply, "Yes, but if you had it to do over again, you'd marry me for love, wouldn't you?" And he admitted it was true.No, Mary Anne wasn't perfect.But Disraeli was wise enough to let her be herself.

As Henry James put it: "The first thing to learn in intercourse with others is noninterference with their own peculiar ways of being happy, provided those ways do not assume to interfere by violence with ours."

That's important enough to repeat: "*The first thing to learn in intercourse with others is noninterference with their own peculiar ways of being happy...*"

Or, as Leland Foster Wood in his book, *Growing Together in the Family*, has observed: "Success in marriage is much more than a matter of finding the right person; it is also a matter of being the right person."

So, if you want your home life to be happy,

Rule 2 is: Don't try to make your partner over.

舒适而变得有价值。她得到的回报呢?她成了他的女神。在玛丽去世后,狄斯累利才受封为伯爵;而当狄斯累利是一介平民时,他就请求维多利亚女王晋封玛丽为贵族。于是,玛丽在 1868 年被封为比肯菲尔德女子爵。

尽管玛丽在公共场合中显得既愚蠢又笨拙,但狄斯累利从来都不批评她。他从未说过一句责怪她的话,如果有人敢讥笑她,他会立即站出来,激烈而忠诚地为她辩护。玛丽并非十全十美,但是 30 年来她总是不知疲倦地谈论她的丈夫,赞美他,夸奖他。结果呢?"我们结婚 30 年,"狄斯累利说,"但是我从来都没有厌烦过她。"(有的人因为玛丽不懂历史,就认为她必定很愚笨。)

就狄斯累利个人而言,他经常说玛丽是他一生中最重要的人。结果呢?"我很感谢他的恩爱,"玛丽经常告诉她的朋友们,"我的生活成了永不谢幕的喜剧。"他们经常会开一个小玩笑。"你知道,"狄斯累利说,"不论如何,我只是为了你的金钱才和你结婚的。"玛丽则会笑着回敬道:"确实不错。但如果你必须再从头开始的话,你就会因为爱情而和我结婚,是不是?"而狄斯累利也明确承认。不,玛丽并非十全十美。但狄斯累利非常聪明,让她保持了自我本色。

正如亨利·詹姆斯所说的:"和别人相处所要学习的第一课,就是不要干涉别人寻找快乐的特殊方式,如果这些方式并没有对我们产生强大妨碍的话。"

这些话非常重要,值得重复一次:"和别人相处所要学习的第一课,就是不要干涉别人寻找快乐的特殊方式,如果这些方式并没有对我们产生强大妨碍的话。"

或者像里兰·弗斯特·伍德在他的著作《在家庭中共同成长》中所说的:"若想婚姻成功,绝不只是找一个好配偶;你自己也要成为一个好配偶。"

因此,如果你想使你的家庭生活幸福快乐,就请记住

第二项原则:不要改变你的伴侣。

3 Do This and You'll Be Looking up the Time-Tables to Reno

Disraeli's bitterest rival in public life was the great Gladstone.These two clashed on every debatable subject under the Empire, yet they had one thing in common; the supreme happiness of their private lives.

William and Catherine Gladstone lived together for fifty-nine years, almost three score years glorified with an abiding devotion.I like to think of Gladstone, the most dignified of England's prime ministers, clasping his wife's hand and dancing around the hearthrug with her, singing this song:

A ragamuffin husband and a rantipoling wife, We'll fiddle it and scrape it through the ups and downs of life.

Gladstone, a formidable enemy in public, never criticized at home.

When he came down to breakfast in the morning, only to discover that the rest of his family was still sleeping, he had a gentle way of registering his reproach.He raised his voice and filled the house with a mysterious chant that reminded the other members that England's busiest man was waiting downstairs for his breakfast, all alone.Diplomatic, considerate, he rigorously refrained from domestic criticism.

And so, often, did Catherine the Great.Catherine ruled one of the largest empires the world has ever known.Over millions of her subjects she held the power of life and death.Politically, she was often a cruel tyrant, waging useless wars and sentencing scores of her enemies to be cut down by firing squads.Yet if the cook burned the meat, she said nothing.She smiled and ate it with a tolerance that the average American husband would do well to emulate.

Dorothy Dix, America's premier authority on the causes of marital unhappiness, declares that more than fifty per cent of all marriages are failures; and she knows that one of the reasons why so many romantic dreams break up on the rocks of Reno is criticism—futile, heartbreaking criticism.

So, if you want to keep your home life happy, remember

Rule 3 is:Don't criticize.

第3章 不要作无用的批评

在政治生涯中,狄斯累利最强有力的对手是格莱斯顿。这两个人对于大英帝国每一件事情都可能会发生冲突。但是他们有一个共同点,他们的私人生活都非常幸福。

格莱斯顿和他妻子凯瑟琳共同生活了59年,在近60年时间里他们一直互敬互爱。我喜欢想象这位英国历史上最尊贵的首相:握着他妻子的手,围着炉边地毯跳舞,唱着这首歌:

丈夫衣衫褴褛,妻子服饰亦陋。人生总有沉浮,需要同甘共苦。

格莱斯顿在公开场合是一位值得敬畏的人物,但他在家里从不批评人。

当他到楼下吃早饭,而全家人却还在睡懒觉时,他就会以温和的方式来表达他的不满。他会提高声音,使整个房屋都充满神秘的歌声,以此提醒他的家人:全英国最忙的人独自一人在楼下等着吃早餐。他总是保持外交家的风度,体谅别人,并竭力自我克制,不在家里批评任何人和事。

俄国女皇凯瑟琳也经常如此。她统治着历史上最大的帝国之一,掌握了千百万人的生杀大权。她在政治上是一个暴君,发动过毫无意义的战争,判处仇敌死刑。但是,如果厨师把肉烤焦了,她却什么也不说,而是微笑着吃下去。她这种宽容的做法,值得做丈夫的学习。

陶乐斯·迪克丝是美国不幸婚姻研究的权威专家, 她认为在所有婚姻中,50%以上是失败的;许多充满浪漫色彩的梦想之所以破灭,原因之一就是那些毫无用处却令人心碎的批评。

所以,如果你想使你的家庭生活幸福快乐,就请记住

第三项原则:不要批评。

4 A Quick Way to Make Everybody Happy

"Most Men when seeking wives," says Paul Popenoe, Director of the Institute of Family Relations in Los Angeles, "are not looking for executives but for someone with allure and willingness to flatter their vanity and make them feel superior. Hence the woman office manager may be invited to luncheon, once. But she quite possibly dishes out warmed-over remnants of her college courses on 'main currents in contemporary philosophy,' and may even insist on paying her own bill. Result: she thereafter lunches alone.

"In contrast, the noncollegiate typist, when invited to luncheon, fixes an incandescent gaze on her escort and says yearningly, 'Now tell me some more about yourself.' Result: he tells the other fellows that 'she's no raving beauty, but I have never met a better talker.'"

Men should express their appreciation of a woman's effort to look well and dress becomingly. All men forget, if they have ever realized it, how profoundly women are interested in clothes. For example, if a man and woman meet another man and woman on the street, the woman seldom looks at the other man; she usually looks to see how well the other woman is dressed.

My grandmother died a few years ago at the age of ninety-eight. Shortly before her death, we showed her a photograph of herself that had been taken a third of a century earlier. Her failing eyes couldn't see the picture very well, and the only question she asked was: "What dress did I have on?" Think of it! An old woman in her last December, bedridden, weary with age as she lay within the shadow of the century mark, her memory fading so fast that she was no longer able to recognize even her own daughters, still interested in knowing what dress she had worn a third of a century before! I was at her bedside when she asked that question. It left an impression on me that will never fade.

The men who are reading these lines can't remember what suits or shirts they wore five years ago, and they haven't the remotest desire to remember them. But women—they are different, and we American men ought to recognize it. French boys of the upper class are trained to express their

第4章 让每个人都高兴的办法

"大多数男子在寻找对象的时候，"洛杉矶家庭关系研究所所长保罗·鲍比诺说，"不是找高级职员，而是想找一位既迷人，又可以满足他们的虚荣心，并使他们感觉超人一等的人。所以，某位办公室女主管可能会被人邀请去吃饭，但也只有一次。她很可能会把她在大学所学的《现代哲学主要思潮》拿出来作为话题，甚至坚持付自己的餐费。结果呢?从此她就一个人吃饭了。

"相反，那些没有上过大学的打字员被人邀请共进午餐的时候，会用热情的眼光注视着她身边的男子，深情地说：'能不能把你的情况多告诉我一些?'结果这个男人会告诉别人：'她并不是很漂亮，但我从未遇到比她更会说话的人。'"

对于女性在追求美丽方面所花的精力，男人应该表示赞赏。所有的男人常常会忘记——尽管他们也知道——女人非常在意自己的衣着打扮。例如，一个男人和一个女人在大街上遇到另一个男人和一个女人时，这女人很少会注意男人，而通常会注意另一个女人的穿着。

几年前，我的祖母在98岁高龄时离开了人世。就在她去世前不久，我们把一张她在30多年前照的照片给她看。尽管她的眼神已经不太好，看不清照片，但她问的唯一问题是："我那时候穿的什么衣服?"请想想! 一位风烛残年的老太太，久病在床，年事已高，近一个世纪的时光将她的全部精力几乎耗尽，记忆力甚至衰退到连自己的女儿都认不出来，可是还想知道她在30多年前穿什么衣服! 她问这个问题的时候，我正好在她床边。这件事给我留下了难以磨灭的印象。

本书的男读者不会记得他们在5年前穿的什么衣服，而且也根本没有心思去记。但是女人

admiration of a woman's frock and chapeau, not only once but many times during an evening. And fifty million Frenchmen can't be wrong!

I have among my clippings a story that I know never happened, but it illustrates a truth, so I'll repeat it:

According to this silly story, a farm woman, at the end of a heavy day's work, set before her men folks a heaping pile of hay. And when they indignantly demanded whether she'd gone crazy, she replied: "Why, how did I know you'd notice? I've been cooking for you men for the last twenty years, and in all that time I am not heard no word to let me know you wasn't just eating hay! "

The pampered aristocrats of Moscow and St Petersburg used to have better manners; in the Russia of the Czars, it was the custom of the upper classes, when they had enjoyed a fine dinner, to insist on having the cook brought into the dining room to receive their congratulations.

Why not have as much consideration for your wife? The next time the fried chicken is done to a tender turn, tell her so. Let her know that you appreciate the fact that you're not just eating hay. Or, as Texas Guinan used to say, "Give the little girl a great big hand."

And while you're about it, Don't be afraid to let her know how important she is to your happiness. Disraeli was as great a statesman as England ever produced; yet, as we've seen, he wasn't ashamed to let the world know how much he "owed to the little woman."

Just the other day, while perusing a magazine, I came across this.

It's from an interview with Eddie Cantor.

"I owe more to my wife," says Eddie Cantor, "than to anyone else in the world. She was my best pal as a boy; she helped me to go straight. And after we married she saved every dollar, and invested it, and reinvested it. She built up a fortune for me. We have five lovely children. And she's made a wonderful home for me always. If I've gotten anywhere, give her the credit."

Out in Hollywood, where marriage is a risk that even Lloyd's of London wouldn't take a gamble on, one of the few outstandingly happy marriages is that of the Warner Baxters. Mrs. Baxter, the former Winifred Bryson, gave up a brilliant stage career when she married. Yet her sacrifice has never been permitted to mar their happiness. "She missed the applause of stage success," Warner

就不同了——我们男人应该注意这一点。法国上层社会的男人就会对女人的衣服帽子表示赞美，而且一个晚上会赞美多次。5000 万法国男人这么做自有道理。

在我的剪报中有一篇故事。尽管我知道这件事从未发生过，但它却说明了一个道理，我复述如下：

这个故事说，一个农村妇女，干了一天的辛苦工作之后，在男人们面前放了一大堆草。当这些男人生气地问她是否发疯时，她回答说："哼！我怎么知道你们会在意？我为你们这些男人做了 20 年饭，可我从未听到你们说过一句话，好让我知道你们吃的不是草。"

从前，莫斯科和圣彼得堡那些养尊处优的上层人物在这方面很有教养。在沙皇俄国时代，上层社会有一种习惯，当他们享受了一顿美味佳肴之后，一定会请来厨师，当面褒奖他们。

为什么不这样对待你的妻子呢？下次她的鸡排做得非常脆嫩可口时，就要这样告诉她，让她知道你非常欣赏她的手艺——你不是在吃草。或者，正如得克萨斯·吉恩常说的："大大地夸奖那个小女人。"

如果你想这样做，不妨让她知道，她对你的幸福多么重要。狄斯累利是英国最伟大的政治家，但如前所述，他会对世人毫不害羞地承认"非常感激那个小女人"。

有一天，我在看一本杂志，看到一段采访艾迪·康德的文字：

"我从我妻子那里获益良多，"艾迪·康德说，"比从任何其他人那里得到的都要多。她是我儿时最好的伙伴，帮助我努力进取。我们结婚之后，她省下每一美元，拿去投资、再投资。她为我积累了一大笔财富。我们有 5 个可爱的孩子，她为我建造了一个温暖舒适的家。假如说我有所成就的话，全都归功于她。"

在好莱坞，婚姻就是一种冒险，即使伦敦的路易保险公司也不敢承保。华纳·巴斯特的婚姻是少数特别幸福的婚姻中的一个。巴斯特夫人婚前的名字是威尼弗雷德·布莱逊，她放弃了如

Baxter says, "but I have tried to see that she is entirely aware of my applause. If a woman is to find happiness at all in her husband, she is to find it in his appreciation, and devotion. If that appreciation and devotion is actual, there is the answer to his happiness also."

There you are. So, if you want to keep your home life happy, one of the most important rules is

Rule 4 is: Give honest appreciation.

日中天的表演生涯，和巴斯特结了婚。但是，她的这种牺牲从未破坏他们的幸福。"她失去了在舞台上成功的机会，"华纳·巴斯特说，"但我已经尽了最大努力，使她知道我对她的赞美。如果一个女人要从她丈夫那里得到幸福，那一定要从他的赞美和热爱中去找。如果这种赞美和热爱发自内心，那么他也会从中得到爱与幸福。"

明白了吗？所以，如果你想使你的家庭生活幸福快乐，一项最重要的原则就是……

第四项原则：给予真诚的欣赏。

5 They Mean So Much to a Woman

From Time immemorial, flowers have been considered the language of love. They don't cost much, especially in season, and often they're for sale on the street corners. Yet, considering the rarity with which the average husband takes home a bunch of daffodils, you might suppose them to be as expensive as orchids and as hard to come by as the edelweiss which flowers on the cloud-swept cliffs of the Alps.

Why wait until your wife goes to the hospital to give her a few flowers? Why not bring her a few roses tomorrow night? You like to experiment. Try it. See what happens.

George M. Cohan, busy as he was on Broadway, used to telephone his mother twice a day up to the time of her death. Do you suppose he had startling news for her each time? No, the meaning of little attentions is this: it shows the person you love that you are thinking of her, that you want to please her, and that her happiness and welfare are very dear, and very near, to your heart.

Women attach a lot of importance to birthdays and anniversaries—just why, will forever remain one of those feminine mysteries. The average man can blunder through life without memorizing many dates, but there are a few which are indispensable: 1492, 1776, the date of his wife's birthday, and the year and date of his own marriage. If need be, he can even get along without the first two—but not the last!

Judge Joseph Sabbath of Chicago, who has reviewed 40,000 marital disputes and reconciled 2,000 couples, says, "Trivialities are at the bottom of most marital unhappiness. Such a simple thing as a wife's waving good-bye to her husband when he goes to work in the morning would avert a good many divorces."

Robert Browning, whose life with Elizabeth Barrett Browning was perhaps the most idyllic on record, was never too busy to keep love alive with little, tributes and attentions. He treated his invalid wife with such consideration that she once wrote to her sisters: "And now I begin to wonder naturally whether I may not be some sort of real angel after all."

第5章 对女人最有意义的事

自古以来，鲜花就被认为是爱情的语言。买花用不了几个钱，尤其是在开花季节，街头巷尾都能买到。但是，一般来说，丈夫很少会买一束水仙花回家。你也许会认为水仙花和兰花一样昂贵，或者像开在高耸入云的阿尔卑斯山陡峭悬崖上的火绒花那样稀有。

为什么要等你妻子住院才给她买花呢?为什么不在明天晚上买一束玫瑰花给她?如果你喜欢，不妨试试，看看结果如何。

乔治·柯恩是百老汇的大忙人，却每天给他母亲通两次电话，直至她去世。你是不是认为他每次都会告诉她一些新鲜事?没有。这种小事的意义在于，向你所爱的人表达你的思念，你想让她幸福快乐；她的幸福快乐对你来说是非常宝贵和重要的。

女人对于自己的生日和纪念日非常在意——为什么呢？这可能永远是一个无人知晓的女性之谜。男人们即使不记得许多有意义的日子，但他们也仍然可以将就地过一辈子，但是有些日子是应该记住的，如 1492 年(哥伦布发现美洲新大陆)、1776 年(美国独立)、妻子的生日以及他自己的结婚纪念日。如果实在记不住，那可以不记前面两个时间——而不是后面两个!

芝加哥大法官塞巴斯曾审过 4 万件离婚案，并使 2000 对夫妇达成和解。他说："大多数婚姻生活的不和，根本原因在于琐事。例如早上丈夫离家上班的时候，如果妻子能向丈夫挥手再见，就可以使许多夫妻免于离婚。"

罗伯特·布朗宁和他妻子伊丽莎白·巴瑞特·布朗宁的婚姻生活，可以说是有史以来最值得称颂的。即使他再忙，也不会忘记从细微之处来体现他的爱意。由于他贴入微地照顾患病的妻子，以至于妻子有一次写信给她妹妹说："现在我很自然地开始觉得，我或许真的是一位

Too many men underestimate the value of these small, everyday attentions. As Gaynor Maddox said in an article in *the Pictorial Review*: "The American home really needs a few new vices. Breakfast in bed, for instance, is one of those amiable dissipations a greater number of women should be indulged in. Breakfast in bed to a woman does much the same thing as a private club for a man."

That's what marriage is in the long run—a series of trivial incidents. And woe to the couple who overlook that fact. Edna St. Vincent Millay summed it all up once in one of her concise little rhymes: "It's not love's going hurts my days, But that it went in little ways."

That's a good verse to memorize. Out in Reno, the courts grant divorces six days a week, at the rate of one every ten marriages.

How many of these marriages do you suppose were wrecked upon the reef of real tragedy? Mighty few, I'll warrant. If you could sit there day in, day out, listening to the testimony of those unhappy husbands and wives, you'd know love "went in little ways".

Take your pocket knife now and cut out this quotation. Paste it inside your hat or paste it on the mirror, where you will see it every morning when you shave:

"I shall pass this way but once; any good, therefore, that I can do or any kindness that I can show to any human being, let me do it now. Let me not defer nor neglect it, for I shall not pass this way again."

So, if you want to keep your home life happy,

Rule 5 is: Pay little attentions.

天使。”

许多男人总是小瞧这种日常关注的重要性。正如盖罗·麦道斯在《图书评论》一篇文章中所说的:“美国家庭真的需要一些新的东西。例如,在床上吃早餐,是许多女人喜欢的一种自我放纵。在床上吃早餐对于女人犹如私人俱乐部对男人一样重要。”

这才是婚姻持续稳定的原因——一连串小事。忽视这些琐事的夫妻必定会出现不幸。艾德娜·圣·文森特·米莱在她的一篇押韵短诗中说得很好:“并不是失去之爱破坏了我的美好时光,而是生活小事导致了爱的消亡。”

这首诗太好了,值得记住。在雷诺,法院每星期有6天办理离婚案件,是结婚登记的1/10。

这些破碎的婚姻,你认为有多少是由于真正的悲剧导致的呢?太少了,我敢保证。如果你有时间从早到晚坐在那里,听那些婚姻不愉快的夫妻们的述说,你就会知道,爱情正是由生活琐事而导致消亡的。

现在,请将下面这段引语剪下来,贴在你的帽子里或镜子上,以便你每天早晨刮脸时都可以看见:

“机会只有一次。因此,凡是我能做的善事或我能向人表达的善心,就让我现在去做。不要拖延,不要疏忽,因为机不可失,时不再来。”

所以,如果你想使你的家庭幸福快乐,就请记住

第五项原则:对小事多加注意。

6 If You Want to Be Happy, Don't Neglect This One

Walter Damrosch married the daughter of James G.Blaine, one of America's greatest orators and one-time candidate for President.

Ever since they met many years ago at Andrew Carnegie's home in Scotland, the Damroschs have led a conspicuously happy life. The secret?

"Next to care in choosing a partner," says Mrs.Damrosch, "I should place courtesy after marriage. If young wives would only be as courteous to their husbands as to strangers! Any man will run from a shrewish tongue."

Rudeness is the cancer that devours love. Everyone knows this, yet it's notorious that we are more polite to strangers than we are to our own relatives. We wouldn't dream of interrupting strangers to say, "Good heavens, are you going to tell that old story again!" We wouldn't dream of opening our friends' mail without permission, or prying into their personal secrets. And it's only the members of our own family, those who are nearest and dearest to us, that we dare insult for their trivial faults.

Again to quote Dorothy Dix: "It is an amazing but true thing that practically the only people who ever say mean, insulting, wounding things to us are those of our own households."

"Courtesy," says Henry Clay Risner, "is that quality of heart that overlooks the broken gate and calls attention to the flowers in the yard beyond the gate." Courtesy is just as important to marriage as oil is to your motor.

Oliver Wendell Holmes, the beloved "*Autocrat of the Breakfast Table*," was anything but an autocrat in his own home. In fact, he carried his consideration so far that when he felt melancholy and depressed, he tried to conceal his blues from the rest of his family. It was bad enough for him to have to bear them himself, he said, without inflicting them on the others as well.

That is what Oliver Wendell Holmes did. But what about the average mortal? Things go wrong at the office; he loses a sale or gets called on the carpet by the boss. He develops a devastating

第6章 如果你想快乐，不要忽视这点

瓦特·丹鲁什娶了詹姆斯·布莱恩的女儿。布雷恩是美国最伟大的演说家之一，曾经是美国总统候选人。

自从他们多年前在苏格兰的安德鲁·卡内基家中相识之后，丹鲁什夫妇就过着非常幸福的生活。他们的秘诀是什么呢?

"除了谨慎地挑选伴侣之外，"丹鲁什夫人说，"我认为婚后的殷勤有礼是最重要的。希望那些年轻的妻子对待她们的丈夫就像对待陌生人那样有礼。如果泼辣蛮横，任何男人都会被吓跑。"

蛮横是腐蚀爱情的毒瘤。每个人都知道这一点，但是我们对待自己的亲人有时竟然不如对陌生人那样有礼貌。我们绝对不会想到打断陌生人的话，说："天啊，你又搬出那些陈芝麻烂谷子的事来了!"如果没有得到允许，我们绝不会拆开朋友的信，或者打听他们的私事。只有我们自己家里的人，也就是我们最亲近的人，我们却会责怪他们的小错误。

再次引用迪克丝的话："令人吃惊却又千真万确的一件事就是，唯一对我们说出那些刻薄难听、带有侮辱性的话的人，正是我们自己家中的人。"

"礼貌，"亨利·克雷·雷森纳说，"是一种内在的品质。它可以弥补服饰和外表的缺陷，使那些比你优越的人也不敢小瞧你。"殷勤有礼对于婚姻就像机油对于发动机一样重要。

奥利弗·温德尔·霍尔姆斯写了广受读者喜爱的《早餐桌上的独裁者》，但是他在自己家里绝不会这样。事实上，他非常体贴别人，即使他心情郁闷，他也总是尽量掩藏，而不让家人知道。既要自己忍受这些痛苦，又不影响其他人，这可真让他难受。

headache or misses the five-fifteen; and he can hardly wait till he gets home—to take it out on the family.

In Holland you leave your shoes outside on the doorstep before you enter the house. By the Lord Harry, we could learn a lesson from the Dutch and shed our workaday troubles before we enter our homes.

William James once wrote an essay called *"On a Certain Blindness in Human Beings."* It would be worth a special trip to your nearest library to get that essay and read it. "Now the blindness in human beings of which this discourse will treat," he wrote, "is the blindness with which we all are afflicted in regard to the feelings of creatures and people different from ourselves."

"The blindness with which we all are afflicted." Many men who wouldn't dream of speaking sharply to a customer, or even to their partners in business, think nothing of barking at their wives. Yet, for their personal happiness, marriage is far more important to them, far more vital, than business.

The average man who is happily married is happier by far than the genius who lives in solitude. Turgenev, the great Russian novelist, was acclaimed all over the civilized world. Yet he said: "I would give up all my genius, and all my books, if there were only some woman, somewhere, who cared whether or not I came home late for dinner."

What are the chances of happiness in marriage anyway? Dorothy Dix, as we have already said, believes that more than half of them are failures; but Dr Paul Popenoe thinks otherwise. He says: "A man has a better chance of succeeding in marriage than in any other enterprise he may go into. Of all the men that go into the grocery business, 70 per cent fail. Of the men and women who enter matrimony, 70 per cent succeed."

Dorothy Dix sums the whole thing up like this: "Compared with marriage," she says, "being born is a mere episode in our careers, and dying a trivial incident.

"No woman can ever understand why a man doesn't put forth the same effort to make his home a going concern as he does to make his business or profession a success.

"But, although to have a contented wife and a peaceful and happy home means more to a man than to make a million dollars, not one man in a hundred ever gives any real serious thought or

这是霍尔姆斯的做法。但是一般人又是怎样做的呢?在办公室出了点差错、丢了一笔业务、被上司责骂了一顿、累得头昏脑涨,或者错过了火车——几乎还没回到家,就想着如何向家人撒气。

在荷兰,进入屋子之前要先把鞋子脱在门外。我们应该向荷兰人学习,在进家门之前,把一天的工作烦恼甩在门外。

威廉·詹姆斯曾写过一篇文章《人类的某种盲目》,很值得去最近的图书馆借来读读。"这篇文章所要讨论的人类的盲目,"他写道,"就是不知道动物和人的感情区别何在。这种盲目使我们都深受其苦。"

"这种盲目使我们都深受其苦。"许多男人绝不会对自己的顾客或业务合伙人说出难听的话,却会对自己的妻子怒吼。然而,就其个人幸福而言,婚姻比事业更重要,也更密切。

婚姻幸福的普通人比独身幽居的天才更加愉快。俄国伟大的小说家屠格涅夫广受文明世界的赞誉,但他也认为:"如果什么地方有个女人关心我是否回家吃晚饭,我情愿放弃我所有的天才和所有的作品。"

婚姻幸福的机会究竟有多少?如前所述,迪克丝认为50%以上的婚姻都是不成功的,但保罗·鲍比诺博士却持相反的观点。他认为:"男人在婚姻上成功的机会,远比在任何行业中成功的机会大。从事杂货生意的男人,70%都会失败;而步入婚姻礼堂的男人和女人,70%会成功。"

迪克丝是这样解释这件事的:"和婚姻相比,出生只不过是人生的一小幕,死亡也不过是小事一桩。

"女人永远都不明白,为什么男人不愿花同样的精力把他的家庭营造成幸福的乐园,就像他在生意或事业上的成功那样。

"但是,对男人而言虽然有一个令人满意的妻子和一个幸福美满的家庭比赚100万美元还

makes any honest effort to make his marriage a success.He leaves the most important thing in his life to chance,and he wins out or loses,according to whether fortune is with him or not.Women can never understand why their husbands refuse to handle them diplomatically,when it would be money in their pockets to use the velvet glove instead of the strong-arm method.

"Every man knows that he can jolly his wife into doing anything,and doing without anything. He knows that if he hands her a few cheap compliments about what a wonderful manager she is, and how she helps him,she will squeeze every nickel.Every man knows that if he tells his wife how beautiful and lovely she looks in her last year's dress,she wouldn't trade it for the latest Paris importation.Every man knows that he can kiss his wife's eyes shut until she will be blind as a bat, and that he has only to give her a warm smack on the lips to make her dumb as an oyster.

"And every wife knows that her husband knows these things about her,because she has furnished him with a complete diagram about how to work her.And she never knows whether to be mad at him or disgusted with him,because he would rather fight with her and pay for it in having to eat bad meals,and have his money wasted,and buy her new frocks and limousines and pearls,than to take the trouble to flatter her a little and treat her the way she is begging to be treated."

So,if you want to keep your home life happy,

Rule 6 is:Be courteous.

重要,可是只有不到百分之一的男人认真地想过或真诚地努力使他的婚姻走向成功。他把自己一生中最重要的事情交给了命运,其成败只能听天由命。女人也永远不明白,为什么她们的丈夫不温和地对待她们,以平息本来可以平息的冲突。

"每个男人都知道,只要让他的妻子高兴,就可以让她不讲条件地干任何事情。他也知道,如果夸她几句把家中安排得井井有条、她帮了他大忙,她也会心甘情愿地掏出最后一分钱。每个男人都知道,如果他告诉妻子,说她穿上去年那件衣服多么美丽可爱,她就会放弃购买从巴黎进口的最新服装。每个男人也都知道,他可以用亲吻让妻子闭上眼睛,直到她像蝙蝠那样看不见东西;他只要在她嘴唇上热情地吻一下,她就会不再说话。

"每一个妻子都知道她丈夫也明白这些,因为她早就将这些明明白白地告诉了他。但是她的丈夫情愿和她争吵,吃难以下咽的饭菜,或者花钱为她买新衣服、汽车、珠宝,却不愿意夸她几句,不愿以她希望的方式来满足她。对此她不知是该喜欢他,还是该讨厌他。"

所以,如果你想使你的家庭幸福快乐,请记住——

第六项原则:要有礼貌。

7 Don't Be a "Marriage Illiterate"

Dr Katherine Bement Davis, general secretary of the Bureau of Social Hygiene, once induced a thousand married women to reply very frankly to a set of intimate questions. The result was shocking—an incredibly shocking comment upon the sexual unhappiness of the average American adult. After perusing the answers she received from these thousand married women, Dr Davis published without hesitation her conviction that one of the chief causes of divorce in this country is physical mismating.

Dr G.V.Hamilton's survey verifies this finding. Dr Hamilton spent four years studying the marriages of one hundred men and one hundred women. He asked these men and women individually something like four hundred questions concerning their married lives, and discussed their problems exhaustively—so exhaustively that the whole investigation took four years. This work was considered so important sociologically that it was financed by a group of leading philanthropists. You can read the results of the experiment in *What's Wrong with Marriage?* by Dr G.V.Hamilton and Kenneth Macgowan.

Well, what is wrong with marriage? "It would take a very prejudiced and very reckless psychiatrist," says Dr Hamilton, "to say that most married friction doesn't find its source in sexual maladjustment. At any rate, the frictions which arise from other difficulties would be ignored in many, many cases if the sexual relation itself were satisfactory."

Dr Paul Popenoe, as head of the Institute of Family Relations in Los Angeles, has reviewed thousands of marriages and he is one of America's foremost authorities on home life. According to Dr Popenoe, failure in marriage is usually due to four causes. He lists them in this order:

1. Sexual maladjustment.
2. Difference of opinion as to the way of spending leisure time.
3. Financial difficulties.
4. Mental, physical, or emotional abnormalities.

第7章 不要做"婚姻的文盲"

社会卫生局总干事凯瑟琳·贝蒙特·戴维斯博士有一次曾说服1000位已婚妇女，请她们毫不隐讳地回答一些个人问题。结果令人吃惊——一般的美国成年人在性生活方面并不愉快。戴维斯博士研究这1000位已婚妇女的回答之后，立刻发表了自己的观点——美国离婚的主要原因之一，就是性生活的不和谐。

乔治·汉密尔顿博士的调查也证实了这一发现。汉密尔顿博士花了4年时间，研究了100个男人和100个女人的婚姻生活。他曾单独问了这些男女400个婚姻生活方面的问题，并对这些问题进行了详细研究——其彻底程度使这项工作花了4年时间。由于这项工作在社会学方面具有重要价值，因此许多著名慈善家出钱赞助了这一活动。你可以从汉密尔顿博士和麦克高文合著的《婚姻的症结》这本书中读到这次调查的结果。

那么，婚姻的症结是什么呢？"只有那些极端偏执或非常莽撞的精神病医生，"汉密尔顿博士说，"才会说婚姻生活的大部分摩擦不是由性生活的不和谐引起的。无论如何，如果性生活本身令人满意，那么许多由其他因素导致的冲突将会迎刃而解。"

洛杉矶家庭关系研究所所长保罗·鲍比诺博士曾分析过几千件婚姻纠纷官司，他是美国家庭生活方面最著名的专家之一。根据他的观点，婚姻的失败常常是由四种因素导致的。他将这些因素排序如下：

1. 性生活不和谐。
2. 对如何休闲娱乐存在分歧。
3. 经济拮据。

Notice that sex comes first; and that, strangely enough, money difficulties come only third on the list.

All authorities on divorce agree upon the absolute necessity for sexual compatibility. For example, a few years ago Judge Hoffman of the Domestic Relations Court of Cincinnati—a man who has listened to thousands of domestic tragedies—announced: "Nine out of ten divorces are caused by sexual troubles."

"Sex," says the famous psychologist, John B. Watson, "is admittedly the most important subject in life. It is admittedly the thing which causes the most ship-wrecks in the happiness of men and women."

And I have heard a number of practicing physicians in speeches before my own classes say practically the same thing. Isn't it pitiful, then, that in the twentieth century, with all of our books and all of our education, marriages should be destroyed and lives wrecked by ignorance concerning this most primal and natural instinct?

The Rev. Oliver M. Butterfield, after eighteen years as a Methodist minister, gave up his pulpit to direct the Family Guidance Service in New York City, and he has probably married as many young people as any man living. He says:

"Early in my experience as a minister I discovered that, in spite of romance and good intentions, many couples who come to the marriage altar are matrimonial illiterates." Matrimonial illiterates!

And he continues: "When you consider that we leave the highly difficult adjustment of marriage so largely to chance, the marvel is that our divorce rate is only 16 per cent. An appalling number of husbands and wives are not really married but simply undivorced: they live in a sort of purgatory."

"Happy marriages," says Dr Butterfield, "are rarely the product of chance: they are architectural in that they are intelligently and deliberately planned."

To assist in this planning, Dr Butterfield has for years insisted that any couple he marries must discuss with him frankly their plans for the future. And it was as a result of these discussions that he came to the conclusion that so many of the high contracting parties were "matrimonial illiterates."

"Sex," says Dr Butterfield, "is but one of the many satisfactions in married life, but unless this

4. 心理、生理或情绪上的反常现象。

请注意，性生活居第一位。非常奇怪的是，经济拮据只排在第三位。

所有研究离婚问题的专家都一致认为，性生活的相互配合绝对必要。例如，几年前，辛辛那提家庭关系法院的哈夫曼法官——他听过几千个家庭悲剧——宣称："离婚的原因，十之八九是性生活不协调。"

著名心理学家约翰·沃特森曾说："性被认为是生活中最重要的事情，而且被认为是导致大部分男女婚姻失败的原因。"

我还听过许多执业医生在我班上的演讲，他们说的几乎相同。那么，在20世纪，我们有这么多的书和教育，却因为对这种最原始自然的本能缺乏了解而导致婚姻失败，难道不可悲吗？

奥利弗·布特费尔博士在担任卫理会18年的牧师之后，放弃了他的传教事业，去纽约市家庭指导服务中心主持工作。他的婚姻也许比许多年轻人的年龄还大，他说：

"根据我早年担任牧师的经验，我发现许多人虽然有着美好的罗曼史和对美好生活的向往，但是他们走进婚姻的殿堂时，仍然是'婚姻的文盲'。"婚姻的文盲！

他又说："当你想到我们对婚姻的极度不协调只能听天由命，而离婚率只有16%时，或许会认为这是个奇迹！其实，许多丈夫和妻子并没有真正结婚，他们只不过没有离婚而已：他们生活在地狱中。"

"幸福的婚姻，"布特费尔博士说，"很少是靠机遇获得的：它们是靠人营造的，而且还要理智、审慎地计划。"

为了帮助制定这种计划，布特费尔博士多年来都坚持一点，即凡是由他主持的婚礼，夫妇双方必须坦诚地和他谈他们未来的计划。他从这些谈话中得出的结论是，许多急于结婚的人其实是"婚姻的文盲"。

"性，"布特费尔博士说，"只是婚姻生活中诸多惬意事情的一种，但只有把这层关系理顺

relationship is right, nothing else can be right."

But how to get it right? "Sentimental reticence"—I'm still quoting Dr. Butterfield—"must be replaced by an ability to discuss objectively and with detachment attitudes and practices of married life. There is no way in which this ability can be better acquired than through a book of sound learning and good taste. I keep on hand several of these books in addition to a supply of my own booklet, *Marriage and Sexual Harmony*.

"Of all the books that are available, the three that seem to me most satisfactory for general reading are: *The Sex Technique in Marriage* by Isabel E. Hutton; *The Sexual Side of Marriage* by Max Exner; *The Sex Factor in Marriage* by Helena Wright."

So, Rule 7 of "How to Make Your Home Life Happier" is:

Read a good book on the sexual side of marriage.

In its issue for June, 1933, *American Magazine* printed an article by Emmet Crozier, "Why Marriages Go Wrong." The following is a questionnaire reprinted from that article. You may find it worthwhile to answer these questions, giving yourself ten points for each question you can answer in the affirmative.

For Husbands:

1. Do you still "court" your wife with an occasional gift of flowers, with remembrances of her birthday and wedding anniversary, or with some unexpected attention, some unlooked-for tenderness?

2. Are you careful never to criticize her before others ?

3. Do you give her money to spend entirely as she chooses, above the household expenses?

4. Do you make an effort to understand her varying feminine moods and help her through periods of fatigue, nerves, and irritability?

5. Do you share at least half of your recreation hours with your wife?

6. Do you tactfully refrain from comparing your wife's cooking or housekeeping with that of your mother or of Bill Jones' wife, except to her advantage?

7. Do you take a definite interest in her intellectual life, her clubs and societies, the books she reads, her views on civic problems?

8. Can you let her dance with and receive friendly attentions from other men without making

了，其他方面才会顺利。"

但如何才能做好呢?"碍于情面而不好意思说，"我还在引用布特费尔博士的话——"必须代之以客观的讨论，并以超然的态度来对待婚姻。要获得这种能力，除了看一本内容丰富的好书之外，别无良方。除了我自己写的《婚姻与性的和谐》这本小册子之外，我手边还有几本这方面的书。

"在所有这类书中，我认为有3本最适合大众阅读：伊莎贝尔·哈顿的《婚姻中的性技巧》，马克思·爱克斯纳的《婚姻中的性》，赫勒拿·莱特的《婚姻中的性因素》。"

所以，如何使你的家庭生活更快乐

第七项原则：读一本关于婚姻中性生活的好书。

在1933年6月出版的一期《美国杂志》中，刊登了埃麦特·克鲁齐尔的一篇文章《为什么婚姻会出问题》。下面这些问题是从这篇文章中转载的，或许你会觉得这些问题值得回答。如果你对某个问题作出肯定回答，可以给自己打10分。

问丈夫的问题：

1. 你是不是还在"追求"你的妻子?偶尔送她一束鲜花，记住她的生日和结婚纪念日?或给她一些出乎意料的体贴?

2. 你是否注意从来不在别人面前批评她?

3. 除了家庭开支以外，你是否还给她一些钱让她随意使用?

4. 你是否尽力了解她各种女性方面的情绪问题，并帮助她度过疲乏、紧张和不安的时期?

5. 你是否至少一半的休闲时间与妻子共处?

6. 除非可以显示她的长处，你是否会巧妙地避免将你妻子的烹饪手艺或理家本领和你母亲或别人的妻子做比较?

7. 你是否对她的学习生活、她的社交、她所读的书和她对公共问题的看法也有一定的兴趣?

jealous remarks?

9. Do you keep alert for opportunities to praise her and express your admiration for her?

10.Do you thank her for the little jobs she does for you, such as sewing on a button, darning your socks, and sending your clothes to the cleaners?

For Wives:

1. Do you give your husband complete freedom in his business affairs, and do you refrain from criticizing his associates, his choice of a secretary, or the hours he keeps?

2. Do you try your best to make your home interesting and attractive?

3. Do you vary the household menu so that he never quite knows what to expect when he sits down to the table?

4. Do you have an intelligent grasp of your husband's business so you can discuss it with him helpfully?

5. Can you meet financial reverses bravely, cheerfully, without criticizing your husband for his mistakes or comparing him unfavourably with more successful men?

6. Do you make a special effort to get along amiably with his mother or other relatives?

7. Do you dress with an eye for your husband's likes and dislikes in colour and style?

8. Do you compromise little differences of opinion in the interest of harmony?

9. Do you make an effort to learn games your husband likes, so you can share his leisure hours?

10. Do you keep track of the day's news, the new books, and new ideas, so you can hold your husband's intellectual interest?

8. 你是否让她和别的男人跳舞并接受他们的殷勤照顾而不说嫉妒话?

9. 你是否经常找机会赞美她,并表达你对她的赞赏?

10. 你是否感激她为你做的各种小事,如钉扣子、补袜子,送你的衣服去洗衣店等?

问妻子的问题:

1. 你是否让你丈夫完全自由地处理公务,绝不批评他的同事,不干涉他选择秘书,或让他有自己的时间?

2. 你是否尽力使你的家庭幸福融洽?

3. 你是否总是变换菜谱,使他坐到饭桌前时还不清楚吃什么?

4. 你是否对丈夫的事业有所了解,并和他进行有益的探讨?

5. 你是否能勇敢、轻松地面对经济困难而不批评你的丈夫,或将他和其他更成功的男人作不利的比较?

6. 你是否特别努力地和他的母亲或其他亲属和睦相处?

7. 你穿衣服时,是否注意你丈夫对颜色及款式的喜好?

8. 为了家庭和睦,你是否会作出一些让步?

9. 你是否努力学习丈夫喜欢的东西,以便和他共度休闲时间?

10. 你是否关注最新新闻、新书和新思想,以使自己在知识、兴趣等方面与丈夫一致?

HOW TO STOP WORRYING AND START LIVING

人性的优点

Preface
How This Book Was Written—and Why

In 1909, I was one of the unhappiest lads in New York. I was selling motor-trucks for a living. I didn't know what made a motor-truck run. That wasn't all: I didn't want to know. I despised my job. I despised living in a cheap furnished room on West Fifty-sixth Street—a room infested with cockroaches. I still remember that I had a bunch of neckties hanging on the walls; and when I reached out of a morning to get a fresh necktie, the cockroaches scattered in all directions. I despised having to eat in cheap, dirty restaurants that were also probably infested with cockroaches.

I came home to my lonely room each night with a sick headache—a headache bred and fed by disappointment, worry, bitterness, and rebellion. I was rebelling because the dreams I had nourished back in my college days had turned into nightmares. Was this life? Was this the vital adventure to which I had looked forward so eagerly? Was this all life would ever mean to me—working at a job I despised, living with cockroaches, eating vile food—and with no hope for the future?... I longed for leisure to read, and to write the books I had dreamed of writing back in my college days. I knew I had everything to gain and nothing to lose by giving up the job I despised. I wasn't interested in making a lot of money, but I was interested in making a lot of living. In short, I had come to the Rubicon—to that moment of decision which faces most young people when they start out in life. So I made my decision—and that decision completely altered my future. It has made the rest of my life happy and rewarding beyond my most utopian aspirations.

My decision was this: I would give up the work I loathed; and, since I had spent four years

序　言
本书是如何写的，为什么要写这本书

1909年，我是纽约最不开心的年轻人。我当时靠推销货车为生。我不了解货车的运转原理。这还不算，我本来就不想了解。我瞧不起我的工作，不愿住在西五十六大街到处都是蟑螂的简陋房间里。我还记得我将一些领带挂在墙上，当我早上伸手去取一条新领带时，蟑螂四处逃散的情景。我厌恨每天不得不去那个廉价而肮脏，或许同样是蟑螂横行的饭馆吃饭。

每天晚上，我都会头痛欲裂地回到那冷冷清清的房间——因失望、忧虑、痛苦和抗争而造成的头痛。我之所以抗争，是因为我大学时代的美好梦想已成为噩梦。这就是生活吗？这就是我热切期望的人生冒险吗？对我来说这就是人生的一切吗——干着自己不喜欢的工作、与蟑螂为伍、吃难以下咽的饭——未来却毫无希望？……我渴望读书的乐趣，渴望写我在大学时代就想写的书。我知道，放弃我不喜欢的工作什么都不会失去，反而可以获益良多。我并不在意赚大把大把的钱，而喜欢让人生富有意义。总之，我已经破釜沉舟——那一刻是大多数年轻人开始人生之旅时都会面临的。因此，我做出了决定——这个决定完全改变了我的前途。它使我后来

studying in the State Teachers' College at Warrensburg, Missouri, preparing to teach, I would make my living teaching adult classes in night schools. Then I would have my days free to read books, prepare lectures, write novels and short stories. I wanted "to live to write and write to live."

What subject should I teach to adults at night? As I looked back and evaluated my own college training, I saw that the training and experience I had had in public speaking had been of more practical value to me in business—and in life—than everything else I had studied in college all put together. Why? Because it had wiped out my timidity and lack of self-confidence and given me the courage and assurance to deal with people. It had also made clear that leadership usually gravitates to the man who can get up and say what he thinks.

I applied for a position teaching public speaking in the night extension courses both at Columbia University and New York University, but these universities decided they could struggle along somehow without my help. I was disappointed then—but now I thank God that they did turn me down, because I started teaching in YMCA night schools, where I had to show concrete results and show them quickly. What a challenge that was! These adults didn't come to my classes because they wanted college credits or social prestige. They came for one reason only: they wanted to solve their problems. They wanted to be able to stand up on their feet and say a few words at a business meeting without fainting from fright. Salesmen wanted to be able to call on a tough customer without having to walk around the block three times to get up courage. They wanted to develop poise and self-confidence. They wanted to get ahead in business. They wanted to have more money for their families. And since they were paying their tuition on an installment basis—and they stopped paying if they didn't get results—and since I was being paid, not a salary, but a percentage of the profits, I had to be practical if I wanted to eat.

I felt at the time that I was teaching under a handicap, but I realise now that I was getting priceless training. *I had to motivate my students. I had to help them solve their problems. I had to make each session so inspiring that they wanted to continue coming.*

It was exciting work. I loved it. I was astounded at how quickly these businessmen developed

的生活变得快乐,而且报酬远远超过我的最高期望。

我的决定是这样的:放弃我厌倦的工作;而且,既然我在密苏里州华伦斯堡州立师范学院读了四年书,并准备去教书,那我可以去夜校教成人课程来谋生。然后我白天就有时间读书、备课,写小说和短篇故事。我希望"为写作而活着,并以写作谋生"。

我晚上能教成年人什么课呢?我回顾并考察了我在大学受过的训练,发现我在公众演讲中所得到的训练和经验对我在商务——而且在人生中更有实际价值,其价值超过了我在大学学到的其他东西的总和。为什么呢?因为它清除了我的胆怯和缺乏自信,给了我与人交往的勇气和自信。它还表明能站起来表达自己想法的人往往具备领导才能。

我向哥伦比亚大学和纽约大学申请一份教公众演讲的晚上函授课程工作,但这两所大学都拒绝了我。我当时有些失望——但我现在庆幸他们拒绝了我,因为我开始在基督教青年会夜校授课,在那里我必须向学员显示立竿见影的具体成效。那是一项多么艰巨的挑战啊!这些成年人来上我的课,并不是想获得大学文凭或社会地位,而是为了一个目的——他们想解决他们的问题。他们想在业务会上站起来说话,而不至于因害怕而昏倒;销售员希望能够拜访难缠的顾客,而不必在街上徘徊,以鼓起勇气;他们希望培养沉着自信;他们希望事业有成;他们希望为家庭多挣一点钱。既然他们以分期付款的方式支付学费——如果他们没有收获就可以停止付费——而且既然我是按利润比例提成(而非支付薪水),所以如果我想吃饭,就必须收到实效。

当时我觉得是在不利条件下授课,但我现在意识到我那是在获得宝贵的训练。我必须激发我的学员,必须帮助他们解决他们的问题,必须让每堂课鼓舞人心,他们才会继续来

self-confidence and how quickly many of them secured promotions and increased pay. The classes were succeeding far beyond my most optimistic hopes. Within three seasons, the YMCAs, which had refused to pay me five dollars a night in salary, were paying me thirty dollars a night on a percentage basis. At first, I taught only public speaking, but, as the years went by, I saw that these adults also needed the ability to win friends and influence people. Since I couldn't find an adequate textbook on human relations, I wrote one myself. It was written—no, it wasn't written in the usual way. It grew and evolved out of the experiences of the adults in these classes. I called it *How to Win Friends and Influence People*. Since it was written solely as a textbook for my own adult classes, and since I had written four other books that no one had ever heard of, I never dreamed that it would have a large sale: I am probably one of the most astonished authors now living.

As the years went by, I realised that another one of the biggest problems of these adults was worry. A large majority of my students were businessmen—executives, salesmen, engineers, accountants: a cross section of all the trades and professions—and most of them had problems! There were women in the classes—businesswomen and housewives. They, too, had problems! Clearly, what I needed was a textbook on how to conquer worry—so again I tried to find one. I went to New York's great public library at Fifth Avenue and Forty-second Street and discovered to my astonishment that this library had only twenty-two books listed under the title WORRY. I also noticed, to my amusement, that it had one hundred eighty-nine books listed under WORMS. *Almost nine times as many books about worms as about worry*! Astounding, isn't it? Since worry is one of the biggest problems facing mankind, you would think, wouldn't you, that every high school and college in the land would give a course on "*How to Stop Worrying*"? Yet, if there is even one course on that subject in any college in the land, I have never heard of it. No wonder David Seabury said in his book *How to Worry Successfully*: "We come to maturity with as little preparation for the pressures of experience as a bookworm asked to do a ballet." The result? More than half of our hospital beds are occupied by people with nervous and emotional troubles.

听课。

这是一项激动人心的工作。我喜欢上了它。这些商务人员获得自信的速度之快,以及他们中的许多人提升销售、增加报酬的速度之快,让我感到震惊。这些课程的发展远远超出了我最乐观的期望。在三个季度内,基督教青年会曾拒绝以薪水的形式支付我一晚上5美元,现在却以提成比例的方式支付我一晚上30美元。起初,我只教公众演讲,但随着时间的流逝,我发现这些成年人还需要赢得朋友、影响他人的能力。由于找不到人际关系方面的合适教材,我就自己写了一本。它写成了——不,它不是以普通形式写成的。它是从这些上课的成年人的经验中成长发展而来的。他给它取名为《人性的弱点》。既然它只是为我自己的成人课程写的教材,而且由于我曾写过四本其他人没听说过的书,所以我从未想过它会畅销:我或许是现在仍活着的最感震惊的作者之一。

随着时间的流转,我发现这些成年人另一个最大的问题是忧虑。我的学员大部分是商务人士——总经理、推销员、工程师、会计——他们大多数人都有问题!班上也有女士——从事商务的女性和家庭主妇。她们也有烦恼!显然,我需要一本如何克服忧虑的书——于是我又努力去找一本这样的书。我去纽约第5大道第42大街的公共图书馆,让我惊讶的是只找到22本与忧虑有关的书。让我觉得有趣的是,我还注意到图书馆却有189本与虫有关的书。这竟然是关于忧虑的书的9倍。令人震惊吧?既然忧虑是人类面临的最大难题之一,你就会想(为什么不想呢?)世界上每一所中学和大学应该开设关于"如何停止忧虑"的课程。然而,我却从未听说过有哪所大学开过一门这样的课。难怪大卫·西伯利在他的作品《如何有效地克服烦恼》中说:"我们成年之后,对于需要应付的各种烦恼,犹如让虫子跳芭蕾舞一样毫无办法。"结果呢?我们医院一半以

I looked over those twenty-two books on worry reposing on the shelves of the New York Public Library. In addition, I purchased all the books on worry I could find; yet I couldn't discover even one that I could use as a text in my course for adults. So I resolved to write one myself.

I began preparing myself to write this book seven years ago. How? By reading what the philosophers of all ages have said about worry. I also read hundreds of biographies, all the way from Confucius to Churchill. I also interviewed scores of prominent people in many walks of life, such as Jack Dempsey, General Omar Bradley, General Mark Clark, Henry Ford, Eleanor Roosevelt, and Dorothy Dix. But that was only a beginning. I also did something else that was far more important than the interviews and the reading. I worked for five years in a laboratory for conquering worry—a laboratory conducted in our own adult classes.

As far as I know, it was the first and only laboratory of its kind in the world. This is what we did. We gave students a set of rules on how to stop worrying and asked them to apply these rules in their own lives and then talk to the class on the results they had obtained. Others reported on techniques they had used in the past.

As a result of this experience, I presume I have listened to more talks on "*How I Conquered Worry*" than has any other individual who ever walked this earth. In addition, I *read* hundreds of other talks on "*How I Conquered Worry*" world talks that were sent to me by mail—talks that had won prizes in our classes that are held throughout the world. So this book didn't come out of an ivory tower. Neither is it an academic preachment on how worry *might* be conquered. Instead, I have tried to write a fast-moving, concise, *documented report on how worry has been conquered by thousands of adults*. One thing is certain: this book is practical. You can set your teeth in it.

I am happy to say that you won't find in this book stories about an imaginary "Mr. B—" or a vague "Mary and John" whom no one can identify. Except in a few rare cases, this book names names and gives street addresses. It is authentic. It is documented. It is vouched for and certified.

"Science," said the French philosopher Valery, "is a collection of successful recipes. "That is

上的床位被那些因神经或情绪而致病的人占据。

我翻看了纽约公共图书馆书架上那22本关于忧虑的书。此外，我还买了我能找到的关于忧虑的书；但我却发现没有一本书适合给我班上的成年人作教材。于是我决定自己写一本。

我在7年前就开始准备写此书了。为什么？我参考了古往今来的哲学家们关于忧虑的论述；还阅读了从孔子到丘吉尔的几百本人物传记。我还拜访了各行业的杰出人物，如杰克·邓普希、奥马尔·布莱德雷将军、马克·克拉克将军、亨利·福特、伊莲娜·罗斯福和陶乐丝·迪克丝。但这只是开始。我还做了比拜访和读书更重要的事情。我在一个克服忧虑的实验室工作了五年——一个在我的成人班上进行的实验室。

据我所知，这是第一个也是唯一一个此类实验室。这就是我们所做的：我们告诉学员一套停止忧虑的原则，要求他们把这些原则用到他们自己的生活中，然后到班上来讲述他们获得的结果。其他人则介绍了他们过去曾用过的技巧。

作为这个实验的结果，我敢说我所听过的"如何克服忧虑"的演讲，比世界上任何其他人都要多。此外，我还读过几百次以信件寄给我的来自世界各地的"如何克服忧虑"的演讲——这些演讲获得了我们在世界各地举办的培训班的奖项。所以这本书不是来自象牙塔，也不是研究如何克服忧虑的学术作品；相反，我尽力将它写成一本快速有效、简洁明了的文件报告，其中包含了成千上万人克服忧虑的真实经历。有一点是明确的：这是一本讲求实效的书。你完全可以照此去做。我很高兴地告诉大家，这本书的每个故事都不是虚构的。除了极少数例子，都是真人真事。本书真实且有据可查，保证可靠。

"科学，"法国哲学家法莱利说，"就是许多成功秘诀的集合体。"本书就是许多成功的、经过

what this book is, a collection of successful and time-tested recipes to rid our lives of worry. However, let me warn you: *you won't find anything new in it, but you will find much that is not generally applied.* And when it comes to that, you and I don't need to be told anything new. We already know enough to lead perfect lives. We have all read the golden rule and the Sermon on the Mount. Our trouble is not ignorance, but inaction. The purpose of this book is to restate, illustrate, streamline, air-condition, and glorify a lot of ancient and basic truths—and kick you in the shins and make you do something about applying them.

DALE CARNEGIE

时间检验的、去除我们烦恼的秘诀的集合体。但是,我要警告你的是:你不会在本书中发现任何新东西,但你会发现许多人们通常不用的东西。如果是那样,你和我都不必学习什么新东西。我们已经足以知道如何过上美好生活。我们都读过黄金法则和耶稣的登山宝训。我们的困难不是无知,而是不去行动。本书的目的就是一再重复、举例说明、精简、调整、发扬光大大量古老而基础性的真理——立即行动,将它们应用到实践中去。

戴尔·卡耐基

Part One
Fundamental Facts You Should Know about Worry

1 Live in "Day-tight Compartments"

In the spring of 1871, a young man picked up a book and read twenty-one words that had a profound effect on his future. A medical student at the Montreal General Hospital, he was worried about passing the final examination, worried about what to do, where to go, how to build up a practice, how to make a living.

The twenty-one words that this young medical student read in 1871 helped him to become the most famous physician of his generation. He organised the world-famous Johns Hopkins School of Medicine. He became Regius Professor of Medicine at Oxford—the highest honour that can be bestowed upon any medical man in the British Empire. He was knighted by the King of England. When he died, two huge volumes containing 1,466 pages were required to tell the story of his life.

His name was Sir William Osler. Here are the twenty-one words that he read in the spring of 1871—twenty-one words from Thomas Carlyle that helped him lead a life free from worry: "*Our main business is not to see what lies dimly at a distance, but to do what lies clearly at hand.*"

Forty-two years later, on a soft spring night when the tulips were blooming on the campus, this man, Sir William Osler, addressed the students of Yale University. He told those Yale students that a man like himself who had been a professor in four universities and had written a popular book was supposed to have "brains of a special quality". He declared that that was untrue. He said that his intimate friends knew that his brains were "of the most mediocre character."

What, then, was the secret of his success? He stated that it was owing to what he called living

第一篇 了解忧虑的基本事实

第1章 活在"完全独立的今天"

1871年春天，有一个年轻人看到一本书，读到了对他的前途产生莫大影响的21个单词。作为蒙特利尔综合医院的一名医科学生，他正担心怎样通过期末考试?将来怎么办？毕业以后去哪里?怎样才能开业?如何谋生?

这位年轻的医科学生在1871年看到的那21个单词，使他成为他那一代最为著名的医学家。他创建了世界著名的约翰·霍普金斯医学院，并且成为牛津大学医学院的钦定教授——这是大英帝国医学人员所获得的最高荣誉。他还被英国国王封为爵士。当他去世时，需要厚达1466页的两册书记述他的一生。

他的名字叫威廉·奥斯勒。下面就是他在1871年春天所看到的那21个单词。它们出自托马斯·卡莱尔，它们使他免除了忧虑的困扰："对我们来说最重要的不是去看远方模糊的事，而是做手边清楚的事。"

42年之后，在郁金香开满校园的一个温和的春夜，威廉·奥斯勒爵士给耶鲁大学的学生作了一次演讲。他对那些耶鲁大学的学生们说，像他这样一位曾在四所大学当过教授，并且写过一本很受欢迎的书的人，似乎应该有一颗"特殊的大脑"，但其实并不是这样。他说他的一些好朋友都知道，他的大脑"最普通不过了"。

in "daytight compartments". What did he mean by that? A few months before he spoke at Yale, Sir William Osler had crossed the Atlantic on a great ocean liner where the captain standing on the bridge, could press a button and—presto! —there was a clanging of machinery and various parts of the ship were immediately shut off from one another—shut off into watertight compartments. "Now each one of you, "Dr. Osler said to those Yale students, "is a much more marvellous organization than the great liner, and bound on a longer voyage. What I urge is that you so learn to control the machinery as to live with 'day-tight compartments' as the most certain way to ensure safety on the voyage. Get on the bridge, and see that at least the great bulkheads are in working order. Touch a button and hear, at every level of your life, the iron doors shutting out the Past—the dead yesterdays. Touch another and shut off, with a metal curtain, the Future—the unborn tomorrows. Then you are safe—safe for today! ... Shut off the past! Let the dead past bury its dead... Shut out the yesterdays which have lighted fools the way to dusty death... The load of tomorrow, added to that of yesterday, carried today, makes the strongest falter. Shut off the future as tightly as the past... The future is today... There is no tomorrow. The day of man's salvation is now. Waste of energy, mental distress, nervous worries dog the steps of a man who is anxious about the future... Shut close, then the great fore and aft bulkheads, and prepare to cultivate the habit of life of 'day-tight compartments'."

Did Dr. Osler mean to say that we should not make any effort to prepare for tomorrow? No. Not at all. But he did go on in that address to say that the best possible way to prepare for tomorrow is to concentrate with all your intelligence, all your enthusiasm, on doing today's work superbly today. That is the only possible way you can prepare for the future.

By all means take thought for the tomorrow, yes, careful thought and planning and preparation. But have no anxiety. During the Second World War, our military leaders *planned* for the morrow, but they could not afford to have any anxiety. "I have supplied the best men with the best equipment we have, "said Admiral Ernest J. King, who directed the United States Navy, "and have given them what seems to be the wisest mission. That is all I can do."

"If a ship has been sunk, "Admiral King went on, "I can't bring it up. If it is going to be sunk, I can't stop it. I can use my time much better working on tomorrow's problem than by fretting about

那么,他成功的秘诀又是什么呢?他认为这完全是因为他生活在"一个完全独立的今天"。这究竟是什么意思呢?就在他去耶鲁大学演讲的几个月之前,奥斯勒爵士搭乘一艘大型海轮横渡大西洋,有一次看见船长站在船舵室中,按下一个按钮,立即听到一阵机械运转的声音,轮船的各个部分立刻彼此隔绝开来,成了几个完全防水的隔离舱。"你们每一个人,"奥斯勒博士对那些耶鲁大学的学生说,"组织都要比那艘大海轮精密得多,所要走的航程也更远。我要求的是你们也必须学习控制一切,活在一个'完全独立的今天',这才是在航程中确保安全的最好方法。到船舵室去,你将会发现那些大的隔离舱至少都可以使用。按下按钮,用铁门隔断过去——已经过去的昨天。再按下另一个按钮,用铁门隔断未来——尚未到来的明天。然后你就保险了——今天安全了!……切断过去,埋葬已逝的过去……切断那些会把傻瓜引到死亡之路的昨天……明天的重担加上昨天的重担,就会成为今天最大的障碍。要把未来像过去一样紧紧地关在门外……未来就在于今天……没有明天。人类得到救赎的日子就是现在。精力的浪费、精神的郁闷、神经的忧虑,都会紧紧跟随着一个担忧未来的人……那么,把船前船后的隔离舱都关掉吧,准备养成活在'完全独立的今天'的习惯。"

奥斯勒博士是不是说我们不必为明天做准备呢?不是,绝对不是。在那次演讲中,他继续说:"为明天做准备的最好方法,就是集中你所有的智慧和热诚,把今天的工作做得尽善尽美,这就是你能应对未来的唯一可能的方法。"

一定要为明天着想——不错,一定要仔细考虑、计划和准备,但不要焦虑。

在第二次世界大战期间,军事领袖要为将来制定计划,可是他们绝不能有任何的焦虑。"把我们最好的装备供应给最优秀的人员,"美国海军上将阿尔耐斯特·金说,"再交给他们似乎是最聪明的任务。我所能做的就是这些。"

"如果一艘船沉了,"金上将继续说,"我不能把它打捞上来。要是船继续下沉,我也没有办

yesterday's. Besides, if I let those things get me, I wouldn't last long."

Whether in war or peace, the chief difference between good thinking and bad thinking is this: good thinking deals with causes and effects and leads to logical, constructive planning; bad thinking frequently leads to tension and nervous breakdowns.

I had the privilege of interviewing Arthur Hays Sulzberger, publisher(1935~1961) of one of the most famous newspapers in the world, *The New* York Times. Mr. Sulzberger told me that when the Second World War flamed across Europe, he was so stunned, so worried about the future, that he found it almost impossible to sleep. He would frequently get out of bed in the middle of the night, take some canvas and tubes of paint, look in the mirror, and try to paint a portrait of himself. He didn't know anything about painting, but he painted anyway, to get his mind off his worries. Mr. Sulzberger told me that he was never able to banish his worries and find peace until he had adopted as his motto five words from a church hymn: One step enough for me.

Lead, kindly Light...
Keep thou my feet:
I do not ask to see The distant scene; one step enough for me.

At about the same time, a young man in uniform—somewhere in Europe—was learning the same lesson. His name was Ted Bengermino, of Baltimore, Maryland—and he had worried himself into a first-class case of combat fatigue.

"In April, 1945, "wrote Ted Bengermino, "I had worried until I had developed what doctors call a 'spasmodic transverse colon'—a condition that produced intense pain. If the war hadn't ended when it did, I am sure I would have had a complete physical breakdown.

"I was utterly exhausted. I was a Graves Registration, noncommissioned Officer for the 94th Infantry Division. My work was to help set up and maintain records of all men killed in action, missing in action, and hospitalised. I also had to help disinter the bodies of both Allied and enemy soldiers who had been killed and hastily buried in shallow graves during the pitch of battle. I had to gather up the personal effects of these men and see that they were sent back to parents or closest relatives who would prize these personal effects so much. I was constantly worried for fear we might be making embarrassing and serious mistakes. I was worried about whether or not I would come

法。与其花时间后悔昨天的失误，还不如去解决明天的问题。何况我若担心这些事情，我也不可能支持很久。"

不论是在战争时期还是在和平年代，好想法和坏想法之间的区别在于：好想法会考虑到原因和结果，从而产生合乎逻辑的、富有建设性的计划；而坏想法通常只会导致精神紧张和崩溃。

我曾荣幸地访问了亚瑟·苏兹伯格，他是世界上最著名的报纸之一《纽约时报》的发行人。苏兹伯格先生告诉我，当第二次世界大战的战火燃烧到欧洲的时候，他非常吃惊，对未来充满了忧虑，几乎无法入睡。他会常常在半夜爬起床，拿着画布和颜料，对着镜子，想给自己画一张自画像。尽管对绘画一无所知，但他还是画着，以此来驱除忧虑。苏兹伯格先生告诉我，他最后是因为一首赞美诗里的一句话才消除了忧虑，得到了平安。这句话是"只要一步就好"。

引导我，仁慈的灯光……
请让你常在我脚旁，
我并不想看远方的风光；只要一步就好。

大概在这个时候，欧洲有个当兵的年轻人，也学到了同一课。他的名字叫泰德·班哲明诺，他住在马里兰州巴尔的摩市——他曾经忧虑得几乎完全丧失了斗志。

"1945年4月，"泰德·班哲明诺写道，"我忧虑得患上了一种医生称为'结肠痉挛'的病，这种病很痛苦。如果战争不在那时结束的话，我想我整个人都会垮掉。

"当时我筋疲力尽。我在第94步兵师担任士官，负责建立和保管在作战中死伤和失踪的士兵名录，还要帮助发掘那些在战争期间被打死而草草掩埋的敌我双方的士兵尸体。我必须收集那些人的私人物品，把这些东西准确地送回到重视这些私人物品的父母或近亲手中。我一直担心自己会造成一些让人难堪的或者严重的错误，还担心我是否撑得过去，担心自己还能不能活着回去搂抱我的独生子——我从来没有见过的儿子已经16个月了。我既担心又疲劳，整整瘦了

through all this. I was worried about whether I would live to hold my only child in my arms—a son of sixteen months, whom I had never seen. I was so worried and exhausted that I lost thirty-four pounds. I was so frantic that I was almost out of my mind. I looked at my hands. They were hardly more than skin and bones. I was terrified at the thought of going home a physical wreck. I broke down and sobbed like a child. I was so shaken that tears welled up every time I was alone. There was one period soon after the Battle of the Bulge started that I wept so often that I almost gave up hope of ever being a normal human being again.

"I ended up in an Army dispensary. An Army doctor gave me some advice which has completely changed my life. After giving me a thorough physical examination, he informed me that my troubles were mental. 'Ted', he said, 'I want you to think of your life as an hourglass. You know there are thousands of grains of sand in the top of the hourglass; and they all pass slowly and evenly through the narrow neck in the middle. Nothing you or I could do would make more than one grain of sand pass through this narrow neck without impairing the hourglass. You and I and everyone else are like this hourglass. When we start in the morning, there are hundreds of tasks which we feel that we must accomplish that day, but if we do not take them one at a time and let them pass through the day slowly and evenly, as do the grains of sand passing through the narrow neck of the hourglass, then we are bound to break our own physical or mental structure.'

"I have practised that philosophy ever since that memorable day that an Army doctor gave it to me. 'One grain of sand at a time... One task at a time.' That advice saved me physically and mentally during the war; and it has also helped me in my present position of public Relations and Advertising Director for the Adcrafters Printing & Off-set Co. Inc. I found the same problems arising in business that had arisen during the war: a score of things had to be done at once—and there was little time to do them. We were low in stocks. We had new forms to handle, new stock arrangements, changes of address, opening and closing offices, and so on. Instead of getting taut and nervous, I remembered what the doctor had told me. 'One grain of sand at a time. One task at a time.' By repeating those words to myself over and over, I accomplished my tasks in a more efficient manner and I did my work without the confused and jumbled feeling that had almost wrecked me on the battlefield."

34磅，而且几乎要发疯了。我眼看着自己的两只手瘦得只剩下皮包骨。一想到自己瘦弱不堪地回家，我就害怕。我崩溃了，像个孩子一样哭了，每当独自一人时我就眼泪汪汪。有一段时间，也就是在大反攻开始不久，我常常哭泣，几乎放弃了做一个正常人的希望。

"最后，我住进了部队医院。一位军医给了我一些忠告，彻底改变了我的生活。在给我做完一次全面检查之后，他告诉我说我的问题纯粹是精神上的。'泰德，'他说，'我希望你把自己的生活想象成一个沙漏。你知道，在沙漏的上半部分有成千上万粒的沙子，它们都缓慢而均匀地流过中间那条细缝。除非把沙漏弄坏，你和我都不能让两粒以上的沙子同时穿过那条窄缝。你和我以及每一个人，都像这个沙漏。每天早上，我们都有许许多多的工作要在这一天之内完成。但是如果我们不是每次只做一件，让它们缓慢而均匀地通过这一天，就像沙粒通过沙漏的窄缝一样，那我们就会损害自己的身体或精神了。'

"从这个值得纪念的日子开始，这位军医告诉我这些之后，我就一直奉行这种哲学。'一次只流过一粒沙子……一次只做一件事。'这个忠告在战时挽救了我的身心；现在它对我在工艺印刷公司的公关广告部中的工作也极有帮助。我发现商场上有时也有和战场上一样的问题：一次要做好几件事情，但却没有时间。例如我们的材料不够用了，有新的表格等待处理，要安排新的资料，要变更地址，新开或关闭分公司，等等。我不再紧张不安，因为我记住了那个军医告诉我的：'一次只流过一粒沙子，一次只做一件事情。'我一再重复这两句话，工作比以前更有效率了，工作时再也不会有那种在战场上几乎使我崩溃的迷惑而混乱的感觉。"

在目前的生活方式中，有一件最可怕的事就是，我们医院一半以上的床位都是给那些大脑神经或者精神上有问题的人留着的。他们都是被日渐累积起来的忧虑压垮的病人。而在这些病人中，只要他们能奉行耶稣的"不要为明天忧虑"，或者信奉威廉·奥斯勒爵士的"生活在一个完全独立的今天"，那他们大多数人就可以过上快乐幸福的生活。

One of the most appalling comments on our present way of life is that at one time half of all the beds in our hospitals were reserved for patients with nervous and mental troubles, patients who have collapsed under the crushing burden of accumulated yesterdays and fearful tomorrows. Yet a vast majority of those people could have avoided those hospitals—could have led happy, useful lives—if they had only heeded the words of Jesus: "*Have no anxiety about the morrow*"; or the words of Sir William Osler: "*Live in day-tight compartments.*"

You and I are standing this very second at the meeting place of two eternities: the vast past that has endured forever, and the future that is plunging on to the last syllable of recorded time. We can't possibly live in either of those eternities—no, not even for one split second. But, by trying to do so, we can wreck both our bodies and our minds. So let's be content to live the only time we can possibly live: from now until bedtime. "Anyone can carry his burden, however hard, until nightfall, "wrote Robert Louis Stevenson. "Anyone can do his work, however hard, for one day. Anyone can live sweetly, patiently, lovingly, purely, till the sun goes down. And this is all that life really means."

Yes, that is all that life requires of us; but Mrs. E. K. Shields, of Saginaw, Michigan, was driven to despair—even to the brink of suicide—before she learned to live just till bedtime. "In 1937, I lost my husband, "Mrs. Shields said as she told me her story. "I was very depressed—and almost penniless. I wrote my former employer, Mr. Leon Roach, of the Roach-Fowler Company of Kansas City, and got my old job back. I had formerly made my living selling *World Book* to rural and town school boards. I had sold my car two years previously when my husband became ill; but I managed to scrape together enough money to put a down payment on a used car and started out to sell books again.

"I had thought that getting back on the road would help relieve my depression; but driving alone and eating alone was almost more than I could take. Some of the territory was not very productive, and I found it hard to make those car payments, small as they were.

"In the spring of 1938, I was working out of Versailles, Missouri. The schools were poor, the roads bad; I was so lonely and discouraged that at one time I even considered suicide. It seemed that success was impossible. I had nothing to live for. I dreaded getting up each morning and facing life. I

你和我在目前的这一瞬间，都站在两个永恒的交叉点上——永远结束了的过去和延伸到无穷无尽的未来。我们都不可能生活在这两个永恒之中——哪怕是一秒钟都不行。如果我们想那样做的话，就会毁掉自己的身心。所以，我们应该满足于目前所生活的这一刻：从现在起直到上床。"不论任务有多重，每个人都能支持到夜晚的来临，"罗伯特·史蒂文森写道，"不论工作有多么辛苦，每个人都能干好一天的工作。每个人都能很甜美、很耐心、很可爱而且很纯洁地活到太阳下山。这就是生命的真谛。"

不错，这也正是生命对我们所要求的。可是住在密歇根州沙支那城的谢尔德夫人，在懂得"只要生活到上床为止"这一道理之前，却深感颓丧，甚至想自杀。"我丈夫在1937年死了，"谢尔德夫人把她的过去告诉我，"我非常颓丧，而且几乎身无分文。我给我以前的东家、堪萨斯市罗区-弗勒公司的老板利奥·罗区先生写信，回去干我以前的工作。我以前给学校推销《世界百科全书》为生。两年前我丈夫生病的时候，我卖掉了汽车；现在我又勉强凑足了钱，分期付款买了一辆旧车，重新开始出去卖书。

"我原想再回去工作或许可以帮助我摆脱颓丧；可是一个人驾车并一个人吃饭，让我几乎无法忍受。有些地方我干得很差，虽然分期付款买车的数额不大，却很难付清。

"1938年的春天，我在密苏里州维萨里市推销。那里的学校都很穷，公路也差，我一个人又孤独又沮丧，有一次甚至想自杀。我觉得成功很难，而活着又没有什么希望。每天早上，我都很怕起床面对生活。我什么都担心：付不起分期付款的车钱，付不出房租，没有足够的东西吃，担心我的健康恶化却没有钱看病。但是，我没有自杀，唯一的理由是我担心我姐姐会因此而难过，而且我又没有足够的钱支付我的丧葬费用。

"然后，有一天，我读到一篇文章，它使我从消沉中振作起来，使我有了继续活下去的勇气。我对那篇文章中一句令人振奋的话永远心存感激：'对一个聪明人来说，每天都是一个新的生

was afraid of everything: afraid I could not meet the car payments; afraid I could not pay my room rent; afraid I would not have enough to eat. I was afraid my health was failing and I had no money for a doctor. All that kept me from suicide were the thoughts that my sister would be deeply grieved, and that I did not have enough money to pay my funeral expenses.

"Then one day I read an article that lifted me out of my despondence and gave me the courage to go on living. I shall never cease to be grateful for one inspiring sentence in that article. It said: 'Every day is a new life to a wise man. 'I typed that sentence out and pasted it on the windshield of my car, where I saw it every minute I was driving. I found it wasn't so hard to live only one day at a time. I learned to forget the yesterdays and to not-think of the tomorrows. Each morning I said to myself: 'Today is a new life. '

"I have succeeded in overcoming my fear of loneliness, my fear of want. I am happy and fairly successful now and have a lot of enthusiasm and love for life. I know now that I shall never again be afraid, regardless of what life hands me. I know now that I don't have to fear the future. I know now that I can live one day at a time—and that 'Every day is a new life to a wise man. '"

Who do you suppose wrote this verse:

Happy the man, and happy he alone,
He, who can call to-day his own:
He who, secure within, can say:
"To-morrow, do the worst, for I have liv'd to-day."

Those words sound modern, don't they? Yet they were written thirty years before Christ was born, by the Roman poet Horace. One of the most tragic things I know about human nature is that all of us tend to put off living. We are all dreaming of some magical rose garden over the horizon—instead of enjoying the roses that are blooming outside our windows today. Why are we such fools—such tragic fools?

"How strange it is, our little procession of life! "wrote Stephen Leacock. "The child says: 'When I am a big boy. 'But what is that? The big boy says: 'When I grow up. 'And then, grown up, he says: 'When I get married. 'But to be married, what is that after all? The thought changes to 'When I'm able to retire. 'And then, when retirement comes, he looks back over the landscape

命。'我用打字机打出这句话,贴在我汽车前面的挡风玻璃上,这样我开车的时候每分钟都能看得见。我发现,每次只活一天并不难。我学会了忘记过去,不再担心未来。每天早上我都会对自己说:'今天又是一个新的生命。'

"我成功地克服了孤寂的恐惧感。我现在过得很快乐,还算比较成功,而且对生命充满了热诚和爱。现在我也知道,不论在生活上碰到什么事情,我都不会再害怕了;我还知道,我不必害怕未来;我还知道,每次只要活一天——而'对一个聪明人来说,每天都是一个新的生命。'"

下面几行诗你猜是谁写的:

这个人很快乐,也只有他才能快乐,
因为他把今天看成是自己的一天;
他在今天会感受到安全,他会这样说:
"不论明天如何,我已经过了今天。"

这几句话听起来很有现代色彩吧?可是却写在基督诞生之前30年,它的作者是古罗马诗人柯瑞斯。

我认为人性之中最可悲的一件事,就是我们所有的人都拖延着不去生活,都梦想着在天边有一座奇妙的玫瑰园,而不能欣赏今天就盛开在我们窗外的玫瑰花。

为什么我们会变成这种傻子,变成这种可怜的傻子呢?

"我们人生的短暂历程多么奇怪啊,"史蒂芬·利科克写道,"小孩子说:'等我成为大孩子的时候。'可是长大之后他又说:'等我长大成人之后。'等长大成人了,他又说:'等我结婚以后。'可是等他结了婚,又会怎么样呢?他的想法随后又变成了'等我退休之后'。然后,等退休之后,他再回顾过去时,似乎有一阵冷风吹过来——他错过了一切,而一切又一去不复返。我们总是无法及早明白:生命就在生活里,就在每一天每一刻。"

traversed; a cold wind seems to sweep over it; somehow he has missed it all, and it is gone. Life, we learn too late, is in the living, in the tissue of every day and hour."

The late Edward S. Evans of Detroit almost killed himself with worry before he learned that life "is in the living, in the tissue of every day and hour." Brought up in poverty, Edward Evans made his first money by selling newspapers, then worked as a grocer's clerk. Later, with seven people dependent upon him for bread and butter, he got a job as an assistant librarian. Small as the pay was, he was afraid to quit. Eight years passed before he could summon up the courage to start out on his own. But once he started, he built up an original investment of fifty-five borrowed dollars into a business of his own that made him twenty thousand dollars a year. Then came a frost, a killing frost. He endorsed a big note for a friend—and the friend went bankrupt. Quickly on top of that disaster came another: the bank in which he had all his money collapsed. He not only lost every cent he had, but was plunged into debt for sixteen thousand dollars. His nerves couldn't take it. "I couldn't sleep or eat, "he told me. "I became strangely ill. *Worry and nothing but worry*, "he said, "*brought on this illness*. One day as I was walking down the street, I fainted and fell on the sidewalk. I was no longer able to walk. I was put to bed and my body broke out in boils. These boils turned inward until just lying in bed was agony. I grew weaker every day. Finally my doctor told me that I had only two more weeks to live. I was shocked. I drew up my will, and then lay back in bed to await my end. No use now to struggle or worry. I gave up, relaxed, and went to sleep. I hadn't slept two hours in succession for weeks; but now with my earthly problems drawing to an end, I slept like a baby. My exhausting weariness began to disappear. My appetite returned. I gained weight.

"A few weeks later, I was able to walk with crutches. Six weeks later, I was able to go back to work. I had been making twenty thousand dollars a year; but I was glad now to get a job for thirty dollars a week. I got a job selling blocks to put behind the wheels of automobiles when they are shipped by freight. I had learned my lesson now. No more worry for me—no more regret about what had happened in the past—no more dread of the future. I concentrated all my time, energy, and enthusiasm into selling those blocks."

Edward S. Evans shot up fast now. In a few years, he was president of the company—the

底特律已故的爱德华·伊文斯在学会“生命就在生活里，就在每一天每一刻”这个道理之前，几乎因为忧虑而自杀。爱德华·伊文斯出生在一个贫苦的家庭，起先是卖报为生，然后在一家杂货店工作。后来，由于家里七口人要靠他吃饭，他找到了一个助理图书管理员的工作，虽然薪水很少，可是他却不敢辞职。直到8年之后，他才鼓足勇气，开始自己的事业。他用借来的55美元干出了一番自己的事业，一年赚进两万美元。随后，厄运降临了：他替一个朋友背书了一张大额支票，而那位朋友却破产了。在这次灾祸之后接着又来了另一次灾祸——他存进所有财产的那家银行垮了。他不但损失了所有的钱财，还负债16000美元。他精神上承受不住了。“我吃不下，睡不着，”他告诉我，“我得了奇怪的病。没有别的原因，只是因为忧虑。有一天，我正走在街上，突然昏倒在路边上，以后就再也不能走路了。我躺在床上，全身都烂了。伤口逐渐往里面烂，连躺在床上都受不了。我日渐虚弱。最后医生告诉我，我只能活两个礼拜。我大吃一惊，写好遗嘱，就躺在床上等死。挣扎或忧虑都没有用了，我只好放弃，开始放松下来，闭目休息。连续好几个星期，我都睡不到两个小时；可是现在一切困难快要结束了，我反而睡得像个婴儿。那些令人疲倦的忧虑渐渐消失了，胃口变好了，体重也开始增加。

“几个星期之后，我就能撑着拐杖走路了。6个星期之后，我又能回去工作了。以前我一年曾赚过两万美元，可是现在我很高兴找到一周30美元的工作。我的工作是推销运送汽车的轮船上用在轮子后面的挡板。这时我已经学会不再忧虑，不再为过去发生的事情后悔，也不再害怕将来。我把所有的时间、精力和热诚都放在推销挡板上。”

爱德华·伊文斯进步非常快。没有几年，他就成了伊文斯工业公司的董事长。多年以来，这家公司一直是纽约股票交易所的一家公司。当他1945年去世时，已成为美国最进步的企业家。如果你乘飞机去格陵兰，很可能降落在伊文斯机场——这个机场是为了纪念他而命名的。

这个故事的启示在于：如果爱德华·伊文斯没有学会“生活在完全独立的今天”的话，他绝

Evans Product Company. It has been listed on the New York Stock Exchange for years. When Edward S. Evans died in 1945, he was one of the most progressive businessmen in the United States. If you ever fly over Greenland, you may land on Evans Field—a flying-field named in his honour. Here is the point of the story: Edward S. Evans would never have had the thrill of achieving these victories in business and in living if he hadn't seen the folly of worrying—if he hadn't learned to live in day-tight compartments.

Five hundred years before Christ was born, the Greek philosopher Heraclitus told his students that "everything changes except the law of change". He said, "You cannot step in the same river twice." The river changes every second; and so does the man who stepped in it. Life is a ceaseless change. The only certainty is today. Why mar the beauty of living today by trying to solve the problems of a future that is shrouded in ceaseless change and uncertainty—a future that no one can possibly foretell?

The old Romans had a word for it. In fact, they had two words for it. Carpe diem. "Enjoy the day." Or, "Seize the day." Yes, seize the day, and make the most of it.

That is the philosophy of Lowell Thomas. I recently spent a weekend at his farm; and I noticed that he had these words from Psalm CXViii framed and hanging on the walls of his broadcasting studio where he would see them often:

This is the day which the Lord hath made
we will rejoice and be glad in it.

The writer John Ruskin had on his desk a simple piece of stone on which was carved one word: TODAY. And while I haven't a piece of stone on my desk, I do have a poem pasted on my mirror where I can see it when I shave every morning—a poem that Sir William Osler always kept on his desk—a poem written by the famous Indian dramatist, Kalidasa:

SALUTATION TO THE DAWN

Look to this day!
For it is life, the very life of life.
In its brief course
Lie all the verities and realities of your existence:

不可能获得这样惊人的成就。

公元前500年,古希腊哲学家赫拉克利特告诉他的学生:"每件事物随时都在变化。"他说,"你不能两次踏进同一条河。"

河每秒都在变化,所以走进河水的人也同样在变化。生命就是一个永不停息的变化过程。

唯一确定的是今天。为什么非要去解决那永远处于变化而尚不能确定的明天的问题,使得今天的美好生活弄得焦头烂额呢?

古罗马人有一句话——其实是两句话。它们是"享受今天"或"抓住今天"。是的,抓住今天,充分过好今天。

这也是罗维尔·托马斯的观点。我最近在他的农场过了一次周末。我注意到他引用了《圣经》第118篇的句子,装在镜框中,挂在他广播电台的墙上,好让他常常看见。

这是耶和华所定的日子,
我们在其中,要高兴欢喜。

作家约翰·罗斯金在他的桌上放了一块石头,石头上只刻有两个字——今天。我的书桌上虽然没有放石头,不过我的镜子上倒贴了一首诗,每天早上刮胡子的时候我都能看见——这也是威廉·奥斯勒爵士一直放在他桌上的那首诗——这首诗的作者是印度一位知名戏剧家卡里达沙:

向黎明敬礼

看着今天!
因为它就是生命,它是生命中的生命。
在它短暂的时间里,有你存在的所有变化与现实:
成长的福佑,行动的荣耀,还有成功的辉煌。

The bliss of growth
The glory of action
The splendour of beauty
For yesterday is but a dream
And tomorrow is only a vision,
But today well lived makes every yesterday a dream of happiness
And every tomorrow a vision of hope.
Look well, therefore, to this day!
Such is the salutation to the dawn.

So, the first thing you should know about worry is this: if you want to keep it out of your life, do what Sir William Osler did—*Shut the iron doors on the past and the future. Live in Day-tight Compartments.*

Why not ask yourself these questions, and write down the answers?

1. Do I tend to put off living in the present in order to worry about the future, or to yearn for some"magical rose garden over the horizon"?
2. Do I sometimes embitter the present by regretting things that happened in the past—that are over and done with?
3. Do I get up in the morning determined to "Seize the day"—to get the utmost out of these twenty-four hours ?
4. Can I get more out of life by"living in day-tight compartments"?
5. When shall I start to do this? Next week?... Tomorrow?... Today?

昨天不过是一场梦,明天只是一个幻影,
但生活在美好的今天,
却能使每一个昨天成为一个快乐的梦,
使每一个明天都充满希望的幻景。
所以,好好看着今天吧,
这就是对黎明的敬礼。

所以,对于忧虑,你应该知道的第一件事就是:如果你不希望它干扰你的生活,就要学习威廉·奥斯勒爵士——“用铁门把过去和未来隔断,生活在完全独立的今天。”

为什么不问自己下面几个问题,然后写下答案?

1. 我是否没有生活在现在,而只担心未来?或者只追求所谓的“遥远奇妙的玫瑰园”?
2. 我是否有时为过去已经发生的事情而后悔,结果使现在更难受?
3. 我早上起来的时候,是否决定“抓住这一天”,尽量利用这24小时?
4. 如果“活在完全独立的今天”,是否能从生命中得到更多的东西?
5. 我应该什么时候开始这么做?是下个星期?明天?还是今天?

2 A Magic Formula for Solving Worry Situations

Would you like a quick, sure-fire recipe for handling worry situations—a technique you can start using right away, before you go any further in reading this book? Then let me tell you about the method worked out by Willis H. Carrier, the brilliant engineer who launched the air-conditioning industry, and who is *now head* of the world-famous Carrier Corporation in Syracuse, New York. it is one of the best techniques I ever heard of for solving worry problems, and I got it from Mr. Carrier personally when we were having lunch together one day at the Engineers' Club in New York.

"When I was a young man, "Mr. Carrier said, "I worked for the Buffalo Forge Company in Buffalo, New York. I was handed the assignment of installing a gas-cleaning device in a plant of the Pittsburgh Plate Glass Company at Crystal City, Missouri—a plant costing millions of dollars. The purpose of this installation was to remove the impurities from the gas so it could be burned without injuring the engines. This method of cleaning gas was new. It had been tried only once before—and under different conditions. In my work at Crystal City, Missouri, unforeseen difficulties arose. It worked after a fashion—but not well enough to meet the guarantee we had made.

"I was stunned by my failure. It was almost as if someone had struck me a blow on the head. My stomach, my insides, began to twist and turn. For a while I was so worried I couldn't sleep.

"Finally, common sense reminded me that worry wasn't getting me anywhere; so I figured out a way to handle my problem without worrying. It worked superbly. I have been using this same anti-worry technique for more than thirty years. It is simple. Anyone can use it. It consists of three steps:

"Step I. *I analysed the situation fearlessly and honestly and figured out what was the worst that could possibly happen as a result of this failure. No one was going to jail me or shoot me. That was certain.* True, there was also a chance that I would lose my position; and there was also a chance that my employers would have to remove the machinery and lose the twenty thousand dollars we

第2章 消除忧虑的魔法公式

你是否想找到一种快速有效地消除忧虑的药方——也就是那种你不必再往下多看之前，就能立即应用的方法?那么，让我告诉你威利·卡瑞尔发明的这个方法。卡瑞尔是一位聪明的工程师，他创建了空调器制造公司，现在是世界闻名的纽约州塞瑞卡斯市卡瑞尔公司的负责人。这是我听过的消除忧虑的最好办法之一，我和卡瑞尔先生在纽约工程师俱乐部吃午饭的时候，亲自从他那里得知的这个方法。

“我年轻的时候，”卡瑞尔先生说，“我在纽约州水牛城的水牛锻造公司工作。有一次，我被派到密苏里州水晶城的匹兹堡玻璃公司———一座花好几百万美元建造的工厂，去安装一台瓦斯清洁机，以便清除瓦斯中的杂质，使瓦斯燃烧时不至于烧坏引擎。这是一种新的清洁瓦斯的方法，以前只试过一次，而且当时的情况很不相同。当我去密苏里州水晶城工作的时候，没有预料到的困难发生了。经过一番调整，机器总算可以用了，但并没有达到我们所保证的程度。

“我对自己的失败非常吃惊，觉得好像有人在我头顶猛击一下。我的胃和整个腹部开始疼痛起来。有好一阵子，我担心得难以入睡。

“最后，常识告诉我，忧虑并不能解决问题；于是我想出了一个不需要忧虑就可以解决问题的办法，结果非常有效。我使用这个办法已经30多年。这个办法很简单，任何人都可以用。它有3个步骤：

“第一步：毫不害怕而且诚恳地分析整个情况，然后找出万一失败将会出现什么最坏的情况。没有人会把我关起来，或者枪毙我，这一点可以肯定。不错，我很可能会丢掉工作，我的老板也可能会拆掉整个机器，使投入的两万美元泡汤。

had invested.

"Step II. *After figuring out what was the worst that could possibly happen, I reconciled myself to accepting it, if necessary.* I said to myself: This failure will be a blow to my record, and it might possibly mean the loss of my job; but if it does, I can always get another position. Conditions could be much worse; and as far as my employers are concerned—well, they realise that we are experimenting with a new method of cleaning gas, and if this experience costs them twenty thousand dollars, they can stand it. They can charge it up to research, for it is an experiment. After discovering the worst that could possibly happen and reconciling myself to accepting it, if necessary, an extremely important thing happened: I immediately relaxed and felt a sense of peace that I hadn't experienced in days.

"Step III. *From that time on, I calmly devoted my time and energy to trying to improve upon the worst which I had already accented mentally.*

"I now tried to figure out ways and means by which I might reduce the loss of twenty thousand dollars that we faced. I made several tests and finally figured out that if we spent another five thousand for additional equipment, our problem would be solved. We did this, and instead of the firm losing twenty thousand, we made fifteen thousand.

"I probably would never have been able to do this if I had kept on worrying, because one of the worst features about worrying is that it destroys our ability to concentrate. When we worry, our minds jump here and there and everywhere, and we lose all power of decision. However, when we force ourselves to face the worst and accept it mentally, we then eliminate all these vague imaginings and put ourselves in a position in which we are able to concentrate on our problem.

"This incident that I have related occurred many years ago. It worked so superbly that I have been using it ever since; and, as a result, my life has been almost completely free from worry."

Now, why is Willis H. Carrier's magic formula so valuable and so practical, psychologically speaking? Because it yanks us down out of the great grey clouds in which we fumble around when we are blinded by worry. It plants our feet good and solid on the earth. We know where we stand. And if we haven't solid ground under us, how in creation can we ever hope to think anything through?

Professor William James, the father of applied psychology, has been dead in 1910. But if he

"第二步:找出可能发生的最坏情况之后,我就让自己在必要时接受它。我对自己说:这次失败对我的人生纪录是一个打击,我可能会丢掉工作。但即使是这样,我还是可以找到另外的工作。而且事情可能更糟。至于我的老板,他们也知道我们现在正在试验一种新的清洁瓦斯的方法,如果这个试验要花两万美元,他们还付得起。他们可以把这笔账记在研究费用上,因为这只是一种试验。当分析到可能发生的最坏情况,并让自己必要时接受它之后,一件非常重要的事情发生了:我马上轻松下来,感受到了几天以来未曾历过的平静。

"第三步:此后,我就平静地把我的时间和精力用于改善我在心理上已接受的最坏情况。

"我努力寻找各种办法,以减少我们目前面临的两万美元的损失。我做了几次实验,最后发现如果我们再多花5000美元加装一些设备,我们的问题就可以解决了。我们按照这个办法去做,公司不但没有损失两万美元,反而赚了15000美元。

"如果我一直担心,恐怕再也不可能做到这一点。因为忧虑的最大害处,就是毁掉我集中精神的能力。当我们忧虑的时候,思想会到处乱转,从而丧失所有的决策能力。然而,当我们强迫自己面对最坏的情况,并且从精神上接受它时,我们就能权衡所有可能的情形,使我们可以集中精力解决问题。

"刚才我所说的这件事发生在很多年以前,因为这种方法非常好,所以我一直使用它。结果,我的生活几乎不再有烦恼了。"

为什么威利·卡瑞尔的魔法公式从心理的角度来讲有这么大的价值,如此实用呢?因为它能够把我们从那巨大的灰暗色云层中拉出来,使我们不再因为忧虑而盲目地摸索;它可以使我们脚踏实地,而我们也都知道自己身处何处。如果我们脚下没有这块结实的土地,又怎么能想通事情呢?

"应用心理学之父"威廉·詹姆斯教授于1910年去世,可是如果他今天还在世,听到这个解

were alive today, and could hear this formula for facing the worst, he would heartily approve it. How do I know that? Because he told his own students: "*Be willing to have it so...* Be willing to have it so, "he said, "*because... acceptance of what has happened is the first step in overcoming the consequences of any misfortune.*"

That's it, exactly! Psychologically, it means a new release of energy! When we have accepted the worst, we have nothing more to lose. And that automatically means—we have *everything* to gain! "After facing the worst, "Willis H. Carrier reported, "I immediately relaxed and felt a sense of peace that I hadn't experienced in days. From that time on, I was able to *think.*"

Makes sense, doesn't it? Yet millions of people have wrecked their lives in angry turmoil, because they refused to accept the worst; refused to try to improve upon it; refused to salvage what they could from the wreck. Instead of trying to reconstruct their fortunes, they engaged in a bitter and "violent contest with experience"—and ended up victims of that brooding fixation known as melancholia.

Would you like to see how someone else adopted Willis H. Carrier's magic formula and applied it to his own problem? Well, here is one example, from a New York oil dealer who was a student in my classes.

"I was being blackmailed! "this student began. "I didn't believe it was possible—I didn't believe it could happen outside of the movies—but I was actually being blackmailed! What happened was this: the oil company of which I was the head had a number of delivery trucks and a number of drivers. At that time, war regulations were strictly in force, and we were rationed on the amount of oil we could deliver to any one of our customers. I didn't know it, but it seems that certain of our drivers had been delivering oil short to our regular customers, and then reselling the surplus to customers of their own.

"The first inkling I had of these illegitimate transactions was when a man who claimed to be a government inspector came to see me one day and demanded hush money. He had got documentary proof of what our drivers had been doing, and he threatened to turn this proof over to the District Attorney's office if I didn't cough up.

"I knew, of course, that I had nothing to worry about—personally, at least. But I also knew that

除忧虑的公式的话，一定也会大加赞同的。我怎么会知道呢?因为他曾经对他的学生说："你们要愿意承担这种情况……因为接受既成事实，是克服随之而来的任何不幸的第一步。"

这就对了，一点也不错。在心理上，你就能发挥出新的能力。当我们接受了最坏的情况时，就不会再损失什么，也就是说一切都可以重新获得。"在面对最坏的情况之后，"威科·卡瑞尔说，"我马上轻松下来，感受到了好几天以来没有经历过的平静。然后，我就能思考了。"

这些话很有道理吧？但仍有千百万人因为愤怒而毁了他们的生活，因为他们不想接受最坏的情况，不愿由此作出改进，不愿在灾难之中尽可能地救出一些可以救出来的东西。他们不但不去重新创造财富，反而参与了"一次冷酷而激烈的斗争"，终于变成了颓丧情绪的牺牲品。

你愿意看其他人如何利用威利·卡瑞尔的魔法公式来解决他们自己的问题吗?好，下面就是一个例子。这个人是一位纽约汽油经销商，他是我班上的学员。

"我被勒索了！"他说，"我不相信这种事情会发生，更不相信会发生在电影以外的现实生活中——可是我真的被勒索了。事情的经过是这样的：我的公司有好几辆运油的卡车和几个司机。当时，战时管理委员会的条例很严，我们只能送给每一个顾客有限的汽油。事情的真相我并不知道，可是确实有一些送油司机克扣顾客的油量，然后再把多余的油卖给其他人。

"一天，一个自称是政府调查员的人找到我，跟我索要红包。他说他拥有我们送油司机违法舞弊的证据，还威胁说如果我不答应他的要求，他就把这些证据转交给地方检察官。我这才发现这些违法交易。

"当然，我知道我不必担心什么，因为这事至少跟我个人无关。但是我也知道法律规定公司应该对员工的行为负责。我还知道万一官司捅到法院，那么这种坏名声就会砸了我的生意。我对自己的生意非常骄傲，那是我父亲在24年前打下的基础。

"我担心得不得了，很快就病了，接连三天三夜吃不下睡不着。我一直担心那件事。我是向那个

the law says a firm is responsible for the actions of its employees. What's more, I knew that if the case came to court, and it was aired in the newspapers, the bad publicity would ruin my business. And I was proud of my business—it had been founded by my father twenty-four years before.

"I was so worried I was sick! I didn't eat or sleep for three days and nights. I kept going around in crazy circles. Should I pay the money—five thousand dollars—or should I tell this man to go ahead and do his damnedest? Either way I tried to make up my mind, it ended in nightmare.

"Then, on Sunday night, I happened to pick up the booklet on *How to Stop Worrying*, which I had been given in my Carnegie class in public speaking. I started to read it, and came across the story of Willis H. Carrier. 'Face the worst', it said. So I asked myself: 'what is the worst that can happen if I refuse to pay up, and these blackmailers turn their records over to the District Attorney?' "The answer to that was: The ruin of my business—that's the worst that can happen. I can't go to jail. All that can happen is that I shall be ruined by the publicity.

"I then said to myself: 'All right, the business is ruined. I accept that mentally. What happens next?' "Well, with my business ruined, I would probably have to look for a job. That wasn't bad. I knew a lot about oil—there were several firms that might be glad to employ me... I began to feel better. The blue funk I had been in for three days and nights began to lift a little. My emotions calmed down... And to my astonishment, I was able to think.

"I was clear-headed enough now to face Step III—*improve on the worst*. As I thought of solutions, an entirely new angle presented itself to me. If I told my attorney the whole situation, he might find a way out which I hadn't thought of. I know it sounds stupid to say that this hadn't even occurred to me before—but of course I hadn't been thinking, I had only been worrying! I immediately made up my mind that I would see my attorney first thing in the morning—and then I went to bed and slept like a log! How did it end? Well, the next morning my lawyer told me to go and see the District Attorney and tell him the truth. I did precisely that. When I finished I was astonished to hear the D. A. say that this blackmail racket had been going on for months and that the man who chimed to be a 'government agent' was a crook wanted by the police. What a relief to hear all this after I had tormented myself for three days and nights wondering whether I should hand over five thousand dollars to this professional swindler!

人付5000美元,还是对那个人说'你爱怎么干就怎么干'呢?我一直下不了决定,每天都做噩梦。

"后来,在一个星期天的晚上,我碰巧拿出一本小书《如何停止忧虑》,这是我上卡耐基公众演讲课时领到的。我开始阅读它,读到了威利·卡瑞尔的故事,里面提到了'面对最坏的情况'。于是我问自己:'如果我不肯向那家伙付钱,他把证据交给地方检察官的话,可能发生的最坏情况是什么?'答案是:这将会砸了我的生意——最坏也就是这样。但我不会被关起来。可能发生的事就是我将被这件事毁了。'

"于是我对自己说:'那好吧,即使生意毁了,但我可以接受它。接下去又会怎样呢?'

"是的,生意毁了之后,我也许得去找工作。这也不坏,我对石油了解很多——有几家大公司可能会乐意雇用我……我开始觉得好多了。接连三天三夜以来,我的忧虑开始消除了一点。我的情绪也稳定下来……而让我感到震惊的是,我能够思考了。

"我清醒地看到了第三步——改善最坏的情况。当我找到了解决办法之后,一个全新的局面展现在我面前:如果我把整个情况告诉我的律师,他可能会帮我找到一条我从未想到的对策。我知道这听起来似乎很笨,因为我刚开始确实没有想到这一点——当然,我起先并没有好好思考,只是一直在担心。我马上决定第二天一大早就去见我的律师——我上床之后,睡得很踏实。

"结果呢?第二天早上,我的律师叫我去见地方检察官,并把真实情况告诉他。我真的那样做了。当我说完之后,竟出乎意料地听地方检察官说这种勒索案已经连续出现几个月了,那个自称是'政府调查员'的人,实际上是警方正在通缉的罪犯。当我因为无法决定是否该把那5000美元交给这个罪犯而担心三天三夜之后,听到这番话我真的松了一口气。

"这次经历给我上了永难忘怀的一课。现在,每当我面临让我忧虑的难题时,我就会应用所谓的'威利·卡瑞尔公式'。"

就在威利·卡瑞尔担心他正在密苏里州水晶城一家工厂安装的瓦斯清除设备时,来自内布

"This experience taught me a lasting lesson. Now, whenever I face a pressing problem that threatens to worry me, I give it what I call 'the old Willis H. Carrier formula'."

At just about the same time Willis H. Carrier was worrying over the gas-cleaning equipment he was installing in a plant in Crystal City, Missouri, a chap from Broken Bow, Nebraska, was making out his will. His name was Earl P. Haney, and he had duodenal ulcers. Three doctors, including a celebrated ulcer specialist, had pronounced Mr. Haney an "incurable case". They had told him not to eat this or that, and not to worry or fret to keep perfectly calm. They also told him to make out his will! These ulcers had already forced Earl P. Haney to give up a fine and highly paid position. So now he had nothing to do, nothing to look forward to except a lingering death. Then he made a decision: a rare and superb decision. "Since I have only a little while to live, "he said, "I may as well make the most of it. I have always wanted to travel around the world before I die. If I am ever going to do it, I'll have to do it now." So he bought his ticket.

The doctors were appalled. "We must warn you, "they said to Mr. Haney, "that if you do take this trip, I would be buried at sea." "'No, I won't, 'I replied. 'I have promised my relatives that I will be buried in the family plot at Broken Bow, Nebraska. So I am going to buy a casket with me.'

"I purchased a casket, put it aboard ship, and then made arrangements with the steamship company—in the event of my death—to put my corpse in a freezing compartment and keep it there till the liner returned home. I set out on my trip, imbued with the spirit of old Omar:

Ah, make the most of what we yet may spend,
Before we too into the Dust descend;
Dust into Dust, and under Dust, to lie,
Sans Wine, sans Song, sans Singer, and—sans End! "

However, he didn't make the trip "sans wine". "I drank highballs, and smoked long cigars on that trip, "Mr. Haney says in a letter that I have before me now. "I ate all kinds of foods—even strange native foods which were guaranteed to kill me. I enjoyed myself more than I had in years! We ran into monsoons and typhoons which should have put me in my casket, if only from fright—but I got an enormous kick out of all this adventure. I played games aboard the ship, sang songs, made new friends, stayed up half the night. When we reached China and India, I realised that the

拉斯加州布罗肯堡的艾尔·汉利也正在写遗嘱。他得了严重的胃溃疡。三位医生,包括一位非常有名的胃溃疡专家,都说汉利先生无药可救了。他们告诉他什么都不必吃,什么都不必担心;还告诉他确立遗嘱。胃溃疡迫使艾尔·汉利放弃了一切希望。现在他无事可干,什么都不指望了,只等着末日到来。然后,他做了一个决定,一个很罕见却很大胆的决定:"既然我只有一点时间可活了,"他说,"不如好好利用它。我一直想在死之前环游世界。如果我还打算做的话,那就现在去做。"于是他买了票。

医生得知了消息。"我们必须警告你,"他们对汉利先生说,"如果你去旅游,将会葬身大海。""'不,我不会的。'我回答说。'我已经答应我的亲友,我要葬在内布拉斯加州我们家族的墓地中,所以我打算买副棺材随身带着。'

"我去买了一副棺材,把它运上船,然后和轮船公司约定好,如果我去世的话,就把我的尸体放在冷冻舱中,一直运到我的老家。我踏上旅程,心里只想着奥玛·凯恩的一首诗:

啊,在我们化作泥土之前,岂能辜负人生?
不拼搏一番,物化为泥,永寐黄泉之下,
没酒没弦没歌伎,而且没有明天!"

但是,他这次旅行可不是没酒为伴。"我喝了老酒,抽了长长的雪茄,"汉利先生在给我的信中说,这封信现在就在我的面前。"我吃了各种东西——甚至包括当地许多奇奇怪怪的食品,而这些据说都是我吃了一定会送命的。多年以来,我从来没有这样享受过生活。我们碰到过季风和台风。这些事情如果内心害怕的话,也会让我躺进棺材,可是我却从这次冒险中得到了极大的乐趣。我在船上做游戏、唱歌、结交新朋友,晚上一直待到深夜。到了中国和印度之后,我发现回去之后需要处理的私事,比起我在东方所见到的贫穷与饥饿简直是天壤之别。我抛弃了所有无聊的担忧,觉得非常舒服。回到美国之后,我的体重很快增加了90磅,我曾患过胃溃疡的事也

business cares that I had faced back home were paradise compared to the poverty and hunger in the Orient. I stopped all my senseless worrying and felt fine. When I got back to America, I had gained ninety pounds and I had almost forgotten I had ever had a stomach ulcer. I had never felt better in my life. I went back to business and haven't been ill a day since."

Earl P. Haney told me he realizes now that he was unconsiously using the selfsame principles that Willis H. Carrier used to conquer worry. "But I realise now," he told me quite recently, "that I was unconsciously using the selfsame principle. I reconciled myself to the worst that could happen—in my case, dying. Third, I tried to improved the situation by getting the utmost enjoyment out of life for the short time I had left... . If, "he continued, "if I had gone on worrying after boarding that ship, I have no doubt that I would have made the return voyage inside of that coffin. But I relaxed—and I forgot all my troubles. And this calmness of mind gave me a new burst of energy which actually saved my life."

So, Rule 2 is: If you have a worry problem, apply the magic formula of Willis H. Carrier by doing these three things—

1. Ask yourself, "What is the worst that can possibly happen?"

2. Prepare to accept it if you have to.

3. Then calmly proceed to improve on the worst.

几乎全忘了。我这一生中从没有这么舒服过。我重新回去工作,此后再也没有病过。"

艾尔·汉利告诉我,他是在无意识中应用了威利·卡瑞尔征服忧虑的办法。"但是我现在认识到,"他最近告诉我,"我是无意识中用到这种方法。我让自己做好最坏的情况,准备接受死亡。第三,我尽力想办法改善这种情况。我开始尽量享受我所剩下的这一点点时间……如果我上船之后还继续忧虑的话,毫无疑问,我一定会躺在棺材里完成这次旅行。可是当我放松下来之后,我忘掉了所有的麻烦。而这种心理上的平静,使我产生了新的力量,挽救了我的生命。"

所以,克服忧虑的第二条规则是:如果你有担忧的问题,就应用威利·卡瑞尔的魔法公式,做好下面三件事情:

第一,问你自己:"可能发生的最坏情况是什么?"

第二,如果你必须接受的话,就准备接受它。

第三,镇定地想办法改善最坏的情况。

3 What Worry May Do to You

Many years ago, a neighbour rang my doorbell one evening and urged me and my family to be vaccinated against smallpox. He was only one of thousands of volunteers who were ringing doorbells all over New York City. Frightened people stood in lines for hours at a time to be vaccinated. Vaccination stations were opened not only in all hospitals, but also in fire-houses, police precincts, and in large industrial plants. More than two thousand doctors and nurses worked feverishly day and night, vaccinating crowds. The cause of all this excitement? Eight people in New York City had smallpox—and two had died. Two deaths out of a population of almost eight million. Now, I have lived in New York for over thirty-seven years, and no one has ever yet rung my doorbell to warn me against the emotional sickness of worry—an illness that, during the same time period, had caused ten thousand times more damage than smallpox. No doorbell ringer has ever warned me that one person out of ten now living in these United States will have a nervous breakdown—induced in the vast majority of cases by worry and emotional conflicts. So I am writing this chapter to ring your doorbell and warn you.

The great Nobel prize winner in medicine, Dr. Alexis Carrel, said: "Businessmen who do not know how to fight worry die young." And so do housewives and horse doctors and bricklayers.

A few years ago, I spent my vacation motoring through Texas and New Mexico with Dr. O. F. Gober—one of the medical executives of the Santa Fe railway. His exact title was chief physician of the Gulf, Colorado and Santa Fe Hospital Association. We got to talking about the effects of worry, and he said: "Seventy per cent of all patients who come to physicians could cure themselves if they only got rid of their fears and worries. Don't think for a moment that I mean that their ills are imaginary, "he said. "Their ills are as real as a throbbing toothache and sometimes a hundred times more serious. I refer to such illnesses as nervous indigestion, some stomach ulcers, heart disturbances, insomnia, some headaches, and some types of paralysis.

"These illnesses are real. I know what I am talking about, "said Dr. Gober, "for I myself

第3章 忧虑会使人短命

许多年前的一个晚上，一个邻居来按我家的门铃，让我和我的家人去接种牛痘，以预防天花。他是整个纽约市几千名志愿者之一。很多人吓坏了，去排了好几个小时的队等待接种牛痘。几乎所有的医院、消防队、警察局和大的工厂里都设有接种站，2000多名医生和护士日夜不停地为人们种痘。为什么这么热闹呢?这是因为纽约市800万人中，有8个人得了天花，而且其中两个死了。我在纽约市已经住了37年，可是并没有一个人来按我的门铃，警告我预防精神忧郁症——这种病在过去37年所造成的伤害，比天花至少要大1万倍。从来没有按门铃的人警告我说目前生活在美国的人，每10个人中就有一个会精神崩溃——这大部分都是因为忧虑和感情冲突所致。所以，我现在写这一章就等于给你按门铃，对你提出警告。

伟大的诺贝尔医学奖获得者亚力西斯·卡瑞尔医生说："不知道如何抗拒忧虑的商人都会短命而死。"家庭主妇、兽医和泥瓦匠也全都如此。

几年前，我在一次度假时曾和郭伯尔博士一同乘车经过得克萨斯和新墨西哥州。郭伯尔博士当时任圣塔菲铁路公司医务处长，他的正式头衔是海湾-科罗拉多-圣塔菲联合医院主治医师。当我们谈到忧虑对人的影响时，他说："那些来看病的人中，70%的人只要能够消除他们的恐惧和忧虑，病就会治好。他们的病都是心理上的。"他说，"他们的病就像你有一颗蛀牙一样，有时候甚至比这要严重上百倍。这种病就像神经性消化不良、某些胃溃疡、心脏病、失眠、头痛和某几种麻痹症等一样严重。"

"这些病都是真的，我不是在胡说，"郭伯尔博士说，"因为我自己就得过12年胃溃疡。恐惧造成忧虑，忧虑使你紧张，并影响到你的胃部神经，使你胃里的胃液变得不正常，于是由此导致

suffered from a stomach ulcer for twelve years. Fear causes worry. Worry makes you tense and nervous and affects the nerves of your stomach and actually changes the gastric juices of your stomach from normal to abnormal and often leads to stomach ulcers."

Dr. Joseph F. Montague, author of the book *Nervous Stomach* Trouble, says much the same thing. He says: "You do not get stomach ulcers from what you eat. You get ulcers from what is eating you." Dr. W. C. Alvarez, of the Mayo Clinic, said "Ulcers frequently flare up or subside according to the hills and valleys of emotional stress."

That statement was backed up by a study of 15,000 patients treated for stomach disorders at the Mayo Clinic. Four out of five had no physical basis whatever for their stomach illnesses. Fear, worry, hate, supreme selfishness, and the inability to adjust themselves to the world of reality—these were largely the causes of their stomach illnesses and stomach ulcers... Stomach ulcers can kill you. According to *Life* magazine, they now stand tenth in our list of fatal diseases.

I recently had some correspondence with Dr. Harold C. Habein of the Mayo Clinic. He read a paper at the annual meeting of the American Association of Industrial Physicians and Surgeons, saying that he had made a study of 176 business executives whose average age was 44.3 years. He reported *that slightly more than a third of these executives suffered from one of three ailments peculiar to high-tension living—heart disease, digestive-tract ulcers, and high blood pressure.* Think of it—a third of our business executives are wrecking their bodies with heart disease, ulcers, and high blood pressure before they even reach forty-five. What price success! And they aren't even buying success! Can any man possibly be a success who is paying for business advancement with stomach ulcers and heart trouble? What shall it profit a man if he gains the whole world—and loses his health? Even if he owned the whole world, he could sleep in only one bed at a time and eat only three meals a day. Even a new employee can do that—and probably sleep more soundly and enjoy his food more than a high-powered executive. Frankly, I would rather be a share-cropper down in Alabama with a banjo on my knee than wreck my health at forty-five by trying to run a railroad or a cigarette company.

The best-known cigarette manufacturer in the world recently dropped dead from heart failure while trying to take a little recreation in the Canadian woods. He amassed millions—and fell dead

胃溃疡。"

约瑟夫·孟塔古博士是《神经性胃病》的作者,他也阐述过同样的道理。他说:"胃溃疡不是因为食物所致,而是正在吞噬你的忧虑所致。"梅育诊所的阿法瑞兹医生说:"胃溃疡通常会根据你的情绪紧张程度而发作或消失。"

在研究了梅育诊所15000例胃病患者的病例记录之后,这种论断得到了证实。4/5的人并不是因为生理上的原因而得胃病;相反,恐惧、忧虑、怨恨、极端自私以及无法适应现实生活,才是他们得胃病和胃溃疡的主要原因……胃溃疡会让你致死。据《生活》杂志的数据,这种疾病在致命疾病中排第十位。

最近我和梅育诊所的哈罗德·海宾医生写过几次信。他曾在全美工业界医生协会年会上宣读过一篇论文,说他研究了176位平均年龄为44.3岁的企业负责人的情况。他报告说:大约有1/3以上的人由于生活过于紧张而导致下列三种病症之一——心脏病、消化系统溃疡和高血压。你想想!在企业领导人中,竟然有1/3以上的人患有这些病!而他们都还不到45岁!成功的代价多大啊!就此而言,他们甚至不是在争取成功!有哪个患胃溃疡和心脏病的人能够成为成功者呢?就算他能赢得整个世界,可是他失去了健康,对他个人又有什么好处?即使他拥有了全世界,可是他一个人每次也只能睡一张床,一天也只吃三餐。即使是一个新员工也可以做到这一点,甚至会比一个很有权力的负责人睡得更安稳,吃得更香。说实话,我情愿做一个在亚拉巴马州租田种地的农夫,弹五弦琴,也不愿在45岁时为了一个铁路公司或烟草公司而毁了我的健康。

一位世界最知名的香烟制造商,最近想在加拿大森林里轻松一下,却因为心脏病发作死了。他拥有几百万的财产,却在61岁死了。他这是用好几年的生命去换取所谓"生意上的成功"。

但是依我看来,这位"香烟大王"的成功还不如我父亲的一半。我父亲是密苏里州的一个农

at sixty-one. He probably traded years of his life for what is called "business success".

In my estimation, this cigarette executive with all his millions was not half as successful as my father—a Missouri farmer—who died at eighty-nine, without a dollar.

The famous Mayo brothers declared that more than half of our hospital beds are occupied by people with nervous troubles. Yet, when the nerves of these people are studied under a high-powered microscope in a post-mortem examination, their nerves in most cases are apparently as healthy as the nerves of Jack Dempsey. Their "nervous troubles" are caused not by a physical deterioration of the nerves, but by emotions of futility, frustration, anxiety, worry, fear, defeat, despair. Plato said that "the greatest mistake physicians make is that they attempt to cure the body without attempting to cure the mind; yet the mind and body are one and should not be treated separately!" It took medical science twenty-three hundred years to recognise this great truth. We are just now beginning to develop a new kind of medicine called *psychosomatic* medicine—a medicine that treats both the mind and the body. It is high time we are doing that, for medical science has largely wiped out the terrible *diseases caused by physical germs*—diseases such as smallpox, cholera, yellow fever, and scores of other scourges that swept untold millions into untimely graves. But medical science has been unable to cope with the mental and physical wrecks caused, not by germs, but by emotions of worry, fear, hate, frustration, and despair. Casualties caused by these emotional diseases are mounting and spreading with catastrophic rapidity.

Doctors figure that one American in every twenty now alive will spend a part of his life in an institution for the mentally ill. One out of every six of our young men called up by the draft in the Second World War was rejected as mentally diseased or defective.

What causes insanity? No one knows all the answers. But it is highly probable that in many cases fear and worry are contributing factors. The anxious and harassed individual who is unable to cope with the harsh world of reality breaks off all contact with his environment and retreats into a private dream world of his own making, and this solves his worry problems.

I have on my desk a book by Dr. Edward Podolsky entitled *Stop Worrying and Get Well.* Here are some of the chapter titles in that book:

What Worry Does To The Heart *High Blood Pressure Is Fed By Worry*

夫，尽管他一文不名，却活到了89岁。

著名的梅育兄弟宣称，医院一半以上的病床被有神经疾病的人占着。但即使是用高倍显微镜，以最现代的方法来检查他们的神经时，却发现他们大部分都非常健康。他们的"神经疾病"并不是由神经反常引起的，而是因为悲观、烦躁、焦急、忧虑、恐惧、挫折、颓丧等。柏拉图曾说："医生所犯的最大错误，就是他们只治疗身体，却不医治思想。可是精神和肉体是一体的，不能分别治疗。"医学界花了2300年的时间，才算明白这个真理。我们正开始发展一种被称为"心理生理医学"的分支，它同时治疗精神和肉体疾病。现在正是做这件事的最佳时机，因为医学科学已经大量消除了由细菌所引起的如天花、霍乱、黄热病以及其他各种曾将数以百万计的人置于死地的传染病。但医学界尚无力治疗精神和身体方面非由细菌引起，而是由情绪忧虑、恐惧、憎恨、烦躁以及绝望所引起的疾病。这种情绪上的疾病所导致的灾难正日渐增加，而且越来越普遍，速度惊人。

医生们估计：现在还活着的美国人，每20人就有一人在某一段时期得过精神疾病。第二次世界大战期间应征入伍的美国年轻人中，每6人就有一人因为精神失常而不能服役。

是什么导致精神失常？没有人知道答案。可是在大多数情况下，极可能是因为恐惧和忧虑导致的。焦虑和烦躁不安的人大都难以适应现实世界，和周围的人没有沟通，退缩到自己的梦幻世界，以此来解决他的忧虑。

我桌上放了爱德华·波多尔斯基医生写的一本书《除忧去病》。下面是这本书中几章的题目：

忧虑对心脏的影响　　忧虑导致高血压
风湿症可能因忧虑而起　　为了你的胃，少些忧虑
忧虑如何使你感冒　　忧虑和甲状腺

Rheumatism Can Be Caused By Worry
How Worry Can Cause A Cold
The Worrying Diabetic
Worry Less For Your Stomach's Sake
Worry And The Thyroid

Another illuminating book about worry is *Man Against Himself* by Dr. Karl Menninger, one of the "Mayo brothers of psychiatry." Dr. Menninger's book is a startling revelation of what you do to yourself when you permit destructive emotions to dominate your life. If you want to stop working against yourself, get this book. Read it. Give it to your friends. It costs four dollars—and is one of the best investments you can make in this life.

Worry can make even the most stolid person ill. General Grant discovered that during the closing days of the Civil War. The story goes like this: Grant had been besieging Richmond for nine months. General Lee's troops, ragged and hungry, were beaten. Entire regiments were deserting at a time. Others were holding prayer meetings in their tents—shouting, weeping and seeing visions. The end was close. Lee's men set fire to the cotton and tobacco warehouses in Richmond, burned the arsenal, and fled from the city at night while towering flames roared up into darkness. Grant was in hot pursuit, banging away at the Confederates from both sides and the rear, while Sheridan's cavalry was heading them off in front, tearing up railway lines and capturing supply trains. Grant, half blind with a violent sick headache, fell behind his army and stopped at a farmhouse. "I spent the night, "he records in his *Memoirs*, "in bathing my feet in hot water and mustard, and putting mustard plasters on my wrists and the back part of my neck, hoping to be cured by morning."

The next morning, he was cured instantaneously. And the tiling that cured him was not a mustard plaster, but a horseman galloping down the road with a letter from Lee, saying he wanted to surrender. When the officer [bearing the message] reached me, "Grant wrote, "I was still suffering with the sick headache, but the instant I saw the contents of the note, I was cured." Obviously it was Grant's worries, tensions, and emotions that made him ill. He was cured instantly the moment his emotions took on the hue of confidence, achievement, and victory.

Seventy years later, Henry Morgenthau, Jr. , Secretary of the Treasury in Franklin D. Roosevelt's cabinet, discovered that worry could make him so ill that he was dizzy. He records in

忧虑的糖尿病患者

另一本讨论忧虑的书是卡尔·明格尔医生写的《自寻烦恼》。明格尔是梅育兄弟精神病院的医生，他的书揭示了一些令人震惊的事实：当你让消极情绪控制你的生活时，你会毁了自己。如果你想远离忧虑，就去买这本书来看。把它送给你的朋友们。它只卖4美元——这是你一生中最好的投资之一。

忧虑甚至会令最强壮的人生病。格兰特将军在南北战争的最后几天发现了这一点。故事是这样的：格兰特围攻瑞奇蒙长达9个月，李将军的军队饥困交加，终于被打败。一时间，整个军队人心惶惶。其余的人在帐营中祈祷——边哭边叫，看到了种种幻象。战争行将结束，李将军的士兵放火烧毁了瑞奇蒙的棉花和烟草仓库，烧了兵工厂，然后在烈焰腾空的黑夜弃城而逃。格兰特乘胜追击，从左右两侧和后方夹击南部联军，另派轻骑兵从正面截击，又拆毁铁路线，缴获了补给车辆。这时，格兰特却剧烈头痛而眼睛半瞎，跟不上队伍，于是只好停在一户农家前。"我过了一夜，"他在回忆录中写道，"把双脚泡在加了芥末的热水里，还把芥末药膏贴在手腕和后颈上，希望第二天早上能够痊愈。"

第二天一大早，他果然好了。可是使他痊愈的并不是什么芥末药膏，而是一个带回来李将军降书的骑兵。"当那个军士来到我面前时，"格兰特写道，"我的头还痛得很厉害，但当我一看到那封信的内容时，我就全好了。"显然，格兰特是因为忧虑、紧张和情绪不安才生病的。一旦从情绪上恢复了自信，想到了他的成就和胜利之后，他就立即好了。

70年后，罗斯福总统的财政部长亨利·摩根索也发现，忧虑会使他头昏眼花。他在日记中写道：为了提高小麦价格，总统下令在一天之内买进440万蒲式耳小麦，这使他非常忧虑。他说："在事情没有结果之前，我头昏眼花。我回到家里，吃完晚饭后只睡了两个小时。"

如果我想知道忧虑对人会产生什么影响，大可不必到图书馆或医院求证。只要从我现在正

his diary that he was terribly worried when the President, in order to raise the price of wheat, bought 4,400,000 bushels in one day. He says in his diary: "I felt literally dizzy while the thing was going on. I went home and went to bed for two hours after lunch."

If I want to see what worry does to people, I don't have to go to a library or a physician. I can look out of the window of my home where I am writing this book; and I can see, within one block, one house where worry caused nervous breakdown—and another house where a man worried himself into diabetes. When the stock market went down, the sugar in his blood and urine went up.

When Montaigne, the illustrious French philosopher, was elected Mayor of his home town—Bordeaux—he said to his fellow citizens: "I am willing to take your affairs into my hands but not into my liver and lungs."

This neighbour of mine took the affairs of the stock market into the blood stream—and almost killed himself.

If I want to be reminded of what worry does to people, I don't need to look at my neighbors' houses. I can look at this very room where I am writing now and be reminded that a former owner of this house worried himself into an untimely grave.

Worry can put you into a wheel chair with rheumatism and arthritis. Dr. Russell L. Cecil, of the Cornell University Medical School, is a world-recognized authority on arthritis; and he has listed four of the *commonest conditions* that bring on arthritis:

1. Marital shipwreck. *2. Financial disaster and grief.*
3. Loneliness and worry. *4. Long-cherished resentments.*

Naturally, these four emotional situations are far from being the only causes of arthritis. There are many different kinds of arthritis—due to various causes. But, to repeat, the commonest conditions that bring on arthritis are the four listed by Dr. Russell L. Cecil. For example, a friend of mine was so hard bit during the depression that the gas company shut off the gas and the bank foreclosed the mortgage on the house. His wife suddenly had a painful attack of arthritis—and, in spite of medicine and diets, the arthritis continued until their financial situation improved.

Worry can even cause tooth decay. Dr. William I. L. McGonigle said in an address before the American Dental Association that "unpleasant emotions such as those caused by worry, fear,

坐着写此书的家里朝窗外看，就能看到在另一条街的一栋房子里，有一个人因为忧虑而精神崩溃；另外一个房子里，有一个人因为忧虑而得了糖尿病。如果股票下跌，他的血和尿里的糖分就会升高。

法国著名的哲学家蒙田当选为家乡波多克斯的市长时，他对市民们说："我愿意用我的双手来处理你们的事情，而不想让它们把我弄得焦头烂额。"

但我的一位邻居却将股票市场搞到他的血液里，差点要了他的老命。

如果想记住忧虑对人会产生什么影响，大可不必去看邻居的房子，只要看看我现在正坐着写此书的这个房间，它以前的主人就因为忧虑而死。

忧虑会使你患风湿症或关节炎而坐进轮椅。康奈尔大学医学院的罗赛尔·赛希尔医生是世界公认的关节炎治疗权威，他曾列举了4种最容易得关节炎的情况：

1.婚姻破裂。 2.财务危机和困难。
3.寂寞和忧虑。 4.长期愤怒。

当然，这4种情绪上的状况并不是导致关节炎的唯一原因。有许多原因会导致关节炎。但产生关节炎的"最常见的原因"，正是赛希尔医生列举的4点。例如，我的一个朋友在经济萧条时期遭到沉重打击，煤气公司切断了他的煤气，银行没收了抵押贷款的房子，他太太突然患了关节炎——虽然经过治疗和加强营养，他太太的关节炎却直到他们的经济条件改善之后才痊愈。

忧虑甚至会使你得蛀牙。威廉·麦克考林格医生曾在全美牙医协会的一次演讲中说："由于焦虑、恐惧等因素所导致的不快情绪，可能会影响人体内的钙质平衡，从而导致蛀牙。"麦克考林格医生还说，他的一个病人原来有一口很好的牙齿，但后来他的夫人得了急病，他开始担心。就在她住院的那3个星期，他突然有了9颗蛀牙——全都是由于焦虑引起的。

nagging... may upset the body's calcium balance and cause tooth decay". Dr. McGonigle told of a patient of his who had always had a perfect set of teeth until he began to worry over his wife's sudden illness.

During the three weeks she was in the hospital, he developed nine cavities—cavities brought on by worry.

Have you ever seen a person with an acutely over-active thyroid? I have, and I can tell you they tremble; they shake; they look like someone half scared to death—and that's about what it amounts to. The thyroid gland, the gland that regulates the body, has been thrown out of kilter. It speeds up the heart—the whole body is roaring away at full blast like a furnace with all of its draughts wide open. And if this isn't checked, by operation or treatment, the victim may die, may "burn himself out".

A short time ago I went to Philadelphia with a friend of mine who has this disease. We went to see a famous specialist, a doctor who has been treating this type of ailment for thirty-eight years. And what sort of advice do you suppose he had hanging on the wall of his waiting-room-painted on a large wooden sign so all his patients could see it? Here it is. I copied it down on the back of an envelope while I was waiting:

RELAXATION AND RECREATION

The most relaxing recreating forces are a healthy religion, sleep, music, and laughter.
Have faith in God—learn to sleep well—
Love good music—see the funny side of life—And health and happiness will be yours.

The first question he asked this friend of mine was: "What emotional disturbance brought on this condition?"He warned my friend that, if he didn't stop worrying, he could get other complications: heart trouble, stomach ulcers, or diabetes. "All of these diseases, "said that eminent doctor, "are cousins, first cousins." Sure, they're first cousins—they're all worry diseases!

When I interviewed film star Merle Oberon, she told me that she refused to worry because she knew that worry would destroy her chief asset on the motion-picture screen: her good looks.

"When I first tried to break into the movies, "she told me, "I was worried and scared. I had just come from India, and I didn't know anyone in London, where I was trying to get a job. I saw a

你是否见过一个人的甲状腺反应过度?我看过。我可以告诉你,他们会发抖、会战栗,看起来就像是吓得半死——事实上也差不多如此。甲状腺的功能是调节生理平衡,一旦反常人的心跳就会加速,整个身体就会亢奋异常,像一个打开了所有炉门的大火炉,如果不做手术或治疗,病人可能会送命,可能"把他自己烧干"。

不久前,我和一个患了这种病的朋友一同去费城。我们去拜访一位专治这种病达38年之久的著名专家。你猜在他候诊室的墙上挂的一块大木板上给病人的忠告写着什么?我把它抄在了一个信封的背面:

轻松和享受

最能让你轻松愉快的,是健康的信仰、睡眠、音乐和欢笑。
要相信神,要学着睡得安稳,
喜欢美妙的音乐,从好的一面来看生活,健康和快乐都会属于你。

他问我朋友的第一个问题就是:"什么情绪问题导致你出现这种情况?"他警告我的朋友说,如果他不停止忧虑,就可能会染上其他并发症:心脏病、胃溃疡或糖尿病等。"所有这些病症,"这位名医说,"都互有关联,甚至是近亲。"没错,它们都是近亲——都是忧虑的疾病。

当我访问电影明星曼尔·奥伯朗的时候,她告诉我她绝不会忧虑,因为她知道忧虑会将她在银幕上的主要资产——美丽容貌摧毁。

"当我起初试图涉足影坛的时候,"她告诉我,"我既担心又害怕。我刚从印度回来,在伦敦举目无亲,却想在那里找到一份工作。我找了几家制片公司,可是没有一家肯录用我。我仅有的一点点钱也快用光了。后来两个星期,我只靠一点饼干和白开水生活。因此我不仅忧虑,还很饥饿。我对自己说:'也许你是个傻瓜,也许你永远也进不了电影界。因为你没有任何经验,也从来没有演过戏——除了一张漂亮的脸蛋,你还有什么?'

few producers, but none of them hired me; and the little money I had began to give out. For two weeks I lived on nothing but crackers and water. I was not only worried now. I was hungry. I said to myself: 'maybe you're a fool. Maybe you will never break into the movies. After all, you have no experience, you've never acted at all—what have you to offer but a rather pretty face?'

"I went to the mirror. And when I looked in that mirror, I saw what worry was doing to my looks! I saw the lines it was forming. I saw the anxious expression. So I said to myself: 'You've got to stop this at once! You can't afford to worry. The only thing you have to offer at all is your looks, and worry will ruin them! '"

Few things can age and sour a woman and destroy her looks as quickly as worry. Worry curdles the expression. It makes us clench our jaws and lines our faces with wrinkles. It forms a permanent scowl.

It may turn the hair grey, and, in some cases, even make it fall out. It can ruin the complexion—it can bring on all kinds of skin rashes, eruptions, and pimples.

Heart disease, is the number one killer in America today. During the Second World War, almost a third of a million men were killed in combat; but during the same period, heart disease killed two million civilians—and one million of those casualties were caused by the kind of heart disease that is brought on by worry and high-tension living. Yes, heart disease is one of the chief reasons why Dr. Alexis Carrel said: "Businessmen who do not know how to fight worry die young."

The Negroes down south and the Chinese rarely have the kind of heart disease brought on by worry, because they take things calmly. Twenty times as many doctors as farm workers die from heart failure. The doctors lead tense lives—and pay the penalty.

"The Lord may forgive us our sins, "said William James, "but the nervous system never does."

Here is a startling and almost incredible fact: more Americans commit suicide each year than die from the five most common communicable diseases. Why? The answer is largely: "*Worry.*"

When the cruel Chinese war lords wanted to torture their prisoners, they would tie their prisoners hand and foot and put them under a bag of water that constantly dripped... dripped... dripped... day and night. These drops of water constantly falling on the head finally became like the

"我去照了照镜子。就在我照镜子的时候,看到了忧虑对我容貌的影响。我看到了皱纹,看见了焦虑的表情。于是我对自己说:'你必须立即停止忧虑!不能再忧虑。你能给别人的只有容貌,而忧虑却会毁了它。'"

再也没有什么比忧虑使一个女人衰老得更快了。忧虑会使我们的表情难看,使我们牙关咬紧,脸上出现皱纹,让人整天愁眉苦脸。

忧虑会使头发灰白,甚至会使头发脱落。忧虑还会使脸上的皮肤长斑点、溃烂和长粉刺。

心脏病现在是美国的头号杀手。在第二次世界大战期间,大约30多万人死于战场,可是在同一时期,心脏病却导致200万人死亡,而其中100万人的心脏病是由于忧虑和过度紧张的生活引起的。也正因为心脏病,亚利西斯·卡瑞尔医生才说:"不知道如何抗拒忧虑的商人,都会短命而死。"

美国南部的黑人和中国人因为处事沉着,所以很少患这种因忧虑而引起的心脏病。死于心脏病的医生是农夫的20倍。因为医生过着紧张的生活,所以才有这样的结果。

"上帝可能原谅我们的罪过,"威廉·詹姆斯说,"但神经系统却不会。"

这里有一个令人吃惊而难以相信的事实:每年因自杀而死的人比各种常见传染病致死的人还要多。为什么呢?答案通常是:"忧虑"。

当残忍的将军想要折磨他们的俘虏时,常常将俘虏绑起来,放在一个不停地往下滴水的袋子下面,水不停地滴着……日夜不停。最后,这些不停地滴落在头上的水变成了槌子敲击的声音,使人精神失常。这种折磨人的方法,以前西班牙的宗教法庭、希特勒的德国集中营都曾用过。

忧虑就像是不停地往下滴的水珠,而那不停地往下滴、滴、滴的忧虑,通常会使人发狂,自杀。

sound of hammer blows—and drove men insane. This same method of torture was used during the Spanish Inquisition and in German concentration camps under Hitler.

Worry is like the constant drip, drip, drip of water; and the constant drip, drip, drip of worry often drives men to insanity and suicide.

When I was a country lad in Missouri, I was half scared to death by listening to Billy Sunday describe the hell-fires of the next world. But he never ever mentioned the hell-fires of physical agony that worriers may have to face here and now. For example, if you are a chronic worrier, you may be stricken someday with one of the most excruciating pains ever endured by man: angina pectoris. Boy, if that ever hits you, you will scream with agony. Your screams will make the sounds in Dante's *Inferno* sound like Babes in Toyland. You will say to yourself then: "Oh, God, oh, God, if I can ever get over this, I will never worry about anything—ever." (If you think I am exaggerating, ask your family physician.)

Do you love life? Do you want to live long and enjoy good health? Here is how you can do it. I am quoting Dr. Alexis Carrel again. He said: "*Those who keep the peace of their inner selves in the midst of the tumult of the modern city are immune from nervous diseases.*"

Can you keep the peace of your inner self in the midst of the tumult of a modem city? If you are a normal person, the answer is "yes." "Emphatically yes." Most of us are stronger than we realize. We have inner resources that we have probably never tapped. As Thoreau said in his immortal book, *Walden*:

"I know of no more encouraging fact than the unquestionable ability of man to elevate his life by a conscious endeavour... If one advances confidently in the direction of his dreams, and endeavours to live the life he has imagined, he will meet with a success unexpected in common hours."

Surely, many of the readers of this book have as much will power and as many inner resources as Olga K. Jarvey has. Her address is Box 892, Coeur d'Alene, Idaho. She discovered that under the most tragic circumstances she could banish worry. I firmly believe that you and I can also—if we apply the old, old truths discussed in this volume. Here is Olga K. Jarvey's story as she wrote it for me: "Eight and a half years ago, I was condemned to die—a slow, agonising death—of cancer. The

当我还是密苏里州一个乡村孩子的时候，星期天听牧师讲地狱中的烈火时会吓得半死，可是他从来没有提到我们因为忧虑而导致的生理上的痛苦。例如，如果你长期忧虑，终有一天会患上最痛苦的冠心病。这种病如果发作，会让你痛得尖声喊叫。你这种尖叫会让但丁的《神曲》"地狱篇"听来就像"娃娃游玩具国"。那时候，你就会对自己说："噢，上帝啊！要是我能好起来，我将不再为任何事忧虑——永远。"（如果你认为我言过其实，不妨去问问你的家庭医生。）

你热爱生活吗?你想健康长寿吗?下面就是你能做到的。我正在引用亚利西斯·卡瑞尔医生的话："在现代城市的混乱中，只有维持内心平静的人才不会变成神经病。"

你能在现代城市的混乱中保持内心的平静吗?如果你是一个正常人，答案是"可以"。"绝对可以"。我们大多数人比我们所认为的都要坚强。我们拥有许多也许从未发现的内在力量，就像梭罗在他不朽的名著《狱卒》里所写的：

"我不知道还有什么比一个人决心改善生活更令人振奋的……要是一个人自信地朝理想的方向努力，决心过他想过的生活，一定会得到意外的成功。"

我相信，本书的许多读者都具有欧嘉·詹维那种意志和内在力量。她住在爱达荷州科尔·达勒的布克斯892号。即使在最悲惨的情况下，她发现自己也能克服忧虑。我坚信，只要我们应用这本书介绍的古老真理，你和我也都能做到。下面就是欧嘉·詹维写给我的故事："8年半以前，医生宣称我将会缓慢而痛苦地死于癌症。国内最有名的医生梅育兄弟也证实了这个诊断。我无药可救了，死亡降临到了我头上。可是我还年轻，还不想死。在绝望之余，我打电话给我住在克洛格的医生，将我内心的绝望告诉他。他不耐烦地拦住我说：'怎么了，欧嘉?难道你一点斗志都没有了?你要是一直这样哭下去，你必死无疑。不错，你是碰上了最坏的情况。好吧！面对现实，不要忧虑，然后想想办法。'就在那时，我立下重誓，指甲都深深地掐进了肉里，而且背上一阵阵

best medical brains of the country, the Mayo brothers, confirmed the sentence. I was at a dead-end street, the ultimate gaped at me! I was young. I did not want to die! In my desperation, I phoned to my doctor at Kellogg and cried out to him the despair in my heart. Rather impatiently he upbraided me: 'What's the matter, Olga, haven't you any fight in you? Sure, you will die if you keep on crying. Yes, the worst has overtaken you. O. K. —face the facts! Quit worrying! And then do something about it! 'Right then and there I took an oath, an oath so solemn that the nails sank deep into my flesh and cold chills ran down my spine: *'I am not going to worry! I am not going to cry! And if there is anything to mind over matter, I am going to win! I am going to LIVE!* '

"The usual amount of X-ray in such advanced cases, where they cannot apply radium, is 101/2 minutes a day for 30 days. They gave me X-ray for 141/2 minutes a day for 49 days; and although my bones stuck out of my emaciated body like rocks on a barren hillside, and although my feet were like lead, *I did not worry*! Not once did I cry! I smiled! Yes, I actually forced myself to smile. I am not so idiotic as to imagine that merely smiling can cure cancer. But I do believe that a cheerful mental attitude helps the body fight disease. At any rate, I experienced one of the miracle cures of cancer. I have never been healthier than in the last few years, thanks to those challenging, fighting words of Dr. McCaffery: 'Face the facts: Quite worrying; then do something about it! '"

I am going to close this chapter by repeating its title: the words of Dr. Alexis Carrel: "Businessmen who do not know how to fight worry die young."

发冷：'我不会再忧虑，不会再哭泣！如果还有什么要想的，就是我一定要赢！一定要活下去！'

"在不能用镭照射的情况下，通常是照10.5分钟的X光，但我却连续49天每天照14.5分钟的X光。虽然我瘦得皮包骨头，双腿重如铅块，我却不忧虑，也没有哭过一次！我面带笑容！不错，我的确是在勉强自己笑。我当然不会傻到相信只要笑就能治好癌症。但我的确相信，愉快的精神状态有助于身体抵抗疾病。总之，我亲身经历了一次癌症治愈的奇迹。在过去几年里，我再也没有像现在这么健康过，多亏了麦卡费雷医生'面对现实，不要忧虑，然后想想办法'这句富于挑战和战斗性的话。"

在这一章就要结束的时候，我要再重复一次亚利西斯·卡瑞尔博士的这句话："不知道抗拒忧虑的商人，会短命而死。"

Part Two
Basic Techniques in Analysing Worry

1 How to Analyse and Solve Worry Problems

Will the magic formula of Willis H. Carrier, described in Part One, Chapter 2, solve all worry problems? No, of course not.

Then what is the answer? The answer is that we must equip ourselves to deal with different kinds of worries by learning the three basic steps of problem analysis. The three steps are:

1. Get the facts. 2. Analyse the facts. 3. Arrive at a decision—and then act on that decision.

Obvious stuff? Yes, Aristotle taught it—and used it. And you and I must use it too if we are going to solve the problems that are harassing us and turning our days and nights into veritable hells.

Let's take the first rule: *Get the facts*. Why is it so important to get the facts? Because unless we have the facts we can't possibly even attempt to solve our problem intelligently. Without the facts, all we can do is stew around in confusion. My idea? No, that was the idea of the late Herbert E. Hawkes, Dean of Columbia College, Columbia University, for twenty-two years. He had helped two hundred thousand students solve their worry problems; and he told me that "*confusion is the chief cause of worry*". He put it this way—he said: "Half the worry in the world is caused by people trying to make decisions before they have sufficient knowledge on which to base a decision. For example, "he said, "if I have a problem which has to be faced at three o'clock next Tuesday, I refuse even to try to make a decision about it until next Tuesday arrives. In the meantime, I concentrate on getting all the facts that bear on the problem. I don't worry, "he said, "I don't agonise over my problem. I don't lose any sleep. I simply concentrate on getting the facts. And by

第二篇　分析忧虑的基本技巧

第1章　解开忧虑之谜

前面提到的威利·卡瑞尔的魔法公式是否能解决所有的忧虑呢?不能,当然不能。

那该怎么办呢?答案是我们一定要学会下面三个分析问题的基本步骤,用它们来解决各种不同的困难。这三个步骤是:

第一步:看清事实。第二步:分析事实。第三步:做出决定,然后依照决定行事。

这是亚里士多德教的方法,他也使用过。如果我们想解决那些压迫我们、使我们成天像生活在地狱中的问题,我们必须应用这些方法。

我们先来看第一步:看清事实。看清事实为何如此重要呢?因为除非我们看清楚事实,否则就不能聪明地解决问题。没有事实,我们只能在混乱中摸索。这是我的理论吗?不,这是哥伦比亚大学哥伦比亚学院已故院长赫伯特·霍基斯说的,他当了20年院长。他曾帮助过20万中学生解决他们忧虑的问题。他告诉我说:"混乱是导致忧虑的主要原因。"他认为:"世界上的忧虑有一半是因为人们没有足够的知识做决定而产生的。例如,"他说,"如果我有一个问题必须在下星期二以前解决,那么在下星期二之前我根本不会去试着做出什么决定。我将在这段时间里集中全力搜集所有的相关事实。我不会发愁,不会为这个问题而难过,更不会失眠,我只是全心全力地搜集事实。等快到星期二的时候,如果我已经搜集了所有的事实,问题本身通常会迎刃而解。"

the time Tuesday rolls around, if I've got all the facts, the problem usually solves itself! "

I asked Dean Hawkes if this meant he had licked worry entirely. "Yes, "he said, "I think I can honestly say that my life is now almost totally devoid of worry. I have found, "he went on, "that *if a man will devote his time to securing facts in an impartial, objective way, his worries will usually evaporate in the light of knowledge.*"

Let me repeat that: "If a man will devote his time to securing facts in an impartial, objective way, his worries will usually evaporate in the light of knowledge."

But what do most of us do? If we bother with facts at all—and Thomas Edison said in all seriousness: "There is no expedient to which a man will not resort to avoid the labor of thinking"—if we bother with facts at all, we hunt like bird dogs after the facts that bolster up what we *already* think—and ignore all the others! We want only the facts that justify our acts—the facts that fit in conveniently with our wishful thinking and justify our preconceived prejudices!

As André Maurois put it: "Everything that is in agreement with our personal desires seems true. Everything that is not puts us into a rage."

Is it any wonder, then, that we find it so hard to get at the answers to our problems? Wouldn't we have the same trouble trying to solve a second grade arithmetic problem, if we went ahead on the assumption that two plus two equals five? Yet there are a lot of people in this world who make life a hell for themselves and others by insisting that two plus two equals five—or maybe five hundred!

What can we do about it? We have to keep our emotions out of our thinking; and, as Dean Hawkes put it, we must secure the facts in"an impartial, objective"manner.

That is not an easy task when we are worried. When we are worried, our emotions are riding high. But here are two ideas that I have found helpful when trying to step aside from my problems, in order to see the facts in a clear, objective manner. 1. When trying to get the facts, I pretend that I am collecting this information not for myself, but for some other person. This helps me to take a cold, impartial view of the evidence. This helps me eliminate my emotions. 2. While trying to collect the facts about the problem that is worrying me, I sometimes pretend that I am a lawyer preparing to argue the other side of the issue. In other words, I try to get all the facts against myself—all the facts that are damaging to my wishes, all the facts I don't like to face.

我问霍基斯院长,这是否表明他可以完全抛除忧虑了?"是的,"他说,"我想我可以老实说,我现在的生活完全没有忧虑。我发现,"他继续说,"如果一个人能把他所有的时间都用在以一种超然、客观的态度去寻找事实的话,那么他的忧虑就会在知识的光芒下消失。"

让我重复一遍:"如果一个人能把他所有的时间都用在以一种超然、客观的态度去寻找事实的话,那么他的忧虑就会在知识的光芒下消失。"

可是,我们大多数人会怎么做呢?如果我们要考虑事实——爱迪生很郑重地说:"一个人为了避免花时间去思想,往往会用各种手段。"——如果我们真的考虑事实,我们通常会像猎狗那样,去找寻那些我们已经想到的,而忽略其他的一切!我们只需要那些适合我们的事实,那些只适合我们的如意算盘、适合我们原有偏见的事实。

正如安德烈·马罗斯所说的:"和我们个人欲望相适合的看来都是真理,而不适合的只会使我们感到愤怒。"

无怪乎我们会觉得,要得到我们问题的答案这么困难。如果我们一直假定2加2等于5,那不是连一个二年级的算术题都不会做了吗? 但事实上, 世界上就有许多人坚持认为2加2等于5——或等于500——以至于弄得自己和别人的日子都不舒服。

对此我们该怎么办呢?我们应该将感情排除于思想之外,就如霍基斯院长所说的,我们必须用"超然客观"的态度来看清事实。

要在忧虑的时候那样做可不是一件简单的事。因为当我们忧虑的时候,会情绪激动。不过,我还是找到了两个有助于我们以清晰客观的态度看清所有事实并克服忧虑的办法:第一,在搜集各种事实的时候,我假装不是为自己搜集这些资料,而是为别人做这事,这样我可以保持冷静超然的态度,也可以帮助自己控制情绪。第二,在搜集造成各种忧虑的事实时,我有时候还将自己假设成对方的律师。换句话说,我也要搜集一些对自己不利的事实——搜集那些有损我的希望以及我所不愿面对的事实。

Then I write down both my side of the case and the other side of the case—and I generally find that the truth lies somewhere in between these two extremities.

Here is the point I am trying to make. Neither you nor I nor Einstein nor the Supreme Court of the United States is brilliant enough to reach an intelligent decision on any problem without first getting the facts. Thomas Edison knew that. At the time of his death, he had two thousand five hundred notebooks filled with facts about the problems he was facing.

So Rule 1 for solving our problems is: *Get the facts*. Let's do what Dean Hawkes did: let's not even attempt to solve our problems without first collecting all the facts in an impartial manner.

However, getting all the facts in the world won't do us any good until we analyse them and interpret them.

I have found from costly experience that it is much easier to analyse the facts after writing them down. In fact, merely writing the facts on a piece of paper and stating our problem clearly goes a long way toward helping us to reach a sensible decision. As Charles Kettering puts it: "A problem well stated is a problem half solved."

Let me show you all this as it works out in practice. Since the Chinese say one picture is worth ten thousand words, suppose I show you a picture of how one man put exactly what we are talking about into concrete action.

Let's take the case of Galen Litchfield—a man I have known for several years; one of the most successful American businessmen in the Far East. Mr. Litchfield was in China in 1942, when the Japanese invaded Shanghai. And here is his story as he told it to me while a guest in my home:

"Shortly after the Japanese bombed Pearl Harbour, "Galen Litchfield began, "they came swarming into Shanghai. I was the manager of the Asia Life Insurance Company in Shanghai. They sent us an 'army liquidator'—he was really an admiral—and gave me orders to assist this man in liquidating our assets. I didn't have any choice in the matter. I could cooperate—or else. And the 'or else' was certain death.

"I went through the motions of doing what I was told, because I had no alternative. But there was one block of securities, worth $750,000, which I left off the list I gave to the admiral. I left that block of securities off the list because they belonged to our Hong Kong organisation and had nothing to do with the Shanghai assets. All the same, I feared I might be in hot water if the

然后，我会把这一边的和另外一边的所有事实都写下来。这时，我通常会发现，真理就存在于这两个极端中间。

这就是我想说明的要点：如果不事先看清楚事实的话，你、我、爱因斯坦，甚至连美国最高法院，也不能对任何问题做出聪明的决定。爱迪生就清楚这一点，他死时留下来的2500本笔记中，记满了他面临的各种问题的事实。

所以，解决我们困难的第一个办法，就是看清事实。让我们仿效霍基斯院长的方法吧：在没有以客观态度搜集所有的事实之前，不要想着如何去解决问题。

然而，如果对事实不加以分析和解释，即使把全世界所有的事实都搜集起来，对我们也没有任何帮助。

根据我个人的经验，把所有的事实都记下来，然后再做分析，事情就会容易得多。事实上，只要在纸上记下各种事实，把我们的问题明明白白地写出来，有助于我们做出合理的决定。正如查尔斯·吉特林所说："把问题写清楚，就已经解决了一半问题。"

让我用实例来告诉你这种方法的成绩，中国有句古话叫"百闻不如一见"。我要告诉你，一个人怎样把上面所说的付诸行动的。

以格兰·李克菲的事情为例——我认识他好几年了，他是远东地区最成功的美国商人之一。1942年，日军侵入上海，李克菲先生正在中国。下面是他在我家做客时告诉我的故事：

"在轰炸珍珠港之后不久，"格兰·李克菲说，"日军攻占了上海。当时我是上海亚洲人寿保险公司的经理。日军派来了一个'军方清算员'(他实际上是一位海军上将)，命令我协助他清算我们的财产。这种事我毫无办法，要么合作，要么算了——而所谓算了，当然是死。

"我只好遵命行事，因为我无路可走。不过，我将一笔大约75万美元的保险费没有填写在清单上。我之所以不填进去，是因为这笔钱属于我们香港的公司，和上海公司的资产无关。但我还

Japanese found out what I had done. And they soon found out.

"I wasn't in the office when the discovery was made, but my head accountant was there. He told me that the Japanese admiral flew into a rage, and stamped and swore, and called me a thief and a traitor! I had defied the Japanese Army! I knew what that meant. I would be thrown into the Bridge house!

"The Bridge house! The torture chamber of the Japanese Gestapo! I had had personal friends who had killed themselves rather than be taken to that prison. I had had other friends who had died in that place after ten days of questioning and torture. Now I was slated for the Bridge house myself!

"What did I do? I heard the news on Sunday afternoon. I suppose I should have been terrified. And I would have been terrified if I hadn't had a definite technique for solving my problems. For years, whenever I was worried I had always gone to my typewriter and written down two questions—and the answers to these questions:

"*1. What am I worrying about?*

"*2. What can I do about it?*

"I used to try to answer those questions without writing them down. But I stopped that years ago. I found that writing down both the questions and the answers clarifies my thinking.

"So, that Sunday afternoon, I went directly to my room at the Shanghai YMCA, and got out my typewriter. I wrote:

"*1. What am I worrying about?*

" I am afraid I will be thrown into the Bridge house tomorrowmorning.

"Then I typed out the second question:

"*2. What can I do about it?*

"I spent hours thinking out and writing down the four courses of action I could take—and what the probable consequence of each action would be.1. I can try to explain to the Japanese admiral. But he"no speak English". If I try to explain to him through an interpreter, I may stir him up again. That might mean death, for he is cruel, would rather dump me in the Bridge house than bother talking about it. 2. I can try to escape. Impossible. They keep track of me all the time. I have to check in and out of my room at the YMCA. If I try to escape, I'll probably be captured and shot. 3. I can stay here in my room and not go near the office again. If I do, the Japanese admiral will be

是担心万一日本人发现了这件事可能会对我不利。他们很快就发现了。

"他们发现的时候,我恰巧不在办公室,但会计部主任在场。他告诉我,日本海军上将大发脾气,还拍桌子直骂人,说我是强盗和叛徒,我侮辱了日本皇军。我知道这是什么意思,我可能会被关进宪兵队。

"宪兵队是日本秘密警察的行刑室。我有几个朋友,他们情愿自杀也不愿被送到那个地方。我还有一些朋友在那里被审问折磨了10天之后,死在那里。而我现在也要被关进宪兵队了。

"我该怎么办?我星期天下午得知的这个消息,我想我当时应该吓得要命。如果我找不到解决问题的方法,我一定会被吓死的。多年来,每当我担心的时候,总会坐在打字机前打出下面两个问题,以及问题的答案:

"第一,我担心什么?

"第二,我能做什么?

"以往我都不把答案写下来,只是在心里回答问题。不过几年前我就不再那样做了。我发现把问题和答案都写下来,会使我的思路变得清晰。所以,在那个星期天的下午,我直接回到我在上海基督教青年会的房间,取出打字机写道:

"第一,我担心什么?

"我担心明天早上会被关进宪兵队里。

"第二,我能做什么?

"我思考了几个小时,写下了我能采取的4种行动,以及每一种行动可能带来的后果。第一,我可以试着向日本海军上将解释。可是他不会说英文,若是我找翻译对他解释,可能会让他再次生气,那可能是死路一条,因为他是个凶残的人,我宁愿被关进宪兵队,也不愿和他谈话。第二,我可以逃走。但这不可能,因为他们一直都在监视我。我从基督教青年会进进出出都要登

suspicious, will probably send soldiers to get me and throw me into the Bridge house without giving me a chance to say a word. 4. I can go down to the office as usual on Monday morning. If I do, there is a chance that the Japanese admiral may be so busy that he will not think of what I did. Even if he does think of it, he may have cooled off and may not bother me. If this happens, I am all right. Even if he does bother me, I'll still have a chance to try to explain to him. So, going down to the office as usual on Monday morning, and acting as if nothing had gone wrong gives me two chances to escape the Bridge house.

"As soon as I thought it all out and decided to accept the fourth plan—to go down to the office as usual on Monday morning—I felt immensely relieved.

"When I entered the office the next morning, the Japanese admiral sat there with a cigarette dangling from his mouth. He glared at me as he always did; and said nothing. Six weeks later—thank God—he went back to Tokyo and my worries were ended.

"As I have already said, I probably saved my life by sitting down that Sunday afternoon and writing out all the various steps I could take and then writing down the probable consequences of each step and calmly coming to a decision. If I hadn't done that, I might have floundered and hesitated and done the wrong thing on the spur of the moment. If I hadn't thought out my problem and come to a decision, I would have been frantic with worry all Sunday afternoon. I wouldn't have slept that night. I would have gone down to the office Monday morning with a harassed and worried look; and that alone might have aroused the suspicion of the Japanese admiral and spurred him to act.

"Experience has proved to me, time after time, the enormous value of arriving at a decision. It is the failure to arrive at a fixed purpose, the inability to stop going round and round in maddening circles, that drives men to nervous breakdowns and living hells. I find that fifty per cent of my worries vanishes once I arrive at a clear, definite decision; and another forty per cent usually vanishes once I start to carry out that decision.

"So I banish about ninety per cent of my worries by taking these four steps:

"*1. Writing down precisely what I am worrying about.*

"*2. Writing down what I can do about it.*

"*3. Deciding what to do.*

记，如果我想逃走，可能被抓住枪毙。第三，我也可以留在房间不再上班。如果这样做，那位日本海军上将就会怀疑，也许会派人来抓我，根本不给我任何说话的机会，直接把我关进宪兵队。第四，我可以星期一早上照常上班。如果我这样做，那位日本海军上将很可能正在忙着，忘掉了我的事情。而且即使他想到了，也可能已经冷静下来，不再找我的麻烦。如果是这样，我就万事大吉了。甚至即使他还来找我，我仍然有机会向他解释。所以我应该和平常一样在星期一早上去办公室，就像什么事也没有发生过，可以给我两个逃避宪兵队的机会。

"等我通盘考虑之后，我决定采取第四个计划——和平常一样，在星期一早上去上班——我大大地松了一口气。

"我第二天早上走进办公室时，那位日本海军上将坐在那里，嘴里叼着香烟，像平常一样看了我一眼，但什么话也没说。6个星期之后——谢天谢地——他调回东京去了，我的忧虑也就此告终!

"就像我前面所说的，我之所以能捡回这条命，大概就因为我在那个星期天下午写出了可以采取各种不同步骤，以及每一个步骤可能产生的后果，然后镇定地做出了决定。如果我不那样做，我可能会思想混乱或者犹豫不决，以至于在紧要关头出错。如果我没有分析我的问题并做出决定，那我整个星期天下午就会心急如焚，那天晚上也睡不着觉，星期一早上上班时可能满面惊慌和愁容——仅此一点，就会使那位日本海军上将起疑心，而使他采取行动。

"以后一次又一次的经验证明，逐渐做出决定的确大有价值。人们正是因为不能实现既定的目的，而且不能控制自己，总是局限在一个令人难以忍受的小圈子里，才会精神崩溃和生活窘迫。我发现一旦做出清楚而明确的决定之后，一半的忧虑会立即消失，而另外的40%通常会在我按照决定去做之后消失。

"采取以下4个步骤，通常就能消除90%的忧虑：

"第一，清楚地写下我们所担心的是什么。

"*4. Starting immediately to carry out that decision.*"

Galen Litchfield is now the Far Eastern Director for Starr, Park and Freeman, Inc., III John Street, New York, representing large insurance and financial interests.

In fact, as I said before, Galen Litchfield today is one of the most important American businessmen in Asia; and he confesses to me that he owes a large part of his success to this method of analyzing worry and meeting it head-on.

Why is his method so superb? Because it is efficient, concrete, and goes directly to the heart of the problem. On top of all that, it is climaxed by the third and indispensable rule: Do something about it.

Unless we carry out our action, all our fact-finding and analysis is whistling upwind—it's a sheer waste of energy.

William James said this, "When once a decision is reached and execution is the order of the day, dismiss absolutely all responsibility and care about the outcome." (In this case, William James undoubtedly used the word "care" as a synonym for "anxiety".) He meant—once you have made a careful decision based on facts, go into action. Don't stop to reconsider. Don't begin to hesitate, worry and retrace your steps. Don't lose yourself in self-doubting which begets other doubts. Don't keep looking back over your shoulder.

I once asked Waite Phillips, one of Oklahoma's most prominent oil men, how he carried out decisions. He replied, "I find that to keep thinking about our problems beyond a certain point is bound to create confusion and worry. There comes a time when any more investigation and thinking are harmful. There comes a time when we must decide and act and never look back."

Why don't you employ Galen Litchfield's technique to one of your worries right now?

Here is:

Question No. 1—What am I worrying about? (Please pencil the answer to that question in the space below.)

Question No. 2—What can I do about it? (Please write your answer to that question in the space below.)

Question No. 3—Here is what I am going to do about it.

Question No. 4—When am I going to start doing it?

"第二,写下我们可以怎么办。

"第三,决定该怎么办。

"第四,马上就照决定去做。"

格兰·李克菲已经成了纽约市第三约翰大街斯塔尔-帕克-弗里曼公司的亚洲区总经理,代表大保险和金融集团的利益。事实上,他现在是亚洲最重要的几位美国商人之一,他诚恳地告诉我:他的成功应归功于这种分析并敢于正视忧虑的方法。

为什么他的方法这么管用?因为它有效可行,直抵问题核心。最重要的是,它遵循了第三项且是不可或缺的原则:采取行动。

除非我们采取行动,否则我们寻找并分析事实的做法都将化为泡影——那真是在白费精力。

威廉·詹姆斯说:"一旦做出决定,当天就要付诸实践,同时不要理会责任问题,也不要关心后果。"他的意思是说一旦你以事实为基础做出了谨慎的决定之后,就要付诸实行,而不是停下来再重新考虑,要毫不迟疑、毫不担忧和犹豫,不要怀疑自己。

我曾问俄克拉荷马州最成功的石油商人之一怀特·菲利浦,他是如何把决心付诸行动的,他回答说:"我发现,如果在超过某种限度之后还一直思考问题的话,一定会导致混乱和忧虑。当调查和思考过度对我们有害的时候,也就是我们必须下定决心、付诸行动、不再犹豫的时候。"

何不马上运用格兰·李克菲的方法来解决你的忧虑?下面就是:

第一个问题——我担忧什么?(请在下面空白处写下你的答案)

第二个问题——我能做什么?(请在下面空白处写下你的答案)

第三个问题——我决定怎么做?

第四个问题——我什么时候开始做?

2 How to Eliminate Fifty Per Cent of Your Business Worries

If you are a businessman, you are probably saying to yourself right now, "The title of this chapter is ridiculous. I have been running my business for nineteen years; and I certainly know the answers if anybody does. The idea of anybody trying to tell me how I can eliminate fifty per cent of my business worries—it's absurd! "

Fair enough—I would have felt exactly the same way myself a few years ago if I had seen this title on a chapter. It promises a lot—and promises are cheap.

Let's be very frank about it: *maybe I won't* be able to help you eliminate fifty per cent of your business worries. In the last analysis, no one can do that, except yourself. But what I can do is to show you how other people have done it—and leave the rest up to you!

You may recall that I quoted the world-famous Dr. Alexis Carrel as saying:

"*Businessmen who do not know how to fight worry die young.*"

Since worry is that serious, wouldn't you be satisfied if I could help you eliminate even ten per cent of your worries?... Yes?... Good! Well, I am going to show you how one business executive eliminated not Fifty per cent of his worries, but seventy-five per cent of all the time he formerly spent in conferences, trying to solve business problems.

Furthermore, I am not going to tell you this story about a "Mr. Jones" or a "Mr. X" or "a man I know in Ohio"—vague stories that you can't check up on. It concerns a very real person—Leon Shimkin, a former partner and general manager of one of the foremost publishing houses in the United States—Simon and Schuster, Rockefeller Centre, New York 20, New York.

Here is Leon Shimkin's experience in his own words:

"For fifteen years I spent almost half of every business day holding conferences, discussing problems.

"Should we do this or that—do nothing at all? We would get tense; twist in our chairs; walk the floor; argue and go around in circles. When night came, I would be utterly exhausted. I fully

第2章 如何减少生意上50%的忧虑

如果你是一个商人,也许你现在正在对自己说:"这章标题实在荒谬,我干这一行已经19年了;如果有谁知道这个答案,当然非我莫属。居然有人想告诉我如何减少生意上50%的忧虑,实在荒谬。"

太对了!如果我在几年前看到这章的标题,也会有同样的感觉。它好像能帮你大忙,但这种空话根本不值钱。

让我们开诚布公吧:也许我不能帮你减少生意上50%的忧虑,因为从我前面的分析来看,除了你自己之外没有人能做到这一点。但我能做到让你看看别人是如何做的,剩下的全看你自己了。

你也许还记得我引用过闻名世界的亚利西斯·卡瑞尔医生的话:"不知道抗拒忧虑的商人,都会短命而死。"既然忧虑这么严重,那么如果我能帮你消除10%的忧虑,你是否会满意呢?会的?很好,我下面就要告诉你一位商人是如何消除忧虑,而且节约了以前用来开会、解决生意问题的70%的时间。

当然,我不会告诉你那些无法查证的故事。这个故事的主人公是活生生的李昂。他是纽约州纽约市洛克菲勒中心著名的西蒙舒斯特出版公司前合伙人兼高层主管。

下面就是李昂自己讲述的经历:

"15年来,我每天几乎用一半的时间开会和讨论问题。

"我们应该这样还是那样?或什么都不管?我们这时会很紧张,坐立不安,或在办公室走来走去,不停地争论绕圈子。到了晚上,我筋疲力尽。我原以为我这辈子大概只能这样了。我干这

expected to go on doing this sort of thing for the rest of my life. I had been doing it for fifteen years, and it never occurred to me that there was a better way of doing it. If anyone had told me that I could eliminate three-fourths of all the time I spent in those worried conferences, and three-fourths of my nervous strain—I would have thought he was a wild-eyed, slap-happy, armchair optimist. Yet I devised a plan that did just that. I have been using this plan for eight years. It has performed wonders for my efficiency, my health, and my happiness.

"It sounds like magic—but like all magic tricks, it is extremely simple when you see how it is done.

"Here is the secret: First, I immediately stopped the procedure I had been using in my conferences for fifteen years—a procedure that began with my troubled associates reciting all the details of what had gone wrong, and ending up by asking: 'What shall we do?' Second, I made a new rule—a rule that everyone who wishes to present a problem to me must first prepare and submit a memorandum answering these four questions:

"Question 1: *What is the problem?*

("In the old days we used to spend an hour or two in a worried conference without anyone's knowing specifically and concretely what the real problem was. We used to work ourselves into a lather discussing our troubles without ever troubling to write out specifically what our problem was.)

"Question 2: *What is the cause of the problem?*

("As I look back over my career, I am appalled at the wasted hours I have spent in worried conferences without ever trying to find out clearly the conditions which lay at the root of the problem.)

"Question 3: *What are all possible solutions of the problem?*

("In the old days, one man in the conference would suggest one solution. Someone else would argue with him. Tempers would flare. We would often get clear off the subject, and at the end of the conference no one would have written down all the various things we could do to attack the problem.)

"Question 4: *What solution do you suggest?*

("I used to go into a conference with a man who had spent hours worrying about a situation

一行已经有15年,从未想过会有更好的办法。如果有人告诉我以减去3/4令人忧虑的会议时间,可以消除3/4的神经紧张,我会认为他是一个盲目的乐观主义者。可是,我现在确实能够拟出一个恰好能做到这一点的计划。这个方法我已经用了8年,对提高效率、健康和快乐都有奇效。

"这像是魔术——可是正如所有的魔术一样,只要你弄清楚是怎么做的,就非常简单了。

"下面就是秘诀:第一,我立即停止了15年来我们会议采取的程序。以往,我的同事先会报告一遍问题的细节,最后会问'我们该怎么办?'第二,我订下一条新规矩——任何人想要问我问题,必须先准备好一份书面报告,回答以下四个问题:

"一是究竟出了什么问题?

("以前我们这种会通常要开一两个小时,可是大家还不清楚真正的问题在哪里。我们总是讨论我们的问题,却不愿提前明确地写出我们的问题是什么。)

"二是问题的起因是什么?

("我回顾了一下,竟然惊奇地发现,我虽然在这种会上浪费了很多时间,却没有清楚地找出问题的根源。)

"三是这个问题可能有哪些解决方法?

("以前,只要有一个人提出一种解决方法,就会有另外一个人跟他辩论,大家也都争论起来,常常扯到题外去,而开完会时还没有找到解决问题的方法。)

"四是你建议用哪一种办法?

("以前和我一起开会的人,往往为一种情况担心几小时,并且不断地绕圈子,却从没有想过什么可行的解决方法,然后写下来:'这是我建议的解决方案。')

"现在,他们很少把他们的问题拿来找我了。为什么呢?因为他们发现要回答上面的四个问题,就必须搜集所有的事实,仔细考虑一遍。当他们做了这些之后,他们会发现大部分问题都不

and going around in circles without ever once thinking through all possible solutions and then writing down: 'This is the solution I recommend.')

"My associates rarely come to me now with their problems. Why? Because they have discovered that in order to answer these four questions they have to get all the facts and think their problems through. And after they have done that they find, in three-fourths of the cases, they don't have to consult me at all because the proper solution has popped out like a piece of bread popping out from an electric toaster. Even in those cases where consultation is necessary, the discussion takes about one-third the time formerly required, because it proceeds along an orderly, logical path to a reasoned conclusion.

"Much less time is now consumed in the house of Simon and Schuster in *worrying and talking* about what is wrong; and a lot more action is obtained toward making those things right."

My friend, Frank Bettger, one of the top insurance men in America, *told* me he not only reduced his business worries, but nearly doubled his income, by a similar method.

"Years ago, "said Frank Bettger, "when I first started to sell insurance, I was filled with a boundless enthusiasm and love for my work. Then something happened. I became so discouraged that I despised my work and thought of giving it up. I think I would have quit—if I hadn't got the idea, one Saturday morning, of sitting down and trying to get at the root of my worries.

"1. I asked myself first: '*Just what is the problem*?'The problem was: *that I was not getting high enough returns for the staggering amount of calls I was making.* I seemed to do pretty well at selling a prospect, until the moment came for closing a sale. Then the customer would say: 'Well, I'll think it over, Mr. Bettger. Come and see me again. 'It was the time I wasted on these follow-up calls that was causing my depression.

"2. I asked myself: '*What are the possible solutions*?'But to get the answer to that one, I had to study the facts. I got out my record book for the last twelve months and studied the figures.

"*I made an astounding discovery*! Right there in black and white, I discovered that seventy per cent of my sales had been closed on the very first interview! Twenty-three per cent of my sales had been closed on the second interview! And only *seven per cent of my sales* had been closed on those third, fourth, fifth, etc. , interviews, which were running me ragged and taking up my time. In

必再来找我商量,因为最合理的解决方案会不断地涌现。即使是那些必须跟我讨论的问题,所花的时间也不过是以前的1/3,因为讨论时有条不紊,最后都能得到明智的结论。

"现在,在我们公司不再花那么多时间去担心、讨论出了什么问题,而是以更多的行动来解决问题。"

我朋友弗兰克·贝特格是美国最了不起的保险业巨头。他曾告诉我,他不仅减少了生意上的忧虑,而且收入几乎增加了一倍,他用的也是类似的方法。

"很多年以前,"弗兰克·贝特格说,"我刚开始推销保险,对自己的工作充满了热情和喜爱。但后来发生了一件事使我很沮丧,让我看不起我的工作,甚至想到过放弃。我几乎都要辞职了,可是我突然想起了一件事。在一个星期六的早晨,我坐下来,想找出忧虑的根源。

"第一,我问自己:'问题到底出在哪里?'我的问题是:我拜访过那么多人,可是业绩并不理想。直到成交之前,我跟那些希望很大的顾客谈得很好。然后顾客会说:'啊!我想再考虑考虑,贝特格先生。什么时候再说吧。'于是我又得再次拜访,这样就浪费掉不少时间,使我觉得很沮丧。

"第二,我问自己:'有什么解决办法?'可是要找出问题的答案,就得研究事实。我拿出过去12个月的记录本,研究上面的数据。

"结果,我有了一个惊人的发现!我所卖的保险有70%是在第一次拜访时成交的,23%是在第二次拜访时成交的!只有7%是在第三、第四甚至第五次才成交的。这让我觉得很难过,因为它很浪费时间。换句话说,我的工作时间几乎有一半浪费在实际上只有7%的业务上。

"第三,'问题的答案是什么?'答案很明显,我立刻停止了第二次以后的所有拜访,多出来的时间用来寻找新的顾客。结果令人难以相信:在很短的时间内,我就把每一次的拜访业绩提高了近一倍。"

other words, I was wasting fully one half of my working day on a part of my business which was responsible for only seven per cent of my sales!

"3. '*What is the answer*?' The answer was obvious. I immediately cut out all visits beyond the second interview, and spent the extra time building up new prospects. The results were unbelievable. In a very short time, I had almost doubled the cash value of every visit I made from a call! "

As I said, Frank Bettger became one of the best-known life-insurance salesmen in America. He is with Fidelity Mutual of Philadelphia, and writes a million dollars worth of policies a year. But he was on the point of giving up. He was on the point of admitting failure—until analyzing the problem gave him a boost on the road to success.

Can you apply these questions to your business problems? To repeat my challenge—they *can* reduce your worries by fifty per cent. Here they are again:

1. What is the problem?
2. What is the CAUSE of the problem?
3. What are all possible solutions to the problem?
4. What solution do you suggest?

弗兰克·贝特格是美国最著名的人寿保险推销员之一，每年推销的保险都在100万美元以上。可是他曾经想要放弃，几乎就要承认自己的失败——分析问题使他走上了成功之路。

你是否也能把这些问题应用到你的业务上呢？重复一下我的挑战——它们能减少你一半的忧虑。

第一，问题是什么？
第二，问题的起因是什么？
第三，解决问题的方法有哪些？
第四，你建议用哪一种解决方法？

Part Three
How to Break the Worry Habit Before It Breaks You

1 How to Crowd Worry out of Your Mind

I shall never forget the night, a few years ago, when Marion J. Douglas was a student in one of my classes. (I have not used his real name. He requested me, for personal reasons, not to reveal his identity.) But here is his real story as he told it before one of our adult-education classes. He told us how tragedy had struck at his home, not once, but twice. The first time he had lost his five-year-old daughter, a child he adored. He and his wife thought they couldn't endure that first loss; but, as he said, "Ten months later, God gave us another little girl—and she died in five days."

This double bereavement was almost too much to bear. "I couldn't take it, "this father told us. "I couldn't sleep, I couldn't eat, I couldn't rest or relax. My nerves were utterly shaken and my confidence gone." At last he went to doctors; one recommended sleeping pills and another recommended a trip. He tried both, but neither remedy helped. He said, "My body felt as if it were encased in a vice, and the jaws of the vice were being drawn tighter and tighter." The tension of grief—if you have ever been paralysed by sorrow, you know what he meant.

"But thank God, I had one child left—a four-year-old son. He gave me the solution to my problem. One afternoon as I sat around feeling sorry for myself, he asked: 'Daddy, will you build a boat for me?' I was in no mood to build a boat; in fact, I was in no mood to do anything. But my son is a persistent little fellow! I had to give in. Building that toy boat took about three hours. By the time it was finished, I realised that those three hours spent building that boat were the first hours of mental relaxation and peace that I had had in months! That discovery jarred me out of my lethargy

第三篇 如何改变忧虑的习惯

第1章 消除思想上的忧虑

我永远都忘不了几年前的一个晚上,当时马利安·道格拉斯是我班上的一个学员。(我没用他的真名。出于个人原因,他要求我不要说出他的身份。)但这是他的真实故事,他在我一个成人教育班上讲过。他告诉我们他家里遭受的不幸——不止一次,而是两次。第一次他失去了5岁的女儿,这是他非常喜爱的孩子。他和他的妻子都以为他们无法承受这个打击;可是,正如他所说的:"10个月之后,上帝又赐给我们另一个小女儿——她只活了5天。"

接连而来的打击几乎使人无法承受。"我受不了,"这个父亲告诉我们,"我睡不着吃不下,也无法休息或放松。我精神上受到了致命的打击,信心全没了。"最后,他去看了医生。有一位医生建议他吃安眠药,而另一位医生则建议去旅行。

他试了这两个方法,可是都没有用。他说:"我的身体犹如夹在一把铁钳子里,而铁钳却愈夹愈紧。"那种悲哀——如果你曾经因为悲哀而感觉麻木的话,就知道是什么感受了。

"不过,感谢上帝,我们还有一个孩子——一个4岁大的儿子。他教我找到了解决问题的方法。一天下午,我悲伤地呆坐着,他问我:'爸爸,你肯不肯给我做一条船?'我实在没有心情;事实上,我没有心情做任何事。可是我的儿子是个很会缠人的小家伙,我不得不屈服。做那条玩具船花了3个小时。等做好之后,我发现这3小时竟成了我这几个月以来第一次心情放松的时间。

and caused me to do a bit of thinking—the first real thinking I had done in months. I realised that it is difficult to worry while you are busy doing something that requires planning and thinking. In my case, building the boat had knocked worry out of the ring. So I resolved to keep busy. The following night, I went from room to room in the house, compiling a list of jobs that ought to be done. Scores of items needed to be repaired: bookcases, stair steps, storm windows, window shades, knobs, locks, leaky taps. Astonishing as it seems, in the course of two weeks I had made a list of 242 items that needed attention.

"During the last two years I have completed most of them. Besides, I have filled my life with stimulating activities. Two nights per week I attend adult-education classes in New York. I have gone in for civic activities in my home town and I am now chairman of the school board. I attend scores of meetings. I help collect money for the Red Cross and other activities. I am so busy now that I have no time for worry."

No time for worry! That is exactly what Winston Churchill said when he was working eighteen hours a day at the height of the war. When he was asked if he worried about his tremendous responsibilities, he said, "I'm too busy. I have no time for worry."

Charles Kettering was in that same fix when he started out to invent a self-starter for automobiles. Mr. Kettering was, until his recent retirement, vice-president of General Motors in charge of the world-famous General Motors Research Corporation. But in those days, he was so poor that he had to use the hayloft of a barn as a laboratory. To buy groceries, he had to use fifteen hundred dollars that his wife had made by giving piano lessons; later, he had to borrow five hundred dollars on his life insurance. I asked his wife if she wasn't worried at a time like that. "Yes, "she replied, "I was so worried I couldn't sleep; but Mr. Kettering wasn't. He was too absorbed in his work to worry."

The great scientist, Pasteur, spoke of "the peace that is found in libraries and laboratories." Why is peace found there?Because the men in libraries and laboratories are usually too absorbed in their tasks to worry about themselves. Research men rarely have nervous breakdowns. They haven't time for such luxuries.

Why does such a simple thing as keeping busy help to drive out anxiety?Because of a law—

这个发现使我从恍惚中惊醒过来,也使我想了许多——这是我几个月来第一次认真思考。我发现,如果你忙着做一些需要计划和思考的事情时,就很难去忧虑了。对我来说,做那条船时忧虑全都消失了,所以我决定让自己忙起来。第二天晚上,我看了看每一个房间,把要做的事情列成一张单子。有许多东西如书架、楼梯、屋顶窗、窗帘、门把、门锁、漏水的龙头都需要修理。让人震惊的是,我在两个星期里竟然列出了242件需要做的事情。

"在过去的两年里,这些事情大部分都已经做完了。此外,我还给我的生活增加了富有启发的活动:每个星期到纽约市参加两晚上成人教育课,并参加了小镇上的一些活动;现在我是校董事会主席,参加过很多会议,并协助红十字会和其他活动募捐。现在我忙得没有时间忧虑。"

没有时间忧虑!这也正是丘吉尔曾说过的,当时战事紧张,他每天工作18个小时。当别人问他是不是担心这一巨大责任时,他说:"我太忙了,没有时间忧虑。"

查尔斯·吉特林着手发明汽车自动点火器的时候,也碰到过类似情形。吉特林先生一直担任通用汽车公司副总裁,主管世界知名的通用汽车研究公司,不久前才退休。可是当年他穷得只能租堆稻草的谷仓做实验室;全家的开销靠他太太教钢琴赚来的1500美元。后来,他不得不用他的人寿保险做抵押借来500美元。我问他太太,她在那段时期是不是很忧虑?"当然,"她回答说,"我担心得睡不着,可是我丈夫一点都不担心。他沉浸在工作中,没有时间忧虑。"

伟大的科学家巴斯特也曾经谈过"在图书馆和实验室找到的平静"。为什么会在那儿找到平静呢?因为在图书馆和实验室工作的人,通常都埋头于工作,没时间为自己担忧。研究人员也很少精神崩溃,因为他们没有时间享受这种奢侈。

为什么"让自己忙着"这么简单的一件事情,就能把忧虑赶走呢?因为有这么一个定理——这是心理学所发现的基本定理之一。这条定理就是:一个人不论多么聪明,都不可能在同一时间想一件以上的事情。不信?让我们来做一个实验:

one of the most fundamental laws ever revealed by psychology. And that law is: *that it is utterly impossible for any human mind, no matter how brilliant, to think of more than one thing at any given time*. You don't quite believe it?Very well, then, let's try an experiment.

Suppose you lean right back now, close your eyes, and try, at the same instant, to think of the Statue of Liberty and of what you plan to do tomorrow morning. (Go ahead, try it.)

You found out, didn't you, that you could focus on either thought in turn, but never on both simultaneously?Well, the same thing is true in the field of emotions. We cannot be pepped up and enthusiastic about doing something exciting and feel dragged down by worry at the very same time.

One kind of emotion drives out the other. And it was that simple discovery that enabled Army psychiatrists to perform such miracles during the Second World War.

When men came out of battle so shaken by the experience that they were called "psychoneurotic", Army doctors prescribed"Keep'em busy"as a cure.

Every waking minute of these nerve-shocked men was filled with activity—usually outdoor activity, such as fishing, hunting, playing ball, golf, taking pictures, making gardens, and dancing. They were given no time for brooding over their terrible experiences.

"Occupational therapy"is the term now used by psychiatry when work is prescribed as though it were a medicine. It is not new. The old Greek physicians were advocating it five hundred years before Christ was born!

The Quakers were using it in Philadelphia in Ben Franklin's time. A man who visited a Quaker sanatorium in 1774 was shocked to see that the patients who were mentally ill were busy spinning flax. He thought these poor unfortunates were being exploited—until the Quakers explained that they found that their patients actually improved when they did a little work. It was soothing to the nerves.

Any psychiatrist will tell you that work—keeping busy—is one of the best anesthetics ever known for sick nerves. Henry W. Longfellow found that out for himself when he lost his young wife. His wife had been melting some sealing-wax at a candle one day, when her clothes caught on fire. Longfellow heard her cries and tried to reach her in time; but she died from the burns. For a while, Longfellow was so tortured by the memory of that dreadful experience that he nearly went insane;

假定你现在靠坐在椅子上，闭上双眼，试着在同一时间去想自由女神以及你明天早上打算做什么事情。

你会发现，你只能轮流想其中的一件事，而不可能同时想两件事，对不对?就你的情感来说也是如此。我们不可能充满热情地想去做一些令人兴奋的事情，同时又因为忧虑而拖延下来。

一种感觉会把另一种感觉赶出去。就是这么简单的发现，使得军方一些心理专家能够在二战时创造出医学奇迹。

当有些人因为在战场上受到打击而退下来时，他们都患上了"心理上的精神衰弱症"。军队医生采取了"保持忙碌"的治疗方法。这些精神受到打击的人每时每刻都在活动，例如钓鱼、打猎、打篮球、打高尔夫球、拍照、种花，跳舞，根本不让他们有时间回想那些可怕的经历。

"职业治疗"是精神病学发明的名词，就是拿工作当作治疗疾病的药。这并不是什么新方法，耶稣诞生前500年古希腊医生就已经使用这种方法。

在富兰克林时代，费城教友会的教徒也使用过这种方法。1774年，有一个人去参观教友会办的疗养院，当他看见那些精神病人正忙着纺纱时，他大为震惊。他认为那些可怜而不幸的人正在被剥削。后来教友会的人向他解释说，他们发现那些病人只有在工作时病情才能真正好转，因为工作能让他们安定。

任何精神病专家都会告诉你：工作——保持忙碌——是治疗精神病的最好良方。亨利·朗费罗在他年轻的妻子去世之后，也发现了这个道理。有一天，他太太在蜡烛上熔化一些封蜡，结果衣服着火了。朗费罗听见她的叫喊声，立即赶过去，但她还是因为烧伤而离开了人世。很长一段时间，朗费罗都忘不掉这件可怕的事情，几乎发疯。幸好他3个幼小的孩子需要他照料。他虽然很伤心，但还是要父兼母职。他带他们散步，给他们讲故事，和他们做游戏，把他们的亲情永存在《孩子们的时间》一诗里。他还翻译了但丁的诗。所有这些使他忙得完全忘了自己，思想上

but, fortunately for him, his three small children needed his attention. In spite of his own grief, Longfellow undertook to be father and mother to his children. He took them for walks, told them stories, played games with them, and immortalised their companionship in his poem *The Children's Hour*. He also translated Dante; and all these duties combined kept him so busy that he forgot himself entirely, and regained his peace of mind. As Tennyson declared when he lost his most intimate friend, Arthur Hallam: "I must lose myself in action, lest I wither in despair."

Most of us have little trouble "losing ourselves in action"while we have our noses to the grindstone and are doing our day's work. But the hours after work—they are the dangerous ones. Just when we're free to enjoy our own leisure, and ought to be happiest—that's when the blue devils of worry attack us. That's when we begin to wonder whether we're getting anywhere in life; whether we're in a rut; whether the boss "meant anything"by that remark he made today; or whether we're getting bald. When we are not busy, our minds tend to become a near-vacuum. Every student of physics knows that "nature abhors a vacuum". The nearest thing to a vacuum that you and I will probably ever see is the inside of an incandescent electric-light bulb. Break that bulb—and nature forces air in to fill the theoretically empty space. Nature also rushes in to fill the vacant mind. With what?Usually with emotions. Why?Because emotions of worry, fear, hate, jealousy, and envy are driven by primeval vigour and the dynamic energy of the jungle. Such emotions are so violent that they tend to drive out of our minds all peaceful, happy thoughts and emotions.

James L. Mursell, professor of education, Teachers College, Columbia, puts it very well when he said: "Worry is most apt to ride you ragged not when you are in action, but when the day's work is done. Your imagination can run riot then and bring up all sorts of ridiculous possibilities and magnify each little blunder. At such a time, "he continued, "your mind is like a motor operating without its load. It races and threatens to burn out its bearings or even to tear itself to bits. The remedy for worry is to get completely occupied doing something constructive."

But you don't have to be a college professor to realise this truth and put it into practice. During the Second World War, I met a housewife from Chicago who told me how she discovered for herself that "the remedy for worry is to get completely occupied doing something constructive." I met this woman and her husband in the dining-car while I was travelling from New York to my farm in

重新得到了平静。这正如丹尼森在他最好的朋友亚瑟·哈兰死的时候曾说过的:"我必须让自己沉浸在工作中,否则我会在绝望中死去。"

对大部分人来说，当日常工作使我们忙得团团转的时候,"沉浸在工作中"不会有多大问题。可是下班以后——也就是我们能够自由自在地享受我们的轻松和快乐的时候——忧虑之魔就会袭击我们。

这时我们会想各种问题:我们的生活有什么成就、我们是不是墨守成规、老板今天说的那句话是不是"有什么特别意思",或者我们是不是开始秃头了……

当我们不忙的时候,大脑常常会变成一片真空。每一个物理专业的学生都知道"自然界没有真空状态"。我们看过的最接近真空状态的是电灯泡。打破灯泡,空气就会进去,充满了从理论上来说是真空的那个空间。

大脑空出来时,也会有东西补充进去。是什么呢?通常是感觉。为什么?因为忧虑、恐惧、憎恨、嫉妒和羡慕等情绪都是受思想控制的,而这些情绪都非常强烈,往往会撵走我们思想中所有平静、快乐的思想和情绪。

詹姆斯·马歇尔是哥伦比亚师范学院教育系教授。他在这方面说得很清楚:"忧虑对你伤害最大的时候,不是在你忙着工作的时候,而是在你干完一天的工作之后。那时,你的想象力会混乱,使你想到各种荒诞不经的事情,夸大每一个小错误。在这个时候,你的思想就像一辆没有载重的汽车,横冲直撞,摧毁一切,甚至把自己撞成碎片。消除忧虑的良方,就是让自己做一些有意义的事情。"

并非成为大学教授才能懂得这个道理,才能将其付诸实践。我在二战时碰到一位住在芝加哥的家庭主妇,她告诉我说,她发现"消除忧虑的良方,就是让自己做一些有意义的事情"。当时我正在由纽约到密苏里州农庄的路上,正好在火车餐车上碰到这位太太和她的先生。(很抱歉

Missouri. (Sorry I didn't get their names—I never like to give examples without using names and street addresses—details that give authenticity to a story.)

This couple told me that their son had joined the armed forces the day after Pearl Harbour. The woman told me that she had almost wrecked her health worrying over that only son. Where was he? Was he safe? Or in action? Would he be wounded? Killed?

When I asked her how she overcame her worry, she replied: "I got busy." She told me that at first she had dismissed her maid and tried to keep busy by doing all her housework herself. But that didn't help much. "The trouble was, "she said, "that I could do my housework almost mechanically, without using my mind. So I kept on worrying. While making the beds and washing the dishes. I realised I needed some new kind of work that would keep me busy both mentally and physically every hour of the day. So I took a job as a saleswoman in a large department store.

"That did it, "she said. "I immediately found myself in a whirlwind of activity: customers swarming around me, asking for prices, sizes, colours. Never a second to think of anything except my immediate duty; and when night came, I could think of nothing except getting off my aching feet. As soon as I ate dinner, I fell into bed and instantly became unconscious. I had neither the time nor the energy to worry."

She discovered for herself what John Cowper Powys meant when he said, in *The Art of Forgetting the Unpleasant*: "A certain comfortable security, a certain profound inner peace, a kind of happy numbness, soothes the nerves of the human animal when absorbed in its allotted task."

And what a blessing that it is so! Osa Johnson, the world's most famous woman explorer, recently told me how she found release from worry and grief. You may have read the story of her life. It is called *I Married Adventure*. If any woman ever married adventure, she certainly did. Martin Johnson married her when she was sixteen and lifted her feet off the sidewalks of Chanute, Kansas, and set them down on the wild jungle trails of Borneo. For a quarter of a century, this Kansas couple travelled all over the world, making motion pictures of the vanishing wild life of Asia and Africa. Back in America nine years ago, they were on a lecture tour, showing their famous films. They took a plane out of Denver, bound for the Coast. The plane plunged into a mountain. Martin Johnson was killed instantly. The doctors said Osa would never leave her bed again. But they didn't know Osa Johnson. Three months later, she was in

我没有他们的姓名,这是增加故事可靠性的细节。我不喜欢不带姓名地址地举例。)

这对夫妇告诉我,他们的儿子在“珍珠港事变”的第二天加入陆军部队。母亲当时很担忧她的独生子,使她的健康严重受损。她常常想他在哪里?是不是安全?是不是在打仗?会不会受伤?会不会阵亡?

我问她是怎么克服忧虑的,她回答说:“我让自己忙着。”她告诉我,她先是把女佣辞退,试图做家务保持忙碌,可是作用不大。“问题是,”她说,“我做家务总是机械式的,完全不用思想。所以当我铺床和洗碟子时,还总是担忧。我发现我需要一些新的工作,才能使我每时每刻都能身心忙碌,于是我去了一家大百货公司当售货员。

“这次好了,”她说,“我马上发现自己身处一个运动的大漩涡:四周全是顾客,问价钱、尺码、颜色等。除了工作,我没有一秒钟想其他问题。到了晚上,我也只能想如何让双脚休息一下。吃完晚饭之后,我躺在床上很快就睡着了。我既没有时间,也没有精力忧虑。”

她发现的这一点,正如约翰·科伯尔·波斯在《忘记不快的艺术》一书中所说的:“一种舒适的安全感, 种内在的宁静,一种因快乐的迟钝,都能使人在专心工作时精神平静。”

能做到这一点的人实在太幸运了!世界最著名的女冒险家奥莎·琼森最近告诉我,她是如何从忧虑悲伤中解脱出来的。你也许读过她的自传《与冒险结缘》。如果说有哪个女人能跟冒险结缘,那就是她。马丁·琼森在她16岁时娶了她,在堪萨斯州查那提镇的街上将她一把抱起,直到婆罗洲的原始森林才把她放下。25年来,这对来自堪萨斯州的夫妇周游了全世界,拍下了亚洲和非洲逐渐绝迹的野生动物的影片。当他们9年前回到美国,到处旅行演讲时,放映了他们的电影。有一次,他们在丹佛城乘飞机前往西海岸,飞机撞在山上,马丁·琼森当场死亡,医生说奥莎也永远不能再下床了。可是他们并不了解奥莎·琼森。3个月后,她就坐着一辆轮椅,当着一大群人演讲。事实上,她在那段时间做了100多场演讲,每次都是坐轮椅去的。当我问她为什么要

a wheel chair, lecturing before large audiences. In fact, she addressed over a hundred audiences that season—all from a wheel chair. When I asked her why she did it, she replied, "I did it so that I would have no time for sorrow and worry."

Osa Johnson had discovered the same truth that Tennyson had sung about a century earlier: "I must lose myself in action, lest I wither in despair."

Admiral Byrd discovered this same truth when he lived all *alone* for five months in a shack that was literally buried in the great glacial ice-cap that covers the South Pole—an ice-cap that holds nature's oldest secrets—an ice-cap covering an unknown continent larger than the United States and Europe combined. Admiral Byrd spent five months there alone. No other living creature of any kind existed within a hundred miles. The cold was so intense that he could hear his breath freeze and crystallise as the wind blew it past his ears. In his book Alone, Admiral Byrd tells all about those five months he spent in bewildering and soul-shattering darkness. The days were as black as the nights. He had to keep busy to preserve his sanity.

"At night, "he says, "before blowing out the lantern, I formed the habit of blocking out the morrow's work. It was a case of assigning myself an hour, say, to the Escape Tunnel, half an hour to leveling drift, an hour to straightening up the fuel drums, an hour to cutting bookshelves in the walls of the food tunnel, and two hours to renewing a broken bridge in the man-hauling sledge...

"It was wonderful, "he says, "to be able to dole out time in this way. It brought me an extraordinary sense of command over myself..." And he adds, "Without that or an equivalent, the days would have been *without purpose; and without purpose they would have ended, as such days always end, in disintegration.*"

Note that last again: "Without purpose, the days would have ended, as such days always end, in disintegration."

If you and I are worried, let's remember that we can use good old-fashioned work as a medicine. That was said by no less an authority than the late Dr. Richard C. Cabot, formerly professor of clinical medicine at Harvard. In his book *What Men* Live By, Dr. Cabot says, "As a physician, I have had the happiness of seeing work cure many persons who have suffered from trembling palsy of the soul which results from overmastering doubts, hesitations, vacillation and

这样做时，她回答说："我这样做，是想让我没有时间悲伤忧虑。"

奥莎·琼森发现了丹尼森先生一个世纪前曾在诗中说的同一真理："我必须让自己沉浸在工作中，否则我会在绝望中死去。"

海军上将拜德也是在覆盖着冰雪的南极小茅屋里单独住了5个月而发现这个道理的。在那冰天雪地里，是一片无人知晓、比美国和欧洲加起来还要大的大陆。拜德上将单独在那里待了5个月，周围100英里以内没有任何生物。天出奇的冷，当风吹过他耳边的时候，他能听见他的呼吸几乎冻住了，结得像水晶一样。他在《孤寂》这本书里，叙述了他在既难过又可怕的黑暗中度过的那5个月。他不得不一直忙着，才不至于发疯。

"在夜晚，"他说，"熄灯之前，我养成了安排第二天工作的习惯。也就是说，我要为自己安排工作。比如，一小时检查逃生隧道，半小时挖横坑，一小时检查燃料罐，一小时在放食物的隧道墙上挖地方放书，再花两小时修整雪橇……

"能把时间分开，"他说，"是一件非常好的事。这使我产生了一种可以主宰自我的感觉……要是没有这些工作，那日子就过得漫无目标了。而没有目标的话，这些日子就会像平常一样，最后崩溃。"

（注意最后那句话："没有目标，这些日子就会像平常一样，最后崩溃。"）

要是我们忧虑的话，就让我们记住，我们可以把工作当作一种很好的古老疗法。原哈佛大学临床医学教授、已故博士理查德·卡伯特在《生活的条件》这本书中也说过："作为一个医生，我很高兴地看到，工作可以治愈很多病人。他们所患的病，是由于过分疑惧、迟疑、踌躇和恐惧造成的。工作带给我们的勇气，就像爱默生永垂不朽的自信一样。"

如果你和我不能一直忙着，如果我们呆坐发愁的话，我们就会孵出许多达尔文称之为"胡思乱想"的东西，而这些"胡思乱想"犹如传说中的魔鬼，会掏空我们的思想，摧毁我们的行动和

fear... Courage given us by our work is like the self-reliance which Emerson has made for ever glorious." If you and I don't keep busy—if we sit around and brood—we will hatch out a whole flock of what Charles Darwin used to call the"wibber gibbers". And the"wibber gibbers"are nothing but old-fashioned gremlins that will run us hollow and destroy our power of action and our power of will.

I know a businessman in New York who fought the "wibber gibbers"by getting so busy that he had no time to fret and stew. His name is Tremper Longman, and his office is at 40 Wall Street. He was a student in one of my adult-education classes; and his talk on conquering worry was so interesting, so impressive, that I asked him to have a late supper with me after class; and we sat in a restaurant until long past midnight, discussing his experiences. Here is the story he told me: "Eighteen years ago, I was so worried I had insomnia. I was tense, irritated, and jittery. I felt I was headed for a nervous breakdown.

"I had reason to be worried. I was treasurer of the Crown Fruit and Extract Company, 418 West Broadway, New York. We had half a million dollars invested in strawberries packed in gallon tins. For twenty years, we had been selling these gallon tins of strawberries to manufactures of ice cream. Suddenly our sales stopped because the big ice-cream makers, such as National Dairy and Borden's, were rapidly increasing their production and were saving money and time by buying strawberries packed in barrels. Not only were we left with half a million dollars in berries we couldn't sell, but we were also under contract to buy a million dollars more of strawberries in the next twelve months! We had already borrowed $350,000 from the banks. We couldn't possibly pay off or renew these loans. No wonder I was worried!

"I rushed out to Watsonville, California, where our factory was located, and tried to persuade our president that conditions had changed, that we were facing ruin. He refused to believe it. He blamed our New York office for all the trouble—poor salesmanship.

"After days of pleading, I finally persuaded him to stop packing more strawberries and to sell our new supply on the fresh berry market in San Francisco. That almost solved our problems. I should have been able to stop worrying then; but I couldn't. Worry is a habit; and I had that habit.

"When I returned to New York, I began worrying about everything: the cherries we were

意志。

我认识纽约的一个商人，他就是用忙碌来赶走"胡思乱想"，使自己没有时间烦恼和忧虑的。他叫查伯尔·朗曼，办公室在40大街；他也是我成人教育班的学员。他征服忧虑的经历非常有意思，也非常特殊，所以上完课之后我请他和我一起去吃宵夜。我们在一间餐馆一直坐到半夜，谈他的经历。下面就是他告诉我的故事："18年前，我因为忧虑患上了失眠症。我紧张不安，爱发脾气。我想我快要精神崩溃了。

"我之所以发愁，是有原因的。当时我是纽约市西百老汇418号皇冠水果制品公司的财务经理。我们投资50万美元，把草莓装在一加仑的罐子里。20年来，我们一直向冰淇淋厂销售这种一加仑装的草莓。

"突然，我们的销售大跌，因为那些大冰淇淋厂商的产量迅速增加，他们为了节省开支和时间，都买桶装草莓。

"我们50万美元的草莓不仅卖不出去，而且根据合同，我们在接下来的一年还要再购买100万美元的草莓。我们已经向银行借了35万美元，既还不出钱，也不能再续借贷款，我当然担忧了！

"我赶到我们在加州华生维里的工厂，想让总经理相信情况有所改变，我们将面临毁灭。但他不肯相信，而是把这些问题都归罪给纽约的公司以及那些可怜的业务员。

"经过几天的协商，我终于说服他不再用这种包装，把新包装投放在旧金山市场上卖。这几乎可以解决我们的问题，因此我应该不再忧虑了；可我还是有些担忧。忧虑是一种习惯，而我已经染上这种习惯了。

"回到纽约后，我开始担心每一件事：在意大利买的樱桃、在夏威夷买的凤梨……我紧张不安，睡不着觉，就像我刚才所说的，简直精神崩溃了。

buying in Italy, the pineapples we were buying in Hawaii, and so on. I was tense, jittery, couldn't sleep; and, as I have already said, I was heading for a nervous breakdown.

"In despair, I adopted a way of life that cured my insomnia and stopped my worries. I got busy. I got so busy with problems demanding all my faculties that I had no time to worry. I had been working seven hours a day. I now began working fifteen and sixteen hours a day. I got down to the office every morning at eight o'clock and stayed there every night until almost midnight. I took on new duties, new responsibilities. When I got home at midnight, I was so exhausted when I fell in bed that I became unconscious in a few seconds.

"I kept up this program for about three months. I had broken the habit of worry by that time, so I returned to a normal working day of seven or eight hours. This event occurred eighteen years ago. I have never been troubled with insomnia or worry since then."

George Bernard Shaw was right. He summed it all up when he said: *"The secret of being miserable is to have the leisure to bother about whether you are happy or not."* So don't bother to think about it! Spit on your hands and get busy. Your blood will start circulating; your mind will start ticking—and pretty soon this whole positive upsurge of life in your body will drive worry from your mind. *Get* busy. *Keep* busy. It's the cheapest kind of medicine there is on this earth—and one of the best.

To break the worry habit, here is:

Rule 1: Keep busy. The worried person must lose himself in action, lest be wither in despair.

"在绝望中,我换了一种新的生活方式,它治好了我的失眠症和忧虑。我一直忙着,忙到必须全力以赴,根本没有时间忧虑。以前我一天工作7小时,现在一天工作十五六个小时。我每天早上8点就到办公室,一直干到半夜。我接下新的工作,担负起新的责任。每当我半夜回家时,总是筋疲力尽地躺在床上,不过几秒钟就浑然入睡。

"这样过了将近3个月,我改掉了忧虑的习惯,恢复到每天工作七八个小时的正常情形。这事情发生在18年前。从那以后,我再也没有失眠和忧虑过。"

萧伯纳说得对,他总结这些说:"人们之所以忧虑,就是有空闲来想自己到底快乐不快乐。"所以,不必去想它!在手掌心吐口唾沫,让自己忙起来,你的血液就会开始循环,你的思想就会变得敏锐——不久这种积极的情绪就会驱除思想上的忧虑。让自己一直忙着!这是世界上治疗忧虑最便宜、最有效的良药。

要改掉忧虑的习惯,下面是第一条规则:

保持忙碌。忧虑的人一定要让自己沉浸在工作中,否则会在绝望中挣扎。

2 Don't Let the Beetles Get You Down

Here is a dramatic story that I'll probably remember as long as I live. It was told to me by Robert Moore, of 14 Highland Avenue, Maplewood, New Jersey.

"I learned the biggest lesson of my life in March, 1945, "he said, "I learned it under 276 feet of water off the coast of Indo-China. I was one of eighty-eight men aboard the submarine *Baya* S. S. 318. We had discovered by radar that a small Japanese convoy was coming our way. As daybreak approached, we submerged to attack. I saw through the periscope a Jap destroyer escort, a tanker, and a mine layer.

"We fired three torpedoes at the destroyer escort, but missed. Something went haywire in the mechanics of each torpedo. The destroyer, not knowing that she had been attacked, continued on. We were getting ready to attack the last ship, the mine layer, when suddenly she turned and came directly at us. (A Japanese plane had spotted us under sixty feet of water and had radioed our position to the Japanese mine layer.) We went down to 150 feet, to avoid detection, and rigged for a depth charge. We put extra bolts on the hatches; and, in order to make our sub absolutely silent, we turned off the fans, the cooling system, and all electrical gear.

"Three minutes later, all hell broke loose. Six depth charges exploded all around us and pushed us down to the ocean floor—a depth of 276 feet. We were terrified. To be attacked in less than a thousand feet of water is dangerous—less than five hundred feet is almost always fatal. And we were being attacked in a trifle more than half of five hundred feet of water—just about knee-deep, as far as safety was concerned. For fifteen hours, that Japanese mine layer kept dropping depth charges.

"If a depth charge explodes within seventeen feet of a sub, the concussion will blow a hole in it. Scores of these depth charges exploded within fifty feet of us. We were ordered'to secure' —to lie quietly in our bunks and remain calm. I was so terrified I could hardly breathe.'this is death,'I kept saying to myself over and over.'This is death! ... This is death! 'With the fans

第2章 不要为小事而垂头丧气

下面这个富有戏剧性的故事我也许终身难忘。讲述这个故事的人叫罗伯特·摩尔,他住在新泽西马普伍德市14大道。

"1945年3月,我学到了我人生当中最重要的一课。"他说,"我是在中南半岛附近276英尺深的海底学到的。当时,我和另外87个人一起在贝雅S.S.318号潜水艇上。我们从雷达上发现正有一小支日本舰队朝我们这边驶来。天将亮的时候,我们浮出水面发动攻击。我从潜望镜里发现了一艘日本驱逐护航舰、一艘油轮和一艘布雷舰。

"我们向那艘驱逐护航舰发射了三枚鱼雷,但未击中目标。那艘驱逐护航舰并不知道正遭受攻击,继续向前驶去。我们又打算攻击最后那艘布雷舰。突然,它转过头径直朝我们驶来。(有一架日本飞机从上空看见我们在深水下,把我们的位置用无线电通知了日本布雷舰。)我们潜到150英尺深处,以免被它探测到,同时做好准备应付深水炸弹:我们在所有的舱盖上都多加了几层铁栓,同时为了让我们的潜艇保持绝对稳定,我们关掉了所有的电扇和冷却系统及发电设备。

"3分钟后,突然天崩地裂:6枚深水炸弹在我们四周爆炸,把我们推到海底276英尺深处。我们吓呆了!在不到1000英尺深的海水里遭受攻击是很危险的——如果不到500英尺几乎难逃厄运。而我们当时却在不到500英尺一半深的水下受到攻击,从安全角度来说,水深等于只到膝盖部分。那艘日本布雷舰不停地投深水炸弹,连续攻击15个小时。

"如果深水炸弹距潜水艇不到17英尺,炸弹可以在潜艇上炸出一个大洞来。大约有十几颗深水炸弹就在离我们50英尺的地方爆炸,我们奉命'固守'——静躺在床上,保持镇定。我吓得

and cooling system turned off, the air inside the sub was over a hundred degrees; but I was so chilled with fear that I put on a sweater and a fur-lined jacket; and still I trembled with cold. My teeth chattered. I broke out in a cold, clammy sweat. The attack continued for fifteen hours. Then ceased suddenly. Apparently the Japanese mine layer had exhausted its supply of depth charges, and steamed away. Those fifteen hours of attack seemed like fifteen million years. All my life passed before me in review.

"I remembered all the bad things I had done, all the little absurd things I had worried about. I had been a bank clerk before I joined the Navy. I had worried about the long hours, the poor pay, the poor prospects of advancement. I had worried because I couldn't own my own home, couldn't buy a new car, couldn't buy my wife nice clothes. How I had hated my old boss, who was always nagging and scolding! I remembered how I would come home at night sore and grouchy and quarrel with my wife over trifles. I had worried about a scar on my forehead—a nasty cut from an auto accident.

"How big all these worries seemed years ago! But how absurd they seemed when depth charges were threatening to blow me to kingdom come. I promised myself then and there that if I ever saw the sun and the stars again, I would never, never worry again. Never! Never!! Never!!! I learned more about the art of living in those fifteen terrible hours in that submarine than I had learned by studying books for four years in Syracuse University."

We often face the major disasters of life bravely—and then let the trifles, the "pains in the neck", get us down. For example, Samuel Pepys tells in his *Diary* about seeing Sir Harry Vane's head chopped off in London. As Sir Harry mounted the platform, he was not pleading for his life, but was pleading with the executioner not to hit the painful boil on his neck!

That was another thing that Admiral Byrd discovered down in the terrible cold and darkness of the polar nights—that his men fussed more about the "pains in the neck"than about the big things. They bore, without complaining, the dangers, the hardships, and the cold that was often eighty degrees below zero. "But, "says Admiral Byrd, "I know of bunkmates who quit speaking because each suspected the other of inching his gear into the other's allotted space; and I knew of one who could not eat unless he could find a place in the mess hall out of sight of the Fletcherist who

几乎无法呼吸。'这下死定了。'我一直不停地对自己说着,'这下死定了……这下死定了。'电扇和冷却系统全都关闭之后,潜水艇内的温度高达华氏100多度,可是我却害怕得全身发冷,虽然穿了一件毛衣,还有一件皮领夹克,可还是冷得发抖。我的牙齿不停地打颤,全身冒出阵阵冷汗。攻击持续了15个小时,然后突然停止。显然,那艘日本布雷舰用光了所有的深水炸弹,这才离开。这15个小时的攻击,就像是1500万年。过去的生活一一呈现在我眼前。

"我记起了以前做过的所有坏事,以及我曾担心的所有小事。在加入海军之前,我是一个银行职员,曾为工作时间太长、薪水太少而且没有多少升迁机会发愁。我曾经因为没有办法买自己的房子、没有钱买新车、没有钱给我太太买好衣服而忧虑。我非常讨厌我以前的老板,他老是给我找麻烦。我还记得,每天晚上回到家里的时候,我总是又累又困,常常因为芝麻小事而跟我太太吵架。我甚至还为我额头上一次车祸留下的伤痕发愁。

"在多年以前,那些令人发愁的事看起来很大!可是在深水炸弹就要夺走我生命的那一刻,这些事情又是多么的荒谬和微不足道。就在那时候,我答应自己,如果我还有机会活下去,永远也不会再忧虑了。永远!永远!!永远!!!在潜艇那15个可怕的小时里,我所学到的生活道理比我在大学4年所学的要多得多。"

我们通常能勇敢地面对生活中的重大危机,可是却会被那些小事情搞得焦头烂额。例如,萨姆尔·白布西在他的日记里写到他曾目睹哈里·维尼爵士在伦敦被砍头的事:当哈里爵士走上断头台的时候,他没有请求饶命,却要求刽子手不要砍他颈上的痛伤之处。

这也是拜德上将在又冷又黑的南极洲的夜晚发现的另外一点——他手下那些人常常为小事情发火,但对大事却不在乎。他们毫无怨言地面对危险和艰苦,在零下80度的寒冷中工作。"可是,"拜德上将说,"我却知道他们之间有好几个人同在一办公室彼此不讲话,因为他们怀疑别人乱放东西,占了他们的地方。我还知道一个人,他一定要在大厅里找一个看不见他的位置

solemnly chewed his food twenty-eight times before swallowing.

"In a polar camp, "says Admiral Byrd, "little things like that have the power to drive even disciplined men to the edge of insanity."

And you might have added, Admiral Byrd, that "little things"in marriage drive people to the edge of insanity and cause"half the heartaches in the world."

At least, that is what the authorities say. For example, Judge Joseph Sabath of Chicago, after acting as arbiter in more than forty thousand unhappy marriages, declared, "Trivialities are at the bottom of most marital unhappiness"; and Frank S. Hogan, former District Attorney of New York County, says, "Fully half the cases in our criminal courts originate in little things. Barroom bravado, domestic wrangling, an insulting remark, a disparaging word, a rude action—those are the little things that lead to assault and murder. Very few of us are cruelly and greatly wronged. It is the small blows to our self-esteem, the indignities, the little jolts to our vanity, which cause half the heartaches in the world."

When Eleanor Roosevelt was first married, she "worried for days"because her new cook had served a poor meal. "But if that happened now, "Mrs. Roosevelt said, "I would shrug my shoulders and forget it." Good. That is acting like an adult emotionally. Even Catherine the Great, an absolute autocrat, used to laugh the thing off when the cook spoiled a meal.

Mrs. Carnegie and I had dinner at a friend's house in Chicago. While carving the meat, he did something wrong. I didn't notice it; and I wouldn't have cared even if I had noticed it. But his wife saw it and lumped down his throat right in front of us. "John, "she cried, "watch what you are doing! Can't you ever learn to serve properly! "

Then she said to us, "He is always making mistakes. He just doesn't try." Maybe he didn't try to carve; but I certainly give him credit for trying to live with her for twenty years. Frankly, I would rather have eaten a couple of hot dogs with mustard—in an atmosphere of peace—than to have dined on Peking duck and shark fins while listening to her scolding.

Shortly after that experience, Mrs. Carnegie and I had some friends at our home for dinner. Just before they arrived, Mrs. Carnegie found that three of the napkins didn't match the tablecloth.

"I rushed to the cook, "she told me later, "and found that the other three napkins had gone to

坐着才能吃下饭。他坚持空腹进食，每口食物一定要嚼过28次才吞下去。

"在南极营地，"拜德上将说，"一些小事情都能把最训练有素的人逼疯。"

拜德上将还可以加上一句话：婚姻中的"小事"也会把人逼疯，造成"世界上半数伤心事"。

至少这话是权威人士说的。例如，芝加哥的约瑟夫·沙巴士法官在仲裁4万多件不愉快的婚姻案件之后说："小事是导致婚姻生活不美满的根本原因。"纽约州前地方检察官弗兰克·霍根也说："在我们的刑事案件里，一半以上都是由小事情引起的：在酒吧里逞英雄，为小事情争吵，讲话侮辱人，措辞不当，行为粗鲁——这些小事情导致了伤害和谋杀。很少有人天性残忍。正是因为自尊心受到了小小的伤害，或受到屈辱，或虚荣心得不到满足，结果造成了世界上半数令人伤心之事。"

罗斯福夫人刚结婚的时候，每天都在担心，因为她的新厨子做饭很差。"可是，如果事情发生在现在，"罗斯福夫人说，"我就会耸耸肩忘了它。"太好了，这才是成年人的做法。就连凯瑟琳这位最专制的俄国女皇，当厨子把饭做坏时，也只是付之一笑。

我和我夫人曾去芝加哥一个朋友家里吃饭。分菜的时候，他出了点差错。我当时并没有注意，而且即使注意到了也不会在意。可是他太太看见了，立即当着我们的面指责他。"约翰，"她尖叫道，"看看你在做什么！难道你永远也学不会如何分菜？"

然后她对我们说："他老是犯错，简直心不在焉。"也许他确实没有好好做，可是我却实在佩服他和他太太相处20年之久。老实说，只要舒服，我情愿只吃抹了芥末的热狗，而不愿一面听她啰嗦，一面吃北京烤鸭和鱼翅。

那件事情之后不久，我夫人和我请了几位朋友到家里来吃晚饭。就在他们快到的时候，我夫人发现有3条餐巾和桌布的颜色没办法相配。

"我冲到厨房，"她后来告诉我，"结果发现另外3条餐巾送出去洗了。客人这时已经到了门

the laundry. The guests were at the door. There was no time to change. I felt like bursting into tears! All I could think was, 'why did this stupid mistake have to spoil my whole evening?' Then I thought—well—why let it? I went in to dinner, determined to have a good time. And I did. I would much rather our friends think I was a sloppy housekeeper," she told me, "than a nervous, bad-tempered one. And anyhow, as far as I could make out, no one noticed the napkins!"

A well-known legal maxim says: *De minimis non curat lex*—"the law does not concern itself with trifles." And neither should the worrier—if he wants peace of mind.

Much of the time, all we need to overcome the annoyance of trifles is to affect a shifting of emphasis—set up a new, and pleasurable, point of view in the mind. My friend Homer Croy, who wrote *They Had to See Paris* and a dozen other books, gives a wonderful example of how this can be done. He used to be driven half crazy, while working on a book, by the rattling of the radiators in his New York apartment. The steam would bang and sizzle—and he would sizzle with irritation as he sat at his desk.

"Then," says Homer Croy, "I went with some friends on a camping expedition. While listening to the limbs crackling in the roaring fire, I thought how much they sounded like the crackling of the radiators. Why should I like one and hate the other? When I went home I said to myself, 'The crackling of the limbs in the fire was a pleasant sound; the sound of the radiators is about the same—I'll go to sleep and not worry about the noise.' And I did. For a few days I was conscious of the radiators; but soon I forgot all about them.

"And so it is with many petty worries. We dislike them and get into a stew, all because we exaggerate their importance..."

Disraeli said, "Life is too short to be little." "Those words," said André Maurois in *This Week* magazine, "have helped me through many a painful experience: often we allow ourselves to be upset by small things we should despise and forget... Here we are on this earth, with only a few more decades to live, and we lose many irreplaceable hours brooding over grievances that, in a year's time, will be forgotten by us and by everybody. No, let us devote our life to worthwhile actions and feelings, to great thoughts, real affections and enduring undertakings. For life is too short to be little."

口。我没有时间再换了。我急得差点哭出来。我当时只想:'为什么会犯这么愚蠢的错误,毁了整个晚上?'然后我又想,为什么要让它毁了呢?于是,我走进去吃晚饭,决定好好享受一下。我真的做到了。我情愿让我的朋友认为我是一个懒散的家庭主妇,"她告诉我,"也不想让他们认为我是一个神经兮兮、脾气暴躁的女人。而且据我所知,根本没有人关心那些餐巾。"

一条众所周知的法律名言说:"法律不管小事。"人也不该为小事而忧虑——如果他希望心理平静的话。

在大多数时间里,要想克服由小事所引起的困扰,只需把重点转移就可以——让你有一个新的、开心的想法。我的朋友荷马·克罗伊是一个作家,写过几本书。他举了一个如何做到这一点的好例子。他以前写作的时候总是被纽约公寓散热器的响声吵得发疯。蒸气会砰然作响,他听到之后会坐在书桌前气得直叫。

"后来,"荷马·克罗伊说,"有一次我和几个朋友一起去露营时,听到了木柴烧得很响的声音,我突然想到这些声音多么像散热器的响声。但我为什么会喜此厌彼呢?回到家以后,我对自己说:'火堆中木头的爆裂声很好听,散热器的声音也差不多,我应该埋头就睡,不必理会这些噪音。'结果,我真的做到了。头几天我还会注意散热器的声音,可是不久我就完全忘了。

"很多其他的小忧虑也是一样,因为我们不喜欢,结果令人颓丧,这都是因为我们夸大了它们的重要性……"

狄斯累利也曾说:"生命如此短暂,不能只顾小事。""这些话,"安德烈·莫瑞斯在《本周》杂志中说,"曾经帮我熬过了很多痛苦的经历:我们常常会因为一些本可不屑一顾的小事而弄得心烦意乱……我们活在这个世上只有短短的几十年,而我们却浪费了许多不可挽回的时间,去为一些一年之内就会被所有人忘了的小事而发愁。不要这样!我们要去实践那些值得做的事情和感觉,想伟大的思想,经历真正的感情,做必须做的事。因为生命如此短暂,不能只顾小事。"

Even so illustrious a figure as Rudyard Kipling forgot at times that "Life is too short to be little". The result?He and his brother-in-law fought the most famous court battle in the history of Vermont—a battle so celebrated that a book has been written about it: *Rudyard Kipling's Vermont Feud.*

The story goes like this: Kipling married a Vermont girl, Caroline Balestier, built a lovely home in Brattleboro, Vermont; settled down and expected to spend the rest of his life there. His brother-in-law, Beatty Balestier, became Kipling's best friend. The two of them worked and played together.

Then Kipling bought some land from Balestier, with the understanding that Balestier would be allowed to cut hay off it each season. One day, Balestier found Kipling laying out a flower garden on this hayfield. His blood boiled. He hit the ceiling. Kipling fired right back. The air over the Green Mountains of Vermont turned blue!

A few days later, when Kipling was out riding his bicycle, his brother-in-law drove a wagon and a team of horses across the road suddenly and forced Kipling to take a spill. And Kipling—the man who wrote, "If you can keep your head when all about you are losing theirs and blaming it on you"—he lost his own head, and swore out a warrant for Balestier's arrest! A sensational trial followed. Reporters from the big cities poured into the town. The news flashed around the world. Nothing was settled. This quarrel caused Kipling and his wife to abandon their American home for the rest of their lives. All that worry and bitterness over a mere trifle! A load of hay.

Pericles said, twenty-four centuries ago: "Come, gentlemen, we sit too long on trifles." We do, indeed!

Here is one of the most interesting stories that Dr. Harry Emerson Fosdick ever told—a story about the battles won and lost by a giant of the forest:

On the slope of Long's Peak in Colorado lies the ruin of a gigantic tree. Naturalists tell us that it stood for some four hundred years. It was a seedling when Columbus landed at San Salvador, and half grown when the Pilgrims settled at Plymouth. During the course of its long life it was struck by lightning fourteen times, and the innumerable avalanches and storms of four centuries thundered past it. It survived them all. In the end, however, an army of beetles attacked the tree and leveled it

即使是吉布林这样有名的人,有时也会忘了"生命如此短暂,不能只顾小事"的道理。结果呢?他和他的舅爷在弗蒙特打了有史以来最有名的一场官司。这场官司如此出名,有一本专辑记载了它,书名叫《吉布林在弗蒙特的领地》。

事情的经过是这样的:吉布林娶了一个弗蒙特女孩凯洛琳·巴里斯蒂尔,在弗蒙特的布拉陀布罗建了一栋很漂亮的房子,在那里定居,准备度过余生。他的舅爷比提·巴里斯蒂尔成了吉布林最好的朋友,他们两个人一同工作,一同游玩。

后来, 吉布林从巴里斯蒂尔那里买了一块地, 事先约定巴里斯蒂尔每一季可以在那里割草。一天,巴里斯蒂尔发现吉布林在那片草地上开了一个花园,他生气了,暴跳如雷。吉布林则反唇相讥。弗蒙特的绿山上乌云笼罩。

几天之后,吉布林骑自行车出去,他的舅爷突然赶着一辆马车和几匹马横穿马路,使吉布林摔了一跤。而吉布林这个曾写过"众人皆醉,你应独醒"的人也昏了头,告到官府,将巴里斯蒂尔关押起来。接下来是一场轰动一时的官司,一些大城市的记者都挤到这个小镇来,这件新闻传遍了全世界。事情无法解决,这次争吵使得吉布林和他的妻子永远离开了他们在美国的家。而这一切忧虑和争吵,仅仅是一件小事——一车干草。

皮瑞克里斯在2400年前说过:"来吧,诸位! 我们在小事上浪费太多时间了。"的确如此!

下面是哈里·爱默生·福斯迪克博士讲的最有意思的一个故事——森林里的一个巨人在战争中如何得胜、又如何失败的。

"在科罗拉多州长山的山坡上,躺着一棵大树的枯枝残躯。自然学家告诉我们,它活了400多年。它发芽时,哥伦布刚登陆美洲;第一批移民来到美国时,它才长一半大。在它漫长的生命历程里,曾被闪电击中14次,无数次狂风暴雨侵袭过它,它都能战胜。但是最后来了一小队甲虫,使它倒在地上。那些甲虫从根部往树里面咬,渐渐伤了树的元气,而它们就只靠细小而持续

to the ground. The insects ate their way through the bark and gradually destroyed the inner strength of the tree by their tiny but incessant attacks. A forest giant which age had not withered, nor lightning blasted, nor storms subdued, fell at last before beetles so small that a man could crush them between his forefinger and his thumb.

Aren't we all like that battling giant of the forest?Don't we manage somehow to survive the rare storms and avalanches and lightning blasts of life, only to let our hearts be eaten out by little beetles of worry—little beetles that could be crushed between a finger and a thumb?

A few years ago, I travelled through the Teton National Park, in Wyoming, with Charles Seifred, highway superintendent for the state of Wyoming, and some of his friends. We were all going to visit the John D. Rockefeller estate in the park. But the car in which I was riding took the wrong turn, got lost, and drove up to the entrance of the estate an hour after the other cars had gone in. Mr. Seifred had the key that unlocked the private gate, so he waited in the hot, mosquito-infested woods for an hour until we arrived. The mosquitoes were enough to drive a saint insane. But they couldn't triumph over Charles Seifred. While waiting for us, he cut a limb off an aspen tree—and made a whistle of it. When we arrived, was he cussing the mosquitoes?No, he was playing his whistle. I have kept that whistle as a memento of a man who knew how to put trifles in their place.

To break the worry habit before it breaks you, here is Rule 2:

Let's not allow ourselves to be upset by small things we should despise and forget. Remember"Life is too short to be little."

不断的攻击。这样一个森林巨人,岁月不曾使它枯萎,闪电不曾将它击倒,狂风暴雨不能伤着它,最后因为一小队大拇指和食指就可以捏死的小甲虫而倒了。"

我们不都像森林中那棵身经百战的大树吗?我们不也经历过生命中无数次狂风暴雨和闪电的打击吗？可是我们却会被心中忧虑的小甲虫咬噬——用大拇指和食指就可以捏死的小甲虫。

几年前，我去了一趟怀俄明州的提顿国家公园。与我同行的是怀俄明州公路局局长查尔斯·谢弗雷德及其朋友。我们本来都想去参观洛克菲勒在那个公园里的一栋房子,可是我坐的那辆车转错一个弯迷了路,等我到达那栋房子时,比其他车晚了一个小时。谢弗雷德先生有打开大门的钥匙,但他却在那个天气又热、蚊子又多的森林里等了一个小时。那里的蚊子多得会让圣人发疯,可是它们不能战胜查尔斯·谢弗雷德。他在等我们时折下一小段白杨树枝,做了一根小笛子。当我们到达时,他是不是正驱赶蚊子呢?不,他正在吹笛子,我认为这个笛子是对一个知道如何避开小事的人的纪念。

要想在忧虑毁了你之前先改掉忧虑的习惯,下面是规则的第二条：

不要让自己因为一些应该抛弃和忘记的小事而忧虑。

要记住:"生命如此短暂,不要为小事而忧虑。"

3 A Law That Will Outlaw Many of Your Worries

As a child, I grew up on a Missouri farm; and one day, while helping my mother pit cherries, I began to cry. My mother said, "Dale, what in the world are you crying about?"I blubbered, "I'm afraid I am going to be buried alive! "

I was full of worries in those days. When thunderstorms came, I worried for fear I would be killed by lightning. When hard times came, I worried for fear we wouldn't have enough to eat. I worried for fear I would go to hell when I died. I was terrified for fear an older boy, Sam White, would cut off my big ears—as he threatened to do. I worried for fear girls would laugh at me if I tipped my hat to them. I worried for fear no girl would ever be willing to marry me. I worried about what I would say to my wife immediately after we were married. I imagined that we would be married in some country church, and then get in a surrey with fringe on the top and ride back to the farm... but how would I be able to keep the conversation going on that ride back to the farm?How?How?I pondered over that earth-shaking problem for many an hour as I walked behind the plough.

As the years went by, I gradually discovered that ninety-nine per cent of the things I worried about never happened.

For example, as I have already said, I was once terrified of lightning; but I now know that the chances of my being killed by lightning in any one year are, according to the National Safety Council, only one in three hundred and fifty thousand.

My fear of being buried alive was even more absurd: I don't imagine that one person in ten million was buried alive; yet I once cried for fear of it.

One person out of every eight dies of cancer. If I had wanted something to worry about, I should have worried about cancer—instead of being killed by lightning or being buried alive.

To be sure, I have been talking about the worries of youth and adolescence. But many of our adult worries are almost as absurd. You and I could probably eliminate nine-tenths of our worries right now if we would cease our fretting long enough to discover whether, *by the law of averages*,

第3章 平均概率可以战胜忧虑

我从小生活在密苏里州的一个农场。一天，我正帮母亲摘樱桃，突然哭了起来。母亲问："戴尔，你哭什么啊?"我哽咽道："我怕被活埋。"

那时我总是充满了忧虑：暴风雨来的时候，我担心被雷电击死；日子困难的时候，我担心东西不够吃；我还怕死了之后会下地狱；我怕一个名叫萨姆·怀特的大男孩会割下我的两只大耳朵——就像他威胁的那样。我还忧虑女孩子在我向她们脱帽鞠躬时取笑我；忧虑将来没女孩子愿意嫁给我；忧虑我们结婚之后我对我太太第一句话该说什么。我想象我们在一间乡下教堂结婚，然后坐一辆上面垂着流苏的马车回农庄……可是在回农庄的路上我该如何不停地跟她谈话呢?怎么办?怎么办?我在耕地时也会常常花几个小时想这些大问题。

一年年过去，我渐渐发现我担心的那些事99%从都不会发生。

例如我刚才说过，我以前怕雷电。可是现在我知道，不论是哪一年，我被雷电击中的概率大概只有三十五万分之一。

我害怕被活埋的忧虑更是荒谬。我没有想到，每1000万人只有一个人被活埋，可是我却因为害怕而哭过。

每8个人就有一个人死于癌症。如果我一定要发愁的话，我应该为癌症发愁——而不应该担心被雷电打死或被活埋。

事实上，我刚才说的都是我童年和少年时代的忧虑。可是许多成年人的忧虑也几乎同样荒谬。要是我们能根据平均概率来评估我们的忧虑，并真正做到长时间不再忧虑，你和我就可以去除90%的忧虑。

全世界最有名的伦敦罗艾得保险公司就靠人们对一些根本很难发生的事情的担忧而大发

there was any real justification for our worries.

The most famous insurance company on earth—Lloyd's of London—has made countless millions of dollars out of the tendency of everybody to worry about things that rarely happen. Lloyd's of London bets people that the disasters they are worrying about will never occur. However, *they don't call it betting. They call it insurance. But it is really betting based on the law of averages.* This great insurance firm has been going strong for two hundred years; and unless human nature changes, it will still be going strong fifty centuries from now by insuring shoes and ships and sealing-wax against disasters that, *by the law of average*, don't happen nearly so often as people imagine.

If we examine the law of averages, we will often be astounded at the facts we uncover. For example, if I knew that during the next five years I would have to fight in a battle as bloody as the Battle of Gettysburg, I would be terrified. I would take out all the life insurance I could get. I would draw up my will and set all my earthly affairs in order. I would say, "I'll probably never live through that battle, so I had better make the most of the few years I have left." Yet the facts are that, according to the law of averages, it is just as dangerous, just as fatal, to try to live from age fifty to age fifty-five in peacetime as it was to fight in the Battle of Gettysburg. What I am trying to say is this: in times of peace, just as many people die per thousand between the ages of fifty and fifty-five as were killed per thousand among the 163,000 soldiers who fought at Gettysburg.

I wrote several chapters of this book at James Simpson's Num-Ti-Gah Lodge, on the shore of Bow Lake in the Canadian Rockies. While stopping there one summer, I met Mr. and Mrs. Herbert H. Salinger, of 2298 Pacific Avenue, of San Francisco. Mrs. Salinger, a poised, serene woman, gave me the impression that she had never worried. One evening in front of the roaring fireplace, I asked her if she had ever been troubled by worry. "Troubled by it?"she said. "My life was almost *ruined* by it. Before I learned to conquer worry, I lived through eleven years of self-made hell. I was irritable and hot-tempered. I lived under terrific tension. I would take the bus every week from my home in San Mateo to shop in San Francisco. But even while shopping, I worried myself into a dither: maybe I had left the electric iron connected on the ironing board. Maybe the house had caught fire. Maybe the maid had run off and left the children. Maybe they had been out on their bicycles and been killed by a car. In the midst of my shopping, I would often worry myself into a cold perspiration and rush out and take the bus

其财。罗艾得保险公司是在跟一般人打赌，说他们担心的灾祸永远不会发生。不过，他们不称此为赌博，而称为“保险”，这实际上是以平均概率为基础的赌博。这家大保险公司已经良性发展200年了，除非人的本性会改变，它至少还可以继续维持5000年，替你保鞋子、船、封蜡的险，利用平均概率向你保证那些灾祸并不像人们想象的那么常见。

如果我们检查平均概率，就会因我们所发现的事实而惊讶。例如，如果我知道在5年之内我必须参加一次像葛底斯堡战役那样惨烈的战役，我一定会吓坏了。我一定会尽力购买所有的人寿保险，会写下遗嘱，把所有的财产安置好。我会说：“我大概挺不过这场战争，所以我最好痛痛快快地度过余生。”但事实上，根据平均概率，和平时代50~55岁之间的人和葛底斯堡战役中战死的人比例相同。也就是说，在和平时代，50~55岁的人每1000个人的死亡人数，和葛底斯堡战役16.3万名士兵每1000人阵亡的人数相同。

本书有几章是我在加拿大落基山弓湖边的辛普森旅馆写的。有一年夏天，我在那里遇到了旧金山市的赫伯特·萨林吉夫妇。萨林吉太太是一个平静沉着的女人，她给我的印象是她从来没有忧虑。一天晚上，我们坐在熊熊的炉火前，我问她是不是曾经因为忧虑而烦恼过。“烦恼?”她说，“我以前的生活几乎被忧虑毁了。在我学会征服忧虑之前，我在自我的苦难中生活了11年。那时我脾气很坏，又很急躁，生活在紧张的情绪中。我每个星期都要从家里搭公共汽车去旧金山买东西，可是即使买东西时，我也会担心得要命：也许我又把电熨斗放在熨衣板上了；也许房子着火了；也许女佣人丢下孩子跑了；也许孩子们骑脚踏车出去被汽车撞死了。我买东西的时候，常常会因为忧虑而冷汗直冒，会冲出店去，搭公共汽车回家，看看一切是否正常。所以我的第一次婚姻没有好结果。

“我第二个丈夫是律师。他是一个很平静、凡事都能仔细分析的人，从不为任何事情忧虑。每当我神情紧张或焦虑时，他就会对我说：‘放松，让我们好好想想……你真正担心的是什么?让我们来看看平均概率，这种事情究竟会不会发生。’

home to see if everything was all right. No wonder my first marriage ended in disaster.

"My second husband is a lawyer—a quiet, analytical man who never worries about anything. When I became tense and anxious, he would say to me, 'Relax. Let's think this out... What are you really worrying about?Let's examine the law of averages and see whether or not it is likely to happen.'

"For example, I remember the time we were driving from Albuquerque, New Mexico, to the Carlsbad Caverns—driving on a dirt road—when we were caught in a terrible rainstorm.

"The car was slithering and sliding. We couldn't control it. I was positive we would slide off into one of the ditches that flanked the road; but my husband kept repeating to me: 'I am driving very slowly. Nothing serious is likely to happen. Even if the car does slide into the ditch, by the law of averages, we won't be hurt.'His calmness and confidence quieted me.

"One summer we were on a camping trip in the Touquin Valley of the Canadian Rockies. One night, we were camping seven thousand feet above sea level, when a storm threatened to tear our tents to shreds. The tents were tied with guy ropes to a wooden platform. The outer tent shook and trembled and screamed and shrieked in the wind. I expected every minute to see our tent torn loose and hurled through the sky. I was terrified! But my husband kept saying: 'Look, my dear, we are travelling with Brewster's guides. Brewster's know what they are doing. They have been pitching tents in these mountains for sixty years. This tent has been here for many seasons. It hasn't blown down yet and, by the law of averages, it won't blow away tonight; and even if it does, we can take shelter in another tent. So relax...'I did; and I slept soundly the balance of the night.

"A few years ago an infantile–paralysis epidemic swept over our part of California. In the old days, I would have been hysterical. But my husband persuaded me to act calmly. We took all the precautions we could: we kept our children away from crowds, away from school and the movies. By consulting the Board of Health, we found out that even during the worst infantile–paralysis epidemic that California had ever known up to that time, only 1,835 children had been stricken in the entire state of California. And that the usual number was around two hundred or three hundred. Tragic as those figures are, we nevertheless felt that, according to the law of averages, the chances of any one child being stricken were remote.

"'By the law of averages, it won't happen.'That phrase has destroyed ninety per cent of my worries; and it has made the past twenty years of my life beautiful and peaceful beyond my highest expectations."

"例如,我记得有一次我们从新墨西哥州的阿布库基开车去卡斯白洞窟,走在一条脏路上,遇到了一场可怕的暴风雨。

"汽车一路打滑,没法控制。我想我们会滑到路边的水沟里,可是我丈夫一直不停地对我说:'我现在开得很慢,不会出事的。即使车子滑到沟里,根据平均概率,我们也不会受伤。'他的镇定和信心使我平静下来。

"有一年夏天,我们去加拿大的落基山区托昆谷露营。一天晚上,我们的营帐扎在海拔很高的地方,突然下起了暴风雨,我们的帐篷都快被撕成碎片了。帐篷用绳子绑在一个木制平台上,外面的帐篷在风中摇晃着,发出尖啸声。我每一分钟都在想:我们的帐篷要被吹垮,吹到天上去了。我真的吓坏了,可是我丈夫不停地说:'亲爱的,我们有好几个布鲁斯特向导,他们对这些了如指掌。他们在这些山地里扎营60年了,这个营帐在这里也过了很长时间,可是至今还没有被吹倒。根据平均概率,今天晚上也不会被吹掉。而且即使被吹掉,我们还可以去另外的营帐,所以请放松……'我放松心情,后半夜睡得很香。

"几年前,小儿麻痹在加利福尼亚我们住的那一带肆虐。要是在以前,我一定会不知所措,可是我丈夫让我镇定,我们尽可能地采取了各种预防方法,不让孩子们出入公共场所,暂时不去上学看电影。与卫生署联系之后,我们得知,到目前为止即使加州曾发生过的最严重的一次小儿麻痹症流行期,整个加州也只有1835名儿童患病。而平常只在二三百人之间。虽然这些数字听起来让人害怕,可是我们觉得,根据平均概率,某一个孩子感染的可能性实在是很小。

"'根据平均概率,这种事不会发生。'这一句话就消除了我90%的忧虑,使我过去20年的生活过得美好而平静,超出了我的最高期望。"

乔治·克鲁克将军——他可能是美国历史上最伟大的印第安战士——在他的自传中说:印第安人"所有的忧虑和不幸来自他们的想象,而非现实"。

General George Crook—probably the greatest Indian fighter in American history—says in his *Autobiography* that "nearly all the worries and unhappiness" of the Indians "came from their imagination and not from reality."

As I look back across the decades, I can see that that is where most of my worries came from also. Jim Grant toll me that that had been his experience, too. He owns the James A. Grant Distributing Company, 204 Franklin Street, New York City. He orders from ten to fifteen car-loads of Florida oranges and grapefruit at a time. He told me that he used to torture himself with such thoughts as: What if there's a train wreck? What if my fruit is strewn all over the countryside? What if a bridge collapses as my cars are going across it? Of course, the fruit was insured; but he feared that if he didn't deliver his f ruit on time, he might risk the loss of his market. He worried so much that he feared he had stomach ulcers and went to a doctor. The doctor told him there was nothing wrong with him except jumpy nerves. "I saw the light then," he said, "and began to ask myself questions. I said to myself: 'Look here, Jim Grant, how many fruit cars have you handled over the years?' The answer was: 'About twenty-five thousand.' Then I asked myself: 'How many of those cars were ever wrecked?' The answer was: 'Oh—maybe five.' Then I said to myself: 'Only five—out of twenty-five thousand? Do you know what that means? A ratio of five thousand to one! In other words, by the law of averages, based on experience, the chances are five thousand to one against one of your cars ever being wrecked. So what are you worried about?'

"Then I said to myself: 'Well, a bridge may collapse!' Then I asked myself: 'How many cars have you actually lost from a bridge collapsing?' The answer was—'None.' Then I said to myself: 'Aren't you a fool to be worrying yourself into stomach ulcers over a bridge which has never yet collapsed, and over a railroad wreck when the chances are five thousand to one against it!'

"When I looked at it that way," Jim Grant told me, "I felt pretty silly. I decided then and there to let the law of averages do the worrying for me—and I have not been troubled with my 'stomach ulcer' since!"

When A1 Smith was Governor of New York, I heard him answer the attacks of his political enemies by saying over and over: "Let's examine the record... let's examine the record." Then he proceeded to give the facts. The next time you and I are worrying about what may happen, let's take a tip from wise old Al Smith: let's examine the record and see what basis there is, if any, for our gnawing anxieties.

That is precisely what Frederick J. Mahlstedt did when he feared he was lying in his grave.

当我回顾过去的几十年时，我发现我的大部分忧虑也来源于此。吉姆·格兰特告诉我，他的经历也是如此。他是纽约富兰克林大街格兰特批发公司的老板。他每次都要从佛罗里达州买10~15车的橘子等水果。他告诉我，他以前常常会因为某些想法而折磨自己：火车失事怎么办？水果滚得满地都是怎么办？如果车子正好经过一座桥时，桥突然垮了怎么办？当然，这些水果都是投了保险的，可他还是担心万一他没有按时把水果送到，就可能失去市场。他甚至担心自己忧虑过度而得了胃溃疡，因此去看医生。医生告诉他，他没有别的毛病，只是太紧张了。"这时我才明白，"他说，"我开始问自己一些问题。我对自己说：'注意，吉姆·格兰特，这么多年你买了多少车水果？'答案是：'大概2.5万车。'然后我问自己：'有多少出过车祸？'答案是：'大概有5次。'然后我对自己说：'一共2.5万次，只有5次出事，你知道这是什么意思？五千分之一。换句话说，根据平均概率，以经验为依据，出事的机会只有5000:1。有什么好担心的？'

"然后我对自己说：'嗯，说不定桥会塌下来。'然后我问自己：'过去究竟有多少车因为桥塌陷而损失了？'答案是：'一次也没有。'然后我对自己说：'那你为了一座根本没有塌过的桥，为了五千分之一的火车失事而忧虑得胃溃疡，不是太傻了吗？'

"当我这样来看时，"吉姆·格兰特告诉我，"我觉得自己太傻了。于是我当时就做出决定，以后让平均概率来替我分忧——从那以后，我再也没有为'胃溃疡'烦恼过。"

当埃尔·史密斯担任纽约州长的时候，我常听到他对攻击他的政敌说："让我们看看纪录……让我们看看纪录。"然后他会说出许多事实。如果下一次你为可能发生的事情而忧虑，就学这位聪明的埃尔·史密斯先生：查一查以前的纪录，看看我们的忧虑是否有道理。

这也正是当年弗雷德里克·马尔斯塔特担心自己躺在坟墓中的时候所做的。下面是他在我们纽约成人教育班所讲的故事：

"1944年6月初，我躺在奥玛哈海滩附近一个狭长的战壕里。我当时正在999信号连服役，部

Here is his story as he told it to one of our adult-education classes in New York:

"Early in June, 1944, I was lying in a slit trench near Omaha Beach. I was with the 999th Signal Service Company, and we had just 'dug in' in Normandy. As I looked around at that slit trench—just a rectangular hole in the ground—I said to myself: 'This looks just like a grave.' When I lay down and tried to sleep in it, it *felt* like a grave. I couldn't help saying to myself: '*maybe this is my grave.*' When the German bombers began coming over at 11 p. m., and the bombs started falling, I was scared stiff. For the first two or three nights I couldn't sleep at all. By the fourth or fifth night, I was almost a nervous wreck. I knew that if I didn't do something, I would go stark crazy. So I reminded myself that five nights had passed, and I was still alive; and so was every man in our outfit. Only two had even been injured, and they had been hurt, not by German bombs, but by falling flak, from our own anti-aircraft guns. I decided to stop worrying by doing something constructive. So I built a thick wooden roof over my slit trench, to protect myself from flak. I thought of the vast area over which my unit was spread. I told myself that the only way I could be killed in that deep, narrow slit trench was by a direct hit; and I figured out that the chance of a direct hit on me was not one in ten thousand. After a couple of nights of looking at it in this way, I calmed down and slept even through the bomb raids!"

The United States Navy used the statistics of the law of averages to buck up the morale of their men. One ex-sailor told me that when he and his shipmates were assigned to high-octane tankers, they were worried stiff. They all believed that if a tanker loaded with high-octane gasoline was hit by a torpedo, it exploded and blew everybody to kingdom come.

But the U. S. Navy knew otherwise; so the Navy issued exact figures, showing that out of one hundred tankers hit by torpedoes sixty stayed afloat; and of the forty that did sink, only five sank in less than ten minutes. That meant time to get off the ship—it also meant casualties were exceedingly small. Did this help morale? "This knowledge of the law of averages wiped out my jitters," said Clyde W. Maas, of 1969 Walnut Street, St. Paul, Minnesota—the man who told this story. "The whole crew felt better. We knew we had a chance; and that, by the law of averages, we probably wouldn't be killed."

To break the worry habit before it breaks you—here is Rule 3:

"Let's examine the record." Let's ask ourselves: "What are the chances, according to the law of averages, that this event I am worrying about will ever occur?"

队刚刚抵达诺曼底。我看了一眼那个狭长战壕——正好在地上成一长方形——然后对自己说：'这看起来像一座坟墓。'当我躺下来准备睡在里面的时候，它更像一座坟墓了。我忍不住对自己说：'也许这就是我的坟墓。'晚上11点，德军轰炸机开始飞过来，炸弹纷纷往下投，我吓得全身僵住了。前两三个晚上，我无法入睡。到了第四天或第五天晚上，我几乎精神崩溃。我知道如果我不想办法的话，我会疯掉。所以我提醒自己说：5个晚上都过了，我还活得好好的，我们这一组的人也都活着，只有两个人受了轻伤。他们不是被德军的炸弹炸伤的，而是被我们自己的高射炮弹碎片打中的。我决定做一些有意义的事情来停止忧虑。于是我在战壕里做了一个厚厚的木头屋顶，保护自己不被碎弹片击中。我计算了一下位置和距离，告诉自己：只有炸弹直接命中，我才有可能被打死在这个又深又窄的战壕里。我又算出了直接命中的比率，不到万分之一。这样，我平静下来，即使敌机来袭也睡得非常安稳。"

美国海军也常常利用平均概率统计出来的数据激励士兵。一位以前当过海军的人告诉我，当他和他船上的伙伴被派到一艘油轮上时，他们都吓坏了。这艘油轮运的是高单位汽油，他们都认为如果油轮被鱼雷击中，每个人都会上西天。

可是美国海军自有办法。海军部队发了一些数据，指出被鱼雷击中的100艘油轮有60艘并没有沉没，而真正沉到海里的40艘中只有5艘是在10分钟之内沉没的。那就是说，有足够的时间跳船，死在船上的可能性非常小。这样对士气有没有帮助呢？"知道了平均法则之后，我的忧虑一扫而光。"明尼苏达州圣保罗市瓦纳特大街1969号的克莱德·马斯说，"船上的人都感觉好多了。我们知道我们有机会，根据平均概率，我们不会死。"

因此，要在忧虑摧毁你之前先改掉忧虑的习惯，下面是规则的第三条：

"让我们看看纪录，让我们根据平均概率问问自己，现在担心会发生的事情，发生的机会是多少？"

4 Cooperate with the Inevitable

When I was a little boy, I was playing with some of my friends in the attic of an old, abandoned log house in north-west Missouri. As I climbed down out of the attic, I rested my feet on a windowsill for a moment—and then jumped. I had a ring on my left forefinger; and as I jumped, the ring caught on a nail-head and tore off my finger.

I screamed. I was terrified. I was positive I was going to die. But after the hand healed, I never worried about it for one split second. What would have been the use?... I accepted the inevitable.

Now I often go for a month at a time without even thinking about the fact that I have only three fingers and a thumb on my left hand.

A few years ago, I met a man who was running a freight elevator in one of the downtown office buildings in New York. I noticed that his left hand had been cut off at the wrist. I asked him if the loss of that hand bothered him. He said, "Oh, no, I hardly ever think about it. I am not married; and the only time I ever think about it is when I try to thread a needle."

It is astonishing how quickly we can accept almost any situation—if we have to—and adjust ourselves to it and forget about it.

I often think of an inscription on the ruins of a fifteenth-century cathedral in Amsterdam, Holland. This inscription says in Flemish: "It is so. It cannot be otherwise."

As you and I march across the decades of time, we are going to meet a lot of unpleasant situations that are so. They cannot be otherwise. We have our choice. We can either accept them as inevitable and adjust ourselves to them, or we can ruin our lives with rebellion and maybe end up with a nervous breakdown.

Here is a bit of sage advice from one of my favourite philosophers, William James. "*Be willing to have it so,* "he said. "*Acceptance of what has happened is the first step to overcoming the consequence of any misfortune.*" Elizabeth Connley, of 2840 NE 49th Avenue, Portland, Oregon,

第4章 接受不可避免的事实

小时候我曾和几个朋友一起在密苏里州西北部一栋荒废的老木屋的阁楼上玩耍。我从阁楼爬下来的时候，我先在窗栏上站住，然后跳下去。我左手的食指戴了一枚戒指。就在我跳下去的时候，那枚戒指钩住了一颗铁钉，我的手指拉断了。

我尖叫着，吓得不知所措，以为必死无疑。可是手好了之后，我再也没有为这件事忧虑过。这又有什么用呢?我接受了这个不可避免的事实。

我现在根本不会想到我的左手只有三个手指和一个大拇指。

几年前，我碰到一个人，他在纽约市中心一家办公大楼开运货电梯。我注意到他的左手被齐腕割断了。我问他缺了那只手是否觉得难过。他说："噢，不会，我根本就不会想到它。我没结婚，只有在穿针的时候才会想起此事。"

如果有必要，我们几乎可以很快接地受任何情况，使自己适应它，然后完全忘了它。这多么令人吃惊啊!

我经常想到一行字，它刻在荷兰阿姆斯特丹一座15世纪老教堂的废墟上："事实就是这样，而不是别样。"

在漫长的岁月里，你和我一定会遇到一些令人不快的事情，既然它们是这样，就不可能是别样。我们也可以有所选择：或者把它们当作不可避免的事实而加以接受并适应它们；或者用忧虑来摧毁我们的生活，最后精神崩溃。

下面是我最喜欢的哲学家之一威廉·詹姆斯的忠告："乐于承认事实如此，" 他说，"接受已经发生的事实，是克服随之而来的任何不幸的第一步。"俄勒冈州波特南市的伊丽莎白·康黎，经过很多困难

had to find that out the hard way. Here is a letter that she wrote me recently: "On the very day that America was celebrating the victory of our armed forces in North Africa, "the letter says, "I received a telegram from the War Department: my nephew—the person I loved most—was missing in action. A short time later, another telegram arrived saying he was dead.

"I was prostrate with grief. Up to that time, I had felt that life had been very good to me. I had a job I loved. I had helped to raise this nephew. He represented to me all that was fine and good in young manhood. I had felt that all the bread I had cast upon the waters was coming back to me as cake! ...

"Then came this telegram. My whole world collapsed. I felt there was nothing left to live for. I neglected my work; neglected my friends. I let everything go. I was bitter and resentful. Why did my loving nephew have to be taken?Why did this good boy—with life all before him—why did he have to be killed?I couldn't accept it. My grief was so overwhelming that I decided to give up my work, and go away and hide myself in my tears and bitterness.

"I was clearing out my desk, getting ready to quit, when I came across a letter that I had forgotten—a letter from this nephew who had been killed, a letter he had written to me when my mother had died a few years ago.

"'Of course, we will miss her, 'the letter said, 'and especially you. But I know you'll carry on. Your own personal philosophy will make you do that. I shall never forget the beautiful truths you taught me. Wherever I am, or how far apart we may be, I shall always remember that you taught me to smile, and to take whatever comes, like a man. '

"I read and reread that letter. It seemed as if he were there beside me, speaking to me. He seemed to be saying to me: 'Why don't you do what you taught me to do?Carry on, no matter what happens. Hide your private sorrows under a smile and carry on. '

"So, I went back to my work. I stopped being bitter and rebellious. I kept saying to myself, 'It is done. I can't change it. But I can and will carry on as he wished me to do. 'I threw all my mind and strength into my work. I wrote letters to soldiers—to other people's boys. I joined an adult-education class at night—seeking out new interests and making new friends. I can hardly believe the change that has come over me. I have ceased mourning over the past that is forever gone. I am

才学到这一道理。下面是她最近写给我的一封信:"在美国庆祝我们陆军在北非获胜的那一天,"信中说,"我接到一封国防部送来的电报:我的侄儿——我最爱的人——在战场上失踪了。没过多久,又一封电报说他死了。

"我悲伤之极。在那之前,我一直觉得命运对我很好。我有自己喜欢的工作,抚养侄儿成人。在我看来,他代表了年轻人一切美好的东西。我觉得自己以前所有的努力现在都得到了回报……

"然后,来了这封电报,我的整个世界碎了,觉得再活下去毫无意义。我开始忽视工作、朋友。我开始抛弃一切,既冷淡又怨恨。为什么我最亲爱的侄儿会死?为什么这么好的孩子,还没有开始生活却要死在战场上?我无法接受这个事实。我悲伤过度,决定放弃工作,远离家乡,把自己埋在泪水和痛苦之中。

"就在我清理桌子,准备辞职的时候,突然看到一封我早已忘了的信。这是我已故侄儿的信。几年前我母亲去世的时候,他给我写了这封信。

"'当然,我们都会想念她,'信上说,'尤其是你。但是我知道你一定能挺过去。以你个人的人生哲学,你能挺过去。我永远都不会忘记你教给我的美好真理:不论在哪里,也不论我们离得多远,我永远都会记得你教我要微笑,要像一个男子汉,勇于承受既成事实。'

"我把那封信读了一遍又一遍,觉得他好像就在我身边,正在对我说话。他好像对我说:'为什么不照你教我的办法去做呢?挺住!不论发生什么事情!把你个人的悲伤掩藏在微笑之下,继续过下去。'

"于是,我又回去工作,不再对人冷淡无礼。我一再告诫自己:'事情既已发生,我不能改变它,但是我能够像他所希望的那样去做。'我将所有的思想和精力都投入到工作上,我给士兵们写信——他们是别人的儿子;晚上,我又参加了成人教育班——寻找新兴趣,结识新朋友。我几乎不敢相信

living each day now with joy—just as my nephew would have wanted me to do. I have made peace with life. I have accepted my fate. I am now living a fuller and more complete life than I had ever known."

Elizabeth Connley, out in Portland, Oregon, learned what all of us will have to learn sooner or later: namely, that we must accept and cooperate with the inevitable. "It is so. It cannot be otherwise." That is not an easy lesson to learn. Even kings on their thrones have to keep reminding themselves of it. The late George V had these framed words hanging on the wall of his library in Buckingham Palace:

"Teach me neither to cry for the moon nor over spilt milk." The same thought is expressed by Schopenhauer in this way: "A good supply of resignation is of the first importance in providing for the journey of life."

Obviously, *circumstances alone do not make us happy or unhappy. It is the way we react to circumstances that determines our feelings.* Jesus said that the kingdom of heaven is within you. That is where the kingdom of hell is, too.

We can all endure disaster and tragedy and triumph over them—if we have to. We may not think we can, but we have surprisingly strong inner resources that will see us through if we will only make use of them. We are stronger than we think.

The late Booth Tarkington always said, "I could take anything that life could force upon me except one thing: blindness. I could never endure that."

Then one day, when he was along in his sixties, Tarkington glanced down at the carpet on the floor. The colours were blurred. He couldn't see the pattern. He went to a specialist. He learned the tragic truth: he was losing his sight. One eye was nearly blind; the other would follow. That which he feared most had come upon him.

And how did Tarkington react to this "worst of all disasters"?Did he feel: "This is *it*! This is the end of my life"?No, to his amazement, he felt quite gay. He even called upon his humour. Floating"specks"annoyed him; they would swim across his eyes and cut off his vision. Yet when the largest of these specks would swim across his sight, he would say, "Hello! There's Grandfather again! Wonder where he's going on this fine morning! "

发生在我身上的变化。我不再为永远过去的事情悲伤。现在我每天都充满了快乐——就像我的侄儿要我做的那样。我的生活已找到宁静港湾。我接受了命运。我现在过着更加充实而有意义的生活。"

伊丽莎白·康黎学到了我们所有人迟早都要学到的道理,那就是我们必须接受和适应不可避免的事实。这一课可不容易学会。就连那些在位的皇帝也必须经常提醒自己这样做。已故的乔治五世在白金汉宫的图书馆墙上挂有下面的名言:

"我不要为月亮哭泣,也不要因事而后悔。"叔本华则也表达了同样的想法,他说:"顺应势事,是踏上人生旅途的最重要的一件事。"

显然，环境本身并不能使我们快乐或不快乐，只有我们对环境的反应才决定了我们的感受。耶稣说天国就在你的心中。而那也是地狱所在之处。

在必要的时候,我们都可以忍受灾难和悲剧,甚至战胜它们。我们会认为自己办不到,但我们有令人惊讶的潜能,只要我们愿意利用,它就能帮助我们克服一切困难。我们比我们想象的更强大。

已故的布斯·塔金顿总是说:"人生加诸我身上的任何事情,我都能承受,但除了一样:那就是失明。我永远无法忍受失明。"

在他60多岁的时候,有一天当他低头看地上的地毯时,发现色彩模糊,看不清图案。他去找了一个眼科专家,证实了不幸的事实:他的视力在衰减,有一只眼睛几乎全瞎,另一只也快瞎了。他最怕的事情终于发生在他身上。

对这种"所有灾难中最可怕的灾难",塔金顿有何反应呢?他是不是觉得"完了,我这一辈子完了"?没有,他自己也没想到他还能非常开心,甚至还能善用他的幽默。以前眼球里面浮动的"黑斑"令他很难过,当它们在眼前游过时,会遮挡他的视线;现在,当那些最大的黑斑从眼前晃

How could fate ever conquer a spirit like that?The answer is it couldn't. When total blindness closed in, Tarkington said, "I found I could take the loss of my eyesight, just as a man can take anything else. If I lost all five of my senses, I know I could live on inside my mind. For it is in the mind we see, and in the mind we live, whether we know it or not."

In the hope of restoring his eyesight, Tarkington had to go through more than twelve operations within one year. With *local* anesthetic! Did he rail against this?He knew it had to be done. He knew he couldn't escape it, so the only way to lessen his suffering was to take it with grace. He refused a private room at the hospital and went into a ward, where he could be with other people who had troubles, too. He tried to cheer them up. And when he had to submit to repeated operations—fully conscious of what was being done to his eyes—he tried to remember how fortunate he was. "How wonderful! "he said. "How wonderful, that science now has the skill to operate on anything so delicate as the human eye! "

The average man would have been a nervous wreck if he had had to endure more than twelve operations and blindness. Yet Tarkington said, "I would not exchange this experience for a happier one." It taught him acceptance. It taught him that nothing life could bring him was beyond his strength to endure. It taught him, as John Milton discovered, that "It is not miserable to be blind, it is only miserable not to be able to endure blindness."

If we rail and kick against it and grow bitter, we won't change the inevitable; but we will change ourselves. I know. I have tried it.

I once refused to accept an inevitable situation with which I was confronted. I played the fool and railed against it, and rebelled. I turned my nights into hells of insomnia. I brought upon myself everything I didn't want. Finally, after a year of self-torture, I had to accept what I knew from the outset I couldn't possibly alter.

I should have cried out years ago with old Walt Whitman:

Oh, to confront night, storms, hunger, ridicule, accident, rebuffs as the trees and animals do.

I spent twelve years working with cattle; yet I never saw a Jersey cow running a temperature because the pasture was burning up from a lack of rain or because of sleet and cold or because her boy friend was paying too much attention to another heifer. The animals confront night, storms,

过时，他却会说："嘿，又是老爷爷来了！今天天气这么好，不知道它要去哪里。"

命运怎么能征服这种乐观呢？当然不能。当塔金顿终于完全失明之后，他说："我发现我也能承受失明的痛苦，就像一个人能承受别的灾难一样。要是我的五种感官完全丧失了，我认为我还能活在我的思想里。因为我们只有在思想中才能看见，只有在思想中才能生活——不论我们是否清楚这一点。"

为了恢复视力，塔金顿在一年之内接受了12次手术。为他做手术的是当地眼科医生。他抱怨了吗?他知道这是必要的，他无法逃避，所以唯一能减轻痛苦的办法就是勇于接受。他拒绝用私人病房，住进普通病房，和其他病人在一起。他试着让其他病人开心，即使在他必须接受好几次手术时——而且他当然很清楚在他眼睛里做什么——他只尽力想他是多么的幸运。"多妙啊，"他说，"多妙啊，现在的科学竟然能为眼睛这么纤细的东西做手术。"

一般人忍受12次以上的手术和长期黑暗的生活，可能会变成神经质了。可是塔金顿却说："我可不愿拿这次经历去换更开心的事。"这件事教会他接受灾难，使他明白生命带给他的没有什么是他不能忍受的；这件事也使他领悟了弥尔顿所说的："失明并不令人难过，难过的是不能忍受失明。"

如果我们抱怨反抗，或者为它难过，也不可能改变不可避免的事实。但是我们可以改变自己，我知道，因为我试过。

有一次，我拒绝接受我遇到的一件不可避免的事情，竟然傻到想反抗它，结果失眠了好几个晚上。我开始让自己想起所有不愿意想的事情，经过一年的自我虐待，我终于接受了不可能改变的事实。

我早就应该喊出沃尔特·惠特曼的名言：

"啊，让我们像树木和牲畜一样，漠视所有不可避免的事实吧！"

and hunger calmly; so they never have nervous breakdowns or stomach ulcers; and they never go insane.

Am I advocating that we simply bow down to all the adversities that come our way?Not by a long shot! That is mere fatalism. As long as there is a chance that we can save a situation, let's fight! But when common sense tells us that we are up against something that is so—and cannot be otherwise—then, in the name of our sanity, let's not look before and after and pine for what is not.

The late Dean Hawkes of Columbia University told me that he had taken a Mother Goose rhyme as one of his mottoes:

For every ailment under the sun.
There is a remedy, or there is none ;
If there be one, try to find it;
If there be none, never mind it.

While writing this book, I interviewed a number of the leading business men of America; and I was impressed by the fact that they cooperated with the inevitable and led lives singularly free from worry. If they hadn't done that, they would have cracked under the strain. Here are a few examples of what I mean:

J. C. Penney, founder of the nation-wide chain of Penney stores, said to me, "I wouldn't worry if I lost every cent I have because I don't see what is to be gained by worrying. I do the best job I possibly can; and leave the results in the laps of the gods."

Henry Ford told me much the same thing. "When I can't handle events, "he said, "I let them handle themselves."

When I asked K. T. Keller, then president of the Chrysler Corporation, how he kept from worrying, he said, "When I am up against a tough situation, if I can do anything about it, I do it. If I can't, I just forget it. I never worry about the future, because I know no man living can possibly figure out what is going to happen in the future. There are so many forces that will affect that future! Nobody can tell what prompts those forces—or understand them. So why worry about them?"K. T. Keller would be embarrassed if you told him he is a philosopher. He is just a good

我曾放了12年的牛，但是从未见过哪条母牛因为草地缺水干枯，或者天气太冷，或者哪条公牛爱上了另一条母牛而恼火。牲畜都能平静地面对一切，所以它们从来不会精神崩溃或者患胃溃疡，也从来不会发疯。

我是不是说碰到任何挫折时，都应该低声下气呢?绝对不是，那就成了宿命论了。只要还有一点机会，我们就要奋斗。可是当常识告诉我们事情已经不可避免，也不会有任何转机时，我们就要保持理智，不要庸人自扰。

哥伦比亚大学已故院长霍基斯曾告诉我，他写了一首打油诗作他的座右铭：

天下疾病多，数都数不清。有些可以救，有的难治愈。
如果有希望，就应把药寻。要是无法治，不如忘干净。

在写这本书的时候，我拜访过美国许多有名的商人。令我印象深刻的是，他们能接受不可避免的事实，过着无忧无虑的生活。如果他们不能这样做，就会在巨大的压力之下垮掉。下面就是几个例子：

潘尼是遍及全国的潘氏连锁商店的创始人，他告诉我："即使我所有的钱都赔光了，我也不会忧虑，因为忧虑并不能让我得到什么。我会尽可能把工作做好；至于结果，就要看老天爷了。"

亨利·福特也告诉过我类似的话："当我碰到无法处理的事情时，我就让它们自己去解决。"

当我问克莱斯勒公司总经理凯勒先生，他是如何避免忧虑的，他说："如果我碰到了棘手的问题，只要我能想出解决办法的，我就去做。否则，我就把它忘了。我从来不替未来担心，因为没有人能知道未来会发生什么，影响未来的因素太多了，也没有人知道这些影响来自哪里。所以，何必为它们担心呢?"如果你认为凯勒是个哲学家，他一定会不安的，他只是一个出色的商人。可是他的这一观念正好与19个世纪以前罗马哲学家爱匹克泰德的理论相近。"快乐的源泉，"他说，"就是不要为我们的意志力所不及的事情而忧虑。"

businessman, yet he has stumbled on the same philosophy that Epictetus taught in Rome nineteen centuries ago. "There is only one way to happiness, "Epictetus taught the Romans, "and that is to cease worrying about things which are beyond the power of our will."

Sarah Bernhardt, the "divine Sarah"was an illustrious example of a woman who knew how to cooperate with the inevitable. For half a century, she had been the reigning queen of the theatre on four continents—the best-loved actress on earth. Then when she was seventy-one and broke—she had lost all her money—her physician, Professor Pozzi of Paris, told her he would have to amputate her leg. While crossing the Atlantic, she had fallen on deck during a storm, and injured her leg severely. Phlebitis developed. Her leg shrank. The pain became so intense that the doctor felt her leg had to be amputated. He was almost afraid to tell the stormy, tempestuous "divine Sarah"what had to be done. He fully expected that the terrible news would set off an explosion of hysteria. But he was wrong. Sarah looked at him a moment, and then said quietly, "If it has to be, it has to be." It was fate.

As she was being wheeled away to the operating room, her son stood weeping. She waved to him with a gay gesture and said cheerfully, "Don't go away. I'll be right back."

On the way to the operating room, she recited a scene from one of her plays. Someone asked her if she were doing this to cheer herself up. She said, "No, to cheer up the doctors and nurses. It will be a strain on them."

After recovering from the operation, Sarah Bernhardt went on touring the world and enchanting audiences for another seven years.

"When we stop fighting the inevitable, "said Elsie Mac-Cormick in a *Reader's Digest* article, "we release energy which enables us to create a richer life."

No one living has enough emotion and vigour to fight the inevitable and, at the same time, enough left over to create a new life. Choose one or the other. You can either bend with the inevitable sleet-storms of life—or you can resist them and break!

I saw that happen on a farm I own in Missouri. I planted a score of trees on that farm. At first, they grew with astonishing rapidity. Then a sleet-storm encrusted each twig and branch with a heavy coating of ice. Instead of bowing gracefully to their burden, these trees proudly resisted and

"神女"莎拉·班哈特可以说是最懂得如何适应不可避免的事实的女性。50年来,她一直是四大州剧院独一无二的"皇后",是全世界最受喜爱的女演员。可是她71岁那一年破产了,所有的钱都没了,而她的医生、巴黎的波兹教授还告诉她必须把腿锯掉。她在横渡大西洋时遇到暴风雨,滑倒在甲板上,腿受了重伤,得了静脉炎和腿痉挛。剧烈的痛苦使医生觉得必须锯掉她的腿。医生害怕把这消息告诉脾气很坏的莎拉。他满以为这个可怕的消息一定会使莎拉大为恼火。可是他错了,莎拉只是看了他一会儿,然后平静地说:"如果非这样不可,也只好这样了。"这就是命运。

当她被推进手术室时,她的儿子站在一边哭泣。她却朝他挥了挥手,开心地说:"不要走开,我马上回来。"

在去手术室的路上,莎拉一直在背她演过的一场戏中的一幕。有人问她是不是在给自己鼓气,她却说:"不是,我是想让医生和护士们高兴,这样他们就不会紧张了。"

手术恢复之后,莎拉继续环游世界,观众又为她着迷了7年。

"当我们不再反抗那些不可避免的事实时,"爱尔西·麦克密克在《读者文摘》的一篇文章中说,"我们就可以节省精力,创造更丰富的生活。"

任何人都不会有足够的情感和精力去抗拒不可避免的事实,同时又创造新的生活。你只能两者选其一:你可以接受生活中不可避免的灾难,或者抗拒它们而被摧毁。

我在密苏里州我的农场就见过这样的事情。我在农场种了几十棵树, 它们起初长得非常快,然后突然下了一场冻雨,每根小树枝上都覆盖着一层厚厚的冰。这些树枝在重压下并没有顺从弯曲,而是骄傲地反抗着,最终在重压之下折断了,然后归于毁灭。它们不如北方的树木那样聪明。我曾在加拿大看过长达几百里的常青树,从未看见一棵柏树或松树被压垮过。这些常青树知道如何顺从,知道如何垂下枝条,适应不可避免的情况。

broke and split under the load—and had to be destroyed. They hadn't learned the wisdom of the forests of the North. I have travelled hundreds of miles through the evergreen forests of Canada. Yet I have never seen a spruce or a pine broken by sleet or ice. These evergreen forests know how to bend, how to bow down their branches, how to cooperate with the inevitable.

The masters of jujitsu teach their pupils to"bend like the willow; don't resist like the oak."

Why do you think your automobile tyres stand up on the road and take so much punishment?At first, the tire manufacturers tried to make a tire that would resist the shocks of the road. It was soon cut to ribbons. Then they made a tire that would absorb the shocks of the road. That tire could"take it". You and I will last longer, and enjoy smoother riding, if we learn to absorb the shocks and jolts along the rocky road of life.

What will happen to you and me if we resist the shocks of life instead of absorbing them? What will happen if we refuse to "bend like the willow"and insist on resisting like the oak?The answer is easy. We will set up a series of inner conflicts. We will be worried, tense, strained, and neurotic.

If we go still further and reject the harsh world of reality and retreat into a dream world of our own making, we will then be insane.

During the war, millions of frightened soldiers had either to accept the inevitable or break under the strain. To illustrate, let's take the case of William H. Casselius, 7126 76th Street, Glendale, New York. Here is a prize-winning talk he gave before one of my adult-education classes in New York:

"Shortly after I joined the Coast Guard, I was assigned to one of the hottest spots on this side of the Atlantic. I was made a supervisor of explosives. Imagine it. Me! A cracker salesman becoming a supervisor of explosives! The very thought of finding yourself standing on top of thousands of tons of TNT is enough to chill the marrow in a cracker salesman's bones. I was given only two days of instruction; and what I learned filled me with even more terror. I'll never forget my first assignment. On a dark, cold, foggy day, I was given my orders on the open pier of Caven Point, Bayonne, New Jersey.

"I was assigned to Hold No. 5 on my ship. I had to work down in that hold with five

日本柔道大师也教他们的学生"像杨柳一样柔顺,不能像橡树那样挺直。"

你知道你的汽车轮胎为什么能在路上跑那么久,承受那么多颠簸吗?最初,轮胎制造商想制造一种轮胎,可以抵抗路上的各种颠簸,可是轮胎不久就成了碎块。然后他们又发明了一种可以吸收路面各种压力的轮胎,这样轮胎就可以"接受一切"。如果我们在坎坷的人生旅途上能够像轮胎那样吸收各种挫折和颠簸的话,我们就能活得更长久,更顺利。

如果我们不顺服,而是反抗生命中的各种挫折,会发生什么情况呢?如果我们不像柳树那样柔顺,而像橡树那样挺直,又会发生什么呢?答案非常简单:我们就会产生一连串矛盾,就会忧虑、紧张、急躁而神经质。

如果我们再进一步,抛弃现实世界的各种不快,退缩到一个我们自己织造的梦幻世界中,我们就会精神错乱。

战时,成千上万心怀恐惧的士兵只有两种选择:要么接受不可避免的事实,要么在压力之下崩溃。让我们以威廉·卡赛流斯为例。下面就是他在纽约成人教育班上所说的一个得奖的故事:

"我加入海岸防卫队之后不久,被派到大西洋一个最热的地方。我负责管炸药。你们想想,我一个卖小饼干的店员,却成了管炸药的!光是想到站在千万吨TNT顶上,就会让我吓得连骨髓都冻住了。我只接受了两天的训练,而我所学到的那些知识更让我害怕。我永远也忘不了我第一次执行任务的情形。那天又黑又冷,还有大雾,我奉命去新泽西州的卡文角露天码头。

"我负责船上的第五号舱,和5个码头工人一起工作。他们身强力壮,但一点都不知道炸药。他们正将那些有上吨重TNT的炸弹往船上装,足够把那条旧船炸成粉碎。我们用两条铁索把这些炸弹吊下船,我不停地对自己说:万一有一条铁索滑溜了,或者是断了,天啊!我害怕极了,浑身颤抖,嘴里发干,膝盖发软,心跳得厉害。可是我不能跑,那样就是逃跑,不但让我丢脸,连我

longshoremen. They had strong backs, but they knew nothing whatever about explosives. And they were loading blockbusters, each one of which contained a ton of TNT—enough explosive to blow that old ship to kingdom come. These blockbusters were being lowered by two cable slings. I kept saying to myself: Suppose one of those cables slipped—or broke! Oh, boy! Was I scared! I trembled. My mouth was dry. My knees sagged. My heart pounded. But I couldn't run away. That would be desertion. I would be disgraced—my parents would be disgraced—and I might be shot for desertion. I couldn't run. I had to stay. I kept looking at the careless way those longshoremen were handling those blockbusters. The ship might blow up any minute. After an hour or more of this spine-chilling terror, I began to use a little common sense. I gave myself a good talking to. I said: 'Look here! So you are blown up. So what! You will never know the difference! It will be an easy way to die. Much better than dying by cancer. Don't be a fool. You can't expect to live forever! You've got to do this job—or be shot. So you might as well like it. '

"I talked to myself like that for hours; and I began to feel at ease. Finally, I overcame my worry and fears by forcing myself to accept an inevitable situation.

"I'll never forget that lesson. Every time I am tempted now to worry about something I can't possibly change, I shrug my shoulders and say, 'Forget it. 'I find that it works—even for a cracker salesman." Hooray! Let's give three cheers and one cheer more for the cracker salesman of the *Pinafore*.

"*Try to bear lightly what needs must be.*" Those words were spoken 399 years before Christ was born; but this worrying old world needs those words today more than ever before: "*Try to bear lightly what needs must be.*"

To break the worry habit before it breaks you, Rule 4 is:

Cooperate with the inevitable.

的父母也不光彩,而且我可能会因为逃跑而被枪毙。我不能跑,只有留下来。我一直看着码头工人毫不在乎地搬运炸弹。船随时可能被炸掉。这样担惊受怕一个多小时之后,我开始运用我所学到的知识。我对自己谈了许久:'你听着,就算你被炸死,又怎么样?反正你也不会有什么感觉了。这样倒死得痛快,总比死于癌症好得多。不要做傻瓜,你不可能永远活着!这件工作不能不做,否则就会被枪毙。所以你还不如开心些。'

"我这样对自己说了好长时间,然后觉得轻松了些。最后,我克服了忧虑和恐惧,让自己接受了不可避免的情况。

"我永远也忘不了这个教训。现在,每当我因为不可能改变的事实而忧虑时,我就会耸耸肩说:'忘了吧。'我发现这很管用——至少对我。"好极了,让我们大声欢呼,再为这位卖饼干的店员多欢呼一声吧!

"对不可避免的事,轻松地去承受。"这句话是在基督出生前399年说的。但是今天这个充满忧虑的世界比以往更需要这句话:"对不可避免的事,轻松地去承受。"

因此,要在忧虑毁了你以前先改变忧虑的习惯,下面是规则的第四条:

接受不可避免的事实。

5 Put a"Stop-Loss"Order on Your Worries

Would you like to know how to make money on the Stock Exchange?Well, so would a million other people—and if I knew the answer, this book would sell for a fabulous price. However, there's one good idea that some successful operators use. This story was told to me by Charles Roberts, an investment counselor with offices at 17 East 42nd Street, New York.

"I originally came up to New York from Texas with twenty thousand dollars which my friends had given me to invest in the stock market, "Charles Roberts told me. "I thought, "he continued, "that I knew the ropes in the stock market; but I lost every cent. True, I made a lot of profit on some deals; but I ended up by losing everything.

"I did not mind so much losing my own money, "Mr. Roberts explained, "but I felt terrible about having lost my friends' money, even though they could well afford it. I dreaded facing them again after our venture had turned out so unfortunately, but, to my astonishment, they not only were good sports about it, but proved to be incurable optimists.

"I knew I had been trading on a hit-or-miss basis and depending largely on luck and other people's opinions. As H.I.Phillips said, I had been 'playing the stock market by ear'.

"I began to think over my mistakes and I determined that before I went back into the market again, I would try to find out what it was all about. So I sought out and became acquainted with one of the most successful speculators who ever lived: Burton S. Castles. I believed I could learn a great deal from him because he had long enjoyed the reputation of being successful year after year and I knew that such a career was not the result of mere chance or luck.

"He asked me a few questions about how I had traded before and then told me what I believe is the most important principle in trading. He said: 'I put a stop-loss order on every market commitment I make. If I buy a stock at, say, fifty dollars a share, I immediately place a stop-loss order on it at forty-five. 'That means that when and if the stock should decline as much as five points below its cost, it would be sold automatically, thereby, limiting the loss to five points.

第5章 让忧虑"到此为止"

你想不想知道如何在股票交易中赚钱?当然,有上百万以上的人都想知道。如果我知道这个问题的答案,那我这本书就要卖个高价了。不过,有一个很好的理念,很多成功炒股者都应用过它。下面这个故事是查尔斯·罗伯兹告诉我的,他是一个投资顾问,在纽约东42大街17号办公。

"我刚从得克萨斯州来纽约的时候带了两万美元,是我朋友给我用来股票市场投资的。"查尔斯·罗伯兹告诉我,"我原以为,我对股票市场很在行,可是我赔得分文不剩。不错!我在某些交易上赚了几笔,可是最后全都赔光了。

"我并不在乎把自己的钱都赔光了。可我认为把我朋友的钱赔光了却不是件好事,虽然他们都很有钱。在我们的投资出现这种不幸结局之后,我很害怕再见到他们,但我没有想到的是,他们对这件事情不仅看得很开,而且还非常乐观。

"我知道我的交易是漫无目标的,大部分靠运气和别人的股评。就像菲利普说的,我'是靠小道消息炒股'。

"我开始仔细研究我的错误,决定在再度进入股票市场之前,一定要先弄明白股票市场到底是何物。于是,我找到一位最成功的预测专家波顿·卡斯特,和他交上了朋友。我相信我能从他那里学到很多东西,因为他多年来一直非常成功,我知道能做出这番事业的人,不可能全靠机遇和运气。

"他先问了我几个问题,并问我以前是如何操作的,然后又告诉我股票交易中最重要的一条原则。他说:'我在股票市场上购买的每一支股票,都设定了一条止损线。例如,我买了一只50

"'If your commitments are intelligently made in the first place, 'the old master continued, 'your profits will average ten, twenty-five, or even fifty points. Consequently, by limiting your losses to five points, you can be wrong more than half of the time and still make plenty of money?'

"I adopted that principle immediately and have used it ever since. It has saved my clients and me many thousands of dollars.

"After a while I realised that the stop-loss principle could be used in other ways besides in the stock market. I began to place a stop-loss order on any and every kind of annoyance and resentment that came to me. It has worked like magic.

"For example, I often have a luncheon date with a friend who is rarely on time. In the old days, he used to keep me stewing around for half my lunch hour before he showed up. Finally, I told him about my stop-loss orders on my worries. I said: 'Bill, my stop-loss order on waiting for you is exactly ten minutes. If you arrive more than ten minutes late, our luncheon engagement will be sold down the river—and I'll be gone. '"

Man alive! How I wish I had had the sense, years ago, to put stop-loss orders on my impatience, on my temper, on my desire for self-justification, on my regrets, and on all my mental and emotional strains. Why didn't I have the horse sense to size up each situation that threatened to destroy my peace of mind and say to myself: "See here, Dale Carnegie, this situation is worth just so much fussing about—and no more"?... Why didn't I?

However, I must give myself credit for a little sense on one occasion, at least. And it was a serious occasion, too—a crisis in my life—a crisis when I stood watching my dreams and my plans for the future and the work of years vanish into thin air. It happened like this. In my early thirties, I had decided to spend my life writing novels. I was going to be a second Frank Norris or Jack London or Thomas Hardy. I was so in earnest that I spent two years in Europe—where I would live cheaply with dollars during the period of wild, printing-press money that followed the First World War. I spent two years there, writing my magnum opus. I called it *The Blizzard*. The title was a natural, for the reception it got among publishers was as cold as any blizzard that ever howled across the plains of the Dakotas. When my literary agent told me it was worthless, that I had no gift, no talent, for fiction, my heart almost stopped. I left his office in a daze. I couldn't have been more

美元的股票，我设定的止损线是45美元。'也就是说，万一这只股票跌价达到5美元时，就立刻卖出去，这样损失就可以限定在5美元。

"'如果你当初买得很聪明的话，'这位大师继续说，'你可能平均赚10~25美元，甚至50美元。因此，在把你的损失限定在5美元以后，即使你有一半以上的判断出现错误，还能赚很多钱。'

"我很快就采用了这个法则，从此一直使用它。这个办法替我的顾客和我挽回了许多钱。

"过了一段时间，我发现这一'到此为止'原则也可以用于股票之外的地方。我开始在每一种烦恼和不快的事情上都加上一个'到此为止'的限制，结果太妙了。

"例如，我经常和一个很不守时的朋友共进午餐。他以前总是在我的午餐时间过去大半后才赶来。而现在我会告诉他我的底线原则，对他说：'以后我只等你10分钟，要是你在10分钟以后才赶到，那我们的午餐就算告吹——我会先走。'"

啊！我真希望在很多年以前就学会将这种"到此为止"的原则用在我的每一个方面：缺乏耐心、脾气、自我适应的欲望、悔恨以及所有精神与情感的压力上。为什么我以前没有想到用它来克服我的忧虑呢?为什么我不会对自己说"这件事情不值得这么担心——不能再去多管"呢?为什么我没有呢?

不过，我觉得自己至少在一件事上做得还不错。那是一次很严重的情况——是我生命中的一次危机。当时，我几乎眼看着我的梦想、我未来的计划以及多年来的工作全都付诸东流。事情是这样的：我刚30岁的时候，我决定一辈子以写小说为职业，梦想做弗兰克·诺瑞斯或杰克·伦敦或哈代第二。我充满了热情，在欧洲住了两年。第一次世界大战结束后的那段时期，用美元在欧洲生活还是很合算的。我在那儿待了两年，完成了我的"杰作"。我给它取名为《暴风雪》。这书名取得太好了，因为所有出版商对它的态度都像呼啸着刮过达科他平原的暴风雪一样冷酷。

stunned if he had hit me across the head with a club. I was stupefied. I realised that I was standing at the crossroads of life, and had to make a tremendous decision. What should I do?Which way should I turn?Weeks passed before I came out of the daze. At that time, I had never heard of the phrase "put a stop-loss order on your worries". But as I look back now, I can see that I did just that. I wrote off my two years of sweating over that novel for just what they were worth—a noble experiment—and went forward from there. I returned to my work of organising and teaching adult-education classes, and wrote biographies in my spare time—biographies and nonfiction books such as the one you are reading now.

Am I glad now that I made that decision?Glad?Every time I think about it now I feel like dancing in the street for sheer joy! I can honestly say that I have never spent a day or an hour since, lamenting the fact that I am not another Thomas Hardy.

One night a century ago, when a screech owl was screeching in the woods along the shore of Walden Pond, Henry Thoreau dipped his goose quill into his homemade ink and wrote in his diary: "The cost of a thing is the amount of what I call life, which is required to be exchanged for it immediately or in the long run."

To put it another way: we are fools when we overpay for a thing in terms of what it takes out of our very existence.

Yet that is precisely what Gilbert and Sullivan did. They knew how to create gay words and gay music, but they knew distressingly little about how to create gaiety in their own lives. They created some of the loveliest light operas that ever delighted the world: *Patience, Pinafore, The Mikado.* But they couldn't control their tempers. They embittered their years over nothing more than the price of a carpet! Sullivan ordered a new carpet for the theatre they had bought. When Gilbert saw the bill, he hit the roof. They battled it out in court, and never spoke to one another again as long as they lived. When Sullivan wrote the music for a new production, he mailed it to Gilbert; and when Gilbert wrote the words, he mailed it back to Sullivan. Once they had to take a curtain call together, but they stood on opposite sides of the stage and bowed in different directions, so they wouldn't see one another. They hadn't the sense to put a stop-loss order on their resentments, as Lincoln did.

Once, during the Civil War, when some of Lincoln's friends were denouncing his bitter

当我的经纪人告诉我说这部作品一文不值，我没有写小说的天才时，我的心跳几乎停止了。我茫然失措地离开了他的办公室。当时即使他用棒子敲打我的脑袋我也不会吃惊——我惊呆了。我发现自己正站在生命的十字路口，必须做一个非常重大的决定。我该怎么办?该往哪一个方向走?几个星期之后，我才从茫然中醒悟过来。当时，我从来没有听过"让你的忧虑'到此为止'"的说法。可是现在回想起来，我当时正好做了这件事。我把自己费尽心血写那本小说看作一次宝贵的教训，然后从那里出发。我重新回去从事成人教育，有时间则写一些传记和非小说类的书，例如你现在正看的这本书。

我是不是很高兴做了这样的决定呢?何止高兴！现在只要是想起它我就会得意地想在大街上跳舞。我可以很坦诚地说，从那以后我从来没有后悔没有成为哈代第二。

100年前的一个夜晚，当一只鸟在瓦尔登湖畔的树林里鸣叫的时候，梭罗用鹅毛笔蘸着自制墨水，在他的日记里写道："一件事物的代价，也即我称之为生活的总值，需要当场交换，或在最后付出。"

用另外一种方式来说：如果我们以生活的一部分来付出代价，而且付得太多的话，那我们就是傻子。

这也正是吉尔伯和苏里文的悲哀。他们知道如何创作快乐的词曲，却完全不知道如何寻找生活中的快乐。他们写过许多世人非常喜欢的轻歌剧，如《宽容》、《围裙》和《麦卡多》，可是却不会控制自己的脾气。他们竟然为了一块地毯的价钱而争吵多年：苏里文为他们剧院买了一块新地毯，当吉尔伯看到账单时，十分生气。他们闹上了公堂，从此到死都没有再交谈过。苏里文为新歌剧写完曲子之后，就把它寄给吉尔伯；而吉尔伯填上歌词之后，再把它寄回给苏里文。一旦他们必须同时上台谢幕，他们就站在舞台的两边分别向不同的方向鞠躬，这样才不至于看见对方。他们不懂得为他们的不愉快设定"到此为止"的底限，而林肯做到了。

enemies, Lincoln said: "You have more of a feeling of personal resentment than I have. Perhaps I have too little of it; but I never thought it paid. A man doesn't have the time to spend half his life in quarrels. If any man ceases to attack me, I never remember the past against him."

I wish an old aunt of mine—Aunt Edith—had had Lincoln's forgiving spirit. She and Uncle Frank lived on a mortgaged farm that was infested with cockleburs and cursed with poor soil and ditches. They had tough going—had to squeeze every nickel. But Aunt Edith loved to buy a few curtains and other items to brighten up their bare home. She bought these small luxuries on credit at Dan Eversole's drygoods store in Maryville, Missouri. Uncle Frank worried about their debts. He had a farmer's horror of running up bills, so he secretly told Dan Eversole to stop letting his wife buy on credit. When she heard that, she hit the roof—and she was still hitting the roof about it almost fifty years after it had happened. I have heard her tell the story—not once, but many times. The last time I ever saw her, she was in her late seventies. I said to her, "Aunt Edith, Uncle Frank did wrong to humiliate you; but don't you honestly feel that your complaining about it almost half a century after it happened is infinitely worse than what he did?"(I might as well have said it to the moon.)

Aunt Edith paid dearly for the grudges and bitter memories that she nourished. She paid for them with her own peace of mind.

When Benjamin Franklin was seven years old, he made a mistake that he remembered for seventy years. When he was a lad of seven, he fell in love with a whistle. He was so excited about it that he went into the toyshop, piled all his coppers on the counter, and demanded the whistle without even asking its price. "I then came home, "he wrote to a friend seventy years later, "and went whistling all over the house, much pleased with my whistle." But when his older brothers and sisters found out that he had paid far more for his whistle than he should have paid, they gave him the horse laugh; and as he said, "I cried with vexation."

Years later, when Franklin was a world-famous figure, and Ambassador to France, he still remembered that the fact that he had paid too much for his whistle had caused him "more chagrin than the whistle gave him pleasure."

But the lesson it taught Franklin was cheap in the end. "As I grew up, "he said, "and came into

南北战争期间,有一次林肯的几位朋友攻击他的一些敌人,林肯说:"你们对私人恩怨的感受比我多,也许我这种感觉太少吧。可是我总觉得这样很不值。一个人没有必要把时间花在争吵上。要是那个人不再攻击我,我也不会再记恨他。"

我真希望我的姑妈伊迪丝也能有林肯的宽恕精神。她和姑父弗兰克住在一栋被抵押的农庄。那里的土质很坏,灌溉条件又差,收成也不好。他们的日子很艰难,每一个小钱都得省着用。可是伊迪丝姑妈却喜欢买一些窗帘和小饰物来装饰那个穷家,她曾向密苏里州马利维里的一家小杂货店赊过这些东西。姑父弗兰克很担心他们的债务,而且不愿意欠债,所以他私下里告诉杂货店老板,不让他太太赊账。当她听说之后,大发怒火——那时离现在差不多50年了,可是她还在大发脾气。我曾经不止一次听她说这件事情。我最后一次见到她时,她将近80岁了。我对她说:"伊迪丝姑妈,弗兰克姑父这样羞辱你确实不对;可是你没有觉得,自从那件事发生之后,你差不多埋怨了半个世纪,是不是有点过分呢?"

伊迪丝姑妈对她这些不愉快的记忆所付出的代价实在太大了——她付出的是她自己内心的平静。

富兰克林小时候也犯了一次他牢记70年的错误。他7岁的时候,看上了一支哨子。他兴奋地跑进玩具店,把所有的零钱放在柜台上,连价钱也不问就把那支哨子买了下来。"然后我回到家,"他70年后写信告诉朋友,"吹着哨子在整个屋子里转,对我的哨子非常得意。"可是当他的哥哥姐姐发现他买哨子多付了钱时,大家都取笑他。正如他所说的:"我懊恼得大哭了一场。"

当富兰克林多年之后成为一位世界知名人物,担任驻法大使时,他还记得因为买哨子而多付了钱,使他从中得到的痛苦远远多过哨子带来的快乐。

富兰克林从中学到了一个道理。"我长大以后,"他说,"见到许多人的行为犹如我当初买哨子多付了钱一样。简而言之,我认为人类的苦难大部分产生于他们错估了事物的价值,也就是

the world and observed the actions of men, I thought I met with many, very many, who gave too much for the whistle. In short, I conceive that a great part of the miseries of mankind are brought upon them by the false estimates they have made of the value of things, and by their giving too much for their whistles."

Gilbert and Sullivan paid too much for their whistle. So did Aunt Edith. So did Dale Carnegie—on many occasions. And so did the immortal Leo Tolstoy, author of two of the world's greatest novels, *War and Peace and Anna Karenina*. According to *The Encyclopedia Britannica*, Leo Tolstoy was, during the last twenty years of his life, "probably the most venerated man in the whole world." For twenty years before he died—from 1890 to 1910—an unending stream of admirers made pilgrimages to his home in order to catch a glimpse of his face, to hear the sound of his voice, or even touch them of his garment. Every sentence he uttered was taken down in a notebook, almost as if it were a "divine revelation". But when it came to living—to ordinary living–well, Tolstoy had even less sense at seventy than Franklin had at seven! He had no sense at all.

Here's what I mean. Tolstoy married a girl he loved very dearly. In fact, they were so happy together that they used to get on their knees and pray to God to let them continue their lives in such sheer, heavenly ecstasy. But the girl Tolstoy married was jealous by nature. She used to dress herself up as a peasant and spy on his movements, even out in the woods. They had fearful rows. She became so jealous, even of her own children, that she grabbed a gun and shot a hole in her daughter's photograph. She even rolled on the floor with an opium bottle held to her lips, and threatened to commit suicide, while the children huddled in a corner of the room and screamed with terror.

And what did Tolstoy do?Well, I don't blame the man for up and smashing the furniture—he had good provocation. But he did far worse than that. He kept a private diary! Yes, a diary, in which he placed all the blame on his wife! That was his "whistle"! He was determined to make sure that coming generations would exonerate *him* and put the blame on his wife. And what did his wife do, in answer to this?Why, she tore pages out of his diary and burned them, of course. She started a diary of her own, in which she made him the villain. She even wrote a novel, entitled *Whose Fault*?in which she depicted her husband as a household friend and herself as a martyr.

他们买哨子多付了钱。"

吉尔伯和苏里文为他们的哨子多付了钱,我姑妈伊迪丝也一样,我自己同样如此。不朽的托尔斯泰,也就是《战争与和平》和《安娜·卡列尼娜》这两部世界最伟大小说的作者也是一样。根据《大英百科全书》记载,在托尔斯泰生命的最后20年,"可能是全世界最受尊敬的人"。在他逝世前20年,他的崇拜者不断地去他家里,希望能见他一面,能听听他的声音,或者哪怕只摸摸他的衣角。有人甚至记下他说的每一句话,就好像那是"神谕"。可是在生活中,托尔斯泰在70岁的时候还不如7岁的富兰克林——他根本没脑筋。

下面就是我这么评价他的原因:托尔斯泰娶了一个他非常喜欢的女孩子。事实上,他们在一起的时候非常开心,常常跪下来向上帝祈祷,希望让他们继续过这种神仙伴侣的生活。然而,托尔斯泰娶的这个女孩子天性善妒,她常常把自己打扮成乡下姑娘,打探他的行动,甚至溜进树林里监视他。他们吵得很厉害,她甚至嫉妒自己的亲生女儿,曾经用枪把她女儿的照片打了一个洞。她会在地板上撒泼,拿着一瓶鸦片,威胁要自杀,孩子们吓得缩在屋子的角落里尖叫。

托尔斯泰是怎么做的呢?如果他暴跳如雷,打烂家具,我不想怪他,因为他有理由这样做。可是他所做的比这更甚,他全部记在私人日记里!将一切都推到了他太太身上——这就是他的"哨子"!他想让他的下一代原谅他,并把所有的错误都推到他太太身上。而他太太又用什么办法来对付他呢?她当然是撕毁并烧掉了他的日记。她自己也写了一本日记,把错误都推在他身上。她甚至写了一本小说,书名为《谁之错》。她把丈夫描写成一个家庭破坏者,而她自己则成了烈士。

这一切的结果呢?为什么他们两个人会把自己家变成托尔斯泰所谓的"疯人院"呢?显然,这里有几个理由,其中之一就是他们都非常希望引起别人的注意。不错,他们最担心的就是别人的意见。我们会不会在乎应该怪谁呢?当然不会,我们只会注意我们自己的问题,而不会浪费

All to what end?Why did these two people turn the only home they had into what Tolstoy himself called “a lunatic asylum”?Obviously, there were several reasons. One of those reasons was their burning desire to impress you and me. Yes, we are the posterity whose opinion they were worried about! Do we give a hoot in Hades about which one was to blame?No, we are too concerned with our own problems to waste a minute thinking about the Tolstoy's. What a price these, two wretched people paid for their whistle! Fifty years of living in a veritable hell—just because neither of them had the sense to say, “Stop! ”Because neither of them had enough judgment of values to say, “Let's put a stop-loss order on this thing instantly. We are squandering our lives. Let's say‘Enough’now! ”

Yes, I honestly believe that this is one of the greatest secrets to true peace of mind—a decent sense of values. And I believe we could annihilate fifty per cent of all our worries at once if we would develop a sort of private gold standard—a gold standard of what things are worth to us in terms of our lives.

So, to break the worry habit before it breaks you, here is Rule 5:

Whenever we are tempted to throw good money after bad in terms of human living, let's stop and ask ourselves these three Questions:

1. How much does this thing I am worrying about really matter to me?

2. At what point shall I set a“stop-loss”order on this worry—and forget it?

3. Exactly how much shall I pay for this whistle?Have I already paid more than it is worth?

时间去想托尔斯泰的事。这两个无知的人为他们的“哨子”付出的代价多大啊!他们50年来住在一个可怕的地狱里,只因为他们都不愿说“不要再吵了”! 因为他们都没有足够的价值判断力说:“让我们在这件事情上打住吧! 我们这是在浪费生命! 让我们现在就说‘够了’吧! ”

我相信“正确的价值观”是获得心理平静的最大秘诀。我也相信,只要我们定出一种个人的标准,我们的忧虑有一半可以立刻消除——就是和我们的生活相比,什么事情才值得。

所以,在忧虑毁了你以前先改变忧虑的习惯,下面是第五项规则:

当我们想掏钱购买的东西不一定合算时,先停下来问自己下面三个问题:

第一,我现在担心的问题,和我到底有什么关系?

第二,这件令我忧虑的事情,我应该如何确定“到此为止”的最低限度,然后忘掉它?

第三,我应该为这支“哨子”付多少钱?我付的钱是不是超过了它的价值?

6 Don't Try to Saw Sawdust

As I write this sentence, I can look out of my window and see some dinosaur tracks in my garden—dinosaur tracks embedded in shale and stone. I purchased those dinosaur tracks from the Peabody Museum of Yale University; and I have a letter from the curator of the Peabody Museum, saying that those tracks were made 180 million years ago. Even a Mongolian idiot wouldn't dream of trying to go back 180 million years to change those tracks. Yet that would not be any more foolish than worrying because we can't go back and change what happened 180 seconds ago—and a lot of us are doing just that. To be sure, we may do something to modify the effects of what happened 180 seconds ago; but we can't possibly change the event that occurred then.

There is only one way on God's green footstool that the past can be constructive; and that is by calmly analyzing our past mistakes and profiting by them—and forgetting them.

I know that is true; but have I always had the courage and sense to do it?To answer that question, let me tell you about a fantastic experience I had years ago. I let more than three hundred thousand dollars slip through my fingers without making a penny's profit. It happened like this: I launched a large-scale enterprise in adult education, opened branches in various cities, and spent money lavishly in overhead and advertising. I was so busy with teaching that I had neither the time nor the desire to look after finances. I was too naive to realise that I needed an astute business manager to watch expenses.

Finally, after about a year, I discovered a sobering and shocking truth. I discovered that in spite of our enormous intake, we had not netted any profit whatever. After discovering that, I should have done two things. First, I should have had the sense to do what George Washington Carver, the Negro scientist, did when he lost forty thousand dollars in a bank crash—the savings of a lifetime. When someone asked him if he knew he was bankrupt, he replied, "Yes, I heard"—and went on with his teaching. He wiped the loss out of his mind so completely that he never mentioned it again.

Here is the second thing I should have done: I should have analyzed my mistakes and learned

第6章 不要锯木屑

就在我写这句话的时候,我可以看见窗外院子里一些留在大石板和石头上的恐龙足迹。这些恐龙足迹是我从耶鲁大学皮尔波蒂博物馆买来的。我还收到一封皮尔波蒂博物馆馆长给我的信,说这些足迹早在1.8亿年前就有了。即使是一个白痴也不会想返回1.8亿年前去改变这些足迹。而一个人的忧虑却会像这种想法一样愚蠢,因为就算是180秒钟以前发生的事情,我们也不可能再回去纠正它——可是我们很多人正在做这种事。说得更确切一点,我们可以想办法改变180秒钟以前的事情所产生的影响,但我们对当时发生的事情却无能为力。

使过去的错误产生价值的唯一方法,就是平静地分析我们过去的错误,并从中吸取教训,然后忘记错误。

我知道这句话很有道理,但我是不是一直有勇气、有思想去这样实践呢?为了回答这个问题,让我告诉你我在几年前的一次奇妙经历吧。当时我白白失去了30多万美元,没有得到一分钱的利润。事情是这样的:我开办了一个规模很大的成人教育班,在很多城市设了分部,并花了许多钱做宣传广告。当时我忙于教课,所以既没有时间、也没有心情去管理财务问题。我过于简单,不知道应该找一个很好的业务经理来支配各项支出。

最后,过了将近一年,我发现了一个很清楚而且很惊人的事实:虽然我们的收入很可观,却没有赚到任何利润。发现这点之后,我本应该做两件事情:

第一,我应该向黑人科学家乔治·华盛顿·卡佛尔学习。当时他破产了,失去了毕生的4万美元积蓄。别人问他是否知道自己破产了,他回答说:"是的,我听说了。"然后继续教书。他把这笔损失从脑子里彻底抹掉,以后再也没有提过。

a lasting lesson.

But frankly, I didn't do either one of these things. Instead, I went into a tailspin of worry. For months I was in a daze. I lost sleep and I lost weight. Instead of learning a lesson from this enormous mistake, I went right ahead and did the same thing again on a smaller scale!

It is embarrassing for me to admit all this stupidity; but I discovered long ago that "it is easier to teach twenty what were good to be done than to be one of twenty to follow mine own teaching."

How I wish that I had had the privilege of attending the George Washington High School here in New York and studying under Mr. Brandwine—the same teacher who taught Allen Saunders, of 939 Woodycrest Avenue, Bronx, New York!

Mr. Saunders told me that the teacher of his hygiene class, Mr. Brandwine, taught him one of the most valuable lessons he had ever learned. "I was only in my teens, "said Allen Saunders as he told me the story, "but I was a worrier even then. I used to stew and fret about the mistakes I had made. If I turned in an examination paper, I used to lie awake and chew my fingernails for fear I hadn't passed. I was always living over the things I had done, and wishing I'd done them differently; thinking over the things I had said, and wishing I'd said them better.

"Then one morning, our class filed into the science laboratory, and there was the teacher, Mr. Brandwine, with a bottle of milk prominently displayed on the edge of the desk. We all sat down, staring at the milk, and wondering what it had to do with the hygiene course he was teaching. Then, all of a sudden, Mr. Brandwine stood up, swept the bottle of milk with a crash into the sink—and shouted: 'don't cry over spilt milk! '

"He then made us all come to the sink and look at the wreckage. 'take a good look, 'he told us, 'because I want you to remember this lesson the rest of your lives. That milk is gone—you can see it's down the drain; and all the fussing and hair-pulling in the world won't bring back a drop of it. With a little thought and prevention, that milk might have been saved. But it's too late now—all we can do is write it off, forget it, and go on to the next thing. '

"That one little demonstration, "Allen Saunders told me, "stuck with me long after I'd forgotten my solid geometry and Latin. In fact, it taught me more about practical living than anything else in my four years of high school. It taught me to keep from spilling milk if I could; but to forget it

我应该做的第二件事是,分析自己的错误,从中吸取教训。

可是坦白地说,这两件事我一件也没有做。相反,我却开始发起愁来。一连好几个月,我都精神恍惚,睡得不好,体重减轻。我不仅没有从这次大错误中吸取教训,反而又犯了一个类似的小错误。

对我来说,要承认这种愚蠢的行为实在难堪。可是我很早就发现一个道理:"教20个人怎么做,比自己一个人去做要容易得多。"

我真希望我也能够到纽约乔治·华盛顿高级中学去向保罗·布兰德温学习——他曾教过住在纽约市布朗士区的亚伦·桑德斯。

桑德斯先生告诉我,教他生理卫生的老师保罗·布兰德温先生给他上了人生中最有价值的一课。"当时我只有十几岁,"亚伦·桑德斯告诉我,"可是我那时候经常忧虑。我常常为自己犯的各种错误而自责;交完考试卷以后,我常常会在半夜里睡不着,咬着指甲,担心不及格。我总是在想我所做过的事情,希望当初没有那样做;想我所说过的话,希望当时能说得更完美些。

"然后,有一天早上,我们全班走进实验室上实验课。布兰德温先生将一瓶牛奶放在桌子边上。我们都坐下来,望着那瓶牛奶,心想这和他所教的生理卫生课有什么关系。这时,布兰德温先生突然站起来,将牛奶瓶打碎,牛奶泼在水槽里——他大声叫道:'不要为打翻的牛奶哭泣。'

"随后他叫我们所有人来到水槽边,看那瓶打碎的牛奶。'好好看着,'他对我们说,'因为我要你们一辈子都记住这一课。牛奶已经没有了!都泼光了!无论你多么着急,多么抱怨,都无法挽回了。只要用一点大脑,加以预防,牛奶就可以保住。可是现在太迟了——我们能做的就是把它忘掉,关注下一件事。'

"那次小小的表演,"亚伦·桑德斯说,"即使是在我忘了几何和拉丁文之后很久,我都会记得。事实上,这件事教给我的实际生活经验,比我在高中4年学的任何知识都管用。它教会我一

completely, once it was spilled and had gone down the drain."

Some readers are going to snort at the idea of making so much over a hackneyed proverb like "Don't cry over spilt milk." I know it is trite, commonplace, and a platitude. I know you have heard it a thousand times. But I also know that these hackneyed proverbs contain the very essence of the distilled wisdom of all ages. They have come out of the fiery experience of the human race and have been handed down through countless generations. If you were to read everything that has ever been written about worry by the great scholars of all time, you would never read anything more basic or more profound than such hackneyed proverbs as "Don't cross your bridges until you come to them" and "Don't cry over spilt milk." If we only applied those two proverbs—instead of snorting at them—we wouldn't need this book at all. In fact, if we applied most of the old proverbs, we would lead almost perfect lives. However, knowledge isn't power until it is applied; and the purpose of this book is not to tell you something new. The purpose of this book is to remind you of what you already know and to kick you in the shins and inspire you to do something about applying it.

I have always admired a man like the late Fred Fuller Shedd, who had a gift for stating an old truth in a new and picturesque way. He was editor of the *Philadelphia Bulletin*; and, while addressing a college graduating class, he asked: "How many of you have ever sawed wood?Let's see your hands." Most of them had. Then he inquired: "How many of you have ever sawed sawdust?"No hands went up.

"Of course, you can't saw sawdust! "Mr. Shedd exclaimed. "It's already sawed! And it's the same with the past. When you start worrying about things that are over and done with, you're merely trying to saw sawdust."

When Connie Mack, the grand old man of baseball, was eighty-one years old, I asked him if he had ever worried over games that were lost.

"Oh, yes, I used to, "Connie Mack told me. "But I got over that foolishness long years ago. I found out it didn't get me anywhere at all. You can't grind any grain, "he said, "with water that has already gone down the creek."

No, you can't grind any grain—and you can't saw any logs with water that has already gone down the creek. But you can saw wrinkles in your face and ulcers in your stomach.

个道理:如何可能,就不要打翻牛奶;万一打翻了牛奶,就要彻底忘掉它。"

有些读者大概会觉得,费这么大精力讲"不要为打翻的牛奶哭泣",未免小题大做。我知道这句话很普通,而且老生常谈,耳朵都听出了老茧。可是这样的老生常谈却包含了所有时代的经验智慧,它们来自人类智慧的结晶,是通过世世代代传承下来的。假设你能读完各个时代伟大学者所写的有关忧虑的书,也不会看到比"船到桥头自然直"和"不要为打翻的牛奶哭泣"更基本、更有用的老生常谈。只要我们能应用这两句老话,不轻视它,我们根本用不着读这本书。然而,如果不能实践,我们就不能过上美好的生活,知识就不能成为力量。本书的目的并不是想告诉你什么新的知识,而是要提醒那些你已经知道的事,并且鼓励你把它们付诸实践。

我一直很佩服已故的弗雷德·富勒·谢德。他有一种天生的本领,能把古老的真理用新颖而吸引人的方法表达出来。他是《费城公报》的编辑。有一次他曾为某大学毕业班演讲,他问道:"有多少人锯过木头?请举手。"结果大部分学生都锯过。然后他又问:"有多少人锯过木屑?"没有一个人举手。

"当然,你们不可能锯木屑!"谢德先生说,"因为它已经被锯下来了。过去的事情也是一样。当你开始忧虑那些已经做完和过去的事情时,你只不过是在锯木屑。"

棒球老将康尼·马克81岁高龄时,我问他是否曾为输了的比赛而忧虑。

"当然。我以前总是这样,"康尼·马克对我说,"可是多年以前我就不再干这种傻事了。我发现这样做对我没有任何好处,因为磨完的细粉不能再磨,水已经把它们冲走了。"

不错,磨完的细粉不能再磨,木屑也不能再锯了。可是,忧虑会让你脸上长皱纹,让你得胃溃疡。

去年感恩节,我和杰克·邓普赛共进晚餐。当我们吃火鸡和酸果酱的时候,他给我讲了他把

I had dinner with Jack Dempsey last Thanksgiving; and he told me over the turkey and cranberry sauce about the fight in which he lost the heavyweight championship to Tunney Naturally, it was a blow to his ego. "In the midst of that fight, "he told me, "I suddenly realised I had become an old man... At the end of the tenth round, I was still on my feet, but that was about all. My face was puffed and cut, and my eyes were nearly closed... I saw the referee raise Gene Tunney's hand in token of victory... I was no longer champion of the world. I started back in the rain—back through the crowd to my dressing-room. As I passed, some people tried to grab my hand. Others had tears in their eyes.

"A year later, I fought Tunney again. But it was no use. I was through forever. It was hard to keep from worrying about it all, but I said to myself, 'I'm not going to live in the past or cry over spilt milk. I am going to take this blow on the chin and not let it floor me.'"

And that is precisely what Jack Dempsey did. How?By saying to himself over and over: "I won't worry about the past"?No, that would merely have forced him to think of his past worries. He did it by accepting and writing off his defeat and then concentrating on plans for the future. He did it by running the Jack Dempsey Restaurant on Broadway and the Great Northern Hotel on 57th Street. He did it by promoting prize fights and giving boxing exhibitions. He did it by getting so busy on something constructive that he had neither the time nor the temptation to worry about the past. "I have had a better time during the last ten years, "Jack Dempsey said, "than I had when I was champion."

Mr. Dempsey told me that he had not read many books; but, without knowing it, he was following Shakespears's advice: "Wise men never sit and wail their loss, but cheerily seek how to redress their harms."

As I read history and biography and observe people under trying circumstances, I am constantly astonished and inspired by some people's ability to write off their worries and tragedies and go on living fairly happy lives.

I once paid a visit to Sing Sing, and the thing that astonished me most was that the prisoners there appeared to be about as happy as the average person on the outside. I commented on it to Lewis E. Lawes—then warden of Sing Sing—and he told me that when criminals first arrive at Sing

重量级拳王头衔输给金的那一场比赛。当然，这对他的自尊是一个打击。"在比赛的中间，"他告诉我，"我突然发现我成了一个老头子……当第十回合结束时，我总算没有倒下去，但仅此而已。我的脸已经被打肿打破了，双眼几乎无法睁开……我只看见裁判员举起金·通利的手，宣布他获胜……我不再是世界拳王了。我在雨中往回走，穿过人群回到我的更衣室。就在我往回走的时候，有些人想来握我的手，另一些人眼含泪水。

"一年之后，我和通利又赛了一场，可是我一点机会也没有，我就这样完了。完全不为这件事情发愁实在太难了，可是我对自己说：'我不想生活在过去里，我不会为打翻的牛奶哭泣。我要承受这次打击，不让它把我打倒。'"

这正是杰克·邓普赛所做的。他是怎么做的呢？一再对自己说"我不再为过去忧虑"吗？不！这样做只会迫使他想起过去的那些忧虑。他的方法是勇于承受一切，忘记失败，然后集中精力筹划未来。他开始经营百老汇的邓普赛餐厅和第57大街的大北方旅店；安排和宣传拳击比赛，举办各种拳赛展览会。他让自己忙着做一些有意义的事情，既没有时间也没有精力为过去担忧。"我过去10年的生活，"杰克·邓普赛说，"比我当拳王的时候好多了。"

邓普赛先生告诉我，他读的书并不多，可是他却在不自觉地照着莎士比亚的忠告行事："聪明人永远不会坐在那里为他们的错误而悲伤；相反，他们会很高兴地找办法来弥补创伤。"

当我读历史和传记并观察人们如何度过难关时，对那些能忘记忧虑和不幸并继续快乐生活的人，我总是既吃惊又羡慕。

我曾参观过星星监狱，最让我吃惊的是那里的囚犯们看起来和外面的人一样快乐。我把我的看法告诉了当时星星监狱的监狱长刘易士·路易斯。他告诉我，这些囚犯刚到星星监狱时，都心怀怨恨，可是几个月之后，他们当中比较聪明的人都能忘掉不幸，平静地接受监狱生活，并尽量过好。路易斯监狱长告诉我，有一个在菜园工作的犯人能做到一边种菜，一边唱歌。

Sing, they are likely to be resentful and bitter. But after a few months, the majority of the more intelligent ones write off their misfortunes and settle down and accept prison life calmly and make the best of it. Warden Lawes told me about one Sing Sing prisoner—a gardener—who sang as he cultivated the vegetables and flowers inside the prison walls.

That Sing Sing prisoner who sang as he cultivated the flowers showed a lot more sense than the most of us do. He knew that:

The Moving Finger writes; and, having writ,
Moves on: nor all your Piety nor Wit
Shall lure it back to cancel half a Line,
Nor all your Tears wash out a Word of it.

So why waste the tears?Of course, we have been guilty of blunders and absurdities! And so what? Who hasn't?Even Napoleon lost one-third of all the important battles he fought. Perhaps our batting average is no worse than Napoleon's. Who knows?

And, anyhow, all the king's horses and all the king's men can't put the past together again. So let's remember Rule 6:

Don't try to saw sawdust.

那个浇花唱歌的犯人比我们大部分人都聪明,因为他知道:

在白纸上写完了一横一竖,
即使你再有能耐也不能抹去半行,
即使洒尽你的眼泪也擦不掉一个字。

所以,为什么要浪费你的眼泪?当然,犯错和疏忽是我们的不对!但这又怎么样呢?谁没有犯过错?就连拿破仑也输掉了1/3的重要战役。也许我们的平均纪录不会比拿破仑差,谁知道呢?何况即使调动所有国王的人马,也不能挽回过去的失误。

所以,让我们记住第六项规则:

不要试着去锯木屑。

Part Four
Seven Ways to Cultivate A Mental Attitude That Will Bring You Peace and Happiness

1 Eight Words That Can Transform Your Life

A few years ago, I was asked to answer this question on a radio programme: "What is the biggest lesson you have ever learned?"

That was easy: by far the most vital lesson I have ever learned is the importance of what we think. If I knew what you think, I would know what you are. Our thoughts make us what we are. Our mental attitude is the X factor that determines our fate. Emerson said, "A man is what he thinks about all day long."... How could he possibly be anything else?

I now know with a conviction beyond all doubt that the biggest problem you and I have to deal with—in fact, almost the *only* problem we have to deal with—is choosing the right thoughts. If we can do that, we will be on the highroad to solving all our problems. The great philosopher who ruled the Roman Empire, Marcus Aurelius, summed it up in eight words—*eight words* that can determine your destiny: "Our life is what our thoughts make it."

Yes, if we *think* happy thoughts, we will be happy. If we think miserable thoughts, we will be miserable. If we think fear thoughts, we will be fearful. If we think sickly thoughts, we will probably be ill. If we think failure, we will certainly fail. If we wallow in serf-pity, everyone will want to shun us and avoid us. "You are not, "said Norman Vincent Peale, "you are not what you think you are; but what you think, you are."

Am I advocating an habitual Pollyanna attitude toward all our problems? No, unfortunately, life isn't so simple as all that. But I am advocating that we assume a *positive* attitude instead of a

第四篇 培养平安快乐的心理

第1章 态度可以改变你的生活

几年前,我在一个电台的广播节目中被主持人问道:"你所学到的最重要的一课是什么?"

这个问题很简单:我所学到的最重要的一课,就是"思想的重要性"。只要知道你在想什么,我就可以知道你是什么人,因为我们的思想造就了我们。我们的命运也取决于我们的心理状态。爱默生曾说:"一个人就是他成天所想象的那种样子。"……他怎么可能成为另一种样子呢?

我现在可以肯定地说,你和我必须面对的最大问题就是如何选择正确的思想——事实上这几乎是我们必须应对的唯一问题。如果我们能够做到这一点,就可以解决一切问题。马尔卡斯·阿理琉斯——这位曾经统治罗马帝国的伟大哲学家,把这些总结成一句话——决定你的命运的话:"生活是由思想形成的。"

不错,如果我们想的都是快乐的东西,我们就会快乐;如果我们想的都是悲伤之事,我们就会悲伤;如果我们想的是恐怖的事情,我们就会恐惧;如果我们想的是不好的念头,我们恐怕就不得安宁了;如果我们想的是失败,我们就会失败;如果我们沉浸在自我哀怜之中,别人都会有意躲开我们。"你并不是,"诺曼·文森特·皮尔说,"你并不是你想象中的那种样子;但你心里想什么,就会成为什么人。"

negative attitude. In other words, we need to be concerned about our problems, but not worried. What is the difference between concern and worry? Let me illustrate. Every time I cross the traffic-jammed streets of New York, I am concerned about what I am doing—but not worried. Concern means realising what the problems are and calmly taking steps to meet them. Worrying means going around in maddening, futile circles.

A man can be concerned about his serious problems and still walk with his chin up and a carnation in his buttonhole. I have seen Lowell Thomas do just that. I once had the privilege of being associated with Lowell Thomas in presenting his famous films on the Allenby-Lawrence campaigns in World War I. He and his assistants had photographed the war on half a dozen fronts; and, best of all, had brought back a pictorial record of T. E. Lawrence and his colorful Arabian army, and a film record of Allenby's conquest of the Holy Land. His illustrated talks entitled "*With Allenby in Palestine and Lawrence in Arabia*" were a sensation in London—and around the world. The London opera season was postponed for six weeks so that he could continue telling his tale of high adventure and showing his pictures at Covent Garden Royal Opera House. After his sensational success in London came a triumphant tour of many countries. Then he spent two years preparing a film record of life in India and Afghanistan. After a lot of incredibly bad luck, the impossible happened: he found himself broke in London. I was with him at the time. I remember we had to eat cheap meals at cheap restaurants. We couldn't have eaten even there if we had not borrowed money from a Scotsman—James McBey, the renowned artist. Here is the point of the story: even when Lowell Thomas was facing huge debts and severe disappointments, he was concerned, but not worried. He knew that if he let his reverses get him down, he would be worthless to everyone, including his creditors. So each morning before he started out, he bought a flower, put it in his buttonhole, and went swinging down Oxford Street with his head high and his step spirited. He thought positive, courageous thoughts and refused to let defeat him. To him, being licked was all a part of the game—the useful training you had to expect if you wanted to get to the top.

Our mental attitude has an almost unbelievable effect even on our physical powers. The famous British psychiatrist, J. A. Hadfield, gives a striking illustration of that fact in his splendid book, *The Psychology of Power*. "I asked three men, "he writes, "to submit themselves to test the effect of mental

我是不是要求以一种习惯性的乐观态度去应对一切困难呢?当然不是。不幸的是,生活不会像这样简单化。但我却希望大家采取积极的态度,而不是消极的态度。换一句话说,我们必须关注我们的问题,但是不能为此而忧虑。关注和忧虑之间区别何在?例如,每当我通过交通拥挤的纽约市街区时,我会对此很注意,可是并不会忧虑。关注指的是了解问题,然后镇定自若地采取办法解决它;而忧虑却是盲目无助地转圈子。

一个人可以关注自己的严重问题,但同时可以将花插在扣眼上昂首阔步。我就曾看过罗维尔·托马斯这样。有一次,我协助罗维尔·托马斯主演一部著名电影,这是有关艾伦贝和劳伦斯在第一次世界大战中出征的电影。他和几个助手在几个战争前线拍摄了战争的镜头,精彩地记录了劳伦斯和他统率的多姿多彩的阿拉伯军队,同时还记录了艾伦贝征服圣地的经过。他那著名演讲《巴勒斯坦的艾伦贝和阿拉伯的劳伦斯》轰动了整个伦敦和全世界,伦敦的歌剧节也因此后推了6星期,以便让他在卡尔文花园皇家歌剧院继续讲述这些冒险故事,并放映电影。在伦敦获得巨大成功之后,他又成功地去了好几个国家。然后,他花了两年的时间,准备拍一部关于在印度和阿富汗生活的纪录片。在一连串令人难以置信的打击之后,不可能的事情发生了:他发现自己已经破产了。当时我恰好和他在一起。我还记得我们不得不在廉价小饭店吃很便宜的东西。要不是一位苏格兰著名画家——詹姆斯·麦克贝借给我们钱的话,我们连饭都没有吃了。这正是这个故事的焦点:当罗维尔·托马斯面临庞大的债务,并极度失望的时候,他很关切此事,可是他并不忧虑。他知道,一旦他被霉运击垮,他就一钱不值了,包括他的债权人也会这么看。所以,他每天早上出门之前,都要买一朵鲜花插在扣眼上,然后昂首走上牛津街头。他想的是积极而勇敢的事情,绝不让挫折击垮他。对他来说,挫折只不过是整个事情的一部分——是你要攀上高峰必须接受的有益锻炼。

我们的精神状态对我们的身体会产生令人难以相信的影响。英国著名的精神学家哈德菲曾

suggestion on their strength, which was measured by gripping a dynamometer." He told them to grip the dynamometer with all their might. He had them do this under three different sets of conditions.

When he tested them under normal waking conditions, their average grip was 101 pounds.

When he tested them after he had hypnotized them and told them that they were very weak, they could grip only 29 pounds—less than a third of their normal strength. (One of these men was a prize fighter; and when he was told under hypnosis that he was weak, he remarked that his arm felt"tiny, just like a baby's".)

When Captain Hadfield then tested these men a third time, telling them under hypnosis that they were very strong, they were able to grip an average of 142 pounds. When their minds were filled with positive thoughts of strength, they increased their actual physical powers almost five hundred per cent.

Such is the incredible power of our mental attitude.

To illustrate the magic power of thought, let me tell you one of the most astounding stories in the annals of America. I could write a book about it; but let's be brief. She is now known to millions of devoted followers as Mary Baker Eddy—the founder of Christian Science.

Yet, until this time, she had known little in life except sickness, sorrow, and tragedy. Her first husband had died shortly after their marriage. Her second husband had deserted her and eloped with a married woman. He later died in a poor-house. She had only one child, a son; and she was forced, because of poverty, illness, and jealousy, to give him up when he was four years old. She lost all track of him and never saw him again for thirty-one years.

Because of her own ill health, Mrs. Eddy had been interested for years in what she called"the science of mind healing". But the dramatic turning point in her life occurred in Lynn, Massachusetts. Walking downtown one cold day, she slipped and fell on the icy pavement—and was knocked unconscious. Her spine was so injured that she was convulsed with spasms. Even the doctor expected her to die. If by some miracle she lived, he declared that she would never walk again.

Lying on what was supposed to be her deathbed, Mary Baker Eddy opened her Bible, and was led, she declared, by divine guidance to read these words from Saint Matthew: "And, behold, they brought to him a man sick of the palsy: lying on a bed: and Jesus... said unto the sick of the palsy;

在他的作品《力量心理学》中解释了这种情况。"我请来三个人,"他写道,"以测试心理暗示对生理的影响。我们采用了握力计来测量。"他要求他们在三种不同的情况下,竭尽全力抓紧握力计。

在正常的清醒状态下,他们的平均握力是101磅。

第二次实验时,则将他们催眠,并告诉他们说他们非常虚弱。结果,他们只能抓29磅——不到他们正常力量的1/3。(这三个人中有一个是拳击获奖者;当他在催眠状态下得知自己很虚弱时,他说他的手臂"就像婴儿的一样小"。)

然后,哈德菲再让这些人做第三次实验:在催眠之后,告诉他们,说他们非常强壮。结果他们的握力平均达到了142磅。当他们积极地认为自己很强壮时,他们的力量几乎增加了500%。

这就是令人难以置信的心理状态。

为了说明心理思想的魔力,我要告诉你美国历史上一个最离奇的故事。我可以就此写一本书,不过让我们长话短说。故事的主人公是众所周知的基督教科学的创始人玛丽·贝克·艾迪。

然而,她当初认为人生只有疾病、愁苦和不幸。她的第一任丈夫婚后不久就死了,第二个丈夫又抛弃了她,和一个已婚女人私奔,后来死在一家贫民收容所。她只有一个儿子,却由于贫穷、疾病和嫉妒而不得不在他4岁那年把他送人。她不知道儿子在哪里,在以后的31年当中再也没有见到他。

因为她自己的身体不好,使她对所谓的"心理治疗法"产生了兴趣。可是她生命中最富戏剧性的转折点却发生在马萨诸塞的理安市。在一个寒冬的日子里,她一个人在城里走着,突然摔倒在结冰的路面上,昏死过去。她的脊椎受损,不停地抽搐,甚至连医生都认为她会死去。医生还说,即使她奇迹般地活了下来,也不可能再行走了。

玛丽·贝克·艾迪躺在一张似乎是送终的床上,打开了《圣经》,被神灵引到了圣马休说的一段话:"有人抬着一个瘫痪的人来到耶稣跟前,耶稣就对瘫痪的人说:'孩子,放心吧,你的罪被宽赦了……起来吧,拿上你的东西回家去吧。'那人就站起来,回家去了。"

Son, be of good cheer; thy sins be forgiven thee... Arise, take up thy bed, and go unto thine house. And he arose, and departed to his house."

These words of Jesus, she declared, produced within her such a strength, such a faith, such a surge of healing power, that she"immediately got out of bed and walked."

"That experience, "Mrs. Eddy declared, "was the falling apple that led me to the discovery of how to be well myself, and how to make others so... I gained the scientific certainty that all causation was Mind, and every effect a mental phenomenon."

Such was the way in which Mary Baker Eddy became the founder and high priestess of a new religion: Christian Science—the only great religious faith ever established by a woman—a religion that has encircled the globe.

You are probably saying to yourself by now: "This man Carnegie is proselytising for Christian Science." No. You are wrong. I am not a Christian Scientist. But the longer I live, the more deeply I am convinced of the tremendous power of thought. As a result of thirty-five years spent in teaching adults, I know men and women can banish worry, fear, and various kinds of illness, and can transform their lives by changing their thoughts. I know! I know!! I know!!! I have seen such incredible transformations performed hundreds of times. I have seen them so often that I no longer wonder at them.

For example, one of these transformations happened to one of my students. Frank J. Whaley, of 1469 West Idaho Street, Saint Paul, Minnesota. He had a nervous breakdown. What brought it on? Worry. Frank Whaley tells me, "I worried about everything: I worried because I was too thin; because I thought I was losing my hair; because I feared I would never make enough money to get married; because I felt I would never make a good father; because I feared I was losing the girl I wanted to marry; because I felt I was not living a good life. I worried about the impression I was making on other people. I worried because I thought I had stomach ulcers. I could no longer work; I gave up my job. I built up tension inside me until I was like a boiler without a safety valve. The pressure got so unbearable that something had to give—and it did. If you have ever had a nervous breakdown, pray God that you never do, for no pain of the body can exceed the excruciating pain of an agonised mind.

"My breakdown was so severe that I couldn't talk even to my own family. I had no control over

她说，正是耶稣这几句话使她产生了一种力量，一种信仰——医治创伤的力量，使她“立刻下床行走”。

“这种经验，”艾迪夫人说，“就像激发牛顿灵感的那个苹果一样，使我发现了自我治疗的方法，并且如何使别人做到这一点。我可以肯定，一切的根源都存在于思想中，这一切都是心理现象。”

就这样，玛丽开创了一种新信仰——基督教科学——唯一由女性创造的伟大信仰——现在已流行于全世界。

至此你也许对自己说：“这个家伙大概是在替基督教科学作宣传吧。”不，你错了，我可不是它的信徒。但是我活得越长，就越相信思想的巨大力量。从事成人教育35年，我知道人们只要改变他们的想法，就能够消除忧虑、恐惧和各种疾病，就能改变他们的生活。我知道！我知道！我知道！这种不可思议的变化，我亲眼目睹过好几百次，因为我见到如此之多，以至于见怪不怪了。

例如，这种转变就曾发生在我的一个学生身上。他是明尼苏达州圣保罗市西伊达荷街1469号的弗兰克·威利。他曾经历了精神崩溃，原因是什么呢？是忧虑。他对我说：“我对什么事情都忧虑。我之所以忧虑，是因为我太瘦了，我发现我正在掉头发，担心我永远都赚不到足够的钱娶老婆，担心我永远做不了一个好父亲，担心会失去我想娶的那个女孩子，担心我现在的生活不够好，担心我给别人的印象不好。我还担心我得了胃溃疡，于是无法再工作，只好辞职。我内心越来越紧张，就像一个没有安全阀的锅炉，终于达到了令人难以忍受的地步，必须有一个退路——结果真的出事了。如果你经历过精神崩溃，祈祷上帝！永远也不要有这种体验吧！因为任何一种肉体上的痛苦都比不上这种精神上的极度痛苦。

“我精神崩溃到不能和我的家人沟通。我无法控制自己的思想，充满了恐惧。只要稍有一点点声响，我就会跳起来。我躲开每一个人，常常无缘无故地哭。

“每天都是一种煎熬。我觉得被所有的人抛弃了——甚至上帝也抛弃了我。我真想跳进河

my thoughts. I was filled with fear. I would jump at the slightest noise. I avoided everybody. I would break out crying for no apparent reason at all.

"Every day was one of agony. I felt that I was deserted by everybody—even God. I was tempted to jump into the river and end it all.

"I decided instead to take a trip to Florida, hoping that a change of scene would help me. As I stepped on the train, my father handed me a letter and told me not to open it until I reached Florida. I landed in Florida during the height of the tourist season. Since I couldn't get in a hotel, I rented a sleeping room in a garage. I tried to get a job on a tramp freighter out of Miami, but had no luck. So I spent my time at the beach. I was more wretched in Florida than I had been at home; so I opened the envelope to see what Dad had written. His note said, 'son, you are 1, 500 miles from home, and you don't feel any different, do you? I knew you wouldn't, because you took with you the one thing that is the cause of all your trouble, that is, yourself. There is nothing wrong with either your body or your mind. It is not the situations you have met that have thrown you; it is what you think of these situations. "As a man thinketh in his heart, so is he." When you realise that, son, come home, for you will be cured. '

"Dad's letter made me angry. I was looking for sympathy, not instruction. I was so mad that I decided then and there that I would never go home. That night as I was walking down one of the side streets of Miami, I came to a church where services were going on. Having no place to go, I drifted in and listened to a sermon on the text: 'He who conquers his spirit is mightier than he who taketh a city. 'Sitting in the sanctity of the house of God and hearing the same thoughts that my Dad had written in his letter—all this swept the accumulated litter out of my brain. I was able to think clearly and sensibly for the first time in my life. I realised what a fool I had been. I was shocked to see myself in my true light: here I was, wanting to change the whole world and everyone in it—when the only thing that needed changing was the focus of the lens of the camera which was my mind.

"The next morning I packed and started home. A week later I was back on the job. Four months later I married the girl I had been afraid of losing. We now have a happy family of five children. God has been good to me both materially and mentally. At the time of the breakdown I

里，一死了之。

"但是我后来决定去佛罗里达旅行，希望换个环境对我有所帮助。我踏上火车之后，父亲交给我一封信，并告诉我到佛罗里达后再拆。我到佛罗里达的时候正值旅游旺季，因为在旅馆订不到房间，就租了一家汽车旅馆的房子住了下来。我想在迈阿密一艘不定期的货船上找一份差事，但没有找到，于是就在海滩上消磨时间。我在佛罗里达比在家更难受。这时，我拆开那封信，看看父亲写了些什么。他写道：'儿子，你现在离家1500里，但你并没有觉得有何不同，对不对?我知道你不会觉得有何不同，因为你还带着你所有麻烦的根源——也就是你自己。其实，你的身体和你的精神都没有问题。并不是你所遇到的环境给了你挫折，而是由你的各种想象造成的。"一个人心里想什么，他就会成为什么样子。"当你理解这点之后，儿子，回家来吧，因为那时你就能恢复了。'

"父亲的信让我生气——我要的是同情，而不是训斥。我非常生气，当时就决定再也不回家。那天晚上，我正路过迈阿密一条小街，经过一个教堂，里面正在举行礼拜。因为没有什么地方好去的，我就晃进了教堂，听了一场布道，题目是'能征服精神的人，比攻城占地更强'。我坐在神殿里，听到了我父亲信中所说的同样的想法——这一切将我脑子里积聚的不快一扫而光。于是，我能清楚而理智地思考了，并发现自己确实是一个大傻瓜。看清楚了自己，这一点实在使我非常震惊，本来我还想改变这个世界以及全世界所有的人呢——但事实上唯一需要改变的，是我大脑中那架思想相机镜头的焦点。

"第二天一大早，我收拾好行李回了家。一个星期以后，我又回去工作了。4个月以后，我娶了我一直害怕失去的那个女孩子，现在我们有了一个快乐的家庭，还有5个子女。无论是在物质还是精神方面，上帝都对我很好。在我精神崩溃的时候，我只是一个小部门的晚班工头，下面有18个工人；现在我成了一家纸箱厂的厂长，管理着450名员工。和以前相比，生活更充实、更美好了。我认为我现在已经了解了生命的真正价值。每当消极思想进入我的大脑(就像每个人遇到

was a night foreman of a small department handling eighteen people. I am now superintendent of carton manufacture in charge of over four hundred and fifty people. Life is much fuller and friendlier. I believe I appreciate the true values of life now. When moments of uneasiness try to creep in (as they will in everyone's life) I tell myself to get that camera back in focus, and everything is Ok.

"I can honestly say that I am glad I had the breakdown, because I found out the hard way what power our thoughts can have over our mind and our body. Now I can make my thoughts work for me instead of against me. I can see now that Dad was right when he said it wasn't outward situations that had caused all my suffering, but what I thought of those situations. And as soon as I realised that, I was cured—and stayed cured." Such was the experience of Frank J. Whaley.

I am deeply convinced that our peace of mind and the joy we get out of living depends not on where we are, or what we have, or who we are, but solely upon our mental attitude. Outward conditions have very little to do with it.

Milton in his blindness discovered that same truth three hundred years ago:

The mind is its own place, and in itself
Can make a heaven of Hell, a hell of Heaven.

Napoleon and Helen Keller are perfect illustrations of Milton's statement: Napoleon had everything men usually crave—glory, power, riches—yet he said at St. Helena: "I have never known six happy days in my life"; while Helen Keller—blind, deaf, dumb—declared: "I have found life so beautiful."

If half a century of living has taught me anything at all, it has taught me that *"Nothing can bring you peace but yourself."*

I am merely trying to repeat what Emerson said so well in the closing words of his essay on *"Self-Reliance"*: "A political victory, a rise in rents, the recovery of your sick, or the return of your absent friend, or some other quite external event, raises your spirits, and you think good days are preparing for you. Do not believe it. It can never be so. Nothing can bring you peace but yourself."

William James, who has never been topped in his knowledge of practical psychology, once

的那样)的时候,我就会告诉自己,只要把相机的焦距调好,一切都好办了。

“坦诚地说,我很高兴我曾经历过那次精神崩溃,因为它使我发现思想对身心两方面所具有的控制力。现在我能使我的思想为我所用,而不会对我造成损伤。我现在才知道我父亲是对的——使我痛苦的不是外在因素,而是我对各种事情的看法。一旦了解这点之后,我完全好了——而且不再生病了。”这就是弗兰克·威利的体验。

我深信,我们内心的平静和我们从生活中所得到的快乐,并不取决于我们在哪里或我们有什么,或我们是谁,而只取决于我们的心境。外在条件并没有多大的影响。

300年前,弥尔顿失明之后,也发现了同样的道理:“思想的运用和思想的本身,既能把地狱变成天堂,也能把天堂变成地狱。”

拿破仑和海伦·凯勒就是弥尔顿这句话的最好例证。拿破仑拥有普通人梦寐以求的一切——荣耀、权力以及财富——可是他却在圣赫勒拿岛说:“我这一辈子从来没有快乐过。”而海伦·凯勒——她既瞎又聋又哑——却宣称:“我发现生活太美妙了。”

如果说半个世纪的生活教会了我什么的话,那就是“除了你自己,没有任何东西可以给你带来平静”。

我想再重复一次爱默生在他的散文《自信》中所写的那句结束语:“不要认为一次政治上的获胜,收入的提高,病体的康复,或分别许久的好友归来,或其他纯粹外在的事物,能提高你的兴致,使你觉得前程美好。不要相信,事情绝不会如此简单。除了你自己,没有任何东西能给你带来平静。”

实用心理学权威威廉·詹姆斯曾发表过这样的理论:“行动似乎产生于感觉之后,可事实上行动和感觉是同时发生的。如果我们能够将由意志控制的行动规律化,那我们也能够间接地使不由意志控制的感觉规律化。”

made this observation: "*Action seems to follow feeling, but really action and feeling go together; and by regulating the action, which is under the more direct control of the will, we can indirectly regulate the feeling, which is not.*"

In other words, William James tells us that we cannot instantly change our emotions just by "making up our minds to"—but that we can change our actions. And that when we change our actions, we will automatically change our feelings.

"*Thus*, "he explains, "*The sovereign voluntary path to cheerfulness, if your cheerfulness be lost, is to sit up cheerfully and to act and speak as if cheerfulness were already there.*"

Does that simple trick work? It works like plastic surgery! Try it yourself. Put a big, broad, honest-to-God smile on your face; throw back your shoulders; take a good, deep breath; and sing a snatch of song. If you can't sing, whistle. If you can't whistle, hum. You will quickly discover what William James was talking about—that it is *physically impossible* to remain blue or depressed while you are acting out the symptoms of being radiantly happy!

This is one of the little basic truths of nature that can easily work miracles in all of our lives. I know a woman in California—I won't mention her name—who could wipe out all of her miseries in twenty-four hours if only she knew this secret. She's old, and she's a widow—that's sad, I admit—but does she try to act happy? No; if you ask her how she is feeling, she says, "Oh, I'm all right"—but the expression on her face and the whine in her voice say, "Oh, God, if you only knew the troubles I've seen! "She seems to reproach you for being happy in her presence. Hundreds of women are worse off than she is: her husband left her enough insurance to last the rest of her life, and she has married children to give her a home. But I've rarely seen her smile. She complains that all three of her sons-in-law are stingy and selfish—although she is a guest in their homes for months at a time. And she complains that her daughters never give her presents—although she hoards her own money carefully, "for my old age". She is a blight on herself and her unfortunate family! But does it have to be so? That is the pity of it—she could change herself from a miserable, bitter, and unhappy old woman into an honored and beloved member of the family—if she *wanted* to change. And all she would have to do to work this transformation would be to start acting cheerful; start acting as though she had a little love to give away—instead of squandering it

换句话说，威廉·詹姆斯告诉我们，我们不能只凭“下定决心”就改变我们的情感——但我们可以改变我们的行为。当我们改变行为的时候，自然就会改变我们的感觉。

“于是，”他解释说，“如果你不快乐，那么找到快乐的唯一的方法，就是振作起来，使你的行动和言词好像已经获得快乐一样。”

这种简单办法是不是有效呢?它就像整形手术一样有效！你不妨试一试：在你脸上露出开心的笑容，挺起胸膛，深呼吸，唱一首小曲；如果你不会唱，那就吹吹口哨；如果你不会吹口哨，那就哼一哼。很快你就会发现威廉·詹姆斯说的意思了——当你用行动显示出你的快乐时，根本就不会再忧虑和颓丧了。

这是大自然的基本真理之一，它能在我们生活中创造奇迹。我认识一个住在加利福尼亚州的女人——我不想提她的名字——如果她知道这条秘诀的话，能在一天之内抛弃所有的哀愁。她已经老了，又是一个寡妇——我承认这很不幸——可是她有没有试过变得快乐些呢?没有。如果你问她觉得怎样，她会说：“哦，我还不错。”但她脸上的表情和哀诉的声音好像在说：“哦，老天爷啊，要是你遇到我的烦恼，就能明白了。”似乎你很快乐地站在她面前都会使她讨厌。有很多女人比她的情况更糟。她丈夫给她留下了足以维生的保险金，她的子女也都已经成家，而且能够奉养她，但是我很少见她笑。她总是埋怨她的3个女婿对她不好——尽管她每次去他们家一住就是好几个月。她还抱怨她女儿从来不送她礼物——但她却不舍得掏出自己的钱，她说是“留着养老”。对她自己和她不幸的家人来说，她的确是个令人讨厌的家伙！但事情必须这样吗?这才是令人遗憾之处——她本来可以使自己从一个忧愁、挑剔而且很不开心的老妇人，变成家里受人敬重和喜爱的成员——只要她愿意。如果她想实现这种转变，只需高高兴兴地活着，觉得她还有一点点爱可以给别人，而不是老谈自己的不快和不幸，一切都好办了。

我认识一个住在印第安纳州的人，印第安纳州泰尔市北街1335号的英格莱特。他现在之所

all on her own unhappy and embittered self.

I know a man in Indiana—H. J. Englert, of 1335 nth Street, Tell City, Indiana—who is still alive today because he discovered this secret. Ten years ago Mr. Englert had a case of scarlet fever; and when he recovered, he found he had developed nephritis, a kidney disease. He tried all kinds of doctors, "even quacks", he informs me, but nothing could cure him.

Then, a short time ago, he got other complications. His blood pressure soared. He went to a doctor, and was told that his blood pressure was hitting the top at 214. He was told that it was fatal—that the condition was progressive, and he had better put his affairs in order at once.

"I went home, "he says, "and made sure that my insurance was all paid up, then I apologised to my Maker for all my mistakes, and settled down to gloomy meditations. I made everyone unhappy. My wife and family were miserable, and I was buried deep in depression myself. However, after a week of wallowing in self-pity, I said to myself, 'You're acting like a fool! You may not die for a year yet, so why not try to be happy while you're here?'

"I threw back my shoulders, put a smile on my face, and attempted to act as though everything were normal. I admit it was an effort at first—but I forced myself to be pleasant and cheerful; and this not only helped my family, but it also helped me.

"The first thing I knew, I began to *feel* better—almost as well as I pretended to feel! The improvement went on. And today—months after I was supposed to be in my grave—I am not only happy, well, and alive, but my blood pressure is down! I know one thing for certain: the doctor's prediction would certainly have come true if I had gone on thinking 'dying' thoughts of defeat. But I gave my body a chance to heal itself, by nothing in the world but a change of mental attitude! "

Let me ask you a question: If merely acting cheerful and thinking positive thoughts of health and courage can save this man's life, why should you and I tolerate for one minute more our minor glooms and depressions? Why make ourselves, and everyone around us, unhappy and blue, when it is possible for us to start creating happiness by merely acting cheerful?

Years ago, I read a little book that had a lasting and profound effect on my life. It was called *As a Man Thinketh* by James Lane Allen, and here's what it said:

"A man will find that as he alters his thoughts towards things and other people, things and

以还活着,正因为他发现了这个秘密。10年前,英格莱特先生患了猩红热病;当他康复以后,又得了肾脏病。他看过许多医生,"甚至江湖医生,"他告诉我,但谁也没治好他。

然后,不久前他又得了另一种并发症,血压变得很高。他去看了医生,医生说他的血压已经达到214的最高值。医生说他已经没救了,情况太严重,最好马上准备后事。

"我回到家,"他说,"查清楚我已经付清了所有的保险费之后,向上帝忏悔我以前的各种错误,坐下来默默沉思。我害得所有人都不开心,我的妻子和家人都非常难受,我自己更是深陷悲观的境地。然而,一个星期的自我怜悯之后,我对自己说:'你这样子像个大傻瓜。你在一年之内可能还不会死,何不趁你还活着的时候快快乐乐的呢?'

"于是,我挺起胸膛,脸上露出微笑,尽力表现出似乎一切正常的样子。我承认刚开始这相当难办,但是我强迫自己开心,这不仅对我的家人有所帮助,对我自己也大有裨益。

"接着,我发现自己开始感觉好多了——几乎好得和我假装的一样好。今天——原以为已经躺在坟墓几个月了——我不仅很快乐,还很健康地活着,而且血压也下降了。有一件事我可以肯定:如果我一直想到自己会死,那么医生的预言就会实现了。可是我给了自己一个自我治愈的机会,别的都没有用,除了改变心情。"

让我问你一个问题:如果只要想着快乐、健康而充满勇气的积极思想就可以拯救人的性命,你和我为什么还要容忍那些小小的不快和颓丧呢?如果让自己快乐就能够产生快乐,那我们又为什么要让自己和身边的人不高兴而遭受痛苦呢?

许多年前,我看过一本小书,它对我的生活产生了长远而深刻的影响,这本书叫《人的思想》,作者是詹姆斯·艾伦,下面是这本书中的话:

"当一个人改变对事物和其他人的看法时,他会发现,事物和其他人也会发生改变……要是一个人把他的思想朝向光明的一面,他就会惊讶地发现他的生活由此受到的巨大影响。人们不能吸

other people will alter towards him... Let a man radically alter his thoughts, and he will be astonished at the rapid transformation it will effect in the material conditions of his life. Men do not attract that which they want, but that which they are... The divinity that shapes our ends is in ourselves. It is our very self... All that a man achieves is the direct result of his own thoughts... A man can only rise, conquer and achieve by lifting up his thoughts. He can only remain weak and abject and miserable by refusing to lift up his thoughts."

According to the book of Genesis, the Creator gave man dominion over the whole wide earth. A mighty big present. But I am not interested in any such super-royal prerogatives. All I desire is dominion over myself—dominion over my thoughts; dominion over my fears; dominion over my mind and over my spirit. And the wonderful thing is that I know that I can attain this dominion to an astonishing degree, any time I want to, by merely controlling my actions—which in turn control my reactions.

So let us remember these words of William James: *"Much of what we call Evil... can often be converted into a bracing and tonic good by a simple change of the sufferer's inner attitude from one of fear to one of fight."*

Let's fight for our happiness!

Let's fight for our happiness by following a daily programme of cheerful and constructive thinking. Here is such a program. It is entitled "Just for Today". I found this program so inspiring that I gave away hundreds of copies. It was written thirty-six years ago by the late Sibyl F. Partridge. If you and I follow it, we will eliminate most of our worries and increase immeasurably our portion of what the French call *la joie de vivre*.

Just For Today

1. Just for today I will be happy. This assumes that what Abraham Lincoln said is true, that "most folks are about as happy as they make up their minds to be." Happiness is from within; it is not a matter of externals.

2. Just for today I will try to adjust myself to what is, and not try to adjust everything to my own desires. I will take my family, my business, and my luck as they come and fit myself to them.

3. Just for today I will take care of my body. I will exercise it, care for it, nourish it, not abuse

引他们想要的,却可以吸引他们所有的……改变气质的神性就存在于我们内心当中,就是我们自己……一个人所能得到的,正是他自己思想的直接结果……一个人只有具备了奋发向上的思想,才能振奋,征服一切并有所成就。如果他不能振作他的思想,只能陷于衰弱和愁苦之中。"

《创世纪》中说,是上帝让人统治整个世界。这是一份贵重的礼物,可是我对这种特权没有什么兴趣。我所希望得到的只是控制我自己——控制我的思想,控制我的恐惧,控制我的内心和精神。最神奇的是,我知道我在这方面可以达到相当高的程度。不论何时,只要我控制自己的行为,就能控制我的反应。

所以,让我们记住威廉·詹姆斯的话:"通常只要把内心感觉由恐惧变成奋斗,就可以把我们所谓的大部分邪恶转变成有益的东西。"

让我们为自己的快乐而奋斗吧!

让我们设计一个能给每天带来快乐并且富有建设性思想的计划,使我们得到快乐吧!下面就是这个计划,名字叫《只为今天》。我认为这种计划非常有用,所以复印了几千份送人。这是由36年前已故的希贝尔·帕特瑞吉写的。如果我们能够照它去做,就能消除大部分忧虑,大大增加"生活上的快乐"。

只为今天

1.只为今天,我要很快乐。如果林肯所说的"大部分人只要下定决心,都能很快乐"这句话是对的,那么快乐是来自人的内心,而不是来自外界。

2.只为今天,我要使自己适应一切,而不是让一切来适应我的欲望。我要以这种态度来接受我的家庭、我的事业和我的运气。

3.只为今天,我要爱惜我的身体。我要多运动,照顾好自己,珍惜自己,不损伤身体,不忽视身体,使它成为我心灵的殿堂。

it nor neglect it, so that it will be a perfect machine for my bidding.

4. Just for today I will try to strengthen my mind. I will learn something useful. I will not be a mental loafer. I will read something that requires effort, thought and concentration.

5. Just for today I will exercise my soul in three ways: I will do somebody a good turn and not get found out. I will do at least two things I don't want to do, as William James suggests, just for exercise.

6. Just for today I will be agreeable. I will look as well as I can, dress as becomingly as possible, talk low, act courteously, be liberal with praise, criticise not at all, nor find fault with anything and not try to regulate nor improve anyone.

7. Just for today I will try to live through this day only, not to tackle my whole life problem at once. I can do things for twelve hours that would appall me if I had to keep them up for a lifetime.

8. Just for today I will have a programme. I will write down what I expect to do every hour. I may not follow it exactly, but I will have it. It will eliminate two pests, hurrying and indecision.

9. Just for today I will have a quiet half-hour all by myself and relax. In this half-hour sometimes I will think of God, so as to get a little more perspective into my life.

10. Just for today I will be unafraid, especially I will not be afraid to be happy, to enjoy what is beautiful, to love, and to believe that those I love, love me.

If we want to develop a mental attitude that will bring us peace and happiness, here is Rule 1:

Think and act cheerfully, and you will feel cheerful.

4. 只为今天，我要加强我的思想。我要学一些有用的知识，不做胡思乱想的人。我要看一些需要精力、思考、专注的书。

5. 只为今天，我要从三方面来锻炼我的灵魂：我要为别人做一件好事，但不要让人家知道；我还要做两件我并不想做的事，就像威廉·詹姆斯建议的，只是为了锻炼自己。

6. 只为今天，我要做个受人欢迎的人。我要尽量修饰外表，尽量穿着得体，说话要低声，行动要优雅，不在乎别人的毁誉。对任何事都不挑毛病，也不干涉或教训别人。

7. 只为今天，我要努力思考如何过好今天，而不是一次解决我一生的问题。虽然我可以持续12小时地工作，但我若一辈子这样做下去的话，就会毁了我。

8. 只为今天，我要制订一个计划。我要写下每小时该做些什么，也许我不会完全照着它去做，但还是要订下这个计划。这样至少可以消除两大缺点——匆忙和犹豫不决。

9. 只为今天，我要为自己留下半小时的安静，轻松下来。在这半小时里，我要感激神，使我的生命更充满希望。

10. 只为今天，我要毫不惧怕，尤其不能害怕快乐，要去欣赏一切美，去爱一切，相信我所爱的那些人也会爱我。

如果我们想培养平安和快乐的心境，下面是规则的第一条：

有了快乐的思想和行为，你就会感受到快乐。

2 The High Cost of Getting Even

One night, years ago, as I was travelling through Yellowstone Park, I sat with other tourists on bleachers facing a dense growth of pine and spruce. Presently the animal which we had been waiting to see, the terror of the forest, the grizzly bear, strode out into the glare of the lights and began devouring the garbage that had been dumped there from the kitchen of one of the park hotels. A forest ranger, Major Martindale, sat on a horse and talked to the excited tourists about bears. He told us that the grizzly bear can whip any other animal in the Western world, with the possible exception of the buffalo and the Kodiak bear; yet I noticed that night that there was one animal, and only one, that the grizzly permitted to come out of the forest and eat with him under the glare of the lights: a skunk. The grizzly knew that he could liquidate a skunk with one swipe of his mighty paw. Why didn't he do it? Because he had found from experience that it didn't pay.

I found that out, too. As a farm boy, I trapped four-legged skunks along the hedgerows in Missouri; and, as a man, I encountered a few two-legged skunks on the sidewalks of New York. I have found from sad experience that it doesn't pay to stir up either variety.

When we hate our enemies, we are giving them power over us: power over our sleep, our appetites, our blood pressure, our health, and our happiness. Our enemies would dance with joy if only they knew how they were worrying us, lacerating us and getting even with us! Our hate is not hurting them at all, but our hate is turning our own days and nights into a hellish turmoil.

Who do you suppose said this: "If selfish people try to take advantage of you, cross them off your list, but don't try to get even. When you try to get even, you hurt yourself more than you hurt the other fellow"?... Those words sound as if they might have been uttered by some starry-eyed idealist. But they weren't. Those words appeared in a bulletin issued by the Police Department of Milwaukee.

How will trying to get even hurt you? In many ways. According to *Life* magazine, it may even wreck your health. "The chief personality characteristic of persons with hypertension [high blood

第2章 报复的代价太高了

多年前的一个晚上,我旅行途经黄石公园,与其他游客一起坐在露天座位上,面对茂密的树林,期望看到森林杀手灰熊的出现。它会到森林旅馆扔弃的垃圾堆中寻找食物。一位森林管理员骑着马告诉了我们这群兴奋的游客有关熊的事情。他告诉我们:灰熊几乎可以击倒西部所有的动物,除了水牛和另一种黑熊之外。但在那天晚上,我却注意到有一只小动物——只有一只——灰熊不但让它从森林里跑了出来,还与它在灯光下共进晚餐。那是一只臭鼬!灰熊很清楚,只需扬起它的巨掌就可以一掌打死臭鼬,但它为什么不那样做呢?因为它从经验里学到那样做得不偿失。

我也知道这个道理。当我还是个乡村孩子的时候,曾在密苏里州的篱笆边抓过这种四只脚的臭鼬;当我长大成人后,在纽约的街头也碰过几个两只脚的臭鼬。我从这些不幸的经历中发现:无论招惹哪一种臭鼬,都不值得。

当我们痛恨我们的敌人时,就等于给了他们取胜的力量。这种力量会影响我们的睡眠、我们的食欲、我们的血压、我们的健康和我们的快乐。如果我们的敌人知道他们是如何让我们忧虑,让我们烦恼,让我们一心只想报复的话,他们一定会高兴得手舞足蹈。我们的恨意完全伤害不到他们,可是却使我们的生活变成了地狱。

你猜这是谁说的?"要是自私的人想占你的便宜,不必理睬他,更不必报复他。当你想跟他扯平的时候,你对自己的伤害远比对那家伙多……"这段话好像是什么理想主义者说的。其实不然。这段话来自一份警察局通告。

报复为什么会伤害你呢?它的伤害可多了。据《生活》杂志说,报复甚至会损害你的健康。

pressure]is resentment, "said *Life*. "When resentment is chronic, chronic hypertension and heart trouble follow."

So you see that when Jesus said, "Love your enemies", he was not only preaching sound ethics. He was also preaching twentieth-century medicine. When He said, "Forgive seventy time seven", Jesus was telling you and me how to keep from having high blood pressure, heart trouble, stomach ulcers, and many other ailments.

A friend of mine recently had a serious heart attack. Her physician put her to bed and ordered her to refuse to get angry about anything, no matter what happened. Physicians know that if you have a weak heart, a fit of anger *can* kill you. *Did* I say can kill you? A fit of anger did kill a restaurant owner in Spokane, Washington, a few years ago. I have in front of me now a letter from Jerry Swartout, chief of the Police Department, Spokane, Washington, saying, "A few years ago, William Falkaber, a man of sixty-eight who owned a café here in Spokane, killed himself by flying into a rage because his cook insisted on drinking coffee out of his saucer. The café owner was so indignant that he grabbed a revolver and started to chase the cook and fell dead from heart failure—with his hand still gripping the gun. The coroner's report declared that anger had caused the heart failure."

When Jesus said, "Love your enemies", He was also telling us how to improve our looks. I know women—and so do you—whose faces have been wrinkled and hardened by hate and disfigured by resentment. All the beauty treatments in Christendom won't improve their looks half so much as would a heart full of forgiveness, tenderness, and love.

Hatred destroys our ability to enjoy even our food. The *Bible* puts it this way, "Better is a dinner of herbs where love is, than a stalled ox and hatred therewith."

Wouldn't our enemies rub their hands with glee if they knew that our hate for them was exhausting us, making us tired and nervous, ruining our looks, giving us heart trouble, and probably shortening our lives?

Even if we can't love our enemies, let's at least love ourselves. Let's love ourselves so much that we won't permit our enemies to control our happiness, our health and our looks. As Shakespeare put it:

"高血压患者的主要特征是容易愤怒,"杂志说,"愤怒不止的话,长期性高血压和心脏病就会随之而来。"

现在你该明白耶稣所说的"爱你的仇人"不只是一种道德教导,而且是在宣扬一种最新医学。当他说"要原谅70个7次"的时候,他正是在教导我们如何避免高血压、心脏病、胃溃疡和其他疾病。

我的一个朋友最近严重心脏病发作,医生要求他躺在床上,不论发生任何事情都不能生气。医生知道患有心脏衰竭症的人,一旦发怒生气就可能送命。几年前,华盛顿州斯泼坎城一家餐馆的老板的确因为生气致死。我面前现在就有一封寄自华盛顿州斯泼坎城警察局局长杰瑞·施瓦脱的信。信中说:"几年以前,68岁的威廉·弗尔坎伯,在斯泼坎城开了一家咖啡馆。因为他的厨师坚持用茶碟喝咖啡,而将他活活气死。当时,那个咖啡馆老板非常恼火,抓起一把左轮手枪去追那个厨师,结果因为心脏病发作倒地死去——他手里还抓着那支手枪。验尸员报告说:他因为愤怒而导致心脏病发作。"

当耶稣说"爱你的仇人"时,他也是在告诉我们如何改进我们的外表。你也和我一样认识一些女性,她们的脸颊因为怨恨而布满了皱纹或变得难看。不管她们如何做美容也不管用,远不及心里充满宽容、温柔和爱的人的容颜。

怨恨会毁坏我们享受食物的美味。《圣经》说:"怀着爱心吃蔬菜,也比怀着怨恨吃牛肉要好。"

假如我们的仇人知道我们对他们的怨恨使我们精疲力竭,使我们紧张不安,使我们的外表受到损伤,使我们患上心脏病,甚至可缩短我们寿命时,他们难道不会拍手欢呼吗?

即使我们不能爱我们的仇人,我们至少也要爱我们自己。要爱自己,不能让仇人控制我们的快乐、我们的健康和我们的外表。正如莎士比亚所说的:"不要因你的敌人而燃起一把怒火,

Heat not a furnace for your foe so hot
That it do singe yourself.

When Jesus said that we should forgive our enemies "seventy times seven", he was also preaching sound business. For example, I have before me as I write a letter I received from George Rona, Fradegata'n 24, Uppsala, Sweden. For years, George Rona was an attorney in Vienna; but during the Second World War, he fled to Sweden. He had no money, needed work badly. Since he could speak and write several languages, he hoped to get a position as correspondent for some firm engaged in importing or exporting. Most of the firms replied that they had no need of such services because of the war, but they would keep his name on file... and so on. One man, however, wrote George Rona a letter saying, "What you imagine about my business is not true. You are both wrong and foolish. I do not need any correspondent. Even if I did need one, I wouldn't hire you because you can't even write good Swedish. Your letter is full of mistakes."

When George Rona read that letter, he was as mad as Donald Duck. What did this Swede mean by telling him he couldn't write the language! Why, the letter that this Swede himself had written was full of mistakes! So George Rona wrote a letter that was calculated to burn this man up. Then he paused. He said to himself, "Wait a minute, now. How do I know this man isn't right? I have studied Swedish, but it's not my native language, so maybe I do make mistakes I don't know anything about. If I do, then I certainly have to study harder if I ever hope to get a job. This man has possibly done me a favour, even though he didn't mean to. The mere fact that he expressed himself in disagreeable terms doesn't alter my debt to him. Therefore, I am going to write him and thank him for what he has done."

So George Rona tore up the scorching letter he had already written, and wrote another that said, "It was kind of you to go to the trouble of writing to me, especially when you do not need a correspondent. I am sorry I was mistaken about your firm. The reason that I wrote you was that I made inquiry and your name was given me as a leader in your field. I did not know I had made grammatical errors in my letter. I am sorry and ashamed of myself. I will now apply myself more diligently to the study of the Swedish language and try to correct my mistakes. I want to thank you for helping me get started on the road to self-improvement."

结果却烧伤自己。"

当耶稣说我们应该原谅我们的仇人"70个7次"时,他也是在教我们做生意。例如,当我写这一段文章的时候,在我面前有一封乔治·罗纳的信,他住在瑞典的艾普苏那。乔治·罗纳在维也纳当了很多年的律师,但是他在第二次世界大战期间逃到了瑞典,身无分文,急需找一份工作。因为他会说会写好几种语言,所以希望在进出口公司找到一份秘书的工作。但绝大多数公司都回说因为现在正在打仗,他们不需要这类人,但他们会将他的名字存在档案中……不过,有一个人给乔治·罗纳写信说:"你完全不了解我的生意。你既蠢又笨,我根本不需要商务秘书。即使我需要,也不会找你,因为你甚至写不好瑞典文,你的信里全是错字。"

当乔治·罗纳看到那封信时,他简直气疯了。那个瑞典人自己的信就错误百出,可是他竟然说罗纳不会瑞典文,是什么意思?于是乔治·罗纳也写了一封信,想使那个人大发一顿脾气。但他接下来对自己说:"慢。我怎么知道这个人说的不是对的?我学过瑞典语,可这并不是我的母语,也许我确实犯了我并不知道的错误。如果真是那样,那么我要想找到工作,就必须更努力学习。这个人可能帮了我一个大忙,虽然他的本意并非如此。他用这么难听的话来表达他的意思,并不表示我不欠他的。所以我应该给他写封信,对他表示感谢。"

于是乔治·罗纳撕毁了他刚写好的那封骂人的信,又另外写了一封信,说:"你不嫌麻烦地给我写信,实在是太好了,尤其是你并不需要商务秘书。我很抱歉弄错了贵公司的业务。我之所以给你写信,是因为我向别人打听到的你,说你是这一行的领袖人物。我并不知道我的信中犯了语法错误,我觉得很惭愧。现在我打算更努力地学习瑞典语,改正我的错误。谢谢你帮助我走上改进之路。"

没过几天,乔治·罗纳就收到了那个人的回信,请罗纳去他那里。罗纳去了,而且得到了一份工作。乔治·罗纳由此发现"温和的回答能消除怒气"。

Within a few days, George Rona got a letter from this man, asking Rona to come to see him. Rona went—and got a job. George Rona discovered for himself that"a soft answer turneth away wrath".

We may not be saintly enough to love our enemies, but, for the sake of our own health and happiness, let's at least forgive them and forget them. That is the smart thing to do. I once asked General Eisenhower's son, John, if his father ever nourished resentments. "No, "he replied, "Dad never wastes a minute thinking about people he doesn't like."

There is an old saying that a man is a fool who can't be angry, but a man is wise who won't be angry.

That was the policy of William J. Gaynor, a former Mayor of New York. Bitterly denounced by the yellow press, he was shot by a maniac and almost killed. As he lay in the hospital, fighting for his life, he said, "Every night, I forgive everything and everybody." Is that too idealistic? Too much sweetness and light? If so, let's turn for counsel to the great German philosopher, Schopenhauer, author of *Studies* in *Pessimism.* He regarded life as a futile and painful adventure. Gloom dripped from him as he walked; yet out of the depths of his despair, Schopenhauer cried, "If possible, no animosity should be felt for anyone."

I once asked Bernard Baruch—the man who was the trusted adviser to six Presidents: Wilson, Harding, Coolidge, Hoover, Roosevelt, and Truman—whether he was ever disturbed by the attacks of his enemies. "No man can humiliate me or disturb me, "he replied. "I won't let him."

No one can humiliate or disturb you and me, either—unless we let him.

Sticks and stones may break my bones,
But words can never hurt me.

Throughout the ages mankind has burned its candles before those Christlike individuals who bore no malice against their enemies. I have often stood in the Jasper National Park, in Canada, and gazed upon one of the most beautiful mountains in the Western world—a mountain named in honour of Edith Cavell, the British nurse who went to her death like a saint before a German firing squad on October 12, 1915. Her crime? She had hidden and fed and nursed wounded French and English soldiers in her Belgian home, and had helped them escape into Holland. As the English chaplain entered her cell in the military prison in Brussels that October morning, to prepare her for

也许我们不能神圣地爱我们的仇人,但为了我们自己的健康和快乐,至少要原谅他们,忘记他们。那才是聪明之举。有一次,我问艾森豪威尔将军的儿子约翰,他父亲是否怨恨别人。"不,"他回答说,"我父亲从来不浪费时间去想他不喜欢的人。"

有句老话说:"不会生气的人是笨蛋,而不生气的人才是智者。"

这也正是纽约州前州长威廉·盖诺的策略。当他被一份街头小报攻击得遍体鳞伤,又被一个疯子打了一枪而几乎送命时,他躺在医院,生命垂危,却仍然说:"每天晚上我都原谅所有的事和所有的人。"这是不是太理想了呢?是不是过于轻松美好了呢?如果是这样,就让我们来看看德国伟大的哲学家、"悲观论"的作者叔本华的理论。他认为生命就是一种毫无价值而又充满痛苦的冒险,当他走过生命中每一刻的时候,全身都散发着痛苦,可是在绝望深处,叔本华却说:"如果可能,不应该怨恨任何人。"

有一次我曾问伯纳德·巴鲁屈——他曾担任过6位总统威尔逊、哈定、柯立芝、胡佛、罗斯福和杜鲁门的顾问——他会不会因为敌人的攻击而烦恼?"没有人能够羞辱或干扰我," 他回答说,"我不会让他们得逞。"

也没有人能够羞辱或困扰你和我——除非我们让他这样做。

"棍棒和石头也许能打断我的骨头,可是语言永远伤害不了我。"

多少年来,人们总是景仰不怀恨其敌人的人。我常去加拿大杰斯帕国家公园,仰望以伊笛丝·卡薇尔的名字命名的山,这是西方最美丽的山。它是为了纪念一位在1915年10月12日被德军行刑队枪毙的英国护士。她犯了什么罪呢?因为她在比利时的家中收容和看护了许多受伤的英法士兵,还帮助他们逃往荷兰。在10月的一天早晨,一位英国教士走进军队监狱她所在的牢房,为她做临终祈祷,伊笛丝·卡薇尔说了两句后来刻在她的纪念碑上的不朽的话:"我知道仅有爱国还不够,我一定不能敌视或怨恨任何人。"4年之后,她的遗体运送到英国,在威斯敏斯特

death, Edith Cavell uttered two sentences that have been preserved in bronze and granite: "I realise that patriotism is not enough. I must have no hatred or bitterness toward anyone." Four years later, her body was removed to England and memorial services were held in Westminster Abbey. Today, a granite statue stands opposite the National Portrait Gallery in London—a statue of one of England's immortals. "I realise that patriotism is not enough. I must have no hatred or bitterness toward anyone."

One sure way to forgive and forget our enemies is to become absorbed in some cause infinitely bigger than ourselves. Then the insults and the enmities we encounter won't matter because we will be oblivious of everything but our *cause*. As an example, let's take an intensely dramatic event that was about to take place in the pine woods of Mississippi back in 1918. A lynching! Laurence Jones, a coloured teacher and preacher, was about to be lynched. A few years ago, I visited the school that Laurence Jones founded—the Piney Woods Country School—and I spoke before the student body. That school is nationally known today, but the incident I am going to relate occurred long before that. It occurred back in the highly emotional days of the First World War. A rumor had spread through central Mississippi that the Germans were arousing the Negroes and inciting them to rebellion. Laurence Jones, the man who was about to be lynched, was, as I have already said, a Negro himself and was accused of helping to arouse his race to insurrection. A group of white men—pausing outside the church—had heard Laurence Jones shouting to his congregation: "Life is a battle in which every Negro must gird on his *armor* and fight to survive and succeed."

"Fight! ""Armor! "Enough! Galloping off into the night, these excited young men recruited a mob, returned to the church, put a rope round the preacher, dragged him for a mile up the road, stood him on a heap of faggots, lighted matches, and were ready to hang him and burn him at the same time, when someone shouted, "Let's make the blankety-blank-blank talk before he hums. Speech! Speech! "Laurence Jones, standing on the faggots, spoke with a rope around his neck, spoke for his life and his *cause*. He had been graduated from the University of Iowa in 1907. His sterling character, his scholarship and his musical ability had made him popular with both the students and the faculty. Upon graduation, he had turned down the offer of a hotel man to set him up in business, and had turned down the offer of a wealthy man to finance his musical education.

大教堂举行安葬仪式。今天,在伦敦国立肖像画廊对面立着伊笛丝·卡薇尔的花岗岩雕像——这是一位英国不朽英雄的雕像。"我知道仅有爱国还不够,我一定不能敌视或怨恨任何人。"

有一个原谅和忘记我们敌人的有效方法,那就是做一些超出我们能力的大事,这样我们所遭受的侮辱和敌意就无关紧要了,因为只有这样,我们才不会去计较其他事情了。举例来说:1918年,密西西比州松树林里发生了一件极富戏剧性的事情,差点引发了一次火刑!劳伦斯·琼斯,一个黑人教师和牧师差点儿被烧死了。我在几年前曾去看过劳伦斯·琼斯创建的松林乡村学校,还对全体学生做了一次演讲。今天那所学校全国皆知,但我下面要说的这件事情却发生在很早以前。它发生在第一次世界大战人们最容易感情冲动的时期。此时,在密西西比州中部流传一种谣言,说德国人正在唆使黑人造反。而那个将被烧死的劳伦斯·琼斯就是黑人,有人控告他带领族人造反。一大群在教堂外面的白人听见劳伦斯·琼斯对人们大声喊道:"生命,就是一场战斗!每一个黑人都要穿上盔甲,以战斗求得生存和成功。"

"战斗!""盔甲!"足够了。于是,这些年轻人趁夜冲出去,纠集了一大群暴徒,回到教堂,拿了一条绳子捆住他,将他拖到一里地以外,让他站在一大堆干柴上面,并点燃了柴堆,准备一面用火烧他,一面把他吊死。这时,有一个人叫起来:"在烧死他之前,我们要让这个喜欢多嘴的人说话。说话啊!说话啊!"

劳伦斯·琼斯站在柴堆上,脖子上套着绳索,为他的生命和理想发表了一篇演说。他于1907年毕业于爱荷华大学,他那纯真的性格和学问以及音乐方面的才华,使得所有的老师和学生都很喜欢他。毕业后,劳伦斯·琼斯拒绝了一个旅馆给留他的职位,还拒绝了一个有钱人资助他继续深造音乐。这是为什么呢?因为他有着非常崇高的理想。当他读完布克尔·华盛顿的传记时,就决定献身教育事业,教育他那些因为贫穷而没有受过教育的族人。因此他回到南方最贫困的地方,也就是密西西比州杰克镇以南25里的一个小地方,用他的手表当了1.65美元,在树林中

Why? Because he was on fire with a vision. Reading the story of Booker T. Washington's life, he had been inspired to devote his own life to educating the poverty-stricken, illiterate members of his race. So he went to the most backward belt he could find in the South—a spot twenty-five miles south of Jackson, Mississippi. Pawning his watch for $1. 65, he started his school in the open woods with a stump for a desk. Laurence Jones told these angry men who were waiting to lynch him of the struggle he had had to educate these unschooled boys and girls and to train them to be good farmers, mechanics, cooks, housekeepers. He told of the white men who had helped him in his struggle to establish Piney Woods Country School—white men who had given him land, lumber, and pigs, cows and money, to help him carry on his educational work.

When Laurence Jones was asked afterward if he didn't hate the men who had dragged him up the road to hang him and burn him, he replied that he *was too busy with his cause to hate—too absorbed in something bigger than himself.* "*I have no time to quarrel,* "he said, "*no time for regrets, and no man can force me to stoop low enough to hate him.*"

As Laurence Jones talked with sincere and moving eloquence as he pleaded, not for himself but his cause, the mob began to soften. Finally, an old Confederate veteran in the crowd said, "I believe this boy is telling the truth. I know the white men whose names he has mentioned. He is doing a fine work. We have made a mistake. We ought to help him instead of hang him." The Confederate veteran passed his hat through the crowd and raised a gift of fifty-two dollars and forty cents from the very men who had gathered there to hang the founder of Piney Woods Country School—the man who said, "I have no time to quarrel, no time for regrets, and no man can force me to stoop low enough to hate him."

Epictetus pointed out nineteen centuries ago that we reap what we sow and that somehow fate almost always makes us pay for our malefactions. "In the long run, "said Epictetus, "every man will pay the penalty for his own misdeeds. The man who remembers this will be angry with no one, indignant with no one, revile no one, blame no one, offend no one, hate no one."

Probably no other man in American history was ever more denounced and hated and double-crossed than Lincoln. Yet Lincoln, according to Herndon's classic biography, "never judged men by his like or dislike for them. If any given act was to be performed, he could understand that his

用树桩做桌子,开始办起了他的露天学校。劳伦斯·琼斯对那些愤怒的、正想要烧死他的人讲述了他所做过的各种奋斗——教育那些没有上过学的男孩和女孩,把他们教成合格的农夫、技工、厨子、家庭主妇。他说到一些白人曾帮助他建立这所学校——这些白人送给他土地、木材、猪、牛和钱,帮助他继续办他的教育事业。

后来有人问劳伦斯·琼斯,他是否恨那些拖他出去准备吊死和烧死的人?他回答说,他正忙于实现他的理想,根本没有时间去恨——他正沉浸于超出他个人能力的大事。"我没有时间吵架,"他说,"没有时间后悔,也没有任何人能强迫我去恨他。"

劳伦斯·琼斯的态度诚恳,令人感动。他没有为自己,而是为了他的事业而乞求。于是,这些暴民开始软下来。最后,人群中一位参加过南北战争的老兵说:"我相信这孩子是在说真话。我认识那些他提到的白人。他是在做好事。我们错了,我们应该帮助他,而不是吊死他。"然后那位老兵把他的帽子在人群中传动,从那些聚集于此准备烧死这位松林乡村学校创建者的人那里,募集了52.4美元,并交给了琼斯这个曾说"我没有时间吵架,没有时间后悔,也没有人能强迫我恨他"的人。

爱匹克泰德在19个世纪前就指出,我们会种因得果,不论如何,我们总会为自己的过错付出代价。"归根结底,"爱匹克泰德说,"每一个人都会为他自己的错误付出代价。能够记住这点的人就不会对任何人生气,也不会和任何人争吵,不会辱骂、斥责、侵犯、痛恨别人。"

在美国历史上,大概没有其他人所受的责难、怨恨和陷害比林肯更多。但是根据赫登的不朽传记记载,林肯"从来不以自己的好恶来评判别人。如果有什么工作要做,他也会想到他的敌人会做得和其他人一样好。如果一个人以前曾羞辱过他或对他个人不敬,但这人却是某个职位的最佳人选的话,林肯也会让他担任该职,就像派他的朋友去做这件事一样……他从未因为某人是他的敌人或者他不喜欢某人而解除其职务。"

enemy could do it just as well as anyone. If a man had maligned him or been guilty of personal ill-treatment, and was the fittest man for the place, Lincoln would give him that place, just as soon as he would give it to a friend... I do not think he ever removed a man because he was his enemy or because he disliked him."

Lincoln was denounced and insulted by some of the very men he had appointed to positions of high power—men like McClellan, Seward, Stanton, and Chase. Yet Lincoln believed, according to Herndon, his law partner, that "No man was to be eulogized for what he did; or censured for what he did or did not do, "because"all of us are the children of conditions, of circumstances, of environment, of education, of acquired habits and of heredity moulding men as they are and will forever be."

Perhaps Lincoln was right. If you and I had inherited the same physical, mental, and emotional characteristics that our enemies have inherited, and if life had done to us what it has done to them, we would act exactly as they do. We couldn't possibly do anything else. As Clarence Darrow used to say: "To know all is to understand all, and this leaves no room for judgment and condemnation." So instead of hating our enemies, let's pity them and thank God that life has not made us what they are. Instead of heaping condemnation and revenge upon our enemies, let's give them our understanding, our sympathy, our help, our forgiveness, and our prayers."

I was brought up in a family which read the Scriptures or repeated a verse from the *Bible* each night and then knelt down and said"family prayers". I can still hear my father, in a lonely Missouri farmhouse, repeating those words of Jesus—words that will continue to be repeated as long as man cherishes his ideals: "Love your enemies, bless them that curse you, do good to them that hate you, and pray for them which despitefully use you, and persecute you."

My father tried to live those words of Jesus; and they gave him an inner peace that the captains and the kings of earth have often sought for in vain.

To cultivate a mental attitude that will bring you peace and happiness, remember that Rule 2 is:

Let's never try to get even with our enemies, because if we do we will hurt ourselves far more than we hurt them. Let's do as General Eisenhower does: let's never waste a minute thinking about people we don't like.

许多被林肯委以高位的人，以前都曾批评或羞辱过他——如麦克里兰、西华、史丹顿和查尔斯。但据赫登记载，林肯认为“没有人会因为他做了什么而被歌颂或受责难。因为我们都会受条件、情况、环境、教育、生活习惯和遗传等因素的影响，由此造就了我们的现在和将来”。

也许林肯是对的。如果你我继承了与我们的敌人同样的生理、心理及情绪特征，如果我们的人生也完全相同，我们就会和他们一样行事。我们不可能做出别的事来。就像克拉伦斯·达罗常说的：“知道了一切就会理解一切，这样我们就不会评判或谴责他人。”所以，不要恨我们的敌人，而是怜悯他们，感谢上帝没有让我们和他们一样经历同样的人生。不要诅咒报复我们的敌人，而是给他们谅解、同情、帮助、宽容和祈祷。

我在一个每天晚上都会念《圣经》并作睡前祈祷的家庭长大。现在，我仿佛还听见密苏里州一个孤寂的农庄中，我父亲正在诵读耶稣的话——只要人类还重视这个理想就会一再重复的话：“爱你的仇人，善待恨你们的人；诅咒你的，要为他祝福，凌辱你的，要为他祷告。”

我父亲按照这些话去做了，也使他的内心得到了一般官员和君主所无法得到的平静。

要想培养平安快乐的心境，请记住第二条规则：

我们永远不要去试图报复我们的仇敌。如果我们那样做的话，我们对自己的伤害将会甚于对敌人的伤害。让我们像艾森豪威尔将军那样去做：不要把时间浪费在去想那些我们不喜欢的人。

3 If You Do This, You Will Never Worry about Ingratitude

I recently met a businessman in Texas who was burned up with indignation. I was warned that he would tell me about it within fifteen minutes after I met him. He did. The incident he was angry about had occurred eleven months previously, but he was still burned up about it. He couldn't speak of anything else. He had given his thirty-four employees ten thousand dollars in Christmas bonuses—approximately three hundred dollars each—and no one had thanked him. "I am sorry," he complained bitterly, "that I ever gave them a penny! "

"An angry man, "said Confucius, "is always full of poison." This man was so full of poison that I honestly pitied him. He was about sixty years old. Now, life-insurance companies figure that, on the average, we will live slightly more than two-thirds of the difference between our present age and eighty. So this man—if he was lucky—probably had about fourteen or fifteen years to live. Yet he had already wasted almost one of his few remaining years by his bitterness and resentment over an event that was past and gone. I pitied him. Instead of wallowing in resentment and self-pity, he might have asked himself why he didn't get any appreciation. Maybe he had underpaid and overworked his employees. Maybe they considered a Christmas bonus not a gift, but something they had earned. Maybe he was so critical and unapproachable that no one dared or cared to thank him. Maybe they felt he gave the bonus because most of the profits were going for taxes, anyway. On the other hand, maybe the employees were selfish, mean, and ill-mannered. Maybe this. Maybe that. I don't know any more about it than you do. But I do know what Dr. Samuel Johnson said: "Gratitude is a fruit of great cultivation. You do not find it among gross people."

Here is the point I am trying to make: this man made the human and distressing mistake of expecting gratitude. He just didn't know human nature.

If you saved a man's life, would you expect him to be grateful? You might—but Samuel Leibowitz, who was a famous criminal lawyer before he became a judge, saved *seventy-eight* men from going to the electric chair! How many of these men, do you suppose, stopped to thank Samuel Leibowitz, or ever

第3章 对人施恩勿望回报

最近,我在得克萨斯州遇到一个商人,他正为某事而发怒。有人警告我说,只要我认识他不到一刻钟,他就会把一切告诉我。果然,令他生气的那件事发生在11个月以前,可是他还在为此生气。他简直控制不住不谈那件事:他给34位员工发了1万美元的年终奖金,大约每人300美元——但是没有一个人感激他。"我实在后悔给他们钱!"他伤心地抱怨说。

"愤怒的人,"孔子说,"心里都会充满怨恨。"这个人就满怀怨恨,我实在是同情他。他大约60岁。人寿保险公司指出,我们每个人可以活到现在的年龄与80岁之间差距的2/3稍强一点,所以这位先生如果运气好的话,也许还可以活十四五年,可是他却浪费了有限的余生中近一年的时间,抱怨一件早已发生的事情。我实在是同情他。他不该总是陷入怨恨和自怜之中,而应该问自己,为什么没有人感激他?也许是他给员工的薪水很低却工作太多;也许员工认为年终奖金并不是什么礼物,而是他们该得的;也许他平常太挑剔、太苛刻,所以没有人敢或者愿意感谢他;也许他们认为他之所以给大家年终奖金,是因为这些收益的大部分得拿去交税。从另一方面来说,那些员工也许都很自私、卑劣而不讲礼貌。也许是这样,也许是那样。我和你一样不知道事情的真相,但我确实知道,塞缪尔·强生博士曾说:"感激是良好教育的结果,这很难在一般人中找到。"

我想说的是,希望别人感恩的人,犯了一般人共有的毛病,可以说他完全不了解人性。

如果你救了某人性命,你是不是希望他感激你?可能会。塞缪尔·利博维兹在担任法官之前,是有名的刑事律师。他曾救过78人的命,使他们不必被电椅处死!你想这些人当中有多少人感激他,或者送他一张圣诞卡呢?有多少?猜猜……不错——一个也没有!

耶稣曾在一个下午治好了10个麻风病人,可是这些人有几个向他道谢了呢?只有一个。你

took the trouble to send him a Christmas card? How many? Guess... That's right—none.

Christ healed ten lepers in one afternoon—but how many of those lepers even stopped to thank Him? Only one. Look it up in Saint Luke. When Christ turned around to His disciples and asked: "Where are the other nine?"they had all run away. Disappeared without thanks! Let me ask you a question: Why should you and I—or this businessman in Texas—expect more thanks for our small favours than was given Jesus Christ?

And when it comes to money matters! Well, that is even more hopeless. Charles Schwab told me that he had once saved a bank cashier who had speculated in the stock market with funds belonging to the bank. Schwab put up the money to save this man from going to the penitentiary. Was the cashier grateful? Oh, yes, for a little while. Then he turned against Schwab and reviled him and denounced him—the very man who had kept him out of jail!

If you gave one of your relatives a million dollars, would you expect him to be grateful? Andrew Carnegie did just that. But if Andrew Carnegie had come back from the grave a little while later, he would have been shocked to find this relative cursing him! Why? Because Old Andy had left 365 million dollars to public charities—and had"cut him off with one measly million, "as he put it.

That's how it goes. Human nature has always been human nature—and it probably won't change in your lifetime. So why not accept it? Why not be as realistic about it as was old Marcus Aurelius, one of the wisest men who ever ruled the Roman Empire. He wrote in his diary one day: "I am going to meet people today who talk too much—people who are selfish, egotistical, ungrateful. But I won't be surprised or disturbed, for I couldn't imagine a world without such people."

That makes sense, doesn't it? If you and I go around grumbling about ingratitude, who is to blame? Is it human nature—or is it our ignorance of human nature? Let's not expect gratitude. Then, if we get some occasionally, it will come as a delightful surprise. If we don't get it, we won't be disturbed.

Here is the first point I am trying to make in this chapter: It is natural for people to forget to be grateful; so, if we go around expecting gratitude, we are headed straight for a lot of heartaches.

I know a woman in New York who is always complaining because she is lonely. Not one of her relatives wants to go near her—and no wonder. If you visit her, she will tell you for hours what she did for her nieces when they were children: she nursed them through the measles and the mumps

可以看《路迦福音》。当耶稣转身问他的门徒"那9个人在哪里"时，发现他们都走了，连"谢谢"都没有说一声就走了。我想问你一个问题：为什么你和我，或者那位得克萨斯州商人，都希望施恩予人之后，就想得到比耶稣更多的感恩呢？

至于钱，就更没指望了。查尔斯·施瓦伯告诉我，有一次他救了一位挪用银行公款投资股票的出纳员。施瓦伯用自己的钱救了那个人，使他不至于受罚。那位出纳员感激他吗？是的，但只是很短一阵时间，很快他就转过身来辱骂和批评施瓦伯——这个使他免受牢狱之灾的人。

要是你给一位亲戚100万美元，你是否希望他感恩？安德鲁·卡内基就做过这样的事。可是，如果卡内基能够死而复生的话，他一定会吃惊地发现他的那位亲戚正在咒骂他。为什么呢？因为卡内基捐给了公共慈善机构3.65亿美元——"只给了他区区100万美元。"所以他要咒骂。

世事就是这样。人性终究是人性——在你的有生之年大概都不会改变，事情就是这样。所以，为什么不接受这个事实？为什么不像曾统治过古罗马帝国的聪明的马可·奥勒留那样现实呢？他曾在日记中写道："我今天就要去见那些多嘴多舌的人——那些自私、以自我为中心、不知感恩的人。可是我既不吃惊也不难过，因为我无法想象，一个没有这种人的世界将会怎样。"

这话很有道理吧？要是你我总是抱怨别人不知感恩，那该怪谁呢？是人性如此，还是我们不了解人性呢？如果我们施恩不望回报，那么，如果我们偶然得到了感恩，那就是一种意外之喜；如果没有得到，也不会难过。

下面是我在这一章要谈的第一个要点：人类的天性是容易忘记对感恩；所以，如果我们施恩予人而期望感恩的话，那我们一定会十分头痛。

我认识一个纽约的女人，她因为孤独而不停地抱怨。她的亲戚没有一个愿意亲近她——这没什么奇怪的。如果你去看她，她就会不停地说她对她的侄女有多好，在她们患麻疹、腮腺炎和百日咳的时候照顾她们；多年来给她们提供吃住，帮其中一个上完了商业学校，另一个也一直在她家住，直到结婚。

and the whooping-cough; she boarded them for years; she helped to send one of them through business school, and she made a home for the other until she got married.

Do the nieces come to see her? Oh, yes, now and then, out of a spirit of duty. But they dread these visits. They know they will have to sit and listen for hours to half-veiled reproaches. They will be treated to an endless litany of bitter complaints and self-pitying sighs. And when this woman can no longer bludgeon, browbeat, or bully her nieces into coming to see her, she has one of her "spells". She develops a heart attack.

Is the heart attack real? Oh, yes. The doctors say she has "a nervous heart", suffers from palpitations. But the doctors also say they can do nothing for her—her trouble is emotional.

What this woman really wants is love and attention. But she calls it "gratitude". And she will never get gratitude or love, because she demands it. She thinks it's her due.

There are thousands of women like her, women who are ill from "ingratitude", loneliness, and neglect.

They long to be loved; but the only way in this world that they can ever hope to be loved is to stop asking for it and to start pouring out love without hope of return.

Does that sound like sheer, impractical, visionary idealism? It isn't. It is just horse sense. It is a good way for you and me to find the happiness we long for. I know. I have seen it happen right in my own family. My own mother and father gave for the joy of helping others. We were poor—always overwhelmed by debts. Yet, poor as we were, my father and mother always managed to send money every year to an orphans' home—the Christian Home in Council Bluffs, Iowa. Mother and Father never visited that home. Probably no one thanked them for their gifts—except by letter—but they were richly repaid, for they had the joy of helping little children—without wishing for or expecting any gratitude in return.

After I left home, I would always send Father and Mother a cheque at Christmas and urge them to indulge in a few luxuries for themselves. But they rarely did. When I came home a few days before Christmas, Father would tell me of the coal and groceries they had bought for some "widder woman" in town who had a lot of children and no money to buy food and fuel. What joy they got out of these gifts—the joy of giving without accepting anything whatever in return!

I believe my father would almost have qualified for Aristotle's description of the ideal man—

她的侄女来看过她吗?是的,她们偶尔会来,只是为了尽义务。但她们都怕来看她,因为她们知道必须在那儿坐好几个小时,听她旁敲侧击地骂人,还得听她那毫无休止的埋怨和自怜的叹息。后来,当这个女人再也无法威逼利诱她的侄女来看她的时候,她使出了一件"法宝"——心脏病发作。

真是心脏病发作吗?是的,医生说她有一个"神经质心脏",才会发生这种病症。可是医生也说他们对此毫无办法,因为她的问题完全是情感上的。

这个女人真正需要的是爱和关切,可是她称之为"感恩"。但她永远得不到感恩和爱,因为她强求它,认为那是应该的。

像她这样的女人太多了。她们都因为别人的忘恩负义、孤独和被人忽视而患病。

她们希望有人爱她们,但这个世界上唯一得到爱的办法,就是不再去强求,而是立即开始付出却不图回报。

这话听上去是不是很荒谬、不切实际、太理想化了?不是的,这只是常识,这是让你我得到我们渴望的快乐的良方。我知道。因为在我自己家里就发生过这样的事情。我的父母乐于助人,我们家很穷,总是债台高筑,不过我们穷归穷,每年我父母总会想办法给爱荷华州布拉夫斯理事会基督之家的孤儿院送点钱去。我父母从未去过那里,或许也没有人为他们的礼物而谢过他们——除了写信之外——但他们得到的回报却非常丰富,因为他们从帮助孤儿中得到了乐趣,而不是希望或等待别人的感恩。

当我离家之后,每年圣诞节我总会给父母寄一张支票,让他们买些比较奢华的东西,但他们很少这样做。当我每年圣诞节前几天回家的时候,父亲就会告诉我,他们又买了些煤和杂货送给镇上那些有一大群孩子却没有钱买食物和柴火的"可怜的女人"。他们从中得到了许多快乐——那就是施恩予人不图回报的快乐。

我相信我父母有资格做亚里士多德所谓的理想的人——也就是最快乐的人。"理想的人,"

the man most worthy of being happy. "The ideal man, "said Aristotle, "takes joy in doing favours for others; but he feels ashamed to have others do favours for him. For it is a mark of superiority to confer a kindness; but it is a mark of inferiority to receive it."

Here is the second point I am trying to make in this chapter: If we want to find happiness, let's stop thinking about gratitude or ingratitude and give for the inner joy of giving.

Parents have been tearing their hair about the ingratitude of children for ten thousand years.

Even Shakespeare's King Lear cried out: "How sharper than a serpent's tooth it is to have a thankless child! "

But why should children be thankful—unless we train them to be? Ingratitude is natural—like weeds. Gratitude is like a rose. It has to be fed and watered and cultivated and loved and protected.

If our children are ungrateful, who is to blame? Maybe we are. If we have never taught them to express gratitude to others, how can we expect them to be grateful to us?

I know a man in Chicago who has cause to complain of the ingratitude of his stepsons. He slaved in a box factory, seldom earning more than forty dollars a week. He married a widow, and she persuaded him to borrow money and send her two grown sons to college. Out of his salary of forty dollars a week, he had to pay for food, rent, fuel, clothes, and also for the payments on his notes. He did this for four years, working like a coolie, and never complaining.

Did he get any thanks? No; his wife took it all for granted—and so did her sons. They never imagined that they owed their stepfather anything—not even thanks!

Who was to blame? The boys? Yes; but the mother was even more to blame. She thought it was a shame to burden their young lives with "a sense of obligation". She didn't want her sons to"start out under debt". So she never dreamed of saying: "What a prince your stepfather is to help you through college! "Instead, she took the attitude: "Oh, that's the least he can do."

She thought she was sparing her sons, but in reality, she was sending them out into life with the dangerous idea that the world owed them a living. And it *was* a dangerous idea—for one of those sons tried to"borrow"from an employer, and ended up in jail!

We must remember that our children are very much what we make them. For example, my mother's sister—Viola Alexander, of 144 West Minnehala Parkway, Minneapolis—is a shining example

亚里士多德说,"以对人施恩而快乐,但却以受恩于人为羞愧。因为待人仁慈者高人一等,而接受别人的恩惠则低人一等。"

下面是我所要说的第二个要点:如果我们想获得快乐,就不要想感恩或忘恩,而只享受施恩的快乐。

几千年来,为人父母者一直为儿女的忘恩负义而悲伤难过。就连莎士比亚笔下的李尔王也叫道:"一个不知感恩的孩子,比毒蛇的牙齿还要尖利。"

可是,孩子们为什么要感恩呢——除非我们教育他们那样。忘恩是人类的天性,就像野草一样;而感恩却如玫瑰,必须给它施肥浇水,给它教养、爱和呵护。

如果我们的子女忘恩负义,该怪谁呢?也许要怪我们。如果我们从来都不教他们感激别人,我们又如何指望他们感激我们呢?

我认识一个芝加哥人,他常常抱怨他的两个养子忘恩负义。他的抱怨自有道理。他在一家纸箱厂工作,一个星期赚不到40美元。他娶了一个寡妇,她要他去借钱供她的两个儿子上大学。他每周40美元的薪水要买吃的、付房租、买燃料、衣服,还要还债。他这样苦苦干了4年,从来没有抱怨过。

他得到感谢了吗?没有,他太太认为这是理所当然的——她两个儿子也这么认为。他们从不认为欠了养父什么,因此连一句谢谢也没有说。

这该怪谁呢?两个孩子?不错,可是更要怪那个母亲。她认为不应该给她的儿子增加"负疚感"。她不想她的儿子"一开始就欠别人的",所以她从来都不曾告诉他们说:"你们养父真是个大好人,他帮你们读完了大学。"她反而采取了这种态度:"这是他该做的。"

她认为她是在保护她的儿子,可这实际上是让他们刚走上人生道路的时候,产生一种全世界都欠他们的危险想法。这的确是很危险的想法——因为她两个儿子中的一个曾想向老板"借钱",结果进了监狱。

of a woman who has never had cause to complain about the "ingratitude" of children. When I was a boy, Aunt Viola took her own mother into her home to love and take care of; and she did the same thing for her husband's mother. I can still close my eyes and see those two old ladies sitting before the fire in Aunt Viola's farmhouse. Were they any "trouble" to Aunt Viola? Oh, often, I suppose. But you would never have guessed it from her attitude. She *loved* those old ladies—so she pampered them, and spoiled them, and made them feel at home. In addition, Aunt Viola had six children of her own; but it never occurred to her that she was doing anything especially noble, or deserved any halos for taking these old ladies into her home. To her, it was the natural thing, the right thing, the thing she wanted to do. Where is Aunt Viola today? Well, she has now been a widow for twenty-odd years, and she has five grown-up children—five separate households—all clamouring to share her, and to have her come and live in their homes! Her children adore her; they never get enough of her. Out of "gratitude"? Nonsense! It is love—*sheer love*. Those children breathed in warmth and radiant human-kindness all during their childhoods. Is it any wonder that, now that the situation is reversed, they *give back* love?

So let us remember that to raise grateful children, we have to be grateful. Let us remember "little pitchers have big ears"—and watch what we say. To illustrate—the next time we are tempted to belittle someone's kindness in the presence of our children, let's stop. Let's never say: "Look at these dishcloths Cousin Sue sent for Christmas. She knit them herself. They didn't cost her a cent!" The remark may seem trivial to us—but the children are listening. So, instead, we had better say: "Look at the hours Cousin Sue spent making these for Christmas! Isn't she nice? Let's write her a thank-you note right now." And our children may unconsciously absorb the habit of praise and appreciation.

To avoid resentment and worry over ingratitude, here is Rule 3:

A. Instead of worrying about ingratitude, let's expect it. Let's remember that Jesus healed ten lepers in one day—and only one thanked Him. Why should we expect more gratitude than Jesus got?

B. Let's remember that the only way to find happiness is not to expect gratitude, but to give for the joy of giving.

C. Let's remember that gratitude is a "cultivated" trait; so if we want our children to be grateful, we must train them to be grateful.

我们必须记住：子女完全是父母教育的结果。例如：我姨妈薇奥拉·亚历山大就是从来不会想到孩子们"忘恩"的光辉榜样。在我小的时候，薇奥拉姨妈把她母亲接到家里来照顾，同样也照顾她婆婆。现在我闭上眼睛还能回想起那两位老太太坐在薇奥拉姨妈家壁炉前的情景。她们会不会给薇奥拉姨妈惹来什么麻烦呢?我想这是常有的。但你从她的态度上一点也看不出来。她爱这两位老太太，所以她顺从她们，关爱她们，让她们过得非常舒适。此外，薇奥拉姨妈还有6个孩子。她从未想到这样做有什么特别的，或者说接两位老太太来家里住有什么值得赞美的。这对她来说是很自然的，也是该做的，并且也是她希望做的。现在薇奥拉姨妈在哪里呢?她现在已经守寡20多年了，而且5个孩子已经成年，组成了自己的小家庭——他们争着要跟她住在一起，让她住他们家。她的孩子们爱戴她，都不想离开她。这是因为"感恩"吗?不是。这是爱，是纯粹的爱。这些孩子在童年时代就懂得了爱心的温暖，现在情形反过来了，他们也回报爱心，这有什么奇怪的?

所以，我们要记住，要教育出感恩图报的孩子，我们必须懂得感恩。我们要记住"小兔子耳朵长"的道理——要注意我们说过的话。例如，当我们下一次在孩子们面前想要贬低别人给我们的好处时，赶快打住。永远也不要说："看，苏表妹送给我们当圣诞礼物的这些桌布，都是她自己钩的，没花一毛钱。"这种话我们也许只是顺口说的，可是孩子们却在听着。我们最好是说："表妹准备这份圣诞礼物，可花了不少时间啊！她真好！我们写封信感谢她！"这样，我们的子女也许就无意中养成了赞美和感恩的习惯。

要避免因为不知感恩而引起的伤心和忧虑，下面是第三条规则：

A. 不要因为别人的忘恩负义而忧伤，忘掉它。记住，耶稣一天之内治好了10个麻风病人，而只有一个人感谢他。为什么我们希望得到比耶稣更多的感恩呢?

B. 要记住，获得快乐的唯一方法，就是施恩予人勿望回报，只为施恩的快乐。

C. 要记住，感恩是"教育"的结果。如果我们希望我们的子女会感恩，我们必须培养他们学会感恩。

4 Would You Take a Million Dollars for What You Have?

I have known Harold Abbott for years. He lives at 820 South Madison Avenue, Webb City, Missouri. He used to be my lecture manager. One day he and I met in Kansas City and he drove me down to my farm at Belton, Missouri. During that drive, I asked him how he kept from worrying; and he told me an inspiring story that I shall never forget.

"I used to worry a lot, "he said, "but one spring day in 1934, I was walking down West Dougherty Street in Webb City when I saw a sight that banished all my worries. It all happened in ten seconds, but during those ten seconds I learned more about how to live than I had learned in the previous ten years. For two years I had been running a grocery store in Webb City, "Harold Abbott said, as he told me the story. "I had not only lost all my savings, but I had incurred debts that took me seven years to pay back. My grocery store had been closed the previous Saturday; and now I was going to the Merchants and Miners Bank to borrow money so I could go to Kansas City to look for a job. I walked like a beaten man. I had lost all my fight and faith. Then suddenly I saw coming down the street a man who had no legs. He was sitting on a little wooden platform equipped with wheels from roller skates. He propelled himself along the street with a block of wood in each hand. I met him just after he had crossed the street and was starting to lift himself up a few inches over the curb to the sidewalk. As he tilted his little wooden platform to an angle, his eyes met mine. He greeted me with a grand smile. 'Good morning, sir. It is a fine morning, isn't it?'he said with spirit. As I stood looking at him, I realised how rich I was. I had two legs. I could walk. I felt ashamed of my self-pity. I said to myself if he can be happy, cheerful, and confident without legs, I certainly can with legs. I could already feel my chest lifting. I had intended to ask the Merchants and Miners Bank for only one hundred dollars. But now I had courage to ask for two hundred. I had intended to say that I wanted to go to Kansas City to try to get a job. But now I announced confidently that I wanted to go to Kansas City to get a job. I got the loan; and I got the job.

第4章 你愿以100万卖尽你拥有的一切吗?

我和哈罗德·艾伯特认识已有好多年了,他住在密苏里州韦伯市南麦迪逊大道820号。他以前是我的教务主任。一天,他在堪萨斯城碰到我,开车把我送到了密苏里州贝尔城我的农庄。我在路上问他是如何避免忧虑的,他给我讲了一个我永远都不会忘记的鼓舞人心的故事。

"以前我常为很多事情忧虑,"他说,"可是,在1934年春天的某一天,我正走在韦伯市的西道提街,看到了一个消除我所有忧虑的场面。这件事情前后只有10秒钟,但我在这10秒钟中内学到的生活哲理,比我过去10年所学的还要多。

"我在韦伯市开过两年杂货店,"艾伯特告诉我这个故事的时候说,"我不仅赔光了所有的积蓄,而且债台高筑,花了7年才还清债务。我的杂货店刚在前一个星期六关门,当时我正准备去工矿银行借钱,以便去堪萨斯城找一份工作。我像个一败涂地的人那样走着,完全丧失了斗志和信心。突然,我对面来了一个没有腿的人,他坐在一个小木板平台上,下面装着从溜冰鞋上拆下来的滑轮。他两手各抓着一块木头,撑着地滑过街来。我看到他的时候,他刚好过了街,正想把自己抬高几英寸上到人行道来。就在他翘起那小木板车的时候,他看见了我。他对我咧嘴一笑说:'你早先生!早上天气真好,是不是?'他开心地说。当我站在那里看着他的时候,我才发现自己多么富有:我有两条腿,我还能走路。我对我的自怜感到羞耻。我对自己说,如果他这个缺了双腿的人都能做到的事,我这个健全的人当然也能做到。我觉得自己的胸膛已经挺直了。本来我只打算向工矿银行借100美元的,但我现在有勇气借200美元了。我本来也只是试着去堪萨斯城找工作,但现在我能自信地说,我要去堪萨斯城找工作。结果,我借到了钱,也找到了工作。

"现在,我在自己浴室的镜子上贴了这几句话,这样我每天早上刮脸时都能够看到:

"I now have the following words pasted on my bathroom mirror, and I read them every morning as I shave:

I had the blues because I had no shoes,
Until upon the street, I met a man who had no feet."

I once asked Eddie Rickenbacker what was the biggest lesson he had learned from drifting about with his companions in life rafts for twenty-one days, hopelessly lost in the Pacific. "The biggest lesson I learned from that experience, "he said, "was that if you have all the fresh water you want to drink and all the food you want to eat, you ought never to complain about anything."

Time ran an article about a sergeant who had been wounded on Guadalcanal. Hit in the throat by a shell fragment, this sergeant had had seven blood transfusions. Writing a note to his doctor, he asked: "Will I live?"The doctor replied: "Yes." He wrote another note, asking: "Will I be able to talk?"Again the answer was yes. He then wrote another note, saying: "*Then what in the* hell am I worrying about?"

Why don't you stop right now and ask yourself: "What in the hell am I worrying about?"You will probably find that it is comparatively unimportant and insignificant.

About ninety per cent of the things in our lives are right and about ten per cent are wrong. If we want to be happy, all we have to do is to concentrate on the ninety per cent that are right and ignore the ten per cent that are wrong. If we want to be worried and bitter and have stomach ulcers, all we have to do is to concentrate on the ten per cent that are wrong and ignore the ninety per cent that are glorious.

The words "Think and Thank"are inscribed in many of the Cromwellian churches of England. These words ought to be inscribed on our hearts, too: "Think and Thank". Think of all we have to be grateful for, and thank God for all our boons and bounties.

Jonathan Swift, author of *Gulliver's Travels*, was the most devastating pessimist in English literature. He was so sorry that he had been born that he wore black and fasted on his birthdays; yet, in his despair, this supreme pessimist of English literature praised the great health—giving powers of cheerfulness and happiness. "The best doctors in the world, "he declared, "are Doctor Diet, Doctor Quiet, and Doctor Merryman."

别人骑马我骑驴,回头看那无腿汉,比上不足比下有余。"

有一次,我问艾迪·雷根伯克,当他和他的同伴在救生筏上漂了21天之久,在太平洋中毫无获救的希望时,他学到的最重要一课是什么。"我从那次经历中学到的最重要一课,"他说,"就是如果你有足够的新鲜水喝,有足够的食物吃,就不该抱怨任何事情。"

《时代》杂志有一篇报道,讲一个士官在某地受了伤,喉部被碎弹片击中,一共输了七次血。他给医生写了一张纸条,问:"我能活下去吗?"医生说:"能。"他又写了一张纸条:"我还能说话吗?"医生又回答可以。然后他又写了一张纸条:"那我还担什么心?"

你为什么不也马上停下来问问自己:"那我还担什么心?"你很可能发现自己担心的事情会变得微不足道了。

我们生活中大概有90%的事情是对的,只有10%是错的。如果我们想要快乐,我们所要做的就是把精力放在那90%正确的事情上,而不要理会那10%的错误。如果我们想担忧、痛苦、胃溃疡,那我们只需把精力集中在那10%的错误上即可,而不必理会那90%的好事。

英国很多新教教堂中都刻有"思考,感恩"两个词,这两个词同样应该铭刻在我们心中。"思考,感恩":要想值得我们感恩的事,并为此而感谢"上帝"。

《格列佛游记》的作者斯维伏特,是英国文学史上最悲观的人。他曾为自己的出生而难过,所以在生日那天他一定会穿黑衣服并绝食一天。可是,即使处于绝望之中,这位英国文学史上最著名的悲观主义者却称颂开心与快乐能给人带来健康。"世界上最好的医生,"他说,"是节食、安静和快乐。"

每一天的每个小时,你和我都能得到"快乐医生"的免费服务,只要我们把精力集中在我们拥有的那么多令人难以置信的财富上——这些财富远远超过了阿里巴巴的珍宝。你愿意以10亿美元出卖你的双眼吗?你愿把你的双腿卖多少钱?还有你的双手、听觉、孩子、家庭?把你所有的

You and I may have the services of "Doctor Merryman"free every hour of the day by keeping our attention fixed on all the incredible riches we possess—riches exceeding by far the fabled treasures of Ali Baba. Would you sell both your eyes for a billion dollars? What would you take for your two legs? Your hands? Your hearing? Your children? Your family? Add up your assets, and you will find that you won't sell what you have for all the gold ever amassed by the Rockefellers, the Fords and the Morgans combined.

But do we appreciate all this? Ah, no. As Schopenhauer said: "We *seldom think of what we have but always of what we lack.*" Yes, the tendency to"seldom think of what we have but always of what we lack"is the greatest tragedy on earth. It has probably caused more misery than all the wars and diseases in history.

It caused John Palmer to turn "from a regular guy into an old grouch", and almost wrecked his home. I know because he told me so.

Mr. Palmer lives at 30 19th Avenue, Paterson, New Jersey. "Shortly after I returned from the Army, "he said, "I started in business for myself. I worked hard day and night. Things were going nicely. Then trouble started. I couldn't get parts and materials. I was afraid I would have to give up my business. I worried so much that I changed from a regular guy into an old grouch. I became so sour and cross that—well, I didn't know it then; but I now realize that I came very near to losing my happy home. Then one day a young, disabled veteran who works for me said: 'Johnny, you ought to be ashamed of yourself. You take on as if you were the only person in the world with troubles. Suppose you do have to shut up shop for a while—so what? You can start up again when things get normal. You've got a lot to be thankful for. Yet you are always growling. Boy, how I wish I were in your shoes! Look at me. I've got only one arm, and half of my face is shot away, and yet I am not complaining. If you don't stop your growling and grumbling, you will lose not only your business, but also your health, your home, and your friends! '

"Those remarks stopped me dead in my tracks. They made me realise how well off I was. I resolved then and there that I would change and be my old self again—and I did."

A friend of mine, Lucile Blake, had to tremble on the edge of tragedy before she learned to be happy about what she had instead of worrying over what she lacked.

资产加在一起,你就会发现你绝不会卖掉现在拥有的一切,即使把洛克菲勒、福特和摩根拥有的黄金都加在一起也不卖。

可是,我们欣赏了这些吗?啊,很难做到。正如叔本华说的:"我们很少想到我们所拥有的,而总是想到我们所没有的。"这正是世界上最大的悲剧,它所造成的痛苦可能比历史上所有的战争和疾病都要多。

正是这一点使约翰·帕尔玛"从一个正常人变成了一个怪老头",几乎毁了他的家庭。我知道这件事,因为他告诉了我。他住在新泽西州帕特森市19大道30号。

"我从军队退伍之后不久,"他说,"就开始做生意。我日夜不停地忙着,一切都干得很好。然后问题来了,我买不到零件和原料。我担心可能会被迫放弃生意,这种担心使我很快由一个正常人变成了一个脾气很坏的人。我变得非常尖酸刻薄——可我当时并不知道,现在才明白我几乎失去了我那个快乐的家。然后,有一天,一个在我这里工作的年轻伤兵对我说:'约翰,你应该感到惭愧。瞧你这副样子,好像全世界只有你一个人遇到了麻烦似的。就算你关门大吉,又会怎么样呢?等到一切恢复正常之后,你还可以东山再起。你有很多值得感激的事,可你却老是抱怨。天啊,我真希望我是你!你看我,我只有一条胳膊,半边脸都受了伤,可我并不抱怨。要是你再这样没完没了地埋怨,你不仅会失去你的生意,还会失去你的健康、家庭和朋友。'

"这些话使我猛然醒悟,使我发现我走上了歧路。我当时就决定必须改变,重新做我自己——而我也做到了。"

我的一位朋友露西莉·布莱克在学会自己知足,不为所缺而忧虑之前,差点儿崩溃了。

我多年前就认识露西莉,当时我们两个都在哥伦比亚大学新闻学院上短篇小说写作课程。9年前,她的生活发生剧变,她当时住在亚利桑那州杜森城,下面是她告诉我的:

"我的生活一直很忙很乱:在亚利桑那大学学习风琴,又在城里办了一个语言学校,还在

I met Lucile years ago, when we were both studying short-story writing in the Columbia University School of Journalism. Nine years ago, she got the shock of her life. She was living then in Tucson, Arizonia. She had—well, here is the story as she told it to me: "I had been living in a whirl: studying the organ at the University of Arizona, conducting a speech clinic in town, and teaching a class in musical appreciation at the Desert Willow Ranch, where I was staying. I was going in for parties, dances, horseback rides under the stars. One morning I collapsed. My heart! 'You will have to lie in bed for a year of complete rest,' the doctor said. He didn't encourage me to believe I would ever be strong again.

"In bed for a year! To be an invalid—perhaps to die! I was terror-stricken! Why did all this have to happen to me? What had I done to deserve it? I wept and wailed. I was bitter and rebellious. But I did go to bed as the doctor advised. A neighbor of mine, Mr. Rudolf, an artist, said to me: 'You think now that spending a year in bed will be a tragedy. But it won't be. You will have time to think and get acquainted with yourself. You will make more spiritual growth in these next few months than you have made during all your previous life.' I became calmer, and tried to develop a new sense of values. I read books of inspiration. One day I heard a radio commentator say: 'You can express only what is in your own consciousness.' I had heard words like these many times before, but now they reached down inside me and took root. I resolved to think only the thoughts I wanted to live by: thoughts of joy, happiness, health. I forced myself each morning, as soon as I awoke, to go over all the things I had to be grateful for. No pain. A lovely young daughter. My eyesight. My hearing. Lovely music on the radio. Time to read. Good food. Good friends. I was so cheerful and had so many visitors that the doctor put up a sign saying that only one visitor at a time would be allowed in my cabin—and only at certain hours.

"Nine years have passed since then, and I now lead a full, active life. I am deeply grateful now for that year I spent in bed. It was the most valuable and the happiest year I spent in Arizona. The habit I formed then of counting my blessings each morning still remains with me. It is one of my most precious possessions. I am ashamed to realize that I never really learned to live until I feared I was going to die."

My dear Lucile Blake, you may not realise it, but you learned the same lesson that Dr. Samuel

我所住的沙漠柳牧场教音乐欣赏课。我还参加各种宴会、舞会,或在星光下骑马。一天早上,我垮了,心脏病犯了。'你得躺在床上静养一年,'医生说。他居然没有鼓励我,让我相信我还能够恢复。

"在床上躺一年,成为一个废人——可能还会死。我吓坏了。为什么我会碰到这种倒霉的事情?我做了什么,会受到这种报应呢?我又哭又叫,满怀怨恨和反抗。不过我还是遵照医生的话躺在了床上。我的一个邻居鲁道夫先生,他是个艺术家,他对我说:'现在你觉得躺在床上一年是个悲剧,但事实上不会的。这样你就有时间思考,真正认识自我。在接下来的几个月,你在思想上的成长会比你前半辈子都要快得多。'我平静下来,开始思考如何培养新的价值观念。我看过许多富有启发的书。一天,我听到一个无线电广播的评论员说:'你只能谈你知道的事情。'这一类话我以前听过许多次,可现在它才真正深入我心,并扎下根来。我决定只想那些我可以赖以生活的快乐而健康的思想。每天早上一起床,我就强迫自己想一些应该感恩的事情:我没有什么伤心的事,有一个可爱的小女儿,眼睛能看见,耳朵能听见收音机里播放的优美音乐,还有时间看书,吃得也很好,有许多好朋友。对此我非常高兴。来医院看我的人太多了,以致医生不得不挂上一个牌子,规定每次只许一个客人探望我,而且只能在某几个特定时间里。

"从那时至今已经9年了,现在我过着丰富多彩的生活。我非常感激我能在床上度过那一年,那是我在亚利桑那州度过的最有价值、最开心的一年。我现在还保持当年养成的习惯,每天早上算算自己值得高兴的事。这是我最珍贵的财富之一。我自觉惭愧,直到我担心自己会死去之前,才真正学会如何生活。"

亲爱的露西莉·布莱克,也许你并不知道,你学到的这一课,正是塞缪尔·约翰逊博士在200多前学到的。"培养只看事物好的一面的习惯,"约翰逊博士说,"比每年赚1000英镑更有意义。"

我想提醒诸位的是,这些话并不是出自一个天生乐观者之口,说这话的人曾经历过痛苦,

Johnson learned two hundred years ago. "The habit of looking on the best side of every event, "said Dr. Johnson, "is worth more than a thousand pounds a year."

Those words were uttered, mind you, not by a professional optimist, but by a man who had known anxiety, rags, and hunger for twenty years—and finally became one of the most eminent writers of his generation and the most celebrated conversationalist of all time.

Logan Pearsall Smith packed a lot of wisdom into a few words when he said: "There are two things to aim at in life: first, to get what you want; and, after that, to enjoy it. Only the wisest of mankind achieve the second."

Would you like to know how to make even dishwashing at the kitchen sink a thrilling experience? If so, read an inspiring book of incredible courage by Borghild Dahl. It is called *I Wanted to See*.

This book was written by a woman who was practically blind for half a century. "I had only one eye, "she writes, "and it was so covered with dense scars that I had to do all my seeing through one small opening in the left of the eye. I could see a book only by holding it up close to my face and by straining my one eye as hard as I could to the left."

But she refused to be pitied, refused to be considered "different". As a child, she wanted to play hopscotch with other children, but she couldn't see the markings. So after the other children had gone home, she got down on the ground and crawled along with her eyes near to the marks. She memorised every bit of the ground where she and her friends played and soon became an expert at running games. She did her reading at home, holding a book of large print so close to her eyes that her eyelashes brushed the pages. She earned two college degrees: an A. B. from the University of Minnesota and a Master of Arts from Columbia University.

She started teaching in the tiny village of Twin Valley, Minnesota, and rose until she became professor of journalism and literature at Augustana College in Sioux Falls, South Dakota. She taught there for thirteen years, lecturing before women's clubs and giving radio talks about books and authors. "In the back of my mind, "she writes, "there had always lurked a fear of total blindness. In order to overcome this, I had adopted a cheerful, almost hilarious, attitude towards life."

缺衣少食地过了20年，终于成为他那个年代最有名的作家，也成为历史上最著名的谈话家。

罗根·皮尔萨尔·史密斯用几句话说出了一番大道理。他说："生活中应该有两个目标：首先，要得到你希望得到的；然后，享受它。只有最聪明的人才能做到第二步。"

你想不想知道如何将在厨房的水槽中洗碗变成一次宝贵的体验呢？如果想知道，可以去看波姬儿·戴尔的书，它主要谈论令人难以置信的勇气，很具有启发性。该书名叫《我希望能看见》。

这本书的作者是一位女性，她失明达50年之久。"我只有一只眼睛，"她写道，"而眼睛上还满是疤痕，只能透过眼睛左边的一个小洞来看外界。看书的时候必须将书移到离脸很近的地方，而且不得不把另一只眼睛往左边斜过去。"

可是她拒绝别人的怜悯，更不愿被认为"与众不同"。小时候，她想和其他小孩一起玩跳房子的游戏，可是她看不见画在地上的线，于是等其他孩子都回家以后，她趴在地上，把眼睛贴在地上察看。她把那块地方的每一处都牢记在心，不久就成为这个游戏的好手了。她在家中看书时，把印有大字的书紧贴眼睛，几乎连眼睫毛都碰到书页上。她获得了两个大学学位：明尼苏达州立大学学士学位和哥伦比亚大学硕士学位。

她开始是在明尼苏达州双谷镇一个小村子里教书，然后逐渐晋升为南达科他州奥格塔那学院的新闻学和文学教授。她在那里工作13年，还在许多妇女俱乐部发表演说，在电台点评图书和作者。"在我的脑海深处，"她写道，"常常怀着一种担心完全失明的恐惧。为了克服这种恐惧，我对生活采取了一种快乐而几近戏谑的态度。"

然后，1943年，在她52岁的时候，奇迹发生了：她去著名的梅育医院做了一次手术，视力比以前清楚了40倍。

一个全新的、令人兴奋而可爱的世界展现在她眼前。现在她发现，即使是在厨房的水槽里

Then in 1943, when she was fifty-two years old, a miracle happened: an operation at the famous Mayo Clinic. She could now see forty times as well as she had ever been able to see before.

A new and exciting world of loveliness opened before her. She now found it thrilling even to wash dishes in the kitchen sink. "I begin to play with the white fluffy suds in the dish-pan, "she writes. "I dip my hands into them and I pick up a ball of tiny soap bubbles. I hold them up against the light, and in each of them I can see the brilliant colours of a miniature rainbow."

As she looked through the window above the kitchen sink, she saw "the flapping grey-black wings of the sparrows flying through the thick, falling snow."

She found such ecstasy looking at the soap bubbles and sparrows that she closed her book with these words: "'Dear Lord, 'I whisper, 'Our Father in Heaven, I thank Thee. I thank Thee.'"

Imagine thanking God because you can wash dishes and see rainbows in bubbles and sparrows flying through the snow!

You and I ought to be ashamed of ourselves. All the days of our years we have been living in a fairyland of beauty, but we have been too blind to see, too satiated to enjoy.

If we want to stop worrying and start living, Rule 4 is:

Count your blessings—not your troubles!

洗碟子,也会让她开心。"我开始玩洗碗槽中的肥皂泡,"她写道,"我把手伸进去,抓起一大把小小的肥皂泡,把它们迎着光举起来,看到了一道小小彩虹般的明亮色彩。"

从水槽上方厨房的窗口望出去,她看到了"振动黑色翅膀飞过厚厚积雪的麻雀"。

能有幸看见肥皂泡和麻雀,因此书中以下面的话作为结尾:"'亲爱的主,'我低语,'我的父啊,我感谢你,我感谢你。'"

想想,因为你能看见洗碗时泡沫中的彩虹和飞过雪地的麻雀,要感谢上帝吧!

你和我都应该感到惭愧。这么多年来,我们每天都生活在一个美丽的童话王国里,可是我们却视而不见,不知珍惜享受。

因此,要想得到快乐,第四条规则是:

想想你得到的恩惠——而不要理会你的烦恼。

5 Find Yourself and Be Yourself: Remember There Is No One Else on Earth Like You

I have a letter from Mrs. Edith Allred, of Mount Airy, North Carolina: "As a child, I was extremely sensitive and shy, "she says in her letter. "I was always overweight and my cheeks made me look even fatter than I was. I had an old-fashioned mother who thought it was foolish to make clothes look pretty. She always said: 'Wide will wear while narrow will tear'; and she dressed me accordingly. I never went to parties; never had any fun; and when I went to school, I never joined the other children in outside activities, not even athletics. I was morbidly shy. I felt I was'different' from everybody else, and entirely undesirable.

"When I grew up, I married a man who was several years my senior. But I didn't change. My in-laws were a poised and self-confident family. They were everything I should have been but simply was not. I tried my best to be like them, but I couldn't. Every attempt they made to draw me out of myself only drove me further into my shell. I became nervous and irritable. I avoided all friends. I got so bad I even dreaded the sound of the doorbell ringing! I was a failure. I knew it; and I was afraid my husband would fired it out. So, whenever we were in public, I tried to be gay, and overacted my part. I knew I overacted; and I would be miserable for days afterwards. At last I became so unhappy that I could see no point in prolonging my existence. I began to think of suicide."

What happened to change this unhappy woman's life? Just a chance remark!

"A chance remark, "Mrs. Allred continued, "transformed my whole life. My mother-in-law was talking one day of how she brought her children up, and she said: 'No matter what happened, I always insisted on their being themselves. '... 'On being themselves. '... That remark is what did it! In a flash, I realised I had brought all this misery on myself by trying to fit myself into a pattern to which I did not conform.

"I changed overnight! I started being myself. I tried to make a study of my own personality. Tried to find out what I was. I studied my strong points. I learned all I could about colors and

第5章 保持自我本色

我有一封伊笛丝·阿雷德夫人的信,她住在北卡罗来纳州艾尔山。"我从小就特别敏感而内向,"她在信中说,"我的身材一直很胖,而我的脸使我比实际看上去还胖得多。我母亲很古板,她认为穿漂亮衣服是愚蠢之举。她总是说:'宽衣舒服,窄衣易破。'她总是照这句话来帮我选衣服。我从来不参加舞会,甚至在学校也不和其他孩子一起做室外活动,甚至不愿上体育课。我非常害羞,觉得我和其他人都不一样,完全不得人喜欢。

"长大之后,我嫁给了一个比我大好几岁的男人。可是我并没有改变,我丈夫全家和睦而自信。他们是我应该成为却没有成为的那种人。我尽了最大的努力要成为他们那样的人,可是没有成功。他们为了使我开心而做的每一件事情,只会让我更加退缩。我变得紧张不安,不敢见所有朋友,情绪极坏,甚至怕听见门铃响。我知道我是一个失败者,但我又怕我丈夫发现这一点。所以每当我们出现在公共场合的时候,我都假装很开心,结果总是做得太过火。我也知道我做得太过火了,所以事后会为此而难过好几天。最后我觉得再活下去也没有什么意思了,开始想自杀。"

到底是什么改变了这个不开心的女人的生活呢?只是一句随口说出的话!

"随口说出的一句话,"阿雷德夫人继续写道,"改变了我的整个生活。有一天,我婆婆正在谈她如何培养她的几个孩子,她说:'不论如何,我总是要求他们保持本色。'……'保持本色。'就是这句话!眨眼之间,我发现我之所以如此苦恼,正是因为我一直在试着让自己去适应一个并不适合我的模式。

"我一夜之间改变了。我开始保持本色,试着研究我自己的个性,试着发现我究竟是怎样的

styles, and dressed in a way that I felt was becoming to me. I reached out to make friends. I joined an organization—a small one at first—and was petrified with fright when they put me on a programme. But each time I spoke, I gained a little courage. It took a long while—but today I have more happiness than I ever dreamed possible. In rearing my own children, I have always taught them the lesson I had to learn from such bitter experience: *No matter what happens, always be yourself*! "

This problem of being willing to be yourself is "as old as history,"says Dr. James Gordon Gilkey, "and as universal as human life."This problem of being unwilling to be yourself is the hidden spring behind many neuroses and psychoses and complexes. Angelo Patri has written thirteen books and thousands of syndicated newspaper articles on the subject of child training, and he says: "Nobody is so miserable as he who longs to be somebody and something other than the person he is in body and mind."

This craving to be something you are not is especially rampant in Hollywood. Sam Wood, one of Hollywood's best-known directors, says the greatest headache he has with aspiring young actors is exactly this problem: to make them be themselves. They all want to be second-rate Lana Turners, or third-rate Clark Gables. "The public has already had that flavor, "Sam Wood keeps telling them, "now it wants something else."

Before he started directing such pictures as *Good-bye, Mr. Chips and For Whom the Bell Tolls*, Sam Wood spent years in the real-estate business, developing sales personalities. He declares that the same principles apply in the business world as in the world of moving pictures. You won't get anywhere playing the ape. You can't be a parrot. "Experience has taught me, "says Sam Wood, "that it is safest to drop, as quickly as possible, people who pretend to be what they aren't."

I recently asked Paul Boynton, employment director for the Socony-Vacuum Oil Company, what is the biggest mistake people make in applying for jobs. He ought to know: he has interviewed more than sixty thousand job seekers; and he has written a book entitled *6 Ways to Get a Job*. He replied: "The biggest mistake people make in applying for jobs is in not being themselves. Instead of taking their hair down and being completely frank, they often try to give you the answers they

人。我研究我的优点，尽我所能去学习色彩和服饰的知识，尽量按照适合我的方式去穿着。我主动交朋友，参加了一个组织——它当初是一个很小的社团——他们让我参加活动，这让我吓坏了。可是我每发一次言，就增加了一些勇气。这件事花了我很长的时间，可是我今天所有的快乐都是我以前从未想到的。在教育我自己的孩子时，我也总是把我从痛苦的经历中所学到的教给他们：不论如何，总要保持自我本色。"

保持本色这个问题"如同人类历史一样古老"，詹姆斯·高登·吉尔基博士说，"也像人生一样普遍。"不能保持本色，正是许多精神和心理疾病的潜在原因。安吉罗·帕特利曾写过13本书和几千篇幼儿教育的文章。他说："再也没有人比那些想做其他人或除他自己以外任何其他东西的人更痛苦的。"

想做与自我不同的人的想法，盛行于好莱坞。山姆·伍德是好莱坞最著名的导演之一。他说，他和某些年轻演员打交道时，遇到的最棘手的问题正是这个；他要让他们保持本色。但他们都想做二流的拉娜，或者是三流的克拉克·盖博。"可这一套观众已经看够了，"山姆·伍德说，"现在需要的是其他东西。"

山姆·伍德在导演《别了，希普斯先生》和《战地钟声》等影片前，曾在房地产业多年，培养了销售员的个性。他认为，商界的规则同样适用于电影界。模仿将一事无成。"经验告诉我，"他说，"最保险的做法是尽快抛弃那些模仿他人的演员。"

最近我向素凡石油公司的人事部经理保罗·鲍尔顿请教，前来求职的人常犯的最大毛病是什么。他应该知道，因为他曾面试过6万多个求职者，还写过一本书《求职的6种方法》。他回答说："求职者所犯的最大错误，就是不能保持本色。他们不敢以真面目示人，不能完全坦诚，经常给你一些他认为你想要的回答。"可是这种做法毫无用处，因为没有人想要伪君子，也从来没有人愿意收假币。

think you want." But it doesn't work, because nobody wants a phony. Nobody ever wants a counterfeit coin.

A certain daughter of a street-car conductor had to learn that lesson the hard way. She longed to be a singer. But her face was her misfortune. She had a large mouth and protruding buck teeth. When she first sang in public—in a New Jersey night-club—she tried to pull down her upper lip to cover her teeth. She tried to act "glamorous". The result? She made herself ridiculous. She was headed for failure.

However, there was a man in this night-club who heard the girl sing and thought she had talent. "See here, "he said bluntly, "I've been watching your performance and I know what it is you're trying to hide. You're ashamed of your teeth." The girl was embarrassed, but the man continued: "What of it? Is there any particular crime in having buck teeth? Don't try to hide them! Open your mouth, and the audience will love you when they see you're not ashamed. Besides, "he said shrewdly, "those teeth you're trying to hide may make your fortune! "

Cass Daley took his advice and forgot about her teeth. *From that time on*, she thought only about her audience. She opened her mouth wide and sang with such gusto and enjoyment that she became a top star in movies and radio. Ot, comedians are now trying to copy *her*!

The renowned William James was speaking of men who had never found themselves when he declared that the average man develops only ten per cent of his latent mental abilities. "Compared to what we ought to be, "he wrote, "we are only half awake. We are making use of only a small part of our physical and mental resources. Stating the thing broadly, the human individual thus lives far within his limits. He possesses powers of various sorts which he habitually fails to use."

You and I have such abilities, so let's not waste a second worrying because we are not like other people. You are something new in this world. Never before, since the beginning of time, has there ever been anybody exactly like you; and never again throughout all the ages to come will there ever be anybody exactly like you again. The new science of genetics informs us that you are what you are largely as a result of twenty-four chromosomes contributed by your father and twenty-four chromosomes contributed by your mother. These forty-eight chromosomes comprise everything that determines what you inherit. "In each chromosome there may be, "says Amran Scheinfeld,

有一位电车司机的女儿,几经努力才懂得这个道理。她想成为歌唱家,但她长得并不好看。她的嘴很大,牙齿暴凸。当她第一次在新泽西州的一家夜总会公开演唱的时候,她想把上嘴唇拉下来,好遮住她的暴牙。她想表演得"很美"。结果呢?她让自己丑态百出,没能逃脱失败的命运。

可是,这家夜总会有一个人听了这女孩的唱歌,认为她有天分。"我想告诉你,"他直率地说,"我一直在观看你的表演,我知道你想遮掩什么。你觉得你的牙齿难看。"这个女孩非常窘迫,但那人继续说:"这有什么?难道长了暴牙就罪大恶极吗?不要去遮掩,张大你的嘴。当观众看到连你都不在乎时,他们就会喜欢你的。再说,"他犀利地说,"你想遮起来的那些牙齿,说不定还会带给你好运呢。"

凯丝·达莉接受了他的忠告,忘了自己的牙齿。从那时候开始,她想到的只有她的观众。她张大了嘴巴,热情奔放地唱歌,成为电影界和广播界一流明星,其他喜剧演员现在还希望学她呢!

著名的威廉·詹姆斯,曾分析过那些从未发现自我的人。他说,一般人只发挥了10%的潜能。"跟我们应该做到的相比,"他写道,"我们只是半醒着。我们只使用了我们身心资源的很小部分。再广而言之,一个人只是活在有限的范围内。他具有各种潜能,却不知道如何利用。"

你和我也有这些潜能,所以我们不该浪费时间,去担心我们不能成为其他人。你是这个世界上的新东西,以前从未有过,从开天辟地以来,从未有过完全跟你一样的人;而且将来直到永远,也不可能再出现一个和你完全一样的人。新的遗传学知识告诉我们,你之所以成为你,主要取决于你父亲的24个染色体和你母亲的24个染色体。"在每一个染色体内",阿伦·舒因费尔德说,"可能有几十到几百个遗传因子——在某些情况下,每一个遗传因子都有可能改变一个人的命运。"不错,我们正是这样"既可怕又奇妙"地制造出来的。

"anywhere from scores to hundreds of genes—with a single gene, in some cases, able to change the whole life of an individual." Truly, we are "fearfully and wonderfully" made.

Even after your mother and father met and mated, there was only one chance in 300,000 billion that the person who is specifically you would be born! In other words, if you had 300,000 billion brothers and sisters, they might have all been different from you. Is all this guesswork? No. It is a scientific fact. If you would like to read more about it, go to your public library and borrow a book entitled *You and Heredity*, by Amran Scheinfeld.

I can talk with conviction about this subject of being yourself because I feel deeply about it. I know what I am talking about. I know from bitter and costly experience. To illustrate: when I first came to New York from the cornfields of Missouri, I enrolled in the American Academy of Dramatic Arts. I aspired to be an actor. I had what I thought was a brilliant idea, a shortcut to success, an idea so simple, so foolproof, that I couldn't understand why thousands of ambitious people hadn't already discovered it. It was this: I would study how the famous actors of that day—John Drew, Walter Hampden, and Otis Skinner—got their effects. Then I would imitate the best point of each one of them and make myself into a shining, triumphant combination of all of them. How silly! How absurd! I had to waste years of my life imitating other people before it penetrated through my thick Missouri skull that I had to be myself, and that I couldn't possibly be anyone else.

That distressing experience ought to have taught me a lasting lesson. But it didn't. Not me. I was too dumb. I had to learn it all over again. Several years later, I set out to write what I hoped would be the best book on public speaking for businessmen that had ever been written. I had the same foolish idea about writing this book that I had formerly had about acting: I was going to *borrow* the ideas of a lot of other writers and put them all in one book—a book that would have everything. So I got scores of books on public speaking and spent a year incorporating their ideas into my manuscript. But it finally dawned on me once again that I was playing the fool. This hodgepodge of other men's ideas that I had written was so synthetic, so dull, that no businessman would ever plod through it. So I tossed a year's work into the wastebasket, and started all over again. This time I said to myself: "You've got to be Dale Carnegie, with all his faults and

即使你母亲和父亲相遇成亲之后，生下的这个人正好是你，但这个机会也是三十亿万分之一。换而言之，即使你有30万亿个兄弟姐妹，也可能完全与你不同。这是猜测吗?不是，这是科学事实。如果你想了解更多的话，不妨去图书馆借一本《遗传与你》，它的作者就是阿伦·舒因费尔德。

我可以和你深入探讨保持本色这个问题，因为我对此感触尤深。我对我正在谈的问题很清楚，因为我为此付出了相当大的代价，有过痛苦的经历。当我从密苏里州的乡下去纽约的时候，我进了美国戏剧艺术学院，希望成为一名演员。当时我有一个自以为非常聪明的想法——一条走向成功的捷径：这个想法如此简单，如此完美，所以我不懂为什么那么多野心勃勃的人居然没有发现这一点。这个想法是这样的：我要学当年那些著名的演员是如何表演的，我要模仿他们每个人的优点，使我自己成为一个集诸人优点于一身的著名演员。多么愚蠢!多么荒谬!我居然浪费那么多时间去模仿别人!最后我终于明白，我一定要保持本色，我不可能变成任何人。

那次痛苦的经历应该使我获得一些教训才对，但并非如此。我并没有接受教训；我太笨了，我得重新学习这个道理。几年之后，我开始写一本书，并希望它成为所有关于当众演讲的书中最好的一本。在写那本书的时候，我又产生了和以前学演戏时一样的愚蠢想法：想"借"来其他作者的观念，放在那本书里，使它无所不包。于是我买了十几本关于当众演讲的书，花了一年时间把它们的概念纳入我的书里，但最后我又一次发现我做了傻事：把别人的观点拼凑在一起写成的东西非常做作枯燥，没有一个人愿意看。所以我把一年的心血都扔进了废纸篓里，又重新开始。

这次我对自己说："你一定要保持自己的本色，保留你的错误和局限。你不可能成为成别人。"于是我不再试着成为其他人的综合体，而是捋起袖子，做了我当初本应该做的事：我以自己的经历和观察，写了一本关于当众演讲的教材，以一个演说家和演讲教师的身份来写。我学

limitations. You can't possibly be anybody else." So I quit trying to be a combination of other men, and rolled up my sleeves and did what I should have done in the first place: I wrote a textbook on public speaking out of my own experiences, observations, and convictions as a speaker and a teacher of speaking. I learned—for all time, I hope—the lesson that Sir Walter Raleigh learned. (I am not talking about the Sir Walter who threw his coat in the mud for the Queen to step on. I am talking about the Sir Walter Raleigh who was professor of English literature at Oxford back in 1904.) "I can't write a book commensurate with Shakespeare, "he said, "but I can write a book by me."

Be yourself. Act on the sage advice that Irving Berlin gave the late George Gershwin. When Berlin and Gershwin first met, Berlin was famous but Gershwin was a struggling young composer working for thirty-five dollars a week in Tin Pan Alley. Berlin, impressed by Gershwin's ability, offered Gershwin a job as his musical secretary at almost three times the salary he was then getting. "But don't take the job, "Berlin advised. "If you do, you may develop into a second-rate Berlin. But if you insist on being yourself, someday you'll become a first-rate Gershwin."

Gershwin heeded that warning and slowly transformed himself into one of the significant American composer of his generation.

Charlie Chaplin, Will Rogers, Mary Margaret McBride, Gene Autry, and millions of others had to learn the lesson I am trying to hammer home in this chapter. They had to learn the hard way—just as I did.

When Charlie Chaplin first started making films, the director of the pictures insisted on Chaplin's imitating a popular German comedian of that day. Charlie Chaplin got nowhere until he acted himself. Bob Hope had a similar experience: spent years in a singing-and-dancing act—and got nowhere until he began to wisecrack and be himself. Will Rogers twirled a rope in vaudeville for years without saying a word. He got nowhere until he discovered his unique gift for humor and began to talk as he twirled his rope.

When Mary Margaret McBride first went on the air, she tried to be an Irish comedian and failed. When she tried to be just what she was a plain country girl from Missouri—she became one of the most popular radio stars in New York.

到了华特·罗里爵士所学到的教训——我希望能永远保持下去。(我不是在谈论把大衣扔在泥地上让女王踩上去的罗里爵士,而是在谈论1904年在牛津大学当英国文学教授的罗里爵士。)"我写不出一本足以和莎士比亚媲美的书,"他说,"但我可以写一本由我自己写成的书。"

成为你自己。就像阿尔文·伯林给已故的乔治·盖歇温的明智忠告那样去做。

当伯林和盖歇温初次见面的时候,伯林已经名声显赫,而盖歇温还是一个未成名的年轻作曲家,一个星期只赚35美元。伯林很欣赏盖歇温的才华,就让他当他的秘书,薪水大概是他当时收入的3倍。"但是不要接受这份工作,"伯林忠告说,"如果你接受这份工作,你可能会成为一个二流的伯林;但如果你坚持保持自己的本色,总有一天你会成为一个一流的盖歇温。"

盖歇温接受了这个忠告,后来终于成为当时美国最重要的作曲家之一。

查理·卓别林、威尔·罗吉斯、玛丽·玛格丽特·麦克布莱德、金·奥特雷以及其他成千上万的人都学过我在此想让各位明白的这一课,而且他们就像我一样也学得很辛苦。

卓别林最初拍电影的时候,电影导演坚持让他模仿当时德国一个非常有名的喜剧演员,但直到卓别林创造出自己的特色之后才开始成名。鲍伯·霍普也有同样的经历。多年来他一直在表演歌舞片,但毫无成就,直到他找到开自己玩笑、表现自我之后,才功成名就。威尔·罗吉斯在一个杂耍团表演抛绳技术,没有任何说话的机会。直到他发现自己有幽默天分,并开始在表演抛绳的时候搞笑时,这才成名。

玛丽·玛格丽特·麦克布莱德刚踏入广播界的时候,想做一名爱尔兰喜剧演员,但她失败了。后来她发挥了自我本色,扮演一个从密苏里州来的平凡农村女孩,结果成为纽约最受欢迎的广播明星。

金·奥特雷刚出道的时候,想改掉他的得克萨斯口音,打扮成城里人,并自称是纽约人,结果大家在背后笑他。后来,他开始弹五弦琴,改唱西部歌曲,开始了演艺生涯,使他成为电影和

When Gene Autry tried to get rid of his Texas accent and dressed like city boys and claimed he was from New York, people merely laughed behind his back. But when he started twanging his banjo and singing cowboy ballads, Gene Autry started out on a career that made him the world's most popular cowboy both in pictures and on the radio.

You are something new in this world. Be glad of it. Make the most of what nature gave you. In the last analysis, all art is autobiographical. You can sing only what you are. You can paint only what you are. You must be what your experiences, your environment, and your heredity have made you. For better or for worse, you must cultivate your own little garden. For better or for worse, you must play your own little instrument in the orchestra of life.

As Emerson said in his essay on *"Self-Reliance"*: "There is a time in every man's education when he arrives at the conviction that envy is ignorance; that imitation is suicide; that he must take himself for better, for worse, as his portion; that though the wide universe is full of good, no kernel of nourishing corn can come to him but through his toil bestowed on that plot of ground which is given him to till. The power which resides in him is new in nature, and none but he knows what that is which he can do, nor does he know until he has tried."

That is the way Emerson said it. But here is the way a poet—the late Douglas Malloch—said it:

If you can't be a pine on the top of the hill.
Be a scrub in the valley—but be
The best little scrub by the side of the rill;
Be a bush, if you can't be a tree.
If you can't be a bush, be a bit of the grass.
And some highway happier make;
If you can't be a muskie, then just be a bass—
But the liveliest bass in the lake!
We can't all be captains, we've got to be crew.
There's something for all of us here.
There's big work to do and there's lesser to do

广播两个行业中最著名的牛仔歌星。

你是这个世界上的新东西,你应该为此而庆幸,并尽力利用大自然赋予你的一切。归根结底,所有艺术都带着自传色彩:你只能唱你自己的歌,只能画你自己的画,只能做一个由你的经历、你的环境和你的家庭所造就的你;不论好坏,你都得创造一个你自己的小花园;不论好坏,你都得在生命的交响乐中演奏你自己的乐器。

正如爱默生在他的散文《自信》中所说的:"每一个人在他的教育过程中,一定会在某个时期发现,羡慕就是无知,模仿就是自杀。不论好坏,他都必须保持自我本色。虽然广袤的宇宙之间全是美好的东西,但除非他耕耘那一块属于自己的土地,否则绝不会有好收成。他所有的能力是自然界的一种新能力,除他之外没有人知道他能做什么,他能知道什么,而这些都必须靠他自己去尝试。"

上面是爱默生的观点。下面是已故诗人道格拉斯·马罗屈说的:

如果你不能成为山顶青松,
就做一丛小树,生长在山谷中,
但必须是溪边最好的一丛小树。
如果你不能成为一棵大树,
就做一丛灌木。
如果你不能成为一丛灌木,
就做一片绿草,
给大路增添几分景致。
如果你不能成为一只麝香鹿,
就做一条鲈鱼,

And the task we must do is the near.
If you can't be a highway, then just be a trail,
If you can't be the sun, be a star;
It isn't by the size that you win or you fail—
Be the best of whatever you are!

To cultivate a mental attitude that will bring us peace and freedom from worry, here is Rule 5:

Let's not imitate others. Let's find ourselves and be ourselves.

但必须是湖里最好的一条鱼。
我们不能都做船长,我们得做海员;
世上的事情多得做不完,
工作有大有小,
我们该做的工作,就在手边。
如果你不能做一条公路,就做一条小径;
如果你不能做太阳,就当一颗星星。
不能凭大小来判断你的输赢,
不论做什么,都要做你自己。

要想培养给你带来平安、消除忧虑的心理,记住第五条规则:

不要模仿别人。让我们找到自我,保持本色。

6 If You Have a Lemon, Make a Lemonade

While writing this book, I dropped in one day at the University of Chicago and asked the Chancellor, Robert Maynard Hutchins, how he kept from worrying. He replied: "I have always tried to follow a bit of advice given to me by the late Julius Rosenwald, President of Sears, Roebuck and Company: 'When you have a lemon, make a lemonade. '"

That is what a great educator does. But the fool does the exact opposite. If he finds that life has handed him a lemon, he gives up and says: "I'm beaten. It is fate. I haven't got a chance." Then he proceeds to rail against the world and indulge in an orgy of self-pity. But when the wise man is handed a lemon, he says: "What lesson can I learn from this misfortune? How can I improve my situation? How can I turn this lemon into a lemonade?"

After spending a lifetime studying people and their hidden reserves of power, the great psychologist, Alfred Adler, declared that one of the wonder-filled characteristics of human beings is "their power to turn a minus into a plus."

Here is an interesting and stimulating story of a woman I know who did just that. Her name is Thelma Thompson, and she lives at 100 Morningside Drive, New York City. "During the war, "she said, as she told me of her experience, "during the war, my husband was stationed at an Army training camp near the Mojave Desert, in New Mexico. I went to live there in order to be near him. I hated the place. I loathed it. I had never before been so miserable. My husband was ordered out on maneuvers in the Mojave Desert, and I was left in a tiny shack alone. The heat was unbearable—125 degrees in the shade of a cactus. Not a soul to talk to but Mexicans and Indians, and they couldn't speak English. The wind blew incessantly, and all the food I ate, and the very air I breathed, were filled with sand, sand, sand!

"I was so utterly wretched, so sorry for myself, that I wrote to my parents. I told them I was giving up and coming back home. I said I couldn't stand it one minute longer. I would rather be in jail! My father answered my letter with just two lines—two lines that will always sing in my

第6章 如果你有一个柠檬,就做一杯柠檬汁

在写这本书的时候，有一天我去芝加哥大学向罗伯特·梅纳德·哈吉斯校长请教如何克服忧虑。他回答说:“我一直都在遵循西尔斯公司已故董事长朱利亚斯·罗森沃德告诉我的忠告。他说:‘如果你只有一个柠檬,就做一杯柠檬汁。’”

这是一个伟大教育家的做法,而傻子却正好相反。要是他发现人生只给他一个柠檬,他就会自暴自弃地说:“我完了。这就是命。我没有任何机会。”然后他就开始诅咒这个世界,沉溺在自怜之中。而聪明人拿到一个柠檬的时候,会说:“我可以从这个不幸中学到什么?我怎样才能改善处境？怎样把这个柠檬做成一杯柠檬汁?”

伟大的心理学家阿尔弗雷德·阿德勒花了毕生精力研究人类未曾开发的潜能之后,认为人类最奇妙的特性之一就是“变负为正的力量”。

下面是一个女人有趣而有意义的故事。我认识她,她正是这样做的。她叫瑟玛·汤普森,住在纽约市黎明街100号。“在战争期间,”她告诉我她的经历,“我先生在新墨西哥州莫嘉佛沙漠附近的陆军训练营驻防。我为了离他近一点,也搬去那里。我讨厌那个地方,我从未这么烦恼过。我先生被派往莫嘉佛沙漠,我一个人留在那间小破屋里。那儿热得难以忍受——大仙人掌的阴影下温度高达华氏125度。除了墨西哥人和印第安人之外,没有人和你谈话,而且这些人又不会说英语。风不停地吹,所有吃的东西和呼吸的空气中全都是沙子！沙子！沙子!

“我极其沮丧,难过得无法描述,就给我父母写了封信,告诉他们我忍受不了,想要回家。我说我连一分钟也住不下去了,还不如待在监狱里。我父亲的回信只有两行字,这两行字一直萦绕在我的记忆当中,彻底改变了我的生活。

memory—two lines that completely altered my life:

Two men looked out from prison bars,
One saw the mud, the other saw stars.

"I read those two lines over and over. I was ashamed of myself. I made up my mind I would find out what was good in my present situation. I would look for the stars.

"I made friends with the natives, and their reaction amazed me. When I showed interest in their weaving and pottery, they gave me presents of their favourite pieces which they had refused to sell to tourists. I studied the fascinating forms of the cactus and the yuccas and the Joshua trees. I learned about prairie dogs, watched for the desert sunsets, and hunted for seashells that had been left there millions of years ago when the sands of the desert had been an ocean floor.

"What brought about this astonishing change in me? The Mojave Desert hadn't changed. The Indians hadn't changed. But I had. I had changed my attitude of mind. And by doing so, I transformed a wretched experience into the most exciting adventure of my life. I was stimulated and excited by this new world that I had discovered. I was so excited I wrote a book about it—a novel that was published under the title *Bright Ramparts*... I had looked out of my self-created prison and found the stars."

Thelma Thompson, you discovered an old truth that the Greeks taught five hundred years before Christ was born: "*The best things are the most difficult.*"

Harry Emerson Fosdick repeated it again in the twentieth century: "Happiness is not mostly pleasure; it is mostly victory." Yes, the victory that comes from a sense of achievement, of triumph, of turning our lemons into lemonades.

I once visited a happy farmer down in Florida who turned even a poison lemon into lemonade. When he first got this farm, he was discouraged. The land was so wretched he could neither grow fruit nor raise pigs. Nothing thrived there but scrub oaks and rattlesnakes. Then he got his idea. He would turn his liability into an asset: he would make the most of these rattlesnakes. To everyone's amazement, he started canning rattlesnake meat. When I stopped to visit him a few years ago, I found that tourists were pouring in to see his rattlesnake farm at the rate of twenty thousand a year. His business was thriving. I saw poison from the fangs of his rattlers being shipped to laboratories to

两个人从监狱的铁窗向外看，
一个只看见烂泥，另一个却看到了星星。

“我把这两行字念了一遍又一遍，自感惭愧。我下定决心，一定要找出那儿还有什么好地方。我要去找星星。

“我和当地人交上了朋友，而他们的反应也令我惊奇不已。当我对他们的织布和陶器表示出兴趣时，他们就把他们最喜欢的、不肯卖给观光客的东西送给我当礼物。我研究仙人掌和各种当地植物，还知道了土拨鼠，看到了沙漠日落，还去寻找300万年前留在这里的贝壳，当时这里还是海床。

“是什么使我产生了如此惊人的改变呢?莫嘉佛沙漠没有变化，印第安人也没有改变。可是我变了。我改变了我的心态。通过改变心态，我把那些令人颓废的境遇变成了我生命中最具刺激的冒险。我所发现的这个崭新的世界，使我感动而兴奋，我为此写了一本小说《光明城堡》……我从自己设下的监狱向外望，看到了星星。”

瑟玛·汤普森，你发现了古希腊人在基督降生之前500年所教的一条真理：“最好的正是最难得到的。”

在20世纪，哈瑞·爱默生·福斯迪克又重复了这句话：“快乐主要并不是享受，而是胜利。”不错，这种胜利来自一种成就感、一种超越、将我们的柠檬做成柠檬汁。

我曾拜访过一位住在佛罗里达的快乐农夫，他甚至把有毒的柠檬做成了柠檬汁。他当初买下那片农场时，非常颓丧。那块地太差了，既不能种水果，也不能养猪，只能生长矮灌木和响尾蛇。然后，他想出了主意，把他所拥有的变成一种资产：他打算好好利用那些响尾蛇。他的做法让大家都很吃惊，因为他开始做起了响尾蛇肉罐头。当我几年前去看他的时候，我发现每年来这里参观他的响尾蛇农场的游客将近两万人。他的生意蓬勃发展。我看到从响尾蛇口里取出

make anti-venom toxin; I saw rattlesnake skins being sold at fancy prices to make women's shoes and handbags. I saw canned rattlesnake meat being shipped to customers all over the world. I bought a picture postcard of the place and mailed it at the local post office of the village, which had been re-christened "Rattlesnake, Florida", in honour of a man who had turned a poison lemon into a sweet lemonade.

As I have traveled up and down and back and forth across America time after time, it has been my privilege to meet dozens of men and women who have demonstrated"their power to turn a minus into a plus".

The late William Bolitho, author of *Twelve Against the Gods*, put it like this: "The most important thing in life is not to capitalise on your gains. Any fool can do that. The really important thing is to profit from your losses. That requires intelligence; and it makes the difference between a man of sense and a fool."

Bolitho uttered those words after he had lost a leg in a railway accident. But I know a man who lost both legs and turned his minus into a plus. His name is Ben Fortson. I met him in a hotel elevator in Atlanta, Georgia. As I stepped into the elevator, I noticed this cheerful-looking man, who had both legs missing, sitting in a wheel-chair in a corner of the elevator. When the elevator stopped at his floor, he asked me pleasantly if I would step to one corner, so he could manage his chair better. "So sorry, "he said, "to inconvenience you"—and a deep, heart-warming smile lighted his face as he said it.

When I left the elevator and went to my room, I could think of nothing but this cheerful cripple. So I hunted him up and asked him to tell me his story.

"It happened in 1929, "he told me with a smile. "I had gone out to cut a load of hickory poles to stake the beans in my garden. I had loaded the poles on my Ford and started back home. Suddenly one pole slipped under the car and jammed the steering apparatus at the very moment I was making a sharp turn. The car shot over an embankment and hurled me against a tree. My spine was hurt. My legs were paralysed.

"I was twenty-four when that happened, and I have never taken a step since."

Twenty-four years old, and sentenced to a wheel-chair for the rest of his life! I asked him

来的毒液被送到各大药厂制造蛇毒血清。我还看到响尾蛇皮以很高的价钱卖出去,用来做女士皮鞋和提包。我还看到响尾蛇肉罐头被运到世界各地的顾客手里。我买了一张印有那个地方照片的明信片,在当地邮局寄了出去。现在这个村子已改名为佛罗里达响尾蛇村,以纪念这位把有毒的柠檬做成甜美柠檬汁的人。

因为我一次又一次在全国各地来回旅行,使我有幸见到许多男人和女人表现出"他们变负为正的能力"。

《十二个以人胜天的人》一书的作者,已故的威廉·波里索曾这样说:"生命中最重要的,就是不要以你的收入为资本。任何傻子都会这样做。真正重要的,是要从你的损失中去获利。这就需要聪明才智,这正是聪明人和傻子的区别。"

波里索是在一次汽车灾难中摔断一条腿后说这些的。但我还知道有一个断了双腿的人,也把他的负面变成了正面。他的名字叫本·福特森。我在佐治亚州大西洋城一家旅馆的电梯里遇到的他。在我进入电梯的时候,我注意到了这个看上去非常开心的人,他断了两条腿,坐在电梯角落的一张轮椅上。当电梯停在他要去的那一层时,他开心地问我是否可以给他让一下,好让他出去。"真对不起,"他说,"给您添麻烦了。"——他说这话的时候,露出了深切而温暖的笑容。

当我出了电梯回到房间时,除了这个开心的残疾人之外,我再也想不起其他事情。于是我去找他,请他把他的故事告诉我。

"事情发生在1929年,"他微笑着告诉我,"我砍了一大堆胡桃木树枝,准备给我花园里的豆子做支架。我把胡桃木枝装在我的福特车上,准备回家。突然一根树枝滑下车,卡在引擎中,当时汽车正急转弯。汽车冲出路外,我撞在了一棵树上。我的脊椎受了伤,两条腿都残了。

"出事那年我才24岁,从那以后我再也没有走过一步路。"

24岁时就被判一辈子依靠轮椅生活。我问他为什么能够这么勇敢地接受这个事实,他说:

how he managed to take it so courageously, and he said: "I didn't." He said he raged and rebelled. He fumed about his fate. But as the years dragged on, he found that his rebellion wasn't getting him anything except bitterness. "I finally realised, "he said, "that other people were kind and courteous to me. So the least I could do was to be kind and courteous to them."

I asked if he still felt, after all these years, that his accident had been a terrible misfortune, and he promptly said: "No." He said: "I'm almost glad now that it happened." He told me that after he got over the shock and resentment, he began to live in a different world. He began to read and developed a love for good literature. In fourteen years, he said, he had read at least fourteen hundred books; and those books had opened up new horizons for him and made his life richer than he ever thought possible. He began to listen to good music; and he is now thrilled by great symphonies that would have bored him before. But the biggest change was that he had time to think. "For the first time in my life, "he said, "I was able to look at the world and get a real sense of values. I began to realise that most of the things I had been striving for before weren't worthwhile at all."

As a result of his reading, he became interested in politics, studied public questions, made speeches from his wheel-chair! He got to know people and people got to know him. Today Ben Fortson—still in his wheel-chair—is Secretary of State for the State of Georgia!

During the last thirty-five years, I have been conducting adult-education classes in New York City, and I have discovered that one of the major regrets of many adults is that they never went to college. They seem to think that not having a college education is a great handicap. I know that this isn't necessarily true because I have known thousands of successful men who never went beyond high school. So I often tell these students the story of a man I knew who had never finished even grade school. He was brought up in blighting poverty. When his father died, his father's friends had to chip in to pay for the coffin in which he was buried. After his father's death, his mother worked in an umbrella factory ten hours a day and then brought piecework home and worked until eleven o'clock at night.

The boy brought up in these circumstances went in for amateur dramatics put on by a club in his church. He got such a thrill out of acting that he decided to take up public speaking. This led him

"我以前并不能这样。"他说他当时充满了怨恨和反抗,抱怨他的命运。但时间仍在一年一年地过去,他发现抱怨不能解决任何问题,只会使他更痛苦。"我终于明白,"他说,"大家都对我很好,很有礼貌,所以我至少应该做到对别人也有礼貌。"

我问他在经过这么多年以后,是否还觉得那次意外是一次巨大的不幸。他当即就说:"不。我现在甚至很高兴有那次经历。"他告诉我,在他克服了懊丧悔恨之后,就开始生活在一个不同的世界。他开始读书,并喜欢上了优秀文学作品。他说,在14年时间里,他至少看了1400多本书,这些书为他开拓了全新的视野,使他的生活比以前更加丰富多彩。他开始欣赏美妙的音乐,以前让他觉得烦闷的伟大交响乐,现在却让他非常感动。但最大的变化是他现在有时间去思考。"我有生以来第一次,"他说,"能仔细地观察这个世界,有了真正的价值观。我开始明白,我以往所追求的事情,实际上大部分一点价值都没有。"

看书的结果,是他对政治产生了兴趣,并研究公共问题,坐在他的轮椅上到处演说,并结识了很多人,很多人也由此认识了他。今天,本·福特森仍然坐在他的轮椅上,却已经成为佐治亚州政府的秘书长。

在过去35年里,我一直在纽约市开办成人教育课程。我发现许多成年人最大的遗憾是他们从来没有上过大学,他们似乎认为没有接受大学教育是一大缺陷。我知道这不一定对,因为我就知道成千上万的成功人士,他们甚至连中学都没有毕业。所以我常常给这些学员们讲一个我认识的人的故事,这个人甚至小学都没有读完。他家里非常穷,当他父亲去世的时候,还是由他父亲的朋友筹款,才把他父亲安葬的。他父亲死后,他母亲在一家制伞厂上班,一天要干10小时,还要带一些活回家,一直干到晚上11点。

在这种环境中成长的这个男孩,曾参加过由当地教堂举办的一次业余戏剧表演。演出时他非常开心,因此决定去学当众演讲。这种能力又引导他步入政坛。30岁时,他当选为纽约州议

into politics. By the time he reached thirty, he was elected to the New York State legislature. But he was woefully unprepared for such a responsibility. In fact, he told me that frankly he didn't know what it was all about. He studied the long, complicated bills that he was supposed to vote on—but, as far as he was concerned, those bills might as well have been written in the language of the Choctaw Indians. He was worried and bewildered when he was made a member of the committee on forests before he had ever set foot in a forest. He was worried and bewildered when he was made a member of the State Banking Commission before he had ever had a bank account, he himself told me that he was so discouraged that he would have resigned from the legislature if he hadn't been ashamed to admit defeat to his mother. In despair, he decided to study sixteen hours a day and turn his lemon of ignorance into a lemonade of knowledge. By doing that, he transformed himself from a local politician into a national figure and made himself so outstanding that *The New York Times* called him "the best-loved citizen of New York."

I am talking about Al Smith.

Ten years after Al Smith set out on his programme of political self-education, he was the greatest living authority on the government of New York State. He was elected Governor of New York for four terms—a record never attained by any other man. In 1928, he was the Democratic candidate for President. Six great universities—including Columbia and Harvard—conferred honorary degrees upon this man who had never gone beyond grade school.

Al Smith himself told me that none of these things would ever have come to pass if he hadn't worked hard sixteen hours a day to turn his minus into a plus.

Nietzsche's formula for the superior man was "not only to bear up under necessity but to love it."

The more I have studied the careers of men of achievement the more deeply I have been convinced that a surprisingly large number of them succeeded because they started out with handicaps that spurred them on to great endeavor and great rewards. As William James said: "Our infirmities help us unexpectedly."

Yes, it is highly probable that Milton wrote better poetry because he was blind and that Beethoven composed better music because he was deaf.

员。可是他对这项职务一点准备也没有。事实上他还告诉我，他甚至不知道这是怎么回事。他开始研究那些他必须投票表决的冗长而复杂的法案——可是这些法案对他来说，就好像是用印第安文字写的。他当选为森林委员会委员时，他从来没有走进过森林，因此他既忧虑又迷惑。当他当选为州议会金融委员会委员时，他同样既担心又惊异，因为他此前甚至不曾在银行开过户。他告诉我，他当时沮丧得差点儿从议会辞职，但他羞于向他的母亲承认他的失败。在绝望之中，他决定每天苦读16个小时，把他一无所知的柠檬变成一杯饱含知识的柠檬汁。结果，他从一个地方政治家变成了一个全国知名的人物，而且使自己变得更加优秀，以至于《纽约时报》称他为“纽约最受欢迎的市民”。

我说的是艾尔·史密斯。

当艾尔·史密斯开始这种自我教育的政治课程10年之后，他成了纽约州政府的活字典。他4次当选为纽约州州长——一个无人打破的纪录。1928年，他成为民主党总统候选人，还有6所大学——包括哥伦比亚大学和哈佛大学——赠予这个甚至连小学都没有毕业的人名誉学位。

艾尔·史密斯亲口告诉我，如果他当年没有一天工作16个小时，把负面转化为正面的话，所有这一切都不可能发生。

尼采对超人的定义是：“不仅在必要的情况下忍受一切，而且还要喜欢这一切。”

我越研究那些有成就的人，就越深刻地相信他们中之所以有许多人能成功，就是因为他们在刚开始的时候有一些缺陷，从而促使他们加倍努力，获得更多的回报。正如威廉·詹姆斯所说的：“我们的缺陷对我们有意外的帮助。”

不错，弥尔顿很可能就是因为双目失明，才写出了更好的诗篇；而贝多芬也可能是因为聋了，才能作出更好的曲子。

海伦·凯勒之所以能有辉煌的成就，也许是因为她的瞎和聋。

Helen Keller's brilliant career was inspired and made possible because of her blindness and deafness.

If Tchaikovsky had not been frustrated—and driven almost to suicide by his tragic marriage—if his own life had not been pathetic, he probably would never have been able to compose his immortal "*Symphonic Pathétique*".

If Dostoevsky and Tolstoy had not led tortured lives, they would probably never have been able to write their immortal novels.

"If I had not been so great an invalid," wrote the man who changed the scientific concept of life on earth—"if I had not been so great an invalid, I should not have done so much work as I have accomplished." That was Charles Darwin's confession that his infirmities had helped him unexpectedly.

The same day that Darwin was born in England another baby was born in a log cabin in the forests of Kentucky. He, too, was helped by his infirmities. His name was Lincoln—Abraham Lincoln. If he had been reared in an aristocratic family and had had a law degree from Harvard and a happy married life, he would probably never have found in the depths of his heart the haunting words that he immortalised at Gettysburg, nor the sacred poem that he spoke at his second inauguration—the most beautiful and noble phrases ever uttered by a ruler of men: "With malice toward none; with charity for all..."

Harry Emerson Fosdick says in his book, *The Power to See it Through*: "There is a Scandinavian saying which some of us might well take as a rallying cry for our lives: 'the north wind made the Vikings.' Wherever did we get the idea that secure and pleasant living, the absence of difficulty, and the comfort of ease, ever of themselves made people either good or happy? Upon the contrary, people who pity themselves go on pitying themselves even when they are laid softly on a cushion, but always in history character and happiness have come to people in all sorts of circumstances, good, bad, and indifferent, when they shouldered their personal responsibility. So, repeatedly the north wind has made the Vikings."

Suppose we are so discouraged that we feel there is no hope of our ever being able to turn our lemons into lemonade—then here are two reasons why we ought to try, anyway—two reasons why

如果柴可夫斯基不是那么痛苦——他那悲惨的婚姻几乎使他自杀——如果他的生活不是那么悲惨,也许他永远创作不出那首不朽的《悲怆交响曲》。

如果陀思妥耶夫斯基和托尔斯泰不是过着痛苦的生活,他们也许永远写不出那些不朽的著作。

"如果我不是有这样的残疾,"达尔文这个改变了生命科学基本概念的人写道,"如果我不是有这样的残疾,也许我不会取得这么大的成就。"达尔文承认,他的残疾对他有意想不到的帮助。

当达尔文在英国出生的那一天,另一个孩子也出生在美国肯塔基州一个森林小木屋里,而他的缺陷也对他产生了帮助。他的名字叫林肯——亚伯拉罕·林肯。如果他出生在一个贵族家庭,从哈佛大学获得法学学位,并且有幸福的婚姻生活的话,也许他永远不可能从内心深处找到在葛底斯堡发表的不朽演说,也不会有他第二次就职演说时如诗般的名言——这是美国统治者曾说过的最美也最高贵的话:"不要对任何人心存恶意,而应喜爱每一个人……"

哈瑞·爱默生·福斯迪克在《洞视一切》这本书中说:"斯堪的那维亚半岛居民有一句俗话,我们可以用来鼓励自己:'北风造就了维京人。'为什么我们会觉得安全舒适的生活,没有任何困难,这些就能够使人变成好人或者变得快乐呢?正好相反,那些可怜自己的人会继续可怜自己,即使他们舒舒服服躺在大垫子上也不例外。可是在历史上,只有不计环境优劣的人才能快乐,他们勇于承担责任。所以让我再说一遍:'北风造就了维京人。'"

假使我们颓丧到了极点,觉得根本不可能把柠檬做成柠檬汁,那么,下面则是我们应该试一试的两条理由——这两条理由告诉我们,为什么我们只会赚而不会赔。

第一条理由:我们可能成功。

第二条理由:即使我们不能成功,但只要我们试着变负为正,就会使我们朝前看,而不会朝后

we have everything to gain and nothing to lose.

Reason one: *We may succeed.*

Reason two: *Even if we don't succeed, the mere attempt to turn our minus into a plus will cause us to look forward instead of backward; it will replace negative thoughts with positive thoughts; it will release creative energy and spur us to get so busy that we won't have either the time or the inclination to mourn over what is past and for ever gone.*

Once when Ole Bull, the world-famous violinist, was giving a concert in Paris, the A string on his violin suddenly snapped. But Ole Bull simply finished the melody on three strings. "That is life, "says Harry Emerson Fosdick, "to have your A string snap and finish on three strings."

That is not only life. It is more than life. It is life triumphant!

If I had the power to do so, I would have these words of William Bolitho carved in eternal bronze and hung in every schoolhouse in the land:

The most important thing in life is not to capitalize on your gains. Any fool can do that. The really important thing is to profit from your losses. That requires intelligence; and it makes the difference between a man of sense and a fool.

So, to cultivate a mental attitude that will bring us peace and happiness, let's do something about Rule 6:

When fate hands us a lemon, let's try to make a lemonade.

看,它将会用肯定的思想来替代否定的思想;将激发你的创造力,让我们忙得根本没有时间、也没有兴趣去为那些已经过去和已经完成的事情担心。

有一次,世界著名的小提琴家欧利·布尔在巴黎举办一场音乐会,他小提琴上的A弦突然断了,但他仍然用另外三根弦演奏完了那支曲子。"这就是生活,"哈瑞·爱默生·福斯迪克说,"如果你的A弦断了,就用其他三根弦演奏完曲子。"

这不仅是生活,它比生活更加可贵——这是一次生命的胜利。

如果我能够做到,我会把威廉·波里索的这些话铭刻在铜牌上,挂在世界上每一所学校里:

"生命中最重要的事情,就是不要把你的收入算资本。任何傻子都会这样做。真正重要的是从你的损失中获利。这就需要有聪明才智,这正是聪明人和傻子的区别。"

所以,要培养能给你带来平安快乐的心理,就要做到第六项规则:

当命运给我们一个柠檬时,我们要试着做一杯柠檬汁。

7 How to Cure Melancholy in Fourteen Days

When I started writing this book, I offered a two-hundred-dollar prize for the most helpful and inspiring true story on"How I Conquered Worry".

The three judges for this contest were: Eddie Rickenbacker, president, Eastern Air Lines; Dr. Stewart W. McClelland, president, Lincoln Memorial University; H. V. Kaltenborn, radio news analyst. However, we received two stories so superb that the judges found it impossible to choose between them. So we divided the prize. Here is one of the stories that tied for first prize—the story of C. R. Burton (who works for Whizzer Motor Sales of Missouri, Inc.), 1067 Commercial Street, Springfield, Missouri.

"I lost my mother when I was nine years old, and my father when I was twelve," Mr. Burton wrote me. "My father was killed, but my mother simply walked out of the house one day nineteen years ago; and I have never seen her since. Neither have I ever seen my two little sisters that she took with her. She never even wrote me a letter until after she had been gone seven years. My father was killed in an accident three years after Mother left. He and a partner bought a café in a small Missouri town; and while Father was away on a business trip, his partner sold the café for cash and skipped out. A friend wired Father to hurry back home; and in his hurry, Father was killed in a car accident at Salinas, Kansas. Two of my father's sisters, who were poor and old and sick took three of the children into their homes. Nobody wanted me and my little brother. We were left at the mercy of the town. We were haunted by the fear of being called orphans and treated as orphans. Our fears soon materialised, too. I lived for a little while with a poor family in town. But times were hard and the head of the family lost his job, so they couldn't afford to feed me any longer. Then Mr. and Mrs. Loftin took me to live with them on their farm eleven miles from town. Mr. Loftin was seventy years old, and sick in bed with shingles. He told me I could stay there 'as long as I didn't lie, didn't steal, and did as I was told.' Those three orders became my *Bible*. I lived by them strictly. I started to school, but the first week found me at home, bawling like a baby. The

第7章 多替他人着想

我在开始写这本书的时候，提出了200美元赏金，以"我如何克服忧虑"为题，征求一则对人最有帮助、最能激励人心的真实故事。

这次征文比赛的3位评审委员，是东方航空公司的董事长艾迪·雷肯贝克、林肯纪念大学的校长史德华·麦克里南博士，以及广播新闻评论家卡坦波恩。但我们最后收到两篇非常好的故事，连3位评审委员也难以取舍。于是我们平分了这笔奖金。

下面就是得到一等奖的故事之一——作者是密苏里州斯普林菲尔德的波顿先生。（他为密苏里韦泽尔汽车销售公司工作。）

"我9岁时没了母亲，12岁时又没了父亲，"波顿先生写道，"我父亲死于意外，我母亲在19年前的某一天离家出走，从此以后我就再也没有见过她，也没有见过被她带走的两个小妹妹。直到离家7年之后，她才给我写了封信。我父亲在母亲离家3年之后死于一次意外。他和一个合伙人在密苏里州一个小镇买了一家咖啡店，这个合伙人趁父亲出差的时候，把咖啡店卖了并卷款潜逃。一个朋友给我父亲发电报，叫他赶快回家。我父亲在匆忙之下，在堪萨斯州沙林那城的一次车祸中丧生。我有两个姑姑，她们又穷又老，而且病魔缠身。她们把我们5个孩子中的3个带到她们家里去。没有人要我和我最小的弟弟，我们只好依靠镇上的人救济度日。我们怕被人家叫孤儿，或被当孤儿来看待，但我们担心的事情很快就发生了。我和一个贫民家庭在镇上共住了一段时间，但日子很艰难，男主人不久又失业，他们没办法再供养我。后来罗福汀先生和夫人收留了我，住在他们一个离镇子11里远的农庄里。当时罗福汀先生70岁，得了带状疱疹躺在床上。他告诉我说，只要我不说谎，不偷窃，能听话做事，我就可以留在那里。这三项要求成了我的圣

other children picked on me and poked fun at my big nose and said I was dumb and called me an 'orphan brat'. I was hurt so badly that I wanted to fight them; but Mr. Loftin, the farmer who had taken me in, said to me: 'Always remember that it takes a bigger man to walk away from a fight than it does to stay and fight.' I didn't fight until one day a kid picked up some chicken manure from the schoolhouse yard and threw it in my face. I beat the hell out of him; and made a couple of friends. They said he had it coming to him.

"I was proud of a new cap that Mrs. Loftin had bought me. One day one of the big girls jerked it off my head and riffled it with water and ruined it. She said she filled it with water so that 'the water would wet my thick skull and keep my popcorn brains from popping'.

"I never cried at school, but I used to bawl it out at home. Then one day Mrs. Loftin gave me some advice that did away with all troubles and worries and turned my enemies into friends. She said: 'Ralph, they won't tease you and call you an "orphan brat" any more if you will get interested in them and see how much you can do for them.' I took her advice. I studied hard; and I soon headed the class. I was never envied because I went out of my way to help them.

"I helped several of the boys write their themes and essays. I wrote complete debates for some of the boys. One lad was ashamed to let his folks know that I was helping him. So he used to tell his mother he was going possum hunting. Then he would come to Mr. Loftin's farm and tie his dogs up in the barn while I helped him with his lessons. I wrote book reviews for one lad and spent several evenings helping one of the girls on her math.

"Death struck our neighbourhood. Two elderly farmers died and one woman was deserted by her husband. I was the only male in four families. I helped these widows for two years. On my way to and from school, I stopped at their farms, cut wood for them, milked their cows, and fed and watered their stock. I was now blessed instead of cursed. I was accepted as a friend by everyone. They showed their real feelings when I returned home from the Navy. More than two hundred farmers came to see me the first day I was home. Some of them drove as far as eighty miles, and their concern for me was really sincere. Because I have been busy and happy trying to help other people, I have few worries; and I haven't been called an 'orphan brat' now for thirteen years."

Hooray for C. R. Burton! He knows how to win friends! And he also knows how to conquer

令，我严格遵守。我开始上学了，可是第一个星期我就像婴儿似的躲在家里号啕大哭。其他孩子都来捉弄我，取笑我的大鼻子，说我是个笨蛋，还说我是个'小臭孤儿'。我伤心得想揍他们一顿，可是收养我的罗福汀先生对我说：'要永远记住，能走开而不打架的人要比打架的人伟大得多。'所以我一直没有和人打过架。直到有一天，有个小孩在学校的院子里抓起一把鸡屎朝我脸上扔来。我狠狠地揍了他一顿，结果交上了好几个朋友，他们都说他是自找苦吃。

"我非常喜欢罗福汀夫人给我买的一顶新帽子。一天，有个大女孩把我的帽子扯了下来，在里面装满了水，弄坏了帽子。她说她之所以往里面装水，是想让那些水弄湿我的大脑瓜，好让我那玉米花似的脑筋不要乱爆。

"我在学校从来没有哭过，但我常常在家里号啕大哭。然后，有一天，罗福汀夫人给了我一些忠告，消除了我所有的烦恼和忧虑，并使我的敌人变成了朋友。她说：'拉尔夫，只要你对他们感兴趣，而且注意你能够为他们做些什么，他们就不会再捉弄你，或叫你"小臭孤儿"了。'我接受了她的忠告。我努力学习，不久就得了第一名。但从来没有人妒忌我，因为我总是尽力帮助别人。

"我帮过好多男孩子写作文，还为好几个男孩子写过完整的报告。有一个孩子不愿让他父母亲知道我在帮他，所以他常常告诉他母亲，说他要去抓田鼠，然后跑到罗福汀先生的农场来，把他的狗关在谷仓中，让我教他功课。我还替一个孩子写过读书报告，还花了好几个晚上帮另一个女孩子学习数学。

"死神来到了我们附近：两个年老的农夫死了，另一位妇女被丈夫抛弃了。我是这4户人家中唯一的男人。我帮了这些寡妇们两年。我上学放学的路上，都会去她们的农场，帮她们砍柴、挤牛奶，给她们的家畜喂饲料喂水。现在，大家都很喜欢我，不再骂我，每个人都把我当朋友。当我从海军退伍回来时，他们向我表达了他们的感情。我到家的第一天，200多个农夫赶来看我，

worry and enjoy life.

So did the late Dr. Frank Loope, of Seattle, Washington. He was an invalid for twenty-three years. Arthritis. Yet Stuart Whithouse of the *Seattle Star* wrote me, saying: "I interviewed Dr. Loope many times; and I *have never known a man more unselfish or a man who got more out of life.*"

How did this bed-ridden invalid get so much out of life? I'll give you two guesses. Did he do it by complaining and criticising? No... By wallowing in self-pity and demanding that he be the centre of attention and everyone cater to him? No... Still wrong. He did it by adopting as his slogan the motto of the Prince of Wales: "*Ich dien*"—"I serve." He accumulated the names and addresses of other invalids and cheered both them and himself by writing happy, encouraging letters. In fact, he organised a letter-writing club for invalids and got them writing letters to one another. Finally, he formed a national organisation called the Shut-in Society.

As he lay in bed, he wrote an average of fourteen hundred letters a year and brought joy to thousands of invalids by getting radios and books for shut-ins.

What was the chief difference between Dr. Loope and a lot of other people? Just this: Dr. Loope had the inner glow of a man with a purpose, a mission. He had the joy of knowing that he was being used by an idea far nobler and more significant than himself, instead of being as Shaw put it: "a self-centred, little clod of ailments and grievances complaining that the world would not devote itself to making him happy."

Here is the most astonishing statement that I ever read from the pen of a great psychiatrist. This statement was made by Alfred Adler. He used to say to his melancholia patients: "You can be cured in fourteen days if you follow this prescription. *Try to think every day how you can please someone.*"

That statement sounds so incredible that I feel I ought to try to explain it by quoting a couple of pages from Dr. Adler's splendid book, *What Life Should Mean to You.* (By the way, there is a book you ought to read.)

"Melancholia, "says Adler in *What Life Should Mean to You*: "is like a long-continued rage and reproach against others, though for the purpose of gaining care, sympathy and support, the

其中还有许多人从80里以外开车过来。他们对我的关怀非常真诚,因为我一直很高兴帮助其他人,所以我没有什么忧虑。而且,13年来再也没有人叫我'小臭孤儿'了。"

让我们为波顿喝彩吧!他知道如何赢得朋友!他也知道如何克服忧虑享受生活。

华盛顿州西雅图市已故博士弗兰克·陆培也是一样。他因为患有风湿病而在床上躺了23年,但是《西雅图之星》的记者史德华·怀特豪斯写信告诉我说:"我访问过陆培博士几次。我从未见过哪个人能像他那样不自私,那样会享受生活。"

像他这样躺在床上的废人怎么能享受生活呢?我让你猜两次。他是否埋怨和批评呢?不……他是不是充满了自怜,想让他成为所有人注意的中心,要求每个人都来照顾他呢?也不是。他的做法是把威尔士亲王的名言"我为民服务"作为座右铭。他搜集了许多病人的姓名和住址,给他们写充满快乐、充满鼓励的信,使他们高兴,并激励他自己。事实上,他创立了一个专供病人通信的俱乐部,使他们能够彼此联络。最后,他创办了一个全国性的组织,即"病房里的社会"。

他躺在床上,每年平均要写1400封信,由别人捐赠给这个组织的收音机和书籍为成千上万的病人带来了快乐。

陆培博士和别人最大的不同是什么呢?就在于他有一种内在的力量,有一种使命感。他知道自己是在为一项高尚而重要的理想服务,并从中获得快乐;他不会做萧伯纳所说的"以自我为中心、又病又苦、成天抱怨这个世界没有好好地使他开心的老家伙"。

下面是我读到的一位伟大的精神病专家所说的最惊人的论断,这句话出自阿尔弗雷德·阿德勒。他常常对那些精神忧郁症患者说:"如果你遵照我开的处方去做,你就可以在两周之内痊愈:每天想想如何让别人高兴。"

这话有些令人难以相信,所以我觉得应该引用阿德勒医生的名著《生命对你意义何在》里

patient seems only to be dejected about his own guilt. A melancholiac's first memory is generally something like this: 'I remember I wanted to lie on the couch, but my brother was lying there. I cried so much that he had to leave.'

"Melancholiacs are often inclined to revenge themselves by committing suicide, and the doctor's first care is to avoid giving them an excuse for suicide. I myself try to relieve the whole tension by proposing to them, as the first rule in treatment, 'Never do anything you don't like.' This seems to be very modest, but I believe that it goes to the root of the whole trouble if a melancholiac is able to do anything he wants, whom can he accuse? What has he got to revenge himself for? 'If you want to go to the theatre, 'I tell him, 'or to go on a holiday, do it. If you find on the way that you don't want to, stop it. 'It is the best situation anyone could be in. It gives a satisfaction to his striving for superiority. He is like God and can do what he pleases. On the other hand, it does not fit very easily into his style of life.

"He wants to dominate and accuse others and if they agree with him there is no way of dominating them. This rule is a great relief and I have never had a suicide among my patients.

"Generally the patient replies: 'But there is nothing I like doing. 'I have prepared for this answer, because I have heard it so often. 'then refrain from doing anything you dislike, 'I say. Sometimes, however, he will reply: 'I should like to stay in bed all day. 'I know that, if I allow it, he will no longer want to do it. I know that, if I hinder him, he will start a war. I always agree.

"This is one rule. Another attacks their style of life more directly. I tell them: '*You can be cured in fourteen days if you follow this prescription. Try to think every day how you can please someone*. 'See what this means to them. They are occupied with the thought. 'How can I worry someone. 'The answers are very interesting. Some say: 'This will be very easy for me. I have done it all my life. 'They have never done it. I ask them to think it over. They do not think it over. I tell them: 'You can make use of all the time you spend when you are unable to go to sleep by thinking how you can please someone, and it will be a big step forward in your health. 'When I see them next day, I ask them: 'Did you think over what I suggested?' They answer: 'Last night I went to sleep as soon as I got to bed. 'All this must be done, of course, in a modest, friendly manner, without a hint of superiority.

面的几页加以解释。

阿德勒在《生命对你意义何在》中说："忧郁症就像一种长年不止的怒气，以及对别人的反感，虽然患者只是想得到照顾、同情和支持，但他们似乎只是因为愧疚而抑郁不乐。忧郁症患者对早期的记忆通常都是这样的：'我记得我想躺在长沙发上，可是我哥哥却躺在那里。我大声哭叫，使他不得不走开。'

"忧郁症患者通常会用自杀来报复他们自己，而医生的第一个方案就是使他们找不到任何自杀的理由。我解除他们情绪紧张的办法——也是治疗的第一条规则——就是建议他们'不要做你不喜欢的事'。这句话听上去似乎非常简单，但我相信它可以深深触及这种病的根源。如果一个忧郁症患者能够做他想做的任何事情，那他还会怪谁呢？他还会报复谁呢？'如果你想去看戏，'我告诉患者说，'或出去度假，那就去吧。如果你走在半路上又不想去了，那就别去。'这是最好的状况，可以满足他所追求的优越感。他就像神仙一样，可以随心所欲。但从另一方面看来，这并不是他所想要的生活方式。

"他想控制别人、责怪别人，而如果大家都随他所愿的话，他就没有办法控制别人了。这种做法可以使人放松。在我的病人当中，从来没有人自杀。

"病人通常会说：'我没有喜欢做的事'。对此我已经准备好了答案，因为我听得太多了。我会说：'那就不要做你不想做的任何事。'不过有时候他们会这样说：'我想整天躺在床上。'这种事我也知道如何回答。如果我说这样很好，他就不会再想这样做了。我知道，如果我反对，他就会和我对着干，所以我总是同意他们。

"这是一种做法。另外一种做法则可以更直接地触动他们的生活方式。我告诉他们：'你可以在两周之内治好，如果你照我的话去做：每天想想如何让别人高兴。'这对他们意味着什么呢？他们满脑子只是想'我怎样才能让别人为我担忧'。他们的回答非常有意思。有的人说：'这

"Others will answer: 'I could never do it. I am so worried. 'I tell them: 'Don't stop worrying; but at the same time you can think now and then of others. 'I want to direct their interest always towards their fellows. Many say: 'Why should I please others? Others do not try to please me. ' 'You must think of your health, 'I answer'The others will suffer later on. 'It is extremely rare that I have found a patient who said: 'I have thought over what you suggested. 'All my efforts are devoted towards increasing the social interest of the patient. I know that the real reason for his malady is his lack of cooperation and I want him to see it too. As soon as he can connect himself with his fellow men on an equal and cooperative footing, he is cured... The most important task imposed by religion has always been 'Love thy neighbour'... It is the individual who is not interested in his fellow man who has the greatest difficulties in life and provides the greatest injury to others. It is from among such individuals that all human failures spring.... All that we demand of a human being, and the highest praise we can give him, is that he should be a good fellow worker, a friend to all other men, and a true partner in love and marriage.

Dr. Adler urges us to do a good deed every day. And what is a good deed?"*A good deed*, "said the prophet Mohammed, "*is one that brings a smile of joy to the face of another.*"

Why will doing a good deed every day produce such astounding effects on the doer? Because trying to please others will cause us to stop thinking of ourselves: the very thing that produces worry and fear and melancholia.

Mrs. William T. Moon, who operates the Moon Secretarial School, 521 Fifth Avenue, New York, didn't have to spend two weeks thinking how she could please someone in order to banish her melancholy. She went Alfred Adler one better—no, she went Adler thirteen better. She banished her melancholy, not in fourteen days, but in one day, by thinking how she could please a couple of orphans.

It happened like this: "In December, five years ago, "said Mrs. Moon, "I was engulfed in a feeling of sorrow and self-pity. After several years of happy married life, I had lost my husband. As the Christmas holidays approached, my sadness deepened. I had never spent a Christmas alone in all my life; and I dreaded to see this Christmas come. Friends had invited me to spend Christmas with them. But I did not feel up to any gaiety. I knew I would be a wet blanket at any party. So, I

对我太容易了。我这一辈子都在做让别人高兴的事。'其实他们从来没有做过。我会要求他们仔细考虑,但他们一般都不愿想。我会告诉他们:'当你睡不着的时候,不妨思考如何让别人高兴。这会大大改善你的健康。'当我第二天再见到他们时,会问他们:'你有没有想过我的建议?'他们会回答:'我昨天晚上一上床就睡着了。'当然,在跟他们谈这些事的时候,一定要诚恳而友善,丝毫不能有优越感。

"其他人会说:'我永远也做不到。我太担心了。'我告诉他们:'你可以继续忧虑下去。不过,你有时候也可以想想别人。'我希望引导他们对别人产生兴趣。很多人会说:'我为什么要让别人高兴呢?别人可从来不会让我高兴。'我回答说:'你一定得考虑你的健康。别人以后也会受苦的。'我很少会碰到病人说:'我曾想过你建议的事。'我这样做只是希望使病人增加对社会的兴趣。我知道他的病根主要是缺乏合作,而我正想使他看到这一点。一旦他能够和其他人在平等合作的基础上接触,他就会治好……宗教中最重要的信条之一就是'爱你的邻居'……那些对别人毫无兴趣的人,在生活中遭到的困难最多,对别人造成的伤害也最大。人类的各种失败也来自这一类人……我们对一个人所要求的,以及我们能给他的最高赞美,就是他应该是一个很合作的人,是其他人的朋友,也是爱情与婚姻生活中的真诚伴侣。"

阿德勒医生要求我们每天都做一件好事,但什么是好事呢?"好事,"先知穆罕默德说,"就是能给别人脸上带来开心微笑的事。"

为什么每天做一件好事就能给人带来这么大的影响呢? 因为当我们努力使别人高兴的时候,就不会只想到自己——这正是产生忧虑和恐惧以及忧郁症的根源。

威廉·孟恩夫人在纽约经营孟氏秘书学校, 她花了不到两周的时间去想如何让别人高兴,就治好了她的忧郁症。她比阿尔弗雷德·阿德勒更高一筹——不对,她比他甚至要高出13倍。她治好忧郁症并没有花14天,只花了一天去想如何让两个孤儿高兴。

refused their kind invitations. As Christmas Eve approached, I was more and more overwhelmed with self-pity. True, I should have been thankful for many things, as all of us have many things for which to be thankful. The day before Christmas, I left my office at three o'clock in the afternoon and started walking aimlessly up Fifth Avenue, hoping that I might banish my self-pity and melancholy. The avenue was jammed with gay and happy crowds—scenes that brought back memories of happy years that were gone. I just couldn't bear the thought of going home to a lonely and empty apartment. I was bewildered. I didn't know what to do. I couldn't keep the tears back. After walking aimlessly for an hour or so, I found myself in front of a bus terminal. I remembered that my husband and I had often boarded an unknown bus for adventure, so I boarded the first bus I found at the station. After crossing the Hudson River and riding for some time, I heard the bus conductor say: 'Last stop, lady.' I got off. I didn't even know the name of the town. It was a quiet, peaceful little place. While waiting for the next bus home, I started walking up a residential street. As I passed a church, I heard the beautiful strains of 'silent Night'. I went in. The church was empty except for the organist. I sat down unnoticed in one of the pews. The lights from the gaily decorated Christmas tree made the decorations seem like myriads of stars dancing in the moonbeams. The long-drawn cadences of the music—and the fact that I had forgotten to eat since morning—made me drowsy. I was weary and heavy-laden, so I drifted off to sleep.

"When I awoke, I didn't know where I was. I was terrified. I saw in front of me two small children who had apparently come in to see the Christmas tree. One, a little girl, was pointing at me and saying: 'I wonder if Santa Clause brought her.' These children were also frightened when I awoke. I told them that I wouldn't hurt them. They were poorly dressed. I asked them where their mother and daddy were. 'We ain't got no mother and daddy,' they said. Here were two little orphans much worse off than I had ever been. They made me feel ashamed of my sorrow and self-pity. I showed them the Christmas tree and then took them to a drugstore and we had some refreshments, and I bought them some candy and a few presents. My loneliness vanished as if by magic. These two orphans gave me the only real happiness and self-forgetfulness that I had had in months. As I chatted with them, I realised how lucky I had been. I thanked God that all my Christmases as a child had been bright with parental love and tenderness. Those two little orphans

事情是这样的："5年前的12月，"孟恩夫人说，"我正陷入一种悲伤而自怜的情绪之中。在多年的快乐婚姻生活之后我失去了丈夫。随着圣诞节的来临，我的病情加深了。我这一辈子从来没有一个人过圣诞节，我害怕这次圣诞节的来临。朋友们来请我和他们一起过圣诞，但我一点也感受不到快乐。我知道，不管在哪里我都会变成令人讨厌的人，所以我拒绝了他们仁慈的邀请。快到圣诞夜的时候，我更觉自己可怜。是的，我是有很多值得感恩的事，就像我们所有的人都有很多值得感恩的事一样。圣诞节的前一天，我在下午3点钟离开办公室，开始在第五大街上漫无目的地走着，希望可以消除我的自怜和忧郁症。大街上到处都是开心的人群——这景象使我回忆起那已经流逝的欢乐岁月。一想到要回那个孤独而空虚的公寓，我就受不了。我不知道该怎么办，忍不住流下眼泪。这样走了大约一个小时之后，我发现自己站在公共汽车站前。我记得以前我丈夫和我常常随意搭上一辆公共汽车瞎玩，于是，我就走上靠站的第一辆公共汽车。汽车过了哈德逊河，又行驶了一段之后，我听到司机说：'到终站了，夫人。'我下了车，但根本不知道这个小镇的名字。那是一个平静、安宁的小地方。在等下一班车回家时，我走到一个住宅区的街上，路过一座教堂，听见里面传来'平安夜'的优美曲调。我走进教堂，发现教堂里面空空的，只有那个弹风琴的人。我静静地坐在一张椅子上，圣诞树上的灯装饰得非常漂亮，使整棵树看上去像无数星星在月光下跳舞。悠扬的乐曲声，加上我从早上到现在一直没有吃东西，使我打起瞌睡来。我觉得身体虚弱而沉重，不久昏睡过去。

"我醒来的时候，不知身在何处。我吓坏了，这时突然看见我面前有两个小孩，他们显然是进来看圣诞树的，其中一个是小女孩，她正指着我说：'是不是圣诞老人把她带来的。'当我醒来时，那两个小孩也吓坏了。我告诉他们我不会伤害他们。他们衣着破旧，我问他们的父母在哪里，他们回答说：'我们没有爸爸妈妈。'原来他们是两个小孤儿，而且比我的境况更差。他们使我对自己的忧伤和自怜感到惭愧。我带他们去看那棵圣诞树，然后带他们去了一个小饮食店吃

did far more for me than I did for them. That experience showed me again the necessity of making other people happy in order to be happy ourselves. I found that happiness is contagious. By giving, we receive. By helping someone and giving out love, I had conquered worry and sorrow and self-pity, and felt like a new person. And I was a new person—not only then, but in the years that followed."

I could fill a book with stories of people who forgot themselves into health and happiness. For example, let's take the case of Margaret Tayler Yates, one of the most popular women in the United States Navy.

Mrs. Yates is a writer of novels, but none of her mystery stories is half so interesting as the true story of what happened to her that fateful morning when the Japanese struck our fleet at Pearl Harbour. Mrs. Yates had been an invalid for more than a year: bad heart. She spent twenty-two out of every twenty-four hours in bed. The longest journey that she undertook was a walk into the garden to take a sunbath. Even then, she had to lean on the maid's arm as she walked. She herself told me that in those days she expected to be an invalid for the balance of her life. "I would never have really lived again, "she told me, "if the Japs had not struck Pearl Harbour and jarred me out of my complacency.

"When this happened, "Mrs. Yates said, as she told her story, "everything was chaos and confusion. One bomb struck so near my home, the concussion threw me out of bed. Army trucks rushed out to Hickam Field, Scofield Barracks, and Kaneohe Bay Air Station, to bring Army and Navy wives and children to the public schools. There the Red Cross telephoned those who had extra rooms to take them in. The Red Cross workers knew that I had a telephone beside my bed, so they asked me to be a clearing-house of information. So I kept track of where Army and Navy wives and children were being housed, and all Navy and Army men were instructed by the Red Cross to telephone me to find out where their families were.

"I soon discovered that my husband, Commander Robert Raleigh Yates, was safe. I tried to cheer up the wives who did not know whether their husbands had been killed; and I tried to give consolation to the widows whose husbands had been killed—and they were many. Two thousand one hundred and seventeen officers and enlisted men in the Navy and Marine Corps were killed and

了一些点心,又给他们买了一些糖果和几样礼物。这时,我的孤独魔幻般地消失了。这两个孤儿给我带来了几个月都不曾体验的真正快乐。当我和他们聊天时,我才发现我是如此幸运。我得感谢上帝,因为我童年时的圣诞节都充满了欢乐,有父母的关爱和照顾。这两个小孤儿带给我的,远比我送给他们的要多得多。这次经历再一次使我认识到,只有让别人快乐才能让我们自己快乐。我发现快乐是有传染性的,在施予的同时得到回报。通过帮助别人,付出自己的爱,我克服了忧虑、悲伤以及自怜,觉得自己像一个新人。我的确是一个新人了——不仅当时是,而且以后一直都是。"

那些忘记自我并由此获得健康与快乐的人的故事,可以写一本书。例如,我们来看玛格丽特·泰勒·叶慈的故事,她是美国海军中最受欢迎的女性之一。

叶慈夫人是一位小说家, 可是她那些神秘小说的趣味性没有一本比得上发生在她身上的真实故事的一半。这件事发生在日本偷袭珍珠港美军舰队的那天早上。

当时,叶慈夫人生病卧床已经一年多了,她得的是严重心脏病,一天要躺在床上22小时。她走过的最长的路,就是去花园晒日光浴。即使在那时,她走路还得由一个女佣搀扶。她告诉我,她当时以为这一辈子全完了。"要不是日本人轰炸珍珠港,把我从这种不良情绪中惊醒过来,"她说,"我绝不可能再有真正的生活。"

"这件事情发生的时候,"叶慈夫人告诉我,"一切都陷入混乱状态。一颗炸弹就落在我家附近,爆炸把我从床上震下来。军队的卡车赶到基地附近,把陆军和海军的家属接到公立学校。在那里,红十字会给那些有多余房间的人打电话收容他们。红十字会的人知道我有一个电话正好放在床边, 因此要求我为他们记录所有的资料。于是我记下所有陆军和海军家属被送到了哪里。红十字会也通知所有的海军和陆军人员给我打电话,打听他们家人的下落。

"我很快就发现,我丈夫罗伯特·叶慈中校安然无恙。我尽量想办法让那些不知道丈夫音讯

960 were reported missing.

"At first I answered these phone calls while lying in bed. Then I answered them sitting up in bed. Finally, I got so busy, so excited, that I forgot all about my weakness and got out of bed and sat by a table. By helping others who were much worse off than I was, I forgot all about myself; and I have never gone back to bed again except for my regular eight hours of sleep each night. I realize now that if the Japanese had not struck at Pearl Harbour, I would probably have remained a semi-invalid all my life. I was comfortable in bed. I was constantly waited on, and I now realize that I was unconsciously losing my will to rehabilitate myself.

"The attack on Pearl Harbor was one of the greatest tragedies in American history, but as far as I was concerned, it was one of the best things that ever happened to me. That terrible crisis gave me strength that I never dreamed I possessed. It took my attention off myself and focused it on others. It gave me something big and vital and important to live for. I no longer had time to think about myself or care about myself."

A third of the people who rush to psychiatrists for help could probably cure themselves if they would only do as Margaret Yates did: get interested in helping others. My idea? No, that is approximately what Carl Jung said. And he ought to know—if anybody does. He said: "About one-third of my patients are suffering from no clinically definable neurosis, but from the senselessness and emptiness of their lives." To put it another way, they are trying to thumb a ride through life—and the parade passes them by. So they rush to a psychiatrist with their petty, senseless, useless lives. Having missed the boat, they stand on the wharf, blaming everyone except themselves and demanding that the world cater to their self-centred desires.

You may be saying to yourself now: "Well, I am not impressed by these stories. I myself could get interested in a couple of orphans I met on Christmas Eve; and if I had been at Pearl Harbour, I would gladly have done what Margaret Tayler Yates did. But with me things are different: I live an ordinary humdrum life. I work at a dull job eight hours a day. Nothing dramatic ever happens to me. How can I get interested in helping others? And why should I? What is there in it for me?"

A fair question. I'll try to answer it. However humdrum your existence may be, you surely meet some people every day of your life. What do you do about them? Do you merely stare through them,

的妻子们高兴，试着安慰那些丈夫牺牲的寡妇——伤亡的人可真不少。海军和陆战队有2117名军官和士兵阵亡，还有960人失踪。

"我刚开始是躺在床上接听所有的电话。然后，我坐在床上接听电话。最后，我忙坏了，完全忘记了我的虚弱，走下床坐在桌子旁边。在帮助那些比我更不幸的人时，我完全忘了自己，除了正常的8小时睡眠以外，再也没有回到床上去。我现在知道，如果没有日本人轰炸珍珠港，我也许终生都是一个半残废者。我舒服地躺在床上，一直都有人照顾；而我现在才知道，我那时正在不知不觉地失去痊愈的希望。

"珍珠港事件在美国历史上是一大悲剧，可是对我个人说来，却是我一生中最幸运的一件事。那次可怕的危机给了我未曾预想的力量。它使我不再只注意我自己，而是去关注别人。它给了我一些非常重要而且不可缺少的东西，并成为我的生活目标。我不再有时间去想自己，或为自己担忧。"

那些找精神病医生看病的人，只要肯按照玛格丽特·叶慈的方法去做，1/3的人都能自我治愈——只要愿意帮助别人。这只是我的看法吗?不，这是著名心理学家卡尔·荣格说的，而他正是这方面的专家。他说，"在我的病人中，大约1/3的人并非真的有病，而是因为他们的生活没有意义和空虚。"换句话说，他们只是想搭别人的顺风车度过一生——可是别人的车子只经过他们却不会停下来，于是他们去找精神病专家，谈他们那些微小的、毫无意义且又毫无用处的生活。他们既上不了船，就只好站在码头上，怪这个或怪那个，却不会怪自己，还要求全世界满足他们以自我为中心的欲望。

你也许正对自己说："哦，我觉得这些故事并没有什么意思。如果圣诞夜遇见孤儿，我也会关心他们；如果我本人在珍珠港的话，我也会很高兴地做玛格丽特·叶慈所做的事。但我的情况不同，我过的是一般人的生活，我做的是一天8小时的枯燥工作，从来没有遇到过任何戏剧性的

or do you try to find out what it is that makes them tick? How about the postman, for example—he walks hundreds of miles every year, delivering mail to your door; but have you ever taken the trouble to find out where he lives, or ask to see a snapshot of his wife and his kids? Did you ever ask him if his feet get tired, or if he ever gets bored?

What about the grocery boy, the newspaper vendor, the chap at the corner who polishes your shoes? These people are human—bursting with troubles, and dreams, and private ambitions. They are also bursting for the chance to share them with someone. But do you ever let them? Do you ever show an eager, honest interest in them or their lives? That's the sort of thing I mean. You don't have to become a Florence Nightingale or a social reformer to help improve the world—your own private world; you can start tomorrow morning with the people you meet!

What's in it for you? Much greater happiness! Greater satisfaction, and pride in yourself! Aristotle called this kind of attitude"enlightened selfishness". Zoroaster said: "Doing good to others is not a duty. It is a joy, for it increases your own health and happiness." And Benjamin Franklin summed it up very simply—"When you are good to others, "said Franklin, "you are best to yourself."

"No discovery of modern psychology, "writes Henry C. Link, director of the Psychological Service Centre in New York, "no discovery of modern psychology is, in my opinion, so important as its scientific proof of the necessity of self-sacrifice or discipline to self-realisation and happiness."

Thinking of others will not only keep you from worrying about yourself; it will also help you to make a lot of friends and have a lot of fun. How? Well, I once asked Professor William Lyon Phelps, of Yale, how he did it; and here is what he said: "I never go into a hotel or a barber-shop or a store without saying something agreeable to everyone I meet. I try to say something that treats them as an individual—not merely a cog in a machine. I sometimes compliment the girl who waits on me in the store by telling her how beautiful her eyes are—or her hair. I will ask a barber if he doesn't get tired standing on his feet all day. I'll ask him how he came to take up barbering—how long he has been at it and how many heads of hair he has cut. I'll help him figure it out. I find that taking an interest in people makes them beam with pleasure. I frequently shake hands with a

事。我怎么会对帮助别人产生兴趣呢?而且我为什么要这样做呢?这对我又有什么好处?"

问得好,我会尽力解答。首先,不管你的处境多么普通,你每天都会碰到一些人。你是如何对待他们的呢?你只是随便看他们一眼,还是试着去了解他们的生活?比如说一位邮递员,他每年要走几百里路,把信送到你家门口,而你是否问过他住在哪里?或者看一看他夫人和孩子的照片呢?你是否问过他的脚累不累?是不是觉得心烦呢?

或者是杂货店送货的孩子、卖报的人、那个在街角为你擦鞋的人?这些人也都是人,都有他们的烦恼、梦想和个人野心,他们也渴望有机会跟其他人来共享快乐,可是你给没给他们机会呢?你是否曾对他们的生活流露出真诚的兴趣呢?这些事情正是我要说的。你不一定要做南丁格尔或做一个社会改革者才能帮助改善这个世界。你可以从明天早上开始,从你碰到的那些人做起。

这对你有什么好处呢?这会给你带来更大的快乐、更多的满足以及更多的自豪。亚里士多德称这种态度为"有益于人的自私"。佐罗亚斯特说:"为别人做好事并不是一种责任,而是一种快乐,因为这能增加你自己的健康和快乐。"富兰克林的说法则更简单:"当你善待别人的时候,就是善待你自己。"

纽约心理治疗中心的负责人亨利·林克说:"照我个人的见解, 现代心理学最重要的发现,就是以科学的方法证明,必须要有自我牺牲精神或者是自我约束思想,才能达到了解自我与快乐。"

多替别人着想,不仅能使你不再为自己忧虑,也能帮助你结交许多朋友,并获得更多的乐趣。怎样做呢?我曾向耶鲁大学的威廉·李昂·费尔浦教授请教他是如何做的,下面就是他说的:"每当我去一家旅馆、理发店或者商店的时候,总会说一些我碰到的每一个人都高兴的话。我会把他们当作一个人,而不只是一台大机器中的一个小零件。有时我会赞美一个在店里向我打招

redcap who has carried my grip. It gives him a new lift and freshens him up for the whole day. One extremely hot summer day, I went into a dining car of the New Haven Railway to have lunch. The crowded car was almost like a furnace and the service was slow. When the steward finally got around to handing me the menu, I said: 'the boys back there cooking in that hot kitchen certainly must be suffering today. 'The steward began to curse. His tones were bitter. At first, I thought he was angry. 'Good God Almighty, 'he exclaimed, 'the people come in here and complain about the food. They kick about the slow service and growl about the heat and the prices. I have listened to their criticisms for nineteen years and you are the first person and the only person that has ever expressed any sympathy for the cooks back there in the boiling kitchen. I wish to God we had more passengers like you. '

"The steward was astounded because I had thought of the coloured cooks as human beings, and not merely as cogs in the organisation of a great railway. What people want, "continued Professor Phelps, "is a little attention as human beings. When I meet a man on the street with a beautiful dog, I always comment on the dog's beauty. As I walk on and glance back over my shoulder, I frequently see the man petting and admiring the dog. My appreciation has renewed his appreciation.

"One time in England, I met a shepherd, and expressed my sincere admiration for his big intelligent sheep dog. I asked him to tell me how he trained the dog. As I walked away, I glanced back over my shoulder and saw the dog standing with his paws on the shepherd's shoulders and the shepherd was petting him. By taking a little interest in the shepherd and his dog, I made the shepherd happy. I made the dog happy and I made myself happy."

Can you imagine a man who goes around shaking hands with porters and expressing sympathy for the cooks in the hot kitchen—and telling people how much he admires their dogs—can you imagine a man like that being sour and worried and needing the services of a psychiatrist? You can't, can you? No, of course not. A Chinese proverb puts it this way: *"A bit of fragrance always clings to the hand that gives you roses."*

If you are a man, skip this paragraph. It won't interest you. It tells how a worried, unhappy girl got several men to propose to her. The girl who did that is a grandmother now. A few years ago, I

呼的小姐,说她的眼睛很漂亮,或者说她的头发很美。我会问一位理发师,他整天这样站着会不会累?我会问他是怎么干上这一行的,干多久了,已经为多少人剃过头?我会帮他算出来。我发现,当你对别人感兴趣的时候,就会使他们非常高兴。我常常和那个帮我搬行李的红帽子握手,这会让他觉得很开心,整天都精神焕发。在一个特别炎热的夏天,我去纽海文铁路餐车吃午饭。餐车中挤满了人,热得难受,服务也非常慢。等到服务员终于把菜单递给我时,我说:'那些在后面闷热的厨房里做饭的人,今天一定很辛苦。'那个服务员开始骂了起来,他的声音充满了怨恨。我开始还以为他是在生气。'天啊!'他大声说,'到这里来的人都埋怨饭菜不好吃,说我们动作太慢,还抱怨这里太热,价钱太高。我听他们这样批评已经有19年了。你是第一个,也是唯一一个对在闷热的厨房里做事的厨师表示同情的人。我真希望上帝让我们多一些像你这样的顾客。'

"这个服务员之所以吃惊,是因为我把后面那些黑人厨师也当人看待,而不是把他们看成一个大铁路机构里的小螺丝。一般人所要的,"费尔浦教授继续说,"只是一点点关注。每次当我在街上看到一个人牵着一条漂亮的狗时,我总是夸那条狗漂亮。当我往前走再回过头去时,通常都会看到那个人正欢喜地拍他的狗——我的赞美使他更喜欢那条狗。

"有一次我在英国碰见一个牧羊人,我非常真诚地赞美了他那只聪明的大牧羊犬。我还请他告诉我是如何训练它的。当我离开以后,回头去看时,看见那只狗前脚竖起搭在牧羊人的肩膀上,牧羊人正拍着它。我对那个牧羊人和他的狗只表示了一点点兴趣,就使得牧羊人很快乐。那条狗很快乐,而我自己也很快乐。"

像这样一个会跟搬运工握手、对在闷热的厨房做饭的厨师表示同情,还告诉别人他多么喜欢他的狗的人——像这样的人,如何不会友好待人,而会满怀忧虑,需要去看精神病医生呢?当然不可能,对不对?是的,当然不可能。中国有一句老话说:"与人玫瑰,手留余香。"

spent the night in her and her husband's home. I had been giving a lecture in her town; and the next morning she drove me about fifty miles to catch a train on the main line to New York Central. We got to talking about winning friends, and she said: "Mr. Carnegie, I am going to tell you something that I have never confessed to anyone before—not even to my husband." (By the way, this story isn't going to be half so interesting as you probably imagine.) She told me that she had been reared in a social-register family in Philadelphia. "The tragedy of my girlhood and young womanhood, "she said, "was our poverty. We could never entertain the way the other girls in my social set entertained. My clothes were never of the best quality. I outgrew them and they didn't fit and they were often out of style. I was so humiliated, so ashamed, that I often cried myself to sleep. Finally, in sheer desperation, I hit upon the idea of always asking my partner at dinner-parties to tell me about his experiences, his ideas, and his plans for the future. I didn't ask these questions because I was especially interested in the answers. I did it solely to keep my partner from looking at my poor clothes. But a strange thing happened: as I listened to these young men talk and learned more about them, I really became interested in listening to what they had to say. I became so interested that I myself sometimes forgot about my clothes. But the astounding thing to me was this: since I was a good listener and encouraged the boys to talk about themselves, I gave them happiness and I gradually became the most popular girl in our social group and three of these men proposed marriage to me." (There you are, girls: that is the way it is done.)

Some people who read this chapter are going to say: "All this talk about getting interested in others is a lot of damn nonsense! Sheer religious pap! None of that stuff for me! I am going to put money in my purse. I am going to grab all I can get—and grab it now—and to hell with the other dumb clucks! "

Well, if that is your opinion, you are entitled to it; but if you are right, then all the great philosophers and teachers since the beginning of recorded history—Jesus, Confucius, Buddha, Plato, Aristotle, Socrates, Saint Francis—were all wrong. But since you may sneer at the teachings of religious leaders, let's turn for advice to a couple of atheists. First, let's take the late A. E. Housman, professor at Cambridge University, and one of the most distinguished scholars of his generation. In 1936, he gave an address at Cambridge University on "The Name and Nature of

如果你是一位男士,就可以跳过这一段,因为你不会有兴趣的。它讲了一个忧虑而不快乐的女孩子如何使好几个男人向她求婚的故事。这个女孩现在已为人祖母。我几年前曾去她家里做客。当时我正在她的小填上演讲,第二天早上她又开车50里送我去搭车前往纽约中央车站。我们谈起了如何交朋友的事, 她说:"卡耐基先生, 我要告诉你一件以前从未跟任何人说过的事——甚至连我丈夫也没说过。"(顺便说一下,这个故事不及想象的一半有趣。)她告诉我,她出生在费城一个很穷的家庭,"我幼年和少年时的不幸,"她说,"就是我家很穷。我不能像其他女孩子那样玩乐,我的衣服料子从来都不是最好的。我长得太快,衣服总是难得合身,而且也不是流行的式样。我一直觉得很丢脸,常常哭着入睡。最后,我在绝望之中想出了一个办法,就是每次参加晚宴的时候,就请我的男伴将他的经历以及他的一些想法,还有他对未来的计划告诉我。我之所以这么做,并不是因为我对他的回答特别感兴趣,而只是不想让他注意到我穿着难看的衣服。可是奇怪的事情发生了:当我听这些年轻人跟我谈话,并对他们有了较多的认识后,我真的愿意听他们说的话了。有时我甚至会忘记了自己的穿着打扮。可是最让我吃惊的事情,是因为我善于倾听,而且鼓励那些男孩子谈他们自己的事情,这使他们非常快乐,于是我渐渐成为我们那里最受欢迎的女孩子,竟然有3个男孩来向我求婚。"

有人看到这里可能会说:"对别人感兴趣,真是胡扯!我才不愿过问别人的事呢!我只想赚钱,得到我想要的东西,可不想管别人的闲事!"

啊,你有选择的权利;不过,如果你是对的,那么自古以来的先贤——耶稣、孔子、佛祖、柏拉图、亚里士多德、苏格拉底、圣弗朗西斯——全都错了。但是如果你对宗教大师有反感,那我们就看看无神论者的忠告吧。先看剑桥大学已故的豪斯曼教授,他是当时最知名的学者。1936年,他在剑桥大学演讲《诗名与其实质》时说道:"历史上最永恒、最深刻的道德发现,就是耶稣说的:'因我而失去生命的人,将得永生。'"

Poetry". In that address, he declared that "the greatest truth ever uttered and the most profound moral discovery of all time were these words of Jesus: 'He that findeth his life shall lose it;and he that loseth his life for my sake shall find it. '"

We have heard preachers say that all our lives. But Housman was an atheist, a pessimist, a man who contemplated suicide; and yet he felt that the man who thought only of himself wouldn't get much out of life. He would be miserable. But the man who forgot himself in service to others would find the joy of living.

If you are not impressed by what A. E. Housman said, let's turn for advice to the most distinguished American atheist of the twentieth century: Theodore Dreiser. Dreiser ridiculed all religions as fairy tales and regarded life as"a tale told by an idiot, full of sound and fury, signifying nothing." Yet Dreiser advocated the one great principle that Jesus taught—service to others. "If he [man] is to extract any joy out of his span, "Dreiser said, "he must think and plan to make things better not only for himself but for others, since joy for himself depends upon his joy in others and theirs in him."

If we are going "to make things better for others"—as Dreiser advocated—let's be quick about it. Time is a wasting. "I shall pass this way but once. Therefore any good that I can do or any kindness that I can show—let me do it now. Let me not defer nor neglect it, for I shall not pass this way again."

So if you want to banish worry and cultivate peace and happiness, here is Rule 7:

Forget yourself by becoming interested in others. Do every day a good deed that will put a smile of joy on someone's face.

我们成天听传教士说这些话,而豪斯曼是无神论者,也是一位悲观主义者,曾想过要自杀,可是他仍旧发现,只想着自己的人不可能活得有意义,他会活得很悲惨。但是忘记自我、为人服务的人,却会发现生命的喜悦。

如果豪斯曼的话也不能打动你,那我们来看看起20世纪美国最杰出的无神论者西奥多·德莱塞的忠告。德莱塞把所有的宗教都看成神话,认为人生只是“傻瓜说的故事,毫无意义”。但是德莱塞却倡导耶稣教给我们的一个伟大真理——为人服务。他说:“如果人想从人生中得到快乐,就不能只想自己,还要为他人着想,因为快乐来自你为他人,他人为你。”

如果我们打算像德莱塞所宣扬的那样“为他人改善一切”,那就赶快去做,时间不容浪费。“这条路我只能走一次,所以我能做到的任何好事,现在就做。不要拖延,也不要忽视,因为我不会再经过这条路。”

所以,如果你想消除忧虑,获得平安与幸福,第七条规则:

要对别人感兴趣,忘掉你自己;每天做一件让别人高兴的事。

Part Five
How to Keep from Worrying about Criticism

1 Remember That No One Ever Kicks a Dead Dog

An event occurred in 1929 that created a national sensation in educational circles. Learned men from all over America rushed to Chicago to witness the affair. A few years earlier, a young man by the name of Robert Hutchins had worked his way through Yale, acting as a waiter, a lumberjack, a tutor, and a clothes-line salesman. Now, only eight years later, he was being inaugurated as president of the fourth richest university in America, the University of Chicago. His age? Thirty. Incredible! The older educators shook their heads. Criticism came roaring down upon the "boy wonder" like a rockslide. He was this and he was that—too young, inexperienced—his educational ideas were cockeyed. Even the newspapers joined in the attack. The day he was inaugurated, a friend said to the father of Robert Maynard Hutchins: "I was shocked this morning to read that newspaper editorial denouncing your son." "Yes, "the elder Hutchins replied, "it was severe, but remember that no one ever kicks a dead dog."

Yes, and the more important a dog is, the more satisfaction people get in kicking him. The Prince of Wales who later became Edward VIII (now Duke of Windsor) had that forcibly brought home to him. He was attending Dartmouth College in Devonshire at the time—a college that corresponds to the Naval Academy at Annapolis. The Prince was about fourteen. One day one of the naval officers found him crying, and asked him what was wrong. He refused to tell at first, but finally admitted the truth: he was being kicked by the naval cadets. The commodore of the college summoned the boys and explained to them that the Prince had not complained, but he wanted to

第五篇 免受批评的忧虑

第1章 没有人会踢一只死狗

1929年，美国发生了一件震惊教育界的大事，美国各地的学者都赶往芝加哥恭逢盛会。几年前，一个名叫罗伯特·霍金斯的年轻人，半工半读从耶鲁大学毕业，他当过服务生、伐木工人、家庭教师和成衣推销员。现在，仅仅8年之后，他就被任命为美国第四富有的大学——芝加哥大学校长。他多大了?30岁！难以置信！老一辈教育人士都大加反对，批评就像山崩石落一样打在这位“神童”头上，说他这样或那样：太年轻了，经验不足。甚至说他的教育观念荒谬，连各大报纸也参与了对他的攻击。在就任的那一天，有一个朋友对霍金斯的父亲说：“我今天早上看见报纸社论攻击你的儿子，真把我吓坏了。”“不错，”老霍金斯回答说，“攻击得很厉害。可是请记住，从来没有人会踢一只死狗。”

是的，这只狗越贵重，踢它的人就越可以获得满足。后来成为英王爱德华八世的威尔士王子，他也有过这种遭遇。他曾就读于帝文夏郡的达特茅斯学院——这个学院相当于美国安那波里斯的海军学院。王子那时只有14岁。一天，一位海军军官发现他在哭，就问他出了什么事。他开始不肯说，但最后终于说了真话：他被一位海军幼校生踢了一脚。指挥官把所有的学生都召集起来，向他们解释王子并没有告状，但是他想弄清楚为什么有人如此粗暴地对待王子。

大家相互推诿了半天，踢人者终于承认说：如果他们自己将来成了皇家海军的指挥官或舰

find out why the Prince had been singled out for this rough treatment.

After much hemming and hawing and toe scraping, the cadets finally confessed that when they themselves became commanders and captains in the King's Navy, they wanted to be able to say that they had kicked the King!

So when you are kicked and criticised, remember that it is often done because it gives the kicker a feeling of importance. It often means that you are accomplishing something and are worthy of attention. Many people get a sense of savage satisfaction out of denouncing those who are better educated than they are or more successful. For example, while I was writing this chapter, I received a letter from a woman denouncing General William Booth, founder of the Salvation Army. I had given a laudatory broadcast about General Booth; so this woman wrote me, saying that General Booth had stolen eight million dollars of the money he had collected to help poor people. The charge, of course, was absurd. But this woman wasn't looking for truth. She was seeking the mean-spirited gratification that she got from tearing down someone far above her. Schopenhauer had said it years ago: "Vulgar people take huge delight in the faults and follies of great men."

One hardly thinks of the president of Yale as a vulgar man; yet a former president of Yale, Timothy Dwight, apparently took huge delight in denouncing a man who was running for President of the United States. The president of Yale warned that if this man were elected President, "we may see our wives and daughters the victims of legal prostitution, soberly dishonoured, speciously polluted; the outcasts of delicacy and virtue, the loathing of God and man." Sounds almost like a denunciation of Hitler, doesn't it? But it wasn't. It was a denunciation of Thomas Jefferson. *Which* Thomas Jefferson? Surely not the *immortal* Thomas Jefferson, the author of the *Declaration of Independence*, the patron saint of democracy? Yes, verily, that was the man. What American do you suppose was denounced as a "hypocrite", "an impostor", and as "little better than a murderer"? A newspaper cartoon depicted him on a guillotine, the big knife read to cut off his head. Crowds jeered at him and hissed him as he rode through the street. Who was he? George Washington.

But that occurred a long time ago. Maybe human nature has improved since then. Let's see. Let's take the case of Admiral Peary—the explorer who startled and thrilled the world by reaching the North Pole with dog sleds on April 6, 1909—a goal that brave men for centuries had suffered

长,他们希望能够告诉别人,他们曾踢过国王。

所以,如果你被别人踢了,或者遭到了批评,请记住,因为这样做可以给踢人者一种自重感,这通常意味着你已经有所成就,并且值得注意。有许多人会从批评比他们学历高或更成功的人中获得某种满足感。例如,在我写这部分内容的时候,就接到一个女人的来信,痛骂创建了救世军的威廉·布慈将军。因为我曾在广播中赞扬过布慈将军,所以这个女人给我写信,说布慈将军侵占了他募集用来救济穷人的800万美元。尽管这种指责非常荒谬,可是这个女人并不想要真相,她只是想击垮一个比她高贵的人,以此获得满足。叔本华多年前曾说过:"庸俗者可以从伟人的错误和愚行中得到巨大的快感。"

很少有人认为耶鲁大学的校长是一个庸俗之辈,但耶鲁大学前校长提摩太·杜威特却显然以贬低某位美国总统候选人为乐。这位耶鲁大学校长警告说,如果这个人当选总统的话,"我们就会看见我们的妻子和女儿成为合法卖淫的牺牲品。我们就会大受羞辱,受到严重伤害,我们的自尊和道德都会消失殆尽,人神共愤。"这些话听上去是在骂希特勒,对不对?但并不是,而是在骂托马斯·杰斐逊! 哪个托马斯·杰斐逊?肯定不是那位不朽的托马斯·杰斐逊吧?是那个起草《独立宣言》,代表民主政体的人物吗?不错,正是这个人。你是否想过哪一个美国人曾经被骂为"伪君子"、"大骗子"、"只比谋杀犯好一点"呢?但的确有家报纸的漫画画着他站在断头台上,一把大刀正准备砍下他的头;在他骑马从街上走过的时候,一大群人围住他又叫又骂。他是谁呢?乔治·华盛顿。

这些都是很久以前的事了。也许从那以后,人性已经有所改进。就让我们拿震惊全球的探险家佩瑞海军上将做例子。他于1909年4月6日乘雪橇到达北极——几百年来,无数勇士为了实现这个目标而挨饿受冻,甚至送命。佩瑞也几乎死于饥寒交迫,他的8个脚趾因为冻伤而不得不切除,他在路上所碰到的各种灾难都使他担心自己会发疯。但是,华盛顿的那些高级海军官员

and died to attain. Peary himself almost died from cold and starvation; and eight of his toes were frozen so hard they had to be cut off. He was so overwhelmed with disasters that he feared he would go insane. His superior naval officers in Washington were burned up because Peary was getting so much publicity and acclaim. So they accused him of collecting money for scientific expeditions and then "lying around and loafing in the Arctic." And they probably believed it, because it is almost impossible not to believe what you want to believe. Their determination to humiliate and block Peary was so violent that only a direct order from President McKinley enabled Peary to continued his career in the Arctic. Would Peary have been denounced if he had had a desk job in the Navy Department in Washington? No. He wouldn't have been important enough then to have aroused jealousy.

General Grant had an even worse experience than Admiral Peary. In 1862, General Grant won the first great decisive victory that the North had enjoyed—a victory that was achieved in one afternoon, a victory that made Grant a national idol overnight—a victory that had tremendous repercussions even in far-off Europe—a victory that set church bells ringing and bonfires blazing from Maine to the banks of the Mississippi. Yet within six weeks after achieving that great victory, Grant—hero of the North—was arrested and his army was taken from him. He wept with humiliation and despair.

Why was General U. S. Grant arrested at the flood tide of his victory? Largely because he had aroused the jealousy and envy of his arrogant superiors.

If we are tempted to be worried about unjust criticism, here is Rule 1:

Remember that unjust criticism is often a disguised compliment.
Remember that no one ever kicks a dead dog.

却因为佩瑞大受欢迎和重视而嫉妒他。于是他们诬告他,说他假借科学探险的名义敛财,然后“无所事事地去北极逍遥”。而且他们可能真的相信,因为人们几乎不可能不相信他们想相信的事情。他们想羞辱和阻挠佩瑞的决心如此强烈,以至于最后必须由麦金利总统直接下令,佩瑞才能在北极继续他的研究工作。如果佩瑞只坐在华盛顿的海军总部工作,他会遭到批评吗?不会,那样他就不会变得如此重要,以致引起嫉妒了。

格兰特将军的经历比佩瑞上将更糟。1862年,格兰特将军赢得了北军第一次决定性的胜利,这使得他立即成为全国的偶像,甚至在遥远的欧洲也引起了强烈的反响。这场胜利,使得从缅因州一直到密西西比河岸,大家都敲钟点火,以示庆贺。但是在这次伟大胜利的6个星期之后,这位北方的英雄却被逮捕,兵权也被剥夺,他屈辱绝望地哭了。

为什么格兰特将军会在胜利之巅被捕呢?绝大部分原因是他引起了那些傲慢的上级对他的嫉妒与羡慕。

所以,如果我们因为遭受不公正的批评而忧虑时,请记住第一条规则:

不公正的批评通常是一种变相的恭维。记住,从来没有人会踢一只死狗。

2 Do This—and Criticism Can't Hurt You

I once interviewed Major-General Smedley Butler—old "Gimlet-Eye". Old "Hell-Devil" Butler! Remember him? The most colourful, swashbuckling general who ever commanded the United States Marines.

He told me that when he was young, he was desperately eager to be popular, wanted to make a good impression on everyone. In those days the slightest criticism smarted and stung. But he confessed that thirty years in the Marines had toughened his hide. "I have been berated and insulted, "he said, "and denounced as a yellow dog, a snake, and a skunk. I have been cursed by the experts. I have been called every possible combination of unprintable cuss words in the English language. Bother me?

"Huh! When I hear someone cussing me now, I never turn my head to see who is talking."

Maybe old"Gimlet-Eye"Butler was too indifferent to criticism; but one thing is sure: most of us take the little jibes and javelins that are hurled at us far too seriously. I remember the time, years ago, when a reporter from the *New York Sun* attended a demonstration meeting of my adult-education classes and lampooned me and my work. Was I burned up? I took it as a personal insult. I telephoned Gill Hodges, the Chairman of the Executive Committee of the *Sun*, and practically demanded that he print an article stating the facts—instead of ridicule. I was determined to make the punishment fit the crime.

I am ashamed now of the way I acted. I realise now that half the people who bought the paper never saw that article. Half of those who read it regarded it as a source of innocent merriment. Half of those who gloated over it forgot all about it in a few weeks.

I realize now that people are not thinking about you and me or caring what is said about us. They are thinking about themselves—before breakfast, after breakfast, and right on until ten minutes past midnight. They would be a thousand times more concerned about a slight headache of their own than they would about the news of your death or mine.

第2章 不要让批评伤害你

有一次我去拜访史密德里·柏特勒少将——就是那个老"锥子眼"、老"地狱恶魔"柏特勒。还记得他吗?他是统帅过美国海军陆战队的最多彩多姿、最会摆派头的将军。

他告诉我,他年轻的时候竭力想成为最受欢迎的人,想使每一个人都对他有好印象。在那段日子里,一点点批评都会让他难受伤心。可是他承认,在海军陆战队工作30年使他变得坚强多了。"我曾被人家责骂和羞辱过,"他说,"被骂成黄狗、毒蛇、臭鼬。我被那些骂人专家骂过,凡是英文中能够想得出来但写不出来的脏字眼都曾被用来骂过我。我伤心吗?哈哈! 我现在要是听到有人骂我,根本不会回头去看是谁在骂我。"

也许只有老"锥子眼"柏特勒对批评不在意。但有一事情是肯定的,那就是大多数人对这种不值一提的小事都过分认真。我还记得在许多年以前,有一个来自纽约《太阳报》的记者参加我举办的成人教育示范教学会,他攻击了我和我的工作。我真的气坏了,认为这是对我的侮辱。我给《太阳报》执行委员会主席吉尔·霍吉斯打电话,特别要求他发表一篇文章澄清事实。我想让那个人受到相应的处罚。

而我现在却对我当时的做法感到惭愧。我现在才明白,买那份报纸的人有一半不会看那篇文章,而看到的人也只有一半会把它视为小事。真正注意到这篇文章的人,又有一半在几个星期之后会忘记它。

我现在才明白,一般人根本就不会想到你和我,或者关注别人对我们的评论。他们只会想他们自己——早饭前,早饭后,一直到半夜12点10分之后。他们对自己的小问题的关注程度,要远远超过对他人大事的上千倍。

Even if you and I are lied about, ridiculed, double-crossed, knifed in the back, and sold down the river by one out of every six of our most intimate friends—let's not indulge in an orgy of self-pity. Instead, let's remind ourselves that that's precisely what happened to Jesus. One of His twelve most intimate friends turned traitor for a bribe that would amount, in our modem money, to about nineteen dollars. Another one of His twelve most intimate friends openly deserted Jesus the moment He got into trouble, and declared three times that he didn't even know Jesus—and he swore as he said it. One out of six! That is what happened to Jesus. Why should you and I expect a better score?

I discovered years ago that although I couldn't keep people from criticising me unjustly, I could do something infinitely more important: I could determine whether I would let the unjust condemnation disturb me.

Let's be clear about this: I am not advocating ignoring all criticism. Far from it. I am talking about *ignoring only unjust criticism.* I once asked Eleanor Roosevelt how she handled unjust criticism—and Allah knows she's had a lot of it. She probably has more ardent friends and more violent enemies than any other woman who ever lived in the White House.

She told me that as a young girl she was almost morbidly shy, afraid of what people might say. She was so afraid of criticism that one day she asked her aunt, Theodore Roosevelt's sister for advice. She said: "Auntie Bye, I want to do so-and-so. But I'm afraid of being criticised."

Teddy Roosevelt's sister looked her in the eye and said: "Never be bothered by what people say, as long as you know in your heart you are right." Eleanor Roosevelt told me that that bit of advice proved to be her Rock of Gibraltar years later, when she was in the White House. She told me that the only way we can avoid all criticism is to be like a Dresden-china figure and stay on a shelf. "Do what you feel in your heart to be right—for you'll be criticised, anyway. You'll be damned if you do, and damned if you don't." That is her advice.

When the late Matthew C. Brush, was president of the American International Corporation at 40 Wall Street, I asked him if he was ever sensitive to criticism; and he replied: "Yes, I was very sensitive to it in my early days. I was eager then to have all the employees in the organisation think I was perfect. If they didn't, it worried me. I would try to please first one person who had been

即使你和我被人耍了,被人当成笑柄,被从后面捅一刀,或者被我们最亲密的朋友出卖了,我们也千万不要沉溺在自怜中。我们应该提醒自己,想想耶稣碰到的那些事。他12个最亲密的友人中,有一个背叛了他,而这个人所得到的赏金如果折算成现在的美元,也不过19美元。他最亲密的友人中,还有一个在他遇到麻烦时公开背弃了他,还三次表白他根本不认识耶稣——还一面说一面发誓。出卖他的人占了1/6! 这就是耶稣所碰到的,为什么你我希望比他更好呢?

我在很多年以前就已经发现,虽然我难以阻止别人对我的不公正批评,但我却可以做更重要的事情:我可以决定是否让自己受不公正的批评干扰。

让我把这一点说得更清楚些吧:我并不赞成漠视所有的批评;相反,我说的是不要理会不公正的批评。有一次我问伊莲娜·罗斯福,她是如何处理不公正的批评的——老天爷知道,她受到的批评太多了。她热心的朋友和凶猛的敌人可能比任何白宫女主人都要多得多。

她告诉我,她小时候非常害羞,害怕别人说她什么。面对批评,她害怕得去向她的姑妈,也就是西奥多·罗斯福的姐姐求助。她说:"姑妈,我想做某件事,可是我担心会受到批评。"

老罗斯福的姐姐正视着她说,"不要怕别人怎么说,只要你自己心里知道你是对的就行了。"伊莲娜·罗斯福告诉我,当她在多年以后住进白宫时,这一忠告还一直是她的行事原则。她告诉我,避免所有批评的唯一方法,就是——"做你心里认为是对的事——因为无论如何你都会受到批评。'做也该死,不做也该死'。"这就是她的忠告。

当已故的马休·布鲁什还在华尔街40号美国国际公司担任总裁的时候,我曾问他是否在意别人的批评?他回答说:"是的,早年我对这种事情非常敏感。当时我急于使公司的每一个人都认为我十全十美。要是他们不这样认为,我就会忧虑。只要某个人对我稍有怨言,我就会想方设法取悦他;可是我讨好他,总会使另外一个人生气。等我再想要满足另一个人的时候,又会惹恼其他的人。最后,我发现我越想讨好别人,以避免别人的批评,就越会使我的敌人增加。所以我

sounding off against me; but the very thing I did to patch it up with him would make someone else mad. Then when I tried to fix it up with this person, I would stir up a couple of other bumble-bees. I finally discovered that the more I tried to pacify and to smooth over injured feelings in order to escape personal criticism, the more certain I was to increase my enemies. So finally I said to myself: 'If you get your head above the crowd, you're going to be criticised. So get used to the idea. 'That helped me tremendously. From that time on I made it a rule to do the very best I could and then put up my old umbrella and let the rain of criticism drain off me instead of running down my neck."

Deems Taylor went a bit further: he let the rain of criticism run down his neck and had a good laugh over it—in public. When he was giving his comments during the intermission of the Sunday-afternoon radio concerts of the New York Philharmonic-Symphony Orchestra, one woman wrote him a letter calling him"a liar, a traitor, a snake and a moron". Mr. Taylor says in his book, *of Men and Musil*: "I have a suspiction that she didn't care for that talk."

On the following week's broadcast, Mr. Taylor read this letter over the radio to millions of listeners. In his book, *Of Men & Music*, he tells us that a few days later he received another letter from the same lady, "expressing her unaltered opinion that I was still a liar, a traitor, a snake and a moron. I have a suspicion, "adds Mr. Taylor, "that she didn't care for that talk." We can't keep from admiring a man who takes criticism like that. We admire his serenity, his unshaken poise, and his sense of humor.

When Charles Schwab was addressing the student body at Princeton, he confessed that one of the most important lessons he had ever learned was taught to him by an old German who worked in Schwab's steel mill. The old German got involved in a hot wartime argument with the other steelworkers, and they tossed him into the river. "When he came into my office, "Mr. Schwab said, "covered with mud and water, I asked him what he had said to the men who had thrown him into the river, and he replied: 'I just laughed.'"

Mr. Schwab declared that he had adopted that old German's words as his motto: "Just laugh."

That motto is especially good when you are the victim of unjust criticism. You can answer the man who answers you back, but what can you say to the man who"just laughs"?

最后对自己说:'只要你出类拔萃,你就一定会遭到批评,所以还是早点习惯为好。'这对我大有帮助。从此以后,我就决定尽最大的努力去做我认为对的事,然后打开我那把旧伞,让批评的雨水从我身上流下去,而不是滴进我的脖子里。"

狄姆斯·泰勒则更进一步:他不但让批评的雨水流进他的脖子,而且当着别人的面对此大笑一番。有一段时间,他每个星期天下午都要在纽约爱乐交响乐团空中音乐会休息时间作音乐方面的评论。有一个女人给他写信,说他是"骗子、叛徒、毒蛇和白痴"。泰勒先生在他的书《人与音乐》中说:"我猜想她只是随便说的。"

在第二个星期的广播里,泰勒先生向几百万听众读了这封信。他在书中说,几天以后,他又接到这个女人写来的另一封信,"表达她丝毫没有改变她的意见,她仍然认为我是一个骗子、叛徒、毒蛇和白痴。我现在觉得她不是随便说说而已。"我们实在佩服他用这种态度来接受批评。我们佩服他的沉着,他那毫不动摇的态度和幽默感。

查尔斯·施瓦伯曾在普林斯顿大学对大学生发表演讲,说他所学到的最重要的一课,是一个在钢铁厂工作的德国老人教给他的。那个德国老人和其他工人发生了争执,那些人把他扔进了河里。"当他走进我的办公室时,"施瓦伯先生说,"满身都是泥水。我问他对那些把他丢进河里的人说了什么,他回答说:'我一笑了之。'"

施瓦伯先生说,后来他就把这个德国老人的话当作他的座右铭——"一笑了之。"

当你成为不公正批评的受害者时,这个座右铭尤其有效。当别人骂你时,你可以回骂他;可是对"一笑了之"的人,你能说什么?

如果林肯没有学会对那些骂他的话置之不理,恐怕他早就受不住内战的压力而崩溃了。他是这样说的:"如果我只是试着去读——更不用说回答所有对我的攻击,那么我不如去做别的。我尽我所知的最好办法去做,也尽我所能去做,而我也想一直这样把事情做完。如果结果证明

Lincoln might have broken under the strain of the Civil War if he hadn't learned the folly of trying to answer all his savage critics. He finally said: "If I were to try to read, much less to answer, all the attacks made on me, this shop might as well be closed for any other business. I do the very best I know how—the very best I can; and I mean to keep on doing so until the end. If the end brings me out all right, then what is said against me won't matter. If the end brings me out wrong, then ten angels swearing I was right would make no difference."

When you and I are unjustly criticised, let's remember Rule 2:

Do the very best yon can;and then put up your old umbrella and keep the rain of criticism from running down the back of your neck.

我是对的,那么不论别人怎么说我,都无关紧要!如果结果证明我是错的,那么即使我花十倍的力气来说我是对的,也没有用。"

所以,当你和我受到不公正的批评时,让我们记住第二条规则:

凡事尽力而为,然后打开你的旧伞,避开批评的雨水。

3 Fool Things I Have Done

I have a folder in my private filing cabinet marked "FTD"—short for "Fool Things I Have Done". I put in that folder written records of the fools things I have been guilty of. I sometimes dictate these memos to my secretary, but sometimes they are so personal, so stupid, that I am ashamed to dictate them, so I write them out in longhand.

I can still recall some of the criticisms of Dale Carnegie that I put in my "FTD"folders fifteen years ago. If I had been utterly honest with myself, I would now have a filing cabinet bursting out at the seams with these "FTD"memos. I can truthfully repeat what King Saul said more than twenty centuries ago: "I have played the fool and have erred exceedingly."

When I get out my "FTD"folders and re-read the criticisms I have written of myself, they help me deal with the toughest problem I shall ever face: the management of Dale Carnegie.

I used to blame my troubles on other people; but as I have grown older—and wiser, I hope—I have realized that I myself, in the last analysis, am to blame for almost all my misfortunes. Lots of people have discovered that, as they grow older. "No one but myself, "said Napoleon at St. Helena, "no one but myself can be blamed for my fall. I have been my own greatest enemy—the cause of my own disastrous fate."

Let me tell you about a man I know who was an artist when it came to self-appraisal and self-management. His name was H. P. Howell. When the news of his sudden death in the drugstore of the Hotel Ambassador in New York was flashed across the nation on July 31, 1944, Wall Street was shocked, for he was a leader in American finance—chairman of the board of the Commercial National Bank and Trust Company, 56 Wall Street, and a director of several large corporations. He grew up with little formal education, started out in life clerking in a country store, and later became credit manager for U. S. Steel—and was on his way to position and power.

"For years I have kept an engagement book showing all the appointments I have during the day, "Mr. Howell told me when I asked him to explain the reasons for his success. "My family never

第3章 我做过的傻事

在我的私人档案柜里有一卷宗夹，上面写着"我做过的傻事"。我把自己做过的所有傻事都记了下来，存在这个夹子里。有时我会用口述方式让我的秘书记录下来。但这些问题有时候太私密，或者太愚蠢，使我不好意思口述，就只好我自己写下来。

我还记得我15年前放在这个夹子里的一些事情。如果我能对我自己绝对诚实，那么我所做过的傻事恐怕会挤破我的档案柜了。我可以在此重复索罗王2000年前所说过的："我曾经做过傻事，做过很多傻事。"

每当我拿出"我做过的傻事"卷宗，重读我对自己的批评时，它们都能帮我解决我所面临的最困难的问题，即如何控制自我。

我以前常常把责任推给别人，可是随着年岁渐长，我发现我所有的不幸几乎都应该怪我自己。很多人在年纪大了之后都会发现这一点。"除了我自己，"拿破仑在被放逐的时候说，"除了我之外，没有任何人应该为我的失败承担责任。我是我自己最大的敌人——也是我不幸命运的根源。"

就让我告诉你一个我熟悉的人的事情吧：他在自我评价和自我控制方面，可以称得上艺术家。他叫霍华。当他1944年7月31日在纽约大使酒店突然去世的消息传遍全美国的时候，整个华尔街都震惊了，因为他是美国金融领袖——美国商业银行和信托公司的董事长，同时也是几家大公司的董事。他小的时候没有受过多少正规教育，从一个乡村小店店员干起，后来成为美国钢铁公司贷款部经理——然后达到了顶峰。

"多年来，我一直保留着一个约会本，上面记了我每天所有的约会，"在我请他解释他的成功原因时，霍华先生对我说，"我的家人也从来不在星期六晚上给我安排活动，因为他们都知道我

makes any plans for me on Saturday night, for the family knows that I devote a part of each Saturday evening to self-examination and a review and appraisal of my work during the week. After dinner I go off by myself, open my engagement book, and think over all the interviews, discussions and meetings that have taken place since Monday morning. I ask myself: 'What mistakes did I make that time? 'What did I do that was right—and in what way could I have improved my performance? 'What lessons can I learn from that experience? 'I sometimes find that this weekly review makes me very unhappy. Sometimes I am astonished by my own blunders. Of course, as the years have gone by, these blunders have become less frequent. This system of self-analysis, continued year after year, has done more for me than any other one thing I have ever attempted."

Maybe H. P. Howell borrowed his idea from Ben Franklin. Only Franklin didn't wait until Saturday night. He gave himself a severe going-over *every* night. He discovered that he had thirteen serious faults. Here are three of them: wasting time, stewing around over trifles, arguing and contradicting people. Wise old Ben Franklin realised that, unless he eliminated these handicaps, he wasn't going to get very far. So he battled with one of his shortcomings every day for a week, and kept a record of who had won each day's slugging match. The next day, he would pick out another bad habit, put on the gloves, and when the bell rang he would come out of his comer fighting. Franklin kept up this battle with his faults every week for more than two years.

No wonder he became one of the best-loved and most influential men America ever produced!

Elbert Hubbard said: "Every man is a damn fool for at least free minutes every day. Wisdom consists in not exceeding that limit."

The small man flies into a rage over the slightest criticism, but the wise man is eager to learn from those who have censured him and reproved him and "disputed the passage with him". Walt Whitman put it this way: "Have you learned lessons only of those who admired you, and were tender with you, and stood aside for you? Have you not learned great lessons from those who rejected you, and braced themselves against you, or disputed the passage with you? "

Instead of waiting for our enemies to criticise us or our work, let's beat them to it. Let's be our own most severe critic. Let's find and remedy ail our weaknesses before our enemies get a chance to say a word. That is what Charles Darwin did. In fact, he spent fifteen years criticising—well, the

每个星期六晚上都要花一些时间自我反省，回顾和检讨我这一星期的工作。晚饭之后，我一个人关在房里，打开约会本，回想周一早上以来所有的会谈、讨论和会议。我会问自己：'我那一次犯了什么错误?''哪些事情我做对了——怎样才能改进?''我能从中学到些什么?' 有时我发现这种每周一次的检讨让我很不高兴，甚至会为自己所犯的过错而吃惊。当然，时间一年年过去，这些错误也渐渐少了。这种自我分析持续了一年又一年，是我曾做过的事情中最有意义的。"

也许霍华的这种做法是从本杰明·富兰克林那里学来的，只不过富兰克林不会等到星期六晚上。他每天晚上都要严厉自省。他发现他有13个严重的错误，下面只是其中三项：浪费时间、为小事烦恼、和别人争论冲突。睿智的富兰克林发现，除非他能减少这类错误，否则他就不可能有出息。因此，他每星期都会用一天时间改正一项缺点，然后把每天的情况做记录。第二天，他会再挑出另一个缺点，准备好了之后，再接下去进行另一场"战斗"。富兰克林这种每周的奋斗持续了两年多时间。

难怪他会成为美国有史以来最受人敬爱，也最具影响力的人。

阿尔伯特·哈伯德说："每个人在每天当中至少有5分钟是个大笨蛋。所谓智慧，就是不超过这5分钟的限制。"

傻子受到一点点批评就会大发脾气，而聪明人却会从责备和反对他，以及"在路上阻碍他"的人那里学到更多的东西。惠特曼这样说："难道你的一切智慧只是从那些羡慕你、讨好你、常常在你身边的人那里学来的吗?你不能从那些反对你、指责你，或站在路上挡拦你的人那里学到更多的东西吗？"

不要等我们的敌人来批评我们或我们的工作，我们要胜过他们。我们要成为自己最严厉的批评者。我们要在敌人有机会指责我们之前就找出并改正我们的弱点。这正是达尔文的做法，事实上，他花了15年时间才做到这点。事情是这样的：当达尔文写完他那本不朽巨著《物种起

story goes like this: When Darwin completed the manuscript of his immortal book, *The Origin of Species*, he realised that the publication of his revolutionary concept of creation would rock the intellectual and religious worlds. So *he became his own critic and spent another fifteen years, checking his data, challenging his reasoning, criticising his conclusions.*

Suppose someone denounced you as"a damn fool"—what would you do? Get angry? Indignant? Here is what Lincoln did: Edward M. Stanton, Lincoln's Secretary of War, once called Lincoln"a damn fool". Stanton was indignant because Lincoln had been meddling in his affairs. In order to please a selfish politician, Lincoln had signed an order transferring certain regiments. Stanton not only refused to carry out Lincoln's orders but swore that Lincoln was a damn fool for ever signing such orders. What happened? When Lincoln was told what Stanton had said, Lincoln calmly replied: "If Stanton said I was a damned fool, then I must be, for he is nearly always right. I'll just step over and see for myself."

Lincoln did go to see Stanton. Stanton convinced him that the order was wrong, and Lincoln withdrew it. Lincoln welcomed criticism when he knew it was sincere, founded on knowledge, and given in a spirit of helpfulness.

You and I ought to welcome that kind of criticism, too, for we can't even hope to be right more than three times out of four. At least, that was all Theodore Roosevelt said he could hope for, when he was in the White House. Einstein, the most profound thinker now living, confesses that his conclusions are wrong ninety-nine per cent of the time!

"The opinions of our enemies, "said La Rochefoucauld, "come nearer to the truth about us than do our own opinions."

I know that statement may be true many times; yet when anyone starts to criticise me, if I do not watch myself, I instantly and automatically leap to the defensive—even before I have the slightest idea what my critic is going to say. I am disgusted with myself every time I do it. We all tend to resent criticism and lap up praise, regardless of whether either the criticism or the praise be justified. We are not creatures of logic. We are creatures of emotions. Our logic is like a canoe tossed about on a deep, dark, stormy sea of emotion.

In previous chapters, I have talked about what to do when you are unjustly criticised. But here

源》的手稿之后，深知要出版这本对生物创造提出了革命性观点的书，一定会动摇整个知识界和宗教界的基础。所以他成了自己的批评者，又花了15年时间检验他的资料，深入研究他的理论，批评他的结论。

假设有人骂你是“一个笨蛋”，你会怎么办呢？生气？觉得受到了侮辱？让我们看林肯是如何做的：有一次，林肯的国防部长爱德华·史丹顿骂林肯是“一个笨蛋”。史丹顿之所以这么恼火，是因为林肯干涉了他的工作。为了取悦一个自私的政客，林肯签发了一项调动军队的命令。史丹顿不仅拒绝命令，还大骂林肯签发这种命令真是愚蠢。结果如何呢？林肯听到史丹顿的话之后，平静地说：“如果史丹顿说我是笨蛋，那我一定是笨蛋，因为他几乎总是对的。我得亲自去看看。”

林肯果然去见了史丹顿。史丹顿让他了解那项命令为何错误，于是林肯收回了成命。只要是以知识为根据并带有建设性的诚恳批评，林肯都欢迎。

你和我也应该欢迎这类批评，因为我们所做的事连3/4的正确率都达不到，而这是罗斯福所希望的，他那时候正入主白宫。爱因斯坦是当今世界最著名的思想家，他也承认他的结论99%是错的。

“我们敌人的意见，”罗切冯卡说，“比我们自己的意见更接近事实。”

有很多次我都知道这话是对的，可是每当有人开始批评我的时候，只要稍不注意，我马上就会本能地辩护——甚至还不知道别人要批评我什么。每当我这样做的时候，我就会后悔。我们都不喜欢被人批评，而是希望听到赞美，也不管这种批评和赞美是否公正。我们不是逻辑生物，而是感情动物。我们的逻辑就像一艘独木小舟，在深不可测的情感海洋中漂荡。

我曾在前面几章介绍过当你受到不公正的批评时该怎么办，下面是另一个办法：当你因为受到不公正的批评而生气时，先停下来说：“等等……我离完美还差很远呢。如果爱因斯坦承认

is another idea: when your anger is rising because you feel you have been unjustly condemned, why not stop and say: "Just a minute... I am far from perfect. If Einstein admits he is wrong ninety-nine per cent of the time, maybe I am wrong at least eighty per cent of the time. Maybe I deserve this criticism. If I do, I ought to be thankful for it, and try to profit by it."

Charles Luckman, president of the Pepsodent Company, spends a millions dollars a year putting Bob Hope on the air. He doesn't look at the letters praising the programme, but he insists on seeing the critical letters. He knows he may learn something from them.

The Ford Company is so eager to find out what is wrong with its management and operations that it recently polled the employees and invited them to criticise the company.

I know a former soap salesman who used even to ask for criticism. When he first started out selling soap for Colgate, orders came slowly. He worried about losing his job. Since he knew there was nothing wrong with the soap or the price, he figured that the trouble must be himself. When he failed to make a sale, he would often walk around the block trying to figure out what was wrong. Had he been too vague? Did he lack enthusiasm? Sometimes he would go back to the merchant and say: "I haven't come back here to try to sell you any soap. I have come back to get your advice and your criticism. Won't you please tell me what I did that was wrong when I tried to sell you soap a few minutes ago? You are far more experienced and successful than I am. Please give me your criticism. Be frank. Don't pull your punches."

This attitude won him a lot of friends and priceless advice.

What do you suppose happened to him? Today, he is president of the Colgate-Palmolive-Peet Soap Company—the world's largest makers of soap. His name is E. H. Little. Last year, only fourteen people in America had a larger income than he had: $240,141.

It takes a big man to do what H. P. Howell, Ben Franklin, and E. H. Little did. And now, while nobody is looking, why not peep into the mirror and ask yourself whether you belong in that kind of company!

To keep from worrying about criticism, here is Rule 3:

Let's keep a record of the fool things we have done and criticise ourselves.

Since we can't hope to be perfect, let's do what E. H. Little did: let's ask for unbiased, helpful, constructive criticism.

他99%的时候都是错的，那我至少有80%是错的。也许我受到这样的批评是应当的。如果确实如此，我应该感谢别人，并想办法从中受益。”

查尔斯·卢克曼是培素登公司的总裁，他每年赞助100万美元给鲍勃·霍伯的节目。他从来不看那些称赞这个节目的信件，而是看那些批评的信件。他知道自己可以从中学到许多东西。

福特公司也希望找出他们在管理和业务方面的缺点，于是公司最近对全体员工做了一次意见调查，请他们来批评公司。

我认识一个以前推销肥皂的人，他甚至常常请人批评他。他刚开始为柯盖公司推销肥皂时，订单非常少。他担心会失去工作。他知道他的肥皂和价格都没有问题，所以他想问题一定出在他身上。因此，每次他没有做成业务的时候，就在街上散步，希望弄清楚问题出在那里：是不是他说话太含糊？他缺乏热情？有时他会回去找客户说：“我这次回来不是向你推销肥皂，是想得到你的建议和批评。你能否告诉我，我在几分钟前向你推销肥皂时，有什么做得不对的？你的经验比我丰富，也比我成功，请你给我批评，坦诚而不加掩饰地告诉我。”

这种态度使他赢得了很多朋友和宝贵的忠告。

你猜他后来如何了？现在他已经是CPP肥皂公司的董事长——这是全世界最大的肥皂公司，他的名字叫李特。去年，全美国只有14个人的收入超过他的。

只有非常了不起的人才能做到霍华、富兰克林、李特所做的事情。现在，既然没有人看着你，你何不自己照照镜子，问问自己到底是哪一种人？

因此，要想不为别人的批评而忧虑，下面是第三条规则：

记下自己做过的傻事，批评自己。

因为我们不可能达到完美的程度，就让我们按照李特的办法去做，请别人给我们坦诚、有益、建设性的批评。

Part Six
Six Ways to Prevent Fatigue and Worry and Keep Your Energy and Spirits High

1 How to Add One Hour a Day to Your Waking Life

Why am I writing a chapter on preventing fatigue in a book on preventing worry? That is simple: because fatigue often produces worry, or, at least, it makes you susceptible to worry. Any medical student will tell you that fatigue lowers physical resistance to the common cold and hundreds of other diseases and any psychiatrist will tell you that fatigue also lowers your resistance to the emotions of fear and worry. So preventing fatigue tends to prevent worry.

Did I say "tends to prevent worry"? That is putting it mildly. Dr. Edmund Jacobson goes much further. Dr. Jacobson has written two books on relaxation: *Progressive Relaxation* and *You Must Relax*; and as director of the University of Chicago Laboratory for Clinical Physiology, he has spent years conducting investigations in using relaxation as a method in medical practice. He declares that any nervous or emotional state "fails to exist in the presence of complete relaxation". That is another way of saying: *You cannot continue to worry if you relax*.

So, to prevent fatigue and worry, the first rule is: *Rest often. Rest before you get tired.*

Why is that so important? Because fatigue accumulates with astonishing rapidity. The United States Army has discovered by repeated tests that even young men—men toughened by years of Army training—can march better, and hold up longer, if they throw down their packs and rest ten minutes out of every hour. So the Army forces them to do just that. Your heart is just as smart as the U. S. Army. Your heart pumps enough blood through your body every day to fill a railway tank car. It exerts enough energy every twenty-four hours to shovel twenty tons of coal onto a platform

第六篇 常保充沛活力的六种方法

第1章 每日多清醒一小时

在这本谈如何防止忧虑的书里,为什么要写如何防止疲劳呢?很简单,因为疲劳容易使人产生忧虑,或者至少使你比较容易忧虑。任何一个医学院的学生都会告诉你,疲劳会降低身体对一般感冒和上百种其他疾病的抵抗力;任何一位精神病专家也会告诉你,疲劳同样会降低你对忧虑和恐惧的抵抗力。所以防止疲劳可以防止忧虑。

我是说"防止忧虑"吗?这样说也许太温和了。艾德蒙·杰科布森医生说得更清楚。他写过两本放松紧张情绪的书《消除紧张》和《你必须放松》,他还担任芝加哥大学实验心理学实验室的主任。他曾用了许多年时间主持研究放松疗法在医学上的用途。他认为,任何一种精神或情绪紧张"在完全放松之后就不复存在了"。也就是说,如果你能放松,就不会再忧虑。

所以,要防止疲劳和忧虑,第一条规则就是:经常休息,在疲劳之前就休息。

这一点为什么如此重要呢?因为疲劳增加的速度非常快。美国陆军曾经做过多次实验,发现即使是经过多年军事训练的强壮年轻人,如果不带背包,而且每一小时休息 10 分钟的话,就会走得更远更持久, 所以陆军总是强行要求他们这样做。你的心脏和美国陆军士兵的一样聪明。从你的心脏每天流出来穿过全身的血液,足够装满一节火车车厢;它 24 小时所供应的能量,足够把 20 吨煤铲到 3 英尺高的台上。你的心脏能完成这些令人难以相信的工作量,可以持

three feet high. It does this incredible amount of work for fifty, seventy, or maybe ninety years. How can it stand it? Dr. Walter B. Cannon, of the Harvard Medical School, explains it. He says: "Most people have the idea that the heart is working all the time. As a matter of fact, there is a definite rest period after each contraction. *When beating at a moderate rate of seventy pulses per minute, the heart is actually working only nine hours out of the twenty-four. In the aggregate its rest periods total a full fifteen hours per day.*"

During World War II, Winston Churchill, in his late sixties and early seventies, was able to work sixteen hours a day, year after year, directing the war efforts of the British Empire. A phenomenal record. His secret? He worked in bed each morning until eleven o'clock, reading papers, dictating orders, making telephone calls, and holding important conferences. After lunch he went to bed once more and slept for an hour. In the evening he went to bed once more and slept for two hours before having dinner at eight. He didn't cure fatigue. He didn't have to cure it. He prevented it. Because he rested frequently, he was able to work on, fresh and fit, until long past midnight.

The original John D. Rockefeller made two extraordinary records. He accumulated the greatest fortune the world had ever seen up to that time and he also lived to be ninety-eight. How did he do it? The chief reason, of course, was because he had inherited a tendency to live long. Another reason was his habit of taking a half-hour nap in his office every noon. He would lie down on his office couch—and not even the President of the United States could get John D. on the phone while he was having his snooze!

In his excellent book, *Why Be Tired*, Daniel W. Josselyn observes: "Rest is not a matter of doing absolutely nothing. *Rest is repair.*" There is so much repair power in a short period of rest that even a five-minute nap will help to forestall fatigue! Connie Mack, the grand old man of baseball, told me that if he doesn't take an afternoon nap before a game, he is all tuckered out at around the fifth inning. But if he does go to sleep, if for only five minutes, he can last throughout an entire *double—header* without feeling tired.

When I asked Eleanor Roosevelt how she was able to carry such an exhausting schedule during the twelve years she was in the White House, she said that before meeting a crowd or

续50年、70年,甚至90年。它怎么承受得了呢?哈佛医学院的瓦尔特·坎农医生解释说:"绝大多数人都认为,心脏整天都在跳动。事实上,在每一次收缩之后它有一段完全静止的时间。当心脏以正常速度每分钟跳70次时,它一天24小时只实际工作9小时。它每天休息了足足15个小时。"

在第二次世界大战期间,丘吉尔快70岁了,却能够每天工作16小时,长年指挥英军作战。太了不起了。他的秘诀呢?他每天早晨在床上工作到上午11点,看文件、口述命令、打电话,开重要会议。午饭后,他再上床睡一个小时。到了晚上8点钟吃晚饭以前,他会再上床休息两个小时。他这样做并不是消除疲劳,因为事先就防止了,所以根本不必消除。由于他经常休息,所以可以精力充沛地一直工作到后半夜。

老约翰·洛克菲勒也创下了两项惊人的纪录:他赚到了当时全世界最庞大的财富,并活到了98岁高龄。他如何做到的呢?最主要的原因当然是他家里的人都很长寿,另外一个原因则是他每天中午要在办公室睡半个小时。他躺在办公室的沙发上,即使是美国总统打来电话,他都不会接。

在《为什么会疲倦》这本书书里,丹尼尔·约西林说:"休息并不是不干任何事;休息就是修补。"短短的休息,具备很强的修补能力,哪怕只打5分钟的盹儿,也有助于防止疲劳。棒球名将康尼·马克曾告诉我,他每次比赛之前如果不睡一个午觉,到第五局他就会觉得筋疲力尽了;可是,如果他睡了午觉,哪怕只睡5分钟,他也能够打完全场——一点也不会感到疲劳。

我曾问过伊莲娜·罗斯福, 在她当白宫第一夫人的12年里是如何应付那么紧张的日程的。她说,每次接见一大群人或发表演说之前,她通常都要坐在一张椅子或沙发上,闭目休息20分钟。

爱迪生认为他之所以具有无穷的精力和耐力,要归功于他随时想睡就睡的习惯。

making a speech, she would often sit in a chair or davenport, close her eyes, and relax for twenty minutes.

Edison attributed his enormous energy and endurance to his habit of sleeping whenever he wanted to.

I interviewed Henry Ford shortly before his eightieth birthday. I was surprised to see how fresh and fine he looked. I asked him the secret. He said: "I never stand up when I can sit down; and I never sit down when I can lie down."

Horace Mann, "the father of modem education", did the same thing as he grew older. When he was president of Antioch College, he used to stretch out on a couch while interviewing students.

I persuaded a motion-picture director in Hollywood to try a similar technique. He confessed that it worked miracles. I refer to Jack Chertock, who is now one of Metro-Goldwyn-Mayer's top directors. When he came to see me a few years ago, he was then head of the short-feature department of M-G-M.

Worn out and exhausted, he had tried everything: tonics, vitamins, medicine. Nothing helped much. I suggested that he take a vacation every day. How? By stretching out in his office and relaxing while holding conferences with his staff writers.

When I saw him again, two years later, he said: "A miracle has happened. That is what my own physicians call it. I used to sit up in my chair, tense and taut, while discussing ideas for our short features. Now I stretch out on the office couch during these conferences. I feel better than I have felt in twenty years. Work two hours a day longer, yet I rarely get tired."

How does all this apply to you? If you are a stenographer, you can't take naps in the office as Edison did, and as Sam Goldwyn does; and if you are an accountant, you can't stretch out on the couch while discussing a financial statement with the boss. But if you live in a small city and go home for lunch, you may be able to take a ten-minute nap after lunch.

If you can't take a nap at noon, you can at least try to lie down for an hour before the evening meal. It is cheaper than a highball; and, over a long stretch, it is 5,467 times more effective. If you can sleep for an hour around five, six, or seven o'clock, you can add one hour a day to your waking life. Why? How? Because an hour's nap before the evening meal plus six hours' sleep at night—a

亨利·福特 80 岁大寿之前不久,我拜访过他。我很惊讶他那么有精神,那么健康。我问他秘诀何在?他说:"能坐着我绝不站着,能躺着我绝不坐着。"

"现代教育之父"柯瑞斯·曼年老之后也是如此。在担任安提奥克大学校长的时候,他总是躺在沙发上接见学生。

我曾建议好莱坞一位动作电影导演也试试类似方法,后来他说这种办法可以创造奇迹。这位导演是杰克·查托克,他是好莱坞最有名的导演之一。几年前他来看我的时候,正担任米高梅公司短片部的经理。

由于疲惫不堪,他试过了一切方法:喝矿泉水、吃维他命和补药,但都无效。于是我建议他每天"度度假"。怎么做呢?那就是当他在办公室开会的时候,躺下来放松。

当我两年之后再见到他时,他说:"出现奇迹了。这是我的医生说的。以前谈论短片时,我总是坐在椅子里,而且非常紧张。现在每次开会的时候,我总是躺在办公室的沙发上。现在我觉得比 20 年前还要棒,每天多工作两个小时,却很少感到疲劳。"

你该如何使用这些方法呢?如果你是打字员,当然不能像爱迪生或萨姆·高尔温那样在办公室休息了;如果你是会计,也不可能躺在沙发上和老板讨论账目。可是,如果你住在一个小城市,每天回家吃午饭的话,那你可以在饭后睡上 10 分钟。

如果你中午不能,至少也要在晚饭之前躺下来休息一小时,这比喝一杯饭前酒要便宜多了。如果算总账,这更有效 5000 多倍。如果你能在下午五六点钟或者七点钟左右睡上一小时,你就可以每天多清醒一小时。为什么呢?因为晚饭前睡一个小时,加上夜里睡 6 个小时,一共是 7 小时,比连续睡 8 个小时更有益。

体力劳动者如果休息时间足够的话,可以干更多的工作。弗雷德里克·泰勒在贝德汉钢铁公司担任科学管理工程师时,就证明了这一道理。他发现每个工人每天可以给货车装大约 12.5

total of seven hours—will do you more good than eight hours of unbroken sleep.

A physical worker can do more work if he takes more time out for rest. Frederick Taylor demonstrated that while working as a scientific management engineer with the Bethlehem Steel Company. He observed that labouring men were loading approximately $12^{1}/_{2}$ tons of pig-iron per man each day on freight cars and that they were exhausted at noon. He made a scientific study of all the fatigue factors involved, and declared that these men should be loading not $12^{1}/_{2}$ tons of pig-iron per day, but forty-seven tons per day! He figured that they ought to do almost four times as much as they were doing, and not be exhausted. But prove it!

Taylor selected a Mr. Schmidt who was required to work by the stop-watch. Schmidt was told by the man who stood over him with a watch: "Now pick up a 'pig' and walk... Now sit down and rest... Now walk... Now rest."

What happened? Schmidt carried forty-seven tons of pig-iron each day while the other men carried only 12 tons per man. And he practically never failed to work at this pace during the three years that Frederick Taylor was at Bethlehem. Schmidt was able to do this because he rested before he got tired. He worked approximately 26 minutes out of the hour and rested 34 minutes. He rested more than he worked—yet he did almost four times as much work as the others! Is this mere hearsay? No, you can read the record yourself in *Principles of Scientific Management* by Frederick Winslow Taylor.

Let me repeat: ***do what the Army does—take frequent rests. Do what your heart does—rest before you get tired, and you will add one hour a day to your waking life.***

吨生铁，而他们到中午时就筋疲力尽了。他对导致疲劳的因素做了科学研究，认为这些工人每天不应该只送 12.5 吨生铁，而是 47 吨！他们应该可以达到目前成绩的 4 倍，而且不会疲劳。不过必须证明这个结论。

于是，泰勒选了一个名叫施密德的人，让他按照马表来工作。一个人站在一边，拿着马表指挥施密德："现在拿起一块生铁，走……现在坐下来休息……现在走……现在休息。"

结果呢?别人每天只能运 12.5 吨生铁，而施密德却能运 47 吨。在泰勒就职于贝德汉钢铁公司的那 3 年里，施密德的工作效力从来都没有降低。他之所以能做到这一点，是因为他在疲劳之前就休息了。他每个小时大约工作 26 分钟，休息 34 分钟。他休息的时间比工作的时间还要多——可是他的工作却是其他人的 4 倍！这是传闻吗？不！你可以从泰勒的《科学管理原理》一书中读到这一记录。

让我再重复一遍：**照美国陆军的办法去做——经常休息；照你心脏的办法去做——在感觉疲劳之前休息，然后你每天可以多清醒一个小时。**

2 What Makes You Tired—and What You Can Do About It

Here is an astounding and significant fact: Mental work alone can't make you tired. Sounds absurd. But a few years ago, scientists tried to find out how long the human brain could labor without reaching "a diminished capacity for work", the scientific definition of fatigue. To the amazement of these scientists, they discovered that blood passing through the brain, when it is active, shows no fatigue at all! If you took blood from the veins of a day labourer while he was working, you would find it full of "fatigue toxins"and fatigue products. But if you took a drop of blood from the brain of an Albert Einstein, it would show no fatigue toxins whatever at the end of the day.

So far as the brain is concerned, it can work "as well and as swiftly at the end of eight or even twelve hours of effort as at the beginning". The brain is utterly tireless... So what makes you tired?

Psychiatrists declare that most of our fatigue derives from our mental and emotional attitudes. One of England's most distinguished psychiatrists, J. A. Hadfield, says in his book *The Psychology of Power*: "the greater part of the fatigue from which we suffer is of mental origin; in fact exhaustion of purely physical origin is rare."

One of America's most distinguished psychiatrists, Dr. A. A. Brill, goes even further. He declares: "One hundred per cent of the fatigue of the sedentary worker in good health is due to psychological factors, by which we mean emotional factors."

What kinds of emotional factors tire the sedentary (or sitting) worker? Joy? Contentment? No! Never! Boredom, resentment, a feeling of not being appreciated, a feeling of futility, hurry, anxiety, worry—those are the emotional factors that exhaust the sitting worker, make him susceptible to colds, reduce his output, and send him home with a nervous headache. Yes, we get tired because our emotions produce nervous tensions in the body.

The Metropolitan Life Insurance Company pointed that out in a leaflet on fatigue: "Hard work by itself, "says this great life-insurance company, "seldom causes fatigue which cannot be cured by

第2章 是什么使你疲劳

这个事实让人吃惊而且非常重要:单纯用脑不会让人疲倦。听起来很荒谬吧?可是科学家们在几年前曾试图了解人的大脑能够工作多久才“工作能量降低”,也就是对疲劳作科学定义,令这些科学家们吃惊的是,他们发现通过活动中的大脑的血液毫无疲劳迹象!但如果你从一个正在做体力劳动的人的血管里抽出血液,就会发现它充满了“疲劳毒素”和各种废物。但如果从爱因斯坦的脑部抽出血来,即使是一天下来也不会有任何疲劳毒素。

就人脑而言,它“在8小时甚至12小时之后,还和开始时一样反应敏捷”,大脑完全不会疲劳……那又是什么使你疲劳的呢?

精神病专家认为,我们的疲劳多半是由精神和情感引起的。英国最著名的精神病专家海德菲在他的《权力心理学》中说:“我们所感受到的绝大部分疲劳源自心理。事实上,纯粹由生理导致的疲劳很少。”

美国一位著名的精神病专家布莱尔医生说得更详细。他说:“一个坐着工作的人如果健康状况良好,他的疲劳完全来自心理因素,也就是情感因素。”

是哪些心理因素使坐着工作的人感到疲劳呢?快乐?满足?都不是,绝不是!而是烦闷、懊悔,一种得不到欣赏的感觉,一种无用、匆忙、焦急、忧虑的感觉——这些都是导致坐着工作的人心力憔悴、使他容易患感冒、降低他的工作成绩、使他回家时神经性头痛的心理因素。不错,我们之所以疲劳,是因为我们的情绪使我们感到紧张。

大都会人寿保险公司在一本讨论疲劳的小册子中指出:“困难工作本身,很少会造成充分休息之后不能消除的疲劳……只有忧虑、紧张和情绪不安,才是导致疲劳的三大因素。通常认

a good sleep or rest... Worry, tenseness, and emotional upsets are three of the biggest causes of fatigue. Often they are to blame when physical or mental work seems to be the cause... Remember that a tense muscle is a working muscle. Ease up! Save energy for important duties."

Stop now, right where you are, and give yourself a check-up. As you read these lines, are you scowling at the book? Do you feel a strain between the eyes? Are you sitting relaxed in your chair? Or are you hunching up your shoulders? Are the muscles of your face tense? Unless your entire body is as limp and relaxed as an old rag doll, you are at this very moment producing nervous tensions and muscular tensions. *You are producing nervous tensions and nervous fatigue!*

Why do we produce these unnecessary tensions in doing mental work? Josselyn says: "I find that the chief obstacle... is the almost universal belief that hard work requires a feeling of effort, else it is not well done." So we scowl when we concentrate. We hunch up our shoulders. We call on our muscles to make the motion of *effort*, which in no way assists our brain in its work.

What is the answer to this nervous fatigue? Relax! Relax! Relax! *Learn to relax while you are doing your work!*

Easy? No. You will probably have to reverse the habits of a lifetime. But it is worth the effort, for it may revolutionise your life! William James said, in his essay "*The Gospel of Relaxation*": "The American over-tension and jerkiness and breathlessness and intensity and agony of expression... are *bad habits, nothing more or less.*" *Tension is a habit. Relaxing is a habit. And bad habits can be broken, good habits formed.*

How do you relax? Do you start with your mind, or do you start with your nerves? You don't start with either. You always begin to *relax with your muscle!*

Let's give it a try. To show how it is done, suppose we start with your eyes. Read this paragraph through, and when you've reached the end, lean back, close your eyes, and *say to your eyes silently*: "Let go. Let go. Stop straining, stop frowning. Let go. Let go." Repeat that over and over very slowly for a minute...

Didn't you notice that after a few seconds the muscles of the eyes *began to obey*? Didn't you feel as though some hand had wiped away the tension? Well, incredible as it seems, you have sampled in that one minute the whole key and secret to the art of relaxing. You can do the same

为由于操心劳力所产生的疲劳,都可以归咎于这三者……请记住!放松你那正在工作的紧张肌肉,储备好能量,以应付重要责任。"

现在就停下来!自己检讨一下:在你念这几行字时,是不是还皱着眉头?是否觉得两眼之间有一种压力?是否正放松地坐在椅子里?还是耸起肩膀?你脸上的肌肉是不是紧张?除非你的全身像破旧的布娃娃一样放松,否则你就是在让你的神经和肌肉紧张,就是在给你制造神经紧张和疲劳。

为什么我们在干脑力工作时会产生这种不必要的紧张?约西林先生说:"我发现主要的原因……就是几乎所有的人都相信,困难的工作需要一种压力感,否则就不能做好。"所以,我们集中精力时就会皱眉,缩肩,让所有的肌肉都来"用力"。但这样做对我们的思考根本没有任何帮助。

一旦出现精神疲劳该怎么办呢?放松!放松!再放松!要学会在工作时放松。

这容易做到吗?不,你也许得改掉一生的习惯才能实现。可是这种努力很值,因为它可以使你的生活发生革命性变化。威廉·詹姆斯在他的文章《论放松情绪》中说:"美国人过度紧张、坐立不安、着急以及紧张痛苦的表情……都是不良习惯,不折不扣的坏习惯。"紧张是一种习惯,放松也是一种习惯。坏习惯可以改掉,好习惯可以培养。

怎样才能放松呢?是先从思想开始,还是先从神经开始呢?都不是。应该先放松你的肌肉。

让我们来试试该怎么做:先从你的眼睛开始,读完这一句。读完之后,头向后靠,闭上双眼。然后默默地对你的眼睛说:"放松!放松!不要紧张!不要皱眉!放松,放松!"这样慢慢地重复一分钟……

你是否注意到,几秒钟之后你双眼肌肉就开始服从命令了?你不觉得有一只无形的手把你的紧张抚平了吗?这看起来虽然难以置信,可是你在这一分钟里却已经试过了放松的全部关键

thing with the jaw, with the muscles of the face, with the neck, with the shoulders, the whole of the body. But the most important organ of all is the eye. Dr. Edmund Jacobson of the University of Chicago has gone so far as to say that if you can completely relax the muscles of the eyes, you can forget all your troubles! The reason the eyes are so important in relieving nervous tension is that they burn up one-fourth of all the nervous energies consumed by the body. That is also why so many people with perfectly sound vision suffer from"eyestrain". They are tensing the eyes.

Vickie Baum, the famous novelist, says that when she was a child, she met an old man who taught her one of the most important lessons she ever learned. She had fallen down and cut her knees and hurt her wrist. The old man picked her up; he had once been a circus clown; and, as he brushed her off, he said: "The reason you injured yourself was because you don't know how to relax. You have to pretend you are as limp as a sock, as an old crumpled sock. Come, I'll show you how to do it."

That old man taught Vicki Baum and the other children how to fall, how to do flip-flops, and how to turn somersaults. And always he insisted: "Think of yourself as an old crumpled sock. Then you've got to relax! "

You can relax in odd moments, almost anywhere you are. Only don't make an effort to relax. *Relaxation is the absence of all tension and effort.* Think ease and relaxation. Begin by thinking relaxation of the muscles of your eyes and your face, saying over and over: "Let go... let go... let go and relax." Feel the energy flowing out of your facial muscles to the centre of your body. Think of yourself as free from tension as a baby.

That is what Galli-Curci, the great soprano, used to do. Helen Jepson told me that she used to see Galli-Curci before a performance, sitting in a chair with all her muscles relaxed and her lower jaw so limp it actually sagged. An excellent practice—it kept her from becoming too nervous before her stage entrance; it prevented fatigue.

Here are five suggestions that will help you learn to relax:

1. Read one of the best books ever written on this subject: *Release from Nervous Tension*, by Dr. David Harold Fink.

2. Relax in odd moments. Let your body go limp like an old sock. I keep an old, maroon-coloured

和秘诀。你可以用同样的办法放松下颌、脸部肌肉、脖子、肩膀、整个身体。但是,最重要的器官还是眼睛。芝加哥大学的艾德蒙·雅科布森博士更是指出,如果你能完全放松眼部肌肉,你就可以忘记所有烦恼。眼睛之所以在消除神经紧张时如此重要,是因为它们消耗了全身能量的 1/4。这也正是许多眼力很好的人总是到"眼部紧张"的原因,因为他们常使眼部感到紧张。

著名作家维基·鲍姆曾说,她小时候遇到一位老人,他教了她人生当中最重要的一课。有一次,她摔了一跤,膝盖碰破了,还扭伤了手腕。那个以前在马戏团演过小丑的老人扶起她,拍干净她身上的灰尘,说:"你之所以会碰伤,是因为你不知道如何放松。你应该把自己想象成一只袜子。来,我教你怎么做。"

老人就教鲍姆和其他孩子如何跑跳、翻斤斗,还一直对他们说:"要把自己想象成一只旧袜子,然后你们就能放松了。"

在任何时候任何地方都要松,但不要太费精力。放松就是要消除所有的紧张和压力,只想到舒适和轻松。刚开始可以放松眼部肌肉和脸部肌肉,不停地对自己说:"放松! 放松! 放松!"要感觉到你的体力正由你的脸部肌肉穿行到你身体的中心。把自己想象成一个没有任何紧张的孩子。

这也是著名女高音嘉莉古琪常用过的方法。海伦·吉普生告诉我,她常常看见嘉莉古琪在演出前坐在一张椅子上,放松全身肌肉,而且下颚松得像脱了臼似的。这种方法非常不错,使她在登台前不会感到太紧张,同时还可以防止疲劳。

下面五项建议可以帮你学会放松:

第一,读一本这方面的最好著作,如大卫·哈罗德·芬克博士的《消除神经紧张》。

第二,随时放松,使你的身体像旧袜子一样柔软。我工作的时候,常常在书桌上放一只红褐色的旧袜子,提醒我应该放松。如果找不到旧袜子,也可以找一只猫。你抱过在太阳底下打盹的

sock on my desk as I work—keep it there as a reminder of how limp I ought to be. If you haven't got a sock, a cat will do. Did you ever pick up a kitten sleeping in the sunshine? If so, both ends sagged like a wet newspaper. Even the yoga in India say that if you want to master the art of relaxation, study the cat. I never saw a tired cat, a cat with a nervous breakdown, or a cat suffering from insomnia, worry, or stomach ulcers. You will probably avoid these disasters if you learn to relax as the cat does.

3. Work, as much as possible, in a comfortable position. Remember that tensions in the body produce aching shoulders and nervous fatigue.

4. Check yourself four or five times a day, and say to yourself: "Am I making my work harder than it actually is? Am I using muscles that have nothing to do with the work I am doing? "This will help you form the habit of relaxing, and as Dr. David Harold Fink says: "Among those who know psychology best, it is habits two to one."

5. Test yourself again at the end of the day, by asking yourself: "Just how tired am I? If I am tired, it is not because of the mental work I have done but because of the way I have done it."

"I measure my accomplishments, "says Daniel W. Josselyn, "not by how tired I am at the end of the day, but how tired I am not." He says:"When I feel particularly tired at the end of the day, or when irritability proves that my nerves are tired, I know beyond question that it has been an inefficient day both as to quantity and quality." If every businessman would learn that same lesson, the death rate from "hypertension"diseases would drop overnight. And we would stop filling up our sanatoriums and asylums with men who have been broken by fatigue and worry.

猫吗？如果抱过，它首尾两头犹如沾湿的报纸一样软。印度的瑜伽术也认为如果你想掌握放松技巧，要向猫学习。我从未见过疲累、精神崩溃、失眠、忧虑或患溃疡的猫。要是你能像猫一样放松自己，就能避免这些问题了。

第三，工作时采取舒适的姿势。记住，身体的紧张会导致肩膀疼痛和精神疲劳。

第四，每天自我检讨四五次，问问自己："我是否使我的工作比实际上更困难？我是否使用了和工作毫无关系的肌肉？"这些都有助于你培养放松的习惯。就像大卫·哈罗德·芬克博士所说的："那些对心理学最了解的人，都知道疲倦是习惯性的。"

第五，每天晚上再检讨一次，问问自己："我有多疲劳？如果我疲劳了，不是我过分操心的缘故，而是因为方法不对。"

"我衡量自己的成绩，" 丹尼尔·约西林说，"不是看我一天下来有多疲倦，而是有多不疲倦。"他说："当一天结束，而我感到特别疲劳时，或者感到精神特别疲乏时，我敢肯定我这一天的工作在质和量上都不理想。"。如果每一位做生意人都能学会这一点，那么由神经紧张而导致的疾病或死亡率马上就会降低。而且我们的精神疗养院再也不会有因为疲劳和忧虑而精神崩溃的人。

3 How The Housewife Can Avoid Fatigue—and Keep Looking Young

One day last autumn, my associate flew up to Boston to attend a session of one of the most unusual medical classes in the world. Medical? Well, yes, it meets once a week at the Boston Dispensary, and the patients who attend it get regular and thorough medical examinations before they are admitted. But actually this class is a psychological clinic. Although it is officially called the Class in Applied Psychology (formerly the Thought Control Class—a name suggested by the first member), its real purpose is to deal with people *who are ill from worry*. And many of these patients are emotionally disturbed housewives.

How did such a class for worriers get started? Well, in 1930, Dr. Joseph H. Pratt—who, by the way, had been a pupil of Sir William Osler—observed that many of the outpatients who came to the Boston Dispensary apparently had nothing wrong with them at all physically; yet they had practically all the symptoms that flesh is heir to. One woman's hands were so crippled with "arthritis"that she had lost all use of them. Another was in agony with all the excruciating symptoms of "cancer of the stomach". Others had backaches, headaches, were chronically tired, or had vague aches and pains. *They actually felt these pains.* But the most exhaustive medical examinations showed that nothing whatever was wrong with these women—in the physical sense. Many old-fashioned doctors would have said it was all imagination—"all in the mind".

But Dr. Pratt realized that it was no use to tell these patients to "go home and forget it". He knew that most of these women didn't want to be sick; if it was so easy to forget their ailments, they would do so themselves. So what could be done?

He opened his class—to a chorus of doubts from the medical doubters on the sidelines. And the class worked wonders! In the eighteen years that have passed since it started, thousands of patients have been "cured"by attending it. Some of the patients have been coming for years—as religious in their attendance as though going to church. My assistant talked to a woman who had hardly missed a session in more than nine years. She said that when she first went to the clinic, she

第3章　家庭主妇如何避免疲劳并青春永驻

去年秋天的一天，我的助手乘飞机去波士顿参加一次全世界最不寻常的医学课程。是医学课吗？不错。它每周在波士顿医院举办一次，参加者进场之前都接受过定期和彻底的身体检查。可是这个课程实际上是一种心理学临床实验，虽然其正式名称叫应用心理学(以前叫思想控制课程)，其真正目的是为忧虑患者提供治疗，而大部分病人都是精神上饱受困扰的家庭主妇。

这种专门为忧虑患者开的课程是怎么开始的呢？1930年，约瑟夫·帕雷特医生——他曾是威廉·奥斯勒爵士的学生——注意到，很多前来波士顿医院求医的病人，生理上根本没有任何毛病，可是他们却认为自己的确患了那种病。例如，有一个女人的两只手因为患"关节炎"而完全无法活动；另一个女人则因为患了"胃癌"而痛苦不堪。其他人有背痛的、头痛的，她们常年感到疲倦或疼痛。事实上，她们真的能感受到这些痛苦。但即使最彻底的医学检查也未能发现她们有任何病。很多年老的医生都认为，这完全是出自心理因素——脑子里的毛病"。

可是帕雷特医生却知道，让那些病人"回家去忘掉这件事"毫无用处。他知道这些女人大多数都不想得病，如果她们的痛苦能够那么容易就忘记，她们早就这样做了。那么，该怎么办呢？

于是他办了这个班——虽然医药界其他同仁都深表怀疑，但却收到了奇效。自从开班以来，18年过去了，成千上万的病人因为参加这个班而治好了病。有些病人参加了好几年，就像去教堂一样虔诚。我的助手曾和一位前后来了9年并且很少缺课的女士交谈过一次。她说她第一次来的时候，深信自己患有肾脏病和心脏病。她既忧虑又紧张，有时会看不清

was thoroughly convinced she had a floating kidney and some kind of heart ailment. She was so worried and tense that she occasionally lost her eyesight and had spells of blindness. Yet today she is confident and cheerful and in excellent health. She looked only about forty, yet she held one of her grandchildren asleep in her lap. "I used to worry so much about my family troubles, "she said, "that I wished I could die. But I learned at this clinic the futility of worrying. I learned to stop it. And I can honestly say now that my life is serene."

Dr. Rose Hilferding, the medical adviser of the class, said that she thought one of the best remedies for lightening worry is "talking your troubles over with someone you trust. We call it catharsis, "she said. "When patients come here, they can talk their troubles over at length, until they get them off their minds. Brooding over worries alone, and keeping them to oneself, causes great nervous tension. We all have to share our troubles. We have to share worry. We have to feel there is someone in the world who is willing to listen and able to understand."

My assistant witnessed the great relief that came to one woman from talking out her worries. She had domestic worries, and when she first began to talk, she was like a wound-up spring. Then gradually, as she kept on talking, she began to calm down. At the end of the interview, she was actually smiling. Had the problem been solved? No, it wasn't that easy. What caused the change was *talking to someone*, getting a little advice and a little human sympathy. What had really worked the change was the tremendous healing value that lies in—*words*!

Psycho analysis is based, to some extent, on this healing power of words. Ever since the days of Freud, analysts have known that a patient could find relief from his inner anxieties if he could talk, just talk. Why is this so? Maybe because by talking, we gain a little better insight into our troubles, get a better perspective. No one knows the whole answer. But all of us know that"spitting it out"or"getting it off our chests"bring almost instant relief.

So the next time we have an emotional problem, why don't we look around for someone to talk to? I don't mean, of course, to go around making pests of ourselves by whining and complaining to everyone in sight. Let's decide on someone we can trust, and make an appointment. Maybe a relative, a doctor, a lawyer, a minister, or priest. Then say to that person: "I want your advice. I have a problem, and I wish you would listen while I put it in words. You may be able to advise me.

东西，因此担心会失明。可是现在她却充满了自信，心情愉快，身体健康。她看上去只有40来岁，可是怀里却抱着熟睡的孙子。“我以前总为家里的事情而忧虑，”她说，“甚至想一死了之。可是我在这里知道了忧虑的害处，学会了如何停止忧虑。现在我可以说，我的生活很平静。”

这个班的医学顾问罗丝·海芬婷医生说，减轻忧虑的最好药剂，就是“跟你信任的人谈论你的问题，我们称之为精神发泄，”她说，“病人到这里来的时候，可以尽量谈她们的问题，直到她们把这些问题完全赶出她们的大脑。忧虑憋在心里而不告诉任何人，会造成极度精神紧张。我们必须让别人分担我们的问题，也必须分担别人的忧虑。我们必须感觉到这个世界还有人愿意倾听和了解我们。”

我的助手就亲眼看到一个女人在说出了忧虑之后，感到了巨大的解脱。她在家事方面有许多烦恼，在她刚开始谈这些问题的时候，就像一个压紧的弹簧，然后一面讲，一面逐渐地平静下来。谈完之后，她居然笑了。她的问题解决了吗?没有，不会这么容易。她之所以出现这样的改观，是因为她能和别人谈心，并得到别人的忠告和同情。而真正造成这种变化的，是具有强大治疗功能的语言。

从某种程度来说，心理分析就是以语言治疗功能为基础的。从弗洛伊德时代开始，心理分析学家就知道，一个病人只要能够说话——仅仅是说话，就能够解除心中的忧虑。为什么呢?这也许是因为通过说话，我们就可以更深入地看到问题，找到更好的解决方法。没有人知道确切答案，可是我们所有人都知道，“畅谈一番”或“发发胸中的闷气”就能使人立刻舒畅。

所以，下一次我们有情感上的困难时，为什么不去找人聊聊呢?当然，我并不是说随便找一个人去大吐苦水和发牢骚。我们要找一个自己信任的人，如找一位亲戚、医生、律师、教士或神

You may see angles to this thing that I can't see myself. But even if you can't, you will help me tremendously if you will just sit and listen while I talk it out."

Talking things out, then, is one of the principle therapies used at the Boston Dispensary Class. But here are some other ideas we picked up at the class—things you, as a housewife, can do in your home.

1. *Keep a notebook or scrapbook for"inspirational"reading.* Into this book you can paste all the poems, or short prayers, or quotations, which appeal to you personally and give you a lift. Then, when a rainy afternoon sends your spirits plunging down, perhaps you can find a recipe in this book for dispelling the gloom. Many patients at the Dispensary have kept such notebooks for years. They say it is a spiritual"shot in the arm".

2. *Donl l蒺 t dwell too long on the shortcomings of others*! Sure, your husband has faults! If he had been a saint, he never would have married you. Right? One woman at the class who found herself developing into a scolding, nagging, and haggard-faced wife, was brought up short with the question: "What would you do if your husband died? "She was so shocked by the idea that she immediately sat down and drew up a list of all her husband's good points. She made quite a list. Why don't you try the same thing the next time you feel you married a tight-fisted tyrant? Maybe you'll find, after reading his virtues, that he's a man you'd like to meet!

3. *Get interested in your neighbours*! Develop a friendly, healthy interest in the people who share the life on your street. One ailing woman who felt herself so "exclusive"that she hadn't any friends, was told to try to make up a story about the next person she met. She began, in the street-car, to weave backgrounds and settings for the people she saw. She tried to imagine what their lives had been like. First thing you know, she was talking to people everywhere—and today she is happy, alert, and a charming human being cured of her"pains".

4. *Make up a schedule for tomorrow's work before you go to bed tonight.* The class found that many wives feel driven and harassed by the unending round of housework and things they must do. They never got their work finished. They were chased by the clock. To cure this sense of hurry, and worry, the suggestion was made that they draw up a schedule each night for the following day. What happened? More work accomplished; much less fatigue; a feeling of pride and achievement; and

父,和他约好时间,然后对他说:"我希望得到你的忠告。我有个问题,我希望你能听我谈谈,也许你可以给我一点忠告。俗话说旁观者清,你也许可以看到我看不到的问题。但即使你做不到这一点,只要你坐在这儿听我谈,也帮了我一个大忙。"

把心里的烦恼说出来,正是波士顿医院课程中最主要的治疗方法之一。下面是我们从那个课程班里整理出来的方法,家庭主妇在家里就可以做。

第一,准备一个"灵感"剪贴本。你可以在上面贴上自己喜欢的令人鼓舞的诗或名人格言。如果你以后感到精神颓丧时,翻开这个本子也许可以找到治疗方法。波士顿医院的很多病人都把这种剪贴本保存好多年,她们说这等于替你在精神上"打了一针"。

第二,不要为别人的缺点太过操心。不错,你丈夫有很多缺点!如果他是个圣人,他根本就不会娶你,对吗?那个班上有一个女人,她发现自己变成了一个尖酸刻薄、整天拉着一张脸的女人,当有人问她"如果你丈夫死了,你怎么办"时,她才惊醒过来,连忙坐下来,把她丈夫所有的优点列举出来。那张单子真是太长了。所以,如果你下一次觉得嫁错了人的话,何不这样试试呢?也许在看过他所有的优点之后,你会发现他正是你希望嫁的那个人呢。

第三,对你的邻居有兴趣。对那些和你共同生活在一条街上的人持一种友善而健康的兴趣。有一个孤独的女人,她觉得自己非常"孤立",一个朋友都没有。有人建议她试着把她下一个将要碰到的人当成主角编个故事。于是,她开始在公共汽车上为她看到的人编故事,设想那个人的生活。后来,她一遇到别人就聊天——现在她活得非常开心,成了一个令人喜欢的人,也治好了她的"痛苦"。

第四,晚上上床之前,安排好明天的工作。很多家庭主妇因为做不完的家务而感到疲倦不堪。她们永远也做不完她们的工作,老是被时间追来赶去。为了治好这种匆忙的感觉和忧虑,她们最好在头一天晚上就把第二天的工作安排好。结果如何呢?她们能完成更多工作,疲

time left over to rest and to"primp". (Every woman ought to take some time out in the course of the day to primp and look pretty. My own guess is that when a woman knows she looks pretty, she has little use for"nerves".)

5. *Finally-avoid tension and fatigue*. *Relax*! *Relax*! Nothing will make you look old sooner than tension and fatigue. Nothing will work such havoc with your freshness and looks! My assistant sat for an hour in the Boston Thought Control Class, while Professor Paul E. Johnson, the director, went over many of the principles we have already discussed in the previous chapter—the rules for relaxing. At the end of ten minutes of these relaxing exercises, which my assistant did with the others, she was almost asleep sitting upright in her chair! Why is such stress laid on this physical relaxing? Because the clinic knows—as other doctors know—that if you're going to get the worry-kinks out of people, they've got to relax!

Yes, you, as a housewife, have got to relax! You have one great advantage—you can lie down whenever you want to, and you can lie on the floor! Strangely enough, a good hard floor is better to relax on than an inner-spring bed. It gives more resistance. It is good for the spine.

All right, then, here are some exercises you can do in your home. Try them for a week—and see what you do for your looks and disposition!

a. Lie flat on the floor whenever you feel tired. Stretch as tall as you can. Roll around if you want to. Do it twice a day.

b. Close your eyes. You might try saying, as Professor Johnson recommended, something like this: "The sun is shining overhead. The sky is blue and sparkling. Nature is calm and in control of the world—and I, as nature's child, am in tune with the Universe." Or—better still—pray!

c. If you cannot lie down, because the roast is in the oven and you can't spare the time, then you can achieve almost the same effect sitting down in a chair. A hard, upright chair is the best for relaxing. Sit upright in the chair like a seated Egyptian statue, and let your hands rest, palms down, on the tops of your thighs.

d. Now, slowly tense the toes—then let them relax. Tense the muscles in your legs—and let them relax. Do this slowly upward, with all the muscles of your body, until you get to the neck. Then let your head roll around heavily, as though it were a football. Keep saying to your muscles

劳却更少了;她们还有了成绩和自豪感;还有时间休息和“打扮”。(每一个女人每天都应该抽出时间来打扮自己,让自己看上去漂亮一些。我认为,当一个女人知道她很漂亮时,就不会紧张了。)

第五,最后,避免紧张和疲劳的唯一办法,就是放松!再没有什么比紧张和疲劳更容易使你苍老的,再也不会有什么对你的外表更有害的。我的助手在波士顿医院举办的那个课程班上坐了一个小时,听负责人保罗·琼森教授谈了许多我们在前面已经讨论过的原则——放松的方法。在10分钟的放松训练结束之后,我的助手也和其他人一起做了这些练习,几乎坐在椅子上睡着了。为什么生理上的放松如此管用呢?因为这家医院知道,如果人们要消除忧虑,就必须放松。

是的,作为一个家庭主妇,一定要放松。你有一个优势——要想躺下随时都可以。而且你还可以躺在地上。奇怪的是,硬地板比里面装着弹簧的床更有助于放松。因为地板的抗力比较大,对脊椎有好处。

下面就是一些你可以在家里做的运动。先试一个星期,看看对你的外表有何好处:

第一,只要你觉得疲倦了,就平躺在地板上。尽量伸展身体,如果想打滚就打滚。每大做两次。

第二,闭上双眼。像琼森教授建议的那样对自己说:“太阳当头照,天空蓝得发亮。大自然一片寂静,控制着全世界——而我是大自然之子,和宇宙协调一致。”或者也可以祈祷!

第三,如果你因为正在炉子上煮菜而没有时间躺下来,那么坐在椅子上效果也相同。硬直背椅子里最适合放松。像古埃及坐像那样,双手掌向下平放在大腿上。

第四,现在,慢慢蜷缩十个脚趾头——然后放松。收紧腿部肌肉——然后放松。慢慢地朝上运动各部分肌肉,最后直到颈部。然后让你的头向四周转动,就像足球一样。不断地对你的肌肉

(as in the previous chapter): "Let go... let go..."

e. Quiet your nerves with slow, steady breathing. Breathe from deep down. The yoga of India were right: rhythmical breathing is one of the best methods ever discovered for soothing the nerves.

f. Think of the wrinkles and frowns in your face, and smooth them all out. Loosen up the worry-creases you feel between your brows, and at the sides of your mouth. Do this twice a day, and maybe you won't have to go to a beauty parlour to get a massage. Maybe the lines will disappear from the inside out!

说:"放松……放松……"

第五,用缓慢而平稳的呼吸来安抚你的神经。从丹田吸气。印度的瑜伽功就很不错:有规律的呼吸是安抚神经的最好方法之一。

第六,想想你脸上的皱纹,尽量抚平它们;松开皱紧的眉头,微微张开嘴巴。这样每天做两次,你也许不必再去美容院做按摩,而这些皱纹就会从此消失。

4 Four Good Working Habits That Will Help Prevent Fatigue and Worry

Good Working Habit No. 1: *Clear Your Desk of All Papers Except Those Relating to the Immediate Problem at Hand.*

Roland L. Williams, President of Chicago and North–western Railway, says: "A person with his desk piled high with papers on various matters will find his work much easier and more accurate if he clears that desk of all but the immediate problem on hand. I call this good housekeeping, and it is the number one step towards efficiency."

If you visit the Library of Congress in Washington, D. C. , you will find five words painted on the ceiling—five words written by the poet Pope:

"Order is Heaven's first law."

Order ought to be the first law of business, too. But is it? No, the average business man's desk is cluttered up with papers that he hasn't looked at for weeks. In fact, the publisher of a New Orleans newspaper once told me that his secretary cleared up one of his desks and found a typewriter that had been missing for two years!

The mere sight of a desk littered with unanswered mail and reports and memos is enough to breed confusion, tension, and worries. It is much worse than that. The constant reminder of "a million things to do and no time to do them" can worry you not only into tension and fatigue, but it can also worry you into high blood pressure, heart trouble, and stomach ulcers.

Dr. John H. Stokes, professor, Graduate School of Medicine, University of Pennsylvania, read a paper before the National Convention of the American Medical Association—a paper entitled "*Functional Neuroses as Complications of Organic Disease*". In that paper, Dr. Stokes listed eleven conditions under the title: "What to Look for in the Patient's State of Mind." Here is the first item on that list: "The sense of must or obligation; the unending stretch of things ahead that simply have to be done."

But how can such an elementary procedure as clearing your desk and making decisions help

第4章 防止疲劳和忧虑的良好工作习惯

第一种良好的工作习惯:将你桌上所有的文件收拾好,只留下正要处理的问题。

芝加哥西北铁路公司董事长罗南·威廉姆斯说:"一个桌上堆满了很多文件的人,如果能把他的桌子清理一下,只留下正要处理的事情,就会发现他的工作更容易,也更有效。我称之为料理家务,这是提高工作效率的第一步。"

如果你参观华盛顿国立图书馆,就会看到天花板上的几个字,这是诗人波浦的话:"秩序是天国的第一法则。"

讲究秩序也应该是做生意的首要法则。但在现实中是否如此呢?不,普通生意人的桌上堆满了几个星期都不会看的文件。新奥尔良一家报纸的老板曾告诉我,他的秘书帮他清理了一张桌子,找到了一部两年来一直没有找到的打字机。

仅仅看到桌上堆满了还没有回的信、报告和备忘录,就足以使人心烦意乱,紧张忧虑。更糟的是,经常想到"有上百万件事情需要去做,可是没有时间去做",不但会使你忧虑和疲倦,还会使你因为忧虑而患高血压、心脏病和胃溃疡。

宾夕法尼亚大学医学院教授约翰·史托克博士曾在美国医学会全国大会上宣读过一篇论文《生理疾病导致的功能性精神并发症》。在这篇论文里,史托克博士在"如何分析病人的心理"中列出了11种病例,下面就是第一种:"一种必要或强迫的感觉,好像必须要做却永远都做不完的事情。"

清理桌子、做各种决定,这些最基本的事情怎么能帮你避免心理重压、"必须做却永远也做不完"的感觉呢?著名精神病专家威廉·桑德尔博士就采用这种简单的办法,使一个病人避免了

you avoid this high pressure, this sense of *must*, this sense of an "unending stretch of things ahead that simply have to be done"? Dr. William L. Sadler, the famous psychiatrist, tells of a patient who, by using this simple device, avoided a nervous breakdown. The man was an executive in a big Chicago firm. When he came to Dr. Sadler's office, he was tense, nervous, worried. He knew he was heading for a tailspin, but he couldn't quit work. He had to have help.

"While this man was telling me his story, "Dr. Sadler says, "my telephone rang. It was the hospital calling; and, instead of deferring the matter, I took time right then to come to a decision. I always settle questions, if possible, right on the spot. I had no sooner hung up than the phone rang again. Again an urgent matter, which I took time to discuss. The third interruption came when a colleague of mine came to my office for advice on a patient who was critically ill. When I had finished with him, I turned to my caller and began to apologise for keeping him waiting. But he had brightened up. He had a completely different look on his face."

"Don't apologise, doctor! "this man said to Sadler. "In the last ten minutes, I think I've got a hunch as to what is wrong with me. I'm going back to my office and revise my working habits... But before I go, do you mind if I take a look in your desk? "

Dr. Sadler opened up the drawers of his desk. All empty—except for supplies. "Tell me, "said the patient, "where do you keep your unfinished business? "

"Finished! "said Sadler.

"And where do you keep your unanswered mail? "

"Answered! "Sadler told him. "My rule is never to lay down a letter until I have answered it. I dictate the reply to my secretary at once."

Six weeks later, this same executive invited Dr. Sadler to come to his office. He was changed—and so was his desk. He opened the desk drawers to show there was no unfinished business inside of the desk. "Six weeks ago, "this executive said, "I had three different desks' in two different offices—and was snowed under by my work. I was never finished. After talking to you, I came back here and cleared out a wagon-load of reports and old papers. Now I work at one desk, settle things as they come up, and don't have a mountain of unfinished business nagging at me and making me tense and worried. But the most astonishing thing is I've recovered completely. There is nothing

精神崩溃。这个病人是芝加哥一家大公司的总经理,他刚去桑德尔博士的诊所时,紧张不安,而且很忧虑。他知道他可能会精神崩溃,但是他不能辞去工作。他需要帮助。

"当这个人正把他的问题告诉我时,"桑德尔博士说,"我的电话响了,是医院打来的。我没有拖延问题,当场作了回答。我总是尽可能立即解决问题。我刚挂上电话,电话又响了。这次是一件很紧迫的事情,我花了一点时间和对方讨论。第三次中断则是我的一个同事,他为了一个重症患者而来我办公室征求我的意见。我和他讨论完了之后,转过身来正想向来访者道歉让他久等了,可是他由阴转晴,显得非常开心。"

"不必道歉了,大夫!"这个人对桑德尔说,"在刚才的那 10 分钟里,我想我已经知道我的问题了。现在我要回办公室,改掉我的工作习惯……可是,在我走之前能不能让我看看你的桌子?"

桑德尔博士打开他办公桌的几个抽屉,里面全都是空的,只放了一些文具。"请告诉我,"那人说,"你没有办完的事情在哪里?"

"都做完了。"桑德尔说。

"那你还没有回的信放在哪里呢?"

"都回了!"山德尔告诉他。"我的原则是,信不回复绝不放下。我一般都是马上向秘书口述回信。"

6 个星期之后,那位总经理把桑德尔博士请到他办公室。他完全变了,他的办公桌也不同以往了。他打开办公桌的抽屉,里面不再有还未完成的工作。"6 个星期以前,"他说,"我在两个办公室有三张写字台,整个人都埋在工作里,事情永远也做不完。那次和你谈过以后,我回到办公室,清理出了一大车的报表和旧文件。现在我只需要一张桌子,事情一出现就立即处理。这样就不再有堆积如山的工作等我去做,让我紧张和忧虑。可是,最让我震惊的是,我完全恢复了健

wrong any more with my health! ”

Charles Evans Hughes, former Chief Justice of the United States Supreme Court, said: “Men do not die from overwork. They die from dissipation and worry.” Yes, from dissipation of their energies—and worry because they never seem to get their work done.

Good Working Habit No. 2: *Do Things in the Order of Their Importance.*

Henry L. Dougherty, founder of the nation-wide Cities Service Company, said that regardless of how much salary he paid, there were two abilities he found it almost impossible to find.

Those two priceless abilities are: first, the ability to think. Second, the ability to do things in the order of their importance.

Charles Luckman, the lad who started from scratch and climbed in twelve years to president of the Pepsodent Company, got a salary of a hundred thousand dollars a year, and made a million dollars besides—that lad declares that he owes much of his success to developing the two abilities that Henry L. Dougherty said he found almost impossible to find. Charles Luckman said: “As far back as I can remember, I have got up at five o'clock in the morning because I can think better then than any other time—I can think better then and plan my day, plan to do things in the order of their importance.”

Frank Bettger, one of America's most successful insurance salesmen, doesn't wait until five o'clock in the morning to plan his day. He plans it the night before—sets a goal for himself—a goal to sell a certain mount of insurance that day. If he fails, that amount is added to the next day—and so on.

I know from long experience that one is not always able to do things in the order of their importance, but I also know that some kind of plan to do first things first is infinitely better than extemporising as you go along.

If George Bernard Shaw had not made it a rigid rule to do first things first, he would probably have failed as a writer and might have remained a bank cashier all his life. His plan called for writing five pages each day. That plan and his dogged determination to carry it through saved him. That plan inspired him to go right on writing five pages a day for nine heartbreaking years, even though he made a total of only thirty dollars in those nine years—about a penny a day.

康,我现在一点病都没有了。”

美国前最高法院大法官查尔斯·伊文斯·休斯说:“人不会死于工作过度，而会死于精力耗费和忧虑。”不错,会死于精力耗费和忧虑,因为他们的工作似乎永远都做不完。

第二种良好的工作习惯:根据事情的重要程度来安排先后。

分公司遍及全美的市务公司的创始人亨利·杜哈提说,不论他出多少钱,都找不到具备两种能力的人。

这两种宝贵能力是:第一,思想能力;第二,按事情的重要程度来安排先后顺序的能力。

查尔斯·卢克曼在12年之内从一个默默无闻的人一跃而成为培素登公司的董事长，年薪10万美元,另外还能赚100万美金。他说这都归功于自己培养了亨利·杜哈提所说的几乎不可能找到的两种能力。查尔斯·卢克曼说:“就我记忆所及,我每天早上都是5点钟起床,因为我那时候比其他时间思考都更清晰。那时我可以考虑周到,计划一天的工作,按事情的重要程度来做事。”

弗兰克·贝特格是美国最成功的保险推销员之一,他不会每天早上5点钟才计划当天的工作,而是在头天晚上就计划好了——给自己订下目标,那天要卖出多少保险。要是没有做到,就将差额加到第二天……依此类推。

通过长期经验,我知道一个人不可能总是按事情的重要程度来做事;但我也知道,按计划做事绝对比随兴趣做事好得多。

如果萧伯纳不严格遵守先做重要事情的原则,他也许不可能成为作家,一辈子只能做一个银行出纳员。他计划每天写5页。这一计划及坚定的决心救了他。他坚持了9年。虽然他在这9年里只存了30美元——每天大约10美分。

第三种良好的工作习惯:当你遇到必须当场做决定的问题时,当场解决,不要拖延。

Good Working Habit No. 3. *When You Face a Problem, Solve It Then and There if You Have the Facts Necessary to Make a Decision. Don't Keep Putting off Decisions.*

One of my former students, the late H. P. Howell, told me that when he was a member of the board of directors of U. S. Steel, the meetings of the board were often long-drawn-out affairs—many problems were discussed, few decisions were made. The result: each member of the board had to carry home bundles of reports to study.

Finally, Mr. Howell persuaded the board of directors to take up one problem at a time and come to a decision. No procrastination—no putting off. The decision might be to ask for additional facts; it might be to do something or do nothing. But a decision was reached on each problem before passing on to the next. Mr. Howell told me that the results were striking and salutary: the docket was cleared. The calendar was clean. No longer was it necessary for each member to carry home a bundle of reports. No longer was there a worried sense of unresolved problems.

A good rule, not only for the board of directors of U. S. Steel, but for you and me.

Good Working Habit No. 4: *Learn to Organise, Deputize, and Supervise.*

Many a business man is driving himself to a premature grave because he has never learned to delegate responsibility to others, insists on doing everything himself. Result: details and confusion overwhelm him. He is driven by a sense of hurry, worry, anxiety, and tension. It is hard to learn to delegate responsibilities. I know. It was hard for me, awfully hard. I also know from experience the disasters that can be caused by delegating authority to the wrong people. But difficult as it is to delegate authority, the executive must do it if he is to avoid worry, tension, and fatigue.

The man who builds up a big business, and doesn't learn to organize, deputize, and supervise, usually pops off with heart trouble in his fifties or early sixties—heart trouble caused by tension and worries. Want a specific instance? Look at the death notices in your local paper.

我以前的一个学员、已故的霍威尔先生告诉我，在他担任美国钢铁公司董事的时候，开董事会总要花很长时间，讨论很多问题，但是达成的决议却很少。结果董事会的每一人都得带一大堆报表回家去看。

最后，霍威尔先生说服董事会，每次开会只讨论一个问题并做出决定，绝不拖延。这样做也许需要看更多的资料，也许会取得成效，也许没有；但无论如何，在讨论下一个问题之前，这个问题一定能够达成某种决议。霍威尔先生告诉我，这样做的结果令人惊讶，也很有效：所有的陈年老账都清理了，工作日历干干净净，董事们再也不必带一大堆报表回家，再也不会为没有解决的问题而忧虑。

这个办法很好，不仅适合美国钢铁公司董事会，也适合你我。

第四种良好的工作习惯：学会组织、授权和监督。

很多商人替自己挖下了一个坟墓，因为他不懂得把责任分给他人，而是事必躬亲，其结果是被琐事包围。他总觉得匆忙、忧虑、焦急和紧张。要学会授权很难。我以前就觉得这个很难——非常难。我也从经验中知道，如果授权不当，将会产生灾难。可是授权虽难，但上司要想避免忧虑、紧张和疲劳，却非得这样做不可。

创建了大企业却不懂得组织、授权和监督的人，通常会在五六十岁死于心脏病——由紧张忧虑导致的心脏病。想要具体例子吗？只看看地方报纸就知道了。

5 How to Banish the Boredom That Produces Fatigue, Worry, and Resentment

One of the chief causes of fatigue is boredom. To illustrate, let's take the case of Alice, a stenographer who lives on your street. Alice came home one night utterly exhausted. She *acted* fatigued. She *was* fatigued. She had a headache. She had a backache. She was so exhausted she wanted to go to bed without waiting for dinner. Her mother pleaded... She sat down at the table. The telephone rang. The boy friend! An invitation to a dance! Her eyes sparkled. Her spirits soared. She rushed upstairs, put on her Alice-blue gown, and danced until three o'clock in the morning; and when she finally did get home, she was not the slightest bit exhausted. She was, in fact, so exhilarated she couldn't fall asleep.

Was Alice really and honestly tired eight hours earlier, when she looked and acted exhausted? Sure she was. She was exhausted because she was bored with her work, perhaps bored with life. There are millions of Alices. You may be one of them.

It is a well-known fact that your emotional attitude usually has far more to do with producing fatigue than has physical exertion. A few years ago, Joseph E. Barmack, Ph. D. , published in the *Archives of Psychology* a report of some of his experiments showing how boredom produces fatigue. Dr. Barmack put a group of students through a series of tests in which, he knew, they could have little interest. The result? The students felt tired and sleepy, complained of headaches and eyestrain, felt irritable. In some cases, even their stomachs were upset. Was it all "imagination"? No. Metabolism tests were taken of these students. These tests showed that the blood pressure of the body and the consumption of oxygen actually decrease when a person is bored, and that the whole metabolism picks up immediately as soon as he begins to feel interest and pleasure in his work!

We rarely get tired when we are doing something interesting and exciting. For example, I recently took a vacation in the Canadian Rockies up around Lake Louise. I spent several days trout fishing along Corral Creek, fighting my way through brush higher than my head, stumbling over

第5章 如何消除烦闷

产生疲劳的主要原因之一就是烦闷。就以住在你附近的速记员艾莉丝为例吧。一天晚上，艾莉丝筋疲力尽地回到家里，头痛，背痛，困得连饭都不想吃就要上床睡觉。她母亲再三恳求，她才坐在饭桌边。这时，电话铃响了，是她男朋友，请她去跳舞。她的眼睛立刻亮了，精神焕发。她飞快地冲上楼，穿上那件天蓝色的洋装，一直跳到凌晨三点钟。当她终于回到家时，却一点也不觉得疲倦，事实上她还兴奋得睡不着觉呢!

8小时以前，也就是艾莉丝的外表和动作看上去精疲力竭的时候，她是否真的那么疲劳呢?不错，她那时之所以疲劳，是因为她厌烦工作，甚至厌倦生活。我们这个世界上有无数艾莉丝这样的人，你也许就是其中之一。

情绪心理比体力劳动更容易让人产生疲劳，这是人尽皆知的事实。几年前，约瑟夫·巴马克博士在《心理学学报》上发表了一篇论文，谈到他的一些实验证明了烦闷会产生疲劳。巴马克博士让一群学生做了一连串实验，而他知道这些实验都是他们不感兴趣的。实验结果呢?所有的学生都觉得疲倦欲睡，头痛，眼睛容易疲劳，容易发脾气，还有几个人甚至觉得胃不舒服。所有这些是"幻觉"吗?不是，这些学生都做过新陈代谢实验，结果显示当一个人烦闷时，体内血压和氧化作用实际上会降低；而一旦他觉得工作有趣时，整个新陈代谢会立刻加速。

当我们做感兴趣而且令人兴奋的事情时很少会疲倦。例如，我最近在加拿大落基山的路易斯湖畔度假，在克莱尔小溪边钓了好几天鲑鱼。为此要穿过比我还高的树丛，爬过横躺在地的原木，爬过倒在地上的木头。可是即使这样辛苦了8小时，我一点都不疲倦。为什么呢?因为我非常兴奋，而且觉得很有成绩：钓到了6条鲑鱼。可是如果我讨厌钓鱼的话，那么你想我会有何

logs, struggling through fallen timber—yet after eight hours of this, I was not exhausted. Why? Because I was excited, exhilarated. I had a sense of high achievement: six cut-throat trout. But suppose I had been bored by fishing, then how do you think I would have felt? I would have been worn out by such strenuous work at an altitude of seven thousand feet.

Even in such exhausting activities as mountain climbing, boredom may tire you far more than the strenuous work involved. For example, Mr. S. H. Kingman, president of the Farmers and Mechanics Savings Bank of Minneapolis, told me of an incident that is a perfect illustration of that statement. In July, 1953, the Canadian government asked the Canadian Alpine Club to furnish guides to train the members of the Prince of Wales Rangers in mountain climbing. Mr. Kingman was one of the guides chosen to train these soldiers. He told me how he and the other guides—men ranging from forty-two to fifty-nine years of age—took these young army men on long hikes across glaciers and snow fields and up a sheer cliff of forty feet, where they had to climb with ropes and tiny foot-holds and precarious hand-holds. They climbed Michaers Peak, the Vice-President Peak, and other unnamed peaks in the Little Yoho Valley in the Canadian Rockies. After fifteen hours of mountain climbing, these young men, who were in the pink of condition (they had just finished a six-week course in tough Commando training), were utterly exhausted.

Was their fatigue caused by using muscles that had not been hardened by Commando training? Any man who had ever been through Commando training would hoot at such a ridiculous question! No, they were utterly exhausted because they were bored by mountain climbing. They were so tarred, that many of them fell asleep without waiting to eat. But the guides—men who were two and three times as old as the soldiers—were they tired? Yes, but not exhausted. The guides ate dinner and stayed up for hours, talking about the day's experiences. They were not exhausted because they were interested.

When Dr. Edward Thorndike of Columbia was conducting experiments in fatigue, he kept young men awake for almost a week by keeping them constantly interested. After much investigation, Dr. Thorndike is reported to have said: "Boredom is the only real cause of diminution of work."

If you are a mental worker, it is seldom the amount of work you do that makes you tired. You

感受呢?我一定会因为在海拔7000英尺高的山上奔波而累垮的。

即使像登山这类消耗体力的活动,可能也不如烦闷那样容易使你疲劳。明尼阿波利斯市农工储蓄银行总裁金曼先生曾告诉我一件事,正好可以说明这一事实:1953年7月,加拿大政府要求加拿大阿尔卑斯登山俱乐部协助威尔斯军团做登山训练。金曼先生当时被选为训练士兵的教练之一。他告诉我,他和其他年龄从42岁到59岁不等的教练带着那些年轻的士兵,长途跋涉经过冰河和雪地,再借用绳索和一些小型登山设备爬上40英尺高的悬崖。他们在加拿大落基山的小月河山谷中爬上了米高峰、副总统峰以及其他许多没有名字的山峰。经过15个小时的登山,那些非常健壮的年轻人全都累垮了——他们刚完成6周的强化突击训练。

他们的疲劳,是因为军事训练时肌肉没有锻炼结实吗?任何一个受过严格军事训练的人都会对这种荒谬的观点嗤之以鼻。他们之所以筋疲力尽,是因为他们厌烦登山。他们太累了,很多人来不及吃饭就睡着了。可是那些年龄比他们要大两三倍的教练是否疲倦呢?不错,可是他们不会筋疲力尽。那教练们吃过晚饭后,还坐了几个小时,谈论这一天的事情。他们之所以没有筋疲力尽,是因为他们喜欢登山。

哥伦比亚大学的爱德华·桑戴克博士在主持疲劳实验时,通过让那些年轻人持续感兴趣的方法,使他们维持清醒长达一星期。经过多次调查,桑戴克博士表示:"工作能量降低的唯一真正原因就是烦闷。"

如果你是一个脑力劳动者,使你感觉疲劳的原因很少是因为工作超量,相反是由于工作量不足。例如,还记不记得上星期那天,你不断地被人打扰,一封信也没有回,约好的事情一件也没有做,到处都是麻烦,所有的事情都不对头,你什么也没做成,可是回到家时却筋疲力尽,而且头痛欲裂。第二天,工作一切顺利。你完成的工作是头一天的40倍,可是回到家却神采奕奕。你一定有过这种经历。我也有过。

may be tired by the amount of work you do not do. For example, remember the day last week when you were constantly interrupted. No letters answered. Appointments broken. Trouble here and there. Everything went wrong that day. You accomplished nothing whatever, yet you went home exhausted—and with a splitting head.

The next day everything clicked at the office. You accomplished forty times more than you did the previous day. Yet you went home fresh as a snowy-white gardenia. You have had that experience. So have I.

The lesson to be learned? Just this: our fatigue is often caused not by work, but by worry, frustration, and resentment.

While writing this chapter, I went to see a revival of Jerome Kern's delightful musical comedy, *Show Boat*. Captain Andy, captain of the *Cotton Blossom*, says, in one of his philosophical interludes: "The lucky folks are the ones that get to do the things they enjoy doing." Such folks are lucky because they have more energy, more happiness, less worry, and less fatigue. Where your interests are, there is your energy also. Walking ten blocks with a nagging wife can be more fatiguing than walking ten miles with an adoring sweetheart.

And so what? What can you do about it? Well, here is what one stenographer did about it—a stenographer working for an oil company in Tulsa, Oklahoma. For several days each month, she had one of the dullest jobs imaginable: filling out printed forms for oil leases, inserting figures and statistics. This task was so boring that she resolved, in self-defence, to make it interesting. How? She had a daily contest with herself. She counted the number of forms she filled out each morning, and then tried to excel that record in the afternoon. She counted each day's total and tried to better it the next day. Result? She was soon able to fill out more of these dull printed forms than any other stenographer in her division. And what did all this get her? Praise? No... Thanks? No... Promotion? No... Increased pay? No... But it did help to prevent the fatigue that is spawned by boredom. It did give her a mental stimulant. Because she had done her best to make a dull job interesting, she had more energy, more zest, and got far more happiness out of her leisure hours. I happen to know this story is true, because I married that girl.

Here is the story of another stenographer who found it paid to act *as if* her work were

我们从中可以学到什么呢?那就是:我们的疲劳通常不是由工作,而是由忧虑、紧张和不快引起的。

在写这一章的时候,我看了重演的杰罗米·凯恩的音乐喜剧《表演船》。剧中的主角安迪船长在一段颇有哲理的话里说:"能做他们喜欢做的事情的人,是最幸运的人。"这种人之所以幸运,是因为他们更有精力,更快乐,而忧虑和疲劳更少。你兴趣所在的地方,也就是你能力所在的地方。陪着一路唠叨不休的太太穿街过巷,一定比陪着心爱的情人走10里路感觉更疲劳。

怎么办?你该采取什么办法呢?下面是俄克拉荷马州托沙城一家石油公司一位速记员的做法。她每个月总有几天要填写一份已经印好的有关石油销售的报表。这是一件最枯燥的工作。为了提高工作情绪,她决定把它变成一件非常有趣的工作。她是怎么做的呢?她每天和自己竞赛,在每天早上点出当天要填的报表数量,然后努力在下午超出纪录;然后再点出当天完成的总数,第二天再努力超出前一天的纪录。结果呢?她比那个部门其他速记员都快得多,很快就把许多很没意思的报表填完了。这样做对她有什么好处吗?赞美?没有……感激?也没有……升迁?也没有……加薪?当然也没有……可是这样做却有助于她防止因烦闷而产生的疲劳,使她能保持很高的兴致。因为她尽了最大的努力,把一件没有意思的工作变得有意思,这样她就有了更多的体力和热情,休息时可以获得更多快乐。我之所以知道这个故事是真的,因为我就娶了这个女孩。

下面是另外一位速记员的故事。她发现假装工作很有意思,会有意想不到的回报。她以前很讨厌她的工作,可是现在变了。她叫维莉·哥顿,住在伊利诺伊州埃默斯特市南凯尼沃斯大道473号。下面就是她在信中告诉我的故事:

"我办公室有4位速记员,每个人都要负责替几个人打印信件,每过一段时间我们就会因为工作太多而忙不过来。有一天,有一个部门的副经理坚持让我把一封长信重打一遍,我非常

interesting. She used to fight her work. But no more. Her name is Miss Vallie G. Golden, and she lives at 473 South Kenilworth Avenue, Elmhurst, Illinois. Here is her story, as she wrote it to me:

"There are four stenographers in my office and each of us is assigned to take letters from several men. Once in a while we get jammed up in these assignments; and one day, when an assistant department head insisted that I do a long letter over, I started to rebel. I tried to point out to him that the letter could be corrected without being retyped—and he retorted that if I didn't do it over, he would find someone else who would! I was absolutely fuming! But as I started to retype this letter, it suddenly occurred to me that there were a lot of other people who would jump at the chance to do the work I was doing. Also, that I was being paid a salary to do just that work. I began to feel better. I suddenly made up my mind to do my work as if I actually enjoyed it—even though I despised it. Then I made this important discovery: if I do my work *as if* I really enjoy it, then I do enjoy it to some extent. I also found I can work faster when I enjoy my work. So there is seldom any need now for me to work overtime. This new attitude of mine gained me the reputation of being a good worker. And when one of the department superintendents needed a private secretary, he asked for me for the job—because, he said, I was willing to do extra work without being sulky! This matter of the power of a changed mental attitude, "wrote Miss Golden, "has been a tremendously important discovery to me. It has worked wonders! "

Without perhaps being conscious of it. Miss Vallie Golden was using the famous "*as if*" philosophy. William James counseled us to act "*as if*" we were brave, and we would be brave; and to act "*as if*" we were happy, and we would be happy, and so on.

Act "*as if*" you were interested in your job, and that bit of acting will tend to make your interest real. It will also tend to decrease your fatigue, your tensions, and your worries.

A few years ago, Harlan A. Howard made a decision that completely altered his life. He resolved to make a dull job interesting—and he certainly had a dull one: washing plates, scrubbing counters, and dishing out ice-cream in the high-school lunch-room while the other boys were playing ball or kidding the girls. Harlan Howard despised his job—but since he had to stick to it, he resolved to study ice-cream—how it was made, what ingredients were used, why some ice-creams were better than others. He studied the chemistry of ice-cream, and became a whiz in the

恼火。我告诉他，这封信只要改一改就可以，不必重打。而他却说，如果我不想干，他就找愿意做的人！我气得不得了！可是当我开始重新打印这封信时，我突然发现其实有很多人都会跳起来抓住这个机会，做我现在正在做的事。而且，人家付我薪水也是要我做这份工作。我感觉好多了。我突然决定，尽管我不喜欢这份工作，但我要假装喜欢它的样子去做。接着，我有了一个重大发现：如果我假装很喜欢我的工作，那我就真的能喜欢到某种程度；我还发现，当我开始喜欢我的工作时，我工作的速度快了许多。所以，我现在很少加班了。这种工作态度使大家都认为我是一个好职员。后来，有一个单位主管需要一位私人秘书，他就让我担任那个职务——因为他认为我很愿意做额外的工作而从不抱怨。转变心态能产生巨大的力量。"哥顿小姐写道，"对我来说这是非常重要的发现。它创造了奇迹。"

哥顿小姐无意中用了著名的"假装"哲学。威廉·詹姆斯建议我们"假装"勇敢，我们就会勇敢；"假装"快乐，我们就会快乐；等等。

如果你"假装"对你的工作感兴趣，这一点点努力就会使你的兴趣变成真的，它会减少你的疲劳和紧张，以及你的忧虑。

许多年前，哈南·霍华德做了一个决定，这个决定完全改变了他的生活，把一个乏味的工作变得富有趣味。他那份工作的确很乏味，就是在高中的食堂洗盘子、擦柜台、装冰淇淋，而其他男孩子则在打球，或与女孩子约会。哈南·霍华德很不喜欢他的工作，可是他必须干下去，于是他决定研究冰淇淋是怎么做成的，里面有什么成分，为什么有些冰淇淋比别的好吃。他研究了冰淇淋的化学成分，结果成为学校化学课的奇才。他还对食物化学产生了极大兴趣，于是进了马萨诸塞州立大学，专门研究食物营养学。后来纽约的可可公司设立了 100 美元奖金，奖励关于可可和巧克力应用的最佳论文。你猜谁得了头奖?不错，哈南·霍华德。

后来他发现工作很难找，就在自己家里的地下室开了一间私人实验室。不久，一项新法案

high-school chemistry course. He was so interested now in food chemistry that he entered the Massachusetts State College and majored in the field of "food technology". When the New York Cocoa Exchange offered a hundred-dollar prize for the best paper on uses of cocoa and chocolate—a prize open to all college students—who do you suppose won it? ... That's right. Harlan Howard.

When he found it difficult to get a job, he opened a private laboratory in the basement of his home at 750 North Pleasant Street, Amherst, Massachusetts. Shortly after that, a new law was passed. The bacteria in milk had to be counted. Harlan A. Howard was soon counting bacteria for the fourteen milk companies in Amherst—and he had to hire two assistants.

Where will he be twenty-five years from now? Well, the men who are now running the business of food chemistry will be retired then, or dead; and their places will be taken by young lads who are now radiating initiative and enthusiasm. Twenty-five years from now, Harlan A. Howard will probably be one of the leaders in his profession, while some of his classmates to whom he used to sell ice-cream over the counter will be sour, unemployed, cursing the government, and complaining that they never had a chance. Harlan A. Howard might never have had a chance, either, if he hadn't resolved to make a dull job interesting.

Years ago, there was another young man who was bored with his dull job of standing at a lathe, turning out bolts in a factory. His first name was Sam. Sam wanted to quit, but he was afraid he couldn't find another job. Since he had to do this dull work, Sam decided he would make it interesting. So he ran a race with the mechanic operating a machine beside him. One of them was to trim off the rough surfaces on his machine, and the other was to trim the bolts down to the proper diameter. They would switch machines occasionally and see who could turn out the most bolts. The foreman, impressed with Sam's speed and accuracy, soon gave him a better job. That was the start of a whole series of promotions. Thirty years later, Sam—Samuel Vauclain—was president of the Baldwin Locomotive Works. But he might have remained a mechanic all his life if he had not resolved to make a dull job interesting.

H. V. Kaltenborn—the famous radio news analyst—once told me how he made a dull job interesting. When he was twenty-two years old, he worked his way across the Atlantic on a cattle

通过:牛奶里面所含的细菌必须计数。于是哈南·霍华德开始为安荷斯特城 14 家牛奶公司数细菌——而且还必须再雇两名助手。

25 年之后,他在哪里呢?是的,这几位现在还从事品化学生意的先生,到那时候或者会退休,或者已经过世,但他们的位置将会由许多刚开始学习并充满了热诚的年轻人来接替。25 年之后,哈南·霍华德很可能成为他这一行的领袖。而当年从他手里买冰淇淋的那些同学,可能穷困潦倒,甚至失业,只会责怪政府,抱怨他们没有机会。哈南·霍华德若不是当初决定将乏味的工作变得有意思,恐怕也不会有什么机会。

几年前,另一个年轻人厌倦了整天站在车床旁边做螺丝的工作。他的名字叫山姆。他想辞职,但是又担心找不到别的工作。既然他必须做这件乏味的工作,他决定把它变得有意思。于是,他开始和旁边另一个管机器的工人比赛,由其中一个先在自己的机器上做出粗坯,再交给另一个把它磨成要求的直径。有时他们也互换机器,看谁做出来的螺丝多。领班对山姆的工作速度和准确度非常欣赏,不久将他调到一个更好的职位,而这只是一连串升迁的开头。30 年后,山姆——塞缪尔·瓦克莱恩——成了包尔温火车头制造公司的董事长。要是他没有想到将乏味的工作变得有意思的话,也许他一辈子只是一名工人。

著名的无线电新闻分析家卡腾堡曾告诉我,他是如何将一件毫无意思的工作变得有趣的。22 岁那年,卡腾堡在一艘横渡大西洋的牲口运输轮船上工作,给牲口喂水喂食。后来他骑脚踏车周游了英国,接着到了巴黎,身无分文,又没有饭吃,就把他的照相机当了 5 美元,在巴黎版的《纽约先驱报》上登了一个求职广告,找到了一份推销立体观测镜的工作。如果你 40 多岁,可能还记得那种老式立体观测镜,我们经常放在眼前看两张完全相同的照片,这时会产生奇迹:观测镜的两个镜头会把两张照片叠合成一张立体照片,可以看出前后的距离,并产生非常真实的立体感。

boat, feeding and watering the steers. After making a bicycle tour of England, he arrived in Paris, hungry and broke. Pawning his camera for five dollars, he put an ad in the Paris edition of *The New York Herald* and got a job selling steropticon machines. If you are forty years old, you may remember those old-fashioned stereoscopes that we used to hold up before our eyes to look at two pictures exactly alike. As we looked, a miracle happened. The two lenses in the stereoscope transformed the two pictures into a single scene with the effect of a third dimension. We saw distance. We got an astounding sense of perspective.

Well, as I was saying, Kaltenborn started out selling these machines from door to door in Paris—and he couldn't speak French. But he earned five thousand dollars in commissions the first year, and made himself one of the highest-paid salesmen in France that year. H. V. Kaltenborn told me that this experience did as much to develop within him the qualities that make for success as did any single year of study at Harvard. Confidence? He told me himself that after that experience, he felt he could have sold *The Congressional Record* to French housewives.

That experience gave him an intimate understanding of French life that later proved invaluable in interpreting, on the radio, European events.

How did he manage to become an expert salesman when he couldn't speak French? Well, he had his employer write out his sales talk in perfect French, and he memorized it. He would ring a door-bell, a housewife would answer, and Kaltenborn would begin repeating his memorized sales talk with an accent so terrible it was funny. He would show the housewife his pictures, and when she asked a question, he would shrug his shoulders and say: "An American... an American." He would then take off his hat and point to a copy of the sales talk in perfect French that he had pasted in the top of his hat. The housewife would laugh, he would laugh—and show her more pictures. When H. V. Kaltenborn told me about this, he confessed that the job had been far from easy. He told me that there was only one quality that pulled him through: his determination to make the job interesting. Every morning before he started out, he looked into the mirror and gave himself a pep talk: "*Kaltenborn, you have to do this if you want to eat. Since you have to do it—why not have a good time doing it? Why not imagine every time you ring a door-bell that you are an actor before the footlights and that there's an audience out there looking at you. After all, what*

卡腾堡刚开始在巴黎挨家挨户地推销这种观测镜时，连法语都不会说，可是他第一年就赚到5000美元，而且使他成为那一年法国收入最高的推销员。卡腾堡告诉我，这次经历对他的成功能力的提升而言，不逊于他在哈佛大学上一年学。自信心呢?他亲口告诉我，有了那次经历以后，他觉得自己可以把《美国国会纪录》推销给法国的家庭主妇们。

这次经历，使他对法国人的生活有了深刻的了解，这对他后来在广播中分析欧洲事件时特别有价值。

他既不懂法语，又怎么能成为推销专家呢?原来，他先请老板用纯正的法语把他该说的那些话写下来，然后他再背下来。当他按响门铃之后，就会有一个家庭主妇来开门，于是卡腾堡开始用滑稽的口音背那一套推销词。他会把那些照片拿给家庭主妇们看。要是对方提问题，他就会耸耸肩说："我是美国人……我是美国人！"然后把帽子脱下来，用手指着贴在他帽子里面的那张用纯正法文写成的推销词。家庭主妇一般会大笑起来，他也一起大笑，然后再让对方看更多的照片。当卡腾堡告诉我这些事情的时候，他承认这份工作实在太难了。他告诉我，他之所以能撑下来，完全是靠一点信念——决心使这份工作变得有意思。每天早上出门之前，他都要对着镜子对自己说："卡腾堡，如果你要吃饭，就必须干好这件事。既然你非做不可，为什么不做得痛快一点呢?为什么不在每次按响门铃的时候，假想自己是一个演员，正站在舞台上，有许多观众正在看着你呢？因为你现在做的事情，也像在舞台上演戏一样滑稽。所以为什么不投入巨大的热情和兴趣呢?"

卡腾堡告诉我，每天给自己打气很有用，这使他把以前既恨又怕的工作变成了喜欢做的事情，而且赚了很多钱。

我问卡腾堡先生是否可以给急于成功的美国年轻人一些忠告?他说："可以。每天早上和自己打一个赌。我们常常觉得需要做一些运动，好让我们从半睡半醒的状态中清醒过来；可是我

you are doing is just as funny as something on the stage. So why not put a lot of zest and enthusiasm into it'? "

Mr. Kaltenborn told me that these daily pep talks helped him transform a task that he had once hated and dreaded into an adventure that he liked and made highly profitable.

When I asked Mr. Kaltenborn if he had any advice to give to the young men of America who are eager to succeed, he said: "Yes, go to bet with yourself every morning. We talk a lot about the importance of physical exercise to wake us up out of the half-sleep in which so many of us walk around. But we need, even more, some spiritual and mental exercises every morning to stir us into action. Give yourself a pep talk every day."

Is giving yourself a pep talk every day silly, superficial, childish? No, on the contrary, it is the very essence of sound psychology. "Our life is what our thoughts make it." These words are just as true today as they were eighteen centuries ago when Marcus Aurelius first wrote them in his book of *Meditations*: "Our life is what our thoughts make it."

By talking to yourself every hour of the day, you can direct yourself to think thoughts of courage and happiness, thoughts of power and peace. By talking to yourself about the things you have to be grateful for, you can fill your mind with thoughts that soar and sing.

By thinking the right thoughts, you can make any job less distasteful. Your boss wants you to be interested in your job so that he will make more money. But let's forget about what the boss wants. Think only of what getting interested in your job will do for you. Remind yourself that it may double the amount of happiness you get out of life, for you spend about one half of your waking hours at your work, and if you don't find happiness in your work, you may never find it anywhere. Keep reminding yourself that getting interested in your job will take your mind off your worries, and, in the long run, will probably bring promotion and increased pay. Even if it doesn't do that, it will reduce fatigue to a minimum and help you enjoy your hours of leisure.

们更需要精神和思想上的运动，使我们每天早上真正行动起来。因此每天要给自己打打气。"

每天早上给自己打打气！是不是很傻、很孩子气？不是；恰好相反，这从心理学来说非常必要。"我们的生活是由我们的思想形成的，"这句话今天仍然像马可·奥勒留 1800 年前在他的《沉思录》中所写的一样真实："我们的生活是由我们的思想形成的。"

每天的每小时都对自己说一遍，你就可以指引自己去想勇敢而快乐的东西和强大而平和的东西。对自己谈一些值得感激的事情，你的脑子就会充满积极向上的思想。

只要你的想法正确，任何工作都会变得不那么讨厌。你的老板希望你对自己的工作感兴趣，那样他才能赚更多的钱；可是我们姑且不管老板需要什么，只需想想，如果你对自己的工作感兴趣的话，你会得到什么好处。常常提醒自己，这样可以使你得到加倍的快乐，因为你每天清醒的时间，有一半以上要花在工作上，如果你在工作中得不到快乐，那么你在别的地方也不可能找到。要不停地提醒自己，对自己的工作感兴趣能使你不再忧虑，最后可能给你带来升迁和加薪。即使没有这么好的结果，也可以使你的疲劳降到最低程度，使你充分享受闲暇时光。

6 How to Keep from Worrying about Insomnia

Do you worry when you can't sleep well? Then it may interest you to know that Samuel Untermyer—the famous international lawyer—never got a decent night's sleep in his life.

When Sam Untermyer went to college, he worried about two afflictions—asthma and insomnia. He couldn't seem to cure either, so he decided to do the next best thing—take advantage of his wakefulness. Instead of tossing and turning and worrying himself into a breakdown, he would get up and study. The result? He began ticking off honours in all of his classes, and became one of the prodigies of the College of the City of New York.

Even after he started to practice law, his insomnia continued. But Untermyer didn't worry. "Nature, "he said, "will take care of me." Nature did. In spite of the small amount of sleep he was getting, his health kept up and he was able to work as hard as any of the young lawyers of the New York Bar. He even worked harder, for he worked while they slept!

At the age of twenty-one, Sam Untermyer was earning seventy-five thousand dollars a year; and other young attorneys rushed to courtrooms to study his methods. In 1931, he was paid—for handling one case—what was probably the highest lawyer's fee in all history: a cool million dollars—cash on the barrelhead.

Still he had insomnia—read half the night—and then got up at five A. M. and started dictating letters. By the time most people were just starting work, his day's work would be almost half done. He lived to the age of eighty-one, this man who had rarely had a sound night's sleep; but if he had fretted and worded about his insomnia, he would probably have wrecked his life.

We spend a third of our lives sleeping—yet nobody knows what sleep really is. We know it is a habit and a state of rest in which nature knits up the raveled sleeve of care, but we don't know how many hours of sleep each individual requires. We don't even know if we *have to* sleep at all!

Fantastic? Well, during the First World War, Paul Kern, a Hungarian soldier, was shot through the frontal lobe of his brain. He recovered from the wound, but curiously enough, couldn't fall

第6章 不要为失眠而忧虑

如果你睡眠不好的话,会不会忧虑呢?那么你也许会乐意知道国际知名大律师撒姆尔·安特梅尔一辈子从来没有好好睡过一晚上。

撒姆尔·安特梅尔上大学的时候,一直担心两件事情——气喘病和失眠症。他这两种病似乎都难以治愈,于是他决定退而求其次——充分利用他的清醒时间。他不再在床上翻来覆去,不再让自己忧虑到精神崩溃的程度,而是起床读书。结果他每门功课都在班上名列前茅,成为纽约市立大学的一位奇才。

即使当了律师以后,他的失眠症仍未治好。然而安特梅尔没有丝毫忧虑。他说:“大自然会照顾我的。”事实果然如此。虽然他每天睡的时间很少,但他的健康却很好,而且能像纽约法律界所有的年轻律师一样工作,甚至超过其他人,因为别人睡觉的时候,他还在工作。

撒姆尔·安特梅尔 21 岁时, 年收入 7.5 万美元, 因此其他年轻律师都去法庭研究他的方法。1931 年, 他在一起诉讼案中得到的酬劳可能是有史以来律师所得酬劳最高——整整 100 万美元,而且全是现金。

可他还是失眠。他晚上一半的时间都在看书,然后早上 5 点钟起床,开始口述信件。当大多数人刚开始工作的时候,他一天的工作几乎干了一半。他一直活到 81 岁,却难得有一天晚上睡得很熟。如果他一直为失眠症忧虑的话,恐怕早就完了。

我们一生中有 1/3 的时间用于睡眠,可是却没有人知道睡眠到底是怎么一回事。我们只知道这是一种习惯,也是一种休息状态,可是我们并不知道每一个人需要几小时的睡眠,甚至不知道人是否非要睡觉。

asleep. No matter what the doctors did—and they tried all kinds of sedatives and narcotics, even hypnotism—Paul Kern couldn't be put to sleep or even made to feel drowsy.

The doctors said he wouldn't live long. But he fooled them. He got a job, and went on living in the best of health for years. He would lie down and close his eyes and rest, but he got no sleep whatever. His case was a medical mystery that upset many of our beliefs about sleep.

Some people require far more sleep than others. Toscanini needs only five hours a night, but Calvin Coolidge needed more than twice that much. Coolidge slept eleven hours out of every twenty-four. In other words, Toscanini has been sleeping away approximately one-fifth of his life, while Coolidge slept away almost half of his life.

Worrying about insomnia will hurt you far more than insomnia. For example, one of my students—Ira Sandner, of 173 Overpeck Avenue, Ridgefield Park, New Jersey—was driven nearly to suicide by chronic insomnia.

"I actually thought I was going insane, "Ira Sandner told me. "The trouble was, in the beginning, that I was too *sound* a sleeper. I wouldn't wake up when the alarm clock went off, and the result was that I was getting to work late in the morning. I worried about it—and, in fact, my boss warned me that I would *have to* get to work on time. I knew that if I kept on oversleeping, I would lose my job.

"I told my friends about it, and one of them suggested I concentrate hard on the alarm clock before I went to sleep. That started the insomnia! The tick-tick-tick of that blasted alarm clock became an obsession. It kept me awake, tossing, all night long! When morning came, I was almost ill. I was ill from fatigue and worry. This kept on for eight weeks. I can't put into words the tortures I suffered. I was convinced I was going insane. Sometimes I paced the floor for hours at a time, and I honestly considered jumping out of the window and ending the whole thing!

"At last I went to a doctor I had known all my life. He said: 'Ira, I can't help you. No one can help you, because you have brought this thing on yourself. Go to bed at night, and if you can't fall asleep, forget all about it. Just say to yourself: "I don't care a hang if I *don't* go to sleep. It's all right with me if I lie awake till morning." Keep your eyes closed and say: "As long as I just lie still and don't worry about it, I'll be getting rest, anyway." '

这奇怪吗?第一次世界大战期间,有一个名叫保罗·柯恩的匈牙利士兵,他的脑前叶被子弹打穿。伤好之后,出现了一件怪事——他再也睡不着了。不论医生用什么办法——他们用过各种镇静剂和麻醉药,甚至催眠术——保罗·柯恩就是睡不着,甚至不觉得困倦。

医生都认为他活不久了,可是他瞒过了所有人。他找到了一份工作,而且非常健康地活了好多年。有时候他会躺下来闭上眼睛休息,可是从未睡着过。他的病例还是医学史上的未解之谜,推翻了我们对睡眠的很多观点。

还有些人比别人睡的时间更长。托斯卡尼尼每天晚上只需要睡 5 个小时,但柯立芝总统却需要两倍的时间,一天睡 11 个小时。换一句话说,托斯卡尼尼的一生大概只睡了 1/5 的时间,而柯立芝却几乎睡掉了他人生的一半时间。

为失眠而忧虑对你的伤害要远远超过失眠本身。就拿我的一个学生、新泽西瑞奇菲尔德公园欧维佩克大道 173 号的伊拉·桑德勒来说吧,他就几乎因为严重的失眠症而自杀。

"我真的以为我会精神失常,"伊拉·桑德勒告诉我,"因为我最初是个睡得很沉的人,就连闹钟响了也不会醒,结果每天早上上班都会迟到。我非常忧虑。事实上,我的老板也警告我必须准时上班。我知道如果我再这样睡过头,就会丢了饭碗。

"我把这件事告诉了我的朋友。有一个人建议我,睡觉时要注意闹钟,结果导致了失眠。那个该死的闹钟的嘀嘀答答声缠着我不放,让我整晚都睡不着,在床上翻来覆去。到了早上,我几乎动弹不了,又疲劳又忧虑。这样持续了 8 个星期,我所受到的折磨难以言表。我深信自己会精神失常。有时候我会在房间走上好几个小时,甚至想从窗口跳下去,一了百了。

"最后,我去看一个我认识的医生。他说:'伊拉,我没有办法帮你,也没有人能帮你,因为这是你自己造成的。每天晚上上床后,如果睡不着,也别理它,只对你自己说:"我才不在乎睡得着睡不着呢,就算是醒着直到天亮也没有关系。"闭上你的眼睛对自己说:"只要我躺在这里不动,

"I did that, "says Sandner, "and in two weeks' time I was dropping off to sleep. In less than one month, I was sleeping eight hours, and my nerves were back to normal."

It wasn't insomnia that was killing Ira Sandner; it was his worry about it.

Dr. Nathaniel Kleitman, professor at the University of Chicago, has done more research work on sleep than has any other living man. He is the world's expert on sleep. He declares that he has never known anyone to die from insomnia. To be sure, a man might worry about insomnia until he lowered his vitality and was swept away by germs. But it was the worry that did the damage, not the insomnia itself.

Dr. Kleitman also says that the people who worry about insomnia usually sleep far more than they realize. The man who swears "I never slept a wink last night"may have slept for hours without knowing it. For example, one of the most profound thinkers of the nineteenth century, Herbert Spencer, was an old bachelor, lived in a boardinghouse, and bored everyone with his talk about his insomnia. He even put"stoppings"in his ears to keep out the noise and quiet his nerves. Sometimes he took opium to induce sleep. One night he and Professor Sayce of Oxford shared the same room at a hotel. The next morning Spencer declared he hadn't slept a wink all night. In reality, it was Professor Sayce who hadn't slept a wink. He had been kept awake all night by Spencer's snoring.

The first requisite for a good night's sleep is a feeling of security. We need to feel that some power greater than ourselves will take care of us until morning. Dr. Thomas Hyslop, of the Great West Riding Asylum, stressed that point in an address before the British Medical Association. He said: "One of the best sleep-producing agents which my years of practice have revealed to me is—*prayer*. I say this purely as a medical man. The exercise of prayer, in those who habitually exert it, must be regarded as the most adequate and normal of all the pacifiers of the mind and calmers of the nerves.

"Let God—and let go."

Jeanette MacDonald told me that when she was depressed and worried and had difficulty in going to sleep, she could always get"a feeling of security"by repeating Psalm XXIII :"The Lord is my Shepherd; I shall not want. He maketh me to lie down in green pastures. He leadeth me beside the still waters..."

But if you are not religious, and have to do things the hard way, then learn to relax by physical

不为这件事担忧,就能得到休息。"'

"我照着他的话去做,"桑德勒说,"不到两个星期我就能安稳地睡着了。不到一个月,我就能每天睡 8 个小时,精神也正常了。"

使伊拉·桑德勒饱受折磨的不是失眠,而是他的忧虑。

芝加哥大学教授萨尼尔·克里特曼博士曾对睡眠问题做过很多研究,他也是全世界研究睡眠问题的专家。他说从来没有听说有人死于失眠症;实际上,可能有人会因为失眠而忧虑,以致体力下降,受到细菌的侵袭。但这种伤害是由忧虑造成的,而不是由失眠本身造成的。

克里特曼博士还说,那些担心失眠的人,睡眠通常比他们想象的要多。那些发誓说"我昨晚上连眼睛都没有闭一下"的人,可能睡了好几个小时却自己不知道。例如,19 世纪最有名的思想家之一斯宾塞先生在老年的时候还是独身一人,住在一间寄宿舍里,整天谈论他的失眠,使周围的人都烦得要命。他甚至会在耳朵里塞上耳塞,以避免外面的吵闹声,有时还吃鸦片催眠。一天晚上,他和牛津大学教授塞士住在一家旅馆的同一个房间。第二天早上,斯宾塞说他整夜没有睡着,可实际上却是塞士教授根本没有睡着,因为斯宾塞的鼾声吵了他一夜。

睡个好觉的首要条件,就是要有安全感。我们必须感到有一种比我们强大得多的力量,它可以一直照顾我们到天亮。托马斯·海斯罗浦医生在英国医药协会的一次演讲中,就特别强调这一点。他说:"我从自己多年行医的经验中发现,使你入睡的最好办法之一就是祈祷。我这纯粹是以一个医生的身份说的。对那些有祈祷习惯的人来说,祈祷是镇定思想和神经的最适当也最常用的方法。

"把自己托付给上帝——然后放松自己。"

詹妮特·麦当娜告诉我说,每当她感觉精神颓丧而忧虑得难以入睡的时候,她就会诵读诗篇第二十三篇,让自己得到"一种安全感":"耶和华是我的牧者,我必不致缺乏。他令我躺在青草地上,将我引到可安憩的水边……"

measures. Dr. David Harold Fink, who wrote *Release from Nervous Tension*, says that the best way to do this is to *talk to* your body. According to Dr. Fink, words are the key to all kinds of hypnosis; and when you consistently can't sleep, it is because you have *talked* yourself into a case of insomnia. The way to undo this is to dehypnotise yourself—and you can do it by saying to the muscles of your body: "Let go, let go—loosen up and relax." We already know that the mind and nerves can't relax while the muscles are tense—so if we want to go to sleep, we start with the muscles. Dr. Fink recommends—and it works out in practice—that we put a pillow under the knees to ease the tension on the legs, and that we tuck small pillows under the arms for the very same reason. Then, by telling the jaw to relax, the eyes, the arms, and the legs, we finally drop off to sleep before we know what has hit us. I've tried it—I know.

If you have trouble sleeping, get hold of Dr. Fink's book, *Release from Nervous Tension*, which I have mentioned earlier It is the only book I know of that is both lively reading and a cure for insomnia.

One of the best cures for insomnia is making yourself physically tired by gardening, swimming, tennis, golf, skiing, or by just plain physically exhausting work. That is what Theodore Dreiser did. When he was a struggling young author, he was worried about insomnia, so he got a job working as a section hand on the New York Central Railway; and after a day of driving spikes and shoveling gravel, he was so exhausted that he could hardly stay awake long enough to eat.

If we get tired enough, nature will force us to sleep even while we are walking. To illustrate, when I was thirteen years old, my father shipped a car-load of fat hogs to Saint Joe, Missouri. Since he got two free railroad passes, he took me along with him. Up until that time, I had never been in a town of more than four thousand. When I landed in Saint Joe—a city of sixty thousand—I was agog with excitement. I saw skyscrapers six storeys high and—wonder of wonders—I saw a street-car. I can close my eyes now and still see and hear that street-car. After the most thrilling and exciting day of my life, Father and I took a train back to Ravenwood, Missouri. Arriving there at two o'clock in the morning, we had to walk four miles home to the farm. And here is the point of the story: I was so exhausted that I slept and dreamed as I walked. I have often slept while riding horseback. And I am alive to tell it!

When men are completely exhausted they sleep right through the thunder and horror and

但你若没有宗教信仰,不能轻松地解决问题的话,你还可以采用另一种方法来放松。大卫·哈罗德·芬克医生写过《消除神经紧张》,提出最好的方法就是和你自己的身体交谈。芬克医生认为,语言是所有催眠法的关键,如果你一直不能睡着,那是因为你自己"说"得太多而使自己得了失眠症。解决的方法,就是使你从这种失眠状态中解脱出来——你可以对你的肌肉说:"放松!放松!放松所有的紧张!"我们已经知道,当人的肌肉紧张的时候,思想和神经就不可能放松。所以,如果我们想要入睡,必须先放松肌肉。芬克医生推荐的有效方法,就是把枕头放在膝盖下,减轻双脚的紧张。然后,把几个小枕头垫在手臂底下,放松下颚、眼睛、两个手臂和两腿,最后我们就会在不知不觉中入睡了。我自己曾经试过,所以知道这个方法很有效。

如果你有失眠症,不妨买一本芬克医生的《消除神经紧张》,这本书我前面也提到过,这是我知道的唯一具有可读性、又能治好失眠症的书。

治疗失眠症的最好办法之一,就是干体力劳动,直到疲倦为止。如种花、游泳、打网球、打高尔夫球、滑雪或做一些需要耗费很多体力的工作。这是著名作家德莱塞的做法。当他还是一个为生活而挣扎的年轻作家时,就为失眠而忧虑。于是他到纽约中央铁路公司找了一份铁路工人的工作,当他每天干完打钉子和铲石子的工作之后,就会累得甚至没有办法坐在那里吃完晚饭。

如果我们疲倦至极的话,即使我们是在走路也会睡着的。例如:我 13 岁那年,我父亲要运一车猪去密苏里州的圣乔城,他当时有两张免费的火车票,所以带了我一同去。我在那之前从来没有去过人口超过 4000 的城市。当我到了有 6 万人的圣乔城时,兴奋得难以形容。我看到了 6 层高的楼——更让我惊奇的是,我还看到了一辆电车。我现在闭上眼睛,好像还能看到、听到那辆电车。在经历了我一生当中最兴奋的一天之后,父亲和我坐火车回家。到家的时候是半夜两点钟,我们还要走 4 里路回到农庄。下面就是这个故事的要点:我疲倦到了一面走一面睡的程度,而且还做着梦。我还常常骑在马背上就睡着了。这些都是我的亲身经历。

danger of war. Dr. Foster Kennedy, the famous neurologist, tells me that during the retreat of the Fifth British Army in 1918, he saw soldiers so exhausted that they fell on the ground where they were and fell into asleep as sound as a coma. They didn't even wake up when he raised their eyelids with his fingers. And he says he noticed that invariably the pupils of the eyes were rolled upward in the sockets. "After that, "says Dr. Kennedy, "when I had trouble sleeping, I would practice rolling up my eyeballs into this position, and I found that in a few seconds I would begin to yawn and feel sleepy. It was an automatic reflex over which I had no control."

No man ever committed suicide by refusing to sleep and no one ever will. Nature would force a man to sleep in spite of all his willpower. Nature will let us go without food or water far longer than she will let us go without sleep.

Speaking of suicide reminds me of a case that Dr. Henry C. Link describes in his book, *The Rediscovery of Man*. Dr. Link is vice-president of The Psychological Corporation and he interviews many people who are worried and depressed. In his chapter"On Overcoming Fears and Worries", he tells about a patient who wanted to commit suicide. Dr. Link knew arguing would only make the matter worse, so he said to this man: "If you are going to commit suicide anyway, you might at least do it in a heroic fashion. Run around the block until you drop dead."

He tried it, not once but several times, and each time felt better in his mind if not in his muscles. By the third night he had achieved what Dr. Link intended in the first place—he was so physically tired (and physically relaxed) that he slept like a log. Later he joined an athletic club and began to compete in competitive sports. Soon he was feeling so good he wanted to live forever!

So, to keep from worrying about insomnia, here are five rules:

1. If yon can't sleep, do what Samuel Untermyer did. Get up and work or read until you do feel sleepy.
2. Remember that no one was ever killed by lack of sleep. Worrying about insomnia usually causes far more damage than sleeplessness.
3. Try prayer—or repeat Psalm XXIII, as Jeanette MacDonald does.
4. Relax your body. Read the book"Release from Nervous Tension".
5. Exercise. Get yourself so physically tired you can't stay awake.

当人们筋疲力尽时,即使是打雷或面临战争的危险,也能够安然入睡。著名的神经科医生弗斯特·肯尼迪告诉我说,当英国第五军在1918年撤退的时候,他就看到过精疲力竭的士兵随地倒下,睡得昏死过去。当他用手拨开他们的眼皮时,他们也没醒过来。他说他注意到所有人的眼球都在眼眶里向上翻去。“从那以后,”肯尼迪医生说,“每当我睡不着的时候,我就会把我的眼珠翻到那个位置。我发现不过几秒钟,我就开始打哈欠,感到困倦难耐。这是一种无法控制的自然反应。”

从来没有人会用不睡觉来自杀。一个人不论毅力多强,大自然都会强迫他入睡。大自然可以让我们长久吃不到东西、喝不到水,却不会让我们不睡觉。

谈到自杀,我想起了亨利·林克博士在他那本《人的再发现》中谈到的一个例子。林克博士是心理问题公司副总裁,曾和很多因为忧虑而颓丧的人交谈过。在“消除恐惧和忧虑”这一章,他谈到了一个想要自杀的病人。林克博士知道争论只会使情况变得更坏,所以他对这个人说:“如果你真的要自杀,至少要做得英雄些。你可以绕着这条街跑到累死为止。”

这个人果然试了,不止一次,而是好几次。结果每一次他都会觉得好过一点,不过这种感觉是在心理上, 而不是在生理上。到第三天晚上, 他终于达到了林克博士最初想要达到的目的——由于体力疲劳(身体放松了),他睡得很沉。后来他参加了某个体育俱乐部,参加各种比赛,不久就开心得想永远活下去。

所以,你若想不为失眠而忧虑,下面是五条规则:

第一,如果睡不着,就起来工作或看书,直到打瞌睡为止。

第二,从来没有人会因为缺乏睡眠而死。担心失眠而忧虑,这种伤害通常比失眠更厉害。

第三,试着祈祷——或者像詹妮特·麦当娜那样诵读诗篇第二十三篇。

第四,放松全身。看看《消除神经紧张》这本书。

第五,运动。参加体力劳动,直到累得酣然入睡。

Part Seven
How to Find the Kind of Work in Which You May Be Happy and Successful

1 The Major Decision of Your Life

(This chapter is addressed to young men and women who haven't yet found the work they want to do.

If you are in that category, reading this chapter may have a profound effect upon the remainder of your life.)

If you are under eighteen, you will probably soon be called upon to make the two most important decisions of your life—decisions that will profoundly alter all the days of your years: decisions that may have far-reaching effects upon your happiness, your income, your health; decisions that may make or break you.

What are these two tremendous decisions? First: How are you going to make a living? Are you going to be a farmer, a mail carrier, a chemist, a forest ranger, a stenographer, a horse dealer, a college professor, or are you going to run a hamburger stand? Second: Whom are you going to select to be the father or mother of your children?

Both of those great decisions are frequently gambles. "Every boy," says Harry Emerson Fosdick in his book, *The Power to See It Through*, "every boy is a gambler when he chooses a vocation. He must stake his life on it."

How can you reduce the gamble in selecting a vocation? Read on; we will tell you as best we can.

First, try, if possible, to find work that you enjoy. I once asked David M. Goodrich, Chairman of the Board, B. F. Goodrich Company—tyre manufacturers—what he considered the first requisite of success

第七篇　找到通往快乐与成功的工作

第1章　人生的重要决定

(这一章是为那些尚未找到理想工作的青年男女写的。如果你现在处于这种状况,阅读本章将会对你未来的生活产生深刻的影响。)

如果你还不到18岁，那么你可能即将面临人生中两项重要的决定——深刻地改变你一生的决定;可能会对你的幸福、收入、健康产生深刻影响的决定;它们既可能造就你,也可能毁灭你。

那么,这两项重大决定是什么?第一,你将如何谋生?你是做一个农夫、邮递员、化学家、森林管理员,还是一名速记员、兽医、大学教授,或是摆一个汉堡摊子?第二,你将选择谁做你孩子的父亲或母亲?

这两项重大决定通常像是赌博。哈瑞·爱默生·福斯迪克在他的著作《透视的力量》中说:"每个男孩在决定如何度过一个假期时,都是赌徒,因为他必须以他的日子做赌注。"

怎样才能降低这种赌博风险呢?读下去,我将尽可能地告诉你。

首先,如果可能的话,要尽量寻找你喜欢的工作。有一次我向轮胎制造商古利奇公司的董事长大卫·古利奇请教,做生意成功的第一要素是什么?他回答说:"快乐地工作。如果你喜欢你的工作,"他说,"你也许工作很长时间,但你却丝毫不会觉得是在工作,而是在做游戏。"

in business, and he replied: "Having a good time at your work. If you enjoy what you are doing, "he said, "you may work long hours, but it won't seem like work at all. It will seem like play. "

Edison was a good example of that. Edison—the unschooled newsboy who grew up to transform the industrial life of America—Edison, the man who often ate and slept in his laboratory and toiled there for eighteen hours a day. But it wasn't toil to him. "I never did a day's work in my life, "he exclaimed. "It was all fun. " No wonder he succeeded!

I once heard Charles Schwab say much the same thing. He said: "A man can succeed at almost anything for which he has unlimited enthusiasm. "

But how can you have enthusiasm for a job when you haven't the foggiest idea of what you want to do? "The greatest tragedy I know of, "said Mrs. Edna Kerr, who once hired thousands of employees for the Dupont Company, and is now assistant director of industrial relations for the American Home Products Company—"The greatest tragedy I know of, "she told me, "is that so many young people never discover what they really want to do. I think no one else is so much to be pitied as the person who gets nothing at all out of his work but his pay. "Mrs. Kerr reports that even college graduates come to her and say: "I have a B. A. degree from Dartmouth [or an M. A. from Cornell]. Have you some kind of work I can do for your firm? "They don't know themselves what they are able to do, or even what they would like to do. Is it any wonder that so many men and women who start out in life with competent minds and rosy dreams end up at forty in utter frustration and even with a nervous breakdown? In fact, finding the right occupation is important even for your health. When Dr. Raymond Pearl, of Johns Hopkins, made a study, together with some insurance companies, to discover the factors that make for a long life, he placed "the right occupation"high on the list. He might have said, with Thomas Carlyle:"Blessed is the man who has found his work. Let him ask no other blessedness. "

I recently spent an evening with Paul W. Boynton, employment supervisor for the Socony-Vacuum Oil Company. During the last twenty years he has interviewed more than seventy-five thousand people looking for jobs, and he has written a book entitled *6 Ways to Get a Job*. I asked him: "What is the greatest mistake young people make today in looking for work? ""They don't know what they want to do, "he said. "It is perfectly appalling to realize that a man will give more thought

爱迪生就是一个很好的例子。这位没有上过什么学的报童，后来却完全改变了美国的工业生活。爱迪生几乎每天在他的实验室辛苦地工作 18 个小时，在里面吃饭睡觉，但他一点也不觉得辛苦。"我一生中从未做过一天工作，"他宣称，"我每天其乐无穷。"怪不得他会成功。

我曾听施瓦伯说过相似的话。他说："一个人从事他无限热爱的工作，就可以成功。"

可是，如果你对自己想做的工作还没有什么概念的话，又怎么能对工作产生热情呢？艾德娜·卡尔夫人曾为杜邦公司雇用过几千名员工，她现在是美国家庭产品公司工业关系部副总经理，她说："我认为这个世界上最大的悲剧就是，许多年轻人从来没有发现他们真正想做什么。我认为，如果一个人从他的工作中得到的除了薪水之外什么也没有，那就可悲了。"甚至有一些大学毕业生到她那儿说："我获得了达特茅斯大学的文学士学位（或康奈尔大学硕士学位），你公司有没有适合我的职位？"他们不知道自己能做什么，也不知道自己想做什么。正因为如此，有许多人刚开始时雄心勃勃，充满了美丽的梦想，但到了 40 岁以后却一事无成，痛苦懊丧，甚至精神崩溃。事实上，选择正确的工作甚至会对你的健康产生重要影响。琼斯·霍普金斯医院的雷蒙·皮尔医生，配合几家保险公司作了一项调查，研究人们长寿的原因，他把"正确的工作"排在了首位。这一结论正好符合卡莱尔的名言："祝福那些找到自己心爱工作的人，他们不需再祈求其他的幸福。"

最近我和素凡石油公司的人事部经理保罗·波恩顿畅谈了一个晚上。他在过去 20 年中至少面试了 7.5 万名求职者，还写了一本名为《获得工作的六个方法》的书。我问他："现在的年轻人求职时所犯的最大错误是什么？"他回答说："他们不知道他们想干什么。这真是让人吃惊，一个人会费尽心思地选一件穿几年就会破的衣服，但在选择关系他将来命运的工作时却马虎得多——而他将来的全部幸福和安宁全都建立在它之上。"

那该怎么办呢？你该如何解决呢？你可以去向"职业指导"寻找帮助。不过，它也许可以成全

to buying a suit of clothes that will wear out in a few years than he will give to choosing the career on which his whole future depends—on which his whole future happiness and peace of mind are based!

"And so what? What can you do about it? You can take advantage of a new profession called vocational guidance. It may help you—or harm you—depending on the ability and character of the counselor you consult. This new profession isn't even within gunshot of perfection yet. It hasn't even reached the Model T stage. But it has a great future. How can you make use of this science? By finding out where, in your community, you can get vocational tests and vocational advice.

Such advice can only take the form of suggestions. You have to make the decisions. Remember that these counselors are far from infallible. The point I am trying to make is that vocational guidance experts, even as you and I, are not infallible.

Perhaps you had better consult several of them—and then interpret their findings in the sunlight of common sense.

You may think it strange that I am including a chapter like this in a book devoted to worry. But it isn't strange at all, when you understand how many of our worries, regrets, and frustrations are spawned by work we despise. Ask your father about it—or your neighbour or your boss. No less an intellectual giant than John Smart Mill declared that industrial misfits are "among the heaviest losses of society". Yes, and among the unhappiest people on this earth are those same "industrial misfits" who hate their daily work!

Do you know the kind of man who "cracked up" in the Army? The man who was misplaced! I'm not talking about battle casualties, but about the men who cracked up in ordinary service. Dr. William Menninger, one of our greatest living psychiatrists, was in charge of the Army's neuro-psychiatric division during the war, and he says: "We learned much in the Army as to the importance of selection and of placement, of putting the right man in the right job... A conviction of the importance of the job at hand was extremely important. Where a man had no interest, where he felt he was misplaced, where he thought he was not appreciated, where he believed his talents were being misused, invariably we found a potential if not an actual psychiatric casualty."

Yes—and for the same reasons, a man may "crack up" in industry. If he despises his business, he can crack it up, too.

你，也许会损害你，这取决于你所找的那位辅导员的能力和个性。这个新行业远远说不上完美，甚至连起步都谈不上，但它的前景十分美好。你该如何利用这项新科学呢？你可以在你家附近找到这类机构，然后接受职业测试，并获得求职指导。

不过他们只能为你提供建议，决定还得由你自己做。要记住，这些辅导员并不一定可靠。我在此想说明的一点是，那些职业指导专家——即使是你我这样的人，也不一定可靠。你也许该多找几位辅导员，然后凭你的常识来判断他们的意见。

你也许会觉得奇怪，为什么我在本章总是说一些令人担心的话。可是一旦你了解到多数人的忧虑、悔恨和沮丧都是由于不重视工作而引起的，那你就不会觉得奇怪了。你可以就此问你的父亲、邻居或老板。最具智慧的人约翰·米勒宣称，工人无法适应工作是"我们这个社会最大的损失之一"。是的，世界上最不快乐的人中就有那些讨厌他们日常工作的"产业工人"。

你认识陆军中"崩溃"的那类人吗？他们就是被分到错误岗位的人！我指的并不是那些在战斗中受伤的人，而是指那些在普通任务中陷入精神崩溃的人。威康·曼尼格医生是当代最伟大的精神病专家之一，他在第二次世界大战期间主管美国陆军精神病诊疗部，他说："我们发现在军队中挑选和安置的重要性，要派适当的人去做适当的工作……最重要的是，要使此人相信他的工作的重要性。当一个人没有兴趣时，就会认为他被放错了地方，并产生不受欣赏和重视的心理，会认为他的才能被埋没了。我们发现，在这种情况下他若没有患上精神病，也会留下隐患。"

由于同样的原因，一个人也会在工业中陷入崩溃；如果他轻视他的工作，他也可以把它弄得一团糟。

菲尔·琼森就是一个很好的例子。菲尔·琼森的父亲开了一家洗衣店，他叫儿子来店里工作，并希望他将来接管这家洗衣店。但菲尔不喜欢洗衣店的工作，所以他有些懒散消极，对工作应付了

Take, for example, the case of Phil Johnson. Phil Johnson's father owned a laundry, so he gave his son a job, hoping the boy would work into the business. But Phil hated the laundry, so he dawdled, loafed, did what he had to do and not a lick more. Some days he was "absent". His father was so hurt to think he had a shiftless, ambitionless son that he was actually ashamed before his employees.

One day Phil Johnson told his father he wanted to be a mechanic-work in a machine shop. What? Go back to overalls? The old man was shocked. But Phil had his way. He worked in greasy dungarees. He did much harder work than was required at the laundry. He worked longer hours, and he whistled at his job! He took up engineering, learned about engines, puttered with machines—and when Philip Johnson died, in 1944, he was president of the Boeing Aircraft Company, and was making the Flying Fortresses that helped to win the war! If he had stuck with the laundry, what would have happened to him and the laundry—especially after his father's death? My guess is he would have ruined the business, cracked it up and run it into the ground.

Even at the risk of starting family rows, I would like to say to young people: Don't feel compelled to enter a business or trade just because your family wants you to do it! Don't enter a career unless you want to do it! However, consider carefully the advice of your parents. They have probably lived twice as long as you have. They have gained the kind of wisdom that comes only from much experience and the passing of many years. But, in the last analysis, you are the one who has to make the final decision.

You are the one who is going to be either happy or miserable at your work.

Now, having said this, let me give you the following suggestions—some of them warnings—about choosing your work:

1. Read and study the following five suggestions about selecting a vocational guidance counselor.

These suggestions are right from the horse's mouth. They were made by one of America's leading vocational guidance experts, Professor Harry Dexter Kitson of Columbia University.

a. "Don't go to anyone who tells you that he has a magic system that will indicate your 'vocational aptitude'. In this group are phrenologists, astrologers, 'character analysts', handwriting experts. Their 'systems' do not work."

b. "Don't go to anyone who tells you that he can give you a test that will indicate what

事,其他事情一概不管。有时他干脆不来店里。为此他父亲十分伤心,认为自己的儿子不求上进,没有野心,使他在员工面前大丢面子。

一天,菲尔告诉父亲,他希望去机械厂当工人。什么?一切从头开始?老人十分惊讶。但菲尔还是坚持自己的意见。最后,他穿上了油腻的粗布工作服,干起了比洗衣店更辛苦的工作,而且工作时间更长,但他在工作中快乐得吹起了口哨。他选修了工程学课程,研究引擎,安装各种机械。当他在1944年去世时,已是波音飞机公司的总裁,并且研制出了"空中飞行堡垒"轰炸机,帮助盟军赢得了第二次世界大战。如果他留在洗衣店,那么他和洗衣店——尤其是他父亲死后——会变成什么样子呢?我想他会毁了这个洗衣店。

即使会引起家庭纠纷,但我仍然想奉劝年轻的朋友们:不要因为你的家人希望你做什么,你就勉强自己进入某一行业。不要贸然从事某一行业,除非你真的想去。不过,你仍然要仔细考虑父母的建议。他们的年纪可能比你大一倍,有丰富的人生阅历。但是到了最后阶段,你还得自己决定。

因为将来工作时,快乐或悲哀的是你自己。

我已说了许多,现在让我给你提供一些关于选择工作的建议——其中有一些是警告:

第一,阅读并研究以下5项关于选择职业辅导员的建议。这些建议是由最权威的人士提供的。它们由美国最成功的职业指导专家、哥伦比亚大学的基森教授拟定。

a. 如果有人对你说他有一套神奇的方法,可以找到你的"职业倾向",千万不要找他。这些人包括摸骨家、星相家、"个性分析家"和笔迹分析家。但他们的方法并不灵。

b. 不要相信这种人,他们说可以给你先作一番测试,然后指出你该选择哪一种职业。这种人违背了职业辅导员必须考虑的原则:被辅导人的健康、社会、经济等各种情况,同时还应该为被辅导人提供就业的具体资料。

occupation you should choose. Such a person violates the principle that a vocational counselor must take into account the physical, social, and economic conditions surrounding the counselee; and he should render his service in the light of the occupational opportunities open to the counselee."

c. "Seek a vocational counselor who has an adequate library of information about occupations and uses it in the counseling process."

d. "A thorough vocational guidance service generally requires more than one interview."

e. "Never accept vocational guidance by mail."

2. Keep out of business and professions that are already jam-packed and overflowing! There are many thousands of different ways of making a living. But do young people know this? Not unless they hire a swami to gaze into a crystal ball. The result? In one school, two-thirds of the boys confined their choices to five occupations—five out of twenty thousand—and four-fifths of the girls did the same. Small wonder that a few business and professions are overcrowded—small wonder that insecurity, worry, and "anxiety neuroses" are rampant at times among the white-collar fraternity! Beware of trying to elbow your way into such overcrowded fields as law, journalism, radio, motion pictures, and the "glamour occupations".

3. Stay out of activities where the chances are only one out of ten of your being able to make a living.

As an example, take selling life insurance. Each year countless thousands of men—frequently unemployed men—start out trying to sell life insurance without bothering to find out in advance what is likely to happen to them! Here is approximately what does happen, according to Franklin L. Bettger, Real Estate Trust Building, Philadelphia. For twenty years Mr. Bettger was one of the outstandingly successful insurance salesmen in America. He declares that ninety per cent of the men who start selling life insurance get so heartsick and discouraged that they give it up within a year. Out of the ten who remain, one man will sell ninety per cent of the insurance sold by the group of ten; and the other nine will sell only ten per cent. To put it another way: if you start selling life insurance, the chances are nine to one that you will fail and quit within twelve months, and the chances are only one in a hundred that you will make ten thousand a year out of it. Even if you remain at it, the chances are only one out of ten that you will be able to do anything more than barely scratch out a living.

c.找一位有丰富的职业资料藏书的职业辅导员，并在接受辅导期间充分利用它。

d.充分的就业辅导服务通常需要面谈两次以上。

e.千万不要接受函授性质的就业辅导。

第二，避免选择那些早就很激烈并且拥挤的职业和行业。在美国，谋生的方法多得是。但年轻人是否知道这一点？除非他们请占卜师透视水晶球，否则他们不会知道。在一所学校内，有2/3的男孩子选择了5种职业——两万种职业中的5种——而4/5的女孩子也是一样。怪不得有少数行业和职业人满为患，也难怪白领阶层会产生不安和忧虑感以及"焦虑性精神病"。需要特别注意的是，如果你想进入法律、新闻、广播、电影以及"光荣职业"等人满为患的行业时，可要费一番功夫。

第三，避免选择只有1/10的生存机会的行业。

例如，推销人寿保险。每年有数以千计的人——往往是失业者——他们事先未打听清楚，就开始推销人寿保险。根据费城房地产信托大厦的弗兰克·贝特格先生的描述，以下就是这个行业的真实情形：在过去20年，贝特格先生一直是美国最杰出而且最成功的人寿保险推销员之一。他指出，90%的推销员首次推销人寿保险时会既伤心又沮丧，会在一年之内放弃。至于那留下来的10个人，只有一个人可以卖出这10个人销售总数的90%，而另外9个人只能卖出10%的保险。换句话说：如果你去推销人寿保险，那你在一年之内放弃而退出的机会比例为9:1，而留下来的机会只有1/10。即使你留下来了，成功的机会也只有10%而已，否则你仅能勉强度日。

第四，如有必要，在你决定从事某个职业之前，先用几周或几个月的时间全面了解该项工作。怎么做呢？你可以去找那些已在这一行业干了10年、20年或40年的人士咨询。

这些面谈对你的将来可能会产生极深的影响。我已经从自己的经历中了解到了这一点。我

4. Spend weeks—even months, if necessary—finding out all you can about an occupation before deciding to devote your life to it! How? By interviewing men and women who have already spent ten, twenty, or forty years in that occupation.

These interviews may have a profound effect on your future. I know that from my own experience.

When I was in my early twenties, I sought the vocational advice of two older men. As I look back now, I can see that those two interviews were turning points in my career. In fact, it would be difficult for me even to imagine what my life would have been like had I not had those two interviews.

How can you get these vocational guidance interviews? To illustrate, let's suppose that you are thinking about studying to be an architect. Before you make your decision, you ought to spend weeks interviewing the architects in your city and in adjoining cities. You can get their names and addresses out of a classified telephone directory. You can call at their offices either with or without an appointment. If you wish to make an appointment, write them something like this:

Won't you please do me a little favor? I want your advice. I am eighteen years old, and I am thinking about studying to be an architect. Before I make up my mind, I would like to ask your advice.

If you are too busy to see me at your office, I would be most grateful if you would grant me the privilege of seeing you for half an hour at your home.

Here is a list of questions I would like to ask you:

a. If you had your life to live over, would you become an architect again?

b. After you have sized me up, I want to ask you whether you think I have what it takes to succeed as an architect.

c. Is the profession of architecture overcrowded?

d. If I studied architecture for four years, would it be difficult for me to get a job? What kind of job would I have to take at first?

e. If I had average ability, how much could I hope to earn during the first five years?

f. What are the advantages and disadvantages of being an architect?

g. If I were your son, would you advise me to become an architect?

If you are timid, and hesitate to face a "big shot"alone, here are two suggestions that will

20多岁时曾向两位老先生请教职业指导。现在回想起来，我发现这两次会谈是我人生的转折点。事实上，如果没有这两次会谈，我的人生将会变成什么样子真的难以想象。

你该如何获得这种职业指导会谈呢?例如，假设你打算当一名建筑师。在你做出决定之前，应该花几个星期去拜访城里和附近的建筑师。你可以从电话簿中找到他们的姓名和住址。不管你事先是否有约定，你都可以去他们办公室找他们。如果你希望约见面时间，你可以给他们写信，内容如下：

"能否麻烦您帮我一个忙?我希望得到您的建议。我现年18岁，正考虑当一名建筑师。在我做出决定之前，希望向您请教。

"如果您太忙，不能在办公室见我，而愿意在您家中给我半小时见我，我将感激不尽。

"以下就是我想向您请教的问题：

"a. 如果您的生命重新开始，您是否愿意再当一名建筑师?

"b. 在您仔细察看我之后，我想请问您是否认为我具备了当一名成功建筑师的条件?

"c. 建筑师这个行业是否已经供过于求?

"d. 如果我学了4年的建筑学课程，要找工作是否困难?我应该先接受哪一类工作?

"e. 如果我的能力中等，在第一个5年我有望赚到多少钱?

"f. 当一名建筑师有什么利弊?

"g. 如果我是您儿子，您愿意鼓励我当一名建筑师吗?"

如果你很害羞而不敢单独去见"大人物"，这里还有两项建议可以帮助你：第一，找一个与你同龄的小伙子一起去。你们可以相互增加对方的信心。如果找不到与你同龄的人，你可以请你父亲一同前往。第二，记住，你去向某人请教，等于是在恭维他。你的请求会使他感觉受到了奉承。记住，成年人往往很乐意向年轻人提忠告。因此你求教的建筑师将会很高兴接

help. First, get a lad of your own age to go with you. The two of you will bolster up one another's confidence. If you haven't someone of your own age to go with you, ask your father to go with you. Second, remember that by asking his advice you are paying this man a compliment. He may feel flattered by your request. Remember that adults like to give advice to young men and women. The architect will probably enjoy the interview.

If you hesitate to write letters asking for an appointment, then go to a man's office without an appointment and tell him you would be most grateful if he would give you a bit of advice.

Suppose you call on five architects and they are all too busy to see you (which isn't likely), call on five more. Some of them will see you and give you priceless advice—advice that may save you years of lost time and heartbreak.

Remember that you are making one of the two most vital and far-reaching decisions of your life. So, take time to get the facts before you act. If you don't, you may spend half a lifetime regretting it.

If you can afford to do so, offer to pay a man for a half-hour of his time and advice.

5. Get over the mistaken belief that you are fitted for only a single occupation! Every normal person can succeed at a number of occupations, and every normal person would probably fail in many occupations. Take myself, for example: if I had studied and prepared myself for the following occupations, I believe I would have had a good chance of achieving some small measure of success and also of enjoying my work. I refer to such occupations as farming, fruit growing, scientific agriculture, medicine, selling, advertising, editing a country newspaper, teaching, and forestry. On the other hand, I am sure I would have been unhappy, and a failure, at bookkeeping, accounting, engineering, operating a hotel or a factory, architecture, all mechanical trades, and hundreds of other activities.

受这次访问。

如果你不愿写信给对方要求见面,那么你不必约定就可直接去他办公室,对他说如果他能为你提供一些就业指导,你将十分感激。

假设你已经拜访了5位建筑师,但他们都因为太忙而不能接见你(这种情形并不多),那么你不妨再去拜访另外5位。他们总会有人愿意接见你,给你提供宝贵的意见——这些意见也许可以使你免去多年的迷失和忧虑。

一定要记住,你这是在做生命中最重要、影响最深远的两项决定中的一项。因此,在采取行动之前,务必多花点时间了解事实真相。如果你不这么做,那么你下半辈子可能会后悔。

如果条件许可,你可以付钱给对方,报答他半小时的时间和忠告。

第五,要克服"你只适合一项职业"的错误观念。每个正常人都可以在多项职业上取得成功,当然也可能在多项职业上失败。拿我自己来说,如果我自己研究并准备从事下列各项职业,我相信成功的机会一定很多,而且会喜欢这些职业,这些工作包括:农艺、水果栽培、科学农业、医药、销售、广告、报纸编辑、教学、林业。另一方面,我敢肯定对于以下工作我一定不会喜欢,而且也会失败:簿记、会计、工程、经营旅馆和工厂、建筑、机械事物以及其他几百项职业。

Part Eight
How to Lessen Your Financial Worries

1 Seventy Per Cent of All Our Worries ...

If I knew how to solve everybody's financial worries, I wouldn't be writing this book, I would be sitting in the White House—right beside the President. But here is one thing I can do: I can quote some authorities on this subject and make some highly practical suggestions and point out where you can obtain books and pamphlets that will give you additional guidance.

Seventy per cent of all our worries, according to a survey made by the *Ladies' Home Journal*, are about money. George Gallup, of the Gallup Poll, says that his research indicates that most people believe that they would have no more financial worries if they could increase their income by only ten per cent. That is true in many cases, but in a surprisingly large number of cases it is not true. For example, while writing this chapter, I interviewed an expert on budgets: Mrs. Elsie Stapleton—a woman who spent years as financial adviser to the customers and employees of Wanamaker's Department Store in New York and of Gimbel's. She has spent additional years as an individual consultant, trying to help people who were frantic with worry about money. She has helped people in all kinds of income brackets, all the way from a porter who earned less than a thousand dollars a year to an executive earning one hundred thousand dollars a year. And this is what she told me: "More money is not the answer to most people's financial worries. In fact, I have often seen it happen that an increase in income accomplished nothing but an increase in spending—and an increase in headaches. What causes most people to worry, is not that they haven't enough money, but that they don't know how to spend the money they have." [You snorted

第八篇　如何减少金钱的烦恼

第1章　百分之七十的烦恼

如果我知道解决每个人的财务困难，我就不会写这本书，而是坐在白宫——坐在总统身边。但我可以给大家做一件事：我可以引述一些权威看法，并提供一些切实可行的建议，提示你可以从何处获得书籍和小册子，给你额外的指导。

根据《妇女家庭月刊》杂志所作的一项调查，我们70%的烦恼都和金钱有关。盖洛普调查公司主席乔治·盖洛普说，根据他的研究显示，大部分人都认为，只要他们的收入增加10%，他们就不会再有经济困难。在很多情况下确实如此，但令人惊讶的是，更多的情况并不是这样。例如，我在写这本书时，曾向预算专家爱尔西·史塔普里顿夫人请教。她曾担任纽约和詹培尔两地华纳梅克百货公司的财政顾问多年；她还以个人指导员身份，帮助过那些受金钱拖累的人。她帮助过不同收入的人，从每年赚不到1000美元的行李搬运工到年薪10万美元的公司经理。她告诉我说："对于大多数人而言，多挣些钱并不能解决他们的财务困难。事实上，我经常看到，在他们的收入增加之后，并没有什么大的作用，反而突然增加了开支——也增加了头痛之事。使大多数人烦恼的，并不是他们没有足够的钱，而是他们不知道如何支配已有的钱！"（你对这最后一句话不屑一听，对不对？好吧，在你再次表示轻视之前，请记住，史塔普里顿夫人并没有说"所有的人"，她只是说"大多数人"。她并不是指你，她指的可能是你兄弟姐妹，他们的人数可就

at that last sentence, didn't you? Well, before you snort again, please remember that Mrs. Stapleton did not say that was true of all people. She said: "most people". She didn't mean you. She meant your sisters and your cousins, whom you reckon by the dozens.]

A lot of readers are going to say: "I wish this guy Carnegie had my bills to meet, my obligations to keep up—on my weekly salary. If he did, I'll bet he would change his tune. "Well, I have had my financial troubles: I have worked ten hours a day at hard physical labor in the cornfields and hay barns of Missouri—worked until my one supreme wish was to be free from the aching pains of utter physical exhaustion. I was paid for that grueling work not a dollar an hour, nor fifty cents, nor even ten cents. I was paid five cents an hour for a ten-hour day.

I know what it means to live for twenty years in houses without a bathroom or running water. I know what it means to sleep in bedrooms where the temperature is fifteen degrees below zero. I know what it means to walk miles to save a nickel car-fare and have holes in the bottom of my shoes and patches on the seat of my pants. I know what it means to order the cheapest dish on a restaurant menu, and to sleep with my trousers under the mattress because I couldn't afford to have them pressed by a tailor. Yet, even during those times, I usually managed to save a few dimes and quarters out of my income because I was afraid not to. As a result of this experience, I realized that if you and I long to avoid debt and financial worries, then we have to do what a business firm does: we have to have a plan for spending our money and spend according to that plan. But most of us don't do that. For example, my good friend, Leon Shimkin, general manager of the firm that publishes this book, pointed out to me a curious blindness that many people have in regard to their money. He told me about a book-keeper he knows, a man who is a wizard at figures when working for his firm—yet when it comes to handling his personal finances! ... Well, if this man gets paid on Friday noon, let us say, he will walk down the street, see an overcoat in a store window that strikes his fancy, and buy it—never giving a thought to the fact that rent, electric lights, and all kinds of "fixed"charges have to come out of that pay envelope sooner or later. No—he has the cash in his pocket, and that's all that counts. Yet this man knows that if the company he works for conducted its business in such a slap-happy manner, it would end up in bankruptcy.

Here's something to consider—where your money is concerned, you're in business for

多了。)

许多读者可能会说:"我希望你这家伙自己来试试:拿我的周薪支付我的账款,维持我应有的开支。只要你试一试,我敢保证你会知道我的困难,不再敢夸口。"不错,我也有我的财务困难:我曾在密苏里州的玉米田和粮仓做过每天10小时的苦力工作。我辛勤地工作,累得腰酸背痛。我当时所做的那些苦活累活,并不是每小时一美元报酬,也不是50美分,甚至不是10美分——而是每小时5美分,每天工作10小时。

我知道持续20年住在没有浴室和自来水的房子里是什么感受;我知道睡在零下15度的卧室中是什么感受;我也知道徒步好几里,以节省10美分,以及鞋底穿洞、袜子打补丁是什么感受;我还尝过在餐厅里只能要最便宜的菜,以及把裤子压在床垫下是什么滋味——因为我没钱把它们拿去洗熨。然而,我在那段时间仍然勉强自己从收入中省下几个铜板,因为我若不那么做的话,心里就会不安。由于有了这段经历,我终于明白,如果你我希望避免负债,不受金钱的困扰,我们就必须和那些公司一样,拟定一个开支计划,然后根据计划花钱。可惜我们大多数人都不能这样做。例如,我的好朋友利奥·西蒙金就向我指出,人们在处理财务问题时,往往表现得十分盲目。他告诉我,他所认识的一个会计在他公司工作时,对金钱十分精明,但他在处理个人财务时……

就让我们举个例子吧:如果这个人在星期五中午领到薪水,他会走到街上,看到商店橱窗中有一件他很喜欢的大衣,就会毫不犹豫地买下来——他从不考虑房租、电费,以及所有杂费迟早都要从这个薪水袋中抽出来支付。不过这个人也知道,如果他所工作的公司也像他这样以贪图目前享受的方式来经营,那么公司一定会破产。

要知道,当某事情涉及你的金钱时,你就是在为自己经营事业。而你如何处理你的金钱,实际上也确实是你"自己"的事。那么,我们管理金钱的原则是什么呢?我们应该如何进行预算

yourself! And it is literally "your business"what you do with your money. But what are the principles of managing our money? How do we begin to make a budget and a plan? Here are eleven rules.

Rule No. 1: *Get the facts down on paper.*

When Arnold Bennett started out in London fifty years ago to be a novelist, he was poor and hardpressed. So he kept a record of what he did with every sixpence. Did he wonder where his money was going? No. He knew. He liked the idea so much that he continued to keep such a record even after he became rich, world-famous, and had a private yacht.

John D. Rockefeller, Sr. , also kept a ledger. He knew to the penny just where he stood before he said his prayers at night and climbed into bed.

You and I, too, will have to get notebooks and start keeping records. For the rest of our lives? No, not necessarily. Experts on budgets recommend that we keep an accurate account of every nickel we spend for at least the first month—and, if possible, for three months. This is to give us an accurate record of where our money goes, so we can draw up a budget.

Oh, you know where your money goes? Well, maybe so; but if you do, you are one in a thousand! Mrs. Stapleton tells me it is a common occurrence for men and women to spend hours giving her facts and figures, so she can get them down on paper—then, when they see the result on paper, they exclaim: "Is that the way my money goes? "They can hardly believe it. Are you like that? Could be.

Rule No. 2: *Get a tailor-made budget that really fits your needs.*

Mrs. Stapleton tells me that two families may live side by side in identical houses, in the very same suburb, have the same number of children in the family, and receive the same income—yet their budgeting needs will be radically different. Why? Because people are different. She says a budget has to be a personal, custom-made job.

The idea of a budget is not to wring all the joy out of life. The idea is to give us a sense of material security—which in many cases means emotional security and freedom from worry. "People who live on budgets, "Mrs. Stapleton told me, "are happier people."

But how do you go about it? First, as I said, you must list all expenses. Then get advice. In

和计划呢?以下有 11 条规则：

规则一:把事实记在纸上。

阿诺德·班尼特 50 年前在伦敦立志当一名小说家时,穷困潦倒,生活压力非常大。所以他把每一便士的用途都作了记录。他是想知道他的钱怎么花掉的吗?不。他想做到心里有数。他很欣赏这个方法,甚至当他成为世界著名作家、富翁,而且拥有一艘私人游艇之后,还保持着这个习惯。

约翰·洛克菲勒也保持了这种习惯。他每天晚上祷告之前,总会记下每便士的用途,然后才上床睡觉。

你和我也一样,应该找一个本子来,开始记录。难道要记一辈子吗?当然没有必要。有关专家建议,我们最起码要记下第一个月的详细开支——如果可能的话,可以记 3 个月。这样做可以让我们保持精确的记录,知道那些钱是如何花掉的,然后我们可以根据它来做预算。

你也许知道你的钱都花在何处了。但即使你知道,每 1000 个人当中也只有一个像你这样的人。史塔普里顿夫人对我说,当人们用几小时记下他们的详细开支之后,他们通常会惊讶地叫道:"天啊! 我的钱难道是这样用掉的?"他们真的不敢相信。你是否也会这样呢?可能吧!

规则二:制定一项真正适合你的财务计划。

史塔普里顿夫人告诉我,假定有两家邻居,他们住同样的房子,同样的社区,甚至连家里的收入和人数也一样,但是他们的财务预算却有很大的差异。为什么会这样呢?因为人各不同。她指出,财务计划必须根据每个人的实际情况来制定。

制定计划并不是想赶走生活的乐趣,它可以给我们一种物质上的安全感——在大多数情况下,物质上的安全可以带来精神上的安全和优越感。史塔普里顿夫人说:"根据计划生活的人,一般都比较幸福。"

many cities of twenty thousand and up, you will find family-welfare societies that will gladly give you free advice on financial problems and help you draw up a budget to fit your income.

Rule No. 3: *Learn how to spend wisely.*

By this I mean: learn how to get the best value for your money. All large corporations have professional buyers and purchasing agents who do nothing but get the very best buys for their firms. As steward and manager of your personal estate, why shouldn't you do likewise?

Rule No. 4: *Don't increase your headaches with your income.*

Mrs. Stapleton told me that the budgets she dreads most to be called into consultation on are family incomes of five thousand dollars a year. I asked her why. "Because, "she said, "five thousand a year seems to be a goal to most American families. They may go along sensibly and sanely for years—then, when their income rises to five thousand a year, they think they have 'arrived'. They start branching out. Buy a house in the suburbs, 'that doesn't cost any more than renting an apartment'. Buy a car, a lot of new furniture, and a lot of new clothes—and the first thing you know, they are runing into the red. They are actually less happy than they were before—because they have bitten off too much with their increase in income."

That is only natural. We all want to get more out of life. But in the long run, which is going to bring us more happiness—forcing ourselves to live within a tight budget, or having dunning letters in the mail and creditors pounding on the front door?

Rule No. 5: *Try to build credit, in the event you must borrow.*

Now, suppose you haven't insurance you can borrow on, and you haven't any bonds, but you do own a house, or a car, or some other kind of collateral. Where do you go to borrow? By all means, to a bank!

Banks all over this land are subject to strict regulation; they have a reputation to maintain in the community; the rate of interest they can charge is fixed firmly by law; and they will deal with you fairly. Frequently, if you are in a financial jam, the bank will go so far as to discuss your problems with you, make a plan, and help you work your way out of your worry and indebtedness. I repeat, I repeat, if you have collateral, go to a bank!

Rule No. 6: *Potect yourself against illness, fire, and emergency expenses.*

你该如何制定计划呢?首先,你必须列出一切开支,然后要求指导。在许多大城市,都有家庭理财机构,他们会很乐意为你提供免费指导,帮助你量身订做预算方案。

规则三:学习如何明智地花钱。

我指的是学习如何使你的金钱体现出最高价值。所有大公司都设有专门的采购员,他们不做别的事,只为公司买到最合适的物品。你作为你个人财产的主人,何不也这样做呢?

规则四:不要因你的收入而多添烦恼。

史塔普里顿夫人告诉我,她最怕的就是被年薪5000美元的家庭请去作财务预算。我问为什么,她说:"因为年收入5000美元似乎是大多数美国家庭的目标。他们可能经过多年的奋斗才实现这一目标——当他们每年的收入达到5000美元后,他们认为自己已经'成功'了,开始大量花销:在郊区买房子,并说'和租房子花一样多的钱';买新车,添新家具和新衣服——等他们发觉时,已经陷于赤字了。实际上他们比以前更不快乐——因为他们增加的收入全花光了。"

这是很自然的事。我们都希望更好地享受生活,但从长远来看,强迫自己在预算之内生活,或是让催账单塞满你的信箱,以及债主猛敲你的大门,到底哪一种方式会带给我们更多的幸福?

规则五:如果你必须借贷,就设法建立个人信誉。

现在假设你没有保险可借,也没有任何有价债券,但是你有房有车或其他担保物,那么你可以到哪里借钱呢?要尽量去银行借。所有银行都很严格规范,它们在社区也有信誉,利率也由法律严格固定,而且会和你公平交易。所以,如果你遇到困难,银行将会与你商讨对策,制定计划,帮你克服忧虑,摆脱财务困境。我必须再次重复——如果你有担保物,就去银行借钱。

规则六:购买疾病、火灾以及意外保险。

对于各种意外、不幸以及可预料的紧急事件,你可以购买小额保险。我并不是建议你对

Insurance is available, for relatively small sums, on all kinds of accidents, misfortunes, and conceivable emergencies. I am not suggesting that you cover yourself for everything from slipping in the bathtub to catching German measles—but I do suggest that you protect yourself against the major misfortunes that you know could cost you money and therefore do cost you worry. It's cheap at the price.

For example, I know a woman who had to spend ten days in a hospital last year and, when she came out, was presented a bill—for exactly eight dollars! The answer? She had hospital insurance.

Rule No. 7: *Do not have your life-insurance proceeds paid to your widow in cash.*

If you are carrying life insurance to provide for your family after you're gone, do not, I beg of you, have your insurance paid in one lump sum.

What happens to "a new widow with new money"? I'll let Mrs. Marion S. Eberly answer that question.

She is head of the Women's Division of the Institute of Life Insurance, 60 East 42nd Street, New York City. She speaks before women's clubs all over America on the wisdom of using life-insurance proceeds to purchase a life income for the widow instead of giving her the proceeds in cash. She tells me one widow who received twenty thousand dollars in cash and lent it to her son to start in the autoaccessory business. The business failed, and she is destitute now. She tells of another widow who was persuaded by a slick real-estate salesman to put most of her life-insurance money in vacant lots that were "sure to double in value within a year". Three years later, she sold the lots for one-tenth of what she paid for them. She tells of another widow who had to apply to the Child Welfare Association for the support of her children—within twelve months after she had been left fifteenth thousand dollars in life insurance. A hundred thousand similar tragedies could be told.

"The average lifetime of twenty-five thousand dollars left in the hands of a woman is less than seven years. "That statement was made by Sylvia S. Porter, financial editor of the *New York Post*, in the *Ladies' Home Journal*.

Years ago, *The Saturday Evening Post* said in an editorial: "The ease with which the average

任何事件都投一份保险,但我郑重地建议你为自己投一些主要的意外险;否则出了事,不但花大笔的钱,也很令人烦恼。这些保险都很便宜。

举个例子吧,我认识一个妇女,去年在医院住了10天。等她出院之后,她收到的账单只有8美元。这是怎么回事呢?因为她有医疗保险。

规则七:不要让保险公司用现金把你的人寿保险支付给你的受益人。

如果你购买人寿险是为了在你死后能使家人有保障,那么我强烈建议你,千万不能一次性支付。

"拥有许多钞票的新寡妇"结局会如何?就让马利翁·艾伯利夫人来解答这个问题。她是纽约市人寿保险研究所妇女部主任。她曾在全国各地的妇女俱乐部演讲,呼吁不让寡妇领取大笔的人寿保险金,而改为领取终身收入。她告诉我,有一位收到2万美元人寿保险金的寡妇,把钱借给儿子从事汽车零件销售,结果失败了,现在她穷困潦倒。她提到另一位寡妇被一位狡猾的房地产经纪人欺骗,把她的大部分人寿保险金拿来购买"保证在一年之内增值一倍"的空地。当她在3年之后卖掉土地时,只拿回当初的1/10。她又说到另一位寡妇,她领取了1.5万美元的人寿保险金12个月以后,就不得不向儿童福利基金会申请补助抚养她的子女。这样的悲剧真是太多了。

"一个女人有2.5万美元,平均不到7年就全部花光了。"这是《纽约邮报》金融编辑施维亚·波特在《妇女家庭月刊》中说的。

多年以前,《星期六晚邮》在一篇社论中说:"由于普通妇女没有受过商业训练,又没有银行人士替她们出主意,因此她们很可能在第一个狡猾的掮客向她们游说之后,就贸然地把她们丈夫的人寿保险金拿去购买股票。任何律师或银行家都可举出许多类似的例子:节俭的丈夫多年来省吃俭用存下来的钱,只因为他的遗孀或孤儿相信某位专骗女人的骗子,而转眼将其花光。"

widow without business training, and with no banker to advise her, can be wheedled into putting her husband's life-insurance money into wildcat stocks by the first slick salesman who approaches her—is proverbial. Any lawyer or banker can cite a dozen cases in which the entire savings of a thrifty man's lifetime, amassed by years of sacrifice and self-denial, were swept away simply because a widow or an orphan trusted one of the slick crooks who rob women for a livelihood."

If you want to protect your widow and your children, why not take a tip from J. P. Morgan—one of the wisest financiers who ever lived. He left money in his will to sixteen principal legatees. Twelve were women. Did he leave these women cash? No. He left trust funds that ensured these women a monthly income for life.

Rule No. 8: *Teach your children a responsible attitude toward money.*

I shall never forget an idea I once read in *Your Life* magazine. The author, Stella Weston Turtle, descried how she was teaching her little girl a sense of responsibility about money. She got an extra cheque-book from the bank and gave it to her nine-year-old daughter. When the daughter was given her weekly allowance, she "deposited"the money with her mother, who served as a bank for the child's funds. Then, throughout the week, whenever she wanted a cent or two, she "drew a cheque"for that amount and kept track of her balance. The little girl not only found that fun, but began to learn real responsibility in handling her money.

This is an excellent method and if you have a son or daughter of school age, and you want this child to learn how to handle money, I recommend it for your consideration.

Rule No. 9: *If necessary, make a little extra money off your kitchen stove.*

If after you budget your expenses wisely you still find that you don't have enough to make ends meet, you can then do one of two things: you can either scold, fret, worry, and complain, or you can plan to make a little additional money on the side. How? Well, all you have to do to make money is to fill an urgent need that isn't being adequately filled now. That is what Mrs. Nellie Speer, 3709 83rd Street, Jackson Heights, New York, did. In 1932, she found herself living alone in a three-room apartment.

Her husband had died, and both of her children were married. One day, while having some ice-cream at a drugstore soda fountain, she noticed that the fountain was also selling bakery pies

如果你想在死后给妻子儿女提供保障,何不向摩根学习呢?他是当代最伟大的金融专家之一。他把自己的遗产分别赠给16位法定继承人,其中12位都是女性。他留给这些人的是现金吗?不,是有价证券!这样可以使这些女人每月都可以得到生活补贴。

规则八:养成子女对金钱负责的态度。

我永远都不会忘记我从《你的生活》杂志中看到的一篇文章。它的作者史蒂拉·威斯顿·图特讲述了她如何教育她的小女儿养成对金钱负责的态度。她从银行要了一本特殊支票簿,将它交给了9岁的女儿。每当女儿得到了每周的零花钱时,就将这些钱"存进"里面,母亲则成了"银行"。然后,在那个星期之中,每当她要用钱时,就从中"提取",把余款记下来。小女孩不仅从中得到了乐趣,而且学会了如何处理金钱。

这是一项特殊方法,如果你有上学的孩子,并想让他学会如何处理金钱,我建议你可以考虑这种方法。

规则九:如果有必要,你可以在家中赚一点额外收入。

如果你制定好开支预算之后,发现仍然无法弥补开支,那么你可以做以下两种选择之一:你可以咒骂、发愁、担心、抱怨;或者你可以想办法赚一点额外的收入。怎么做到呢?要想赚钱,可以寻找人们最需要而目前供应不足的东西。家住纽约杰克森山庄的赖莉·斯皮尔夫人就是这么做的。她1932年一个人住在一套有3个房间的公寓里。

她的丈夫已经死了,两个儿子也已经结婚。一天,她去一家杂货店的苏打水柜台买冰淇淋,发现那里还卖水果饼,但那些水果饼看上去实在让人不敢恭维。她问老板愿不愿向她买一些真正的家制水果饼,结果他订了两份。

"虽然我是个好厨师,"斯皮尔夫人对我说,"但以前我们住在佐治亚州时,一直有女佣,我亲自烘制饼干的次数也不过10多次。在得到两份订单之后,我向一位邻居请教了如何做苹果

that looked sad and dreary. She asked the proprietor if he would buy some real home-made pies from her. He ordered two. "Although I was a good cook, "Mrs. Speer said, as she told me the story, "I had always had servants when we lived in Georgia, and I had never baked more than a dozen pies in my life. After getting that order for two pies, I asked a neighbor woman how to cook an apple-pie. The soda fountain customers were delighted with my first two home-baked pies, one apple, one lemon. The drugstore ordered five the next day. Then orders gradually came in from other fountains and luncheonettes. Within two years, I was baking five thousand pies a year—I was doing all the work myself in my own tiny kitchen, and I was making a thousand dollars a year clear, without a penny's expense except the ingredients that went into the pies."

The demand for Mrs. Speer's home-baked pastry became so great that she had to move out of her kitchen into a shop and hire two girls to bake for her: pies, cakes, bread, and rolls. During the war, people stood in line for an hour at a time to buy her home-baked foods.

"I have never been happier in my life, "Mrs. Speer said. "I work in the shop twelve to fourteen hours a day, but I don't get tired because it isn't work to me. It is an adventure in living. I am doing my part to make people a little happier. I am too busy to be lonesome or worried. My work has filled a gap in my life left vacant by the passing of my mother and husband and my home."

When I asked Mrs. Speer if she felt that other women who were good cooks could make money in their spare time in a similar way, in towns of ten thousand and up, she replied: "Yes—of course they can!"

Mrs. Ora Snyder will tell you the same thing. She lives in a town of thirty thousand—Maywood, Illinois. Yet she started in business with the kitchen stove and ten cents' worth of ingredients. Her husband fell ill. She had to earn money. But how? No experience. No skill. No capital. Just a housewife. She took the white of an egg and sugar and made some candy on the back of the kitchen stove; then she took her pan of candy and stood near the school and sold it to the children for a penny a piece as they went home. "Bring more pennies tomorrow, "she said. "I'll be here every day with my home-made candy. "During the first week, she not only made a profit, but had also put a new zest into living. She was making both herself and the children

饼的方法。结果,那家杂货店的顾客对我最初的两份水果饼赞不绝口——一份是苹果饼,一份是柠檬饼。第二天杂货店又预订了5份,接着其他杂货店也陆续向我订货。两年之内,我发展到一年必须烘制5000份饼。我单独一人在我自己的小厨房里做这些,我一年纯收入达1000美元。除了一些做饼的原料,我一分钱都不乱花。"

由于对斯皮尔夫人家烘烤饼的需求量愈来愈大,她不得不搬出厨房,租下一间店铺,还雇了两个女孩子帮忙。在世界大战期间,人们常常排一个小时的长队买她的家制食品。

"在我一生中,从未有如此快乐,"斯皮尔夫人说,"我一天在店里工作12~14小时,但我从不觉得累,因为对我来说这不是什么工作。那可真是生活中的奇异体验。我只是尽我所能使人们更加快乐。我如此忙碌,以至于无暇忧愁或寂寞。我的工作弥补了自我母亲和丈夫去世后给我留下来的空白。"

我问斯皮尔夫人,是否其他烹调技术高明的家庭主妇也可以在闲暇时以同样的方式在一个1万人以上的小镇上赚钱,她回答说:"可以。当然可以。"

奥拉·斯林达夫人也会告诉你同样的故事。她住在伊利诺伊州一个3万人口的梅梧小镇。她就在厨房以10美分的原料开创了自己的事业。由于她丈夫病了,她必须赚钱。怎么办?她既没有经验,也没有技术,又没有资金,只不过是个家庭主妇。她从一颗鸡蛋中取出蛋清,加上一些白糖,在厨房里做了一些饼干,然后将这些饼干带到学校附近,卖给正放学回家的学生,一块饼干只卖一分钱。"明天多带点钱来,"她说,"我每天都会带自制饼干来这儿。"在第一周,她不仅赚了钱,也找到了生活的乐趣。她为自己和孩子们带来了欢乐,再也没有时间忧虑了。

这位来自伊州梅梧镇的文静家庭主妇有着很大的抱负,她决定往外扩展,找个代理人在繁华的芝加哥市卖她的家制饼干。她羞怯地找到一个在街头卖花生的意大利人。他耸耸肩,说他的顾客只要花生,而不是饼干。她给了他一块样品,他很喜欢,于是开始替她出售饼干,第一天

happy. No time now for worry.

This quiet little housewife from Maywood, Illinois, was so ambitious that she decided to branch out—to have an agent sell her kitchen-made candy in roaring, thundering Chicago. She timidly approached an Italian selling peanuts on the street. He shrugged his shoulders. His customers wanted peanuts, not candy. She gave him a sample. He liked it, began selling her candy, and made a good profit for Mrs.

Snyder on the first day. Four years later, she opened her first store in Chicago. It was only eight feet wide. She made her candy at night and sold it in the daytime. This erstwhile timid housewife, who started her candy factory on her kitchen stove, now has seventeen stores—fifteen of them in the busy Loop district of Chicago.

Here is the point I am trying to make. Nellie Speer, in Jackson Heights, New York, and Mrs. Ora Snyder, in Maywood, Illinois, instead of worrying about finances, did something positive. They started in an extremely small way to make money off the kitchen stove—no overhead, no rent, no advertising, no salaries. Under these conditions, it is almost impossible for a woman to be defeated by financial worries.

Look around you. You will find many needs that are not filled. For example, if you train yourself to be a good cook, you can probably make money by starting cooking classes for young girls right in your own kitchen. You can get your students by ringing door-bells.

Rule No. 10: *Don't gamble-ever.*

I am always astounded by the people who hope to make money by betting on the ponies or playing slot machines. I know a man who makes his living by owning a string of these "one armed bandits", and he has nothing but contempt for the foolish people who are so naive as to imagine that they can beat a machine that is already rigged against them.

I also know one of the best known bookmakers in America. He was a student in my adult-education classes. He told me that with all his knowledge of horse racing, he couldn't make money betting on the ponies. Yet the facts are that foolish people bet six billion dollars a year on the races—six times as much as our total national debt back in 1910. This bookmaker also told me that if he had an enemy he despised, he could think of no better way of ruining him than by getting him to bet on the

就为她赚了不少钱。4 年后,她在芝加哥开了第一间店铺,只有 8 尺宽。她晚上做饼,白天销售。这位以前羞怯的家庭主妇,从厨房的炉灶开创饼干工厂,现在拥有 17 家店铺——其中 15 家在芝加哥市最热闹的鲁普区。

我在此想说的是,赖莉·斯皮尔和奥拉·斯林达不仅没有为金钱而烦恼,反而采取积极主动的做法。她们以最小的方式,从厨房开始,没有租金,没有广告费,也没有薪水。在这种情况下创业的女人,是不可能被财务忧虑拖垮的。

看看你四周,你也许会发现许多尚未达到饱和的行业。例如,如果你自己是一名优秀的厨师,你可以开一个烹饪培训班,就在你自己的厨房里教年轻女孩子,说不定上门的学生络绎不绝呢。

规则十:不要赌博——永远不要。

我总是不理解那些想从赌赛马和玩吃角子机器上赢钱的人。我认识一个人,他有多台"单手土匪"游戏机,并依靠这些机器为生。他对于那些天真地想打败这些骗钱机器的傻瓜,除了蔑视之外,别无同情。

我还认识美国最出色的一名赌赛马的老手。他是我成人教育班的一名学员。他告诉我,根据他的经验,他并不能从赌赛马中赚到钱。然而,事实是每年都有许多傻瓜在赛马中赌掉了 60 亿美元——刚好是美国 1910 年全国总债务的 6 倍。这位赛马赌徒还告诉我,如果他想毁灭他的敌人,最好的办法就是让对方去赌赛马。我问他,如果有人根据赛马的内部情报来下赌注,那结果会如何?他回答说:"照这种方式来赌,会输掉整个美国造币厂。"

规则十一:如果我们不能改善自己的经济状况,不妨宽恕自己。

如果我们不能改善自己的经济状况,也许我们可改进我们的心态。记住,别人也有他们的财务烦恼。我们可能会因为经济条件不如别人而烦恼,但别人也可能因为比不上另一家而烦

races. When I asked him what would happen to the man who played the races according to the tipster sheets, he replied: "You could lose the Mint by betting that way. "

Rule No. 11: *If we can't possibly improve our financial situation, let's be good to ourselves and stop resenting what can't be changed.*

If we can't possibly improve our financial situation, maybe we can improve our mental attitude towards it. Let's remember that other people have their financial worries, too. We may be worried because we can't keep up with the Joneses; but the Joneses are probably worried because they can't keep up with the Ritzes; and the Ritzes are worried because they can't keep up with the Vanderbilts.

Some of the most famous men in American history have had their financial troubles. Both Lincoln and Washington had to borrow money to make the trip to be inaugurated as President.

If we can't have all we want, let's not poison our days and sour our dispositions with worry and resentment. Let's be good to ourselves. Let's try to be philosophical about it. "If you have what seems to you insufficient, "said one of Rome's greatest philosophers, Seneca, "then you will be miserable even if you possess the world. "

And let's remember this: even if we owned the entire United States with a hog-tight fence around it, we could eat only three meals a day and sleep in only one bed at a time.

恼，而这另一家又因为比不上另一家而烦恼。

即使美国历史上最著名的人物也有他们的财务烦恼。例如，林肯和华盛顿都必须向人借钱，才能上路就任总统。

如果我们得不到我们想要的东西，最好不要让忧虑和悔恨来打搅我们的生活。我们要善待自己。古罗马最伟大的哲学之一塞尼加说："如果你一直觉得不满足，那么即使你拥有整个世界，你也会伤心。"

记住，即使我们拥有整个世界，我们一天也只吃三餐，一次也只睡一张床。

Part Nine
"How I Conquered Worry—32 True Stories"

Six Major Troubles Hit Me All at Once

By C. I. Blackwood

Proprietor, Blackwood-Davis Business College Oklahoma City

In the summer of 1943, it seemed to me that half the worries of the world had come to rest on my shoulders.

For more than forty years, I had lived a normal, carefree life with only the usual troubles which come to a husband, father, and business man. I could usually meet these troubles easily, but suddenly—wham! wham!! wham!!! wham!!!! WHAM!!!!! WHAM!!!!!! Six major troubles hit me all at once. I pitched and tossed and turned in bed all night long, half dreading to see the day come, because I faced these six major worries:

1. My business college was trembling on the verge of financial disaster because all the boys were going to war; and most of the girls were making more money working in war plants without training than my graduates could make in business offices with training. 2. My older son was in service, and I had the heart-numbing worry common to all parents whose sons were away at war. 3. Oklahoma City had already started proceedings to appropriate a large tract of land for an airport, and my home—formerly my father's home—was located in the centre of this tract. I knew that I would be paid only one tenth of its value, and, what was even worse, I would lose my home; and because of the housing shortage, I worried about whether I could possibly find another home to shelter my family of six. I feared we might have to live in a tent. I even worried about whether we would be able to buy a tent. 4. The water well on my property went dry because a drainage canal had been dug near my home. To dig a new well would be throwing five hundred dollars away because the land was probably being appropriated. I had to carry water to my livestock in buckets every morning for two months, and I feared I would have to continue it

第九篇　克服忧虑的真实故事

困扰我的6大烦恼

戴卫斯商业学院创始人　C. I. 布莱克伍德

1943年夏天,似乎这个世界的一半烦恼都降临到了我身上。

40多年来,我一直过着正常而无忧无虑的生活,平时遇到的是作为一个丈夫、父亲、商人所遇到的小问题。我通常都可以轻易地处理好这些,但突然间,我的天啊! 竟然有6项主要烦恼突然同时打击着我。我整夜在床上辗转反侧,害怕白天的到来。因为我所面临的是下面六大忧虑:

第一,我的商学院濒临破产边缘,因为所有的男孩子都参军了,而大部分女孩子即使没有接受商业训练,她们在军火厂所赚的钱也比在我的商学院毕业后去公司赚的还多。第二,我的大儿子正在服役,跟所有父母一样,我十分担心。第二,俄克拉荷马市政府已开始计划征收一大片土地建造机场,我家的房子——以前是我父亲的房子——正好位于这片土地的中央。我知道我只能得到1/10的补偿;更糟糕的是,我将失去我的房子;加上当时房源缺乏,我担心能不能找到另一栋房子让一家六口度日。我担心我们也许必须住在帐篷里;我甚至担心我们是否有能力购置帐篷。第四,由于我家附近刚刚挖了一条大排水沟,使得我土地上的水井干了。若是再挖一口新井,等于浪费500美元,因为这块土地也许会被征收。我已经接连两个月每天早上提水喂牲口,我担心在战争结束以前必须每天都这么做。第五,我的住处离学校有10里远,而我领的是"B级汽油卡",这表明我不能购买任何新轮胎。因此,我担心一旦我那辆过时的福特车的

during the rest of the war. 5. I lived ten miles away from my business school and I had a class B petrol card: that meant I couldn't buy any new tyres, so I worried about how I could ever get to work when the superannuated tyres on my old Ford gave up the ghost. 6. My oldest daughter had graduated from high school a year ahead of schedule. She had her heart set on going to college, and I just didn't have the money to send her. I knew her heart would be broken.

One afternoon while sitting in my office, worrying about my worries, I decided to write them all down, for it seemed no one ever had more to worry about than I had. I didn't mind wrestling with worries that gave me a fighting chance to solve them, but these worries all seemed to be utterly beyond my control. I could do nothing to solve them. So I filed away this typewritten list of my troubles, and, as the months passed, I forgot that I had ever written it. Eighteen months later, while transferring my files, I happened to come across this list of my six major problems that had once threatened to wreck my health. I read them with a great deal of interest—and profit. I now saw that not one of them had come to pass. Here is what had happened to them:

1. I saw that all my worries about having to close my business college had been useless because the government had started paying business schools for training veterans and my school was soon filled to capacity. 2. I saw that all my worries about my son in service had been useless: he was coming through the war without a scratch. 3. I saw that all my worries about my land being appropriated for use as an airport had been useless because oil had been struck within a mile of my farm and the cost for procuring the land for an airport had become prohibitive. 4. I saw that all my worries about having no well to water my stock had been useless because, as soon as I knew my land would not be appropriated, I spent the money necessary to dig a new well to a deeper level and found an unfailing supply of water. 5. I saw that all my worries about my tyres giving out had been useless, because by recapping and careful driving, the tyres had managed somehow to survive. 6. I saw that all my worries about my daughter's education had been useless, because just sixty days before the opening of college, I was offered—almost like a miracle—an auditing job which I could do outside of school hours, and this job made it possible for me to send her to college on schedule.

I had often heard people say that ninety-nine per cent of the things we worry and stew and fret about never happen, but this old saying didn't mean much to me until I ran across that list of

轮胎爆了,我就无法上班了。第六,我大女儿提前一年高中毕业,她想上大学,但我没有钱供她上大学。我知道她一定很伤心。

一天下午,我正在办公室担心这些烦恼,于是将它们全部记下来,因为似乎没有人比我的烦恼更多了。只要有机会,我并不在乎花时间和精力去解决它们,但现在这一切困难似乎超出了我的能力。我根本无法解决。所以我就用打字机把这些困难全部写出来。几个月之后,我忘了这件事。18 个月之后,当我整理文件时,碰巧又看到了这张列有一度令我几乎崩溃的六大困难的单子。我极感兴趣地看了一遍,获益不少。现在我发现所有的困难都不复存在了。这是它们后来的变化:

第一,我发现担心商学院会被迫关门是瞎操心。因为政府开始拨款补助商学院,代为培训退伍军人,我的学校很快又恢复了活力。第二,我发现担心我儿子也没有用。他安然无恙地接受了战争洗礼。第三,我发现担心土地被征收也是多余的,因为在我农场附近找到了石油,建造机场的计划停了下来。第四,我发现担心没有水井打水喂牲口也是不必要的,因为当我得知土地不再被征收之后,就立刻花钱打了一口新井,水源不绝。第五,我发现担心我的轮胎破裂也是不必要的。因为我将那个旧轮胎改新之后,只要小心驾驶,它绝对没问题。第六,我发现担心我女儿上大学的事也是不必要的。因为在开学前 6 天,我获得了一个查账的工作机会——这简直是个奇迹——这使我能够即时送她上大学。

我常听人说,我们所担心的事 99%都不会发生,但我对这种说法一直不以为然,直到我看见我在 18 个月之前那个可怕的下午打的那张单子之后,才明白这一道理。

虽然我白白为这些烦恼而忧虑,但我现在十分感激。因为这段经历给了我永难磨灭的教训,它使我明白,成天担心永远不会发生的事情是多么悲哀啊!

记住,今天就是你昨天担心的明天。一定要问自己:我怎样才能"知道"我现在所担心的事

worries I had typed out that dreary afternoon eighteen months previously.

I am thankful now that I had to wrestle in vain with those six terrible worries. That experience has taught me a lesson I'll never forget. It has shown me the folly and tragedy of stewing about events that haven't happened—events that are beyond our control and may never happen.

Remember, today is the tomorrow you worried about yesterday. Ask yourself: How do I KNOW this thing I am worrying about will really come to pass?

I Can Turn Myself into a ShoutingOptimist Within an Hour

By Roger W. Babson

Famous Economist Babson Park, Wellesley Hills, Massachusetts

When I find myself depressed over present conditions, I can, within one hour, banish worry and turn myself into a shouting optimist.

Here is how I do it. I enter my library, close my eyes, and walk to certain shelves containing only books on history. With my eyes still shut, I reach for a book, not knowing whether I am picking up Prescott's *conquest of Mexico* or Suetonius' *Lives of the Twelve Caesars*. With my eyes still closed, I open the book at random. I then open my eyes and read for an hour; and the more I read, the more sharply I realize that the world has always been in the throes of agony, that civilisation has always been tottering on the brink. The pages of history fairly shriek with tragic tales of war, famine, poverty, pestilence, and man's inhumanity to man. After reading history for an hour, I realise that bad as conditions are now, they are infinitely better than they used to be. This enables me to see and face my present troubles in their proper perspective as well as to realize that the world as a whole is constantly growing better.

Here is a method that deserves a whole chapter. Read history! Try to get the viewpoint of ten thousand years—and see how trivial your troubles are, in terms of eternity.

How I Got Rid of an Inferiority Complex

By Elmer Thomas

Former United States Senator from Oklahoma

When I was fifteen I was constantly tormented by worries and fears and self-consciousness. I

真的会发生?

做一个乐观的人

著名经济学家 罗杰·巴伯森

每当我发现自己对眼前的景况感到沮丧时,我可以在一小时之内抛弃所有的烦恼,使自己成为一个高高兴兴的乐观者。

下面就是我的办法:

我走进书房,闭上眼睛,走向专放历史书的书架前。我仍旧闭着眼睛,随手取出一本书——根本不知道是普里斯科特写的《墨西哥征服史》,还是史东尼所著的《恺撒传》。我仍然把眼睛闭上,随便翻到一页。然后,我睁开眼睛,读上一个小时。我越往下读,就越能体会到这个世界总是痛苦不断,人类文明总是濒临毁灭的边缘。历史上充满了悲剧故事:战争、饥荒、穷困、瘟疫、惨无人道。

读了一小时的历史之后,我就会明白,即使是目前处境恶劣,实际上也比以前好许多。这使我能够朝好的方面看我现在所遇到的困难,明白这个世界正在不断地朝着更好的方向发展。

上述方法值得用一整章来介绍。读读历史吧!试着将你的眼光扩展到1万年——从永恒的角度来看,“你的”烦恼真是微不足道。

克服自卑的心理

美国前参议员 艾玛·托马斯

在我15岁时,经常遭受烦恼、恐惧、自卑的折磨。当时我的身高相对我的年龄来说实在太高了,而且我瘦得像竹竿一样。我身高6.2英尺,而体重只有118磅。虽然我长得这么高,但身

was extremely tall for my age and as thin as a fence rail. I stood six feet two inches and weighed only 118 pounds. In spite of my height, I was weak and could never compete with the other boys in baseball or running games. They poked fun at me and called me "hatchet-face". I was so worried and self-conscious that I dreaded to meet anyone, and I seldom did, for our farmhouse was off the public road and surrounded by thick virgin timber that had never been cut since the beginning of time. We lived half a mile from the highway; and a week would often go by without my seeing anyone except my mother, father, and brothers and sisters.

I would have been a failure in life if I had let those worries and fears whip me. Every day and every hour of the day, I brooded over my tall, gaunt, weak body. I could hardly think of anything else. My embarrassment, my fear, was so intense that it is almost impossible to describe it. My mother knew how I felt. She had been a school-teacher, so she said to me: "Son, you ought to get an education, you ought to make your living with your mind because your body will always be a handicap."

Since my parents were unable to send me to college, I knew I would have to make my own way; so I hunted and trapped opossum, skunk, mink, and raccoon one winter; sold my hides for four dollars in the spring, and then bought two little pigs with my four dollars. I fed the pigs slop and later corn and sold them for forty dollars the next fall. With the proceeds from the sale of the two hogs I went away to the Central Normal College—located at Danville, Indiana. I paid a dollar and forty cents a week for my board and fifty cents a week for my room. I wore a brown shirt my mother had made me. (Obviously, she had used brown cloth because it wouldn't show the dirt.) I wore a suit of clothes that had once belonged to my father. Dad's clothes didn't fit me and neither did his old congress gaiter shoes that I wore—shoes that had elastic bands in the sides that stretched when you put them on. But the stretch had long since gone out of the bands, and the tops were so loose that the shoes almost dropped off my feet as I walked. I was so embarrassed to associate with the other students, so I sat in my room alone and studied. The deepest desire of my life was to be able to buy some store clothes that fit me, clothes that I was not ashamed of.

Shortly after that, four events happened that helped me to overcome my worries and my feeling of inferiority. One of these events gave me courage and hope and confidence and completely changed all the rest of my life. I'll describe these events briefly:

体却很弱,一直都不能和其他男孩在棒球或田径比赛上竞争。他们嘲笑我,叫我“瘦脸”。我十分忧愁,非常自卑,几乎不敢见人。而我确实也很少与人见面,因为我们的农场离公路很远,四周全都是茂密的树林。我们的住处离公路有半里远,所以我经常是一连七八天都看不到陌生人,只能看见我的父母和兄弟姐妹。

如果我被动地让这些烦恼和恐惧打击我,那我可能终生都是一个失败者。每一天的每一小时,我总是在担心自己那高瘦虚弱的身体。我无法想其他事情。我的自卑与恐惧如此严重,简直难以描述。我母亲知道了我的感觉。她曾经当过学校老师。她对我说:“孩子,你应该去读书。你应该靠你的大脑生活,因为你的身体不好。”

由于我父母没有能力送我去读大学,因此我知道自己必须努力奋斗。有一年冬天,我去打猎:铺设陷阱捕捉负鼠、臭鼬、貂和浣熊。到了春天,我把这些兽皮卖了 4 美元,然后用那些钱买了两头小猪。我先用流质饲料喂养小猪,然后改用玉米。第二年秋天,两只猪卖了 40 美元。我带了这笔钱,到位于印第安纳州丹维市的中央师范学院。我每周的伙食费是 1.4 美元,房租每星期是 0.5 美元。穿着母亲给我缝制的棕色衬衫。(显然,她用棕色布是因为不容易脏。)我穿了一套以前父亲穿的西服——父亲的衣服我穿不合身。我脚上穿的那双鞋也是父亲的,同样不合适——那种鞋子两侧有松紧带,你一拉紧它们就松开,但是父亲那双鞋的松紧带早就没了弹性,加上前端又很宽松,因此我一走起路来鞋子就会从脚上掉下来。我觉得很难堪,不敢和其他学生往来,所以独自一人关在房间看书。当时我最大的欲望就是有能力买一些衣服,既合我身材,又不会让我感到羞耻。

没过多久,发生了几件事,使我克服了忧虑和自卑感。其中一件事不仅给了我勇气、希望和信心,还完全改变了我以后的生活。我简单描述一下这几件事。

第一件:在进入师范学院 8 个星期之后,我参加了一项考试,获得一份“三等证书”,这样

First: After attending this normal school for only eight weeks, I took an examination and was given a third-grade certificate to teach in the country public schools. To be sure, this certificate was good for only six months, but it was fleeting evidence that somebody had faith in me—the first evidence of faith that I ever had from anyone except my mother.

Second: A country school board at a place called Happy Hollow hired me to teach at a salary of two dollars per day, or forty dollars per month. Here was even more evidence of somebody's faith in me.

Third: As soon as I got my first cheque I bought some store clothes—clothes that I wasn't ashamed to wear. If someone gave me a million dollars now, it wouldn't thrill me half as much as that first suit of store clothes for which I paid only a few dollars.

Fourth: The real turning point in my life, the first great victory in my struggle against embarrassment and inferiority occurred at the Putnam County Fair held annually in Bain-bridge, Indiana. My mother had urged me to enter a public-speaking contest that was to be held at the fair. To me, the very idea seemed fantastic. I didn't have the courage to talk even to one person—let alone a crowd. But my mother's faith in me was almost pathetic. She dreamed great dreams for my future. She was living her own life over in her son. Her faith inspired me to enter the contest. I chose for my subject about the last thing in the world that I was qualified to talk on: "The Fine and Liberal Arts of America". Frankly, when I began to prepare a speech I didn't know what the liberal arts were, but it didn't matter much because my audience didn't know, either. I memorised my flowery talk and rehearsed it to the trees and cows a hundred times. I was so eager to make a good showing for my mother's sake that I must have spoken with emotion. At any rate, I was awarded the first prize. I was astounded at what happened. A cheer went up from the crowd. The very boys who had once ridiculed me and poked fun at me and called me hatchet-faced now slapped me on the back and said: "I knew you could do it, Elmer. " My mother put her arms around me and sobbed.

As I look back in retrospect, I can see that winning that speaking contest was the turning point of my life. The local newspapers ran an article about me on the front page and prophesied great things for my future. Winning that contest put me on the map locally and gave me prestige, and, what is far more important, it multiplied my confidence a hundredfold. I now realize that if I had not won that contest, I probably would never have become a member of the Linked States Senate,

我就可以在乡村公立学校教书。说得更明确一点，这份证书的期限只有6个月，但它可以使别人对我有信心——这是除了我母亲之外，第一次有人对我有信心。

第二件：一所位于“快乐谷”的乡村学校的董事会聘请了我，每天的薪水是2美元，或者月薪40美元。这更表明有人相信我。

第三件：领到第一份薪水之后，我从商店里买了衣服，穿上这衣服使我不再觉得羞耻。如果现在有人给我100万美元，我也不会像当初花几美元买那些衣服那么兴奋。

第四件：我生命中真正的转折点——我克服自卑和忧愁的第一次伟大胜利，发生在印第安纳州班桥镇每年举行一次的“普特南郡博览会”上。我母亲鼓励我参加一项将在博览会上举行的演讲赛。对我来说，这可是个幻想。我甚至没有勇气当着一个人的面谈话——更不用说面对一群人了。但母亲对我的信心几乎令人心酸。她对我的前途期望很高，她是为她的儿子而活的。她的信任使我决定参加比赛。

我选择了我唯一有资格演讲的题目《美国的自由艺术》。老实说，我刚开始准备这次演讲时，并不知道什么是自由艺术。不过，因为我的听众也不懂，所以我将我那份辞藻华丽的演讲词全部背了下来，并对着树木和牛练习了不下一百遍。由于我想在母亲面前好好表现一下，因此我一定是带着深厚的感情作那次演讲的——无论如何，我得了第一名。

我不禁呆了！听众中间响起一片欢呼。而那些曾讥笑我、称我为“瘦脸”的男孩子，现在却拍着我的背说：“艾玛，我早知道你能行。”母亲抱着我哭了。

回顾过去，可以看出那次演讲比赛获胜是我人生的转折点。当地报纸在头版刊登了一篇报道，预言我前途无量。

在那次比赛中获胜，使我在当地声名鹊起。更重要的是，这极大地增加了我的信心。现在我很清楚，如果我不是在那次比赛中获胜，恐怕我一辈子也进不了美国参议院，因为它开启了我

for it lifted my sights, widened my horizons, and made me realize that I had latent abilities that I never dreamed I possessed. Most important, however, was the fact that the first prize in the oratorical contest was a year's scholarship in the Central Normal College.

I hungered now for more education. So, during the next few years—from 1896 to 1900—I divided my time between teaching and studying. In order to pay my expenses at De Pauw University, I waited on tables, looked after furnaces, mowed lawns, kept books, worked in the wheat and cornfields during the summer, and hauled gravel on a public road-construction job.

In 1896, when I was only nineteen, I made twenty-eight speeches, urging people to vote for William Jennings Bryan for President. The excitement of speaking for Bryan aroused a desire in me to enter politics myself. So when I entered De Pauw University, I studied law and public speaking. In 1899 I represented the university in a debate with Butler College, held in Indianapolis, on the subject "Resolved that United States Senators should be elected by popular vote." I won other speaking contests and became editor-in-chief of the class of 1900 College Annual, *The Mirage*, and the university paper, *The Palladium*.

After receiving my A. B. degree at De Pauw, I took Horace Greeley's advice—only I didn't go west, I went southwest. I went down to a new country: Oklahoma. When the Kiowa, Comanche, and Apache Indian reservation was opened, I home-steaded a claim and opened a law office in Lawton, Oklahoma. I served in the Oklahoma State Senate for thirteen years, in the lower House of Congress for four years, and at fifty years of age, I achieved my lifelong ambition: I was elected to the United States Senate from Oklahoma. I have served in that capacity since March 4, 1927. Since Oklahoma and Indian Territories became the state of Oklahoma on November 16, 1907, I have been continuously honoured by the Democrats of my adopted state by nominations—first for State Senate, then for Congress, and later for the United States Senate.

I have told this story, not to brag about my own fleeting accomplishments, which can't possibly interest anyone else. I have told it wholly with the hope that it may give renewed courage and confidence to some poor boy who is now suffering from the worries and shyness and feeling of inferiority that devastated my life when I was wearing my father's cast-off clothes and gaiter shoes that almost dropped off my feet as I walked.

的视野,使我明白自己具有以前想都不敢想的潜力。不过,最重要的是,我在那场演讲比赛中得到的第一名奖品,是中央师范学院一年的奖学金。

那时,我渴望多学一点东西。因此,在以后的几年当中,我把我的时间分为教和学两部分。为了支付我在迪保大学的费用,我当过服务生,看过锅炉,剪过草,当过记账员,暑假还去麦田和玉米田工作,并在公路上挑石子修路。

1896 年,当时我只有 19 岁,但我已作了 28 次演说,呼吁人们投票选威廉·杰宁斯·布利恩当总统。为布利恩竞选拉选票的经历,使我产生了从政的兴趣。因此,在我进入迪保大学之后,就选修法律和公开演说两门课程。1899 年,我代表学校参加了和巴特勒学院的辩论赛,这次比赛在印第安纳波利斯举行,题目是《美国参议员是否应由大众选举》。我还赢得了其他演讲比赛,成为班刊和校刊的总编辑。

在迪保大学获得学士学位之后,我接受柯雷斯·格莱利的建议,去了西南方。我来到一个新地方俄克拉荷马。当基俄瓦、康曼奇、阿帕奇的印第安人保留区开放之后,我也申请到一块土地,并在俄克拉荷马的罗顿市开了一家法律事务所。我在州参议院干了 13 年,在州下议院干了 4 年。在我 50 岁那年,我终于实现了一生最大的愿望:从俄克拉荷马州被选入美国参议院。从 1927 年 3 月 4 日起,我一直担任该职。自从俄克拉荷马和印第安区于 1907 年 11 月 16 日合并成为俄克拉荷马州之后,我一直获得了该州民主党的光荣提名——先是进入州参议院,然后进入州议会,最后进入美国参议院。

我讲这些往事,并不是炫耀我小小的成就,因为人们不会感兴趣。我这样做只是希望给那些目前受烦恼和自卑感所苦的可怜小伙子们增添一些勇气和自信心。想当初,在我穿着父亲那身旧衣服以及那双走路几乎要脱落的鞋子时,那种烦恼和羞怯以及自卑几乎毁了我。

(编者注:有件事十分有趣,艾玛·托马斯年轻时因为衣服不合身而大为苦恼,但他后来却

(Editor's note: It is interesting to know that Elmer Thomas, who was so ashamed of his ill-fating clothes as a youth, was later voted the best-dressed man in the United States Senate.)

I Lived in The Garden of Allah

By R. V. C. Bodley

Descendant of Sir Thomas Bodley, founder of the Bodleian Library, Oxford Author of *Wind in the Sahara*, *The Messenger*, and fourteen other volumes

In 1918, I turned my back on the world I had known and went to northwest Africa and lived with the Arabs in the Sahara, the Garden of Allah. I lived there seven years. I learned to speak the language of the nomads. I wore their clothes, I ate their food, and adopted their mode of life, which has changed very little during the last twenty centuries. I became an owner of sheep and slept on the ground in the Arabs' tents. I also made a detailed study of their religion. In fact, I later wrote a book about Mohammed, entitled *The Messenger*.

Those seven years which I spent with these wandering shepherds were the most peaceful and contented years of my life.

I had already had a rich and varied experience: I was born of English parents in Paris; and lived in France for nine years. Later I was educated at Eton and at the Royal Military College at Sandhurst. Then I spent six years as a British army officer in India, where I played polo, and hunted, and explored in the Himalayas as well as doing some soldiering. I fought through the First World War and, at its close, I was sent to the Paris Conference as an assistant military attaché. I was shocked and disappointed at what I saw there. During the four years of slaughter on the Western Front, I had believed we were fighting to save civilisation. But at the Paris Peace Conference, I saw selfish politicians laying the groundwork for the Second World War—each country grabbing all it could for itself, creating national antagonisms, and reviving the intrigues of secret diplomacy.

I was sick of war, sick of the army, sick of society. For the first time in my career, I spent sleepless nights, worrying about what I should do with my life. Lloyd George urged me to go in for politics. I was considering taking his advice when a strange thing happened, a strange thing that

被选为美国参议院着装最佳先生。)

我住在安拉的乐园

《撒哈拉之风》、《先知》作者　伯德莱

我于1918年离开我所熟悉的世界，前往非洲西北部，和阿拉伯人住在撒哈拉这个“安拉的乐园”。我在那儿住了7年，掌握了那些游牧民族的语言。我穿他们的服装，吃他们的食物，按照他们的方式生活，过去20年间很少改变。我成了羊群的主人，睡在阿拉伯人的帐篷里。我还深入研究了他们的宗教。事实上，我后来写了一本有关穆罕默德的书，书名为《先知》。

和这群流浪牧羊人在一起的7年，是我一生中最安详充实的日子。

我本来过着富裕而多姿多彩的生活：我父母是英国人，而我却出生在巴黎，在法国待了9年。后来，我在伊顿学院和皇家军事学院上学。然后，我以英国陆军军官的身份在印度待过6年，在那里打马球、打猎，并到喜马拉雅山探险。我参加过第一次世界大战，战争结束时，我被选派参加巴黎和会，当了一名助理军事武官。在当地的所见所闻，令我震惊和失望。我在西方前线的4年战斗中，深信我们是为了维护人类文明而战。可是在巴黎和会上，我亲眼目睹了自私自利的政客给第二次世界大战埋下了导火线——每个国家都在竭力为自己争夺土地，制造国家之间的仇恨，并再度掀起秘密外交的各种阴谋活动。

我开始厌倦战争，厌倦军队，并厌倦这个社会。我生命中第一次无法入睡，不知该做什么。洛伊·乔治建议我从政当官，我考虑接受他的劝告，可是这时候发生了一件奇怪的事，它改变了我后来7年的人生道路。这件事发生在一次不到4分钟的谈话中——这次的谈话对象是“泰德”劳伦斯，也即第一次世界大战中最富浪漫色彩的“阿拉伯的劳伦斯”。他曾同阿拉伯人一起住在沙漠里，他还建议我也这么做。起初，这个建议有些奇异。

shaped and determined my life for the next seven years. It all came from a conversation that lasted less than two hundred seconds—a conversation with "Ted"Lawrence, "Lawrence of Arabia", the most colourful and romantic figure produced by the First World War. He had lived in the desert with the Arabs and he advised me to do the same thing. At first, it sounded fantastic.

However, I was determined to leave the army, and I had to do something. Civilian employers did not want to hire men like me—ex-officers of the regular army—especially when the labour market was jammed with millions of unemployed. So I did as Lawrence suggested: I went to live with the Arabs. I am glad I did so. They taught me how to conquer worry. Like all faithful Moslems, they are fatalists.

They believe that every word which Mohammed wrote in the Koran is the divine revelation of Allah. So when the Koran says: "God created you and all your actions, "they accept it literally. That is why they take life so calmly and never hurry or get into unnecessary tempers when things go wrong. They know that what is ordained is ordained; and no one but God can alter anything. However, that doesn't mean that in the face of disaster, they sit down and do nothing. To illustrate, let me tell you of a fierce, burning windstorm of the sirocco which I experienced when I was living in the Sahara. It howled and screamed for three days and nights. It was so strong, so fierce, that it blew sand from the Sahara hundreds of miles across the Mediterranean and sprinkled it over the Rhone Valley in France. The wind was so hot I felt as if the hair was being scorched off my head. My throat was parched. My eyes burned. My teeth were full of grit. I felt as if I were standing in front of a furnace in a glass factory. I was driven as near crazy as a man can be and retain his sanity. But the Arabs didn't complain. They shrugged their shoulders and said: "*Mektoub*! "... "It is written."

But immediately after the storm was over, they sprang into action: they slaughtered all the lambs because they knew they would die anyway; and by slaughtering them at once, they hoped to save the mother sheep. After the lambs were slaughtered, the flocks were driven southward to water. This was all done calmly, without worry or complaining or mourning over their losses. The tribal chief said:"It is not too bad. We might have lost everything. But praise God, we have forty per cent of our sheep left to make a new start."

I remember another occasion, when we were motoring across the desert and a tire blew out.

不过,我已经决定离开军队,所以必须再找点事情做。私人老板可不想雇用像我这种从正规军队退伍的军官——尤其当时求职者多如牛毛。所以我听了劳伦斯的建议,和阿拉伯人住在一起。我很高兴这么做。他们教会了我如何克服忧虑。

他们相信穆罕默德在《古兰经》上写的每一句话,都是安拉的圣言。因此,当《古兰经》上说"上帝创造了你及你所有的行为"时,他们完完全全地接受下来。这也正是他们能够安详地生活,当事情出了差错时也不发火的原因。他们知道,除了上帝,没有人能够改变任何事情。不过,这并不是说他们在面临灾难时只坐在那里毫不作为。我可以把我住在撒哈拉时经历的一场炙热暴风的事情告诉大家。那场暴风连续刮了三天三夜,风势强劲而猛烈,甚至把撒哈拉的沙子带过地中海,吹到了几百里远的法国的隆河河谷。那次暴风酷热难耐,我觉得我的头发似乎烧焦了,喉咙又干又痛,眼睛刺痛,嘴里全都是沙子。我觉得自己好像站在玻璃厂的熔炉前,被折磨得几近疯狂,但还勉强保持着清醒。不过阿拉伯人并不抱怨,他们只是耸耸肩说:"麦克托伯!"……"一切都已注定。"

暴风过后,他们立即行动开来:杀死所有的羊羔,因为他们知道那些小羊反正活不下去了,杀死小羊还可以挽救母羊。在杀死小羊之后,他们就把羊群赶到南方喝水。所有这一切都是在平静中完成的,他们对于自己的损失没有任何抱怨或哀伤。一位部落酋长说:"这还算不错的。我们本来会损失一切,但是感谢上帝,我们还留下了40%的羊群,一切可以从头开始。"

我还记得另外一件事:有一次我们乘车横越大沙漠,一只汽车轮胎爆裂,而司机又忘了修备用胎,所以我们的汽车只剩下三只轮胎。我又急又怒,烦躁不已,问阿拉伯人我们该怎么办。他们对我说,着急也无济于事,只会让人更加燥热。他们说,车胎爆裂是安拉的意思,别无办法。于是,我们就靠三只轮胎又开始往前走,没过多久,车又停了下来——原来汽油没有了。但酋长只说了一声:"麦克托伯!"他们并没有对司机所带的汽油不足而向他大声怒吼,而是保持冷静。

The chauffeur had forgotten to mend the spare tyre. So there we were with only three tires. I fussed and fumed and got excited and asked the Arabs what we were going to do. They reminded me that getting excited wouldn't help, that it only made one hotter. The blown-out tire, they said, was the will of Allah and nothing could be done about it. So we started on, crawling along on the rim of a wheel. Presently the car spluttered and stopped. We were out of petrol! The chief merely remarked: "*Mektoub*! "And, there again, instead of shouting at the driver because he had not taken on enough petrol, everyone remained calm and we walked to our destination, singing as we went.

The seven years I spent with the Arabs convinced me that the neurotics, the insane, the drunks of America and Europe are the product of the hurried and harassed lives we live in our so-called civilisation.

As long as I lived in the Sahara, I had no worries. I found there, in the Garden of Allah, the serene contentment and physical well-being that so many of us are seeking with tenseness and despair.

Many people scoff at fatalism. Maybe they are right. Who knows? But all of us must be able to see how our fates are often determined for us. For example, if I had not spoken to Lawrence of Arabia at three minutes past noon on a hot August day in 1919, all the years that have elapsed since then would have been completely different. Looking back over my life, I can see how it has been shaped and moulded time and again by events far beyond my control. The Arabs call it *mektoub*, *kismet*—the will of Allah. Call it anything you wish. It does strange things to you. I only know that today—seventeen years after leaving the Sahara—I still maintain that happy resignation to the inevitable which I learned from the Arabs. That philosophy has done more to settle my nerves than a thousand sedatives could have achieved.

You and I are not Mohammedans: we don't want to be fatalists. But when the fierce, burning winds blow over our lives—and we cannot prevent them—let us, too, accept the inevitable.(see part Ⅲ, chapter 9) And then get busy and pick up the pieces.

Five Methods I Use to Banish Worry

By Professor William Lyon Phelps

[I had the privilege of spending an afternoon with Billy Phelps, of Yale, shortly before his

我们徒步到达目的地,一路上高歌不停。

和阿拉伯人在一起的7年,使我相信发生在美国和欧洲的精神错乱、疯狂和酗酒,都是由于我们所谓的匆忙、烦扰的文明生活造成的。

只要我住在撒哈拉,我就不会有烦恼。我在这个"安拉的乐园"找到了心理满足和肉体健康,而这正是我们许多人努力寻找却难以找到的。

许多人讥笑宿命论。也许他们有道理。谁知道呢?但是,我们大家一定可以从许多事情上看出,我们的命运是早已注定的。例如,如果我不在1919年8月一个闷热的下午和"阿拉伯的劳伦斯"交谈3分钟,那么我以后的人生道路也许将完全不同。回顾过去,我发现我的生活一直受到许多我无法控制的事情的影响。阿拉伯人认为这就是"麦克托伯,吉斯米特"——安拉的意旨。你可以按照你的方式来称呼它。它对你的确有奇异的影响。我只知道,在我离开撒哈拉17年后的今天,我依然保持着从阿拉伯人那里学来的处事态度:愉快地接受不可避免的事情。这种人生哲理比上千支镇静剂更能安抚我的紧张和不安。

也许你和我都不是伊斯兰教徒。但当猛烈而酷热的狂风吹进我们的生活中,而我们又无法阻止时,那我们不妨接受这种不可避免的命运,(见本书第三篇第九章)然后再收拾残局。

驱逐烦恼的五个方法

威廉·利奥·费尔普教授

(耶鲁大学的费尔普教授在去世之前不久,我曾和他畅谈了一个下午。下面就是他驱除烦恼的五个方法,这是我在那次会谈中记下来的。——戴尔·卡耐基)

方法一:

在我24岁时,我的视力突然变得很差。看书三四分钟,眼睛就觉得扎满了针一样;即使不看书,眼

death. Here are the five methods he used to banish worry—based on the notes I took during that interview. Dale carnegie]

1. When I was twenty-four years old, my eyes suddenly gave out. After reading three or four minutes, my eyes felt as if they were full of needles; and even when I was not reading, they were so sensitive that I could not face a window. I consulted the best occultists in New Haven and New York. Nothing seemed to help me. After four o'clock in the afternoon, I simply sat in a chair in the darkest corner of the room, waiting for bedtime. I was terrified. I feared that I would have to give up my career as a teacher and go out West and get a job as a lumberjack. Then a strange thing happened which shows the miraculous effects of the mind over physical ailments. When my eyes were at their worst that unhappy winter, I accepted an invitation to address a group of undergraduates. The hall was illuminated by huge rings of gas jets suspended from the ceiling. The lights pained my eyes so intensely that, while sitting on the platform, I was compelled to look at the floor. Yet during my thirty-minute speech, I felt absolutely no pain, and I could look directly at these lights without any blinking whatever. Then when the assembly was over, my eyes pained me again.

I thought then that if I could keep my mind strongly concentrated on something, not for thirty minutes, but for a week, I might be cured. For clearly it was a case of mental excitement triumphing over a bodily illness.

I had a similar experience later while crossing the ocean. I had an attack of lumbago so severe that I could not walk. I suffered extreme pain when I tried to stand up straight. While in that condition, I was invited to give a lecture on shipboard. As soon as I began to speak, every trace of pain and stiffness left my body; I stood up straight, moved about with perfect flexibility, and spoke for an hour. When the lecture was over, I walked away to my stateroom with ease. For a moment, I thought I was cured. But the cure was only temporary. The lumbago resumed its attack.

These experiences demonstrated to me the vital importance of one's mental attitude. They taught me the importance of enjoying life while you may. So I live every day now as if it were the first day I had ever seen and the last I were going to see. I am excited about the daily adventure of living, and nobody in a state of excitement will be unduly troubled with worries. I love my daily work as a teacher. I wrote a book entitled *The Excitement of Teaching*. Teaching has always been

睛也十分敏感,甚至不敢面对窗口。我去向纽哈芬和纽约市最出色的眼科大夫求医,但收效甚微。

每天下午 4 点以后,我只能坐在房子里最暗的角落的椅子上,等着上床睡觉。我真的吓坏了,害怕自己必须放弃教师职业,去西部当一名伐木工人。

接着,发生了一件奇怪的事,显示了精神意志对肉体疾病的奇迹般影响。

在那个悲惨的冬天,我的眼睛实在是差到了极点,我应邀为一群大学生作演讲。当时,演讲厅的天花板上悬挂了许多大灯,强烈的灯光刺得我的眼睛疼痛难忍,当我坐在台上,等待被介绍上去演讲之前,只能被迫盯着地板。然而,在 30 分钟的演讲时间里,我完全忘了疼痛,同时还可以直接看那几盏灯却不眨眼。但在演讲结束之后,我的眼睛又开始疼痛了。

当时我就想,如果我能专心致志地做某件事——不是短短的 30 分钟,而是一个星期的话,也许我就可以痊愈。很明显,心理上的兴奋战胜了肉体上的不适。

后来,我有一次乘船经过大西洋时,又有过一次类似的经历。那一次,我的腰突然痛得很厉害,走不了路。如果我站直身子,更是痛到了极点。正是在那种情况下,我应邀在甲板上作了一次演许。当我开始演讲时,所有的疼痛都不见了。我站得笔直,完美地表达自己,讲了一个小时。演讲结束之后,我轻松地走回我的房间。这时,我以为自己已经痊愈了。但那只是暂时的,腰痛不久又来了。

这些经历使我深深领悟到,一个人的心理状态非常重要。它们教导我,要尽一切可能享受生活的美好。所以,我现在每天都在努力地生活,把每一天都当作我一生中的第一天,同时也是最后一天。对于每天这种新奇而冒险的生活,我一直都很兴奋,而一个情绪兴奋的人是永远不会有烦恼的。我很喜欢每天的教学工作,我还写了一本书《教学的乐趣》。对我来说,教学不仅仅是一种艺术或职业,它更是一种爱好。我像画家喜爱绘画、像歌手喜爱唱歌一样喜爱着教学。我每天早上下床之前,只要想到我的学生,心里就充满了无限的喜悦。我一直以为人生成功的最大因素就是“热情”。

方法二:

more than an art or an occupation to me. It is a passion. I love to teach as a painter loves to paint or a singer loves to sing. Before I get out of bed in the morning, I think with ardent delight of my first group of students. I have always felt that one of the chief reasons for success in life is enthusiasm.

2. I have found that I can crowd worry out of mind by reading an absorbing book. When I was fifty-nine, I had a prolonged nervous breakdown. During that period I began reading David Alec Wilson's monumental *Life of Carlyle*. It had a good deal to do with my convalescence because I became so absorbed in reading it that I forgot my despondency.

3. At another time when I was terribly depressed, I forced myself to become physically active almost every hour of the day. I played five or six sets of violent games of tennis every morning, then took a bath, had lunch, and played eighteen holes of golf every afternoon. On Friday night I danced until one o'clock in the morning. I am a great believer in working up a tremendous sweat. I found that depression and worry oozed out of my system with the sweat.

4. I learned long ago to avoid the folly of hurry, rush, and working under tension. I have always tried to apply the philosophy of Wilbur Cross. When he was Governor of Connecticut, he said to me: "Sometimes when I have too many things to do all at once, I sit down and relax and smoke my pipe for an hour and do nothing."

5. I have also learned that patience and time have a way of resolving our troubles. When I am worried about something, I try to see my troubles in their proper perspective. I say to myself: "Two months from now I shall not be worrying about this bad break, so why worry about it now? Why not assume now the same attitude that I will have two months from now?"

I Stood Yesterday. I Can Stand Today

By Dorothy Dix

I have been through the depths of poverty and sickness. When people ask me what has kept me going through the troubles that come to all of us, I always reply: "I stood yesterday. I can stand today. And I will not permit myself to think about what might happen tomorrow."

I have known want and struggle and anxiety and despair. I have always had to work beyond

我发现我可以通过读一本吸引人的书，将烦恼抛除。在我59岁那年，曾经历了相当长时间的精神崩溃。在那段日子里，我开始阅读大卫·威尔逊的伟大作品《卡莱尔传》。这对我的恢复很有用，因为我被深深吸引，以至于忘记了精神上的消沉。

方法三：

还有一次，我十分沮丧，因此我强迫自己每天每小时做一次剧烈的运动。我每天早上都要打五六场激烈的网球，然后洗澡，吃中午饭，下午再打18洞的高尔夫球。星期五晚上，我会一直跳舞跳到凌晨1点。我强迫自己流了许多汗，发现沮丧和忧愁全都随汗水流走了。

方法四：

我很早以前就知道如何避免匆忙，如何避免在紧张的状态下工作。我一直想尝试应用韦伯·克洛斯的哲学。他担任康涅狄格州的州长时曾对我说："我有时候要同时处理很多工作，我会先坐下来放松，抽根烟，在一个小时之内什么事也不干。"

方法五：

我也知道，耐心和时间能解除我们的烦恼。当我为某事而烦恼时，我就从积极的角度来看待它。我会告诉自己："两个月以后，我就不会再为这事烦恼了。所以，我现在又何必为它烦恼呢?为什么我现在不采取两个月以后我会采取的那种态度呢?"

既然昨天已经度过，今天也不会难熬

陶乐丝·迪克斯

我曾经历过极其严峻的贫困和疾病。有人问我是如何度过那些难关的，我总是回答说："我已经度过了昨天，今天也不会难熬。我不会让自己去猜想明天将发生什么。"

我深知什么是需要、奋斗、焦虑和失望。我经常会以超乎自己的能力拼命地工作。我回顾自

the limit of my strength. As I look back upon my life, I see it as a battlefield strewn with the wrecks of dead dreams and broken hopes and shattered illusions—a battle in which I always fought with the odds tremendously against me, and which has left me scarred and bruised and maimed and old before my time.

Yet I have no pity for myself; no tears to shed over the past and gone sorrows; no envy for the women who have been spared all I have gone through. For I have lived. They only existed. I have drank the cup of life down to its very dregs. They have only sipped the bubbles on top of it. I know things they will never know. I see things to which they are blind. It is only the women whose eyes have been washed clear with tears who get the broad vision that makes them little sisters to all the world.

I have learned in the great University of Hard Knocks a philosophy that no woman who has had an easy life ever acquires. I have learned to live each day as it comes and not to borrow trouble by dreading the morrow. It is the dark menace of the future that makes cowards of us. I put that dread from me because experience has taught me that when the time comes that I so fear, the strength and wisdom to meet it will be given me. Little annoyances no longer have the power to affect me. After you have seen your whole edifice of happiness topple and crash in ruins about you, it never matters to you again that a servant forgets to put the doilies under the finger bowls, or the cook spills the soup.

I have learned not to expect too much of people, and so I can still get happiness out of the friend who isn't quite true to me or the acquaintance who gossips. Above all, I have acquired a sense of humor, because there were so many things over which I had either to cry or laugh. And when a woman can joke over her troubles instead of having hysterics, nothing can ever hurt her much again. I do not regret the hardships I have known, because through them I have touched life at every point I have lived. And it was worth the price I had to pay.

Dorothy Dix conquered worry by living in "day-tight" compartments.

I Did Not Expect to Live to See the Dawn

By J. C. Penney

[On April 14, 1902, a young man with five hundred dollars in cash and a million dollars in determination opened a drygoods store in Kemmerer, Wyoming—a little mining town of a thousand

己的生活，觉得像是一个战场，它充满了破灭的梦想、残败的希望和残缺的幻想——在那场战斗中，我的获胜机会非常小，我在战斗中全身是伤，手脚残缺，显得苍老了许多。

然而，我没有为自己哀怜，也不为过去的烦恼而哭泣，也不嫉妒那些不曾遭遇我这些苦难的女性。因为我确实生活过了，而她们只是一种简单的存在。我已饮尽了生活的苦酒，而她们只是尝到上面的一层泡沫。我经历的事情她们永远不会理解。我看到的东西她们永远不会看到。只有泪水洗净了眼睛的妇人，视野才会开阔。

我从这种困苦的环境中学到了一种哲学，而这是那些生活在舒适环境中的女人所学不到的。我学会了珍惜每一天，不必因为担心明天的来到而自寻烦恼。恐惧只会令人懦弱。我将恐惧感从自己身上排除出去，因为经验告诉我，当我害怕的那一刻来临时，我自然而然地会产生勇气和智慧去应对它。那些小的不愉快不再对我有任何影响。当你经历过这种极度的不幸之后，即使是仆人服侍不周，或者是厨师弄坏了一锅汤，你也不会再恼怒了。

我已经学会不要对人期望太高，因此当有朋友对我不忠，或是有人说我的坏话时，我也不会介意，仍然乐于和他们交往。除此之外，我还学会了幽默，因为让我哭笑不得的事情实在是太多了。而当一个女人遇到烦恼时，如果能不焦急，就能变不利为有利，没有东西可以伤害她了。

对于遭遇的困难，我并不遗憾，因为通过这些东西，我可以接触生活的每一个层面。而这已经值得我为之付出了。

陶乐丝·迪克斯通过生活在今天克服了忧虑。

我以为活不到明天

J.C.潘尼

(1902 年 4 月 14 日，一个只有 500 美元现金的年轻人立志要赚 100 万美元，他在怀俄明州

people. situated on the old covered-wagon trail laid out by the Lewis and Clark Expedition. That young man and his wife lived in a half-storey attic above the store, using a large empty drygoods box for a table and smaller boxes for chairs. The young wife wrapped her baby in a blanket and let it sleep under a counter while she stood beside it, helping her husband wait on customers. Today the largest chain of drygoods stores in the world bears that man's name: the J. C. Penney stores—over sixteen hundred of them covering every state in the Union. I recently had dinner with Mr. Penney, and he told me about the most dramatic moment of his life.]

Years ago, I passed through a most trying experience. I was worried and desperate. My worries were not connected in any way whatever with the J. C. Penney Company. That business was solid and thriving; but I personally had made some unwise commitments prior to the crash of 1929. Like many other men, I was blamed for conditions for which I was in no way responsible. I was so harassed with worries that I couldn't sleep, and developed an extremely painful ailment known as shingles—a red rash and skin eruptions. I consulted a physician—a man with whom I had gone to high school as a boy in Hamilton, Missouri: Dr. Elmer Eggleston, a staff physician at the Kellogg Sanatorium in Battle Creek, Michigan. Dr. Eggleston put me to bed and warned me that I was a very ill man. A rigid treatment was prescribed. But nothing helped. I got weaker day by day. I was broken nervously and physically, filled with despair, unable to see even a ray of hope. I had nothing to live for. I felt I hadn't a friend left in the world, that even my family had turned against me. One night, Dr. Eggleston gave me a sedative, but the effect soon wore off and I awoke with an overwhelming conviction that this was my last night of life. Getting out of bed, I wrote farewell letters to my wife and to my son, saying that I did not expect to live to see the dawn.

When I awoke the next morning, I was surprised to find that I was still alive. I can't explain it. I can only call it a miracle. I felt as if I had been instantly lifted out of the darkness of a dungeon into warm, brilliant sunlight. I felt as if I had been transported from hell to paradise. I realized then that I alone was responsible for all my troubles. From that day to this, my life has been free from worry. I am seventy-one years old.

J. C. Penney learned to overcome worry almost instantaneously, because he discovered the one perfect Cure.

的克莫勒镇开了一家绸布店——克莫勒是一个只有 1000 人的矿业小镇,位于以前开发西部所必经的篷车道上。这个年轻人和他的妻子住在商店上面的小阁楼里,用一个装绸布的大木箱作桌子,再用小木箱作椅子。年轻的妻子用毯子裹住婴儿,将他放在柜台底下睡觉,而她站在柜台旁边,帮助丈夫招呼客人。今天,全世界最大的一家绸布连锁店就以这个人的姓名为名——J.C.潘尼百货店——它一共有 1600 家分店,遍布美国各州。最近我和潘尼先生共进晚餐,他把他生活中最富戏剧性的经历告诉了我。)

几年前,我经历了一段最痛苦的时光。当时我既忧虑又绝望——我的忧虑和公司的业务完全没有关系。当时公司业务十分稳定,而且蒸蒸日上,但我个人却做出了一些不明智的举措,导致我于 1929 年破产。和其他人一样,我遭到了别人的指责,忧虑得无法入睡,终于发展成一种疼痛难忍的疾病,即"带状疱疹"——这是一种突发性的红疹。我向密歇根州巴托卫生局的伊格斯顿大夫求治,他是和我从小一起长大的老朋友。伊格斯顿大夫让我躺在床上,并警告说,我病得十分严重。我接受了一次严格的治疗,但没有什么效果。我的身体越来越虚弱,精神和肉体都开始崩溃,我绝望至极,一丝希望也没有。我活得毫无寄托,认为自己在这世界上没有一个朋友,甚至连家里人也反对我。一天晚上,伊格斯顿大夫给我服了一剂镇静剂,但它的功效很快就消失了,我痛得醒了过来,心想这可能是我生命中最后一个晚上了。我爬起床,给我夫人和儿子写了诀别书,说我活不到天亮了。

当我第二天早上醒来时,我惊异地发现自己仍然活着。对此我无法解释,只能说那是一个奇迹。我觉得自己似乎一下子被人从黑暗的地牢中接到了温暖、明亮的阳光之下,立即从地狱进入了天堂。我恍然大悟,原来我所有的烦恼都是自找的。从那以后直到今天,我的生活中一直没有任何烦恼。现在我已经 71 岁了。

(潘尼学会了在瞬间克服忧虑,因为他找到了一种极好的治疗方法。)

I Go to The Gym to Punch the Bag or Take a Hike Outdoors

By Colonel Eddie Eagan

New York Attorney, Rhodes Scholar Former Chairman,
New York State Athletic Commission,
Former Olympic Light-Heavyweight
Champion of the World

When I find myself worrying and mentally going round in endless circles like a camel turning a water wheel in Egypt, a good physical work-out helps me to chase those "blues"away. It may be running or a long hike in the country, or it may be a half-hour of bag punching or squash tennis at the gymnasium. Whichever it is, physical exercise clears my mental outlook. On a weekend I do a lot of physical sport, such as a run around the golf course, a game of paddle tennis, or a ski weekend in the Adirondacks. By my becoming physically tired, my mind gets a rest from legal problems, so that when I return to them, my mind has a new zest and power.

Quite often in New York, where I work, there is a chance for me to spend an hour at the Yale Club gym. No man can worry while he is playing squash tennis or skiing. He is too busy to worry. The large mental mountains of trouble become minute molehills that new thoughts and acts quickly smooth down.

I find the best antidote for worry is exercise. Use your muscles more and your brain less when you are worried, and you will be surprised at the result. It works that way with me—worry goes when exercise begins.

I Was"The Worrying Wreckfrom Virginia Tech"

By Jim Birdsall

Plant Superintendent C. F. Muller Company 180
Baldwin Avenue, Jersey City, New Jersey

Seventeen years ago, when I was in military college at Blacksburg, Virginia, I was known as "the worrying wreck from Virginia Tech". I worried so violently that I often became ill. In fact, I was ill so often that I had a regular bed reserved for me at the college infirmary at all times.

锻炼可以消除忧虑

奥林匹克前次重量级拳王　艾迪·伊甘上校

如果我发现自己有了烦恼,或者在精神上像埃及骆驼寻找水源那样猛绕圈子转个不停,我就会利用激烈的体能训练来帮助我驱除这些烦恼。这些活动可能是跑步,或是在乡村徒步远足,或是打半个小时的沙袋,或是去体育馆打网球。不管是什么体育活动,都会使我的精神为之振奋。

每到周末,我就去做多项运动,例如绕高尔夫球场跑一圈,打一场激烈的网球,或去阿第伦达克山滑雪。当我的肉体疲倦时,我的精神也会随之得到休息,因此等我再度回去工作时,我就会神清气爽,充满活力。

在我工作的纽约,我经常有机会去俱乐部健身房,在那里待上一个小时。没有任何人会在滑雪或激烈运动的时候还会烦恼。因为他忙得没时间去忧虑。这时,烦恼的大山很快就变成微不足道的小丘,一个新念头和新行动很容易就能将它"抚平"。

我发现,运动是烦恼的最佳"消毒剂"。当你烦恼时,就多用肌肉,少用大脑,其结果将会令你惊讶不已。这种方法对我来说极其有效——当我开始运动时,烦恼就会消失。

我曾是"烦恼大王"

穆勒公司工厂主任　吉姆·勃德索

17 年前,当我在弗吉尼亚州的布莱克斯堡军事学院上学时,是人人皆知的"弗吉尼亚烦恼大王"。我的烦恼如此严重,以至于经常生病。事实上,由于我常常生病,所以学校的医院经常为我保留一张病床。每当护士看到我又上门时,就会跑上前来为我注射一针。我对任何事情都会忧虑。有时我甚至会忘了自己担心什么。我会担心因为成绩不好而被学校开除,我的

When the nurse saw me coming, she would run and give me a hypo. I worried about everything. Sometimes I even forgot what I was worrying about. I worried for fear I would be busted out of college because of my low grades. I had failed to pass my examinations in physics and other subjects, too. I knew I had to maintain an average grade of 75–84. I worried about my health, about my excruciating attacks of acute indigestion, about my insomnia. I worried about financial matters. I felt badly because I couldn't buy my girl candy or take her to dances as often as I wanted to. I worried for fear she would marry one of the other cadets. I was in a lather day and night over a dozen intangible problems.

In desperation, I poured out my troubles to Professor Duke Baird, professor of business administration at V. P. I.

The fifteen minutes that I spent with Professor Baird did more for my health and happiness than all the rest of the four years I spent in college. "Jim, "he said, "you ought to sit down and face the facts. If you devoted half as much time and energy to solving your problems as you do to worrying about them, you wouldn't have any worries. Worrying is just a vicious habit you have learned."

He gave me three rules to break the worry habit: Rule 1. Find out precisely what is the problem you are worrying about. Rule 2. Find out the cause of the problem. Rule 3. Do something constructive at once about solving the problem.

After that interview, I did a bit of constructive planning. Instead of worrying because I had failed to pass physics, I now asked myself why I had failed. I knew it wasn't because I was dumb, for I was editor–in–chief of *The Virginia Tech Engineer*. I figured that I had failed physics because I had no interest in the subject. I had not applied myself because I couldn't see how it would help me in my work as an industrial engineer. But now I changed my attitude. I said to myself: "If the college authorities demand that I pass my physics examination before I obtain a degree, who am I to question their wisdom? " So I enrolled for physics again. This time I passed because instead of wasting my time in resentment and worrying about how hard it was, I studied diligently.

I solved my financial worries by taking on some additional jobs, such as selling punch at the college dances, and by borrowing money from my father, which I paid back soon after graduation.

I solved my love worries by proposing to the girl that I feared might marry another cadet. She

物理学和其他科目考试不及格,我知道我的平均分必须维持在75~84分之间。我还担心我的健康:急性消化不良、失眠。我担心我的收入状况。我还会因为不能经常买礼物送给我的女朋友,或是带她去跳舞而烦恼。我担心她会嫁给另外一位军校学生。我整天整夜地担心各种无形的问题。

在绝望之下,我向杜克·巴德教授倾诉了我的烦恼。巴德教授是企业管理学教授。

见巴德教授的那15分钟,对我的健康及幸福的帮助远远超过我在大学4年所学的一切。"吉姆,"他说,"你应该坐下来,面对现实。如果你能把你用于烦恼的一半时间和精力去解决你的问题,那么你将不会再有烦恼。而你以前只学会烦恼这一项不良习惯。"

他为我订了三项消除烦恼的规则:第一,准确查明忧虑的究竟是什么问题。第二,找出问题的真正原因。第三,立刻采取建设性的行动,以解决问题。

这次会谈之后,我拟定了一些积极的计划。我不再因为物理考试不及格而烦恼,而是反问自己为什么会不及格。我知道那并不是因为我天资愚笨,因为当时我已经当上了校刊的总编辑。我发现我之所以考试不及格,是因为我对这门功课没有什么兴趣。而我之所以对它不感兴趣,是因为我认为它对我将来从事工业工程师并没有多大帮助。但我现在改变了态度。我告诉自己:"如果学院要求我们通过物理考试才能取得学位,我怎么能对他们的智慧产生怀疑呢?"所以,我又埋头研究物理。这一次我通过了考试,因为我不再花时间去想物理多么困难,改而专心致志地学习。

我还以打工的方式——例如在学院的舞会上推销果汁——解决了我的经济困难。同时我又向父亲贷款,毕业不久就还清了贷款。

我还解决了我的爱情难题:我向当初担心她会移情别嫁的女子求婚,现在她已是吉姆·勃德索夫人。

is now Mrs. Jim Birdsall.

As I look back at it now, I can see that my problem was one of confusion, a disinclination to find the causes of my worry and face them realistically.

Jim Birdsall learned to stop worrying because he ANALYZED his troubles. In fact, he used the very principles described in the chapter"How to Analyze and Solve Worry Problems."

I Have Lived by This Sentence

By Dr. Joseph R. Sizoo

President, New Brunswick Theological Seminary
New Brunswick, New Jersey,
The oldest theological seminary in the United States,
founded in 1784

Years ago, in a day of uncertainty and disillusionment, when my whole life seemed to be overwhelmed by forces beyond my control, one morning quite casually I opened my *New Testament* and my eyes fell upon this sentence: "He that sent me is with me—the Father hath not left me alone."

My life has never been the same since that hour. Everything for me has been for ever different after that. I suppose that not a day has passed that I have not repeated it to myself. Many have come to me for counseling during these years, and I have always sent them away with this sustaining sentence. Ever since that hour when my eyes fell upon it, I have lived by this sentence. I have walked with it and I have found in it my peace and strength. To me it is the very essence of religion. It lies at the rock bottom of everything that makes life worth living. It is the Golden Text of my life.

I Hit Bottom and Survived

By Ted Ericksen

16,237 South Cornut a Avenue, Bellflower,
California Southern California Representative
National Enameling and Stamping Company

I used to be a terrible "worry wart". But no more. In the summer of 1942, I had an experience

现在回想起来，我发现我当时的问题在于不愿去寻找烦恼的原因，并勇敢地面对它们。

（吉姆·勃德索因为分析了他的烦恼而学会了停止忧虑。事实上，他应用的正是"如何分析和解除烦恼"这一章规则。）

一句经文救了我

新布鲁恩斯威克神学院院长　乔瑟夫·希祖博士

多年以前，我总是迷惘而惶惑，认为生活中似乎充满了许多我无法掌控的力量。一天早上，我很偶然地打开《新约》，眼光落在其中一句经文上："他派我来，并和我在一起——天父并没有忘记我。"

从那以后，我的生活就大不相同了。对我来说，所有的事物都和以前不同了。我想我现在几乎每天都在对自己重复这句经文。在这几年当中，许多人前来向我请教，我就送给他们这句经文。自从我第一次看到这句经文以后，我就把它奉为我的座右铭。我与它同行，并从它那里发现了平和与力量。对我来说，它是宗教的根本，它使我的生活变得更加有价值，它成了我生活中的金科玉律。

我做过最苦的工作

国家搪瓷与打印机公司南加州代表　泰德·埃瑞克森

我以前是个糟透了的"烦恼大王"。不过我现在不再是了。1942 年夏天，我有过一次经历，它消除了我所有的忧虑烦恼——我希望今后也能永远如此。那次经历，使我所有的烦恼相比之下都显得微不足道。

多年以来，我一直希望能在阿拉斯加的一艘渔船上工作一个夏天。因此，在 1942 年夏天，

that banished worry from my life—for all time, I hope. That experience made every other trouble seem small by comparison.

For years I had wanted to spend a summer on a commercial fishing craft in Alaska, so in 1942 I signed on a thirty-two-foot salmon-seining vessel out of Kodiak, Alaska. On a craft of this size, there is a crew of only three: the skipper who does the supervising, a No. 2 man who assists the skipper, and a general work horse, who is usually a Scandinavian. I am a Scandinavian.

Since salmon seining has to be done with the tides, I often worked twenty hours out of twenty-four. I kept up that schedule for a week at a time. I did everything that nobody else wanted to do. I washed the craft. I put away the gear. I cooked on a little wood-burning stove in a small cabin where the heat and fumes of the motor almost made me ill. I washed the dishes. I repaired the boat. I pitched the salmon from our boat into a tender that took the fish to a cannery. My feet were always wet in rubber boots. My boots were often filled with water, but I had no time to empty them. But all that was play compared to my main job, which was pulling what is called the "cork line". That operation simply means placing your feet on the stem of the craft and pulling in the corks and the webbing of the net. At least, that is what you are supposed to do. But, in reality, the net was so heavy that when I tried to pull it in, it wouldn't budge. What really happened was that in trying to pull in the cork line, I actually pulled in the boat. I pulled it along on my own power, since the net stayed where it was. I did all this for weeks on end it was almost the end of me, too. I ached horribly. I ached all over. I ached for months.

When I finally did have a chance to rest, I slept on a damp lumpy mattress piled on top of the provisions locker. I would put one of the lumps in the mattress under the part of my back that hurt most—and sleep as if I had been drugged. I was drugged by complete exhaustion.

I am glad now that I had to endure all that aching and exhaustion because it has helped me stop worrying. Whenever I am confronted by a problem now—instead of worrying about it, I say to myself: "Ericksen, could this possibly be as bad as pulling the cork line? "And Ericksen invariably answers: "No, nothing could be that bad! "So I cheer up and tackle it with courage. I believe it is a good thing to have to endure an agonising experience occasionally. It is good to know that we have hit bottom and survived. That makes all our daily problems seem easy by comparison.

我签约之后，上了阿拉斯加科地亚克的一艘长32英尺的鲑鱼拖网渔船工作。这艘船上只有3名船员：船长负责督导，另外一个副手协助船长，剩下那一个则是日常打杂的水手，这通常都由北欧人担任，而我正好是北欧人。由于用拖网捕捞鲑鱼必须配合潮汐进行，因此我经常要连续工作20小时。有一次，我这样工作了一个星期。我干的是其他人都不愿意干的工作：洗甲板、保养机器、在小船舱里用一个烧木材的小炉子做饭。小船舱里马达的热气和恶臭令我作呕。我还要洗碗修船，把鲑鱼从我们的船抛到另一艘小船，将它们送去制成罐头。尽管我穿着长统胶鞋，但两脚总是湿漉漉的。我的胶鞋里面经常有水，但我却没有时间倒水。但上述这些工作跟我的主要工作比起来只能算是游戏，我的主要工作就是所谓的"拉网"——这个工作看起来很简单：你只需站在船尾，把渔网的浮标和边线拉上来即可。我的工作就是这些。但是，由于渔网太重了，当我想把它拉上来时，它却怎么也拉不动。我本想把渔网拉上来，但实际上却把船给拉了下去。由于渔网拉不动，我只好用尽全力，沿路拖住不放。我这样做了好几个星期，累得浑身酸痛，而且一连痛了好几个月。

最后，当我好不容易有时间休息时，我就在一个临时拼成的柜子上放好潮湿的被褥，倒头就睡。我浑身上下无处不疼，但我却睡得烂熟，像服用了安眠药一样。其实，极度的劳累就是我的安眠药。

我很高兴当初能吃那些苦头，因为它们使我不再烦恼。现在，如果我遭遇了困难，我不会再烦恼，我会反问自己："埃瑞克森，还有什么比拖网更辛苦的吗？"我总是回答说："不，没有比它更辛苦的！"于是，我振作起来，勇敢地接受这项挑战。我认为，偶尔体验一下痛苦是件好事。我很高兴自己能做世界上最辛苦的工作并挺了过来。它使得我日常生活中的所有问题相比之下，都显得微不足道。

I Used to Be One Of the World's Biggest Jackasses

By Percy H. Whiting

Author of the *Five Rules of Selling* Managing Director,
Dale Carnegie and Company 50 East 42nd Street, New York

I have died more times from more different diseases than any other man, living, dead, or half dead.

I was no ordinary hypochondriac. My father owned a drug-store, and I was practically brought up in it. I talked to doctors and nurses every day, so I knew the names and symptoms of more and worse diseases than the average layman. I was no ordinary hypo—I had symptoms! I could worry for an hour or two over a disease and then have practically all the symptoms of a man who was suffering from it. I recall once that, in Great Barrington, Massachusetts, the town in which I lived, we had a rather severe diphtheria epidemic. In my father's drug-store, I had been selling medicines day after day to people who came from infected homes. Then the evil that I feared came upon me: I had diphtheria myself. I was positive I had it. I went to bed and worried myself into the standard symptoms. I sent for a doctor. He looked me over and said: "Yes, Percy, you've got it." That relieved my mind. I was never afraid of any disease when I had it—so I turned over and went to sleep. The next morning I was in perfect health.

For years I distinguished myself and got a lot of attention and sympathy by specialising in unusual and fantastic disease—I died several times of both lockjaw and hydrophobia. Later on, I settled down to having the run-of-mill ailments—specialising on cancer and tuberculosis.

I can laugh about it now, but it was tragic then. I honestly and literally feared for years that I was walking on the edge of the grave. When it came time to buy a suit of clothes in the spring, I would ask myself: "Should I waste this money when I know I can't possibly live to wear this suit out? "

However, I am happy to report progress: in the past ten years, I haven't died even once.

How did I stop dying? By kidding myself out of my ridiculous imaginings. Every time I felt the dreadful symptoms coming on, I laughed at myself and said: "See here, Whiting, you have been dying from one fatal disease after another now for twenty years, yet you are in first-class health today. An insurance company recently accepted you for more insurance. Isn't it about time, Whiting,

我曾是世界上最大的笨蛋

纽约卡耐基公司总经理　波希·惠廷

我比这个世界上任何一个人——包括活的、死的、奄奄一息的——都得过更多的疾病。

我并不是那种普通的忧郁症患者。我父亲开了一家药铺,我从小就在那种环境中长大。每天我都和大夫、护士聊天,所以我比普通人知道更多的疾病名称和病症。尽管我并不是忧郁症患者,但我有时确实有某些病症!我可以为某种疾病而担心一两个小时,于是在不知不觉中就有了那种疾病的全部病症。有一次,在我居住的马萨诸塞州的巴林顿镇,流行相当严重的白喉。我每天都在父亲的药铺里给受传染的病人卖药。接着,我所害怕的事情降临到了我身上。我敢肯定我是感染上了。我躺到床上,忧虑万分,结果真的出现了一些标准症状。我请来医生。他给我检查了一遍,说:“不错,波希,你已经感染上了。”这使我心情为之一松。当我得病之后,我不再害怕任何疾病了。于是,我翻过身,呼声如雷地睡着了。当我第二天早上醒来时,我发现自己健康如初。

有好几年,我都成为人们注意和同情的重点,因为我得了一些不寻常而且很怪异的疾病——我曾多次“死”于狂犬病和牙关紧闭症。后来,我又发展到一些更加恐怖的疾病,特别是癌症和肺结核。

现在我可以笑对这一切,但我当时的情景却十分悲惨。我多年来一直心存恐惧,总害怕自己走在坟墓边缘上。例如,到了春天我该给自己买衣服的时候,我总是问自己:“我既然已经知道自己不能再活着穿这些衣服了,为什么还要浪费钱呢?”

不过,我很高兴地告诉你,我已经大有进步:在过去10年中,我甚至连一次都没有“死”过。

我是如何取得进步的呢?那就是对自己这些荒唐的想象大加嘲笑。每当我觉得那些恐怖的病症又降临到我身上时,我就会笑着对自己说:“嘿!惠廷,过去20年来,你一次又一次地‘死’

that you stood aside and had a good laugh at the worrying jackass you are? "

I soon found that I couldn't worry about myself and laugh at myself at one and the same time. So I've been laughing at myself ever since.

The point of this is: Don't take yourself too seriously. Try "just laughing"at some of your sillier worries, and see if you can't laugh them out of existence.

I Have Always Tried to Keep My Line of Supplies Open

By Gene Autry

The World's Most Famous and Beloved Singing Cowboy

I figure that most worries are about family troubles and money. I was fortunate in marrying a small-town Oklahoma girl who had the same background I had and enjoyed the same things. We both try to follow the golden rule, so we have kept our family troubles to a minimum.

I have kept my financial worries to a minimum also by doing two things. First, I have always followed a rule of absolute one hundred per cent integrity in everything. When I borrowed money, I paid back every penny. Few things cause more worry than dishonesty.

Second, when I started a new venture, I always kept on ace in the hole. Military experts say that the first principle of fighting a battle is to keep your line of supplies open. I figure that that principle applies to personal battles almost as much as to military battles. For example, as a lad down in Texas and Oklahoma, I saw some real poverty when the country was devastated by droughts. We had mighty hard scratching at times to make a living. We were so poor that my father used to drive across the country in a covered wagon with a string of horses and swap horses to make a living. I wanted something more reliable than that. So I got a job working for a railway-station agent and learned telegraphy in my spare time. Later, I got a job working as relief operator for the Frisco Railway. I was sent here, there, and yonder to relieve other station agents who were ill or on vacation or had more work than they could do. That job paid $150 per month. Later, when I started out to better myself, I always figured that that railroad job meant economic safety. So I always kept the road open back to that job. It was my line of supplies, and I never cut myself off from it until I

于一些致命的疾病,但你目前却身体健康。一家保险公司最近甚至还同意你为自己买更多的人寿保险。惠廷,难道你不认为,现在正是你嘲笑自己是个大笨蛋的时候吗?"

很快,我就发现如果我能嘲笑自己,就不会有时间去烦恼了。于是,从那以后,我就一直嘲笑自己。

(这篇故事的意义是:不要太过严肃地对待自己。对自己一些愚蠢的忧虑,不妨"开怀一笑",然后看看是否可以将它们笑得不见踪影。)

我的补给线永远畅通

著名牛仔歌手　吉尼·奥特里

我认为大部分忧虑都和家庭事务及金钱有关。我很幸运地娶了俄克拉荷马一个小镇的女子为妻,她的家庭背景和我的很相似,我们的兴趣爱好也大致相同。我们两人都尽量遵守这些"金律",所以我们的家庭烦恼也降到了最低限度。

我通过两种方法使我的金钱烦恼减到了最低限度:第一,我总是坚持一条原则,对任何事情都要百分之百地诚实。如果我向别人借了钱,就必须全部偿还。诚实可以使人免去许多烦恼。

第二,每当我开拓一项新事业时,我总会给自己预留后路。军事专家曾指出,作战的第一原则,就是保持补给线的畅通。我认为这项原则同样可以用于个人的"战斗"。例如,我从小生活在得克萨斯和俄克拉荷马,在那里遭受干旱侵袭时,我才真正领略到了贫穷。我们辛勤地劳作着。我们太穷了,我父亲必须驾着敞篷车,带着交换得来的马匹,到处不停地奔波谋生。我希望找一份比较稳定的工作,所以在一家火车站找了一份差事,在闲暇时学习发电报。后来,我找到另一项工作,在佛里斯科铁路公司当一名轮班员。我经常被派往各处,接替其他生病或休假的火车站站员,或在他们忙不过来时提供支援。这份工作的月薪是150美元。后来,当我准备开创更美

was firmly established in a new and better position.

For example, back in 1928, when I was working as a relief operator for the Frisco Railway in Chelsea Oklahoma, a stranger drifted in one evening to send a telegram. He heard me playing the guitar and singing cowboy songs and told me I was good—told me that I ought to go to New York and get a job on the stage or radio. Naturally, I was flattered; and when I saw the name he signed to his telegram, I was almost breathless: *Will Rogers*.

Instead of rushing off to New York at once, I thought the matter over carefully for nine months. I finally came to the conclusion that I had nothing to lose and everything to gain by going to New York and giving the old town a whirl. I had a railroad pass: I could travel free. I could sleep sitting up in my seat, and I could carry some sandwiches and fruit for my meals.

So I went. When I reached New York, I slept in a furnished room for five dollars a week, ate at the Automat, and tramped the streets for ten weeks—and got nowhere. I would have been worried sick if I hadn't had a job to go back to. I had already worked for the railway five years. That meant I had seniority rights; but in order to protect those rights, I couldn't lay off longer than ninety days. By this time, I had already been in New York seventy days, so I rushed back to Oklahoma on my pass and began working again to protect my line of supply. I worked for a few months, saved money, and returned to New York for another try. This time I got a break. One day, while waiting for an interview in a recording-studio office, I played my guitar and sang a song to the girl receptionist: "Jeannine, I Dream of Lilac Time". While I was singing that song, the man who wrote it—Nat Schildkraut—drifted into the office. Naturally, he was pleased to hear anyone singing his song. So he gave me a note of introduction and sent me down to the Victor Recording Company. I made a record. I was no good—too stiff and self-conscious. So I took the advice of the Victor Recording man: I went back to Tulsa, worked for the railway by day, and at night I sang cowboy songs on a sustaining radio programme. I liked that arrangement. It meant that I was keeping my line of supplies open—so I had no worries.

I sang for nine months on radio station KVOO in Tulsa. During that time, Jimmy Long and I wrote a song entitled *"That Silver-Haired Daddy of Mine"*. It caught on. Arthur Sattherly, head of the American Recording Company, asked me to make a recording. It clicked. I made a number of

好的前途时,我总觉得在铁路公司工作有经济保障,所以我总是保留了回到那项工作的退路,这就是我的补给线,我从来不会关闭那条路,除非我已建立了更稳定、更可靠的位置。

例如,1928 年,当时我就职于佛里斯科铁路公司,被派往俄克拉荷马的切尔西市工作。一天晚上,一个陌生人走进火车站办公室发一封电报。他听到我正在弹吉他,唱着牛仔歌曲,就对我说我弹得不错,歌也唱得不错——还告诉我,说我应该去纽约,去电台或戏院工作。我当然觉得他是在奉承我。但是当我看到他在电报上的签名时,我几乎惊呆了——威尔·罗吉斯。

我并没有立刻去纽约。我把这件事前后仔细地考虑了 9 个月。最后我得出结论:去纽约,我绝无损失,而且一定会有收获。我有铁路通行证,可以免费乘车。我还可以坐在火车上睡觉,而且可以带一些三明治和水果当一日三餐。

于是我去了纽约。到达纽约之后, 我找到一间每周房租 5 美元并带有家具的房间住了下来,在快餐厅吃饭,在街上流浪了 10 个星期,可是一无所获。如果我回去没有工作可干的话,那我一定会急出病来的。我已在铁路公司工作了 5 年,这意味着我有优先权;但要想保留这项优先权,我不能离职超过 90 天。而我那时已在纽约呆了 70 天,于是我充分利用我的铁路通行证,立即赶回俄克拉荷马,又回去开始工作,以保证我的补给线不至于中断。我工作了几个月,存了一点钱,又到纽约去碰运气。这一次,我有了新的进展。一天,我在一家录音房等待面试时,弹吉他为那些女接待员唱了一首歌《珍妮,我梦到了紫丁香》。当我正在唱那首歌时,恰巧歌曲作者纳特·史切克劳特走进办公室。他当然很高兴听到别人唱他的歌曲。于是他写了一张条子,要我去维克多唱片公司试试。我录了一首歌,但成绩不很理想——说是太生硬了,显得不自然。于是我接受了唱片公司录音师的劝告,回到图尔萨,白天在铁路公司上班,晚上去当地电台唱牛仔歌曲。我很喜欢这种安排,这使得我的补给线始终敞开着,因此我没有了烦恼。

我在图尔萨 KVOO 电台演唱了 9 个月。在那段时间内,吉米·朗和我合写了一首歌《我那白

other recordings for fifty dollars each, and finally got a job singing cowboy songs over radio station WLS in Chicago. Salary: forty dollars a week. After singing there four years, my salary was raised to ninety dollars a week, and I picked up another three hundred dollars doing personal appearances every night in theatres.

Then in 1934, I got a break that opened up enormous posstibilities. So Hollywood producers decided to put on cowboy pictures; but they wanted a new kind of cowboy—one who could sing. The man who owned the American Recording Company was also part owner of Republic Pictures. "If you want a singing cowboy, "he said to his associates, "I have got one making records for us." That is how I broke into the movies. I started making singing-cowboy pictures for one hundred dollars a week. I had serious doubts about whether I would succeed in pictures, but I didn't worry. I knew I could always go back to my old job.

My success in pictures exceeded my wildest expectations. I now get a salary of one hundred thousand a year plus one half of all the profits on my pictures. However, I realize that this arrangement won't go on forever. But I am not worried. I know that no matter what happens—even if I lose every dollar I have—I can always go back to Oklahoma and get a job working for the Frisco Railway. I have protected my line of supplies.

I Heard a Voice in India

By E. Stanley Jones

One of America's Most Dynamic Speakers and
The Most Famous Missionary of His Generation

I have devoted forty years of my life to missionary work in India. At first, I found it difficult to endure the terrible heat plus the nervous strain of the great task that stretched before me. At the end of eight years, I was suffering so severely from brain fatigue and nervous exhaustion that I collapsed, not once but several times. I was ordered to take a year's furlough in America. On the boat returning to America, I collapsed again while speaking at a Sunday morning service on the ship, and the ship's doctor put me to bed for the remainder of the trip.

After a year's rest in America, I started back to India, but stopped on the way to hold

发的父亲》,结果颇受好评。美洲唱片公司老板亚瑟·萨德利甚至要求我灌一张唱片,也获得了成功。我另外又灌制了许多唱片,每张50美元,最后终于在芝加哥WLS电台找到了一份演唱牛仔歌曲的工作,薪水为每周40美元。我在那家电台唱了4年,薪水提高到了每周90美元;同时我每天晚上又在戏院登台表演,另外有300美元的收入。

1934年,我的机会来了。当时好莱坞的制片商决定拍摄牛仔影片,但他们需要的是一种会唱歌的新型牛仔。美洲唱片公司的老板——同时也是"共和电影公司"的老板之一说:"如果你们想找一个会唱歌的牛仔,我的唱片公司里正好有这么一个人。"我就是这样闯进电影圈的。我开始拍牛仔歌曲电影时,每周薪水为100美元。我对拍电影是否能够成功十分怀疑,但我并不担心。因为我知道,我随时可以回到干原来的工作。

我在电影上的成就远远超出了我的期望。我现在的年薪为10万美元,另外加上我所有影片的一半红利。不过,我知道这种情况并不能永远保持下去,但我并不忧虑。我知道,无论发生什么——即使我失去了所有的金钱——我也可以随时回到俄克拉荷马, 在佛里斯科铁路公司里找到一份工作——我的补给线永远畅通。

我听到了神的召唤

著名演说家兼传教士　史坦利·琼斯

我在印度传教已经有40年。刚开始时,我很难忍受当地那令人恐怖的热气;再加上任务艰巨,使我精神十分紧张。8年之后,我心力交瘁,精神疲惫,竟致精神崩溃,而且不止一次,是接连多次。最后我接到命令,回美国休养一年。在乘船返回美国的途中,我在船上作周日早晨的布道时,又精神崩溃,船上的医生要求我躺在床上,直至抵达美国。

在美国休养一年之后,我再次返回印度。但我在路经马尼拉时停了下来,为当地大学生作

evangelistic meetings among the university students in Manila. In the midst of the strain of these meetings, I collapsed several times. Physicians warned me that if I returned to India, I would die. In spite of their warnings, I continued on to India, but I went with a deepening cloud upon me. When I arrived in Bombay, I was so broken that I went straight to the hills and rested for several months. Then I returned to the plains to continue my work. It was no use. I collapsed and was forced to return to the hills for another long rest. Again I descended to the plains, and again I was shocked and crushed to discover that I couldn't take it. I was exhausted mentally, nervously, and physically. I was completely at the end of my resources. I feared that I would be a physical wreck for the balance of my life.

If I didn't get help from somewhere, I realized that I would have to give up my missionary career, go back to America, and work on a farm to try to regain my health. It was one of my darkest hours. At that time I was holding a series of meetings in Lucknow. While praying one night, an event happened that completely transformed my life. While in prayer—and I was not particularly thinking about myself at the time—a voice seemed to say: "Are you yourself ready for this work to which I have called you?"

I replied: "No, Lord, I am done for. I have reached the end of my resources."

The Voice replied: "If you will turn that over to Me and not worry about it, I will take care of it."

I quickly answered: "Lord, I close the bargain right here."

A great peace settled into my heart and pervaded my whole being. I knew it was done! Life—abundant life—had taken possession of me. I was so lifted up that I scarcely touched the road as I quietly walked home that night. Every inch was holy ground. For days after that I hardly knew I had a body. I went through the days, working all day and far into the night, and came down to bedtime wondering why in the world I should ever go to bed at all, for there was not the slightest trace of tiredness of any kind. I seemed possessed by life and peace and rest—by Christ Himself.

The question came as to whether I should tell this. I shrank from it, but I felt I should—and did. After that it was sink or swim before everybody. More than a score of the most strenuous years of my life have gone by since then, but the old trouble has never returned. I have never had such health. But it was more than a physical touch. I seemed to have tapped new life for body, mind, and

了一次布道。在接连举行几次这类会议之后，我又崩溃了几次。医生警告我说，如果我坚持去印度，将必死无疑。但我不顾他们的警告，继续赶往印度，但心头的隐忧愈来愈深。当我抵达孟买时，已濒临崩溃的边缘。于是，我直接到一座山上休养了几个月，然后又回到平原，继续开展我的工作。但这不管用。我又精神崩溃了，只好再次回到山上休养。然后，我又下了山，惊讶地发现我忍受不了山下的环境。我身心疲惫，几乎到了山穷水尽的地步。我害怕自己会瘫倒，悲惨地度过余生。

我知道如果我不能从别的地方获得帮助，就只能放弃传教生涯，回到美国去农场工作，那样就可以恢复健康。那是我最悲惨的一段时期。当时，我正在鹿克诺主持一系列会议。一天晚上，我在做祈祷的时候，发生了一件事，它完全改变了我的生活。在我祈祷的时候——我当时并没特别想到自己——似乎有一个声音在说："你自己是否已做好准备，接受我交给你的工作？"

我回答："不，主呀，我已尽力了。我到了山穷水尽地步。"

那个声音说："如果你把它交还给我，不再为它烦恼，我可以为你好好照顾它。"

我立即回答："主呀，我接受你的建议。"

这时，我心中无比祥和，那种感觉迅即遍布全身。我知道一切都解决了！生命——多姿多彩的生命——已经回到我身上来了。那天晚上，我异常兴奋，在回家的路上飘飘然的，仿佛漂浮在云层之间，踩不到路面。在那件事发生之后的几天，我几乎忘记了自己的存在。一连好几天，我都夜以继日地工作着；到了上床就寝的时间，我竟然会奇怪我为什么还要上床睡觉，因为我一点儿疲倦的感觉也没有。我似乎为生命、和平、休养以及上帝所占有。

我不知道是否应该把这件事情讲出来。我有些迟疑，但觉得应该这么做——而且我真的说了。从那以后直到今天，这件事已经过去了几十年，虽然我的壮年时代已经过去，但以前的那些烦恼永远都不再出现，我的健康状况也更好了。我不仅是肉体上获得了健康，我的身体、精神、

spirit. After that experience, life for me functioned on a permanently higher level. And I had done nothing but take it!

During the many years that have gone by since then, I have traveled all over the world, frequently lecturing three times a day, and have found time and strength to write *The Christ of the Indian Road* and eleven other books. Yet in the midst of all this, I have never missed, or even been late to, an appointment. The worries that once beset me have long since vanished, and now, in my sixty-third year, I am overflowing with abounding vitality and the joy of serving and living for others.

I suppose that the physical and mental transformation that I have experienced could be picked to pieces psychologically and explained. It does not matter. Life is bigger than processes and overflows and dwarfs them.

When the Sheriff Came in My Front Door

By Homer Croy

Novelist, 150 Pinehurst Avenue, New York

The bitterest moment of my life occurred one day in 1933 when the sheriff came in the front door and I went out the back. I had lost my home at 10 Standish Road, Forest Hills, Long Island, where my children were born and where I and my family had lived for eighteen years. I had never dreamed that this could happen to me. Twelve years before, I thought I was sitting on top of the world. I had sold the motion-picture rights to my novel *West of the Water Tower* for a top Hollywood price. I lived abroad with my family for two years. We summered in Switzerland and wintered on the French Riviera—just like the idle rich.

I spent six months in Paris and wrote a novel entitled *They Had to See Paris*. Will Rogers appeared in the screen version. It was his first talking picture. I had tempting offers to remain in Hollywood and write several of Will Rogers' pictures. But I didn't. I returned to New York. And my troubles began!

It slowly dawned on me that I had great dormant abilities that I had never developed, I began to fancy myself a shrewd businessman. Somebody told me that John Jacob Astor had made millions

意志也似乎全都获得了新生命。自从那次经历之后，我的生命到了一个更高的永恒境界，而我只是坦然地接受它。

那件事发生之后的许多年中，我去世界各地旅行，经常一天做3次演讲，而且还有精力和时间写《印度的基督》及另外11本书。而在这么繁忙的情况下，我从未错过一次约会，甚至连迟到都不会有。困扰我的那些烦恼早已消失，现在我都63岁了，但我仍能享受生命的无穷乐趣。

我想，我所经历的肉体及精神上的变化，也许可以从心理学的观点来解释。但这并没有什么关系，因为生命包罗万象，是难以解释得清的。

当我突然一无所有时

小说家　荷马·克洛伊

我一生中最悲惨的时刻是在1933年的一天。这天，警长来到我家的前门口，而我则从后门溜了出去。我失去了在长岛佛罗里斯特山的家，我的孩子都出生在那儿，我和家人在那里住了18年。我从未想到这种事情竟然会降临到我头上。12年前，我认为我处于世界顶端。我的小说《水塔之西》的电影版权以最高价格卖给了好莱坞。我和家人在国外待了两年，去瑞士避暑，在法国南部过冬——过着标准的富翁生活。

我在巴黎住了6个月，写了一本小说《他们必须来巴黎观光》。它后来被改编成电影，由威尔·罗吉斯主演，这也是他的第一部有声电影。他们要求我留在好莱坞为罗吉斯写几部电影剧本，但我还是回到了纽约。我的麻烦从此开始了！

我渐渐地认为自己拥有一些尚未开发的潜能，开始幻想自己是一个精明的商人。有一个人告诉我，约翰·嘉科布·亚斯特在纽约投资购买空地而成为百万富翁。亚斯特是什么人呢?他只不过是一个带着口音的移民商贩。如果他能成功，为什么我就不能?……我马上就要发大财了!

investing in vacant land in New York. Who was Astor? Just an immigrant peddler with an accent. If he could do it, why couldn't I?... I was going to be rich! I began to read the yachting magazines.

I had the courage of ignorance. I didn't know any more about buying and selling real estate than an Eskimo knows about oil furnaces. How was I to get the money to launch myself on my spectacular financial career? That was simple. I mortgaged my home, and bought some of the finest building lots in Forest Hills. I was going to hold this land until it reached a fabulous price, then sell it and live in luxury—I who had never sold a piece of real estate as big as a doll's handkerchief. I pitied the plodders who slaved in offices for a mere salary. I told myself that God had not seen fit to touch every man with the divine fire of financial genius.

Suddenly, the great depression swept down upon me like a Kansas cyclone and shook me as a tornado would shake a hen coop.

I had to pour $220 a month into that monster-mouthed piece of Good Earth. Oh, how fast those months came! In addition, I had to keep up the payments on our now-mortgaged house and find enough food. I was worried. I tried to write humor for the magazines. My attempts at humour sounded like the lamentations of Jeremiah! I was unable to sell anything. The novel I wrote failed. I ran out of money. I had nothing on which I could borrow money except my typewriter and the gold fillings in my teeth. The milk company stopped delivering milk. The gas company turned off the gas. We had to buy one of those little outdoor camp stoves you see advertised; it had a cylinder of gasoline; you pump it up by hand and it shoots out a flame with a hissing like an angry goose.

We ran out of coal; the company sued us. Our only heat was the fireplace. I would go out at night and pick up boards and leftovers from the new homes that the rich people were building... I who had started out to be one of these rich people.

I was so worried I couldn't sleep. I often got up in the middle of the night and walked for hours to exhaust myself so I could fall asleep.

I lost not only the vacant land I had bought, but all my heart's blood that I had poured into it.

The bank closed the mortgage on my home and put me and my family out on the street.

In some way, we managed to get hold of a few dollars and rent a small apartment. We moved in the last day of 1933. I sat down on a packing case and looked around. An old saying of my

我开始读游艇杂志。

我空有无知的勇气，对于房地产却一无所知。我应该如何开始这方面的事业呢?很简单。我抵押了我的房子，然后买下佛罗里斯特山一些位置最好的建筑用地。我想保留这块地，直到地价涨到最高时再将它卖掉，去过奢华的生活——我这个人从未卖过巴掌大的一块地。我同情那些在办公室为一点点薪水而忙碌的职员。我告诉自己，上帝并未赋予每个人特殊的创富才能。

经济危机突然像堪萨斯的旋风摇荡鸡笼一样袭击了我。

我每个月必须为那块地支付 220 美元。唉，那几个月过得真快啊!除外，我还必须为那座被抵押的房子还款，要养活一家人。

我十分烦恼，想为杂志社写一些幽默小说。但我的幽默小品颇似《旧约》中的哀歌。我没有卖出任何稿子。我写的小说也没人要。我的钱全用光了，除了打字机和我口中的金牙之外，我没有任何东西可抵押借款的。牛奶公司停止为我送奶，燃气公司也关掉了燃气，我只好买了一个广告宣传的露营用的小火炉，它有一个汽油缸，要用手举着，喷出嘶嘶响的火焰，就像发怒的鹅在叫唤。

我们没有煤了，煤炭公司起诉了我们。唯一取暖的东西是那个壁炉。我会在晚上出去，到那些有钱人正在建造的房子附近捡一些废木头……而我本来是想跻身这些有钱人行列的。

我忧虑得难以入睡，经常在半夜起床，走上几个小时，直到疲倦入睡。

我不仅失去了我买的那块空地，连我花在上面的全部心血也都付诸东流。银行中止了我的抵押，把我和家人全赶到了大街上。

我们好不容易找到几美元，租了一小间公寓，在 1933 年的最后一天搬过去。我坐在行李箱上，抬头四处张望。这时，我母亲的一句老话涌入我的脑海："不要为打翻的牛奶哭泣! "

mother's came back: "Don't cry over spilt milk."

But this wasn't milk. This was my heart's blood!

After I had sat there a while I said to myself: "Well, I've hit bottom and I've stood it. There's no place to go now but up."

I began to think of the fine things that the mortgage had not taken from me. I still had my health and my friends. I would start again. I would not grieve about the past. I would repeat to myself every day the words I had often heard my mother say about spilt milk.

I put into my work the energy that I had been putting into worrying. Little by little, my situation began to improve. I am almost thankful now that I had to go through all that misery; it gave me strength, fortitude, and confidence. I know now what it means to hit bottom. I know it doesn't kill you. I know we can stand more than we think we can. When little worries and anxieties and uncertainties try to disturb me now, I banish them by reminding myself of the time I sat on the packing case and said: "I've hit bottom and I've stood it. There is no place to go now but up."

What's the principle here? Don't try to saw sawdust! Accept the inevitable! If you can't go lower, yon can try going up.

The Toughest Opponent I Ever Fought Was Worry

By Jack Dempsey

During my career in the ring, I found that Old Man Worry was an almost tougher opponent than the heavyweight boxers I fought. I realized that I had to learn to stop worrying, or worry would sap my vitality and undermine my success. So, little by little, I worked out a system for myself. Here are some of the things I did:

1. To keep up my courage in the ring, I would give myself a pep talk during the fight. For example, while I was fighting Firpo, I kept saying over and over: "Nothing is going to stop me. He is not going to hurt me. I won't feel his blows. I can't get hurt. I am going to keep going, no matter what happens." Making positive statements like that to myself, and thinking positive thoughts, helped me a lot. It even kept my mind so occupied that I didn't feel the blows. During my career, I have had my lips smashed, my eyes cut, my ribs cracked—and Firpo knocked me clear through the

但这并不是牛奶,而是我的心血!

我在那里坐了一会儿,然后对自己说:"好吧!我已经历过最悲惨的遭遇,而且熬了过去。现在,情况只会好转,而不会变坏。"

我开始想到好的方面,被抵押的房子还在。我的身体依旧健康,还有朋友。一切都可以重新再来。我不再为过去而哀伤,我将每天重复我过去常听到的母亲说的那句话。

我把精力用在工作上,不再自寻烦恼。渐渐地,我的情况开始改善。对于我以前的那段悲惨遭遇,我现在充满了感激:它给了我力量、坚忍和信心。现在我知道什么是最困苦的生活,我还知道天无绝人之路,更知道我们能忍受更多的苦难。现在,当我遇到小烦恼、焦虑和障碍时,我就会提醒自己当年坐在行李箱上对自己说的话:"我已经历过最悲惨的遭遇,而且熬过去了。现在,情况只会好转,而不会变坏。"

(这篇故事的规则是什么?不要锯木屑!接受不可避免的事实!如果你的境况已经糟至极点,那就试着往上爬吧!)

我最大的对手是忧虑

杰克·邓普赛

在我的拳击生涯中,我发现"忧虑"比我所遇到的任何重量级拳手都更难对付。我知道我必须学会停止忧虑,否则忧虑会削弱我的活力,毁坏我的成就。于是,我给自己草拟了一项制度,以下就是其中的几部分:

第一,为了保持在比赛中的勇气,我总是在比赛时自我打气。例如,当我和佛波比赛时,我不断地告诉自己:"没有人打得过我!他伤不了我!他的拳头伤不了我!我不会受伤!不论发生什么事,我一定要勇往直前!"这样不断地为自己鼓气,使内心的想法变得主动积极,对我帮助

ropes, and I landed on a reporter's typewriter and wrecked it. But I never felt even one of Firpo's blows. There was only one blow that I ever really felt. That was the night Lester Johnson broke three of my ribs. The punch never hurt me, but it affected my breathing. I can honestly say I never felt any other blow I ever got in the ring.

2. Another thing I did was to keep reminding myself of the futility of worry. Most of my worrying was done before the big bouts, while I was going through training. I would often lie awake at nights for hours, tossing and worrying, unable to sleep. I would worry for fear I might break my hand or sprain my ankle or get my eye cut badly in the first round so I couldn't coordinate my punches. When I got myself into this state of nerves, I used to get out of bed, look into the mirror, and give myself a good talking to. I would say: "What a fool you are to be worrying about something that hasn't happened and may never happen. Life is short. I have only a few years to live, so I must enjoy life." I kept saying to myself: "Nothing is important but my health. Nothing is important but my health." I kept reminding myself that losing sleep and worrying would destroy my health. I found that by saying these things to myself over and over, night after night, year after year, they finally got under my skin, and I could brush off my worries like so much water.

3. The third—and best—thing I did was pray! While I was training for a bout, I always prayed several times a day. When I was in the ring, I always prayed just before the bell sounded for each round. That helped me fight with courage and confidence. I have never gone to bed in my life without saying a prayer; and I have never eaten a meal in my life without first thanking God for it... Have my prayers been answered? Thousands of times!

I Prayed to God to Keep Meout of an Orphan's Home

By Kathleen Halter

Housewife, 1074 Roth, University City 14, Missouri

As a little child, my life was filled with horror. My mother had heart trouble. Day after day, I saw her faint and fall to the floor. We all feared she was going to die, and I believed that all little girls whose mothers died were sent to the Central Wesleyan Orphans' Home, located in the little

很大,甚至使我不觉得对方的拳头打到了我。在我的拳击生涯中,我的嘴唇曾被击裂,眼睛被打伤,肋骨被打断,而且佛波有一次还将我打出场外,摔倒在一位记者的打字机上,压坏了打字机。但我对佛波的拳头甚至没有任何感觉。只有一次,我真的感觉到了拳击。那天晚上,李斯特·约翰逊一拳打断了我三根肋骨。虽然那一拳伤不了我,但影响到了我的呼吸。我可以坦白地说,除此之外,我从未在比赛中对任何拳击有过感觉。

第二,另外一个方法就是不断地提醒自己,烦恼毫无益处。我的大部分烦恼都出现在大型比赛之前,也就是我接受训练期间。我经常会在半夜醒来,一连好几个钟头辗转反侧,无法入睡。我担心自己会在第一回合被对方打断手,或扭伤脚,或眼睛被严重击伤,这样我就不能尽情发挥攻势了。当我有了这种烦恼时,我总是爬下床,对着镜子,好好训斥自己一顿。我会说:"你真是一个大笨蛋,竟然会为一些尚未发生而且可能永远都不会发生的事情担心!人生苦短,你的时间只有几年,所以你必须尽情享受。"我又对自己说:"你的健康是最重要的。除了你的健康,没有任何东西比它更重要。"我不断地提醒自己,失眠和忧虑会损害我的健康。我发现,当我不停地提醒自己这些事的时候,它们最后终于渗透到我的内心当中了,因此我可以很容易地消除所有的烦恼。

第三,最后一种方法——也是最好的——就是祈祷!在接受比赛训练时,我每天会祈祷好几次。在比赛中,我总是会在每一回合铃响之前祈祷,这使我有了继续比赛的信心和勇气。我从未不祈祷就睡觉,也从未不祈祷就吃饭……我的祈祷有用吗?千百次事实已做了回答!

摆脱烦恼的秘诀

家庭主妇　凯瑟琳·哈尔特

在我小的时候,生活充满了恐惧。我的母亲患有心脏病,我经常看见她晕倒在地板上。我们

town of Warrenton, Missouri, where we lived. I dreaded the thought of going there, and when I was six years old I prayed constantly: “Dear God, please let my mummy live until I am old enough not to go to the orphans' home.”

Twenty years later, my brother, Meiner, had a terrible injury and suffered intense pain until he died two years later. He couldn't feed himself or turn over in bed. To deaden his pain, I had to give him morphine hypodermics every three hours, day and night. I did this for two years. I was teaching music at the time at the Central Wesleyan College in Warrenton, Missouri. When the neighbors heard my brother screaming with pain, they would telephone me at college and I would leave my music class and rush home to give my brother another injection of morphine. Every night when I went to bed, I would set the alarm clock to go off three hours later so I would be sure to get up to attend to my brother. I remember that on winter nights I would keep a bottle of milk outside the window, where it would freeze and turn into a kind of ice-cream that I loved to eat. When the alarm went off, this ice cream outside the window gave me an additional incentive to get up.

In the midst of all these troubles, I did two things that kept me from indulging in self-pity and worrying and embittering my life with resentment. First, I kept myself busy teaching music from twelve to fourteen hours a day, so I had little time to think of my troubles; and when I was tempted to feel sorry for myself, I kept saying to myself over and over: “Now listen, as long as you can walk and feed yourself and are free from intense pain, you ought to be the happiest person in the world. No matter what happens, never forget that as long as you live! Never! Never! ”

I was determined to do everything in my power to cultivate an unconscious and continuous attitude of gratefulness for my many blessings. Every morning when I awoke, I would thank God that conditions were no worse than they were; and I resolved that in spite of my troubles I would be the happiest person in Warrenton, Missouri. Maybe I didn't succeed in achieving that goal, but I did succeed in making myself the most grateful young woman in my hometown—and probably few of my associates worried less than I did.

This Missouri music teacher applied two principles descried in this book: she kept too busy to worry, and she counted her blessings. The same technique may be helpful to you.

都很害怕她会死，而且我认为那些失去母亲的小女孩都会被送到位于我们所住的密苏里州华林顿镇的卫斯里中心孤儿院。只要一想到被送到那儿，我就非常害怕。当我还只有6岁时，我就经常祈祷：“亲爱的上帝，请让我母亲继续活下去，直到我长大了，可以不用去孤儿院。”

20年后，我哥哥梅勒受了重伤，遭受极大的痛苦，直到20年后才去世。他不能吃东西，也不能在床上翻身。为了减轻他的痛苦，无论白天或晚上，我每隔3小时必须为他注射一针吗啡。我这样做了两年。那时，我在镇上的卫斯里中心学院教音乐。当邻居们听到我哥哥痛苦得大声呼叫时，就打电话到学院找我，我会立即放下手中的工作，跑回家再为我哥哥注射一针吗啡。每天晚上上床时，我会把闹钟拨到3小时之后，以便起床照料哥哥。我记得在一个冬天的晚上，我总是把一瓶牛奶放在窗外，好让它结成冰，变成我最喜欢吃的冰淇淋。当闹钟响时，窗外的冰淇淋也就成了我起床的另一种动力了。

在这么艰苦的情况下，我采取了两项措施，使自己避免陷入自怜自艾，也免受烦恼和悔恨之苦。第一，我让自己每天忙着教12~14小时的音乐课，因此没有时间去想我的忧虑。而当我为自己感到难过时，我会一再对自己说：“听着，只要你还能走路，还能自己吃饭，身上又没有大病大痛，那么你就是这个世界上最快乐的人。千万不要忘记，不管遇到什么困难，只要你还活着，那你就是最幸运的人！不要忘记！”

第二，我决定为我所获得的这些幸福培养一种永远感激的态度。当我每天早晨醒来时，我就会感谢上帝：情况没比以前更糟。我深深地感到，尽管我遇到了许多困难，但我仍然是密苏里州华林顿最快乐的人。也许我并未成功地实现这一目标，但我的确成功地使自己成为这个镇上最知道感恩的年轻女子——而我的同事中可能没有几人会像我这样没有忧虑。

(这位密苏里州的音乐教师应用了本书介绍的两条原则：使自己保持忙碌而没有时间去忧虑；对自己的幸福心存感激。这两条原则对你也许同样有用。)

I Was Acting Like a Hysterical Woman

By Cameron Shipp

Magazine Writer

I had been working very happily in the publicity department of the Warner Brothers studio in California for several years. I was a unit man and feature writer. I wrote stories for newspapers and magazines about Warner Brothers stars.

Suddenly, I was promoted. I was made the assistant publicity director. As a matter of fact, there was a change of administrative policy, and I was given an impressive title: Administrative Assistant.

This gave me an enormous office with a private refrigerator, two secretaries, and complete charge of a staff of seventy-five writers, exploiters, and radio men. I was enormously impressed. I went straight out and bought a new suit. I tried to speak with dignity. I set up filing systems, made decisions with authority, and ate quick lunches.

I was convinced that the whole public relations policy of Warner Brothers had descended upon my shoulders. I perceived that the lives, both private and public, of such renowned persons as Bette Davis, Olivia De Havilland, James Cagney, Edward G. Robinson, Errol Flynn, Humphrey Bogart, Ann Sheridan, Alexis Smith, and Alan Hale were entirely in my hands.

In less than a month I became aware that I had stomach ulcers. Probably cancer.

My chief war activity at that time was chairman of the War Activities Committee of the Screen Publicists Guild. I liked to do this work, liked to meet my friends at guild meetings. But these gatherings became matters of dread. After every meeting, I was violently ill. Often I had to stop my car on the way home, pulling myself together before I could drive on. There seemed to be so much to do, so little time in which to do it. It was all vital. And I was woefully inadequate.

I am being perfectly truthful—this was the most painful illness of my entire life. There was always a tight fist in my vitals. I lost weight. I could not sleep. The pain was constant.

So I went to see a renowned expert in internal medicine. An advertising man recommended him. He said this physician had many clients who were advertising men.

This physician spoke only briefly, just enough for me to tell him where I hurt and what I did

我曾像个疯女人

杂志作家　卡梅龙·希普

我曾在加利福尼亚州的华纳兄弟影片公司宣传部愉快地工作了几年。我是个专栏作家，一个人单独写作，为几家报纸和杂志撰写文章，报道华纳公司的明星动态。

我曾在突然之间获得升迁，被提拔为宣传部副主任。事实上，公司的行政策略有所改变，我被授予了一项重要头衔——行政助理。

这个新头衔使我拥有了一间大办公室、一台私人冰箱和两位秘书，并负责指挥75名撰稿人员、开发人员以及无线电人员。我自以为一路顺风，马上买了一套新衣服。我以威严的口气说话，建立起档案制度，做出权威的决定，吃饭也匆匆忙忙。

我觉得华纳公司的整个公共关系政策全部托付在我身上，我甚至以为公司的一些大明星，如贝蒂·戴维斯、奥利维尔·哈维兰德、詹姆斯·卡格尼、爱德华·鲁滨逊……全都在我掌握之中。

可是不到一个月，我就觉得自己得了胃溃疡，甚至是癌症。

当时我的另一项主要工作，是任银幕宣传指导委员会的策划小组主席。我很喜欢这个工作，很高兴能在各种会议中和老朋友见面。但这些聚会后来却让我害怕，因为每次开完会之后，我总是很不舒服。我必须经常在回家的半路上将汽车停在路边，好使自己轻松一下，再继续开车。我似乎有许多工作要做，但是时间却不够。由于这些工作都很重要，我却难以胜任。

我生来为人诚实——我认为这是我一生中最大的痛苦。我总觉得精神压抑，体重减轻，开始失眠，而且经常觉得疼痛。

于是我去看了一位著名的内科大夫。一位广告商向我推荐的他，他说这名大夫有许多患者都是广告商。

for a living. He seemed more interested in my job than in my ailments, but I was soon reassured: for two weeks, daily, he gave me every known test. I was probed, explored, X-rayed, and fluoroscoped. Finally, I was instructed to call on him and hear the verdict.

"Mr. Shipp, "he said, leaning back and offering me a cigarette, "we have been through these exhaustive tests. They were absolutely necessary, although I knew *of course* after my first quick examination that you *did not have stomach ulcers*.

"But I knew, because you are the kind of man you are and because you do the kind of work you do, that you would not believe me unless I showed you. Let me show you."

So he showed me the charts and the X-rays and explained them. He showed me I had no ulcers.

"Now, "said the doctor, "this costs you a good deal of money, but it is worth it to you. Here is the prescription: *don't worry*.

"Now"—he stopped me as I started to expostulate—"now, I realise that you can't follow the prescription immediately, so I'll give you a crutch. Here are some pills. They contain belladonna. Take as many as you like. When you use these up, come back and I'll give you more. They won't hurt you. But they will always relax you.

"But remember: you don't need them. All you have to do is quit worrying.

"If you do start worrying again, you'll have to come back here and I'll charge you a heavy fee again. How about it? "

I wish I could report that the lesson took effect that day and that I quit worrying immediately. I didn't. I took the pills for several weeks, whenever I felt a worry coming on. They worked. I felt better at once.

But I felt silly taking these pills. I am a big man physically. I am almost as tall as Abe Lincoln was—and I weigh almost two hundred pounds. Yet here I was taking little white pills to relax myself. I was acting like an hysterical woman. When my friends asked me why I was taking pills, I was ashamed to tell the truth. Gradually I began to laugh at myself. I said: "See here, Cameron Shipp, you are acting like a fool. You are taking yourself and your little activities much, much too seriously. Bette Davis and James Cagney and Edward G. Robinson were world-famous before you started to handle their publicity; and if you dropped dead tonight, Warner Brothers and

这位大夫说话简短，只让我告诉他哪里不舒服，以及从事什么工作。他对我的工作似乎比对我的病情更感兴趣，不过我后来发现并不是这样的。接连两个星期，他给我做了各种检查。最后，他通知我去见他，告诉我检查的结果。

“希普先生，”他说，同时向椅背上一靠，并递给我一支烟，“我们已经做了各种检查。这些检查对你来说是绝对必要的，虽然我第一天为你做了大致的检查之后，就知道你并没有患胃溃疡。

“不过我知道，就你的个性和你目前所从事的工作而言，你是不会轻易相信我的，除非我能向你证明。让我来告诉你。”

于是，他拿来各项检查表及X光片为我解释，说我并未患胃溃疡。

“听着，”大夫说，“虽然这些会花你不少钱，但是很值。给你的药方是：不要烦恼。”

我正想对他发火，但他制止了我，继续说道：“注意听我说：我知道你无法立刻遵照这个药方去做，所以我给你开了一些药。这些药你想服用多少，尽管放心服用。用完了你再到我这儿来，我会再给你开一些。它们不会对你有害，但能使你经常保持轻松愉快。

“但要记住：你不是非服用不可。你所要做的就是抛除烦恼。

“如果你又有了烦恼，那你必须回我这儿来。那时，我可又要向你要一大笔治疗费了。你可愿意？”

我希望能告诉各位，这位医生的话在我身上生效了，我立刻停止了烦恼。然而，这一切并没有发生。我连续服用了好几个星期的药。而它们确实有效，我立刻觉得好多了。

但我觉得服用这些药实在可笑。我已经是一个成年人，几乎和林肯总统一样高，体重也将近200磅，而我却还在服用这种白色小药片使自己放松。我觉得自己像个歇斯底里的妇人。当朋友们问我为何服药时，我都不好意思说出真相。慢慢地，我开始嘲笑自己。我说：“喂，卡梅龙·

their stars would manage to get along without you. Look at Eisenhower, General Marshall, Macarthur, Jimmy Doolittle and Admiral King—they are running the war without taking pills. And yet you can't serve as chairman of the War Activities Committee of the Screen Publicists Guild without taking little white pills to keep your stomach from twisting and turning like a Kansas whirlwind."

I began to take pride in getting along without the pills. A little while later, I threw the pills down the drain and got home each night in time to take a little nap before dinner and gradually began to lead a normal life. I have never been back to see that physician.

But I owe him much, much more than what seemed like a stiff fee at the time. He taught me to laugh at myself. But I think the really skilful thing he did was to refrain from laughing at me, and to refrain from telling me I had nothing to worry about. He took me seriously. He saved my face. He gave me an out in a small box. But he knew then, as well as I know now, that the cure wasn't in those silly little pills—the cure was in a change in my mental attitude.

The moral of this story is that many a man who is now taking pills would do better to read Chapter 7, and relax.

I Learned to Stop Worrying by Watching My Wife Wash Dishes

By Reverend William Wood

204 Hurlbert Street, Charlevoix, Michigan

A few years ago, I was suffering intensely from pains in my stomach. I would awaken two or three times each night, unable to sleep because of these terrific pains. I had watched my father die from cancer of the stomach, and I feared that I too had a stomach cancer—or, at least, stomach ulcers. So I went to Byrne's Clinic at Petosky, Michigan, for an examination. Dr. Lilga, a stomach specialist, examined me with a fluoroscope and took an X-ray of my stomach. He gave me medicine to make me sleep and assured me that I had no stomach ulcers or cancer. My stomach pains, he said, were caused by emotional strains. Since I am a minister, one of his first questions was: "Do you have an old crank on your church board? "

He told me what I already knew; I was trying to do too much. In addition to my preaching

希普,你的举止像个大傻瓜。你把自己和你那不起眼的工作看得太重要了。贝蒂·戴维斯、詹姆斯·卡格尼、爱德华·鲁滨逊早在你开始做他们的宣传之前,就已经闻名世界了。假如你今晚突然暴亡,华纳公司和它所有的明星没有你也照样能过下去。艾森豪威尔、马歇尔、麦克阿瑟、吉米·杜立特,虽然他们主持全球的战争,但却不必服药。而你却必须吞下那些小白药丸,才能使你保持平静,才能干好你的工作。"

我开始不服药,并以此为荣。没过多久,我就把那些药扔进马桶,晚上准时回家,先小睡一会儿,然后吃晚饭。我渐渐开始恢复了正常生活,再也没有去看过那位大夫。

但我欠他的太多了,这远非我那次付的高昂诊费所能比。他教会了我如何放松。但我认为,他真正高明之处在于避免嘲笑我,也没有直接告诉我实际上没有什么好担心的——相反,他郑重地接纳了我,给我留了面子。他只给我一小盒药丸,但他早已知道——而我现在也知道——并不是那些令人发笑的小药丸治好了我,而是我改变了自己的心态。

不要把烦恼叠加在一起

牧师 威廉·伍德

多年来,我因为患上了严重的胃病而十分痛苦。我每晚会痛醒两三次,无法入睡。我曾见到我父亲死于胃癌,我担心自己也会得胃癌——或者至少也是胃溃疡。因此,我去了一家诊所接受检查。胃科专家利伽医生用荧光镜和X光检查了我的胃部。他给我开了一些药帮助我入睡;并且向我保证,我并没有得胃溃疡或胃癌,他说我的胃痛是由精神紧张所引起的。由于我是牧师,因此他的第一个问题是:"你在教堂是不是很忙?"

他问我的我其实早已知道:我总是想做太多的事。除了每个星期天的讲道及主持教堂的各种活动之外,我还担任了红十字会主席、吉瓦尼斯俱乐部会长;同时每周还要主持两三次葬礼

every Sunday and carrying the burdens of the various activities of the church, I was also chairman of the Red Cross, president of the Kiwanis. I also conducted two or three funerals each week and a number of other activities.

I was working under constant pressure. I could never relax. I was always tense, hurried, and high–strung. I got to the point where I worried about everything. I was living in a constant dither. I was in such pain that I gladly acted on Dr. Lilga's advice. I took Monday off each week, and began eliminating various responsibilities and activities.

One day while cleaning out my desk, I got an idea that proved to be immensely helpful. I was looking over an accumulation of old notes on sermons and other memos on matters that were now past and gone. I crumpled them up one by one and tossed them into the wastebasket. Suddenly I stopped and said to myself: "Bill, why don't you do the same thing with your worries that you are doing with these notes? Why don't you crumple up your worries about yesterday's problems and toss them into the wastebasket? "That one idea gave me immediate inspiration—gave me the feeling of a weight being lifted from my shoulders. From that day to this, I have made it a rule to throw into the wastebasket all the problems that I can no longer do anything about.

Then, one day while wiping the dishes as my wife washed them, I got another idea. My wife was singing as she washed the dishes, and I said to myself: "Look, Bill, how happy your wife is. We have been married eighteen years, and she has been washing dishes all that time. Suppose when we got married she had looked ahead and seen all the dishes she would have to wash during those eighteen years that stretched ahead. That pile of dirty dishes would be bigger than a barn. The very thought of it would have appalled any woman."

Then I said to myself: "The reason my wife doesn't mind washing the dishes is because she washes only one day's dishes at a time." I saw what my trouble was. I was trying to wash today's dishes and yesterday's dishes and dishes that weren't even dirty yet.

I saw how foolish I was acting. I was standing in the pulpit, Sunday mornings, telling other people how to live, yet I myself was leading a tense, worried, hurried existence. I felt ashamed of myself.

Worries don't bother me any more now. No more stomach pains. No more insomnia. I now crumple up yesterday's anxieties and toss them into the wastebasket, and I have ceased trying to

以及各种其他活动。

我在持续压力下工作，永远都无法放松。我总是紧张匆忙地生活着，几乎到了凡事皆烦恼的地步。我一直生活在紧张不安中，因此当然乐于接受医生的忠告。我每个星期一都自动休假，同时减少了各种社会工作及活动。

一天，我在清理桌子时，突然产生一个念头，结果证明这个念头极其有效。当时，我正在看抽屉里一大堆以前讲道的旧笔记，以及一些已经过时的备忘录。我将它们全都拿出来，然后扔进了废纸篓里。突然，我停了下来对自己说："为什么你对自己的烦恼不能像对这些旧笔记一样呢?为什么不将昨天的全部烦恼捡出来扔进废纸篓呢?"这个念头立刻起了作用——我顿时觉得肩头的重担减轻了不少。从那天起直到今天，我已将它当成一项铁则：把我无力解决问题都扔进废纸篓。

接着，有一天，我太太在洗盘子，我帮她擦干，我又产生了另一个念头。当时我太太一面洗盘子，一面唱着歌。我对自己说："瞧，你太太多么快乐。我们已结婚 18 年，而她洗盘子也洗了 18 年。假如我们结婚时，她就看到她在这期间要洗的盘子堆起来可以装满一个谷仓的话，一定会吓走任何一个女人。"

然后，我告诉自己："我太太之所以不介意洗盘子，是因为她一次只洗一天的盘子。"我终于找到了我的问题所在——我企图一次洗完今天和昨天甚至尚未使用的盘子。

我发现我的行动实在是太傻了。每个星期天的早晨，我都会站在讲台上，告诉人们如何生活，而我自己却一味地紧张、匆忙和烦恼。我对自己感到惭愧。

从此以后，烦恼再也不来打扰我了，胃也不再痛了，而且不再失眠。我现在将昨天的烦恼全揉成一团，然后将它们扔进废纸篓；同时，我开始停止为未来担忧。

你是否还记得这句话："明天的烦恼，加上昨天的烦恼，和今天的合起来，于是造成了最沉

wash tomorrow's dirty dishes today.

Do you remember a statement quoted earlier in this book? "The load of tomorrow, added to that of yesterday, carried today, makes the strongest falter."... Why even try it?

I Found the Answer—keep Busy!

By Del Hughes

Public Accountant, 607 South Euclid Avenue, Bay City, Michigan

In 1943 I landed in a veterans' hospital in Albuquerque, New Mexico, with three broken ribs and a punctured lung. This had happened during a practice Marine amphibious landing off the Hawaiian Islands. I was getting ready to jump off the barge, onto the beach, when a big breaker swept in, lifted the barge, and threw me off balance and smashed me on the sands. I fell with such force that one of my broken ribs punctured my right lung.

After spending three months in the hospital, I got the biggest shock of my life. The doctors told me that I showed absolutely no improvement. After some serious thinking, I figured that worry was preventing me from getting well. I had been used to a very active life, and during these three months I had been flat on my back twenty-four hours a day with nothing to do but think. The more I thought, the more I worried: worried about whether I would ever be able to take my place in the world. I worried about whether I would remain a cripple the rest of my life, and about whether I would ever be able to get married and live a normal life.

I urged my doctor to move me up to the next ward, which was called the "Country Club" because the patients were allowed to do almost anything they cared to do.

In this "Country Club"ward, I became interested in contract bridge. I spent six weeks learning the game, playing bridge with the other fellows, and reading Culbertson's books on bridge. After six weeks, I was playing nearly every evening for the rest of my stay in the hospital. I also became interested in painting with oils, and I studied this art under an instructor every afternoon from three to five. Some of my paintings were so good that you could almost tell what they were! I also tried my hand at soap and wood carving, and read a number of books on the subject and found it fascinating. I kept myself so busy that I had no time to worry about my physical condition. I even found time to read books on psychology

重的负担。"为什么要这样做呢？

我找到了答案

会计师 迪尔·休斯

我在 1943 年住进了新墨西哥州阿布奎基市一家军队医院。当时我的肋骨三根折断，肺部穿孔。这发生在夏威夷岛的一次陆战队两栖登陆大演习中。当时我正准备从小艇跳到沙滩上，碰巧一阵大浪扑来，托起了小艇，我失去了平衡，跌倒在沙滩上。由于摔下来力量很大，我折断了肋骨，并且其中一根刺进了我的右肺。

我在医院待了 3 个月之后，经历了一生中最严重的惊吓——医生说我的伤势绝不可能好转。在经过谨慎思考之后，我认为是过度的烦恼使我无法康复。我以前的生活活跃而多姿多彩，可是这三个月我却必须一天 24 小时躺在病床上，无事可做，只能胡思乱想。想得愈多，就愈烦恼：担心自己是否能恢复以前的地位；担心是否会终生残废，以及是否还能结婚并过正常的生活。

于是我要求医生将我安排到隔壁病房，这是一间被称为"乡间俱乐部"的病房，因为那儿的病人几乎可以完全自由地活动。

在这个"乡村俱乐部"病房，我对"合约桥牌"发生了兴趣。我用了 6 个星期学会这个游戏，和其他伙伴一起搭档，还阅读了一些桥牌书。6 个星期之后，我几乎每天晚上都打桥牌。我还对油画产生了兴趣：在每天下午 3~5 点，我都在一位老师的指导下学习画画。我的一些作品画得极好，你甚至一眼就可以看出我画的是什么。我还尝试雕刻肥皂和木头，并读了许多有关的书籍，觉得十分有趣。我让自己变得十分忙碌，因此没有时间去担心我的伤势。我甚至花许多时间阅读红十字会赠送给我的心理学书。到了第 3 个月末，全体医护人

given to me by the Red Cross. At the end of three months, the entire medical staff came to me and congratulated me on "making an amazing improvement". Those were the sweetest words I had ever heard since the days I was born. I wanted to shout with joy.

The point I am trying to make is this: when I had nothing to do but lie on the flat of my back and worry about my future, I made no improvement whatever. I was poisoning my body with worry. Even the broken ribs couldn't heal. But as soon as I got my mind off myself by playing contract bridge, painting oil pictures, and carving wood, the doctors declared I made "an amazing improvement".

I am now leading a normal, healthy life, and my lungs are as good as yours.

Remember what George Bernard Shaw said? "The secret of being miserable is to have the leisure to bother about whether you are happy or not." Keep active, keep busy!

Time Solves a Lot of Things

By Louis T. Montant, Jr.

Sales and Market Analyst, 114 West 64th Street, New York

Worry caused me to lose ten years of my life. Those ten years should have been the most fruitful and richest years of any young man's life—the years from eighteen to twenty-eight.

I realize now that losing those years was no one's fault but my own.

I worried about everything: my job, my health, my family, and my feeling of inferiority. I was so frightened that I used to cross the street to avoid meeting people I knew. When I met a friend on the street, I would often pretend not to notice him, because I was afraid of being snubbed.

I was so afraid of meeting strangers—so terrified in their presence—that in one space of two weeks I lost out on three different jobs simply because I didn't have the courage to tell those three different prospective employers what I knew I could do.

Then one day eight years ago, I conquered worry in one afternoon—and have rarely worried since then. That afternoon I was in the office of a man who had had far more troubles than I had ever faced, yet he was one of the most cheerful men I had ever known. He had made a fortune in 1929, and lost every cent. He had made another fortune in 1933, and lost that; and another fortune

员来向我道贺，说我伤势恢复极佳。那是我自出生以来所听见的最甜蜜的话。我高兴得真想放声大叫。

我在此想说明的一点是，当我无所事事，成天只能躺在床上为我的将来烦恼时，我没有任何进步。我那只是用烦恼来残害我的身体，甚至折断的肋骨也难以好起来。但等我专心地打桥牌、画画、雕刻，忘记了身体的伤痛时，医生就说我“进步极大”。

我现在过着正常而健康的生活，我的肺也和你的一样好。

你是否还记得萧伯纳说过的一句话?“悲哀的根源，在于你有余暇去想你是否快乐。”活跃起来，让自己忙起来！。

时间可以解决许多问题

市场销售分析专家　路易斯·蒙坦特

“忧虑”使我丧失了10年光阴，而这10年本来应该是年轻人最有收获、最丰富多彩的岁月——18~28岁的时间。

现在我已经明白，失去这10年不是别人的错，而是我自己造成的。

我对所有的事情忧虑：我的工作、健康、家庭、自卑感。为此，我经常不得不躲避我认识的人。当我在街上碰到某位朋友时，我会假装没有看见，因为我害怕遭到嘲笑。

我非常害怕见到陌生人——在陌生人面前我就会不自在——因此有一次在两个星期当中，我接连失去了3个工作机会，只因为我没有勇气对未来的老板说我能干什么。

然后，8年前的某一天下午，我征服了一切烦恼——从那时开始，我就很少有烦恼了。那天下午，我去了某人办公室。那人似乎没有任何烦恼，而且是我所认识的人当中最快乐的一个。他在1929年发了一笔大财，可是后来却分文不剩。1932年他又东山再起，可是又赔光了。然后在

in 1939, and lost that, too. He had gone through bankruptcy and had been hounded by enemies and creditors. Troubles that would have broken some men and driven them to suicide rolled off him like water off a duck's back.

As I sat in his office that day eight years ago, I envied him and wished that God had made me like him.

As we were talking, he tossed a letter to me that he had received that morning and said: "Read that."

It was an angry letter, raising several embarrassing questions. If I had received such a letter, it would have sent me into a tailspin. I said: "Bill, how are you going to answer it? "

"Well, "Bill said, "I'll tell you a little secret. Next time you've really got something to worry about, take a pencil and a piece of paper, and sit down and write out in detail just what's worrying you. Then put that piece of paper in the lower right-hand drawer of your desk. Wait a couple of weeks, and then look at it. If what you wrote down still worries you when you read it, put that piece of paper back in your lower right-hand drawer. Let it sit there for another two weeks. It will be safe there. Nothing will happen to it. But in the meantime, a lot may happen to the problem that is worrying you. I have found that, if only I have patience, the worry that is trying to harass me will often collapse like a pricked balloon."

That bit of advice made a great impression on me. I have been using Bill's advice for years now, and, as a result, I rarely worry about anything.

Times solves a lot of things. Time may also solve what you are worrying about today.

I Was Warned Not to Try to Speakor to Move Even a Finger

By Joseph L. Ryan

Supervisor, Foreign Division, Royal Typewriter Company 51 Judson Place, Rockville Centre, Long Island, New York

Several years ago I was a witness in a lawsuit that caused me a great deal of mental strain and worry.

After the case was over, and I was returning home in the train, I had a sudden and violent

1939年他又大赚一笔,可是又赔光了。他曾多次破产,遭到敌人和债主的逼压。他遇到的烦恼可以使任何人精神崩溃,甚至自杀。

8年前的那一天,我坐在他的办公室,对他充满了羡慕,希望上帝将我也改造得像他一样。

在我们谈话的时候,他把那天早晨收到的一封信递给我,说:"你看看这封信。"

那是一封愤怒的来信,提出了一些令人难堪的问题。如果我收到这样一封信,我可要烦死了。我说:"比尔,你打算如何回复?"

"哦,"比尔说,"我告诉你一个小秘密。当你下一次碰到令你烦恼的事时,取出一支铅笔和一张纸,详细地写下你的烦恼,然后将那张纸放在你右手下方的抽屉里。一两个礼拜之后,再取出来看看。如果你第二次阅读时,认为那些事情仍让你烦恼,那么再将它放回原来的抽屉,再放上一两个星期。它在那儿绝对安全,不会有什么变化。但与此同时,你的烦恼可能会发生许多变化。而且我发现,只要我有耐心,烦恼总会自动消失。"

比尔的忠告给了我极深的印象。我已经使用比尔的忠告许多年了,结果我真的烦恼少多了。

时间可以解决许多问题。时间也许可以解决你今天的烦恼。

逃脱死亡

罗亚尔打字机公司国外部经理　约瑟夫·瑞恩

多年前,我曾在一件官司中担当一名证人,结果导致我精神紧张和烦恼。官司结束之后,我搭火车回到家,突然间病倒了,而且病得非常厉害。心脏病!我发现我几乎喘不过气来。

我回家以后,医生给我打了一针。当时我并不是躺在床上——我只能支撑到客厅,再也走不动了。当我神智恢复之后,发现教区的牧师已经在为我准备最后的洗礼。

physical collapse. Heart trouble. I found it almost impossible to breathe.

When I got home the doctor gave me an injection. I wasn't in bed—I hadn't been able to get any farther than the living-room settee. When I regained consciousness, I saw that the parish priest was already there to give me final absolution!

I saw the stunned grief on the faces of my family. I knew my number was up. Later, I found out that the doctor had prepared my wife for the fact that I would probably be dead in less than thirty minutes. My heart was so weak I was warned not to try to speak or to move even a finger.

I had never been a saint, but I had learned one thing—not to argue with God. So I closed my eyes and said: "Thy will be done ... If it has to come now, Thy will be done."

As soon as I gave in to that thought, I seemed to relax all over. My terror disappeared, and I asked myself quietly what was the worst that could happen now. Well, the worst seemed to be a possible return of the spasms, with excruciating pains—then all would be over. I would go to meet my Maker and soon be at peace.

I lay on that settee and waited for an hour, but the pains didn't return. Finally, I began to ask myself what I would do with my life if I didn't die now. I determined that I would exert every effort to regain my health. I would stop abusing myself with tension and worry and rebuild my strength.

That was four years ago. I have rebuilt my strength to such a degree that even my doctor is amazed at the improvement my cardiograms show. I no longer worry. I have a new zest for life. But I can honestly say that if I hadn't faced the worst—my imminent death—and then tried to improve upon it, I don't believe I would be here today. If I hadn't accepted the worst, I believe I would have died from my own fear and panic.

Mr. Ryan is alive today because he made use of the principle described in the Magic Formula—FACE THE WORST THAT CAN HAPPEN.

I Am a Great Dismisser

By Ordway Tead

Chairman of the Board of Higher Education New York

Worry is a habit—a habit that I broke long ago. I believe that my habit of refraining from

我看到了家人脸上的悲伤。我知道我的生命已到了最后时刻。后来,我又发现医生要我妻子面对现实:我可能会在30分钟之内死去。我的心脏如此衰弱,医生警告我不得说话,甚至连手指头也不得动弹。

我并不是什么圣徒,但我学会了一件事——不要和上帝争论!所以,我闭上眼睛,对自己说:"该来的,总是会来的。"

有了那个想法之后,我似乎全身放松了。我的恐惧消失了,我镇静地问自己,现在可能会发生的最糟糕的事情是什么?嗯,大不了是心脏痉挛,让我疼痛好一阵子,然后一切都过去了。我知道我马上就要去见上帝,永远安息了。

我躺在沙发上,等了1小时,但是疼痛并没有再次袭击我。最后,我开始问自己,如果我现在不死,我将对生活作何打算。我决定尽一切努力恢复健康,不再用紧张和烦恼来毁灭自己,要重建自己的力量。

那已经是4年前的事了。我的身体恢复得很快,甚至连医生也对我的进步大加赞扬。我不再自寻烦恼,对生命有了新的感受。但我必须承认,如果我不是曾经在死亡线上挣扎过,然后努力进步,我不相信我今天还会健在。如果我没有接受最糟糕的情况,我相信我会因自身的恐惧和惊慌而死去。

(瑞恩先生今天之所以还活着,是因为他采用了"魔法公式"中介绍的法则——勇于面对可能发生的最坏局面。)

消除忧虑的良方

纽约高等教育委员会主席　欧德威·梯德

忧虑是一种习惯,而我在许久以前就打破了这种习惯。我认为我之所以能解除烦恼,应当

worrying is due largely to three things.

First: I am too busy to indulge in self-destroying anxiety. I have three main activities—each one of which should be virtually a full-time job in itself. I lecture to large groups at Columbia University. I am also chairman of the Board of Higher Education of New York City. I also have charge of the Economic and Social Book Department of the publishing firm of Harper and Brothers. The insistent demands of these three tasks leave me no time to fret and stew and run around in circles.

Second: I am a great dismisser. When I turn from one task to another, I dismiss all thoughts of the problems I had been thinking about previously. I find it stimulating and refreshing to turn from one activity to another. It rests me. It clears my mind.

Third: I have had to school myself to dismiss all these problems from my mind when I close my office desk. They are always continuing. Each one always has a set of unsolved problems demanding my attention. If I carried these issues home with me each night, and worried about them, I would destroy my health; and, in addition, I would destroy all ability to cope with them.

Ordway Tead is a master of the Four Good Working Habits. Do you remember what they are? (see part Ⅶ, chapter 26)

If I Had Not Stopped Worrying, I Would Have Been in My Grave Long Ago

By Connie Mack

The Grand Old Man of Baseball

I have been in professional baseball for over sixty-three years. When I first started, back in the eighties, I got no salary at all. We played on vacant lots, and stumbled over tin cans and discarded horse collars. When the game was over, we passed the hat. The pickin's were pretty slim for me, especially since I was the main support of my widowed mother and my younger brothers and sisters. Sometimes the ball team would have to put on a strawberry supper or a clambake to keep going.

I have had plenty of reason to worry. I am the only baseball manager who ever finished in last

归功于三项举措。

第一,我太忙了,以至于没有时间沉溺于自我毁灭的焦虑之中。我有三项主要活动:在哥伦比亚大学讲课,担任纽约市高等教育委员会主席,又掌管哈泼出版公司的经济及社会丛书部。每一项活动都是全天性的工作。这三项主要工作,使我根本没有时间去自寻烦恼。

第二,我是一个放得开的人。当我放下一项工作去干另一项工作时,我会完全抛开以前所想的问题。我发现,变换新的活动可以令人振奋,使我得到休息,神志清醒。

第三,当我离开办公桌之后,我就让自已把所有的烦恼从大脑中剔除出去。这些问题都是连贯性的,如果我每天晚上都把这些问题带回家,并且为它们而烦恼的话,那我的健康就全完了,同时也将失去解决烦恼的能力。

(欧德威·梯德是良好工作习惯的大师。你还记得这些习惯吗?)

康尼·迈克的原则

棒球老将　康尼·迈克

我在职业棒球界已经 63 年多了。当我首次加入球队时,完全没有薪水。我们在空地上打球,常常被地上的废弃物绊倒。比赛结束之后,我们就摘下帽子,传过去向大家收钱。但是这些钱实在太少了。尤其是我,承担养活寡母及弟弟妹妹的责任。有时候,球队为了赚钱,必须做一些逗笑的演出,才能使球赛继续下去。

我有许多可以烦恼的原因。我曾是连续 7 年都排在最末位的唯一一位棒球队经理,而且曾在 8 年之内输了 800 场球。经过一连串失败,我愁得吃不下饭,睡不着觉。但我在 25 年前就不再烦恼了。我相信,如果我不停止烦恼,那么我早就进棺材了。

现在回忆我漫长的生命历程 (我是在林肯总统时代出生的), 我认为我之所以能够征服忧

place for seven consecutive years. I am the only manager who ever lost eight hundred games in eight years. After a series of defeats, I used to worry until I could hardly eat or sleep. But I stopped worrying twenty-five years ago, and I honestly believe that if I hadn't stopped worrying then, I would have been in my grave long ago.

As I looked back over my long life (I was born when Lincoln was President), I believe I was able to conquer worry by doing these things:

1. I saw how futile it was. I saw it was getting me nowhere and was threatening to wreck my career.

2. I saw it was going to ruin my health.

3. I kept myself so busy planning and working to win games in the future that I had no time to worry over games that were already lost.

4. I finally made it a rule never to call a player's attention to his mistakes until twenty-four hours after the game. In my early days, I used to dress and undress with the players. If the team had lost, I found it impossible to refrain from criticising the players and from arguing with them bitterly over their defeats. I found this only increased my worries. Criticising a player in front of the others didn't make him want to cooperate. It really made him bitter. So, since I couldn't be sure of controlling myself and my tongue immediately after a defeat, I made it a rule never to see the players right after a defeat. I wouldn't discuss the defeat with them until the next day. By that time, I had cooled off, the mistakes didn't loom so large, and I could talk things over calmly and the men wouldn't get angry and try to defend themselves.

5. I tried to inspire players by building them up with praise instead of tearing them down with faultfinding. I tried to have a good word for everybody.

6. I found that I worried more when I was tired; so I spend ten hours in bed every night, and I take a nap every afternoon. Even a five-minute nap helps a lot.

7. I believe I have avoided worries and lengthened my life by continuing to be active. I am eighty-five, but I am not going to retire until I begin telling the same stories over and over. When I start doing that, I'll know then that I am growing old.

Connie Mack never read a book on *HOW TO STOP WORRYING* so he made out his own rules. Why don't YOU make a list of the rules you have found helpful in the past—and write them out here?

虑，得益于下面这些方法：

第一，我认为烦恼毫无益处。除了对我的棒球生涯造成威胁之外，烦恼对我毫无帮助。

第二，我认为烦恼会损害我的健康。

第三，我让自己忙着准备在将来的比赛中获胜，因此没有时间为已经失败的球赛去自寻烦恼。

第四，我给自己定了一个规则：球赛过后24小时内，不得批评球员所犯的过错。以前我总是和球员们一起穿衣、更衣。如果球队在比赛中输了，我总会忍不住批评球员们，而且毫不留情地与他们争论为什么会失败。后来我发现这样只会增加我的烦恼；而且在其他球员面前批评某位球员，只会使他以后更不愿合作，因为这确实使他大丢面子。因此，既然我没有把握在球赛刚结束时控制自己，那我只好给自己立下一个规则：比赛失败之后，绝不立刻和球员见面；一直要等到第二天，才和他们讨论失利问题。到那时候，我已经冷静下来，不会扩大错误，而且可以和球员们冷静地讨论事实，球员也不会生气或为自己辩护。

第五，我会赞扬球员们，激励他们，而不是像以前那样总是挑他们的毛病。我想对每个人都说些赞扬的话。

第六，我发现，当我身体疲倦时，烦恼就更多。所以，我每天晚上要休息10小时，每天下午还要睡一会儿。即使是5分钟的小睡，对我也大有帮助。

第七，我相信，由于我不断地忙着，使我不再受各种烦恼的干扰，因而延长了我的寿命。我已经85岁，但我还不想退休，而是要把同样的故事讲一遍又一遍。那时，我才知道自己确实已经老了。

（康尼·迈克并没有读过《人性的优点》这一类书，但他能够给自己订下一些规则。你为什么不把你以前觉得很有帮助的一些规则列成一张表并写下来呢？）

One at a Time Gentleman, One at a Time

By John Homer Miller

Author of *Take a Look at Yourself*

I Discovered years ago that I could not escape my worries by trying to run away from them, but that I could banish them by changing my mental attitude toward them. I discovered that my worries were not outside but inside myself.

As the years have gone by, I have found that time automatically takes care of most of my worries. In fact, I frequently find it difficult to remember what I was worrying about a week ago. So I have a rule: never to fret over a problem until it is at least a week old. Of course, I can't always put a problem completely out of mind for a week at a time, but I can refuse to allow it to dominate my mind until the allotted seven days have passed, either the problem has solved itself or I have so changed my mental attitude that it no longer has the power to trouble me greatly.

I have been greatly helped by reading the philosophy of Sir William Osler, a man who was not only a great physician, but a great artist in the greatest of all arts: *The Art of Living*. One of his statements has helped me immensely in banishing worries. Sir William said, at a dinner given in his honor: "More than to anything else, I owe whatever success I have had to the power of settling down to the day's work and trying to do it well to the best of my ability and letting the future take care of itself."

In handling troubles, I have taken as my motto the words of an old parrot that my father used to tell me about. Father told me of a parrot that was kept in a cage hanging over the doorway in a hunting club in Pennsylvania. As the members of the club passed through the door, the parrot repeated over and over the only words he knew: "One at a time, gentlemen, one at a time." Father taught me to handle my troubles that way: "One at a time, gentlemen, one at a time." I have found that taking my troubles one at a time has helped me to maintain calm and composure amidst pressing duties and unending engagements. "One at a time, gentlemen, one at a time."

Here again, we have one of the basic principles in conquering worry: LIVE IN DAY-TIGHT COMPARTMENTS. Why don't you turn back and read that chapter again?

一次只做一件事

《自我反思》作者 约翰·荷马·米勒

几年前我发现我并不能以逃避忧虑的方式来摆脱忧虑，但我可以改变心态来消除忧虑。我发现我的忧虑不是来自外部，而在我自身。

岁月流逝，我发现时间会自动消除我大部分忧虑。事实上，我经常发现要记住一个星期以前的忧虑很难。于是我定下一条原则：绝不为一个问题而烦恼一个星期。当然，我不可能一次就将一个问题从大脑中清除一个星期，但我不会让它控制我的思想，或者让问题自行解决，或者我改变心态，让它不再来烦我。

读威廉·奥斯勒爵士的名言对我助益匪浅。他不仅是伟大的医生，还是生活这门最伟大的艺术的艺术家。他的一句话对我消除忧虑帮助极大。在一次欢迎晚宴上，他说："我的成就归功于有能力解决今天的问题，尽力干好工作，让将来去照料它。"

在处理烦恼时，我将父亲常对我讲的一只老鹦鹉说的话当作我的座右铭。父亲告诉我，在宾夕法尼亚，有一只挂在猎人俱乐部门廊上方笼子里的鹦鹉。每当俱乐部的成员穿过门廊时，这只鹦鹉会一再重复它唯一会说的话："一次只做一件事，先生！一次只做一件事！"父亲教我那样处理我和烦恼："一次只做一件事！"我发现一次处理一件事情有助于我保持平静，承受重压和繁杂的工作。"一次只做一件事！"

（我们在此又看到了克服忧虑的基本原则："活在完全独立的今天。"为什么不再翻回去看那一章呢？）

I Now Look for The Green Light

By Joseph M. Cotter

1534 Fargo Avenue, Chicago, Illinois

From the time I was a small boy, throughout the early stages of young manhood, and during my adult life, I was a professional worrier. My worries were many and varied. Some were real; most of them were imaginary. Upon rare occasions I would find myself without anything to worry about—then I would worry for fear I might be overlooking something.

Then, two years ago, I started out on a new way of living. This required making a self-analysis of my faults—and a very few virtues—a "searching and fearless moral inventory"of myself. This brought out clearly what was causing all this worry.

The fact was that I could not live for today alone. I was fretful of yesterday's mistakes and fearful of the future.

I was told over and over that "today was the tomorrow I had worried about yesterday". But it wouldn't work on me. I was advised to live on a twenty-four-hour program. I was told that today was the only day over which I had any control and that I should make the most of my opportunities each day. I was told that if I did that, I would be so busy I would have no time to worry about any other day—past or future. That advice was logical, but somehow I found it hard to put these darned ideas to work for me.

Then like a shot from out of the dark, I found the answer—and where do you suppose I found it? On a Northwestern Railroad platform at seven P. M. on May 31, 1945. It was an important hour for me. That is why I remember it so clearly.

We were taking some friends to the train. They were leaving on *The City of Los Angeles*, a streamliner, to return from a vacation. War was still on—crowds were heavy that year. Instead of boarding the train with my wife, I wandered down the tracks towards the front of the train. I stood looking at the big shiny engine for a minute. Presently I looked down the track and saw a huge semaphore. An amber light was showing. Immediately this light turned to a bright green. At that moment, the engineer started clanging a bell; I heard the familiar "All aboard! "and, in a matter of seconds, that huge streamliner began to move out of

寻找人生的绿灯

约瑟夫·柯特

从我还是个小男孩时开始,直到我成年之初,以及在成年阶段,我一直是个"烦恼大王"。我的烦恼太多了,而且千奇百怪。有些是真烦恼,但大部分却是胡思乱想。我几乎很少发现自己没有什么事不烦恼的——从那时起,我就担心我是否遗漏了什么东西。

接着,在两年前,我开始了新的生活方式。这种生活方式要求我对自己的过错及极少数美德作自我分析,对我自己进行全面了解。这样一来,我就把所有烦恼的原因弄清楚了。

事实是这样的:我并不只是为今天而活着;我为昨天的错误而后悔,又对将来心存恐惧。

不断地有人这样告诫我:"今天就是你昨天所忧虑的明天。"但这句话对我并不管用。还有人建议我,只活在今天。也有人说,今天是我唯一能掌握并好好利用的时间。还有人说,尽量让自己忙碌起来,这样就没有时间去烦恼了。这些说法都很有道理,但我发现很难把它们用到我身上来。

接着,我像从黑暗中突然冲出来一般,终于找到了答案。你知道我是在哪儿找到的吗?那是在 1945 年 5 月 31 日晚上 7 点, 在西北铁路公司的一个站台上。对我来说那是如此重要的时刻,因此我一直记得很清楚。

我们当时在送朋友上火车。他们刚度完假,准备搭"洛杉矶市"号快车离开。当时战争还未结束,车站上人潮涌动。我没有和太太一起送朋友上车,而是沿着轨道向火车头走去。我站在那里看闪着亮光的庞大引擎,然后目光移向铁道的前方,发现了一座巨大的信号灯台,当时正好显示的是黄灯。

突然,黄灯变成了绿色。这时,火车鸣起了汽笛,我听见站务人员高喊"全部上车!"接着,在几秒钟之内,那巨大的列车开始驶出车站,踏上了 2300 英里的旅程。

that station on its 2,300-mile trip.

My mind started spinning. Something was trying to make sense to me. I was experiencing a miracle. Suddenly it dawned on me. The engineer had given me the answer I had been seeking. He was starting out on that long journey with only one green light to go by. If I had been in his place, I would want to see all the green lights for the entire journey. Impossible, of course, yet that was exactly what I was trying to do with my life—sitting in the station, going no place, because I was trying too hard to see what was ahead for me.

My thoughts kept coming. That engineer didn't worry about trouble that he might encounter miles ahead. There probably would be some delays, some slowdowns, but wasn't that why they had signal systems? Amber lights—reduce speed and take it easy. Red lights—real danger up ahead—*stop*. That was what made train travel safe. A good signal system.

I asked myself why I didn't have a good signal system for my life. My answer was—I did have one. God had given it to me. He controls it, so it has to be foolproof. I started looking for a green light. Where could I find it? Well, if God created the green lights, why not ask Him? I did just that.

And now by praying each morning, I get my green light for that day. I also occasionally get amber lights that slow me down. Sometimes I get red lights that stop me before I crack up.

No more worrying for me since that day two years ago when I made this discovery. During those two years, over seven hundred green lights have shown for me, and the trip through life is so much easier without the worry of what color the next light will be. No matter what color it may be, I will know what to do.

How John D. Rockefeller Lived on Borrowed Time for Forty-five Years

John D. Rockefeller, Sr., had accumulated his first million at the age of thirty-three. At the age of forty-three, he had built up the largest monopoly the world has ever seen—the great Standard Oil Company. But where was he at fifty-three? Worry had got him at fifty-three. Worry and high-tension living had already wrecked his health. At fifty-three, he "looked like a mummy,"

我的大脑开始旋转——似乎要向我证明什么。我正在经历一次奇迹，一切突然真相大白——原来那位火车司机已经为我提供了我一直在找寻的答案。他只看见一盏绿灯，就开始了漫长的旅程。但若换了是我，我会希望整段旅程全都是绿灯。当然，这是不可能的，但我对生活的期望却正是那样——坐在人生的车站里，结果哪儿也去不了，因为我一直想看清楚前面是什么。

我思潮澎湃。那位火车司机并没有为前面旅程中可能遇到的麻烦而忧虑。火车可能会出现延误、故障，但不正是因此而有了信号灯系统吗？黄灯——减速慢行。红灯——前方危险——停车。这可以保证火车安全，因此是一种很好的系统。

我问自己，为什么不为自己的生活制定一套良好的信号灯系统呢？我找到了答案——我本来就有。这是上帝赐给我的。由他进行操纵，因此我会步步安全。

我开始找寻人生的绿灯。到哪里去找呢？如果上帝创造了绿灯，为什么不问他？我也那样做了。

现在，我每天早晨都要为当天祈祷绿灯。有时我也会遇到黄灯，那么我会慢下来。有时我会遇到红灯，我会立即停止，以免崩溃。

当我在两年前发现这个奥秘之后，就不再忧虑了。在这两年中，我遇到了大约700多盏绿灯，使我不必担心下一盏灯是什么颜色，我的人生之旅也更为轻松愉快。不管前面的信号灯是什么颜色，我已经知道怎么办了。

洛克菲勒的快乐法则

约翰·洛克菲勒在33岁时就赚到了第一个100万。43岁时，他建立了世界上前所未有的最大垄断企业——庞大的标准石油公司。但是当他到了53岁时情况又怎么样呢？他被烦恼搞惨了，各种烦恼和高度紧张的生活已经破坏了他的健康。这时，他“看起来像个木乃伊”，为他写

says John K. Winkler, one of his biographers.

At fifty-three, Rockefeller was attacked by mystifying digestive maladies that swept away his hair, even the eyelashes and all but a faint wisp of eyebrow. "So serious was his condition, "says Winkler, "that at one time John D. was compelled to exist on human milk." According to the doctors, he had alopecia, a form of baldness that often starts with sheer nerves. He looked so startling, with his stark bald dome, that he had to wear a skullcap. Later, he had wigs made—at $ 500 a piece—and for the rest of his life he wore these silver wigs.

Rockefeller had originally been blessed with an iron constitution. Reared on a farm, he had once had stalwart shoulders, an erect carriage, and a strong, brisk gait.

Yet at only fifty-three—when most men are at their prime—his shoulders drooped and he shambled when he walked. "When he looked in a glass, "says John T. Flynn, another of his biographers, "he saw an old man. The ceaseless work, the endless worry, the streams of abuse, the sleepless nights, and the lack of exercise and rest"had exacted their toll; they had brought him to his knees. He was now the richest man in the world; yet he had to live on a diet that a pauper would have scorned. His income at the time was a million dollars a week—but two dollars a week would probably have paid for all the food he could eat. Acidulated milk and a few biscuits were all the doctors would allow him. His skin had lost its color—it looked tike old parchment drawn tight across his bones. And nothing but medical care, the best money could buy, kept him from dying at the age of fifty-three.

How did it happen? Worry. Shock. High-pressure and high-tension living. He"drove"himself literally to the edge of the grave. Even at the age of twenty-three, Rockefeller was already pursuing his goal with such grim determination that, according to those who knew him, "nothing lightened his countenance save news of a good bargain." When he made a big profit, he would do a little war dance—throw his hat on the floor and break into a jig. But if he lost money, he was ill! He once shipped $40,000 worth of grain by way of the Great Lakes. No insurance. It cost too much: $150. That night a vicious storm raged over Lake Erie. Rockefeller was so worried about losing his cargo that when his partner, George Gardner, reached the office in the morning, he found John D. Rockefeller there, pacing the floor.

传记的作家约翰·温克勒说。

洛克菲勒53岁时患了奇怪的消化性疾病，不仅头发全掉光了，甚至连眼睫毛也一样，只剩下一绺淡淡的眉毛。“他的情况十分严重。”温克勒说，“有一段时间，他靠喝人奶维持生存。”根据医生们的说法，他得了“脱毛症”，这种病通常是由过度紧张造成的。他的头光秃秃的，模样很是古怪，他不得不戴上帽子。后来，他订制了一些假发，每顶假发500美元，从此他就一直戴着这些假发。

洛克菲勒的身体本来十分强健。他从小在农场长大，肩膀又宽又壮，腰杆笔直，并且步伐稳健有力。

可是在53岁的时候——这正是大多数男人的壮年时期——洛克菲勒却双肩下垂，走起路来摇摇晃晃的。据另一位传记作家佛林说：“当他照镜子时，看见的是个老头。没完没了的工作、无穷无尽的烦恼、长期的不良生活习惯、经常失眠以及缺乏运动和休息，夺走了他的健康，使他挺不起腰来。”虽然他现在成了世界上最富有的人，但他只能吃些连穷人都不屑一顾的食物。当时他每周收入100万美元，而他每周所吃的食物只需2美元就可以解决。因为医生只允许他吃一些酸牛奶和饼干。他的皮肤早已失去光泽，看起来像是老羊皮包在骨头上。金钱这时候也没有用了，只能为他付医疗费用，使他不至于在53岁就死去。

这是怎么回事呢?忧虑、惊吓、高度紧张的生活！他自己把自己“推”到了坟墓的边缘。洛克菲勒早在23岁的时候，就全身心地追求他的目标。据他的朋友说：“除生意上的好消息，没有任何事情能令他开怀大笑。”当他赚到了一大笔钱时，他会高兴得把帽子摔到地上，开心地跳起舞来。但如果失败了，那他也会随之病倒。有一次，洛克菲勒在五大湖上托运一批价值4万美元的谷物，但他没有买保险。因为保险费太高了——要150美元。那天晚上，暴风雨袭击伊利湖。洛克菲勒十分担心，怕他的货物遭遇不测。在第二天早上，当他的合伙者乔治·加德勒来到办公室

"Hurry, "he quavered. "Let's see if we can take out insurance now, if it isn't too late! " Gardner rushed uptown and got the insurance; but when he returned to the office, he found John D. in an even worse state of nerves. A telegram had arrived in the meantime: the cargo had landed, safe from the storm. He was sicker than ever now because they had "wasted"the $150! In fact, he was so sick about it that he had to go home and take to his bed. Think of it! At that time, his firm was doing gross business of $500,000 a year—yet he made himself so ill over $150 that he had to go to bed!

He had no time for play, no time for recreation, no time for anything except making money and teaching Sunday school. When his partner, George Gardner, purchased a second-hand yacht, with three other men, for $2,000, John D. was aghast, refused to go out in it. Gardner found him working at the office one Saturday afternoon, and pleaded: "Come on, John, let's go for a sail. It will do you good. Forget about business. Have a little fun." Rockefeller glared. "George Gardner, "he warned, "you are the most extravagant man I ever knew. You are injuring your credit at the banks—and my credit too. First thing you know, you'll be wrecking our business. No, I won't go on your yacht—I don't ever want to see it! "And he stayed plugging in the office all Saturday afternoon.

The same lack of humor, the same lack of perspective, characterized John D. all through his business career. Years later he said: "I never placed my head upon the pillow at night without reminding myself that my success might be only temporary."

With millions at his command, he never put his head upon his pillow without worrying about losing his fortune. No wonder worry wrecked his health. He had no time for play or recreation, never went to the theatre, never played cards, never went to a party. As Mark Hanna said, the man was mad about money. "Sane in every other respect, but mad about money."

Rockefeller had once confessed to a neighbor in Cleveland, Ohio, that he"wanted to be loved"; yet he was so cold and suspicious that few people even liked him. Morgan once balked at having to do business with him at all. "I don't like the man, "he snorted. "I don't want to have any dealings with him." Rockefeller's own brother hated him so much that he removed his children's bodies from the family plot. "No one of my blood, "he said, "will ever rest in land controlled by John D."

时,发现洛克菲勒已在那里,正来回走动。

"快,"他发抖地说:"看现在是否还能投保,否则来不及了!"加德勒立即冲到城里,买好了保险;可是当他回到办公室时,却发现洛克菲勒的情况更严重了。这时恰好来了一封电报:货物已经卸下,未受到暴风雨袭击。但洛克菲勒这时反而更沮丧了,因为他已经"浪费"了150美元!事实上,他太伤心了,只好回家去躺下来休息。想想看,那时他的公司每年做着50万美元的生意,可是他却为150美元而失魂落魄,甚至病倒在床。

他没有时间玩,也没有时间休息,除了赚钱和教堂生活,没有时间做其他事情。当他的合伙人加德勒和其他三个朋友花了2000美元买下一艘二手游艇时,洛克菲勒几乎吓坏了,拒绝搭乘那艘游艇出航。在一个星期六的下午,加德勒发现洛克菲勒还在办公室工作,就对他说:"走吧,约翰!我们乘船出海吧。暂时忘掉工作,轻松一下!"但洛克菲勒对他怒目而视。"乔治·加德勒,"他警告说,"你是世界上最浪费的人了!你正在破坏你在银行的信用,包括我的信用。将来你会把我们的生意毁掉。不行,我可不乘你的游艇,我永远也不愿见到它!"于是,他整个星期六下午都留在办公室工作。

缺乏幽默感和安全感,这是洛克菲勒一生的特征。几年之后,他说:"每天晚上,我一定会先提醒自己,我的成功也许只是暂时性的!然后才躺下来睡觉。"

这时他已经有几百万美元可以支配,但他仍然担心会失去一切财富。怪不得忧虑会拖垮他的身体。他没有时间游玩或娱乐,也从未进过戏院,没打过纸牌,没参加过宴会。正如马克·汉纳所说的,他为金钱而疯狂,"他在别的事情上都很正常,唯独为金钱疯狂"。

洛克菲勒曾在俄亥俄州克利夫兰市向一位邻居承认,他"希望有人爱",但是他太冷漠多疑了,很少有人喜欢他。有一次摩根大发怨言,说不愿意和他打交道。"我不喜欢那种人,"他不屑地说,"我不愿再和他有任何往来。"洛克菲勒的亲弟弟对他也深恶痛绝,甚至把自己孩子的棺

Rockefeller's employees and associates lived in holy fear of him, and here is the ironic part: *He* was afraid of *them*—afraid they would talk outside the office and "give secrets away". He had so little faith in human nature that once, when he signed a ten-year contract with an independent refiner, he made the man promise not to tell anyone, not even his wife! "Shut your mouth and ran your business"—that was his motto.

Then at the very peak of his prosperity, with gold flowing into his coffers like hot yellow lava pouring down the sides of Vesuvius, his private world collapsed. Books and articles denounced the robber-baron war of the Standard Oil Company! — secret rebates with railroads, the ruthless crashing of all rivals.

In the oil fields of Pennsylvania, John D. Rockefeller was the most hated man on earth. He was hanged in effigy by the men he had crushed. Many of them longed to tie a rope around his withered neck and hang him to the limb of a sour-apple tree. Letters breathing fire and brimstone poured into his office—letters threatening his life. He hired bodyguards to keep his enemies from killing him. He attempted to ignore this cyclone of hate. He had once said cynically: "You may kick me and abuse me provided you will let me have my own way." But he discovered that he was human after all. He couldn't take hate—and worry too. His health began to crack. He was puzzled and bewildered by this new enemy—illness—which attacked him from within. At first "he remained secretive about his occasional indispositions," tried to put his illness out of his mind. But insomnia, indigestion, and the loss of his hair—all physical symptoms of worry and collapse—were not to be denied. Finally, his doctors told him the shocking truth. He could take his choice: his money and his worries—or his life. They warned him he must either retire or die. He retired. But before he retired, worry, greed, fear had already wrecked his health. When Ida Tarbell, America's most celebrated female writer of biographies, saw him, she was shocked. She wrote: "An awful age was in his face. He was the oldest man I have ever seen." Old? Why, Rockefeller was then several years younger than General Macarthur was when he recaptured the Philippines! But he was such a physical wreck that Ida Tarbell pitied him. She was working at that time on her powerful book which condemned the Standard Oil and

木从家族的祖坟中移走。他说:“在我的亲骨肉之中,不允许任何一个人在约翰控制的土地上安息。”洛克菲勒的职员和同事也很敬畏他。但令人好笑的是,他竟然也怕他们——怕他们在办公室以外随意说话,“泄露公司的秘密”。他对人类天性没有任何信心。有一次,他和一位独立制造商签订了 10 年合作协议,但他要那位商人保证不告诉任何人,甚至他的妻子。“闭紧你的嘴,努力工作”——这就是他的座右铭。

正当他的事业达到顶峰, 他的财富像维苏维火山的金黄色岩浆那样源源不断地流入他的保险库时,他的私人世界却崩溃了。许多书和文章都公开谴责标准石油公司不择手段攫取财富的财阀行为——因为它和铁路公司之间的秘密回扣,无情地压击垮了所有竞争者。

在宾夕法尼亚产油区,当地居民最痛恨的就是洛克菲勒。被他击败的竞争对手甚至把他的像挂在树上解恨。他们当中有许多人都恨不得亲手将绳子套在他那萎缩的脖子上,并将他吊死在酸苹果树上。充满火药气味的信件也如雪花般地飞进他的办公室,威胁要他的命。因此他雇用了许多保镖,以防遭对手杀害。他试图忽视这些仇恨之火。有一次,他曾以讽刺的口吻说:“你们尽管踢我骂我,但我还是按我自己的方式行事。”但他最后还是发现,自己毕竟是一个普通人,无法忍受人们对他的仇恨,也受不了忧虑的侵扰。他的身体开始不行了。这个新的敌人——疾病——从内部向他发起进攻,令他措手不及,惶恐不安。刚开始,“他试图对自己偶尔的不适保密”。但是,失眠、消化不良、掉头发——这些烦恼和精神崩溃的肉体上的病症却无法遮掩。最后,医生只好将惊人的实情告诉他:他只有两种选择:财富和烦恼——或是性命。他们警告他:必须在退休和死亡之间做出抉择。他选择了退休。在退休之前,烦恼、贪婪、恐惧已经破坏了他的健康。美国著名传记女作家伊达·塔贝尔看见他的时候,几乎吓坏了。她写道:“他的脸上显示的是可怕的苍老,我从未见过他那样苍老的人。”老人?为什么?洛克菲勒可比当时重新收回菲律宾的麦克阿瑟将军还要年轻几岁呀!但他的身体如此衰弱,使得伊达·塔贝尔为他深感悲哀。

all that it stood for; she certainly had no cause to love the man who had built up this "octopus". Yet, she said that when she saw John D. Rockefeller teaching a Sunday school class, eagerly searching the faces of all those around him—"I had a feeling which I had not expected, and which time intensified. I was sorry for him. I know no companion so terrible as fear."

When the doctors undertook to save Rockefeller's life, they gave him three rules—three rules which he observed, to the letter, for the rest of his life. Here they are:

1. *Avoid worry. Never worry about anything, under any kind of circumstances.*
2. *Relax, and take plenty of mild exercise in the open air.*
3. *Watch your diet. Always stop eating while you're still a little hungry.*

John D. Rockefeller obeyed those rules; and they probably saved his life. He retired. He learned to play golf. He went in for gardening. He chatted with his neighbors. He played games. He sang songs.

But he did something else too. "During days of torture and nights of insomnia,"says Winkler, "John D. had time for reflection." He began to think of other people. He stopped thinking, for once, of how much money he could *get*; and he began to wonder how much that money could buy in terms of human happiness.

In short. Rockefeller now began to *give* his millions away! Some of the time it wasn't easy. When he offered money to a church, pulpits all over the country thundered back with cries of "tainted money! "But he kept on giving. He learned of a starving little college on the shores of Lake Michigan that was being foreclosed because of its mortgage. He came to its rescue and poured millions of dollars into that college and built it into the now world-famous University of Chicago. He tried to help the Negroes. He gave money to Negro universities like Tuskegee College, where funds were needed to carry on the work of George Washington Carver. He helped to fight hookworm. When Dr. Charles W. Stiles, the hookworm authority, said: "Fifty cents' worth of medicine will cure a man of this disease which ravages the South—but who will give the fifty cents? "Rockefeller gave it. He spent millions on hookworm, stamping out the greatest scourge that has ever handicapped the South. And then he went further. He established a great international

她当时正在撰写她那本有名的著作，揭发标准石油公司的罪恶，她当然不喜欢这个一手建造了这个庞大组织的人。但是，她又说，当她看见洛克菲勒在主日学校教书，焦急地搜寻他四周的脸孔时，“我有一种前所未有的感觉。这种感觉与日俱增。我真为他悲哀。我知道，一个人没有知心的伙伴是一件很恐怖的事。”

医生开始挽救洛克菲勒的性命，他们为他制定了三条规则——这成为他后来奉行不渝的三条规则。这就是：

第一，避免烦恼。在任何情况下都不为任何事而烦恼。

第二，放松，多做适当的户外运动。

第三，注意节食，随时保持半饥饿的状态。

洛克菲勒严格遵守这三条规则，保住了自己的性命。他退了下来，学打高尔夫球，修整庭院，和邻居聊天，还打牌、唱歌。

但他同时也做一些其他的事。温克勒说：“在那段痛苦的日子和失眠的夜晚，洛克菲勒终于有时间进行自我反省。”他开始为别人着想，一度停止去想还能赚多少钱，并开始思考如何用这些钱换取人类的幸福。

简而言之，洛克菲勒现在开始考虑把数百万财富捐出去。有时候这可真不容易。例如，当他准备向一座教堂捐款时，全国各地的传教士一致发出反对的怒吼：“腐败的金钱！”但他继续捐献。当他获悉密歇根湖岸的一家学院因为抵押权而被迫关闭时，他立刻做出了援助行动，捐出几百万美元给这家学院，将它建设成目前举世闻名的芝加哥大学。他还尽力帮助那些黑人。例如塔斯基吉黑人大学需要一笔基金来实现黑人教育家华盛顿·卡尔文的志愿，洛克菲勒捐出了巨款。他还出资协助消灭钩虫。当著名的钩虫专家史泰尔博士说：“50 美分的药就可以为一个人治好这种在南方肆虐的病。可是谁会捐这些钱呢？”洛克菲勒立即捐了出来。他捐

foundation—the Rockefeller Foundation—which was to fight disease and ignorance all over the world.

I speak with feeling of this work, for there is a possibility that I may owe my life to the Rockefeller Foundation. How well I remember that when I was in China in 1932, cholera was raging all over Peking. The Chinese peasants were dying like flies; yet in the midst of all this horror, we were able to go to the Rockefeller Medical College in Peking and get a vaccination to protect us from the plague. Chinese and "foreigners" alike, we were able to do that. And that was when I got my first understanding of what Rockefeller's millions were doing for the world.

Never before in history has there ever been anything even remotely like the Rockefeller Foundation. It is something unique. Rockefeller knew that all over the world there are many fine movements that men of vision start. Research is undertaken; colleges are founded; doctors struggle on to fight a disease—but only too often this high-minded work has to die for lack of funds. He decided to help these pioneers of humanity—not to "take them over", but to give them some money and help them help themselves. Today you and I can thank John D. Rockefeller for the miracles of penicillin, and for dozens of other discoveries which his money helped to finance. You can thank him for the fact that your children no longer die from spinal meningitis, a disease that *used to* kill four out of five. And you can thank him for part of the inroads we have made on malaria and tuberculosis, on influenza and diphtheria, and many other diseases that still plague the world.

And what about Rockefeller? When he gave his money away, did he gain peace of mind? Yes, he was contented at last. "If the public thought of him after 1900 as brooding over the attacks on the Standard Oil," said Allan Kevins, "the public was much mistaken."

Rockefeller was happy. He had changed so completely that he didn't worry at all. In fact, he refused even to lose one night's sleep when he was forced to accept the greatest defeat of his career!

The defeat came when the corporation he had built, the huge Standard Oil, was ordered to pay "the heaviest time in history". According to the United States Government, the Standard Oil was a

出数百万美元消除了钩虫,解除了曾经使美国南方陷于瘫痪的这种疾病。然后,他又采取了更进一步的行动,成立了一个庞大的国际性基金会"洛克菲勒基金会",致力于消灭全世界各地的疾病、文盲。

我谨向这一伟大工程致敬,因为洛克菲勒基金会曾救过我一命。我还记得很清楚,1932 年我在中国,当时霍乱蔓延整个北平,农民们像苍蝇一样死去。而在这种恐怖之中,我们仍然能够去洛克菲勒医学院接受预防注射,这才使我们免受感染。那时我才第一次明白,洛克菲勒的百万美元财富对全世界的贡献。

洛克菲勒基金会这种壮举,在历史上前所未有,在全世界也绝无仅有。洛克菲勒深知世界各地有许多有识之士正在进行各种有意义的活动:进行研究工作,建立学校,医生则致力于和某些疾病做斗争,但是这些高尚的工作却经常因为经费短缺而中止。他决定帮助这些人道主义的开拓者,但并不是"将他们接收过来",而是资助他们一笔钱,帮助他们完成工作。今天,你和我都应该感谢约翰·洛克菲勒先生,因为在他的资助下,人类发现了盘尼西林和其他多种新事物。你也应该感谢他,因为是他使你的孩子不再因患上"脊髓性脑膜炎"而死亡。你更应该感谢他的是,他使我们克服了疟疾、肺结核、流行性感冒、白喉和目前仍在危害世界的其他疾病。

洛克菲勒自己又怎么样了?他把钱捐出去之后,是否已获得了心灵上的平安?不错,他最后终于满足了。"如果人们仍然认为,他在 1900 年以来因为人们对标准石油公司的攻击而一蹶不振的话,"亚伦·凯文斯说,"那可就大错特错了。"

洛克菲勒十分快乐。他已经完全改变了,不再烦恼。事实上,在他被迫接受生命中最大的一次失败时,他甚至不愿失去一个晚上的睡眠。

那次失败是这样的:他一手创建的标准石油公司被政府勒令支付"历史上最重的罚款"。根

monopoly, in direct violation of the antitrust laws. The battle raged for time years. The best legal brains in the land fought on interminably in what was, up to then, the longest court war in history. But Standard Oil lost.

When Judge Kenesaw Mountain Landis handed down his decision, lawyers for the defense feared that old John D. would take it very hard. But they didn't know how much he'd changed.

That night one of the lawyers got John D. on the phone. He discussed the decision as gently as he could, and then said with concern: "I hope you won't let this decision upset you, Mr. Rockefeller. I hope you'll get your night's sleep! "

And old John D. ? why, he crackled right back across the wire: "Don't worry, Mr. Johnson, I intend to get a nights sleep. And don't let it bother you either. Good night! "

That from the man who had once taken to his bed because he had lost $150! Yes, it took a long time for John D. to conquer worry. He was "dying" at fifty-three—but he lived to ninety-eight!

Reading a Book on Sex Prevented My Marriage from Going on the Rocks

By B. R. W.

I hate to make this story anonymous. But it is so intimate that I could not possibly use my name.

However, Dale Carnegie will vouch for the truth of this story. I first told it to him twelve years ago.

After leaving college, I got a job with a large industrial organization, and five years later, this company sent me across the Pacific to act as one of its representatives in the Far East. A week before leaving America, I married the sweetest and most lovable woman I have ever known. But our honeymoon was a tragic disappointment for both of us—especially for her. By the time we reached Hawaii she was so disappointed, so heartbroken, that she would have returned to the States, had she not been ashamed to face her old friends and admit failure in what can be—and should be—life's most thrilling adventure.

We lived together two miserable years in the Orient. I was so unhappy that I had sometimes

据美国政府的说法，标准石油公司是一个垄断性企业，直接违反了《反托拉斯法案》。这场官司打了好几年。全美国最优秀的法律人才全都投入到了这场看来似乎永无休止的官司，但标准石油公司最后还是败诉。

在南迪斯法官宣布了他的判决之后，辩方律师担心洛克菲勒无法接受这个坏消息。但他们却不知道他已经完全变了。

那天晚上，一位律师打电话给洛克菲勒。他尽量委婉地把判决告诉他，然后关切地问："洛克菲勒先生，我希望这项判决不至于让你沮丧，希望你睡个好觉。"

洛克菲勒怎么说的?哦，他毫不迟疑地回答："不要担心，约翰逊先生。我本来就想好好睡一觉。希望你也不要不安。晚安！"

这些话竟出自一个曾因损失了150美元而病倒在床的人之口?不错。洛克菲勒花了很长时间才克服了忧虑。他曾"死于"53岁，但他活到了98岁。

一本书挽救了我的婚姻生活

B.R.W

我恨自己只能用假名来写这个故事。但由于这件事太具有隐私性，所以我不可能使用自己的真名。

但无论如何，卡耐基先生可以为这个故事的真实性作证。我在12年前第一次把我的故事告诉了他。

大学毕业之后，我在一家大公司找到了一份工作。5年后，公司派我到太平洋彼岸的远东地区，担任公司驻该地区的代表。在离开美国的前一个星期，我娶了一位最可爱、最甜蜜的女郎为妻。但对我俩，尤其是对她来说，我们的蜜月却是一次悲伤的失望。当我们抵达夏威夷时，她

thought of suicide. Then one day I chanced upon a book that changed everything. I have always been a lover of books, and one night while visiting some American friends in the Far East, I was glancing over their well-stocked library when I suddenly saw a book entitled *Ideal Marriage*, by Dr. Van de Velde. The title sounded like a preachy, goody—goody document. But, out of idle curiosity, I opened it. I saw that it dealt almost entirely with the sexual side of marriage—and dealt with it frankly and without any touch of vulgarity.

If anyone had told me that I ought to read a book on sex, I would have been insulted. Read one? I felt I could write one. But my own marriage was such a bust that I condescended to look this book over, anyway. So I got up the courage to ask my host if I could borrow it. I can truthfully say that reading that book turned out to be one of the important events of my life. My wife also read it. That book turned a tragic marriage into a happy, blissful companionship. If I had a million dollars, I would buy the rights to publish that book and give free copies of it to the countless thousands of bridal couples.

I once read that Dr. John B. Watson, the distinguished psychologist, said: "Sex is admittedly the most important subject in life. It is admittedly the thing which causes the most shipwrecks in the happiness of men and women."

If Dr. Watson is correct—and I am persuaded that his statement, sweeping as it is, is almost, if not wholly, true—then why does civilization permit millions of sexual ignoramuses to marry each year and wreck all chances for married happiness?

If we want to know what is wrong with marriage, we ought to read a book entitled *What is Wrong With Marriage*? by Dr. G. V. Hamilton and Kenneth MacGowan. Dr. Hamilton spent four years investigating what is wrong with marriage before writing that book, and he says: "It would take a very reckless psychiatrist to say that most married friction doesn't find its sources in sexual maladjustment. At any rate, the frictions which arise from other difficulties would be ignored in many, many cases if the sexual relation itself were satisfactory." I know that statement is true. I know from tragic experience.

The book that saved my marriage from shipwreck, Dr. Van de Velde's *Ideal Marriage*, can be found in most large public libraries, or bought at any bookshop. If you want to give a little gift to

失望至极。若不是因为她不好意思面对老朋友,并承认婚姻生活的失败的话,她可能早就回美国了。

我们在远东度过了两年不幸的日子。我很不开心,好几次都想自杀。有一天,我偶然看到了一本书,它改变了一切。我一向喜欢读书。一天晚上,我去拜访一些住在远东的美国朋友,在浏览他们藏书丰富的图书室时,我突然看到了一本《理想婚姻》,作者是韦尔迪博士。从书名来看,这是一本说教式的论文报告。但出于好奇,我将它翻开看了看,结果发现里面讨论的几乎都是婚姻生活中的"性"问题——开诚布公地讨论性问题,但没有任何粗俗之谈。

如果有人告诉我应该去阅读有关"性"的书,我会认为那是对我的侮辱。看那种书?我觉得我甚至可以写一本。但我自己的婚姻如此失败,我决定好好看这本书。所以,我鼓起勇气,问主人是否可以借那本书。现在我可以说,读那本书其实正是我一生中最重要的一件大事。我太太也读了那本书。那本书使一次濒临破裂的婚姻变得既快乐又幸福。如果我有 100 万美元,我会买下那本书的版权,印刷之后免费送给所有的夫妇。

我曾读过著名心理学家沃特逊博士的一段话:"性,无疑是人生中最重要的主题。导致绝大多数男女婚姻触礁的,也正是这件事。"

如果沃特逊博士是对的——我也由此得到建议,并且它几乎(即使不是完全)正确的话,我们为什么每年还要让千百万对性无知的年轻人结婚,从而破坏婚姻生活的幸福机会呢?

如果我们希望知道婚姻生活中的问题,我们应该去看看《婚姻的问题》。这是由汉密尔顿博士和麦克高文博士合著的。汉密尔顿博士花了 4 年时间调查婚姻的问题究竟出在哪儿,然后写成这本书。他说:"只有最愚蠢的精神病学家才会否认婚姻生活的不美满不是由性生活的不协调造成的。无论如何,如果性生活本身获得了满足,则婚姻生活中其他的许多不美满都好解决。"

some bride and groom, don't give them a carving set. Give them a copy of *Ideal Marriage*. That book will do more to increase their happiness than all the carving sets in the world.

I Was Committing Slow Suicide Because I Didn't Know How to Relax

By Paul Sampson

Direct-Mail Advertising, 12815 Sycamore, Wyandotte, Michigan

UP to six months ago, I was rushing through life in high gear. I was always tense, never relaxed. I arrived home from work every night worried and exhausted from nervous fatigue. Why? Because no one ever said to me: "Paul, you are killing yourself. Why don't you slow down? Why don't you relax? "

I would get up fast in the morning, eat fast, shave fast, dress fast, and drive to work as if I were afraid the steering wheel would fly out the window if I didn't have a death grip on it. I worked fast, hurried home, and at night I even tried to sleep fast.

I was in such a state that I went to see a famous nerve specialist in Detroit. He told me to relax. (By the way, he gave me the same principles for relaxation that are advocated in Chapter 24 of this book.) He told me to think of relaxing all the time—to think about it when I was working, driving, eating, and trying to go to sleep. He told me that I was committing slow suicide because I didn't know how to relax.

Ever since then I have practised relaxation. When I go to bed at night, I don't try to go to sleep until I've consciously relaxed my body and my breathing. And now I wake up in the morning rested—a big improvement, because I used to wake up in the morning tired and tense. I relax now when I eat and when I drive. To be sure, I am alert when driving, but I drive with my mind now instead of my nerves. The most important place I relax is at my work. Several times a day I stop everything and take inventory of myself to see if I am entirely relaxed. When the phone rings now, no longer do I grab it as though someone were trying to beat me to it; and when someone is talking to me, I'm as relaxed as a sleeping baby.

The result? Life is much more pleasant and enjoyable; and I'm completely free of nervous

韦尔迪博士这本挽救了我婚姻的书在许多大图书馆都能找到,或在书店买到。如果你想送给某对新人礼物,不要送雕塑,就送这本书给他们,它会比雕塑更有助于他们的幸福。

紧张就等于慢性自杀

直邮广告商　保罗·辛普森

在6个月以前,我的生活高度紧张。我总是紧紧张张的,从不会轻松。我每天晚上下班回到家时,总是忧心忡忡,精疲力竭。这是为什么呢?因为从来没有人对我说:“保罗,你正在自杀。为什么不慢慢来?为什么不放松?”

每天早上,我总是急急忙忙地起床、吃早餐、刮脸、穿衣服,然后又匆匆忙忙地开车上班。我紧握方向盘,好像它随时会飞出窗外一样。我迅速工作,又匆匆忙忙地赶回家。到了晚上,我甚至匆匆忙忙地入睡。

我这种状况太严重了,因此我去找了底特律一位著名的精神科专家。他建议我放松,还建议我随时都要想到放松——也就是在工作、开车、吃饭、入睡时,都要想到放松。他说,我正在慢性自杀,因为我不知道如何放松。

从那时候起,我就开始学习放松。我每天晚上上床时,并不急着入睡,而是先使自己的身体和呼吸放松。现在,我每天早上醒来时会觉得休息充分。这是一大进步,因为我以前每天早上醒来时总觉得又累又紧张。而现在,我开车、吃饭时也很轻松。为了安全,我驾车时提高了注意力,却不如以前那样紧张。最重要的是,我上班时也能放松。一天当中,我总要将手中的工作停几次,仔细检讨自己是否已经彻底放松了。现在,当电话铃响时,我不再像以前那样急着去接听;有人对我讲话时,我也会使自己轻松得像熟睡的婴儿一样。

结果呢?我的生活更轻松愉快了,我完全不再紧张烦恼了。

fatigue and nervous worry.

A Real Miracle Happened to Me

By Mrs. John Burger

3,940 Colorado Avenue, Minneapolis, Minnesota

Worry had completely defeated me. My mind was so confused and troubled that I could see no joy in living. My nerves were so strained that I could neither sleep at night nor relax by day. My three young children were widely separated, living with relatives. My husband, having recently returned from the armed service, was in another city trying to establish a law practice. I felt all the insecurities and uncertainties of the postwar readjustment period.

I was threatening my husband's career, my children's natural endowment of a happy, normal home life, and I was also threatening my own life. My husband could find no housing, and the only solution was to build. Everything depended on my getting well. The more I realized this and the harder I would try, the greater would be my fear of failure. Then I developed a fear of planning for any responsibility. I felt that I could no longer trust myself. I felt I was a complete failure.

When all was darkest and there seemed to be no help, my mother did something for me that I shall never forget or cease being grateful for. She shocked me into fighting back. She upbraided me for giving in and for losing control of my nerves and my mind. She challenged me to get up out of bed and fight for all I had. She said I was giving in to the situation, fearing it instead of facing it, running away from life instead of living it.

So I did start fighting from that day on. That very weekend I told my parents they could go home, because I was going to take over; and I did what seemed impossible at the time. I was left alone to care for my two younger children. I slept well, I began to eat better, and my spirits began to improve. A week later when they returned to visit me again, they found me singing at my ironing. I had a sense of well-being because I had begun to fight a battle and I was winning. I shall never forget this lesson... If a situation seems insurmountable, face it! Start fighting! Don't give in!

From that time on I forced myself to work, and lost myself in my work. Finally I gathered my

生活中的奇迹

约翰·伯格夫人

烦恼已将我完全击败。我大脑中一片混乱，觉得生活毫无乐趣。我的精神十分紧张，不但晚上睡不着觉，连白天也无法休息。我的三个孩子都和亲戚住在一起，和我隔得很远。我丈夫最近刚从军队退役，一个人住在外地，正准备成立一家法律事务所。我认为自己完全感染了战后恢复时期的那种不安全、惶惑的情绪。

我的情绪影响了我丈夫的事业，以及我们正常的家庭生活，同时也严重影响了我自己的生活。我丈夫找不到房子，唯一的解决方法就是自己建一栋。现在，万事皆备，就等我恢复健康了。我对这种情况知道得愈多，愈想努力恢复，对失败的恐惧也就愈甚。于是，我对任何事情都怀有一种深切的负罪感。我觉得我再也无法相信自己，觉得自己完全失败了。

在最黯淡无助的时期，我母亲帮助了我，使我永远难忘，终生感激。她鼓励我和生活奋斗。她责怪我消极放弃，失去了对神经和大脑的控制。她让我爬起床去拼搏。她说我这是对生活妥协，不敢直面人生，是在逃避生活。

于是，从那天起，我开始振作起来。到了那个周末，我对父母说他们可以回家了，因为我就要恢复了。那时，我完成了一些几乎不可能的工作：我一个人照顾两个幼小的孩子，睡得很好，食欲也开始好转，精神也大有进步。一个星期之后，当他们再来看我时，发现我正在熨衣服，还哼着歌曲。我有一种富裕满足的感觉，因为我已经展开一场自我战斗，而且正在获胜。我将永远记住这个教训……如果情况似乎很难克服，就勇敢地面对它！开始奋斗！永不放弃！

从那时起，我强迫自己工作，让自己沉浸在工作中。最后，我把孩子全部接回家来，和我丈夫一起住在我们新房子里。我知道我可以恢复，使我这个可爱的家庭有一位健康、快乐的母亲。我将全

children together and joined my husband in our new home. I resolved that I would become well enough to give my lovely family a strong, happy mother. I became engrossed with plans for our home, plans for my children, plans for my husband, plans for everything—except for me. I became too busy to think of myself. And it was then that the real miracle happened.

I grew stronger and stronger and could wake up with the joy of well-being, the joy of planning for the new day ahead, the joy of living. And although days of depression did creep in occasionally after that, especially when I was tired, I would tell myself not to think or try to reason with myself on those days—and gradually they became fewer and fewer and finally disappeared.

Now, a year later, I have a very happy, successful husband, a beautiful home that I can work in sixteen hours a day, and three healthy, happy children—and for myself, peace of mind!

Setbacks

By Ferenc Molnar

Noted Hungarian Playwright"Work is the best narcotic! "

Exactly fifty years ago my father gave me the words I have lived by ever since. He was a physician. I had just started to study law at the Budapest University. I failed one examination. I thought I could not survive the shame so I sought escape in the consolation of failure's closest friend, alcohol, always at hand: apricot brandy to be exact.

My father called on me unexpectedly. Like a good doctor, he discovered both the trouble and the bottle, in a second. I confessed why I had to escape reality.

The dear old man then and there improvised a prescription. He explained to me that there can be no real escape in alcohol or sleeping pills—or in any drug. For any sorrow there is only one medicine, better and more reliable than all the drugs in the world: work!

How right my father was! Getting used to work might be hard. Sooner or later you succeed. It has, of course, the quality of all the narcotics. It becomes habit-forming. And once the habit is formed, sooner or later, it becomes impossible to break one's self of it. I have never been able to break myself of the habit for fifty years.

部身心放在了家庭、孩子、丈夫以及所有事情上——除了我自己。我太忙了,根本没时间去想自己。就在这时,真正的奇迹出现了。

我越来越强健,每天早上起床时都充满喜悦:富足的喜悦,为新的一天到来的喜悦,生活的喜悦。虽然我偶尔也有沮丧的时候,特别是疲倦之时,但我告诉自己,不必在沮丧的时候想那么多——于是,这种情况逐渐愈来愈少,终于完全消失。

现在,一年之后,我有了一位非常快乐成功的丈夫,一个美丽的家庭和三个健康快乐的孩子——而我自己,也快乐安详。

挫　折

著名匈牙利剧作家　费伦斯·莫尔纳

50年前,我父亲给了我一句话,自那以后我靠它生活至今。父亲是医生。我刚开始在布达佩斯大学学习法律,有一次考试不及极。我受不了这种羞辱,不想见朋友,并借酒浇愁,手中总是拿着杏味白兰地。

父亲意外地来看我了。就像一位善良的医生,他立即看出了我的麻烦和酒瓶。我承认了为何要逃避现实。

这可爱的老人立即给我开了一个处方。他向我解释说:酒精和安眠药都不能解决问题——任何药物都不能。治疗不幸的药只有一种,世界上比药物更好、更可靠的东西就是——工作。

父亲太对了!投入工作可能很难。但你迟早会做到这一点。工作当然拥有所有麻醉剂的功效。它是一种习惯的培养。一旦这种习惯养成,就不可能剔除。我这种习惯就保持了50年。

I Was So Worried I Didn't Eat a Bite of Solid Food for Eighteen Days

By Kathryne Holcombe Farmer

Sheriff's Office, Mobile, Alabama

Three months ago, I was so worried that I didn't sleep for four days and nights; and I did not eat a bite of solid food for eighteen days. Even the smell of food made me violently sick. I cannot find words to describe the mental anguish I endured. I wonder whether hell has any worse tortures than what I went through. I felt as if I would go insane or die. I knew that I couldn't possibly continue living as I was.

The turning point of my life was the day I was given an advance copy of this book. During the last three months, I have practically lived with this book, studying every page, desperately trying to find a new way of life. The change that has occurred in my mental outlook and emotional stability is almost unbelievable. I am now able to endure the battles of each passing day. I now realize that in the past, I was being driven half mad not by today's problems but by the bitterness and anxiety over something that had happened yesterday or that I feared might happen tomorrow.

But now, when I find myself starting to worry about anything, I immediately stop and start to apply some of the principles I learned from studying this book. If I am tempted to tense up over something that must be done today, I get busy and do it immediately and get it off my mind.

When I am faced with the kind of problems that used to drive me half crazy, I now calmly set about trying to apply the three steps outlined in Chapter 2, Part One. First, I ask myself what is the worst that can possibly happen. Second, I try to accept it mentally. Third, I concentrate on the problem and see how I can improve the worst which I am already willing to accept—if I have to.

When I find myself worrying about a thing I cannot change—and do not want to accept—I stop myself short and repeat this little prayer:

"*God grant me the serenity to accept the things I cannot change, the courage to change the things I can, and wisdom to know the difference.*"

Since reading this book, I am really experiencing a new and glorious way of life. I am no longer destroying my health and happiness by anxiety. I can sleep nine hours a night now. I enjoy

我生命的转折点

亚拉巴马州莫比市副警长 霍尔康摩·法摩

3个月之前,我心烦意乱,一连四天四夜都睡不着觉,连续18天吃不下任何固体食物。甚至食物的气味也会让我极不舒服。我无法找到适当的字眼来描述我的精神痛苦,我怀疑地狱中是否还有比这更痛苦的折磨。我觉得自己似乎要发疯或死掉。我知道我不可能再这样活下去。

我生命中的转折点,是在我收到一本《人性的优点》之后。在过去3个月,我实际上是依赖这本书活下来的;我详细研读了每一页,急于找到新的生活方式。这本书带给我的心理安定,其功效简直令人难以相信。

现在我已经可以应付每天的生活挑战。我已经明白,我过去之所以差点疯掉,是因为我不仅为今天的问题而烦恼;还为昨天发生的事情,或明天也许会发生的某些事情而忧虑。

现在,当我发现自己又开始为某件事情烦恼时,我会立刻下来停,并运用我从这本书中学到的某些原则。如果是今天必须完成的工作,那我就立刻去做,然后将它从我的大脑中清除。

当我再遇到以前那些迫使我几乎发狂的问题时,我能镇静地运用这本书所教的方法来解决。第一,我问自己,可能发生的最糟糕的情况是什么。第二,我试着从内心去接受它。第三,我专注于研究问题本身,看看如何才能改进最糟糕的情况。

如果我发现自己为一件无法改变,而我又不愿意接受的事情而烦恼时,我会让自己反复诵读这段简短的祈祷:

"愿主赐给我安宁,接受我无法改变的事物;赐给我勇气,改变我无法改变的事物;赐给我智慧,洞悉其中的差异。"

读过这本书之后,我真正享受到了新的精彩生活。我不再让焦虑来破坏我的健康和幸福。现在我每天晚上都能够安睡9个小时,吃东西也津津有味。障碍已经消除,大门已经打开。我现

my food. A veil has been lifted from me. A door has been opened. I can now see and enjoy the beauty of the world which surrounds me. I thank God for life now and for the privilege of living in such a wonderful world.

May I suggest that you also read this book over: keep it by your bed: underscore the parts that apply to your problems. Study it; use it. For this is not a "reading book"in the ordinary sense; it is written as a"guide book"—to a new way of life!

在可以看到身边世界的美丽,并尽情享受它。我感谢上帝赐给我生命,并让我生活在如此美丽的世界。

我建议你也去看这本书:把它放在床边,划出那些可以解决你问题的部分。研究并运用它,因为这可不是一本普通的"闲书",而是一本生活"指南"——通向新生活的宝典。

THE QUICK AND EASY WAY TO EFFECTIVE SPEAKING

语言的突破

Part One
Fundamentals of Effective Speaking

1 Acquiring the Basic Skills

I started teaching classes in public speaking in 1912, the year the Titanic went down in the icy waters of the North Atlantic. Since then, more than seven hundred and fifty thousand people have been graduated from these classes.

In the demonstration meetings preceding the first session of the Dale Carnegie Course, people are given the opportunity of telling why they intend to enroll and what they hope to gain from this training. Naturally, the phraseology varies; but the central desire, the basic want in the vast majority of cases, remains surprisingly the same: "When I am called upon to stand up and speak, I become so self-conscious, so frightened, that I can't think clearly, can't concentrate, can't remember what I intended to say. I want to gain self-confidence, poise, and the ability to think on my feet. I want to get my thoughts together in logical order, and I want to be able to talk clearly and convincingly before a business or social group."

Doesn't this sound familiar? Haven't you experienced these same feelings of inadequacy? Wouldn't you give a small fortune to have the ability to speak convincingly and persuasively in public? I am sure you would. The very fact that you have begun reading the pages of this book is proof of your interest in acquiring the ability to speak effectively.

I know what you are going to say, what you would say if you could talk to me: "But Mr. Carnegie, do you really think I could develop the confidence to get up and face a group of people and address them in a coherent, fluent manner?"

第一篇 高效演讲的基本原则

第1章 获得演讲的基本技巧

我于1912年,也就是"泰坦尼克号"沉没在北大西洋冰海的那一年,开始教授当众讲话这门课程。如今,已经有75万多学员从我这里毕业了。

当众讲话教程的第一堂课是示范表演。一些学员会上台讲他们为什么选这门课程,以及期望从这一训练中学到什么。尽管每个人都有不同的说法,但大多数人的原因和基本需求几乎如出一辙:"面对众人讲话时,我会觉得浑身不自在,总担心不能清晰地思考,不能集中精力,甚至不知道自己究竟想说什么。我希望获得自信,能随心所欲地思考问题,逻辑清晰地归纳自己的思想,在商业场合和社交场合侃侃而谈,思路清晰而又不乏语言魅力。"

这番话听起来不觉得耳熟吗?你是否有过这种心有余而力不足的感觉?你不希望自己在演讲时口若悬河,侃侃而谈,令人折服吗?现在你正在翻开这本书,说明你也希望获得这种成功演讲的能力。

我知道你想说什么。我猜想你一定会问我:"卡耐基先生,你真的认为我能培养自信,面对众人而口齿流利地对他们演讲吗?"

我这一生几乎全都用于帮助人们消除恐惧、培养勇气和自信。在我班上发生的种种奇迹,可以写出几十本书。因此,你问的问题不在于我"认为";如果你能根据书中的方法和建议去练

I have spent nearly all my life helping people get rid of their fears and develop courage and confidence. I could fill many books with the stories of the miracles that have taken place in my classes. It is not, therefore, a question of my *thinking.* I know you can, if you practice the directions and suggestions that you will find in this book.

Is there the faintest shadow of a reason why you should not be able to think as well in a perpendicular position before an audience as you can sitting down? Is there any reason why you should play host to butterflies in your stomach and become a victim of the "trembles" when you get up to address an audience? Surely, you realize that this condition can be remedied, that training and practice will wear away your audience-fright and give you self-confidence.

In order to get the most out of this book, and to get it with rapidity and dispatch, you will find these four guideposts useful:

FIRST/ TAKE HEART FROM THE EXPERIENCE OF OTHERS

There is no such animal, in or out of captivity, as a born public speaker. In those periods of history when public speaking was a refined art that demanded close attention to the laws of rhetoric and the niceties of delivery, it was even more difficult to be born a public speaker. Now we think of public speaking as a kind of enlarged conversation. Gone forever is the old grandiloquent style and the stentorian voice. What we like to hear at our dinner meetings, in our church services, on our TV sets and radios, is straightforward speech, conceived in common sense and dedicated to the proposition that we like speakers to talk with, and not at, us.

Despite what many school texts would lead us to believe, public speaking is not a closed art, to be mastered only after years of perfecting the voice and struggling with the mysteries of rhetoric. I have spent almost all of my teaching career proving to people that it is *easy* to speak in public, provided they follow a few simple, but important, rules.

I wish I could give you a chance to browse through the files of testimonial letters in my home or in the offices of my representatives in various parts of the world. They come from industrial leaders whose names are frequently mentioned in the business section of *The New York Times and The Wall Street Journal*, from governors of states and members of parliaments, from college

习,那么你一定能做到。

为什么站在众人面前就不能像坐着那样冷静地思考呢?为什么当众站起来讲话,你的胃部就会翻腾,身体就会不停地发抖呢?这些问题肯定是可以克服的,只要接受训练和练习,你就会消除面对听众的恐惧,并充满了自信。

为了从本书获得最大教益,并对它有一个快速了解,以下四条指引十分有用:

一、学习别人的经验,激发自己的勇气

不论是否处于被囚禁的状态,没有任何一种动物是天生的大众演讲家。在历史上某些时期,当众演讲是一门精致的艺术,要求谨遵修辞法与优雅的演讲方式,因此想成为一名优秀的演讲家十分困难。但现在我们却将当众讲话看作一种范围有所扩大的交谈,从前边说边唱的演讲方式和如雷贯耳的声音已经永远过去了。我们无论是在晚餐聚会上,还是在教堂做礼拜、在家里看电视听收音机,都更愿意听到率真的语言,根据常理来思考,诚恳地交流,而不是对着我们夸夸其谈。

当众讲话并不是一门封闭的艺术,它并不像许多教科书中所说的那样,必须经过多年的美化声音以及艰苦的修辞训练之后才能掌握。我的教学生涯几乎全都致力于向人们证明:当众讲话很容易,只要遵循一些简单却又重要的规则就可以。

我希望大家有机会去我家或我在世界各地的代表的办公室,看看学员寄给我的信。这些信来自企业界的领袖,他们的大名常常见诸各大报纸,如《纽约时报》和《华尔街日报》,有的来自州长、国会议员、大学校长和娱乐圈明星,还有更多的信来自家庭主妇、牧师、教师和青年男女,他们全都是一些默默无闻的普通人,以及企业中已经接受训练或尚未接受训练的主管人员、技术娴熟或生疏的工人、工会成员、大学生和职业女性。所有这些人都觉得自己需要足够的自信

presidents, and from celebrities in the world of entertainment. There are thousands more from housewives, ministers, teachers, young men and women whose names are not well known yet, even in their own communities, executives and executive trainees, laborers, skilled and unskilled, union men, college students, and business women. All of these people felt a need for self-confidence and the ability to express themselves acceptably in public. They were so grateful for having achieved both that they took the time to write me letters of appreciation.

Of the thousands of people I have taught, one example comes to mind as I write because of the dramatic impact it had on me at the time. Some years ago, shortly after he joined my course, D. W. Ghent, a successful businessman in Philadelphia, invited me to lunch. He leaned across the table and said: "I have sidestepped every opportunity to speak to various gatherings, Mr. Carnegie, and there have been many. But now I am chairman of a board of college trustees. I must preside at their meetings. Do you think it will be possible for me to learn to speak at this late date in life?"

I assured him, on the basis of my experience with men in similar positions who had been members of my classes, that there was no doubt in my mind that he would succeed.

About three years later we lunched together again at the Manufacturers' Club. We ate in the same dining room and at the very same table we had occupied at our first meeting. Reminding him of our former conversation, I asked him whether my prediction had come true. He smiled, took a little red-backed notebook out of his pocket, and showed me a list of speaking engagements for the next several months.

"The ability to make these talks," he confessed, "the pleasure I get in giving them, the additional service I can render in the community—these are among the most gratifying things in my life."

But that was not all. With a feeling of justifiable pride, Mr. Ghent then played his ace card. His church group had invited the prime minister of England to address a convocation in Philadelphia. And the Philadelphian selected to make the introduction of the distinguished statesman, on one of his rare trips to America, was none other than Mr.D.W. Ghent.

This was the man who had leaned across that same table less than three years before and asked me whether I thought he would ever be able to talk in public!

心和在公众场合表达自己的能力。他们在这两方面都取得了一定成效而心存感激,所以给我写信表示感谢。

当我开始写这本书的时候,有一个人立刻闪现在我的脑海里。在我教过的几千名学员中,我对他的印象很深。根特先生是费城一名成功的企业家,刚参加我的训练班不久就邀请我和他共进午餐。在餐桌上,他倾身向前,对我说:"卡耐基先生,我曾有许多机会在公众场合说话,但我总是试图逃避。现在我是一家大学的董事会主席,必须经常主持各种会议。你认为我在迟暮之年是否还能学会当众讲话?"

由于在我的训练班上像他这样的人很多,因此,我向他保证,他一定能够成功。

大约3年后,我们又一次在企业家俱乐部共进午餐。我们在以前那个餐厅的同一张桌上吃饭,又谈起了从前谈过的话。我问他我的预言是否实现了,他微微一笑,从口袋里面掏出了一个红色的小笔记本,向我展示了未来几个月已经预定的演讲日程表。"有能力做这些演讲,"他承认,"演讲时所获得的快乐,以及我能为社会提供更多的服务——这些都是我人生中最高兴的事。"

事情还远不仅于此。根特先生还得意地告诉我,他所在的教区曾邀请英国首相来费城演讲,负责向人们介绍这位旅美之行的杰出政治家的人不是别人,正是根特先生。

正是这个人,3年前还在这张桌子旁问我,他将来是否能够当众畅谈自如?

还有另外一个例子:已故的格力屈公司董事长大卫·格力屈先生,有一天来我的办公室说:"在我的一生中,每次面对众人讲话时总是惊恐万状。而我作为董事长,又不能不主持会议。我和各位董事都十分熟悉;大家围着桌子谈话时我能够对答如流。但是当我站起身时,就会有一种恐惧,一个字也说不出来。这种情况已存在多年了。我现在想知道你是否能给我一些帮助。我觉得十分严重,这种情况持续多年了。"

Here is another example. The late David M. Goodrich, Chairman of the Board of the B. F. Goodrich Company, came to my office one day. "All my life," he began, "I have never been able to make a talk without being frozen with fear. As Board Chairman I have to preside at our meetings. I have known all the board members intimately for years, and I have no trouble talking to them when we are sitting around the table. But the moment I stand up to talk, I am terrified. I can hardly say a word. I have been that way for years. I don't believe you can do anything for me. My trouble is too serious. It has existed too long."

"Well," I said, "if you don't think I can do anything for you, why did you come to see me?"

"For one reason only," he replied. "I have an accountant who takes care of my personal accounting problems. He is a shy chap, and to get into his little office, he has to walk through my office. He has been sneaking through my office for years, looking at the floor and hardly ever saying a word. But lately, he has been transformed. He walks into my office now with his chin up, a light in his eye; and he says, 'Good morning, Mr. Goodrich,' with confidence and spirit. I was astonished at the change. So, I said to him: 'Who has been feeding you meat?' He told me about taking your course of training; and it is only because of the transformation that I have witnessed in that frightened little man that I have come to see you."

I told Mr. Goodrich that if he attended the classes regularly and did what we asked him to do, within a few weeks he would enjoy speaking before audiences.

"If you can do that," he replied, "I'll be one of the happiest men in the country."

He joined the course, made phenomenal progress, and three months later, I invited him to attend a meeting of three thousand people in the ballroom of the Hotel Astor, and talk to them on what he had gotten out of our training. He was sorry—couldn't come—a previous engagement. The next day he phoned me. "I want to apologize," he said. "I have broken that engagement. I'll come and speak for you. I owe it to you. I'll tell the audience what this training did for me. I'll do it with the hope that my story will inspire some of the listeners to get rid of the fears that are devastating their lives."

I asked him to speak for two minutes only. He spoke to three thousand people for eleven minutes.

I have seen thousands of similar miracles worked in my courses. I have seen men and women whose lives were transformed by this training, many of them receiving promotions far beyond their

“噢,”我说,“既然你怀疑我是否能给你帮助,那你为什么还来找我呢?”

“只有一个原因,”他回答说,“我有一个会计,他专门为我处理私人账目。他原本是一个害羞的小伙子,每天进自己的办公室时必须经过我的办公桌。许多年来,他一直都是蹑手蹑脚的十分小心,双眼紧盯着地面,也难得说一个字。但是他最近却改头换面了,变得神采奕奕,走进办公室时也敢抬头挺胸了,并且还大大方方地问候我。我对他的这种变化十分惊讶,于是问他为什么会发生这种改变。他告诉我说他参加了你的训练课程。正是因为我亲眼目睹了这个小伙子的改变,我才来寻求你的帮助的。”

我对格力屈先生说,如果他能定期来上课,并且按照我的要求训练,不出几个星期,他就敢在大众面前讲话了。

“如果你真的能改变我,”他回答说,“那我可真的是全美国最快乐的人了。”

他坚持上课,并且进步神速。3个月后,我请他参加了一次宴会,地点是在阿斯特饭店舞厅,参加者有3000人。我让他谈谈在演讲训练中的获益情况。由于他事先有约会,他对自己不能前来表示歉意,但是第二天他又给我打电话说自己要来。他说:“我把约会取消了。我很高兴为你演讲。我要告诉人们这次训练带给我的好处,用我自己的故事来激励人们,消除那正在摧毁他们生活的恐惧。”

我只让他讲两分钟时间,结果他面对3000人说了11分钟。

类似的奇迹,我曾在班上亲眼目睹过几千次。我看到了许多人的人生也因为参加了这项训练而得以改观:一些人获得了梦寐以求的提升,而另一些人则在商场、工作和沟通中大大获利。有时候,一场演讲就足以办成一件重要的事情。我们来看玛利欧·拉卓的故事。

几年前,我意外地收到了一封寄自古巴的电报。电报中说:“除非你给我发电报阻止我,否则我将立即赶往纽约,接受演讲训练。”落款人是玛利欧·拉卓。我不知道这个人是谁,从前也没

dreams or achieving positions of prominence in their business, profession, and community. Sometimes this has been done by means of a single talk delivered at the right moment. Let me tell you the story of Mario Lazo.

Years ago, I received a cable from Cuba that astonished me. It read: "Unless you cable me to the contrary, I am coming to New York to take training to make a speech." It was signed: "Mario Lazo." Who was he? I wondered! I had never heard of him before.

When Mr. Lazo arrived in New York, he said: "The Havana Country Club is going to celebrate the fiftieth birthday of the founder of the club; and I have been invited to present him with a silver cup and to make the principal talk of the evening. Although I am an attorney, I have never made a public talk in my life. I am terrified at the thonght of speaking. If I fail, it will be deeply embarrassing to my wife and myself socially; and, in addition, it might lower my prestige with my clients. That is why I have come all the way from Cuba for your help. I can stay only three weeks."

During those three weeks, I had Mario Lazo going from one class to another speaking three or four times a night. Three weeks later, he addressed the distinguished gathering at the Havana Country Club. His address was so outstanding that Time Magazine reported it under the head of foreign news and described Mario Lazo as a "silver-tongued orator."

Sounds like a miracle, doesn't it? It is a miracle—a twentieth-century miracle of conquering fear.

SECOND/ KEEP YOUR GOAL BEFORE YOU

When Mr. Ghent spoke of the pleasure his newly acquired skill in public speaking gave him, he touched upon what I believe (more than any other one factor) contributed to his success. It's true he followed the directions and faithfully did the assignments. But I'm sure he did these things because he wanted to do them, and he wanted to do them because he saw himself as a successful speaker. He projected himself into the future and then worked toward bringing that projection into reality. That is exactly what you must do.

Concentrate your attention on what self-confidence and the ability to talk more effectively will mean to you. Think of what it may mean to you socially, of the friends it will bring, of your increased capacity to be of service in your civic, social, or church group, of the influence you will

有听说过他。

拉卓先生到了纽约。他说:"哈瓦那乡村俱乐部准备为创始人的50岁生日举行庆祝大会,安排我在晚会上担任主持人,并为他颁发纪念杯。虽然我是一名律师,但从来没有公开发表过演讲。一想到要当众讲话我就害怕。如果把事情办砸了,我和我太太该有多难为情啊!这将会大大影响我在我的委托人面前的形象。因此,我特意从古巴来向你求助。但我只能待3周。"

在那3周时间内,我让玛利欧从一个班换到另一个班,每晚都要作三四次演讲。3个星期之后,他在哈瓦那乡村俱乐部的盛大宴会上发表了一场演讲,这场演讲如此精彩,《时代周刊》还专门在国外新闻栏目中做了特别报道,称他为"银舌演讲家"。

听起来像是奇迹,是吗?它的确是一个奇迹——20世纪的人们克服恐惧的奇迹。

二、时刻不忘自己的目标

当根特先生说到他新掌握的当众讲话的技巧给他带来的极大乐趣时,我认为这也正是他获得成功的原因(这一因素比其他因素更为重要)。他的确遵循了我们的指导,毫不懈怠地完成了任务。但是,我相信他之所以能坚持下来,完全是出于一种自我需要,他想让自己成为一名成功演讲家。他将自己投入了未来的良好形象中,然后不懈地努力,终于梦想成真。这也是你必须做的。

集中全部精力,时刻不忘自信与侃侃而谈的演讲能力,对你而言十分重要:想想由此结交的朋友在社交方面对你的重要性,想想自己为大众、为社会服务的能力将大大增强,想想它对你的人生和事业所产生的深远影响。总之,它将为你领袖群伦铺平道路。

国家现金注册公司董事会主席、联合国教科文组织主席艾林,在《演讲季刊》中发表了一篇文章《演讲与领导在事业上的关系》。他说:"在历史上从事商业的人当中,有不少人是凭借在演讲方面的杰出表现而获得赏识的。许多年前,有一位青年,他当时主管堪萨斯一个小分行,但是

be able to exert in your business. In short, it will prepare you for leadership.

In an article entitled "Speech and Leadership in Business," S.C. Allyn, Chairman of the Board of the National Cash Register Company and Chairman of UNESCO, wrote in the *Quarterly Journal of Speech*: "In the history of our business, many a man has drawn attention to himself by a good job done on the platform. A good many years ago a young man, who was then in charge of a small branch in Kansas, gave a rather unusual talk, and is today our vice-president in charge of sales." I happen to know that this vicepresident is now the president of the National Cash Register Company.

There is no predicting how far the ability to speak on your feet will take you. One of our graduates, Henry Blackstone, President of the Servo Corperation of America, says, "The ability to communicate effectively with others and win their cooperation is an asset we look for in men moving to the top."

Think of the satisfaction and pleasure that will be yours when you stand up and confidently share your thoughts and feelings with your audience. I have traveled around the world several times, but I know of few things that give greater delight than holding an audience by the power of the spoken word. You get a sense of strength, a feeling of power. "Two minutes before I begin," said one of my graduates, "I would rather be whipped than start; but two minutes before I finish, I would rather be shot than stop."

Begin now to picture yourself before an audience you might be called upon to address. See yourself stepping forward with confidence, listen to the hush fall upon the room as you begin, feel the attentive absorption of the audience as you drive home point after point, feel the warmth of the applause as you leave the platform, and hear the words of appreciation with which individual members of the audience greet you when the meeting is over. Believe me, there is a magic in it and a never-to-be-forgotten thrill.

William James, Harvard's most distinguished professor of psychology, wrote six sentences that could have a profound effect on your life, six sentences that are the open sesame to Ali Baba's treasure cave of courage: "In almost any subject, your passion for the subject will save you. If you care enough for a result, you will most certainly attain it. If you wish to be good, you will be good. If you wish to be rich, you will be rich. If you wish to be learned, you will be learned. Only then you must really wish these things and wish them with exclusiveness and not wish one hundred other incompatible things just as strongly."

当他发表了一场精彩的演讲之后,今天成了我们公司负责业务的副总裁。"我正好还知道,这位副总裁是现任国家现金注册公司总裁。

能够从容不迫地站起来演讲,将使你的前途不可估量。我的一名学员亨利·布莱克斯通是美国舍弗公司的总裁。他说:"和别人进行有效的交谈,并争取他们的合作,是我们所寻找的追求进步的人应具备的宝贵财富。"

想想,当你充满了自信,站起来与听众们共同分享你自己的思想和感觉时,该是多么的满足和舒畅啊!我曾多次做环球旅行,深知一个道理,那就是用语言的力量影响全场听众的那种愉悦感是其他任何事物都不能相比的。你会有一种力量感、一种强大感。有一位毕业生曾这样说:"在演讲开始的前两分钟,即使用鞭子抽打我也无法开口。但到结束前的两分钟,我情愿挨枪子儿也不愿停下来。"

现在,闭上你的眼睛想象一下:面对听众,充满自信地走上演讲台,听听开场后全场的鸦雀无声,感觉一下听众们在你深入浅出、一语中的时的那种全神贯注,感受一下当你离开演讲台时听众们掌声的温馨,并带着微笑接受大家对你的赞赏。请相信我,这里有一种魔力和一种永难忘怀的惊喜。

哈佛大学最卓越的心理学教授威廉·詹姆斯曾写过六句话,它们对你的一生可能会产生深远的影响。这六句话就是阿里巴巴勇探藏宝穴的开门秘诀:"不论什么课程,只要充满热情,就可以顺利完成。如果你对结果足够关注,你就一定会得到它。只要你想做好,你就一定能做好。如果你渴望致富,你便会拥有财富。如果你想博学,你就会学富五车。只有真正地渴望这些事情,你才会心无旁骛,而不会白费心思、胡思乱想许多不相干的杂事。"

学习有效地当众讲话,其好处不仅仅是可以做正式的公开演讲。事实上,即使你一辈子都不需要正式公开演讲,但接受这种训练仍有许多好处。例如,当众演讲训练可以帮助你培养自

Learning to speak effectively to groups brings other benefits than merely the ability to make formal public speeches. As a matter of fact, if you never give a formal public speech in your life, the benefits to be derived from this training are manifold. For one thing, public speaking training is the royal road to self-confidence. Once you realize that you can stand up and talk intelligently to a group of people, it is logical to assume that you can talk to individnals with greater confidence and assurance. Many men and women have taken my course in Effective Speaking primarily because they were shy and self-conscious in social groups. When they found they were capable of speaking on their feet to their fellow class members without having the roof fall in, they became aware of the ridiculousness of self-consciousness. They began to impress others, their families, friends, business associates, customers, and clients, with their newly found poise. Many of our graduates, like Mr. Goodrich, were impelled to take the course by the remarkable change in the personalities of those around them.

This type of training also affects the personality in ways that are not immediately apparent. Not long ago I asked Dr. David Allman, the Atlantic City surgeon and former president of the American Medical Association, what in his opinion were the benefits of public speaking training in terms of mental and physical health. He smiled and said he could best answer that question by writing a prescription that "no drugstore can fill. It must be filled by the individual; if he thinks he can't, he is wrong."

I have the prescription on my desk. Every time I read it, I am impressed. Here it is, just as Dr. Allman jotted it down:

> Try your best to develop an ability to let others look into your head and heart. Learn to make your thoughts, your ideas, clear to others, individually, in groups, in public. You will find, as you improve in your effort to do this, that you—your real self—are making an impression, an impact, on people such as you never made before.
>
> You can reap a double benefit from this prescription. Your self-confidence strengthens as you learn to speak to others, and your whole personality grows warmer and better. This means that you are better off emotionally, and if you are better off emotionally, you are better off physically. Public speaking in our modern world is for everybody, men and women, young and elderly. I do not know personally about its advantages to one in business or industry. I only hear that they are great. But I do know its advantages in health. Speak when you can, to a few or to

信。因为一旦你发现自己能够站起来,有条不紊地对着众人说话,那么当你和别人谈话时,一定会更有信心和勇气。很多来上我的"高效演讲"课程的人,大多是因为在社交场合中感到害羞和拘束。当他们发现自己站着和同事讲话天也不会塌下来时,便会发现自己的拘束是多么可笑。他们在训练中培养出来的自然洒脱,让他们的家人、朋友、事业伙伴和顾客刮目相看。许多毕业的学员也都是因为看到身边的人个性发生了巨大的变化才来上课的。如格力屈先生就是这样。

这种类型的训练,也会在不同方面影响人的个性,但不会立即显现出来。不久前,我曾问大西洋城一位外科医生、美国医学会会长大卫·奥尔曼博士,就心理和生理健康而言,接受当众演讲训练有什么好处?他笑着说:"回答这个问题,最好是开一个处方,这个处方在药房里是抓不到药的,每个人得自己给自己配药;如果他认为自己不行,那他就错了。"

我桌上就放着这份处方,我每读一次,就觉得有所收获。以下便是奥尔曼博士开的处方:

> 努力培养一种能力,让别人走进你的脑海和心灵。试着面对单独的人,或者在大众面前清晰地表达你的思想和理念。当你通过这种努力获得进步时,你便会发觉:你——你真正的自我——正在塑造一个别人以前从未见过的崭新的形象。
>
> 你可以从这个处方中获得双倍的益处。当你试着和别人讲话时,你的自信心也会随之增强,你的性格也会变得越来越温柔美好。这就意味着你的情绪已经渐入佳境。既然情绪渐入佳境,那么身体也就会随之好起来。在我们这个世界,不论男女老少都需要当众讲话。我并不清楚这在工商业中究竟会带来什么利益,但我听说它们有无穷的好处。不过我的确了解它对于健康的益处。只要一有机会,就对几个人或许多人说话——你将会越说越好,我自己就是这样。同时,你会感到神清气爽,觉得自己完美无缺,而这是你从前所感受不到的。
>
> 这是一种美妙的感觉,没有任何药物能给你这种感受。

因此,第二项指引便是想象你自己正在成功地做着你目前所害怕的事,想象你已经能够当

many; you will do it better and better, as I have found out, myself; and you will feel a buoyancy of spirit, a sense of being a whole, rounded person, such as you never felt before.

It is a wonderful sense to have, and no pill ever made can give it to you.

The second guidepost, then, is to picture yourself as successfully doing what now you fear to do, and to concentrate on the benefits you will receive through your ability to talk acceptably before groups. Remember the words of William James: "If you care enough for a result, you will most certainly attain it."

THIRD / PREDETERMINE YOUR MIND TO SUCCESS

I was asked once, on a radio program, to tell in three sentences the most important lesson I have ever learned. This is what I said: "The biggest lesson I have ever learned is the stupendous importance of what we think. If I knew what you think, I would know what you are, for your thoughts make you what you are. By changing our thoughts, we can change our lives."

You have set your sights on the goal of increased confidence and more effective communication. From now on, you must think positively, not negatively, about your chances to succeed in this endeavor. You must develop a buoyant optimism about the outcome of your efforts to speak before groups. You must set the seal of determination upon every word and action that you devote toward the development of this ability.

Here is a story that is dramatic proof of the need for resolute determination on the part of anyone who wants to meet the challenge of more expressive speaking. The man I am writing about has come up the management ladder so far that he has become a big business legend. But the first time he stood up to speak in college, words failed him. He couldn't get beyond the middle of the five-minute talk his teacher had assigned. His face went white, and he hurried off the platform in tears.

The man who had that experience as a young student didn't let that failure frustrate him. He determined to become a good speaker and didn't stop in that determination until he became a world-respected economic consultant to the government. His name is Clarence B. Randall. In one of his thoughtful books, *Freedom's Faith*, he has this to say about public speaking: "I have service stripes all the way up one sleeve and all the way down the other from appearances before luncheons and dinners of manufacturers' associations, Chambers of Commerce, Rotary Clubs, fund-raising

众说话并且被接纳，由此获得了很多益处。牢记威廉·詹姆斯的话："假如你对结果足够关心，你一定会实现它。"

三、下定成功的决心

有一次在一个广播节目中，我被要求用三句话来说明我曾学到的最重要的一课。我是这么说的："我所学过的最重要的一课，就是我们的思想非常重要。如果我知道你的所思所想，就能了解你这个人，因为正是你的思想造就了你。通过改变我们的思想，就能改变我们的一生。"

你的目标已经指向了建立自信和进行有效交谈。那么，从现在开始，你就要积极地设想自己的这些努力终将会成功。你必须对自己当众演讲的努力成果保持轻松乐观的态度。一定要把你的决心烙在每个词句、每项行动上，竭尽全力培养这种能力。

这里有一个故事，可以作为这一观点的强有力证明：任何人如果希望迎接语言表达的挑战，就一定要具备坚毅的决心。这个故事里的这个人，现在已经登上了企业最高层而成为商界的传奇人物。但是他在大学第一次站起来讲话时，却因为不善言辞而失败了。老师规定每个人5分钟的演讲，他讲了不到一半，就脸色发白，不得不含着眼泪匆匆走下讲台。

虽然有这样的不幸经历，但他不甘心被击倒。他决心要成为一个优秀的演讲家，并且不懈地努力，最终成了世人尊敬的政府经济顾问。他名叫克劳伦斯·蓝道尔。在他富有思想性的作品之一《自由的信念》中，他提到了当众演讲的情况："我的演讲安排十分紧凑，要参加各种聚会，如厂商协会、商务部、扶轮社、基金筹募会、校友会以及其他团体举办的聚会。我曾在密歇根州的艾斯肯那巴发表爱国主义演讲，谈到我投身于第一次世界大战；我还和米基·龙尼进行巡回慈善演讲，与哈佛大学校长詹姆士·布朗特·柯南及芝加哥大学校长罗伯特·哈钦斯进行教育宣传；我甚至还曾以糟糕的法语发表过一次餐后演讲。

campaigns, alumni organizations, and all the rest. I talked myself into World War I by a patriotic address in Escanaba, Michigan; I have barnstormed for charity with Mickey Rooney, and for education with President James Bryant Conant of Harvard and chancellor Robert M.Hutchins of the University of Chicago; and I have even made an after-dinner speech in very bad French.

"I think I know something about what an audience will listen to, and how they want it said. And there *is nothing whatever about it that a man worthy to bear important business responsibility cannot learn if he will.*"

I agree with Mr. Randall. The will to succeed must be a vital part of the process of becoming an effective speaker. If I could look into your mind and ascertain the strength of your desire and the light and shadow of your thought I could foretell, almost with certainty, the swiftness of your progress toward your goal of improved communicative skills.

In one of my classes in the Middle West, a man stood up the first night and unabashedly said that as a builder of homes he wouldn't be content until he became a spokesman for the American Home Builders' Association. He wanted nothing more than to go up and down this country and tell everybody he met the problems and achievements of his industry. Joe Haverstick meant what he said. He was the kind of class member that delights an instructor: he was in dead earnest. He wanted to be able to talk, not on local issues only, but on national ones, and there was no halfheartedness about his desires. He prepared his talks thoroughly, practiced them carefully, and never missed a single session, though it was the busy season of the year for men in his business. He did precisely what such a class member always does—he progressed at a rate that surprised him. In two months he had become one of the outstanding members of the class. He was voted its president.

The instructor handling that class was in Norfolk, Virginia, about a year later, and this is what he wrote: "I had forgotten all about Joe Haverstick back in Ohio when, one morning while I was having breakfast, I opened the *Virginia Pilot*. There was a picture of Joe and a write-up about him. The night before, he had addressed a large meeting of area builders, and I saw that Joe was not just a spokesman for the National Home Builders' Association; he was its president."

So, to succeed in this work, you need the qualities that are essential in any worthwhile endeavor: desire amounting to enthusiasm, persistence to wear away mountains, and the self-

"我认为我了解听众想听什么,以及他们喜欢听到这些内容如何被讲出来。对于肩负重任的人来说,这里面的窍门就是,只要愿意学,就没有什么学不会的。"

我与蓝道尔先生深有同感。成功的决心,正是决定了你能不能成为一个有效说话者的关键因素。如果我了解你的心思,知道你的意志强度,以及你是否有乐观的态度,那么我就几乎可以准确地预测你在改进沟通技巧上会有多快的进步。

在我中西部的一个班上,一位学员在第一天晚上就站起来信心十足地说,他不满足于当一名房屋建造商,他要做"全美房屋建筑协会"的发言人。他最想做的是在全国各地奔走,将他在房屋建筑业中遭遇的问题与获得的成就告诉人们。乔·哈弗斯蒂真的说到做到,他也正是那种让老师高兴的学生,有着狂热的追求。

他想讲的,不仅仅包括地方性的问题,还包括全国性的问题。对于这个想法,他没有三心二意,而是详细地准备自己的演讲,并认真地练习,从没有耽搁一堂课,即使是遇上一年中最忙的时节,他仍然一丝不苟地按照要求去做——结果他的进步连他自己都感到吃惊。在两个月内,他就成为班上的佼佼者,被选为班长。

大约一年以后, 在弗吉尼亚州的诺佛克市管理这个班的教师这样写道:"我已经完全忘了来自俄亥俄州的乔·哈弗斯蒂。有一天早晨,我正在吃早餐,我打开了《弗吉尼亚指南》,里面竟然有一幅乔的照片和一篇称赞他的报道。前天晚上,他在一次地区建筑商的盛大聚会中发表了精彩的演讲。我看到这时的乔可不仅仅是全国房屋建筑协会的发言人,简直就是会长!"

因此,要想成功演讲,就必须有强烈的欲望:高度的热忱,翻越高山的坚强毅力,以及相信自己一定会成功。

当裘里斯·恺撒从高卢奔驰而来,穿越海峡,率领他的军团登陆英格兰时,他是怎样确保自己的军队成功的呢?他想出了一个非常聪明的办法:他把军队带到了多佛海峡的白岩石悬崖

assurance to believe you will succeed.

When Julius Ceasar sailed over the channel from Gaul and landed with his legions in what is now England, what did he do to insure the success of his army? A very clever thing: he halted his soldiers on the chalk cliff, of Dover; and, looking down over the waves two hundred feet below, they saw red tongues of fire consume every ship in which they had crossed. In the enemy's Country, with the last link with the Continent gone, the last means of retreat burned, there was but one thing left for them to do: to advance, to conquer. That is precisely what they did.

Such was the spirit of the immortal Ceasal. Why not make it yours, too, as you set out to conquer your fear of audiences? Throw every shred of negative thought into the consuming fires and slam doors of steel upon every escape into the irresolute past.

FOURTH / SEIZE EVERY OPPORTUNITY TO PRACTICE

The course I gave in the 125th Street YMCA before World War I has been changed almost beyond recognition. Every year new ideas have been woven into the sessions and old ones cast away. But one feature of the course remains unchanged. Every member of every class must get up once, and in the majority of cases, twice, and give a talk before his fellow members. Why? Because no one can learn to speak in public without speaking in public any more than a person can learn to swim without getting in the water. You could read every volume ever written about public speaking—including this one—and still not be able to speak. This book is a thorough guide. But you must put its suggestions into practice.

When George Bernard Shaw was asked how he learned to speak so compellingly in public, he replied: "I did it the same way I learned to skate—by doggedly making a fool of myself until I got used to it." As a youth, Shaw was one of the most timid persons in London. He often walked up and down the embankment for twenty minutes or more before venturing to knock at a door. "Few men," he confessed, "have suffered more from simple cowardice or have been more horribly ashamed of it."

Finally, he hit upon the best and qnickest and surest method ever yet devised to conquer timidity, cowardice, and fear. He determined to make his weak point his strongest asset. He joined

上,让士兵们望着自己脚底下两百英尺的海面上曾运送他们渡海的船只被火焰吞没。由于置身敌国,与大陆的最后联系已经断绝,退却的工具已经被焚毁,唯一可做的事情就只有前进! 征服! 恺撒和他的军团就这样成功了。

这正是不朽的恺撒精神。当你想征服面对听众的恐惧时,为何不把这种精神用于自己身上呢?把消极思想全都扔进熊熊烈火中,并把身后通往犹豫退缩的大门紧紧关上。

四、抓住一切练习演讲的机会

第一次世界大战前,我在第125大街青年基督教协会教的课程已经有了变化,不再像当年的情况。每年都会有新观念加入课程,而那些旧思想则被淘汰。但是有一点却一直没有改变,那就是每个学员至少要当众演讲一次,很多时候都是两次。为什么这样做呢?因为不当众说话,谁都不可能学会如何当众演讲,这好比一个人不下水就永远学不会游泳一样。就算你读遍了所有关于当众演讲的著作,包括本书,也仍然开不了口,对你也没有任何帮助。本书只是指引,你得付诸实践。

当有人问萧伯纳是如何获得气势逼人的当众演讲的经验时, 他说:"我借鉴了自己学滑冰的方法——固执地让自己一个劲儿地出丑,直到学会为止。"萧伯纳年轻时,是伦敦最胆小的人之一,当他去找人时,常常在走廊上徘徊20分钟或更长时间,才敢鼓起勇气敲门。他承认:"很少有人仅仅因为胆小而痛苦,或者深深地为它感到羞耻。"

终于,他无意中使用了最好、最快而且最有效的方法来克服羞怯、胆小和恐惧。他决定把这个弱点变成自己最强有力的资本。他参加了一个辩论学会,只要伦敦有公众讨论的集会他都会参加。萧伯纳全身心地投入到社会主义事业中,四处演讲,终于把自己变成了20世纪上半叶最有信心、也最出色的演讲家之一。

a debating society. He attended every meeting in London where there was to be a public discussion, and he always arose and took part in the debate. By throwing his heart into the cause of socialism, and by going out and speaking for that cause, George Bernard Shaw transformed himself into one of the most confident and brilliant speakers of the first half of the twentieth century.

Opportunities to speak are on all sides. Join organizations and volunteer for offices that will require you to speak. Stand up and assert yourself at public meetings, if only to second a motion. Don't take a back seat at departmental meetings. Speak up! Teach a Sunday School class. Become a Scout leader. Join any group where you will have an opporunity to participate actively in the meetings. You have but to look around you to see that there is scarcely a single business, community, political, professional, or even neighborhood activity that does not challenge you to step forward and speak up. You will never know what progress you can make unless you speak, and speak, and speak again.

"I know all about that," a young business executive once said to me, "but I hesitate to face the ordeal of learning."

"Ordeal!" I replied. "Put that thought out of your mind. You've never thought of learning in the right—the conquering—spirit."

"What spirit is that?" he asked.

"The spirit of adventure." I told him, and I talked to him a little about a path to success, through public speaking, and the warming up, the unfolding, of one's personality.

"I'll give it a try," he finally said. "I'll head into this adventure."

As you read on in this book, and as you put its principles into practice, you, too, will be heading into adventure. You will find it is an adventure in which your power of self-direction and your vision will sustain you. You will find it is an adventure that can change you, inside and out.

说话的机会随处都有,你不妨参加一些组织,从事一些需要讲话的工作。你可以在聚会上站起来说上几句,哪怕只是附议他人也好。开会时不要躲在角落里。说话吧!去教堂为人讲道!或者做一个童子军的领队,或者加入一个有机会活跃地参加各种聚会的团体。你只要看看自己周围,便会发现没有哪个工作和活动是不需要开口说话的,甚至连住宅小区里的活动也是如此。如果你不说话,就永远不知道自己会有怎样的进步。

"这些我也都明白,"一位年轻的商务主管曾对我说,"可我总是担心学习的严峻考验。"

"严峻考验?"我说,"赶快丢掉这种想法。否则你永远不会用正确的征服性的精神来看待这个问题。"

"那是什么精神?"他问。

"就是冒险精神呀!"我告诉他。接着我又对他谈了一些通过当众演讲而获得成功,并且使个性也因此开朗起来的真实例子。

"我也要试试,"他最后说,"我要去从事这项冒险。"

当你继续阅读此书,并将其付诸实践的时候,你也是在冒险。你将会发现,在这项冒险活动中,你的自我引导力量和观察力将会给你帮助。你还会发现,这项冒险会从里到外彻底改变你。

2 Developing Confidence

"Five years ago, Mr. Carnegie, I came to the hotel where you were conducting one of your demonstrations. I walked up to the door of the meeting room and then stopped. I knew if I entered that room and joined a class, sooner or later I'd have to make a speech. My hand froze on the doorknob. I couldn't go in. I turned my back and walked out of the hotel.

"If I had only known then how you make it easy to conquer fear, the paralyzing fear of an audience, I wouldn't have lost these past five years."

The man who spoke these revealing words wasn't talking across a table or a desk. He was directing his remarks to an audience of some two hundred people. It was the graduation session of one of my courses in New York City. As he gave his talk, I was particularly impressed by his poise and self-assurance. Here was a man, I thought, whose executive skills will be tremendously increased by his newly acquired expressiveness and confidence. As his instructor, I was delighted to see that he had dealt a death blow to fear, and I couldn't help thinking how much more successful, and what is more, how much happier this man would have been if his victory over fear had come five or ten years before.

Emerson said, "Fear defeats more people than any other one thing in the world." Oh, how I have been made aware of the bitter truth of that statement. And how grateful I am that during my life I have been able to rescue people from fear. When I started to teach my course in 1912, little did I realize that this training would prove to be one of the best methods ever yet devised to help people eliminate their fears and feelings of inferiority. I found that learning to speak in public is nature's own method of overcoming self-consciousness and building up courage and self-confidence. Why? Because speaking in public makes us come to grips with our fears.

In years of training men and women to speak in public, I have picked up some ideas to help you quickly overcome stage fright and develop confidence in a few short weeks of practice.

第2章 培养演讲的信心

“卡耐基先生,我5年前来到你举办演讲的饭店,走近了大门却不敢进去。我知道如果进去参加了训练班,迟早就要当众演讲。因此我的手僵在门把上,不敢进去;最后,我只好转身离开了。

“当时假如我知道你能让我轻易克服恐惧,克服那种面对听众的恐惧的话,我就不会浪费这5年了。”

说这番肺腑之言的人不是在桌对面讲话,而是正在对大约200名听众大发感慨。这是纽约一个培训班的毕业聚会,这位学员发表讲话时,我对他的镇定和自信印象极深。我想,这个人一定能凭借他学到的语言表达能力和自信心,极大地提高处理各项事务的技巧。作为他的老师,我很高兴看到他能勇敢地战胜恐惧。想想吧,如果他在5年或10年前就战胜了恐惧,那么他现在肯定会有更多的成功和更多的快乐。

爱默生说:“和任何其他事物相比,恐惧更能击溃人类。”这是多么让人无奈的事实啊!感谢上天,它使我有能力帮助人们从恐惧中解脱出来。我于1912年刚开始授课时,一点也不知道这项训练竟然是帮助人们消除恐惧和自卑的最好方法之一。我发现学习当众说话,是一种天然的方法,它可以帮助人们克服紧张,建立勇气和自信心。为什么呢?因为当众说话让我们控制了自己的恐惧感。

通过多年来的训练,我获得了一些方法,可以帮助你很快克服上台演讲的恐惧,在短短几周练习之后就会有信心。

FIRST / GET THE FACTS ABOUT FEAR OFSPEAKING IN PUBLIC

Fact Number One: *You are not unique in your fear of speaking in public.* Surveys in colleges indicate that eighty to ninety per cent of all students enrolled in speech classes suffer from stage fright at the beginning of the course. I am inclined to believe that the figure is higher among adults at the start of my course, almost one hundred per cent.

Fact Number Two: *A certain amount of stage fright is useful!* It is nature's way of preparing us to meet unusual challenges in our environment. So, when you notice your pulse beating faster and your respiration speeding up, don't become alarmed. Your body, ever alert to external stimuli, is getting ready to go into action. If these physiological preparations are held within limits, you will be capable of thinking faster, talking more fluently, and generally speaking with greater intensity than under normal circumstances.

Fact Number Three: *Many professional speakers have assured me that they never completely lose all stage fright.* It is almost always present just before they speak, and it may persist through the first few sentences of their talk. This is the price these men and women pay for being like race horses and not like draft horses. Speakers who say they are "cool as a cucumber" at all times are usually as thick-skinned as a cucumber and about as inspiring as a cucumber.

Fact Number Four: *The chief cause of your fear of public speaking is simply that you are unaccustomed to speak in public.* "Fear is misbegotten of ignorance and uncertainty," says Professor Robinson in The Mind in the Making. For most people, public speaking is an unknown quantity, and consequently one fraught with anxiety and fear factors. For the beginner, it is a complex series of strange situations, more involved than, say, learning to play tennis or drive a car. To make this fearful situation simple and easy: practice, practice, practice. You will find, as thousands upon thousands have, that public speaking can be made a joy instead of an agony merely by getting a record of successful speaking experiences behind you.

The story of how Albert Edward Wiggam, the prominent lecturer and popular psychologist, overcame his fear, has been an inspiration to me ever since I first read it. He tells how terror-struck he was at the thought of standing up in high school and delivering a five-minute declamation.

"As the day approached," he writes, "I became positively ill. Whenever the dreadful thought

一、了解当众讲话恐惧的根源

实情之一:害怕当众讲话并不只是个别现象。大学调查表明,上演讲课的学生十之八九刚上课的时候都会有上台的恐惧。在我的成人教育班里,课程刚开始的时候,学员登台的恐惧比例更高,几乎达到了百分之百。

实情之二:一定程度的登台恐惧是有利的。它是让我们具备应付环境挑战能力的自然方法。所以,当你感到自己的脉搏加快、呼吸急促时,一定不要紧张。这是你的身体对外来刺激保持的警惕,它正在为即将到来的行动做准备。假如这种生理上的准备正好适度,你会因此而思考得更快,话也说得更流畅,反而会比在普通情况下说得更精彩。

实情之三:很多职业演讲者都承认,他们从来都没有完全消除登台的恐惧。几乎每一次演讲前他们都会感到害怕,而且会持续到刚开头的几句话。要想当赛马而不当驮马,演讲者必须付出这样的代价。有些演讲者常把自己比喻成"像黄瓜一样冰凉",其实更确切地说是像黄瓜一样皮厚和富有激情。

实情之四:你之所以害怕当众讲话,主要是因为你不习惯。鲁滨逊教授在《思想的酝酿》一书中说:"恐惧源于无知与不确定。"对大多数人来说,当众讲话正是一个不确定的因素,因此心里就不免焦虑和恐惧。特别是对新手来说,这是一连串陌生而复杂的环境,这远比学打网球或开汽车困难。只有通过千万次的练习、练习、再练习,才能把这种恐惧的状况变得单纯而轻松。那时你就会发现,只要有了成功演讲的经验,当众讲话就不再是一种痛苦,而是一种快乐了。

杰出演讲家、著名心理学家阿尔伯特·爱德华·威格玛克服恐惧的故事,自我初读以后就一直激励着我。他说,在读中学时,他被叫起来做5分钟的演讲,一想到这件事他就非常害怕。

他写道:"当演讲的日子快要到时,我就病倒了。只要一想到那件可怕的事情,我就会血冲

occurred to me, my whole head would flush with blood and my cheeks would burn so painfully that I would go out behind the school building and press them against the cold brick wall to try to reduce their surging blushes. It was the same way with me in college.

"On one occasion, I carefully memorized a declamation beginning, 'Adam and Jefferson are no more.' When I faced the audience, my head was swimming so I scarcely knew where I was. I managed to gasp out the opening sentence, stating that 'Adams and Jefferson have passed away.' I couldn't say another word, so I bowed, and walked solemnly back to my seat amid great applause. The president got up and said, 'Well, Edward, we are shocked to hear the sad news, but we will do our best to bear up under the circumstances.' During the uproarious laughter that followed, death would surely have been a welcome relief. I was ill for days afterward.

"Certainly the last thing on earth I ever expected to become was a public speaker."

A year after he left college, Albert Wiggam was in Denver. The political campaign of 1896 was raging over the issue of Free Silver. One day he read a pamphlet explaining the proposals of the Free Silverites; he became so incensed over what he considered the errors and hollow promises of Bryan and his followers, that he pawned his watch for enough money to get back to his native Indiana. Once there, he offered his services to speak on the subject of sound money. Many of his old school friends were in the audience. "As I began," he writes, "the picture of my Adams and Jefferson speech in college swept over me. I choked and stammered and all seemed to be lost. But, as Chauncey Depew often said, both the audience and I managed somehow to live through the introduction; and encouraged by even this tiny success, I went on talking for what I thought was about fifteen minutes. To my amazement, I discovered I had been talking an hour and a half!

"As a result, within the next few years, I was the most surprised person in the world to find myself making my living as a professional public speaker.

"I knew at first hand what William James meant by the habit of success."

Yes, Albert Edward Wiggam learned that one of the surest ways of overcoming the devastating fear of speaking before groups is to get a record of successful experiences behind you.

You should expect a certain amount of fear as a natural adjunct of your desire to speak in public, and you should learn to depend on a limited amount of stage fright to help make you give a better talk.

脑门,脸颊发烧,只好跑到学校后边去,把脸贴在那冰凉的砖墙面上,好让脸上的绯红尽快消退。读大学时我还是这样。

"有一次,我小心地背下了一篇演讲词的开头。但是当我面对听众时,脑袋里突然轰的一下,就不知身处何处了。我好不容易才勉强挤出开场白:'亚当斯与杰斐逊已经过世……'然后再也说不出一句话了,我只好向听众鞠躬,在如雷般的掌声中心情沉重地回到我的座位上。校长站起来说:'唉,爱德华,我们听到这则悲伤的消息真是太震惊了。不过,我们会尽量节哀的。'接着是哄堂大笑。当时我真想以死来解脱,然后我又病了几天。

"我在这世上最不敢期望的,就是当一名大众演讲家。"

离开大学一年后,他到了丹佛市。1896年。掀起了一场"自由银币铸造"政治运动。他对"自由银币主义者"布莱安及其支持者的错误和空洞承诺很不满,因此他把自己的手表当了足够的盘缠,回到家乡印第安纳州。一到那里,他就自告奋勇地就健全的币制发表演讲。听众当中有不少人是他的老同学。"刚开始时,"他写道,"我在大学演讲'亚当斯和杰斐逊'的那一幕又掠过我的脑海,我感到窒息,讲话结巴,什么都忘了。不过,就如乔西·德普常说的那样,听众和我都勉强挺过了绪论部分,这小小的成功鼓舞了我,我继续往下说了自以为大约只有15分钟的时间。让我惊讶的是,我说了一个半小时。

"结果,在以后的几年里,我成了全世界最感惊奇的人。我发现我竟然把当众演讲当成了谋生的职业。

"我终于体会到威廉·詹姆斯所说的'成功的习惯'的含义了。"

阿尔伯特·爱德华·威格玛终于认识到,要想克服当众讲话的那种灭顶之灾的恐惧,最好的办法就是获取成功的经验,并以此为后援。

要学会当众讲话,应该有一定程度的恐惧,同时你也要学会凭借这种适度的恐惧感,使你说得更好。

If stage fright gets out of hand and seriously curtails your effectiveness by causing mental blocks, lack of fluency, uncontrollable ties, and excessive muscular spasm, you should not despair. These symptoms are not unusual in beginners. If you make the effort, you will find the degree of stage fright soon reduced to the point where it will prove a help and not a hindrance.

SECOND / PREPARE IN THE PROPER WAY

The principal speaker at a New York Rotary Club luncheon several years ago was a prominent government official. We were looking forward to hearing him describe the activities of his department.

It was obvious almost at once that he had not planned his speech. At first he tried to talk impromptu. Failing in that attempt, he pulled out of his pocket a sheaf of notes which evidently had no more order than a flatcar full of scrap iron. He fumbled awhile with these, all the time becoming more embarrassed and inept in his delivery. Minute by minute he became more helpless, more bewildered. But he kept on floundering, apologizing, trying to make some semblance of sense out of his notes and raising a glass of water with a trembling hand to his parched lips. He was a sad picture of a man completely overcome by fright, due to almost total lack of preparation. He finally sat down, one of the most humiliated speakers I have ever seen. He made his talk as Rousseau says a love letter should be written: he began without knowing what he was going to say, and finished without knowing what he had said.

Since 1912, it has been my professional duty to evaluate over five thousand talks a year. From that experience, one great lesson stands out like Mt. Everest, towering above all the others: *only the prepared speaker deserves to be confident.* How can anyone ever hope to storm the fortress of fear if he goes into battle with defective weapons, or with no ammunition at all? "I believe," said Lincoln, "that I shall never be old enough to speak without embarrassment when I have nothing to say."

If yon want to develop confidence, why not do the one thing that will give you security as a speaker? "Perfect love," wrote the Apostle John, "casted out fear." So does perfect preparation. Daniel Webster said he would as soon think of appearing before an audience half-clothed as half-prepared.

NEVER MEMORIZE A TALK WORD FOR WORD

By "perfect preparation" do I mean that you should memorize your talk? To this question I give

即使这种登台的恐惧有时会一发而不可收，造成心灵障碍和言辞不畅、肌肉痉挛，你也不必绝望。这些症状在初学者中都很常见。只要你肯努力，就会发现这种恐惧很快就会减少到适当的程度，成为一种助力而不是阻力。

二、做好适当的准备

几年前，有一位地位显赫的政府官员在纽约扶轮社的午餐会上担任主讲人。大家都在等他介绍他部里的一些情况。

显然，他没有做好准备。他开始想发表一番即兴演讲，结果却不知该说些什么。于是，他从口袋里掏出一叠笔记。然而笔记非常杂乱，就像一卡车碎铁片。他手忙脚乱地翻着笔记，说话时更显得尴尬而笨拙。时间一分一秒地过去，他越来越绝望迷惑。他不停地向大家道歉，还想从笔记里找出一点头绪来。他用颤抖的手端起一杯开水，凑到发干的唇边。此情此景实在是惨不忍睹——他完全被恐惧击倒了，就因为他没有提前做好准备。最后，他只好坐下来。我看到的是一个最没面子的演讲家。他的演讲正像卢梭所说的某些人写的情书："始于不知何所云，止于不知已所云。"

1912年以来，出于职业原因，我每年都要担任5000多次演讲的评委。这给我上了最重要的一课，就像圣母峰高于群山之上一样：只有做好充分准备的演讲者，才会拥有自信。这好比上战场却带着不能用的武器，或者不带半点儿弹药，又何谈攻城略地呢？林肯说："如果我无话可说，就算是年纪一大把也会难为情的。"

假如你想培养自信，为什么不为演讲做好充分的准备呢？圣约翰说："完全的爱，会将恐惧置之度外。"丹尼尔·韦伯斯特也说，如果他不做好准备就出现在听众面前，就像是没有穿衣服一样。

1. 不要逐字背诵演讲

"充分的准备"是逐字背诵演讲吗？当然不是。为了保护自己，以免在听众面前大脑一片空

back a thunderous NO. In their attempts to protect their egos from the dangers of drawing a mental blank before an audience, many speakers fall headlong into the trap of memorization. Once a victim of this type of mental dope addiction, the speaker is hopelessly bound to a time-consuming method of preparation that destroys effectiveness on the platform.

When H.V. Kaltenborn, the dean of American news commentators, was a student at Harvard University, he took part in a speech contest. He selected a short story entitled "Gentlemen, the King." He memorized it word for word and rehearsed it hundreds of times. The day of the contest he announced the title, "Gentlemen, the King." Then his mind went blank. It not only went blank; it went black. He was terrified. In desperation he started telling the story in his own words. He was the most surprised boy in the hall when the judges gave him first prize. From that day to this, H.V. Kaltenborn has never read nor memorized a speech. That has been the secret of success in his broadcasting career. He makes a few notes and talks naturally to his listeners without a script.

The man who writes out and memorizes his talks is wasting his time and energy, and courting disaster. All our lives we have been speaking spontaneously. We haven't been thinking of words. We have been thinking of ideas. If our ideas are clear, the words come as naturally and unconsciously as the air we breathe.

Even Winston Churchill had to learn that lesson the hard way. As a young man, Churchill wrote out and memorized his speeches. Then one day, while delivering a memorized talk before the British Parliament, he stopped dead in his mental tracks. His mind went blank. He was embarrassed, humiliated! He began his last sentence all over again. Again his mind went blank and his face scarlet. He sat down. From that day to this, Winston Churchill has never attempted to deliver a memorized talk.

If we memorize our talk word for word, we will probably forget it when we face our listeners. Even if we do not forget our memorized talk, we will probably deliver it in a mechanical way. Why? Because it will not come from our hearts, but from our memories. When talking with people privately, we always think of something we want to say, and then we go ahead and say it without thinking of words. We have been doing that all our lives. Why attempt to change it now? If we do write out and memorize our talks, we may have the same experience that Vance Bushnell had.

Vance was a graduate of the Beaux Arts School in Paris, and later became vice-president of

白,许多演讲者会首选背诵演讲词。一旦犯了这种毛病,就会浪费时间做这样的准备,而这只会毁掉整个演讲。

美国新闻评论家卡腾堡还在哈佛大学读书时,曾参加过一次演讲比赛。他选了一则短篇故事,题目叫《先生们,国王》。他把它逐字逐句背诵下来,并预讲了好几百次。比赛那天,他刚说出题目"先生们,国王",然后脑子里就一片空白。岂止是空白?简直是一片漆黑。他差点儿吓蒙了。绝望之余,他只好用自己的语言来讲这个故事。当评委把第一名颁给他时,他简直不敢相信。从那天起,他再也不去背诵演讲稿了。这正是他在广播事业上取得成功的秘诀。他只做些简单的笔记,然后自然地对听众谈话。

写好演讲稿并背下来的人,不但浪费时间和精力,而且容易导致失败。我们平时与人说话都是很自然的事,从不会费心思推敲字眼。我们随时都在思考,当思想清晰时,语言就会像我们呼吸的空气,不知不觉地自然流出。

温斯顿·丘吉尔也是通过经验教训才学到这一课的。丘吉尔年轻时也会写讲稿、背讲稿。有一天,他正在英国国会背诵演讲稿,突然思路中断,大脑一片空白。他感到尴尬和羞辱。他重复了一遍上 句,但还是什么也想不起来,他的脸立即变成了猪肝色。他只好颓然坐下。从那以后,丘吉尔再也不背演讲稿了。

如果我们逐字背诵演讲词,面对听众的时候会忘记。而且即使没有忘记,讲出来可能也很呆板。为什么呢?因为它不是发自我们的内心,只是出于记忆。我们私下与别人交谈时,总是会一心想着要说的事,然后直接说出来,并不会特别留心词句。既然我们平时都是这么做的,现在为什么要改变呢?如果我们非要写演讲稿、背演讲词,很可能会重蹈凡斯·布什奈尔的覆辙。

凡斯毕业于巴黎波欧艺术学校, 后来成为世界上最大的保险公司之一——平衡人寿保险公司的副总裁。多年前,他应邀在西弗吉尼亚的白磺泉召开的平衡人寿公司代表会议中发表演

one of the largest insurance companies in the world—the Equitable Life Assurance Society. Years ago, he was asked to address a conference of two thousand Equitable Life representatives from all over America at a meeting in White Sulphur Springs, West Virginia. At that time, he had been in the life insurance business for only two years, but he had been highly successful, so he was scheduled to make a twenty-minute talk.

Vance was delighted to do so. He felt it would give him prestige. But, unfortunately, he wrote out and memorized his talk. He rehearsed forty times in front of a mirror. He had everything down pat: every phrase, every gesture, every facial expression. It was flawless, he thought.

However, when he stood up to deliver his address, he was terrified. He said: "My part in this program is..." His mind went blank. In his confusion, he took two steps backward and tried to start all over again. Again, his mind went blank. Again he took two steps back and tried to start. He repeated this performance three times. The platform was four feet high; there was no railing at the back; and there was a space five feet wide between the back of the platform and the wall. So, the fourth time he stepped back, he toppled backwards off the platform and disappeared into space. The audience howled with laughter. One man fell off his chair and rolled in the aisle. Never before nor since in the history of the Equitable Life Assurance Society has anyone ever given such a comic performance. The astonishing part of the story is that the audience thought it was really an act. The old-timers of the Equitable Life are still talking about his performance.

But what about the speaker, Vance Bushnell? Vance Bushnell himself told me it was the most embarrassing occasion of his life. He felt so disgraced that he wrote out his resignation.

Vance Bushnell's superiors persuaded him to tear up his resignation. They restored his self-confidence; and Vance Bushnell, in later years, became one of the most effective speakers in his organization. But he never memorized a talk again. Let us profit by his experience.

I have heard countless scores of men and women try to deliver memorized talks, but I don't remember even one speaker who wouldn't have been more alive, more effective, more human, if he had tossed his memorized talk into the waste basket. If he had done that, he might have forgotten some of his points. He might have rambled, but at least he would have been human.

Abe Lincoln once said: "I don't like to hear a cut-and-dried sermon. When I hear a man preach, I like

讲，来自全美的两千名代表参加了大会。当时，他从事人寿保险才两年，可是已经非常成功，所以他被安排发表20分钟的演讲。

凡斯十分兴奋，他知道这会让他声望大增。然而，不幸的是，他却把演讲词写下来再去背。他对着镜子演练了40次，对一切都做了精心准备：每句话、每个手势、每个表情……他认为自己完美无瑕。

可是，当他站起来演讲的时候，他感到一阵恐惧。他说："我在本计划里的职位是……"然后大脑一片空白。慌乱之中，他后退了两步，想重新开始，但脑子里仍一片空白。于是他再退后两步，想再次开始，他这样重复了三次。演讲台有4英尺高，后边没有栏杆，距墙只有5英尺宽。所以，当他第四次后退时，掉下了演讲台，跌进了隔缝中。听众们哄然大笑，有一个人还笑得跌下椅子，滚到了走道上。在平衡人寿保险公司出现这种滑稽表演，可谓前无古人。更让人拍案叫绝的是，听众真的以为这是公司特意安排的助兴节目。平衡人寿公司的一些资深员工现在还津津乐道他的演出！

可是凡斯·布什奈尔的感受如何呢？他亲口对我说，那是他一生中最没面子的事。他觉得万分羞愧，当即写了辞呈。

但是凡斯的上司说服了他，撕掉辞呈，并帮助他重建自信。后来，凡斯成了公司数一数二的演讲高手。不过，他再也不背演讲词了。我们应该以此为鉴。

我听说过很多人都背演讲稿，却不知道有谁把演讲稿扔进废纸篓后，反而说得更生动、更有效果，也更富有人性。其实，扔掉演讲稿，或许会忘掉其中几点，说起来也有些散乱，但至少会更有人情味。

林肯曾说过："我不喜欢听枯燥乏味的说教。当我听人布道时，我喜欢看到他像在跟蜜蜂搏斗。"他喜欢听演讲者自由随意且激情澎湃的演讲。背演讲稿是绝不会表现得跟蜜蜂拼命似的。

to see him act as if he were fighting bees." Lincoln said he wanted to hear a speaker cut lose and get excited. No speaker ever acts as if he were fighting bees when he is trying to recall memorized words.

ASSEMBLE AND ARRANGE YOUR IDEAS BEFOREHAND

What, then, is the proper method of preparing a talk? Simply this: search your background for significant experiences that have taught you something about life, and assemble your thoughts, your ideas, your convictions, that have welled up from these experiences. True preparation means brooding over your topics. As Dr. Charles Reynold Brown said some years ago in a memorable series of lectures at Yale University: "Brood over your topic until it becomes mellow and expansive... then put all these ideas down in writing, just a few words, enough to fix the idea... put them down on scraps of paper—you will find it easier to arrange and organize these lose bits when you come to set your material in order." This doesn't sound like such a difficult program, does it? It isn't. It just requires a little concentration and thinking to a purpose.

REHEARSE YOUR TALK WITH YOUR FRIENDS

Should you rehearse your talk after you have it in some kind of order? By all means. Here is a surefire method that is easy and effective. Use the ideas you have selected for your talk in everyday conversation with your friends and business associates. Instead of going over the ball scores, just lean across the luncheon table and say something like this: "You know, Joe, I had an unusual experience one day. I'd like to tell you about it." Joe will probably be happy to listen to your story. Watch him for his reactions. Listen to his response. He may have an interesting idea that may be valuable. He won't know that you are rehearsing your talk, and it really doesn't matter. But he probably will say that he enjoyed the conversation.

Allan Nevins, the distinguished historian, gives similar advice to writers: "Catch a friend who is interested in the subject and talk out what you have learned at length. In this way you discover facts of interpretation that you might have missed, points of arguments that had been unrealized, and the form most suitable for the story you have to tell."

THIRD / PREDETERMINE YOUR MIND TO SUCCESS

In the first chapter, you remember, this sentence was used in reference to building the right

2. 预先汇集整理你的思想

那么,准备演讲的恰当方法是什么呢?很简单:要留心生活中那些有意义的、曾经给过你人生指导的经验,然后对这些经验中的思想、理念、感悟等进行汇集整理。真正的准备,是对演讲题目的思考。查尔斯·雷诺·布朗博士多年前曾在耶鲁大学演讲时说:"谨慎思考你的题目,酝酿成熟之后,它会散发出思想的馨香……再把这些思想简要地写下来,表达清楚概念即可……通过这样的整理,那些零散的片断就很容易安排和组织了。"这听起来并不难吧?事实上也确实不难,只需要一点专注和思考就行了。

3. 在朋友面前预讲

当你准备好之后,要不要试讲一下呢?完全必要。这可以保证万无一失。用日常交谈的话语,把你的想法告诉朋友或同事,没有必要全部讲出来,只需要在吃午餐时朝他倾过身去,这样说:"乔,你知道我那天遇到了一件不同寻常的事。我想告诉你。"乔可能愿意听你的故事。这时你要观察他的反应,听听他的想法,说不定他会给你提出有价值的建议。他并不知道你是在预演,而且即使知道也没关系,他或许会说"聊得真痛快"。

杰出的历史学家艾兰·尼文斯对作家也有类似的忠告:"找一个对你的题材感兴趣的朋友,把你的想法详尽地告诉他。通过这种方式,你可以发现可能遗漏的见解、无法预料的争论,并找到最适合讲述这个故事的形式。"

三、给予积极的暗示

在第一章,你可能还记得这句话被用来指导建立对当众讲话训练的正确态度。现在你又面临用同样的法则去完成特定的目标,那就是将每一次演讲的机会当成一次成功的体验。有三种方法可以实现这一目标。

attitude toward public speaking training in general. The same rule applies to the specific task now facing you, that of making each opportunity to speak a successful experience. There are three ways to accomplish this:

LOSE YOURSELF IN YOUR SUBJECT

After you have selected your subject, arranged it according to plan, and rehearsed it by "talking it out" with your friends, your preparation is not ended. You must sell yourself on the importance of your subject. You must have the attitude that has inspired all the truly great personages of history—a belief in your cause. How do you fan the fires of faith in your message? By exploring all phases of your subject, grasping its deeper meanings, and asking yourself how your talk will help the audience to be better people for having listened to you.

KEEP YOUR ATTENTION OFF NEGATIVE STIMULI THAT MAY UPSET YOU

For instance, thinking of yourself making errors of grammar or suddenly coming to an end of your talk somewhere in the middle of it is certainly a negative projection that could cancel confidence before you started. It is especially important to keep your attention off yourself just before your turn to speak. Concentrate on what the other speakers are saying, give them your wholehearted attention and you will not be able to work up excessive stage fright.

GIVE YOURSELF A PEP TALK

Unless he is consumed by some great cause to which he has dedicated his life, every speaker will experience moments of doubt about his subject matter. He will ask himself whether the topic is the right one for him, whether the audience will be interested in it. He will be sorely tempted to change his subject. At times like these, when negativism is most likely to tear down self-confidence completely, you should give yourself a pep talk. In clear, straightforward terms tell yourself that your talk is the right one for you, because it comes out of your experience, out of your thinking about life. Say to yourself that you are more qualified than any member of the audience to give this particular talk and, by George, you are going to do your best to put it across. Is this old-fashioned Coué teaching? It may be, but modern experimental psychologists now agree that motivation based on autosuggestion is one of the strongest incentives to rapid learning, even when simulated. How much more powerful, then, will be the effect of a sincere pep talk based on the truth?

1. 确信自己的题目有意义

题目选好之后，根据计划进行整理，并和朋友聊聊，但这样的准备还不是很充分。你还要让自己确信这个题材是有意义的，必须具备坚定的态度，以此来激励自己，坚信自己。怎样才能让自己确信这一点呢?这就要详细研究题材，抓住更深层的意义，问你自己，你的演讲将如何帮助听众在听过你的演讲之后会成为更优秀的人。

2. 避免想那些使你不安的事情

举例来说，假如你设想自己可能会犯语法错误，或中间突然讲不下去，这些消极想法很可能会使你在开始之前便没有了信心。演讲之前，尤其重要的是要将注意力从自己身上移开。集中精力听别的演讲者在说什么，把全部身心放在他们身上，这样就不会给你造成过度的登台恐惧了。

3. 自己给自己鼓气

除非有可以为之牺牲的远大目标，否则每一位演讲者都会对自己的题材产生怀疑。他会问自己是否适合这个题目，听众会不会感兴趣等，因此很可能一念之间就更改题目。这时候，消极的思想极有可能彻底毁灭自信，所以你应该给自己打气，用清晰明确的话告诉自己：这次演讲很适合你，因为它来自你的经验，来自你对生活的思考；告诉自己，你比任何一个听众都更适合做这番特殊的演讲；你也会全力以赴把它说清楚。这是一种古老的自我暗示法吗？也许是。但现代实验心理学家们都同意，这种由自我暗示而产生的动机，即使是假装的，也会成为人们快速学习的最有力的诱因之一。那么，根据事实所做的真诚的自我激励，效果就会更好了。

四、表现得信心十足

美国最著名的心理学家威廉·詹姆斯曾作过这样一番论述：

FOURTH / ACT CONFIDENT

The most famous psychologist that America has produced, Professor William James, wrote as follows:

"Action seems to follow feeling, but really action and feeling go together; and by regulating the action, which is under the more direct control of the will, we can indirectly regulate the feeling, which is not.

"Thus the sovereign voluntary path to cheerfulness, if our spontaneous cheerfulness be lost, is to sit up cheerfully and to act and speak as if cheerfulness were already there. If such conduct does not make you feel cheerful, nothing else on that occasion can.

"So, to feel brave, act as if we were brave, use all of our will to that end, and a courage-fit will very likely replace the fit of fear."

Apply Professor James' advice. To develop courage when you are facing an audience, act as if you already had it. Of course, unless, you are prepared, all the acting in the world will avail but little. But granted that you know what you are going to talk about, step out briskly and take a deep breath. In fact, breathe deeply for thirty seconds before you ever face your audience. The increased supply of oxygen will buoy you up and give you courage. The great tenor, Jean de Reszke, used to say that when you had your breath so you "could sit on it" nervousness vanished.

Draw yourself up to your full height and look your audience straight in the eyes, and begin to talk as confidently as if every one of them owed you money. Imagine that they do. Imagine that they have assembled there to beg you for an extension of credit. The psychological effect on you will be beneficial.

If you doubt that this philosophy makes sense, you would change your mind after a few minutes' conversation with almost any of the class members who have preceded you in following the ideas on which this book is based. Since you can't talk to them, take the word of an American who will always be a symbol of courage. Once he was the most timorous of men; by practicing self-assurance, he became one of the boldest; he was the trust-busting, audience-swaying, Big-Stick-wielding President of the United States, Theodore Roosevelt.

"Having been a rather sickly and awkward boy," he confesses in his autobiography, "I was, as a young man, at the first both nervous and distrustful of my powers. I had to train myself painfully and laboriously not merely as regards my body but as regards my soul and spirit."

Fortunately, he has disclosed how he achieved the transformation. "When a boy," he wrote, "I

"行动似乎产生于感觉之后,但事实上却是与感觉并行的。行动在意念的直接控制之下,通过制约行动,我们也可以间接地制约不受意念直接控制的感觉。因此,假如我们失去了自然的快乐,那么,变得快乐的最佳方法就是快快乐乐地坐着或者说话,好像快乐本来就存在一样。如果这种方法还不能让你快乐,那就没有别的办法了。所以,要让自己感觉很勇敢,就要表现得真的勇敢,运用所有的意念去达到这个目标,那么勇气就很可能会取代恐惧。"

接受詹姆斯教授的忠告吧。为了培养勇气,面对观众的时候,不妨表现得你已经拥有了勇气。当然,除非你做好了准备,否则再怎么表现也不起作用。如果你对自己要讲的内容已经了然于胸,那就轻松地走出来,做一次深呼吸。深呼吸30秒,可以给你提神,给你信心和勇气。杰出的男高音简·德·雷斯基常说,如果你气充于胸,可以"胸有成竹",紧张就会消失。

身体站直,看着听众的眼睛,然后开始信心十足地演讲,好像他们每个人都欠你的钱,他们聚在那儿只不过是请求你宽限还债的时间。这种心理作用将会对你大有帮助。

如果你怀疑这种理论,可以找我班上任何一个同意这种观点的学员谈谈,不出几分钟,就会让你消除疑虑。如果你没有机会和他们交谈,就听听一个美国人说的话吧。他常常被视为勇气的象征。他也曾经非常胆小,通过这种自我鼓励的训练之后,才成为最勇敢的人——他便是反托拉斯斗士、常常左右听众、挥舞着巨杖的美国总统西奥多·罗斯福。

他在自传里说:"小时候我总是病怏怏的,又很笨拙。年轻时,我最初既紧张又没有自信,因此不得不艰难而辛苦地训练自己,不只对身体,而且对灵魂和精神进行各种训练。"

幸运的是,他揭示了自己蜕变的经过:"孩提时代,我在马利埃特的一本书里读到一段话,给我的印象极深。这段话中,一艘小型英国军舰的舰长向别人讲述如何才能做到无畏无惧。他说:刚开始的时候,每个人想有所行动,但都会感到害怕。应该学会驾驭自己,让自己表现得好像毫无畏惧。这样持之以恒,原先的假装就会变成事实,通过这种练习,就会在不知不觉中真的

read a passage in one of Marryat's books which always impressed me. In this passage, the captain of some small British man-of-war is explaining to the hero how to acquire the quality of fearlessness. He says that at the outset almost every man is frightened when he goes into action, but that the course to follow is for the man to keep such a grip on himself that he can act just as if he were not frightened. After this is kept up long enough, it changes from pretense to reality, and the man does in very fact become fearless by sheer dint of practicing fearlessness when he does not feel it.

"This was the theory upon which I went. There were all kinds of things of which I was afraid at first, ranging from grizzly bears to 'mean' horses and gunfighters; but by acting as if I were not afraid I gradually ceased to be afraid. Most men can have the same experience if they choose."

Overcoming fear of public speaking has a tremendous transfer value to everything that we do. Those who answer this challenge find that they are better persons because of it. They find that their victory over fear of talking before groups has taken them out of themselves into a richer and fuller life.

A salesman wrote: "After a few times on my feet before the class, I felt that I could tackle anyone. One morning I walked up to the door of a particularly tough purchasing agent, and before he could say no, I had my samples spread out on his desk, and he gave me one of the biggest orders I have ever received."

A housewife told one of our representatives: "I was afraid to invite the neighbors in for fear that I wouldn't be able to keep the conversation going. After taking a few sessions and getting up on my feet, I took the plunge and held my first party. It was a great success. I had no trouble stimulating the group along interesting lines of talk."

At a graduating class, a clerk said: "I was afraid of the customers, I gave them a feeling that I was apologetic. After speaking to the class a few times, I found that I was speaking up with more assurance and poise, I began to answer objections with authoritativeness. My sales went up forty-five per cent the first month after I started to speak to this class."

They discovered that it was easy to conquer other fears and anxieties and to be successful where before they may have failed. You, too, will find that speaking in public will enable you to face what each day presents with a sure touch that confidence brings. You will be able to meet the problems and conflicts of life with a new sense of mastery. What has been a series of insoluble situations can become a bright challenge to increased pleasure in living.

变成无所畏惧的勇者。

"这便是我训练自己的理论依据。刚开始的时候,我害怕的事情太多了,从大灰熊到野马,还有枪手,可是我故意假装不怕,慢慢地我就真的不再害怕。大家若是愿意,也能像我一样做到。"

克服当众讲话的恐惧,对我们做任何事情都会产生极大的影响。那些敢于接受这项挑战的人,会发现自己的人品正渐臻完善,战胜当众说话的恐惧会使自己脱胎换骨,进入更丰富、更美满的人生。

有一位推销员这样写道:"在班上站起来几次之后, 我觉得可以应付任何人了。一天早上,我走到一个平时特别凶悍的买主面前,当他还没来得及说'不'时,我已经把样品摊开在他的桌上了。结果他给了我一份最大的订单!"

一位家庭主妇也说:"原来我不敢请邻居来我家里,我怕和客人不能融洽地谈话。但是上了几次课并站起来讲话之后,我决定开一次家庭舞会。那次舞会非常成功,我往来于宾客之间,尽情地与他们谈笑。"

在一个毕业班上,一名职员说:"我很害怕和顾客说话,每次总是战战兢兢的。在班上演讲几次之后,我觉得有自信而且从容不迫了。我开始理直气壮地说出不同的意见。我在班上演讲后的第一个月,销售业绩便上升了45%。"

他们发现,他们已经能够很容易地克服恐惧或焦虑;从前可能失败的事现在却成功了。你也会发现当众讲话会让你满怀信心地面对每一天的献礼。你也可以获得一种新的胜利感,迎接生活的挑战。那么,那些曾经接二连三地袭来的困境,就会变成生活中增添情趣的愉快挑战。

3 Speaking Effectively the Quick and Easy Way

I seldom watch television in the daytime. But a friend recently asked me to listen to an afternoon show that was directed primarily to housewives. It enjoyed a very high rating, and my friend wanted me to listen because he thought the audience participation part of the show would interest me. It certainly did. I watched it several times, fascinated by the way the master of ceremonies succeeded in getting people in the audience to make talks in a way that caught and held my attention. These people were obviously not professional speakers. They had never been trained in the art of communication. Some of them used poor grammar and mispronounced words. But all of them were interesting. When they started to talk they seemed to lose all fear of being on camera and they held the attention of the audience.

Why was this? I know the answer because I have been employing the techniques used in this program for many years. These people, plain, ordinary men and women, were holding the attention of viewers all over the country; they were talking about themselves, about their most embarrassing moments, their most pleasant memory, or how they met their wives or husbands. They were not thinking of introduction, body, and conclusion. They were not concerned with their diction or their sentence structure. Yet they were getting the final seal of approval from the audience—complete attention in what they had to say. This is dramatic proof of what to me is the first of three cardinal rules for a quick and easy way to learn to speak in public:

FIRST / SPEAK ABOUT SOMETHING YOU HAVE EARNED THE RIGHT TO TAIK ABOUT THROUGH EXPERIENCE OR STUDY

The men and women whose live flesh-and-blood stories made that television program interesting were talking from their own personal experience. They were talking about something they knew. Consider what a dull program would have resulted if they had been asked to define communism or to describe the organizational structure of the United Nations. Yet that is precisely

第3章 简单而有效的演讲方法

我平时很少看电视,但最近有一位朋友建议我看看下午的某个电视节目,这个节目是专门针对家庭主妇的,收视率很高。这位朋友之所以让我收看,是因为他认为该节目中的观众参与可能会引起我的兴趣。的确如此,我看了几次,很欣赏那位主持人请观众参与谈话的方式,而观众的说话方式也引起了我的注意:这些人显然都不是职业演讲家,而且也没有受过什么沟通艺术方面的训练,甚至语法很差,还说错字。可是他们全都说得十分有趣,他们说话时似乎全没有那种上镜头的恐惧,还能吸引观众的注意力。

这是为什么呢?我找到了答案,因为我后来长期在训练中采用这种方法。这些普普通通的男人和女人,抓住了全国电视观众的注意力,他们谈的是自己:自己最困难的时刻,自己最美好的回忆,或是最初与自己的妻子或丈夫约会等等。他们根本就没有想到什么绪论、正文和结论,也不在乎遣词造句,然而他们却获得了观众的赏识,他们完全倾注于他们所要说的事情。我认为,这正是当众讲话三个简单而有效的法则。

一、讲述自己的亲身经历或知识

那些男男女女自己活生生的故事,使那个电视节目变得生动有趣,他们谈的全都是自己的亲身经历和自己精通的知识。如果他们被要求解释共产主义或描述美国的组织结构,想象一下这个节目会有多么单调乏味!但这正是无数演讲者在许多聚会中常犯的主要错误。他们认为必须讲一些自己毫无个人经历或个人兴趣与关注的东西。他们会随便拿起一个如爱国主义、民主或公正的题目,然后花上几小时无头绪地搜索什么格言集或各种场合的演讲者手册,又将他们

the mistake that countless speakers make at countless meetings and banquets. They decide they must talk about subjects of which they have little or no personal knowledge and to which they have devoted little or no attention. They pick a subject like Patriotism, or Democracy, or Justice, and then, after a few hours of frantic searching through a book of quotations or a speaker's handbook for all occasions, they hurriedly throw together some generalizations vaguely remembered from a political science course they once took in college, and proceed to give a talk distinguished for nothing other than its length. It never occurs to these speakers that the audience might be interested in factual material bringing these high-flown concepts down to earth.

At an area meeting of Dale Carnegie instructors in the Conrad Hilton Hotel in Chicago some years ago, a student speaker started like this: "Liberty, Equality, Fraternity. These are the mightiest ideas in the dictionary of mankind. Without liberty, life is not worth living. Imagine what existence would be like if your freedom of action would be restricted on all sides."

That is as far as he got, because he was wisely stopped by the instructor, who then asked him why he believed what he was saying. He was asked whether he had any proof or personal experience to back up what he had just told us. Then he gave us an amazing story.

He had been a French underground fighter. He told us of the indignities he and his family suffered under Nazi rule. He described in vivid language how he escaped from the secret police and how he finally made his way to America. He ended by saying: "When I walked down Michigan Avenue to this hotel today, I was free to come or go, as I wished. I passed a policeman and he took no notice of me. I walked into this hotel without having to present an identification card, and when this meeting is over I can go anywhere in Chicago I choose to go. Believe me, freedom is worth fighting for." He received a standing ovation from that audience.

TELL US WHAT LIFE HAS TAUGHT YOU

Speakers who talk about what life has taught them never fail to keep the attention of their listeners. I know from experience that speakers are not easily persuaded to accept this point of view—they avoid using personal experiences as too trivial and too restrictive. They would rather soar into the realms of general ideas and philosophical principles, where unfortunately the air is too rarefied for ordinary mortals to breathe. They give us editorials when we are hungry for the news.

曾在大学上的政治课中记住的一些模糊不清的通俗性概念拼凑在一起，然后上台发表一次毫无意义的冗长演讲。这些演讲者不知道，听众可能对产生这些高扬在上的概念的真实故事更感兴趣。

几年前，卡耐基成人教育班的教师们在芝加哥的康拉德·希尔顿大饭店聚会。一位学员是这样开场的："自由、平等、博爱，这些都是人类词典中最伟大的思想。没有自由，生命就没有存在的价值。设想一下，如果我们的行动处处受到限制，将是一种什么样的生存状况？"

他讲到这儿的时候，指导教师立即请他停止，问他是否有什么证据或亲身经历可以支持他刚才所说的观点。于是，他讲了一个动人心弦的故事。

他曾是一名法国的地下革命者，他讲了他和家人在纳粹统治下受尽屈辱。他以生动形象的语言，描述了自己是如何躲过秘密警察的追捕逃到美国的。最后他说："今天，当我从密歇根街来到这家饭店时，可以自由地来去。我经过一位警察身边时，他也并不注意我。我可以不用出入卡就可以走进饭店。会议结束之后，我可以按自己的意愿去芝加哥的任何地方。因此，请相信，自由是值得奋斗的。"他刚一说完，就获得了全场起立欢呼。

1. 阐释生命对自己的启示

演讲者阐释生命的启示，绝不会没有人愿意听。但是经验也告诉我，这个观点很不容易让人接受——因为人们会极力避开个人经历，认为这些事情太琐碎、太局限。他们宁愿说一些一般概念或者哲理，可惜这些更让平凡的我们无法接受。这好比我们渴望新闻，可是他们却给我们社论。我们并不反对听社论，但是这应该由那些有资格的人来说，例如报纸编辑或发行者。因此，还是谈谈生命对你的启示吧，我将会成为你的忠实听众。

据说爱默生总是喜欢听人谈话，而不论其地位多么卑微，因为他觉得自己可以从任何人身上学到一些东西。我听过的成人谈话，或许比任何人都多。说实话，一个演讲者叙述生命给他

None of us is averse to listening to editorials, when they are given by a man who has earned the right to editorialize—an editor or publisher of a newspaper. The point, though, is this: Speak on what life has taught you and I will be your devoted listener.

It was said of Emerson that he was always willing to listen to any man, no matter how humble his station, because he felt he could learn something from every man he met. I have listened to more adult talks, perhaps, than any other man west of the Iron Curtain, and I can truthfully say that I have never heard a boring talk when the speaker related what life had taught him, no matter how slight or trivial the lesson may have been.

To illustrate: Some years ago, one of our instructors conducted a course in public speaking for the senior officers of New York City banks. Naturally, the members of such a group, having many demands upon their time, frequently found it difficult to prepare adequately, or to do what they conceived of as preparing. All their lives they had been thinking their own individual thoughts, nurturing their own personal convictions, seeing things from their own distinctive angles, living their own original experiences. They had spent forty years storing up material for talks. But it was hard for some of them to realize that.

One Friday a certain gentleman connected with an uptown bank—for our purposes we shall designate him as Mr. Jackson—found four-thirty had arrived, and what was he to talk about? He walked out of his office, bought a copy of *Forbes' Magazine* at a newsstand, and in the subway coming down to the Federal Reserve Bank where the class met, he read an article entitled, "You Have Only Ten Years to Succeed." He read it, not because he was interested in the article especially, but because he had to speak on something to fill his quota of time.

An hour later, he stood up and attempted to talk convincingly and interestingly on the contents of this article.

What was the result, the inevitable result?

He had not digested, had not assimilated what he was trying to say. "Trying to say" —that expresses it precisely. He was *trying*. There was no real message in him seeking for an outlet; and his whole manner and tone revealed it unmistakably. How could he expect the audience to be any more impressed than he himself was? He kept referring to the article, saying the author said so and

的启示时,不论他说的多么琐碎、多么微不足道,我从不会觉得厌烦。

例如,几年前,我们的一位教师替纽约市一些资深的银行官员开了一门当众讲话的课程。当然,这些人的事情多得不能分身,常常感到要做好充分准备或他们心目中认为的准备很难。其实,他们一直都在思考自己的问题,有个人的信念,会从自身的角度看问题,而且积累了原始的经验。他们已经积累了40年的谈话资料,但他们有些人却不知道这一点。

在某个星期五,一位来自上区银行的先生来到训练班——因为某种原因,我们姑且叫他杰克逊先生——有45个人参加了这次训练。他准备讲什么呢?他离开办公室时,在报摊上买了一份《福布斯杂志》。在前往联邦储备银行上课所在地的地铁上,他看了杂志中的一篇文章《十年成功秘诀》。他读它并不是因为对它特别感兴趣,而是想找点谈资,以便上课时有内容可讲。

一小时后,他离开地铁,准备把这篇文章讲得妙趣横生。

可是结果呢?不可避免的结果是什么样的?

他并没有把阅读的东西消化,也没有吸收到自己想要说的东西。"想要说"这个词形容得很准确,因为他只是"想要"。他并没有想挖掘一些有深度的内容来谈,他的整个仪态和音调明显地透露了这一点。他怎么能期望听众比他自己更受感动呢?他不断地提到那篇文章,说那位作者如何如何。他的演讲里,我们了解了《福布斯杂志》很多,遗憾的是对杰克逊先生自己的东西却了解太少。

他演讲完后,指导老师说:"杰克逊先生,我们对你讲的那位作者并不感兴趣,他不在这里,我们也看不到他。我们倒是对你和你的观点感兴趣。不妨告诉我们你是怎么想的,不要谈别人怎么讲。把更多的有关你自己的事情放在演讲里,下星期再用同样的题目演讲好吗?请把那篇文章再读一遍,问问你自己是否同意那位作者的论点。如果同意,就以你自己的经验来论证。如果不同意,告诉我们为什么。就让这篇文章作为一个引子,引出你自己的演讲。"

so. There was a surfeit of *Forbes' Magazine* in it, but regrettably little of Mr. Jackson.

After he finished his talk, the iustructor said, "Mr. Jackson, we are not interested in this shadowy personality who wrote that article. He is not here. We can't see him. But we are interested in you and your ideas. Tell us what you think, personally, not what somebody else said. Put more of Mr. Jackson in this. Would you take this same subject next week? Read this article again, and ask yourself whether you agree with the author or not. If you do, illustrate the points of agreement with observatious from your own experience. If you don't agree with him, tell us why. Let this article be the starting point from which to launch your own talk."

Mr. Jackson reread the article and concluded that he did not agree with the author at all. He searched his memory for examples to prove his points of disagreement. He developed and expanded his ideas with details from his own experience as a bank executive. He came back the next week and gave a talk that was full of his own convictions, based on his own background. Instead of a warmed-over magazine article, he gave us ore from his own mine, currency coined in his own mint. I leave it to you to decide which talk made a stronger impact on the class.

LOOK FOR TOPICS IN YOUR BACKGROUND

Once a group of our instructors were asked to write on a slip of paper what they considered was the biggest problem they had with beginning speakers. When the slips were tallied, it was found that "getting beginners to talk on the right topic" was the problem most frequently encountered in early sessions of my course.

What is the right topic? You can be sure you have the right topic for you if you have lived with it, made it your own through experience and reflection. How do you find topics? By dipping into your memory and searching your background for those significant aspects of your life that made a vivid impression on you. Several years ago, we made a survey of topics that held the attention of listeners in our classes. We found that the topics most approved by the audience were concerned with certain fairly defined areas of one's background:

Early Years and Upbringing. Topics that deal with the family, childhood memories, schooldays, invariably get attention, because most of us are interested in the way other people met and overcame obstacles in the environment in which they were reared.

杰克逊先生重读了那篇文章,发现自己根本不同意作者的观点。他从记忆里搜寻事例来反驳,并以自己担任银行主管的经验详尽阐述论证自己的观点。因此,他的第二次演讲不再是翻抄杂志文章的内容,而是充满了根据他自身背景所得的理念,他给我们的是他自己矿场里的矿石,是他自己铸币厂里铸造的钱币。你想这两场演讲哪一场更能给班上学员强烈的印象?

2. 根据自己的经历寻找题目

有一次,有人请教我们的指导教师,初学演讲者所遇到的最大问题是什么?据统计发现,"教初学者根据适合的题目演讲"是初学演讲者最常碰到的问题。

什么才是适合的题目呢?假使你的生活中经历过它,或者是你经过思考使它属于你的,你就可以肯定这个题目适合你。那又该如何找题目呢?不妨翻开自己的记忆,从自己的生活背景中去搜寻生命中那些有意义,并且给你留下深刻印象的事情。几年前,我们曾在班上就能够吸引听众注意的题目做了一次调查,发现最受听众欣赏的题目都与某些特定的个人背景有关:

早年与成长的历程:与家庭、童年回忆、学校生活有关的题目,一定会引起人们的注意,因为别人在成长过程中如何应对艰难的经历,最能引起我们的兴趣。

不论何时,只要有可能,都应该把自己早年的故事融进演讲中。许多脍炙人口的戏剧、电影和故事讲的都是人们早年遇到的挑战,这就足以证明关于成长历程的题材是很有价值的,当然也适用于演讲。但是如何验证别人会对你小时候经历的事感兴趣呢?有个很简单的方法:多年以后,只要某件事情依旧鲜明地印在你的脑海中,随时都可能呼之欲出,那几乎可以保证听众会感兴趣。

早年出人头地的奋斗:这是充满了人情味的经历。例如,回忆自己早期为追求成功所做的努力,一定能吸引听众。你是如何从事某种特别的工作或行业的?是什么机遇造就了你的事业?告诉人们,你在这竞争激烈的世界创业时所遭遇的挫折、你的希望以及你的成功。如果谦虚地

Whenever possible, work into your talks illustrations and examples from your early years. The popularity of plays, movies, and stories that deal with the subject of meeting the challenges of the world in one's early years attests to the value of this area for subject matter of talks. But how can you be sure anyone will be interested in what happened to you when you were young? There's one test. If something stands out vividly in your memory after many years have gone by, that almost guarantees that it will be of interest to an andience.

Early Struggles to Get Ahead. This is an area rich in human interest. Here again the attention of a group can be held by recounting your first attempts to make your mark on the world. How did you get into a particular job or profession? What twist of circumstances accounted for your career? Tell us about your setbacks, your hopes, your triumphs when you were establishing yourself in the competitive world. A real-life picture of almost anyone's life—if told modestly—is almost surefire material.

Hobbies and Recreation. Topics in this area are based on personal choice and, as such, are subjects that command attention. You can't go wrong talking about something you do out of sheer enjoyment. Your natural enthusiasm for your particular hobby will help get this topic across to any audience.

Special Areas of Knowledge. Many years of working in the same field have made you an expert in your line of endeavor. You can be certain of respectful attention if you discuss aspects of your job or profession based on years of experience or study.

Unusual Experiences. Have you ever met a great man? Were you under fire during the war? Have you gone through a spiritual crisis in your life? These are experiences that make the best kind of speech material.

Beliefs and Convictions. Perhaps you have given a great deal of time and effort to thinking about your position on vital subjects confronting the world today. If you have devoted many hours to the study of issues of importance, you have earned the right to talk about them. But when you do, be Certain that you give specific instances for your convictions. Audiences do not relish a talk filled with generalizations. Please don't consider the casual reading of a few newspaper articles sufficient preparation to talk on these topics. If you know little more about a subject than the people in your audience, it is best to avoid it. On the other hand, if you have devoted years of study to some subject, it is undoubtedly a topic that is made to order for you. By all means, use it.

描述一些个人的真实生活，几乎是最保险的题材。

爱好及娱乐：这方面的题目可以根据个人的不同来定，因此，也是能引起听众注意的题材。讲一件完全是个人喜欢的事，一般不会出现失误。你对某一项特殊的爱好发自内心的热诚，有助于你把这个题目讲得生动有趣。

特殊领域的知识：如果你多年在同一个领域里工作，会使你成为这个领域的专家。如果你能用多年的经验或研究来讲述自己的工作或职业方面的事情，也会引起听众的注意与尊敬。

不同寻常的经历：你有没有见过名人？你有没有经历过战争？你有没有经历过精神上的危机？这些经历都可以成为最佳的演讲材料。

信仰与信念：你或许花了许多时间和精力去思考自己应该对当今世界所面临的重大问题持何种态度。那么，你当然有资格谈论它们。不过，在这样做的时候，你一定要举例子来说明你的论点，因为听众并不爱听空泛的演讲。千万不要以为随意读些报纸文章，就可以谈论这些题目。如果你自己所知的不比听众的多，还是避而不谈为妙。反过来说，既然你曾经投入了多年的时间研究某个问题，这显然是你该说的题目，因此你绝对要用它。

前面我已经指出，准备演讲并不只包括在纸上写些字，或者背诵一连串的字句，也不是从匆忙读过的书或报纸文章中抽取别人第二手的观点。而是要在你自己的脑海及心灵深处挖掘，并将贮藏在那儿的信念随时提取出来。不必怀疑那里有没有材料！那里当然有，而且贮藏丰富，正等待你去发掘。也不要以为这样的题材太个人化、太轻微，听众可能不会喜欢听。其实，正是这样的演讲才让我感到快乐和深受感动，甚至比我听过的那些职业演讲家的演讲更让我快乐，更让我感动。

只有讲那些你有资格谈论的事情，才能会使你达到学习快速有效地当众讲话的第二个要求。下面就是这一要求：

As was pointed out in Chapter Two, the preparation of a talk does not consist merely in getting some mechanical words down on paper, or in memorizing a series of phrases. It does not consist in lifting ideas secondhand from some hastily read book or newspaper article. But it does consist in digging deep into your mind and heart and bringing forth some of the essential convictions that life has stored there. Never doubt that the material is there. It is! Rich stores of it, waiting for you to discover it. Do not spurn such material as too personal, too slight for an audience to hear, I have been highly entertained and deeply moved by such talks, more entertained and more moved than I have been by many professional speakers.

Only by talking about something you have earned the right to talk about will you be able to fulfill the second requirement for learning to speak in public quickly and easily. Here it is:

SECOND / BE SURE YOU ARE EXCITED ABOUT YOUR SUBJECT

Not all topics that you and I have earned the right to talk about make us excited. For instance, as a do-it-yourself devotee, I certainly am qualified to talk about washing dishes. But somehow or other I can't get excited about this topic. As a matter of fact, I would rather forget about it altogether. Yet I have heard housewives—household executives, that is—give superb talks about this same subject. They have somehow aroused within themselves such a fury of indignation about the eternal task of washing dishes, or they have developed such ingenious methods of getting around this disagreeable chore, that they have become really excited about it. As a consequence, they have been able to talk effectively about this subject of washing dishes.

Here is a question that will help yon determine the suitability of topics you feel qualified to discuss in public: if someone stood up and directly opposed your point of view, would you be impelled to speak with conviction and earnestness in defense of your position? If you would, you have the right subject for you.

Recently, I came across some notes I had written in 1926 after I had visited the Seventh Session of the League of Nations in Geneva, Switzerland. Here is a paragraph: "After three or four. lifeless speakers read their manuscripts, Sir George Foster of Canada took the floor. With immense satisfaction I noted that he had no papers of notes of any kind. He gestured almost constantly. His

二、对演讲的题目充满热情

并不是你我有资格谈论的话题就一定会让我们充满热情。例如,我是一个天天干家务的忠实丈夫,我确实有资格谈谈关于洗盘子的事。可是我对此并没有热情,事实上我根本不愿想它,你想我能把这个题目讲好吗?但是,我却听过家庭主妇们把这个题目说得精彩极了。她们内心当中或许对永远洗不完的盘子有一股怒火,或许发现了一种新方法可以处理这恼人的工作——不管怎样,她们对这个题材更喜欢,所以她们可以对这个题目说得津津有味。

这里有个问题,可以帮你确认某个题目是否适合你演讲:如果有人站起来直接反对你的观点,你是否有百分之百的信心为自己激烈地辩护?如果有的话,这题目一定适合你。

我1926年曾去瑞士的日内瓦参观国际联盟第七次大会,后来对当时的情形做了笔记。最近我无意间翻看了这些笔记。以下是其中一段:"在三四个死气沉沉的演讲者念完手稿之后,加拿大的乔治·佛斯特爵士上台发言。他没有带任何纸张或字条,我不禁大为欣赏。他对他要讲的事情非常专注,常常通过手势来强调他的观点。他很想让自己的思想被听众了解,热切地把那些珍贵的理念传达给听众。这种情形十分清楚,犹如窗外澄明的日内瓦湖。我一直在教学上倡导的那些法则,在他的演讲中展现得完美无缺。"

我常常想起乔治爵士的演讲。他真诚而热心。因此,只有对演讲的题目有真实感受,才会有如此的感情显露。富尔顿·辛主教是美国最具震撼力的演讲家之一,他从早年的生活中也学到了这一课。

他在《不虚此生》一书中写道:"我被选出来参加学院的辩论队。在一次辩论的前一晚,我们的辩论教授把我喊到办公室,责骂了我一顿。

heart was in what he was saying. He had something he very much wanted to get across. The fact that he was earnestly trying to convey to the audience certain convictions that he cherished in his own heart was as plain as Lake Geneva outside the windows. Principles I have been advocating in my teaching were beautifully illustrated in that talk."

I often recall that speech by Sir George. He was sincere; he was earnest. Only by choosing topics which are felt by the heart as well as thought out by the mind will this sincerity be made manifest. Bishop Fulton J. Sheen, one of America's most dynamic speakers, learned this lesson early in life.

"I was chosen for the debating team in college," he wrote in his book, *Life Is Worth Living*, "and the night before the Notre Dame debate, our professor of debating called me to his office and scolded me."

"'You are absolutely rotten. We have never had anybody in the history of this college who was a worse speaker than yourself.'

"'Well,' I saki, trying to justify myself, 'if I am so rotten why did you pick me for the team?'

"'Because,' he answered, 'you can think; not because you can talk. Get over in that corner. Take a paragraph of your speech and go through it.' I repeated a paragraph over and over again for an hour, at the end of which he said, 'Do you see any mistake in that?' 'No.' Again an hour and a half, two hours, two and a half hours, at the end of which I was exhausted. He said, 'Do you still not see what is wrong?'

"Being naturally quick, after two hours and a half, I caught on. I said, 'Yes. I am not sincere. I am not myself. I do not talk as if I meant it.'"

At this point, Bishop Sheen learned a lesson he always remembered: *he put himself into his talk*. He became excited about his subject matter. Only then the wise professor said, "Now, you are ready to speak!"

When a member of one of our classes says, "I don't get excited about anything, I lead a humdrum sort of life," our instructors are trained to ask him what he does in his spare time. One goes to the movies, another bowls, and another cultivates roses. One man told his instructor that he collected books of matches. As the instructor continued to question him about this unusual hobby, he gradually became animated. Soon he was using gestures as he described the cabinets in which

"'你真是饭桶！本院有史以来还没有一个演讲者比你更差的！'

"'那，'我说，我想替自己辩解，'既然我是一个大饭桶，为什么还挑我参加辩论队？'

"'因为你会思考，而不是你会讲。'他回答道，'到那边去，从演讲词中抽出一段，把它讲出来。'我把这段话反反复复地讲了一个钟头，然后他说：'你看出其中的错误了吧？''没有。'于是接下来又是两个半钟头。最后我筋疲力尽。他说：'你还看不出错在哪里吗？'

"过了两个半钟头，我终于找到了问题的关键。我说：'看出来了，我没有诚意。我心不在焉，没有真实的情意。'"

就这样，辛主教学到了他永生难忘的一课：把自己沉浸在演讲中。他开始让自己对演讲的题材产生热情。直到这时，博学的教授才说："现在你可以讲了！"

如果我班上有学员说"我对什么事都不感兴趣，我过的是平凡单调的生活"，我们的指导老师便会问他闲暇时都做些什么。有人说看电影，有人说打保龄球，有人则说种玫瑰花。有一位学员告诉指导老师，他收集有关火柴的书籍。于是，老师继续问他这个不寻常的嗜好，他渐渐来了精神。不一会儿，他便兴致勃勃地描述起自己收藏火柴书的小书柜来。他告诉老师，他几乎收藏了世界各国关于火柴的书。等他对自己最喜爱的话题产生兴趣之后，指导老师打断他："为什么不谈谈这个话题呢？我觉得挺有意思的。"他说他从来没想到会有人感兴趣！这个人几乎耗尽了一生的心血，对自己这一嗜好充满了感情，几乎成了一种狂热，而他却否定它的价值，认为它不值一谈。指导老师告诉他，要想知道一个话题有没有趣味和价值，最好的方法就是问自己对它有多感兴趣。后来，他以收藏家的姿态兴高采烈地畅谈了一个晚上。后来我又听说他去参加各种午餐俱乐部，向人们演讲有关火柴书籍收藏的话题，因此得到了地方人士的推崇。

如果你希望迅速而轻易地学会当众讲话，那么这个例子正好可以引出第三条法则。

he stored his collection. He told his instructor that he had match books from almost every country in the world. When he became excited about his favorite topic, the instructor stopped him: "Why don't you tell us about this subject? It sounds fascinating to me." He said that he didn't think anyone would be interested! Here was a man who had spent years in pursuit of a hobby that was almost a passion with him; yet he was negative about its value as a topic to speak about. This instructor assured this man that the only way to gauge the interest value of a subject was to ask yourself how interested you are in it. He talked that night with all the fervor of the true collector, and I heard later that he gained a certain amount of local recognition by going to various luncheon clubs and talking about match book collecting.

This illustration leads directly to the third guiding principle for those, who want a quick and easy way to learn to speak in public.

THIRD / BE EAGER TO SHARE YOUR TALK WITH YOUR LISTENERS

There are three factots in every speaking situation: the speaker, the speech or the message, and the audience. The first two rules in this chapter dealt with the interrelationships of the speaker to a speech. Up to this point there is no speaking situation. Only when the speaker relates his talk to a living audience will the speaking situation come to life. The talk may be well prepared; it may concern a topic which the speaker is excited about; but for complete success, another factor must enter into his delivery of the talk. He must make his listeners feel that what he has to say is important to them. He must not only be excited about his topic, but he must be eager to transfer this excitement to his listeners. In every public speaker of note in the history of eloquence, there has been this unmistakable quality of salesmanship, evangelism, call it what you will. The effective speaker earnestly desires his listeners to feel what he feels, to agree with his point of view, to do what he thinks is right for them to do, and to enjoy and relive his experience with him. He is audience-centered and not self-centered. He knows that the success or failure of his talk is not for him to decide—it will be decided in the minds and hearts of his heaters.

I trained a number of men in the New York City Chapter of the American Institute of Banking to speak during a thrift campaign. One of the men in particular wasn't getting across to his audience. The

三、激发听众的共鸣

演讲由三种因素构成:演讲者、演讲内容和听众。本章的前两条法则讨论了演讲者和演讲内容之间的相互关系,但仅止于此,还不是真正的演讲。只有当演讲者把自己的演讲与听众发生联系以后,演讲才真正完成。演讲也许准备周详、演讲者也许对自己的话题充满热情,然而要真正演讲成功,却还有另一个因素必须考虑:演讲者必须使听众觉得他所说的对他们很重要。他不仅要自己对这个话题富有热情,还必须把这种热情传达给听众。历史上那些著名的雄辩家都具有这样的王婆卖瓜的本领,或者是传播福音之术。高明的演讲者总是热切地希望听众感受到他的感受,同意他的观点,并做他认为该做的事,与他一同分享他的快乐,一同分担他的忧愁。他会以听众为中心,而不是以自我为中心。他明白自己演讲的成败不是由他来决定,而是由听众的头脑和心灵来决定。

在推行节俭运动期间,我到美国银行学会纽约分会培训了一批人。其中有一个人无法和听众沟通。要帮助他,首先要让他对自己的题目燃起热情之火。我告诉他,先一个人静静地待在一边,把自己的题目反复想几遍,直到对它产生热情。我要让他记住这样一个事实:纽约遗嘱公证法庭记录显示,85%的人去世时没有留下分文,只有3.3%的人留下1万美元或更多的财产。我还让他明白,他现在不是去求别人施舍,或者要求别人做根本无法做到的事。他应该这样对自己说:"我是在替这些人着想,要使他们老了以后衣食无忧,过上舒适安逸的生活,并且给妻儿留下安全的保障。"我还让他相信,他是在做一项了不起的社会服务工作。总之,他必须把自己当作一名斗士。

他考虑了这些事实,终于使自己热血沸腾,激发出兴趣和热情,并开始觉得自己的确是身担重任。于是,他外出演讲时,那满载信念的语言感染了人们。他将节俭的利益告诉大家,因为

first step in helping that man was to fire up his mind and heart with zeal for his subject. I told him to go off by himself and to think over this subject until he became eathusiastic about it. I asked him to remember that the Probate Court Records in New York show that more than 85 per cent of the people leave nothing at all at death; that only 3.3 per cent leave $10,000 or over. He was to keep constantly in mind that he was not asking people to do him a favor or something that they could not afford to do. He was to say to himself: "I am preparing these people to have meat and bread and clothes and comfort in their old age, and to leave their wives and children secure." He had to remember he was going out to perform a great social service. In short, he had to be a crusader.

He thought over these facts. He burned them into his mind. He aroused his own interest, stirred his own enthusiasm, and came to feel that he, indeed, had a mission. Then, when he went out to talk, there was a ring to his words that carried conviction. He sold his listeners on the benefits of thrift because he had an eager desire to help people. He was no longer just a speaker armed with facts; he was a missionary seeking converts to a worthwhile cause.

At one time in my teaching career I relied considerably on the textbook rules of public speaking. In doing this I was merely reflecting some of the bad habits that had been instilled into me by teachers who had not broken away from the stilted mechanics of elocution.

I shall never forget my first lesson in speaking. I was taught to let my arm hang loosely at my side, with the palm turned to the rear, fingers half-closed and thumb touching my leg. I was drilled to bring the arm up in a picturesque curve, to give the wrist a classical turn, and then to unfold the forefinger first, the second finger next, and the little finger last. When the whole aesthetic and ornamental movement had been executed, the arm was to retrace the course of the curve and rest again by the side of the leg. The whole performance was wooden and affected. There was nothing sensible or honest about it.

My instructor made no attempt to get me to put my own individuality into my speaking; no attempt to have me speak like a normal, living human being conversing in an energetic manner with my audience.

Contrast this mechanistic approach to speech training with the three primary rules I have been discussing in this chapter. They are the basis of my entire approach to training in effective speaking. You will come across them again and again in this book. In the next three chapters each of these rules will be explained in detail.

他热切地想帮助他们。他不再是个只知道陈述事实的演讲者,他已经成了一名为理想事业而改变信仰的传教士。

在我的教学生涯中,曾经非常依赖教科书中的教条。我只是照搬我的老师们长年灌输给我的一些坏习惯,而他们也没能从虚浮的演讲风气中有所突破。

我永远都忘不了我的第一次演讲课:老师让我将双臂轻轻地垂放在身体两侧,手掌朝后,所有手指都蜷曲一半,大拇指轻触大腿。然后,举起手臂,画出优美的弧线,以便让手腕优雅地转动。接着张开食指,然后是中指,最后是小指。当这一整套合乎美学的、装饰性的动作完成之后,手臂还必须回溯刚才的那道弧线,再放于双腿两侧。这整套表演显得虚假而做作,既没有意义,也不真实。

我的老师并未教我将个性融于演讲之中, 也不让我像平常人那样富有朝气地与听众谈天说地。

请把这种机械的演讲训练方式与我在这一章所介绍的三项主要原则互相对比一下。这三项原则是我"高效演讲训练"全套方法的根本。你将会在本书中一再看到它们。在下面三章中,将逐条详细解释这些法则。

Part Two
Speech, Speaker, and Audience

1 Earning the Right to Talk

Many years ago, a Doctor of Philosophy and a rough-and-ready fellow who had spent his youth in the British Navy were enrolled in one of our classes in New York. The man with the degree was a college professor; the ex-tar was the proprietor of a small side-street trucking business. His talks were far better received by the class than those given by the professor. Why? The college man used beautiful English. He was urbane, cultured, refined. His talks were always logical and clear. But they lacked one essential—concreteness. They were vague and general. Not once did he illustrate a point with anything approaching a personal experience. His talks were usually nothing more than a series of abstract ideas held together by a thin string of logic.

On the other hand, the trucking firm proprietor's language was definite, concrete, and picturesque. He talked in terms of everyday facts. He gave us one point and then backed it up by telling us what happened to him in the course of his business. He described the people he had to deal with and the headaches of keeping up with regulations. The virility and freshness of his phraseology made his talks highly instructive and entertaining.

I cite this instance, not because it is typical of college professors or of men in the trucking business, but because it illustrates the attention-compelling power of rich, colorful details in a talk.

There are four ways to develop speech material that guarantees audience attention. If you follow these four steps in your preparation you will be well on the way to commanding the eager

第二篇 演讲、演讲者和听众

第1章 做好演讲前的准备

多年以前,有两个人同时参加了我在纽约的一个训练班。一个是哲学博士,在大学当教授;另一个是在街头流动的小摊贩,他年轻的时候曾是一名英国海军,为人豪爽而粗鲁。但令人奇怪的是,那位流动摊贩的演讲远比大学教授的更吸引人。这是为什么呢?大学教授上台演讲时,总是以漂亮的词汇发言,台风优雅,讲话条理清楚;但是他缺少了一个必备的因素——具体化。他的谈话太不明确了,太过空泛了。他从未用个人经历解释过什么观点。他的演讲只不过是用一条逻辑的绳子连接在一起的抽象的理念。

至于那位流动摊贩,却正好相反:他开口之后,就可以立即抓住问题的核心,内容具体而明确。他的演讲充满了生活气息。他说出一个观点,然后用他生意中发生的真实事件来证明。他讲了他与之打交道的人,以及遵守各项规则的头痛之事。他那男人的气质和新奇的词句,使他的演讲非常吸引人。

我之所以举这个例子,并不是因为它是大学教授或流动摊贩的典型,而是因为它正好说明只有充满生气、说话具体而且明确的人,才会吸引别人的注意力。

有四种组织演讲材料的方法, 保证可以获得听众的注意。如果你在演讲时遵循这四个步骤,你就可以十拿九稳地调动听众的热切关注。

attention of your listeners.

FIRST/ LIMIT YOUR SUBJECT

Once you have selected your topic, the first step is to stake out the area you want to cover and stay strictly within those limits. Don't make the mistake of trying to cover the open range. One young man attempted to speak for two minutes on the subject of "Athens from 500 B.C. to the Korean War". How utterly futile! He barely had gone beyond the founding of the city before he had to sit down, another victim of the compulsion to cover too much in one talk. This is an extreme example, I know; I have heard thousands of talks, less encompassing in scope, that failed to hold attention for the same reason—they covered far too many points. Why? Because it is impossible for the mind to attend to a monotonous series of factual points. If your talk sounds like the World Almanac you will not be able to hold attention very long. Take a simple subject, like a trip to Yellowstone Park. In their eagerness to leave nothing out, most people have something to say about every scenic view in the Park. The audience is whisked from one point to another with dizzying speed. At the end, all that remains in the mind is a blur of waterfalls, mountains, and geysers. How much more memorable such a talk would be if the speaker limited himself to one aspect of the Park, the wildlife or the hot springs, for example. Then there would be time to develop the kind of pictorial detail that would make Yellowstone Park come alive in all its vivid color and variety.

This is true of any subject, whether it be salesmanship, baking cakes, tax exemptions, or ballistic missiles. You must limit and select before you begin, narrow your subject down to an area that will fit the time at your disposal.

In a short talk, less than five minutes in duration, all you can expect is to get one or two main points across. In a longer talk, up to thirty minutes, few speakers ever succeed if they try to cover more than four or five main ideas.

SECOND/ DEVELOP RESERVE POWER

It is far easier to give a talk that skims over the surface than to dig down for facts. But when

一、限定题材范围

演讲的题目一旦选好，第一步就是要确定演讲所包含的范围，并且把话题严格限定在其中。不要妄想讲一个无所不包的话题。例如有一个年轻人想用两分钟的时间就“从公元前500年至朝鲜战争时期的雅典”这个题目发表看法。这几乎是痴人说梦话！因为他刚讲完雅典城的建造就该下台了。他想在一场演讲中包含太多的东西，最终却只有失败，而且不明不白。当然，这只是个极端的例子。我曾听过许多演讲，都因为范围不确定，结果都出于同样的原因——包含了太多的论点，以致无法吸引听众的注意力。为什么呢?因为人们的注意力不可能一直放在一连串单调的事实上。如果你的演讲听起来像是一部世界年鉴，那么你根本无法长时间抓住听众的注意力。假设你选了一个简单的题目，如“黄石公园之旅”，那么大多数演讲者都会十分详细地介绍公园中每个景色，不肯遗漏半点东西。虽然这样听众会被引导着由这一点到另一点，但最后只能记住一些模糊的瀑布、山岭和喷泉。如果演讲者把自己的话题限定在公园的某一个方面，例如野生动物或者温泉，这场演讲将会令人难以忘怀！这样，你便有时间来介绍那些生动而有趣的细节，将黄石公园那鲜明的颜色和无穷的变化栩栩如生地展现在听众眼前。

这个道理用于任何题目都很有效，不论它讲的是销售术、烤蛋糕、减免税赋或者是炸弹。在演讲开始以前先对题材加以限制和选择，把题目缩小至某一个范围，这样就会适合自己的时间。

在短短的不超过5分钟的演讲里，我们只能期望说明一两点。就算是30分钟的演讲，但演讲者若想包含4个或5个以上的主要概念，也很少会成功。

二、深入思考题材

做浮光掠影的演讲，要比深入事实的演讲容易得多。但前者仅能让听众获得很少的印象，

you take the easy way you make little or no impression on the audience. After you have narrowed your subject, then the next step is to ask yourself questions that will deepen your understanding and prepare you to talk with authority on the topic you have chosen: "Why do I believe this? When did I ever see this point exemplified in real life? What precisely am I trying to prove? Exactly how did it happen?"

Questions like these call for answers that will give you reserve power, the power that makes people sit up and take notice. It was said of Luther Burbank, the botanical wizard, that he produced a million plant specimens to find one or two superlative ones. It is the same with a talk. Assemble a hundred thoughts around your theme, then discard ninety.

"I always try to get ten times as much information as I use, sometimes a hundred times as much," said John Gunther not long ago. The author of the bestselling "Inside" books was speaking of the way he prepared to write a book or give a talk.

On one occasion in particular, his actions bore out his words. In 1956, he was working on a series of articles on mental hospitals. He visited institutions, talked to supervisors, attendants, and patients. A friend of mine was with him, giving some small assistance in the research, and he told me they must have walked countless miles up stairs and down, along corridors, building to building, day after day. Mr. Gunther filled notebooks. Back in his office, he stacked up government and state reports, private hospital reports, and reams of committees' statistics.

"In the end," my friend told me, "he wrote four short articles, simple enough and anecdotal enough to make good speeches. The paper on which they were typed weighed, perhaps, a few ounces. The filled notebooks, and everything else he used as the basis for the few ounces of product, must have weighed twenty pounds".

Mr. Gunther knew that he was working with pay dirt. He knew he couldn't overlook any of it. An old hand at this sort of thing, he put his mind to it, and he sifted out the gold nuggets.

A surgeon friend of mine said: "I can teach you in ten minutes how to take out an appendix. But it will take me four years to teach you what to do if something goes wrong." So it is with speaking: Always prepare so that you are ready for any emergency, such as a change of emphasis

甚至全无印象。因此，在题目范围确定之后，下一步就要问自己一些问题，加深自己的了解，使自己可以用权威的口吻来讲述这个题目："我为什么会相信这一点？我在现实生活中有没有看到？我究竟想要证明什么？它是怎样发生的？"

像这样一类问题的答案可以使你深入思考演讲题材，让听众集中注意力。据说植物界的天才路德·伯班克，为了寻找一两种高级品种而培养了100万种植物品种。演讲也是如此，围绕主题汇集100种思想，然后舍去其中90种。

"我总是搜集比我要使用的材料多10倍的东西，有时甚至达到上百倍，"约翰·甘德不久前这样说。他是畅销书《内涵》的作者。他在这里说的是准备写作或演讲的方法。

有一次，他的行动恰好印证了他的话。当时，他正准备写一系列关于精神病院的文章。他前往各地的医院，和院长、护士及病人分别谈话。我的一位朋友跟随他，为他的研究工作提供了一些小的帮助。后来我朋友告诉我，他们从这栋大楼到另外一栋大楼，不停地上下楼梯，日复一日地沿着走道不知走了多少路。甘德先生记录了许多笔记本。在他的办公室，到处都放了政府与各州的报告、私立医院的报告、各委员会的统计资料。

"最后，"我朋友说，"他写了4篇短文，简单而又趣味横生，是很好的演讲题材。写成文章的几张纸也许只有几盎司。可是，那些密密麻麻的笔记本以及其他材料，也即他创作出这几盎司产品的依据，却超过了20磅。"

甘德先生知道自己的回报不值一提，但他也知道自己不应该忽视任何一部分。他是这一行业的资深专家，他把心思全放在上面，然后筛选出金块。

我的一位外科医生朋友也说："我可以在10分钟内教会你如何取出盲肠。然而，要教你出了差错时该如何应付，却要花4年时间。"演讲也是如此：必须做好周密准备，以应付变化。例如，可能由于前一名演讲者的观点，你不得不当场决定改变自己观点的重心；或者是在演讲后的讨论

because of a previous speaker's remarks, or a well-aimed question from the audience in the discussion period following your talk.

You, too, can acquire reserve power by selecting your topic as soon as possible. Don't put it off until a day or two before you have to speak. If you decide on the topic early you will have the inestimable advantage of having your subconscious mind working for you. At odd moments of the day when you are free from your work, you can explore your subject, refine the ideas you want to convey to your audience. Time ordinarily spent in reverie while you are driving home, waiting for a bus, or riding the subway, can he devoted to mulling over the subject matter of your talk. It is during this incubation period that flashes of insight will come, just because you have determined your topic far in advance and your mind subconsciously works over it.

Norman Thomas, a superb speaker who has commanded the respectful attention of audiences quite opposed to his political point of view, said: "If a speech is to be of any importance at all, the speaker should live with the theme or message, turning it over and over in his mind. He will be surprised at how many useful illustrations or ways of putting his case will come to him as he walks the street, or reads a newspaper, or gets ready for bed, or wakes up in the morning. Mediocre speaking very often is merely the inevitable and the appiopriate reflection of mediocre thinking, and the consequence of imperfect acquaintance with the subject in hand."

While you are involved in this process you will be under strong temptation to write your talk out, word for word. Try not to do this, for once you have set a pattern, you are likely to be satisfied with it, and you may cease to give it any more constructive thought. In addition, there is the danger of memorizing the script. Mark Twain had this to say about such memorization: "Written things are not for speech; their form is literary; they are stiff, inflexible, and will not lend themselves to happy effective delivery with the tongue. Where their purpose is merely to entertain, not to instruct, they have to be limbered up, broken up, colloquialized, and turned into the common form of unpremeditated talk; otherwise they will bore the house—not entertain it."

Charles F. Kettering, whose inventive genius sparked the growth of General Motors, was one of America's most renowned and heartwarming speakers. Asked if he ever wrote out any part or all

时间里,回答听众关注的更多问题。

选好题目之后,应尽快对其深入思考。千万不能等到演讲的前一两天才去做。如果及早确定了题目,你的潜意识便能为你发挥很大的作用,这对你大有好处。在每天工作完成后的零散时间里,你可以深入思考自己的题材,提炼你想传达给听众的理念。在驾车回家的途中、在等候公共汽车或乘地铁时,你也可以将这些时间用来思考自己的演讲题材。也许灵光一闪的顿悟,正巧来自这段孕育的过程,因为你已经提前思考了题材,你的大脑早已对它做了潜意识的加工。

诺曼·托马斯是世界一流的演讲家,即使面对强烈反对他的政治观点的听众他也能驾驭自如,获得他们的敬佩。他说:"如果一篇演讲真的十分重要,演讲者就应该和其主题或内涵融为一体。他必须在头脑里反复思考。他会惊讶地发现,不管是走在街上,还是在看报纸,或者准备睡觉,或者清晨醒来时,自己观点的例证和演讲方式就会自动涌现。平庸的思考只能产生平庸的演讲;这种不可避免的现象,正是因为对题目认识不清楚的结果。"

当你置身于这一过程中时,你会感到一种强烈的诱惑,总想把自己的演讲内容写下来。但千万不要这样做,因为你一旦写下来,它就成了一个固定的形式,你自己也许会觉得很满意了,就会停止更有价值的思考。而且,你甚至会陷入背诵的陷阱。马克·吐温曾这样评论背诵讲稿:"笔写的东西不是为演讲而准备的;因为它的形式是文学的,生硬而缺乏灵活性,无法再通过嘴来愉悦而有效地传达。如果演讲的目的是想让听众感到快乐,而不是说教,就需要把它们变得温和、简洁,使之尽量口语化,使用一种就像平时并不怎么经过认真思考就说出来的方式。否则,就会烦死整屋子的人,而不是让他们高兴。"

查尔斯·吉特林的发明天才促成了通用汽车公司的成长,他也是美国最著名、最真诚的演讲家之一。当他被问到有没有把演讲的内容部分或全部写下来的时候,他说:"我认为,由于我要讲的话实在太重要了,所以我不能在纸上写下来。我必须把自己一丝一毫的东西都写进听众

of his talks, he replied: "What I have to say is, I believe, far too important to write down on paper. I prefer to write on my audience's mind, on their emotions, with every ounce of my being. A piece of paper cannot stand between me and those I want to impress."

THIRD/ FILL YOUR TALK WITH ILLUSTRATIONS AND EXAMPLES

In the Art of Readable Writing, Rudolf Flesch begins one of his chapters with this sentence: "Only stories are really readable." He then shows how this principle is used by Time and Reader's Digest. Almost every article in these top-circulation magazines either is written as pure narrative or is generously sprinkled with anecdotes. There is no denying the power of a story to hold attention in talking before groups as well as writing for magazines.

Norman Vincent Peale, whose sermons have been heard by millions on radio and television, says that his favorite form of supporting material in a talk is the illustration or example. He once told an interviewer from the Quarterly Journal of Speech that "the true example is the finest method I know of to make an idea clear, interesting, and persuasive. Usually, I use several examples to support each major point."

Readers of my books are soon aware of my use of the anecdote as a means of developing the main points of my message. The rules from How to Win Friends and Influence People can be listed on one and a half pages. The other two hundred and thirty pages of the book are filled with stories and illustrations to point up how others have used these rules with wholesome effect.

How can we acquire this most important technique of using illustrative material? There are five ways of doing this: Humanize, Personalize, Specify, Dramatize, and Visualize.

HUMANIZE YOUR TALK

I once asked a group of American businessmen in Paris to talk on "How to Succeed." Most of them merely listed a lot of abstract qualities and gave preachments on the value of hard work, persistence, and ambition.

So I halted this class, and said something like this: "We don't want to be lectured to. No one enjoys that. Remember, you must be entertaining or we will pay no attention whatever to what you are saying. Also remember that one of the most interesting things in the world is

的脑子里，写进他们的情感中。在我和我尽力想感动的听众之间，纸条是没有存在的空间的。”

三、列举实例使演讲生动有趣

在《流畅的写作艺术》一书中，鲁道夫·弗烈奇在其中一章这样开篇写道：“只有故事才真正具有可读性。”然后他引用了《时代杂志》和《读者文摘》来作为例子。他说，在这两份雄踞畅销排行榜首位的杂志中，几乎每一篇文章都充满了趣闻轶事。因此，在当众讲话中，要想具备驾驭听众注意的能力，也应该学习这两本杂志中文章的写作方法。

诺曼·文森特·皮尔牧师的讲道，曾通过收音机和电视机而被无数人接受。他说，在演讲中，他最喜欢举出实例来支持自己的论点。他对《演讲季刊》的采访者说：“用真实的例子，是我知道的最好的方法。它可以使一个观点变得清晰而有趣，更具有说服力。我通常同时采用好几个例子来证明每一个主要论点。”

凡是看过我的书的读者很快也会发现，我同样喜欢用有趣的事情来概括总结我的观点。《人性的弱点》一书中的法则，列出来其实只有一页半，而其余230页全都是故事和例证，解释别人是如何使用这些法则取得实效的。

那么，在演讲中应该怎么做呢？概括起来有5种方法：人性化、个人化、翔实化、戏剧化和视觉化。

1. 使演讲富有人性

有一次，我要求一群在巴黎的美国商人以“成功之道”为题做演讲。他们大多数人都只列举了一大串抽象的东西，给了一大堆勤奋工作、持之以恒或者远大目标的说教。

于是，我打断了他们：“我们都不想听别人说教，也没有人会喜欢。记住，你的话必须让我们感到愉快和有趣，否则不论你说什么我们都不会听的。同时要记住，世界上最有趣的事情，

sublimated, glorified gossip. So tell us th [illegible] of two men you have known. Tell why one succeeded and why the othe [illegible] y listen to that, remember it, and possibly profit by it."

There was a cer [illegible] invariably found it difficult to interest either himself or his audien [illegible] d the human interest suggestion and told us of two of his classmate [illegible] en so conservative that he had bought shirts at the different stores i [illegible] which ones laundered best, wore longest, and gave the most servi [illegible] was always on pennies; yet, when he was graduated—it was an e [illegible] a high opinion of his own importance that he was not willing to beg [illegible] ay up, as the other graduates were doing. Even when the third ann [illegible] e was still making laundry charts of his shirts, while waiting for s [illegible] come his way. It never came. A quarter of a century has passed s [illegible] tisfied and soured on life, still holds a minor position.

The speaker then con [illegible] ry of one of his classmates who had surpassed all expectations.T [illegible] ixer. Everyone liked him. Although he was ambitious to do big thin [illegible] an. But he was always on the lookout for opportunity. Plans were t [illegible] k World's Fair. He knew engineering talent would be needed there [illegible] n in Philadelphia and moved to New York. There he formed a partn [illegible] in the contracting business. They did considerable work for the telep [illegible] s finally taken over by that concern at a large salary.

I have recorded here only [illegible] speaker told. He made his talk interesting and illuminating wit [illegible] an interest details. He talked on and on—this man who could n [illegible] three—minute speech—and he was surprised to learn, when h [illegible] e floor on this occasion for ten minutes.The speech had been so [illegible] o everyone. It was his first real triumph.

都是那些精致典雅、妙语连珠的趣 [illegible] 识的两个人的故事，并分析为什么一个人会成功，而另一个人却 [illegible] 样的故事，会记住它，可能还会从中获益。”

这个班有个学员，他总觉得要提起自己的兴趣或激发别人的兴趣太难了。可是这天晚上，他就抓住“人的兴趣”的建议，给大家讲了他大学两个同学的故事：一个人小心谨慎，以至于买衬衫也要在不同的商店各买一件，并制出表格显示哪一件最经得起洗熨，穿得最久，以便让每一块钱的投资获得最大的效用。他的心思只在钱上。可是，这个人从工学院毕业后，自视甚高，不愿像别的毕业生那样从基层开始做起。因此当3年后同学聚会时，他仍旧在画他的衬衫洗熨表，还在等待好差事凭空降临，结果什么也没有等到。从那时候起，过了25年，那个人满腹怨恨与不满，一辈子都在一个小职位上。然后演讲者将这个失败者与另一个同学相比。现在这个同学已经超越了当初的自我期望。他与人相处融洽，大家都喜欢他。他不乏雄心壮志，想成就一番事业，但却从绘图员做起。不过他一直在寻找机会。当时，纽约世界博览会正处在规划阶段，他知道那儿需要工程人才，所以辞去了费城的职务，迁往纽约。他与人合伙，搞起了承包工程的业务，承揽了很多电话公司的业务，最后被博览会高薪聘请。

我这里写下来的，仅仅是那位演讲者所说的概述。他本人的讲述中还有许多有趣而充满人情味的细节，使他的演讲妙趣横生。他不停地说着——这个人平时是说不了3分钟的——这次他却吃惊地发现自己讲了足足有10分钟。由于讲得太精彩了，大家似乎都觉得太短了。这也是他第一次演讲成功。

每个人都可以从这个故事中得到一些启示：如果平淡的演讲能穿插一些富含人性的趣味故事，将会引人入胜。演讲者应该只提出自己的论点，然后用具体的事例来作为例证。这样的演讲，肯定能抓住听众的注意力。当然，这种人性化故事最丰富的源泉，正是你自己的生活背景。

Almost everyone can profit by this incident. The average speech would be far more appealing if it were rich with human interest stories. The speaker should attempt to make only a few points and to illustrate them with concrete cases. Such a method of speechbuilding can hardly fail to get and hold attention.

Of course, the richest source of such human interest material is your own background. They are the surest means of holding attention; don't neglect them.

PERSONALIZE YOUR TALK BY USING NAMES

By all means, when you tell stories involving others, use their names, or, if you want to protect their identity, use fictitious names. Even impersonal names like "Mr. Smith" or "Joe Brown" are far more descriptive than "this man" or "a person." The label identifies and individualizes. As Rudolf Flesch points out, "Nothing adds more realism to a story than names; nothing is as unrealistic as anonymity." Imagine a story whose hero has no name.

If your talk is full of names and personal pronouns you can be sure of high listenability, for you will have the priceless ingredient of human interest in your speech.

BE SPECIFIC—FILL YOUR TALK WITH DETAIL

You might say at this point, "this is all very fine, but how can I be sure of getting enough detail into my talk?"There is one test. Use the 5-W formula every reporter follows when he writes a news story: answer the questions When? Where? Who? What? and Why? If you follow this formula your examples will have life and color. Let me ill ustrate this with an anecdote of my own, one that was published by the Reader's Digest:

"After leaving college, I spent two years traveling through South Dakota as a salesman for Armour and Company. I covered my territory by riding on freight trains. One day I had to lay over in Redfield, S.D.,for two hours to get a train going south. Since Redfield was not in my territory I couldn't use the time for making sales. Within a year I was going to New York to study at the American Academy of Dramatic Arts, so I decided to use this spare time practicing speaking. I wandered down through the train yards and began rehearsing a scene for Macbeth. Thrusting out my arms, I cried dramatically: ' Is this a dagger which I see before me, the handle toward my hand? Come, let me clutch thee: I have thee not, and yet I see thee still.'

亲身经历是抓住听众注意力最可靠的方法,千万不要忽视。

2. 用人名使演讲富有个性

如果讲故事的时候要提到某个人,那就一定要讲出他的名字。不过,为了保护别人的隐私,可以用个假名。即使用的是"史密斯先生"或"乔·布朗"这种不具个人特性的名字,也比使用"这个人"或"一个人"更能使故事生动有趣。姓名有证明和显现个体的功能,就像鲁道夫·弗烈屈指出的:"没有什么更能比名字增加故事的真实性了。隐姓埋名是最虚假不过的。"试想一下,如果故事里的主角没名没姓,将是什么样子?

如果你的演讲中使用具体的名字与个人的代称,你的演讲将会有很强的可听性,因为它已经具备了人性化这一可贵的要素。

3. 使演讲充满细节

对此你可能会存有疑惑:"这确实不错, 可是我如何才能让我的演讲有足够多的细节?"有一个方法可以作个测试——即使用新闻记者写新闻故事时遵循的"5W":何时(When)? 何地(Where)? 何人(Who)? 何事(What)? 为何(Why)? 如果你依照这五要素来准备,你的举例便会详尽周到,栩栩如生。让我拿自己一件趣事来加以说明吧。这则趣事曾刊登在《读者文摘》上:

"离开大学后,我在铁甲公司当了两年销售员,一直在南达科他州四处跑。我搭乘运货卡车来完成我的旅途。有一次,我正在莱德菲尔,两小时后才能搭上一列南行的火车。由于这里不是我负责的区域,所以我不能利用这段时间去推销。再过不到一年我就要去纽约美国戏剧艺术学院读书,所以我决定利用这段空闲来练习台词。我漫无目的地走过车场,开始演练莎士比亚的戏剧《麦克白》中的一幕。我举起双臂,戏剧性地高呼:'难道我眼前所见是匕首吗?它的手柄正朝着我。来吧,让我抓住你! 我抓不着你,但我依然看见了你!'

"正当我沉浸在表演中时,4名警察突然朝我扑来,问我为什么恐吓妇女?就算他们指控我

"I was still immersed in the scene when four policemen leaped upon me and asked why I was frightening women. I couldn't have been more astounded if they had accused me of robbing a train. They informed me that a housewife had been watching me from behind her kitchen curtains a hundred yards away. She had never seen such goings-on. So she called the police, and when they approached they heard me ranting about daggers.

"I told them I was ' practicing Shakespeare, ' but I had to produce my order book for Armour and company before they let me go."

Notice how this anecdote answers the questions posed in the 5-W formula above.

Of course, too much detail is worse than none. All of us have been bored by lengthy recitals of superficial, irrelevant details. Notice how in the incident about my near-arrest in a South Dakota town there is a brief and concise answer to each of the 5-W questions. If you clutter your talk with too much detail, your audience will blue-pencil your remarks by refusing to give you their complete attention. There is no blue-pencil more severe than inattentiveness.

DRAMATIZE YOUR TALK BY USING DIALOGUE

Suppose you want to give an illustration of how you succeeded in calming down an irate customer by using one of the rules of human relations. You could begin like this:

"The other day a man came into my office. He was pretty mad because the appliance we had sent out to his house only the week before was not working properly. I told him that we would do all we could to remedy the situation. After a while he calmed down and seemed satisfied that we had every intention to make things right." This anecdote has one virtue—it is fairly specific—but it lacks names, specific details, and, above all, the actual dialogue which would make this incident come alive. Here it is with these added qualities:

"Last Tuesday, the door of my office slammed and I looked up to see the angry features of Charles Blexam, one of my regular customers. I didn't have time to ask him to take a seat. 'Ed, this is the last straw, ' he said, 'you can send a truck right out and cart that wash machine out of my basement.'

"I asked him what was up. He was too willing to reply.

"'It won't work, ' he shouted, ' the clothes get all tangled, and my wife's sick and tired

抢劫火车,我都不会这么惊异的。他们告诉我,有一个家庭主妇在30米远的厨房窗帘后面一直看着我。她从没有见过这样的情况,所以打电话给警方。他们到达时,正好听到我在狼哭鬼嚎地表演关于匕首的情节。

"我告诉他们我是在演练莎士比亚戏剧,但是直到我出示了铁甲公司的订货簿以后,他们才放我走。"

请注意,这则故事是如何体现上述五要素的。

不过,细节过多又比没有细节更糟。每个人都会被冗长而肤浅的细节搞得厌烦透顶。你们看,我叙述自己在南达科他州差点儿被捕的经历时,对每一个要素只作了简明扼要的叙述。因此,如果你的演讲全是鸡毛蒜皮的事,听众必然会不耐烦,不会听你讲话。最糟糕的演讲,莫过于不能抓住听众的注意力了。

4. 利用对话使演讲戏剧化

假设你要举例说明自己如何应用人际关系的原则成功地平息了一位顾客的愤怒,你可能会这样开始:

"前几天,有个人闯进了我的办公室。他非常愤怒,因为我们上一周送到他家里去的洗衣机不能正常工作。我对他说,我们将竭尽所能弥补失误。过了一会儿,他平静下来,对我们全心全意要把这件事情做好显得很满意。"这则小故事有个优点,就是十分详细。可是它缺少姓名、特殊的过程,而且最关键的是缺少能使这件事活生生地呈现在人们面前的真实对话。这里就给它添加一些对话材料:

"上星期二,我办公室的门砰的一声被推开。我抬起头来,只看见查尔斯·伯烈克逊先生怒气冲天。他是我的一位常客。我还没有来得及请他坐下,他劈头就说:'艾德,我要让你帮我做最后一件事:你马上派一辆卡车去,把那台洗衣机给我从地下室运回来。'

of it.'

"I asked him to sit down and explain it in more detail.

"'I haven't got time to sit down. I'm late for work and I wish I'd never come in here to buy an appliance in the first place. Believe me, I'll never do it again.' Here he hit the desk with his hand and knocked over my wife's picture.

"' Look, Charley,' I said,' if you will just sit down and tell me all about it, I promise to do whatever you want me to do.' With that, he sat down, and we calmly talked it over."

It isn't always possible to work dialogue into your talk, but you can see how the direct quotation of the conversation in the excerpt above helps to dramatize the incident for the listener. If the speaker has some imitative skill and can get the original tone of voice into the words, dialogue can become more effective. Also, dialogue gives your speech the authentic ring of everyday conversation. It makes you sound like a real person talking across a dinner table, not like a pedant delivering a paper before a learned society or an orator ranting into a microphone.

VISUALIZE BY DEMONSTRATING WHAT YOU ARE TALKING ABOUT

Psychologists tell us that more than eighty-five per cent of our knowledge comes to us through visual impressions.No doubt this accounts for the enormous efectiveness of television as an advertising as well as entertainment medium. Public speaking, too,is a visual as well as auditory art.

One of the best ways to enrich a talk with detail is to incorporate visual demonstration into it. I remember a talk given in an industrial class that was a masterpiece of visual detail. The speaker was poking good-natured fun at inspectors and efficiency experts. His mimicry of the gestures and bodily antics of these gentlemen as they inspected a broken-down machine was more hilarious than anything I have ever seen on television. What is more, visual detail made that talk memorable—I for one shall never forget it, and I am sure the other members of that class are still talking about it.

It is a good idea to ask yourself, "How can I put some visual detail into my talk?" Then proceed to demonstrate, for, as the ancient Chinese observed,one picture is worth ten thousand

"我问他出了什么事。他气急了,几乎无法清楚地回答。

"'它根本不能用,'他大吼道,'衣服全缠在一起,我老婆讨厌死它,烦死它了。'

"我请他坐下来,让他解释得更清楚些。

"'我才没时间坐呢。我上班已经迟到了!我想我以后再也不会来你这里买电器了。请相信,我再也不买了。'说到这儿,他伸出手来又是拍打桌子,又是敲我太太的照片。

"'听我说,查理,'我说,'你坐下来把情况都告诉我,我愿意替你做你要我做的一切事,好吧?'听了我这话,他这才坐下,我们总算平静地把事情讨论个清楚。"

当然,不可能每次都能把对话加进演讲。不过,你应该可以看出来,上面例子直接引用对话,对于听众有助于增加戏剧性。如果演讲者还有模仿技巧,把原来的声调语气表现出来,那么这些对话就更见效果了。而且,对话是日常生活中的会话,可以使演讲更为真实可信。它使你听起来像个充满了真情实意的人,是在隔着桌子说话,而不是像个老学究在学富五车的学会会员面前宣读论文,或像个大演讲家对着麦克风穷吼。

5. 使演讲内容视觉化

心理学家告诉我们,85%以上的知识是通过视觉印象传递给我们的。这正好解释了电视成为广告与娱乐的主要媒介并收效显著的原因。当众讲话也是一样,是一种听觉艺术,同时还是一种视觉艺术。

采用细节来丰富演讲,最好的方法就是在其中加入有利于视觉吸收的展示。我记得在一个工业界人士培训班上的一场演讲,其中的视觉细节实在是一篇杰作。演讲者模仿视察员和效率专家们检查损坏的机器时所做的各种手势与滑稽动作,比我在电视上所看过的一切都形象生动得多。这些视觉细节使那场演讲很难忘记——至少我是忘不了的。我也相信,其他学员至今一定还会谈到它。

words.

FOURTH/ USE CONCRETE, FAMILIAR WORDS THAT CREATE PICTURES

In the process of getting and holding attention, which is the first purpose of every speaker, there is one aid, one technique, that is of the highest importance. Yet, it is all but ignored. The average speaker does not seem to be aware of its existence. He has probably never consciously thought about it at all. I refer to the process of using words that create pictures. The speaker who is easy to listen to is the one who sets images floating before your eyes. The one who employs foggy, commonplace, colorless symbols sets the audience to nodding.

Herbert Spencer, in his famous essay on the "Philosophy of Style," pointed out long ago the superiority of terms that call forth bright pictures:

"We do not think in generals but in particulars... We should avoid such a sentence as:

"'In proportion as the manners, customs, and amusements of a nation are cruel and barbarous, the regulations of their penal code will be severe!'

"And in place of it, we should write:

"'In proportion as men delight in battles, bull fights, and combats of gladiators, will they punish by hanging, burning, and the rack.'"

Picture-building phrases swarm through the pages of the Bible and through Shakespeare like bees around a cider mill. For example, a commonplace writer would have said that a certain thing would be "superfluous," like trying to improve the perfect. How did Shakespeare express the same thought? With a picture phrase that is immortal: "To gild refined gold, to paint the lily, to throw perfume on the violet."

Did you ever pause to observe that the proverbs that are passed on from generation to generation are almost all visual sayings? "A bird in the hand is worth two in the bush." "It never rains but it pours." "You can lead a horse to water but you can't make him drink." And you will find the same picture element in almost all the similes that have lived for centuries and grown hoary with too much use: "Sly as a fox." "Dead as a doornail." "Flat as a pancake." "Hard as a rock."

问问自己"我怎样才能给我的谈话加入一些视觉细节"是个好主意。然后就会像古代中国人所观察到的那样,证明"百闻不如一见"的道理。

四、充分利用具体熟悉的语言

演讲者的第一目标是把握听众的注意力。在此过程中,还有一项极为重要的技巧,然而,它却完全被忽视了。一般的演讲者似乎并没有注意到它的存在,恐怕也从未有意识地想到过它。我所指的这一技巧,就是使用能形成图画般鲜明景象的字眼。能够让听众听来轻松愉快的演讲者,最善于在听众眼前塑造鲜明的景象。使用模糊不清、繁琐乏味语言的演讲者,只会让听众打瞌睡。

赫伯特·斯宾塞早就在他那篇著名的论文《风格哲学》中指出,优秀的文字能够激发读者对鲜明图画的联想:

"我们并不做一般性的思考,而是要做特殊性的思考……我们应该尽量避免这样的句子:

"'一个国家的民族性、风俗及娱乐如果残酷而野蛮,那么,他们的刑罚必然也很严厉。'

"我们应该把它改写成:

"'一个国家的老百姓如果喜爱战争、斗牛,并从奴隶公开格斗中取乐,那么他们的刑罚将包括绞刑、烧烙及拷打。'"

《圣经》和莎士比亚著作中同样充满了图画般的字句,就像蜂蜜围着苹果汁一样多。例如,一位平凡的作家在评论某件事是多余时,他会说这种努力完全是想把已经很完美的事情再加以改善。但莎士比亚又会怎样表达呢?他可以写出不朽的图画般的字句:"替精炼过的黄金镀金,替百合花上彩油,把香水洒在紫罗兰上。"

你有没有注意到,那些世代相传的谚语几乎全都具有视觉效果?"一鸟在手,胜过两鸟在林"、"不鸣则已,一鸣惊人"、"你可以把马牵到水边,却不能逼它喝水"。在那些流传了好几个世

Lincoln continually talked in visual terminology. When he became annoyed with the long, complicated, red-tape reports that came to his desk in the White House, he objected to them, not with colorless phraseology, but with a picture phrase that it is almost impossible to forget. "When I send a man to buy a horse," he said, "I don't want to be told how many hairs the horse has in his tail. I wish only to know his points."

Make your eye appeals definite and specific. Paint mental pictures that stand out as sharp and clear as a stag's antlers silhouetted against the setting sun. For example, the word "dog" calls up a more or less definite picture of such an animal—perhaps a cocker spaniel, a Scottish terrier, a St. Bernard, or a Pomeranian. Notice how much more distinct an image springs into your mind when a speaker says "bulldog" —the term is less inclusive. Doesn't "a brindle bulldog" call up a still more explicit picture? Is it not more vivid to say "a black Shetland pony" than to talk of "a horse"? Doesn't "a white bantam rooster with a broken leg" give a much more definite and sharp picture than merely the word "fowl"?

In The Elements of Style, William States, Jr., states: "If those who have studied the art of writing are in accord on any one point, it is on this: the surest way to arouse and hold the attention of the reader is by being specific, definite, and concrete. The greatest writers—Homer, Dante, Shakespeare—are effective largely because they deal in particulars and report the details that matter. Their words call up pictures." This is as true of speaking as of writing.

I once devoted a session years ago in my course in Effective Speaking to an experiment in being factual. We adopted a rule that in every sentence the speaker must put either a fact or a proper noun, a figure, or a date. The results were revolutionary. The class members made a game of catching one another on generalities; it wasn't long before they were talking, not the cloudy language that floats over the head of an audience, but the clear-cut, vigorous language of the man on the street.

"An abstract style," said the French philosopher Alain, "is always bad. Your sentences should be full of stones, metals, chairs, tables, animals, men, and women."

This is true of everyday conversation as well. In fact, all that has been said in this chapter about the use of detail in talks before groups applies to general conversation. It is detail that makes

纪而且被广泛使用的比喻里,我们也不难发现同样的图画效果:"如狐狸般狡猾"、"僵死得像一枚钉子"、"像薄煎饼那样平"、"硬得像石头"。

林肯也一直使用有视觉效果的语言来讲话。当他厌烦每天送到他白宫办公桌上的冗长而复杂的官方报告时,他并不是用毫无色彩的话来反对,而是用几乎不可能忘记的图像词句来反对。"当我派一个人出去买马时,"他说,"我并不想这个人告诉我这匹马的尾巴有多少根毛,我只希望知道它有什么特点。"你看,他并没有用那种平淡的语句来表达他的意思。

我们要用具体、耳熟能详的语言描绘出内心的景象,使它突出、显著、分明,就像落日余晖映照着公鹿头角的长影。例如,"狗"这个词一般会让人想起某种动物的具体形象——也许是只短腿、长毛、大耳下垂的小猎犬;也许是一只苏格兰犬;也许是一只圣伯纳犬,或者是一只波密雷尼亚犬。但是演讲者如果说出"牛犬"时(一种短毛、方嘴、勇敢而顽强的犬),请注意你的脑海里浮出的形象会更加具体。"一只有斑纹的牛犬"是不是让你有了更鲜明的印象?"一匹黑色的雪特兰小马",是不是比说"一匹马"形象得多?"一只白色、断了一条腿的矮种公鸡",是不是比"鸡"这个词更能给人具体的图像效果?

小威廉·史特茨在《风格之要素》中说道:"那些研究写作艺术的人,如果说他们的观点有一致的地方,那么这个观点就是:能够抓住读者注意力的最稳妥的方法就是要具体、明确而详细。像荷马、但丁、莎士比亚等最伟大的作家,他们的高明之处,就在于他们在处理特殊的情境和关键的细节时,他们的语句能唤起读者脑海里的景象。"写作是这样,讲话也同样如此。

多年以前,我和参加"高效演讲"课程班的学员进行了一项实验:讲述事实。我们订了一个规则:演讲者必须在每个句子里加入一个事实、一个专有名词、一个数字或一个日期。这次实验极其成功。学员们拿它当游戏,彼此指出对方的毛病。没花多长时间,他们便不再说那些只会让人感到晦涩不明的语言了,他们说的全都是大街上普通人都能明白的活泼的语言。

conversation sparkle. Anyone who is intent upon making himself a more effective conversationalist may profit by following the advice contained in this chapter. Salesmen, too, will discover the magic of detail when applied to their sales presentations. Those in executive positions, housewives, and teachers will find that giving instructions and dispensing information will be greatly improvet by the use of concrete, factual detail.

法国哲学家艾兰说:“抽象的风格总是不好的。在你的句子里,应该全是石头、金属、椅子、桌子、动物、男人和女人。”

日常对话也是如此。事实上,本章所说的一切有关当众讲话的技巧,同样也适用于日常交谈。正是细节使谈话充满了光彩。任何人要想成为一个高超的谈话者,只要牢记这些忠告,就会大有收获。销售员使用它,会发现它特有的魔力;那些公司主管、家庭主妇和教师也将会发现,自己在下达命令和传播知识、传达消息时,因为使用了具体、翔实的细节,效果会大大改进。

2 Vitalizing the Talk

Right after the First World War, I was in London working with Lowell Thomas, who was giving a series of brilliant lectures on Allenby and Lawrence of Arabia to packed houses. One Sunday I wandered into Hyde Park to the spot near Marble Arch entrance where speakers of every creed, color, and political and religious persuasion are allowed to air their views without interference from the law. For a while I listened to a Catholic explaining the doctrine of the infallibility of the Pope, then I moved to the fringes of another crowd, intent upon what a Socialist had to say about Karl Marx. I strolled over to a third speaker, who was explaining why it was right and proper for a man to have four wives! Then I moved away and looked back at the three groups.

Would you believe it? The man who was talking about polygamy had the fewest number of people listening to him! There was only a handful. The crowds around the other two speakers were growing larger by the minute. I asked myself why? Was it the disparity of topics? I don't think so. The explanation, I saw as I watched, was to be found in the speakers themselves. The fellow who was talking about the advantages of having four wives didn't seem to be interested in having four wives himself. But the other two speakers, talking from almost diametrically opposed points of view, were wrapped up in their subjects. They talked with life and spirit. Their arms moved in impassioned gestures. Their voice, rang with conviction. They radiated earnestness and animation.

Vitality, aliveness, enthusiasm—these are the first qualities I have always considered essential in a speaker. People cluster around the energetic speaker like wild turkeys around a field of autumn wheat.

How do you acquire this vital delivery that will keep the attention of your audience? In the course of this chapter I will give you three sovereign ways to help you put enthusiasm and excitement into your speaking.

第2章 赋予演讲生命力

第一次世界大战刚结束，我就到伦敦，和罗维尔·托马斯共事。他当时正在为阿拉伯的阿伦比和劳伦斯发表一连串精彩绝伦的演讲，听众连连爆满。有一个星期天，我散步走进海德公园。在公园的大理石拱门入口附近，各种思想、种族、政治、宗教信仰的演讲者都可以畅所欲言，不受法律的干预。我先是听了一位天主教徒解释教皇无谬论，然后我又向前走，听到一位社会主义者在谈论卡尔·马克思主义。后来我又走到第三个演讲者那里，他正在阐释一个男人应该有4个妻子才算恰当！然后我站在远处，观察那三群人。

反正信不信由你，那个鼓吹一夫多妻制的家伙听众是最少的，屈指可数。另外两个演讲者身边的人群却越来越多。我问自己这是为什么?难道是因为不同的题目吗?我想不是。我观察后认识到，问题出在三位演讲者身上。那位大谈娶4个老婆如何好的家伙，自己却不像有兴趣讨4个老婆的样子；而另外两个演讲者，却针对所有对立的观点来阐释观点，沉浸在自己的演讲中。他们在拼命地演讲，舞动双臂做着激烈的手势，声音高昂而充满信念，散发出无穷的热情与活力。

生命力、活力及热情——这三种因素我一直认为是演讲者首先必须具备的条件。人们聚集在生龙活虎的演讲者四周，就像野雁围着秋天的麦田旋转。

那么，怎样才能做到这种富有活力的演讲，牢牢地吸引听众的注意力呢?本章将教你3个妙方，帮助你将自己的热情和激情融入演讲中。

FIRST/ CHOOSE SUBJECTS YOU ARE EARNEST ABOUT

In Chapter Three was stressed the importance of feeling deeply about your subject. Unless you are emotionally involved in the subject matter you have chosen to talk about, you cannot expect to make your audience believe in your message. Obviously, if you select a topic that is exciting to you because of long experience with it, such as a hobby or recreational pursuit, or because of deep reflection or personal concern about it (as, for instance, the need for better schools in your community), you will have no difficulty in talking with excitement. The persuasive power of earnestness was never more vividly demonstrated to me than in a talk made before one of my classes in New York City more than two decades ago. I have heard many persuasive talks, but this one, which I call the Case of Blue Grass vs. Hickory Wood Ashes, stands out as a kind of triumph of sincerity over common sense.

A top-flight salesman of one of the best-known selling organizations in the city made the preposterous statement that he had been able to make blue grass grow without the aid of seeds or roots. He had, according to his story, scattered hickory wood ashes over newly plowed ground. Presto! Blue grass had appeared! He firmly believed that the hickory wood ashes, and the hickory wood ashes alone, were responsible for the blue grass.

Commenting on his talk, I genfiy pointed out to him that his phenomenal discovery would, if true, make him a millionaire, for blue grass seed was worth several dollars a bushel. I also told him that it would make him the outstanding scientist of all history. I informed him that no man, living or dead, had ever been able to perform the miracle he claimed to have performed: no man had ever been able to produce life from inert matter.

I told him that very quietly, for I felt that his mistake was so palpable, so absurd, as to require no emphasis in the refutation. When I had finished, every other member of the course saw the folly of his assertion; but he did not see it, not for a second. He was in earnest about his contention, deadly in earnest. He leaped to his feet and informed me that he was not wrong. He had not been relating theory, he protested, but personal experience. He knew whereof he spoke. He continued to talk, enlarging on his first remarks, giving additional information, piling up additional evidence, sincerity and honesty ringing in his voice.

一、选择熟悉的话题

在第三章一再强调，对自己的演讲题目要有深刻的感受。除非你对这个题目有特别的偏爱，否则别想让听众相信你。道理很简单，如果你对这个题目有实际接触和经验，对它充满了热情，或者是你已经对题目做过深入思考，有个人的关注(例如你的社区需要更好的学校)，那你就会满腔热情，不愁演讲时不会热心了。我至今还记得20多年前的一场演讲，因为演讲者的热诚而造成的说服力现在还鲜明地呈现在我的眼前，还没有一场演讲比它更精彩的。我听过很多令人心服的演讲，可是这个被我称之为“兰花和山胡桃木灰”的演讲实例，却因为以热诚战胜常识而独树一帜。

原来，纽约一家极具知名度的销售公司，有一位极优秀的销售员提出了一个反常的观点，说他已经能够使“兰花”在既无花种、又无草根的情况下生长。据说他曾将山胡桃木灰撒在新犁过的地里，然后兰花在眨眼间便长出来了！所以他坚信山胡桃木灰——而且只有山胡桃木灰——才是兰花草长出来的原因。

评论时，我温和地向他指出，如果他这种非凡的发现是真的，将使他在一夜之间暴富，因为兰花的种子价值不菲，而且这项发现还将使他成为人类历史上杰出的科学家。但是我告诉他，事实上没有一个人曾经完成，或有能力完成这个奇迹——从无机物中培植出生命。

这个错误是如此明显，以至于根本没有必要反驳，所以我平静地告诉了他这些。我说完后，其他学员也看出了他谈话的荒谬之处，但是他却不这么看。他想都没有想，立刻站起来告诉我说他没有错。他对自己的发现极其热衷，甚至到了不可思议的地步，他还大声说没有引用论据，只是陈述了他自己的经验而已。他知道自己在说什么。然后他继续往下说，并扩大了原先的论述，提出了更多的资料，举出了更多的证据，声音中透露出了完完全全的真诚。

Again I informed him that there was not the remotest hope in the world of his being right or even approximately right or within a thousand miles of the troth. In a second he was on his feet once more, offering to bet me five dollars and to let the U.S.Department of Agriculture settle the matter.

And do you know what happened? Several members in the class were won over to his side. Many others were beginning to be doubtful. If I had taken a vote I am certain that more than half of the businessmen in that class would not have sided with me.I asked them what had shaken them from their original position. One after another said it was the speaker's earnestness, his belief, so energetically stated, that made them begin to doubt the common sense viewpoint.

Well, in the face of that display of credulity I had to write the Department of Agriculture. I was ashamed, I told them to ask such an absurd question. They replied, of course, that it was impossible to get blue grass or any other living thing from hickory wood ashes, and they added that they had received another letter from New York asking the same question. That salesman was so sure of his position that he sat down and wrote a letter, too!

This incident taught me a lesson I'll never forget. If a speaker believes a thing earnestly enough and says it earnestly enough, he will get adherents to his cause, even though he claims he can produce blue grass from dust and ashes. How much more compelling will our convictions be if they are arrayed on the side of common sense and truth!

Almost all speakers wonder whether the topic they have chosen will interest the audience. There is only one way to make sure that they will be interested: stoke the fires of your enthusiasm for the subject and you will have no difficulty holding the interest of a group of people.

A short time ago, I heard a man in one of our classes in Baltimore warn his audience that if the present methods of catching rock fish in Chesapeake Bay were continued the species would become extinct. And in a very few years! He felt his subject. It was important. He was in real earnest about it. Everything about his matter and manner showed that. When he arose to speak, I did not know that there was such a creature as a rock fishin Chesapeake Bay. I imagine that more of the audience shared my lack of knowledge and lack of interest. But before the speaker finished, all of us would probably have been willing to sign a petition to the legislature to protect the rock fish by law.

我只好再次告诉他，他不可能是正确的，他正确的可能性是零。他马上又站了起来，提出要和我赌5美元，让美国农业部来解答这件事。

你猜想发生了什么?这个班的若干学员站到了他那一边，另外还有许多人犹疑不定。我相信，要是来一次表决的话，这个班有一半以上的商务人士不会同意我的观点。我问他们为什么改变自己最初的观点?他们异口同声地说，是演讲者的热诚和确信使他们对常识产生了怀疑。

既然这样，我只好给农业部写了一封信。我对他们说，问这样幼稚的问题很不好意思。他们当然回答说，要使兰花或其他东西从山胡桃木灰里长出来，是根本不可能的。他们还说收到了另一封同样的信，原来那位销售员真的很相信他自己的发现，因此也给农业部写了信。

这件事给了我一个永难忘记的启发——如果演讲者真的确信某件事，并充满热情地谈论它，便能让人们相信，即使是宣称自己能从尘土和灰烬中培植出兰花也没有关系。既然这样，如果我们大脑中归纳、整理出来的信念是正确的常识和真理，那该会多么令人信服啊!

几乎所有的演讲者都会对自己选择的题目能否引起听众的兴趣心存疑虑。其实，要让人们对你的题目感兴趣，方法很简单：激发你自己对题目的狂热之情，就不愁没有办法激发人们的兴趣。

不久前，我们巴尔的摩培训班的一位学员警告人们，说如果继续用现在捕捞奇沙比克湾石鱼的方法捕石鱼的话，这里的石鱼将会绝迹。他真的非常关注这个问题，因为这件事很重要。他的一言一行无不表明了这一点。在他讲话之前，我并不知道在奇沙比克湾有什么石鱼，我想大多数听众也所知甚少，而且也不怎么感兴趣。可是，由于他表现得如此热切，他还没有讲完，我们都愿意联名，向立法机关请求立法保护石鱼。

有人曾问美国前驻意大利大使理查·华胥本·乔尔德，作为一个意趣无穷的作家，他成功的秘诀是什么?他回答说："我非常热爱生命，所以不能静止不动。我只是觉得必须告诉人们这点

Richard Washburn Child, the former American Ambassador to Italy, was once asked the secret of his success as an interesting writer. He replied: "I am so excited about life that I cannot keep still. I just have to tell people about it." One cannot keep from being enthralled with a speaker or writer like that.

I once went to hear a speaker in London; after he was through, one of our party, Mr. E. F. Benson, a well-known English novelist, remarked that he enjoyed the last part of the talk far more than the first. When I asked him why, he replied: "The speaker himself seemed more interested in the last part, and I always rely on the speaker to supply the enthusiasm and interest."

Here is another illustration of the importance of choosing your topics well.

A gentleman, whom we shall call Mr. Flynn, was enrolled in one of our classes in Washington, D.C. One evening early in the course, he devoted his talk to a description of the capital city of the United States. He had hastily and superficially gleaned his facts from a booklet issued by a local newspaper. They sounded like it—dry, disconnected, undigested. Though he had lived in Washington for many years, he did not present one personal instance of why he liked the city. He merely recited a series of dull facts, and his talk was as distressing for the class to hear as it was agonizing for him to give.

A fortnight later, something happened that touched Mr. Flynn to the core: an unknown driver had smashed into his new car while it was parked on the street and had driven away without identifying himself. It was impossible for Mr. Flynn to collect insurance and he had to foot the bill himself. Here was something that came hot out of his experience. His talk about the city of Washington, which he laboriously pulled out sentence by sentence, was painful to him and his audience; but when he spoke about his smashed-up car, his talk welled up and boiled forth like Vesuvius in action. The same class that had squirmed restlessly in their seats two weeks before now greeted Mr. Flynn with a heartwarming burst of applause.

As I have pointed out repeatedly, you cannot help but succeed if you choose the right topic for you. One area of topics is sure-fire: talk about your convictions! Surely you have strong beliefs about some aspect of life around you. You don't have to search far and wide for these subjects—they generally lie on the surface of your stream of consciousness, because you often

罢了。"每个人都会被这样的演讲者或作家情不自禁地吸引。

我有一次在伦敦听人演讲,演讲完后,我的一个同伴本森先生评论说,这场演讲的最后一部分比第一部分更精彩。本森先生是位知名的英国小说家。我问他为什么,本森先生回答说:"演讲者自己对最后一部分的兴趣似乎更大一些,而我一向都很注重演讲者的热情和兴趣。"

这里还有一个例子,说明了选择演讲题目的重要性。

有一位先生,我们姑且叫他弗莱恩先生,参加了我们在华盛顿的训练班。在课程开始的一天晚上,他要介绍首都华盛顿。他从一家地方报纸发行的一本小册子里匆匆忙忙地搜集了一些资料,然后为我们演讲。虽然他在华盛顿住了许多年,但却没有举出一个亲身经历来说明他为什么喜欢这个地方,所以听起来十分的枯燥、无序而生硬。他只是一味地陈述一连串枯燥无趣的事实,大家听了不舒服,他自己也很别扭。

但是在两个星期后发生了一件事情让他感触极深:他刚买的新车停放在路边上,被人开车撞坏了,并且驾车逃逸。弗莱恩先生不可能要求保险理赔,只得自掏腰包。这件事来自他的亲身经历。当他介绍华盛顿时语言枯燥,让自己和听众都很难受。当他说起自己的车被撞坏时,却讲得十分真切,滔滔不绝,好似维苏威火山爆发。两星期前,大家听他的演讲时还觉得枯燥无味,现在却发出了热烈的掌声。

我一再指出,如果演讲题目选好了,想不成功也很难。比如谈自己的信念这种题目,就很容易吸引听众!你对自己的生活必然会有强烈的信仰,因此你不必再四处寻找,它们通常就在你的意识当中,你时常都会想到它们。

不久以前,电视台播出了立法委员就死刑举行的听证会。许多证人出席了这次会议,对这个问题提出正反两方面的意见。其中一个证人是洛杉矶警员,他显然对这个议题很有想法。他有11位警察同事都死于和罪犯的搏斗中,所以他曾对这个问题再三思考,产生了需要死刑的强

think about them.

Not long ago, a legislative hearing on capital punishment was presented on television. Many witnesses were called to give their viewpoints on both sides of this controversial subject. One of them was a member of the police department of the city of Los Angeles, who had evidently given much thought to this topic. He had strong convictions based on the fact that eleven of his fellow police officer, had been killed in gun battles with criminals. He spoke with the deep sincerity, of one who believed to his heart's core in the righteousness of his cause.

The greatest appeals in the history of eloquence have all been made out of the depths of someone's deep convictions and feelings. Sincerity rests upon belief, and belief is as much a matter of the heart and of warmly feeling what you are saying as it is of the mind and coldly thinking of what to say. "The heart has reasons that the reason does not know." In many classes I have had frequent occasions to verify Pascal's trenchant sentence. I remember a lawyer in Boston who was blessed with a striking appearance and who spoke with admirable fluency, but when he finished speaking people said: "Clever chap." He made a surface impression because there never seemed to be any feeling behind his glittering facade of words. In the same class, there was an insurance salesman, small in stature, unprepossessing in appearance, a man who groped for a word now and then, but when he spoke there was no doubt in any of his listeners' minds that he felt every word of his talk.

It is almost a hundred years since Abraham Lincoin's assassination in the presidential box of Ford's Theatre in Washington, D.C., but the deep sincerity of his life and his words still lives with us. As far as knowledge of law is concerned, scores of other men of his time outstripped him. He lacked grace, smoothness, and polish. But the honesty and sincerity of his utterances at Gettysburg, Cooper Union, and on the steps of the Capitol in Washington, have not been surpassed in our history.

You may say, as one man once did, that you have no strong convictions or interests. I am always a little surprised at this, but I told this man to get busy and get interested in something. "What, for instance?" he asked. In desperation I said, "Pigeons." "Pigeons?" he asked in a bewildered tone. "Yes," I told him, "pigeons. Go out on the square and look at them, feed them, go to the library and read about them, then come back here and talk about them." He did. When

烈信念。他饱含真情地说出了自己的理由,引起了听证会上人们的轰动。

历来最伟大的雄辩都来自于演讲者的强烈信念和感觉。真诚是建立在信仰之上的,而信仰则出自内心当中对自己所要说的话题的热爱,出于头脑的冷静思考。"心灵会拥有连理性都不知晓的理性。"我在许多班上都曾见证了帕斯卡这句犀利的话。我记得有一位波士顿律师,他仪表出众,说话畅达,但是他演讲完了之后大家都说:"好一个精明的家伙。"原来,他给人一种虚浮的表面印象,在他漂亮词句的背后人们看不到一点真的情感。同一个班上有一个保险公司的推销员,个子很小,长得毫不起眼,说话当中还不时停下来思索接下来该说什么。可是当他演讲时,没有人怀疑不是出自他的真心。

林肯在华盛顿福特戏院遇刺几乎有100年了,但是他的一生、他的言辞和真诚情感,却永远留在了我们的记忆里。如果只就法律知识而言,他同时代的许多人都远远超过了他。他缺少优雅、顺畅和精致,但是他在葛底斯堡、古柏联盟和华盛顿国会山上发表演讲的真诚,历史上却无人能够超越。

你可能会说,就像有个学员对我说的,自己没有强烈的信念和兴趣。对此我总是很惊讶。我对他说,让自己忙碌起来,让自己对事情产生兴趣!"对什么事,比如说?"他问我。我告诉他说:"就鸽子吧。""鸽子?"他有些不明白。"是的!"我告诉他,"就是鸽子。你可以到广场上去看看它们,给它们喂东西,到图书馆去阅读有关鸽子的书,再回来讲你对鸽子的看法。"

他真的这样做了。当他回来演讲时,没有什么能阻止他了。他刚一开始便以养鸟者的狂热来谈鸽子。当我想要他停下来时,他正说到有关鸽子的40本书,他把它们都读了一遍!他作了我曾听过的最有趣味的演讲之一。

我还有一个建议:对自己认为很好的演讲题目,要尽量多了解一些。你对某件事了解越多,便会越热情。《销售的五大法则》的作者帕西·华廷告诉推销员,对自己推销的东西必须有所了

he came back there was no holding him down. He started to talk about pigeons with all the fervor of a fancier. When I tried to stop him he was saying something about forty books on pigeons and he had read them all. He gave one of the most interesting talks I have ever heard.

Here is another suggestion: Learn more and more about what you now consider a pretty good topic. The more you know about something the more earnest and excitedly enthusiastic you will become. Percy H. Whiting, the author of the Five Great Rules of Selling, tells salesmen never to stop learning about the product they are selling. As Mr. Whiting says, "The more you know about a good product, the more enthusiastic you become about it." The same thing is true about your topics—the more you know about them, the more earnest and enthusiastic you will be about them.

SECOND/ RELIVE THE FEELINGS YOU HAVE ABOUT YOUR TOPIC

Suppose you are telling your audience about the policeman who stopped you for going one mile over the speed limit. You can tell us that with all the cool disinterestedness of an onlooker, but it happened to you and you had certain feelings which you expressed in quite definite language. The third-person approach will not make much of an impression on your audience. They want to know exactly how you felt when that policeman wrote out that ticket. So, the more you relive the scene you are describing, or recreate the emotions you felt originally, the more vividly you will express yourself.

One of the reasons why we go to plays and movies is that we want to hear and see emotions expressed. We have become so fearful of giving vent to our feelings in public that we have to go to a play to satisfy this need for emotional expression.

When you speak in public, therefore, you will generate excitement and interest in your talk in proportion to the amount of excitement you put into it. Don't repress your honest feelings; don't put a damper on your authentic enthusiasms. Show your listeners how eager you are to talk about your subject, and you will hold their attention.

THIRD/ ACT IN EARNEST

When you walk before your audience to speak, do so with an air of anticipation, not like a

解。他说:"对一项优良产品知道得越多,便会对它越热情。"这同样适用于演讲题目——对它们懂得越多,你对它们也就越充满热情。

二、表达自己的真实感受

如果你想告诉听众由于你开车超速,警察把你拦下来的经历,你可以以一个旁观者的身份来讲述。但这事发生在你身上,你会有某种切身感受,这种感受会使你的讲述更加明确。以第三人称的方式表述,是不能给听众留下什么深刻印象的。他们想知道的是,当那个警察开罚单给你时,你是什么感受。所以,你越清楚地描述当时的情形和你当时的感受,你就越能生动逼真地表达自己。

我们去看话剧、电影的原因之一,就是因为我们想要见到或听到感情的表露。我们很害怕当众表露自己的感情,因此去看话剧,以满足这种感情表达的需要。

所以,当众说话时,你就可以根据自己倾注于谈话中的热心程度,来表现自己的热诚与兴趣。不要抑制自己的真挚情感,也不要在自己真实感人的热情上面加个闭气阀。要让听众们看到你对自己谈论的题目有多热诚,你就会抓住他们的注意力。

三、表现出十足的热情

当你走到听众面前准备演讲时,应该表现出对演讲的企盼神态,而不要像一个登上绞刑架的犯人。轻快的步伐也许大部分是假装出来的,但它却能为你创造奇迹,让听众感受到你有东西渴望交流谈论。演讲之前,再深吸一口气。不要靠着讲桌。抬起头,仰起下颚,告诉自己:你现在就要给听众讲一些有价值的事情, 因此你全身的每一部分都应该清楚无误地让他们知道这一点。要把自己想象成大权在握,就像威廉·詹姆斯所说的那样,要表现得好像是这样。如果能

man who is ascending the gallows. The spring in your walk may be largely put on, but it will do wonders for you and it gives the audience the feeling that you have something you are eager to talk about. Just before you begin, take a deep breath. Keep away from furniture or from the speaker's stand. Keep your head high and your chin up. You are about to tell your listeners something worthwhile, and every part of you should inform them of that clearly and unmistakably. You are in command, and as William James would say, act as if you are. If you make an effort to send your voice to the back of the hall, the sound will reassure you. Once you begin making gestures of any kind, they will help to stimulate you.

This principle of "warming up our reactivity," as Donald and Eleanor Laird describe it, can be applied to all situations that demand mental awareness. In their book Techniques for Efficient Remembering, the Lairds point to President Theodore Roosevelt as a man who "breezed through life with a bounce, vigor, dash, and enthusiasm which became his trademark. He was absorbingly interested, or effectively pretended he was, in everything he tackled." Teddy Roosevelt was a living exponent of the philosophy of William James: "Act in earnest and you will become naturally earnest in all you do."

Above all, remember this: ***acting in earnest will make you feel earnest.***

将你的声音传到大厅的后方,这样的音效会让你更有信心。如果一开始就能使用手势,它们更能令你振奋。

杜纳德和伊林诺·雷尔德把这项法则描述为“预热我们的反应”。它适用于任何需要心灵感觉的场合。在他们的著作《有效记忆的技巧》中,雷尔德夫妇认为西奥多·罗斯福总统是这样一个人:“活泼而愉快地度过了一生,充满了雀跃、活力、冲撞和热情。这些正是他的标记。他总是对自己要处理的一切事情兴趣浓厚,浑然忘我,或者假装得就像这个样子。”罗斯福也的确是威廉·詹姆斯哲学“表现得热烈,你对自己所做的一切自然便会热烈起来”的活生生的阐释者。

总之,要牢牢记住这句话:**表现出热情,你就会感受到热情。**

3 Sharing the Talk with the Audience

Russell conwell's famous lecture, "Acres of Diamonds," was given nearly six thousand times. You would think that a talk repeated so often would become set in the speaker's mind, that no word or intonation would vary in delivery. That was not the case. Dr. Conwell knew that audiences differ. He recognized that he had to make each successive audience feel that his talk was a personal, living thing created for it, and it alone. How did he succeed in keeping this interrelationship between speaker, speech, and audience alive from one speaking engagement to the next? "I visit a town or city," he wrote, "and try to arrive there early enough to see the postmaster, the barber, the hotel manager, the principal of the schools, some of the ministers, and then go into the stores and talk with people, and see what has been their history and what opportunities they had. Then I give my lecture and talk to those people about the subjects that apply to them locally."

Dr. Conwell was thoroughly aware that successful communication depends upon how well the speaker can make his talk a part of the listeners and the listeners a part of the talk. That is why we have no true copy of "Acres of Diamonds," one of the most popular talks ever given from a lecture platform. With his clever insight into human nature and his painstaking industry, Dr. Conwell did not give the same lecture twice, although he addressed almost six thousand different audiences on the same subject. You can profit from his example by making certain that your talks are always prepared with a specific audience in mind. Here are some simple rules that will help you to build up a strong feeling of rapport with your listeners.

FIRST/ TALK IN TERMS OF YOUR LISTENERS' INTERESTS

That is exactly what Dr. Conwell did. He made a point of working into his lecture plenty of local allusions and examples. His audiences were interested because his talk concerned them, their interests, their problems. This linkage with what your hearers are most interested in,

第3章 与听众融为一体

鲁塞·康威尔著名的演讲《钻石宝地》,总共发表过近6000次。你或许会想,重复这么多次的演讲,可能已经根深蒂固地刻在演讲者的脑海里,演讲时的字句音调该不会再变了吧?事实却并非如此。康威尔博士知道,听众的情况各不相同,因此他明白必须让听众感到他的演讲是个性化的、活生生的东西,是特意为他们准备的。他是如何在一场接一场的演讲中成功地维系演讲者、演讲和听众之间轻松愉快的关系的呢?"当我到了某个城市或某个镇时,"他写道,"总是先去拜访那些邮政局长、理发师、旅馆经理、学校校长、牧师,然后走进店里同人们交谈,了解他们的历史和他们所拥有的发展机会。然后,我才发表我的演讲,对那些人谈论适合他们当地的话题。"

康威尔博士很清楚,成功的沟通有赖于演讲者使他的演讲成为听众的一部分,并且使听众成为演讲的一部分。这也正是《钻石宝地》成为最受欢迎的演讲,但我们却找不到一本演讲词的副本的原因。由于康威尔博士聪敏、洞察人性,而且又勤奋谨慎,所以这一相同的题材尽管已经给大约6000场的听众讲过,但同一次演讲不会说两次。从他的例子中你应该有所领悟:准备演讲时,头脑里应该想着特定的听众。这里有一些简单的法则,可以帮助你建立起与听众之间和谐密切的关系。

一、根据听众的兴趣演讲

这正是康威尔博士采用的方法。他会在自己的演讲中加入许多当地俗谈和实例。听众之所以对他感兴趣,就是因为他的谈话与他们有关,与他们的兴趣有关,与他们的问题有关。这种与

namely, themselves, will insure attention and guarantee that the lines of communication will remain open. Eric Johnston, former head of the United States Chamber of Commerce and now president of the Motion Picture Association, uses this technique in almost every talk he gives. Note how resourcefully he employed local interests in a commencement address at the University of Oklahoma:

You Oklahomans are well acquainted with goosepimple peddlers. You don't have to think back too far to remember when they were writing Oklahoma off the books as a hopeless risk forever.

Why, in the 1930's, all the ravens of despair were telling the crows to bypass Oklahoma unless they could pack along their own rations.

They consigned Oklahoma to an everlasting future as part of a new American desert. Nothing would ever bloom again—they said. But in the 1940's Oklahoma was a garden spot—and the toast of Broadway. For, once again, there was "waving wheat that sure smells sweet when the wind comes right behind the rain."

In one short decade, the dustbowl was smothered with corn stalks as high as the elephant's eye.

Here was a pay-off for faith—and calculated risk...

But it is always possible to see our own times in better perspective against the backdrop of yesterday.

So I looked up the files of the *Daily Oklahoman* for the spring of 1901 in preparation for my visit here. I wanted to sample the flavor of life in the territory fifty years ago.

And what did I discover?

Why, I found the big accent was all on Oklahoma's future. The big stress was on hope.

Here is an excellent example of talking in terms of audience interest. Eric Johnston used instances of calculated risk right out of his listeners' back yards. He made them feel that his talk was no mimeographed copy—it was freshly created for them. No audience can withhold attention from a speaker who talks in its interests.

Ask yourself how knowledge of your subject will help the members of your audience solve their problems and achieve their goals. Then proceed to show them that, and you will have their

听众本身及其兴趣相关联的内在联系，能够牢牢抓住听众的注意力，保证沟通渠道的畅通无阻。艾力克·琼斯顿是美国前商会会长，现为动作电影协会会长，在他的每一场演讲中几乎都应用了这种技巧。下面来看看他在俄克拉荷马大学的毕业典礼上是如何巧妙地使用这个方法的：

各位俄克拉荷马的公民，对于那些习惯危言耸听的小商小贩们应是再熟悉不过了。各位只需稍稍回想一下，便会想起来，他们一向将俄克拉荷马州排除在外，认为它是永远绝望的冒险。

噢，在20世纪30年代，所有绝望的乌鸦都告诉其他乌鸦，最好是避开俄克拉荷马，除非他们自己携带干粮。

他们认为俄克拉荷马是美洲新沙漠中永远难以改变的一部分。他们这样形容道："这里永远都不会有东西开花。"但是到了20世纪40年代，俄克拉荷马却成了花园，连百老汇也要举杯为它祝福。因为在那儿，"当雨后微风吹来，便有小麦波浪起伏，散发出清香。"

在短短的10年之内，这个曾经干旱肆虐的地区，到处都是茂盛的玉米秆。

这是信仰的结果——也是有计划地冒险的结果……

因此，我们在考察自己时代的时候，应该总是看到美好的远景，而不是停留在昨天的阴影之中。

当我准备访问这里的时候，我先看过了《俄克拉荷马日报》卷宗，知道了这里1901年春天的景象。我想体会一下50年前本地的生活。

结果我发现了什么？

噢，我发现它描述的全是俄克拉荷马的未来，重心都放在了将来的希望上。

这是一个根据听众兴趣来演讲的极好例子。艾力克·琼斯顿采用的这一有计划的冒险事例源自听众身边，使听众们觉得他的演讲不是油印出来的拷贝文件，而是特意为他们准备的。演

complete attention. If you are an accountant and you start your talk by saying something like this, "I am going to show you how to save from fifty to a hundred dollars on your tax return," or you are a lawyer and you tell your listeners how to go about making a will, you will be certain to have an interested audience. Surely, there is some topic in your special fund of knowledge that can be of real help to members of your audience.

When asked what interests people, Lord Northcliffe, the William Randolph Hearst of British journalism, replied, "themselves." He built a newspaper empire on that single truth.

In *Mind in the Making*, James Harvey Robinson describes reverie as "a spontaneous and favorite kind of thinking." He goes on to say that, in reverie, we allow our ideas to take their own course, and this course is determined by our hopes and fears, our spontaneous desires, their fulfillment or frustration; by our likes and dislikes, our loves, hates, and resentments. There is nothing so interesting to ourselves as ourselves.

Harold Dwight, of Philadelphia, made an extraordinarily successful talk at a banquet which marked the final session of our course. He talked about each person in turn around the entire table, how he had spoken when the course started, how he had improved; he recalled the talks various members had made, the subjects they had discussed; he mimicked some of them, exaggerated their peculiarities, had everyone laughing, had everyone pleased. With such material, he could not possibly have failed. It was absolutely ideal. No other topic under the blue dome of heaven would have so interested that group. Mr. Dwight knew how to handle human nature.

Some years ago I wrote a series of articles for the *American Magazine*, and I had the opportunity of talking with John Siddall, who was then in charge of the Interesting People Department.

"People are selfish," he said. "They are interested chiefly in themselves. They are not very much concerned about whether the government should own the railroads; but they do want to know how to get ahead, how to draw more salary, how to keep healthy. If I were editor of this magazine," he went on, "I would tell them how to take care of their teeth, how to take baths, how to keep cool in summer, how to get a position, how to handle employees, how to buy homes, how to remember, how to avoid grammatical error, and so on. People are always interested in human

讲者根据听众的兴趣来演讲，听众当然不会转移注意力。

要先问问自己，你的演讲如何帮助听众解决他们的问题，怎样才能达到他们的目标?然后开始讲给他们听，就会让他们全神贯注。如果你是个会计师，你的开场白可以这样："我现在要教你们如何节省50到100美元税收。"或者如果你是一位律师，你可以告诉听众如何立遗嘱。你肯定会让听众兴致勃勃。事实上，在每个人的知识积累中，必然会有某个题目能对听众有所帮助。

曾有人问英国报业巨子诺斯克利夫爵士，什么东西能够激发人们的兴趣，他回答说："人们自己。"他就是根据这一单纯的事实建立了一个报业帝国。

詹姆斯·哈维·鲁滨逊在《思想的酝酿》一书中，形容幻想是"一种出于自然的、最受欢迎的思想"。他接下去说，在幻想中，我们允许自己的思想各自沿着它的方向前进，而它的方向又取决于人们的希望或恐惧；取决于人们的成功或幻灭；取决于人们的喜、怒、哀、乐等情绪。世上再也没有比我们自己更令我们感兴趣的事了。

来自费城的哈罗德·杜怀特，在一次毕业宴会上做了一场非常成功的演讲。他依次谈到了桌边的每个人。他说刚上演讲课的时候，自己并不善于讲话，而现在进步多了。他一边回忆同学们所做的演讲和讨论过的题目，一边夸张地模仿其中一些人，逗得大家开怀大笑。像他这样的演讲，是不可能失败的，这是绝对理想的谈话题材。天底下没有什么题目比这更能令大家感兴趣的。杜怀特先生真是通晓人性。

几年前，我替《美国杂志》写过一系列文章，有幸和约翰·西德达先生交谈。当时他正主持杂志的《有趣人物》专栏。"人都是自私的，"他说，"他们只对自己感兴趣。他们并不怎么关心政府是否应该把铁路收归国有，但他们却想知道如何才能获得晋升，如何才能得到更多的薪水，如何保持健康。如果我是这家杂志的总编辑，我将告诉读者如何保护好他们的牙齿，如何洗澡，如

interest stories, so I would have some rich man tell how he made a million in real estate. I would get prominent bankers and presidents of various corporations to tell the stories of how they battled their ways up from the ranks to power and wealth."

Shortly after that, Siddall was made editor. The magazine then had a small circulation. Siddall did just what he said he would do. The response? It was over whelming. The circulation figures climbed up to two hundred thousand, three, four, half a million. Here was something the public wanted. Soon a million people a month were buying it, then a million and a half, finally two million. It did not stop there, but continued to grow for many years. Siddall appealed to the selfinterests of his readers.

The next time you face an audience, visualize them as eager to hear what you have to say—as long as it applies to them. Speakers who fail to take this essential egocentricity of their listeners into account are apt to find themselves facing a restless audience, one squirming in boredom, glancing at wristwatches, and looking hopefully toward the exit doors.

SECOND/ GIVE HONEST, SINCERE APPRECIATION

Audiences are composed of individuals, and they react like individuals. Openly criticize an audience and they resent it. Show your appreciation for something they have done that is worthy of praise, and you win a passport into their hearts. This often requires some research on your part. Such fulsome phrases as "this is the most intelligent audience I have ever addressed," are resented as hollow flattery by most audiences.

In the words of a great speaker, Chauncey M. Depew, you have to "tell them something about themselves that they didn't think you could possibly know." For example, a man who spoke before the Baltimore Kiwanis Club recently could find nothing unusual about that club except that it had in its membership a past international president and an international trustee. This was no news to the members of the club. So he tried to give it a new twist. He started his talk with this sentence: "The Baltimore Kiwanis Club is one club in 101,898!" The members listened. This speaker was certainly wrong—because there were only 2,897 Kiwanis Clubs in the world. The speaker then went on:

何在夏天保持清凉,如何找到一份好工作,如何应付雇员,如何买房子,如何记忆,如何避免文法错误,等等。另外,人们也总是对别人有趣的经历感兴趣,所以我会邀请一些大富翁谈谈他们如何在房地产中赚进几百万美元。我还要请一些著名的银行家及各大公司的总裁,谈谈他们是如何从底层奋斗到有权有势的地位的。"

不久,西德达真的当上了总编辑。当时这家杂志的销量很小。西德达立即按照自己的构想开展工作。结果怎样呢?情况发生了巨大变化,销售量急剧上升,达到20万份、30万份、40万份、50万份,以至于更多,因为它的内容是一般民众想知道的。没多久,杂志每个月销售量就达到了100万份,然后是150万份,最终达到了200万份。但它并没有就此停住,而是持续上升了许多年。西德达满足了读者们的兴趣,因此获得了成功。

当你下次面对听众时,要把他们想象成急切地想听你说什么——只要对他们有用就行。演讲者如果不考虑听众自我中心的天然倾向,就会发现自己面对的是一群烦躁不安的听众。他们会局促不安,表现出不耐烦,不时地看手表,并且渴望离开。

二、真心诚意地赞美听众

听众由单个的人组成,他们的反应亦如个人的反应。公然批评听众,必然会导致愤懑。如果你对他们所做的值得称赞的事情表示赞美,你就会赢得通往他们心灵的护照。但这常常需要你去认真研究。例如这样肉麻的句子"各位是我曾见过最有智慧的听众",也许会被大多数听众认为是空洞的谄媚而招致反感。

我想引用著名演讲家琼西·德普的话:你必须"告诉他们一些有关他们的事,这些事情他们没想到你可能会知道"。例如,有个人最近要在巴尔的摩的基瓦尼俱乐部发表演讲,却找不到该俱乐部的特殊资料,只知道在该俱乐部会员里曾有一位出任国际会长、一位出任国际董事。这

"Yes, even if you don't believe it, it is still a fact that your club, mathematically at least, is one in 101,898. Not one club in 100,000 or one in 200,000, but just exactly one in 101,898.

"How do I figure that out? Kiwanis International has only 2,897 member clubs. Well, the Baltimore club has a past president of Kiwanis International and an international trustee. Mathematically, the chances that any Kiwanis club will have both a past president and an international trustee at the same time are one in 101,898—and the reason I know it's right is that I got a Johns Hopkins Ph.D. in mathematics to figure it out for me."

Be exactly one hundred per cent sincere. An insincere statement may occasionally fool an individual, but it never fools an audience. "This highly intelligent audience..." "This exceptional gathering of the beauty and chivalry of HoHokus, New Jersey..." "I'm glad to be here because I love each one of you." No, no, no! If you can't show sincere appreciation, don't show any!

THIRD/ IDENTIFY YOURSELF WITH THE AUDIENCE

As soon as possible, preferably in the first words you utter, indicate some direct relationship with the group you are addressing. If you are honored by being asked to speak, say so. When Harold Macmillan spoke to the graduating class at De Pauw University in Greencastle, Indiana, he opened up the lines of communication in his first sentence.

"I am very grateful for your kind words of welcome," he said. "For a Prime Minister of Great Britain to be invited to your great university is an unusual occasion. But I feel that my present office was not the only nor, indeed, perhaps the main reason for your invitation."

Then he mentioned that his mother was an American, born in Indiana, and that her father had been one of De Panw's first graduates.

"I can assure you that I am proud to be associated with De Pauw University," he said, "and to renew an old family tradition."

You may be sure that Macmillan's reference to an American school and to the American way of life which his mother and her pioneer father knew made friends for him at once.

Another way to open the lines of communication is to use the names of people in the audience. I once sat next to the main speaker at a banquet and I was amazed at his curiosity concerning

些情况对俱乐部的人来说并不是新闻。但这个人却使大家感到了与众不同的东西。他是这样开场的:"巴尔的摩基瓦尼俱乐部是101898个基瓦尼俱乐部中的一个! "会员们听了有些奇怪:这个演讲者大错特错——因为全球只有2897个基瓦尼俱乐部。然后这位演讲者接着说:

"就算各位不相信,它仍然是事实,至少在数学方面是这样。各位的俱乐部是101898个当中的一个,不是10万或20万个当中的一个,而确实是101898当中的一个。

"我是如何计算出来的呢?不错,国际基瓦尼组织只有2897个俱乐部。但是,巴尔的摩俱乐部过去曾出过一位国际会长和一位国际董事。从数学的观点来看,任何一个基瓦尼俱乐部想同时出一个国际会长和董事的几率是1:101898。我有琼斯·霍普金斯大学的数学博士学位,可以证明我计算出来的数字的准确性。"

表示赞美的时候要确实出自真心诚意。没有诚意的话偶尔会骗过一两个人,却不能永远欺骗听众。例如"这样高度智慧的听众……"、"来自霍霍柯斯、新泽西的美女和侠士的特别聚会……"、"我真高兴在这儿,因为我爱你们每一位"……千万不要这样肉麻! 如果你表示不出真心诚意的赞美,最好什么也别说。

三、与听众建立友谊的桥梁

演讲时,要尽快指出你正与之谈话的听众之间存在某种直接的关系。如果你感到被邀请很荣幸,不妨说出来。哈罗德·麦克米兰在印第安纳州绿堡的德堡大学跟毕业班学生讲话时,一开始就这样建立了沟通的纽带。

"我很感激各位亲切的欢迎词,"他说,"身为大不列颠首相,我应邀前来贵校,的确非比寻常。不过我感到,我现在就任的政府职位,恐怕不是各位盛情邀请我的主要原因。"

接着,他提到自己的母亲是美国人,出生在印第安纳州,而他的父亲则是德堡大学首届毕业生。

various people in the hall. All through the meal he kept asking the master of ceremonies who the person in the blue suit at one table was, or what was the name of the lady in the flowered hat. When he arose to speak, it became evident at once why he was curious. He very cleverly wove some of the names he had learned into his talk, and I could see the evident pleasure on the faces of the persons whose names were used and I sensed the warm friendliness of the audience that this simple technique won for the speaker.

Notice how Frank Pace, Jr., speaking as the president of the General Dynamics Corporation, worked in a few names to advantage. He was speaking at an annual dinner of Religion in American Life, Inc., in New York:

"This has been a delightful and meaningful evening for me in many ways," he said. "First, I have my own minister, the Reverend Robert Appleyard, here in the audience. By his words, deeds, and leadership he has been an inspiration to me personally, to my family, and to our entire congregation ... Secondly, to sit between Lewis Strauss and Bob Stevens, men whose interest in religion has been amplified by their interest in public service... is again a source of great personal pleasure..."

One word of caution: If you are going to work strange names into your talk, having learned them through inquiries made for the occasion, be sure you have them exactly right; be sure you understand fully the reason for your use of the names; be sure you mention them only in a favorable way; and use them in moderation.

Another method of keeping the audience at peak attentiveness is to use the pronoun "you" rather than the third-person "they." In this way you keep the audience in a state of self-awareness, which I have pointed out earlier cannot be overlooked by the speaker if he is to hold the interest and attention of his listeners. Here are some excerpts from a talk on Sulphuric Acid by one of our students in a New York City class:

> Suphuric acid touches you in your life in a score of ways. If it were not for sulphuric acid, your car would stop, for it is used extensively in the refining of kerosene and gasoline. The electric lights that illuminate your office and your home would not be possible without it.
>
> When you turn on the water for your bath, you use a nickel-plated faucet, which requires

"我可以向各位保证,能和德堡大学有些关系,使我感到无上光荣,"他说,"并以能重温故乡的传统而骄傲。"

可以肯定,麦克米兰提到这所美国学校,以及母亲和身为该校先驱的父亲,立刻为自己赢得了友谊。

另一种建立友谊的方法,就是提及听众中某些人的名字。在一次宴会上,我紧挨着坐在主讲人边上。我很奇怪他对每一个人都非常好奇。他不停地向宴会的主人打听,比如那个穿蓝色西装的人是谁,或那位帽子缀满了鲜花的女士芳名叫什么。直到他站起来讲话时,我才了解他为什么好奇——他非常巧妙地把他刚才打听到的名字用到了自己的演讲中,我看到那些名字被他提到的人脸上洋溢着欢乐,而这个简单的技巧也为演讲者赢得了听众温暖的友情。

再来看看通用动力公司总裁小弗兰克·佩斯是如何使用几个名字便使演讲产生效果的。他在纽约美国生活宗教公司一年一度的晚宴上做的演讲:

"从很多方面来讲,今晚对我而言是一个愉快而且很有意义的晚上,"他说,"首先,我的牧师罗伯·阿勃亚便坐在听众席中。他的语言、行为和领导,已使他成为我个人、我的家人以及我们所有听众的一种激励和启示……其次,路易·施特劳斯和鲍伯·史蒂文斯两人对宗教的热诚,已从他们对公共事业的热情支持上表露无遗。能坐在他们二位中间,是我莫大的快乐……"

不过有一点需要小心:如果你准备在演讲用到陌生的名字,而这些名字是你通过询问得知的,那你必须确保正确无误,必须确实了解自己使用这些名字的原因,而且只能以友好的方式提到它们,当然还得有一定的节制。

让听众始终保持高度注意力的另一个方法,就是在演讲中使用第二人称代词"你们",而不是使用第三人称"他们",这样可以让听众保持一种亲自参与的感觉。我在前面已经指出,演讲者如果想抓住听众的注意力和兴趣,是不能忽视这一点的。下面摘录了我们纽约培训班一位学

sulphuric acid in its manufacture. The soap you use has possibly been made from greases or oils that have been treated with the acid. The bristles in your hairbrush and your celluloid comb could not have been produced without it. Your razor, no doubt, has been pickled in it after annealing.

You come down to breakfast. The cup and saucer, if they are other than plain white, could not have come into being without it. Your spoon, knife and fork have seen a bath of sulphuric acid if they are silver-plated.

And so on through the whole day sulphuric acid affects you at every turn. Go where you will, you cannot escape its influence.

By skillfully using "you" and inserting his listeners into the picture, this speaker was able to keep attention alive and glowing. There are times, however, when the pronoun "you" is dangerous, when it may establish a cleavage between speaker and audience rather than a bridge. This occurs when it might seem as though we were talking down to our audience or lecturing it. Then it is better to say "we" instead of "you."

Dr. W.W.Bauer, Director of Health Education of the American Medical Association, often used this technique in his radio and television talks. "We all want to know how to choose a good doctor, don't we?" he said in one of his talks. "And if we are going to get the best service from our doctor, don't we all want to know how to be good patients?"

FOURTH/ MAKE YOUR AUDIENCE A PARTNER IN YOUR TALK

Did it ever occur to you that you can keep an audience hanging on every word by using a little showmanship? The moment you choose some member of the audience to help you demonstrate a point or dramatize an idea, you will be rewarded by a noticeable rise in attention. Being aware of themselves as an audience, the members of it are keenly conscious of what happens when one of its own is brought into "the act" by the speaker. If there is a wall between the man on the platform and the people out there, as many speakers say, the use of audience participation will break that wall down. I remember a speaker who was explaining the distance it takes to stop a car after the brakes have been applied. He asked one of his listeners in the front

员题为《硫酸》的演讲词的几段来作为实例。

硫酸和我们的生活联系密切。如果没有硫酸,你们的汽车就不能行驶,因为提炼汽油和制造汽车时,必须用到硫酸。不论是你们办公室的电灯,还是你们家里的灯,如果没有硫酸就不会点亮。

在你们放水洗澡时,那镍质的水龙头在制造过程中也要使用硫酸。你们使用的肥皂也可能是用油脂和硫酸制成的。你们发刷上的鬃毛和假象牙梳子,如果没有硫酸也制造不出来。你们的刮胡刀在经过锤炼后,也一定要浸在硫酸中做处理。

你们下楼用早餐时,如果你们使用的杯子和盘子刚好不是纯白色的,那就更少不了它。如果你们的汤匙、刀叉是镀银的,也要在硫酸中浸过。

总之,在一整天的时间里,硫酸会从各个方面影响你们。不管走到哪儿,你们都无法逃过它的影响。

这位演讲者通过巧妙地使用"你们",把听众融入到具体的情景中,因此吸引了听众的持续注意。不过,有些时候使用"你们"却是很危险的,它可能不是在你和听众之间建立友谊的桥梁,而是会造成分裂。例如,当你以智者的身份居高临下地对听众讲话或说教时,这种情形便会发生。这时候,最好是说"我们",而不是"你们"。

美国医药协会健康教育主任保尔博士,在广播和电视演讲中就经常使用这种技巧。"我们都想知道如何选个好医生,是不是?"他在一次谈话中说,"如果我们想从医生那里获得最好的服务,那我们是不是需要知道如何做个好病人呢?"

四、鼓励听众参与演讲

你是否想过,怎样用点小小的表演技巧,就能让听众紧跟着你的讲话?如果你在演讲时让

row to stand and help demonstrate how this distance varied with the speed of the car. The man in the audience took the end of a steel tape measure and carried it forty-five feet down the aisle, where he stopped on a signal from the speaker. As I watched this procedure I couldn't help but notice how the whole audience became engrossed in the talk. I said to myself that the tape measure, in addition to being a graphic illustration of the speaker's point, was certainly a line of communication between that speaker and this audience. Without that touch of showmanship the audience might still be concerned with what it was going to have for dinner or what programs would be on TV that evening.

One of my favorite methods of getting audience participation is simply to ask questions and to get responses, I like to get the audience on its feet, repeating a sentence after me, or answering my questions by raising their hands. Percy H. Whiting, whose book *How to Put Humor in Your Speaking and Writing* contains some valuable advice on the subject of audience participation, suggests having your listeners vote on something, or inviting them to help you solve a problem. "Get yourself in the right state of mind," says Mr. Whiting, "a state of mind that recognizes that a speech is unlike a recitation—that it is designed to get audience reaction—to make the audience a partner in the enterprise." I like that description of the audience as "a partner in the enterprise." It is the key to what this chapter is all about. If you use audience participation you confer the rights of partnership on your listeners.

FIFTH/ PLAY YOURSELF DOWN

Of course, nothing will take the place of sincerity in this speaker-audience relationship. Norman Vincent Peale once gave some very useful advice to a fellow minister who was having great difficulty keeping the audience intent upon his sermons. He asked this minister to question his feelings about the congregation he addressed each Sunday morning—did he like them, did he want to help them, did he consider them his intellectual inferiors? Dr. Peale said that he never ascended the pulpit without feeling a strong sense of affection for the men and women he was about to face. An audience is quick in taking the measure of a speaker who assumes that he is superior in mental accomplishment or in social standing. Indeed, one of the best ways for a speaker to endear himself

听众协助你展示某个观点，或者把你的观点戏剧化地表现出来，那么听众对你的注意力就会明显提升。这是因为当听众中的一个人被演讲者带入"表演"中时，听众们就会敏锐地注意所发生的事。如果在讲台上的人和讲台下的人之间有一堵墙——就像许多演讲者说的那样——利用听众的参与就可以推倒这堵墙。我还记得，有个演讲者为了说明汽车在刹车后，还必须前进多长的距离才能够停住，请了前排一位听众出来，帮他展示汽车在不同速度下这个距离有什么变化。这个听众拿着钢卷尺的一端，沿着走道把它拉长到45尺处演讲者示意他停下来的地方……在这位听众演示的过程中，我注意到其他听众也是全神贯注。我对自己说，那条卷尺除了能生动地展现演讲者的论点之外，还成了演讲者与听众之间一座沟通的桥梁。若不是使用这一展示方法，听众可能还在想着晚饭吃什么，或者晚上看什么电视节目！

我最喜欢使用的让听众参与演讲的方法，就是提问并让听众回答。我喜欢请听众站起来，跟着我重复一句话，或举手回答我的问题。帕西·华廷有一本书叫《如何在演讲和写作中运用幽默》，也提出了一些如何让听众参与进来的忠告。他建议让听众对一些事情进行表决，或邀请他们共同解决问题。"确保自己的思想是正确的，"华廷先生说，"正确的思想会让演讲不像在背诵，它可以引起听众的反应，把听众变成企业的伙伴。"我很喜欢他把听众描述为"企业的伙伴"。这是本章所讨论的重点。如果能让听众参与进来，你就把合伙人的权利送给了他们。

五、保持谦虚谨慎的态度

在演讲者和听众之间的所有关系中，真诚是最重要的。诺曼·文生特·皮尔给了一位牧师一些有用的忠告——那个牧师讲道时简直没有办法抓住听众的注意力。他让牧师问自己，他对每个星期天早晨都要布道的人们怀有什么样的感情——是否喜欢他们？是否愿意帮助他们？是否认为自己比他们智力高出一等？皮尔博士说，他登上讲坛时，每次都对即将面对的男男女女怀

to an audience is to play himself down.

Edmund S. Muskie, then U.S. Senator from Maine, demonstrated this when he spoke to the American Forensic Association in Boston.

"I approach my assignment this morning with many doubts," he said. "In the first place, I am conscious of the professional qualifications of this audience, and question the wisdom of exposing my poor talents to your critical view. In the second place, this is a breakfast meeting—an almost impossible time of day for a man to be on guard effectively; and failure in this respect can be fatal to a politician. And thirdly, there is my subject—the influence which debating has had on my career as a public servant. As long as I am active politically, there is likely to be a sharp division of opinion among my constituents as to whether that influence has been good or bad.

"Facing these doubts, I feel very much like the mosquito who found himself unexpectedly in a nudist colony. I don't know where to begin."

Senator Muskie went on, from there, to make a fine address.

Adlai E. Stevenson played himself down at the beginning of a commencement exercise address at Michigan State University. He said:

"My feeling of inadequacy on these occasions brings to mind Samuel Butler's remark when he was once asked to talk about how to make the most out of life. I think his reply was: 'I don't even know how to make the most out of the next fifteen minutes.' And I feel that way about the next twenty minutes."

The surest way to antagonize an audience is to indicate that you consider yourself to be above them. When you speak, you are in a showcase and every facet of your personality is on display. The slightest hint of braggadocio is fatal. On the other hand, modesty inspires confidence and good will. You can be modest without being apologetic. Your audience will like and respect you for suggesting your limitations as long as you show you are determined to do your best.

The world of American television is a demanding one, and every season top-rated performers fall under the withering fire of competition. One of the survivors who comes back year after year is Ed Sullivan, who is not a television professional, but a newspaper man. He is an amateur in this fiercely competitive field and he survives because he doesn't presume to be anything but an

着强烈的感情。演讲者如果自认为在智力或社会地位上比别人高出一等，听众一听就会很清楚。所以，如果演讲者想得到听众的爱戴，最好保持谦虚谨慎的低姿态。

艾德蒙德·穆斯基担任缅因州参议员时，曾在波士顿的美国辩论协会的一次讲话中展示了这种技巧。

"今天，我被派来履行自己的职责，心里确实有一些担心。"他说，"首先，我很清楚你们全都是专家，我在这里是班门弄斧，在你们犀利的目光下只会暴露自己的愚蠢，不知我这样做是不是明智之举。第二，这是一次早餐会，而早晨又是一个人警觉性最差的时候，对于一位政客来说，如果失败，后果将不堪设想。第三，我要讲的题目是'辩论对我公仆生涯的影响'。由于我在政坛上比较活跃，这对我的选民的影响很可能会形成尖锐的意见分歧。

"面对这些担心，我感觉自己就像一只蚊子，无意间闯入了天体营，不知从哪儿开始才好。"

穆斯基议员就这样开始，发表了一场精彩的演讲。

阿德莱·史蒂文生在密歇根州立大学毕业典礼上的演讲，一开始也采取了低姿态。他说：

"在这样的场合，我总是感到心有余而力不足。我想起了有一次塞缪尔·巴特勒被问到如何充分利用生命时的谈话。他说：'我甚至不知道如何很好地利用下面的15分钟呢。'现在我对这20分钟也有相同的感觉。"

如果你想让听众敌视你，最好的办法就是让他们感觉你高高在上。演讲时，就如同把自己放在橱窗里展示，你人性中的每一侧面都暴露出来了，只要你稍稍有一点自夸，就注定要失败。但你若表现出患得患失、没有信心，那也是很糟糕的。你可以谦虚，但不能表现出患得患失、没有信心的样子。只要你表示出要尽力讲好，并说自己才识有限，听众就会喜欢你，尊敬你。

美国电视界竞争非常残酷，每一季收视率最高的演员都要陷入这种竞争。在这里能够保持常胜的演员只有艾德·萨利文。他不是电视专业人员，而是一位新闻从业人员。他在竞争激烈的

amateur. Some of his mannerisms on camera would have been handicaps for anyone with less natural appeal. He cups his chin in his hand, hunches his shoulders, tugs at his necktie, stumbles over words. But these failings are not fatal for Ed Sullivan. He doesn't resent people for criticizing these faults. At least once a season he hires the services of a talented mimic who caricaturizes him to perfection, exaggerating all his faults. Ed Sullivan laughs as unaffectedly as everyone else when this performer holds the mirror up to nature. He welcomes criticism, and audiences love him for it. Audiences like humility. They resent the show-off, the egotist.

Henry and Dana Lee Thomas, in their book *Living Biographies of Religious Leaders*, said of Confucius: "He never tried to dazzle people with his exclusive knowledge. He merely tried to enlighten them with his inclusive sympathy." If we have this inclusive sympathy, we have the key that unlocks the door to the audiences' heart.

电视圈里只算是个业余选手。他之所以能够在竞争中取胜,是因为他没有把自己看得很高,只认为自己就是业余的。他在镜头前会有些不自然的举动,别人也都可能会认为是一种失误,他会手撑下巴,弓着两肩,拉扯领带,说话结巴……但这些缺陷都无损于他;即使有人批评他,他也不计较。他每个季度至少要请一位模仿高手在电视里惟妙惟肖地模仿自己,并夸大自己的缺点。他会和别人一样对这些可笑的动作哈哈大笑。他欢迎批评,观众也因此而喜欢他。因为观众喜欢谦逊,厌恶自大自夸的卖弄者。

亨利和丹纳·李·托马斯在他们的著作《现代宗教领袖传》中这样评述孔子:"他从不向人们炫耀自己的知识。他只是用自己的仁德之心,设法启迪人们。"如果我们能有这样的包容,我们便掌握了打开听众心扉的钥匙。

Part Three
The Purpose of Prepared and Impromptu Talks

1 Making the Short Talk to Get Action

A famous english bishop, during World War I, spoke to the troops at Camp Upton. They were on their way to the trenches; only a very small percentage of them had any adequate idea why they were being sent. I know; I questioned them. Yet the Lord Bishop talked to these men about "International Amity," and "Serbia's Right to a Place in the Sun." Why, half of them did not know whether Serbia was a town or a disease. He might just as well have delivered a learned disquisition on the nebular hypothesis. However, not a single trooper left the hall while he was speaking; military police were stationed at every exit to prevent their escape.

I do not wish to belittle the bishop. He was every inch a scholar, and before a body of churchmen he would probably have been powerful; but he failed with these soldiers, and he failed utterly. Why? He evidently knew neither the precise purpose of his talk nor how to accomplish it.

What do we mean by the purpose of a talk? Just this: every talk, regardless of whether the speaker realizes it or not, has one of four major goals. What are they?

1. To persuade or get action. 2. To inform.
3. To impress and convince. 4. To entertain.

Let us illustrate these by a series of concrete examples from Abraham Lincoln's speaking career.

Few people know that Lincoln once invented and patented a device for lifting stranded boats

第三篇 成功发表商务演讲

第1章 激励听众采取行动的演讲

第一次世界大战期间,一位著名的英国主教在厄普顿营对即将奔赴战场的士兵发表讲话。只有一些士兵明白作战的意义,这一点我很清楚,因为我和他们聊过。可是,这位主教先生却对他们大谈什么"国际亲善",以及"塞尔维亚在太阳底下应占有一席之地",而士兵们有一半却对塞尔维亚在哪里都不清楚。所以,他不如发表一篇谁也不懂的"星云假说"的学术演讲,反正效果完全一样。不过,在他演讲的过程中没有一个士兵跑开的,因为有宪兵站在每个出口,防止他们跑出去。

我无意取笑这位主教,他是一位真正的学者,在宗教人士面前他很可能令人折服;但面对这些军人他却失败了,而且是彻底失败。为什么呢?因为他不知道自己演讲的真正目的,当然不知道怎么做了。

讲话的目的是什么呢?不论你自己是不是了解,任何讲话一般包括以下所列的四个目的中的一个。它们是什么呢?

1. 说服听众采取行动。 2. 说明情况。
3. 增强印象,使人信服。 4. 给人们带来欢乐。

我们就以林肯总统一系列具体的演讲为例来说明吧。

off sand bars and other obstructions. He worked in a mechanic's shop near his law office making a model of his apparatus. When friends came to his office to view the model, he took no end of pains to explain it. The main purpose of those explanations was to inform.

When he delivered his immortal oration at Gettysburg, when he gave his first and second inaugural addresses, when Henry Clay died and Lincoln delivered a eulogy on his life—on all these occasions, Lincoln's main purpose was to impress and convince.

In his talks to juries, he tried to win favorable decisions. In his political talks, he tried to win votes. His purpose, then, was action.

Two years before he was elected president, Lincoln prepared a lecture on inventions. His purpose was to entertain. At least, that should have been his goal; but he was evidently not very successful in attaining it. His career as a popular lecturer was, in fact, a distinct disappointment. In one town, not a person came to hear him.

But he succeeded notably in his other speeches, some of which have become classics of human utterance. Why? Largely because in those instances he knew his goal, and he knew how to achieve it.

Because so many speakers fail to line up their purpose with the purpose of the meeting at which they are speaking, they often flounder and come to grief.

For example: A United States congressman was once hooted and hissed and forced to leave the stage of the old New York Hippodrome, because he had—unconsciously, no doubt, but nevertheless, unwisely—chosen to make an informative talk. The crowd did not want to be instructed. They wanted to be entertained. They listened to him patiently, politely, for ten minutes, a quarter of an hour, hoping the performance would come to a rapid end. But it didn't. He rambled on and on; patience snapped; the audience would not stand for more. Someone began to cheer ironically. Others took it up. In a moment, a thousand people were whistling and shouting. The speaker, obtuse and incapable as he was of sensing the temper of his audience, had the bad taste to continue. That aroused them. A battle was on. Their impatience mounted to ire. They determined to silence him. Louder and louder grew their storm of protest. Finally, the roar of it, the anger of it, drowned his words—he could not have been heard twenty feet away. So he was forced to give

很少有人知道林肯曾发明过一种装置，它可以将搁浅在沙滩或其他阻碍物中的船只吊起来，并获得了专利。他在他的律师事务所办公室附近一家机械厂制作了这种装置的模型，每当有朋友来看模型时，他就不厌其烦地讲解它。这种讲解的主要目的，就是说明情况。

他在葛底斯堡发表不朽的演讲，第一次和第二次总统就职演讲，在亨利·柯雷去世时做的悼词……所有这些演讲的主要目的是增强听众的印象，使他们信服。

他对陪审团讲话时，想赢得有利的决定；发表政治演讲时，想赢得选票。这种演讲的目的，就是要让听众采取行动。

而在林肯当选总统的两年前，他曾精心准备了一场关于发明的演讲。他本想给人们带来一些欢乐，这至少是他的目的，可惜他在这方面没有成功。他原本想当一个大众演讲家，结果遭到了挫折。甚至有一次，竟然没有一个人来听他的演讲。

但是林肯的许多演讲获得了神奇的成功，其中一些演讲已经成为人类语言中的经典之作。为什么他能成功呢?因为在这些演讲中，他明白自己的目的，并且知道怎样达到这个目的。

但是有许多演讲者却不能把自己的目标与听众的目标相结合，所以手忙脚乱，说话结巴，演讲也就难免失败了。

有一位美国国会议员曾被强行轰赶下了纽约旧马戏场的演讲台，因为他很不明智地选择了要做一次说明性演讲。听众可不想听什么教训，他们只想得到快乐。他们刚开始时耐心而有礼貌地听他讲了10分钟，但在后15分钟，大家都希望他最好尽快结束。可是他却不理会这些，仍然没完没了地说个没完。听众们再也不愿忍受了，开始有人嘲讽地喝彩，其他人接着起哄，立刻就有上千人吹起口哨，甚至大声吼叫起来。这位议员真是太愚蠢了，居然还感觉不到听众的心情，仍然继续讲他的话。这激怒了听众。一场战斗展开了。人们的不耐烦立即激化成怒火，他们决定让他闭嘴。于是，抗议声越来越大。最终，吼叫和愤怒淹没了他的声音——20英尺处都听不

up, acknowledge defeat, and retire in humiliation.

Profit by his example. Fit the purpose of your talk to the audience and the occasion. If the congressman had decided in advance whether his goal of informing the audience would fit the goal of the audience in coming to the political rally, he would not have met with disaster. Choose one of the four purposes only after you have analyzed the audience and the occasion which brings them together.

To give you guidance in the important area of speech construction, this entire chapter is devoted to the short talk to get action. The next three chapters will be devoted to the other major speech purposes: to inform, to impress and convince, and to entertain. Each purpose demands a different organizational pattern of treatment, each has its own stumbling blocks that must be hurdled. First, let's get down to the brass tacks of organizing our talks to get the audience to act.

Is there some method of marshaling our material so that we will have the best chance for successful follow through on what we ask the audience to do? Or is it just a matter of hit-and-miss tactics?

I remember discussing this subject with my as sociates back in the thirties when my classes were beginning to catch on all over the country. Because of the size of our groups we were using a two-minute limit on the talks given by class members. This limitation did not affect the talk when the purpose of the speaker was merely to entertain or inform. But when we came to the talk to actuate, that was something else. The talk to get action just didn't get off the ground when we used the old system of introduction, body, and conclusion—the organizational pattern followed by speakers since Aristotle. Something new and different was obviously needed to provide us with a sure-fire method of obtaining results in a two-minute talk designed to get action from the listeners.

We held meetings in Chicago, Los Angeles, and New York. We appealed to all our instructors, many of them on the faculties of speech departments in some of our most respected universities. Others were men who held key posts in business administration. Some were from the rapidly expanding field of advertising and promotion. From this amalgam of background and brains, we hoped to get a new approach to speech organization, one that would be streamlined, and one that would reflect our age's need for a psychological as well as a logical method for influencing the listener to act.

到他的声音了。他被吼叫和嘘叫声轰下了台，简直羞辱难当。

我们要以此为鉴，让自己的演讲适合听众和场合。那位议员如果事先斟酌一下自己演讲的目的是否适合前来参加政治集会的听众的目的，他就不会有如此惨败了。所以，一定要事先分析听众和场合之后，才可以从四种目的中选择一种来进行你的演讲。

为了让读者获得“搭建演讲架构”方面的指导，本章专门介绍如何“说服听众采取行动”。接下来的三章则着重讨论演讲的其他几个重要目标：说明情况；增强印象令人信服；带给听众欢乐。每一个目标都需要采取不同的组织方式，各自都有其易犯的错误和必须克服的障碍。首先，我们谈谈如何组织演讲素材，使听众乐意采取行动。

有没有什么方法，肯定可以把我们要演讲的材料组织好，让听众能轻松地抓住我们要求他们去做的事情呢?或者它只不过是一种偶尔有效的方法呢?

我记得在20世纪30年代曾和同事们讨论过这个话题。当时我的课程在全国各地开始受到欢迎。由于班上人数众多，我们便要求每个学员的演讲只有两分钟。如果演讲者的目标只定位在娱乐或说明情况，这个限制对演讲并不会造成影响。但是，当我们学习“鼓励听众采取行动”的演讲时，情况就不一样了。如果采用自亚里士多德以来就被演讲者遵循的传统的演讲模式——绪论、本论和结论，这种激励听众采取行动的演讲便无法展开。我们显然需要一些新鲜的东西为我们提供一个稳妥有效的方法，在两分钟之内得到结果，并从听众那里获得反应。

我们分别在芝加哥、洛杉矶和纽约举行会议，向所有的老师请教。他们当中有在名牌大学演讲系执教的；有在事业经营方面占有举足轻重地位的；也有来自正在快速扩张的广告和促销界的。我们希望结合这些背景和智慧，找到一种新的组织演讲结构的方法——一个合理的、能反映我们时代需要的、符合心理学和逻辑学的方法，以影响听众并让他们采取行动。

天道酬勤，我们从这些讨论中终于研究出组织演讲结构的“魔术公式”。这个方法在班上采

We were not disappointed from those discussions came the Magic Formula of speech construction. We began using it in our classes and we have been using it ever since. What is the Magic Formula? Simply this: Start your talk by giving us the details of your Example, an incident that graphically illustrates the main idea you wish to get across. Second, in specific clearcut terms give your Point, tell exactly what you want your audience to do; and third, give your reason, that is, highlight the advantage or benefit to be gained by the listener when he does what you ask him to do.

This is a formula highly suited to our swiftpaced way of life. Speakers can no longer afford to indulge in long, leisurely introductions. Audiences are composed of busy people who want whatever the speaker has to say in straightforward language. They are accustomed to the digested, boiled-down type of journalism that presents the facts straight from the shoulder. They are exposed to hard-driving Madison Avenue advertising that shoots the message in forceful, clear terms from signboard, television screen, magazine, and newspaper. Every word is measured and nothing is wasted. By using the Magic Formula you can be certain of gaining attention and focusing it upon the main point of your message. It cautions against indulgence in vapid opening remarks, such as: "I didn't have time to prepare this talk very well," or "When your chairman asked me to talk on this subject, I wondered why he selected me." *Audiences are not interested in apologies or excuses, real or simulated.* They want action. In the Magic Formula you give them action from the opening word.

The formula is ideal for short talks, because it is based upon a certain amount of suspense. The listener is caught up in the story you are relating but he is not aware of what the point of your talk is until near the end of the two—or three-minute period. In cases where demands are made upon the audience, this is almost necessary for success. No speaker who wants his audience to dig deep in their pocketbooks for a cause, no matter how worthy, will get very far by starting like this: "Ladies and gentlemen. I'm here to collect five dollars from each of you." There would be a scramble for the exits. But if the speaker describes his visit to the Children's Hospital, where he saw a particularly poignant case of need, a little child who lacked financial help for an operation in a distant hospital, and then asks for contributions, the chances of getting support from his audience

用后,我们一直使用到今天。这个“魔术公式”是什么呢?很简单:一开始就描述实例的细节,生动地说明你希望传达给听众的意念;其次,详细而清晰地表达你的观点,确切地说出你想让听众做什么;第三,陈述缘由,向听众强调,如果按照你所说的去做,他们会获得什么好处。

这个公式非常适合当今快节奏的生活。演讲者不能再沉湎于冗长而闲散的绪论之中。人们越来越忙,他们希望讲演者以直接的言语,一针见血地说出要说的话。他们习惯于听精简而浓缩的新闻报道,使他们不必转弯抹角便能直接获得事实。他们全都被淹没在麦迪逊大街上铺天盖地的广告中。这些广告使用了招牌、电视、杂志和报纸上的一些鲜明有力的词语,把信息一股脑儿倾出;它们一字千金,没有半点儿浪费。所以利用这个“魔术公式”,可以保证引起听众的注意,并可以将焦点对准演讲的重点。它可以避免“我没有时间把这场演讲准备得很好”,或“你们的主席请我谈论这个题目时,我在想他为何要挑选我”之类毫无意义的开场白。听众对道歉或辩解不感兴趣,不论你的道歉或辩解是出于真心还是假意。他们要的是行动。在这个“魔术公式”里,你一开口便给了他们行动。

这套公式用于简短演讲时非常理想,因为其中有着某种程度的悬念。在你开始叙述时,听众就会被你的故事所吸引,但要等到两三分钟之后,他们才能知道你的重点。如果你希望听众照你的要求去做,这一招就很有必要。演讲者如果想让听众为某件事而慷慨解囊,却这样开口:“各位女士,各位先生,我来这儿是想向各位每人收取5美元。”那么,不管这件事多么值得他们掏钱,他们一定会争先恐后地夺门而逃。相反,如果演讲者描述自己去探访儿童医院的时候,看到迫切待援的病例:一个幼童在偏远的医院里,因为缺乏经济援助而无法动手术,然后向听众呼吁救助,肯定会获得听众的支持。为期望中的行动铺路的,正是生动的故事和实例。

让我们再看看列兰·史脱先生是怎样通过事件或事例来打动听众,让他们支持联合国儿童救援行动的:

would be immeasurably enhanced. It is the story, the Example, that prepares the way for the desired action.

Note how the incident-example is used by Leland Stowe to predispose his audience to support the United Nations' Appeal for Children:

> I pray that I'll never have to do it again. Can there be anything much worse than to put only a peanut between a child and death? I hope you'll never have to do it, and live with the memory of it afterward. If you had heard their voices and seen their eyes, on that January day in the bombscarred workers' district of Athens... Yet all I had left was a half-pound can of peanuts. As I struggled to open it, dozens of ragged kids held me in a vise of frantically clawing bodies. Scores of mothers, with babes in their arms, pushed and fought to get within arm's reach. They held their babies out toward me. Tiny hands of skin and bone stretched convulsively. I tried to make every peanut count.
>
> In their frenzy they nearly swept me off my feet. Nothing but hundreds of hands: begging hands, clutching hands, despairing hands; all of them pitifully little hands. One salted peanut here, and one peanut there. Six peanuts knocked from my fingers, and a savage scramble of emaciated bodies at my feet. Another peanut here, and another peanut there. Hundreds of hands, reaching and pleading; hundreds of eyes with the light of hope flickering out. I stood there helpless, an empty blue can in my hand... Yes, I hope it will never happen to you.

The Magic Formula can be used also in writing business letters and giving instructions to fellow employees and subordinates. Mothers can use it when motivating their children, and children will find it useful when appealing to their parents for a favor or privilege. You will find it a psychological tool that can be used to get your ideas across to others every day of your life.

Even in advertising the Magic Formula is used every day. Eveready Batteries recently ran a series of radio and television commercials built upon this Formula. In the Example step, the announcer told of someone's experience of being trapped, for instance, in an overturned car late at night. After giving the graphic details of the accident, he then called upon the victim to finish the story by telling how the beams of the flashlight, powered by Eveready Batteries, brought help in time. Then the announcer went on to the Point and Reason: "Buy Eveready Batteries and you may

> 我祈祷自己再也不要为此而奔走呼吁了:一个孩子和死亡之间,只差一颗花生。请想想,还有比这更凄惨的吗?我希望在座诸位也永远不要这样奔走呼吁,永远不要活在这种悲惨的记忆里。如果某一天,你在雅典被炸得千疮百孔的工人居住区里,听到了他们的声音,见到了他们的眼睛……可是,我的记忆中所留下的一切,只有半磅重的一罐花生。当我费力地打开它时,一群群衣衫褴褛的孩子把我团团围住,朝我伸出他们的手。还有大批的母亲,怀抱婴儿在推挤争抢……她们都把婴儿伸向我,婴儿那只剩皮包骨的小手抽搐地伸张着。我尽力使每颗花生都能起作用。
>
> 在他们疯狂地挤拥之下,我几乎被撞倒。我举目一望,只见上百只手:乞求的手、抓握的手、绝望的手——全都是瘦小得可怜的手。他们这里分一颗盐花生,那里分一颗盐花生。有六颗花生从我手里掉了下来,那些瘦弱的身体在我脚下争抢着。他们在这里分一颗,再在那里分一颗。数以百只的手伸向我,请求着;数以百只的眼睛闪射着希望的光芒。我无助地站在那里,手中只剩下一个蓝色的空罐子……啊,我希望这种情况永远都不会发生在诸位身上。

这套"魔术公式"还可运用于写商业书信和对员工作指示。母亲可以利用它来激励孩子,而孩子也会发现利用它向父母要求什么也很容易。你会发现它就像一把心理利器,在日常生活中,你可以通过它把自己的理念传达给别人。

即使在广告界,这套"魔术公式"每天也都被使用着。伊弗雷迪电池公司最近在广播和电视上做了一系列广告,就是根据这套公式设计的。首先是主持人讲一个故事:某个人因事故而在深夜被困在一辆翻倒的汽车里。主持人绘声绘色地描述这个意外之后,又请出受害者告诉观众,他是如何通过使用伊弗雷迪电池的手电筒发出亮光,及时为他带来援助的。然后,主持人再回到他的目标,点出"重点和缘由":"购买伊弗雷迪电池,你就可以在类似的紧急事故中生存。"

survive a similar emergency." These stories were all true experiences out of the Eveready Battery Company's files. I don't know how many Eveready Batteries this particular advertising series sold, but I do know that the Magic Formula is an effective method of presenting what you want an audience to do, or to avoid. Let us take up the steps, one at a time.

FIRST/ GIVE YOUR EXAMPLE, AN INCIDENT FROM YOUR LIFE

This is the part of your talk that will take up the major portion of your time. In it you describe an experience that taught you a lesson. Psychologists say we learn in two ways: one, by the Law of Exercise, in which a series of similar incidents leads to a change of our behavioral patterns; and two, by the Law of Effect, in which a single event may be so startling as to cause a change in our conduct. All of us have had this type of unusual experience. We do not have to search long for these incidents because they lie close to the surface of our memories. Our conduct is guided to a large extent by these experiences. By vividly reconstructing these incidents we can make them the basis of influencing the conduct of others. We can do this because people respond to words in much the same way that they respond to real happenings.

In the Example part of your talk, then, you must recreate a segment of your experience in such a way that it tends to have the same effect upon your audience as it originally had upon you. This places upon you the obligation to clarify, intensify, and dramatize your experiences in a way that will make them interesting and compelling to your listeners. Below are a number of suggestions which will help to make the Example step of your action talk clear, intense, and meaningful.

BUILD YOUR EXAMPLE UPON A SINGAE PERSONAL EXPERIENCE

The incident type of example is particularly powerful when it is based upon a single event that had a dramatic impact upon your life. It may not have taken more than a few seconds, but in that short span of time you learned an unforgettable lesson. Not long ago a man in one of our classes told of a terrifying experience when he tried to swim to shore from his overturned boat. I am sure that everyone in his audience made up his mind that, faced with a similar situation, he would follow this speaker's advice and stay with the capsized boat until help came. I remember another

这些故事都来自伊弗雷迪电池公司的真实档案资料。我不知道这套广告帮助伊弗雷迪公司卖了多少电池，但我可以确信这套“魔术公式”真的很有用，可以有效地向听众陈述你要他们去做或避免去做的事情。

现在，我们还是一步步地进行讨论吧。

一、用自己生活中的事件作例证

你生活中的事例是演讲的一部分，应该占你演讲的大部分时间。在这个阶段，应该描述曾给你带来启示的经验。心理学家说，人们学习的方式有两种：一是练习律，即让一连串的类似事件来改变人的行为模式；二是效应律，即让单一的事件产生强烈的震撼力，并造成人们行为的改变。我们每个人都有过这种不同寻常的经验，这是不需要花太多的时间去苦苦搜寻的。我们的行为也多半受这些经验的引导。如果能把这些事件重新组织起来，就可以把它们变成影响别人行为的事实基础。这一点我们应该很容易做到，因为人们对言辞的反应和对实际发生的事情的反应都差不多。

在举例的时候，一定要把自己经验中的东西重新改造，使听众产生与你当初一样的感受。为了达到这个效果，你可以把你的经验清楚地叙述出来，突出其特点，并使之富有戏剧化，让它们听起来更有趣，也更有力量。下面的建议，可以让你举例的步骤清晰有力，具有意义。

1. 根据个人经验举例

如果这种例子曾经是对你的生活造成强烈冲击的单一事件，将会很有威力。事情的发生也许不超过几秒钟，可是在那短短的一瞬间，你已经学到了难忘的一课。比如，不久前我们班上一个学员讲了他竭力从翻转的船边游上岸的可怕经历。我相信每个听众都会这样想，如果自己遇到了类似的情况，一定会听从他的忠告而留在船边，等待救援人员的到来。我还记得另一个演

example of a speaker's harrowing experience involving a child and an overturned power mower. That incident was so graphically etched in my mind that I will always be on guard when children are hovering near my power mower.

Many of our instructors have been so impressed by what they have heard in their classes that they have acted promptly to prevent similar accidents around their homes. One keeps a fire extinguisher handy in his kitchen, for instance, because of a talk he heard which vividly recreated a tragic fire that started from a cooking accident. Another has labeled all bottles containing poison, and has seen to it that they are out of the reach of his children. This action was prompted by a talk detailing the experience of a distraught parent when she discovered her child unconscious in the bathroom with a bottle of poison clutched in her hand.

A single personal experience that taught you a lesson you will never forget is the first requisite of a persuasive action talk. With this kind of incident you can move audiences to act—if it happened to you, your listeners reason, it can happen to them, and they had better take your advice by doing what you ask them to do.

START YOUR TALK WITH A DETAIL OF YOUR EXAMPLE

One of the reasons for starting your talk with the example step is to catch attention at once.

Take a tip from top-flight magazine and newspaper writers: begin right in your example and you will capture the attention of your audience immediately.

Here are some opening sentences that drew my attention like a magnet: "In 1942, I found myself on a cot in a hospital"; "Yesterday at breakfast my wife was pouring the coffee and..."; "Last July I was driving at a fast clip down Highway 42..."; "The door of my office opened and Charlie Vann, our foreman, burst in"; "I was fishing in the middle of the lake; I looked up and saw a motor boat speeding toward me."

If you start your talk with phrases that answer one of the questions, Who? When? Where? What? How? or Why? you will be using one of the oldest communication devices in the world to get attention—the story. "Once upon a time" are the magic words that open the floodgates of a child's imagination. With this same human interest approach you can captivate the minds of your listeners with your first words.

讲者讲的经历:这是关于一个孩子和一台翻转过来的电动剪草机的悲惨事件,这在我的脑海里留下了鲜明深刻的印象,以后只要有孩子在我的电动剪草机附近玩耍时,我就会提高警觉。

我们很多讲师,因为他们对在班上听到的事情印象深刻,所以回家后便立即采取行动,防止家庭再发生类似的意外。例如,有一个人因为听了一场关于烹饪意外而引起的火灾的演讲之后,就立即将灭火器放在厨房内。另一个人也从演讲中吸取教训,把家中所有装毒品的瓶子贴上标签,并特别留意把它们放在孩子们拿不到的地方。这是因为他听了一场演讲:一个母亲发现她的孩子不省人事地躺在浴缸里,手里拿着一瓶毒药。当时这位母亲真是心神发狂了。

一次使你永远都不会忘记的教训,是说服性演讲必备的条件。利用这种事件,可以打动听众并让他们采取行动——因为听众会这样推理,如果你会遭遇到,他们也可能会遭遇到,那么最好是听你的忠告,做你希望他们做的事。

2. 开门见山叙述事例的细节

在演讲一开始就进入举例阶段,这样做可以立即抓住听众的注意力。

请记住某位一流报纸杂志作者的一句忠言:直接开始你的例证,就可以立即抓住听众的注意力。

我在这里列出一些开场白,它们都像磁石一样吸引着我的注意力:"1942年,我发现自己躺在医院的病床上";"昨天早饭时,我妻子正在倒咖啡……";"去年7月,当我快速驾车驶下42号公路时……";"我办公室的门被打开了, 我们的领班查理·冯闯了进来";"我正在湖中央钓鱼;我一抬起头,看到一艘快艇正朝我快速开来"。

如果在开场白中讲清楚了人物、时间、地点、事件和发生的原因,那么你就是在使用最古老的获取听众注意力的沟通方式。"从前"是一个很有魔力的字眼,它可以打开孩子们幻想的水闸。采用相同的趣味方式,你也能一开口就抓住听众的注意力。

FILL YOUR EXAMPLE WITH RELEVANT DETAIL

Detail, of itself, is not interesting. A room cluttered with furniture and bric-a-brac is not attractive. A picture filled with too many unrelated details does not compel the eyes to linger upon it. In the same way, too many details—unimportant details—make conversation and public speaking a boring test of endurance. The secret is to select only those details that will serve to emphasize the point and reason of the talk. If you want to get across the idea that your listeners should have their cars checked before going on a long trip, then all the details of your example step should be concerned with what happened to you when you failed to have your car checked before taking a trip. If you tell about how you enjoyed the scenery or where you stayed when you arrived at your destination, you will only succeed in clouding the point and dissipating attention.

But relevant detail, couched in concrete, colorful language, is the best way to recreate the incident as it happened and to picturize it for the audience. To say merely that you once had an accident because of negligence is bald, uninteresting, and hardly likely to move anyone to be more careful behind the wheel of a car. But to paint a word picture of your frightening experience, using the full range of multisensory phraseology, will etch the event upon the consciousness of the listeners.

For instance, here is the way one class member developed an Example step that points up vividly the need for great caution on wintry roads:

> I was driving north on Highway 41 in Indiana one morning just before Christmas, in 1949. In the car were my wife and two children. For several hours we had been creeping along on a sheet of mirror-like ice; the slightest touch on the steering wheel sent the rear of my Ford into a sickening slide. Few drivers got out of line or attempted to pass, and the hours seemed to creep as slowly as the cars.
>
> Then we came to an open stretch where the ice was melted by the sun and I stepped on the accelerator to make up for lost time. Other cars did the same. Everybody suddenly seemed in a hurry to get to Chicago first. The children began to sing in the back seat as the tension of danger subsided.
>
> The road suddenly went uphill and into a wooded area. As the speeding car reached the top I saw, too late, that the northern slope of the hill, still untouched by the sun's rays, was

3. 使事例充满相关细节

细节本身并不具备趣味性。例如,到处散置着家具和古董的房间并不好看,一幅图画全是不相关的细物也不能让人们停留注视。同样,无关紧要的细节太多,也会让当众演讲成为无聊的活动。所以,你必须选择那些能强调你的演讲重点和缘由的细节。如果你想告诉大家,在长途旅行前应该先检查车辆的性能状况,那么你应该详细讲述某次旅行前,因为你没有事先检查车辆而发生的悲剧。相反,如果你先讲怎样观赏风景,或者到达目的地后在什么地方过夜,就只会遮盖重点,分散听众的注意力。

如果你能围绕话题重点,用相关细节来渲染你的故事,这确实是最好的方法。它可以重现当时的情况,让听众感觉如在眼前。相反,只说你从前因疏忽而发生意外,就很难让听众小心驾车,因为这样的方法不会让人感到有吸引力。如果你把惊心动魄的经历转化为语言,使用各种辞藻来表达你的切身感受,那么就能把这件事深深地烙在听众的大脑中。

请看下面的实例,这是一个训练班的学员讲的例子,生动地指出了在寒冬时开车要多么小心:

> 1949年圣诞节前一天的早上,我在印第安纳州41号公路上往北行驶,我的妻子和两个孩子也在车里。我们已经沿着一段平滑如镜的冰路,缓慢地行驶了好几个小时。稍稍触及方向盘,我的福特车就会任意打滑。很少有司机会离线超车,时间就这样一小时一小时地慢慢过去。
>
> 我们来到一处开阔的转弯处。这儿的冰雪已经被阳光照射得开始融化,所以我就加大了油门,想弥补失去的时间。其他人也和我一样,大家似乎都很匆忙,想第一个抵达芝加哥。由于不再紧张了,孩子们也开始在车后座上唱起歌来。
>
> 汽车突然走上一段上坡路, 进了一处森林地带。当汽车急驰到顶端时, 我突然看到——可是太迟了——北边的山坡因为没有阳光照射,所以路面的冰还没有融化。我看到我们前面有两辆车疯狂地侧翻了下去,然后我们的车也滑了下去。我们飞过路沿,完全失

like a smooth river of ice. I had a fleeting glance of two wildly careening cars in front of us and then we went into a skid. Over the shoulder we went, hopelessly out of control, and landed in a snowbank, still upright; but the car that had been following us went into a skid, too, and crashed into the side of our car, smashing in the doors and showering us with glass.

The abundance of detail in this example made it easy for the audience to project themselves into the picture. After all, your purpose is to make your audience see what you saw, hear what you heard, feel what you felt. The only way you can possibly achieve this effect is to use an abundance of concrete details. As was pointed out in Chapter Four, the task of preparation of a talk is a task of reconstructing the answers to the questions Who? When? Where? How? and Why? You must stimulate the visual imagination of your listeners by painting word pictures.

RELIVE YOUR EXPERIENCE AS YOU RELATE IT

In addition to using picturesque details, the speaker should relive the experience he is describing. Here is where speaking approaches its sister field of acting. All great speakers have a sense of the dramatic, but this is not a rare quality, to be found only in the eloquent. Most children have a plentiful supply of it. Many persons of our acquaintance are gifted with a sense of timing, facial expression, mimicry, or pantomime that is a part, at least, of this priceless ability to dramatize. Most of us have some skill along these lines, and with a little effort and practice we can develop more of it.

The more action and excitement you can put into the retelling of your incident, the more it will make an impression on your listeners. No matter how rich in detail a talk may be, it will lack punch if the speaker does not give it with all the fervor of recreation. Are you describing a fire? Give us the feeling of excitement that ran through the crowd as the firemen battled the blaze. Are you telling us about an argument with your neighbor? Relive it; dramatize it. Are you relating your final struggles in the water as panic swept over you? Make your audience feel the desperation of those awful moments in your life.

For one of the purposes of the example is to make your talk memorable. Your listeners will remember your talk and what you want them to do only if the example sticks in their minds. We recall George Washington's honesty because of the cherry tree incident popularized in the Weem's

去了控制，然后落进雪堆里，仍然直立着。但紧跟着我们的车也滑了下来，正好撞到我们车的一侧，我们的车门被撞碎了，我们身上全是碎玻璃。

这个事例中丰富的细节，很容易让听众身临其境。毕竟你的目的就是要让听众看到你所看到的，让听众听到你所听到的，让听众感觉到你所感觉到的。而要做到这一点，唯一的方法就是使用丰富而具体的细节。正如第四章提到的，准备一场演讲就是回答如下问题：何人？何时？何地？如何？为什么？你必须用图画般的词汇去激发听众的想象力。

4. 叙述事例时让经验重现

除了运用图画般的细节之外，演讲者还应该让情景再现。演讲和“表演”有相近的地方。所有伟大的演讲家都有一种表演的天分，但这并非只能在雄辩家身上找到的稀有特质，孩童们大多具有这种才能。我们所认识的许多人也都有这样的天赋，他们富于面部表情，善于模仿或做手势，这都是表演的宝贵资质。我们多数人也都有这样的技巧，只要稍微努力和练习，就能有一定的发展。

在描述事件时，如果能加入越多的动作和激动的情感，就越能给听众留下深刻的印象。演讲不论多么富于细节，如果演讲者不能以再创造的热情来讲述，就是没有力量的。例如，你想描述一场大火吗?那不妨为我们讲述消防队与火焰搏斗时人们感受到的激烈、焦灼、兴奋、紧张的感觉，并把这些传递给我们。你想告诉我们你同邻居之间的一场争吵吗?那就把它再现出来，戏剧化地表现出来。你想描述在水中做最后挣扎时的惊恐情绪吗?那就让我们感受到你生命中那些可怕时刻的绝望吧。

举例的目的之一，就是让听众对你的演讲牢记不忘。只有让事例深刻在听众的脑海中，他们才会记住你的演讲，以及你希望他们去做的事。我们之所以记得华盛顿的诚实，是由于他小时候砍樱桃树的事情，已经通过韦姆斯的传记而深入人心。《圣经·新约》是嘉言懿行的丰富宝

biography. The New Testament is a rich storehouse of principles of ethical conduct reinforced by examples full of human interst—for instance, the story of the Good Samaritan.

In addition to making your talk more easily remembered, the incident-example makes your talk more interesting, more convincing, and easier to understand. Your experience of what life has taught you is freshly perceived by the audience: they are in a sense, predetermined to respond to what you want them to do. This brings us right to the doorstep of the second phase of the Magic Formula.

SECOND/ STATE YOUR POINT, WHAT YOU WANT THE AUDIENCE TO DO

The Example step of your talk to get action has consumed more than three-quarters of your time. Assume you are talking for two minutes. You have about twenty seconds in which to hammer home the desired action you wish the audience to take and the benefit they can expect as a result of doing what you ask. The need for detail is over. The time for forthright, direct assertion has come. It is the reverse of the newspaper technique. Instead of giving the headline first, you give the news story and then you headline it with your Point or appeal for action. This step is governed by three rules:

MAKE THE POINT BRIEF AND SPECIFIC

Be precise in telling the audience exactly what you want them to do. People will do only what they clearly understand. It is essential to ask yourself just exactly what it is you want the audience to do now that they have been disposed to action by your example. It is a good idea to write the point out as you would a telegram, trying to reduce the number of words and to make your language as clear and explicit as possible. Don't say: "Help the patients in our local orphanage." That's too general. Say instead: "Sign up tonight to meet next Sunday to take twenty-five children on a picnic."

It is important to ask for an overt action, one that can be seen, rather than mental actions, which are too vague. For instance, "Think of your grandparents now and then," is too general to be acted upon. Say instead: "Make a point of visiting your grandparents this weekend." A statement such as, "Be patriotic," should be converted into "Cast your vote next Tuesday."

MAKE THE POINT EASY FOR LISTENERS TO DO

No matter what the issue is, controversial or otherwise, it is the speaker's responsibility to word his point, the request for action, in such a way that it will be easy for his listeners to

库,其中的道德操守原则都是通过富有人情味的故事来传达和强化的,例如“善良的撒马利亚人”的故事。

这种事例,除了可以让你的演讲更容易被记住之外,还可以使你的演讲更加有趣,更具有说服力,也更容易理解。生活教给你的经验,已经被听众重新感知:就某种意义而言,他们已经下定决心按照你的意思去做。这样,我们就到了“魔术公式”第二道门前。

二、直接提出问题,提出诉求

在说服听众行动的演讲中,举例阶段已经用去了四分之三以上的时间。假设你只讲两分钟,那你就只剩下20秒钟来表达你期望听众采取的行动,以及他们采取这种行动会有什么好处。这时不再需要讲述细节了,该做直截了当的声明。这与报纸消息的技巧相反,你不是先说标题,而是先讲故事,再以自己的目的或对听众行动的诉求作为标题。这一阶段要注意三条法则:

1. 使重点简明扼要

要简明扼要地告诉听众,你希望他们做什么。人们一般只会做他们清楚地了解的事情。所以,你最好先问自己,你究竟要在听众听了你的例证之后,他们该做什么?像写电报稿一样把重点写下来,是个很不错的主意,应该尽可能精简字数,又要使其清楚明白。不要说:“帮助我们本地孤儿院的病童吧。”因为这样太笼统。应该这样说:“今晚就签名,下星期天集合,带25名孤儿去野餐。”

要求采取公开行动很重要,这个行动应该是看得见的,而不是心理活动,否则就太含混了。例如“时时想想祖父母吧!”就太含糊而不好采取行动;而这样说“本周末就去看望祖父母吧!”则要更明确些。再比如说“要爱国”,如果改成“下星期二就请投下你的一票”,就更明确了。

2. 使重点简单易行

不论问题是什么,不论人们是不是还在争论不休,演讲者必须把自己的重点和对行动的请

understand and to do. One of the best ways to do this is to be specific. If you want your listeners to improve their ability to remember names, don't say: "Start now to improve your memory of names." That is so general it is difficult to do. Say instead: "Repeat the name of the next stranger you meet five times within five minutes after you meet him."

Speakers who give detailed action points are more apt to be successful in motivating their audiences than those who rest upon generalities. To say: "Sign the get well card in the back of the room" is far better than to urge your listeners to send a card or write a letter to a hospitalized fellow class member.

STATE THE POINT WITH FORCE AND CONVICTION

The Point is the entire theme of your talk. You should give it, therefore, with forcefulness and conviction. As a headline stands out in block letters, your request for action should be emphasized by vocal animation and directness. You are about to make your last impression on the audience. Make it in such a way that the audience feels the sincerity of your appeal for action. There should be no uncertainty or diffidence about the way you ask for the order. This persuasiveness of manner should carry over to your last words, in which you give the third step of the Magic Formula.

THIRD/ GIVE THE REASON OR BENEFIT THE AUDIENCE MAY EXPECT

Here again, brevity and economy are necessary. In the reason step you hold out the incentive or reward the listeners may expect if they do what you have asked in the Point.

BE SURE THE REASON IS RELEVAN TO THE EXAMPLE

Much has been written about motivation in public speaking. It is a vast subject and a useful one for anyone engaged in persuading others to act. In the short talk to get action, on which we are centering our attention in this chapter, all you can hope to do is highlight the benefit in a sentence or two and then sit down. It is most important, however, that you focus upon the benefit that was brought out in the Example step. If you tell of your experience in saving money by buying a used car, and urge your listeners to buy a secondhand car, you must emphasize in your reason that they, too, may enjoy the economical advantages of buying secondhand. You should not deviate

求讲得让听众容易理解和实行。最好的方法之一就是要明确。例如,你想让听众加强记忆人名的能力,千万不要说"现在便开始加强你对人名的记忆",因为这样太笼统了,让人无从做起。不如说:"在你遇到下一个陌生人的5分钟之内,就把他的姓名重复5次。"

演讲者对听众给予明确的行动指示,比概略的言辞更容易成功地引发听众的行动。例如"去讲堂后面,在祝贺康复的卡片上签名",要比劝听众寄一张慰问卡,或写信给一位住院的同学更好。

3. 强烈而满怀信心地表明观点

演讲的核心是观点,因此你应该强烈而且信心十足地陈述出来。就像标题应该特别突出显著一样,你对听众行动的请求也应该通过激烈的演讲,直接表达出来。你现在就要给听众留下积极的印象,让听众感觉到你的诚意。你的请求不应有不确定或信心不足的语气,游说的态度也应该持续到最后一个词,然后再进行"魔术公式"的第三步。

三、说明原因或听众可能获得的利益

在这个阶段,简短扼要依然是必要的。在这第三步,你必须说出自己演讲的动机;或者告诉听众,如果按照你的要求去做,他们会有什么益处。

1. 使缘由与事例相关

本书已经阐述了很多当众讲话的动机。这是个范围很大的题目,对于想说服听众采取行动的演讲者很有用处。在这一章我们谈的只是关于"获得听众行动的简短演讲",你所要做的,就是用一两句话把好处说出来,然后坐下。不过,最重要的是你所强调的好处应该是从你所举的事例引出来的。如果你想说自己买旧车省钱的经验,然后力劝听众买二手货,那么你必须强调他们买了二手车会有何经济益处。千万不可偏离事例,说有些旧车的样式比最新的汽车要好。

from the example by giving as your reason the fact that some used cars have better styling than the latest models.

BE SURE TO STRESS ONE REASON AND—ONE ONLY

Most salesmen can give a half-dozen reasons why you should buy their product, and it is quite possible that you can give several reasons to back up your Point and all of them may be relevant to the Example you used. But again it is best to choose one outstanding reason or benefit and rest your case on it. Your final words to the audience should be as clearcut as the message on an advertisement in a national magazine. If you study these ads upon which so much talent has been expended, you will develop skill in handling the point and reason of your talk.

No ad attempts to sell more than one product or one idea at a time. Very few ads in the big circulation magazines use more than one reason why you should buy. The same company may change its motivational appeal from one medium to another, from television to newspapers, for instance, but rarely will the same company make different appeals in one ad, whether vocal or visual.

If you study the ads you see in magazines and newspapers and on television and analyze their content you will be amazed at how often the Magic Formula is used to persuade people to buy. You will become aware of the ribbon of relevancy which binds the whole ad or commercial together into a unified package.

There are other ways of building up an example, for instance, by using exhibits, giving a demonstration, quoting authorities, making comparisons, and citing statistics. These will be explained more at length in Chapter Thirteen, where the longer talk to persuade will be discussed. In this chapter, the formula has been restricted to the personal incident type of example because, in the short talk to get action, it is by far the easiest and most interesting, dramatic, and persuasive method a speaker can use.

2. 必须强调一个理由,仅仅一个就足够

许多推销员可以举出半打理由,劝说你为什么应该购买他们的产品;你也能举出好几个理由,来支持你自己的观点,并且全都与你所使用的事例有关。然而,最好还是选一个最突出的理由或利益。说给听众的最后几句话应该清楚而明确,就像刊登在全国性的杂志里的广告词那样。如果你对这些融入了许多人的智慧设计出来的广告加以研究,你将会获得处理演讲中的"重点和缘由"的技巧。

没有哪个广告会一次推销两种或两种以上的产品或理念。在销售量很大的杂志中,也没有一个广告使用两个以上的理由来说明你为什么应该买某种商品。同一个公司也许会从一种媒介改为另一种媒介来刺激消费者的动机,如从电视改成报纸,但是同一家公司却很少在一个广告中做不同的诉求,不论是口头上的还是视觉上的。

如果你能研究一下报纸杂志和电视中的广告,分析它们的内容,你就会惊讶地发现,在劝说人们购买商品时,这一"魔术公式"被使用的次数实在是太多了。你可以由此体会到,"切题"是让整个广告成为一个统一整体的经纬线。

还有其他的方式来举例,例如陈列、展示、引述权威评论、比较和引用统计数字等。这些将在后面的章节详细介绍。本章中的"魔术公式"仅限于个人式的事例,因为在"获得听众行动的简短演讲"中,这套公式是迄今为止最简易、最有趣、最戏剧性而且最具说服力的方法。

2 Making the Talk to Inform

Probably you often have heard speakers like one who once made a United States Senate investigating committee squirm with annoyance. He was a high-ranking government official, but he did not know any better than to talk on and on, vaguely, without ever making his meaning clear. He was pointless and obscure, and the committee's confusion mounted by the moment. Finally one of its members, Samuel James Ervin, Jr., speaking as the senior Senator from North Carolina, got a chance to say a few words—and they were telling ones.

He said the official reminded him of a husband he knew back home. The husband notified his lawyer he wanted to divorce his wife, although he conceded she was beautiful, a fine cook, and a model mother.

"They Why do you want to divorce her?" his lawyer asked.

"Because she talks all the time." the husband replied.

"What does she talk about?"

"That's the trouble," the husband answered, "she never says ! "

This is the trouble, too, with many speakers, both women and men. Their hearers don't know what such speakers are talking about. They never say. They never make their meaning clear.

In Chapter Seven, you received a formula for making short talks to get action from your listeners. Now, I am going to give you methods to help make your meaning clear when you set out to inform, and not motivate, your listeners.

We make informative talks many times every day: giving directions or instructions, making explanations and reports. Of all the types of talks given every week to audiences everywhere, the talk to inform is second only to the talk to persuade or get action. The ability to speak clearly precedes the ability to move others to action. Owen D. Young, one of America's top industrialists, emphasizes the need for clear expression in today's world:

As one enlarges his ability to get others to understand him, he opens up to that extent his

第2章 说明性演讲

有一次,一位政府高级官员把美国参议院调查委员会搞得坐立不安,如坠雾里,也许就像你经常看到的某些演讲者那样。此人不停地说着,却含混不清,毫无重点,根本没有把他自己的意思讲清楚。整个委员会的困惑也逐渐增加。最后,一位来自北卡罗莱纳州的参议员小撒姆尔·詹姆斯·艾尔文终于抓住机会,说了几句精彩的比喻。

他说,这位官员让他想起家乡一个男人来。这个男人通知律师,说要和他老婆离婚,不过他却承认她很漂亮,是个好厨子,而且还是个模范母亲。

"那你为何还要和她离婚?"律师问他。

"因为她总是说个不停。"这个男人说。

"她都说些什么呢?"

"就是这个让我讨厌呀,"男人说,"因为她从来没说清楚过。"

这正是许多演讲者(无论男女)的问题所在。大家根本不知道他们在说些什么,他们也从来没有说清楚过,也从来没把自己的意思讲明白过。

在第七章中,介绍了一套做简短演讲并从听众那里获得行动的公式。现在,我还要教给你一些方法,帮助你在告知他人某一信息时,把自己的意思表达清楚。

我们每天都要做许多说明性的谈话,比如提出说明或指示,提出解释和报告。每星期在各地举行的各种类型的演讲中,说明性演讲仅次于说服性演讲或获得行动的演讲。清楚说话的能力,其实也是打动听众采取行动的能力。欧文·杨是美国工业巨子之一,他也强调了清晰的表达能力在当今社会的重要性:

opportunity for usefulness. Certainly in our society, where it is necessary for men even in the simplest matters to co-operate with each other, it is necessary for them first of all to understand each other. Language is the principal conveyor of understanding, and so we must learn to use it, not crudely but discriminatingly.

In this chapter are some suggestions to help you see language so clearly and discriminately that your audience will have no difficulty understanding you. "Everything that can be thought at all," said Ludwig Wittgenstein, "can be thought clearly. Everything that can be said, can be said clearly."

FIRST/ RESTRICT YOUR SUBJECT TO FIT THE TIME AT YOUR DISPOSAL

In one of his talks to teachers, Professor William James pauses to remark that one can make only one point in a lecture, and the lecture he referred to lasted an hour. Yet I recently heard a speaker, who was limited by a stop watch to three minutes, begin by saying that he wanted to call our attention to eleven points. Sixteen and a half seconds to each phase of his subject! Seems incredible, doesn't it, that an intelligent man should attempt anything so manifestly absurd? True, this is an extreme case but the tendency to err in that fashion, if not to that degree, handicaps almost every novice. He is like a Cook's guide who shows Paris to the tourist in one day. It can be done, just as one can walk through the American Museum of Natural History in thirty minutes. But neither clearness nor enjoyment results. Many a talk fails to be clear because the speaker seems intent upon establishing a world's record for ground covered in the allotted time. He leaps from one point to another with the swiftness and agility of a mountain goat.

If, for example, you are to speak on Labor Unions, do not attempt to tell us in three or six minutes why they came into existence, the methods they employ, the good they have accomplished, the evil they have wrought, and how to solve industrial disputes. No, no; if you strive to do that, no one will have a very clear conception of what you have said. It will be all confused, a blur, too sketchy, too much of a mere outline.

Wouldn't it be the part of wisdom to take one phase, and one phase only, of labor unions, and cover that adequately and illustrate it? It would. That kind of talk leaves a single impression. It is lucid, easy to listen to, easy to remember.

当一个人扩大了使他人了解自己的能力时,他也拓展了自己的作用。在我们的社会,即使是最简单的事情,也需要人们的彼此合作,所以他们首先必须相互了解。语言是沟通的主要传递媒介,所以我们必须学会使用它,不是粗略地学会,而是精确地学会。

本章的各项建议,将让你清晰、精确地使用语言,让听众毫无困难地了解你。罗德威·威根斯坦说:"凡是可以想到的事情,都是可以清楚地思考的。而凡是可以说出来的事,也是可以清楚地表述出来的。"

一、限制演讲题材,以适合特定的时间

威廉·詹姆斯教授曾向一些教师指出,一个人在一次演讲中只能针对一个要点。他所说的演讲,是指那种时间限定为一个小时的演讲。而我最近却听过一位演讲者所做的3分钟的演讲,他一开始就说,他想谈11个要点。平均用16.5秒钟来说明一个要点!怎么会有这样"聪明"的人,居然想做如此荒谬的事情,有些不可思议吧?当然,这也只是个别极端的例子,但是即使情况没有这么严重,对于任何新手来说,论点太大也注定会出差错。这就像一个导游,带着一群游客一天之内看完巴黎所有的风光,这当然不是办不到。但就像一个人也可以在30分钟之内看完美国国家历史博物馆一样,根本不记得看到了什么。许多演讲之所以讲不清楚,就是因为演讲者企图在指定的时间内创下世界纪录。因此,他就像只敏捷的山羊,飞快地从这一点跳到那一点。

假设你现在就以劳工联盟作为演讲的题目,你根本不可能在3分钟或6分钟内告诉我们这个组织成立的原因,它们所采用的方法,它们的建树和缺失,以及它们怎样解决工业争端等。如果你坚持这样做,没有人会对你所说的留下清晰印象。它将只是一片混乱和含糊,而且只是一些太过简单的大纲。

如果你只谈它的一个方面,并且仅此一个,对它进行详细讲述,这样做是不是更明智呢?当然是的。这样将给听众留下一个单一的印象,但透彻易懂,也容易记住。

When I went to call one morning on a company president whom I know, I found a strange name on his door. The personnel director, an old friend of mine, told me why.

"His name caught up with him." my friend said.

"His name?" I repeated. "He was one of the Joneses who control the company, wasn't he?"

"I mean his nickname," my friend said. "It was ' Where-Is-He-Now?' Everyone called him ' Where-Is-He-Now' Jones. He didn't last long. The family put a cousin in his place. He never took the pains to know what this business is all about. He'd put in a good long day, all right, but doing what? Popping in here, popping in there, all over the place, all the time. Just sort of covering ground. He thought it was more important for him to see that a shipping clerk turned out an electric light or that a stenographer picked up a paper clip than it was for him to study a big sales campaign. He wasn't in his office much. That's why we called him ' Where-Is-He-Now.'"

"Where-Is-He-Now" Jones reminds me of many speakers who could do much better than they do. They don't do better because they won't discipline themselves. They are the ones who, like Mr. Jones, try to cover too much ground. Haven't you heard them? And in the midst of a talk, haven't you wondered. "Where is he now?"

Even some experienced speakers are guilty of this fault. Perhaps the fact that they are capable in many other ways blinds them to the danger in dispersed effort. You need not be like them. Hold fast to your main theme. If you are to make yourself clear, your hearers must always be able to say, "I understand him.I know where he is now! "

SECOND/ ARRANGE YOUR IDEAS IN SEQUENCE

Almost all subjects can be developed by using a logical sequence based on time, space, or special topics. In the time sequence, for instance, you might consider your subject under the three categories of past, present, and future, or you might begin at a certain date and move backward or forward from that date. All process talks, for example, should begin at the raw-material stage and move through the various manufacturing steps that produce the finished product. How much detail you bring in will, of course, be governed by the time you have.

In the space sequence, you arrange your ideas according to some central point and go

有一天早晨,我去拜访一家公司的总经理,却发现他的门上挂着一个陌生的名字。这家公司的人事部长是我的老朋友,他告诉我为何换了人。

“他的名字害苦了他。”我这位朋友说。

“他的名字?”我不太明白,“他不是控制这家公司的董事之一吗?”

“我说的是他的绰号,”这位朋友说,“他的绰号叫‘他现在在哪里?’人们都叫他‘他现在在哪里’·琼斯。因为我们总找不到他,不知道他在哪里。他从来不肯花心思去了解公司的整个业务概况。他每天待在公司的时间很长,但是在忙什么呢?他只是这里蹿一下,那里蹿一下,这样打发漫漫长日。他认为看到船运部门的职员关掉一盏灯,或见到速记员拾起一张纸,比他研究一桩大买卖更重要。他很少坐在办公室,因此我们叫他‘他现在在哪里’。”

“他现在在哪里”·琼斯让我想起很多演讲者,他们本来可以表现得更好些的。他们之所以不能表现得更优秀,就因为他们没有抓住原则。他们像琼斯先生一样,想包揽更大的范围。你听过他们的演讲吗?在他们演讲的时候,你有没有想过“他现在在哪里”?

即使是那些经验丰富的演讲者有时也会犯这样的错误。也许他们具备多方面的才华,所以看不到精力分散的危险。但你可不要向他们学习,而是要紧扣主题。如果你让自己清楚明了,听众就会说:“我懂他所说的,我知道他现在在说什么! ”

二、遵循一定的顺序

几乎所有的演讲题材都可以利用一定的时间顺序、空间顺序或者事物的逻辑顺序来展开。比如时间顺序,可以按照过去、现在、将来“三段式”的顺序来处理材料,也可以从某一天开始进行倒叙或向前叙述。演讲的过程,都是从最粗糙的原材料开始,然后经过各种各样的制造阶段,最后完成真正的产品。至于其中加入多少细节,就取决于演讲的时间了。

outward from there or you cover the material directionally, north, south, east, and west. If you were to describe the city of Washington, D. C., you might take your listeners to the top of the capitol building and indicate the points of interest in each direction. If you are describing a jet engine or an automobile, for example, you might best discuss it by breaking it down into its component parts.

Some subjects have a built-in sequence. If you set out to explain the structure of the United States Government, you will do well to follow this inherent organizational pattern and discuss it according to the legislative, executive, and judicial branches.

THIRD/ ENUMERATE YOUR POINTS AS YOU MAKE THEM

One of the simplest ways to keep a talk shipshape in the minds of your listeners is to mention plainly as you go along that you are taking up first one point and then another.

"My first point is this: ..."You can be as blunt as that. When you've discussed the point, you can say frankly that you are going to the second one. You can keep on that way to the end.

Dr. Ralph J. Bunche, when assistant secretarygeneral of the United Nations, began an important talk sponsored by the City Club of Rochester, New York, in this straightforward manner:

"I have chosen to speak tonight on the topic, 'the Challenge of Human Relations,'for two reasons," he said. He went on at once to add, "In the first place..."He continued soon, "In the second place..."Throughout the talk, he was careful to make clear to his audience that he was leading it, point by point, to his conclusion:

"We must never lose faith in man's potential power for good."

The same method was given an effective twist when the economist, Paul H. Douglas, spoke to a congressional joint committee struggling with means to stimulate business when it once was lagging in this country. He spoke both as a tax expert and as Senator from Illinois.

"My theme," he began, "is this: The quickest and most effective way to act is by means of a tax cut for lower and middle income groups—that is, those groups which tend to spend almost all their income."

"Specifically..." he went on.

在空间顺序上,可以立足于某个点,然后由此向外拓展;或者按照方位来处理,例如北方、南方、东方和西方。假设你要描述华盛顿城,你可以领着听众,从国会山庄的顶端,按照各个方向来叙述有趣的地方。如果你要说明一架喷气引擎或一辆汽车,最好是把它分解成各部分的组成零件,再来逐一谈论。

而有些演讲题材本身就具有自己的内在顺序。例如,如果你要介绍美国政府的结构,不妨按照立法、行政、司法三部门的内在结构来介绍,效果必然很好。

三、逐一列举你的要点

要想让演讲给听众一种井然有序、条理分明的印象,最简单的方法之一,就是在演讲过程中明白地表示:现在你先讲哪一点,接下来再讲哪一点。

"我要讲的第一点是……"你完全可以这样开门见山地说。讨论完这一点,你可以明确地说将要谈第二点,就这样一直说到结尾。

拉尔夫·布切博士担任联合国助理秘书长的时候,在纽约罗切斯特城市俱乐部主办的一次重要演讲上,这样直截了当地说:

"今晚我选择的演讲题目是'人际关系的挑战',是因为以下两个原因,"然后他又说,"首先……其二……"从头到尾,他都小心翼翼地让听众明白他的每一个重点。他引领听众,最后得出结论:

"我们不能对人类向善的天性失去信心。"

在美国国会联合委员会想方设法试图刺激一度停滞不前的商业会议上,经济学家道格拉斯以税务专家和伊利诺伊州参议员的身份演讲,巧妙而有效地使用了相同的办法。

他是这样开始的:"我的演讲主题是:最迅速、最有效的行动方式,是对中低收入阶层减税,因为这些群体几乎会花光他们所有的收入。"

"Further ..."he continued.

"In addition..." he continued.

"There are three principal reasons: ... First ... Second ... Third...

"To summation, what we need is an immediate tax cut for low and middle income groups in order to increase demand and purchasing power."

FOURTH/ COMPARE THE STRANGE WITH THE FAMILIAR

Sometimes you will find yourself floundering in a vain attempt to explain your meaning. It's something quite: clear to you but requiring involved explanation if your hearers are to be clear about it too. What to do? Compare it with something your hearers do understand; say one thing is like the other, the strange like the familiar.

Suppose you are discussing one of chemistry's contributions to industry—a catalyst. It is a substance that causes changes to occur in other substances without changing itself. That's fairly simple. But isn't this better? It is like a little boy in a schoolyard, tripping, punching, upsetting, poking all the other children there, and never being touched by a blow from anyone else.

Some missionaries once had to face this problem of putting strange statements into familiar terms when they translated the Bible into the dialect of a tribe living in equatorial Africa. Should they translate literally? They realized that if they did, the words at times would be meaningless to the natives.

They came, for example, to the lines: "Though your sins be as scarlet, they shall be white as snow." Should they translate this literally? The natives didn't know snow from jungle moss. But they had often climbed coconut trees and had shaken down nuts for lunch. The missionaries likened the unknown to the known. They changed the lines to read:

"Though your sins be as scarlet, they shall be white as the meat of a coconut."

Under the circumstances, it would be hard to improve on that, wouldn't it?

TURN A FACT INTO A PICTURE

How far away is the moon? The sun? The nearest other star? Scientists are apt to answer spacetravel questions with a lot of mathematics. But science lecturers and writers know this is no way to make a fact clear to an average audience. They turn the figures into pictures.

然后他继续说:"具体说……进一步说……此外……有三个主要的理由:第一……第二……第三……"

他最后说:"总之,我们需要的,是立即对中低收入阶层实行减税措施,以增加需求与购买力。"

四、将陌生题材与听众熟悉的相比较

有时候你会有这种感觉:你辛辛苦苦地忙了半天,仍然没有把自己的意思解释清楚。你本来是很清楚这件事的,可是要让听众也明白它,就需要深入的解说。这该怎么办呢?不妨把它和听众熟悉的事情相比较,告诉他们这件事和另一件事一样,和他们所熟悉的事一样。

假设你要介绍催化剂在化学中对工业的贡献。你如果告诉人们这是一种物质,它能让别的物质改变而不会改变其本身,这说起来很简单;但是如果你说它正像个小男孩,在校园里又跳又打又闹,还推别的孩子,而他自己却安然无恙,从没有被人打过、碰过,这不是更好吗?

还有一个令人惊奇而有趣的例子:一些传教士在把《圣经》翻译成赤道非洲土著部落的土话时,面临着将陌生语言翻译成他们熟悉语言的难题。是逐字逐句照翻过来吗?他们意识到如果那样做,这些句子对土著人将毫无意义。

例如,他们遇到了一句话:"虽然你的罪恶一片鲜红,但它们终将白如雪花。"这一句怎样翻译呢?这些土著人从来分不清雪和丛林苔藓的区别,但他们经常爬椰子树,摇下椰子当午餐。因此,传教士就把陌生的词语和他们熟悉的东西联系起来,把那句话改译成:

"虽然你的罪恶一片鲜红,但它们终将白如椰肉。"

在这种情况下,再也找不到比这更好的翻译了,不是吗?

1. 将事实变成图画

月亮有多远?太阳呢?最近的星星呢?科学家们一般都会用一大堆数字来回答这些问题。可

The famous scientist Sir James Jeans was particularly interested in mankind's yearnings to explore the universe. As a scientific expert, he knew the mathematics involved, and he also knew that he would be most effective in writing or speaking if he dropped in a figure only here and there.

Our sun (a star) and the planets around us are so near that we do not realize how far away other objects whirling in space are, he pointed out in his book, *The Universe Around Us.* "Even the nearest star (Proxima Centauri) is 25,000,000,000,000 miles away," he said. Then, to make this figure more vivid, he explained that if one were to take off from the earth at the speed of light—186,000 miles a second—it would take him four and a quarter years to reach Proxima Centauri.

In this way, he made the vast distances in space seem more real than did another speaker whom I once heard describe such a simple thing as distances in Alaska. He said Alaska's area was 590,804 square miles, and dropped the attempt to show its size right there.

Does this give you any kind of picture of the size of the 49th State? It didn't give me one. To visualize its bigness, I had to wait until I learned from another source that its area more than equals the combined areas of Vermont, New Hampshire, Maine, Massachusetts, Rhode Island, Connecticut, New York, New Jersey, Pennsylvania, Delaware, Maryland, West Virginia, North Carolina, South Carolina, Georgia, Florida, Tennessee, and Mississippi. Now the 590,804 square miles take on a new meaning, don't they? You realize that in Alaska there's plenty of room to move around.

Some years ago a member of one of our classes described the fearful toll of fatal accidents on our highways by this appalling picture: "You are driving across the country from New York to Los Angeles. Instead of highway markers, imagine coffins standing upright in the earth, each containing a victim of last year's slaughter on the roads. As you speed along your car passes one of these gruesome markers every five seconds, for they are spaced twelve to a mile from one end of the country to the other!"

I never take a ride in a car very far before that picture comes back to me with startling realism.

Why is that so? Because ear impressions are hard to retain. They roll away like sleet striking the smooth bark of a beech tree. But eye impressions? I saw, a few years ago, a cannon ball imbedded in an old house standing on the banks of the Danube—a cannon ball that Napoleon's

是科普作家都知道,这种方法很难让普通听众了解,因此他们经常会将数字转化成图画。

著名科学家詹姆·吉恩斯爵士对人们探测宇宙的渴望特别感兴趣。身为科学家,他自然懂得高深的数学,但是他也明白,自己在写作或演讲中若只偶尔用上几个数字,效果将会最好。

虽然太阳和我们周围的行星如此靠近,但我们并不了解在太空中旋转的其他物体离我们究竟有多远,因此他在《我们周围的宇宙》一书中这样写道:"即使是最近的星(普洛西玛·森多里星),也在25万亿英里以外。"为了使这数字更鲜明些,他解释说:"假如一个人从地球上起飞,以光速飞行——每秒18.6万英里——他也需要4年零3个月才能到普洛西玛·森多里星。"

他以这种方式来说明太空的广阔浩瀚,比我曾听另一个人解说阿拉斯加的面积这一类似问题时要真实多了。他说阿拉斯加的面积是590804平方英里,然后就丢下不管了,不再去解释它究竟大到什么程度。

这能给你美国第49个州的规模任何图像概念吗?显然不会。我是后来通过其他资料才知道这个地区有多大的。它比佛蒙特、新罕布什尔、缅因、马萨诸塞、罗德岛、康乃狄克、纽约、新泽西、宾夕法尼亚、德拉维尔、马里兰、西弗吉尼亚、北卡罗莱纳、南卡罗莱纳、佐治亚、佛罗里达、田纳西及密西西比等州加起来还要稍微大一点。现在这590804平方英里才有了新的意义,对不对?你会发现,在阿拉斯加还有许多土地可开发的。

几年前,我们训练班的一位学员曾惊心动魄地描述了高速公路上因车祸而死亡的人数多得可怕:"你现在驾车横穿全国,从纽约前往洛杉矶。假设路边上立着的不是路标,而是一些棺材的话,每一具棺材里面就装有一个在去年公路大屠杀中的受害者。那么当你驱车疾驶时,每隔5秒钟就会经过这样一个阴森恐怖的标志,自这头至那头,每1英里立12个!"

因此,以后我每次开车都不敢离家太远,因为这一景象总会清晰地浮现在我的脑海里。

为什么会产生这样的效果呢?因为耳朵听来的印象不容易持久,它们就像雹子打在榉树光

artillery had fired at the battle of Ulm. Visual impressions are like that cannon ball; they come with a terrific impact. They imbed themselves. They stick. They tend to drive out all opposing suggestions as Bonaparte drove away the Austrians.

AVOID TECHNICAL TERMS

If you belong to a profession the work of which is technical—if you are a lawyer, a physician, an engineer, or are in a highly specialized line of business—be doubly careful, when you talk to outsiders, to express yourself in plain terms and to give necessary details.

Be doubly careful, for, as a part of my professional duties, I have listened to hundreds of speeches that failed right at this point, and failed woefully. The speakers appeared totally unconscious of the general public's widespread and profound ignorance regarding their particular specialties. So what happened? They rambled on and on, uttering thoughts, using phrases that fitted into their experience and were instantly and continuously meaningful to them; but to the uninitiated, they were about as clear as the Missouri River after the June rains have fallen on the newly plowed cornfields of Iowa and Kansas.

What should such a speaker do? He ought to read and heed the following advice from the facile pen of former Senator Beveridge of Indiana:

> It is a good practice to pick out the least intelligent-looking person in the audience and strive to make that person interested in your argument. This can be done only by lucid statements of fact and clear reasoning. An even better method is to center your talk on some small boy or girl present with parents.
>
> Say to yourself—say out loud to your audience, if you like—that you will try to be so plain that the child will understand and remember your explanation of the question discussed, and after the meeting be able to tell what you have said.

A physician in one of our classes remarked in a talk that "diaphragmatic breathing is a distinct aid to the peristaltic action of the intestines and a boon to health." He was about to dismiss that phase of his talk with that one sentence and to rush on to something else. The instructor stopped him, and asked for a show of hands of those who had a clear conception of how diaphragmatic breathing differs from other kinds of breathing, why it is especially beneficial to physical well-

滑的树皮上,会随即掉落。但是用眼睛看到的印象呢?很多年前,我曾亲眼看到了一颗嵌入一幢位于多瑙河岸边老屋的炮弹,这颗炮弹是拿破仑的炮兵部队在乌尔姆战役中所发射的。视觉印象就像那颗炮弹,它们以排山倒海之势扑面而来,深深地嵌入了我的大脑,牢牢地附着在上面,驱走了一切反面的提示,就像拿破仑赶走奥地利人一样。

2. 避免使用专业术语

如果你是从事某项技术性的专业工作——例如律师、医生、工程师,或是高度专业化的行业——那么当你向外行人演讲时,必须加倍小心地使用浅显易懂的语言来解释,同时还注意加上必要的细节。

之所以要加倍小心,是因为我的专业责任的关系。我已经听过几百场演讲,它们正是因此而失败,而且败得那么惨痛。这些演讲者显然完全不知道,一般听众对他们的特殊行业普遍缺乏了解。这样的结果会如何呢?虽然他们滔滔不绝地高谈阔论,用他们工作中常用的那些只对他们有意义的词句,但对于外行来说,却是云山雾罩,不知所云。

这时演讲者应该怎样做呢?他应该去读一读并留意印第安纳州前参议员贝佛里奇下面的建议:

> 一个好办法,就是从听众中选一个看上去最不聪明的人,然后努力让那个人对你的演讲感兴趣。你只能用清晰易懂的话语来叙述,并清楚地说明你的观点,才能做到这一点。另一个更好的办法,就是把你的演讲目标放在那些由父母陪着的小男孩或小女孩身上。
>
> 你要在心里对自己说——当然,你也可以大声对你的听众说出来,如果你喜欢的话——你会尽量讲得简单明白一些,让小孩子也能够了解并记住你的解释,而且会后还能够把你所讲的告诉别人。

我训练班上的一个医生在一场演讲中这样说道:"用膈膜呼吸对肠子的蠕动将产生显著的帮助,这是对健康的一种恩赐。"他本想用这句话概括这部分内容,然后再讲述别的东西。但指

being, and what peristaltic action is. The result of the vote surprised the doctor; so he went back, explained, enlarged in this fashion:

> The diaphragm is a thin muscle forming the floor of the chest at the base of the lungs and the roof of the abdominal cavity. When inactive and during chest breathing, it is arched like an inverted washbowl.
>
> In abdominal breathing every breath forces this muscular arch down until it becomes nearly flat and you can feel your stomach muscles pressing against your belt. This downward pressure of the diaphragm massages and stimulates the organs of the upper part of the abdominal cavity—the stomach, the liver, the pancreas, the spleen, the solar plexus.
>
> When you breathe out again, your stomach and your intestines will be forced up against the diaphragm and will be given another massage. This massaging helps the process of elimination.
>
> A vast amount of ill health originates in the intestines. Most indigestion, constipation, and autointoxication would disappear if our stomachs and intestines were properly exercised through deep diaphragmatic breathing.

It is always best to go from the simple to the complex in giving explanations of any kind. For example, suppose you were trying to explain to a group of housewives why refrigerators must be defrosted. This would be the wrong way to go about it:

> The principle of refrigeration is based on the fact that the evaporator pulls heat from the inner portion of the refrigerator. As the heat is pulled out, the accompanying humidity clings to the evaporator, piling up into a thickness which insulates the evaporator and necessitates more frequent turning on of the motor to compensate for the thickening frost.

Notice how much easier it is to understand if the speaker starts with what the housewives are familiar with:

> You know where you freeze meat in your refrigerator. Well, you know, too, how the frost gathers on that freezer. Every day the frost gets thicker and thicker until the freezer must be defrosted to keep the refrigerator in good working order. You see, frost around the freezer is really like a blanket covering you in bed or like rock wool between the walls insulating your house. Now

导老师打断了他，并请那些听懂了膈膜式呼吸与其他呼吸方式有何不同、为什么它会对健康特别有益，以及蠕动作用是什么这三个问题有明确概念的听众举手。结果让这位医生大吃一惊。于是他回头重新讲解：

> 膈膜是一层薄薄的肌肉，它位于肺的底部和腹腔的顶部，形成了胸腔的底层。当胸腔呼吸时，它会收缩，像只上下倒置的洗涮盆。
>
> 在做腹腔式呼吸时，每一次呼吸都会迫使膈膜往下推，使它几乎成平面状，此时便会感觉胃肠受到了腰带的挤压。膈膜这种向下的压力会按摩并刺激腹腔的上部器官——胃、肝、胰、脾等。
>
> 当把气呼出时，胃和肠又往上挤迫膈膜，相当于再做一次按摩，这种按摩有助于排泄过程。
>
> 绝大多数疾病都来自肠胃不适。假如我们的肠胃因为膈膜的深呼吸而有适当的运动，那么大部分的消化不良、便秘以及体内积毒现象都会消失。

不论你如何解说，总是由简入繁最佳不过。比如，你想对一群家庭主妇解释为什么冰箱必须除霜，如果这样开始你可就糟了：

> 冷冻的原理，是蒸发器从冰箱内部吸收热气。当热量被吸出来的时候，伴随它的湿气就会附着在蒸发器上，形成厚厚的一层，造成蒸发器绝热，并使马达频频开动工作，以补偿逐渐增厚的霜层形成的绝热。

请注意，如果演讲者从家庭主妇们所熟悉的事物开始，就更容易让她们明白了：

> 各位都知道肉类应该放在冰箱的哪一层。那么，各位也一定知道霜是如何聚结在冰冻器上的。这些霜一天天越结越厚，最后冰冻器就得除霜，以保持冰箱运转良好。冰冻器四周的霜，就像你躺在床上时盖的毯子，或者像墙里用于隔热的石棉。这些霜结得越厚，冰冻器越难从冰箱中吸出热气，以保持冰箱的冷度。于是冰箱的马达就必须频繁开动，这样才能保持冰箱内的冷度。如果

the thicker the frost gets, the harder it is for the freezer to pull the warm air out of the rest of the refrigerator and keep the refrigerator cold. The refrigerator motor then must work more often and longer to keep the box cold. But with an automatic defroster on your refrigerator, the frost never gets a chance to build up thickly. Consequently, the motor works less often and for shorter periods.

Aristotle gave some good advice on the subject: "Think as wise men do, but speak as the common people do." If you must use a technical term, don't use it until you have explained it so everybody in the audience knows what it means. This is especially true of your keystone words, the ones you use over and over.

I once heard a stock broker speak to a group of women who wanted to learn fundamentals of banking and investment. He used simple language and he put them at ease in a conversational way. He made everything clear except his foundation words, which were strange to them. He spoke of the "clearing house," "puts and calls," "refunding mortgages," and "short sales and long sales," what could have been a fascinating discussion became a puzzle because he did not realize his hearers were unfamiliar with the words that were part and parcel of his trade.

There is no reason to avoid a keystone word which you know will not be understood. Just explain it as soon as you use it. Never fail to do this, the dictionary is all yours.

Do you want to say something about singing commercials? Or about impulse buying? About liberal arts courses, or cost accounting? About government subsidies, or automobiles that pass on the wrong side? Would you like to advocate a permissive attitude toward children, or the LIFO system of valuing inventories? Merely make sure that your hearers accept your keystone words in these specialized fields in the same sense in which you accept them.

FIFTH/ USE VISUAL AIDS

The nerves that lead from the eye to the brain are many times larger than those leading from the ear; and science tells us that we give twenty-five times as much attention to eye suggestions as we do to ear suggestions.

"One seeing," says an old Japanese proverb, "is better than a hundred times telling about."

So, if you wish to be clear, picture your points, visualize your ideas. That was the plan of

在冰箱里装一个自动除霜器,霜就不会结厚,马达运转的次数和时间也可以减少了。

关于这个方法,亚里士多德曾有一句名言:"思维如智者,说话如常人。"如果你必须使用专业术语,那只有在给听众解释过后使用,这样才能让他们都听懂。所以,你需要一再使用的关键词更应该这样。

我曾听过一位证券经纪商对一群妇女演讲。这些妇女想了解一些银行与投资的基本原则。他使用了简单的语言和轻松的谈话方式让她们放松下来。本来他每件事情都说得清清楚楚的,但对于一些基本词却没说清楚,而这些词对她们而言却很陌生。比如他提到了"票据交换所"、"课税与偿付"、"退款抵押"以及"短期买卖和长期买卖"。结果,本来是一场精彩动人的讨论却变成了一团雾水,因为他不明白听众对他的专业术语不熟悉。

不过,有时候即使你知道某个关键词听众不会了解,也没必要避免它,只需在使用时尽快解释就可以。不要害怕这样做,你完全可以去查词典。

你对歌唱广告有意见要发表吗?或者对冲动式购物、文学艺术课程或者成本会计、政府津贴或逆向行驶汽车有什么意见?你愿倡导一种对待孩子的宽容态度,或评估价值的体系吗?不论上述什么题材,你都一定要让听众对这些专业术语或关键词的了解与你一样。

五、使用视觉辅助工具

通过眼睛通往脑部的神经,比从耳朵通往脑部的神经要多好几倍;而且科学实验发现,人们对眼睛暗示的注意力是对耳朵暗示的25倍。

日本有一句俗语:"百闻不如一见。"

因此,如果你想清楚表达自己,应该用图像来描绘你的要点,把你的观点视觉化。这正是美国现金注册公司创始人帕特森采用的方法。他为《系统杂志》写了一篇论文,简要说明了他

John H. Patterson, founder of the National Cash Register Company. He wrote an article for *System Magazine*, outlining the methods he used in speaking to his workmen and his sales forces:

> I hold that one cannot rely on speech alone to make himself understood or to gain and hold attention. A dramatic supplement is needed. It is better to supplement whenever possible with pictures which show the right and the wrong way: diagrams are more convincing than mere words, and pictures are more convincing than diagrams. The ideal presentation of a subject is one in which every subdivision is pictured and in which the words are used only to connect them. I early found that in dealing with men, a picture was worth more than anything I could say.

If you use a chart or diagram, be sure it is large enough to see, and don't overdo a good thing. A long succession of charts is usually boring. If you make the diagram as you go along, be careful to sketch roughly and swiftly on the blackboard or flip chart. Listeners are not interested in great art work. Use abbreviations; write largely and legibly; keep talking as you draw or write; and keep turning back to your audience.

When you use exhibits, follow these suggestions and you will be assured of the rapt attention of your audience.

1. Keep the exhibit out of sight until you are ready to use it.
2. Use exhi bits large enough to be seen from the very last row. Certainly your audience can't learn from any exhibit unless they see it.
3. Never pass an exhibit around among your listeners while you are speaking. Why invite competition?
4. When you show an exhibit, hold it up where your listeners can see it.
5. Remember, one exhibit that moves is worth ten that don't. Demonstrate if practicable.
6. Don't stare at the exhibit as you talk—you are trying to communicate with the audience, not with the exhibit.
7. When you have finished with the exhibit, get it out of sight if practicable.
8. If the exhibit you are going to use lends itself to "mystery treatment," have it placed on a table which will be at your side as you speak. Have it covered. As you talk, make references to it

向工人和销售人员演讲时使用的方法：

> 我认为，一个人不能仅仅通过言语就希望别人了解他的想法，或是抓住别人的注意力。我们需要一些具有戏剧性的辅助工具，最好的方法是使用图片，用图片来表现对和错的两面。图表比仅用语言文字更具有说服力，而图片又比图表更具有说服力。表现某一主题最理想的方法，就是给每一部分配上图片，而语言文字只是与图片配合的手段。我很早就发现，和人们交谈时，一张图片往往要胜过我的任何话。

如果你使用一张图表，一定要让它足够大，让人们可以看清楚。不过，还要注意千万别做过了头。一长串的图表有时也会令人感觉无聊。如果是边讲边画，那就一定要在黑板上简单而快速地画，听众可对伟大的艺术作品并不都感兴趣。使用缩略语时，要写得大而容易辨认；在画图或写字的时候，不要停止你的讲话，要随时转身面对听众。

利用展示物时，要注意以下建议，这可以保证你能抓住听众的注意力。

1. 展示物应先藏好，直到使用时再拿出来。
2. 使用的展示物应该足够大，使最后一排的人都能看清楚。听众如果看不见展示物，展示物就不能起到应有的作用。
3. 演讲的时候，不要将展示物在听众中间传阅。你大概不想给自己找个对手进行竞争吧？
4. 展示物品时，把它举到听众看得见的高度。
5. 记住，一件能打动听众的展示物要胜过10件不能打动人的东西。所以如果可以，不妨先示范一下。
6. 演讲时不要紧盯着展示物——你应该与听众沟通，而不是和展示物沟通。
7. 展示完后，尽快收起展示物，不再让听众看见。
8. 如果展示物非常适合做“隐蔽处理”，就把它放在桌子边上，演讲时把它盖住。演讲时，不

that will arouse curiosity—but don't tell what it is. Then, when you are ready to unveil it, you have aroused curiosity, suspense, and real interest.

Visual materials are becoming more and more prominent as devices to promote clarity. There is no better way to insure that your audience will understand what you have to say than to go before them prepared to show as well as to tell them what you have in mind.

Two American presidents, both masters of the spoken word, have indicated that the ability to be clear is the result of training and discipline. As Lincoln said, we must have a passion for clarity. He told Dr. Gulliver, the President of Knox College, how he developed this "passion" in early life:

> Among my earliest recollections I remember how, when a mere child, I used to get irritated when anybody talked to me in a way I could not understand. I don't think I ever got angry at anything else in my life. But that always disturbed my temper, and has ever since. I can remember going to my little bedroom, after hearing the neighbors talk of an evening with my father, and spending no small part of the night walking up and down and trying to make out the exact meaning of some of their, to me, dark sayings. I could not sleep, though I often tried to, when I got on such a hunt after an idea, until I had repeated it over and over, until I had put it in language plain enough as I thought for any boy I knew to comprehend. This was a kind of passion with me, and it has since stuck by me.

The other distinguished president, Woodrow Wilson, wrote some words of advice that strike the right note to end this chapter on making your meaning clear:

> My father was a man of great intellectual energy. My best training came from him. He was intolerant of vagueness, and from the time I began to write until his death in 1903, when he was eighty-one years old, I carried everything I wrote to him.
>
> He would make me read it aloud, which was always painful to me. Every now and then, he would stop me. "What do you mean by that?" I would tell him, and, of course, in doing so would express myself more simply than I had on paper. "Why didn't you say so?" he would go on. "Don't shoot at your meaning with birdshot and hit the whole countryside; shoot with a rifle at the thing you have to say."

妨多提它几次,这会引发听众的好奇心——不过不要告诉听众它是什么。当你展示它的时候,你早就引发了听众的好奇心、猜想和真正的兴趣。

视觉材料在增强演讲效果方面,已越来越显得重要。除非你早就胸有成竹,否则与其用言词表达你的意思,还不如展示给听众看,除此之外没有更好的方法能保证听众会听明白。

有两位美国总统——林肯和威尔逊——同为语言大师。他们指出,清晰的表达能力是训练与自我控制的结果。林肯说:"我们必须狂热地追求明晰。"他对诺克斯学院院长嘉利佛博士说了他在早年是如何培养这种"狂热"的:

> 我记得,当我还是个孩子的时候,遇到有人用我听不懂的方式跟我说话时,我就会非常不舒服。在我一生当中,还没有对别的事情生过气。可是,听不懂别人的讲话总会让我发脾气,现在仍然是这样。记得有一次,我在听邻居和我父亲欢谈了一个晚上之后,我走回自己的小卧室,大半夜里都在不停地走来走去,企图思考一些语言的确切意义。在我刚开始这样做的时候,常常是到了该睡觉的时间,可就是睡不着,直到我能把它用浅显易懂的语言说出来,自认为可以让我所认识的每个男孩都能了解才肯罢休。这是我的一种狂热,它一直紧紧地跟着我。

另一位杰出的总统伍德罗·威尔逊,有一些忠告正好为本章画上一个注脚:

> 我父亲是一位具有大智慧的人,我所受过的最好的训练都来自于他。他不能容忍含混隐晦。从我开始提笔写字到他903年81岁高龄时去世,我总是随身携带自己写给他的所有东西。
>
> 他会让我大声读出来。这对我来说真是一件苦差事。他会时不时打断我:"你这是什么意思?"我就会告诉他为什么这样说。为此我就得用比写在纸上更简洁明了的方式来表达。"那你为何不这样说?"他会继续训下去,"别用鸟枪来瞄射自己的意思,那样只会击得一片凌乱;要用来福枪瞄射自己想说的话,让人一听就明白。"

3 Making the Talk to Convince

There was once a small group of men and women who found themselves in the path of a hurricane. Not a real hurricane, but the next thing to it. In short, a hurricane of a man named Maurice Goldblatt. Here is how one of that group described it:

We were sitting around a luncheon table in Chicago. We knew this man was reputed to be a powerful speaker. We watched him intently as he stood up to speak.

He began quietly—a spruce, pleasant man of middle age—thanking us for inviting him. He wanted to talk about something serious, he said, and he hoped we would forgive him if he disturbed us.

Then, like a whirlwind, he struck. He leaned forward and his eyes transfixed us. He didn't raise his voice, but it seemed to me that it crashed like a gong.

"Look around you," he said. "Look at one another. Do you know how many of you sitting now in this room are going to die of cancer? One in four of all of you who are over forty-five. One in four!"

He paused, and his face lightened. "That's a plain, harsh fact, but it needn't be for long," he said. "Something can be done about it. This something is progress in the treatment of cancer and in the search for its cause."

He looked at us gravely, his gaze moving around the table. "Do you want to help toward this progress?" he asked.

Could there have been an answer except "Yes!" in the minds of any of us then? "yes!" I thought, and I found later that so did the others.

In less than a minute, Maurice Goldblatt had won us. He had drawn us personally into his subject. He had us on his side, in the campaign he was waging for a humanitarian cause.

Getting a favorable reaction is every speaker's objective any time, anywhere. As it happened, Mr. Goldblatt had a dramatically good reason for wanting to get one from us.

第3章　说服性演讲

有一次，一小群男女发现自己正置身于一场风暴的通路上。这并不是一场真正的风暴，但也可以这样来比喻它。说得清楚一点，这场风暴来自一个名叫毛里斯·格伯莱的人。其中一个人这样描述说：

我们围坐在芝加哥一张午餐桌旁。我们早听说过这个人的大名，他是一个声名远扬的演讲家。他站着演讲时，每个人都目不转睛地望着他。

他开始安详地讲话——他是一个整洁而儒雅的中年人——他首先感谢我们的邀请。他说他想对我们谈一件严肃的事，如果这打扰了我们，就请我们原谅。

接着，他像一阵龙卷风一样席卷过来。他身体前倾，双眼牢牢盯住我们。他并未提高声音，但我却似乎感觉到了铜锣爆裂的声音。

"向你四周瞧瞧，"他说，"彼此瞧一瞧。你们知不知道，现在坐在这房间里的人，将有多少死于癌症?55岁以上的人中，每四个人就有一个。四个人中就有一个！"

他停下来，但脸上散发出光彩。"这是常见而残酷的事实，不过不会长久这样，"他说，"我们可以找到办法，寻求治疗癌症的方法，研究它们产生的病因。"

他神情凝重地望着我们，目光绕着桌子逐一移动。"你们愿意共同努力吗?"他问道。

在我们脑海中，除了"愿意"之外，还会有别的回答吗?"愿意！"我想。事后，我发现别人和我的想法一样。

不到一分钟，毛里斯·格伯莱就赢得了我们的心。他已经把我们每个人都拉进了他的话题，让我们站在他那一边，共同投入到为人类谋求幸福的运动中。

He and his brother, Nathan, starting with little more than nothing, had built up a department store chain doing a business of more than $100,000,000 a year. Fabulous success had come to them after long, hard years, and then Nathan, ill only a short time, had died of cancer. After that, Maurice Goldblatt saw to it that the Goldblatt Foundation gave the first million dollars to the University of Chicago's cancer research program, and he gave his own time—retiring from business—to the work of interesting the public in the fight against cancer.

These facts, together with Maurice Goldblatt's personality, won us. Sincerity, earnestness, enthusiasm—a blazing determination to give himself to us for a few minutes, just as he was giving himself year in and out to a great cause—all of these factors swept us up into a feeling of agreement with the speaker, a friendliness for him, a willingness to be interested and moved.

FIRST/ WIN CONFIDENCE BY DESERVING IT

Quintilian described the orator as "a good man skilled in speaking." He was talking about sincerity and character. Nothing said in this book, nor anything which will be said, can take the place of this essential attribute of speaking effectiveness. Pierpont Morgan said that character was the best way to obtain credit; it is also the best way to win the confidence of the audience.

"The sincerity with which a man speaks," said Alexander Woolcott, "imparts to his voice a color of truth no perjurer can feign."

Especially when the purpose of our talk is to convince, it is necessary to set forth our own ideas with the inner glow that comes from sincere conviction. We must first be convinced before we attempt to convince others.

SECOND/ GET A YES-RESPONSE

Walter Dill Scott, former president of Northwestern University, said that "every idea, concept, or conclusion which enters the mind is held as true unless hindered by some contradictory idea." That boils down to keeping the audience yes-minded. My good friend

不论何时何地，获得赞同是每个演讲者的目标。正如已经发生的情况一样，格伯莱先生有非常充足的理由要我们做出这样的反应：他和他的兄弟纳逊白手起家，建立了一个连锁百货公司，年收入超过1亿美元。在历经长期的艰辛之后，他们终于获得了神话般的成功，不料纳逊却在短短的时间里因为患癌症而去世。这之后，毛里斯·格伯莱特意安排格伯莱基金会，捐出第一个100万美元给芝加哥大学癌症研究中心。他退休后，又把自己的时间投入到提醒民众共同抗癌的斗争中。

这些事实，加上毛里斯·格伯莱的个性，赢得了我们的心。这种真诚、关切、热情——这种火一般的热烈的决心，让他在短短的几分钟内就把自己展现给了我们，正如把他长期献身给这个伟大目标一样——所有这一切都让我们对他产生了一种赞同、友谊、感兴趣和被打动的感情。

一、以真诚赢得信心

公元1世纪罗马著名的演说家昆体良称演讲家是“一个擅长讲话的好人”。在这里，他指的是真诚和个性。本书已经说过和将要说的一切，没有一个能取代这一高效演讲的必要条件。约翰·皮尔庞特·摩根说，个性是获取听众信任的最好方法，同时也是获取听众信心的最好方法。

“一个人说话时的那种真诚态度，”亚历山大·伍柯特说，“会让他的声音焕发出真实的光彩，那是虚伪的人假装不出来的。”

如果我们的目的是想要说服别人，那就特别需要发自内心的诚挚的自信，以这种内在的光辉来宣讲自己的理念。我们只有自己先说服自己，然后才能设法说服别人。

二、获得听众的赞同

前美国西北大学校长华特·狄尔·斯科特说：“每个新的意见、观念或结论被提出来时，都会

Professor Harry Overstreet brilliantly examined the psychological background of this concept in a lecture at the New School for Social Research in New York City:

> The skillful speaker gets at the outset a number of yes-responses. He has thereby set the psychological processes of his listeners moving in the affirmative direction. It is like the movement of a billiard ball. Propel it in one direction, and it takes some force to deflect it, far more force to send it back in the opposite direction.

The psychological patterns here are quite clear. When a person says "No" and really means it, he is doing far more than saying a word of two letters. His entire organism—glandular, nervous, muscular—gathers itself together into a condition of rejection. There is, usually in minute but sometimes in observable degree, a physical withdrawal, or readiness for withdrawal. The whole neuromuscular system, in short, sets itself on guard against acceptance. Where, on the contrary, a person says "Yes," none of the withdrawing activities takes place. The organism is in a forward-moving, accepting, open attitude. Hence the more "Yesses" we can, at the very outset, induce, the more likely we are to succeed in capturing the attention for our ultimate proposal.

It is a very simple technique—this yes-response. And yet how much neglected! It often seems as if people get a sense of their own importance by antagonizing at the outset. The radical comes into a conference with his conservative brethren; and immediately he must make them furious! What, as a matter of fact, is the good of it? If he simply does it in order to get some pleasure out of it for himself, he may be pardoned. But if he expects to achieve something, he is only psychologically stupid.

Get a student to say "No" at the beginning, or a customer, child, husband, or wife, and it takes the wisdom and patience of angels to transform that bristling negative into an affirmative.

How is one going to get these desirable "yes-responses" at the very outset? Fairly simple. "My way of opening and winning an argument," confided Lincoln, "is to first find a common ground of agreemeat." Lincoln found it even when he was discussing the highly inflammable subject of slavery. "For the first half hour," declared *The Mirror*, a neutral paper reporting one of his talks, "his opponents would agree with every word he uttered. From that point he began to lead them off, little by little, until it seemed as if he had got

被认为是真理,除非有相反的理念阻碍,则另当别论。"这其实就是要求争取获得听众的赞同。我的好友哈瑞·奥佛斯特里特教授在纽约社会研究中心的演讲中,很清晰地阐释了这种说法的心理背景:

> 有技巧的演讲者,一开始便能获得许多赞同的反应。他能够借此引导听众朝着赞同的方向前进。它就像撞球游戏中的弹子运动,把它往一个方向推动后,若想让它转一个方向就要费一些力气;如果想把它推到相反的方向,则需要花更大的力气。

在这里,心理的转变可以看得很清楚。当一个人说"不",而且内心真的反对的时候,他所做的不仅仅是说"不"这个简简单单的字了。他的整个身体——腺体、神经、肌肉——都会把自己包裹起来,进入一种抵抗状态。通常,他会有微小的身体上的撤退,或做好撤退的准备,有时甚至表现得非常明显。这就是说,整个神经、肌肉系统都戒备起来拒绝接受。相反,当一个人说"是"时,他就绝无撤退的行为发生。这时他的整个身体会处在一种前进、接纳、开放的状态。所以,如果从一开始我们就能获得越多的"是",就越有可能成功地抓住听众的注意力,让他们接受我们的建议。

获得听众的赞同,是非常简单的技巧,但往往容易被忽视。人们常常以为,如果一开始就采取一种敌对的姿态,似乎就能显示自己的重要性,于是激进派和保守派的人在一起开会时,不用片刻大家就都火冒三丈了。说实话,这样做究竟有什么好处呢?如果这样做仅仅是为了找点刺激的话,还情有可原;可是如果希望这样做能达成什么目标的话,未免太愚蠢了。

如果一开始就让学生、顾客、孩子、丈夫或妻子说"不",然后再想把这种有增无减的否定转变为肯定,恐怕需要神一样的智慧和耐心了。

那么,怎样一开始就获得你所希望的"赞同反应"呢?这很简单。让我们看看林肯说的秘密:"我展开一场讨论并最终获胜的秘诀,是先找到一个大家都赞同的基准点。"例如,即使在讨论

them all into his fold."

Is it not evident that the speaker who argues with his audience is merely arousing their stubbornness, putting them on the defensive, making it wellnigh impossible for them to change their minds? Is it wise to start by saying, "I am going to prove so and so"? Aren't your hearers liable to accept that as a challenge and remark silently, "Let's see you do it"?

Is it not much more advantageous to begin by stressing something that you and all of your hearers believe, and then to raise some pertinent question that everyone would like to have answered? Then take your audience with you in an earnest search for the answer. While on that search, present the facts as you see them so clearly that they will be led to accept your conclusions as their own. They will have much more faith in some troth that they have discovered for themselves. "The best argument is that which seems merely an explanation."

In every controversy, no matter how wide and bitter the differences, there is always some common ground of agreement on which a speaker can invite everyone to meet. To illustrate: On February 3, 1960, the prime minister of Great Britain, Harold Macmillan, addressed both houses of the Parliament of the Union of South Africa. He had to present the United Kingdom's nonracial viewpoint before the legislature body at a time when apartheid was the prevailing policy. Did he begin his talk with this essential difference in outlook? No. He began by stressing the great economic progress made by South Africa, the significant contributions made by South Africa to the world. Then, with skill and tact he brought up the questions of differing viewpoints. Even here, he indicated that he was well aware that these differences were based on sincere conviction. His whole talk was a masterly statement reminding one of Lincoln's gentle but firm utterances in the years bofore Fort Sumter.

"As a fellow member of the commonwealth," said the Prime Minister, "it is our earnest desire to give South Africa our support and encouragement, but I hope you won't mind my saying frankly that there are some aspects of your policies which make it impossible for us to do this without being false to our deep convictions about the political destinies of free men to which in our own territories we are trying to give effect. I think we ought as friends to face together,

尖锐对立的奴隶问题时,他都能找到这种共同的基准点。《明镜》这家中立的报纸在报道他的一场演讲时,这样叙述道:"前半个小时,他的反对者几乎会同意他所说的每一个词。然后,他会抓住这一点,开始领着他们向前走,一点一点地,最后把他们全部引入自己的目的地。"

演讲者与听众争辩,只会激发听众的固执,使他们拼命防守,几乎不可能改变他们的思想。这不是很明显的事实吗?宣称"我要证明这样是否明智",是否明智呢?听众就会认为这是一种挑衅,并且无声地说:"那咱们不妨走着瞧! "

如果一开始就强调一些听众和你都相信的事情,再提一个每个人都愿意回答的问题,这样是不是有利得多?然后,你可以带着听众一起去寻找答案。在这个过程中,把你十分清楚的事实陈列在他们面前,他们就会接受你的引领,同意你的结论。这种由他们自己发现的事实,会让他们有更多的信心。"看似一场解说的辩论,才是一流的辩论。"

在各种争议中,不论分歧有多大、有多尖锐,总会有一些共同的地方可以使演讲者和听众都产生心灵的共鸣。例如,1960年2月3日,大不列颠首相哈罗德·麦克米兰曾向南非联邦国会的两院发表演讲。当时,南非当局采取的是种族隔离政策,而他必须面对南非立法团体,陈述英国无种族歧视的观点。他是不是一开始就阐述双方的这种分歧呢?没有。他开始只是强调南非在经济上取得了不起的成就,对世界做出了重大的贡献。然后,他才巧妙而机智地提出了双方有分歧的问题。但即使讲到这一点,他还是指出,他非常了解这些分歧都来自双方各自真诚的信念。这场演讲非常精彩,可以与林肯在苏姆特堡所发表的那些温和却坚定的言辞相比。

"身为大不列颠国的一位成员,"麦克米兰首相说,"我们真诚地希望,能给予南非支持和鼓励,不过希望各位不要介意我的直言:在我们大不列颠的领土上,我们正在设法给予自由人政治前途——这是我们坚定的信念,所以,我们无法在支持和鼓励各位的同时,不违背自己的信念。我认为,不论谁是谁非,我们都应该像朋友一样,共同面对一个事实,那就是我们今天还存

without seeking to apportion credit or blame, the fact that in the world of today this difference of outlook lies between us."

No matter how determined one was to differ with a speaker, a statement like that would tend to convince you of the speaker's fair-mindedness.

What would have been the result had Prime Minister Macmillan set out immediately to emphasize the differenee in policy rather than the common ground of agreement? Professor James Harvey Robinson's enlightening book, *The Mind in the Making*, gives the psychological answer to that question:

> We sometimes find ourselves changing our minds without any resistance or heavy emotion, but if we are told we are wrong we resent the imputation and harden our hearts. We are incredibly heedless in the formation of our beliefs, but find ourselves filled with an illicit passion for them when anyone proposes to rob us of their companionship. It is obviously not the ideas themselves that are dear to us, but our selfesteem which is threatened... The little word my is the most important one in human affairs, and properly to reckon with it is the beginning of wisdom. It has the same force whether it is *my* dinner, *my* dog, and *my* house, or *my* faith, *my* country and *my* God. We not only resent the imputation that our watch is wrong, or our car shabby, but that our conception of the canals of Mars, of the pronunciation of "Epictetus," of the medicinal value of salicine, or of the date of Sargon I, are subject to revision... We like to continue to believe what we have been accustomed to accept as true, and the resentment aroused when doubt is cast upon any of our assumptions leads us to seek every manner of excuse for clinging to it. The result is that most of our so-called reasoning consists in finding arguments for going on believing as we already do.

THIRD/ SPEAK WITH CONTAGIOUS ENTHUSIASM

Contradicting ideas are much less likely to arise in the listener's mind when the speaker presents his ideas with feeling and contagious enthusiasm. I say "contagious," for enthusiasm is just that. It thrusts aside all negative and opposing ideas. When your aim is

在分歧。"

不论一个人多么坚决地想和演讲者对抗,但是若听到这样的言论,他也会相信演讲者公正的坦诚之心。

假设麦克米兰首相一开始就强调双方在政策上的差异,而不是提出双方共同的赞同点,后果将会怎样呢?詹姆斯·哈维·鲁滨逊教授在他富有启迪的《思想的酝酿》一书中,对这个问题做出了心理学上的解答:

> 有时,我们会发现自己在毫无抵抗、情绪毫不激动的状况下改变自己的思想。但是,如果有人说我们错了,我们就会讨厌这样的责备,便无论如何也不同意对方了。在信仰形成的过程中,我们不会刻意留心;可是一旦有任何人表示与我们的信仰不同时,我们就会对自己的信仰怀有偏激的狂爱。显然,我们所珍爱的并非理念本身,而是我们那正在遭受威胁的自尊……这小小的"我",是人类最重视的一个词,可能也是人类智慧的起源。不论它是我的晚餐、我的狗、我的家、我的信仰、我的国家,还是我的神,都具有相同的力量。我们不仅憎恨别人指责我们的手表走时不准,或我们的汽车破旧不堪,甚至厌恶别人指责我们的某些观念,如火星运河论、某个字的发音或水杨酸的药效、萨尔恭王一世的年代需要修正……我们喜欢相信自己作为真理而接受的东西,因此一旦我们的任何假设受到别人的怀疑时,由此导致的愤怒会促使我们寻找一切借口来坚持它。这样,我们所谓的大多数"讲理",其实就是找出一大堆借口来让自己继续相信已经相信的东西。

三、热情而富有感染力

当演讲者用富有感情和感染力的热情来讲述自己的信念时,听众很少会产生相反的想法。我说"感染力",因为热情就来自于此。它会将一切否定和相反的理念抛到一边。你的目标是说

to convince, remember it is more productive to stir emotions than to arouse thoughts. Feelings are more powerful than cold ideas. To arouse feelings one must be intensely in earnest. Regardless of the petty phrases a man may concoct, regardless of the illustrations he may assemble, regardless of the harmony of his voice and the grace of his gestures, if he does not speak sincerely, these are hollow and glittering trappings. If you would impress an audience, be impressed yourself, *Your* spirit, shining through your eyes, radiating through your voice, and proclaiming itself through your manner, will communicate itself to your audience.

Every time you speak, and especially when your avowed purpose is to convince, what you do determines the attitude of your listeners. If you are lukewarm, so will they be; if you are flippant and antagonistic, so will they be. "When the congregation ·falls asleep," wrote Henry Ward Beecher, "there is only one thing to do; provide the usher with a sharp stick and have him prod the preacher."

I was once one of three judges called on to award the Curtis medal at Columbia University. There were half a dozen undergraduates, all of them elaborately trained, all of them eager to acquit themselves well. But—with only a single exception—what they were striving for was to win the madal. They had little or no desire to convince.

They had chosen their topics because these topics permitted oratorical development. They had no deep personal interest in the arguments they were making. And their successive talks were merely exercises in the art of delivery.

The exception was a Zulu Prince. He had selected as his theme "The Contribution of Africa to Modern Civilization." He put intense feeling into every word he uttered. His talk was no mere exercise; it was a living thing, born of conviction and enthusiasm. He spoke as the representative of his people, of his continent; with wisdom, high character, and good will, he brought us a message of his people's hopes and a plea for our understanding.

We gave him the medal, although he was possibly no more accomplished in addressing a large group than two or three of his competitors. What we judges recognized was that his talk had the true fire of sincerity; it was ablaze with truth. Beside it, the other talks were only flickering

服别人,因此请记住,动之以情比晓之以理的效果更好。情绪要比冷静的思维更有威力。要激发听众的情感,你自己必须先热烈如火。即使一个人能够编造精美的词句,能够搜集许许多多的例证,声音有多么和谐,手势有多么优雅,但若不能以真诚的态度来讲述,这些全都会变成空洞而无用的装饰。要让听众印象深刻,你自己就应该先有深刻的印象。你的精神会由于你的双眼而闪现出光彩,会由于你的声音而向四面辐射,会由于你的态度而自我抒发,于是它便得以和听众沟通。

每次演讲,特别是发表说服性演讲时,你的行为决定了听众的态度。你若冷淡,他们也同样如此;你若轻率而不够包容,他们会同样如此。"当听众昏昏欲睡时,"亨利·沃德·毕彻尔这么写道,"只有一件事可做:给服务员一根尖棒,让他去猛刺演讲者。"

有一次,我应哥伦比亚大学之邀担任"科蒂斯奖章"的三位裁判之一。有6位毕业生,他们在经过精心准备之后,急于好好表现自己。可是他们当中除了一人之外,都只想赢得奖章,因而很少有或根本没有说服听众的欲望。

他们之所以选择那些演讲题目,就是这些题目可以让他们滔滔不绝地说下去。可是他们对自己的话题却没有一点兴趣,他们一连串的演讲也仅仅是表达艺术的练习而已。

唯一的例外是一位来自非洲祖鲁族的王子。他选的题目是"非洲对现代文明的贡献"。他每个字里都饱含着强烈的情感,他的演讲不是在机械练习,而是出于自身坚定的信念和热情的宣言。他把自己当作本族人民的代表,当作他那片大陆的代表。他以自己的智慧、高尚品格和善良愿望,向听众诉说了他的人民的希望,并热切希望得到我们的了解。

虽然在讲话技巧方面他不一定比另外两三位竞争者表现得更好,但我们还是把奖章颁给了他。因为我们裁判看到的是他的演讲中的真诚之火,它闪现出了真实的光芒。同这相比,其他演讲都只不过是煤气炉上微弱的火苗。

gas-logs.

The Prince had learned in his own way in a distant land that you can't project your personality in a talk to others by using reason alone; you have to reveal to them how deeply you yourself believe in what you say.

FOURTH/ SHOW RESPECT AND AFFECTION FOR YOUR AUDIENCE

"The human personality demands love and it also demands respect," Dr. Norman Vincent Peale said as a prelude to speaking of a professional comedian. "Every human being has an inner sense of worth, of importance, of dignity. Wound that and you have lost that person forever. So when you love and respect a person you build him up and, accordingly, he loves and esteems you.

"At one time I was on a program with an entertainer. I did not know the man well, but since that meeting I read that he was having difficulty, and I think I know why.

"I had been sitting beside him quietly for I was about to speak. 'You aren't nervous, are you?' he asked.

"'Why, yes,' I replied. 'I always get a little nervous before I stand up before an audience. I have a profound respect for an audience and the responsibility makes me a bit nervous. Don't you get nervous?'

"'No,' he said, 'Why should I? Audiences fall for anything. They are a lot of dopes.'

"'I don't agree with you,' I said. 'they are your sovereign judges. I have great respect for audiences.'"

When he read about this man's waning popularity, Dr. Peale was sure the reason lay in an attitude that antagonized others instead of winning them.

What an object lesson for all of us who want to impart something to other people!

FIFTH / BEGIN IN A FRIENDLY WAY

An atheist once challenged William Paley to disprove his contention that there was no Supreme Being. Very quietly Paley took out his watch, opened the case, and said: "If I were to tell you that those levers and wheels and springs made themselves and fitted themselves together and started

这位王子以他自己的方式学得了一课：演讲中仅仅运用理智，而不把自己的个性展现出来，是没有说服力的；必须展现你对自己信念的诚挚之情。

四、对听众表示尊敬

"人类的天性需要爱，也需要尊敬，"诺曼·文生特·皮尔博士在谈到专业喜剧家时经常这样说。"每个人都有一种内在的价值感、重要感和尊严感。你若伤害了它，便永远失去了那个人。因此，当你爱一个人、尊敬一个人时，你也成就了他；而且，他也同样爱你、尊敬你。

"有一次，我和一位艺人同时表演一个节目。我和他当时并不十分熟悉，但自从那次以后，我从报纸杂志上得知了他正声誉下跌，陷入了困境。我想我明白其中的原因。

"当时，我安静地坐在他旁边，等待演讲时刻的来临。'你好像不紧张嘛?'他问。

"'啊，不，'我说，'每当我在听众面前站起来之前，总是稍微有点紧张。我尊敬听众，这种责任感令我略感紧张。难道你不紧张吗?'

"'不会，'他说，'为什么要紧张呢?他们是一群傻瓜，会照单全收的，他们全都是瘾君子。'

"'我不同意，'我说，'他们是你至高无上的裁判，是你的上帝。我对听众怀着莫大的尊敬。'"

当他得知有关此人声望下跌的消息时，皮尔博士确信，原因在于这人采取的是与听众敌对的态度，而不是赢得人心的态度。

因此，如果我们想让别人接受我们的观点，一定要记住这个教训。

五、以友好的态度开始演讲

曾有一位无神论者向威廉·巴利挑战，要证明宇宙中并不存在超自然现象。巴利非常安详

runing on their own account, wouldn't you question my intelligence? Of course, you would. But look up at the stars. Every one of them has its perfect appointed course and motion—the earth and planets around the sun, and the whole group pitching along at more than a million miles a day. Each star is another sun with its own group of worlds, rushing on through space like our own solar system. Yet there are no collisions, no disturbance, no confusion. All quiet, efficient, and controlled. Is it easier to believe that they just happened or that someone made them so?"

Suppose he had retorted to his antagonist at the outset: "No God? Don't be a silly ass. You don't know what you are talking about." What would have happened? Doubtlessly a verbal joust—a wordy war would have ensued, as futile as it was fiery. The atheist would have risen with an unholy zeal upon him to fight for his opinions with all the fury of a wildcat. Why? Because, as Professor Overstreet has pointed out, they were his opinions, and his precious, indispensable selfesteem would have been threatened; his pride would have been at stake.

Since pride is such a fundamentally explosive characteristic of human nature, wouldn't it be the part of wisdom to get a man's pride working for us, instead of against us? How? By showing, as Paley did, that the thing we propose is very similar to something that our opponent already believes. That renders it easier for him to accept than to reject your proposal. That prevents contradictory and opposing ideas from arising in the mind to vitiate what we have said.

Paley showed delicate appreciation of how the human mind functions. Most men, however, lack this subtle ability to enter the citadel of a man's beliefs arm in arm with the owner. They erroneously imagine that in order to take the citadel, they must storm it, batter it down by a frontal attack. What happens? The moment hostilities commence, the drawbridge is lifted, the great gates are slammed and bolted, the mailed archers draw their long bows—the battle of words and wounds is on. Such frays always end in a draw; neither has convinced the other of anything.

This more sensible method I am advocating is not new. It was used long ago by Saint Paul. He employed it in that famous address of his to the Athenians on Mars Hill—employed it with an adroitness and finesse that compels our admiration across nineteen centuries. He was a man of

地拿出他的怀表来,打开了表盒,说:"如果我告诉你,这些小杆、小齿轮、小弹簧是它们自己制造出来,再把它们自己拼凑在一起并开始运行的,你是不是要怀疑我的智慧?当然,你一定会怀疑的。但是,请抬头瞧瞧天空的那些星星:它们每一颗都有自己完美而特定的轨道和运动——犹如地球与行星围绕着太阳,每天在太阳的周围以100多万英里的速度运行一样。每颗星星其实也都是另一个太阳,它们都有自己的世界,在宇宙中和我们的太阳系一样运行,却不必担心它们之间会碰撞、干扰或者出现混乱,一切都安静而高效,而且很有节奏。这样的现象,你相信它们是自己发生的,还是有人特意将它造成这样的?"

假设他一开始就反驳对手说:"没有神? 别再像头倔驴了, 你根本不知道自己在胡说些什么。"那么会发生什么呢?一定会引起一场咬文嚼字的大战,而这根本于事无补。这位无神论者可能会在一怒之下,疯狂地为自己的意见而战,就像一只被激怒的山猫。为什么?因为就像奥佛斯特里特教授所说的那样,这是他自己的意见,他那珍贵而不可缺少的自尊受到了威胁,他的骄傲已岌岌可危,所以他必须反抗到底。

既然骄傲是人性中一个基本的,而且容易被激怒的特性,如果我们足够聪明的话,是不是应该充分尊重并利用这一点,而不是去和它作对呢?那该怎样做呢?不妨按照巴利的做法,给我们的对手展示一下,我们的建议与他已经相信的某些事情也很相似,这样他就容易接受了,而不至于拒我们于千里之外。这可以使他们不致产生相反或对立的理念,从而破坏我们的演讲。

巴利对人的心理活动相当了解, 然而大多数人都缺少这种进入对方充满防卫的心理的本领。他们错误地认为,要攻占敌人的城堡,必须狂轰滥炸,把它夷为平地。这会产生什么结果呢?这时,敌意一旦产生,对方的吊桥会立刻收起,并且紧闭大门,身披盔甲的武士拉弓射箭——一场头破血流的战争开始了。而在双方逞勇斗狠之后,总以平手结束,因为任何一方都难以说服对方。

我现在推荐的这种方法其实并不新颖,它很早就被圣徒保罗使用过。他在马斯山上对雅典

finished education; and, after his conversion to Christianity, his eloquence made him its leading advocate. One day he arrived at Athens—the post-Pericles Athens, an Athens that had passed the summit of its glory and was now on the decline. The Bible says of it at this period: "All the Athenians and strangers which were there spent their time in nothing else but either to tell or to hear some new thing."

No radios, no cables, no news dispatches; those Athenians must have been hard put in those days to scratch up something fresh every afternoon. Then Paul came. Here was something new. They crowded about him, amused, curious interested. Taking him to the Aeropagus, they said: "May we know what this, new doetrline, whereof thou speakest, is? For thou bringest certain strange things to our ears: we would know therefore what these things mean."

In other words, they invited a speech; and, nothing loath, Paul agreed. In fact, that was what he had come for. He probably stood up on a block or stone, and, being a bit nervous, as all good speakers are at the very outset, he may have given his hands a dry wash, and have cleared his throat before he began.

However, he did not altogether approve of the way they had worded their invitation; "New doctrines... strange things." That was poison. He must eradicate those ideas. They were fertile ground for the propagating of contradictory and clashing opinions. He did not wish to present his faith as something strange and alien. He wanted to tie it up to, liken it to, something they already believed. That would smother dissenting suggestions. But how? He thought a moment; hit upon a brilliant plan; he began his immortal address: "Ye men of Athens, I perceive that in all things ye are very superstitious."

Some translations read, "Ye are very religious." I think that is better, more accurate. They worshipped many gods; they were very religious. They were proud of it. He complimented them, pleased them. They began to warm toward him.

One of the rules of the art of effective speaking is to support a statement by an illustration. He does just that:

"For, as I passed by, and beheld your devotions, I found an altar with this inscription, TO THE UNKNOWN GOD."

人所做的著名演讲中就曾用过它——而且非常熟练,即使是过了19个世纪的今天,我们仍然赞叹不已!他接受过完整的教育,改信基督后,他凭借自己激情洋溢的辩才,成为基督教的主要拥护者。一天,他来到了伯里克利统治之后的雅典,此时的雅典已经越过了光荣的巅峰,开始走下坡路了。据《圣经》记载:"所有的雅典人和寄居在该地的异乡人,都把全部时间用在传闻和打听奇闻轶事上。"

没有收音机,没有电报,也没有新闻传播渠道,这一时期的雅典人总是在每日的午后不得不找点新鲜事来谈论。这时保罗来到雅典,他们当然也就有了新鲜事啦!他们挤在保罗的周围,觉得又好玩又好奇。他们带他到艾罗培哥斯,他们说:"我们能不能知道你所说的新教义是什么?因为你为我们带来了新鲜的东西,我们想知道它究竟是什么。"

换句话说,他们在邀请他演讲。保罗一口答应下来。事实上,他正是因为这些才来的。他大概是站在一个拍卖台上或一方石块上,像所有优秀的演讲家一样,刚开始时有点紧张,或许双手还搓了几下,开口前还清了清嗓子。

然而,保罗却不能完全赞同他们的话:"新教义……新鲜的事物",这实在是可怕的东西。他必须让他们把这些概念彻底抛弃,否则他们就会成为宣传相反意见的支持者。他当然不希望把自己的信仰当成新奇的、怪异的事情来讲。因此,只有把自己的信仰和雅典人已经相信的事实联系起来,才能避免雅典人的异议。应该如何开始呢?保罗想了一会儿,然后展开了他那千古不朽的演讲:"你们雅典人,我知道你们非常具有宗教热诚。"

有些《圣经》版本这样写道:"你们都非常虔诚。"我认为这样说更好更准确,因为雅典人信奉多神,非常虔敬,并且以此为荣。保罗先称赞他们,让他们喜欢,他们就会对他感到亲切。

高效演讲艺术中还有一条法则,就是要用例证来支持论点,保罗当然也这样做了:

"当我路过这里时,发现了你们的虔诚。我看到有一处神坛,上面题有'献给不知名的神'。"

That proves, you see, that they were very religious. They were so afraid of slighting one of the deities that they had put up an altar to the unknown God, a sort of blanket insurance policy to provide against all unconscious slights and unintentional oversights. Paul, by mentioning this specific altar, indicated that he was not dealing in flattery; he showed that his remark was a genuine appreciation born of observation.

Now, here comes the consummate rightness of this opening: "Whom therefore ye ignorantly worship, him declare I unto you."

"New doctrine... strange things?" Not a bit of it. He was there merely to explain a few truths about a God they were already worshipping without being conscious of it. Likening the things they did not believe, you see, to something they already passionately accepted—such was his superb technique.

He pronounced his doctrine of salvation and resurrection, quoted a few words from one of their own Greek poets; and he was done. Some of his hearers mocked, but others said, "We will hear thee again on this matter."

Our problem in making a talk to convince or impress others is just this: to plant the idea in their minds and to keep contradicting and opposing ideas from arising. He who is skilled in doing that has power in speaking and influencing others. Here is precisely where the rules in my book *How to Win Friends and Influence People* will be helpful.

Almost every day of your life you are talking to people who differ from you on some subject under discussion. Aren't you constantl trying to win people to your way of thinking, at home, in the office, in social situations of all kinds? Is there room for improvement in your methods? How do you begin? By showing Lincoln's tact and Macmillan's? If so, you are a person of rare diplomacy and extraordinary discretion. It is well to remember Woodrow Wilson's words, "If you come to me and say, 'Let us sit down and take counsel together, and, if we differ from one another, understand why it is that we differ from one another, just what the points at issue are,' we will presently find that we are not so far apart after all, that the points on which we differ are few and the points on which we agree are many, and that if we only have the patience and the candor and the desire to get together, we will get together."

你瞧,这就证明了他们非常虔诚。雅典人害怕忽略了任何一位神,竟然建立神坛献给不知名的神。这真有点像一种保险,也就是为一切没有察觉到的疏忽或无意识的遗漏提供保险。保罗提到了这座特殊的神坛,表明自己不是在奉承,而是说明自己的评论是经过观察后的真心赞赏。

这样,保罗就可以有一个再适合不过的开场了:"对于你们一无所知但崇拜的这位神,我将把他宣示给你们。"

保罗对"新教义、新鲜的事物"只字未提。他只是向雅典人解释了有关某位神(基督)的一些事实,而这位神是他们早就信奉但还不了解的。你看,保罗把他们原本不相信的事情和他们已经狂热接受的东西联系在一起——这便是他的高明之处。

他在宣讲了基督教救赎与复活的教义之后,引述了希腊人自己一位诗人的一些诗句来结束他的演讲。有听众嘲笑他,但其他人却说:"我们还想听听你讲这些事。"

在说服他人加深印象的演讲中,我们的问题只是:如果想把自己的理念灌进听众的心里,就要避免让听众产生相反或对立的想法。长于此道的人,说起话来魅力无穷,并且会深深影响他人。这就是我的另一本书《人性的弱点》中讲的一些法则可以派上用场的地方。

在你每天的生活中,几乎都可能会遇到和你意见不同的人并和他们进行交谈。你不想在家里、办公室、各种各样的社交场合赢得人心,并让别人和你的想法一致吗?那就想想你的方法有没有需要改进的地方呢?你应该怎么开始?你有没有使用林肯和麦克米兰的智慧?要是你的回答是肯定的,你就是一位少有的外交人才,是一位心思缜密的高手。请记住伍德罗·威尔逊总统的话吧:

"如果你对我说:'让我们坐下来谈谈吧。如果我们意见不合,先让我们寻找彼此的原因,究竟存在什么问题。'我们立即就会感到彼此之间没有了距离,感觉我们分歧很少,而共同点倒很多。而且我们会发现,只要我们有耐心,有诚意,希望彼此之间进行沟通,我们就会相聚相合。"

4 Making Impromptu Talks

Not long ago a group of business leaders and government officials met at the dedication of a pharmaceutical corporation's new laboratory. One after another, half a dozen subordinates to the research director arose and told of the fascinating work being done by chemists and biologists. They were developing new vaccines against communicable diseases, new antibiotics to fight viruses, new tranquilizers to ease tension. Their results, first with animals and then with human beings, were dramatic.

"This is marvelous," an official said to the research director. "Your men are really magicians. But why aren't you up there, speaking, too?"

"I can talk to my feet—not to an audience," the research director said gloomily.

A little later, the chairman took him by surprise.

"We haven't heard from our director of research," he said. "He doesn't like to give a formal speech. But I'm going to ask him to say a few words to us."

It was pitiful. The director stood up and managed no more than a couple of sentences. He apologized for not speaking at length, and that was the gist of his contribution.

There he was, a brilliant man in his field, and he seemed as awkward and confused as a man could be. This was not necessary. He could have learned to speak impromptu on his feet. I have never seen a serious and determined member of our classes who couldn't learn this. At the start, it takes what this research director hadn't given it—a resolute and brave rejection of one's defeatist attitude. Then, perhaps for quite a while, it takes an unwavering will to do the job no matter how hard it may be.

"I get along all right if I've prepared my talk and practiced it," you may say. "But I'm at a loss for words if I'm asked to talk when I don't expect it."

The ability to assemble one's thoughts and to speak on the spur of the moment is even more important, in some ways, than the ability to speak only after lengthy and laborious

第4章 即兴演讲

不久前,一群商界领袖和政府官员共同出席了一家制药公司新实验室的落成典礼。该公司研究处处长的6名属下逐一站起来做了发言,介绍了他们的化学家和生物学家们正在进行一些了不起的工作——他们正在研究抵抗传染性疾病的新疫苗、对抗过滤性病毒的新抗生素、缓解紧张的新镇静剂;他们先用动物做实验,然后在人身上做试验,结果都令人非常满意。

一位官员对研究处处长说:"真是太神奇了,你的手下简直是魔术师。但是你为什么不上去讲呢?"

"我只能对着自己的脚讲话,而不敢面对听众。"这位研究处处长黯然神伤地说。

但是后来大会主席让他吃惊不小。

这位主席说:"我们还没有听到我们的研究处处长讲话。他不喜欢发表正式演讲,那么就请他给我们随便说几句话吧。"

这真是令人尴尬。处长站了起来,很费劲地挤出了几句话。他为自己没有详细解说而道歉,而这就是他在台上所说的全部内容。

他呆呆地站在那里。像他这样一个在自己行业中杰出的人才,却与普通人一样显得笨拙而迷惘。其实本不该这样的,他本来可以学会即兴演讲。我还没有发现我训练班上任何一个有决心的学员不能学会这一招。他们一开始所拥有的,正是这位研究处处长所没有的——坚决而勇敢地击退失败的态度。然后,也许要花一定时间,需要一种毫不动摇的意志,无论多么困难都要坚决讲出来。

"若是先有准备并做好了练习,那就没有什么困难,"你可能会这样说,"可是如果在意料之

preparation. The demands of modern business and the current casualness with which modern oral communication is carried on make it imperative to be able to mobilize our thoughts quickly and verbalize fluently. Many of the decisions that affect industry and government today are made, not by one man, but around the conference table. The individual still has his say, but what he has to say has to be forcefully stated in the forum of group opinion. This is where the ability to speak impromptu comes alive and produces results.

FIRST/ PRACTICE IMPROMPTU SPEAKING

Anyone of normal intelligence who possesses a fair portion of self-control can make an acceptable, often a brilliant, impromptu talk—which simply means "talking off the cuff." There are several ways you can improve your ability to express yourself fluently when called upon suddenly to say a few words. One method is to use a device that some famous movie actors used.

Years ago Douglas Fairbanks wrote an article for *American Magazine* in which he described a game of wits he, Charlie Chaplin, and Mary Piekford played almost every night for two years. It was more than a game. It was practice in that most difficult of all speaking arts—thinking on one's feet. As Fairbanks wrote, the "game" went like this:

> Each of us would write a subject on a slip of paper. Then we folded the slips and shook them up. One would draw. Immediately he would have to stand and talk for sixty seconds on that subject. We never used the same subject twice. One night I had to talk on "lampshades." Just try it if you think it is easy. I got through somehow.
>
> But the point is all three of us have sharpened up since we began the game. We know a lot more about a variety of miscellaneous subjects. But, far better than that, we are learning to assemble our knowledge and thoughts on any topic at a moment's notice. We are learning how to think on our feet.

Several times during my course the class members are asked to talk impromptu. Long experience has taught me that this kind of practice does two things: (1) it proves to the people in the class that they can think on their feet, and (2) this experience makes them much more secure and confident when they are giving their prepared talks. They realize that, if the worst should happen

外即兴讲话,我真的不知所措了。"

然而,在情急之下整理自己的思路并发表讲话,有时甚至比经过长时间准备的演讲更加重要。由于现代商业的需要,以及现代人口头沟通的自由随意性,使得这种即兴发言的能力不可缺少。这时,我们需要迅速组织自己的思想,并流畅地遣词造句。许多影响今天工业和政府的决定,都不是出于一个人,而是在会议桌上当场商定的。每个人都可以发言,然而在这群策群议的会议里,他的话必须强劲而有力,才能对集体决策产生影响。这也正是即兴演讲能力如此重要并发挥效力的原因所在。

一、勤加练习

任何能够控制自己的智力正常的人,都能够发表令人接受、有时还非常精彩的即席演讲——也就是"不假思索地说出来"的意思。我们当然有办法,可以帮助你在突然被人邀请讲几句话时,流畅地表达自己的思想。其中之一就是采用一些著名演员曾使用过的一种方法。

许多年以前,道格拉斯·费尔班克为《美国杂志》写了一篇文章,介绍了一种益智游戏,查理·卓别林、玛丽·皮克福和他有两年时间几乎每个晚上都玩这种游戏。这不仅仅是一种游戏,它还包含了所有演讲技巧中最困难的练习——站立思考。根据费尔班克写的,这个"游戏"是这样进行的:

> 我们每个人各自在一张小纸条上写下一个题目,然后把纸条折好,混在一起。当一个人抽出题目后,要求马上站起来,用那个题目说上一分钟。同一题目不会使用两次。一天晚上,我必须谈"灯罩"。如果你以为这很容易,那就试试。我好歹算过了关。
>
> 重要的是,自从我们开始玩这个游戏以来,我们全都变得思维敏捷了。对于五花八门的题目我们也有了更多的了解。但是,更有用的是,我们学会了在瞬间根据任何题目整理自己知识和思想,学会了怎样站着思考。

and they experience a blackout while giving their prepared material, they still can talk intelligently on an impromptu basis until they get back on the track again.

So, at one time or another, the class member hears, "tonight each of you will be given a different subject on which to talk. You won't know what it is until you stand up to speak. Good luck!"

What happens? An accountant finds he is called on to speak about advertising. An advertising salesman has to talk on kindergartens. A schoolteacher's topic may be banking, and a banker's topic may be schoolteaching. A clerk may be assigned to talk on production, and a production expert may be asked to discuss transportation.

Do they hang their heads, and give up? Never! They don't pretend to be authorities. They work the subjects around to fit their knowledge of something familiar to them. In their first efforts, they may not give a fine talk. But they *do* get up; they *do* talk. For some it is easy; for some it is hard, but they don't give up; they all find that they can do far better than they'd thought they would. This is thrilling to them. They see that they can develop an ability which they didn't believe they had.

I believe that if they can do this, anybody can do it—with will power and confidence—and that the more often one tries to do it, the easier it will be.

Another method we use to train people to speak on their feet is the linkage technique of impromptu speaking. It is a stimulating feature of one of our class sessions. One class member is told to begin a story in the most fantastic terms he can invent. For instance he might say, "The other day I was piloting my helicopter when I noticed a swarm of flying saucers approaching. I started to descend. But a little man in the nearest saucer started to open fire. I ..."

At this point a bell sounds indicating the end of this speaker's time, and the next class member in line must continue the story. By the time everyone in the class has contributed his share, the action may end along the canals of Mars or in the halls of Congress.

This method of developing skill in speaking without preparation is admirable as a training device. The more such practice a person gets the better he win be qualified to meet the real situations that may arise when he has to speak "for keeps" in his business and social life.

在我的训练班里,学员会经常被要求站起来即席演讲。长期经验告诉我,这种练习有两个作用:一是可以向学员证明,他们能够站着思考;二是这种经验可以使他们在做有准备的演讲时,更加沉着自信。他们知道,当他们在做有准备的演讲时,即使不幸大脑突然一片空白,他们还有即席演讲的基础,能条理清晰地谈话,直到重新回到原来的话题上。

所以,我们总会给学员这样的通知:"今晚将给你们每个人不同的题目做演讲。直到站起来演讲时你们才会知道要讲什么。祝大家好运!"

结果如何呢?会计师发现自己要讲如何做广告,而广告销售员要讲幼儿园;也许老师的题目是谈论银行业务,而银行家的题目也许是学校的教学工作;员工也许要谈论生产,而生产专家则要讨论运输问题。

他们是不是觉得很难而放弃了呢?从来没有!他们没有把自己当权威,而是在经过深思熟虑之后,把题目和他们熟悉的知识联系起来。他们刚开始也许讲得不是很好,可是他们有勇气站起来,并且开口讲话了!对此有些人觉得很简单,有些人觉得很困难,但他们没有放弃。他们都发现自己比想象的讲得好。这让他们很兴奋。他们发现自己竟然也能培养这种连自己都不敢相信的能力。

我相信他们都能做到这些,每个人也可以做到——用你的意志与信心——尝试越多,就会越容易。

我们训练学员站着讲话所使用的另一个方法,是即席演讲的联结技巧。这是我们训练班一个十分刺激的特点。我们会告诉一个学员,用他能想到的最奇妙的方式开始讲述一个故事。例如,他可能会说:"前几天,我正驾着直升机。突然,一大群飞碟朝我飞来,我被迫下降。不料最近的一座飞碟里有一个小人开始向我开火。我……"

这时,铃声响起,这个人的时间到了,然后由另一个学员继续说这个故事。等到每个人都讲完之后,这个故事也许会结束在火星的运河边,或是在国会大厅里。

SECOND/ BE MENTALLY READY TO SPEAK IMPROMPTU

When you are called on to speak without preparation usually you are expected to make some remarks about a subject upon which you can speak with authority. The problem here is to face up to the situation of talking and to decide what exactly you want to cover in the short time at your disposal. One of the best ways to become adept at this is to prepare yourself mentally for these situations. When you are at a meeting keep asking yourself what you would say now if you were called upon. What aspect of your subject would be most appropriate to cover at this time? How would you phrase your approval or rejection of the proposals now being put forth on the floor?

So the first bit of advice I offer is this: condition yourself mentally to speak impromptu on all occasions.

This requires thinking on your part, and thinking is the hardest thing in the world to do. But I am certain that no man ever made a reputation as an impromptu speaker who did not prepare himself by devoting hours of analysis to every public situation in which he was a participant. Just as an airline pilot readies himself to act with cool precision in an emergency by continually posing to himself problems that could arise at any moment, the man who shines as an impromptu speaker prepares himslef by making countless talks that are never given. Such talks really are not "impromptu"; they are talks with general preparation.

Because your subject is known, your problem is one of organization to fit the time and the occasion. As an impromptu speaker you will naturally speak for only a short time. Decide what aspect of your topic would fit the situation. Don't apologize because you are unprepared. This is the expected thing. Launch into your topic as soon as possible, if not immediately, and please, I beg you, follow this advice.

THIRD/ GET INTO AN EXAMPLE IMMEDIATELY

Why? For three reasons: (1) You will free yourself at once of the necessity to think hard about your next sentence, for experiences are easily recounted even in an impromptu situation. (2) You will get into the swing of speaking, and your first-moment jitters will fly away, giving you the opportunity to warm up to your subject matter. (3) You will enlist the attention of your

这种培养即席演讲技巧的方法很好。如果一个人获得这种练习越多,那么当他必须在商务或社交场合发表演讲时,就越能轻车熟路地应对可能发生的任何情况。

二、做好即兴演讲的心理准备

当你在毫无准备的情况下被邀请演讲时,一般是希望你对属于你的领域的事物发表一些看法。所以你此时此刻的问题是,要勇于面对这种情况,并决定在这短短的时间里谈些什么。要想成为这方面的高手,有个非常好的方法,那就是要从心理上做好准备。在开会时,不妨问问自己,如果你被邀请站起来讲话,你应该讲些什么?这时最适合讲哪方面的问题?对于你要谈论的问题,应该怎样措辞以表示赞同或反对?

所以我的第一个忠告就是从心理上做好在各种场合即席讲话的准备。

这就需要你去思考。思考才是世界上最难的事情。不过我确信,没有哪一位有"即兴演讲家"美称的人,是不需花费时间就能够做好准备的。他必须像一个飞行员,不断向自己提出任何可能发生的问题,以随时准备在紧急状况下做出冷静而精确的反应。一位令人瞩目的即兴演讲家,也是在经过无数次演讲以后,才使自己准备就绪的。其实,这样的演讲并不能算是真正的"即兴演讲",而是平时就有所准备的演讲!

既然演讲题目已知,剩下来的便是怎样组织材料,以使它们适合时间、场合了。即兴讲演时间一般不会太长,因此首先要决定什么演讲题目适合这种场合。你不必道歉自己没有准备,这是意料之中的事情。要尽快进入主题。如果你还不能立即做到这点,那么一定要听听下面的忠告。

三、立刻举例说明

为什么这样做呢?有3个理由:第一,你可以从考虑下一句应该说什么的困境中立即解脱出

audience at once. As pointed out in Chapter Seven, the incident-example is a sure-fire method of capturing attention immediately.

An audience absorbed in the human interest aspect of your example will give you reassurance when you need it most—during the first few moments of speaking. Communication is a two-way process; the speaker who captures attention is immediately aware of it. As he notes the receptive forces and feels the glow of expectancy, like an electric current, play over the heads of his audience, he is challenged to go on, to do his best, to respond. The rapport thus established between speaker and audience is the key to all successful speaking—without it true communication is impossible. That is why I urge you to begin with an example, especially when you are called on to say a few words.

FOURTH/ SPEAK WITH ANIMATION AND FORCE

As has been said several times before in this book, if you speak with energy and forcefulness, your external animation will have a beneficial effect upon your mental processes. Have you ever watched a man in a conversational group who suddenly begins to gesture as he speaks? Soon he is talking fluently, sometimes brilliantly, and he begins to attract a group of eager listeners. The relation of physical activity to the mind is a close one. We use the same words to describe manual and mental operations: for instance, we say "we grasp an idea," or "we clutch at a thought." Once we get the body charged up and animated, as William James pointed out, we very soon will get the mind functioning at a rapid pace. So my advice to you is to throw yourself with abandon into your talk and you will help to insure your success as an impromptu speaker.

FIFTH/ USE THE PRINCIPLE OF THE HERE AND NOW

The time will come when someone will tap you on the shoulder and say "How about a few words?" Or it might come without warning at all. You are relaxed and enjoying the remarks of the master of ceremonies when suddenly you realize he is talking about you. Everybody turn in your direction and before you know it you are introduced as the next speaker.

In this kind of situation your mind is apt to shoot off, like Stephen Leacock's famous but

来,因为即使在即兴场合下经验也很容易复述;第二,你可以渐渐进入状态,刚开始的紧张会慢慢消失,使你有机会把自己的题材逐渐酝酿成熟;第三,你可以立即吸引听众的注意,因为正如第七章指出的,事例是立刻抓住注意力的万无一失的良方。

听众聚精会神地听你讲述充满人情味的故事,在你最需要的时候会给你重新肯定——尤其是在演讲开始后的极短时间内。沟通是一种双向过程,善于吸引别人注意力的人会立即注意这一点。当他注意到听众接纳他的观点,并且如电流般在听众之间交流时,他就会感受到挑战,从而尽最大的能力来回应。演讲者与听众之间建立和谐关系,是一切演讲成功的关键——没有这种关系,真正的沟通就不可能出现。这就是我一直建议用事例开始演讲的原因,当人家请你说几句话时尤其要这样做。

四、保持蓬勃旺盛的精力

我曾多次讲过,如果你演讲时精力充沛,那么你蓬勃向上的朝气就会对你的心理过程产生非常好的影响。你是否注意到,在交谈的人群里面,如果有个人忽然指手画脚地讲起来,他很快就会头头是道地说个不停了,有时精彩纷呈,而且还会引来一群热心的听众?身体活动与心理活动是紧密相连的。我们常用相同的词来描述手和心理活动。比如,我们说"我们抓住了一个概念",或"我们掌握了一个思想"。一旦身体充起电来——充满了蓬勃的生气,我们很快就能让心灵迅速开展活动,正如威廉·詹姆斯教授所说的那样。所以,我要给你的忠告是,忘我地投入演讲中,你就很容易成为一名成功的即兴演讲家。

五、从此时此地开始

常常会有这样的情况,一个人拍拍你的肩头说:"讲几句吧?"或者事先根本没有一点信

befuddled horseman, who got on his horse "and made off in all directions." Now, if ever, is the time to remain calm. You can get a breather as you address the chairman. Then it is best to stay close to the meeting in the remarks you make. Audiences are interested in themselves and what they are doing. There are three sources therefore, from which you can draw ideas for an impromptu speech.

First is the audience itself. Remember this, I pray you, for easy speaking. Talk about your listeners, who they are and what they are doing, especially what specific good they perform to the community or for humanity. Use a specific example.

The *second* is the occasion. Surely you can dwell on the circumstances that brought the meeting about. Is it an anniversary, a testimonial, an annual meeting, a political or patriotic occasion?

Lastly, if you have been an attentive listener, you might indicate your pleasure in something specific another speaker said before you and amplify that. The most successful impromptu talks are those that are really impromptu. They express things that the speaker feels in his heart about the audience and the occasion. They fit the situation like hand in glove. They are tailor-made for this occasion, and this occasion alone. Therein lies their success: they flower out of the moment and then, like rare-blossoming roses, they fade from the scene. But the pleasure enjoyed by your audience lives on, and sooner than you think you begin to be looked upon as an impromptu speaker.

SIXTH/ DON'T TALK IMPROMPTU—GIVE AN IMPROMPTU TALK

There is a difference as implied in the statement above. It is not enough just to ramble on and string together a series of disconnected nothings on a flimsy thread of inconsequence. You must keep your ideas logically grouped around a central thought which might well be the point you want to get across. Your examples will cohere to this central idea. And again, if you speak with enthusiasm, you will find that what you say off the cuff has a vitality and punch that your prepared talks do not have.

You can become a competent impromptu speaker if you take to heart some of the suggestions made in this chapter. You can practice along lines of the classroom techniques explained in the early part of this chapter.

At a meeting you can do a little preliminary planning and you can keep yourself aware of the

号——当你正轻松愉快地欣赏大会主持人讲话时，却突然发现他竟然谈起你来了，于是每个人都望着你。你还没弄清楚是怎么回事时，主持人就介绍说你是下一个演讲者了。

在这种情况下，你的心思很容易混乱，就像斯蒂芬·里柯克笔下那位著名而迷惑的马术师那样，跳上马"四下里乱窜"。如果说有什么时刻最需要保持平静，那就是这个时刻。你不妨先向主持人致意，以争取喘息的机会。然后，最好是讲和这次大会关系密切的话题，因为听众只对自己和自己正在做的事情感兴趣。所以，你可以从下面3个来源抓取题材进行即兴演讲。

一是听众本身。要想让演讲轻松进行，千万要记住这一点。谈论你的听众，说说他们是谁，他们正在做什么，特别是他们对社会和人类做了什么贡献等等。当然，还要用一个实例来说明。

二是场合。当然你也可以讲讲这次聚会的缘由，例如它是周年纪念日?还是表扬大会?是年度聚会?是政治性或爱国主义集会?

最后，如果你曾认真听了演讲，你可以表达对另一位演讲者在你之前谈到的某件事件很感兴趣，并将它再详述一遍。最成功的即兴演讲，都是真正当场演讲的。它们所表达的内容，是演讲者内心对听众和场合的感想，做到了因地、因人制宜，就像手和手套这样关系密切。这种演讲是专为这种场合量身定做的，它们在特殊的时刻绽放，像昙花一现，花开之后很快就凋谢不见了。然而，听众享受到的愉悦却远不止于此，在你还没有想到之前，他们早就将你当成即兴演讲家了。

六、不要随兴而讲——要即兴而谈

上面这句话是有区别的。仅仅是不着边际地胡说八道，用不合乎逻辑的方式把那些根本不相关而且毫无意义的事扯在一起，这样做是行不通的。你必须围绕一个中心，把自己的理念进行合理的归纳。这个中心思想，必须是你要说明的。你所举的事例要和这个中心一致。同时再提醒一次，如果你能以真诚的态度演讲，你就会发现自己在演讲时会精力充沛，效果显著，即使

possibility of being called upon at any moment. If you think you may be asked to contribute your comments or suggestions, pay careful attention to the other speakers. Try to be ready to condense your ideas into a few words. When the time comes, say what you have in mind as plainly as you can. Your views have been sought. Give them briefly, and sit down.

Norman Bel-Geddes, the architect and industrial designer, used to say that he couldn't put his thoughts into words unless he was on his feet. Pacing up and down his office, as he talked to associates about complex plans for building or exhibit, he was at his best. He had to learn how to speak when sitting down, and of course he did.

With most of us, it's the other way around; we have to learn to speak standing up, and of course we can. The chief secret lies in making a start—giving one short talk—and then making another start, and another, and another.

We will find that each successive talk comes more easily. Each talk will be better than its predecessors. We will realize in the end speaking impromptu to a group is merely an extension of the same thing we do when we speak impromptu to friends in our living room.

有准备的演讲也不能与之相比。

牢记本章的各项建议,即兴演讲就可以得心应手。同时,按照本章前面的课堂技巧,勤奋地进行练习。

遇到集会时,应该事前稍作计划,以准备随时可能被人邀请上台演讲。如果你认为自己可能会被邀请讲话,那最好是仔细留心别的演讲者。设法把自己的理念概括成简洁的话,演讲时间一到,就尽量把它简单明了地讲出来。只要预先思考好了主题,现在只需要简明地说出来就可以了。

建筑师兼工业设计家诺曼·贝尔格德常常说,如果不站起来,他简直就不能把自己的思想表达出来。当他向同事们说明某个建筑或展览计划时,总是要在办公室来回走动才能讲清楚。他要学的是如何坐着讲话。当然,他学会啦!

至于我们大多数人,则恰好相反——我们得学会如何站着讲话。当然,我们也能学会,主要诀窍就是要有一个开端——例如做一次简短的讲话——然后再进行另一个开端,又一个,又一个……

只要坚持努力,我们将会发现,会一场比一场更轻松,一场比一场更精彩。最后我们终于明白,对着一群人即兴演讲,其实就像在自己的客厅里和朋友即兴谈话一样,只不过范围有所扩大而已。

Part Four
The Art of Communicating

1 Delivering the Talk

When i first started to teach public speaking classes, I spent a great deal of time on the use of vocal exercises to develop resonance, increase the range of voice, and enhance inflectional agility. It wasn't long, however, before I began to see the utter futility of teaching adults how to project their tones into the upper sinuses and how to form "liquid" vowels. This is all very fine for those who can devote three or four years to improving themselves in the art of vocal delivery. I realized that my students would have to settle for the vocal equipment they were born with. I found that if I expended the time and energy I formerly devoted to helping class members to "breathe diaphragmatically" and worked on the far more important objectives of freeing them from their inhibitions and general reluctance to let themselves go, I would achieve quick and lasting results that were truly amazing. I thank God I had the sense to do this.

FIRST/ CRASH THROUGH YOUR SHELL OF SELF-CONSCIOUSNESS

It is not easy to be natural before an audience. Actors know that. When you were a child, say, four years old, you probably could have mounted a platform and talked naturally to an audience. But when you are twenty-and-four, or forty-and-four, what happens when you mount a platform and start to speak? Do you retain that unconscious naturalness that you possessed at four? You may, but it is dollars to doughnuts that you will become stiff and stilted and mechanical, and draw back into your shell like a snapping turtle.

第四篇 沟通的艺术

第1章 发表演讲的技巧

刚开始教当众演讲课的时候，我花了大量的时间来进行发声训练，为的是产生共鸣、增大音量、增强婉转活力。但是不久前，我开始认识到，教学员如何正确发音，如何产生“圆润”的声音，是绝对失策的。对他们来说，能够花三四年时间来提高演讲发音技巧固然不错，但是我意识到，我的学员只能靠天生的发音系统。我发现，如果把以前帮助学员“运气”，且偏离更重要目标的大量时间和精力，用来帮助他们从压抑和紧张的情绪中解脱出来，会有很快的成效，还会保持惊人的结果。感谢上帝，让我有了这样的智慧。

一、摆脱自我束缚

在听众面前保持轻松自然是不容易的。演员很了解。如果你是一个孩子，假如4岁，或许会站上讲台，自然地对听众演说。但如果你24岁或44岁，登上讲台演讲时，会发生什么呢？你会保持4岁时具有的天真烂漫吗？或许会，但将变得迂回、呆板、虚伪、机械，像乌龟一样缩进壳里。

教授演讲的关键不在于增加他们的特长，主要是消除他们的障碍，使之做到就算有人打扰，也能展现同样的自然本色。

有多少次，我中途打断他们演讲，恳求他们“像人一样说话”。有多少个夜晚，我回到家里苦

The problem of teaching or of training adults in delivery is not one of superimposing additional characteristics; it is largely one of removing impediments, of getting them to speak with the same naturalness that they would display if someone were to knock them down.

Hundreds of times I have stopped speakers in the midst of their talks and implored them to "talk like a human being." Hundreds of nights I have come home mentally fatigued and nervously exhausted from trying to drill members of my classes to talk naturally. No, believe me, it is not so easy as it sounds.

In one of the sessions of my course I ask the class to act out portions of dialogue, some of which is in dialect. I ask them to throw themselves into these dramatic episodes with abandon. When they do, they discover to their amazement that, though they may have acted like a fool, they didn't feel badly when they were doing it. The class too is amazed at the dramatic ability some of the class members display. My point is that once you let your hair down before a group you are not likely to hold yourself back when it comes to the normal, everyday expression of your opinions whether to individuals or before groups.

SECOND/ DON'T TRY TO IMITATE OTHERS—BE YOURSELF

We all admire speakers who can put showmanship into their speaking, who are not afraid to express themselves, not afraid to use the unique, individual, imaginative way of saying what they have to say to the audience.

Shortly after the close of the First World War, I met two brothers in London, Sir Ross and Sir Keith Smith. They had just made the first aeroplane flight from London to Australia to win a fifty-thousand-dollar prize offered by the Australian government. They had created a sensation throughout the British Empire and had been knighted by the King.

Captain Hurley, a well-known scenic photographer, had flown with them over a part of their trip, taking motion pictures; so I helped them prepare an illustrated travel talk of their flight and trained them in the delivery of it. They gave it twice daily for four months in Philharmonic Hall, London, one speaking in the afternoon, the other at night.

They had had identically the same experience, they had sat side by side as they flew halfway

思冥想,如何把学员训练得可以自然地表达。不,相信我,这可不像听起来那么容易。

有一次课上,我要求学员进行对话表演,有一些是用方言。我要求他们抛开顾虑,进入剧情。这时,他们才感到惊讶,自己像傻子一样在表演,却浑然不觉。面对某些学员展现出的表演才能,大家也相当惊叹。我的建议是,一旦你能在人群面前放松,那么不管面对个人还是群众发言,都不会感到压抑了。

二、不要刻意模仿别人,做你自己

我们都羡慕有些演讲家善用演讲技巧。对听众演讲时,他们无所畏惧地表达,大胆地运用独特、个性、富有想象力的方式。

第一次世界大战结束不久,我在伦敦遇到兄弟俩,罗斯爵士和基思·史密斯爵士。他们刚刚结束从伦敦到澳大利亚的旅行,这是他们生平头一回飞行,获得了澳大利亚政府授予的5万美元奖金。他们在英国制造了轰动,并获得英王的授勋。

著名的风景摄影师赫尔利上尉,与这兄弟俩度过了一段旅程,还拍了一些动作照片,所以我帮他们准备了一份有插图的飞行游讲座,并教他们怎样表达。他们在伦敦的交响乐厅进行了4个月,每天两场演讲,安排在下午和晚上,每人负责一场。

他们经历相同,并携手飞遍了大半个世界。他的演讲内容一样,几乎一字不差。然而,听上去完全不同。

演讲中除了用词外,还要注意一些其他的事情。也就是演讲的风格。说什么和怎么说是截然不同的两回事。

俄罗斯大画家布鲁洛夫有一次纠正学生的作业。那学生惊喜地看着修改的绘画,兴奋地说:“为什么您只改动了一点点,效果却完全不同了?”布鲁洛夫回答:“艺术就在于细微之处。”

around the world, and they delivered the same talk, almost word for word. Yet, somehow it didn't sound like the same talk at all.

There is something besides the mere words in a talk which counts. It is the flavor with which they are delivered. It is not so much just what you say as how you say it.

Brulloff, the great Russian painter, once corrected a pupil's study. The pupil looked in amazement at the altered drawing, exclaiming: "Why, you have touched it only a tiny bit, but it is quite another thing." Brulloff replied, "Art begins where the tiny bit begins." That is as true of speaking as it is of painting and of Paderewski's playing.

"All Fords are exactly alike," their maker used to say, "but no two men are just alike. Every new life is a new thing under the sun; there has never been anything just like it before, and never will be again. A young man ought to get that idea about himself; he should look for the single spark of individuality that makes him different from other folks, and develop that for all he is Worth. Society and schools may try to iron it out of him; their tendency is to put us all in the same mold but, I say, don't let that spark be lost; it's your only real claim to importance."

All that is doubly true of effective speaking. There is no other human being in the world like you. In other words, you have an individuality. As a speaker, it is your most precious possession. Cling to it. Cherish it. Develop it. It is the spark that will put force and sincerity into your speaking. "It is your only real claim to importance." Please, I beg you, do not attempt to force yourself in a mold and thereby lose your distinctiveness.

THIRD/ CONVERSE WITH YOUR AUDIENCE

Let me give you an illustration that is typical of the fashion in which thousands of persons talk. I happened on one occasion to be stopping in Murren, a summer resort in the Swiss Alps. I was living at a hotel operated by a London company; and they usually sent out from England a couple of lecturers each week to talk to the guests. One of them was a wellknown English novelist. Her topic was "The Future of the Novel." She admitted that she had not selected the subject herself; and the long and short of it was that she had nothing she cared to say about it to mate it worthwhile expressing. She had hurriedly made some rambling notes; and she stood before the audience,

演讲就和绘画以及巴德列夫斯基的演奏一样,于细微处显示差异。

"所有的福特汽车都十分相像。"福特制造商说。"但是没有两个人是完全相像的。每一个新生命都是阳光下的新事物,以前不存在,以后也不会有。年轻人应该有自己的想法,探寻个性的火花,使自己与众不同,发展自己的价值观。社会和学校应该尽力纠正他们的不良习惯。他们趋向于把所有人看作同一种模式,但我认为不应该让这类激情少年消失。因为那是能说明你的重要性的唯一证据。"

上述建议对成功演讲是相当管用的。世界上没有一个人会和你一样。换句话说,你是独一无二的。作为一位演讲者,这就是你最宝贵的优势,要坚持,要珍惜,要发扬。正是这个闪光点,会给你的演讲增加魅力和真实感。"那是能说明你的重要性的唯一证据。"我恳求你们,请不要把自己变成一种模式,因为那会失去你的特征。

三、和听众交谈

先说一个例子,它是大多数人谈话的一种典型风格。我曾经在瑞士阿尔卑斯山的一个避暑胜地缪伦度假。我住在一家伦敦公司开的旅馆。他们经常每周从英格兰派出演讲者为旅客演讲。其中有一位是著名的英国小说家。她的演讲题目是《小说的未来》。她承认,这个题目不是自己选择的,所以显得无话可说,甚至不敢肯定它是否值得演讲。她草草地列了几项不着边际的要点。她站在听众面前,却忽视了他们,甚至根本不敢正视他们。她有时越过听众的头顶,凝视前方;有时盯着自己的笔记;有时看着地板。她用机械的声音念着每个字,眼神闪烁游离,声音飘忽不定。

那不是演讲,是在自言自语,没有一点沟通的感觉。成功演讲的首要条件是——沟通的感觉。听众必须感受到,有一个信息正在从演讲者的意识和心里传到他们的意识和心里。我刚才

ignoring her hearers, not even looking at them, staring sometimes over their heads, sometimes at her notes, sometimes at the floor. She unreeled words into the primeval void with a far-away look in her eyes and a far-away ring in her voice.

That isn't delivering a talk at all. It is a soliloquy. It has no *sense of communication*. And that is the first essential of good talking: a *sense of communication*. The audience must feel that there is a message being delivered straight from the mind and heart of the speaker to their minds and their hearts. The kind of talk I have just described might as well have been spoken out in the sandy, waterless wastes of the Gobi desert. In fact, it sounded as if it were being delivered in some such spot rather than to a group of living human beings.

A modern audience, regardless of whether it is fifteen people at a business conference or a thousand people under a tent, wants the speaker to talk just as directly as he would in a chat, and in the same general manner he would employ in speaking to one of them in conversation, in the same *manner*, but with greater force or energy. In order to appear natural, he has to use much more energy in talking to forty people than he does in talking to one, just as a statue on top of a building has to be of heroic size in order to make it appear of lifelike proportions to an observer on the ground.

At the close of one of Mark Twain's lectures in a Nevada mining camp, an old prospector approached him and inquired: "Be them your natural tones of eloquence?"

That is what the audience wants: "your natural tones of eloquence," enlarged a bit.

The only way to acquire the knack of this enlarged naturalness is by practice. And, as you practice, if you find yourself talking in a stilted manner, pause and say sharply to yourself mentally: "Here! What is wrong? Wake up! Be human." Then mentally pick out a person in the audience, someone in the back or the least attentive person you can fred, and talk to this person. Forget there is anyone else present at all. *Conrevse* with this person. Imagine that he has asked you a question and that you are answering it, and that you are the *only* one who can answer it. If he were to stand up and talk to you, and you were to talk back to him, that process would immediately and inevitably make your speaking more conversational, more natural, more direct. So, imagine that is precisely what is taking place.

You may go so far as actually to ask questions and answer them. For example, in the midst of your talk, you may say, "and you ask what proof have I for this assertion? I have adequate proof and here it

说的那个演讲可能适合于干涸的戈壁滩。事实上,这种演讲听起来好像是对荒漠,而不是对人。

无论是商务会中的十几个人,还是帐篷里的上千人,只要是一个现代听众,都希望演讲者能像聊天那样直截了当,采用的风格也像和某个人交谈一样轻松自然。形式可以一样,不过声音的力量要更大些。为了表现得自然,他必须耗费更多的能量,因为他面对的听众是40个,而不是一个。这就好比建筑物顶上的一座雕像,不得不显现出英雄的伟大,底下的参观者才能觉得它真切。

马克·吐温在内华达州的一个矿厂进行演讲。结束后,一位老矿工走近他,问:"这就是你平时演讲的风格吗?"

那正是听众想要的:"你平时演讲的风格!"再稍微增强一点。

增强这份亲切自然感的诀窍,唯一的方式是练习。在练习的时候,如果你发现自己的演讲有点虚伪,要马上停下来,对自己说:"这里!什么搞错了?清醒!要人性化。"然后,想象着从观众中挑出一个人,可以是最后一排的人,也可以是一点都不专心听的人,和他聊一聊。忘掉这里的其他人。只和选定的这位听众聊。设想他在提问,你在回答,你是唯一能回答的人。假设他立论,你驳论。这个过程会立即、无一例外地把你的演讲变得更像交流,更自然,更直接。所以,可以想象当时会发生什么。

你可以切实地问一些问题,并给予回答。例如,在演讲时,你可以说:"你们会问,我能为这种说法拿出什么证据?我有足够的证据,那就是……"然后继续提问。这件事可以做得很自然,它能打破一个人演讲的单调气氛,从而变得直接、愉悦、易于沟通。

在商会上发言,就应该像对老朋友聊天一样。什么是商会呢,不也是朋友的聚会吗?与单个朋友交流可行的方式,难道不可以同样用于一帮朋友吗?

本章前面讲了一位小说家的演讲情况。后来,在她曾经演讲过的大厅里,我们却非常愉快

is ..."Then proceed to answer the question. That sort of thing can be done very naturally. It will break up the monotony of one's delivery; it will make it direct and pleasant and conversational.

Speak to the Chamber of Commerce just as you would to John Henry Smith. What is a meeting of the Chamber of Commerce, after all, but a collection of John Henry Smiths? Won't the same methods that are successful with those men individually be successful with them collectively?

Earlier in this chapter was descried the delivery of a certain novelist. In the same ballroom in which she had spoken, we had the pleasure, a few nights later, of hearing Sir Oliver Lodge. His subject was "Atoms and Worlds." He had devoted to this subject more than half a century of thought and study ant experiment and investigation. He had something that was essentially a part of his heart and mind and life, something that he wanted very much to say. He forgot that he was trying to make a "speech." That was the least of his worries. He was concerned only with telling the audience about atoms, telling us accurately, lucidly, and feelingly. He was earnestly trying to get us to see what he saw and to feel what he felt.

And what was the result? He delivered a remarkable talk. It had both charm and power. It made a deep impression. He was a speaker of unusual ability. Yet I am sure he didn't regard himself in that light. I am sure that few people who heard him over thought of him as a "public speaker" at all.

A good window does not call attention to itself. It merely lets in the light. A good speaker is like that. He is so disarmingly natural that his hearers never notice his manner of speaking: they are conscious only of his matter.

FOURTH/ PUT YOUR HEART INTO YOUR SPEAKING

Sincerity and enthusiasm and high earnestness well help you, too. When a man is under the influence of his feelings, his real self comes to the surface. The bars are down. The heat of his emotions has burned all barriers away. He acts spontaneously. He talks spontaneously. He is natural.

So, in the end, even this matter of delivery comes back to the thing which has already been emphasized repeatedly in these pages: namely, *put your heart into your talks.*

"I shall never forget," said Dean Brown in his Lectures on Preaching before the Yale Divinity School, "the description given by a friend of mine of a church service which he once attended in the

地聆听了奥利弗·洛奇爵士的演说。他的题目是《原子与世界》。半个多世纪以来，他致力于这个题目的思考、研究、实践和调查。有些东西已经成为了他内心、思想和生命中不可或缺的一部分，有些东西是他迫切想要说出来的。他忘了自己是在“演讲”。他根本不担心无话可说。他只是想告诉听众有关原子的一些情况，他的演讲准确、清楚、富有感情。他热切地要让我们看到他所看到的，感受到他所感受到的。

结果如何呢？当然是做了一场与众不同的演讲。这次演讲充满魅力，跌宕激昂，给人留下深刻的印象。他是一位能力超群的演讲家。不过，我确信他不一定会看到自己的这个闪光点。我敢说听过他演讲的人，没有谁会认为他是“公众演讲家”。

一扇好窗户不会引起别人的注意，它只会让阳光照射进来。一位杰出的演讲者也是如此。他会尽可能地放松，以至于听众根本不去注意他的演讲神态：因为他们只关心他的内容。

四、全身心地投入演讲

真诚、热情和高度的热诚也会有益于你的演讲。当一个人受到情感的影响时，他真实的自我就会浮上表面，一切障碍都会消除。他的热情会燃烧掉所有的障碍。他行动自然，演讲自然。他完全是出乎自然。

所以，最终即使是演讲的内容，还是要回到本书前面反复强调的——也就是全身心地投入到演讲中。

布朗校长在耶鲁大学神学院的演讲中说：“我永远不会忘记，一位朋友向我描述的他曾经在伦敦参加过的一次教堂仪式。传教士是乔治·麦克唐纳。那天早晨，他读的经文是《希伯来人书》的第11章。布道时，他说：‘你们都听过信徒们的事迹。我不准备告诉你们什么是信仰。因为神学教授会比我解释得更清楚。我在这里是要帮助你们去相信。’随后，他以简单、真诚、庄重的

city of London. The preacher was George MacDonald; he read for the Scripture lesson that morning the eleventh chapter of Hebrews. When the time came for the sermon, he said: 'You have all heard about these men of faith. I shall not try to tell you what faith is. There are theological professors who could do that much better than I could do it. I am here to help you believe.' Then followed such a simple, heartfelt, and majestic manifestation of the man's own faith in those unseen realities which are eternal, as to beget faith in the minds and hearts of all his hearers. *His heart was in his work, and his delivery was effective because it rested upon the genuine beauty of his own inner life.*"

"His heart was in his work." That is the secret. Yet I know that advice like this is not popular. It seems vague. It sounds indefinite. The average person wants foolproof rules, something definite, something he can put his hands on, rules as precise as the directions for operating a car.

That is what he wants; that is what I would like to give him. It would be easy for him and it would be easy for me. There are such rules, and there is only one little thing wrong with them: they just don't work. They take all the naturalness and spontaneity and life and juice out of a man's speaking. I know. In my younger days, I wasted a great deal of energy trying them. They won't appear in these pages for, as Josh Billings observed in one of his lighter moments: "There ain't no use in knowin so many things that ain't so."

Edmund Burke wrote speeches so superb in logic and reasoning and composition that they are today studied as classic models of oratory in the colleges of the land; yet Burke, as a speaker, was a notorious failure. He didn't have the ability to deliver his gems, to make them interesting and forceful; so he was called "the dinner bell" of the House of Commons. When he arose to talk, the other members coughed and shuffled and either went to sleep or went out in droves.

You can throw a steel-jacketed bullet at a man with all your might, and you cannot make even a dent in his clothing. But put powder behind a tallow candle and you can shoot it through a pine board. Many a tallow-candle speech with powder makes, I regret to say, more of an impression than a steel-jacketed talk with no force, no excitement, behind it.

FIFTH/ PRACTICE MAKING YOUR VOICE STRONG AND FLEXIBLE

When we are really communicating our ideas to our listeners we are making use of many

表现形式，表达出对看不见而又永恒存在的事物的信任，唤起在场听众从意识和心中对它们的信任。他全心投入演讲，收效甚好，因为演讲展现了他内在生命的真正的美。”

“他在用心演讲。”那就是秘密所在。然而，我知道这种建议是不受欢迎的，似乎太笼统了，听起来很模糊。一般人都想要简单的法则，明确的规定，可以触摸得到，就像驾车指南一样精确。

人人都想要那些，我也希望提供那些。这对他容易，对我也容易。这样的法则是有的，但是存在弊病：它们根本起不到作用。它们会让演讲失去轻松自然的感觉、生活的气息，以及演讲的精髓。我很清楚这点。年轻时，我浪费了大量的精力去寻找法则。它们不会出现在本书中，正如乔希·比林斯回顾一次辉煌的时刻时说：“知道太多没用的东西也是枉然。”

埃德蒙·伯克写的演讲稿，逻辑、推理和组织上都相当有水平，甚至在今天这些稿件仍作为本土大学演讲范本在学习。但是伯克作为一名演讲家，却是声名狼藉、一败涂地的。他没有能力展示自己的珍宝，使之有趣、有魅力，所以他被人称为下议院的“晚钟”。当他站起来发言时，其他人会咳嗽、拖着脚步走路、睡觉或者陆续出去。

你可能朝某人投掷一枚钢甲子弹，而不在他衣服上留下一丝痕迹。但随着蜡烛抛洒出去的香粉，却能够射穿松木板。我只能遗憾地说，与软弱无力、没有激情的钢铁般的演讲相比，含有香粉的蜡烛般的演讲更会给听众留下深刻的印象。

五、练习，让你的声音强劲而富有弹性

当我们真正同听众交流思想时，要充分利用各种语言和动作要素。我们可以耸耸肩，动动胳膊，皱皱眉毛，提高音量，改变音调，并根据场合与主题说得或快或慢。但最好记住，这些只是效果，不是原因。所谓的音调的改变或调节，都是受我们思想和情绪状态的影响的。这正好说明

elements of vocal and physical variety. We shrug our shoulders, move our arms, wrinkle our brows, increase our volume, change pitch and inflection, and talk fast or slow as the occasion and the material may dictate. It is well to remember that all these are effects and not causes. The so-called variables, or modulations of tone, are under the direct influence of our mental and emotional state. That is why it is so important that we have a topic we know and a topic we are excited about when we go before an audience. That is why we must be so eager to share that topic with our listeners.

Since most of us lose the spontaneity and naturalness of youth as we grow older, we tend to slip into a definite mold of physical and vocal communication. We find ourselves less ready to use gestures and animation; we rarely raise or lower our voices from one pitch to another, In short, we lose the freshness and spontaneity of true conversation. We may get into the habit of talking too slowly or too rapidly, and our diction, unless carefully watched, tends to become ragged and careless. In this book you have been repeatedly told to act natural, and you may suppose that I therefore condone poor diction or monotonous delivery provided it is natural. On the contrary, I say that we should be natural in the sense that we express *our* ideas and express them with spirit. On the other hand, every good speaker will not accept himself as incapable of improvement in breadth of vocabulary, richness of imagery and diction, and variety and force of expression. These are areas in which everyone interested in self-improvement will seek to improve.

It is an excellent idea to evaluate oneself in terms of volume, pitch variation, and pace. This can be done with the aid of a tape recorder. On the other hand, it would be useful to have friends help you make this evaluation. If it is possible to secure expert advice, so much the better. It should be remembered, however, that these are areas for practice away from the audience. To concern yourself with technique when you are before an audience will prove fatal to effectiveness. Once there, pour yourself into your talk, concentrate your whole being on making a mental and emotional impact on your audience, and nine chances out of ten you will speak with more emphasis and force than you could ever get from books.

了为什么在演讲前一定要了解题目并对其产生激情，那也正是我们为何如此热切地与听众分享这个话题的缘故。

随着年龄的增长，我们大多数人会失去年轻时代的率真和自然，会陷入肢体和语言表达的固定模式。我们会发现自己不再愿意做手势，没了生气。说话时也很少抑扬顿挫，缺乏激情。总而言之，我们失掉了沟通的新鲜感和动力。我们可能会养成太快或太慢的说话习惯。除非仔细审查，否则我们的措辞也会变得散乱无序。在本书中，我反复告诉大家，注意表达要自然。你可能认为，我会因此原谅贫乏的词句和单调的演讲。正相反，我说的是我们要在表达思想的感觉上保持自然，要带有感情的表达。另外，每一位杰出的演讲家都不承认自己的词汇不用扩充，表意和措辞无需丰富，表达方式不必多样化，表达的力度不用加强。这些都是每个有志于自我提高的人努力完善的地方。

根据音量、变化和语速来自我测评，是一个好主意。这可以借助一台录音机来完成。另外，找个朋友帮你评估，是非常有用的。如果可以得到专家的建议，就更好了。不过，应该记住，这是脱离听众的训练。当你站在听众面前时，如果只关心技巧，对演讲的影响将是致命的。一旦站在讲台上，就要把自己融入演讲之中，集中全部精力，带给听众精神和情感上的冲击，你的演讲将会更强劲有力。

Part Five
The Challenge of Effective Speaking

1 Introducing Speakers, Presenting and Accepting Awards

When you are called upon to speak in public, you may introduce another speaker or make a longer talk to inform, entertain, convince, or persuade. Perhaps you are program chairman of a civic organization or a member of a women's club and you face the task of introducing the main speaker at your next meeting, or perhaps you are looking forward to the time when you will address the local PTA, your sales group, a union meeting, or a political organization. In Chapter Thirteen, I will give you hints on preparing the longer type of talk, and this chapter will help you to prepare a speech of introduction. I shall give you also some valuable hints on presenting and accepting awards.

John Mason Brown, the writer and lecturer, whose lively talks have won audiences everywhere in the country, was speaking one night with the man who was to introduce him to his audience.

"Stop worrying about what you are going to say," the man told Mr. Brown. "Relax. I don't believe in preparing a speech. Nope, preparation's no good. Spoils the charm of the thing; kills gaiety. I just wait for the inspiration to come to me when I'm on my feet—and it never fails."

These reassuring words let Mr. Brown look forward to a fine introduction, he recalls in his book, *Accustomed As I Am*. But when the man arose to make it, it came out this way:

> Gentlemen, may I have your attention, please? We have bad news for you tonight. We wanted to have Isaac F. Marcosson speak to you, but he couldn't come. He's sick. (Applause.) Next we asked Senator Bledridge to address you... but he was busy. (Applause.) Finally we tried in vain to get Doctor Lloyd Grogan of Kansas City to come down to speak to you. (Applause.) So, instead,

第五篇 接受成功演讲的挑战

第1章 介绍演讲者、颁奖和领奖

当你被邀请当众发言时，你可以推荐另一个人，或者自己作一番介绍，以便向听众说明情况，取悦或者令他们信服。假如你是民间组织的节目主持人，或者某妇女俱乐部的成员，你就面临着介绍下次会议主讲人的任务。或许，你有机会在当地的家庭教师协会、销售小组、同盟会或政治组织中发表演讲。在第13章，我将给你们一些准备长篇演讲的提示。本章旨在帮助你们如何准备介绍词。我也会提供一些有关颁奖和领奖的实用性建议。

约翰·梅森·布朗是作家和演讲家。他生动的演讲赢得了全国各地的听众。一天晚上，他和一名主持人交谈。

"别为你的演讲担心，"主持人对布朗先生说，"放松点，我认为演讲不用准备。不用，准备没什么用。只会破坏美感，扼杀好的氛围。我只期望临场发挥——从没出过纰漏。"

这番安抚之词让布朗先生期待主持人会有一个精彩的介绍，他在《积习难改》这本书中这样回忆。但是，这位主持人站起来介绍时，却这样说：

> 先生们，能请您注意一下吗？今晚我们有个坏消息要告诉大家。我们原打算邀请艾萨克·马克森先生为大家演讲，但是他因病不能来了。（鼓掌）后来我们又邀请伯莱维基议员……但是他也很忙。（鼓掌）最后我们邀请堪萨斯州的劳埃德·葛罗根博士也未成功。（鼓

we have—John Mason Brown. (Silence.)

Mr. Brown, recalling this disaster, said only: "At least my friend, that inspirationalist, got my name correctly."

Of course you can see that this man, who was so sure his inspiration would carry him through, couldn't have done much worse if he had tried to do so. His introduction violated every obligation he had both to the speaker whom he was introducing and to the audience which was to hear the speaker. There aren't many of these obligations, but they are important, and it is astonishing how many program chairmen fail to realize this.

The speech of introduction serves the same purpose as a social introduction. It brings the speaker and the audience together, establishes a friendly atmosphere, and creates a bond of interest between them. The man who says, "You don't have to make a speech, all you have to do is introduce the speaker," is guilty of under—statement. No speech is more mangled than the speech of introduction, probably because it is looked upon as unimportant by many chairmen who are entrusted with the duty of preparing and delivering it.

An introduction—that term was fashioned from two Latin words, *intro*, to the inside, and *ducere*, to lead—ought to lead us to the inside of the topic sufficiently to make us want to hear it discussed. It ought to lead us to the inside facts regarding the speaker, facts that demonstrate his fitness for discussing this particular topic. In other words, an introduction ought to "sell" the topic to the audience and it ought to "sell" the speaker. And it ought to do these things in the briefest amount of time possible.

That is what it ought to do. But does it? Nine times out of ten, no—emphatically no. Most introductions are poor affairs, feeble and inexcusably inadequate. They do not have to be. If the speaker making the introduction realizes the importance of his task and goes about doing it in the right way he will soon be in demand as a chairman or master of ceremonies.

Here are some suggestions to help you make a well organized speech of introduction.

FIRST/ THOROUGHLY PREPARE WHAT YOU ARE GOING TO SAY

Even though the introductory talk is short, hardly ever exceeding one minute, it demands careful

掌)所以,在不得已的情况下,我们只能请——约翰·梅森·布朗。(沉默)

布朗先生回忆这次遭遇时,只说:"至少我的朋友,那位灵感家,把我的名字念得一字不差。"

你肯定能看明白,这位坚信自己的灵感可以应付一切的主持人,如果稍加准备一下,是不可能会弄得这么糟的。他的介绍词已经背离了对待演讲者和听众的职责。尽管主持人的这类职责不多,却很重要。令人不解的是,有那么多节目主持人都没有意识到这一点。

介绍词的作用与交际介绍一样。它把演讲者和听众联系在一起,为的是建立良好的气氛,让彼此发生兴趣。认为"你不必说什么,只要介绍演讲者就足矣"的人,是不成熟的。没有哪种演讲比介绍词更容易被搞砸的,或许正是因为它不被许多主持人重视的缘故。

介绍——这个词由两个拉丁字组成。intro表示内部,ducere表示领导,意思应该是:带领我们充分深入事物的内部,听听要讨论的内容。它应该引领我们深入了解演讲者,并认为他足以胜任探讨这个特别的话题。换句话说,介绍应该是向听众"推销"演讲主题和演讲者。它应该以最简明的语言来介绍。

那就是介绍词所要做的。但是做到了吗?十有八九没做到——真的没做到。大多数介绍词都很平庸、不堪一击、更不充分。该做的他们没有做到。如果主持人意识到自己任务的重要性,并立即给予更正,他很快就会成为广受欢迎的典礼和仪式的主持人。

下面是一些建议,可以帮你较好地组织介绍词。

一、做好充分准备

即使介绍词很简短,甚至不到一分钟,也应该好好准备。首先,必须收集事实。这些事实可以围绕三点:演讲的题目、演讲者对该话题的资历及演讲者的姓名。有时再加上第四点——为

preparation. First, you must gather your facts. These will center around three items: the subject of the speaker's talk, his qualifications to speak on that subject, and his name. Often a fourth item will become apparent—why the subject chosen by the speaker is of special interest to the audience.

Be certain that you know the correct title of the talk and something about the speaker's development of the subject matter. There is nothing more embarrassing than for the speaker to take exception to the introduction by disclaiming part of it as untrue of his stand on the subject. This can be obviated by making sure you know what the speaker's subject is and refraining from trying to predict what he will say. But your duty as introducer demands that you give the title of the speaker's talk correctly and point out its relevancy to the audience's interests. If at all possible, try to get this information directly from the speaker. If you have to rely on a third party, a program chairman, for instance, try to get the information in writing and check with the speaker just before the meeting.

But perhaps most of your preparation will involve getting the facts on the speaker's qualificalions. In some cases you will be able to get an accurate listing from *Who's Who* or a comparable work, if your speaker is nationally or regionally well known. On the local level you can appeal to the public relations or personnel office of the concern where he works, or in some cases verify your facts by calling a close friend or a member of his family. The main idea is to get your biographical facts correct. People close to your speaker will be glad to furnish you with material.

Of course, too many facts will become boring, especially when one degree implies the speaker's acquisition of lesser degrees. To say that a man received a B.S. and an M.A. degree is superfluous when you indicate that he is a Doctor of Philosophy. Likewise, it is best to indicate the highest and most recent offices a man has held rather than to string out a catalogue of the positions he has held since leaving college. Above all, do not pass over the most distinguished achievements of a man's career instead of the less important.

For example, I heard a well-known speaker—a man who ought to have known better—introduce the Irish poet W.B. Yeats. Yeats was to read his own poetry. Three years prior to that he had been awarded the Nobel Prize in literature, the highest distinction that can be bestowed upon a man of letters. I am confident that not ten per cent of that particular audience knew of the award or its significance. Both ought, by all means, to have been mentioned. They ought to have been

什么演讲的题目特别有趣。

你一定要知道确切的演讲主题,以及演讲者对该主题的发挥。最尴尬的事情莫过于演讲者对主持人的介绍有异议,认为其中有与他立场不一致的地方。这种情况是可以避免的,只要主持人确切知道演讲者的主题是什么,且不妄加猜测。但是主持人的职责要求准确把握演讲主题,并指出它是听众感兴趣的话题。如果可能的话,尽量直接从演讲者那里获取信息。如果需要依靠第三方的帮助,节目主持人就应该在演讲开始之前,努力收集书面资料,并与演讲者进行核实。

但是,你准备最多的内容应该是演讲者的资历。如果演讲者是享誉全国或者当地知名的人物,你可以从名人录或者出色人物中获取准确的信息。如果他是当地的名人,你可以求助他的公众关系和单位的人事部门,也可以拜访他的好友或家人,主要目的是让你的信息准确。演讲者的亲朋好友一定会很乐意给你提供资料的。

当然,介绍得过多也会令人讨厌,尤其是没必要详细介绍演讲者所获得的各种学历。比如,如果已经介绍一个人是哲学博士,又说他获得了学士和硕士学位是多余的。同理,最好是介绍他最高和最近的职位,而不是说出他大学毕业后的各种职务。最重要的是,不能忽略他最杰出的成就,无关紧要的部分则可以省去。

例如,我曾经听过一位著名的演讲家——此人本应该更著名的——介绍爱尔兰诗人W·B·叶慈。叶慈准备朗诵一首自己的诗歌。三年前,他获得了诺贝尔文学奖,这是授予文艺工作者的最高荣誉。我相信,只有不到百分之十的人知道这个奖项及其意义。但是无论如何,应该值得一提。即使别的内容不说,这些也应该说出来。但是主持人做了什么呢?他完全忽略了这些,而是去谈论神话和希腊诗歌。

最重要的是,牢记演讲者的姓名,当即熟悉它的发音。约翰·梅森·布朗说,他曾被人介绍成

announced even if nothing else were said. But what did the chairman do? He utterly ignored these facts, and wandered off into talking about mythology and Greek poetry.

Above all, be certain of the speaker's name and begin at once to familiarize yourself with its pronunciation. John Mason Brown says that he has been introduced as John Brown Mason and even John Smith Mason. In his delightful essay, *"We Have with Us Tonight,"* Stephen Leacock, the distinguished Canadian humorist, tells of one introduction he received in which the introducer said:

> There are many of us who have awaited Mr. Learoyd's coming with the most pleasant anticipations. We seemed from his books to know him already as an old friend. In fact I do not think I exaggerate when I tell Mr. Learoyd that his name in our city has long been a household word. I have very, very great pleasure in introducing to you—Mr. Learoyd.

The main purpose of your research is to be specific, for only by being specific will the introduction achieve its purpose—to heighten the audience's attention and make it receptive to the speaker's talk. The chairman who comes to a meeting poorly prepared usually comes up with something as vague and soporific as this:

> Our speaker is everywhere recognized as an authority on, —on, his subject. We are interested in hearing what he has to say on this subject, because he comes from a, —a great distance. It gives me great pleasure to present, let's see now, —oh, here it is, —Mr. Blank.

By taking a little time to prepare we can avoid the sad impression such an introduction makes upon both speaker and audience.

SECOND/ FOLLOW THE T-I-S FORMULA

For most introductions, the T-I-S formula serves as a handy guide in organizing the facts you have collected in your research:

1.T stands for Topic. Start your introduction by giving the exact title of the speaker's talk.

2. I stands for Importance. In this step you bridge over the area between the topic and the particular interests of the group.

3. S stands for Speaker. Here you list the speaker's outstanding qualifications, particularly those that relate to his topic. Finally, you give his name, distinctly and clearly.

约翰·布朗·梅森,甚至约翰·史密斯·梅森。加拿大著名的幽默大师斯蒂芬·里柯克在他那篇轻快的散文《我们相聚在今晚》中,提到了一位主持人对他的介绍:

> 在座的各位都热情地期待里罗德先生的大驾光临。通过他的书,我们似乎已经将他当作老朋友。事实上,我可以毫不夸张地说,里罗德先生的大名在本市是家喻户晓。我非常非常荣幸地向大家介绍——里罗德先生。

收集信息的主要目的应该明确,因为只有明确,才能达到介绍的目的——提高听众的注意力,使之接受下面的演讲。主持人如果准备欠佳,常常会发生下面这样含糊不清、令人昏昏欲睡的情况:

> 演讲者是这个论题公认的权威。我们都想聆听他的高见,因为他来自一个——一个遥远的地方。这让我很想一睹风采,现在有请——哦,这位——布兰克先生。

只要稍加准备,我们就能避免这类介绍给演讲者和听众双方造成的不良印象。

二、采用T-I-S模式

对大多数介绍词来说,T-I-S格式是一个很好的提纲,可以用来组织收集的资料:

T表示主题。介绍词的开头要说出准确的演讲主题。

I表示重要性。在这一部分,要建立起演讲主题和听众兴趣之间的桥梁。

S表示演讲者。需要列举演讲者突出的资历,特别是那些与主题相关的部分。最后准确清楚地说出他的姓名。

这种格式提供了许多供你发挥想象的空间。介绍词未必是一成不变的。下面用一个例子说明,采用这种格式,而又全然不落俗套。下面是纽约市的一名编辑霍默·卓恩向一群新闻工作者对纽约电话公司总裁乔治·韦伯先生的介绍:

There is plenty of room in this formula for using your imagination. The introduction need not be cut and dried. Here is an example of an introduction that follows the formula without giving the effect of a formula at all. It was given by a New York City editor, Homer Thorne, when he introduced a New York Telephone Company executive, George Wellbaum, to a group of newspaper men and women:

Our speaker's topic is "The Telephone Serves You".

It seems to me that one of the world's big mysteries—like love and a horse player's persistence—is the mystery of what happens when you make a telephone call.

Why do you get a wrong number? Why can you sometimes make a call from New York to Chicago quicker than from your own home town to another town just over the hill? Our speaker knows the answers, and all the others to telephone questions. For twenty years it has been his job to digest all sorts of details about the telephone business and to make this business clear to other people. He is a telephone company executive who has earned his title by work.

He will speak to us now about the ways his company serves us. If you are feeling friendly toward the service today, look on him as a patron saint. If you've recently been annoyed by your telephone, let him be a spokesman for the defense.

Ladies and Gentlemen, the vice-president of the New York Telephone Company, Mr. George Wellbaum.

Notice how cleverly the introductory speaker gets the audience thinking about the telephone. By asking questions he excites their curiosity and then indicates that the speaker will answer these questions and any others the audience may have.

I doubt that this introduction was written out or memorized. Even on paper it sounds conversational and natural. An introduction should never be memorized. Cornelia Otis Skinner was once introduced by a chairman of the evening whose memorized words she forgot as she began. She took a deep breath and then said: "Due to the exorbitant price of Admiral Byrd, we have with us this evening, Miss Cornelia Otis Skinner."

The introduction should be spontaneous, seemingly arising out of the occasion, not strait-laced and severe.

我们演讲者这次的题目是“电话为你服务”。

对我而言,世界上像爱情、赌马者的执著一样最神秘的事情之一,就是打电话时发生的神秘事件。

为什么你会拨错号?为什么有时拨通纽约到芝加哥的电话比一山之隔的两个镇要快?我们的演讲者知道这些答案,也能解答其他电话方面的问题。20多年来,这一直是他的工作:整理各种电话资料,让用户了解电话中的问题。现在他因工作出色而成为一家电话公司的总裁。

他将会介绍他们公司为我们服务的方法。如果大家对电话服务感到满意,就请把他当作一位仁慈的圣徒吧。如果你最近为电话而烦心,就让他做一个辩解人。

女士们、先生们,这位就是纽约电话公司的副总裁,乔治·韦伯先生。

可以看到,主持人多么巧妙地让听众想到了电话。通过提问,他燃起了听众的好奇心,然后指出演讲者将会回答这些问题,以及他们想知道的所有问题。

我不认为这份介绍词是事先写好了记住的。或者即使是在纸上写好的,它读起来也那么熟练自然。介绍词不应该死记硬背。在一次晚会上,主持人介绍科妮莉亚·奥蒂斯·斯金纳时,把背的内容全忘了。于是她深吸了一口气,然后说:“由于拜德上将要价过高,所以今晚,我们邀请了科妮莉亚·奥蒂斯·斯金纳小姐。”

介绍词应该是自发形成的,随即产生的,不受任何约束和局限。

前面引用过的介绍韦伯先生的例子,并没有“我荣幸地”、“我有幸为大家介绍”之类的陈词滥调。介绍演讲者的最好方式是说出他的姓名,或者说“我要介绍”后面加上他的姓名。

有一些主持人失败之处在于说得太多,让听众反感。另一些主持人则沉浸于高谈阔论之中,想让演讲者和听众留下深刻印象,证明自己的重要性。还有一些主持人会说些笑话,有的还

In the introduction of Mr. Wellbaum, quoted above, there are no clichés, such as, "it gives me great pleasure," and "it is a great privilege to introduce to you." The best way to present a speaker is to give his name or to say, "I present," and give his name.

Some chairmen are guilty of talking too long and making the audience restive. Others indulge in flights of oratorical fancy in order to impress the speaker and the audience with a sense of their importance. Still others make the sad error of dragging in "canned jokes," sometimes not in the best taste, or of using humor that patronizes or deprecates the speaker's profession. All of these faults should be avoided by the man who is desirous of achieving the purposes of an effective introduction.

Here is another example of an introduction that closely follows the T-I-S formula and yet has an individuality all its own. Note especially the way Edgar L. Schnadig blends the three phases of the formula as he introduces the distinguished science educator and editor, Gerald Wendt:

> "Science Today," our speaker's topic, is a serious business. It reminds me of the story of the psychopathic patient who suffered from the hallucination that he had a cat in his insides. Unable to disprove this, the psychiatrist simulated an operation. When the man came out of the ether, he was shown a black cat, and was told his troubles were over. He replied, "I'm sorry, doctor, but the cat that is bothering me is gray."
>
> So it is with science today. You reach for a cat called U-235, and you come up with a flock of kittens called neptunium, plutonium, uranium 233 or something else. Like a Chicago winter, the element, are overpowered. The alchemist of old, the first nuclear scientist, on his deathbed begged for one more day to discover the secrets of the universe. Now scientists produce secrets of which the universe never dreamed.
>
> Our speaker today is one who knows about science as it is, and as it may be. He has been a professor of chemistry at the University of Chicago, dean of the Pennsylvania State College, director of the Battelle Institute of Industrial Research at Columbus, Ohio. He has been a scientist in the government service, and editor and author. He was born in Davenport, Iowa, and received his professional degree at Harvard. He completed his training in war plants, and has traveled extensively in Europe.

很没品位,或者以幽默的方式来抬高或贬低演讲者的职业。所有这些做法都是极端错误的。如果主持人想要一个出色的介绍词,上面的错误就应该避免。

下面是一个遵从T–I–S模式的例子,完全彰显了它的个性。在介绍著名的科学家、教育家和编辑杰罗德·温迪时,埃德加·L·史纳迪采用了这个三段式。请特别注意他使用的方法:

> 我们演讲者的题目《今日科学》是一个非常严肃的话题。它让我们想起了某个精神病患者的故事,他幻想自己体内有一只猫。因为无法证明这是错觉,心理学家只好给他进行模拟手术。等他从麻醉中苏醒过来后,医生给他看了一只黑猫,并告诉他麻烦解决了。他却回答说:"很抱歉,医生,可是折磨我的那只猫是灰色的。"
>
> 今天的科学也是如此。你要抓的是一只叫铀–235的猫,却抓来一群小猫,镎、钚、铀–233或别的什么。就像芝加哥的冬天,这些元素都被一一击败了。古时候的炼金术士,也是最初的核能科学家,在临终前还苦苦哀求老天,多给一天时间去探寻宇宙间的秘密。现在的科学家创造了宇宙间许多原本不敢想象的秘密。
>
> 今天的演讲者,通晓当今科学的情况和未来发展趋势。他是芝加哥大学化学系的教授,宾夕法尼亚学院的院长,也是俄亥俄州哥伦布巴德尔工业研究所的所长。他一直是政府部门的科学顾问,更是编辑和作家。他出生在爱荷华州的达文波特,在哈佛大学获得专业学位。他参加了军工厂的培训,还曾经遍游欧洲。
>
> 演讲者是几个学科的许多教科书的作者和主编。他最著名的书是《未来世界的科学》,此书出版时,他正担任纽约世界博览会的科技部主任。作为《时代》、《生活》、《财富》和《时局》等杂志的顾问,他对科学新闻的诠释吸引了一大批读者。他的《原子时代》于1945年出版,正是原子弹轰炸日本广岛后的第10天。他的口头禅是"最好的就要来了。"我很自豪地介绍,各位也一定会高兴地听到,《科学画报》的主编——杰罗德·温迪博士。

Our speaker is author and editor of numerous textbooks in several sciences. His best-known book is *Science for the World of Tomorrow*, published when he was director of science at the World's Fair in New York. As consulting editor to *Time*, *Life*, *Fortune*, and *March of Time*, his interpretation of scientific news reached a wide audience. The *Atomic Age* by our speaker appeared in 1945, ten days after the bomb hit Hiroshima. His pet phrase is "The best is yet to come," and so it is. I am proud to present, and you will be happy to hear, the editorial director of *Science Illustrated*, Dr. Gerald Wendt.

Not many years ago it was a kind of oratorical fashion to over-praise the speaker in the introduction. Bouquets of flowers were heaped upon the speaker by the chairman. The poor speaker was often overwhelmed by the heavy odor of flattery.

A popular humorist, Tom Collins, of Kansas City, Missouri, told Herbert Prochnow, author of *The Toastmaster's* Handbook, that "it is fatal to a speaker who intends to be humorous to promise his audience they soon will be rolling in the aisles with uncontrollable mirth. When a toastmaster begins to mumble about Will Rogers, you know you might just as well cut your wrists and go home, because you are ruined."

On the other hand, don't under-praise either. Stephen Leacock recalls the time he had to respond to introductory remarks that ended in this manner:

This is the first of our series of lectures for this winter. The last series, as you all know, was not a success. In fact, we came out at the end of the year with a deficit. So this year we are starting a new line and trying the experiment of cheaper talent. May I present Mr. Leacock.

Mr. Leacock dryly comments: "Judge how it feels to crawl out in front of the audience labelled ' cheaper talent.'"

THIRD/ BE ENTHUSIASTIC

In making an introduction of a speaker, manner is quite as important as matter. You should try to be friendly, and instead of saying how happy you are, be genuinely pleasant making your talk. If you give the introduction with a sense of building to a climax at the end when you announce the speaker's name, the sense of anticipation will be increased and the audience will applaud the

几年前，在介绍演讲者时，盛行过分追捧的风气。主持人会给演讲者增加许多光环。可怜的演讲者常常被过度的奉承弄得昏眩不堪。

密苏里州堪萨斯市著名的幽默大师汤姆·柯林斯曾告诉《主持人手册》的作者赫伯特·普洛克罗："如果一个演讲者希望幽默风趣，对听众许诺，他们不久就会大笑不止地前俯后仰，这是相当致命的。当主持人开始支支吾吾地提到威尔·罗杰斯时，你就知道还不如回家割脉自杀，因为你已经完蛋了。"

另外，也不要贬低演讲者。斯蒂芬·里柯克回忆起有一次他不得不对介绍词进行反击。那次介绍是以如下方式结尾的：

这是今年冬天我们举办的首次演讲。众所周知，上次一系列的演讲开展得并不成功。事实上，我们去年年底已经出现了赤字。所以本年度我们开始采用一套新的思路，邀请要价稍低的人来演讲。现在请让我介绍里柯克先生。

里柯克先生沮丧地评价说："打上了'廉价人才'的烙印，缓步来到听众面前，想想会是怎样的感觉。"

三、充满热情

介绍演讲者时，表情和内容一样重要。你应该尽量表现得友善，愉快地进行介绍，而不必说出自己多么的高兴。如果你在介绍的过程中营造了热烈的气氛，那么最后你宣布演讲者姓名的时候，听众的期待会增加，也会给演讲者以更热烈的掌声。反过来，听众良好状态的表现，将有助于激励演讲者发挥最佳状态。

当你最后公布演讲者姓名时，切记要"停顿"、"中断"和"力度"。停顿，指的是在说出姓名前，稍作沉默，这样可以增加听众的期待。中断，指的是姓和名应该稍稍分隔，以便听众清楚地

speaker more enthusiastically. This display of the audience's good feeling will in turn help to stimulate the speaker to do his best.

When you do pronounce the speaker's name at the very end of the introduction it is well to remember the words, "pause," "part," and "punch." By *Pause* is meant that a little silence just before the name is given will give an edge to anticipation; by *part* is meant that the first and last names should be separated by a slight pause so that the audience gets a clear impression of the speaker's name; by *punch* is meant that the name should be given with vigor and force.

There is one more caution: please, I beg of you, when you do enunciate the speaker's name, don't turn to him, but look out over the audience until the last syllable has been uttered; *then* turn to the speaker. I have seen countless chairmen give fine introductory speeches that were ruined at the end because they turned toward the speaker, pronouncing his name for him alone and leaving the audience in total ignorance of his identity.

FOURTH/ BE WARMLY SINCERE

Lastly, be sure to be sincere. Do not indulge in deprecatory remarks or snide humor. A tongue-in-cheek type of introduction is often misinterpreted by some members of the audience. Be warmly sincere, because you are in a social situation that demands the highest kind of finesse and tact. You may be on familiar terms with the speaker, but the audience isn't, and some of your remarks, innocent though they be, may be misconstrued.

FIFTH/ THOROUGHLY PREPARE THE TALK OF PRESENTATION

"It has been proved that the deepest yearning of the human heart is for recognition—for honor!"

When Margery Wilson, the author, wrote this she expressed a universal feeling. We all want to get along well in life. We want to be appreciated. Someone else's commendation, if it is only a word—let alone a gift presented at a formal affair—lifts the spirit magically.

Althea Gibson, the tennis star, managed to get this "yearning of the human heart" most aptly into the title of her autobiography. She called it, *I Wanted To Be Somebody.*

记住演讲者的姓名。力度,指的是姓名应该着重有力地说出来。

还有一件事要注意:请你——我恳求——当你大声说出演讲者姓名时,不要转向他,而是应该面对听众,直到说出姓名的每一个音节,然后再转向演讲者。我见过无数的主持人,介绍词讲得十分精彩,却因转向演讲者而功败垂成。这样等于是只对演讲者宣布姓名,而让听众感到被彻底忽视了。

四、表现出真诚

最后,必须要表现出真诚。不要滥用贬低之词或者不诚实的幽默。夸夸其谈的介绍总是令许多听众产生误解。要表现真诚。因为你处于一个社交环境,需要最高水平的策略和技巧。你可能与演讲者很熟悉,但是听众不一定。你的一些评论,尽管是无心的,却可能会造成误解。

五、认真准备颁奖词

"已经证实,人类心里最深的渴望是被认可——得到荣誉!"

作家玛约莉·威尔逊在书中写到这一点,表达了一个普遍存在的感觉。我们都希望和平共处。我们渴望被人欣赏。别人的评论,哪怕只有一个字——更不要说是正式场合下颁发的奖品,会鬼使神差地让人飘飘然。

网球明星阿尔泰亚·吉普森,成功地把"人类心里最深的渴望"巧妙地选为她自传的标题。她称之为《我想做名人》。

当我们做颁奖祝词时,可以确定,此人一定是名人:他因努力而获得成功,他值得褒奖。颁奖词应当简明,但也要谨言慎行。对那些经常获奖的人来说,可能没什么,但对不这么幸运的人而言,这可能很重要,会铭记一辈子。

When we make a speech of presentation, we reassure the recipient that he really is *somebody*. He has succeeded in a certain effort. He is deserving of honor. We have come together to pay him this honor. What we have to say should be brief but we should give it careful thought. It may not mean much to those who are used to receiving honors, but to others less fortunate it may be something to be remembered brightly all the rest of a lifetime.

We, therefore, should give serious consideration to our choice of words in presenting the honor. Here is a time-tested formula:

1. Tell why the award is made. Perhaps it is for long service, or for winning a contest, or for a single notable achievement. Explain this simply.
2. Tell something of the group's interest in the life and activities of the person to be honored.
3. Tell how much the award is deserved and how cordially the group feels toward the recipient.
4. Congratulate the recipient and convey everyone's good wishes for the future.

Nothing is so essential to this little talk as sincerity. Everyone realizes this, perhaps without saying so. So if you have been chosen to make a speech of presentation you, as well as the recipient, have been honored. Your associates know you can be trusted with the task that demands a heart as well as a head. This must not tempt you to make certain mistakes that some speakers make. They are mistakes concerned with exaggeration.

At a time such as this, it is easy to exaggerate someone's virtues far beyond their real measure. If the award is deserved, we must say so, but we should not add words of over-praise. Exaggerated praise makes the recipient uncomfortable and it doesn't convince an audience which knows better.

We also should avoid exaggerating the importance of the gift itself. Instead of stressing its intrinsic value, we should emphasize the friendly sentiments of those who are giving it.

SIXTH/ EXPRESS YOUR SINCERE FEELINGS IN THE TALK OF ACCEPTANCE

This should be even shorter than the speech of presentation. It certainly shouldn't be anything we have memorized: yet being ready to make it will be a advantage. If we know we are to be given a present, with a speech of presentation, we shouldn't be at a loss for words of acknowledgment

因此在颁奖时,我们应该注意用词。这里是一个长盛不衰的公式:

第一,说明为什么要颁奖。或者是因获奖者长期的服务,或者赢得比赛,或者是一项重大的成就。简要地说明一下。

第二,说一些听众感兴趣的事情,如获奖者的生活和贡献。

第三,说明颁奖是多么有价值,大家对此人感到多么热切。

第四,祝贺获奖者,把每个人的祝愿转达给他。

对于这类演讲,没有什么比真诚更重要的。不用说,人人都知道这一点。所以如果被选来说颁奖词,那么和领奖人一样,也是很荣幸的。你的团队知道,你是值得信任的,能够完成这件费心费神的任务。这就要求你不能犯某些演讲者那样夸大其词的错误。

在这种场合下,很容易把获奖者的优点夸得言过其实。如果颁奖是值得的,我们必须说出来,但不应该过分吹嘘。过分赞美会让获奖者深感不安,也不能使了解实情的听众信服。

我们还应该避免夸大奖品本身的重要性。不要强调它自身的价值,应该着重于获奖者善意的感情。

六、答词的技巧

获奖感言应该比颁奖词要短。它不可能是预先背好的,但提前准备也很有好处。如果知道要领奖,听到要发表颁奖词后,我们就不会无所适从了。

只说些“谢谢”、“这是我一生中最幸福的日子”、“这是我有生以来最荣耀的事”之类的话,并不太好。和颁奖词一样,也存有夸大其词的危险。“最幸福的日子”和“最荣耀的事”太泛指了。如果用更加适中的词,可能会更好地表达心声。下面是一个参考模式:

第一,真诚地对大家“致谢”。

that will be a credit to us.

Just to mumble, "Thank you" and "greatest day in my life" and "most wonderful thing that ever happened to me," is not very good. Here, as in the speech of presentation, a danger of exaggeration lurks. "Greatest day" and "most wonderful thing" take in too much territory. You can express heartfelt gratiude better in more moderate terms. Here is a suggested format:

1. Give a warmly sincere "thank you" to the group.
2. Give credit to others who have helped you, your associates, employers, friends, or family.
3. Tell what the gift or award means to you. If it is wrapped, open it and display it. Tell the audience how useful or decorative it is and how you intend to use it.
4. End with another sincere expression of your gratitude.

In this chapter we have discussed three special types of talks, any one of which you may be called upon to give in the course of your work or your affiliation with some organization or club.

I urge you to follow these suggestions carefully when making any of these talks and you will have the satisfaction that comes from saying the right thing at the right time.

第二,把荣誉归功于帮助过你的人,你的团队、老板、朋友或者家庭。

第三,指明这个奖品或荣誉对你的意义。如果奖品是包起来的,当场打开并展示给大家。告诉听众它是多么有用,多么精致,以及你打算怎样用它。

第四,再说一些表示真诚感谢的话来结尾。

在本章,我们已经讨论了三种类型的演讲,每一种都可能在你的工作、组织或俱乐部中碰到。

我极力推荐,你在做这些演讲时,要认真遵循以上建议。在适当的场合说适当的话,你将会有满意的收效。

2 Organizing the Longer Talk

No sane man would start to build a house without some sort of plan; but why will he begin to deliver a talk without the vaguest notion of what he wishes to accomplish?

A talk is a voyage with a purpose, and it must be charted. The man who starts nowhere, generally gets there.

I wish that I could paint this saying of Napoleon's in flaming letters of red a foot high over every doorway on the globe where students of effective speaking foregather: "The art of war is a science in which nothing succeeds which has not been calculated and thought out."

That is just as true of speaking as of shooting. But do speakers realize it—or, if they do, do they always act on it? They do not. Many a talk has just a trifle more plan and arrangement than a bowl of Irish stew.

What is the best and most effective arrangement for a given set of ideas? No one can say until he has studied them. It is always a new problem, an eternal question that every speaker must ask and answer himself again and again. No infallible rules can be given; but we can, at any rate, indicate the three major phases of the longer talk to get action: the attention step, the body, and conclusion. For each, there are some timetested methods of developing each phase.

FIRST/ GET ATTENTION IMMEDIATELY

I once asked Dr. Lynn Harold Hough, formerly president of Northwestern University, what was the most important fact his long experience as a speaker has taught him. After pondering a moment, he replied, "To get an arresting opening, something that will seize favorable attention immediately." Dr. Hough struck at the heart of the matter of all persuasive speaking: how to get the audience "tuned in" right from the speaker's first words. Here are some methods which, if applied, will give high attention value to your opening phrases.

第2章 如何发表长篇演讲

明智的人绝不会不做计划就开始建房。但是为什么他在没有想好明确目的之时,就发表演讲呢?

演讲就好比有目标的航行,必须规划航线。一个从某处随意出发的人通常会毫无目标。

我想把拿破仑这句话铸成一尺高的大字,并染成火红的颜色,挂在世界上每个高效演讲班的门口——那就是"战术是一门科学,未经计划和思考就不会成功"。

演讲和射击一样。但是演讲者认识到这一点吗?如果认识到,又是否会付诸行动呢?他们不会。许多演讲不过是一件小事,演讲者对它的计划和安排比一道爱尔兰炖菜多不了多少。

怎样才是对既定题目最好、最有效的安排?只有经过研究才能了解。这是每一个演讲者必须反复问自己的一个既新而又永恒的问题。尽管我们不能给出一套完全正确的理论,但是,不管怎么样,我们还是能说出有关长篇演讲的三点注意事项:吸引听众注意力、正文内容和结论。每一方面,都有一些历久弥新的方法。

一、开场白要立即引起听众的注意

我曾经问过西北大学前任校长林恩·哈罗德·哈夫教授,以他长期的演讲经验,最重要的事情是什么?经过片刻的沉思,他回答说:"要有一个引人入胜的开场白,可以立即吸引听众的注意。"哈夫教授揭开了所有说服性演讲的核心问题:如何从一开始就让听众把自己"交给"演讲者。下面列出一些方法,只要巧妙使用,就会对你的开场白大有裨益。

BEGIN YOUR TALK WITH AN INCIDENT-EXAMPLE

Lowell Thomas, who has made a world-wide reputation as a news analyst, lecturer, and motion picture producer, began a talk on Lawrence of Arabia with this statement:

> I was going down Christian Street in Jerusalem one day when I met a man clad in the gorgeous robes of an oriental potentate. At his side hung the curved gold sword worn only by the descendants of the prophet Mohammed ...

And he was off—off with a story from his experience. That is what hooks attention. That kind of opening is almost foolproof. It can hardly fail. It moves, it marches. We follow because we identify ourselves as part of a situation and we want to know what is going to happen. I know of no more compelling method of opening a talk than by the use of a story.

One of my own talks which I have given many times begins with these words:

> Just after I had finished college, I was walking one night down a street in Huron, south Dakota, and I saw a man standing on a box talking to a crowd of people. I was curious, so I became part of the group listening to him. "Do you know," the speaker was saying, "that you never see a baldheaded Indian? Or you never see a bald-headed woman, do you? Now, I'm going to tell you why ..."

No stalling. No "warm-up" statements. By launching directly into an incident, you can make it easy to capture an audience's attention.

A speaker who begins a talk with a story from his experience is on safe ground, for there is no groping for words, no loss of ideas. The experience he is relating is his, a recreation, as it were, of part of his life, the very fiber of his being. The result? A self-assured, relaxed manner which will help a speaker establish himself on a friendly basis with an audience.

AROUSE SUSPENSE

Here is the way Mr. Powell Healy began a talk at the Penn Athletic Club in Philadelphia:

> Eighty-two years ago, there was published in London a little volunme, a story, which was destined to become immortal. Many people have called it "the greatest little book in the world." When it first appeared, friends meeting one another on the Strand or Pall Mall asked the question, "Have you read it?" The answer invariably was: "Yes, God bless him, I have."

1. 以实例开始

罗威尔·托马斯是一位誉满全球的新闻分析家、学者和电影制片人。在讲“阿拉伯的劳伦斯”时,他以下面这段话开场:

> 一天,我走在耶路撒冷的基督街上。这时我碰到一个人,身穿东方皇族的华丽袍子。在他腰侧,别着一把金制的弯刀。这种刀只有先知穆罕默德的后裔才有……

他以自己的亲身经历开场。那是吸引听众注意的话题。这类开场白通常是可行的,不会有什么问题。它鼓舞人心,引人入胜。我们之所以愿意继续听,是因为我们把自己看成是某个圈子的一分子,想知道接下去会发生什么事。我不知道还有什么方法比引用一个故事开场更有用。

我有一次演讲是这样开始的:

> 刚大学毕业时,一天晚上,我走在南达科他州的休伦街上,看见一名男子站在一只箱子上,对人群说些什么。我很好奇,所以也加入听众的行列。那人说:“你们从没见过秃顶的印第安人吧?没见过秃顶的印第安妇女吧?现在,我告诉你为什么……”

不用停顿,无须作预热的陈述。直接以说笑的方式引用故事,你就可以轻易地抓住听众的注意力。

演讲者以他亲身经历的故事开场是有效的。因为他不用挖空心思去琢磨说什么,也不用担心主题的丧失。他所阐述的是自己的经历,是生活中娱乐的一部分,是身体中的肌纤维。结果呢?自信而轻松的方式会让演讲者在听众中建立友好的基础。

2. 制造悬念

在费城的佩恩运动俱乐部时,鲍威尔·希利先生的演讲是这样开始的:

> 82年前,伦敦出版了一本小册子,讲了一个故事。这个故事注定是要流芳百世的。许多人称它“世界上最伟大的小书”。在它刚刚问世时,朋友们在斯特兰德大道或者帕码街碰到

The day it was published a thousand copies were sold. Within a fortnight the demand had consumed fifteen thousand. Since then it has run into countless thousands of editions and has been translated into every language under heaven. A few years ago, J.P. Morgan purchased the original manuscript for a fabulous sum and it now reposes among the priceless treasures in his magnificent art gallery. What is this world famous book? It is...

Are you interested? Are you eager to know more? Has the speaker captured the favorable attention of his listeners? Do you feel this opening has held your attention, heightened your interest as it progressed? Why? Because it aroused your curiosity and held you in suspense.

Curiosity! Who is not susceptible to it?

Perhaps you, too! You are asking just who is the author and what is the book mentioned above? To satisfy your curiosity, here is the answer: The author: Charles Dickens: the book: *A Christmas Carol.*

Creating suspense is a sure-fire method of getting your listeners interested. Here is how I try to arouse suspense in my lecture on "How to Stop Worrying and Start Living." I begin like this: "In the spring of 1871, a young man who was destined to become a world-famous physician, William Osler, picked up a book and read twenty-one words that had a profound effect upon his future."

What were the twenty-one words? And how did these words affect his future? These are the questions your listeners will want answered.

STATE AN ARRESTING FACT

Clifford R. Adams, director of the Marriage Counseling Service of the Pennsylvania State College, began an article in *The Reader's Digest*, entitled "How to Pick a Mate," with these startling facts—facets that make you gasp, facts that make an arresting opener:

> Today the chances that our young people will find happiness through marriage are slim indeed. The rise of our divorce rate is frightening. One marriage in five or six landed on the rocks in 1940. By 1946, it is expected to be one in four. And if long range trends continue, the rate in fifty years will be one in two.

Here are two other examples of "arresting facts" openers:

"The War Department predicts that, in the first night of an atomic war, twenty million

时,总会问:"你读过它吗?"回答总是千篇一律:"是的,上帝保佑,我读了。"

出版的当天,它卖出了1000册。两周内,销售量达到1.5万册。此后,它又进行了无数次再版,并被译成各种语言。几年后,J·P·摩根以巨额买下了原稿。现在,它安坐在他富丽堂皇的艺术长廊之中。这本举世瞩目的书是什么?它是……

你想知道更多吗?演讲者抓住了听众的注意力吗?你是否感觉这样的开场已经吸引了你的注意,增加了继续听下去的兴趣呢?为什么?因为它诱发了你的兴趣,让你产生了悬念。

好奇之心,谁没有呢?

或许你也一样!你会问此书的作者是谁?这是一本什么书?为了满足你的好奇心,把答案告诉你:作者是查尔斯·狄更斯,书名是《圣诞欢歌》。

制造悬念是让听众产生兴趣的一种必胜方法。请看我在演讲《人性的优点:怎样消除烦恼,开始生活》时,是如何制造悬念的。我是这样开始的:"在1871年春,一个年轻的小伙子,威廉·奥斯勒,他注定要成为世界闻名的内科医生。他拿起一本书,读到21个字。它们对他的将来产生了重大影响。"

这21个字是什么?对他的未来又有怎样的影响呢?这些都是你的听众想知道的问题。

3. 讲述引人注意的事情

克利福德·亚当斯是宾夕法尼亚大学婚姻咨询服务处的主任。他在《读者文摘》中发表了一篇题为《如何择偶》的文章,其中就引用了一些令人震惊的实例,足以让你有语惊四座之感,营造了一个出色的开场氛围。他写道:

> 今天,我们青年人想通过婚姻来找到幸福的机会真是渺茫。离婚率的增长速度令人胆寒。1940年,每五六件婚姻会有一件失败。到了1946年,估计变成了四分之一。如果这种趋势长此下去,要不了50年,离婚率就上升为二分之一。

Americans will be killed."

"A few years ago, the Scripps-Howard newspapers spent $176,000 on a survey to discover what customers disliked about retail stores. It was the most costly, the most scientific, the most thorough survey ever made of retail selling problems. Questionnaires were sent into 54,047 homes in sixteen different cities. One of the questions was: What do you dislike about the stores in this town?

"Almost two-fifths of all the answers to that question were the same: Discourteous clerks! "

This method of making startling statements at the beginning of a talk is effective in establishing contact with the listener because it jars the mind. It is a kind of "shock technique" that enlists attention by using the unexpected to focus attention upon the subject matter of the talk.

One of our class members in Washington, D.C., used this method, arousal of curiosity, as effectively as anyone I have ever heard. Her name, Meg Sheil. Here is her opening:

"I was a prisoner for ten years. Not in an ordinary prison, but in one whose walls were worry about my inferiority and whose bars were the fear of criticism."

Don't you want to know more about this true-life episode?

A danger of the startling opener must be avoided, that is, the tendency to be over-dramatic or too sensational. I remember one speaker who started his talk by shooting a pistol into the air. He got attention all right, but he also blasted the eardrums of his listeners.

Make your opening conversational in manner. An efficient way to discover whether you have an opener that is conversational is to try it out across the dinner table. If the way you open your talk isn't conversational enough to be spoken across the dinner table, it probably won't be conversational enough for an audience either.

Frequently, however, the opening of the talk that is supposed to get the listeners' interest is, in reality, the dullest part of the talk. For example, I recently heard a speaker begin like this: "Trust in the Lord and have faith in your own ability..." A preachy, obvious way to begin a talk! But note his second sentence; it is interesting; it has heart throb in it. "My mother was left a widow in 1918 with three children to support, and no money..." Why, oh why, didn't that speaker begin in his first sentence by telling about the struggles of his widowed mother with three little children to support!

If you want to interest your listeners, don't begin with an introduction. Begin by leaping right

还有两个以"令人震惊的事实"开场的例子:

"国防部预测,原子能战争的第一夜,将会有2000万美国人丧生。"

"几年前,《斯克瑞普斯-霍华德》报社动用17.6万美元,调查客户不喜欢零售店的什么方面。这是有史以来,对零售店问题进行的最昂贵、最科学、最彻底的调查。这次调查向16个城市的54047户家庭发送了调查问卷。有一个问题是:你不喜欢本市零售店的什么?

"关于这个问题,几乎有五分之二的回答都是一样的:态度不好的店员!"

这种以令人震惊的陈述开场的方式,可以与听众有效地建立沟通,因为它能震撼人的思想。正是这种"震撼技巧",采用出人预料的形式,使听众集中注意力来听你的演讲论题。

我们在华盛顿演讲培训班的一个学员,曾用过这种方法激发听众的好奇心,也一样有效。她的名字是梅格·希尔。她的开场白是这样的:

"我做了10年的囚犯。那并不是一个普通的监狱,而是由于我担心自己能力低,受批评而从心理上建造的监狱。"

对这段真实生活的插曲,你不想了解更多吗?

令人震惊的开场中,有一种风险应该回避,那就是避免趋于过分戏剧化或者太煽情。我记得有位演讲者,朝空中射了一枪作为开场。他当即吸引了听众注意,但是也震坏了他们的耳膜。

应该让你的开场彬彬有礼。要想知道你的开场是否得体,有效的方式是在晚宴上实践一下。如果它不够合宜,在餐桌上都通不过,那么多半也不适合你的听众。

然而,在许多时候,本该调动听众兴趣的开场白,事实上却成了演讲中最无趣的部分。例如,我最近听过一位演讲者是这样开场的:"相信上帝,相信自己的能力……"多么说教而无趣的开场方式啊!但是第二句,越听越有趣,令人怦然心动。"1918年我母亲成了寡妇,带着三个孩子,没有钱……"为什么?哦,为什么?那位演讲者不第一句话就说,他寡居的母亲与命运抗争,

into the heart of your story.

That is what Frank Bettger does. He is the author of *How I Raised Myself From Failure to Success in Selling.* He is an artist when it comes to creating suspense in his first sentence. I know, because he and I traveled together all over the United States giving talks on selling under the auspices of the United States Junior Chamber of Commerce. I always admired the superb way he opened his talk on enthusiasm. No preaching. No lecturing. No sermonizing. No general statements. Frank Bettger leaped right into the heart of his subject in his first sentence. He began his talk on enthusiasm like this:

"Shortly after I started out as a professional baseball player, I got one of the biggest shocks of my life."

What effect did this opening have on his audience? I know, I was there. I saw the reaction. He had everyone's attention instantly. Everyone was eager to hear why and how he was shocked, and what he did about it.

ASK FOR A SHOW OF HANDS

A splendid way to get interested attention is to ask the audience to raise their hands in answer to a question. For example, I have opened my talk on "How to Prevent Fatigue" with this question:

"Let's see your hands. How many of you get tired more quickly than you feel you ought to?"

Note this point: When you ask for a show of hands, usually give the audience some warning that you are going to do so. Do not open a talk with: "How many people here believe the income tax should be lowered? Let's see your hands." Give the audience a chance to be ready for the vote by saying, for instance: "I am going to ask for a show of hands on a question of importance to you. This is the question: 'How many of you believe that trading stamps benefit the consumer?'"

The technique of asking for a show of hands gets a priceless reaction known as "audience participation." When you use it, your talk is no longer a one-sided affair. The audience is participating in it now. When you ask, "How many of yon get tired more quickly than you feel you ought to?" everyone starts thinking of his favorite topic: himself, his aches, his fatigue. He lifts his hand and possibly looks around to see who else has his hand up. He forgets that he is listening to a talk. He smiles. He nods to a friend sitting next to him. The ice is broken. You, the speaker, are at

养育着三个孩子呢？

如果你想让听众产生兴趣，就不要一开始就介绍细节，而应该直奔故事的中心思想。

弗兰克·贝特格做到了。他是《我是如何在销售中从失败走向成功的》一书的作者。他是一位语言艺术家，书中的第一句话，他就制造了悬念。我知道此事，因为在美国青年基督会的资助下，他和我一起就销售的话题进行了全国巡回演讲。我总是很钦佩他充满热情的、绝妙的开场方式。不唠叨、不训诫、不讲大道理、不笼统。弗兰克·贝特格开篇就点了题。他是这样饱含感情地开始的：

"我成为一名职业篮球队员之后不久，遇上了一生中最让我震惊的事。"

这样的开场会对听众产生什么样的效果呢？我知道，因为我就在现场。我看到了下面的反应。他立刻吸引了每个人的注意。大家都想听听他为什么，是多么震惊，以及如何处理的。

4. 要求听众举手参与

抓住听众注意力的一个绝好的方法就是要求他们举手回答问题。例如，在演讲"如何防止疲劳"这个题目时，我就以这个问题开始：

"请举手，让我看看你们中有多少人，在感到自己应该疲劳之前就已经疲劳了？"

请注意：当你要求听众举手时，应该带给他们一些提示，让他们知道你想做什么。不要开口就问："在座的各位有多少人认为税收应该降低？请举手！"在语言上，要给听众准备投票的机会。可以这样说："我想请大家举手来回答一个很重要的问题。这个问题就是：'你们中有多少人认为商业赠券对消费者有利？'"

要求听众举手参与的技巧可以得到宝贵的反应，即"听众参与"。当你采用这种方法时，你的演讲就不再是独角戏了。因为听众参与进来了。当你问"你们中有多少人，在感到自己应该疲劳之前就已经疲劳了？"每个人都开始寻思他关心的方面：自己、疼痛、劳累。他会举手，可能还

ease, and so is the audience.

PROMISE TO TELL THE AUDIENCE HOW THEY CAN GET SOMETHING THEY WANT

An almost unfailing way to get alert attention is to promise to tell your listeners how they can get what they want by doing what you suggest. Following are some illustrations of what I mean:

"I am going to tell you how to prevent fatigue. I am going to tell you how to add one hour a day to your waking life."

"I'm going to tell you how you can materially increase your income."

"I Promise that, if you will listen to me for ten minutes, I'll tell you one sure way to make yourself more popular."

The "promise" type of opener is sure to get attention because it goes straight to the self-interests of the audience. All too often speakers neglect to tie their topics to the vital interests of their hearers. Instead of opening the door to attention, they slam it shut with dull openings that trace the history of the subject matter or laboriously dwell upon the background necessary to an understanding of the topic.

I remember one talk I heard a few years ago on a topic which, in itself, was important to the audience: the necessity of periodic health examinations. How did the speaker begin his talk? Did he add to the natural attractiveness of his subject by an effective opening? No. He started with a colorless recital of the history of his topic and the audience began to lose interest in him and in his subject. An opening built around the "promise" technique would have been admirably appropriate. For instance:

> Do you know how long you are expected to live? Life insurance companies can predict this by means of life expectancy tables which have been compiled from the lives of millions of persons. You can expect to live two-thirds of the time between your present age and eighty... now, is this long enough for you to live? No, no! We are all passionately eager to live longer and we want to prove that this prediction is wrong. But how, you ask, can this be done? How can I extend my life beyond the shockingly small number of years statisticians say remain for me? Well, there is an answer, a possible way this can be done, and I shall tell you how to do this...

I leave it to you to decide whether this type of opening captures your interest, if it compels you to listen to the speaker. You *must* listen to him because he not only is talking about you, about your

会环顾一下会有谁举手。他忘了自己是在听演讲。他笑了,向邻座的朋友点点头。冷场的局面化解了。你,演讲者轻松自如,听众也一样。

5. 告诉听众如何获得他们想要的

抓住听众注意力,还有一种屡试不爽的方式,那就是承诺他们,采用你的建议,可以得到自己想要的东西。下面是一些例子:

"我会告诉你们怎样避免疲劳。我会告诉你们怎样做,能让你每天清醒的时间增加1小时。"

"我会告诉你们怎样从根本上增加收入。"

"我可以承诺,如果愿意听我说10分钟的话,我会告诉你们一种让自己成名的好办法。"

"承诺"的开场方式必定是能吸引听众注意力的,因为它直接调动了听众的兴趣。演讲者常常忽视把自己的话题与听众的兴趣联系起来。他们不去开启听众注意力的大门,反而用无趣的开场白将其封闭,追溯话题的来由,述说背景对理解主旨的必要性。

记得我几年前听过的一次演讲,论题本身对听众很重要:定期健康检查的必要性。演讲者是如何开场的呢?他是否通过一个有效的开场,增添了话题的自然魅力?不是。他是以对主题背景了无生气的叙述开始的,听众一开始就对他的话题没了兴趣。如果以"承诺"的技巧开场,一定相当有效。例如:

> 你知道自己能活多久吗?人寿保险公司将几百万人的寿命进行了汇总,制成了生命期望表,通过这种方式,可以预测人的寿命。你的寿命大约是你现在年龄至80岁之间的三分之二……那么现在,你是否觉得时间够长呢?不,不!我们都渴望活得更长一点,我们总想证明这个预测是错误的。但是,怎样才能做到呢?如何将自己的生命,延续得比统计数据所说的那个骇人听闻的数字更长?当然有方法,有一种方法能办到。我会告诉你们怎样做……

life, but he has promised to tell you something of the most intense personal value to you. No dull recital of impersonal facts here! Such an opening as this is almost impossible to resist.

USE AN EXHIBIT

Perhaps the easiest way in the world to gain attention is to hold up something for people to look at. Almost any creature, from the simplest to the most complex, will give heed to that kind of stimulus. It can be used sometimes with effectiveness before the most dignified audience. For example, Mr. S.S. Ellis, of Philadelphia, opened one of his talks in one of our classes by holding a coin between his thumb and forefinger, and high above his shoulder. Naturally everyone looked. Then he inquired: "Has anyone here ever found a coin like this on the sidewalk? It announces that the fortunate finder will be given a lot free in such and such a real estate development. He has but to call and present this coin..." Mr. Ellis then proceeded to condemn the misleading and unethical practices involved.

All of the foregoing methods are commendable. They may be used separately or they may be combined. Recognize that how you open a talk largely determines whether the audience is going to accept you and your message.

SECOND/ AVOID GETTING UNFAVORABLE ATTENTION

Please, please, I urge you, remember that you must not only capture the attention of your audience, but you must capture their *favorable* attention. Please note that I said *favorable* attention. No rational person would begin a talk by insulting his audience or by making any obnoxious or disagreeable statement that would turn them against him and his message. Yet how frequently speakers begin talks by attracting attention through the use of one of the following devices.

DO NOT OPEN WITH AN APOLOGY

To begin a talk with an apology does not get you off to a good start either. How often we all have heard speakers begin by calling the attention of the audience to their lack of preparation or their lack of ability. If you are not prepared, the audience will probably discover it without your assistance. Why insult your audience by suggesting that you did not think them worth preparing for, that just any old thing you had on the fire was good enough to serve them? No, we don't want to hear apologies; we want to be informed and interested—to be *interested*: remember that. Let your

你看,这样开场能不能引起听众的兴趣,能否让你想听演讲者讲下去?你必须听,因为他不仅在谈论你,谈论你的生命,也承诺会告诉你一切有价值的知识,而不是无趣地叙述无聊的事实!像这样的开场几乎是难以抵抗的。

6. 采用展示物

或许世界上抓住注意力最容易的方法就是举起一件东西,给大家看。从最低级到最高级,几乎所有生物都会注意那种刺激性的举动。即使面对最严肃的听众,这种方法有时也很管用。例如,费城的S·S·艾利斯先生在我们的一次演讲培训班上,演讲前拇指和食指夹着一枚硬币,并将手举过肩膀。本能地,大家都盯着看。然后,他问:"在场的各位,有谁曾在人行道上发现过这样的硬币吗?据说,拾到过的幸运者将可以在购置房产时享受许多免税政策。只要他能交出这枚硬币……"艾利斯先生接下来继续谴责这种误导和不道德的行为。

上述方法都是可行的。它们既可以独立使用,也可以相互组合。要知道,如何开场很大程度上决定了听众是否会接受你和你的演说。

二、避免引起不利的注意

我再三地请你记住,不仅要抓住听众的注意力,而且必须抓住积极的注意力。请记住我说的是积极的注意力。理性的人不会一开始就侮辱听众,或是说出令人不愉快的话。这势必会让听众对演讲者和他的话题产生反感。然而,通过使用下面的方法之一,演讲者通常就能抓住听众的注意力。

1. 不要以道歉开场

以道歉开场并不能让你有一个很好的开始。我们总是听说,有些演讲者想抓住听众注意力,可是缺乏准备和能力。如果你没有准备好,不用道歉,可能听众也会察觉到。为什么要暗示听众,认为他们不值得你提前准备?你在火炉边听说的故事足以应付他们?这不是轻视他

opening sentence capture the interest of your audience. Not the second sentence. Not the third sentence. *The first*!

AVOID THE "FUNNY" STORY OPENING

You may have noticed that there is one method of opening a talk, and one much favored by speakers, that is not recommended here: the so-called "funny" story opening. For some lamentable reason, the novice feels that he ought to "lighten up" his talk by telling a joke; he assumes that the mantel of Mark Twain has descended upon his shoulders: Do not fall into this trap; you will discover to your embarrassment the painful truth that the "funny" story is more often pathetic than funny—and the story may be known to persons in your audience.

A sense of humor, though, is a prized asset for any speaker. A talk need not begin, nor be, heavyfooted, elephantine, and excessively solemn. Not at all. If you have the ability to tickle the risibilities of your audience by some witty reference to a local situation or to something arising out of the occasion or the remarks of a previous speaker, then by all means do so. Observe some incongruity. Exaggerate it. That type of humor is more likely to succeed than stale jokes about Pat and Mike, or mothers-in-law, or shaggy dogs, because it is *relevant* and because it is original.

Perhaps the easiest way to create merriment is to tell a story on yourself. Depict yourself in some ridiculous and embarrassing situation. That gets down to the very essence of humor. Jack Benny has used this device for years. He was one of the first major radio comedians to "poke fun" at himself. By making himself the butt of jokes concerning his ability to play the violin, his miserliness, and his age, Jack Benny works a rich vein of humor that keeps his ratings high from year to year.

Audiences open their hearts, as well as their minds, to speakers who deliberately deflate themselves by calling attention to some deficiency or failing on their part, in a humorous sense, of course. On the other hand, creating the image of the "stuffed shirt" or the visiting expert with all the answers leaves an audience cold and unreceptive.

THIRD/ SUPPORT YOUR MAIN IDEAS

In the longer talk to get action you will have several points; the fewer the better, but all of

们吗？不，我们不想听到道歉的话。我们希望听到一些新闻趣事——感到有趣的事：记住这一点。要让自己第一句话就捕获听众的兴趣。而不是等到第二句、第三句，而是一开口！

2. 慎用"幽默"故事开场

你可能已经注意到，有一种开场方式很受演讲者青睐，那就是众所周知的所谓的"幽默"故事。由于某些不愉快的原因，初学者感到他应该借用一个笑话来渲染演讲气氛。他幻想马克·吐温的天赋降临在他的身上——千万不要掉在这个陷阱里。你很快会发现自己处于尴尬的境地。"幽默"故事可能把气氛搞得很惨——因为听众可能早就知道这个故事。

尽管对任何演讲者而言，幽默感都是一笔珍贵的资产，但演讲开始是否一定要气氛沉重、严肃？并非如此。如果你有能力调起听众的幽默感，引用一些当前的实例，或者以往演讲家举过的例子或发表的言论，那么也是十分适宜的。观察一些不适宜的社会现象，然后加以夸大；相比陈芝麻烂谷子的笑话，这种幽默方法是很管用的。因为它事关当前社会，是新鲜事。

或许最简便的活跃气氛的方法是讲一个关于你自己的故事。可以描述你处于荒诞可笑、进退两难境地的情况。那样可以打下很好的幽默基础。杰克·本尼这个绝活用了多年。他是最早的广播喜剧演员之一，懂得以"嘲弄"自己来博得观众。由于把自己拉小提琴的能力、吝啬和年龄等素材制成笑料，他成了一代幽默巨星，人气指数与日俱增。

如果演讲者有意贬低自己，说出自己的缺点和失意，当然是以幽默的方式，听众就会向他敞开心扉和思想。相反，如果将自己打造成"自命不凡"的形象，或者一副专家的样子，听众会表情冷漠，不愿接受。

三、突出主要论点

在做长篇演讲时，需要注意几点：越简明越好，而且一切都必须支持演讲题材。在第七章

them will require support material. In Chapter Seven we discussed one method of supporting the Point of a talk, which is what you want the audience to do, by illustratinng it with a story, an experience out of your life. This type of example is popular because it appeals to a basic drive in people, summed up by the slogan, "Everybody Loves a Story." An incident or happening is the kind of example most often used by the average speaker, but it is by no means the only way your point can be supported. You might also use statistics, which are nothing more than illustrations scientifically grouped, expert testimony, analogies, exhibits, or demonstrations.

USE STATISTICS

Statistics are used to show the proportion of instances of a certain kind. They can be impressive and convincing, especially as evidence where an isolated example might not do as well. The effectiveness of the Salk anti-poliomyelitis vaccine program was measured by statistic gathered in all parts of the country. Isolated cases of ineffectiveness were the exceptions that proved the rule. A talk based on one of these exceptions would not, therefore, convince a parent that the Salk vaccine program would not protect his child.

Statistics, of themselves, can be boring. They should be judiciously used, and when used they should be clothed in a language that makes them vivid and graphic.

Here is an example of how statistics can be impressive by comparing them with things familiar to us. In backing up his point that a vast amount of time is lost by New Yorkers, neglecting to answer telephones promptly an executive said:

> Out of each one hundred telephone connections made, seven show a delay of more than a minute before the person called answers. Every day 280,000 minutes are lost in this way. In the course of six months, this minute delay in New York is about equal to all the business days that have elapsed since Columbus discovered America.

Mere numbers and amounts, taken by themselves, are never very impressive. They have to be illustrated; they ought, if possible, to be put in terms of our experiences. I remember listening to a lecture by a guide in the vast power room under Grand Coulee Dam. He could have given us the square-foot figures of the room's size, but that would not have been so convincing as the method he used. He told us that the room was large enough for a crowd of 10,000 people to view a football

我们介绍了一种支持论点的方法,即通过你生活中的故事、经历来说明,让听众去做你希望的事情。这类例子很受欢迎,因为它满足了人类基本的冲动,用一句话概括就是"人人都爱听故事"。意外和事件是一般演讲者广为使用的例子。但这绝不是支持你论点的唯一方法。你还可以引用统计数据,那不过是经过科学处理的图表、专家意见、类比、展示或者演示。

1. 使用统计数据

统计数据用来显示某类事情的比例结果。它们可以给人留下深刻印象,也令人信服,尤其可以作为一项证据,是单个的例子所不及的。索尔克的抗小儿麻痹症疫苗技术的有效性,在全美各州进行统计后得到证实。个别无效例子是许可之内的例外。因此,以这些例外为基础的言论,并不能让父母认为索尔克的抗小儿麻痹症疫苗技术不能保护他的孩子。

统计本身是枯燥的,应该理智地使用。用到它们时,应该穿上语言的外衣,使之生动形象。

这里有一个例子,如何通过把统计数据与我们熟悉的事情相比较,达到令人印象深刻的效果。一位总裁认为纽约人不注意立即接电话,浪费了大量时间,为了支持这一观点,他说:

> 在接电话前,每100个电话,有7个就要耽误1分钟。每天有28万分钟就这样浪费了。6个月,纽约浪费的时间,大约相当于自哥伦布发现美洲以来的所有工作日时间。

光是数字和数量,是不能令人印象深刻的。还需要举例子。如果可能,例子应该依据生活经验来举出。我记得在一座大坝的发电房,听过一位向导的解说。他本可以告诉我们房间的面积形状,但那样实在没有说服力。他告诉我们房间相当大,足可容纳1万人在标准场地观看足球赛,而且四周还能划出几个网球场地!

许多年前,我们布鲁克林中心基督教青年会的演讲培训班的一名学员,在一次演讲时,说到去年因火灾而损毁的房屋的数量。他进一步说,如果把这些被毁的建筑一个挨一个地排起来,可以从纽约延伸到芝加哥;如果把在火灾中丧生的人每隔半英里放一个,这条可怕的线路

game on a regulation field and, in addition, there would be room left over for several tennis courts at each end!

Many years ago, a student in my course at the Brooklyn Central YMCA told in a talk the number of houses destroyed by fire during the previous year. He further said that, if these burned buildings had been placed side by side, the line would have reached from New York to Chicago, and that if the people who had been killed in those fires had been placed half a mile apart, that gruesome line would reach back again from Chicago to Brooklyn.

The figures he gave I forgot almost immediately but years have passed, and, without any effort on my part, I can still see that line of burning buildings stretching from Manhattan Island to Cook County, Illinois.

USE THE TESTIMONY OF EXPERTS

Frequently you can effectively back up the points you want to make in the body of your talk by the use of the testimony of an expert. Before using testimony it should be tested by answering these questions:

1. Is the quotation I am about to use accurate?

2. Is it taken from the area of the man's expert knowledge? To quote Joe Louis on economics would obviously be exploiting his name but not his forte.

3. Is the quotation from a man who is known and respected by the audience?

4. Are you sure that the statement is based on firsthand knowledge, not personal interest or prejudice?

One of the members of my class at the Brooklyn Chamber of Commerce many years age opened a talk on the need for specialization with a quotation from Andrew Carnegie. Did he choose wisely? Yes, because he accurately quoted a man, who was respected by the audience as one who had earned the right to speak on business success. That quotation is still worth repeating today:

> I believe the true road to prominent success in any line is to make yourself master in that line. I have no faith in the policy of scattering one's resources, and in my experience I have rarely if ever met a man who achieved pre-eminence in money-making—certainly never one in manufacturing—who was interested in many concerns. The men who have succeeded are the

又能从芝加哥返回布鲁克林。

他给出的数据，我很快就忘了。但是这么多年过去了，不费吹灰之力，我依然能看见烧毁建筑的那条线路，从曼哈顿岛到伊利诺伊州的库克县。

2. 引用专家建议

引用一位专家的言论，你可以有效地支持自己演讲中的论点。不过在引用之前，必须先回答这几个问题：

第一，准备引用的话是否准确？

第二，它是否来源于专业知识领域？在经济学问题上引用乔·路易斯的话，显然是注重了他的名字而非专长。

第三，引用的话是否出自一位知名的、受听众尊敬的人士？

第四，你确信这些话是一手资料，没有掺杂个人兴趣和偏见？

多年前，布鲁克林商会培训班中有一个学员，谈到专业化的必要性时，引用了安德鲁·卡内基的话。他的选择明智吗？是的，因为选准了人，卡内基被听众尊为有资格谈论经商之道。现在，那段引言也值得一提：

> 我认为在各行各业中取得成功的正确途径是精通自己的业务。我不赞成分割自己精力的做法。依照我的经验，在制造业，我很少甚至没有遇见过，有人在赚钱方面很卓越，而在其他许多方面也饶有兴趣。凡有成就的人必是选准一条路，坚持做下去的。

3. 采用类比

根据韦伯斯特的观点，类比是“两个事物中相似的关系……所指的相似，不是事物本身，而是特征、环境或效果。”

采用类比是支持主题的很好技巧。担任内政部助理秘书时，C·吉拉德·戴维森做过一篇题

men who have chosen one line and stuck to it.

USE ANALOGIES

An analogy, according to Webster, is a "relation of likeness between two things...consisting in the resemblance not of the things themselves but of two or more attributes, circumstances, or effects."

The use of an analogy is a fine technique for supporting a main idea. Here is an excerpt from a talk on "The Need for More Electric Power," by C. Girard Davidson when he was Assistant Secreatary of the Interior. Note how he employs a comparison, an analogy, to back up his point:

> A prosperous economy has to keep moving forword or it goes into a tailspin. There is a parallel with the airplane, which is a useless collection of nuts and bolts standing still on the ground. When moving forward in the air, however, it comes into its own and serves as a useful function. To stay up, it has to keep going forward. If it doesn't move , it sinks—and it can't move backward.

Here is another, perhaps one of the most outstanding analogies in the history of eloquence; it was used by Lincoln in answer to his critics during a crucial period of the Civil war:

> Gentlemen, I want you to suppose a case for a moment. Suppose that all the property you were worth was in gold, and you had put it in the hands of Blondin, the famous rope-walker, to carry across the Niagara Falls on a tightrope. Would you shake the rope while he was passing over it, or keep shouting to him. "Blondin, stoop a little more! Go a little faster! " No, I am sure you would not. You would hold your breath as well as your tongue, and keep your hands off until he was safely over. Now the government is in the same situation. It is carrying an immense weight across a stormy ocean. Untold treasures are in its hands. It is doing the best it can. Don't badger it! Just keep still, and it will get you safely over.

USE A DEMONSTRATION WITH OR WITHOUT AN EXHIBIT

When executives of the Iron Fireman finn were talking to dealers, they needed some way of dramatizing the fact that fuel should be fed into a furnace from the bottom rather than from the top. So they hit on this simple but striking demontration. The speaker lights a candle. Then he says:

> See how clearly the flame burns—how tall it is. Since virtually all the fuel is being converted into heat, it gives off practically no smoke.

为《对更多电力的需求》的演讲,下面给出一段摘录。请注意他是怎样使用比较、类比来支持自己观点的:

> 繁荣的经济必须不断前进,否则就会衰退。就像是飞机,停在地面时,只是一堆毫无用处的螺母和螺钉的组合。可是在空中飞行时,它就变成了真正的自己,发挥了有效的作用。为了飞行,它必须前进。如果它不动,就会下落——它不会后退。

还有一个例子,可能是雄辩历史上最精彩的类比。它是在内战的一个关键时期,林肯用来回击批判者的。

> 先生们,我希望你们设想一下:假如把你所有值钱的财富换成金子,交到著名的走钢丝选手布洛丁的手里,让他带着这些金子走钢丝穿过尼亚加拉瀑布。那么当他走在钢丝上时,你会不会晃动绳索,或者冲他大喊:"布洛丁,再低点!走快点!"不,我相信你不会。你会屏住呼吸,握紧拳头,直到他安全通过。现在,政府也处于同样的境地。它正背负着巨大的重担,穿行在狂风巨浪的海洋中。数不清的财富在手里攥着。它正在尽其所能地努力着。不要打扰它!保持安静,它会带着你安全渡过。

4. 使用展示物

当钢铁公司的主管与经销商谈论业务时,他们总是采用表演的形式,来说明燃料应该从底部而不是从顶部加入。他们找到了这种简单而又形象的说明方式。演讲者点着一根蜡烛。然后,他说:

> 看这火苗多亮——多旺啊。其实是因为所有的燃料都转化为热量,不产生烟。
> 蜡烛的燃料是从底部提供的,就像钢铁锅炉一样,也是从底部添加燃料。
> 假如蜡烛是从上面加燃料,就像人工加料炉一样。(这时,演讲者把蜡烛倒过来。)
> 注意火苗是怎么熄灭的。闻到烟味,听见噼啪声,看到火苗发红,这是由于不完全燃

The fuel of the candle is fed in from below, just as the Iron Fireman feeds fuel into a furnace.

Suppose that this candle was fueled from above, as hand-stoked furnaces are. (*Here the speaker turns the candle upside down.*)

Notice how the flame dies down. Smell the smoke. Hear it sputter. See how red the flame is because of incomplete combustion. And finally the flame goes out, as a result of inefficient fueling from above.

Some years ago, Henry Morton Robinson wrote an interesting article on "How Lawyers Win crees" for *Your Life* magazine. In it, he describes how a lawyer named Abe Hummer is credited with a telling dramatic demonstration of showmanship while representing an insurance company in a damage suit. The plaintiff, a Mr. Postlethwaite, stated that as a result of falling down an elevator shaft his shoulder had been so severely injured that he was unable to raise his right arm.

Hummer appeared to be gravely concerned. "Now Mr. Postlethwaite," he said confidently, "show the jury how high you can raise your arm." Gingerly, Postlethwaite brought his arm up to ear level "Now show us how high you could raise it before you were injured," urged Hummer. "As high as this," said the plaintiff, shooting his arm at full length over his head.

You may draw your own conclusion regarding the reaction of the jury to this demonstration.

In the longer talk to secure action you might make three, or at most, four points. They could be uttered in less than a minute. To recite them to an audience would be dull and boring. What makes these points come alive? It is the support material you use. This is what gives sparkle and interest to your talk. By the use of incidents, comparisons and demonstrations, you make your main ideas clear and vivid; by the use of statistics and testimony you substatiate the truth and emphasize the importance of your main points.

FOURTH/ APPEAL FOR ACTION

I dropped in to talk a few minutes one day with George F. Johnson, the industrialist and humanitarian. He was President of the great Endicott-Johnson Corporation at the time. More interesting to me, though, was the knowledge that he was a speaker who could make his hearers

烧所致。最终火苗灭了，因为从顶部不能有效地添加燃料。

几年前，亨利·莫顿·鲁滨逊为杂志《你的生活》写了一篇有趣的文章《律师如何胜诉》。在文中，他讲述了一位名叫亚伯·胡莫的人的故事，此人在受理一家保险公司的伤害案时，是怎样进行技艺高超的展示表演的。原告波斯特维特先生声称，由于电梯掉下来，他的肩膀严重受伤，胳膊都抬不起来了。

胡莫表示十分关切。他自信地说："现在，波斯特维特先生，你让陪审团看看你的胳膊能抬多高。"波斯特维特先生小心翼翼地，把胳膊举到耳朵的位置。胡莫催促着："现在，再让我们看看你受伤之前能举多高。"原告随即把手臂举过头顶说："这样高。"

从陪审团对这个示范动作的反应，你可以知道结果如何。

进行长篇演讲时，你可以列举三条，最多四条。这些要在一分钟之内说完。如果照着念下去，将是无聊而沉闷的。什么能让它们生动起来呢？那就是引入支持观点的材料。通过引用事例、类比和展示，你可以把主题思想变得生动鲜明；引用统计数据和名言，可以阐明真理，突出主题的重要作用。

四、在实践中检验

一天，我和企业家和人道主义者乔治·F·约翰逊聊了几分钟。当时他是实力雄厚的恩迪科特-约翰逊公司的总裁。不过令我更感兴趣的是，他是一位杰出的演讲家，能控制听众的悲喜情绪，并长久地记住他的话。

他没有专属于自己的办公室，而是在一间宽大而忙碌的工厂的一个角落办公。他处事态度就和那张旧书桌一样谦恭。

"你来得正好。"他起身招呼我说，"我正有一件特别的工作要安排。今晚对工人们说的结尾

laugh, and sometimes cry, and often remember for a long time what he said.

He didn't have a private office. He had a corner of a big, busy factory, and his manner was as unpretentious as his old wooden desk.

"You've come at a good time," he said as he stood up to greet me. "I've just got a job out of the way. I've jotted down what I want to say at the end of a talk I'm going to give to the workers tonight."

"It's always a relief to get a talk ship-shape in your mind from beginning to end," I told him.

"Oh, I haven't got it all in mind yet," he said. "Just the general idea and the specific way I want to finish it."

He was not a professional speaker. He never went in for ringing words or fine phrases. From experience, however, he had learned one of the secrets of successful communication. He knew that if a talk is to go over well, it has to have a good ending. He realized that the conclusion of a talk is the part toward which all that precedes it must reasonably move if an audience is to be impressed.

The close is really the most strategic point in a talk, what one says last, the final words left ringing in the ears when one ceases—these are likely to be remembered longest. Unlike Mr. Johnson, beginners seldom appreciate the importance of this; their endings often leave much to be desired.

What are their most common errors? Let us discuss a few and search for remedies.

First, there is the man who finishes with: "That is about all I have to say on the matter, so I guess I shall stop." This speaker usually throws a smoke screen over his inability to end a talk satisfactorily by lamely saying "thank you." That is not an ending. That is a mistake. It reeks of the amateur. That is almost unpardonable. If that is all you have to say, why not round off your talk, and promptly take your seat and stop without talking about stopping. Do that, and the inference that that is all you have to say may, with safety and good taste, be left to the discernment of the audience.

Then, there is the speaker who says all he has to say, but he does not know how to stop. I believe it was Josh Billings who advised people to take the bull by the tail instead of the horns, since it would be easier to let go. This speaker has the bull by the frontal extremities, and wants to part company with him, but try as hard as he will, he can't get near a friendly fence or tree. So he finally thrashes about in a circle, covering the same ground, repeating himself, leaving a bad impression ...

The remedy? An ending has to be planned sometime, doesn't it? Is it the part of wisdom to try

部分,我草拟了一下。"

"把要讲的东西从头至尾在脑海里过一遍,会让你觉得很轻松的。"我告诉他。

"哦,我还没有进行全面构思呢,"他说,"我只是搭了框架,还有一个专门的结尾。"

他不是一个职业的演讲家。他也从来不追求响亮的词语或者华丽的句子。然而,从实践中他学到了成功沟通的秘诀。他明白演讲要成功,必须有一个精彩的结尾。他认识到,要让听众印象深刻,演讲的结论应该将全文合理地推进得出。

结尾是演讲中最画龙点睛的一笔。演讲者结束发言之后,他说的最后一席话还能在听众耳边萦绕——这些话可能会被记住得更久。与约翰逊先生不同,初学者很少在意这一点的重要性。他们的结尾常常留下一些遗憾。

他们最常犯的错误是什么呢?我们来探讨一下,寻找补救办法。

首先,有人是这样结尾的:"关于这件事情,这就是我想说的。到此,我想我该结束了。"这类演讲者经常放出一阵烟雾,心虚地说一句"谢谢各位"来掩盖自己未能令人满意的无能,那不是结尾,只会显示出你是个生手。那几乎是不可原谅的。如果你要说的说完了,为什么不立刻停止,什么都不用多说。这样做,效果会很好,听众自然明白你说完了。

还有的演讲者讲完之后,不知道怎样结尾。乔希·比林斯建议人们捉公牛时,要抓牛尾而不是牛角,因为牛尾更容易抓到。演讲者总是从正面去抓牛角,想努力甩开,却不能逃到附近的篱笆或树上。所以他最终只能是绕着原地转圈子,说着重复的话,给听众留下极差的印象……

如何补救呢?结尾必须提前构思,不是吗?你在面对听众的时候,是处于紧张和压力之下的,而且思想还集中在说话的内容上,那么这时你去思考如何结尾明智吗?如果预先在心态平和的时候去想,不是很好吗?

你打算怎样获得一个精彩的结尾呢?下面是一些建议:

to do it after you are facing an audience, while you are under the strain and stress of talking, while your mind must be intent on what you are saying? Or does common sense suggest the advisability of doing it quietly, calmly, beforehand?

How do you go about bringing your talk to a climactic close? Here are a few suggestions:

SUMMARIZE

In the longer talk a speaker is very apt to cover so much groud that at the close the listeners are a little hazy about all his main points. However, few speakers realize that. They are misled into assuming that because these points are crystal clear in their own minds, they must be equally lucid to their hearers. Not st all. The speaker has been pondering over his ideas for some time. But his points are all new to the audience; they are flung at the audience like a handful of shot. Some may stick, but most are liable to roll off in confusion. The hearers are liable, in the words of Shakespeare, to "remember a mass of things but nothing distinctly."

Some anonymous Irish politician is reported to have given this recipe for making a speech: "First, tell them what you are going to tell them; then tell them; then tell them what you have told them." It is often highly advisable to "tell them what you have told them."

Here is a good example. The speaker, a traffic manager for one of Chicago's railways, ends his talk with this summary:

> In short, gentlemen, our own back-door yard experience with this block device; the experience in its use in the East, in the West, in the North; the sound operating principles underlying its operation; the actual demonstration in the money saved in one year in wreck prevention—move me most earnestly and unequivocally to recommend its immediate installation on our Southern branch.

You see what he has done? You can see it and feel it without having heard the rest of the talk. He has summed up in a few sentences, in sixty-two words, practically all the points he had made in the entire talk.

Don't you feel that a summary like that helps? If so, make that technique your own.

ASK FOR ACTION

The closing just quoted is also an excellent illustration of the ask-for-action ending. The

1. 总结观点

长篇演讲包含很多的内容，以致到了最后，听众对主题都感到模糊。可是，很少有演讲者认识到这一点。他们被自己的假想误导了，因为这些要点在自己的脑海里透彻明了，所以认为听众也一样明晰。但事实并非如此。演讲者一直思考着他的观点。但是这些观点对听众来说是全新的，就像一梭子弹，突然掠过。有一些可能击中目标，但是大多数都错过了。用莎士比亚的话来说，听众可能“记得很多事情，但一件也记不清。”

据说，有位不知名的爱尔兰政客给出了一套演讲提纲：“首先，告诉听众你想说什么，然后说出具体内容，最后对上面的内容进行总结。”最值得采纳的是：“告诉他们，你刚讲了什么。”

有一个很好的例子。一位演讲者是芝加哥某铁道交通部的经理，他是这样总结收尾的：

> 总之，先生们，依据我们在自己后院使用这套设备的经验，以及在东部、西部和北部使用的经验，其操作原理简单，再有每年预防事故而又节省费用的实例——这些都让我强烈而又坚定地建议，立即在南部使用这套设备。

你们明白他的精妙之处了吗？你们不用听懂前面的演讲，可能就知道其内容了。他只用了几句话，几十个字，就概括出了全文所有的要点。

你不觉得像这样的总结很好吗？如果认同，不妨采用这个技巧。

2. 倡议听众采取行动

上面引用的那个结尾，也是以倡议行动结尾的好例子。演讲者想劝服听众有所行动：在铁路线南部地区安装一套设备。他请求行动是基于此设备可以预防事故进而节省费用。演讲者希望听众行动起来。他成功了。这不只是一个演讲练习，这次演讲是面对铁路部门董事会的，并取得了成功。

speaker wanted something done: a block device installed on the Southern branch of his road. He based his request for action on the money it would save on the wrecks it would prevent. The speaker wanted action, and he got it. This was not a mere practice talk. It was delivered before the board of directors of a railway, and it secured the installation of the block device for which it asked.

In your final words of a talk to secure, action the time has come to ask for the order. So ask for it! Tell your audience to join, contribute, vote, write, telephone, buy, boycott, enlist, investigate, acquit, or whatever it is you want them to do. Be sure to obey these caution signs, however:

Ask them to do something specific. Don't say, "Help the Red Cross." That's too general. Say, instead, "Send your enrollment fee of one dollar tonight to the American Red Cross, 125 Smith Street in this city."

Ask the audience for some response that is within their power to give. Don't say, "Let us cast our ballot against the Demon Rum." It can't be done. At the moment, we aren't ballotting on the Demon Rum. You could, instead, ask them to join a temperance society or to contribute to some organization which is fighting for prohibition.

Make it as easy as you can for your audience to act on your appeal. Don't say, "Write your congressman to vote against this bill." Ninety-nine per cent of your listeners won't do it. They are not vitally interested; or it is too much trouble; or they will forget. So make it easy and pleasant to act. How? By writing a letter yourself to your congressman, saying, "We, the undersigned, urge you to vote agninst Bill No.74321." Pass the letter around with a fountain pen, and you will probably get a lot of signers—and perhaps lose your fountain pen.

在演讲的最后几句话,要说明行动的时机已经到来。所以应该提出要求!倡议听众参与、捐助、投票、写信、去电、购买、抵制、赞助、调查、偿还,或者任何你想要他们做的。不过,一定要遵从以下原则:

要求他们做的事必须明确。不要说:"请帮助红十字协会。"那太笼统了。可以说:"请你今晚就把入会费送到美国红十字协会,本市的史密斯街125号。"

要求听众在能力范围之内有所行动。不要说:"让我们投票反对酒鬼。"那样是没用的,因为当时我们不是在现场进行投票。你可以要求他们加入一个戒酒协会,或者向禁酒组织提供支持。

尽力让听众接受你的倡议。不要说:"写信给议员,投票反对这项议案。"百分之九十九的听众都不会这么做。他们一点都不感兴趣,或者嫌麻烦,或者根本就忘了。所以要让事情轻松完成,该怎么做呢?你可以自己给议员写封信,说:"我们联名,请您投票反对第74321号议案。"把此信和钢笔在听众间传递,你会得到许多签名——甚至会连笔都丢了。

3 Applying What You Have Learned

At the fourteenth session of my course I have often heard with pleasure students tell how they used the techniques in this book in their everyday lives. Salesmen point to increased sales, managers to promotions, executives to a widened span of control, all due to the increased skill with which they gave instructions and solved problems using the tools of effective speech.

As N. Richard Diller wrote in *Today's Speech*: "Talk, the type of talk, the amount of talk, and the atmosphere for such talk.., can act as the very life blood of an industrial communication system." R. Fred Canaday, in charge of the General Motors Dale carnegie Course in Effective Leadership, wrote in the same magazine: "One of the basic reasons we at General Motors are interested in speech training is our recognition that every supervisor is a teacher to a greater or lesser degree. From the time he interviews a prospective employee, through the orientation phase of early employment, on through regular assignment and possible promotion, a supervisor is continually called upon to explain, describe, reprimand, inform, instruct, review, and discuss myriads of subjects with each person in his department."

As we proceed up the ladder of oral communication to those areas that come closest to public speaking discussions, decision-making, problem-solving and policy-formulating conferences—we see again how the skills of effective speaking as taught in this book can be transferred to everyday speech activities. The rules for effective speaking before groups are directly applicable to conference participation and conference leadership.

Organization of the idea to be presented, the choice of the right words to launch it, the earnestness and enthusiasm used in delivering it are elements that will guarantee the idea's life in the final stage of solution. All these elements have been thoroughly discussed in this book. It remains for the reader to apply what he has learned in every conference in which he pariticipates.

You are wondering when to begin applying what you perhaps have learned in the previous thirteen chapters of this book. You may be surprised if I answer that query by one word:

第3章 在实践中应用

上第十四堂课时，我经常会高兴地听到一些学员说，他们如何把本书的知识应用于日常生活之中。销售员增加了业务量，经理人获得了晋升，总裁扩大了权力范围，这些都归功于语言技能的增强。利用这个有效的语言工具，他们可以提供建议，并解决问题。

正如N·理查德·迪勒在《今日语言》中所说的："说、说的方式、说的长短，还有说的语气……是商务沟通的生命线。"R·弗雷德·卡内德在通用汽车公司负责卡耐基高效领导课程的培训，他也在这本杂志中写道："我们对通用汽车的口头表达训练感兴趣，原因之一是我们发现，这里每个主管都是老师，都有一定的水平。当他面试一位应聘人员时，会考虑此人以前的工作方式，会考虑对此人进行怎样的安排和提供可能的晋升。一位主管总免不了解释、说明、申斥、通知、指示、评论，还要和本部门中的每一个成员讨论各个项目。"

只要我们继续攀登口头沟通的楼梯，就会到达更高的境界，有能力参加一些会议，并当众演说、做决定、解决问题，阐明方法——我们还可以看到，正如本书中所讲的那样，高效演讲技巧还可以应用到日常表达中。当众高效演讲的法则，可直接应用到普通例会和领导会议中。

思想的组织表达、正确的遣词造句、充满热情和真诚，这些都是思想能够得到完美表达的要素。所有这些技巧都在本书中进行了详细的介绍，以后就要看读者们在各种场合如何灵活应用了。

你现在可能会想，什么时候开始应用前13章中所学的知识。也许你会奇怪，因为我的回答只有一个词：立刻。

Immediately.

Even though you are not planning to make a speech in public for some time, if at all, I am certain you will find that the principles and techniques in this book are applicable every day. When I say start using these techniques now, I mean in the very next speaking situation in which you find yourself.

If you analyze the speaking that you do every day, you will be amazed by the similarity of purpose between your daily speaking and the type of formal communication discussed in these pages.

In Chapter Seven, you were urged to keep in mind one of four general purposes when you speak before groups; you may want to give them information, entertain them, convince them that your position is right, or persuade them to take action of some kind. In public speaking we try to keep these purposes distinct, both as to the content of the talk and the manner of out delivery.

In daily speaking, these purposes are fluid, merging with one another and constantly changing through the course of the day. At one moment we may be indulging in friendly chitchat and then suddenly we may be using speech to sell a product or persuade a child to put his spending money in the bank. By applying the techniques describebed in this book to everyday conversation we can make ourselves more effective, get our ideas across more efficiently, and motivate others with skill and fact.

FIRST/ USE SPECIFIC DETAIL IN EVERYDAY CONVERSATION

Take just one of these techniques, for instance. Remember in Chapter Four I appealed to you to put detail in your talk. In that way you make your ideas come alive, in a vivid and graphic way. Of course I was thinking mainly of speaking before groups. But isn't the use of detail just as important in everyday conversation? Just think for a moment of the really interesting conversationalists of your acquaintance. Aren't they the ones who fill their talk with colorful, dramatic details, who have the ability to use picturesque speech?

Before you can begin to develop your conversational skills you must have confidence. So almost all that was said in the first three chapters of this book will be useful in giving you the security to

就算你根本用不着准备当众演讲,我敢肯定,你会发现本书中的法则和技巧每天都能用得上。我说现在就开始使用这些技巧,指的是从你说下一句话起就应用。

如果仔细分析你每天说的话,你会惊讶地发现,日常会话和本书中涉及的正式交流,其目的非常相似。

在第4章,我曾力劝你在当众发言时,要牢记四个目的中的一点,也就是传递信息、制造娱乐、说服别人同意你的观点,或者劝他们采取某个行动。当众演讲时,我们务必明确上述目的,也必须明确谈话的内容和表达方式。

在日常会话中,说话的目的并非一成不变,而是相互作用,不断变化的。也许在这一刻,我们可以肆无忌惮地聊天,下一刻突然要吆喝着兜售货品,或者劝说一个孩子把零花钱存到银行。将本书介绍的技巧应用到日常交流中,我们可以变得更加高效,也可以更好地表达自己的思想,巧妙地激励他人。

一、在日常交流中应用

就以其中的一个技巧为例。记得在第4章,我让你们说话时插入细节,这样你就能以生动形象的方式表达你的思想。当然,我这里指的主要是当众演讲。但是,难道使用细节在日常交流中就不重要吗?现在请想想你所熟悉的有趣的演讲家。难道他们不是在谈话中加入精彩生动的细节,不具有独特的演讲才能吗?

在展现你的演讲才能之前,你必须先要有信心。关于这一点,前3章中几乎都有介绍。它很管用,能给你安全感,让你敢同别人打成一片,也敢在非正式的场合发表自己的观点。一旦你急于想表达自己的想法时,即使是面对一个很小的场合,你也会动手搜集一些资料,作为演讲素材。这样,一件伟大的事情就此发生了——你的视野变得开阔,你对自己的人生会有

mix with others and to voice your opinions in an informal social group. Once you are eager to express your ideas even on a limited scale, you will begin to search your experience for material that can be converted to conversation Here a wonderful thing happens—your horizons begin to expand and you see your life take on new meaning.

Housewives, whose interests may have become somewhat restricted, have been most enthusiastic in reporting what happens when they begin to apply their knowledge of speaking techniques to small conversational groups. "I realize that my newly found confidence gave me courage to speak up at social functions," Mrs. R. D. Hart told her classmates in Cincinnati, "and I began taking an interest in current events. Instead of withdrawing from the give and take of the group I eagerly joined it. Not only that, but everything I did became grist for the conversational mill and I found myself becoming interested in a host of new activities."

To an educator there is nothing new in Mrs. Hart's grateful report. Once the drive to learn and to apply what has been learned is stimulated, it starts a whole train of action and interaction that vivifies the entire personality. A cycle of achievement is set up and, like Mrs. Hart, one gets the feeling of fulfillment, all through putting into practice just one of the principles taught in this book.

Though few of us are professional teachers, all of us use speech to inform others on many occasions during the day. As parents instructing our children, as neighbors explaining a new method of pruning roses, as tourists exchanging ideas on the best route to follow, we constantly find ourselves in conversational situations that require clarity and coherence of thought, vitality and vigor of expression. What was said in Chapter Eight in relation to the talk to inform is applicable in these situations as well.

SECOND/ USE EFFECTIVE SPEAKING TECHNIQUES IN YOUR JOB

Now we enter the area of the communicative process as it affects our jobs. As salesmen, managers, clerks, department heads, group leaders, teachers, ministers, nurses, executives, doctors, lawyers, accountants, and engineers, we are all charged with the responsibility of explaining specialized areas of knowledge and giving professional instructions. Our ability to make these instructions in clear, concise language may often be the yardstick used by our superiors in

新的感悟。

家庭主妇的兴趣总是受到一些限制。可是当她们开始采用演讲技巧时，总是热衷于对小范围人群宣扬自己的心得体会。“我能感觉到，刚找到的自信让我有勇气在社交场合大声发言。”R·D·哈特夫人在辛辛那提时，对她的同学说，“我开始对时事发生兴趣。我不会再害怕与人交流，而是踊跃地加入。不仅如此，我还发现自己的各种经历能变为交流的资本。我感到自己对一些新活动越来越有兴趣。”

对一位传授演讲技巧的教师来说，哈特夫人的感激一点也不新鲜。一旦激发了学习和应用技巧的动力，它就会引发一连串的行为和交互作用，活跃整个人性，从此建立一个良性循环。就像哈特夫人一样，只要把本书介绍的某一条法则付诸实践，就能收获充实的感觉。

尽管我们大都不是职业教师，可是我们时常要对别人说明意图。比如，父母教导孩子，邻居间传授一种修剪玫瑰的新方法，游客对最佳线路交换意见，我们经常会碰到这些情况，这时需要清晰严整的思路，形象生动的表达。第八章介绍的演讲技巧也适用于这些场合。

二、在工作中有效地应用

接下来，我们谈谈演讲技巧对工作的影响。不论是销售员、经理、职员、主任、总裁、教师、牧师、护士、总经理、医生、律师、会计，还是工程师，我们都肩负着责任，解说专业知识，给出专业指导。以简单明了的语言进行解释的能力，通常是上司用来衡量我们工作水平的标准。如何敏捷地思考、流利地表达是一种技巧，可以从演讲的练习中获得。但是这种技巧绝不仅限于正式演讲——人人都能用，每天都可以用。今天，在企业界、政府机构和各职业领域中纷纷涌现的关于沟通交流的课程，更充分地说明了当今社会对清晰地进行语言表达的需求。

judging our competence. How to think quickly and verbalize adroitly is a skill acquired in presenting speeches of information, but this skill is by no means limited to formal speaking—it can be used every day by every one of us. The need for clarity in business and professional speech today is highlighted by the recent spate of oral communications courses in industry, government, and professional organizations.

THIRD/ SEEK OPPORTUNITIES TO SPEAK IN PUBLIC

In addition to using the principles of this book in everyday speech, where incidentally you will reap the greatest rewards, you should seek every opportunity to speak in public. How do you do this? By joining a club where public speaking of some sort goes on. Don't just be an inactive member, a mere looker-on Pitch in and help by doing committee work. Most of these jobs go begging. Get to be program chairman. That will give you an opportunity to interview good speakers in your community, and you certainly will be called upon to make speeches of introduction.

As soon as possible, develop a twenty-to thirtyminute talk. Use the suggestions in this book as a guide. Let your club or organization know that you are prepared to address them. Offer your services to a speaker's bureau in your town. Fund-raising campaigns are looking for volunteers to speak for them. They provide you with a speaker's kit which will be of great help in preparing your talk. Many speakers of consequence have begun in this way. Some of them have risen to great prominence. Take Sam Levenson, for example, the radio and TV star and a speaker whose services are sought all over the country. He was a high school teacher in New York. Just as a sideline he began making short talks about what he knew best, his family, relatives, his students, and the unusual aspects of his job. These talks took fire, and he was soon asked to address so many groups it began to interfere with his teaching chores. But, by this time he was a guest on network programs and it wasn't long before Sam Levenson transferred his talents entirely to the entrtainment world.

FOURTH/ YOU MUST PERSIST

When we learn any new thing, like French or golf or speaking in public, we never advance

三、寻找当众发言的机会

把本书的法则运用到日常会话中,你会有一些意外的收获。不过除此之外,你还应该寻找每一个当众发言的机会。怎样做到这一点呢?可以参加一个俱乐部,在那里有一些当众演讲的活动。不要光做一个默默无闻的成员或仅仅是一个观众,应该投入进去,从事一些组织性的工作。这些工作的大部分内容是去请求别人。如果成为节目主持,你将有机会接触到周围的语言大家。你理所当然地要对他们进行一番介绍。

只要有可能,就应该争取连续二三十分钟的演说。注意采用本书的一些建议。让你的俱乐部或组织知道,你的演讲是经过准备的。你也可以到镇上的宣传部门去争取演讲的机会。募集基金的活动需要一些志愿者为他们代言。他们会教你一堆说话的技巧,这对于锻炼你的口才大有裨益。许多演讲家都是从这里开始的。他们中的一些人取得了巨大的成就。以萨姆·利文森为例,他是广播和电视明星,也是一位演讲家,他的演讲受到全国人民的敬仰。他是纽约的一位高中教师。作为业余活动,他会以简短的方式,谈一些自己最熟悉的话题,比如家庭、亲戚、学生,还有工作。这些话题居然很受欢迎,不久他就被邀请到各处进行演说,甚至开始影响教学。而那时他还只是网络节目的嘉宾。不久,萨姆·利文森把他的全部精力都投入到了娱乐圈。

四、必须持之以恒

我们学习任何新事物,像法语、高尔夫或者当众演说,都不可能一帆风顺。我们会遭遇波折,突遇障碍,甚至停滞不前。然后我们会有一段时间原地踏步,甚至倒退,还会丢掉从前占有的领地。对于这段停滞或退步的时期,所有心理学家都很清楚,并称之为"学习曲线图中的台阶部分"。练习演讲的学员有时会受到挫折,这个过程可能会持续几个星期。他们可能会感到困难

steadily. We do not improve gradually. We do it by waves, by abrupt starts and sudden stops. Then we remain stationary a time, or we may even slip back and lose some of the ground we have previously gained. These periods of stagnation, or retrogression, are well known by all psychologists: they have been named "plateaus in the curve of learning." Students of effective speaking will sometimes be stalled, perhaps for weeks, on one of these plateaus. Work as hard as they may, they cannot seem to get off it. The weak ones give up in despair. Those with grit persist, and they find that suddenly, almost overnight, without knowing how or why it has happened, they have made great progress. They have lifted from the plateau like an airplane. Abruptly they have acquired naturalness, force, and confidence in their speaking.

You may always, as has been stated elsewhere in these pages, experience some fleeting fear, some shock, some nervous anxiety, the first few moments you face an audience. Even the greatest musicians have felt it in spite of their innumerable public appearances. Paderewski always fidgeted nervously with his cuffs immediately before he sat down at the piano. But as soon as he began to play, all of his audiencefear vanished quickly like a mist in August sunshine.

His experience will be yours. If you will but persevere, you will soon eradicate everything, including this initial fear; and that will be initial fear, and nothing more. After the first few sentences, you will have control of yourself. You will be speaking with positive pleasure.

One time a young man who aspired to study law wrote to Lincoln for advice. Lincoln replied: "If you are resolutely determined to make a lawyer of yourself, the thing is more than half done already ... Always bear in mind that your own resolution to succeed is more important than any other one thing."

Lincoln knew. He had gone through it all. He had never, in his entire life, had more than a total of one year's schooling. And books? Lincoln once said he had walked and borrowed every book within fifty miles of his home. A log fire was usually kept going all night in the cabin. Sometimes he read by the light of that fire. There were cracks between the logs in the cabin, and Lincoln often kept a book sticking there. As soon as it was light enough to read in the morning, he rolled over on his bed of leaves, rubbed his eyes, pulled out the book and began devouring it.

He walked twenty and thirty-miles to hear a speaker and, returning home, he practiced his

重重，似乎没有办法克服。意志薄弱者会因绝望而放弃。那些意志坚定的人会坚持下去，他们会发现突然豁然开朗，在不知不觉中，他们取得了重大的进步。他们宛如一架飞机轻松越过高原。突然之间，他们不再腼腆，有了说话的力量和信心。

或许你会像本书中某些地方所说的，在刚开始面对听众时，会感到有些害怕、激动和紧张。甚至最伟大的音乐家，尽管经历了无数次的公演，也会如此。巴德列夫斯基坐在钢琴旁之前，总是神经紧张，不停地翻动袖口。但是只要他一开始演奏，所有的怯场都会烟消云散。

他的经历你也有。如果你能坚持不懈，相信很快就能战胜一切，包括最初的恐惧。也就是最初的一点恐惧，没什么大不了的。一旦说出前几句话，接下来你就能控制自己，就能轻松自如地说了。

有一次，一位想学法律的年轻人给林肯写信征求建议。林肯回信说："如果你下定决心要让自己成为一名律师，这件事就已经成功一半了……永远记住，要想成功，你的决心比其他任何事情更重要。"

林肯很明白。他早就经历了这些。他一生从都没有好好上过一年学。至于书，林肯曾经说，他每次都是走50英里路才借到的。小木屋里总是整夜点看一对柴火。他就借着这火光读书。小木屋墙上的木头上有许多裂缝，林肯常常把书插在那里。一到早上，天色亮得能够看书了，他就从树叶铺的床上爬起来，揉揉眼睛，抓起书就开始贪婪地读起来。

他会走二三十英里路，去听别人演讲。回来后，他会在每一个地方练习——田间、树林，以及吉利维尔村琼斯的杂货店那儿聚集的人群前。他参加了新塞勒姆和斯普林菲尔德的文学辩论社团，探讨时事。他在女人面前很腼腆。他向玛丽·托德求爱时，总是坐在客厅，害羞得一句话也说不出来，所以总是听她说。然而就是这样一个人，经过不懈地努力和勤奋地学习，终于使自己成为一名演讲家，还敢和当时最卓越的雄辩家道格拉斯议员进行辩论。就是这样一个人，在

talks everywhere—in the fields, in the woods, before the crowds gathered at Jones' grocery at Gentryville; he joined literary and debating societies in New Salem and Springfield, and practiced speaking on the topics of the day. He was shy in the presence of women; when he courted Mary Todd he used to sit in the parlor, bashful and silent, unable to find words, listening while she did the talking. Yet that was the man who, by faithful practice and home study, made himself into the speaker who debated with the most accomplished orator of his day, Senator Douglas. This was the man who, at Gettysburg, and again in his second inaugural address, rose to heights of eloquence that have rarely been attained in all the annals of mankind.

Small wonder that, in view of his own terrific handicaps and pitiful struggle, Lincoln wrote: "If you are resolutely determined to make a lawyer out of yourself, the thing is more than half done already."

An excellent picture of Abraham Lincoln hangs in the President's office in the White House. "Often when I had some matter to deckle," said Theodore Roosevelt, "something involved and difficult to dispose of, something where there were conflicting rights and interest, I would look up at Lincoln, try to imagine him in my place, try to figure out what he would do in the same circumstances. It may sound odd to you, but, frankly, it seemed to make my troubles easier of solution."

Why not try Roosevelt's plan? Why not, if you are discouraged and feeling like giving up the fight to make a more effective speaker of yourself, why not ask yourself what he would do under the circumstances? You know what he would do. You know what he did do. After he had been beaten by Stephen A. Douglas in the race for the U.S. Senate, he admonished his followers not to "give up after one or one hundred defeats."

FIFTH/ KEEP THE CERTAINTY OF REWARD BEFORE YOU

How I wish I could get you to prop this book open on your breakfast table every morning until you had memorized these words from Professor William James:

Let no youth have any anxiety about the upshot of his education, whatever the line of it may be. If he keeps faithfully busy each hour of the working day, he may safely leave the final

葛底斯堡发表第二次就职演说，精彩程度真是绝无仅有。

相比他所经历的艰难挫折和辛苦奋战，这实在不足为道。林肯写道："如果你下定决心要让自己成为一名律师，这件事就已经成功一半了。"

亚伯拉罕·林肯的画像挂在白宫总统的办公室。西奥多·罗斯福总统说："当我要对某件事做出决定时，尤其是那些很难应对的事情，它们牵涉到各方的利害关系，我就会看一看林肯，想想如果他在我这种处境会怎么做。这听起来有点不可思议，但是，坦白说，这会让我的难题更容易解决。"

为什么不试试罗斯福的方法呢？为什么不呢？在你努力想成为一名杰出的演说家时，如果受到挫折而打算放弃时，为什么不问林肯在这时会做什么呢？你知道他会怎么做。你知道他是怎么做的。在美国议会选举时，他败给斯蒂芬·A·道格拉斯之后，他安慰同伴不要"因为一次或一百次的失败而放弃"。

五、坚信付出就有回报

我多么希望，能让你每天早晨都把这本书摊在餐桌上，直到你熟记威廉·詹姆斯教授的话：

年轻人不要为学历的高低而烦恼，不管它处于哪个层次。只要真正用好每一天的每小时，他就会得到最好的结果。他可以带着无比的自信，期待某个美妙的早晨，突然发现自己成了曾经追求的同辈中的佼佼者。

现在，借着著名的詹姆斯教授的这些话，我也想说，只要你勤于练习，就能自信十足地期望在一个美好的早晨醒来，发现自己变成了本市或社区中的一位演讲高手。

无论你现在听起来觉得有多么的异想天开，它却是一个普遍存在的真理。当然，例外也是有的。一个人如果心理素质很差、性格怯懦、知识匮乏，也就不可能成为像丹尼尔·韦伯斯特这

result to itself. He can, with perfect certainty, count on waking up some fine morning to find himself one of the competent ones of his generation, in what ever pursuit he may have singled out.

And now, with the renowned Professor James to fall back upon, I shall go so far as to say that if you keep right on practicing intelligently, you may confidently hope to wake up one fine morning and find yourself one of the competent speakers of your city or community.

Regardless of how fantastic that may sound to you now, it is true as a general principle. Exceptions, of course, there are. A man with an inferior mentality and personality, and with nothing to talk about, is not going to develop into a local Daniel Webster; but, with reason, the assertion is correct.

Let me illustrate: former Governor Stokes of New Jersey attended the closing banquet of one of our classes at Trenton. He remarked that the talks he had heard that evening were as good as the speeches that he had heard in the House of Representatives and Senate at Washington. These Trenton "speeches" were made by businessmen who had been tongue-tied with audience-fear a few months previously. They were not incipient Ciceros, these New Jersey businessmen; they were typical of the businessmen one finds in any American city. Yet they woke up one fine morning to find themselves among the competent speakers of their city, and probably in the country.

I have known and carefully watched literally thousands of persons trying to gain self-confidence and the ability to talk in public. Those that succeeded were, in only a few instances, persons of unusual brilliancy. For the "most par't, they were the ordinary run of businessmen you will find in your own home town. But they kept on. More exceptional men sometimes got discouragingly they did not get very far; but the ordinary individual with grit and singleness of purpose, at the end of the road, was at the top."

That is only human and natural. Don't you see the same thing occurring all the time in commerce and the professions? John D. Rockefeller, Sr., said that the first essential for success in business was patience and the knowledge that reward is ultimately certain. It is likewise one of the first essentials for success in effective speaking.

A few summers ago, I started out to scale a peak in the Austrian Alps called the *Wilder*

样的杰出人物。但是,一般而言,这个观点还是适用的。

我举个例子吧:新泽西州前州长斯托克斯先生参加了我们在特伦顿培训班的毕业晚宴。他评论说,那天晚上听到的演讲,毫不逊色于在华盛顿的参议院和众议院上听到的。这些特伦顿的"演讲家"由商人组成,几个月以前他们还因为害怕听众而紧张得说不出话来。他们不是古代的西塞罗,只是新泽西州的商人,是美国任何一个城市都可见到的普通商人。然而,他们一夜醒来,发现自己成了本市、甚至可能是全国著名的演说家。

我逐渐认识并且发现,成千上万的人正在尽力让自己增强当众讲话的信心和能力。成功者当中只有小部分是聪明绝顶的人,而绝大多数都是普通商人,但是他们坚持不懈。有点天赋的人有时会因气馁而不能坚持到底。但是普通人只要肯吃苦,肯坚持,最终都会到达顶峰的。

那是符合人类和自然法则的。你没发现在各行各业都有这样的事情吗?约翰·D·洛克菲勒先生说,要在事业上取得成功,首要的是耐心和坚信付出终有回报。对于成功的演讲,这条法则也同样适用。

几年前,我想攀登奥地利的阿尔卑斯山怀尔德·恺撒峰。《贝德克尔旅行指南》说攀登很困难,所以对于一个业余登山员来说,有必要找一位向导。我和一位朋友都没找向导,当然我们都是业余爱好者,所以另一个朋友问我俩是否能成功。"当然了。"我们回答说。

"你们凭什么这样自信?"他问。

"别人没找向导也成功了,"我说,"所以我知道一定行,而且我从来不会去考虑失败。"

那是做任何事都应该具备的正常心态,不论是演讲还是攀登珠穆朗玛峰。

你获得成功的大小,很大程度上取决于演讲前的思考。因此不妨想象一下,你正以极好的自控能力同别人谈话。

Kaiser. Baedeker said that the ascent was difficult, and a guide was essential for amateur climbers. A friend and I had none, and we were certainly amateurs; so a third party asked us if we thought we were going to succeed. "Of course," we replied.

"What makes you think so?" he inquired.

"Others have done it without guides," I said, "so I know it is within reason, and I never undertake anything thinking defeat."

That is the proper psychology for anything from speaking to an assault on Mt. Everest.

How well you succeed is largely determined by thoughts you have prior to speaking. See yourself in your imagination talking to others with perfect selfcontrol.

It is easily in your power to do this. Believe that you succeed. Believe it firmly, and you will then do what is necessary to bring success about.

During the Civil War, Admiral Dupont gave half a dozen excellen reasons why he had not taken his gunboat into Chadeston harbor. Admiral Farragut listened intently to the recital "But there was another reason that you have not mentioned," he replied.

"What is that?" questioned Admiral Dupont.

The answer came: "You did not believe you could do it."

The most valuable thing that most members acquire from training in our classes is an increased confidence in themselves, an additional faith in their ability to achieve. What is more important for one's success in almost any undertaking?

Emerson wrote, "Nothing great was ever achieved without enthusiasm." That is more than a well-turned literary phrase; it is the road map to success.

William Lyon Phelps was probably the most beloved and the most popular professor ever to teach at Yale University. In his book The Excitement of Teaching, he states, "With me, teaching is more than an art or an occupation. It is a passion. I love to teach, as a painter loves to paint, as a singer loves to sing, as a poet loves to write. Before I get out of bed in the morning, I think with ardent delight of my group of students."

Is there any wonder a teacher so filled with enthusiasm for his job, so excited about the work ahead of him achieved success? Billy Phelps exerted a tremendous influence on his students,

这是在你能力范围内容易办到的。相信自己会成功。坚信这一点,你才能做好成功路上的事情。

内战时期,海军上将都庞特为自己没把炮船驶入查斯顿港摆出了大堆的理由。法拉格上将专注地听着这些说辞,"但是还有一个原因你没提到。"他回答说。

"是什么?"都庞特上将问。

"还有你认为自己根本做不到。"

在我们演讲班中,大多数学员从训练中获得的最有用的东西,就是增强了自信心,对自己走向成功的一份额外的自信。在通常情况下,一个人要取得成功,更重要的是什么呢?

爱默生写道:"没有热情,什么大事也做不成。"那不仅仅是一句措辞巧妙的文学用语,更是一幅通向成功的地图。

威廉·莱昂·费尔普斯可能是耶鲁大学最受爱戴和欢迎的教授。在他的《教书热》一书中,他说:"对我而言,教书更胜于艺术和其他职业。那是一种激情。我热爱教书,就像画家喜欢绘画,歌唱家钟情歌唱,诗人爱好写诗。每天早晨起床之前,我总会热情洋溢地想着那群学生。"

一位老师对他的事业充满热情,对工作极具兴趣,并取得了成功,这奇怪吗?费尔普斯对他的学生产生了巨大的影响,主要是因为他在教学中投入了爱心和激情,还有热情。

如果你在学习如何有效演讲的过程中加入一点热情,就会发现前进路上的障碍会消失。把你全部的天赋和潜力都用来与人进行有效的交流,这是一种挑战。想想你可能会有的自信、肯定和镇定,以及吸引别人注意、煽动他人情感、说服众人采取行动所具有的控制力,你将会发现,自我表达的能力也会带来其他方面的能力,因为训练自己能言善辩是一条光明的大道,可以在工作和生活的各个方面获得自信。

戴尔·卡耐基课程的教师指南手册中有这样的话:"一旦学员们发现,他们抓住了听众的注

largely by the love and excitement, by the enthusiasm, he put into his teaching.

If you put enthusiasm into learning how to speak more effectively you will find that the obstacles in your path will disappear. This is a challenge to focus all your talent and power on the goal of effective communication with your fellow men. Think of the self-reliance, the assurance, the poise that will be yours, the sense of mastery that comes from being able to hold the attention, stir the emotions, and convince a group to act. You will find that competence in self-expression will lead to competence in other ways as well, for training in effective speaking is the royal road to self-confidence in all the areas of working and living.

In the manual for the guidance of instructors who teach the Dale Carnegie Course are these words: "When class members discover that they can hold the attention of an audience and receive an instructor's praise, and the applause of the class—when they are able to do that, they develop a sense of inner power, courage, and calm that they have never before experienced. The result? They undertake and accomplish things that they never dreamed possible. They find themselves longing to talk before groups. They take active parts in business and professional and community activities, and become leaders."

The word "leadership" has been used often in the chapters that have gone before this one. Clear, forceful, and emphatic expressiveness is one of the marks of leadership in our society. This expressiveness must govern all the utterances of the leader from private interview to public pronouncements. Properly applied the material in this book will help to develop leadership—in the family, the church group, the civic organization, the corporation, and the government.

意力，得到了教师的表扬，以及同学的掌声，一旦得到这些，就会开发出以前从未有过的潜力、勇气和镇定。结果呢？他们尝试并完成了做梦也不敢想的事情。他们发现自己敢当众发言了。他们积极参加商业、专业和公共活动，并成为领袖人物。"

"领导力"一词在前面章节中频繁引用。在我们的社会中，清晰、有力、强劲的表达正好是领导力的特征之一。从私人会面到公众演讲，表达必须涵盖领导者的全部思想。巧妙地应用本书中的方法，将有助你在家庭、教会、社区、公司和政府等领域，发挥领导作用。

译后记

戴尔·卡耐基是20世纪最伟大的成功学导师。他运用心理学和社会学知识，对人类共同的心理特点进行探索和分析，开创和发展了一套独特的融演讲、推销、为人处世及智力开发于一体的成人教育方式，接受卡耐基教育的有社会各界人士，他们从中获益匪浅。

卡耐基成人教育通过培养学员的自信心，使他们过上了更丰富、更满足的生活。这种成功，可以从成千上万名毕业学员写来的信中得到证明。写这些信的学员有工厂工人、家庭主妇、政界人士、公司负责人、教师及传教士等等，他们的职业遍及各行各业。很多公司还把他们的职员送来接受卡耐基训练，或者干脆请卡耐基机构为他们公司开设课程，直接训练他们的职员。这些知名公司包括美国假日酒店、强生公司、麦当劳公司以及通用汽车公司……著名的"石油大王"洛克菲勒也曾因为忧虑而濒临死亡，但在接受卡耐基的课程之后，他征服了忧虑，得到了快乐，获得了健康，又多活了半个世纪。

卡耐基于1955年11月1日去世，华盛顿一家报纸曾这样评价他说："千百万人受到他的影响，他的这些哲理如文明一样古老，如'十诫'一般简明，但是对于人们在这个狂乱的年代里获得快乐和成就极有帮助。"

卡耐基一生勤于著述，他的作品如《人性的弱点》、《人性的优点》、《语言的突破》等，都是非常畅销的成功励志作品，在世界各地广受读者的欢迎。时至今日，在教导人们追求自我进步和获得成功的书籍中，这些书仍然是必读的。

这本书的翻译工作由刘祐组织，李发、刘爽、韩少阳、康健、永琦、赵悦、李小龙、孙晔、宋保仁、杨滢、戴忠东、兆海、瑞静、郝伟林、殷俊、胡明峰、吴良平、宋艳丽、张源、张勇、赵永安、朱苒、张岩、赵星烁、梁淑霞、龙科锋、李平、王志刚、宏韬等参与了各章的整理。若有不妥之处，请读者不吝指正。我们衷心希望这本书的出版，能帮助您跨越前进道路上的各种障碍，实现自己的人生理想，早日走向成功的人生。